Nineteenth-Century Literature Criticism

Guide to Gale Literary Criticism Series

For criticism on	Consult these Gale series
Authors now living or who died after December 31, 1959	*CONTEMPORARY LITERARY CRITICISM (CLC)*
Authors who died between 1900 and 1959	*TWENTIETH-CENTURY LITERARY CRITICISM (TCLC)*
Authors who died between 1800 and 1899	*NINETEENTH-CENTURY LITERATURE CRITICISM (NCLC)*
Authors who died between 1400 and 1799	*LITERATURE CRITICISM FROM 1400 TO 1800 (LC)* *SHAKESPEAREAN CRITICISM (SC)*
Authors who died before 1400	*CLASSICAL AND MEDIEVAL LITERATURE CRITICISM (CMLC)*
Black writers of the past two hundred years	*BLACK LITERATURE CRITICISM (BLC)*
Authors of books for children and young adults	*CHILDREN'S LITERATURE REVIEW (CLR)*
Dramatists	*DRAMA CRITICISM (DC)*
Hispanic writers of the late nineteenth and twentieth centuries	*HISPANIC LITERATURE CRITICISM (HLC)*
Native North American writers and orators of the eighteenth, nineteenth, and twentieth centuries	*NATIVE NORTH AMERICAN LITERATURE (NNAL)*
Poets	*POETRY CRITICISM (PC)*
Short story writers	*SHORT STORY CRITICISM (SSC)*
Major authors from the Renaissance to the present	*WORLD LITERATURE CRITICISM, 1500 TO THE PRESENT (WLC)*

ISSN 0732-1864

Volume 54

Nineteenth-Century Literature Criticism

Criticism of the
Works of Novelists, Poets, Playwrights,
Short Story Writers, Philosophers, and Other
Creative Writers Who Died between 1800
and 1899, from the First Published Critical
Appraisals to Current Evaluations

James E. Person, Jr.
Editor

Denise Kasinec
Marie Lazzari
Mary L. Onorato
Contributing Editors

GALE

DETROIT • NEW YORK • TORONTO • LONDON

STAFF

James E. Person, Jr., *Editor*

Dana Ramel Barnes, Denise Kasinec, Marie Lazzari,
and Mary L. Onorato, *Contributing Editors*

Gerald R. Barterian, *Associate Editor*

Susan M. Trosky, *Managing Editor*

Marlene S. Hurst, *Permissions Manager*
Margaret A. Chamberlain and Maria Franklin, *Permissions Specialists*
Diane Cooper, Michele Lonoconus, Maureen Puhl, Susan Salas, Shalice Shah,
Kimberly F. Smilay, and Barbara A. Wallace, *Permissions Associates*
Sarah Chesney, Edna Hedblad, Margaret McAvoy-Amato, Tyra Y. Phillips,
Lori Schoenenberger, and Rita Velázquez, *Permissions Assistants*

Victoria B. Cariappa, *Research Manager*
Alicia Noel Biggers, Julia C. Daniel, Tamara C. Nott, Michele P. Pica,
Tracie A. Richardson, and Cheryl Warnock, *Research Associates*

Mary Beth Trimper, *Production Director*
Deborah L. Milliken, *Production Assistant*

Sherrell Hobbs, *Macintosh Artist*
Randy Bassett, *Image Database Supervisor*
Robert Duncan and Mikal Ansari, *Imaging Specialists*
Pamela A. Hayes, *Photography Coordinator*

∞™
  This book is printed on acid-free paper that meets the minimum requirements of American National Standard for Information Sciences—Permanence Paper for Printed Library Materials, ANSI Z39.48-1984.

Library of Congress Catalog Card Number 84-643008
ISBN 0-8103-6437-9
ISSN 0732-1864
Printed in the United States of America

10 9 8 7 6 5 4 3 2 1

Contents

Preface vii

Acknowledgments xi

Preface

Since its inception in 1981, *Nineteenth-Century Literature Criticism* has been a valuable resource for students and librarians seeking critical commentary on writers of this transitional period in world history. Designated an "Outstanding Reference Source" by the American Library Association with the publication of its first volume, *NCLC* has since been purchased by over 6,000 school, public, and university libraries. The series has covered more than 300 authors representing 26 nationalities and over 15,000 titles. No other reference source has surveyed the critical reaction to nineteenth-century authors and literature as thoroughly as *NCLC*.

Scope of the Series

NCLC is designed to introduce students and advanced readers to the authors of the nineteenth century, and to the most significant interpretations of these authors' works. The great poets, novelists, short story writers, playwrights, and philosophers of this period are frequently studied in high school and college literature courses. By organizing and reprinting commentary written on these authors, *NCLC* helps students develop valuable insight into literary history, promotes a better understanding of the texts, and sparks ideas for papers and assignments. Each entry in *NCLC* presents a comprehensive survey of an author's career or an individual work of literature and provides the user with a multiplicity of interpretations and assessments. Such variety allows students to pursue their own interests; furthermore, it fosters an awareness that literature is dynamic and responsive to many different opinions.

Every fourth volume of *NCLC* is devoted to literary topics that cannot be covered under the author approach used in the rest of the series. Such topics include literary movements, prominent themes in nineteenth-century literature, literary reaction to political and historical events, significant eras in literary history, prominent literary anniversaries, and the literatures of cultures that are often overlooked by English-speaking readers.

NCLC continues the survey of criticism of world literature begun by Gale's *Contemporary Literary Criticism (CLC)* and *Twentieth-Century Literary Criticism (TCLC)*, both of which excerpt and reprint commentary on authors of the twentieth century. For additional information about *TCLC, CLC,* and Gale's other criticism series, users should consult the Guide to Gale Literary Criticism Series preceding the title page in this volume.

Coverage

Each volume of *NCLC* is carefully compiled to present:

- criticism of authors, or literary topics, representing a variety of genres and nationalities
- both major and lesser-known writers and literary works of the period
- 6-10 authors or 4-6 topics per volume
- individual entries that survey critical response to an author's work or a topic in literary history, including early criticism to reflect initial reactions, later criticism to represent any rise or decline in reputation, and current retrospective analyses.

Organization

An author entry consists of the following elements: author heading, biographical and critical introduction, list of principal works, excerpts of criticism (each preceded by a bibliographic citation and an annotation), and a bibliography of further reading.

■ The **Author Heading** consists of the name under which the author most commonly wrote, followed by birth and death dates. If an author wrote consistently under a pseudonym, the pseudonym will be listed in the author heading and the real name given in parentheses on the first line of the biographical and critical introduction. Also located at the beginning of the introduction to the author entry are any name variations under which an author wrote, including transliterated forms for an author whose language uses a nonroman alphabet.

■ The **Biographical and Critical Introduction** outlines the author's life and career, as well as the critical issues surrounding his or her work. References are provided to past volumes of *NCLC* in which further information about the author may be found.

■ Most *NCLC* entries include a **Portrait** of the author. Many entries also contain reproductions of materials pertinent to an author's career, including manuscript pages, title pages, dust jackets, letters, and drawings, as well as photographs of important people, places, and events in an author's life.

■ The list of **Principal Works** is chronological by date of first publication and identifies the genre of each work. In the case of foreign authors with both foreign-language publications and English translations, the English-language version is given in brackets. Unless otherwise indicated, dramas are dated by first performance, not first publication.

■ **Criticism** in each author entry is arranged chronologically to provide a perspective on changes in critical evaluation over the years. All titles of works by the author featured in the entry are printed in boldface type to enable the user to easily locate discussion of particular works. Also for purposes of easier identification, the critic's name and the publication date of the essay are given at the beginning of each piece of criticism. Unsigned criticism is preceded by the title of the journal in which it appeared. Publication information (such as publisher names and book prices) and some parenthetical numerical references (such as page and line references to specific editions of works) have been deleted at the editors' discretion to provide smoother reading of the text.

■ A complete **Bibliographic Citation** provides original publication information for each piece of criticism.

■ Critical excerpts are prefaced by **Annotations** providing the reader with a summary of the critical intent of the piece. Also included, when appropriate, is information about the critic's reputation, individual approach to literary criticism, and particular expertise in an author's works, as well as information about the relative importance of the critical excerpt. In some cases, the annotations cross-reference excerpts by critics who discuss each other's commentary.

■ An annotated list of **Further Reading** appearing at the end of each entry suggests secondary sources on the author. In some cases it includes essays for which the editors could not obtain reprint rights.

Cumulative Indexes

- Each volume of *NCLC* contains a cumulative **Author Index** listing all authors who have appeared in Gale's Literary Criticism Series, along with cross-references to such biographical series as *Contemporary Authors* and *Dictionary of Literary Biography*. Useful for locating authors within the various series, this index is particularly valuable for those authors who are identified with a certain period but who, because of their death dates, are placed in another, or for those authors whose careers span two periods. For example, Fyodor Dostoevsky is found in *NCLC*, yet Leo Tolstoy, another major nineteenth-century Russian novelist, is found in *TCLC* because he died after 1899.

- Each *NCLC* volume includes a cumulative **Nationality Index** which lists all authors who have appeared in *NCLC*, arranged alphabetically under their respective nationalities.

- Each new volume in Gale's Literary Criticism Series includes a cumulative **Topic Index**, which lists all literary topics treated in *NCLC, TCLC, LC 1400-1800*, and the *CLC* Yearbook.

- Each new volume of *NCLC*, with the exception of the Topics volumes, contains a **Title Index** listing the titles of all literary works discussed in the volume. In response to numerous suggestions from librarians, Gale has also produced a **Special Paperbound Edition** of the *NCLC* title index. This annual cumulation lists all titles discussed in the series since its inception. Additional copies of the index are available on request. Librarians and patrons have welcomed this separate index: it saves shelf space, is easy to use, and is recyclable upon receipt of the following year's cumulation. Titles discussed in the Topics volume entries are not included in the *NCLC* cumulative index.

Citing *Nineteenth-Century Literature Criticism*

When writing papers, students who quote directly from any volume in Gale's Literary Criticism Series may use the following general forms to footnote reprinted criticism. The first example pertains to material drawn from periodicals, the second to material reprinted from books:

[1]T.S. Eliot, "John Donne," *The Nation and Athenaeum*, 33 (9 June 1923), 321-32; excerpted and reprinted in *Literature Criticism from 1400-1800*, Vol. 10, ed. James E. Person, Jr. (Detroit: Gale Research, 1989), pp. 28-9.

[2]Clara G. Stillman, *Samuel Butler: A Mid-Victorian Modern* (Viking Press, 1932); excerpted and reprinted in *Twentieth-Century Literary Criticism*, Vol. 33, ed. Paula Kepos (Detroit: Gale Research, 1989), pp. 43-5.

Suggestions Are Welcome

In response to suggestions, several features have been added to *NCLC* since the series began, including annotations to excerpted criticism, a cumulative index to authors in all Gale literary criticism series, entries devoted to criticism on a single work by a major author, more illustrations, and a title index listing all literary works discussed in the series.

Readers who wish to suggest authors, single works, or topics to appear in future volumes, or who have other suggestions, are cordially invited to write: The Editors, *Nineteenth-Century Literature Criticism*, 835

Penobscot Bldg., 645 Griswold St., Detroit, MI 48226-4094; call toll-free at 1-800-347-GALE; or fax to 1-313-961-6599.

Acknowledgments

The editors wish to thank the copyright holders of the excerpted criticism included in this volume and the permissions managers of many book and magazine publishing companies for assisting us in securing reprint rights. We are also grateful to the staffs of the Detroit Public Library, the Library of Congress, the University of Detroit Mercy Library, Wayne State University Purdy/Kresge Library Complex, and the University of Michigan Libraries for making their resources available to us. Following is a list of the copyright holders who have granted us permission to reprint material in this volume of *NCLC*. Every effort has been made to trace copyright, but if omissions have been made, please let us know.

COPYRIGHTED EXCERPTS IN *NCLC*, VOLUME 54, WERE REPRINTED FROM THE FOLLOWING PERIODICALS:

The Atlantic Monthly, v. 225, April, 1970 for "Puppet's Progress" by Martha Bacon. Copyright 1970 by The Atlantic Monthly Company, Boston, MA. Reprinted by permission of the author.—*Forum for Modern Language Studies*, v. XXVI, July, 1990 for "The Poem, the Gloss and the Critic: Discourse and Subjectivity in 'The Rime of the Ancient Mariner'" by Lindsay Davies. Copyright © 1990 by *Forum for Modern Language Studies* and the author. Reprinted by permission of the publisher and the author.—*Heine-Jahrbuch*, v. 27, 1988. Reprinted by permission of the publisher.--*The Illustrated London News*, v. CLXXXV, August 4, 1934. Copyright 1934 The Illustrated London News & Sketch Ltd. Reprinted by permission of the publisher.—*The Lion and the Unicorn*, v. 12, December, 1988 for "Carlo Collodi as Translator: From Fairy Tale to Folk Tale" by Esther Zago. Copyright © 1988 *The Lion and the Unicorn*. Reprinted by permission of the publisher and the author.—*Monatshefte*, v. 73, Winter, 1981. Copyright © 1981 by the Board of Regents of the University of Wisconsin System. Reprinted by permission of The University of Wisconsin Press.—*Poetics Today*, v. 13, 1992. Copyright 1992 by the Porter Institute for Poetics and Semiotics, Tel Aviv University. Reprinted with the permission of the publisher.—*The Saturday Review of Literature*, v. XXI, February 17, 1940. Copyright 1940, renewed 1968 *Saturday Review* magazine. Reprinted by permission of Saturday Review Publications, Ltd.—*The Ukrainian Quarterly*, v. XXXVII, Spring, 1981. Reprinted by permission of the publisher.

COPYRIGHTED EXCERPTS IN *NCLC*, VOLUME 54, WERE REPRINTED FROM THE FOLLOWING BOOKS:

Adams, Charles Hansford. From *"The Guardian of the Law:" Authority in James Fenimore Cooper*. Pennsylvania State University Press, 1990. Copyright © 1990, The Pennsylvania State University Press, University Park, PA. Reproduced by permission of the publisher.—Berman, Russell A. From "Poetry for the Republic: Heine and Whitman," in *Heinrich Heine and the Occident: Multiple Identities, Multiple Receptions*. Edited by Peter Uwe Hohendahl and Sander L. Gilman. University of Nebraska Press, 1991. Copyright © 1991 by the University of Nebraska Press. All rights reserved. Reprinted by permission of the publisher.—Bloom, Edward A. From an introduction to *Evelina or the History of a Young Lady's Entrance into the World*. By Frances Burney. Edited by Edward A. Bloom. Oxford University Press (London), 1968. © Oxford University Press 1968. Reprinted by permission of the publisher.—Boulger, James D. From "Christian Skepticism in 'The Rime of the Ancient Mariner'," in *From Sensibility to Romanticism: Essays Presented to Frederick A. Pottle*. Edited by Frederick W. Hilles and Harold Bloom. Oxford University Press, Inc., 1965. Copyright © 1965, renewed 1993 by Harold Bloom. Reprinted by permission of the publisher.—Bowra, C. M. From *The Romantic Imagination*. Cambridge, Mass.: Harvard University Press, 1949. Copyright 1949 by the President and Fellows of Harvard College. Renewed © 1977 by the Literary Estate of Cecil Maurice Bowra. Excerpted by permission of Harvard University Press.—Brooks, Van Wyck. From *The World of Washington Irving*. Dutton, 1944. Copyright, 1944, by Van Wyck Brooks. All rights reserved. Used by permission of the publisher, E. P. Dutton, an imprint of New American Library, a division of Penguin Books USA Inc.—Brown, Martha G. From "Fanny Burney's Feminism: Gender or Genre?," in *Fettered or Free? British Women Novelists, 1670-1815*. Edited by Mary Anne Schofield and Cecilia Macheski. Ohio University Press, 1986. Copyright © 1986 by Ohio University Press. Reprinted

PHOTOGRAPHS AND ILLUSTRATIONS APPEARING IN *NCLC*, VOLUME 54, WERE RECEIVED FROM THE FOLLOWING SOURCES:

Fanny Burney

1752-1840

(Born Frances Burney; later Madame d'Arblay) English novelist, dramatist, letter writer, and diarist.

For additional information about Burney's life and career, see *NCLC,* Volume 12.

INTRODUCTION

Burney is remembered for her contribution to the English novel of manners, most notably with *Evelina; or, A Young Lady's Entrance into the World* (1778). *Evelina* achieved renown for its humor, simple prose, and insightful depiction of a young woman's coming of age in eighteenth-century England. While her novels have been overshadowed by the writings of Jane Austen, who perfected the novel of manners, Burney is considered a significant transitional figure who employed the methods of Samuel Richardson and Henry Fielding to create a new subgenre that made possible the domestic novels of Austen, Maria Edgeworth, and countless other successors.

Biographical Information

Burney was born in London to Esther Sleepe and Charles Burney. Her mother died when Burney was ten, and she became very attached to her father, a prominent musician and England's first musicologist. Although Burney was a shy child and received little formal education, she met a number of artists and intellectuals through her father. She read extensively and, though her father preferred that she devote herself to more serious activities than writing, she began to experiment secretly with poems, plays, and fiction. In 1767, however, apparently in response to her father's disapproval of her writing, Burney destroyed all her manuscripts. Among these early manuscripts was the novel "The History of Caroline Evelyn." When Burney began to write again several years later, the novel formed the basis of the first part of *Evelina.* To Burney's surprise, the success of *Evelina* delighted her father; ironically, Dr. Burney had read and enjoyed *Evelina,* which had been published anonymously, without knowing that his daughter was the author. He introduced Fanny to such prominent literary figures as Samuel Johnson and Edmund Burke, who warmly welcomed her into London's literary circles and encouraged her to continue writing. However, because Dr. Burney privately pronounced her next work, a drama entitled "The Witlings," a failure, it was never produced or published. Several critics now contend

that her father objected to this parody of bluestocking society for its controversial subject.

Despite Burney's popularity as an author, her family continued to be concerned about her unmarried status and future financial security. When she was offered a position as second keeper of the robes to Queen Charlotte in 1786, she accepted the prestigious post at her father's urging. However, Burney's estrangement from the society that inspired her novels made her miserable. She recorded her experience in journals and letters, published posthumously in the *Diary and Letters of Madame d'Arblay* (1842-46), that are today considered a telling account of the rigors and restrictions of life at court. Several tragedies that she composed during this period also bear witness to Burney's increasing unhappiness and frustration. Eventually, she became ill and Dr. Burney obtained her release from royal service. She left court in 1791, receiving a pension of one hundred pounds a year. Soon after, Burney married Alexandre d'Arblay, a penniless French exile. The marriage was evidently very happy and, in 1794, she gave birth to their son, Alexander. Burney resumed her novel-writing career in 1796 with *Camilla*, a satirical examination of the social restrictions of marriage. The work yielded sufficient funds to build the d'Arblays a new home, Camilla Cottage. Burney's days at Camilla Cottage were her happiest; there she wrote several unpublished comedies before traveling to France with her family in 1802. Though they intended to visit briefly, they were forced to stay until 1812 because of the outbreak of war between France and England. Upon their return to England, Burney wrote her last novel, *The Wanderer* (1814). In 1815, during Napolean's Hundred Days, d'Arblay aided the forces against Napolean while Burney fled to Brussels for the duration of the conflict; they returned to England later that year and settled in Bath. After d'Arblay's death in 1818, Burney moved back to London, where she began to revise her journals to add her experiences in exile during wartime. She died at the age of eighty-eight.

Major Works

Burney published *Evelina* anonymously, aided by her brother Charles, who disguised himself when submitting the manuscript. An epistolary novel with a focus on female identity, the novel met with immediate acclaim. In Evelina, Burney created a heroine who is considered one of the most vibrant and realistic in English literature. Burney next wrote *Cecilia; or, Memoirs of an Heiress* (1782), in which she continued to explore the social mores of her era with wit and satire. It was also her first experiment in third-person narrative, which she employed in both her subsequent novels. While not as great a success as *Evelina*, *Cecilia* was generally well received. Critics favorably compared it with the works of Richardson, Fielding, and Laurence Sterne, but argued that it lacked the spontaneity of *Evelina*, a flaw also detected in *Camilla; or, A Picture of Youth* (1796) and *The Wanderer; or, Female Difficulties* (1814), her last two novels. Though most commentators fault *Camilla* as a sensational work written purely for financial reasons, it was extremely popular. *The Wanderer* was the most poorly received of her novels, criticized as dated and awkwardly constructed. The novel's depiction of a nineteenth-century woman struggling to earn her own living, however, has prompted considerable critical commentary in recent years, particularly from a feminist standpoint. During the final years of her life, Burney edited her father's memoirs and correspondence, *Memoirs of Dr. Burney, Arranged from His Own Manuscripts, from Family Papers, and from Personal Recollections* (1832). Though she claimed to have carefully edited sections to avoid including any slanderous material, detractors have charged that Burney chose to incorporate material that illuminates her own life rather than her father's. Her *Diary and Letters*, published by her niece over a period of several years after Burney's death, generated so much public interest that well into the twentieth century she was remembered more as a diarist than as a novelist.

Critical Reception

Of Burney's novels, *Evelina* is consistently the most admired and is considered the best evidence of her keen social observation and ear for dialect. Since the novel's publication, critics have praised its characterization, humor, and engrossing plot. Most scholars agree, too, that in her first novel Burney created her most consummately human and believable heroine. They also concur that Burney never recaptured the fresh, spontaneous prose of *Evelina* and that her later works suffer from a labored style. Though *Cecilia* and *Camilla* appealed to eighteenth-century readers, critics today consider both dated and stilted. Ironically, *The Wanderer*, which was dismissed by contemporary commentators, has recently received the greatest share of critical attention for its focus on the status and condition of women. Burney's journals and letters have elicited almost as much positive critical response as *Evelina*; today, they are considered both engaging depictions of her era and valuable historical documents. Though her harshest critic, her contemporary John Wilson Croker, derided the *Diary* as egocentric, most commentators, including Thomas Babington Macaulay, George Saintsbury, and Lytton Strachey, have assessed the work as insightful and historically accurate. In the twentieth century, however, Gamaliel Bradford argued that the *Diary* merely depicted Burney's obsession with the superficial in society. In recent years, such literary figures as the novelist Margaret Drabble have termed Burney a perceptive correspondent and diarist and praised her description of life in the late eighteenth and early nineteenth centuries. Today, Burney's stature has been eclipsed by that of her successors, most notably Austen. While most critics concur that Burney's talent as a novelist blossomed early and then faded, they also hail *Evelina* as a landmark work that initiated the tradition of the domestic novel and the novel of manners. It seems likely that Burney's importance in years to come will continue to derive from her spirited depiction of Evelina's maturation into womanhood.

PRINCIPAL WORKS

Evelina; or, A Young Lady's Entrance into the World (novel) 1778
Cecilia; or, Memoirs of an Heiress (novel) 1782
Camilla; or, A Picture of Youth (novel) 1796
Edwy and Elgiva (drama) 1796
The Wanderer; or, Female Difficulties (novel) 1814
Memoirs of Dr. Burney, Arranged from His Own Manuscripts, from Family Papers, and from Per-

sonal Recollections (memoirs) 1832
Diary and Letters of Madame d'Arblay. 7 vols. (diary and letters) 1842-46
The Early Diary of Frances Burney, 1768-1778. 2 vols. (diary) 1889
The Journals and Letters of Fanny Burney (Madame D'Arblay). 12 vols. (diaries and letters) 1972-84
*A Busy Day (drama) 1984

*Written c. 1800.

CRITICISM

Joyce Hemlow (essay date 1958)

SOURCE: "*Cecilia*," in *The History of Fanny Burney*, Oxford at the Clarendon Press, 1958, pp. 139-68.

[*In the following essay, Hemlow chronicles the historical context that prompted Burney's writing* Cecilia.]

> Heavens! what a life of struggle between the head
> and the heart!
>
> *Cecilia*, v. x. 6

The publication of *Evelina*, which introduced Fanny Burney into the Streatham group and thus into the London world, put an end to her fortunate and spontaneous habit of writing for its own happy ends. No one can know, of course, what work she might have produced if she had been left to her own quiet ways. The protests that she made on being thrust into public notice indicate that one of the genial conditions of her growth had been the screen that shielded her from the disapproval or opprobrium easily incurred by the wit or novelist. Anonymity had afforded temporary security and made for uninhibited writing. She had launched her first craft on a lee shore.

In *Cecilia*, however, Miss Burney must meet the full tide of public criticism. Where the earlier novel had been based on the girlish adventures and dreams of Poland Street and St. Martin's Street and took ten years to develop, *Cecilia* was the product of Streatham, Brighton, Bath, and the larger world, which at this time Fanny was getting to know, but which she was allowed no time to assimilate. Finally, the new work was not a spontaneous but a forced production, written largely because Dr. Burney thought that the new author should seize and capitalize on the shining hour of her first success. *Cecilia*, in short, took form under pressures of time and compulsion that had never entered into the composition of *Evelina* and, as Fanny's complaints to her sisters indicate, the book often proceeded with great travail.

I go on but indifferently,—I don't write as I did, the certainty of being known, the high success of Evelina, which, as Mr. Crisp says, to fail in a 2d would *tarnish*,—these thoughts worry & depress me,—& a desire to do more than I have been able, by writing at unseasonable Hours, & never letting my Brains rest even when my *corporeal machine* was succumbent.

Dr. Burney and Mr. Crisp had allowed her no respite; having condemned her play, they urged her first to begin and then to hurry on with a novel. Mrs. Thrale insisted that she visit Streatham and accompany parties to the watering-places. Fanny herself wished to journalize, but for a time she attempted to satisfy all demands at once, and we have as a result the first outline of *Cecilia* and a volume of Streatham, Brighton, and Bath *Journals*.

Early in April, 1780, Mrs. Thrale obtained Dr. Burney's permission to have Fanny at Bath ('I can't go without her & there's an End'). The Thrales took a house at the corner of the South Parade overlooking the Avon, and Fanny, Queeney, and Mrs. Thrale went to plays, the pump-room, and countless evening parties, where they met the bluestockings. Mrs. Montagu and Mrs. Carter, Mr. Anstey (author of *The New Bath Guide*), the Bowdlers, the infidel Miss W—, Beau Travell, the poet Edward Jerningham, the wit Lord Mulgrave, and, finally, Mrs. Macartney (nicknamed Mrs. McDevil), the notorious Bath Queen. They made a satiric visit to an alderman, Mr. Ferry, in order to see furniture that emerged and dropped out of sight through trapdoors and the mechanical eagle that swooped from the ceiling to remove the table-cloth. There was a merry walk home across the meadows. 'Indeed we laughed all the way.'

Mr. Crisp was very glad to have Fanny in the 'midst of the Bath circle'.

> Your time could not be better employed, for all your St. Martin's daddy wanted to retain you for some other purpose. You are now at school, the great school of the world, where swarms of new ideas and new characters will continually present themselves before you,
>
> which you'll draw in,
> As we do air, fast as 'tis ministered!

Just so had 'old Sarah Marlborough' read men and cards, not books. Yet the old monitor could not refrain from jogging Fanny's memory and conscience about a character-sketch that she had sent him and a plot that he thought would present a large field for unhackneyed characters and give ample scope for satire and ridicule. Just now Fanny had little time for writing anything except the memoranda from which the Bath Journal of 1780 (some hundred pages) was afterwards constructed. She had scarcely a moment to herself.

In June the Gordon Riots reached Bath. 'We saw the flames & heard the shouts together, one whole dreadful night.' Mr. Thrale, dubbed a papist and threatened because in 1778 he had voted in Parliament for the Bill for the Relief of Roman Catholics, was in immediate danger. In the morning (June 10) the family set out for Brighton, choosing a devious route in order to avoid crowds, travelling in a coach-and-four with two postilions and two footmen on horseback, intending, Fanny said, if the rioting grew worse, to embark for Holland. Frantic with fears for the Burney families in London, Fanny could take little joy in the leisurely progress of the route. The Thrales arrived in Brighton on the 18th. With the news that reached them there of the bonfires and pillage that marked the rioting not only in London but in Leicester Fields and St. Martin's Street itself, Fanny felt even worse. At Brighton they may have received Susan's horrific journal of the lurid sights she watched from the observatory, and her explanation of the acute peril the Burneys were in because of threats to a Roman Catholic china-dealer who rented some part of Dr. Burney's premises at the back, and because of proximity to the Orange Street Chapel that the rioters for a time mistook for a Catholic chapel. Fanny was happy when Mrs. Thrale took her to London on June 23 and consented to leave her at home. Long absence had made her feel almost 'an *alien* of late'. She was not ungrateful to the Thrales, but she explained to her father: 'As I should not even *wish* to leave them when they are in sickness or in sorrow, if I also stay with them when they are in Health & in spirits, I am neither *yours* nor *my own*, but *theirs*.' The letters marked Fanny's decision to remain a Burney, rather than accept the hospitality of the Thrales and become a permanent appendage to their household.

In August Dr. Burney with Fanny and Charlotte, and later Susan in exchange, spent about five weeks at Chessington, and Fanny promised Mr. Crisp to return in the winter and work hard on the novel. It was at this time that the Thrales with Dr. Johnson visited Chessington with invitations to Fanny (and *en passant* to Mr. Crisp and Dr. Burney) to accompany them to Brighton, but Fanny felt that she must decline. In late October and in November she was at home incognita—'only stumping out, muffled up & early now & then of a frosty & dry morning into the Park'. The illness of Mr. Thrale delayed her return to Chessington, but for part of December and through January and most of February she was there at work on the early and miscellaneous fragments that were to become *Cecilia.* At the end of January a draft of the first volume was completed.

By February she was worn out by weeks of hard work and longed to return to London.

> One way or other my Hand scarce rests an Hour in the whole Day. Whenever this work is done—if

ever that Day arrives, I believe I shall not write another word for 3 years! however, I really believe I must still publish it *in part,* for I begin to grow horribly tired, & yet am by no means *near* any thing *bordering* upon an end. And the eternal fagging of my mind & Brains does really much mischief to my Health.

She chafed at the separation from Mrs. Thrale and especially from Susan, whose engagement to one of the heroes of Cook's last expedition, Lieutenant Molesworth Phillips, waited only Dr. Burney's consent. The 'eternal book' that kept her from home at such an exciting crisis had become 'a drudgery'. In mid-February, with the first volume of *Cecilia* scarcely finished, she fell ill of her chief enemy, a lurking fever. Mr. Crisp believed that her 'close application' to writing had 'contributed not a little to her present Illness', for she was like her father, he said, 'indefatigable and ardent in all her pursuits'. Mrs. Thrale with excitable kindness drove over the winter roads to Chessington, viewed Fanny's state with alarm, and on her return undertook to upbraid Dr. Burney

> & told him that your anxious earnestness to oblige him had caused much of the Illness we lamented— Why says he I did tease her to write while she was away &c that the Book so long expected might at length be done.

Before the end of February Daddy Crisp, far from well himself, accompanied Fanny in a chaise across the bare frozen common to the doors of St. Martin's Street. Mrs. Thrale was waiting on the doorstep with a physician that she had brought along to prescribe remedies. Fanny knew that her father would be disappointed that the novel was unfinished.

> He will expect me to have just *done,* when I am so behind hand as not even to see land!—yet I have written a great deal, but the work will be a long one, & I cannot without ruining it make it otherwise. . . . I am *afraid* of seeing my father. Think of a whole volume not yet *settled,* not yet begun! & that so important a one as the last! . . . I cannot sleep half the night for planning what to write next Day, & then next day am half dead for want of rest!

Obviously all was over with the book for a time. Though 'the vile & irksome fever' was soon conquered, it threatened to return. March was almost sped before Fanny was up and about again at St. Martin's Street, paying frequent visits to the Thrales in Grosvenor Square, busy with dinners and assemblies, and soon much concerned with the sorrows and changes that followed Mr. Thrale's death in April—agitations that, with new troubles nearer home, put her health again in 'a state of precariousness'. Her 'slight machine' was not made for 'rough encounters', the old gentleman at Chessington noted, but he bided his time. Just now, he conceded, Mrs. Thrale had the first claim.

During most of 1781 domestic joys and distresses filled Fanny's mind. Charles Burney, though now an M.A. from Aberdeen, tarried long in the north after he was expected at home. In love again, he was filling pages with love verses. He was again in debt and his light-hearted gaiety savoured, the family thought, of levity. They almost foresaw and certainly feared what happened in December when the Bishop of London refused him ordination. James, on the other hand, had returned in October, 1780, with the remnant of Cook's last and tragic expedition, sailing up the Thames as 'Master & commander of the ship "The Discoverer"', of which he went out first Lieut'. But even so patronage did not come his way, and his next ship, a miserably armed brig, was much below his captain's dignity. His sisters worried over his independent and Whiggish attitudes and the vicissitudes of patronage scarcely less than over the dangers of the sea—and these, Fanny knew, were not slight:

> wretched weather, much danger, infinite sickness, & no prize! but he is *safe* now . . . in the Humber, *50* of his men sick with Fevers, from wet, hard watching, & fatigue!

In the summer Fanny worried over Esther's health, her careworn state, and her cares—too many children on an income insufficient to support them. In August she helped nurse both Esther and a newly born infant that lived only a few weeks. Somehow she managed to go on with the Streatham Journal, her passages at arms with Crutchley, Johnsonian annals, and the last of the immortal days there.

In September she again succumbed to fever. 'Why, what a slight piece of machinery is the terrestrial part of thee, our Fannikin!' wrote Mr. Crisp a few years previously—'a mere nothing, a Blast, a Vapour, disorders the Spring of thy Watch; & the Mechanism is so fine, that it requires no common hand to set it a going again.' This time she was attended at Streatham by the physician Sir Richard Jebb, advised to leave off 'asses milk as too *nourishing*', blooded ('a thing I mortally dislike'), and required to exist on 'Turnips, with a little dry Bread, & odious rennet whey', thus avoiding, as she gratefully believed, 'another long and tedious Illness'. Except for Charles, 'not one of us could boast of much strength', Susan remarked. Fanny, with a constitution that, like her father's, enabled her to live almost eighty-eight years, was often feverishly ill. 'She has no radical complaints', Susan explained.

> If she has no particular fatigue or any anxiety of mind to cope with she is lively, active, & well—but her Frame is certainly delicate & feeble—She is quickly sensible of fatigue & cannot long resist it &

still more quickly touched by any anxiety or distress of mind.

In the first week of November the novelist left Streatham for Chessington. On the 22nd Mrs. Thrale was giving her opinion of the new novel—expecting to cry herself blind over it—''tis so excessively pathetic'. Mr. Crisp, who had at last won over Streatham, had made up his mind to keep Fanny till the book was finished, but by December she was again chafing at the bit. 'I *have* hinted to him a design of eloping', she told Susan, 'but his arguments were *rage*, & his *rage*, at the same Time, I must own, was *argument.*'

This time it was Susan's approaching marriage that diverted Fanny's heart and mind from her work. Dr. Burney, fearing that there might not be '*de quoi manger* very plentifully', had at first opposed the match, but by December the Captain's relatives, the Shirleys, had evidently come forward, for by then Dr. Burney spoke with satisfaction of their kindness and of plans that seemed to go on 'very smoothly & happily'. He must have been brought to consent to the marriage, which in its tragic ending was to cause Fanny more lasting grief and regret than any other trouble in the Burney saga. But all this was for the future. Phillips was then gay and loving and true, and Fanny was happy at the glad news, though at the same time a little sad.

> There is something to me in the thought of being so near parting with you as the Inmate of the same House, Room—Bed—confidence & life, that is not very *merrifying,* though I would by no means have things altered.

She longed to go to St. Martin's Street, but had to throw into the balance the 'villainous draw backs to all comforts' at home, where the jealous and irate stepmother still played her proverbial role. Fanny found it difficult to write there. Again there was the conflict between the head and the heart.

> Mr. Crisp will not *hear* of 6 weeks, or *any given* Time, but insists most solemnly upon the propriety & necessity of my staying where I am, till the Book is actually finished. But in this I will be guided wholly by your affairs. If I cannot be of *use* to you, I shall take his advice, as I know well it is my Father's wish equally, & as I know but too well the many interruptions from ill management, inconvenience, & ill nature I must meet with when I go, will retard me most cruelly, & keep me back I know not how long.

On December 15 the 'melancholy news' about Charles and the refusal of the Bishop of London to ordain him had reached Chessington, and Fanny could work no more. ''Tis a vile thing', she lamented, 'that I have such pitiful Brains they will never be content without keeping a correspondence with the Heart, & hanging so upon it, that they catch all its infirmities!' Dr. Burney, realizing the effect of such family disasters on Fanny, desired her to quiet her mind and 'stay peaceably to finish!' 'How to *quiet* it', was another matter,

> yet, at the rate I went on, I do believe but for this melancholy affair, I should have written the Finis by this Evening.

She wished only to finish the book and go home, and she appealed to Susan for help.

> Sweetest Girl, assist *me* now!—What shall I do with my *Father,* to prevent displeasure or cold looks at my return?—they would half break my Heart, after the most kind Letter he has sent me not to *budge* or *fudge*!

'I will scrawl Night & Day, if I *can.*' And so she must have done and thus obtained permission to go to London. On December 22 she excitedly wrote to Susan that on Sunday or Monday alike she would be ready. She was back in the fold for Christmas Day and for a family party given early in the New Year (1782), when 'a prodigious Tribe of Burneys' were invited to dine at St. Martin's Street. 'Mighty disagreeable arrangement for Susan', she commented, 'but hardly to be avoided.' The wedding took place at St. Martin-in-the-Fields on January 10. Molesworth Phillips, seaman, sportsman, and gentleman-farmer, was, according to Mr. Crisp, 'a fine made, tall, stout, active, manly-looking young fellow as you shall see. I think Susan has great luck.' 'He seems perfectly to adore her, which She returns very properly.' The honeymoon was spent at Chessington, though in February Phillips was ordered to join a recruiting party at Ipswich. Susan's letters, for a time 'full of Content', were not for over ten years to be filled with sorrow. All who knew her paid tribute to her talents in music, both vocal and instrumental, and to her judgement and taste in all the arts. In intelligence—in almost every way—she, more than her brothers and sisters, resembled the Doctor. The marriage made no interruption in the flow of confidences between Susan and Fanny. Besides 'alives' (short reports on health and the like), they continued to exchange long, confidential journal-letters and sometimes undertook to dispatch them regularly at the end of every month. As Pacchierotti had observed, there seemed to be '*but one soul—but one mind*' between them.

Apparently Fanny had accompanied the wedding-party to Chessington, but had returned to St. Martin's Street before January 22. In the interval arrangements had been made for the publication of her book. So casually and so often does the name *Payne* occur in the Burney letters—the visits of Patty and Sally Payne to St. Martin's Street and Chessington, James's new 'Beauism', his visits to Castle Street, and his *devoirs* to Sally (ending later in marriage)—that one is hardly

surprised to learn that 'honest Tom Payne', 'Old Payne', as the Doctor called him, was to publish Fanny's new work. Fanny had noted that when the publisher had visited Chessington in February, 1781, he seemed to be looking for an opportunity to speak to her in private, but since she was then too ill to discuss business he wrote to Mr. Crisp about the new work, which he did not doubt would be excellent. Apparently the Doctor closed the contract. An old receipt shows that the copyright of *Cecilia* was sold to Payne and Cadell for £250. When Fanny later realized that, whereas Lowndes had printed 500 copies at first, Payne and Cadell had issued 2,000, she was very indignant. Perhaps neither the Burneys nor the Paynes suspected even then how well the £250 was invested, or that, like Lowndes, 'honest Tom Payne' was to get a good novel at a bargain. Mr. Crisp thought the price fair enough, indeed, 'a pretty Spill' for a girl to earn in a few months only by sitting quietly by a good fire and consulting nothing but her own brains.

> You see how triumphantly she goes on. If she can coin gold at such a Rate, as to sit by a warm Fire, and in 3 or 4 months (for the real time she has stuck to it closely, putting it all together, will not amount to more, tho' there have been long Intervals, between) gain £250 by scribbling the Inventions of her own Brain—only putting down in black and white whatever comes into her own head, without labour drawing singly from her own Fountain, she need not want money.

What could be simpler?

Through the London winter Fanny was seen occasionally at concerts or operas, but for the most part 'denied' to everyone except Mrs. Thrale and Hetty. In February she is too 'dreadfully busy', as she says in a letter to Susan, to 'write to any human Being but yourself for any pay, so horribly aches my Hand with copying'. On February 12 she had 'just finished that drudgery to the 1st volume'.

She was often seized with 'fits of terror' about her work. 'But for my Father', she wrote Mrs. Thrale, 'I am sure I should throw it behind the Fire!—as, when he knew nothing of the matter, was the case with many of its Predecessors; *all,* indeed, but Evelina.' 'But for my Father' may be taken as the operative phrase for *Cecilia.* Dr. Burney and Mr. Crisp had insisted that she begin; and now the novel, written at headlong speed, was too long; but she was allowed no time to write a short one. She complained later that her book was advertised in the newspapers before she had begun to copy or revise the fifth volume and while the end was still unwritten. Mrs. Thrale could twit her that, like Dr. Johnson himself, she was plagued for copy by her booksellers (i.e. publishers). Many pages of the first draft that she had no time to copy still stand among the copied pages in the *Cecilia* manuscript. Apart from the changes in names (Albina Wyerly to Cecilia Beverley, Mr. Vaughan to Mr. Briggs, *et al.*), the revisions are usually curtailments of the text or attempts to avoid circumlocution. If she had been allowed time for a little more excision, or if she had been advised to delete duplicated trends in the plot, *Cecilia* would now be more popular. Incidents, words, and dialogue came easily and rapidly to her. Such fecundity was wonderful, as everybody thought; but it was a pity too that the work had not been subjected to a little more classical pruning and more control. In February of 1782 she found some recompense for her labour in her father's pleasure in the first volume. 'He is quite *infatuated* with fondness for it,—not only beyond my most sanguine hopes, but almost beyond credibility.'

By March, 1782, the first volume of *Cecilia* was in the press and Fanny was at work revising and copying the second and third. Mr. Crisp, who had seen much of the work in the rough, was impatient to see the changes. He had questioned the credibility of the behaviour of the Delviles—a criticism that Fanny took great pains to refute. She wished her book to be 'true to life'—not a mere sentimental thing—a romance—

> I meant in Mrs. Delvile to draw a great, but not a perfect character; I meant, on the contrary, to blend upon paper, as I have frequently seen blended in life, noble and rare qualities with striking and incurable defects.

Later she was able to defend the verisimilitude of the Delviles through the authority of people of rank, who shared their views and testified that, placed in the same position, they would have acted in the same way. Nothing could have been more disturbing to the new realist than that Mr. Crisp should have found her characters unnatural. She found it necessary also to defend the conclusion, which she thought somewhat new in fiction, 'for the hero and the heroine are neither plunged in the depths of misery, nor exalted to UN*human* happiness. Is not such a middle state more natural, more according to real life, and less resembling every other book of fiction?' 'I shall think I have rather written a farce than a serious history, if the whole is to end, like the hack Italian operas, with a jolly chorus that makes all parties good and all parties happy!' Mr. Crisp will find that she will 'fight a good battle here'. Unless she is allowed an ending more consonant with human experience, she told him, 'the last page of any novel in Mr. Noble's circulating library may serve for the last page of mine, since a marriage, a reconciliation, and some sudden expedient for great riches, concludes them all alike'. The monitor was, for the moment, subdued. Fanny 'is so deep in her present Work that I quite let her alone at present', wrote the old gentleman to his sister on May 7. 'I believe the 1st is printed off, and Mr. Payne is about the 2d. She is now hard upon cor-

recting the 3d which he will have soon; the whole 5 Vols. are to come out together.' Later he agreed wholeheartedly with changes she had made. 'How will this go down?' he had asked himself as he read. 'The tribunal of the Inquisition itself is not more inflexible than I endeavoured to be on this occasion. Every other mode of proceeding is only delusive, and what is called making one's market at home.'

In April the second volume of *Cecilia* was circulating freely in manuscript and everybody except Mrs. Thrale, who preferred the *ton* parties at the beginning, liked it even better than the first. The work was to be printed volume by volume as fast as copy could be supplied. On May 23 Mr. Crisp was proudly announcing that 'great Expectations' were raised about Fanny's book, which was to come out after the royal Birthday. There was the possibility, too, that 'if the work answer'd' Mr. Payne might give an additional £50. 'A pretty Spill (£300) for a young girl in a few months to get by sitting still in her Chamber by a good Fire!'

Cecilia, or Memoirs of an Heiress (5 volumes) came out on June 12, 1782, and sold so rapidly that the booksellers, the lordly gentlemen in the full-powdered white wigs, could not supply their clientèle. Miss Reynolds told Miss Burney that 'the circulating library people have had it bespoken by old customers for months to come'. If the first edition had been kept at 2,000 copies, according to Dr. Johnson's knowledgeable calculations Tom Payne could have made a profit from July to October of £500. Friends of the Burneys began to scold: 'Miss Cholmondeley told me she understood I had behaved like a poor *simple thing* again, & had a Father *no wiser than myself!'*

In 1782 Fanny sometimes accepted invitations to accompany her father, and wherever she went she heard comments on her book. At Sir Joshua Reynolds's in June she had met Mr. Burke and fallen 'quite desperately & outrageously in love'. At another party at Sir Joshua's in July, Dr. Johnson told Fanny that he had read the first volume of her novel and that he considered Hobson 'a very *perfect* character'. He had kind words also for characters like Simkins and Miss Larolles and for the scene in Vauxhall Gardens: 'I have again read Harrel's death, it is finely done,—it is *very* finely done!' 'One likes one part, another prefers another part', reported Mrs. Thrale; 'but *Johnson* says, most judiciously, that the grand merit is in the *general Power of the whole.'*

Meanwhile Susan and Phillips had been begging Fanny to contrive a visit to them at Ipswich. One difficulty was that she could not ask her father for money since she already owed him some, but in mid-July, when the resourceful Phillips secured her an advance of £100 from Mr. Payne, she was on her way. Susan was now pregnant, and Fanny would congratulate her more cheerfully, if (thinking, no doubt, of Esther) she could but stipulate her 'future number'. She wrote gaily in anticipation of delights and enjoyments not to be had at home—bread and butter with her tea, and a blazing fire annihilating all the black coals in the grate. Her enumeration of other luxuries was an oblique comment on life at St. Martin's Street:

> If I find myself in good spirits, I shall not have the fear of wrath before my Eyes because I may happen to simper: if I am grave, & have had cause for gravity, I shall not conclude that you will be gayer than usual: if I ask you a common question, I shall not expect a stern look for an answer; if I make you a common reply, I shall not take it for granted you will pervert my words into an affront: if I talk of some favourite friend, I shall not prepare myself for hearing him or her instantly traduced; nor yet if I relate something that has made me happy, shall I know my conversation is the fore-runner of an Head-ache.

If such indulgences are refused, Fanny will only be where she was. From Ipswich she wrote happily to her father and to Mrs. Thrale about Susan's happiness. 'Poor thing, she has been little used to such serene comfort as she now enjoys!' Every day the sisters made 'thankful comparisons of the past with the present'.

> Capt. P., when he listens to us, is seized with such fits of alternate indignation against *somebody*, & rapture that *he* was the deliverer, that it is impossible not to be diverted by such eager & honest transitions.

Fanny had asked Susan not to begin **Cecilia** before she arrived, for she anticipated reading it with her as 'one of the most pleasant & heartfelt satisfactions' of her life. The quiet readings were interrupted one day by a letter from no less a person than Edmund Burke. Fanny longed to send it to her father but had no frank. 'For elegance of praise no such a one was ever written before.' No one else except her father, thought Fanny,

> could, at a Time of Business, disappointment, care & occupation such as His are now, have found time to read with such attention, & to commend with such good nature, a work so totally foreign to every thing that just now can come Home to his Business & bosom.

Few authors, perhaps, will deny the justice of these remarks, for Burke had indeed taken the trouble to point out and praise the three components already discussed at some length in connexion with **Evelina**, 'the natural vein of humour, the tender pathetic, [and] the comprehensive and noble moral'.

On August 9 Fanny reported her return to St. Martin's Street, where she

found Charlotte alone, & more glad to see me than I ever yet saw her after the longest separations, for she could hardly speak for crying,—I always knew her to be very affectionate, but never before surprised her in such a trick of sensibility.

Fanny resolved for the future to take 'more comfort' in Charlotte's society than her loss of Susan had hitherto given her spirit to attempt. But the honest and affectionate Charlotte, who meant to fill Susan's place, had not as yet 'the *powers*,'

> our tastes do not naturally accord, our likings and dislikings, are often dissimilar,—we don't admire the same people, we don't read the same Books, we don't search the same amusements, we don't adore the same Pacchierotti,—with *you* all seemed the same as with myself.

Charlotte's turn was to come later.

In 1782 the Doctor published the second volume of his *History of Music* and began the third.

> My father is all himself—gay, facile, and sweet. He comes to all meals, writes without toiling, and gives us more of his society than he has done many years.

In July he had gone to Chessington, accompanied by Mrs. Burney and Miss Young. Though they had planned to return in a few days, Mrs. Burney, as Mr. Crisp wrote to his sister, was taken so ill that she could not go back. Her case was thought 'desperate',

> insomuch that the famous Dr. Warren, the King's favourite Physician, was sent for hither from London, who when he came gave but little hopes. She has ever since lain struggling between Life and Death, and has been thought actually dying more than once: particularly a week ago Mr. Hemming saw her, and said she would not live till morning; for that the Death Sweats were upon her. How it will end, God knows. She still lives, but without sleep, and almost without food. . . . It is absolutely impossible for her to be mov'd, it seems; as Hemming says she would dye upon the Road; so that we are in for it to some purpose.

This crisis also passed. Mrs. Burney slowly recovered, convalescing through the month of August at Chessington. Mrs. Gast arrived, and on August 12 Fanny came with her cousin Edward in a chaise 'well loaded with canvasses, pencils, and painting materials'. Edward had been invited to paint Mr. Crisp and Mrs. Gast, and to Fanny's surprise plans had been laid for a portrait of her own *'pauvre petite personne'*. 'My sweet father came down Gascoign Lane to meet us, in very good spirits and very good health. Next came dear Daddy Crisp, looking vastly well, and, as usual, high in glee and kindness at the meeting. Then the affectionate Kitty, the good Mrs. Hamilton, the gentle Miss Young, and the enthusiastic Mrs. Gast.' The unhappy Invalid waited inside. The pleasant scenes over, Fanny repaired, as she says,

> to the *Lady of the Manor*,—not such was here our performance,—she was cold,—I was civil,—she looked artificial, I felt heartless! Shabby doings! as Mr. Blakeney says,—that we cannot live apart from those who love not us, & whom we yet more dislove.

The letters of the summer reveal characteristic tensions and attitudes.

> The Lady Herself is almost well; she will not, however, confess as much this Twelve month, for she finds the attendance & distinction of an Invalide the *only* attendance & distinction she has any chance to meet.

On many occasions Fanny described her mother's unhappiness and 'eternal restlessness'. 'She wants more amusement to keep off the foul fiend than any human being I ever saw.' At Chessington she did not know how to fill up her time.

> She goes out to walk, & returns in 3 minutes. She retires to her own Room, & comes back before we recover Breath, she takes up a Book, & throws it down before she has read one paragraph. My father has bought for her a very pretty Garden chair, in which he drags her himself every Day; & though she will suffer him, or any one else, to work like a plough man in pulling it without resting, she always finds it too hot or too cold, & only goes into it, with an air of reluctance, as if she were compelled.

As usual there was a treasonable quarter where none but rebels were welcome, this time the painting-room, where Edward had caricatured the poor Lady '& that with not more keen severity of exaggeration, than acuteness of humorous observation'. How many would 'esteem his sketch invaluable!' But Mr. Crisp had seized upon it and would not give it up for anything that could be offered in return. As for Fanny, she had never found her stepmother more 'supportable' than at this time.

> You well know she never behaves so kindly to any of us as when alone with her, her eternal jealousy of our affection & comfort from each other having then less power to torment her.

Meanwhile Edward toiled with loving care over the well-known portrait of Fanny. He succeeded, she thought, too well, and her troubled comments on his efforts are still extant.

> I believe if I am not under written, no one would guess he ever saw me, much less that I sat for the Picture called mine. Never was Portrait so violently flattered. I have taken pains incredible to make him *magnify* the Features, & darken the complection, but he is impenetrable in action, though fair & docile in promise. I shall still, however, work at him, for it really makes me uneasy to see a Face in which the smallest resemblance of my own can be traced looking almost *perfectly* handsome. In his 3 portraits of Mr. Crisp he has succeeded beyond all his former works; they are all different, yet all strikingly like, animated, expressive & handsome. I never saw likenesses more agreeable, yet more just. Mrs. Gast is like à faire rire!—which it is impossible not to do when looking at her Picture, which, however, is by no means flattered. His flattery, as I reproach him eternally, is all for *me*; not only in the phiz, but the back Ground, which he has made very beautiful; & as to my Dress, which I have left to himself, he has never been tired of altering & gracing it. It is now the black vandyke Gown, with slashed lilac sleeves, & very elegant.

Edward probably thought that he was presenting an artistic truth, even if, to make it apparent, he must paint a fairer flesh. What he captured was a modest, elusive, Evelina-like quality, probably that which in its day disarmed Dr. Johnson and charmed old gentlemen like Mr. Crisp, Sir Joshua Reynolds, Jacob Bryant, Owen Cambridge, Windham, and George III, captivated even such honest knuckle-heads as Mr. Barlow, or the shy, retiring Edward Francesco himself.

In late September Fanny returned to Ipswich, but a few weeks after the birth of Susan's child (October 5, 1782) she joined Mrs. Thrale, who had been waiting for her at Brighton, where Fanny remained till near the end of November. For the first time in over two years she could take 'a change of air' without an inquiry from Chessington about the progress of her book or qualms of conscience about disappointing her father. Mr. Belfield's complaints to Cecilia about the pangs and sufferings of the hack writer coincide so exactly with those expressed by Fanny herself in her letters of the previous years to her sisters, that the passage may be considered no less dramatic than autobiographical. It may serve as her final comment on the composition of the *opus* in which it occurs:

> . . . to write by rule, to compose by necessity, to make the understanding, nature's first gift, subservient to interest, that meanest offspring of art!—when weary, listless, spiritless, to rack the head for invention, the memory for images, and the fancy for ornament and allusion; and when the mind is wholly occupied by its own affections and affairs, to call forth all its faculties for foreign subjects, uninteresting discussions, or fictitious incidents!— Heavens! what a life of struggle between the head and the heart! how cruel, how unnatural a war between the intellects and the feelings!

Yet fame followed fast upon her effort. So reliable a witness as Mrs. Barbauld testified that 'next to the balloon Miss B[urney was] the object of public curiosity'. In the public rooms at Brighton Fanny could feel the pointing fingers. 'Most violent was the staring and whispering as I passed and repassed.' 'That's the famous Miss Burney! That's she!' 'Had any body told her 2 or 3 years ago', remarked Susan, that 'such a *misfortune* would have befallen *her,* the most shy & retired of human creatures, could she even have believed it?', The favour of the 'Blues & the Tons' was contagious. 'Oh, ma'am, you don't know what a favour this is, to see you!' said Mrs. Thrale's milliner. 'I have longed for it so long. It is quite a comfort to me, indeed!' Apparently everyone was reading her book, from the Queen to mantua-makers and tradeswomen, who, seeing all the ladies they served 'quite distracted' about *Cecilia,* procured copies for themselves. Mrs. Twining read it *'twice in a breath.* As soon as she had finished she began again.' 'Who will read our Histories of Music & our commentaries upon *Aristotle* at *this* rate?' archly asked Mr. Twining. Mrs. Chapone also read the novel twice—once for the story, and once more for the moral sentiments. Not even the opera house, which in November, 1782, Dr. Burney found so much improved that he thought himself in Italy ('so much symmetry & Elegance!'), not even the music pleased him more than the praise he heard of *Cecilia.* Everyone there had read *Cecilia,* even his old friend Lady Mary Duncan, who he suspected had read no other book except the Bible.

One evening in December, 1782, at Miss Monckton's fashionable house in Charles Street, Berkeley Square, it seemed to Mr. Burke that Fanny Burney's fame must have reached its zenith. So fashionable was her book and so much was she mentioned that the aged Dowager Lady Galway, who usually kept to her seat by the fire, receiving nobody, hobbled across the room to peek at the little figure who also kept quietly to one place, and who was so gallantly supported by kind old Sir Joshua, the witty and satiric Mr. Metcalfe, Miss Monckton herself, Dr. Johnson, and Mr. Burke. Among them they managed to tell her that Mr. Crisp's former acquaintance, the Dowager Duchess of Portland, who had read 'no Modern Book of entertainment for so long', had praised *Cecilia*; that the aged Mrs. Delany, who no longer expected any pleasure from novels, had read it three times; and finally that Mr. Gibbon had gone through the five volumes in a day. Here were laurels enough! And Fanny described them in full for Susan's pleasure and the satisfaction of the old gentleman at Chessington: 'My dear daddy and Kitty, are you not doubly glad you so kindly hurried me upstairs to write?'

The time was still good for a novel. 'Good novels amongst the bad, "*apparent rari nantes in gurgite vasto*".' So artfully, moreover, was *Cecilia* contrived, that through one or another of its components—the satire on the manners of the times, moral lessons, the 'tender pathetic', or the story—it seemed to please everywhere.

In the eighteenth century only the lost souls did not weep. The response of tears was the indication of benevolence and of the right feeling heart, and the ability of the author to evoke them was one criterion of success. 'Misses must cry or it's nothing!' Here *Cecilia* did not fail. 'It has drawn iron tears down cheeks that were never wetted by pity before', said Mr. Twining. 'As to myself, Cecilia has done just what she pleas'd with me; I laughed & cried, (for I am one of the blubberers—) when she bade me.' There were ladies unnumbered appearing late at balls and dinners with red eyes and noses; Lord Ferrars, who 'cried violently'; and many others, who, like the Dowager Duchess of Portland and Mrs. Delany, read and wept together. 'Oh, Mrs. Delany, shall you ever forget how we cried?'

Fanny Burney knew the literature of her age, the theatre, and the public who went to weep over Mrs. Siddons as Belvidera or Jane Shore. She knew at least one source of contemporary tears and she tended to fashion the crises and harrowing denouements of her novels on the pathetic finales of the she-tragedies of Nicholas Rowe and others or on the mad scenes of eighteenth-century Shakespeare. How much the stage was in her mind as she wrote such melodramatic scenes is indicated in the closing chapters of *Cecilia,* where the heroine emerges as an Ophelia-like creature of innocence and beauty gone mad with harsh usage and pain, and where her lover (and husband) young Delvile, the immediate source of her late miseries and distress, finds words for his contrition in utterances reminiscent of Hamlet. 'Well, then,—I may grieve, perhaps, hereafter.' Shades of Shakespeare hover again as Delvile stands over the expiring girl so much ill-used of late but 'sweet even in the arms of death and insanity'. Scarcely indeed is the eighteenth-century lover outdone by the Prince of Denmark: 'Peace and kindred angels are watching to receive thee.' In the end Cecilia does not die, or remain mad, or float dead upon the waters, but the reader, having wept tremendously, is the better for having endured such crises—crises that had a functional as well as a cathartic effect, since partly through them the elder Mr. Delvile was constrained to abandon his objections to the marriage and the long woes could close.

Such scenes no longer move us to tears, but may appear overwrought, hollow, farcical, and falsely heroic. Having their origin in the stage rather than in life, they must be at least once removed from reality. If Fanny Burney had succeeded in depicting emotional crises or great emotions as accurately after 'life and nature' as she had been able to draw minor characters and situations, she would indeed have added many cubits to her stature as a novelist. Even as it was, not all of her high action failed. The Vauxhall scene with its hurrying excitement, its lurid and desperate merry-making in the teeth of ruin, and the abrupt cessation with Harrel's suicide are credible even now.

The laughter that, according to contemporary testimony, made amends for the tears was confined largely to the minor action, where characters like Miss Larolles, Honoria Pemberton, Mr. Meadows, Mrs. Belfield, Hobson, and Simkins afford comic relief, choric comment, and, at the same time, a telling satire on manners. Here, as in the journals, new or absurd personages were introduced by a *character* in the technical sense followed by revealing specimens of dialogue exhibiting the character in action.

Formal character-sketches were sometimes given to a fictional commentator, Mr. Gosport, 'a man of good parts, and keen satire',—one who, 'minute in his observations', like Mrs. Thrale or Miss Burney herself, made 'the *minutiae* of absurd characters' his study. He divided the *ton*-misses into two classes, the SUPERCILIOUS and the VOLUBLE, and, as 'chronologer of the modes', supplied a sketch of the rude and negligent fop Mr. Meadows and of Captain Aresby, who belonged to the sect of the JARGONISTS. The *ton* thus anatomized was made to reveal itself in lively dialogue. Nothing had struck Mr. Burke more in reading Fanny's book than 'the admirable skill' with which she made her 'ingenious characters' known 'by their own words'. Thus the voluble Miss Larolles:

'Lord, my dear creature, who'd have thought of seeing you here? I was never so surprised in my life! I really thought you was gone into a convent, it's so extreme long since I've seen you. But of all things in the world, why was you not at Lady Nyland's last assembly? I thought of asking Mrs. Harrel fifty times why you did not come, but it always went out of my head. You've no notion how excessively I was disappointed.'

'You are very obliging,' said Cecilia laughing, 'but I hope, since you so often forgot it, the disappointment did not much lessen your entertainment.'

'O Lord no! I was never so happy in my life. There was such a crowd, you could not move a finger. Every body in the world was there. You've no idea how delightful it was. I thought verily I should have fainted with the heat.'

'That was delightful indeed! And how long did you stay?'

'Why we danced till three in the morning. We began with Cotillions, and finished with country dances. It was the most elegant thing you ever saw in your life; every thing quite in style. I was so monstrously fatigued, I could hardly get through the last dance. I really thought I should have dropped down dead. Only conceive dancing five hours in such a monstrous crowd! I assure you when I got home my feet were all blisters. You have no idea how they smarted.'

Her sprightliest conversation, however, is provoked by the languid fop, Mr. Meadows ('a real and common character'). The reciprocal effect of his absent-mindedness (he is 'so excessive absent you've no notion') and Miss Larolles's loquacity is one of the sources of laughter in the comic sections.

The foibles, philosophy, and idiom of the London citizenry were represented in Mr. Hobson, a retired 'man of business' (formerly a bricklayer and a landlord), and his cringing friend Mr. Simkins. According to contemporary testimony Mr. Hobson was drawn with no less verisimilitude than Miss Larolles, and is in his own right and in his role as choric commentator a truly comic figure. Though his function is the somewhat traditional one of the clown in tragedy, he comes stalwart and fresh from the London streets and pleasure-gardens of the seventies—just such a character as Garrick may have acted out for the amusement of the young Burneys on one of his morning visits to Poland Street or St. Martin's Street. Cecilia first caught sight of Mr. Hobson at the Vauxhall Gardens:

A fat, sleek, vulgar-looking man, dressed in a bright purple coat, with a deep red waistcoat, and a wig bulging far from his head with small round curls, while his plump face and person announced plenty and good living, and an air of defiance spoke the fullness of his purse, strutted boldly up to Mr. Harrel, and accosting him in a manner that shewed some diffidence of his reception, but none of his right, said 'Sir your humble servant'.

His criteria of values ('what i'n't fit for business, i'n't of no value'), his shrewdness, litigiousness, natural prejudices (patriotism and contempt for foreigners), his good-heartedness (where his rights, monetary or civil, were not infringed), his sturdy independence, self-indulgence, and the senticious absurdity of some of his choric comment all appear in self-revealing and discursive conversation. In spite of his respect for money he will have no part of the self-denial and miserliness of Mr. Briggs.

'Let every man have his own proposal . . . for my part, I take every morning a large bowl of water, and souse my whole head in it; and then when I've rubbed it dry, on goes my wig, and I am quite fresh and agreeable: and then I take a walk in Tottenham Court Road as far as the Tabernacle, or thereabouts, and snuff in a little fresh country air, and then I come back, with a good wholesome appetite, and in a fine breathing heat, asking the young lady's pardon; and I enjoy my pot of fresh tea, and my round of hot toast and butter, with as good a relish as if I was a Prince.'

He by no means approves of Mr. Briggs, who tries to live on water-gruel.

> 'When a man's got above the world, where's the harm of living a little genteel? as to a round of toast and butter, and a few oysters, fresh opened, by way of a damper before dinner, no man need be ashamed of them, provided he pays as he goes.'

He is the free-born Englishman:

> 'For what I say is this, what a man earns, he earns, and it's no man's business to enquire what he spends, for a free-born Englishman is his own master by the nature of the law, and as to his being a subject, why a Duke is no more, nor a Judge, nor the Lord High Chancellor, and the like of those; which makes it tantamount to nothing, being he is answerable to nobody by the right of Magna Charta: except in cases of treason, felony, and that.'

As for a Lord,

> 'I am one of them that lay no great stress upon that, unless he has got a good long purse of his own, and then, to be sure, a Lord's no bad thing. But . . . nothing, in comparison of a good income. . . . A man's a man, and for one man to worship another is quite out of law.'

A man's a man for a' that:

> 'I've got a fair character in the world, and wherewithal to live by my own liking. And what I have is my own, and all I say is, let every one say the same, for that's the way to fear no man, and face the d—l.'

If Mr. Hobson were to speak his notion, his last word would be this:

> 'The best way to thrive in the world is to get money; but how is it to be got? Why by business: for business is to money, what fine words are to a lady, a sure road to success.'

In the opinion of the *Monthly Review,* 'the self-importance of a rich tradesman is represented to the life'; and there was no lack of contemporary testimony to the verisimilitude of Mr. Hobson. Dr. Johnson supported him 'at the Head of the tribe'; Mrs. Thrale had often seen him and his friend the cringing Simkins in the Borough. 'I am confident they were both canvassed last year; they are not representations of life, they are the life itself.' Mr. Twining thought them 'admirable pieces of nature. Characters that every soul must rec-

ognize, & nobody has drawn.' He also praised the lawyer from the Egglestons as another 'portrait of *exact* nature': 'not in the whole book, nor in any other book is there a juster piece of natural delineation.'

Mrs. Belfield was 'so grossly natural, so mean in her Ideas, so confined, so determined' as to resemble, according to Mrs. Thrale, 'half the *decent* women of the Borough'. Mr. Hobson with all his absurd sententiousness was not without common sense and a certain square-footed dignity. Mrs. Belfield, according to Fanny Burney's conception, lacked good sense, and appeared in *Cecilia* as the vulgar exponent of ambition and folly. She had encouraged her son to forsake his father's shop and 'proper station' and to rise in the world. The career of young Belfield himself is an extended study based on notions that Fanny had imbibed from current literature, the semi-ethical courtesy-books, didactic works like the *Rambler,* and of late, of course, from conversations at Streatham, where an Old Philosopher sat discoursing with his Mistress and her company on order and subordination versus anarchy and savagery, on reason versus the imagination, genius, or enthusiasm. Young Belfield is a speaking picture of the woes to be incurred by the rebel, the genius, and the enthusiast—a son, said Mrs. Belfield regretfully,

> 'that I thought to have seen living like a prince, and sending his own coach for me to dine with him! . . . for when he was quite a child in arms, the people used all to say he was born to be a gentleman, and would live to make many a fine lady's heart ache.'

Such were the characters drawn from both high and low life that impressed Fanny Burney's contemporaries by their realism. So exactly were they represented that *Cecilia* seemed to many, as it seemed to Mrs. Thrale, 'a Camera Obscura in a Window of Piccadilly'. 'No character appears (Miss Beverley and Albany excepted) that every day's experience does not discover a similar', wrote Miss Burney's critic in the *English Review.* 'To her own observation she appears to be solely indebted for the characters of the novel. All of them seem fairly purchased at the great work-shop of life, and not the second-hand, vamped-up shreds and patches of the Monmouth-street of modern romance.'

Yet Fanny Burney always affirmed that the characters in her novels and plays were copies of *nature* rather than of *individuals.* As preliminary sketches that have survived often show, she first envisaged her fictitious personages as *types* or *abstracts,* epitomizing some phenomenon of manners, a condition, quality, or set of follies or foibles. If one may judge from the extant scraps of paper showing tentative lists of *dramatis personae* for her later novels and plays and from the internal evidence of *Cecilia* itself, the preliminary cast for the minor action of that novel was almost certainly first filled with such bloodless cyphers as a Miss Rattle, a Miss Voluble, a Miss Supercilious, a Mr. Nonchalant, a Mrs. Vulgarity, and a retired tradesman (a 'rich business leaver-off')—a cast who only later appeared as Honoria Pemberton, Miss Larolles, Miss Leeson, Mr. Meadows, Mrs. Belfield, and Mr. Hobson. Having first conceived the social scene in the abstract, and having thus secured representatives of general or universal truth, she had next to put the shadowy states, faults, foibles, or qualities into action. Here she could rely on her long habits of observation, her keen ears, and her retentive memory, and she succeeded in supplying action and dialogue so credible, natural, and realistic that her readers took many of her characters for what they were not, copies of individuals, and were forever looking about for the originals. As Lady Hales read the book, she thought she could 'hear some people chattering their nonsense at random'.

> 'O, . . . said Mrs. Walsingham, . . . I meet her characters every Day: Miss Larolles in particular.'

> 'O, said Mrs. Pery, I have seen more Miss Larolles's than any character I ever saw drawn in my life.'

> 'All the Misses that go to see Mrs. Siddons, said Mrs. Walsingham, talk like Miss Larolles, they are so *hot*, & so *delighted*, they *cry* so & find it so *charming*. And then Mr. Meadows—'

> 'O, the *Meadows* are a tribe as numerous as it is hateful, said Mrs. Montagu.'

Even Albany, who resembles Dr. Burney's Moravian friend Mr. Hutton and who seems to have a literary antecedent in Sir Launcelot Greaves, had a counterpart suggested for him. Mr. George Cambridge knew just such a philanthropist in a benevolent 'old half-pay officer', who wandered about St. James's Park looking for persons in distress and relieving poverty with borrowed funds.

Mr. Briggs, a caricature of a miser (probably suggested by the sculptor Nollekens), the villain Mr. Delvile (said to exist only by virtue of his Ruling Passion, Pride), the exponents of low life, even the members of the lively social set, have all at times been criticized as mere sets of foibles and must, perhaps, yield to the charge. Taken separately, they are not, indeed, great characters, but slight characters are not without very good effect in the large satiric canvas that Fanny wished to paint. In large canvases, like those of Dickens, for instance, the use of caricature makes for greater clarity. It makes also for the ready comprehension on which comic effect must depend. By the photographic depiction of ridiculous foibles, speech, and action, Fanny hoped indeed to amuse the reader, but she intended also to castigate follies. By 1782 she had had an op-

portunity to observe the social scene at Bath, Brighton, and, to some extent, in the London drawing-rooms, and her second novel mirrors the fashionable people she met there. Cecilia's comment on 'how ill the coldness of their hearts accorded with the warmth of their professions' matches Fanny's impression as given in a journal-letter to Susan: 'My coldness in return to all these sickening, heartless, *ton*-led people, I try not to repress.' She proceeded, therefore, to castigate heartlessness and, after that, insincerity and affectation. In low life she discerned the same heartlessness and, in addition, selfishness, meanness, turbulence, and frequent recourse to litigation. Her pen—pictures of vulgarity are attacks on such propensities. In spite of the moral purpose, the lively actors of the comic scenes seem to walk straight from life to the page, and they are as entertaining today as they ever were.

The central action of ***Cecilia, or Memoirs of an Heiress*** follows the adventures of Cecilia Beverley for two years, from the age of twenty-one when she emerged from the country estates of her family to reside with her guardians in London, until she marries young Delvile. The terminal point of the action is marriage. The chief retarding factor is family pride: first, that of the Beverleys (in particular, that of an uncle, who bequeathed Cecilia a fortune of £3,000 per annum on condition that, if she should marry, her husband must take her name); and, secondly, that of the elder Delvile, scion of a noble family, who, though impoverished, values his son's name above Cecilia's fortune or, of course, the happy culmination of young love. This resolution is delayed further by the machinations of a self-interested (if rather unreal) villain Monckton, by the forwardness of Mrs. Belfield, and finally by errors and indiscretions on the part of the heroine herself, who, though closer to the courtesy-book girl than Evelina was, is still subject to human failings.

Now that Fanny was known, her original impulse to draw her heroines from nature seemed almost stultified by the compulsion to invent a novel and a heroine meeting the indispensable qualification for novels and novelists in her time, that is, *moral utility*. She felt that she must draw a model of behaviour, but the twofold purpose, to draw a paragon and to draw from nature, could not be easily reconciled. Moreover, the paragon of behaviour was not without great difficulty made to enter into interesting action. As the *Monthly Review* of 1782 noted, it was odd to see such a girl as Cecilia in the company of the Harrels at Vauxhall. Cecilia had lost the natural youthfulness, demureness, and piquancy of Evelina. Leaves from the courtesy-books cling about her, sometimes making odd contrasts not only with *nature* but also with violent scenes reminiscent of the she-tragedies of the age. Improving paragraphs on reason (with which, we are assured, Cecilia was endowed) scarcely prepare the way for imprudent love, temporary madness, and distresses worthy of Belvidera or Jane Shore. Fanny's inventive muse had frequented quiet and sheltered places, had liked slyness and 'snugness'. But now Fanny had been dragged into the limelight, and Cecilia was the result. Happily, at least, we have the testimony of 'that honest gentlewoman' Mrs. Chapone that Miss Burney was 'more like her first Heroine than her second'.

Through the exigencies of a plot that took Cecilia into the homes of three guardians and on many another round of visits, as well as to assemblies, masquerades, and routs, and on excursions to the opera, the theatre, bookstalls, and the pleasure-gardens of Vauxhall and Ranelagh, the novelist secured an opportunity to depict a varied social scene, a cross-section of the London of her time, still valuable as a genuine record of customs and manners. According to Dr. Johnson, moreover, one could hear in *Cecilia* 'the free full flow of London talk'. The conversational pieces taking place in the City, the comic dialogue of the pump-room (though probably not Cecilia's stilted idiom) may be taken as tape-recordings of contemporary speech.

By the criterion of the age, moral utility, *Cecilia* came off very well. Many young ladies, usually forbidden access to so dangerous a genre as the novel, were allowed to read it. Even the Princesses, as Fanny discovered later, were permitted to read *Cecilia*—at least after it was 'sanctioned by a Bishop's recommendation,—the late Dr. Ross of Exeter'. Even Cecilia's faults were useful, for the sufferings they entailed came tearfully home to the business and bosoms of young ladies and served as warning guides.

The crowning praise of the work was, in Fanny's opinion, that of Mrs. Delany and the Duchess of Portland.

> 'If you speak of the Harrels, and of the morality of the book,' cried the Duchess, with a solemn sort of voice, 'we shall, indeed, never give Miss Burney her due: so striking, so pure, so genuine, so instructive.'

> Mrs. Delany, with the eagerness of fifteen—though 83!—exclaimed: '*No* Book ever was so *useful* as this; because none other that is so *good*, has been so universally read by young as well as old.'

It was only with the greatest difficulty that Mrs. Delany had gained the unwilling consent of the Duchess to have the authoress presented to her, so chary was she of artists, writers, and their kind. She had 'a prejudice against female novel writers, which *almost* amounted to a *horror of them*'; yet the moral tone of *Cecilia* and unlooked-for modesty in the authoress undermined old prejudices a little. This novel could not be dismissed as the trash common to the circulating libraries or be banned for its immorality. On the contrary, said the Duchess, 'it should be the study of youth Both for Precept & Example'.

> 'It is so innocent, & as [Mr. Burke] says, so pure, with all its contrasts of gaiety & humour, that if I had now the care of any young persons, it should be the first Book I would put into their hands.'

One citadel at least had been taken. Old prejudices began to give a little, though for the wrong reason. Fanny could scarcely keep the tears from her eyes 'at so solemn a sanction'. This accurate analysis and the appreciation of her purpose by 'characters so respectable, so moral, so high in public estimation, & so aged, with Mr. Burke as their Guide', constitute the last words, as she told Mr. Crisp, 'hear what I may, that I can ever write upon Cecilia'. 'I close forever my Pen as Panegyric Recorder.'

Edward A. Bloom   (essay date 1968)

SOURCE: An introduction to *Evelina; or, the History of a Young Lady's Entrance into the World*, by Frances Burney, edited by Edward A. Bloom, Oxford University Press, 1968, pp. vii-xxxi.

[*In the following essay, Bloom dissects* Evelina, *evaluating its characterization, structure, and critical reception.*]

'This year was ushered in by a grand and most important event! At the latter end of January, the literary world was favoured with the first publication of the ingenious, learned, and most profound Fanny Burney! I doubt not but this memorable affair will, in future times, mark the period whence chronologers will date the zenith of the polite arts in this island!' Thus the author of *Evelina* announced in her diary for 1778 the appearance of her novel. And thus—playfully ironic—she continued the game writing had been for her since her tenth year. Despite herself she was a better prophet than she would have ever dared hope; yet, morbidly timid, she shrank from the success that threatened her privacy and stigmatized herself as 'the very cowardly Writer'. When, in that historic first year, Mrs. Thrale added her to the collection of Streatham celebrities, Fanny was horrified to find *Evelina* on display. 'I *hid* it under other Books,' she confessed, 'for I should *Die*,—or *Faint* at least,—if any body was to pick it up innocently while I am here.'

To be sure, Fanny Burney could hug herself in silent pleasure while overhearing the praises of her novel. But she thought of fame as an enchantment that must end; and she dreaded the harsher reality of being exposed as the creator of *Evelina*. 'What will all this come to?—where will it end? and when and how shall I wake from the vision of such splendid success? for

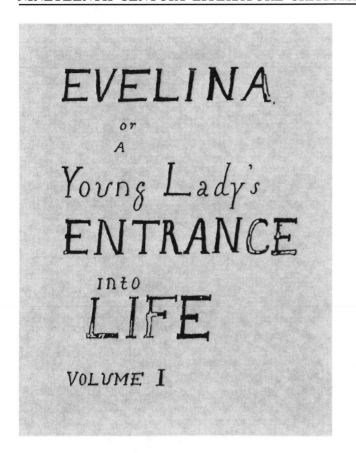

Burney's draft of a title page for her first novel.

I hardly know how to believe it real.' Anonymity, her 'dear old obscurity', was an illusory shield against public criticism. 'I am frightened out of my wits from the terror of being attacked *as an author,* and therefore *shirk,* instead of *seeking,* all occasions of being drawn into notice.' And in the journal which she kept for her sympathetic younger sister Susan she wrote: 'But pray Heaven may spare me the horror irrecoverable of personal abuse! Let them criticise, cut, slash without mercy my book, and let them neglect me; but may God avert my becoming a public theme of ridicule!'

Macaulay's assumption is far too facile, even cynical, when he associates Fanny's passion for concealment with an intention of safely avoiding disgrace while seeking fame. Her love of privacy was obsessive, despite the undeniable and natural pleasure of seeing her words in print. Like many shy and talented persons, she discovered resources of self-expression in art which otherwise would have remained buried under the inhibitions of personality and breeding. In the Burney household she had been brought up prudishly, like her own heroine, to respect the virtues of discretion and correct conduct; and her fear was that these could not be reconciled with a public performance such as *Evelina*. Had she been more self-confident and less the child of a culture that still looked askance at fiction, she

would have grasped that her novel was as blameless as her life.

She learned to read late. Writing, however—or at least invention—was an early accomplishment, for by the age of ten she was already afflicted by *cacoethes scribendi,* 'an incurable itch to write'. Before long she was pouring forth an indiscriminate stream of poems, plays, and stories; but fearing ridicule, she confided at first only in Susan. Her delight in writing was alloyed by a phobia that her secret pastime was unworthy. Hence when she was fifteen, '*the silent observant Miss Fanny*' performed the melancholy ritual of destroying all of her scribblings in a bonfire. Included in this prudential sacrifice was **The History of Caroline Evelyn**, whose heroine was the unfortunate mother of Evelina. Happily, however, the infant survived the flames: the idea took a new form and eleven years later the irresistibly beautiful young woman from Berry Hill entered the world.

Impersonally, in **The Memoirs of Doctor Burney**, Fanny said she 'had written the little book, like innumerable of its predecessors that she had burnt, simply for her private recreation. She had printed it for a frolic, to see how a production of her own would figure in that author-like form. But that was the whole of her plan.' She was motivated by the same spirit of fun when she drew her sisters and brother Charles into the innocent conspiracy. She thus wrote the first two volumes of Evelina's history in a disguised hand; for having transcribed Dr. Burney's *General History of Music*, she wished to avoid any possibility of identification. Now the game was too good to be delayed, and Charles, with more ebullience than wisdom, acted as Fanny's agent to find a publisher for the incomplete novel. Their first choice, the reputable bookseller Dodsley, refused to consider the anonymous work. Thereupon the family cabal, 'half-amused, half-provoked', decided to 'forego the *eclat* of the west end of town, and to try their fortune with the urbanity of the city'.

Still insisting upon anonymity, the casual and ingenuous cabalists next offered the book to Thomas Lowndes. His answer, they requested, was to be addressed to 'Mr. King' and left at the Orange Coffee House. Thus, in December 1776, the publication of *Evelina* became assured. Lowndes, who dealt widely in novels and perhaps had a shrewder instinct than Dodsley for the popular tastes of the day, was willing to gamble with his time. On 23 December he agreed to read the manuscript, optimistically noting that 'now is the time for a Novel'. And then, only six days later, he wrote tersely, man to man: 'Sir, I've read and like the Manuscript and if you'll send the rest I'll soon run it over.' What he saw, in other words, must have been only a part of the two volumes. Lowndes's speedy reply obviously was bracing; and Charles, preposterously disguised, at once delivered the remainder of the manuscript to Fleet Street.

By 17 January the bookseller had read the material and agreed to publish it, but only if that final volume were submitted. 'I would rather,' he wrote, 'print in July than now to Publish an Unfinished book.' More than fifty years later Fanny recalled being so disappointed by Lowndes's 'priggish punctilio' that she almost lost her zest for authorship. Her account in the *Memoirs,* however, is more restrained than that in her private *Juvenile Journal* for 1777 where she recorded the physical difficulties of stealthy composition. 'Now, this man,' she complained, 'knowing nothing of my situation, supposed, in all probability, that I could seat myself quietly at my bureau, and write on with all expedition and ease, till the work was finished. But so different was the case, that I had hardly time to write half a page in a day; and neither my health nor inclination would allow me to continue my *nocturnal* scribbling for so long a time as to write first, and then copy, a whole volume. I was therefore obliged to give the attempt and affair entirely over for the present.' Fanny Burney's 'writing mania' was not easily suppressed, however, and regardless of her private feelings she accepted Lowndes's terms, 'though I should have been better pleased to have *felt the pulse* of the public' before proceeding with the final volume.

The return to authorship was complicated by scruples about taking this irrevocable step without her father's knowledge. Apprehensively, therefore, she told him about 'her secret little work' and begged that he would not ask to see it. Far from being disturbed, Dr. Burney was amused by his daughter's whim to appear in print and restrained his curiosity to defer to her modesty. He asked only that her agent, Charles, be discreet and that she preserve her anonymity.

As Fanny reported the confrontation in her *Juvenile Journal*: 'He made no sort of objection to my having my own way in total secrecy and silence to all the world. Yet I am easier in not taking the step, without his having this little knowledge of it, as he is contented with my telling him I shall never have the courage to let him know its name.' Armed with this parental tolerance (which Macauley severely reproved) Fanny went back to her writing table. In due time the third volume was completed. Her cousin Edward (in the absence of Charles) delivered it. On 11 November 1777 Lowndes offered twenty guineas (a sum amended in the printed account to twenty pounds), and promised that he would 'without loss of time put it to press'. So the deed was done; the author and her fellow conspirators began an anxious wait. Unconsciously perhaps she had been thinking of herself as well as of her heroine when she wrote the final letter of the novel: 'All is over my dearest Sir, and the fate of your Evelina is decided!'

On 7 January Lowndes sent unbound sheets (though not all) to 'Mr. Grafton' at the Orange Coffee House, making evident his keenness for early publication. But he asked that the author 'should first revise it, or the reviewers may find a flaw'. Fanny prepared a list of errata which Lowndes, too much in haste to make the corrections inserted at the beginning of the first volume. Later on 2 July she requested that 'if ever the book went through another Edition' she be given 'timely notice', because she 'had some corrections and alterations to propose'. This is a more confident Fanny Burney, finally responding to success with a degree of pride and even authority: her desire to perfect the text is obvious. Implicitly also—though actually prompted by her father—she is reproaching Lowndes for seeming indifference to a best-selling author: he had not told her the publication date of the first edition (a fact which she discovered only accidentally through a newspaper advertisement); and he had delayed sending her a bound set of *Evelina.* The bookseller was both reasonable and placatory. After all, he had been unable to get in touch with the elusive author (who he still thought was a man). Flatteringly he added: 'the Great World send here to buy Evelina. A polite Lady said Do, Mr. Lowndes, give me Evelina, I am treated as unfashionable for not having read it. I think the Impression will be sold by Christmas.' Reporting this to Susan a few days later, Fanny crowed: 'Did you ever know the like?—pray tell my dear Father all this.—no, don't mention it, for I'll write to him myself.'

By now Dr. Burney, aware of his daughter's triumph was angered by Lowndes's inattention and by the small sum he had paid her. Eventually, after the third edition, she realized a total of thirty pounds for this extraordinarily popular novel, but at the time she was satisfied. The cost of the three volumes was 7*s.* 6*d.* sewed, or 9*s.* bound in calf. Before the end of 1779 five editions of *Evelina* (one of them pirated in Dublin) had gone out to an intrigued public, a record which justified Lowndes's acumen if not his niggardliness. The novel, she wrote to the family friend Samuel ('Daddy') Crisp on 4 May 1779, 'continues to sell in a most wonderful manner; a fourth edition is preparing, with cuts, designed by [John Hamilton] Mortimer just before he died, and executed [i.e. engraved] by [John] Hall and [Francesco] Bartolozzi'.

Fanny recalled for her father in 1796 that the first edition of *Evelina* consisted of 800 copies, the second of 500, and the third of 1,000. 'What the following have been I have never heard. The sale from that period became more flourishing than the publisher cared to announce.' Her memory was not quite accurate, to judge from a letter Lowndes wrote to Dr. Burney, in January 1779, when her authorship had become common knowledge. The bookseller at this time was preparing 1,500 copies of which 500 would be a third edition, and 1,000—with the cuts—a fourth. He complained that Bartolozzi was being laggard and asked Dr. Burney to speed him along. Lowndes, who had just rejected the manuscripts of three novels after cursory readings, obviously knew he had a bargain in *Evelina*. But had he been more generous, his bargain would have been greater: *Cecilia* was brought out in 1782 by another publisher, who paid Fanny £250 for the copyright and—capitalizing on the reputation of the earlier novel—issued a first edition of 2,000 copies.

The popularity of *Evelina* was not confined to English-speaking readers; editions began to appear almost at once on the Continent. For instance, a Leipzig publishing firm brought out in 1779 a German translation, *Evelina oder eines jungen Frauenzimmers Eintritt in die Welt*. And in Amsterdam the first volume of *Evelina; eene Engelsche Geschiedenis* appeared in 1780, the second in 1782, and the third in 1785. Both translations are complete except for the omission of the dedicatory poem and the letter to the reviewers. An edition in English also, this one issued in Dresden in 1788, included on the title-page the fact that *Evelina* was 'By Miss Burney'. The 'dear old obscurity' had long since vanished.

Personal detachment, as Fanny Burney had been afraid, became an impossible luxury. A much greater ego than hers was needed to cope with the invasion of privacy that always accompanies public status. Hence we find Crisp attempting to rally his 'Fannikin' in November of 1778. Understanding her timidity, he also argued that 'surely these painful feelings ought to go off when the salts of general applause are continually held under the nose. It is then time to follow your friend Johnson's advice, and learn to be a swaggerer, at least so far as to be able to face the world, and not be ashamed of the distinction you have fairly earned, especially when it is apparent you do not court it.' Johnson's advice had been stated somewhat more trenchantly when he was arming Fanny for a meeting with the redoubtable Elizabeth Montagu. 'Down with her, Burney!' he cried, '—down with her!—spare her not!—attack her, fight her, and down with her at once! . . . always fly at the eagle!'

Such counsel, while well meant, was too militant for one who regretted, 'the more the book is drawn into notice, the more exposed it becomes to criticism and remark'. Like Crisp and Johnson, Mrs. Thrale tried to fortify her, to make her less afraid of notoriety. After a pamphlet, *Warley: a Satire* [by the Reverend George Huddesford], named 'dear little Burney' the author of *Evelina*, Fanny was extravagantly upset; and Mrs. Thrale futilely urged that she consider the matter dispassionately. 'And is that an injury?' she said. 'Surely you are not yet to learn how highly that little sweet book has been praised, admired, and esteemed by people whose good word should at least weigh with you

against such a wretch as I hear this is, who has mentioned your name irrevently—for I do not perceive he had done anything else at last.' Still, as Fanny told Crisp early in 1779, she was 'shocked, mortified, grieved, and confounded' to learn about the pamphlet, which apparently she had not seen. 'I had always dreaded as a real evil my name's getting into print—but to be lugged into a pamphlet! . . . So now the murder's out!'

Cry 'murder' all she would, Fanny simply could not draw a curtain between herself and the world: her fame was not hers to control, and life was becoming complex. Understandably, the novice anticipated the public reviews with a terror that she would 'be horribly mauled' and—even worse—identified. But she had to admit that she had 'come off with flying Colours'. In February 1778 the *London Review* noticed *Evelina* favourably; and in April the influential *Monthly Review* pronounced it 'one of the most sprightly, entertaining, and agreeable productions of this kind, which has of late fallen under our notice'. The reviewer did not like the characterization of Captain Mirvan, but this was only a minor cavil and Fanny copied the review into her journal. Then, in September, the *Critical Review* made flattering comparisons with Richardson, and stressed both the moral and comic vitality of *Evelina*.

Many years later Fanny recalled the critical reception of her first novel with gratification, although in retrospect she lamented the brevity of her notices. There was no doubt about it: *Evelina* had made a lasting mark; everyone was reading it; and some were even writing fan letters. One anonymous correspondent, from Snow Hill, requested a fourth volume. Rather snobbishly, Fanny commented, 'one would think the people on Snow Hill might think three volumes enough for what they are the better, and not desire a fourth to celebrate more Smiths and Branghtons'. Whether in admission or in irony, she also said about Snow Hill, 'I never knew the Public's place of residence before.'

She could write to Susan, '—you can't think how I tremble for what all this will end in! I verily think I had best stop where I am, and never again attempt writing: for after so much honour, so much success, how shall I bear a downfall?' But if success frightened it also titillated, serving as the source of both pride and amusement. Frequently, before her authorship was made public, her confederates in the Burney household would report to her the praises of *Evelina*'s readers; or she herself would silently listen to animated discussions about various characters and situations. For all her embarrassment, she was so delighted that occasionally she almost gave herself away. Later, as the centre of attention in the Streatham circle, she was left speechless by the praise of formidable personalities. In the private records of those visits, however, she released the buoyancy and excitement to which the triumph entitled her.

Sometimes, indeed, she played the game of being an uninvolved spectator and enjoyed herself with innocent egoism. Thus it was when Fanny and her mother went incognita to Lowndes's that they might hear what was being said about the author. When the bookseller admitted that he once thought *Evelina* had been written by Horace Walpole (as once Miss Humphries had attributed it to Christopher Anstey, author of *The New Bath Guide*), Fanny, almost overcome with merriment, 'was obliged to look out at the shop-door' until they were ready to leave. Another time she went with Edward to Bell's Circulating Library. She was too bashful to inquire about the book, but her cousin learned that *Evelina* was in all the circulating libraries. 'I have an exceeding odd sensation', she wrote on 26 March 1778, 'when I consider that it is now in the power of *any* and *every* body to read what I so carefully hoarded even from my best friends, till this last month or two,—and that a work which was so lately lodged, in all privacy in my bureau, may now be seen by every butcher and baker, cobler and tinker, throughout the three Kingdoms, for the small tribute of three pence.' From Charles, who was then in Reading, came word that *Evelina* was the craze of the provinces.

But being the restrained witness of her own celebrity could at times be unpleasant and even annoying. When, for instance, she had to read her novel to the unsuspecting Daddy Crisp, she lost her composure. Yet she was wryly amused—at least in her diary—when he alluded to it as 'only a trumpery novel', the work of an unknown writer. After all, this venerable friend whom she could forgive anything, had been 'greedily eager to go on with' the story. She was less tolerant of the vulgar reactions of some ladies who were thrilled to discover Fanny was the author of the novel. '"Very extraordinary, indeed!" said one—"Dear heart, who'd have thought it?" said another—"I never saw the like in my life!" said a third.' Contemptuous and snobbish as she at times tended to be, Fanny 'had almost thrown [herself] out of the window, in [her] eagerness to get out of the way of this gross and noisy applause'.

During the first six months of 1778, while most of the Burney family were gleefully following the fortunes of *Evelina*, Dr. Burney remained majestically oblivious to his daughter's achievement. The whispers, the knowing glances, the surreptitious 'confabulations', all these escaped him. Although he had not at first taken seriously either Fanny's literary ambition or the secrecy in which it was cloaked, he was anything but an indifferent parent. And he was distracted at this time by personal trials which were intensified by illness, first his own and then hers. While she was convalescing in Samuel Crisp's country home, Chessington Hall, her sister Charlotte wrote that their father had somehow got wind of Fanny's authorship.

The account of that discovery, described in the *Memoirs* and *Diary*, reveals Dr. Burney agitatedly reading the review in the *Monthly*, sending a servant to Lowndes's for *Evelina*, and beginning the novel with tear-filled eyes. Two female acquaintances, Lady Hales and Miss Coussmaker, thereafter read the novel with him and shared his enthusiasm. 'Upon my word,' he told Susan, 'I think it the very best novel I know excepting Fielding's, and, in some respects, *better* than his!' Dr. Burney, whose library (as Fanny notes in *The Wanderer*) contained one novel—*Amelia*—may of course be excused a father's partiality. However uninformed his critical judgements of fiction, he was always the fond champion of 'my daughter, the young Novelist', whether he was talking about *Evelina* or *Camilla*. In the former he particularly liked the letters of Villars and the characterization of Orville, but he was disturbed by Mirvan's roughness. As for Lady Hales and Miss Coussmaker, the tragic sadness of the encounter between Evelina and Sir John Belmont 'made them quite ill'.

In a manner worthy of Evelina herself the invalid reacted to her father's admiration 'with feelings of strong—and yet living gratitude'. His own natural pride was inflated during a weekly visit to the Thrale residence in Streatham, when Dr. Johnson (who had not yet read the novel) repeated the praises he had heard of it. Unable to contain himself, Dr. Burney came to Chessington and told his daughter, 'I have read your book, Fanny!—but you need not blush at it—it is full of merit—it is, really,—extraordinary!' Already in emotional turmoil, she was joyously stunned by his proposal, if Mrs. Thrale were pleased with the novel, to tell her the secret of its authorship. Hitherto she had been known vaguely to Mrs. Thrale as one of Dr. Burney's daughters. Now, unexpectedly, she was to be granted a seat in distinguished company. Nothing in her book, she remarked in the *Memoirs* of her father could be closer to romance.

With the introduction to Mrs. Thrale's sophisticated set, her world expanded immeasurably. The shy author was petted and lionized, a celebrity among celebrities. Privately her hostess characterized her as one 'who certainly must be a Girl of good Parts and some Knowledge of the World too'. *Evelina*, on the other hand, she thought 'flimzy'. Still, neither she nor the regular procession of visitors to Streatham seemed ever to have enough of the novel. Fanny noted with discomfort that Mrs. Thrale quoted endlessly; 'some or other part of the Book is àpropos to everything.' And as Dr. Burney reported, she was full of '*Ma foi's* jokes, the Captain's brutality, Squire Smith's gentility, Sir Clement's audaciousness, the Branghton's vulgarity, and Mother Selwyn's sharp knife, &c, &c.'

When eminent figures like Sir Joshua Reynolds and Edmund Burke joined the growing company of *Evelina*'s admirers, Fanny was elated. But no one's approbation meant more to her than that of Dr. Johnson: upon learning that he had read the book, she ran out on to the lawn at Chessington and danced around a mulberry tree. The elderly Johnson was indeed so intrigued by the characters—especially the vulgar ones—that he memorized their scenes and was convulsed with laughter. His favourite was Mr. Smith, whom he called 'the Holborn Beau' and by whose 'vulgar gentility' he was so taken that he ponderously imitated him. Although he liked the comedy, he rejoiced to find in the novel a seriousness of meaning worthy of Richardson. 'And all this comic humour of character . . . owes its effect to contrast; for without Lord Orville and Mr. Villars, and that melancholy and gentleman-like half-starved Scotchman, poor Macartney, the Branghtons, and the Duvals, would be less than nothing; for vulgarity, in its own unshadowed glare, is only disgusting.' He teased Fanny for having created 'that Scotch dog, Macartney', but he respected *Evelina* for the impression it gave of 'long experience and deep and intimate knowledge of the world'.

Despite the discrepancy in their ages, a friendship developed between Fanny and Johnson that transcended literary achievement. Yet *Evelina* was always there as a bond which somehow solidified their mutual esteem and affection. He recommended her book generously, but reproached her for neglecting him. 'She no more minds me', he complained to Mrs. Thrale, 'than if I were a Branghton.' Amusedly he wrote (in 1781), 'whatever Burney may think of the celerity of fame, the name of Evelina had never been heard at Lichfield, till I brought it. I am afraid my dear Townsmen will be mentioned in future days as the last part of this nation that was civilised.'

Almost twenty years after *Evelina* was published, Fanny gratefully recollected Johnson's 'powerful influence' on behalf of her novel. *Evelina*, she wrote to Dr. Burney, made its way without any significant help from the reviews. 'It was circulated only by the general public, till it reached, through that unbiased medium, Dr. Johnson and Mr. Burke, and thence it wanted no patron.' There is a nice irony in the association of these two great names; for, as she observed in the dedicatory epistle of *The Wanderer*, the merit of *Evelina* was one of the very few subjects on which they could agree.

When Evelina, in the sentimentalized words of her creator, made 'her first appearance upon the great and busy stage of life', she had 'a virtuous mind, a cultivated understanding, and a feeling heart'. At the same time, she revealed an 'ignorance of the forms, and inexperience in the manners, of the world'. Fanny Burney thus allowed her beautiful heroine (aged seventeen) about seven months in which to discover herself; to relate herself to the external demands of society and confirm the incorruptibility of disciplined innocence. Towards the achievement of this victory, as much social as moral, Evelina can draw upon dual resources: her own nature and the guidance of such high-minded teachers as the Reverend Arthur Villars and Lord Orville. Throughout the novel indeed, there is little doubt that she will succeed. The suspense—from incident to incident—inheres in the means, since the successful resolution of the conflict is assumed from the start.

Fanny Burney therefore built her novel upon a series of 'little incidents' which test Evelina's response to the newly found joys and frustrations, the tensions and satisfactions of worldliness. Although the situations are entertaining in and of themselves, their appeal is as much to the moral sense as to the imagination. Each episode becomes a tutorial adventure, providing Evelina with new experiences 'in the manners of the world'. These she must assimilate in a way that will bring wisdom to herself and honour to her teachers. More protected and so more fortunate than other fictional young women who had gone into the world—Defoe's Moll and Roxana, Marivaux's Marianne, or Richardson's Pamela—Evelina is never far from benign counsel or a sheltering friend. When distance reduces Villars's influence to affectionate abstraction, there are always Mrs. Mirvan and Lord Orville to abet her instinctive goodness with practicality.

Like any education, hers is cumulative, with virtue and self-awareness directed to social fulfillment. Being already endowed with virtue, she must now assure its preservation by storing up and applying the lessons of her moral odyssey. By the end of seven months her education, if not complete, has prepared her to take on the responsibilities of adulthood. No longer a child, she has come to learn—often painfully—the value of prudence. And all of the incidents in the novel, all of the concern with setting and manners, corroborate the means by which the prudent individual may attain harmony with himself and his social group.

That Evelina has reached this enviable state is symbolized in her marriage, which guarantees feeling as well as status and security. Not that she is now invulnerable to all temptation. She has, however, come to appreciate the efficacy of prudence in human affairs. And while she will doubtless err from time to time, her educational progress is certain: Orville, who is now her guide, is a paragon of wise, deliberate conduct; and Villars, as the final letter makes amusingly plain, will not relinquish his spiritual guardianship simply because Evelina is married.

The plot, disarmingly simple, is an effective vehicle for the subject of initiation. Like most eighteenth-century fiction the story is enlivened by variety of incident, contrivance, and mood; yet the plot moves steadily towards the inculcation of its moral premise. Almost from the beginning, Fanny Burney employs a double narrative vision: that of Villars, who supplies expository details as well as moral reflections; and that of Evelina, who in her dramatic movement gives Villars the bases for exhortation and advice. However reluctant he had been to release her from Berry Hill, he understood in the spirit of Johnson's Imlac that 'the time draws on for experience and observation to take place of instruction'. As she tests her values empirically, discarding the naïve for those more sophisticated, she shares with her guardian the responsibility for confirming the worth of prudence. At the outset, in other words, Villars establishes the problem as in the opening act of a drama; thereafter Evelina takes a dominant position, involving herself in complications, being involved in them, and generally creating a climate of discovery.

She is not only an individual, however; she is a representative of feminine decorum, so that Villars may admonish her, 'nothing is so delicate as the reputation of a woman: it is, at once, the most beautiful and most brittle of all human things'. It is her duty to protect such fragility, and social induction puts her to the proof. Her entrance into the world parallels the temptation of Eve; unlike the biblical figure, however, she will be able to bridle her impulses and thus reach for prudential maturity. But initially the confusion and the wavering are there. Because of the 'artlessness of [her] nature, and the simplicity of [her] education', she is weak enough to enjoy flattery. She is young enough to relish the social round, to implicate herself in white lies and desires that strain against caution. She herself, aware of her occasional immoderacy, is troubled by 'heedless indiscretion[s] of temper' which balk discipline. Yearning for the revels of Ranelagh and the Pantheon, she writes to Villars: 'I believe I am bewitched! I made a resolution when I began, that I would not be urgent; but my pen—or rather my thoughts, will not suffer me to keep it—for I acknowledge, I must acknowledge, I cannot help wishing for your permission.'

This is the credible reaction of a naïve but obedient girl. That she is not ready for the lures of a false Eden is obvious; that she is moving towards sophisticated prudence is equally obvious. In time her experiences increase. Proportionately her vulnerability and dependence diminish; her capacity for sound judgement grows. Throughout the dramatic story of Evelina's evolving education, there runs a moralistic leitmotive which never alters: judicious conduct offers safety and sound reputation; intemperance only uncertainty and sorry consequences.

Villars's letters, as a result, are crucial both to the structural and thematic development of the novel. At the first level they are the link between the social universe Evelina has just entered and the world of Berry Hill. They assure the permanence of affection and prudential order; and they help Evelina to widen her vision, to exemplify her own understanding of incident and character. To this extent, the Villars—Evelina correspondence is integral to the plot. At the second level, however, his correspondence with Lady Howard—though still within the framework of the plot—serves a frankly hortatory function. These observations sometimes go beyond the immediate range of Evelina's adventures. And because they are addressed to another adult rather than to an impressionable child, their contents—unlike the euphemisms which fill his letters to Evelina—are more forthright. They stress without camouflage the necessity of prudence.

For instance, he is restrained in acknowledging Mme Duval's faults to Evelina and insists upon the former's right to her grand-daughter's respect. But in writing to Lady Howard, he is vehement about the Frenchwoman's impertinence and prejudices, her 'unruly and illiberal passions', which are the antitheses of prudence. It is to Lady Howard that he speaks of the tragic consequences to 'the mother of this dear child,—who was led to destruction by her own imprudence, the hardness of heart of Madame Duval, and the villainy of Sir John Belmont'. The sharp tonal differences between his letters to Evelina and those to Lady Howard give breadth to the novel. They also illuminate the character of Villars, and, perhaps above all else, impress upon the reader more stringently than is possible in general discourse with Evelina the author's pervasive moral intention.

That intention is best summed up by Evelina herself: 'Alas, my dearest Sir, that my reflections should always be too late to serve me! dearly, indeed, do I purchase experience! and much I fear I shall suffer yet more severely, from the heedless indiscretion of my temper, ere I attain that prudence and consideration, which, by foreseeing distant consequences, may rule and direct in present exigencies.' Prudence thus relates the individual to what Johnson (in *Idler*, No. 57) called the 'cursory business of common life', sensible preparation for everyday existence. But for Johnson, and for Fanny Burney as well, prudence was more than merely pragmatic. An intellectual faculty also, it was (as in Aristotle's *Ethics*) 'practical wisdom' and so a guard to virtue. To pursue the Aristotelian definition, 'a man has practical wisdom not by knowing only but by being able to act'. And proper action is inseparable from a capacity for proper judgement.

That is why Villars persistently reminds Evelina that she must learn to judge and act for herself. Now judgement entails two collateral powers: inner understanding or self-knowledge, and apprehension of external reality, the 'forms' and 'manners, of the world'. Evelina gropes toward this complex goal and—despite near-disastrous blunders—she preserves her reputation and finds her way. She comes to learn that self-concealment is 'the foe of tranquility', that appearances often belie reality, that the 'amiable' is not necessarily the 'good'. She learns to discriminate between what is lasting and worthy and what is transient and meaningless, not by the promptings of the heart but by the discipline of the mind, by the training of 'discretion' and 'thought'.

From the beginning her education has aimed at the achievement of virtue in action; that is, the moral sense at work in diverse social relationships. Its truths unfold gradually for her. Each new situation or individual she meets enlarges her capacity to make ethical judgements or choices; exposure to negative activity is paradoxically as essential to her development as the positive. Thus, once in the glittering atmosphere of London and Bristol Hotwells, she is introduced to varieties of imprudence: the ill temper of Mme Duval, the vulgarity of the Branghtons and Smith, the crudity of Captain Mirvan, the passion of Willoughby, the foppishness of Lovel, the 'villainy' of Belmont. She recognizes that these people have imperfections which she cannot always escape and which she must, therefore, endure, transcend, and in the case of her father forgive. But in this same world, so dynamic after Berry Hill, is Orville, who by loving example teaches her that virtue may flourish in sophistication as well as in rustic simplicity.

'Generous, noble Lord Orville!' she describes him, 'how disinterested his conduct! how delicate his whole behavior!' And how passionless the attraction between them. Evelina, indeed, thinks of him as brother and father; he calls her 'sister'. Sensuousness is in fact erased by spiritual compatibility. She—meek, obedient, chaste, forgiving—has the traits, despite minor venial failings, of a Christian heroine. Through her idealizing vision he takes on the superior virtues of a Christian hero—'civility, courtesy, obligingness'. He is the rational altruist, offering 'compassion' and 'service even to people unknown'. Although he controls his passions and so every situation, he escapes self-righteousness; he conducts himself with a good nature which 'knows no intermission, and makes no distinction, is as unassuming and modest, as if he had never mixed with the great, and was totally ignorant of every qualification he possesses'.

Evelina is no philosopher, of course; but she does intuit Orville's consummate goodness in action. Socially pre-eminent and worldly, as Villars is not, he nevertheless translates all of the older man's admirable qualities into a secular context. As an exemplar of moderation, he is the enemy of cruelty and injustice. On the occasion of the footrace between the two ancient women, for instance, he shows in his inimitably reserved

way that he can be 'angry at the right things and with the right people'. As a lover he is notable for propriety if not for ardour. His declaration of love, when it finally comes, is correctly ritualistic. It is a social form to be enacted on bended knees, and the sardonic interruption of Mrs. Selwyn barely disturbs his aplomb. Even jealousy does not provoke him into being other than polite and restrained.

Among readers to whom such exquisite sensibility is two hundred years removed from their coarser reality, Orville is almost incredibly perfect. And to be sure he does border upon a stereotype of consideration and social finesse. Some allowance must be made for Fanny Burney's reticence and inexperience, that is, her limitation in painting a masculine portrait whole. But even as she created him, he is the ideal companion for Evelina while she learns the rules of discretion. For her he is as much mentor as lover, a sentimental guide who gladly assumes the task of ordering her 'feeling heart' with wisdom, of refining the lessons of prudence which Villars had begun years before in Berry Hill.

A novel, according to Fanny Burney, 'is, or it ought to be, a picture of supposed, but natural and probable human existence. It holds, therefore, in its hands our best affections; it exercises our imaginations; it points out the path of honour; and gives to juvenile credulity knowledge of the world, without ruin, or repentance; and the lessons of experience, without its tears'. Although she published this statement in 1814, when dedicating *The Wanderer* to her father, she could have attached it just as readily to *Evelina* thirty-six years earlier. In her theory of fiction, as in her novels, she indicates a proper respect for the inventive faculty but nothing which suggests a depth of aesthetic and technical concern. Rather, very much in tune with eighteenth-century moralism, she saw the novel as a perceptive vehicle. That is wily she insisted, 'whatever, in illustrating the characters, manners, or opinions of the day, exhibits what is noxious or reprehensible, should scrupulously be accompanied by what is salubrious, or chastening'.

The fictional intention of *Evelina* evolved from the orderly pattern of a tranquil existence. The standards clearly delimited in the 'Author's Preface' are probability, reason, and natural simplicity; and these not unexpectedly obviate the fantasy of romance. Furthermore, because Fanny wished to enlarge and generalize the implications of her narrative materials, she deliberately chose to draw social types, 'characters from nature, though not from life, and to mark the manners of the times'.

Her first novel is the product of a singularly uncomplicated personality. Long before writing *Evelina*, when Fanny was sixteen, she was shocked by the pessimism of *Rasselas*; but (after initial misgivings) she was intrigued by the "rural felicity" of *The Vicar of Wakefeld*. Unrelieved human wickedness, such as she found in Walpole's *Mysterious Mother*, was to her at once incomprehensible and unbearable. Always pronouncedly affective in her response to literature, she made her own writings a register of personal emotions and values. Realism, which she consequently related to her early serenity, becomes a triumph of benevolence with social propriety and unaffected goodness inseparable virtues. In her fictional practice, hence, she worked from a broadly humanistic base while at the same time symbolically projecting her own optimism.

The comic spirit which has pleased readers of *Evelina* for almost two centuries is a by-product of that optimism. It would be wrong, however, to assume (as does an uncomprehending moralist like Mrs. Barbauld) that her comedy either bars or corrupts serious purpose. *Evelina* is, in fact, a serio-comic novel which partakes of two narrative movements, one intellectual or thematic and the other situational or structural, but both operating at the same time. In its thematic movement *Evelina* focuses upon the adventures of its heroine: and though many of them are laughable, they often bring her perilously close to disaster. Through it all she manages to skirt the pitfalls. Each escape, in short, becomes one more step in her progress towards self-knowledge and in the assurance of a happy resolution. In its structural movement the novel is neatly—too neatly—defined by a system of balance and counter-balance, point and counterpoint. No amusing episode is contrived for its own sake; rather, each is juxtaposed to another that is notable for its serious implications, or it is followed by an edifying, hortatory statement. Whatever is 'noxious', or at least deserving of censure, is 'scrupulously . . . accompanied by what is salubrious, or chastening'.

This controlled tidiness of meaning and plot is complemented by settings which blend with but never dominate actions or characters. While Fanny Burney gives impressions of tangible locations, she seldom if ever provides minute details. Critics like Paul Elmer More and Austin Dobson were perhaps right in complaining about her visual deficiency, but there are compensations in this lack which they failed to take into account. By suggesting rather than delineating place, Fanny keeps her people in the foreground at all times and lets them play their roles in appropriate but muted settings. We may regret the absence of vivid pictures, but the narrator's hints, flurries of action, and dialogue stimulate our own imaginations to fill in the outlines. If we do not really see place, we are always aware of it as a social force. As a novelist Fanny appreciated setting, but she thought it less important than her shifting clusters of people and their interaction.

She was nevertheless carefully selective in matching character or situation with place. The vaguely pastoral Berry Hill, for example, is an appropriate environment for elderly, slow-paced wisdom. Howard Grove, though also rural, emphasizes a lively, youthful prelude to the city. Here too we find the seeds of contrast and conflict; these anticipate and vivify the London experiences as Captain Mirvan and Mme Duval disrupt the order of the country with their brawls. On a more radical scale London is a kaleidoscope of confusion and gaiety—sparkling and sordid, artificial and dirty, treacherous and wanton. In a welter of topsy-turvy values the opera is a place where one goes to be seen, the parks playgrounds for would-be seducers. The disorder of the city is symbolized by the untidy Branghton house, the broken carriage, the muddy and rain-drenched streets. Yet urban life is not all bad: the London round has its charms, and it has Orville too. Furthermore there is the provincial setting—in some ways the most important in the novel—of Bristol Hotwells and Clifton, where town and country meet on elegant terms. Against this fashionable but faintly drawn backdrop Evelina undergoes her final tests and resolves all her problems.

Even as setting reinforces the schematized balance of *Evelina*, the precisely ordered structure as a whole contributes to the same effect. Coincident with the division of the novel into three volumes, the narrative centre is tripartite. Three units, comparable in length, are separated by actions of less magnitude, entr'actes that provide useful moments of contrast and stasis. Part one is preparatory, with Evelina's visit to the Mirvans logically succeeded by the first trip to London; here she discovers high and low social groupings, the modish set and the vulgar one of Mme Duval and the Branghtons. The climax of part one, vividly told by Evelina (16 April, Letter XXI), is the embarrassing episode at the opera. An interval at Howard Grove juxtaposes the rough-house comedy of the Captain (assisted by Willoughby) and the refinements of London society. The main action of part two then returns Evelina to London (beginning with the letter of 6 June) and emphasizes her exposure to the coarseness of Mme Duval and her mercantile relatives. The climactic episode (described in the letter of 3 July) deals with the former's impertinent appropriation of Orville's coach and ends in Evelina's imprudent letter of apology to Orville. This misadventure leads to the dark interlude at Berry Hill (starting with the letter of 14 July). Here, upon receipt of the false love letter supposedly from Orville, Evelina broods over the unreliability of appearances. Part three is centered in Bristol Hotwells and Clifton where she goes to recover from the deception. At the spa ferocity is camouflaged by gentility, and Evelina encounters decadence at its worst; in this setting she is also at the lowest point in her search for familial identity. Now, however, the wheel is turning upward, and she is about to enjoy her greatest triumphs:

she and Orville come to recognize their love—that is, their mutual esteem; she discovers a father and a brother.

Climax thus builds upon climax, advancing through a series of misunderstandings, discomfitures, and complexities. The plot moves steadily against a background of social extremes, comic mishaps, and near-tragedy. The search for a father, while a necessary complication which threads its way through the entire novel, is less significant than the search for practical wisdom and its correlative, the pursuit of a 'proper' marriage. In its serio-comic theme, then, *Evelina* at least partially fulfills Lionel Trilling's concept of the novel as 'a perpetual quest for reality, the field of its research being always the social world, the material of its analysis being always manners ["a culture's hum and buzz of implication"] as the direction of man's soul'. To develop the tensions which are the measure of her own quest for reality, Fanny Burney methodically set the comic against the serious. The result, if one were to make a chart of the double movement, might look like this: the thematic strain, pervading the entire book, would be represented by a single, continuous line, its course gradually upward; the structural elements, enforcing the thematic, would appear to be a pendulant line swinging with more or less regularity from a fixed point between the serious and the comic.

Once the thematic direction of *Evelina* is understood—and this is early in the novel—it does not invite particularly subtle analysis; it is ingenuously straightforward. The situations may oscillate between the grave and the amusing; but they are tightly controlled by the stability of the argument. For example, Evelina's letter of 27 June is a grateful confirmation of her respect for Villars. After a hiatus of two days, however, she renews her letter with an abrupt shift in mood from her sober reflections to a dramatization of the vulgar conduct of Smith, Mme Duval, and the Branghtons before and at the Hampstead Assembly. On the surface, as Evelina describes their speech and actions, they are ludicrous figures, ridiculous copies of their social betters. Their apishness, as the core of a narrative situation, is exploited for its comedy. And in so far as they can be divorced from Evelina, their antics provoke involuntary laughter. Our sympathies, however, are so closely bound with her that even while we laugh we see them through her disapproving eyes as vulgarians who deny decorum and, hence, moral substance. In this way, through a reversal of approved values, the theme is corroborated. The overtly serious mood is then quickly restored by Macartney's letter; this not only has melodramatic overtones and conveniently implies his blood relationship with Evelina, but also points up the consequences of his own imprudence.

The device of balance and reversal occurs so frequently in *Evelina* as to be almost mechanical. That the comic will be succeeded by the serious is a constant expectation, and as a result the moral purpose preempts a large portion of the reader's attention. Even when the author refrains from explicit statement, irony of situation supplies the missing hortatory element. The first letter of 16 April, for example, centres in the Captain's crudely amusing torment of Mme Duval. The initial impression is farcical because we have no reason to mind seeing her mauled by the rough nationalist. But Willoughby's mannered subtlety emphasizes the ill breeding of the sailor, and—more significantly—implies that his own good breeding is illusory. This alliance of two disparate social types thus converts broad comedy into an ironical censure of indecorous behaviour. The point is underscored in the next letter with the appearance of Lovel and Lord Orville. The former, of course, adds to Evelina's distaste for bad manners, while his lordship clarifies for her the nature of rational gentlemanliness.

Without such balance, the humour and horseplay which abound in the novel would be aimlessly cruel and even awkward. Unlike Smollett, whose influence lurks behind the farce of *Evelina*, Fanny Burney does not have a talent for sustaining boisterously savage exchanges. More like Fielding, she is at her best in the controlled play of social affection, in the adumbration of what is ridiculous and not painful. Generally, thus, her comic scenes are intervals between the grave ones; and not only do they serve her thematically through ironic reversal, but they often contribute to structural development. The comic introduction of Mme Duval, in the letter of 13 April, is replete with Captain Mirvan's anti-Gallicisms. The real issue, however, is Evelina's shocked discovery of her grandmother. Comparably, the footrace between the two old women will seem to most modern readers questionable fun. Yet by contrasting the cruelty of Lord Merton and Mr. Coverley with the benevolence of Lord Orville, Fanny tightens the affinity between the latter and Evelina.

Apart from the thematic interest of the novel, much of its lasting appeal derives from both characterization and particular comic scenes. The value of the moral lessons depends upon the immediate, subjective relevance of the people who enact them. According to Fanny's own terms, ideas must be exemplified. Once she questioned philosophy as 'an endurance of events in which we have no share—any thing, every thing—but Feeling and Nature!' Without a capacity for philosophical abstraction, she none the less had ideas which, with a sensitivity for 'Feeling and Nature', she incorporated in her characters. Most of them—even within the confining limits of what they represent—provoke us to a response, whether it be to their hypocrisy and vanity or to their good nature and charity. The characters of worth are paradoxically less interesting than those who perform with eccentric crudity or selfishness. Such goodness as we see in Villars, Orville,

Macartney, Evelina herself, often taxes even the latitude implicit in moral realism. The fops and posturers are likewise exaggerated, but their credibly comic dialogue and actions soften didactic intention. Human imperfections, if we allow for the author's inflation, are more assimilable than superhuman virtues. But the bad and the low are as necessary to Fanny's scheme as the good and the high.

In the creation of her comic characters she observed a precedent set by Fielding. That is, she too—without his consciously satiric thrust—recognized affectation as the 'source of the true Ridiculous'. Plot—and hers is a frail one—was ultimately less important to the intention of *Evelina* than characterization. More precisely Fanny was absorbed in the problem of making her heroine see and come to grips with varieties of personality and behavior. Such preoccupation tends to produce type-figures, two-dimensional or 'flat' figures (as E. M. Forster would have it) who exist for their predominant traits. Yet out of the interplay of types—the balance of attitudes—emerges Fanny Burney's distinct if contracted image of humanity.

There are times when we wish the 'flatness' to be less pronounced: sometimes the triflers are too trifling, the vulgarians too vulgar, the snobs too snobbish. The occasional inadequacy of portraiture is one of execution (and perhaps even of experience) rather than of intention, for Fanny herself thought her portraiture was realistic. A common complaint in her own day, for instance, was that Captain Mirvan's grossness went beyond credibility. In her *Diary* she comforted herself with the retaliatory thought, 'that the more I see of sea captains, the less reason I have to be ashamed of Captain Mirvan; for they have all so irresistible a propensity to wanton mischief,—to roasting beaux, and detesting old women, that I quite rejoice I showed the book to no one ere printed, lest I should have been prevailed upon to soften his character'.

Narrative writing was almost second nature for Fanny Burney, whose diaries, letters, and scrapbooks give the impression of one who is always self-consciously playing the author. During a visit to the country in 1777, for instance, she wrote to Susan: 'Indeed, for the future, I must beg leave to visit places with which you are wholly unacquainted; for here my genius is perpetually curbed, my fancy nipped in the bud; and the whole train of my descriptive powers cast away, like a ship upon a desert island! . . . a marvelous good simile!' Descriptions of people and events—particularly the odd and eccentric—are confided to these private pages: a marriage between the family cook and a glassblower (or polisher) much her junior; a masquerade; a coach accident in London; a sea-storm; a pig race and a rowing match between women (germs perhaps of the footrace in *Evelina*); visits to the theatre.

On other pages she captured social types—coxcombs, gentlemen, fops, ardent suitors—traces of whom appear in the novel. Or occasionally she tried her hand at vignettes which emphasize female vanity: Miss Pogelandel, Miss Digget, Miss Hasty. The last, a seventeen-year-old girl, is intriguing as the antithesis of Evelina. Through these early jottings Fanny shows herself to be adept in the rendering of suspense, responsive to the minutiae of character and episode.

Her creative imagination led her inevitably to *Evelina* and a firm place in the tradition of eighteenth-century fiction. As a bridge from the earlier novelists—Fielding, Richardson, Smollett—to Maria Edgeworth and Jane Austen, she served both as pupil and teacher. Under the influence of Fielding, she refined her comic and social perceptions; even her thematic interest owes much to him. Her purpose in *Evelina* is not unlike Fielding's in *Tom Jones*. 'I have endeavoured', he wrote in his dedication to George Lyttleton, 'strongly to inculcate that virtue and innocence can scarce ever be injured but by indiscretion; and that is this alone which often betrays them into the snares that deceit and villainy spread for them.' From Fielding also she doubtless learned a good deal about the careful ordering of plot. But there were additional lessons for her in the epistolary techniques of Richardson and Smollett, to say nothing of the violent comedy of the latter and the moral, sentimental gravity of the former. To these debts, of course, must be added those which she herself ascribed to Rousseau, Johnson, and Marivaux.

Looking ahead to those who followed her closely in time, we see the resemblance of Maria Edgeworth's Lord Colambre and Grace Nugent (of *The Absentee*) to Lord Orville and Evelina. That the line of influence culminates superbly in Jane Austen is a critical commonplace which needs no enlargement. With her superior comic vision, acute psychological understanding, and sheer craftsmanship Jane has overshadowed her predecessor. But it is pleasant to realize that Fanny, though somewhat obscured by Jane's lustre, continues to glow softly in the light of her own memorable achievement.

Martha G. Brown (essay date 1986)

SOURCE: "Fanny Burney's 'Feminism': Gender or Genre?" in *Fettered or Free? British Women Novelists, 1670-1815,* edited by Mary Anne Schofield and Cecilia Macheski, Ohio University Press, 1986, pp. 29-39.

[In the following essay, Brown answers feminist interpretations of Burney by insisting that seemingly feminist themes result from the romance tradition from which Burney drew her inspiration.]

Reading older literature with modern glasses is a pervasive tendency. In the nineteenth century, this approach resulted in a propensity to judge eighteenth-century poetry by Romantic standards and to find it wanting. The novel too, has suffered from this sort of self-congratulatory measurement in the twentieth century, in which the yardstick was Jamesian realism. In the past few years, a different manifestation of this approach has been gaining in popularity as critics sift through the fiction of the eighteenth- and nineteenth-century women novelists, looking for evidence of latent feminism. Recent interpretations of Fanny Burney's novels, in which feminist readings are becoming fashionable, reflect this tendency. Critics point to the trials the heroine in each novel endures, including her loss of fortune, and to the marriage at the end as expressions, however repressed or even unconscious, of the frustrations and resentment Burney felt in her role as a woman in a male-dominated society. Each heroine does suffer a series of trials in which she falls prey to an assortment of villainous males who attack her virtue, her heart, or her purse; each novel is also concluded with a marriage. This is, however, a matter of genre, rather than gender, since these plot features, which some critics trace to feminism, are instead debts to the romance tradition, from which Burney drew heavily for plot, theme, and character.

All feminist readings of Burney's fiction center around one recurring theme—dependence. All stress three central plot features that these critics see as evidence that Burney visualized women as dependent—economically, physically, and psychologically—on men. The first of these arguments for Burney's feminism is that the heroine in each novel is denied her proper rank and fortune—at least until the end, a fact which they interpret as a feminist resentment of women's financial dependence on men. [In "Defiant Women: The Growth of Feminism in Fanny Burney's Novels," *Studies in English Literature, 1500-1900* 17 (1977): 519-30,] Rose Marie Cutting argues that "all are cut off from their rightful inheritance—a situation that serves as a good metaphor for the historic poverty and economic dependence of women."

The first part of this statement is undeniably true. Evelina, the unacknowledged but legitimate daughter of a nobleman, has been abandoned by her father, a libertine who burned the marriage certificate. Aware of her questionable parentage, Evelina calls herself an "orphan," "motherless," and "worse than fatherless." Throughout the novel, as she is forced to live in the vulgar world of Madame Duval and her Branghton relatives, the possibility that she may be accepted by her true father seems remote, as Villars recognizes when he asks, "only child of a wealthy baronet, whose person she has never seen, whose character she has reason to abhor, and whose name she is forbidden to claim; entitled as she is to lawfully inherit his fortune and

estate, is there any probability that he will properly own her?"

Cecilia's situation also focuses on the question of inheritance. Orphaned young, she has been reared by an uncle whose recent death has left her alone except for three guardians. Unlike Evelina's, Cecilia's pedigree is public. Cecilia, however, is marked by a different stigma—the name clause, which requires her to retain her family name forever and her husband to relinquish his. Since the Delviles' pride in their family name makes it impossible for them to approve their son Mortimer's taking Cecilia's maiden name of Beverly, this clause blocks the lovers' marriage. After an abortive first attempt at a secret marriage, they are finally married secretly, but with Mrs. Delvile's approval. A condition of the marriage is, of course, that Cecilia must give up her fortune of £3,000 per year rather than Mortimer his name, making her "portionless, though an HEIRESS."

In *Camilla*, the inheritance theme takes a different form. No mystery surrounds Camilla's birth; no clause blocks her inheritance, which is denied her instead through an even more bizarre circumstance. The daughter of a poor clergyman, she is heir to her uncle's estate until a series of accidents that leave her sister terribly crippled cause her uncle to make this unfortunate niece his heiress. Dependent on a small allowance from her father, Camilla, because of her own imprudence, is in economic distress throughout the novel, distress which is alleviated only through her union with the wealthy Edgar Mandlebert.

In *The Wanderer*, Burney returns to a more traditional use of the inheritance theme. Juliet's birth and identity are shrouded in mystery. The daughter of a nobleman by his first and secret marriage to a commoner, she has been reared in France by a bishop in an arrangement that stipulates that she inherit only if she remains in France, keeping her identity secret. Escaping a forced marriage, she comes to England where she is forced to conceal her name as she struggles to support herself in a series of demeaning occupations until she is acknowledged by her father and receives the standard reward—name, money, and a husband.

Although inheritance is an important focus in all four novels, the assertion that this "serves as a good metaphor for the historic poverty and economic dependency of women" is unconvincing. Fielding's Joseph Andrews and Tom Jones are both cut off from their rightful inheritance; so is Smollett's Humphrey Clinker. Are we, therefore, to assume that Fielding and Smollett meant this as a "metaphor" for men's "economic dependence"? Of course not. The inheritance theme in so many eighteenth-century novels is clearly traceable to the romance tradition, a tradition whose influence on the novel has recently been recognized by several critics.

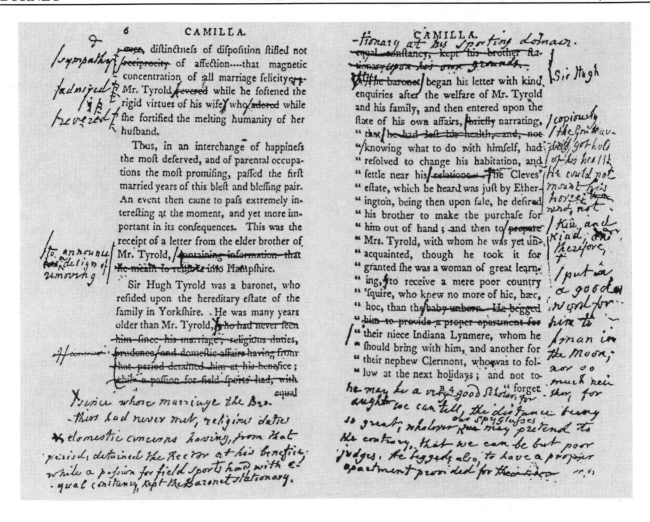

Burney's revisions of proofs of Camilla.

The typical romance plot, beginning with the Greek prose romances of Heliodorus, Longus, and Tatius, centers on an infant who is abandoned, or "exposed," by his parents, rescued and reared by a kindly shepherd. After the child reaches maturity, he falls in love, a romance that is blocked, often by the mystery surrounding the hero's birth. After a series of trials, the lovers are finally united when their true identities are revealed, their inheritance is restored, and they are married. Variations on this story have supplied the plot for prose and verse romances for many centuries; they continued to do so in the eighteenth-century novel.

In Burney's novels, as in romance in general, the denial of the hero's birthright has important implications for plot and theme. At the superficial level of plot, the hero's mysterious origin and lack of both rank and fortune make possible the adventures so necessary for romance. Evelina and Juliet are forced on their journeys or quests by the dubious circumstances of their birth and by their rights to inherit. The economic plights of all four heroines make them vulnerable, which is necessary to set them up for the trials and tests that they must endure. Mr. Villars says of Evelina's vulnerability, "The supposed obscurity of your birth and situation makes you liable to a thousand disagreeable adventures." The "disagreeable adventures" multiply in *The Wanderer*, where Juliet's namelessness and poverty subject her to humiliation and danger.

The disinheritance of the heroines also has important thematic implications, and these are moral and psychological, rather than economic. The quest for identity ending in the self-recognition so central in romance is really, as Northrop Frye suggests [in *The Secular Scripture: A Study of the Structure of Romance*], "attaining one's original identity." This attainment is especially apparent in *Evelina* and *The Wanderer*. Because Evelina has been stripped of her fortune and her name she must seek to discover who she is before she can claim her place in society. She must also seek to discover where and to whom she belongs. Her position makes her all *potentia*. Because she is nobody and belongs to nobody, she may be anybody and belong to anybody.

Her quest for identity involves a series of moral tests and moral choices through which she proves herself worthy of the inheritance and name she has been denied. Juliet, too, must undertake such a quest in order to discover her proper identity and claim her fortune. Because her name and fortune have been denied her, she is forced to leave her home and is thrust into the world, nameless, friendless, and fortuneless, to undergo a bizarre series of trials, including the obligatory incest threat, which tests her prudence, courage, and virtue. Her well-deserved reward is the return of her rightful identity and fortune. Since Cecilia's paternity is not in question, the idea of inheritance becomes even more urgently connected with the theme of identity, which is underlined by the name clause. And when Camilla is stripped of her inheritance, confusion arises about which of the Tyrold daughters is the true heiress—a question that helps to reveal motive and character. A heroine who is secure in both her identity and her inheritance would simply not be an effective heroine of romance, where the quest is essential to both plot and meaning. Romance demands instead a heroine who is poised at the threshold of initiation into experience, who is ready to undergo the symbolic *rite de passage*, which involves testing and self-discovery. The lack of name and fortune are necessary plot devices embodying central thematic concerns.

And finally the economic distresses of all four heroines serve to reinforce not only the theme of identity, but also a second major theme—prudence. Characters in Burney's novels are judged by the way they handle their money as well as by the way they order their passions. Each learns in the course of the quest the financial prudence that will enable her to be a careful mistress of her fortune. Although this is not a pressing concern in *Evelina*, it becomes an increasingly urgent theme in each succeeding novel. Cecilia, who like her friend Mrs. Calton has a "generous foible," is seduced into supporting Mr. Harrel's decadent extravagance. By the end of her quest, however, "she had learnt the error of profusion, even in charity and beneficence." Camilla's misguided generosity has even more dire consequences, resulting ultimately in her uncle's ruin and her father's imprisonment. And Juliet's lesson is hardest of all; she must learn not only to save money, but also to make it. It is not surprising to find the question of inheritance linked so closely with prudence since wealth or treasure as a symbol central to romance often, according to Frye [in *Anatomy of Criticism*], "means wealth in its ideal forms, power and wisdom."

A second argument for Burney's feminism—closely related to the first—is that the heroines in the novels suffer abuse because they exist in a world where women are powerless and oppressed. Cutting sees the cruelty in Burney's novels "as a manifestation of feminine sensibility: she was, after all, describing a world in which women had little power." It is true that each heroine suffers abuse at the hands of a malicious man. Evelina is at the mercy of her chief tormentor, Sir Clement Willoughby, throughout and occasionally falls prey to a cast of minor villains who accost her physically in the alleys of Vauxhall and Marylebone gardens. Cecilia is the victim of the machinations of an arch villain, Mr. Monckton; the greed of Mr. Harrel and Mr. Briggs; and the pride of Mr. Delvile. In *Camilla*, the heroine's tormentors, Sir Sedley Clarendel and her own brother Lionel, are less wicked than the utterly vile Bellamy, who heartlessly tortures Eugenia. Because of her deformities, which are the result of her uncle's carelessness, Eugenia is constantly brutalized.

Feminist readings of the cruelty in Burney's novels have two main weaknesses. First, the heroines are victimized by women as often as by men. Evelina's wicked "stepmother," Madame Duval, uses and abuses her as often and as maliciously as Sir Clement. In *Cecilia*, each male tormentor has his female counterpart—Mr. Monckton's cruelty is rivaled by that of Mrs. Monckton, Mr. Delvile's by that of Mrs. Delvile, Mr. Harrel's by that of Mrs. Harrel. In *Camilla* Eugenia is frequently victimized by women, such as Indiana or the nameless country women, who taunt her about her dwarfed and crippled body. And finally, in *The Wanderer*, Juliet's nightmarish trials are caused largely by Mrs. Ireton, Mrs. Maple, Selina, and other vicious women.

If the malice is general, we must seek a source other than feminism; that source is the romance tradition, where the hero's mettle is tested by a series of trials. In the Greek romance, the heroine undergoes a bizarre series of adventures in which she is shipwrecked, kidnapped, tortured by pirates and savages—who are, by the way, males. Does this suggest that Heliodorus, Longus, and Tatius were avant-garde feminists? The idea is too absurd to entertain. But it is no more reasonable to attribute the trials of Burney's heroines to feminism when they are so clearly a feature of the genre in which she was working. As Frye explains [in *Anatomy of Criticism*], the quest in romance has three stages: "the stage of the perilous journey and the preliminary minor adventures, the crucial struggle . . . and the exaltation of the hero." Burney's novels, all of which fall roughly into three parts analogous to these three stages, concern the "perilous journey" of the heroine. The "preliminary minor adventures" are typically social skirmishes, while the "crucial struggles" are moral and spiritual.

The quest is necessary for the heroine's moral growth because each is, at the beginning, virtuous but untried. All four heroines have been reared in seclusion and are of just that age when their innocence must be tested by experience. The theme of the initiation or *rite de pas-*

sage is implied in the title **Evelina; or, The History of a Young Lady's Entrance into the World**, and it is made explicit by the narrator who says in the first chapter of **Camilla**:

> The experience which teaches the lesson of truth, and the blessings of tranquillity, comes not in the shape of warning nor of wisdom; from such they turn aside, defying or disbelieving. 'Tis in the bitterness of personal proof alone, in suffering and in feeling, in erring and repenting, that experience comes home with conviction, or impresses to any use.

Each heroine, then, must be thrust out of the rural world of innocence into the urban world of experience so that her virtue can be tried and perfected. On one level the tests involve manners, as the heroine is placed in social situations in which her choices are invested with symbolic and ritualistic significance. In speaking of the perilous journey of romance, Kathleen Williams says [in "Romance Tradition in *The Faerie Queene*," *Research Studies* 32 (1964)], "the hero's fate depends upon whether he takes a certain seat, asks or answers a certain question."

On another level, the tests are moral. Basically virtuous, each heroine has only to add good judgment to a good heart. *Prudentia*, involving the ability to make moral choices leading to virtuous action, is what each heroine must acquire. And she can acquire this only through a series of tests in which her failure to judge well and to act wisely brings her perilously near disaster again and again. The more serious assaults on the heroine are a necessary part of the ritual initiation in which the quester must meet and slay the dragon. [In *Anatomy of Criticism*,] Frye explains that in romance, "the hero travels perilously through a dark labyrinthine underworld full of monsters" and that this often becomes "a structural principle of fiction." In Burney's fiction the obligatory dragons and monsters of romance are transformed into a gallery of fops and rakes; the labyrinth becomes the dark alleys of Marylebone and Vauxhall.

The centrality of the quest to romance also provides the refutation for the third feminist argument, which is that the marriage at the end of each novel suggests a surrender to male power. [In "Evelina: Or, the History of a Young Lady's Entrance into the Marriage Market," *Modern Language Studies* 6 (Spring 1976): 48-56,] Judith Newton calls Evelina's entrance into the world an "entrance into the marriage market" and argues that by marrying she abdicates adult responsibility and power. Cutting asserts that "if a woman's whole life (and 'fortune') depend on pleasing and winning a man, then Camilla's story is also a fitting parable for the general fate of women." And Patricia Meyer Spacks argues [in *The Female Imagination*] that in Burney

novels, the heroine's "'growth' leads her back toward childhood" and that "the 'happy endings' of Burney novels reassert the charm and irresponsibility of the child as the greatest achievement to be hoped for by adolescents." These are odd criticisms to make of Burney; indeed, they would be odd criticisms to make of any eighteenth-century novel, since, with the exception of *Clarissa*, all major novels of the period end in just this way—happily, and with marriage, or better yet, a set of marriages. In the romance tradition in all its different incarnations, including the eighteenth-century novel, marriage signifies in two essential ways. First of all, marriage and treasure are the two standard rewards awaiting the hero at the end of the successful quest. With the exception of Juliet, who is perfect from the beginning, each of the heroines is unfit at the onset of the quest to manage either marriage or money; these are rights that must be won. The marriage is also a way of placing the hero's individual moral maturation into a social and communal context, making it more symbolic than personal. As Henry Knight Miller suggests [in *Henry Fielding's Tom Jones*], "romance and comedy traditionally conclude with the celebration of a marriage, not because that marks the end but precisely because it celebrates a new beginning, the sacramental emblem of a new world of maturity and hope, the assertion of life and continuity as against the 'reality' of isolation and death." Marriage, then, is not a matter of giving up, but of growing up.

And Burney is no more fettered by the tradition in which she was working than her heroines are fettered by the tradition of marriage that they all enter. In fact, working within a tradition is freeing for an artist in a very real sense. Because the romance tradition supplies plot and character types, Burney was freed from these decisions, which enabled her to concentrate on other narrative areas, such as dialogue and setting. Of course another way a writer may use tradition is to react against it openly or, more subtly, to turn it to his or her own purposes. So that if one accepts the contention that these plot features—the heroine's lack of her rightful rank and fortune, her trials, and finally her marriage—are drawn straight from romance, it is possible to argue that Burney took these stock features of romance and put them to feminist uses. There is, however, no evidence, at least in the first three novels, to support this; there is instead ample evidence to refute it.

In the first place, as I suggested earlier, the numbers of villainous men and women are roughly equivalent. The moral types, too, are as often men as women. Each heroine has her chivalrous knight to protect her. Evelina is guarded and guided by Orville, who is a paragon of courtesy and morality. Cecilia has Mortimer Delvile, Camilla has Edgar Mandlebert, and Juliet has Harleigh—all of whom are versions of Orville. In addition, there are several wise, kindly, father figures—the

Reverend Villars in *Evelina* and the Reverend Tyrold in *Camilla*—and a variety of decent men who befriend the heroines—Mr. Macartney in *Evelina*, Hal Westwyn in *Camilla*, Mr. Arnot in *Cecilia*, and Lord Melbury in *The Wanderer*.

In addition, in each novel, Burney creates one more-or-less liberated lady and clearly disapproves of her. Mrs. Selwyn in *Evelina* is such a character. Although she serves the positive function of occasionally protecting Evelina, she is too aggressively outspoken to suit Burney. Evelina says of this intelligent, independent, and sharp-tongued woman, "her understanding, indeed, may be called *masculine*; but, unfortunately, her manners deserve the same epithet; for in studying to acquire the knowledge of the other sex, she has lost all the softness of her own."

Lady Honoria in *Cecilia* is a free-spirited, strong-willed woman, whose wit and charm are outweighed by the confusion and embarrassment she causes. That Fanny Burney sternly disapproved of such behavior is amply evident in her early diary where she writes of a Miss Allen, "she is too sincere: she pays too little regard to the world; and indulges herself with too much freedom of raillery and pride and disdain toward those whose vices and follies offend her."

In *Camilla*, Mrs. Arlery, who flaunts convention and is "guilty of no vices, but utterly careless of appearances," has sullied her reputation by her lack of prudent behavior. Again the early diary evidences Burney's distaste for this sort of behavior among women. Writing of a certain Miss Bowdler who lives "exactly as she pleases" and scandalizes all by visiting single men, Burney declares herself in agreement with Mr. Rishton, who believes that a woman "who despises the customs and manners of the country she lives in must, consequently, conduct herself with impropriety." To this Burney adds, "I can by no means approve so great a contempt of public opinion."

The most complex and interesting example of this type of "new woman" is *The Wanderer*'s Elinor Joddrel, who is a spokeswoman for personal and political freedom. An ardent admirer of the French Revolution, she declares, "I hold no one thing in the world worth living for but liberty!" But if her love of freedom is attractive, it is also dangerous and destructive. The narrator explains that what "was termed by Elinor the love of independence" is actually the "spirit of contradiction," and that although she has "a solid goodness of heart," "quickness of parts," and "liberality of feeling," she is also "alarming and sarcastic, aiming rather to strike than to please, to startle than to conquer." She is so headstrong and so saturated with a sort of self-destructive willfulness that she cannot love Albert's brother, Dennis, who loves her, but only Albert, who does not. Not only does she take masochistic pleasure

in her unrequited love, but she also delights in her own histrionics, especially her theatrical suicide attempts.

Although Burney certainly does not completely approve of Elinor and does not intend her as a model of female virtue, there is some sympathy and even admiration in her portrayal of this "new woman," who is complex and interesting, although finally unsatisfactory. Many of her comments are perceptive and fair. She says, for example, "the Rights of Woman . . . are the Rights of human nature," and rebukes Juliet when she is complaining of the difficulties of being an unprotected female by saying, "Debility and folly! Put aside your prejudices, and forget that you are a dawdling woman, to remember that you are an active human being, and your FEMALE DIFFICULTIES will vanish into the vapour of which they are formed."

This ambivalent attitude toward Elinor is indicative of a subtle change in Burney's attitude in *The Wanderer*. Although this novel is clearly influenced, as the first three are, by the romance in plot, character, style, and theme, there is a new note of anxiety and dissatisfaction with women's lot in life and a new focus on problems that are particularly female. This new concern is evidenced from the beginning by the subtitle, "Female Difficulties," which seems to have gynecological connotations, as well as social implications. Although Juliet is accomplished and educated, there is simply no way she, as an unprotected and unknown female, can make her own way in the world. First of all, Juliet's situation draws attention to a woman's dependence on social status, especially that provided by men, to ratify her worth. She observes:

> 'How insufficient . . . is a FEMALE to herself! How utterly dependent upon situations—connexions—circumstances! how nameless, how for ever fresh-spring are her DIFFICULTIES, when she would owe her existence to her own exertions! Her conduct is criticized, not scrutinized; her character is censured, not examined; her labours are unhonoured, and her qualifications are but lures to ill will! Calumny hovers over her head, and slander follows her footsteps!'

If social ostracism is humiliating to the unprotected female, economic distresses are still more pressing and dangerous. Juliet, who is well-educated, talented, and intelligent, is forced to undertake a series of degrading and poorly paid occupations. First, she gives harp lessons, which is respectable but hardly lucrative, since her pupils refuse to pay and are incensed that she expects to be paid "just as if she were a butcher, or a baker; or some useful tradesman." Next, she is saved from the humiliation of a public performance only by Elinor's suicide attempt, after which Juliet employs herself with needlework of various kinds. Finally, she is forced into the most devastating occupation of all as she becomes Mrs. Ireton's "toad-eater," which is, as

Mr. Giles Arbe defines it, "a person who would swallow any thing, bad or good; and do whatever he was bid, right or wrong: for the sake of a little pay." It is significant that Juliet is the only one of Burney's heroines who is forced to work for a living.

If there is indeed such a change, however subtle, in Burney's attitude and intentions in *The Wanderer* there are two possible causes for it. The first is that in the years between the writing of *Camilla* and *The Wanderer*, Burney suffered many personal defeats and disappointments that may have seemed to her especially womanly ones. For one thing, she watched her favorite sister Susan abused by a cruel husband. She also experienced pain and humiliation when her brother James abandoned his wife and children to run away with his half-sister, Sally. Burney herself had been crushed by economic hardships, by a painful separation from her family, and by poor health. In 1811 she underwent a mastectomy, performed with no anesthetic; this was a female difficulty which may have scarred Burney emotionally as well as physically. A second explanation may be found in a shifting social consciousness and intellectual climate typified by the publication—twenty-two years before *The Wanderer* was written—of Mary Wollstonecraft's *A Vindication of the Rights of Woman*.

Perhaps this apparent "feminism" in *The Wanderer* has led some critics into reading these tendencies, if they actually exist, back into the earlier novels. Because the novels are so similar on the surface in basic plot, characterization, and even in theme, it is tempting to lump them together and to generalize about them almost as though they were one novel. To do so, however, is reductive and slights the richness, the complexity, and the diversity of Burney's work. The young girl who wrote *Evelina* was different in many and important ways from the mature woman who wrote *The Wanderer*, which embodies new concerns and new attitudes.

Judy Simons   (essay date 1987)

SOURCE: "Fanny Burney's Heroines," in *Fanny Burney,* Macmillan Education Ltd, 1987, pp. 24-42.

[In the following essay, Simons compares the heroines in Burney's novels and discusses her treatment of women's issues.]

The two modes of writing that Burney principally employed seem to reflect the separate worlds that she inhabited, the public and the private. Whereas her journals are unrestrained and direct—they confront emotion without melodrama and their style is fresh and effortless—her novels, reliant on conventions, are deeply indebted to contemporary literary models. Such disparity of method endorses the idea of the tensions of personality that Fanny Burney experienced, her struggle to blend self and society, and it is a struggle that all her writing in some way affirms.

The novels share a common theme, a theme which was to become increasingly familiar to readers of nineteenth-century fiction. It is identified in the subtitle to *Evelina—A Young Lady's Entrance into the World—*and was a subject of fundamental importance to eighteenth-century women, whose situation and status was in the process of being reassessed and debated. The theme of the ingenue's first encounter with society was not in itself a female prerogative. Fielding's Tom Jones was perhaps the most influential of the literary innocents whose values, in many ways superior to those of his fellows, must yet be tempered by prudence before he could become fully integrated. Samuel Richardson's Clarissa had become an archetypal figure of female victimisation, suffering at the hands of an unscrupulous and powerful male aggressor. The impact of this legacy on Fanny Burney cannot be overestimated. For by the late eighteenth century, the topic of social initiation had acquired a special relevance for women and was put to particular use by Burney, who probed so searchingly the uncertainties and anomalies of a woman's position in a man's world. Each of her novels contains a study of an adolescent heroine and progressively charts stages in her efforts to gain social recognition, beginning with Evelina's naivety as she tentatively negotiates metropolitan values on her first visit to London. This variant on the favourite eighteenth-century theme of the opposition between nature and art was developed by Fanny Burney so as to have specific implications for women, perplexed as they were about their social roles. For, like Cecilia and Juliet in *The Wanderer*, Evelina is a girl without parental support, unprotected in a powerful and exclusive society. How can she best survive? That is the question posed by all the novels, as Burney's heroines try to adapt their own intuitive sense of value to the practical demands of existence that confront them.

All Burney's heroines are alone. All journey away from a secure base into unknown territory. This movement, so popular in eighteenth-century fiction, of a journey away from a father's house, reflects in Burney's novels a metaphorical estrangement from familiar and supportive values. Evelina keeps in touch with her moral centre via her letters to her safe and reliable guardian, the Rev. Mr Villars, but Cecilia, Burney's second heroine, has no such prop. All apparent sources of support are one by one removed from her and, as her guardians prove successively unreliable, she is forced back on her own judgement, facing the undeniable fact of her own isolation. In the third novel, Camilla, unlike the other heroines, is provided with a family but in becoming separated from them she too becomes the victim of misunderstandings. When familial sympathy is removed she stands to lose everything. The later novels' departure from the spontaneous personal narrative of *Evelina* is accompanied by a progressively darkening vision, as the dangers resulting from social rejection are made ferociously explicit. The melodramatic fates of the heroines, however, have their parallels in actual social documentation and historical fact. Destitution, imprisonment, incarceration in a lunatic asylum were all real possibilities for women who strayed from the path of virtue. In *The Wanderer*, the portrayal of Juliet, the fair Incognita, expands this sense of victimisation. Through her disguise and her refusal to give her real name, attention is forced on her representative function and, as the threats magnify, the real instability of women's social identity is disclosed.

Clearly, the continuing dialogue about women's position in contemporary society is mirrored in these novels, which articulate the central issues of the controversy. The works after *Evelina*, in particular, demonstrate an awareness of the problematic nature of women's roles. Burney's heroines do not exist solely in domestic situations but are presented always in a wider social context. They are never seen as wives and mothers (although Camilla's filial duties are sternly put to the test) but as potentially independent beings. Burney is concerned with problems of inheritance and questions of economics. She agonises over Cecilia's fortune and her helplessness in the face of unscrupulous men determined to defraud her. Her other heiress, Eugenia Tyrold, is shown as dreadfully at risk because she is quite unaware of the value of the money which turns her into a marketable object. In the same book, Camilla's financial ignorance is used to demonstrate the evils of gambling and the desperate consequences of debt. Money is the hallmark of Fanny Burney's society and women are shown to be woefully inadequate in handling it. The growth of the commercial society had given middle-class women leisure and respectability which ironically removed them from the source of the activity which shaped their position. Anticipating this situation, Defoe, half a century earlier, had complained that certain trades were becoming not 'proper' for women, 'such as linen and woollen drapers, mercers and goldsmiths, all sorts of dealers by commission and the like. Custom I say, has made these trades so effectually to shut out the women, that what with custom and the women's generally thinking it below them, we never or rarely see any women in such shops and warehouses.'

This gradual exclusion of women from the commercial world resulted naturally in their increased ignorance of business matters and their consequent helplessness and dependence on men. At the time of writing *Camilla*, Fanny Burney was herself peculiarly alert to the problems of earning a living. Marriage to D'Arblay, an unemployed, impecunious foreigner, meant that she was the one now responsible for supporting her family. From

this unusual viewpoint, she was able to visualise without sentimentality the limitations of education in equipping girls to deal with the harsh realities of economic existence. *The Wanderer* of course clarifies and intensifies the nature of this problem as Juliet acknowledges the difficulties of finding employment.

> 'How few', she cried, 'how circumscribed are the attainments of women! and how much fewer and more circumscribed still are those which may, in their consequences, be useful as well as ornamental to the higher or educated!'

Juliet is required to perform a delicate balancing act. She must ward off starvation while still maintaining her respectability. Her gentility is one potential avenue to eventual social acceptance and she has to be careful not to compromise it. She learns bitterly not only the inadequacy of her own skills but also how few are 'those through which, in the reverses of fortune, a FEMALE may reap benefit without abasement!'

All Fanny Burney's heroines find themselves in precarious positions and have to tread warily over the abyss of social disapproval in order to secure the rich husband who will give them a name and protection. In Burney's world, no other realistic solution can guarantee both freedom of movement and dinner on the table. Without society, Fanny Burney's women have no identity; society is the all-powerful authority which can make or break their futures. Social errors form the main sources of fear for her heroines. Recognising the weight carried by social codes, Burney portrays her upper-class English communities as if they are alien tribes, with strange rituals which have to be learned by the initiate before full acceptance can take place.

If the emphasis in the novels on problems of courtesy seems trivial to our twentieth-century consciousness, we must remember that for Fanny Burney and her heroines, etiquette was the only currency available. Her interest in manners is by no means frivolous but part of a deep understanding of the social mechanisms that exert such influence in shaping the lives of individuals. The warning of *Evelina*'s serious-minded clergyman, Mr Villars, that 'nothing is so delicate as the reputation of a woman; it is at once the most beautiful and most brittle of all human things,' relates crucially to Burney's perception of social and sexual roles, and her understanding of women's essential vulnerability. Evelina's faux pas at the ball, for instance, when she refuses one partner and then accepts another, exposes a complicated network of male-female relationships and their far-reaching political effects.

In stressing the importance of conduct, Fanny Burney reflects one of the major preoccupations of her age. From the beginning of the century, essays on social behaviour had appeared in the pages of *The Tatler* and

The Spectator, the latter advertising itself as a 'work which endeavours to cultivate and polish human life,' and both periodicals illustrating the contemporary interest in the relationship between manners and morals. The self-consciousness of the newly educated middle class and its need for confidence-strengthening is evident not only in the witty pamphleteering of Addison and Steele, and later in Johnson's *The Rambler* and *The Idler*, but also in the plethora of courtesy books, aimed particularly at women, that began to appear as the century wore on. Dr Fordyce's *Sermons to Young Women,* which was first published in 1765, was still thought worthy when Jane Austen described Lydia Bennet's truculent reaction to its moralistic tedium thirty years later. Almost as enduring were Mrs Chapone's *Essays on the Improvement of the Mind* (1772) and Dr Gregory's *A Father's Legacy to His Daughters* (1774). These, together with a spate of lesser known works, combined religious precepts with detailed advice on domestic conduct and were highly recommended for their improving educational value. Girls were taught to avoid coquetry and artifice and instead to cultivate the virtues of modesty, obedience and (significantly) silence, for 'a very young woman can hardly be too silent and reserved in company.' They were advised on dress, on deportment and on which accomplishments were considered suitable. Behaviour was seen as an accurate indicator of ethical principles. 'Modesty and unassuming carriage in people of talent and fame, are irresistible,' wrote Fanny Burney to Mr Crisp after one evening party. 'How much do I prefer for acquaintance the well-bred and obliging Miss Davies to the self-sufficient and imperious Bastardini, though I doubt not the superiority of her powers as a singer.' And she was later to condemn the apparently worthy Mr Barlow who applied for her hand because he had 'no elegance of manners.'

Gradually conduct books attempted to enliven their sermonising with brief illustrative narratives and, as fiction increased its appeal, a series of novels were produced with overt didactic messages. As J. M. S. Tompkins has pointed out, the titles alone are sufficient to announce the motives of books such as *The Exemplary Mother* (1769), *Victim of Fancy* (1787) and *The School for Widows* (1791), which trailed in the wake of the courtesy book wave. Time and again minor novels of the period such as these portrayed the model young lady, an assiduous pupil of Dr Fordyce and his followers, artless, elegant and submissive. Burney's heroines similarly indicate their origins. Evelina, Cecilia, Camilla and Juliet are all innocents, untainted by show or forward behaviour. Their natural impulses inspire modesty: they cast their eyes downward: they do not gaze boldly: they blush easily. But one of Burney's greatest achievements was that she was able to manipulate these conventions for her own ends and to transcend the formulae that she also exploited.

In probing the intricate relationship between self and society, Fanny Burney equips her women with many of the characteristics of sentimental fiction. Sentimentalism, the cult of sensibility, had arisen in mid-century as a result of the expanding interest in the values of personal experience. In an age when the court itself was becoming increasingly domesticated (Burney's diary shows us a king who drinks barley-water after hunting, a queen who does embroidery and a princess who gets 'the snuffles') Burney's novels depict accurately the shift of emphasis from thinking big to thinking small. Her heroines have to ensure social acceptance it is true but the society she envisages is one composed of family gatherings, shopping, evening parties and theatre visits. Her characters spend much of their time reading, drawing, sewing and going for walks. Her social politics focus on the dynamics of personal relationships.

For the true sentimentalist, the quality of life was observed to reside in trivial occasions and the mind capable of appreciating the finer details of experience was thought of as possessing a degree of sophistication beyond the vulgarian's reach. To be responsive to the delicacy of momentary sensations, to recognise the significance of the casual glance, touch or minute, was to realise in oneself the true refinements of sensibility. In Mary Wollstonecraft's words sensibility was 'the most exquisite feeling of which the human soul is capable, . . . acute senses, finely fashioned nerves which vibrate at the slightest touch, and convey such clear intelligence to the brain that it does not require to be arranged by the judgement.' Such extreme sensitivity became endowed with moral properties, as the feeling heart was seen as a reliable guide for action. Compassion and benevolence for those less fortunate than oneself were emotions engendered by the extension of the bonds of human sympathy. Evelina's pity for the desolate Mr Macartney is aroused by a chance encounter as they pass one another on the stairs. She is attracted by his air of melancholy, an obvious give-away to his own highly developed sensibility, and by the notion that she might be able to relieve his sufferings. But benevolence remained in the eighteenth century a private action, capable of giving as much satisfaction to the donor as to the recipient, and in **Evelina** her charitable impulses are an illustration of the heroine's own sensitivity as much as anything else.

All Burney's young women are emotionally responsive, highly susceptible to trivial stimuli and easily moved. Their tears flow but Burney makes sure that they flow only with good cause. She was particularly scathing about the excesses of sentimentalism. When one evening in company at Mrs Thrale's she met the beautiful Sophy Streatfeild, who wept on request to demonstrate her extreme tenderness of heart, she records how 'two crystal tears came into the soft eyes of the S.S. and rolled gently down her cheeks! Such a sight

I never saw before, nor could I have believed. She offered not to conceal or dissipate them; on the contrary she really contrived to have them seen by everybody. . . . Loud and rude bursts of laughter broke from us all at once. How indeed could they be restrained?' There is for Burney a sharp distinction to be drawn between the melting, instinctive response of the genuinely soft heart and the deliberate cultivation of its more showy effects. So although her heroines weep easily there is always proper occasion and while they incorporate many of the stereotypic features of other literary models, Burney is insistent on their capacity for rational thought.

It is judgement which operates in Evelina's and Cecilia's censure of the attitudes of polite society. They are critical of foppishness, of extravagant behaviour and of slavish followers of fashion. Cecilia receives cynically her instructions on how to converse in the approved mode. 'So much,' she chaffs her tutor, 'for sorrow and for affectation. Proceed next to stupidity; for that in all probability, I shall most frequently encounter.' And Evelina can 'scarce forbear laughing' when asked to dance by a young man whose fashionable behaviour seems to her only outlandish and affected. As well as independent thought, these women are also quite capable of independent action. Evelina, for instance, has no hesitation in snatching at loaded pistols, when there is no strong man around to tell her not to. The sensibility of Burney's heroines is always carefully balanced by an active intelligence. The heart and the head combine in their portrayal.

Fanny Burney was a realist. Her attitude towards the literary clichés she employs is sceptical and her novels easily assimilate the melodramatic elements into the overall comic scenario. Her plots for instance incorporate many of the features of conventional romance. *Evelina* and *Camilla* are merely versions of the Cinderella theme, a staple ingredient of eighteenth-century novels since Richardson's brilliant adaptation of it in *Pamela.* The story of the Princess and the Pea, gentility in rags, is retold through the experiences of Cecilia and Juliet, the discovery of their true identity allowable only after a series of tests and a highly prolonged and extravagant denouement. Characters are painfully rejected by their loved ones and then gloriously reunited. They are threatened with penury, starvation, madness, abduction and they encounter suicide attempts and deathbed scenes. The heroines marry elitist and aristocratic heroes, who frequently have little but their station in life to recommend them. Yet although the narrative direction of her novels follows these well tried formulae, Burney's main interest is not in the contrivances of the plot nor in romance but in the social comedy and its illumination of individual dilemmas.

It is not the action but the heroine's response to the action which is foregrounded. Like their sentimental predecessors, the characters are confronted with experience that they cannot immediately control. Their social circumstances, where they live, whom they meet are all matters dictated for them, so that major choices are removed from them but their capacity for judgement is not. Thus it is the characters' minds which become the focus of interest and the quality of their experience which provides the narrative dynamic. This view of the mind as a sensitive receptacle which absorbed experience and responded accordingly was not in itself new. The sentimental emphasis on the values of individualism had produced a range of central characters who were required to make sense of the chaotic flux of experience which surrounded them—notably Sterne's Uncle Toby in *Tristram Shandy* and Yorick in *A Sentimental Journey* or the heroes of Henry Mackenzie. In these novels, coherent action reduced to a minimum, the sensations and intricacies of personality sustained the overall direction. Burney of course does not aspire to Sterne's literary or philosophical sophistication, nor does she wish to dispense in any way with the formal structures. The observance of the proprieties remained vital to her. She develops rather the interest in women's roles initially stimulated by Richardson, suggesting that the female mind is as worthy of attention as the male and that feminine experience has a unique dimension which justifies serious analysis. Less radical than Richardson, she has one advantage which was denied him: her own experience of growing up as a woman in a restrictive society. She seeks ways of best liberating the self and allowing the individual personality to find full expression without disturbing the social forms which necessarily provide constraints but which also provide structure.

In initiating what was to become the 'woman's novel,' Fanny Burney adopts a mode which presents her readers with the very texture of women's lives and by so doing, establishes herself as a literary pioneer. William Hazlitt's comment that she 'is a quick, lively and accurate observer of persons and things' is sharpened by the recognition that 'she always looks at them with a consciousness of her sex, and in that point of view in which it is the particular business and interest of women to observe them.' With no female vocabulary available to them previous women writers had fallen back on male techniques. Charlotte Charke, for instance, in her autobiography created a persona reminiscent of Defoe's Moll Flanders, a woman who could survive only by being like a man, adopting male disguise, travelling round the country, fighting and asserting her equality by partaking in traditionally male activities. Novelists, such as Eliza Haywood or Mary de la Rivière Manley, also employed a largely masculine tenor in recounting their histories. Action took precedence over character in their tales of adventure, fantastic exploits and broad panoramic scenes. The complexities of the personality were ignored, together with any idea of the shared and special nature of women's experience. But Fanny Burney discloses the essential fibre of women's daily lives as lives composed of trivia, where the choice of dress, the petty matters of conversation, the technicalities of hairdressing or reserving theatre seats are seen to carry significance. The extreme situations and creaking plot mechanisms are merely pegs on which to hang this material. Burney moves away from the episodic novels which preceded her to the coherence of *Evelina*, which uses the epistolary method so successfully employed by Richardson to blend thematic and narrative elements, and maintains the close focus on detailed experience which was to identify the common approach of so many later women novelists.

Apart from *Camilla*, Fanny Burney's novels are not conventionally didactic and even *Camilla* departs from its orthodox moralistic direction with a subtext which offers a challenge to certain prevailing standards. But Burney is deeply concerned with behavioural codes and in considering the nature of female lives her books illustrate a fundamentally prudential morality. Reworking her own experience through her novels, she demonstrates her own anxieties about doing the right thing and introduces a distinctively feminine perspective on the male hierarchy. Men appear as they impinge on women's experience. They are seen in their domestic roles, as fathers, brothers, potential husbands, all of whom can arbitrarily withhold love and deny support. They also appear as guardians, lawyers, bankers, the figureheads of officialdom with bureaucratic power. Frequently their roles overlap. The aristocratic Lord Orville represents for Evelina both the material security and social status that she craves and the love and moral constancy that will sustain her personal confidence. The power of masculine values is recognised and accepted, however inimical it might be to women's own sense of priorities.

As Patricia Meyer Spacks has observed [in *Imagining a Self*, 1976], Burney's women are dominated by a sense of fear, an emotion which shapes their attitudes and inspires their actions. The fear which projected itself in the Gothic novels of the period as deep-seated psychological phantasmagoria is transmuted in Burney's fiction into a setting of deceptively reassuring familiarity. The terror experienced by Burney's heroines is located in the minutiae of polite society. Evelina worries about her lack of polish and her vulgar relatives. Juliet is nervous about playing the harp in public. Camilla is distraught about her lover's discovery of innocently committed misdemeanours. Ignorance, exposure, misinterpretation—these are the anxieties that dog Burney's women and reveal their fundamental confusion about how to conduct themselves. 'I have been,' cries Cecilia at a late stage in the novel, 'too facile and too unguarded!' Despite her original determination to 'think and live for herself,' she is forced to recognise the duplicity of her society and to learn

that she can never be fully independent of the community which carries the power to destroy her. She is helpless in the face of legal demands on her inheritance and defenceless in the face of insidious rumours about her moral character. Circumstances combine against her to initiate the cumulative disasters of *Cecilia*'s final volume. In examining the problems which beset social conformity, Burney's attitude is how can women possibly survive in a society which is so obviously and heavily weighted against them.

For Fanny Burney, women's social vulnerability is closely associated with their sexual fragility. The novels are fraught with sexual menace. The London of pleasure gardens and bourgeois residential streets contains dangers as perilous and as real as Mrs Radcliffe's wild foreign landscapes and isolated castles with their antique chambers. Evelina's panic, lost in the subliminally sinister dark alleys at Vauxhall dramatises women's basic fear of personal violation. Evelina is 'terrified to death,' 'frightened exceedingly,' 'distracted with terror.' Attacked by a group of strange men who see her as legitimate sexual game, she is rescued by another who, under the guise of friendship, tries to seduce her and proves to be equally as treacherous. It seems as if there is no escape. In stressing the precariousness of the situation of the single woman, Burney reveals that sexuality is an ambivalent attribute. It is both a trap and a shield for the sex who can so easily be reduced to gender characteristics. The veneer of polite society conceals an atavistic violence against which women must constantly be on their guard.

The dividing line between respectability and degradation is always presented as a very narrow one. 'It is impossible and improper to keep up acquaintance with a female who has lost her character, however sincerely she may be an object of pity,' Burney noted in her diary of 1775, having just snubbed a rather shady young lady in the park. 'Much is to be said in excuse of a poor credulous young creature whose person is attractive while her mind is unformed' but there was no way that such sympathy could be corroborated by action. Burney was a creature of her time and her novels continually assert the tenuous nature of the hold women have on the world's approbation. Cecilia and Camilla are both mistaken for prostitutes when male protection is removed. Juliet and Cecilia are reluctantly inveigled into secret marriages against their better judgement. Confusion prevails. All these heroines are shrouded in mystery at some stage in their stories. Without men, their identity remains an enigma. The popular fictional motifs of unknown parentage, disguise, disinheritance and reconciliation are invested with a new dimension as Burney lays bare the problematics of self. Women's identity is seen as being reliant on male status but this in itself is shown as a hazardous source of refuge.

The burden of this examination of women's experience does not rest with the heroines alone. The novels contain a host of minor female characters who have independent contributions to make to the fabric of enquiry. All provide variants on the ideas of conformism and role-playing. Burney creates immature adolescents who marry without fully understanding what that means; she exposes the plight of old maids; she mocks girls who are over demonstrative and those who follow fashion unthinkingly; she ridicules women who are ignoramuses and women who are too educated for their own good; she paints women who are forceful and aggressive and women who attempt to live without male mentors. Her young lord who complains, 'I don't know what the devil a woman lives for after thirty; she is only in other folks' way,' is a perfect prototype of male arrogance and an illustration of the tendency to classify women as dispensable items. Her heroines learn by bitter experience how to avoid this categorisation but Burney's lesser characters often indicate quite fully realised alternatives. They are not, as in many other contemporary novels, used merely as warning examples, foils for that moral paragon, the heroine, but are frequently presented with a degree of imaginative sympathy that intensifies the pattern of the whole.

This sympathy necessarily affects the portrayal of her male characters too. Much of Fanny Burney's critical reputation in the past has rested with these brilliantly vivid caricatures and satiric portraits but it is perhaps worthwhile noting that her men only seem to come alive when they are objects of attack. Her heroes are pale and uninteresting, spineless representatives of a dead value system. They engage her only as symbolic figures, providing the conventional disciplines of romance and moral authority which her lively heroines must ultimately acknowledge. Much of the time they are in fact absent from the narrative, remaining only in spirit as a guiding principle of the culture they embody, inspiring terror in the hearts of the heroines who seek their approval and directing their movements from a position offstage. But the clowns, fops, villains and fools have a stature and vitality that is instantly absorbing. Burney's comic sense, derived from the traditions of eighteenth-century satire, owes much to Fielding, Smollett and the Hogarthian tradition of the social cartoon. She scrutinises the details of manner and dress, notes the precision of idiomatic speech and the impact of visual idiosyncrasies. These methods of observation were trained during her long apprenticeship to Mr Crisp, who demanded that her letters should provide him with a graphic reconstruction of events in London to enliven the solitude of his quiet country evenings. 'He is indeed very ill-favoured,' begins her sharp dissection of Dr Johnson. 'Is tall and stout; but stoops terribly; he is almost bent double.' Each detail continues the process of devastation. 'His mouth is almost constantly opening and shutting, as if he was chewing. He has a strange method of frequently twirling his fingers, and twisting his hands. His body is in continual agitation, *see-sawing* up and down; his feet are never a moment quiet and in short, his whole person is in *perpetual motion.*' Burney's genuine delight in the originality of individuals evolves as a genius for trenchant character demolition in her novels, in targets such as the bumptious social climber, Mr Smith, the inspired lunatic, Mr Dubster and the filthy miser, Mr Briggs, whose personalities are fleshed from her perception of physical curiosities.

It is Fanny Burney's comic flair which helps to distinguish her novels from those of her contemporaries. A keen lover of theatre, she was obviously influenced by dramatic practice, not only in characterisation but in her conception of the comic possibilities of situation. Despite her image of ladylike propriety, her humour is raucous and often outrageous. Her novels contain scenes of wild farce, unthinkable for later women writers with their controlled decorousness. The dropping of an old woman's wig and the overturning of a carriage provide Burney with occasions for laughter, if they demonstrate the discomfiture of haughty or vulgar individuals. She had a keen sense of the ridiculous, but it became tempered more and more by notions of artistic decorum, as she grew older and became more urgently aware of the effects of public notice. After the success of *Evelina*, Sir Joshua Reynolds had recommended her to write 'anything in the dialogue way,' a proposal strongly endorsed by Sheridan's enthusiastic encouragement. Mrs Thrale's Streatham set were quick to recognise the dramatic potential of *Evelina*, and the result of this heady influence, chasing quickly on *Evelina*'s heels, was the glittering and acerbic *The Witlings*, a tight little play, with highly individualised 'humour' characters: Mrs Voluble, Lady Smatter, Mrs Sapient and Mrs Wheedle. On the title page of this onslaught on the pretensions of female literati, Fanny Burney signed herself 'A Sister of the Order' of Witlings, a self irony which disappointingly vanishes in her later work. Perhaps it was the anxious condemnation of her father and Mr Crisp that awakened her to the thorns in the path of public scrutiny, and made her so nervous about the future reception of her writing. Certainly her native talent for dialogue never diminished. It remained for her an instinctive approach in the visualisation of events, and many of her letters are written in dialogue form, set out like the script of a play, as action acquires meaning through the perception of its participants.

Certainly one of the reasons for the great success of *Evelina* was its dramatised technique, a technique which Burney was to discard in her other novels. In selecting the method she used in her journals for her fiction, she was able to amalgamate most closely the aspects of her divided sensibility, the private and the public selves. When, in her subsequent fiction, she had to find an authoritative voice to describe the events taking place, the efforts of depersonalisation progressively obliterated the essential spontaneity of vision and *The Wanderer*, her last novel, which contains some of the most penetrating political insights, is actually the dullest and most tedious of her books. Both Burney's journals and her first novel, however, assert overpoweringly the centrality of the self in defining the nature of experience. It is personality which shapes our response here, rather than events, and both the diaries and *Evelina* embody the triumph of contingency over form.

These two aspects of her writing, the novels and the diaries, illuminate the difference between material moulded to fit a conventional pattern and material which defines and creates its own pattern. And there is always present in the novels themselves a tension between the dominant moral strictures and the imaginative evocation of personal impressions. This can be detected in the narrative organisation which tries to accommodate both formal, often derivative, motifs and individual subjective insights. The sequence of the four novels demonstrates this tension quite strikingly. *Evelina* freely adapts the techniques of the personal diary to the disciplines of fiction and much of its charm is in the very freshness which the epistolary method throws into prominence, as Evelina's perceptions establish the means by which we see the story. The next three novels, however, reverse this procedure. Burney, much more conscious of the possible criticism from her readers, submerges her heroines' voices beneath an impersonal, authorial commentary. Events therefore gain consequence and become increasingly insistent. Cecilia, for example, moves to London from the country at the beginning of the novel because under the terms of her guardian's will she has no alternative not, like Evelina, because she is invited. As circumstances take over, the quality of the characters' experience is reported rather than enacted. The diction too becomes more dignified, as Fanny Burney seems to lose touch with any direct involvement in the activities she recounts. 'It is not very early in life we learn how little is performed, for which no precaution is taken,' the narrator of *Camilla* admonishes her audience. 'Care is the offspring of disappointment; and sorrow and repentance commonly hang upon its first lessons.' This is typical of Burney's later fictional style. Passive constructions, abstract nouns, the didactic tone all combine to try to deny the force of the subjective experience which *Evelina* had so keenly tried to convey. The language moves further and further from the intimacy we find both there and in the letters and journals. Only in the dramatic comedies does it recur, where the genre itself dictates the author's absence and characters can speak freely in their own idiom.

Once again we are faced with Fanny Burney's own difficulty in finding an appropriate role for herself. Her natural genius for dramatisation, like her own gift

for mimicry which she suppressed in polite company, became squashed beneath her urge to conform to the proprieties and her attempt to synchronise her own responses with the persona she believed it was her duty to adopt led inevitably to literary disaster. It was as if the freedom to think and speak as she liked was a reward she granted herself for good behaviour; certainly her mischievous opinions were saved for unguarded moments with her diary, her close friends and her family. She screened her private personality, her lifeline, from intrusive public eyes as, dominated by her consciousness of expected codes of feminine reticence, she sensed that her own ideas were at odds with the contemporary ethos.

The forms of her writing mirror their subjects. The examination of how to adapt the private self to a required public role is central to all her work. The problem of how to synthesise individualism with the social ethic can be solved for her only through the device of secrecy. It is important both for Burney and her heroines, to keep hidden the true impulses of the soul, which are essentially uncontained and free. When she was an old lady, she went through her journals, erasing sections and destroying whole years of memories, for fear of possible publication. The fact that private and public lives could never satisfactorily merge became increasingly apparent to her as her work developed. Female freedom is the subject of all her novels and it is a subject which is reflected in the forms those novels take, as they move towards a public voice, a reduction of the writer's own personality and a tone of objective neutrality. As she became more conscious of the demands of the all powerful system which determined the conditions of women's lives, she found that secrecy was her only recourse. Both Fanny Burney's life and her writings ultimately affirm this course of action.

Margaret Drabble (essay date 1988)

SOURCE: An introduction to *The Wanderer or, Female Difficulties,* by Fanny Burney, Pandora, 1988, pp. vii-xiv.

[*In the following essay, Drabble reevaluates* The Wanderer, *claiming that "Fanny Burney's common sense and common humanity survive the machinery of her own plot and counterbalance the melodrama with affectionate observation and a real optimism."*]

The Wanderer is the fourth and last novel of Fanny Burney, and the least known. It was published in 1814 after a silence of fourteen years, and was eagerly—perhaps too eagerly—awaited by the many celebrated admirers, friends and critics who had so highly praised its predecessors, *Evelina* (1778), *Cecilia* (1782) and *Camilla* (1796). But for various reasons it disappointed expectations, and has since been little read except by scholars of the period: this is the first reprint since 1814. We can now ask ourselves: does it deserve the oblivion into which it fell? Is it merely a historical curiosity or may we now discern in it qualities which its contemporary readers failed to note? Before considering some of these questions, and attempting to place the novel in its social and political context, may I pay it the tribute of an innocent reader who read it in the somewhat cumbersome form of a bulky photocopy nearly a foot thick (the text is 60,000 words longer even than the lengthy *Cecilia*) which I carried around with me in sections. At one point I found I had underestimated my reading capacity and had finished the wad of pages I had with me: I was two hundred miles from the continuation, frustrated and miserable because I could not immediately pursue the mysterious adventures of the 'black, patched and penniless' heroine. I could not wait to get back to the story; I longed to know what was going to happen next. Burney's narrative power survives the decades, and she keeps us guessing at her dénouement through five volumes. This is no small achievement. But the book also has other attractions which make it a welcome addition to the Mothers of the Novel series.

The story of Fanny Burney's precocious success as the anonymous author of *Evelina* is well known. She had been writing stories and diaries from girlhood onwards, discouraged by her stepmother (who believed that writing was not a suitable career for a woman), but encouraged tacitly and openly by other members of her family, despite some attempts at secrecy. It was her brother Charles who negotiated with her publishers for her. Her father, the musicologist Dr Charles Burney, when informed that Fanny wanted his consent to publish merely (in Macaulay's words) 'stared, burst out a-laughing, kissed her, gave her leave to do as she liked, and never even asked the name of her work.' Macaulay considered his behaviour grossly negligent, but it certainly cannot be construed as hostile. Gradually her identity became known and she received the praise and friendship of the most eminent literary and intellectual figures of her day, including Burke, Mrs Delany, Joshua Reynolds, Dr Johnson and Mrs Thrale. While protesting her timidity and modesty, she found herself a celebrity, increasingly drawn into social and public life. Success followed success and *Cecilia* was also warmly received. She seemed set for a full and rewarding career as a writer when, in 1786, she accepted an invitation to become Second Keeper of the Robes to Queen Charlotte, a post which inflicted upon her what now seem grotesque constraints of behaviour for very little reward, apart from the material which enriched her Diary for the entertainment of posterity. Royal service made her as ill and as unhappy as any heroine of a Gothic novel imprisoned in a cobwebbed castle, and she escaped in 1791 with a pension of £100 a year. Two years later, at the age of forty-one, she

met and married Alexandre d'Arblay, the exiled Adjutant-General of Lafayette, and it was through him and his circle of fellow *émigrés* in Surrey that she embarked on the adventures that provide much of the background of *The Wanderer*.

The Wanderer opens dramatically, as a small boat puts off at dead of night from the coast of France during the reign of terror under Robespierre. It is hailed by and picks up a mysterious dark bandaged stranger, a young female 'Hottentot' whose real identity continues to intrigue her rescuers and the reader as she progressively sheds her disguise and discloses her many graces. It is only gradually revealed in successive volumes, inch by inch, in a web of melodrama which at times is reminiscent of the exploits of the Scarlet Pimpernel of Baroness Orczy. Delay is used to an extreme and apparently exaggerated degree: the Wanderer resists with the utmost vehemence and at some risk to herself the increasingly pressing attempts to discover her name, and is known in the first chapters by those who take pity on her inexplicable plight as the 'Incognita'. She then becomes known as 'Miss Ellis', or plain 'Ellis' after the initials 'L.S.' which appear on a letter she receives, a letter which is her only link with the outside world. Her first name, Juliet, is revealed to the reader but not to her associates at the beginning of Volume 3, and the full explanation of her provenance and her reasons for remaining so obstinately nameless and friendless are revealed only in the last pages. Thus for nearly five volumes we follow, and at a certain narrative distance, the misadventures of a penniless unidentified stranger, distinguished only by her grace, beauty, gentlewoman's manners, and artistic and musical skills.

It must at once be admitted that there is much that is implausible and ridiculous in the difficulties which the lovely Juliet endures during the course of the novel, and that her misfortunes—in losing her purse at crucial moments of the plot not once but twice, in finding herself in embarrassing social positions or overencumbered with undesirable admirers, in discovering herself bewildered in forests or surprised in inns—are not always such as invite sympathy. The subtitle of the whole work is 'Female Difficulties', a phrase repeated with emphasis many times in the plot, and the reader at times is compelled to agree with Hazlitt, who commented in the *Edinburgh Review* (February 1815) that 'The difficulties in which [Miss Burney] involves her heroines are indeed "Female Difficulties";—they are difficulties created out of nothing.' The excessive decorum and excessive sensibility of Juliet seem at times a strained development of Burney's more robust though equally beleaguered early heroines, and the language of some of the passages—particularly those between Juliet and her admirer Harleigh, or her beloved Lady Aurora Granville—reach heights of circumlocution and affectation that justify all Macaulay's censure, though perhaps not his vehemence. Macaulay, in his well-known essay on Burney, condemned the language of her later work as 'a sort of broken Johnsonese, a barbarous *patois*, bearing the same relation to the language of *Rasselas* which the gibberish of the negroes of Jamaica bears to the English of the House of Lords.' He ascribes the deterioration of her style not only to the damaging influence of Johnson, but also to her ten years' residence in enforced exile in France (from 1802 to 1812) when she had little chance for intercourse with speakers of what Macaulay would have considered acceptable English.

Nevertheless, the book does not deserve the blanket dismissal of Hazlitt and Macaulay. It has fine things in it, and even the parts which are not fine are of interest. When reading it, one is tempted to forget that in writing of the hardships of *émigrés* from France during the Revolution, Fanny Burney was not exploiting a distant romantic past of fantastic exploits, as was Orczy, but was writing of her own firsthand experience. Even the composition of *The Wanderer* took place against a background of intrigue and violence: she had the unfinished manuscript of it with her when she sailed surreptitiously after long delays and struggles with the police from Dunkirk in 1812 on an American smuggling vessel, the *Mary Ann*. The ship was seized in the Channel by a British sloop but Fanny eventually arrived safely in England with her book and her son Alexander to kiss the beach of Deal when she landed. One may feel she had had good reason to fear that the 'Fourth Child' of her brain might be 'destroyed ere it was Born'. Her vivid diary account of the five weeks she spent trying to leave Dunkirk reminds us of the very real dangers of the times she lived in.

Her later life could hardly have been more different from that of her distinguished successor and admirer Jane Austen, in whose works, notoriously, the French wars make hardly a whisper of an appearance. Burney, both in England and France, was at the centre of the political and historical revolutions of the period, and her immediate acquaintance included many who had fled certain death and whose relatives had died in battle or by the guillotine. She exchanged the stifling prison of the English court for a world of change and challenge, and some of this makes its way into her work.

Not, perhaps, enough: one of the explanations of the disappointing reception of *The Wanderer* undoubtedly lies in the fact that readers had very high expectations of its author, not only from her previous works but also—as Burney was well and apprehensively aware—from the fact that they expected a portrait of life in Paris under Napoleon and did not get one. This may indeed be reasonably regretted: had she used some of her French material (such as, for example, the exquisitely funny 1802 Journal descriptions of the way in which 'des Dames françoises' kiss one another upon

greeting) in a comedy of manners in the style of *Evelina* we would have inherited both a fine comic novel and a fine social document. But this was not her intention in *The Wanderer*, and she may well have had diplomatic as well as artistic reasons for choosing not to write in too much detail of her experience of France. As it was she was taken to task in the *Quarterly Review* and by other critics for failing to condemn 'the gigantic despotism, the ferocious cruelty, the restless and desolating tyranny of Buonaparte,' and for mildly and tactfully expressing in her Preface her gratitude to the 'honour and liberality' of her husband's country in which she had lived (at times somewhat unwillingly, it must be admitted) for so many years. Indeed, she claims that she has no interest in stoking political controversy and national animosity: her choice of a refugee heroine is not intended to be politically provocative.

What, then, in the career of Juliet and her 'female difficulties', is she attempting to portray? One of her principal aims is surely to display to the reader the innumerable obstacles which any young, unprotected, poor woman encounters when she tries to earn her own living honourably and preserve her independence. The modern reader, while perhaps driven to impatience by the author's and heroine's acceptance of most of the sexual and social codes of the day, can sympathize with some of the humiliations which Juliet endures. We know from Burney's notebook that she had a schematic view of these, and that she wished to present Juliet successively as a victim of various social conventions and prejudices. She is shown as suffering as a dependent 'toad-eater' and semi-servant from the arrogance of Mrs Maple and Mrs Ireton: when she tries to earn her living by teaching music or as a milliner she suffers from the financial whims and selfishness of her customers and employers. Through her we learn that a girl needs capital even to embark on a lowly career as a needlewoman: Juliet does not have the premium to pay her employer for an apprenticeship, and anyway there are several other young women already on a waiting list. Running a small shop as her friend Gabrielle tries to do is not easy either. The lives of working girls are portrayed with sympathy and some sharpness. Some of the best, wittiest and most feeling passages in the book are those which describe the unthinking negligence with which the gentry treat tradespeople and servants. Mr Giles's lectures on this subject to Juliet are well argued, and we note with interest that the vulgar grocer Mr Tedman, who had earlier offended the refined Juliet by over-friendly grossness and greasy cakes, is the only one who pays his debts. Juliet, although an implausible paragon of beauty and accomplishment, is not perfect and, in the course of the novel, she has much to learn, not only about others but also about herself.

She learns, for example, that it is not enough to be a talented amateur musician, admired by young men in drawing rooms: to earn one's living as a professional performer requires hard work, dedication, a lack of false modesty. The scenes in which she attempts a career as a singer foreshadow, perhaps, the similar attempts and similar disappointments of Gwendolen Harleth in George Eliot's *Daniel Deronda*, though Fanny Burney's attitude to her heroine's musical ambitions and to the proprieties is more ambiguous than George Eliot's, and more unresolved.

Indeed, there is something intriguingly unresolved throughout **The Wanderer** in Burney's attitude towards female difficulties, as there was in her attitude towards royalty, towards sexual decorum, and towards the politics of revolutionary and Napoleonic France. Nowhere is it more striking than in her portrait of Juliet's counterpart and foil in the novel, Elinor Joddrel, who is passionately in love with Juliet's admirer, the virtuous and almost wholly colourless Harleigh. Elinor is a New Woman of her time, influenced by the philosophy of the French Revolution and the Enlightenment, intellectually interested in the Rights of Man and more specifically in the Rights of Woman: she is bold, emotional, reckless, capricious. She is portrayed as part ridiculous, part heroic: her lack of modesty and judgment is condemned, and her behaviour (which includes various melodramatic and highly public suicide attempts) is grotesque and unstable. She is a character who could never have appeared in the pages of Jane Austen; she belongs to another world. Yet it is not a wholly fictitious world, and Elinor relates to real historical models, to women whom Fanny Burney knew either by repute or as friends and acquaintances.

One of these models, proposed by Claire Tomalin in her biography, *The Life and Death of Mary Wollstonecraft* (1974) is Mary Wollstonecraft herself, the notorious author of *A Vindication of the Rights of Women* (1792), who had, like Elinor, visited France during the revolutionary period and sympathised with its revolutionary ideals. She had, like Elinor, no maidenly inhibitions about taking an active part in declaring her love for a man, and, like Elinor, she made suicide attempts when she was rejected—with the significant difference that she had lived with and had a child by the lover who abandoned her. Elinor is not allowed such licence. Mary died in 1797, after marrying the radical philosopher William Godwin and giving birth to the future Mary Shelley, and we have evidence that Fanny Burney was already at this period planning the novel that was to become **The Wanderer:** it is more than likely that the doubtful example of Mary's life and death was in Fanny's mind when she created Elinor.

Another possible and probable model is the French writer, Madame de Staël (1766-1817), author of two 'advanced' feminist novels (*Delphine*, 1802 and *Corinne*, 1807) and various important critical and philo-sophic works. Fanny met her in 1793 at Juniper Hall, Surrey: Germaine de Staël was a member of the circle of French *émigrés* which included Fanny's future husband, General D'Arblay. Fanny was at first captivated by her intellect, charm and conversation, but the friendship dwindled under pressure from her father and a belated realisation that Madame de Staël was the mistress of her fellow *émigré,* Louis de Narbonne. Fanny was afraid of losing her court pension if she mixed with such politically and morally unacceptable characters and succumbed to propriety, though she continued to write with admiration of her old friend. De Staël was to comment caustically to Fanny's sister Susan Phillips that in England women were treated as minors all their lives: 'It seems to me that your sister behaves like a girl of fourteen.' Like Elinor Joddrel and Mary Wollstonecraft, de Staël made various suicide attempts, as did her lover Benjamin Constant, who always seemed to have a handy threatening bottle of opium in his pocket. It was the age of sentiment, of the flamboyant gesture, of passion and intensity: Romanticism had succeeded the Age of Reason, and the vogue for suicide and 'Wertherism', which had swept Europe in the wake of Goethe's immensely influential *Sorrows of Young Werther* (1774), had not yet ebbed. Fanny Burney's portrait of Elinor Joddrel represents what she saw as the dangers of crossing the frontiers of known and approved conduct, and the folly of believing in the perfectibility of man and the liberation of women. 'Boundless licence' of thought can only lead, as Harleigh proclaims, to disaster; a moral that the aftermath of the French Revolution illustrated only too well to the apprehensive English across the Channel. We see in Fanny's ambivalence towards Mme de Staël the seeds of Victorian prudery, the growth of what we would now call a 'moral backlash'. Fanny is poised between two worlds. One might note, as a marker, the fact that the pure Juliet is allowed to appear as an amateur actress to universal applause and without forfeiting her respectability in a performance of a restoration comedy, *The Provoked Wife*, whereas in a novel published that same year, *Mansfield Park*, Jane Austen judges with some harshness the indelicacy of those who take part in amateur theatricals. The climate was changing: Mary Wollstonecraft had lost the battle, if not the war.

Burney nervously condemns Elinor, but she gives her some good lines and reveals that despite her own scruples she had been deeply engaged and stimulated by the intellectual speculations of de Staël. In Book Five there is a long culminating debate between Elinor and Harleigh on the ethical implications of suicide (a subject on which de Staël published a treatise in 1813, retracting her own earlier Wertherian views). Elinor cries, 'O, if ever that wretched thing called life has a noble moment, surely it must be that of its voluntary sacrifice! lopping off, at a blow, that hydra-headed monster of evil upon evil, called time; bounding over the imps of superstition; dancing upon the pangs of

disease; and boldly, hardily mocking the senseless legends that would frighten us with eternity!—Eternity? to poor, little, frail finite beings like us! . . . Nature comes but for succession; though the pride of man would give her resurrection. Mouldering all together we go, to form new earth for burying our successors.'
It is hard to find this argument as 'horrible' as Harleigh professes to find it, and hard not to suspect that Fanny Burney was more sympathetic to and intrigued by the adventurous Elinors of this world than she dared to show.

It is hard, too, to believe that she did not have some sympathy with Elinor's expressed feminism. Elinor exclaims, 'Why, for so many centuries, has man alone been supposed to possess, not only force and power for action and defence, but even all the rights of taste; all the fine sensibilities which impel our happiest sympathies, in the choice of our life's partners?' Why indeed? Fanny as a young woman had known what it was to be persuaded towards an unwelcome but 'suitable' marriage by those whom she loved and trusted, as she had known what it was to be a toady at court. But she had also, uncharacteristically for her time, tasted independence: she had earned money of her own, had chosen her own man (and a Frenchman and a Catholic at that), and had enjoyed status in her own right as an author. Juliet, more representatively, is more unfortunate. Juliet's career is nothing but an illustration of the difficulties which beset the single girl in a hostile and hypocritical society, where her only hope of happiness and status appears to lie in a marriage for which she must passively wait, pure and uncompromised. It cannot have escaped her creator's notice that Juliet, in order to remain pure and uncompromised and to evade the insulting and threatening attentions of various lascivious pursuers, is obliged to expose herself to all sorts of unnecessary dangers and to roam the wild countryside, a wanderer indeed, when a word of rational explanation might have brought the whole plot to a sudden and simple end. The contrasts between the dangers of polite society in Brighthelmstone (i.e., Brighton), the dangers of France under Robespierre, and the dangers of the English countryside are implicit rather than explicit, and some of the comedy and irony are lost in solemnity and pious moralising, but the fundamental 'difficulty' of being a woman in a man's world is forcefully portrayed. Fanny Burney may have been timid and conservative in her expressed morality, but nevertheless she in real life and her heroines in her novels manage to find themselves in some wildly unconventional situations, and a certain tough spirit of survival manifests itself even in the modest, shrinking Juliet. She survives ordeal after ordeal, from sitting in a crowded carriage tormented by a spoiled child and a hot dog to sleeping in a forest hut full of smugglers, and although she emerges as a heroine should to a fairy-tale happy ending, her wanderings provide opportunity for a wide range of incident and satiric comment.

Fanny Burney insisted that this novel was not a love story, and indeed its romantic interest is now perhaps the least appealing of its ingredients. It may be read now as a series of reflections on the ambiguous attitudes of society to the independence and employment of women, and on the dangers to which they are exposed because of that society's rigid expectations of them. And it survives on a simple level as a tale of suspense and intrigue. But it also, almost incidentally, offers us some fresh and appealing portraits of odd corners of English rural life: we find Juliet singing old ballads in a dame's school in Hampshire; Juliet shrinking fastidiously from the boisterous fun of a farmer's fair; Juliet puzzled by a mysterious poacher's pie called 'chicky-biddy', Juliet comparing the farmer's lot with the shepherd's and wondering if either admire the beauties of nature. Some of the best moments are the outdoor moments, when we escape altogether from the stifling pettiness of the rigid class system and the ludicrous sexual mores of the polite world of Granvilles and Maples and Iretons into another, broader, greener world. Dame Fairfield's defence of the people of the New Forest rings out loud and clear against the pretensions and trickeries of Brighton and the dark suspicions of the romantically nervous Juliet.

> Why sure, and sure, there be no daunger to nobody in our Forest! We do go up it and down it, noight and day, with no manner of fear; and though I do come from afar myself, being but a stranger in these parts, till I was married; my feather-in-law, who has lived in them, mon and boy, better than ninety odd years,—for, though a be still as fresh as a rose, a be a'most a hundred; he do tell me that a would carry his gold watch, if a had one, in his open hand, from top to bottom of our nine walks, in the pitch of the night; and a should aunswer to come to no harm; for a had never heard of a traveller as had so much as a hair of his head hurt in the New Forest.

That 'if a had one' is masterly, and this is far, far better stuff than the novel's somewhat tired caricatures of French villains or English seducers. Fanny Burney's common sense and common humanity survive the machinery of her own plot and counterbalance the melodrama with affectionate observation and a real optimism. Her prose may have become convoluted with age but her heart remained kind.

Joanne Cutting-Gray (essay date 1992)

SOURCE: "*Evelina*: Writing Between Experience and Innocence," in *Woman as 'Nobody' and the Novels of Fanny Burney*, University Press of Florida, 1992, pp. 9-30.

[*In the following essay, Cutting-Gray claims that Evelina's writing serves as a means of transcending societally imposed restrictions on women.*]

Thus ought a chaste and virtuous woman . . . lock up her very words and set a guard upon her lips, especially in the company of strangers, since there is nothing which sooner discovers the qualities and conditions of a woman than her discourse.

—Plutarch

A worldly wise, often subversive, journalist-narrator who represents herself as an inexperienced young rustic has intrigued, if not puzzled, the readers of Burney's first novel, *Evelina*. The fact that Evelina's innocence can only be seen from the narrator's perspective beyond innocence, that innocence is a reductive concept within the broader, reflexive context of writing is an important clue to the quixotic conduct of Burney's first heroine. If, as T. B. Macaulay notes, "novel" was a name that produced shudders from respectable people so that a novelist sometimes risked social ostracism, then a female novelist, much like her fictional counterpart, risked even more. It is no wonder then, that young Burney, single, genteel, and shy, kept her authorship a secret. No one, except perhaps her father, was more astonished than she at the immediate popularity of *Evelina*.

Aside from its popular reception, Burney's first novel also charmed the arbiters of eighteenth-century taste—Johnson, Reynolds, Burke, and Sheridan—and delighted Mrs. Thrale and Lady Mary Montagu. Mrs. Thrale, relieved to discover that *Evelina* was not "mere sentimental business," commented that "it's writ by somebody that knows *the top and the bottom,* the *highest* and *lowest* of mankind." Early reviewers of *Evelina* praised its charming, unaffected glimpse into the social life of London, its satire of class and individual character, and its broad humor and pathos even as they cited its contrived plot and flatly conceived heroine as instances of its conventionality. Modern commentary, however, is more likely to laud *Evelina*'s publication in 1778 as a frontier: "Behind it are centuries of silence; in front of it, that 'damned mob of scribbling women' who seized upon the novel as a means of subsistence and self-expression and thereby challenged the masculine perspective that had previously dominated literature."

As circumspect forerunner of what was called that "mob of scribbling women," Burney explained the innocent character of Evelina to her sister Susan by saying that she "had been brought up in the strictest retirement, that she knew nothing of the world, and only acted from the impulses of Nature." Quoting from her own preface, she added that the heroine was the "offspring of Nature in her simplest attire." Though Evelina incarnates artlessness in a world of duplicity and evil, she nonetheless requires "observation and experience" to make her "fit for the world." Evelina under the guardianship of the Reverend Mr. Villars is the innocent in a private world of innocence until she sallies forth into a disjunctive, public world where, affronted by male assertiveness, she, as female, becomes a problem to herself. Unless one hears in Evelina's discourse a misguided effort to maintain the "simplest attire" of innocence, one will too often see only female compliancy. As long as she insists upon preserving her innocence-passivity (a symbol for the stasis of her being), she cannot assimilate experience. Compliancy thus becomes for Evelina a deviant form of prudence that violates any practical wisdom.

Knowing nothing of the world suggests a state of unreflective union with nature prior to knowledge. This state of unselfconsciousness contrasts with a succeeding stage of irretrievable loss in which the emergent self stands over against the world. Indeed, to act only from the "impulses of Nature" accords with those older patriarchal notions of the feminine as well as our common sense precept of innocence ("Nature in her simplest attire"). Within such a limited, cultural stereotype for female behavior Evelina authors her journal-diary and retrieves in the act of writing a richness of experience otherwise denied to her. In the gap between her speech and action, between her disclaimers of experience and her writing of a journal-diary, one can hear a frustrated desire that seeks to be recognized: what will emerge as both problem and promise is Evelina's namelessness as a metonym for her absence from patriarchal language. Through the social void opened up by that gap, Evelina discovers that both she and her history can be (re)figured by her own act of writing. For that reason, writing an account of her experiences shatters the rigid concept of woman that she begins with. Writing her journal-letters will liberate Evelina from the alienating self-consciousness that divides her from herself; it will release her to the company of the two-in-one of thought—a process denied the rest of Burney's represented heroines.

What needs to be carefully traced before one can understand the significance of Evelina's journal is how, at first, she relinquishes experience for the sake of concealing herself in innocence. In her early forays into the world, the assailed heroine's intentional focus upon artlessness obscures the transparency of the natural self that she wishes to project. In effect, to act only from "the impulses of Nature" is to perform, as well as to invite, oppression. Furthermore, any binary economy of female innocence-male oppression overlooks Evelina's calculated innocence and concealed experience. Only at a point of crisis near to hysteria, when she is forced to write on her own behalf, does Evelina begin to understand how concealment does not prevent her from revealing herself—to herself, as well as to others. Even as Evelina narrates a representational myth in which the one narrated is caught in the female self-identity/male repression dichotomy, as writer she questions the essentialism underlying that binary economy.

The novel opens with the cultural definition that outlines Evelina's intrinsically innocent character. Reverend Villars describes his adopted ward, setting forth in little the problem of the female in eighteenth-century society: "This artless young creature, with too much beauty to escape notice, has too much sensibility to be indifferent to it; but she has too little wealth to be sought with propriety by men of the fashionable world." He explains the "peculiar cruelty of her situation" as "only child of a wealthy Baronet, whose person she has never seen, whose character she has reason to abhor, and whose name she is forbidden to claim; entitled as she is to lawfully inherit his fortune and estate, is there any probability that he will *properly* own her?" Artlessness and beauty without wealth and name is not only Evelina's global condition; it is also the charm of her appeal, the only marketable asset she has, and the greatest danger to her character.

Evelina's social position teeters precariously between legitimacy and bastardy; although she is the legitimate daughter of a baronet, her mother's legal marriage remains unacknowledged by her father. Adopted by a country parson, she can't claim social rank with such modest means. Her namelessness—a form of social silence—creates the conflict in the novel. More than a social deficiency, namelessness functions symbolically for the patriarchy that constitutes the "named." As a metonym for woman, it stands in the way of Evelina's social acceptance and inhibits her ability to name herself other than within the category of innocence, the character given to her by her culture.

The question of character and its rival conceptions immediately emerge. Is Evelina to be described as a traditional fictional entity created and controlled by an author—even an author in the form of a dominant culture who authors her? Is she an autonomous person, a "real identity," who speaks and acts by her own authority? Is she a purely linguistic construction? Each of these notions of character fails to describe adequately the generative power of naming that multiplies the company of Evelina within the free play of writing.

Preserving Evelina's singularly innocent name seems mandated by all those in the novel concerned with the continuity of the social order. For example, Villars's wish to have Evelina returned from her social experiences unchanged, still "all innocence," implies sacrificing the seasoning of practical knowledge on the patriarchal altar of pristine ignorance. All he asks from Lady Howard in sending her his Evelina as "innocent as angel, and artless as purity itself," is that she will return his child "as you receive her." Lady Howard reassuringly agrees with Villars that Evelina is indeed "truly ingenuous and simple" with "a certain air of inexperience and innocency." Launched into the world, Evelina should somehow expand her experience, but without the loss of her intrinsic, encapsulated inno-

cence. "The world," says Villars to Evelina, "is the general harbour of fraud and of folly, of duplicity and of impertinence" where "the artlessness of your nature, and the simplicity of your education alike *unfit* you for its thorny path." A properly feminine, bourgeois "education" assures one of a perspective "unfit" for the intrigues of society. Villars holds an unshakable belief in Evelina's essentialistic innocence and hopes that she may be an "ornament" of delight to family, friends, and neighbors, "employing herself in useful and innocent occupations." Above all else, he cautions her to retain her "genuine simplicity." But we will see by Evelina's own account of her first social forays that she is not as devoid of practical wisdom or as unfit for society as she, and everyone else, assumes.

In writing about her first ball to Villars, Evelina finds male behavior so "provoking" that she determines not to dance at all rather than seem to be "humouring" male condescension. Her reaction is more than the shock of innocence at the disportment of behavior outside the bounds of her experience, for she interprets what she sees as an assumption of superiority toward women. Rather than lacking awareness about the situation at hand, she is lacking information about social propriety. The fact that her account to Villars focuses not on ignorance of social sanctions but on her interpretation of human incivility proves this point. In this respect, her response is spontaneous but not discriminating, intuitively just, but not socially correct.

Evelina's reflexive ability to read more than one possible meaning in otherwise socially correct behavior refutes any Lockean notion that innocence is a tabula rasa upon which an accumulating experience is engraved. Although Evelina recognizes hypocrisy (Mr. Lovel), bad taste (the Branghtons), male impertinence (Willoughby), and female constraints (codes of propriety), time and again she retreats into the blankness of self-conscious confusion, silence, and the unformed feature of innocence, as when she meets Lord Orville:

> How will he be provoked, thought I, when he finds what a simple rustic he has honoured with his choice! one whose ignorance of the world makes her perpetually fear doing something wrong!

But while castigating her own behavior, Evelina exhibits an assimilative, interpretive grasp, as when the thought occurs to her that Orville did choose her, "insignificant as I was, compared to a man of his rank and figure." This ready adaptability to fit herself to new social situations is belied by the way her letters attire her in an innocence bordering on the hysterical. Furthermore, that correct social appearance includes a contradictory comportment of innocence: unworldly enough to appear guileless or different, yet sophisticated enough to recognize dissimulation and artifice; subtle enough to discern deception and fraud, and poised enough to withstand male aggression.

From Evelina's writing about her very first ball, we can see that though ignorant of social decorum, she is not devoid of perception. We are led to think otherwise when Villars's letters array her in artlessness. Whenever Evelina is abashed with shyness or outraged at male impropriety toward her person, she does the same. On such occasions, she cloaks her feelings in the more artless raiment of silence even as she discloses them in her writing: "But I was silent, for I knew not what I ought to say." As she enters an already established symbolic order and submits her desire to the pressures of that order, adopting a conventional conceptual wardrobe, furnishing herself with a language that has already determined who she is, she allows her reflections to be covered over by the veneer of naïveté.

This acquiescence, a very imprudent prudence, precipitates her disasters. Lord Orville's attentions, in part an attempt to test her capability to speak, merely create a restraint that causes her to lapse into silence. Ignorant of the impropriety entailed in refusing one dance partner and accepting another, Evelina generates male judgments ranging from "beautiful" to "ill-bred," "intelligent" to "rustic," or in Orville's case, from "ignorant or mischievous" to "a poor weak girl." To submit to the pressure for female silence contributes to her appearance of artlessness, a commodity valuable to the patriarchal appetite for the natural, as, for example, when Orville later says of Evelina that "she is too young for suspicion, and has an artlessness of disposition I never saw equalled." She discovers early, however, that an uncalculated artlessness is unreadable by others without the accompanying signs of reflection in her that would prevent misreading *artless* for *artifice.* Smarting from the effects of her own innocent guise, Evelina writes that she wishes to flee London, convincing herself that she now finds it "tiresome."

If Evelina's inexperience causes her embarrassment and real anguish, so does pretending to an experience that would conceal her genuine lack of worldly tempering. This posturing reveals itself when she attempts to elude the impertinent attentions of the lecherous Sir Clement Willoughby. She imitates fashionable manners, but her artifice cannot match Willoughby's rakishness. Here is a much keener male adversary than any she has met before, and one who epitomizes the fraud and duplicity Villars worries about. Her "peevish" indignation only charms the rake into further importunities toward one whose "airs" heighten her beauty. Merely exchanging innocence for sophistication does not solve the problem of being turned—or turning oneself—into an object for exploitation.

Evelina concludes her London letters to Villars with the plaint: "I am too inexperienced and ignorant to conduct myself with propriety in this town, where everything is new to me, and many things are unaccountable and perplexing." Though her comment testifies to the inadequacy of *any* concept of female innocence that excludes an experiential understanding, it also clearly demonstrates a view that oscillates between the perspectives of innocence and experience. Claiming confusion admits to an articulated need for understanding experience—and therefore admits to how much she already understands it.

Even when displeased with her narrated ignorance, Villars is quite aware of Evelina's narrative understanding; her persuasive writing is enough to convince him of her budding wisdom. Nevertheless, he answers her letter with a postscripted prayer that artlessness or "gaiety of heart" will remain hers. It is not only Evelina who feels compelled to overwrite her experience with the inscription of innocence—it is Villars's religious and moral clothing as well.

The contrast between Evelina's practical wisdom and others' dullness sharpens when she meets her wealthy but vulgar grandmother and her middle-class shopkeeping relatives. The Branghtons display all the ignorant excesses of grasping bourgeois social climbers without any of the intelligence that could redeem them. Their vulgarity and lack of manners vividly contrast Evelina's grace, refinement, modesty, and quickness. Willfully ignorant of decorum governing opera, they embarrass Evelina with their stingy selection of seats, lack of civility and proper attire. Offensive at every turn, they even arouse our sympathy for her when she rushes into Willoughby's arms to escape them. At the same time, however, the Branghtons' doggedly unrefined appetites attest to Evelina's fuller understanding of those social nuances that remain unarticulated. Indeed, such outrageous, low, and vulgar behavior spontaneously prompts her will, passion, and tongue: "This family is so low-bred and vulgar, that I should be equally ashamed of such a connection in the country, or anywhere."

When straining to recommend herself to males, however, Evelina postures in the language and comportment of the idealized female for whom discrimination is forbidden. She fails to distinguish between acquiring the accoutrements of innocence and *being* innocent, a standard that forces her into an anxious mode and wears away her spontaneity. Even though Evelina can understand a bold stare, even from a mighty lord, to be a "look of libertinism toward women," she seems almost willfully to overlook sexual dangers. Her awareness, significantly, does not extend to the sexual-social threat in accepting, although under some duress, Willoughby's offer to drive her home unescorted or in accompanying the Branghton girls into the darkened alleys of Vauxhall. This gap in her understanding points to the broader issue of how the conceptual model of vulnerable innocence conceals from a female not only her own sexual desire but her sexual power as well. The patriarchal model for female virtue appears to posit innocence merely in order to assault it, so that lecherous Willoughby can silence Evelina's objections by invoking the patriarchal code designed to protect her. Thus, when Orville discovers her alone with the rake, she "was not at liberty to assign any reason" for her ambiguous behavior. An unarticulated injunction against understanding, as well as interpreting, herself to others lies at the core of her repressed desperation and anguish. Merely deferring to male authority encourages misinterpretation, accedes to an unconscious presumption of her own innocence, and attests to the ambiguity inherent in consciously maintaining a vicious form of female virtue: permanent naïveté.

We learn then, very early in the novel that Evelina is persuasively observant, often aware of the role she plays in creating equivocal situations. Evelina and those representing her culture have mutually, though not always overtly, collaborated to grant her a character that denies the richness of archetype by confining it to stereotype. Above all else, reflective thought must be excluded from a conception of female virtue. It is no surprise then that attending Congreve's *Love for Love* puts her out of countenance, paralyzes her with silence, prevents her from observing. This is not a play, Orville says, that "can be honoured with their [the ladies'] approbation"; the young ladies in question must keep their observations to themselves in order to keep their innocence intact. Despite Orville's injunction against honoring the risqué play with female approbation, Evelina *writes* that it was "fraught with wit and entertainment." She also admits to Villars in another letter how her own virtue "must seem rather to invite than to forbid the offers and notice I received; and yet, so great was my apprehension of this interpretation, that I am sure, my dear Sir, you would have laughed had you seen how proudly grave I appeared."

In spite of such astute reasoning, in every situation where Lord Orville sees but does not hear her, her represented (cultivated) artlessness veils her in an ambiguous silence that invites attack. Overlooking the obvious sexual threat, Evelina reluctantly agrees to accompany the vulgar Branghton girls into the darkened alleys of Vauxhall. Accosted by a group of rowdy wags bent upon the plunder of innocence, Evelina once again flies off with Willoughby into an even darker alley. Although outraged at his predatory impertinence, at the implied sexual innuendo that seeks to cut off her response, she cannot refute the stinging correctness of his satire: "Is this a place for Miss Anville?—these dark walks!—no party! no companions!" Mr. Branghton puts it more bluntly: "You must all of you have had a mind to be affronted." "A mind to be affronted" rationalizes its complicity by taking refuge in the role of female victim. We can be outraged at Willoughby's

verbal power play, but we cannot discount the truth of what he says. Willoughby himself testifies to Evelina's wisdom: "Let Miss Anville look to herself; she has an excellent understanding, and needs no counselor." But the weight of social codes and conceptual models is too much for someone who must adhere to a narrow female standard.

Whenever Evelina relinquishes the authority of her own experience in favor of a naive sexual facade, she draws from others an opposing aggressiveness. After a fireworks display at Marybone Gardens, Evelina once again rushes off in a fright, heedless of remaining with her companions. Various "bold and unfeeling" men accost her, and she runs hastily to some questionable women for refuge. It is revealing that she protests her inability to free herself from their strong grip, and yet as soon as she is recognized by Orville, she finds the strength to tear herself away. With consternation and a measure of disingenuousness she later writes, "How strangely, how cruelly have all appearances turned against me! Had I been blessed with any presence of mind, I should instantly have explained to him the accident which occasioned my being in such terrible company:—but I have none!" If courage has deserted her in this incident, so has the memory of similar experiences. To Villars, she deplores her lack of "presence of mind," while forgetting that "presence of mind" responds spontaneously to the situation at hand, but persistently believing what she ought to be supersedes what she needs to do. If further proof that Evelina has guessed full well what kind of "ladies" she has been with is needed, she provides it when amused at Madame Duval's ignorance of them: "Indeed, it is wonderful to see how easily and how frequently she is deceived."

Doomed to fly from one dangerous and improper situation into another, Evelina seems inflexibly passive in her resignation to "properly own" the female name she has adopted, in spite of growing experiential evidence that this name does not serve her best interests any more than her namelessness does. If Evelina needs to learn to overcome a passive role, she also needs to acknowledge that passivity and innocence are anything but powerless. Mrs. Selwyn, a delightfully satirical version of woman, comments that Evelina's appearance seems coquettish and creates confusion: "You, innocent as you pretend to look, are the cause." When Evelina departs from Clifton in order to flee Orville, the same event viewed from Mrs. Selwyn's perspective is seen as "the logic of coquetry" crafted to captivate Orville. Seeing herself as a victim only, that is, as an unaccountable participant, however involuntary that participation may be, reduces the richer possibilities for action that would fit Evelina *for* the world and not just *to* it. In the social arena where she must display herself as a nameless (valueless) commodity until she can acquire nameability, however, she is often overwhelmed by the harshness of a world based upon a conceptual model that categorizes her by gender, calculates her visible worth, names her as nameless, and thereby condemns her to a passive silence by speaking for her.

The Evelina so named (represented) in the journal, however, is not the one who intrigues us as much as the who that narrates and orders the events by writing about them. The Evelina who writes reveals a much more evaluative knowledge of her world than the Evelina she writes about. As the account of Mrs. Stanley's ball has shown, Evelina is not without judgment, wit, and quick intelligence. As her accounts of the Branghtons show, she is brighter, more sensitive, and perceptive than they could ever hope to be. Her journal reveals that the most intelligent men, Orville and Willoughby, do appreciate her understanding in spite of her inexperience. Furthermore, when describing the witty Mrs. Selwyn's satirical forays, the Evelina who writes is more discriminating than the older lady who seems unaware of the censure her bent for irony invites. The ability to converse by writing to "two in good company," the oneself who asks and the oneself who answers, by traveling back and forth through the gap created by speech and writing, enables Evelina to find a path through the horrific void that namelessness implies.

A central episode involving the use and authority of Evelina's name marks a turn in her understanding of herself, a turn away from any self constructed as a singular entity, and also marks the intersection between the Evelina narrated and the who that narrates. The Branghtons learn of her acquaintance with Lord Orville and insist upon taking advantage of that relationship in order to usurp the social meaning of her name when they call on Lord Orville to solicit his business for the family shop. She writes to Villars: "I could have met with no accident that would so cruelly have tormented me." This threat is even more serious than the sexual dangers she has encountered. Until now, Evelina's own essentialistic awareness of herself as an innocent has prevented her from fully recognizing the self-objectification enforced by that definition. The overt reification of her as a "device" available to the utility and consumption of bourgeois economy, another form of namelessness, presses upon her what she would otherwise wish to conceal from herself. She cries out: "By what authority did you take such a liberty," and, "who gave you leave?—who desired you?" At this instance the subdued and repressed hysteria percolating at the edges of the narrative boils to the surface. For perhaps the first time in the novel, Evelina claims her own right to the disclosing as well as the concealing power of name and discourse. To speak importunately to Orville "as comes from one Miss Anville," makes her name an item in the Branghton trade. It forces her to act to lay the disguise of female passivity.

Usurping and reifying Evelina's name graphically illustrates how a narrowly defined, passive female role but poorly serves her, causing her to forfeit Orville's good opinion and giving him "reason to suppose I presumed to boast of his acquaintance!" "Half frantic," driven "wild," suffering an "irreparable injury," Evelina eschews the codes of both female decorum and virtue and writes to Orville directly. Forced to assert herself to prevent an inauthentic mode of discourse, namely reification, she nonetheless is impeded when her status as a nameless female undercuts her authority to name, that is, to articulate and interpret herself to others. To the Branghtons she may insist, "I must take the liberty to request, that my name may never be made use of without my knowledge," but in experience her name as female consists of those qualities and traits attributed *to* her rather than *by* her. Evelina closes her letter to Orville with a plaintive acknowledgment that she was used as the "instrument, however innocently, of so much trouble." When the letter is purloined by Willoughby just as her name was usurped by the Branghtons, it erupts from the silence relegated to a female, domestic circle of family and friends and into the din of a male, public circulation. The letter and its erratic and unforeseen postings radically alter the message Evelina has been sending about herself—to others as well as herself.

This central episode introduces the purloined letter and the forged reply. The letter never reaches Orville because Willoughby purloins it, forges an impertinent answer, and signs Orville's name. Woman's letter, her "name" is purloined through Willoughby by the patriarchal "name of the father."

When Evelina's letter is diverted from its path, it becomes purloined in another sense. *Pur-loigner* in the French means to put aside or put amiss, to suffer, a letter in sufferance trapped in a discourse it does not initiate, a letter effectively silenced. So trapped, Evelina herself becomes a letter in sufferance. Nonetheless, when the letter is diverted from its "proper" course, it does not cease to function. Evelina's letter overreaches authorial intention and male possession, initiating a chain of unpredictable changes in whoever comes to read it. She intends her letter to represent her "truely" to Orville, whereas Willoughby intends his letter persuasively to present Orville as different from the man himself. In each case, the one who comes to possess the letter is determined by it. Although the forged reply at first delights Evelina, Evelina's letter comes to possess Willoughby. In holding her letter, Willoughby hides her and her possibilities and becomes possessed by what he possesses without authority. In holding the false letter, Evelina comes to a clearer understanding of the real Orville. The letter stirs desire and, in some sense, rewrites all their lives. Even at the end of the novel, Evelina's letter still has the power to cost someone's life in a duel.

At first perusal, as Evelina ruefully admits, the forged reply delights her. She marks only its expressions of regard because they answer to her own desires:

> It gave me no sensation but of delight. . . . I only marked the expressions of his own regard . . . repeating to myself, 'Good God, is it possible?— am I then loved by Lord Orville?'

In a second reading, "every word changed,—it did not seem the same letter." She recalls, furthermore, the circumstances surrounding the receipt of the letter:

> Had this letter been the most respectful that could be written, the clandestine air given to it, by his proposal of sending his servant for my answer, instead of having it directed to his house, would effectually have prevented my writing.

In the forgery, Willoughby speaks for Orville, in his name, to discredit his authority and to conceal Evelina's "capacity": "I concealed your letter to prevent a discovery of your capacity; and I wrote you an answer, which I hoped would prevent your wishing for any other." It bears a "clandestine air" because it tries to divert her response, to prevent her from "having it directed to [Orville's] house." Once again the forged letter conceals Evelina, requiring her to envelop herself in innocence, to post herself into danger. In purloining her letter he silences her, denies her voice and name.

Nevertheless, words are changed by changing contexts, and when she and Orville meet in Bristol, Evelina rejects the forgery, rejects Villars's abstractions about character, and lets observation guide her judgment. Accordingly, she can interpret the letter more accurately in writing about it. Evelina recognizes in this concrete event how innocence can be a "false delicacy which occasioned my silence." Writing opens to her a horizon of experience beyond the literal reading of the text, beyond the sense corresponding to her desire, beyond the sense of the "Orville" presented to her. Although the words in the forged letter remain unchanged, the meaning of them does not. When she rethinks the situation by writing about it, Villars's reply and Orville's past actions change the significance of the false letter.

When Evelina meets Orville face to face, her proper, intended coldness and reserve melt away and she writes Villars:

> It was my intention, nay, my endeavour, to support them with firmness: but when I formed the plan, I thought only of the letter,—not of Lord Orville.

In rejecting the false letter as a misrepresentation of Orville, Evelina acts from the stronger conviction that she knows him through a broader context of experience—character, regard, comportment.

The meaning, then, of the letter resides in the relations among sender, receiver, and holder, a communal bond that enmeshes in its web whoever comes in contact with it. When Willoughby purloins Evelina's letter, he is only the most outrageous (and hence useful) instance of a social order that in speaking for her, in owning the signs that signify her, in using namelessness as a sign of woman as currency, purloins her letter. In *The Rape of Clarissa*, Terry Eagleton conjoins writing and woman:

> The problem of writing is in this sense the problem of the woman: how is she to be at once decorous and spontaneous, translucently candid yet subdued to social pressure? Writing, like women, marks a frontier between public and private, at once agonized outpouring and prudent stratagem.

Through the dialogic agency of a letter as both "agonized outpouring and prudent stratagem" and of her own journal, "decorous and spontaneous, translucently candid yet subdued to social pressure," Evelina better understands the consequences of her misrepresentation. Moreover, she recognizes that silence transforms her into a victim and exacerbates her sufferings; silence does not prevent her self-revelation when she admits that behavior, mood, and other nonverbal gestures create a horizon of possible meaning for Orville to interpret: "I tremble lest he should misconstrue my reserve for embarrassment!" And again, "I could not endure he should make his own interpretation of my silence."

Writing gives Evelina an opportunity to speak, lending her a voice that the world not only denies but insists she doesn't have. She does not simply record what confounds her in London—a form of spectatorship— she participates in reordering what puzzles and frightens her. In writing, Evelina learns that she is capable of thought and therefore capable of speech, and she says this in the very process of denying it: "I will talk,—write,—think of him no more!" These disclaimers cause Villars to miss the strength and achievement of Evelina's letters. He unwittingly acknowledges their authority by simply accepting them as representational, as veridical accounts. The persuasive power of her narration compensates for the authority that silences her. She corresponds because her experiences do not— *discordia concors.*

At times the dazzling power of narration causes Evelina to fall back upon that reductive concept of female innocence, laying claim to the unambiguous and literal, draping herself in self-illusion. To discover that writing uncovers what has been carefully concealed from oneself can be very disconcerting: "I will not write any longer; for the more I think . . . the less indifferent . . . I find myself." Writing begins to find for her, her self. What she cannot see, perhaps what at times she *will* not see is that transparency and innocence are available only within experience. The greater her vocabulary of experience, the broader her perspective on a situation, the more she understands the power and attendant dangers of innocence. Writing enables Evelina to share in the composition of her own destiny, to see that the role of innocent bystander is often complicitous with that of active participant.

Writing as act precludes her being a passive spectator: she is enmeshed in a web of discourse that calls for her response, that connects her to her particular place in culture. Writing reliably guides or opens her to possible modes of female conduct. When Villars warns Evelina against "those regions of fancy and passion whither her new guide conducted her," he also implies that writing informs experience, since her new "guide" is her imaginative pen—not patriarchal advice. Since the letters themselves not only reside in but *are* the "regions of fancy and passion," they are not as easily subject to the discursive control of patriarchal logic. Neither are they limited to the linear movement of a conventional plot, a sending that asks for no reply. In fact, the episodic zigzag movement of epistolary narrative resists any overarching structure targeted as plot. The epistolary shapes pathos, terror, emotion in such a way as to discourage the reader from building theoretical constructions of analysis upon it. Her letters are not a form for imperatives, statements of facts, or assertions. The indirection of the culturally unsayable opens "regions of fancy and passion."

Feelings are less a subject Evelina takes *up* than an affective condition that takes *her*. "I made a resolution, when I began, that I would not be urgent; but my pen—or rather my thoughts, will not suffer me to keep it—." Writing does not merely record her feelings for Orville, it shapes them, gives space for the feelings that draw her into dark alleys. Writing reveals to her—and others—the pattern of her desires. Villars, Maria, and we are sure she is in love, even though she has never admitted to it openly: "Long . . . have I perceived the ascendancy which Lord Orville has gained upon your mind." Evelina writes to Villars but finds herself addressing Orville:

> Oh! Lord Orville!—it shall be the sole study of my happy life, to express, better than by words, the sense I have of your exalted benevolence and greatness of mind!

As Evelina's writing becomes a displacement for her concealed desires, it opens her to more than one identity, more than one version of character. It draws her out of the stifling closet of female reserve and into multiple chambers of thought.

The company of thought is available to Evelina through the conversation of her writing. This conversation enables Evelina to discover a counter-authority to that of the patriarchy. Usually when Evelina's discourse falls silent due to lack of authority, it is Villars, much like Burney's father, who feels authorized to speak for her. His letters to Evelina are filled with maxims, exhortations, and the highest sentiments of concern and moral propriety. Ever admonishing, he simply cannot forbear talking about "the right line of conduct," the same for both sexes, "though the manner in which it is pursued may somewhat vary." The varied "manner" in which "the right line of conduct" is pursued not only attests to the inadequacy of any "right line of conduct" as a guide for females but also to the impossibility of only one "right line." Nonetheless, even Villars is persuaded by Evelina's narrative power so that, when she writes about male importunity, he admonishes her to take authority in the sense of responsibility to her own experience to learn from it:

> But you must learn not only to *judge* but to *act* for yourself; if any schemes are started, any engagements made, which your understanding represents to you as improper, *exert* yourself resolutely in avoiding them; and do not, by a *too passive* facility, risk the censure of the world, or your own future regret. (emphasis added)

In an astonishing admission, Villars explains to Evelina that innocence *conceals* the approach of duplicity: "Guileless yourself, how could you prepare against the duplicity of another? Your disappointment has but been proportioned . . . to the innocence which hid its approach." He repines: "That innocence . . . should, of all others, be the blindest to its own danger,—the most exposed to treachery,—and the least able to defend itself, in a world where it is little known, less valued, and perpetually deceived!" Innocence, he implies, nurtures hysteria. Evelina's persuasive narration holds an authority that forces Villars to redefine his cherished concept of female innocence.

The dialogue generated by these letters shows how writing addresses an important issue far beyond the need to express or the purpose of guidance—especially since Evelina often does not respond in her letters to the advice he gives. Her realistic descriptions and astute assessments of human behavior convince Villars of the authority of her writing even as he tries to maintain the fiction of her artlessness. He consistently displaces Evelina's authority, standing *in* for her but not letting her stand *up* for herself. Renouncing such a patriarchal version of authority can be the means for woman to name herself rather than let others name her.

Although Villars may speak for Evelina when she cannot, *speaking for* is not the same as *letting* speak. Evelina's letters are authoritative precisely to the extent to which they are filled with concrete, but ever-changing, interpretations of particular events. When pressed by Evelina's details concerning actual events, Villars is forced to relinquish his abstractions for more practical considerations that are attuned to the present need. Her authority corresponds to the way her letters say what *is* rather than what ought to be. Evelina's letter about Willoughby is so persuasive that it even moves Villars to relinquish the patriarchal mandate for female reserve:

> It is not sufficient for you to be reserved: his conduct even calls for your resentment; and should he again, as will doubtless be his endeavour, contrive to solicit your favour in private, let your disdain and displeasure be so marked, as to constrain a change in his behaviour.

In other words, female virtue encompasses more than a silent reserve; virtue takes the active form of a disdain and displeasure so marked that it will force a behavioral change in others. Concealing the strength of a woman's own desires and intelligence diminishes her human richness; she remains one-dimensional as long as she is complicitous with the representational model.

In writing, Evelina finds the connections, the parallels, and the patterns of events that shape her experience to herself and her co-respondents. In writing, Evelina can explain and defend how she behaved at her first ball, although she could never do so by speaking directly to those who received a wrong impression of her. In a letter she can discuss her disapprobation of people, places, and events, expressing attitudes and opinions that she must otherwise hide or dissemble. The letter privately gratifies, frees her discourse from what must otherwise adhere to social strictures. Eagleton states that a decorum of who may write to whom, and under what conditions, provides an internal censorship, since the epistle is at heart an appeal to another. Since Evelina writes the bulk of her letters to Villars who represents the authority of patriarchy, she allows the dialogue to speak for her rather than give him the impression she is making judgments. By seeming to record whole conversations, she lets the rhetoric of the letter ameliorate the impertinence of its own intimate revelation. Her epistles subversively charm more than her strained efforts to be artless; the more her letters express a deeply felt private sentiment, the more they snare the reader into a reciprocal intimacy.

Evelina allows the dialogue to speak indirectly for her rather than playing author in the patriarchal sense. She criticizes the authorial model, nonetheless, when she, like Burney, deliberately conceals her authority by editing or merely recording events in the form of private letters. Evelina's (non)authority becomes a viable alternative not only to the power exercised by males,

but to that of the other women as well. Madame Duval's access to society rests entirely upon her patrilineal name and money, for which she is more tolerated than accepted. Lady Howard can speak with the authority of the patrilineal name, money, and position. She therefore does not test the limits of masculine authority. Though Mrs. Selwyn thrives on satirical challenges to authority, she is indulged for the sake of name and position. These versions of female power rely on an idea of identity coextensive with patriarchy. The forced race of the nameless old women servants, so often puzzling to readers, demonstrates the plight of woman without resource to male legitimation. The argument here is that Evelina, by contrast, opens up a non-patriarchal path for identity and authority through the company of the letter's conversation.

The novel is about sendings, letters; hence a novel without author(ity), only an editor. In both Burney's preface and Evelina's narrative, authority is renounced. What is true of the letters is true of the novel: neither Evelina, the one narrated and the one narrating, nor Burney authors it in the sense of origin and closure. They send letters—one sends to Berry Hill, one into the world—but they do not speak for others. They let others speak for themselves and keep the conversation going. They listen to the world and send letters as a function of listening. Evelina narrates: in letting the others speak she must listen and understand them better perhaps than they understand themselves. She makes Mrs. Selwyn's irony her own, makes Branghton vulgarity part of her world even as she dismisses it; she even assimilates the aggression of the male and the displacement of woman to this narrated world. She is author in the ancient sense of *auctor*, one who augments the conversation underway, one who need not command or coerce to make herself heard.

With the help of her new guide, Evelina discovers how she can resist any "plot" ready formed for her. It enables her to say who she is in spite of cultural limits upon her discourse. The intimacy of the letter creates the impression of saying what was not intended to be heard, what she is not authorized to say. Thus, she can use writing as a form of cultural power to disarm cherished notions rather than wresting them from the grip of the opposition. The patriarchal authorities, those "magistrates of the press, and Censors for the public" (original preface), merely assert what ought to be, while Evelina describes what is, that is, what appears. This opening for what appears, for further dialogue, prevents any determinant meaning. The Evelina narrated and the one who narrates, Villars, Maria, Burney, and imagination, the new guide, all symbolize the intersubjective relations that expropriate the individual.

Narrating names who she is long before her father or her husband give her an authorized, patrilineal name. But the narrative is not public, else it couldn't be written—or is public only by editorial intervention. Like Evelina's unauthorized being, her letters are unauthorized, private appeals to another, protected by an internal censorship:

> I gave over the attempt of reading . . . and, having no voice to answer the enquiries of Lord Orville, I put the letter into his hands, and *left it to speak both for me and itself.* (emphasis added)

Otherwise they would be indecorous, even impertinent. Thus the narrating Evelina outgrows the already narrated innocent angel whom others wish to preserve.

Burney may purloin Evelina's letters by editing them, and we may eavesdrop. Like Willoughby, we may be claimed, drawn into the narrative conversation by overhearing her, but she does not intend the world to hear what she is not authorized to say. Instead, Evelina's authority is revealed as that of character in the ancient sense of ethos. It is based upon everything we as readers know about her: her represented and representing self, her shrewdness in oscillating between those two selves. Ethos emerges as a provisional identity, in between the narrator/narrated, in between author/editor Burney, between the different seedings. Burney's narrative about Evelina writing a narrative about herself is not properly named or fathered; like that of Evelina, it is "unnamed, unknown without any sort of recommendation" (original preface), an "other" message. Evelina's letter was purloined at birth, and her search is for a legitimate name, a voice that is authentically her own.

Evelina cannot authenticate her own narrative according to the patriarchal standards for authority and legitimacy. To do so would open her to dangers which patrilineal name, position, and money would otherwise circumvent. It would also open her to the censure that Mrs. Selwyn's irony receives. Jean-François Lyotard helps us say what is at stake in this narrative at a high level of generality, and hence, at a broad level of applicability. Legitimation, he observes, is the process of deciding the true and the false. Representation and its rational criterion of adequacy or accuracy is masculine—an Enlightenment ideal. In the Enlightenment culture of Burney's age, [according to Lyotard,] narrative knowledge lacks legitimacy and belongs to "fables, myths, legends; fit only for women and children." However, narrative knowledge lies behind, is presupposed by, such rational discourse. It reveals the significant shape of human life in that all questions of truth are situated in events that have enough coherence to be told as a narrative. The events and their connections are not veridical; rather they are events of vision, the a priori context for representational discourse.

It is no accident that women who, like Evelina, cannot control signification write letters that forestall closure and keep the conversation in good company. As Evelina's letters displace her as a constituted entity, they become communally constitutive. Each sending replaces the previous one so that ideological structures cannot censor them. Thus they mediate all conceptual boundaries—public, private, self, world. Instead of embalming the world in patriarchy's sterile discourse, the name of the father, these generative women—Evelina, Caroline Evelyn, Fanny Burney—give it birth, even beyond their own mortality.

Women's purloinable letter, like an unnamed child without a legitimating birthright, reveals there is no fixed identity at either end of the co-respondence. Evelina's birthright cannot be subject to such a public or legal claim, for if it were, it would violate the rule of female propriety, damage her father's honor, and call her own legitimacy into question. She must rely, instead, on private intercession by others who speak on her behalf. Yet, what convinces Sir John Belmont that Evelina is his daughter is not Mrs. Selwyn's argument, not a legal claim, not even an appeal to pathos. It is Evelina's resemblance to her mother, a truth that destroys his narrative by substituting another—by refiguring his life. That is, her most convincing proof is neither a document nor a form of patriarchal speech that bears the silencing authority of a truth statement. She posts a likeness of her mother that lacks any of those patrilineal seals of legitimation. Caroline Evelyn's letter, read by John Belmont years after her death, is shattering: "Ten thousand daggers could not have wounded me like this letter." Evelina's legitimacy rests on a revolutionary displacement of the criterion of legitimacy inherent in patriarchal culture. It rests upon her own renunciation of the patriarchal authority that diminishes rather than augments when it insists upon power over discourse. Though she seems to sink into the conventional patrilineal family and ends her story, "I have time for no more [writing]," her lack of name and of the means by which her name is recovered opens a countercultural possibility for narrating ourselves without the authoritative subject at either end of the writing and conversing process. The representative heroine is subverted by her own act of representing.

We have seen that any notion of the female as a singular, stable entity is radically altered by Evelina's writing. In writing, the representational Evelina is exposed as a reductive concept, a product of the narrowly mediated, patriarchal code. Uncritically assuming that the individual is fully present as given, that representation is the ontological determination of woman, ensures an utterly predictable crisis for, and plot against, women. That plot, woman's silence, her repressed hysteria, hides possible self-discovery when it makes her nameable, sayable only by the linguistically mediated form available to her. As long as woman lacks a voice in the sense of sharing in the cultural figuration of who she is, she can never be an active conveyor of meaning. Indirection by means of writing without closure allows the forbidden unsayable to be said. Julia Kristeva writes: "In 'woman' I see something that cannot be represented, something that is not said, something above and beyond nomenclature and ideologies." Yet, every time "nomenclature and ideologies" fail women, they speak indirectly of woman's inexhaustibility and subvert their own representation of woman. Revealed and concealed in any concept of woman is the open possibility for an ongoing, ever incomplete and incompletable identity. That possibility lies in writing, for, more than marks upon a page, writing calls forth the generative power of name—all that woman is and can be and is not yet; all about her that has been overlooked and yet is to be said.

Claudia L. Johnson (essay date 1995)

SOURCE: "Statues, Idiots, Automatons: *Camilla*," in *Equivocal Beings: Politics, Gender, and Sentimentality in the 1790s: Wollstonecraft, Radcliffe, Burney, Austen,* The University of Chicago Press, 1995, pp. 141-64.

[*In the following essay, Johnson contends that Burney's heroines characterize her ideal of feminine propriety.*]

Frances Burney's heroines have a passion for abjection. Their careers evince it with an extravagance at once grotesque and festive. At times, their suffering is nuanced enough to be a credit to sensibility. When they blush with exquisitely intense embarrassment over *faux pas* and *contretemps*—take Evelina's evolving sensitivity to the manners of high life, for example—they show that their affective lives are perfectly calibrated to the social practices of their culture, practices whose worldliness, venerated by the "ton," seems to call for the sophistication the English associate with the French. More often, however, their affliction burgeons beyond all seemly proportions, as when Cecilia loses her mind and grovels deliriously among clumps of straw; or as when Camilla—convinced that her father has been imprisoned, her uncle pauperized, and his estate closed up, and all, *all* because of her—does not merely retreat to her bed, but actually "crawl[s]" there, expecting never to rise again. What differentiates such exorbitant affliction from that of other eighteenth-century heroines—no slouches when it comes to suffering—is that it is not protested. Clarissa dies underscoring woman's duty to "BEAR AND FORBEAR," to be sure, but she never surrenders the moral confidence that makes friends love and persecutors quail before her: the severity of her father, the weakness of her mother, the acquisitiveness of her brother, and the jealousy of her sister should not be. In a similar way, gothic heroines are often feisty in the midst of their suffering. The extremity of their hardship not only li-

censes but requires them to defy their tormentors. Careful as she is to distinguish herself from Madame Montoni, a great complainer, Emily St. Aubert sounds a bit like Wollstonecraft herself when she pleads her "rights" against Montoni, and she is even willing (as Clarissa is not) to entertain the idea of litigation.

But Burney's heroines, far from protesting their wretchedness, vindicate its justice and embrace it with all the strenuousness of real commitment. This enthusiasm imparts that characteristically masochistic edge to her fiction, and her last two novels take such enthusiasm to the outer limits. The plots of the earlier *Evelina, or, A Young Woman's Entrance into the World* (1778) and *Cecilia, or Memoirs of an Heiress* (1782) lodge trenchant social criticisms, even if the heroines might demur: *Evelina* assails patriarchs who shirk the offices of paternity, and though the docile little daughter trembles before her father's dread power, the novel bearing her name brings him to her knees. Gradually stripped of all her patrimony as well as her memory, Cecilia is likewise a casualty of a patriarchal system which con-

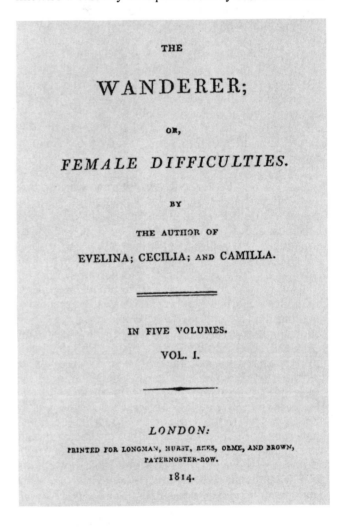

Title page of The Wanderer; or, Female Difficulties.

tinues to be honored despite its decay, and which keeps its iron hold by erasing the names and squelching the identities of females such as herself. By contrast, the later *Camilla, or, a Picture of Youth* (1796) and *The Wanderer; or, Female Difficulties* (1814) go to elaborate lengths to make sure that no damaging criticism falls on the hoary heads of men who are dear. In *The Wanderer*, Ellis/Juliet affirms the dignity of the "reverend, aged, infirm" Bishop even though his paternal powerlessness is the precondition of her panoramic miseries. In *Camilla* as well, the Tyrold children suffer as a result of failures of paternal authority that are gross yet curiously unforegrounded: an extortionist and fraud, Lionel leeches from anyone he can, even pimping his sister to cover his debts; Eugenia is mangled by her uncle, from whose singularly inept hands she is easily abducted and forced into marriage; and finally, preyed upon by her brother and disastrously ill-advised by her father, Camilla has no idea how to anticipate or manage expenses in public places. Yet, unlike Burney's previous works, *Camilla* never encourages us to wonder how parents, clergymen, and baronets go wrong, but rather asks how children can be so bad as to disappoint persons so good. Consequently and bizarrely, no one in the novel is troubled by the insanely exaggerated sense of guilt that makes Camilla, whose debts are so modest, shoulder criminally intense responsibility for her family's ruin, while the massive depredations of Lionel and Clermont, legitimate heirs, receive scant mention.

Burney's later fiction forces her heroines into shoring up persons and institutions who cause their tribulations because it was composed amidst an intensely repressive period of political reaction. The reaction made it urgent to venerate the men of feeling who, as conservative ideologues would argue, ensured the durability of the social order by virtue of the sentimental sway—the eliciting of loyalty, gratitude, deference, solicitude, endearment—they exerted over subordinates. Coming at the end of a sentimental tradition which had been strategically deployed in order to redefine masculinity and re-form political subjects, Burney's later novels unfold amidst conditions that both promote and prohibit female suffering: having appropriated legitimate affectivity, male sentimentality throws female feeling, indeed female subjectivity itself, into doubt—as faked, frivolous, undutiful, wayward. Engrafted onto the unassailable patterns of Christian martyrdom, Clarissa's agony had been her glory, and her passive fortitude in face of injustice had demonstrated the grandeur of feminine heroism. But a character like Camilla must deny not only the injustice of her excruciation but also the fact of that excruciation itself. Pushed to the breaking point by Lionel's assumption that a brother's financial embarrassments take precedence over a sister's distress, she asks, "What can I ever say, to make you hear me, or feel for me?" The extremity of her final harrowing is necessitated by the impossibility of an-

swering that question. In this novel, "good" women are exhorted to self-control; nothing short of their evacuation by death or madness can both authenticate their suspect distress and exonerate them from the charge of shameful self-indulgence. From the depths of her misery, Camilla heads the note she has scrawled to Edgar with the portentous words, "*Not to be delivered till I am dead*," because she realizes that only annihilation can make credible and pardonable her obtrusion into speech, absolve her from the bother her subjectivity has caused. The extraordinary abjection of Burney's last two heroines is thus both a result of and a response to the problem of femininity under the dispensation of male sentimentality.

Burney's late fiction is marked by an ambivalence that derives from the very privilege of her position as a novelist whose career developed in close association with the men who were then (as now) recognized to be at the forefront of English art, literature, and politics—men such as Reynolds, Johnson, Burke, Sheridan, Garrick, not to mention her father Charles. At first, this filiation, a major preoccupation of Burney's life as well as her fiction, seemed protective. The young author of *Evelina* was careful not only to honor her father, the "author of [her] being," but also to clarify her relation or nonrelation to the other authors—Rousseau, Johnson, Marivaux, Fielding, Richardson, and Smollett—who made up the canonical tradition of prose fiction. With astonishing confidence considering the timidity often (with some justice) attributed to her, the then anonymous Burney imagines it possible to be sheltered by such forefathers—the title "novelist" cannot seem ignominious if she shares it with them—without being overborne by them: since they have not written about a young lady's "Entrance into the World," *Evelina* will not cover "the same ground which they have tracked," and their examples need not intimidate her.

But such confidence would dissipate as Burney's success bound her to sustain her fame beneath an increasingly more exacting critical gaze, and as the very concept of authority itself became more vexed. Nowhere is this more painfully evident than in *Camilla*. Conceived amidst the turmoil of the 1790s and dedicated to the Queen of England, *Camilla* is haunted by crises of authority—paternal, political, and literary. This may seem a strange claim given the novel's studied reticence about matters political. Discussing *Camilla* with her royal acquaintances at Court, Burney returned Princess Sophia's scandalized observation that "the Writers are all turned Democrats, they say" by assuring her—and evidently with complete sincerity—that "*Politics* were, *all ways*, left out" of her fiction because she believed that "they were not a *feminine* subject for discussion." Even if we give Burney credit for not denouncing "Democrats," as the conversation seemed to invite—and as her father often did—her "feminine" claim to apoliticality contradicts the accomplishment of her last two novels and alerts us to her profound uneasiness about risking direct criticism. Burney's "*Directions for coughing, sneezing, or moving, before the King and Queen*" horribly if hilariously demonstrates that self-mutilating repression is the price one pays for the privilege of royal favor. But although Burney's novels attest, as Julia Epstein has eloquently put it, to the "volcanic spillage" that is produced when "female desire is yoked to the service of social propriety," Burney never frontally challenges the system that required this of her. The recent renaissance in Burney studies has tended sometimes to overstate Burney's confidence as a social critic, as if she were Wollstonecraft's ideological sister, whereas it seems to me that Burney is distinctive precisely for her retreat from the explicitly oppositional.

Burney appears to have wished not to recognize the critical character of her own fiction, but her "silence" about politics is still more apparent than real. Political crisis had already become so thoroughly intertextualized in the fiction of the 1790s that its presence need not be signaled by any polemical announcements. In *Camilla*, the pressure which political reaction placed even upon loyal subjects is discernible in small but pervasive ways. Irked by his sister's disapproval of the impiety with which he has spoken of their uncle, Lionel scolds Camilla in a speech that would seem unremarkable if it weren't for the allusion with which it concludes: "Don't you know it's a relief to a man's mind to swear, and say a few cutting things when he's in a passion? when all the time he would no more do harm to the people he swears at, than you would, that mince out all your words as if you were talking treason, and thought every man a spy that heard you." While Austen's Henry Tilney likes being surrounded by "a neighbourhood of voluntary spies," Lionel Tyrold resents eavesdroppers who would abrogate a man's right to vent his anger in speech. Their shared awareness of the antitreason acts of 1795 reminds us that the authority of the state was considered so shaky that subjects were monitored, that such surveillance was felt to reach intimately into neighborhood life, and that even sweet-tempered daughters and feckless sons felt obliged to watch what they said. Relating Camilla's exacting internal as well as external monitor (Edgar) to the spies scattered around the neighborhood sniffing out those who do not revere authority as they ought, Lionel's asseveration helps us account for the intensity of Camilla's paranoia and the crippling guilt that she suffers over filial infractions which would not seem to warrant such a fuss if we regarded them as merely private.

Lionel's allusion tells us much about the political pressure under which Camilla labors to be dutiful, but it also tells us much about how the same internal pressures dampened Burney's criticism. As her diaries

show, people in high places read and discussed her work, and vetted its politics. Having lived at Court during the first years of the French Revolution, Burney could not regard treason as an abstraction. But having married an émigré Constitutionalist, on the likes of whom her father was content to pin the worst excesses of the Terror, neither could she wholeheartedly countenance the vigorously repressive agendas of the reaction. Her position vis-à-vis conservative deployments of sentimental ideology is of interest precisely because of the discomfort with which she endorses as well as resists it. Unlike Wollstonecraft and Radcliffe, Burney was an insider, and her career was very long—long enough in fact for her to have outlived the writers who had been brought up on her own *Evelina* and *Cecilia*, and Wollstonecraft and Radcliffe were surely among them. Burney shared their uneasiness about the masculinization of sentiment brought about in response to the French Revolution. But precisely because her place was so privileged, she could not launch her criticism from the same position they did, though her final two novels clearly do start where they left off. In the next chapter, I shall argue that *The Wanderer* refutes Wollstonecraft as Burney stunningly misread her in *The Wrongs of Woman*. *Camilla*, by contrast, rewrites Radcliffe's *Mysteries of Udolpho*. "Why should not I have my mystery, as well as Udolpho," Burney asked her father in a letter dated 18 June 1795. Why indeed? Although she crafted *Camilla* into five "*Udolphoish* volumes*," and depicted, as Margaret Doody has pointed out, Radcliffean characters who "approach death and guilt circuitously, working upon hypotheses, inferences, and clues," *Camilla* is actually an anti-*Udolpho*. This is partly because, situated squarely within the authorized literary tradition, Burney cannot avail herself of subliterary generic strategies which enable the crises of the present to be projected backwards and defamiliarized, as Radcliffe did. But it is also, and more crucially, because Radcliffean gothic attempts initially at least to dignify female complaint, even though it is compelled finally to trivialize it retrospectively. In *Camilla*, the regime of male sentimentality is so strict that it extends to Camilla's unconscious, prohibiting her even from fantasizing exactly what sentimental ideology requires of her: the spectacle of her own suffering and disfigurement.

For this reason, Burney's social criticism in *Camilla* is decentered, conducted dramatically without narratorial commentary, and largely through what, given the novel's pervasive concern with the theatricality of gender, may not inappropriately be called stylistic drag. Sentimentality, of course, is normatively excessive. And in the world of Burney's imagination, the already excessive stranglehold of sentimental propriety can be loosened only by excessive compliance. This makes her fiction campy where it is most dutiful, for norms here are so saturated with excess that they lose their sway as norms. Masquerading in a variety of authoritative discursive modes—for example, the sermon, the Johnsonian sentence, Shakespearean tragedy, classical learning, even dicta from conduct books—*Camilla* saturates them with disruptive surplus. Ringing disastrously false, the sermon aggravates Camilla's problems by encouraging concealment; Johnsonian parallelisms wobble, unable to contain their subjects; performed in dialects drawn from throughout the kingdom, the performance of *Othello* becomes a national travesty of male melodrama; classical learning and the virtue it underwrites, once the flower of civilized manhood, are here the domain of women; continually excoriating the ethereal Camilla with ponderous and clearly misplaced opprobria, conduct-book maxims get smothered by their own pomposity.

In part because of this densely textured irony, *Camilla* is Burney's most arduous novel. *Cecilia* is practically as long, variegated, and densely peopled, and yet because the course of action that divests the heroine of all her money and all her identity is at once so simple and so inexorable, the plot reads smoothly despite its multifariousness. Working by complicating accretion rather than progression, the narrative flow of *Camilla*, by contrast, is fitful, impeded, constantly breaking down. There was a time when critics chalked this unsteadiness up to bad writing, and the bad writing in turn up to any number of causes, such as stuffy didacticism, financial necessity, and the dreary exhaustion of advancing age, the stilling influence of Samuel Johnson. But as Burney's own chapter heading "Offs and Ons" indicates, the novel's abrupt starts and halts are contrived according to the intricacy and inconsistency of what the prefatory paragraph announces to be its central subject: "the Heart of man."

Somewhat in defiance of eighteenth-century usage, I read "Heart of man" here in all its gendered specificity. For even though the narrator talks in universal terms about the mazelike complexity of the "human heart," virtually all of the maddening impactions of the ensuing chapters arise from the "contrarieties" of male sentiment—the "Heart of *man*" [my emphasis]—in particular. At the same time as male sentimentality has vitiated customary practices of authority—thus giving rise to the complications narrated throughout the novel—its excesses upset all indices of gender, casting women's various modes of femininity into radical doubt as histrionic, extreme, grotesque. A profoundly conflicted novel, *Camilla* suggests two responses to this disruption. On the one hand, it wants men to be men again so that women can be (women) too, not only vis-à-vis men but also, and even more importantly, vis-à-vis other women. Functioning beneath the conflicting disciplinary regimes of the clerical males—her father, Marchmont, Edgar—Camilla must be almost entirely emptied before she is accepted and loved, and both by the too sensitive man who has monitored her in an agony all along and by her severe mother, who cannot

indulge maternal warmth until Camilla is half-dead. And yet, on the other hand, read with attention to the peripheries, *Camilla* allows for the enjoyment of sentimental excess when it is not bounded by domesticity. Burney is the last major novelist to be at home with a courtly, ludic ethos of theatricality which, in privileging artificiality over artlessness, stylishness over sincerity, is in part the origin of camp. The ease with which fops like Sir Sedley and grand ladies of fashion like Mrs. Arlbery indulge the *outré* can be liberating for her seemlier heroines. In these contexts, the sex and gender disruptions caused by sentimentality itself can prove thrilling for women—who to this day are not generally considered the principal beneficiaries of camp. Burney's fiction is utterly unique in representing this possibility, although it is wary about it as well.

Camilla begins by setting forth the gender disruptions which, as we have already seen, typify the practice of male sentimentality. Among the first things we learn about Camilla's parents in the opening chapter, "A Family Scene," is that stereotypes about affectivity have been systematically regendered. A tender susceptibility to feeling now distinguishes the moral authority of the father of the household:

> Mr. Tyrold, gentle with wisdom and benign in virtue, saw with compassion all imperfections but his own, and there doubled the severity which to others he spared. Yet the mildness that urged him to pity blinded him not to approve; his equity was unerring, though his judgment was indulgent. His partner had a firmness of mind which nothing could shake: calamity found her resolute; even prosperity was powerless to lull her duties asleep. The exalted character of her husband was the pride of her existence. . . . Mr. Tyrold revered while he softened the rigid virtues of his wife, who adored while she fortified the melting humanity of her husband.

Here, while the once classically masculine virtues of severity, firmness, resolution, and fortitude fall to the sturdy wife, the good husband is "exalted" in his possession of virtues such as gentleness, compassion, mildness, indulgence, and softness. Such a reversal might appear empowering, or at the very least, dignifying for women. The stoic virtues Mrs. Tyrold practices—particularly her endeavor "to be superior to calamity"—were profoundly attractive to late-century moralists, preeminently Samuel Johnson, even though these virtues were ultimately passed over in preference of the more amiable virtue Mr. Tyrold practices: "melting humanity." But in a world which privileges the sensitivity of men, anything bordering on stoic self-possession and indifference in a woman, far from being regarded as a virtue, is held in much suspicion. Mrs. Arlbery, for example, is judged by Edgar Mandlebert to be a dangerous companion for Camilla because she is "alone" and possesses "a decided superiority to all she saw, and a perfect indifference to what opinion she incurred in return." Self-assurance, independence, reliance upon one's own judgment—these may sometimes be masculine virtues, but in the eighteenth century they are never feminine ones: when catastrophe forces Burney's last heroine, the Wanderer, to be independent, she finds herself utterly unsexed in the eyes of the world, and she refuses to charge the world with injustice on this score. For her part, Mrs. Tyrold clears herself from the taint of unfeminine independence by submitting to the guidance of her adoring husband. Given his weakness this requires enormous effort. *His* obviously erring—and erring because too tender—heart, rather than *her* rigorous and infallible judgment is to serve as "her standard excellence." But because the two are so often at odds, this submission chafes. Mrs. Tyrold reasonably opposes Sir Hugh's foolish schemes, schemes to which her fond husband yields, and with ruinous results. In her, the rationalist's haughty but accurate sense of her rightness conflicts with the wife's duty of obedience. And yet such is the rigor of her virtue that Mrs. Tyrold unconditionally observes the "vow taken at the altar to her husband" which requires that there be "no dissent in opinion" from him. She yields to the promptings of his fondness without "murmur," but with covert frustration, retiring "to her own room, to conceal with how ill a grace she complied."

Comparing his mother's penetration to his uncle Relvil's "weak parts," Lionel opines that "there was some odd mistake in their births, and that my mother took away the brains of the man, and left the woman's for the noddle of my poor uncle." Mrs. Tyrold's virilescence, as a result, far from carrying any prestige, underscores frustration rather than procures fulfillment. Gender is thus disrupted in Mrs. Tyrold's case by inversion rather than by reversal, for rendering them grotesque, women's immasculation only aggravates the problem of female subjectivity. While avuncular figures like Sir Hugh and Relvil take hysterically to their beds and while good Mr. Tyrold is immobilized in prison, Mrs. Tyrold becomes the guardian of a system which negates her agency on any other terms except the ones which make her dreadful. It is not the mild father, but the rigorous mother who is "deeply feared by all her children," and as we shall see, at last most dramatically by Camilla herself. In a novel whose central images recur to statuary, Mrs. Tyrold embodies the rigidity of the law, a rigidity which is crippling and scary. The emphasis in the opening "A Family Scene" remains squarely on the exemplary preciousness of Mr. Tyrold's sensitivity which Mrs. Tyrold must honor even where it errs, not on the excellence of her capability.

In classic sentimental fashion, then, paternal authority here and throughout the novel secures itself by staging its weakness rather than its might. Virtually every male character here relies, as Mr. Tyrold does, on the disciplinary properties of this weakness. Indeed, one of the few specimens of English manhood *not* touched by

this system is the birdkeeper, who outrages Camilla by the corporal punishment he inflicts upon the diminutive bullfinch to teach it tricks. He acquires and sustains his dominion over the caged bird by, in his own words, "the true old way, Miss; I licks him." Everyone, the birdkeeper continues with a menacing grin, is "the better for a little beating, as I tells my wife. There's nothing so fine set, Miss, but what will bear it, more or less." Comprehending bullfinches, wives, and impulsive young daughters, who are always trespassing without knowing it, the birdkeeper's words are a threatening reminder to her of what, according to "the true old way," lay in store for delicate creatures who displeased their monitors. Unembarrassed by charges of brutality (six or seven bullfinches die under his pedagogy for each one that graduates), the birdkeeper does not regard his birds as unfortunate. Indeed, he is the one put upon, for their own ungovernability necessitates his stern measures: they are so shy and cunning that "one's forced to be pretty tough with 'em."

Having forsaken the "true old way," modern male authority, by contrast, wins its sway by asserting not its legitimacy as the agent of discipline but its status as the object of pity, much as Parson Yorick absorbs the plaintive starling into his own name (Sterne), transforming it into a figure for his sensitivity. In *Camilla* sentimentality is a more violent affair, in which men gain sway by a passive-aggressive display of susceptibility. The most conspicuous example of this, of course, is Alphonso Bellamy, alias Nicholas Gwigg, who gets his way with the credulous Eugenia by pleading a passion for her so desperate that he will kill himself rather than live without her. Not until she is within his clutches will he drop the sentimental mask and adopt the birdkeeper's directness—"I shall lock you up upon bread and water for the rest of your life." But even after their marriage he threatens suicide, and such is his underlying effeminacy that he botches his threat and dies accidentally by his own hand. Other men also make a spectacle of their immolation. Persistently vaunting his unique stature as a "man" of spirit who swears, spends, drinks, without unmanly restraint—he scoffs at Melmond as "just a girl's man . . . all sentiment, and poetry, and heroics"—Lionel Tyrold may appear to be an exception to this rule, but he too tyrannizes by his weakness. Coercing his sister by convincing her he feels too much rather than too little, he supplements his increasingly importunate demands for money with suicide threats: "I have no great *gusta* for blowing out my brains," he declares, implying however, that he will have no other choice unless Camilla comes up with money for him. The fiery Macdersey likewise woos Indiana by telling her "he'd shoot himself through the brains" if she were so "cruel" as to refuse his suit, and his hero, the clownish Othello, that man-of-action turned man-of-feeling, cries out in piteous dialect, "I must veep!"

Camilla never gets a chance to watch this Othello off himself for the edification of the assembled, as it turns out, because she must rush home to another sentimental male, Sir Hugh, who is at that moment enacting his own (premature) deathbed scene which the whole family has been called to witness. The novel's principal figurehead of authority, Sir Hugh is the man of feeling writ large, to whom Mr. Tyrold fondly and Mrs. Tyrold reluctantly defer, and in crafting him Burney has taken care to stress his Englishness. Among a long line of "amiable humorists" running from Roger de Coverley to Uncle Toby and beyond, Sir Hugh is a national figure—the eccentric but endearing head of the family, the keeper of its inherited wealth, the diffuser of its good name through munificence. In the 1790s, active, distinctively English good nature such as his was increasingly invoked as a means of differentiating the wholesomeness of the English ruling class from the decadence of the French. Sir Hugh's stature as a national type was quite apparent to Burney's politically discriminating readers. An indefatigable projector for the counterrevolution, Frances Anne Crewe had already enlisted Burney to write a charity sermon on behalf of French priests fleeing the Terror, and she tried to convince Burney to contribute to an antijacobin weekly magazine. Slated to appear under titles as diverse as "The Breakfast Table," "The Modern Nestor," "The Old Gentleman," or (more ominously) "The Spying Glass," this periodical was to feature Sir Hugh himself animadverting on the times, and as Crewe assumed, opposing newfangled Frenchified speculative systems with old-fashioned English virtues of the heart.

Professing herself "gratified" by Crewe's purposes and "flattered" by her request, Burney still declined the proposal. But though she did so pleading her unfitness for political journalism, she might just as easily have pleaded Sir Hugh's unfitness as a figure for national salvation. Despite his idealization, Sir Hugh is also a figure of mismanagement, directly responsible for many of the most serious ills of the novel precisely because of the affective drag in which sentimentality has invested him. As if to emphasize this, Burney puts him in women's clothes. In a passage which encapsulates much of the plot, Sir Hugh celebrates the little Camilla's birthday with all the absurd guilelessness that marks him as a man of feeling, a child in the eyes of the world:

> [He] suffered his darling little girl [Camille] to govern and direct him at her pleasure. . . . She metamorphosed him into a female, accoutring him with her fine new cap, while she enveloped her own small head in his wig; and then, tying the maid's apron round his waist, put a rattle into his hand, and Eugenia's doll upon his lap, which she told him was a baby that he must nurse and amuse.

Sir Hugh gladly becomes a spectacle—a "comical sight" and "grotesque figure" which children, servants, and "their numerous guests" behold with glee. But this lord of misrule, wielding a rattle instead of a sceptre, rules nonetheless, as the double sense of "suffer" makes clear. The apparently humiliating reversal he embodies when dressed as a woman is authorized by his permission, and any subversive potential it seems to portend is thus circumscribed and absorbed. Little Camilla's "pleasure" seems to be at stake, but ultimately it is his pleasure that she and all the children serve—they are, after all, severally scuttled from Etherington to Beech Park and back again, enriched or disinherited according to his whims. Yet the other sense of "suffer" is also crucial here, for in this novel about male suffering, the humiliation he seems to take on enlarges the sphere of his power. Sir Hugh isn't "metamorphosed" into just any sort of woman by donning female clothing; it is the maternal part he appropriates. Nursing is a variously gendered phenomenon throughout this novel. When Edgar watches Camilla nursing little children, he finds that she may not be a degraded flirt after all. But the tenderness which sensibility opens out to men makes them more effectually maternal than women are. Unlike Wollstonecraft, Burke, we recall, has nothing to say on the subject of Marie-Antoinette's maternity, stressing instead Louis XVI's anxiety as a father, and sentimental literature in general cedes maternal softness to men. In *Camilla*, fathers too are active nurses— Mr. Tyrold, for instance, shares in the nursing of the sick Eugenia, and one suspects that his ministrations are gentler than his wife's. Nevertheless, male nurturance, like all other forms of authoritative guidance (think of Marchmont's tutelage, or Mr. Tyrold's sermon) always bungles here. In the case at hand, Sir Hugh, wearying of the maternal part, cries out "Do take away poor Doll, for fear I should let it slip," and he is right, though the creature he eventually does let slip is not, unfortunately, a doll. Soon he unwittingly exposes Eugenia to a disease that will scar her for life, and then he drops her from the seesaw and leaves her dwarfed and crippled. Without casting him as a monster, as Radcliffe would, or as a coarse bully botching his daughter's life while quaffing claret with a neighboring squire, in the Wollstonecraftean mode, Burney dramatizes the ruinous ineptitude of a figure beloved as a national institution. She thus assails sentimental authority for maintaining the offices and the prerogatives of power without possessing the competencies of it, exposing the perverse logic which obliges us to love him more with every failure.

Mangled by male nurturance, Eugenia Tyrold exemplifies in the most blatant way possible the mutilation of the female subject under male sentimentality. But what is even more shocking than her injury is its systematic erasure from discourse. As the little Eugenia grows up, no one lets her look in a mirror, and no one in the family is permitted to refer to her disfigurement, which we are constantly being given to understand is egregiously hideous. Withheld from any means of beholding or thinking about herself, she is raised in complete ignorance of her condition. The manifest rationale for this prohibition on self-reflexivity, of course, is a wish to spare her feelings. But this wish to keep Eugenia from feeling on her own behalf is exactly what is so sinister. From the beginning, Sir Hugh has treated Eugenia's misfortune in such a way as to render himself the chief subject of it, the passionate inflation of his rhetoric actually guaranteeing the diminishment of his guilt. Weeping and wailing, in a frenzy of passive aggression, he enjoins his brother and sister to "Hate me . . . for you can't help it!" or to "Kill me in return," though his ramblings remain childishly self-exculpatory even when most apparently self-responsible: "It's all my doing; though innocently enough, as to any meaning, God knows."

Eugenia must be kept in the dark about her suffering because that knowledge would unsettle the allegiance she owes to men of feeling. Not accidentally, Eugenia's giddy male relatives lack the discipline for classical education. Since its immasculating rigors are not functional for sentimental manhood, they form female manhood instead. Inspiring Eugenia with a pious reverence for the father and his laws, as well as with stoic self-command, classical education becomes the basis of Eugenia's virtue and at the same time really does deform her. Having "read no novels"—the sort of "women's" literature on which pedants like Orkborne and moralists like Marchmont frown—Eugenia cannot anticipate the machinations of fortune hunters. She is vulnerable because she takes her duty seriously: she defers to the spectacle of male feeling ("Tears in a man. . . . How touching!" she exclaims credulously about Bellamy's performance as a lovesick suitor), and she honors promises, perhaps the single most important obligations of political subjects, even if made under duress. Sometimes chided for this quixotism, Eugenia only does what every dutiful daughter ought to do: efface herself before her obligations. Burney's defamiliarizing excess thus discloses the unbearable oddness of the exemplary.

Under male sentimentality, the female in distress, as we have seen, is an object either of suspicion or derision, not of a tender compassion that testifies to the male onlooker's goodness of heart. True, when the preternaturally beautiful Indiana emits "little shrieks, and palpitations," the quixotically gallant Melmond is captivated: "What feminine, what beautiful delicacy!—How sweet in terror!—How soul-piercing in alarm." But Indiana's alarm is phony; her only real fear is losing her audience. Just as the calamities of the poor make up the amusement of the gentry, so is genuine female suffering greeted with the gleeful, unrelenting cruelty Burney is unsurpassed at depicting: officers ridicule Eugenia's hellish ugliness in Camilla's hearing; Dubster calls her "that limping little body"; the market women call her a scarecrow to her face; Cler-

mont considers her a "wizen little stump"; and even her own brother feels no compunction about describing her as "a little dowdy thing" whose misfortune, in his view, makes her a less fitting object of Sir Hugh's bounty than himself. The most innocent and outrageously severe suffering in the novel, then, has no place in the sentimental economy, and it is especially off-limits to the woman whose experience it is.

In *Camilla*, imperviousness to suffering is woman's cardinal virtue. Even though Mr. Tyrold assures Eugenia that "sympathy springs spontaneously for whatever is unfortunate, and respect for whatever is innocent," we never see such sympathy. It is Eugenia's duty to "steel [her]self," and to prove herself a good daughter by not feeling her distress and thus sparing the sympathetic feelings of the uncle and parents who are responsible for it. Once she discovers and laments her condition, her father, bedewing her cheeks with his tears, effects her desensitization by taking her to spy upon a ravishingly beautiful young woman. Inviting her and Camilla to gaze upon this "beautiful creature" whose "face" is "perfect" and whose "chin" a "statuary might have wished to model," Mr. Tyrold remarks that since even the greatest beauty must survive the decay of her charms, women must cultivate a heroic indifference to pain: "The soldier who enters the field of battle requires not more courage, though of a different nature, than the faded beauty who enters an assembly-room" and to prepare for this eventuality a woman must withstand the "flatteries" that would "enervate" and feminize her when she should instead be inuring herself with martial "fortitude." Despite her respect for the heroic mode, Eugenia is not content with this comfort. Only when the young woman begins to slobber and to burst into "loud, shrill, and discordant laughter" do Eugenia and Camilla realize that Mr. Tyrold has set up an object lesson in the inappropriateness of self-pity rather than a *vanitas* sermon on the evanescence of beauty:

> The sisters now fearfully interchanged looks that shewed they thought her mad, and both endeavoured to draw Mr. Tyrold from the gate, but in vain; he made them hold by his arms, and stood still.

> Without seeming giddy, she next began to jump; and he now could only detain his daughters, by shewing them the gate, at which they stood, was locked.

> In another minute, she perceived them, and, coming eagerly forward, dropt several low courtesies, saying, at every fresh bend—"Good day!—Good day!—Good day!"

> Equally trembling, they now both turned pale with fear; but Mr. Tyrold, who was still immovable, answered her by a bow, and asked if she were well.

Although anxiety about what Johnson dubbed "the uncertain continuance of reason" was endemic to the culture of late-eighteenth-century England—George III's insanity could never be very far from Burney's, as from any informed subject's mind—the lovely madwoman is a trope of sentimental literature. In this episode, an instance of gendered reading, Burney is glancing at Sterne, whose *Sentimental Journey* is an intertextual presence throughout the novel. Like Mr. Tyrold, whose interest in female beauty is chiefly and avowedly in its "effect upon the beholder," whom he assumes to be male, Parson Yorick, as we have already seen, indulges his sympathy for the mad Maria, and the "undescribable emotions" welling in him make him "positive I have a soul." Burney characteristically raises the tension of this topos several notches, rendering the madness of her "fair afflicted" more turbulent and gross: her autistic babble is violent, self-mutilating, and obscene. But curiously enough, Parson Tyrold, though transfixed, looks on with perfect equanimity rather than with the Sternean effusions we might expect: he can moralize upon her condition because he need not partake of it. His daughters, on the other hand, are pained to the quick by the display of a woman with whom they must identify, and they try repeatedly to draw away their adamantine father. He remains "immovable," the gate is "locked," and thus the refrain of Sterne's songbird ("I can't get out—I can't get out") suits Camilla and Eugenia as much as it does the idiot and the other encaged creatures here.

Mr. Tyrold contrives this spectacle in order to teach Eugenia to be thankful that her mind is lucid no matter how deformed her body, and indeed the stalwart Eugenia takes it like a soldier, vowing to think about the lovely idiot whenever she is "discontented," and to "submit, at least with calmness, to [her] lighter evils and milder fate." The "fair afflicted" is thus clearly supposed to embody what every woman should fear becoming: in Eugenia's words, a "spectacle of human degradation." And yet, as *Camilla* amply shows, the lesson is not nearly so simple as this because of the ways in which that spectacle is gendered. As Mr. Tyrold remarks, because the woman "was born an idiot," she is "insensible to her terrible state." Insensibility is actually what is required of Eugenia and Camilla. To possess "beauty, without mind," far from being dreadful, is all-too-desirable. For Parson Yorick, madness enhances rather than degrades Maria's charm: with her vacant gaze, she is still so "feminine" that she possesses "all that the heart wishes, or the eye looks for in a woman." In *Camilla*, what Eugenia considers to be the spectacle of human degradation many gentlemen see as the picture of ideal femininity: Indiana Lynmere. Yet Indiana personifies "beauty, without mind" almost as much as the idiot does, and the two figures are linked by signifiers of internal deficiency. Perfect as "statuary," they are each without volition: the "mind-dependent" Indiana is called an "automaton" by Mrs.

Arlbery, and the idiot is described as a "machine." Despite inhuman vacancy—Melmond finally deplores the "vacancy of [Indiana's] soul's intelligence," and the "shocking imbecility" of the idiot's utterances resemble "nothing human"—they are also compelling spectacles of "sensibility personified."

The figure of the female automaton, then, is abhorred as well as desired, and the contradictions circulating around her derive from uncertainties about female inferiority which sentimentality gives rise to, or better, from men's anxiety concerning these uncertainties: is the woman in distress faking it? does her suffering signify? Yorick, as we recall, fears that the starling's heartrending song, taught by the servant of its aristocratic owner and hence carrying with it the portentous affectivity of the underclass, may not be credible, and hence that Yorick's pity for it may be wasted or misplaced. And yet Maria's madness seems to him credible and truly feminine because her dementia puts her beyond the possibility of looking back, and hence beyond the suspicion of staging her sorrow in order to seduce him. Because she has no interiority, she can conceal nothing. Camilla is present in this scene because her subjectivity presents the same problem to Edgar, who despite Mrs. Arlbery's characterization of him as "frozen composition of premature wisdom," is the quintessentially sensitive male spectator. Not coincidentally, when Camilla's identity caves in under his scrutiny, she becomes an idiot woman too: her "intellects" become "shattered," her "eyes" become "dim," her "faculties confused," her compliance "mechanical," and her demeanor "vacant," "lost alternately in misery and absence." Only then can he love her.

With the exception of the perfectly dutiful Lavinia—who has no desires and hence no narrative—the Tyrold sisters trouble their father with untoward feeling, and he encourages them to suppress it by inviting them into a martial, heroicized vision of femininity which in Camilla's case especially is of national import. Often reprinted in reviews and conduct books, Mr. Tyrold's "little sermon upon the difficulties and the conduct of the female heart" admonishes Camilla to modesty by linking her conduct to the well-being of the nation, for in the 1790s conservative ideologues considered regulation of "decent" sexuality a political priority. Appearing to accept as noncontroversial those arguments which proponents of democratic reform had made about the moral equality of the sexes, Mr. Tyrold's sermon finesses them by framing them as a very loaded question about sexual propriety: should "women as well as men . . . be allowed to dispose of their own affections"? Like Maria Edgeworth, who dodged controversy by declaring herself more interested in the "happiness" than in the "rights" of women, Mr. Tyrold concurs with reformers like Wollstonecraft "in theory" only to dismiss their proposals as more "curious than important" given the presumed absence of any "practicability." Part of his argument is prudential, claiming to make women content with what is likely to be their lot, marriage. Living as she does in what Mr. Tyrold calls "this doubly appendant state," the modest female, recognizing her dependence upon first her parents and then her husband, must exist in a state of affective equipoise. The engagement of her desires or cultivation of her mind might render her unsuitable for and unhappy with "the husband into whose hands she may fall" and on whose "humour" she must subsist.

But other aspects of Mr. Tyrold's argument enforce modesty with a more coercive sting. Sidestepping Wollstonecraft's critique of modesty, Mr. Tyrold asks, "Since Man must choose Woman, or Woman Man, which should come forward to make the choice? Which should retire to be chosen," but the question is purely rhetorical: no good girl would favor the prerogative of choice. A "modest and reasonable young woman," inspired by "all her feelings of delicacy, all her notions of propriety," will of course wish to wait (as Lavinia Tyrold does) until asked by a gentleman her parents approve. Despite his paternal kindness, Mr. Tyrold's implication cannot be missed: Camilla ought never have formed a wish for Edgar's hand without being asked, and having illicitly done so, she must now stifle her desire, and "combat against a positive wish." The world, monitoring female propriety, will consider "unreturned female regard" as evidence of a woman's immodestly "ungoverned passions," and even if the imputation of what amounts to promiscuous excess is not fair, a woman who has had so little respect for herself as to form an unsolicited passion cannot "reasonably demand" anything like "consideration and respect from the community."

Like the "altered female" whose entrance into an assembly room where she once reigned is as heroic as that of a soldier onto the battlefield, Camilla is true to her Virgilian pedigree: she must "struggle" against herself as she would struggle "against an enemy." But if Mr. Tyrold's call to warfare within pushes Camilla towards the idiot's madness, it also urges a cessation of affect that pushes her towards Indiana's statued coldness. The difference is that while Indiana's insensibility is real—she has no feelings—Camilla's is an act, for she possesses feelings which are to be invested in the drapery of decency. Mr. Tyrold's recommendation of female discretion and reserve resonates with Burkean subtexts. Far from encouraging the vice of hypocrisy or part-playing, the concealment of her frailty, Mr. Tyrold explains, is a "conciliation to virtue" and carries a national agenda: "It is the bond that keeps society from disunion; the veil that shades our weakness from exposure, giving time for that interior correction, which the publication of our infirmities would else, with respect to mankind, make of no avail."

Men like Sir Hugh or Mr. Tyrold can be loved for wearing their hearts on their sleeves because sentimentality licenses their excess. Their effusions extend their authority by demonstrating the mildness of their yoke. The same sort of overflow is not permitted Camilla, even though, as her name indicates, it is her birthright. The drapery of decency seems to be a peculiarly feminine costume, requiring that a woman both have and conceal her feeling. Not to have any, of course, is to threaten the sentimental economy by failing to cede to it the veneration, awe, loyalty, and love it requires. Accordingly, men first adore the vacancy that ensures the unclouded radiance of Indiana's brow, finally to recoil from her indifference. Camilla, on the other hand, is doubly bound because the frailty of warmth is required. Had she been insensible to Edgar, she would be unworthy because unfeeling. But having given way to her feelings and formed a wish, she is scolded for weakness and exhorted to stony constraint, to "shut up every avenue by which a secret which should die untold can further escape you." Camilla, then, must masquerade as a statue, conscious that reserve such as hers is "the bond that keeps society from disunion."

The injunction to have and to stifle emotion seems bad enough. But, from Edgar's point of view, it is too lenient, allowing a dangerous degree of control to women in the conduct of their inner life and licensing a concealment which can impose upon and thereby undo the authority of male onlookers. The novel's chief policeman of bourgeois notions of femininity, Edgar Mandlebert prohibits women even the narcissistic pleasure in their spectacularity that Rousseau granted them as coquettes by nature. Having appointed himself Camilla's "monitor," he is constantly spying or listening in on her in order to trace her sensibility to its wellsprings, to discover her "real" disposition, and to assess her worthiness as a wife. Camilla is far from resenting this watchfulness. Indeed, so long as their watching is reciprocal, the system seems fair. To her, his watchfulness proves that her behavior is of intimate consequence to him; and to him, her compliancy gratifies his authority and betokens a wifely sweetness of temper.

The hideous logic of this familiar system whereby (to recall Mr. Tyrold's formulation) a man chooses a woman and a woman retires to be chosen, is disclosed through the exaggerated suspicion authorized by Marchmont. A two-time loser in marriage, Marchmont suspects the waywardness and inscrutability of women's inferiority, of which a husband must possess himself entirely. After the death of his first wife, Marchmont discovers that she had written not his own name, but that of another man over and over again in her private diary; having been caught just before committing the act of adultery that would oblige him to cast her off, the second wife wastes away. The stories of Marchmont's wives could easily be imagined as radically charged sentimental novels in potentia, the first about a dutiful young girl dying of disappointed love after consenting to a marriage without affection; the second, about a far less dutiful woman who wastes her life away in a loveless marriage until she, rather mysteriously, is "no more." But although the redundancy of dead wives—Dubster also has survived the decease of two—invites resistant counterreadings in the toxicity of husbands' love, the readings of Marchmont and Edgar underwrite the legitimacy of a husband's dominion over the inner life of his wife. Upon the decease of his first wife, Marchmont is mortified by her dead body: a "lifeless, soulless, inanimate frame was all she had bestowed upon me," he remarks, in words which place her in the company of the other female automatons of **Camilla** whose vacancy is deplored, even as it is also desired. Persuaded that a husband must be in "entire possession of the heart" of the woman *before* he proposes, Marchmont adjures Edgar to watch Camilla with a distrustful eye for consummate self-referentiality, asking of her every move not "'Is this right in her'" but rather "'Would it be pleasing to me'.".

In a brilliant discussion drawing on game theory, Doody has illuminated the impossible position in which Camilla has been placed by guardians of feminine virtue—her father on one hand, and her "monitor" Edgar on the other. Unworthy of her father's regard if she exposes an affection that has not been solicited, and unable to gain Edgar's if she does not, Camilla cannot find any manner of being *not* liable to severe reproach. Much in the spirit of Othello, who imagines Desdemona to have slept with the entire army, Edgar convicts her of "the common dissipation of coquetry," pruriently recurring to fantasies about her degradation, her "perverted" and "spoilt" delicacy. By Edgar's lights, the problem with coquettes like Camilla (and by extension, Indiana) is not that they possess "beauty without mind" but rather that their minds are not vacant enough. Lamenting that she is too conscious by far, Edgar nostalgically recalls the time before Camilla lost that "clear transparent singleness of mind, so beautiful in its total ignorance of every species of scheme, every sort of double measure, every idea of secret view and latent expedient." The transparency and ignorance he yearns for recall, once again, the idiot's vacancy. Surface without depth, beauty without mind are for him constitutive of female excellence.

Enjoined by her father to soldierly self-command over the same somatic signs of sensibility (tears, fainting spells, blushes, starts) that Edgar requires on the grounds that they bypass faculties of artful self-control, Camilla is brought to an impasse towards the end of the novel, and death and madness are her only ways out. As she learns that her father has been incarcerated and her uncle's estate relinquished for her unconfessed debts, her mind and body snap: "Words of alarming incoherency proclaimed the danger menacing her in-

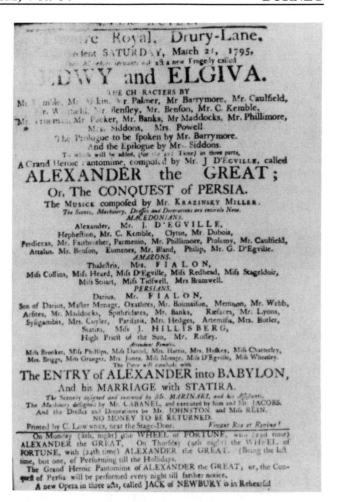

Playbill for the only performance of Edwy and Elgiva.

tellects, while agonies nearly convulsive distorted her features, and writhed her form." Camilla's misery is necessarily overdetermined, for given the dual prohibitions under which she labors, nothing less than total devastation could, on the one hand, legitimize her loss of self-control and, on the other, authenticate her feelings. It takes a crisis of national proportions to bring this about. At a time when the neighborhood was still the basic political unit and the squire's manor the basic site of law, the desolation of Sir Hugh's estate ("naked and forlorn, despoiled of its hospitality, bereft of its master,—all its faithful old servants unrewarded dismissed") is fraught with import which aggravates Camilla's guilt. Female manners must be awfully momentous if it takes only a few debts at the milliner's shop to devastate one's entire family and all the dependents in its environs. And yet since Camilla's guilt itself is an abscess of forbidden egoism, her immolation is reprehensibly self-indulgent. Indeed as Camilla herself learns from Lavinia, Mrs. Tyrold refuses Camilla's wish to come home on the grounds that she only wants "to abandon herself to her feelings."

Insofar as it underscores the prohibition on female distress, then, the climactic moment of **Camilla** inverts the initiatory moment of *Udolpho*. The scene where the overwrought Camilla looks at what turns out to be Bellamy's corpse demonstrably adapts Emily St. Aubert's horrifying view of the body behind the veil in *Udolpho*. The sight of "a dead body" is what finally, in the landlady's words, makes Camilla go "out of her mind" and sink into a deathly delirium. Like Emily, Camilla cannot resist confronting the spectacle of a dead body "stretched out upon a table." Driven by a curiosity that is stronger than her dread, she too must lift a "cloth" which "covered the face" if she is to get the view she both fears and desires. But the similarities stop there. In Radcliffe's novel, Emily is permitted misrecognitions that disclose truths contrary to those authorized by the official discourses of the novel, and thus her vivid imagination of Laurentini's rotting corpse, abetted by servants' stories, enables Emily to figure her own suffering as nothing else will. But whereas in *Udolpho*, as we have seen, the sex of the body is not transparent, in Burney's novel Camilla is never allowed even the fleeting fancy that the body could be her own. For Camilla, the body is decidedly male—"Dismal is its view; grim, repulsive, terrific its aspect"—and as such more formidable than it was when alive, for like all the spectacles of male distress we have seen so far, it incriminates Camilla through its very recumbency. Coming upon it when she has considered vying with it by committing suicide, Camilla looks upon the supposedly murdered body only to condemn herself for criminally "blamable self-desertion" that renders her guiltier even than Bellamy's (nonexistent) murderer because she should have known better than to make a spectacle of her suffering.

Camilla renounces the guilty agency of suicide, but unwilled mental and physical collapse accomplish what everyone has wanted. Camilla does everything a woman can do to die short of dying itself, and this extremity gives her in abundance what everyone has refused all along: pity, and the permission to feel that it carries with it. Having been compelled to *her* bed much as her uncles have taken to theirs, but with none of the fanfare, Camilla herself becomes the figure stretched out behind the curtain, and her condition is judged so hopeless that servants call for a clergyman (who turns out to be Edgar himself) to read the prayer for the dead over her expiring body. Proof positive that she is without subterfuge, Camilla's dying exposes the "true feelings of her heart." Accordingly, Edgar "moisten[s]" her hand "with his tears," a "testimony of his sensibility." The murderousness of Marchmont's caution, then, is not renounced but fully satisfied and then some. Edgar may safely marry Camilla because, reading over letters marked "*Not to be delivered until I am dead*," he can be sure that he is "the constant object of every view, the ultimate motive to every action." And as if this weren't assurance enough, ever the monitor he

then (with the authorization of the teary-eyed Mr. Tyrold) actually eavesdrops on Camilla's confessions to her mother, without coming forward and renewing his suit until he hears her avow her undying love. Clearly, scenes of reconciliation that should, if conventions were allowed to function normally, feel satisfying and appropriate instead pall by an excess that keeps reasserting rather than resolving the problems that have generated the crises to begin with.

As central as the Edgar-Camilla conflict has been in the plotting of **Camilla**, however, in some ways Camilla's relations to other women are of equal if not more weight to Camilla herself. Burney is unparalleled in her readiness to investigate relationships other than the love plot, and in her exceedingly capacious novels women's relations to other women are depicted with a richness and consequence that in some cases rival the sway men are supposed to have in their affective lives. In **Camilla**, the very derelictions of sentimental men sometimes make it possible for women to assume new relationships to each other, as when Camilla displays her "courage" by coming to the "rescue" of the distressed "youth, sensibility, and beauty" of Mrs. Berlinton, under ineffectual attack by a fop standing "a few yards off, taking a pinch of snuff, and humming an opera air." And like the chivalric male, Camilla becomes endeared to the object of her courageous exertions. More often, however, the disruption of gender markers authorized by sentimentality has, in problematizing virtually every mode of femininity, rendered women hard to love. The following description cannot keep from painting women with the same brush it paints fops:

> Clermont Lynmere so entirely resembled his sister in person, that now, in his first youth, he might almost have been taken for her, even without change of dress: but the effect produced upon the beholders bore not the same parallel: what in her was beauty in its highest delicacy, in hind seemed effeminacy in its lowest degradation. The brilliant fairness of his forehead, the transparent pink in his cheeks, the pouting vermilion of his lips, the liquid lustre of his languishing blue eyes, the minute form of his almost infantine mouth, and the snowy whiteness of his small hands and taper fingers, far from bearing the attraction which, in his sister, rendered them so lovely, made him considered by his own sex as an unmanly fop, and by the women, as too conceited to admire any thing but himself.

Assailing the effeminacy of the modern male, this passage fairly bristles with a homophobic determination to reaffirm the very markers of gender which sentimentality elsewhere blurs: we are to love Sir Hugh when he is in woman's clothing or when he fails to master ancient languages, but we are to despise Clermont for looking like a woman and preferring newspapers to the classics. And yet, even though this passage purportedly despises Clermont for not being a woman—i.e., for being a caricature of a woman, effeminate rather than feminine—it clearly despises women as well. The novel everywhere insists that Indiana's femininity is effeminacy, every bit as put on, caricatured, hyperconventional, theatrical, and undesirable as her brother's. As we have amply seen, other modes of femininity—Eugenia's duty, Camilla's liveliness—appear equally extravagant and maiming in their own way.

Given her heroines' yearning for intimacy with women—Burney's attachment to her sisters and her intense but ill-fated intimacy with Mrs. Thrale surely figure here—the unsettling of feminine roles feels like a heavy loss, at times even a betrayal. This is especially so where mothers are concerned. Like Cecilia, whose enthrallment to Mrs. Delvile is the central and most absorbing subject of *Cecilia*, Camilla desires a mother's tenderness with passion that leaves Edgar far behind, and yet sentimentality has so alienated women from their "natural" roles, the novel appears to complain, that maternal love between women is scarcely possible. Camilla's penitential return to Etherington is prevented because one person is there whose voice she no sooner overhears than she must flee, whose wrathful face she would sooner die than behold, and from whose terrible malediction she shrinks with dread as from Yahweh Himself. This potent figure is Mrs. Tyrold, licensed by male sentimentality to be awesome on its behalf, while it arrogates to itself the sweetness typically assigned to feminine beauty. While Wollstonecraft likes to imagine a nation of manly women exerting their power productively to control, guide, admonish, and discipline, Burney is embarrassed at best and horrified at worst by virile women. Where they are respected as effectual guardians and negotiators, as with Mrs. Selwyn in *Evelina*, they are kept at arm's length as "unfeminine," and when their power is exercised under the banner of patriarchy, as with Mrs. Delvile in *Cecilia* or Mrs. Tyrold here, they are ferociously equivocal. Having aggravated Camilla's distress by doubting its reality, Mrs. Tyrold still enjoins her daughter to stifle her transgressive sentience: "Repress, repress . . . these strong feelings. . . . It is time to conquer this impetuous sensibility." Camilla, "[s]truck with extreme dread of committing yet further wrong," is ready as always to consent to yet another round of browbeating even though she has only just returned from the brink of death. She obeys, soon to give way (helplessly and uncomplainingly, of course) to the "weak state of her body." Only when confronted with her daughter's corporeal dissolution does Mrs. Tyrold finally believe her, and take to her bosom the child she has banished, becoming a fantasy of maternal misericordia, "softly solicitous, and exquisitely kind," profuse with all of the intimacies of tenderness—the hovering solicitude, the soothing words, the enfolding embraces, the incessant caresses—for which Camilla has been desperate. The extremity of Camilla's abjection thus both reproaches Mrs. Tyrold's disciplinary ire and temporarily restores her, as the novel nostalgically implies, to womanly sympathy outside the sentimental economy.

But not all women in *Camilla* circulate within this economy, and as a result not all are so tainted. Mrs. Arlbery, a widow, is a woman of wit rather than of feeling. As her name suggests—"Arlbery" is an anagram of sorts for Burney's married name, "Arblay"—Mrs. Arlbery is in part a projection of Burney herself. Burney's portrait is largely captivating: the "commanding air of her countenance, and the easiness of her carriage" are allowed to speak "a confirmed internal assurance, that her charms and her power were absolute." What is so unusual about Mrs. Arlbery's conscious power is that it is as free from the taint of excess towards the feminine (i.e., coquettishness) as it is from excess towards the masculine (i.e., inversion), and accordingly it makes possible relations of desire to other women that are not mediated by heterosexual gender codes, as Mary's relation to Ann is in Wollstonecraft's *Mary*, for example. Mrs. Arlbery's pursuit of Camilla has all the earmarks of seduction: having perceived Camilla's "youthful wonder, and felt a propensity to increase it," Mrs. Arlbery turns on all her charms with no other end in view than to become "a violent favourite with" Camilla. Burney's novels and journals are full of the delights of hetero- as well as homoerotic flirtation, even though these delights cannot generally be very frequently, very freely, or very safely indulged. Mrs. Arlbery's flirtation is conducted with the physical intimacy Burney's heroines pine for—she "lean[s] her hand on the shoulder of Camilla" or "pat[s] her cheek," for example—and its results are enjoyed with a pleasure and ease that have a clear erotic charge: "Mrs. Arlbery, charmed with all she observed [in Camilla], and by all she inspired, felt such satisfaction in her evident conquest, that before the *tête-à-tête* was closed, their admiration was become nearly mutual." In a novel where all other versions of femininity are disfiguring—from the self-mutilation in the service of soldierly valor that is Camilla's amazonian birthright, to the moral and physical deformities voluntarily undertaken by Mrs. Tyrold and Eugenia—Mrs. Arlbery is the only woman who experiences her "equivocal being" as pleasure, and it is small wonder that Camilla takes some of that pleasure in.

Most of the excess in the novel generates pain. But it is also possible, of course, to take pleasure in excess and in the subversion it promotes, as campy excess typically does. In the case of Mrs. Arlbery, Burney appears willing to consider this possibility and the emancipatory potential it may hold for women. True, in the interests of symmetry, Burney halfheartedly attempts to make Mrs. Arlbery take responsibility for meddling with Camilla, much as Marchmont had interfered with Edgar. But because most of Mrs. Arlbery's judgments about Edgar stand as accurate, the attempt is not successful. Mrs. Arlbery is permitted to take a pure pleasure in raillery that Camilla and the reader alike are invited to share. Not that her sallies are completely unbounded, of course. Indeed, careful to differentiate her from Mrs. Berlinton, Burney goes to some lengths to establish the unassailability of her reputation and to circumscribe her diversions by her conviction that "vice is detestable." Still, her flamboyance— note that her dress is perversely "fantastic and studied . . . in the same proportion as that of every other person present was more simple and quiet," and her manners conspicuously unconventional—menaces the hyperorthodox. Mrs. Arlbery's sharp wit, then, is bounded by morality, but not by heterosexuality, and sentimentality insists on the linkage of the two. Not surprisingly, although Mr. Tyrold is charmed by her humor, and Sir Hugh impressed with the care she shows to the servants and horses of neighboring gentry, the ever-strict Edgar, alarmed by her irreverence, wants Camilla to be friends instead with women happily tethered within heterosexual disciplinary structures, women like Lady Isabella Irby.

Of course, this independence from the heterosexual economy is what makes Mrs. Arlbery's penchant for the ludicrous so attractive. The same holds true for the foppish Sir Sedley, a "bachelor" similarly detached from domestic ideology, and who appears as a fixture in the highly unconventional household at the Grove. Though spared the homophobic opprobrium that befalls Clermont, he is supposed to seem feminine and frivolous rather than manly and serious. Yawning and lounging rather than attentively ceding his chair to ladies, Sedley is anything but a chivalrous male. Indeed, once he becomes one, he loses all his charm. When Sedley rescues Camilla from runaway horses, his sensibility is masculinized. And while this episode implies a solidly natural basis for gender—in vigorously exerting his good nature on behalf of a lady in distress, Sir Sedley casts aside "the effeminate part he was systematically playing" and restores his heart to its original, unaffected state—it also reinitiates the same old problem, for brought within the heterosexual economy, Sir Sedley becomes irksome to Camilla. Until then, however, the excesses of his sensibility, indulged frankly as play, are enjoyed without harmful consequences. Compared to the duty-driven repression that obtains elsewhere, the freedom with which Arlbery and Sir Sedley banter appears positively wholesome. Though their alliance, like Edgar's and Camilla's, is on-again-off-again, their sparring is conducted openly as a game, and accordingly calls our attention to the younger pair's inability to talk to one another. The campy hyperbole that particularly marks Sir Sedley's mock disapproval of Mrs. Arlbery—"O shocking! shocking! killing past resuscitation! Abominably horrid, I protest!"—serves as a foil to the dourer anguish Edgar feels looking upon Camilla, anguish which he never registers as the excess it is.

Disdaining the categories "romance" and "novel" on the grounds that they signify "a mere love story," Burney preferred to think of *Camilla* as "*sketches of Characters & morals, put in action.*" But her "sketches" finally yield to the romantic plot after all, and in the process put Mrs. Arlbery and the Grove out of Camilla's reach. The vastness of Burney's canvases here and elsewhere enables her to articulate subversive counterpossibilities, but these are always left suspended in outlying areas, while the central composition affirms dominant values. In *Camilla*, as I have argued, that affirmation comes at such a high cost that it seems to take away with one hand what it has (too) profusely granted with the other. The plethora of concluding marriages, for example, flouts the convention by glutting it incredibly: Indiana's elopement with Macdersey, ironically, makes sense enough; but Lavinia compliantly accepts Hal Westwyn, whom she does not know; Eugenia is paired with Melmond, the worshiper of female beauty; and Camilla's marriage to Edgar is more or less posthumous, her conciliatory story, "the fullest, most candid, and unsparing account of every transaction of her short life," sounding for all the world as though she had already died. Yet precisely because *Camilla* purports to be a sober sketch of manners as they occur in the historical present, its critique of sentimentality comes up against the same difficulty female camp generally does: given the currency of already excessive norms, how can the monstrous excess it depicts be recognized as such? In *Udolpho*, Radcliffe solved this problem not only by availing herself of the defamiliarizing properties of gothic genre, but also by textualizing rupture, compelling the reader to register the unbridgeable difference between Emily's story and the true "HISTORY OF SIGNORA DI LAURENTINI."

But *Camilla* does not solve the problem because the problem itself offers a solution to Burney's own ambivalence. *Camilla* makes it possible not to stumble over the shifting ground. Without any of the self-discrediting irony of the Austenian narrator of *Mansfield Park* who quits the "odious subjects" of "guilt and misery," Burney's narrator here commends "the virtuous Tyrolds" and "the beneficent Sir Hugh," and even restores to favor the repentant Marchmont, as though the bases on which they have functioned as norms had not been called into doubt by the foregoing tome. Although Burney is now typically read as a satirist of propriety, contemporary reviewers, to say nothing of a number of distinguished scholars of our own century, read *Camilla* as a contribution to conduct literature, and their view is not completely wrong. Wounded by the less than enthusiastic reception of her novel in the *Monthly Review*, Burney appears to have been flattered by the acknowledgment of her stature as an instructress of young females: "The recommendation at the conclusion [of the review] of the Book as a warning Guide to Youth would recompense me, upon the least reflection, to whatever strictures might precede it." If it is possible to read the monstrosity of dutifully endured pain in *Camilla* as a testament of extravagant loyalty to dominant values rather than as a protest against them, it is because Burney herself was equivocal.

───────────

FURTHER READING

Bibliography

Grau, Joseph A. *Fanny Burney: An Annotated Bibliography.* New York: Garland Publishing, 1981, 210 p.

A detailed primary and secondary bibliography.

Biography

Adelstein, Michael E. *Fanny Burney.* Twayne's English Authors Series, edited by Sylvia E. Bowman, No. 67. New York: Twayne Publishers, 1968, 169 p.

Examines Burney's life and work.

Dobson, Austin. *Fanny Burney (Madame D'Arblay).* English Men of Letters. London: Macmillan & Co., 1904, 216 p.

The standard biography of Burney until the publication of Joyce Hemlow's *The History of Fanny Burney* (see annotation below).

Edwards, Averyl. *Fanny Burney: 1752-1840, A Biography.* London: Staples Press, 1948, 170 p.

Briefly examines Burney's life.

Gosse, Edmund. "The Age of Wordsworth: 1780-1815." In *English Literature, an Illustrated Record: From the Age of Johnson to the Age of Tennyson*, Vol. IV, rev. edition, pp. 1-106. New York: Macmillan Co., 1923.

An illustrated biography of Burney.

Hahn, Emily. *A Degree of Prudery: A Biography of Fanny Burney.* Garden City, N.Y.: Doubleday & Co., 1950, 179 p.

A biographical study widely regarded as condescending in approach.

Hemlow, Joyce. *The History of Fanny Burney.* Oxford: Oxford at the Clarendon Press, 1958, 528 p.

The definitive biography by the foremost Burney scholar.

Hill, Constance. *Fanny Burney at the Court of Queen Charlotte.* London: John Lane, The Bodley Head, 1912, 364 p.

A biography covering the years 1786 to 1791.

Jeaffreson, J. Cordy. "Frances D'Arblay." In *Novels and Novelists from Elizabeth to Victoria*, Vol. I, pp. 312-39. London: Hurst and Blackett, 1858.

A lengthy biographical sketch with a few derogatory comments about Burney's novels.

Masefield, Muriel. *The Story of Fanny Burney: Being an Introduction to the "Diary and Letters of Madame d'Arblay."* New York: Haskell House Publishers, 1974, 160 p.

An account of Burney's life and times.

Tourtellot, Arthur Bernon. *Be Loved No More: The Life and Environment of Fanny Burney.* Boston: Houghton Mifflin Co., 1938, 381 p.

A biographical and historical study based largely on Burney's diary.

Criticism

Agress, Lynne. "Wives and Servants: Proper Conduct for One's Proper Place." In *The Feminine Irony: Women on Women in Early-Nineteenth-Century English Literature*, pp. 114-45. Rutherford, N.J.: Fairleigh Dickinson University Press, 1978.

Discusses Burney's work, especially focusing on *Evelina*. The critic contends that the novel's message is that a young woman must marry well in order to lead a happy life.

Backscheider, Paula R. "Woman's Influence." *Studies in the Novel* XI, No. 1 (Spring 1979): 3-22.

Analyzes the means by which Evelina learns to influence the men around her.

Bradbrook, Frank W. "The Feminist Tradition." In *Jane Austen and Her Predecessors*, pp. 90-119. Cambridge: Cambridge at the University Press, 1966.

Acknowledges Austen's literary debt to Burney.

Cutting-Gray, Joanne. "Writing Innocence: Fanny Burney's *Evelina*." *Tulsa Studies in Women's Literature* IX, No. 1 (Spring 1990): 43-57.

Contends that Burney's Evelina characterizes a state of natural innocence.

Doody, Margaret Anne. "Deserts, Ruins and Troubled Waters: Female Dreams in Fiction and the Development of the Gothic Novel." *Genre* X, No. 4 (Winter 1977): 529-72.

Discusses the significance of female dreams and madness in a number of eighteenth-century novels, devoting several pages to *Cecilia* and *Camilla*.

Gruner, Elisabeth Rose. "The Bullfinch and the Brother: Marriage and Family in Frances Burney's *Camilla*." *Journal of English and Germanic Philology* XCIII, No. 1 (January 1994): 18-34.

Examines Burney's exploration in *Camilla* of female self-discovery and identity "within a family and a world controlled by men."

Hale, Will Taliaferro. "Madame D'Arblay's Place in the Development of the English Novel." *Indiana University Studies* III, No. 28 (January 1916): 5-35.

Perceives in Burney's style an increasing artificiality for which he blames the influence of Johnson and Burney's father.

Hemlow, Joyce. "Fanny Burney: Playwright." *University of Toronto Quarterly* XIX, No. 2 (January 1950): 170-89.

Discusses Burney's dramatic writings and their role in her literary career.

——. "Fanny Burney and the Courtesy Books." *PMLA* LXV, No. 5 (September 1950): 732-61.

Demonstrates the influence on Burney's novels of contemporary works discussing the conduct of young ladies.

[Hunt, J. H. Leigh.] "Men and Books." *The New Monthly Magazine* XXXVII, No. CXLV (January 1833): 48-59.

Discusses the *Memoirs of Dr. Burney*, contending that Johnson's influence on Burney "spoilt her style."

MacCarthy, B. G. "The Domestic Novel—The Novel of Manners." In *The Female Pen: The Later Women Novelists, 1744-1818*, Vol. 2, pp. 87-128. Cork: Cork University Press, 1947.

Documents Burney's literary decline following the publication of *Evelina*.

McMaster, Juliet. "The Silent Angel: Impediments to Female Expression in Frances Burney's Novels." *Studies in the Novel* XXI, No. 3 (Fall 1989): 235-52.

Claims that Burney's novels dramatize restrictions on the female voice in the eighteenth and nineteenth centuries.

Rogers, Katharine M. "Fanny Burney: The Private Self and the Published Self." *International Journal of Woman's Studies* VII, No. 2 (March/April 1984): 110-17.

Contends that although she shared several qualities with her heroines Burney shaped her novels so that her heroines would not display such independence as she did in her life.

Saintsbury, George. "The New Paradise of the Novel." In *The Peace of the Augustans: A Survey of Eighteenth-Century Literature as a Place of Rest and Refreshment*, pp. 105-76. London: G. Bell and Sons, 1916.

An overview of Burney's works, with special attention paid to *The Wanderer*. Saintsbury terms Burney's last novel "a clumsy and immensely long ado about nothing."

Staves, Susan. "*Evelina*; or, Female Difficulties." *Modern Philology* 73, No. 4, Part 1 (May 1976): 368-81.

Contends that the focus of *Evelina* is the heroine's powerful anxiety. Staves believes the book's psychological implications render it a far more serious work than it is often considered to be.

Stevenson, Lionel. "Terror and Edification (1775-1800)." In *The English Novel: A Panorama*, pp. 148-76. Boston: Houghton Mifflin, Riverside Press, 1960.

Details the historical circumstances under which Burney composed her novels.

Voss-Clesly, Patricia. *Tendencies of Character Depiction in the Domestic Novels of Burney, Edgeworth, and Austen: A Consideration of Subjective and Objective World*. 3 vols. Salzburg Studies in English Literature: Romantic Reassessment, edited by James Hogg, No. 95. Salzburg: Universität Salzburg, 1979.

A comparative analysis of selected works. Voss-Clesly states that her intention is "to demonstrate the perfection of technique in character depiction in the domestic novels of Burney, Edgeworth, and Austen."

Wagenknecht, Edward. "The Romance of the Tea-Table: Fanny Burney, the First 'Lady Novelist'." In *Cavalcade of the English Novel*, revised edition, pp. 134-38. New York: Henry Holt and Co., 1954.

Assesses *Evelina* and *Cecilia*. While Wagenknecht considers *Cecilia* to be the more successful from a technical standpoint, he also admires the freshness of *Evelina* and asserts that Burney's greatest strength is her ability to recreate accurately the life of London society.

White, Eugene. *Fanny Burney, Novelist; A Study in Technique: "Evelina," "Cecilia," "Camilla," "The Wanderer."* Hamden, Conn.: Shoe String Press, 1960, 93 p.

Studies Burney's novels, focusing on plot, characterization, style, and narrative technique.

Woolf, Virginia. "Fanny Burney's Half-Sister." In *Collected Essays*, Vol. III, pp. 147-57. London: The Hogarth Press, 1967.

Sketches the life of Maria Allen Rishton, who Woolf suggests was the model for Evelina.

Additional coverage of Burney's life and career is contained in the following sources published by Gale Research: *British Novelists, 1660-1800*; *Dictionary of Literary Biography*, Volume 39; and *Nineteenth-Century Literature Criticism*, Volume 12.

Samuel Taylor Coleridge

The Rime of the Ancient Mariner

The following entry presents criticism of Coleridge's poem *The Rime of the Ancient Mariner* (1798). For a discussion of Coleridge's complete career, see *NCLC*, Volume 9.

INTRODUCTION

A major work of the English Romantic movement, *The Rime of the Ancient Mariner* is considered one of the most significant and famous poems in the English language. While the poem was poorly received during Coleridge's lifetime, it is now praised as a classic example of imaginative poetry, characterizing Coleridge's poetic theories, of which he said in the *Biographia Literaria*, "My endeavors should be directed to persons and characters spiritual and supernatural, or at least romantic."

Biographical Information

In 1796 Coleridge met the poet William Wordsworth, with whom he had corresponded casually for several years. Their rapport was instantaneous, and the next year Coleridge moved to Nether Stowey in the Lake District, where he, Wordsworth and Robert Southey became known as "the Lake Poets." Much of Coleridge's most admired work was composed between the years 1798 and 1800, his most prolific period as a poet. During that time, Wordsworth and Coleridge collaborated on *Lyrical Ballads, with a few Other Poems* (1798), in which *The Rime of the Ancient Mariner* appears. *Lyrical Ballads* marks the beginning of the Romantic movement in England, and is a landmark of world literature.

Plot and Major Characters

Coleridge's *The Ancient Mariner* appears in *Lyrical Ballads* in a purposefully "archaic" form, with words spelled in the manner of an earlier day. Coleridge changed some of the archaic diction of the original *Ancient Marinere* for the second edition of *Lyrical Ballads* and added glosses in the margins when it was included in *Sibylline Leaves* (1817). In its original form and in the modified version that followed, the poem describes an elderly mariner who, compelled to wander the Earth repeating his tale of woe, narrates his story to a wedding guest he meets in a village street. The story he tells relates how, in his youth, the mariner had set out on a sea voyage to the Southern Hemisphere with two hundred other men aboard a sailing ship. During the voyage, the ship is shadowed by an albatross, a huge seabird considered an omen of good fortune by seafarers. For no good reason, the mariner shoots the albatross dead with his crossbow, to the horror of his companions. In a short time, the ship is becalmed, and soon all the crew members die of thirst—all except the mariner. Before they died, the angry crew hung the dead albatross around the mariner's neck for his folly; and now, stricken with the horror of his deed's consequences, the mariner spends his time watching the phosphorescent trails of slimy creatures who writhe and coil in the night waters in the ship's shadow. In his heart, he blesses these humble creatures for their life and beauty, and at that moment, as he leans over the ship's side, the curse on his life begins to lift, as the albatross falls from his neck and sinks into the sea. The rest of the poem tells of the supernatural events that took place as spirits and angels propel the ship north into the snug harbor of the mariner's home town and his rescue by a holy hermit, who pronounces the terms of the mariner's penance upon him. The poem presents a variety of religious and supernatural images to depict a moving spiritual journey of doubt, sin, punishment, renewal, and eventual redemption.

Major Themes

The Ancient Mariner begins with almost the sense of classical Greek tragedy, with a man who has offended against pagan forces condemned to wander the world and repeat his tale to passersby when the daemon within him moves him. There is much in this poem concerning luck, fate, and fortune; this and the theme of death-in-life appear throughout the poems first half, with death-in-life, graphically symbolized by the revivified crew of corpses, appearing from the poem's mid-point almost too the end. There is a point of transition between pagan and Christian elements in the poem, falling at the moment the mariner blesses the sea-snakes in his heart. Death-in-life continues, and elemental spirits converse in the poet's conscious. Yet now, a redemptive presence is at work in the mariner's life, and even the elemental spirits and the living dead are subservient to it, as it becomes apparent that angelic beings have taken over the bodies of the dead crew and are bringing the ship into port. Christian themes and imagery become more pronounced as the poem nears its end, with the mariner declaiming about the quiet, longed-for joy of walking to church with his friends in the village, and then uttering one of the most-quoted stanzas in the entire poem: "He prayeth best who loveth best / All things both great and small; / For the dear God who loveth us, / He made and loveth all"—lines expressing sentiments endorsed by even so formidable an agnostic as Theodore Dreiser. Much of the poem's Biblical and medieval Catholic imagery has sparked radically different interpretations, and several commentators consider it an allegorical record of Coleridge's own spiritual pilgrimage. Coleridge himself, however, commented that the poem's major fault consisted of "the obtrusion of the moral sentiment so openly on the reader. . . . It ought to have had no more moral than the *Arabian Nights'* tale of the merchant's sitting down to eat dates."

Critical Reception

The Rime of the Ancient Mariner was initially disliked and, because it was the longest poem in the collection, helped keep *Lyrical Ballads* from success. In a review shortly after its first publication, Southey called it "a Dutch attempt at German sublimity," and even Wordsworth disliked the negative appraisal the poem seemed to garner their entire volume. Although critical estimation of *The Ancient Mariner* increased dramatically after Coleridge's death, relatively little positive commentary was written on it until the turn of the century. Today, most critics agree that the poem constitutes a seminal contribution to English literature. Perhaps the most important twentieth-century study of *The Ancient Mariner* appeared in 1927 in John Livingston Lowes's magisterial work *The Road to Xanadu: A Study in the Ways of the Imagination.* Here, Lowes brought his broad and deep knowledge of poetic history, poetic diction, and the imagination to bear on Coleridge's early poetry in general and *The Ancient Mariner* in particular. Of Coleridge's first major poem, Lowes harked to themes from the works of Apuleius, Josephus, Michael Psellus, Marsilio Ficino, and many others to "make it clear—where for daemons of the elements, or water-snakes, or sun, or moon—that the rich suggestiveness of a masterpiece of the imagination springs in some measure from the fact that infinitely more than reached expression lay behind it in the shaping brain, so that every detail is saturated and irradiated with the secret influence of those thronged precincts of the unexpressed. . . ." Other major scholars who have written at length on *The Ancient Mariner* include E. M. W. Tillyard, C. M. Bowra, Robert Penn Warren, A. E. Dyson, and Julian Lovelock. In response to critics such as Warren, who have read moral overtones into the poem, Camille Paglia has ruminated upon *The Ancient Mariner* as an expression of pagan visions of sexuality and possession—what T. S. Eliot termed "fear of fear and frenzy" and "fear of possession"—layered over with a veneer of Christian symbols. To Paglia, writing in her *Sexual Personae: Art and Decadence from Nefertiti to Emily Dickinson*

(1990), the Mariner is a "male heroine," who is the receptor of all the active forces of nature which bear him down during the course of the poem's story. The symbols that recur in *The Ancient Mariner*, discussed by Paglia and others, have inspired critical debate over their aptness and Coleridge's use of them. James Stephens has written that "this poem is extreme, its fantasy is extreme, its knowledge of music and colour and pace is extreme," concluding, "No miracle of talent or technique can quite redeem untruth from being initially and persistently inhuman in both life and letters." Other critics, notably Lowes and Bowra, have found otherwise, with the latter writing that the poem succeeds because it is nevertheless "founded on realities in the living world and in the human heart." While a few commentators consider the poem overrated, contemporary scholars generally look to the poem as one of the greatest works of the English Romantic movement.

CRITICISM

William Norman Guthrie (essay date 1898)

SOURCE: "The *Rime of the Ancient Mariner* as Prophecy," in *The Sewanee Review,* Vol. VI, No. 2, April, 1898, pp. 200-13.

[*In the following essay, Guthrie discusses Coleridge's poetry, claiming that it expresses a clear Christian ethic.*]

I. THE ALLEGORY.

If ever a great poet set about his work with a deliberate religious purpose, Coleridge is that man. He believed a new and happier age had begun. His studies in the great philosophic systems of Germany, then new to the world, equipped him, he thought, for the task of reconciling science, political liberty, and the "Truth in Christ." He had, as he tells us in his glorious ode entitled **"Dejection,"** the "Fancy" that made him "dreams of happiness" out of "all misfortunes;" and the "shaping spirit of Imagination" that could give living utterance to subtlest thought and feeling—utterance whereby they obtained a new dignity and a new power. Only when this "spirit" deserted him (for cause) did he turn to mere "abstruse research," the poet dying into critic, expounder of philosophy, and theologian.

It is, of course, as the poet of the ***Rime of the Ancient Mariner*** that he is most renowned. Had he written nothing else, he would not have been born in vain. Not merely as a stirring ballad, nor for its picturesque qualities, the skilful handling of the supernatural it evinces, does the average reader prize the famous ***Rime.*** Somehow he feels so much "more is meant than meets the ear" or even the mental eye. No doubt he loves it most for the light, mysterious play, as of heavenly fingers over the secret keys of his soul, so that unheard music thrills his being through and through.

An allegory it is, but an essentially poetic one, and as such irreducible to plain prose. The poet has always to choose, when attempting to convey abstract thought in concrete form, as for instance, in a narrative, between two evils, that which seems to him least. Either his tale will not be forcible, faithful, plausible enough, as such to interest the reader, save as a vehicle for doctrines that gain his assent; or the doctrine will be forced to recede from the foreground and, now and then, be wholly lost to the sight even of the keenest eye. The charm of the "Faëry Queene" is just this: that Una, Sir Guyon, Britomart, and all Spenser's other delightful figures, are no mere personifications; that often he himself forgets their sense and the sense of their doings and sufferings to take a tale-teller's delight in them and their adventures. Hence, while in Milton's words, "more is meant than meets the ear," it is not always so. At times the story is meaningless—story, and nothing more. When it becomes again significant, our joy in the "sense" is the keener for its brief absence. Allegory, then, rather gains by discreet introduction of meaningless details. For the very reason that they are meaningless, they appear to be full of meaning too deep and wonderful for words. The inexpressible, elusive is suggested. The reader is "teased out of thought," as by Keats's "Grecian Urn" and set to musing for himself. This is surely legitimate poets' charlatanry. At times, to be sure, it has been somewhat maliciously practised, as by the great and shrewd Goethe, who was not above tempting over-ingenious readers to discover marvelous senses in his occasional flashes of deliberate nonsense. And may it not perhaps be true that even our serious Browning set a cunning snare for ultrazealous interpreters now and then out of sheer mischievous delight in watching them sink up to their pensive, hand-supported chins in the quagmire of their own profundity.

A mechanical exegesis of the poem—line by line—would then deservedly expose a critic to ridicule. For surely never was allegory more artistically fashioned by its poet to satisfy first and foremost the demands made of a thrilling tale. Its message is like the perfume of a flower, invisible to the eye that delights in the color and form, and quite unnecessary, so to speak. The beauty suffices that sense. There are no frostbitten petal edges that have to seek for an excuse in the perfume. The perfume is absolutely over and above the perfect pleasure of the eye, a free gift to another, more intimate sense. It is to the spirit, rather than to the intellect, that the doctrine of the *Rime* is addressed. But surely it will gain for us every way if we acquaint ourselves with the philosophy and theology of the poet, constituting, so to speak, the atmosphere in which bloomed this perfect, rare-scented, sevenfold flower of a ballad.

Skilfully, the whole weird tale of wondrous incident and experience is told, so that the closing, lines leave one in doubt:

> A sadder and a wiser man
> He rose the morrow morn.

Perhaps after the astounding relation, you think, do you, that the wedding-guest slept? Such a tale, so told, under the glittering eye of such a teller, could well be expected to scare sleep away for one night at least from the weariest eyelids in the world. But then, it may have been all a dream—that walk with two friends to the wedding-feast, that weird arrest by the seaman, that spell-bound hearing of his yarn—and then how natural would be his waking with the moral well digested, that made him a "wiser" man, and "sadder" only in the sense of not being able to deceive himself as hitherto with regard to what is really "love." He had rightly thought "love" the best thing in the world. He had thought love was chiefly present at the romantic wedding-feast. Has he now no doubt that what is there is always—"love?" *that* divine love that is the most precious thing in the world?

At all events, in the *Rime*, the killing of the albatross in a mood of recklessness, for the mere display of skill, brought on the mariner a curse. The Polar Spirit, whose bird it was, demanded the life of its slayer. The law of nature is: "An eye for an eye, a tooth for a tooth!" His fellows openly disapproved of the deed. They were thus not guilty with the mariner, and the Polar Spirit could not punish him without punishing them; so the fair breeze went on blowing.

But these men judged not of a deed as a deed; they did not refer it to its motive, or half-conscious impulse, and condemn it for that. For the mariner's guilt as such they cared nothing. It was not the lack of love that allowed of his thoughtless cruelty, or his marksman's vanity that outran his love, which shocked them. They did not judge of the bird-victim by its actual character, and pity its undeserved fate. So when their fears seemed vain—for the favorable wind kept blowing—they ceased to believe the bird one of good omen, in spite of its old friendliness, and ascribed to it the mists that now had cleared. They therefore congratulated the mariner, and his crime passed for a meritorious piece of prowess. So the Polar Spirit was free now to exact a penalty. All on board were alike guilty of a lack of "love," and the mariner's fellows, most of all, as was proved by the fact that he at least was "plagued" from the start by fiends of remorse, whilst they—approvers of the deed if its issues only were fortunate—tried to fix the whole guilt on the remorseful doer as soon as the general punishment began.

Death reaches them. The mariner falls to the lot of life-in-death. His remorse will make him a useful instrument of God, in spreading the true doctrine of "love." His fellows could be of no service whatever. Could they be released from danger, they would never pray to be "shriven" of any sin. The moral they would have carried away would have been: "If any one, by a loveless deed to God's creatures brings wrath upon us (who, though quite as loveless, have abstained from actual deeds), let us hate him, and then our hatred will purchase us pardon of the God of love!"

But the death of his fellows seems to the mariner himself an inexplicable mystery—an unjust doom visited on them for his own sin. He does not realize their guilt, greater even than his. He himself still thinks the reckless deed was his sin, not the lack of love. So to him they seem innocent. Their hatred, he had incurred, torments him. He sympathizes almost in their hatred of him. He hates his life, that is continued, when so many were stricken dead for his crime. And the continued life of the low creatures of the sea, his only quick companions, now seems but another form of the same monstrous injustice. He would have them dead too, with himself, or his old shipmates alive and hale.

But at last he looks up to the moon, and then to the quiet stars. An ecstasy of joy in their beauty comes over him. He looks down and sees these same sea creatures which in the bitterness of his insane remorse he had cursed. Their beauty, their happiness, dazzles him. He blesses them:

> A spring of love gushed from my heart,
> And I blessed them unaware.

His sin had been an unconscious one. His atonement, too, was unconscious. The remorse had only deepened his lack of love into a general hatred of life. But God's beauty stole over his spirit—emitted as divine light from all his creatures, stars and snakes alike—and the spell was lifted, the sin was blotted out, because the lovelessness whence it proceeded was neutralized by the new love. All that remained for him was such an expiation of his fault as should render the cure permanent; as should make indelible the impression produced by that vision of universal beauty—namely, the new deep-saving obligation of love to all that lives—and render him a lifelong apostle of the doctrine; conscious of a terrible "woe is me" if he preach it not everywhere and always to him that the Spirit should point out.

II. The Philosophy.

Often among a poet's works are found artistic failures, valuable only because they furnish the reader with a convenient commentary on his artistic successes. The latter usually maintain proud—nay, haughty—silence if cross-questioned as to the opinions of their author. A poet's prose works are not half so reliable. Often the man and the poet differ considerably. But these unhappy children of the poet are, nevertheless, a poet's children. They are brothers of his best offspring. In the case of Coleridge, **"Religious Musings"** and the **"Destiny of Nations"** are poems from which lines may be culled which give definite expression to his spiritual philosophy, and a number of quotations will now be made with a current comment. It is not the part of the present writer to criticize, but merely to interpret.

What marks the higher man from the lower is chiefly a fuller development of what is nowadays termed the "social sense." Among the higher animals homes exist, monogamous lifelong relations of mates, and devoted care of the young. Villages of prairie-dogs or beavers, monarchical states and military republics among bees and ants, witness to this capacity for organization. With man alone does it bear spiritual fruits in a religious faith.

> The savage roams,
> Feeling himself, his *own* low *self, the whole.*
> —**"Religious Musings."**

If anything else enters into his notion of the "whole," it is the fear of fellow savage and the hope of plentiful game. Only after long experience of ever-enlarging horizons, as he climbs the great Mount of Vision, does he come to realize how

> 'Tis the sublime in man
> Our noontide majesty, to know our*selves*
> Parts and proportions of *one* wondrous
>   *whole.*
> —**"Religious Musings"**.

The thought of a universe dawns on him. The thought of a universal consciousness brings the full spiritual day. Law and order everywhere the condition of beauty; everywhere this law and order the evidence of one living Will! Man himself part of this universe! If he put himself, then, in the right attitude toward it, he becomes one with it. As a hero's deeds are appropriated by his proud people, so the mountains, the plains, the seas, the beasts, the flowers, the dews, the skies, the sun, moon, and stars become man's very own.

> The savage roams,
> Feeling himself, *his own* low *self,* the *whole,*
> When he by sacred sympathy might make
> The *whole* ONESELF.
> —*Ib.*

This attitude of mind is called "sacred sympathy." Why so? Actually (according to the philosophy of

Coleridge), the unity of all things is the result of a Will holding them together, dwelling in each part as its life, and making out of them a larger whole, of which He is again the Life in a more intimate sense. But because men's physical organs are separately impressed by things each in turn, things seem not only distinct but separate entities. Here is a stone; there, a tree. Only after much experience do we learn that they are parts of one planet. Here is our earth; there in the heavens are Mars, Venus, and Saturn. Only after centuries of study have we learned that they are part of one solar system. Here is the sun; there is Sirius or Aldebaran. Only in the future will we understand how they constitute one stellar universe. Now we *know* things are united. We utter our conviction whenever we use the word "universe." But we continue to perceive things separate. God makes them *be*, in fact, one whole. We can make them *appear* to us as God makes them be. For this we must share the divine mood; we must be in "sacred sympathy" with him; we must do in our little world of thoughts and feelings that correspond to the external things what He does with the things themselves: unify them, and impart to them of our *one life*.

But from the great unity men's minds are not excluded.

> As one body seems the aggregate
> Of atoms numberless, each organized,
> So by a strange and dim similitude
> Infinite myriads of *self-conscious minds*
> *Are one all-conscious* SPIRIT.
> > **—"Destiny of Nations."**

When the man has become sufficiently spiritual to hold a conception of this substantial unity of the soul with God, he becomes eager to realize the conception. He will not have it remain a barren piece of philosophic speculation. We are self-conscious. We only infer God. Why are we not as directly conscious of God as we are of ourselves? Because our eyes are impure? How shall we then, purify them?

> The drowsed soul
> . . . Of its nobler nature 'gan to feel
> Dim recollections, and thence soared to
>   hope; . . .
> From hope and firmer faith to perfect love
> Attracted and absorbed; and centered there,
> God only to behold and know and feel,
> Till, by *exclusive consciousness of God*
> (All self-annihilated), *it shall make*
> GOD *its identity*—GOD all in all,
> We and our Father ONE.
> > **—"Religious Musings."**

This is but a poetical description of the old method common to all the saints of the Catholic Church, that of devout meditation. Mystical systems differ in nomenclature; specific methods differ also in details; but,

directly or indirectly, all aim at denial as forgetfulness of self. Self stands out against self, mutually repellent forever. What is mine cannot be thine; what is thine must be mine. To affirm and remember self (the opposite of self-denial or self-forgetfulness) involves eternal warfare. How shall the self be denied effectually or forgotten? Only by the affirmation and perpetual remembrance of One who includes both, who is *me* more truly than I am, and yet is as really my friend and my foe alike. The thought of my origin in God makes me wonder at my possibilities. I hope to be other than I am. I trust I shall indeed become all that I vaguely descry, and more. I love That whence I came, whither I go, and which upholds me now upon my way. I feel this God as my *very* SELF. Do I who believe myself a child of God dare call this man that I appear to be, myself? If I remember him, I deny him. Probably, however, I am so attracted and absorbed by the supreme beauty that I have utterly forgotten him. So the old *self*-love has become SELF-love; the old selfishness, selflessness—the love of all in ONE.

What becomes of the sensible world to one so rapt in the vision of God?

> All that meet the bodily sense
> I deem *symbolical*.
> > **—"Destiny of Nations."**

Far indeed is he from growing indifferent to it. He shall (Coleridge's wish for his infant son)

> Wander like a breeze
> By lakes and sandy shores, beneath the
>   crags
> Of ancient mountains, and beneath the
>   clouds
> Which image in their bulk both lakes and
>   shores
> And mountain crags: so shalt thou see and
>   hear
> The lovely shapes and sounds intelligible
> Of that *eternal language,* which thy God
> Utters, who from eternity doth teach
> Himself in all, and all things in himself.
> Great Universal Teacher! He shall mold
> Thy Spirit, and by giving make it ask.
> > **—"Frost at Midnight".**

In a certain sense, to be sure, the mystic will despise all things. He will not, at all events, prize the sound of the eternal language more than its sense. He will never wish to rest in things. He will spurn them under foot, yet only because he is

> Treading . . . all visible things
> As steps that upward to the Father's throne
> Lead—
> > **—"Religious Musings."**

Should there come, however, a time when he can see, not feel, how beautiful they are, all the glorious things in earth and sky, will any diligent contemplation of their beauty make him once more "feel" what he only "sees." Surely not. "Outward Forms" cannot yield

> The passion and the life whose fountains
>   are within.
>
> —*Ib.*

For, of a truth, "we receive but what we give," and to us at least

> In our life alone does nature live.
>   —**"Dejection."**

If we are to behold God in nature, or aught of his glory,

> Oh, from the soul itself must issue forth
> A light, a glory, a fair luminous cloud
> Enveloping the earth.
>
> —*Ib.*

This beautiful and beauty-making power may best be called "joy," "life and life's effluence."

> We in ourselves rejoice.
>
> —*Ib.*

And this "joy" the pure in heart have given to them of God, as a babe the milk from its mother. Of this inner "joy" comes the power to see in nature a divine, continuous sacrament. For this "joy" itself is the witness of the Spirit, and reveals God in us and nature, and makes of all that is in turn a vehicle of our fervent worship—the prayer becoming visible to the eye as Mt. Blanc that cleaves with his peak of sunlit snows the heaven of heavens.

III. THE HOMILY.

To many it may perhaps prove an unwelcome thought that a poem they have enjoyed merely as a poem should have anything to teach them. There are those who irreverently remark that the poets probably see no farther than their respective noses. If so, I fear some have noses that will considerably damage the classic profile of their poetic owners. Not a few give evidences of being exceptionally far-sighted. Things close at hand they do not see. Things at a great distance seem close at hand. They live in anticipated joys. In winter-time for them the trees are full-leaved, the bushes in blossom, the air shivering with song, and richly charged with manifold fragrance. Social conditions that the wildest theorist regards as possibly existing on the earth centuries hence are to the poet, if only he perceives their causes at work, already realized. We have the habit of estimating distances by the relative dis-

tinctness of the objects fixed by the eye; what we see in detail we imagine near, what appears blurred and indefinite we suppose to be far off. Now the poet, as man, does what we all do in this matter. When, however, the poetic fury assails him, he becomes preternaturally keen sighted. The indefinite defines itself, the vague stands out boldly, the neutral tints give birth to many brilliant colors; but his old habit of judging of distances remains in force, and so he cries, "Behold! it is at hand! it is at the very doors!" And such has been always the custom of prophets, not that for rhetorical effect they eliminated the element of time, and deliberately represented processes as finished products, but that they themselves were ignorant of "times and seasons."

Just because a poet is free to speak what he thinks, feels, and fancies, without any sense of obligation to his past self, to logic or structural consistency; because he is by common consent emancipated from the tyranny of premises, as one is in dreams; just because no sane reader will call him to account for every word, or expect him to define his terms and avoid equivocation, or explain away the difficulties he seems to create in his progress; for these very reasons is he fitted to promulgate difficult doctrines. We often know the truth before we can prove it; the facts are not all given, the premises cannot even be framed, yet the conclusion is already certain. Should one appear as a witness to such "transcendental truths" in the garb and guise of a moral philosopher, we should undoubtedly subject him to the severest cross-questioning; and if we succeeded in confusing him by our impertinences and technical objections, we should declare him perjured, and scoff at his difficult doctrine as false and absurd. But a poet we treat more graciously. He comes to give us pleasure. If incidentally in pleasing us he insinuates a bit of doctrine, we blink the fact in case the doctrine is not such as we favor. But the skilfulest poet will cunningly oblige the reader to assume the doctrine just for the nonce, because otherwise the full pleasure of the poem cannot be obtained. He does not insist that you shall believe the doctrine, much less put it into practise! He may himself do neither. He himself may only have "assumed" it.

When Coleridge makes the ancient mariner prefer

> To walk together to the kirk
> With a goodly company!
> To walk together to the kirk,
> And all together pray,

to the marriage-feast and all its "loud uproar" the "bridesmaids singing," and in the garden bower the bride; "when he goes farther yet, and prefers simple philanthropy and gentle consideration for animals to the formal worship, saying:

He prayeth well who loveth well
Both man and bird and beast.
He prayeth best who loveth best
All things both great and small;
For the dear God who loveth us,
He made and loveth all—

when Coleridge says these things, so earnestly but so picturesquely, and has them not on his own lips, but puts them in the mouth of a wise old madman, why of course no one presumes to contradict him!

Perhaps some reader may remember the savage words of a certain critic to the effect that poor Coleridge "had no morals;" another will recall his shiftlessness, his incapacity of continuous devotion to duty, his practical desertion of wife and children, his unfortunate opium habit! And all this is, alas! too true. An apology can be framed. He who knows the intoxication of the Spirit, and who for personal faults has in some manner driven him away, may be tempted to obtain from drugs a stimulation that shall deceive him momentarily into believing himself once more visited from heaven. Our *Rime*, however, dates from his best year, his twenty-seventh. The "shaping spirit of the imagination" walked with him often. For companion besides he had his friend Wordsworth, and his home was sunny with hope. This man, who could philosophize so acutely, and hold all England spellbound by his strange eloquence, knew well that "abstruse research," whatever his demands, did not require inspiration, not even the exercise of strenuous will, while good poetry assuredly does.

Now the lines beginning "He prayeth well" are not a homiletic after-thought. They constitute the very germ of the whole poem. But Coleridge, with an artist's true cunning, does not betray the secret of his *Rime* till it is well-nigh ended.

Accept for one moment as true the thought of a conscious omnipotent Source of Being, a God who is truly the universal Father. All that he has made must be well made. All must reflect his character, all must be very good. If not, he would not preserve it with loving care. Grant, furthermore, that a relation with this God is possible to his intelligent creature man; that he is given some natural mode of access, no matter how difficult; that he is, therefore, competent to form some conception of His being, and to feel love for Him. How can you now escape the doctrine of the *Rime*? The true worshiper finds that, whether he will or no,

From himself he flies
Stands in the sun, and with no partial gaze
Views all creation; and he *loves* it *all*
And blesses it, and calls it very good.
—**"Religious Musings"**.

God's universal fatherhood implies a universal brotherhood of all created things. Conversely he who, from abounding "joy" within, calls all very good, blesses it, and loves it all, finds himself, whether he will or no, transported to the central Sun, sees things from the divine point of view, and so enters into "sacred sympathy" with that "Sun," that he is at length wholly rapt in the thought of "God all in all," and in the feeling for which there are no words; "he and his Father—ONE." From the universal brotherhood of created things, which to the poet, when in poetic mood, is axiomatic, one can reason transcendentally to a universal Father.

From God to nature; from nature to God.

Nature . . . may well employ
Each faculty of sense, and keep the heart
Awake to love and beauty.
No sound is dissonant which tells of *life*.
—**"This Lime-Tree Bower My Prison"**.

For is not all life from the Father of lives? Is not biology in a certain sense theology? Even the "foal of an ass" would the poet take with him

In the dell
Of peace and mild equality to dwell.
—**"To a Young Ass"**.

Wherefore not? Is not God seen as well in least as in greatest? Indeed, what tests a worshiper's sincerity? Humble before God when conscious of his presence? or rather, tender to His weaker creatures where

So lovely 'twas, that God himself
Scarce seemed there to be?

To love them that love us is surely no wonderful virtue! To love them that can help us may be mere selfish prudence. But love for God's sake is most distinctly seen when it goes out to those whose need is greatest, and therefore whose own claims are least. The love at the wedding-feast, if it be really love, goes out to bride and—albatross! Not merely the love that after long loneliness "hails it in God's name," "as if it had been a Christian soul;" but the love that makes murder as difficult as suicide; that considers the dignity of life, and the glory of the Life-Giver, rather than the use of the individual living thing for us; the love that makes the unnecessary killing of fellow beast as loathsome as the unnecessary killing of fellow man.

Somewhat fanatical doctrine, you object? Is not war an honorable calling? Is not hunting of animals a most respectable manly sport? The poet has no answer to make to your objections or to mine. If he hears us, he shrugs his shoulders, and smiles ironically. He is bound to poetical logic alone. The germ of his poem was love. If God loves all, and we love God, we must love all. If we love all, we would harm none. Do we then love God? Such is the question the poet insists on asking. And he reminds us that we, to whom he has told his tale, need it:

> I know the man that must hear me;
> To him my tale I teach.

We are wedding-guests? We are in haste? So much the worse for us. We shall have to wait. His glittering eye will hold us. He will hint that we are wedding-guests indeed, bidden by another Bridegroom. Long afterward, whether we agree with them or not, his words will go on obstinately ringing in our ears:

> O happy living things! no tongue
> Their beauty might declare;
> A spring of love gushed from my heart
> And I blessed them unaware!
> The self-same moment I could pray!

>   . . . . .

> He prayeth well who loveth well
> Both man and bird and beast.
> He prayeth best who loveth best.
> All things both great and small;
> For the dear God who loveth us,
> He made and loveth all.

John Livingston Lowes   (essay date 1927)

SOURCE: "The Bird and the Dæmon," in *The Road to Xanadu: A Study in the Ways of the Imagination,* 1927. Reprint by Vintage Books, 1959, pp. 201-20.

[*In the following essay, Lowes discusses the source material that inspired* The Rime of the Ancient Mariner, *insisting that its dæmonic imagery exemplifies "the voyaging, Neoplatonizing, naively scientific spirit of the closing eighteenth century."*]

Across the course of the voyage, just where its great loop swings around the southern termination of the continent, the albatross comes through the fog. And the shooting of the albatross sets the forces of the invisible world in motion. And the action of those forces is in turn bound up with the normal evolution, in experience, of cause and consequence. The albatross, in a word,— "that white phantom [which] sails in all imaginations," as Herman Melville in an eloquent passage calls it— binds inseparably together the three structural principles of the poem: the voyage, and the supernatural machinery, and the unfolding cycle of the deed's results.

It is the second of the three which we must now take into account. And the supernatural machinery, like the architectonic conception of the voyage, falls into our scheme, not as a series of interesting and often singular details, but as a controlling imaginative design. It determines, in a word, the *action* of the poem, precisely as the ground-plan of the voyage set its course and fixed its background. And like the voyage, the unfolding of the action stirs to life, and sweeps within its compass, and fuses into unity, the latent imagery of those deep-lying tracts which we have called "the Well"—"that lifeless, twilight, realm of thought," in Coleridge's phrase, which is, for thoughts, "the confine, the *intermundium*" between consciousness past and consciousness perhaps to come. We are simply approaching from a fresh angle our old theme—the assimilating and incorporative power of the shaping spirit. And the ingredients with which that spirit this time had to work were these: the figure of the Mariner himself; the shooting of the albatross; the "spectral persecution"; the skeleton bark; the navigation of the ship by the dead sailors; and the angelic interposition at the end. Those are the constituent elements of the action, and the fortuitous fashion in which, on a dark November evening, they combined, is matter of curious record. And that record we must first be clear about. But more important far than the quaint accessories of their conjunction are the operations of these ethereal chemicals (to paraphrase John Keats) upon the potential stuff of poetry in Coleridge's brain. And upon that interplay of masses of associations falls the emphasis in the three chapters now to come.

I

The day, almost the hour, when fragmentary hints of birds and ships and mariners and spectres flashed back and forth from mind to mind and swiftly wove a shining plan, along a road that went down to the sea— this eventful day is fixed for us by Dorothy Wordsworth, who wrote November 20, 1797:

> We have been on another tour: we set out last Monday evening at half-past four. The evening was dark and cloudy; we went eight miles, William and Coleridge employing themselves in laying the plan of a ballad, to be published with some pieces of William's.

November 20 fell that year on Monday. "Last Monday," accordingly, was the 13th. Of the two other members of the party, Coleridge has left one brief comment on the expedition, but Wordsworth reverted to it often in his later years.

In the long prefatory note to "We are Seven," dictated to Miss Fenwick in or about 1843, Wordsworth, with the privileged inconsequence of age, broke into his account of the little girl at Goodrich Castle, and of the joke before the "little tea-meal" about "dear brother

Jem," to tell a less domestic story. It is ancient history, but every word of it is needed:

> In the autumn of 1797, he [Coleridge], my sister, and myself, started from Alfoxden pretty late in the afternoon, with a view to visit Linton, and the Valley of Stones near to it; and as our united funds were very small, we agreed to defray the expense of the tour by writing a poem . . . Accordingly we set off, and proceeded, along the Quantock Hills, towards Watchet; and in the course of this walk was planned the poem of the "Ancient Mariner," founded on a dream, as Mr. Coleridge said, of his friend Mr. Cruikshank. Much the greatest part of the story was Mr. Coleridge's invention; but certain parts I suggested; for example, some crime was to be committed which should bring upon the Old Navigator, as Coleridge afterwards delighted to call him, the spectral persecution, as a consequence of that crime and his own wanderings. I had been reading in Shelvocke's Voyages, a day or two before, that, while doubling Cape Horn, they frequently saw albatrosses in that latitude, the largest sort of sea-fowl, some extending their wings twelve or thirteen feet. "Suppose," said I, "you represent him as having killed one of these birds on entering the South Sea, and that the tutelary spirits of these regions take upon them to avenge the crime." The incident was thought fit for the purpose, and adopted accordingly. I also suggested the navigation of the ship by the dead men, but do not recollect that I had anything more to do with the scheme of the poem. . . . We began the composition together, on that to me memorable evening. . . . As we endeavoured to proceed conjointly (I speak of the same evening), our respective manners proved so widely different, that it would have been quite presumptuous in me to do anything but separate from an undertaking upon which I could only have been a clog.

A few years earlier, in a significant connection, Wordsworth had given to the Reverend Alexander Dyce substantially the same account, which was first made public in a note to *The Ancient Mariner* in the *Poems* of 1852:

> When my truly honoured friend Mr. Wordsworth was last in London, soon after the appearance of De Quincey's papers in "Tait's Magazine," he dined with me in Gray's Inn, and made the following statement, which, I am quite sure, I give you correctly: "*The Ancient Mariner* was founded on a strange dream, which a friend of Coleridge had, who fancied he saw a skeleton ship, with figures in it. . . . I had very little share in the composition of it, for I soon found that the style of Coleridge and myself would not assimilate. . . . The idea of *'shooting an albatross' was mine; for I had been reading Shelvocke's Voyages, which probably Coleridge never saw.* I also suggested

the reanimation of the dead bodies, to work the ship."

The signal importance of Wordsworth's contributions to the scheme of *The Ancient Mariner* admits no question. He suggested the shooting of the albatross, the "spectral persecution," and the navigation of the ship by the dead men. The first two are the mainsprings of the action, and the third is an essential stage in its development. Yet Wordsworth was not so generous as just, when he declared that "much the greatest part of the story was Mr. Coleridge's invention." The "skeleton ship, with figures in it," of Cruikshank's dream, and the "Old Navigator" himself were clearly in Coleridge's mind from the beginning, and they are presupposed in Wordsworth's suggestion of the crime and of its supernatural avenging. And granting unreservedly that Wordsworth supplied the links which knit the loose materials of narrative into a story, and fanned to flame a smouldering conception, it remains no less true that the magnificent imaginative elaboration of the jointly assembled ingredients of a plot is Coleridge's own, as truly as *Hamlet* and *Lear* and *Anthony and Cleopatra,* on grounds essentially the same, are Shakespeare's. Wordsworth, in fact, had builded far better than he knew. His suggestions stirred to life the throngs of dormant memories which had been gathering for just this fateful hour, and before the evening which saw the poem's birth was ended, he had recognized that the spirits which he had evoked called Coleridge master but not him.

Five of the six determining factors of the action, then, fell into place while talk flew fast in the nipping air, and the tang of the sea grew sharper, as Watchet neared. Two owed their origin to Coleridge, three to Wordsworth, and the part played by angelic intervention may or may not have been an afterthought. Each of the six tapped a brimming reservoir, and the shooting of the albatross comes logically first.

II

The albatross brings us to Shelvocke, and the history of Wordsworth's copy of the *Voyage* suggests an irresistible postscript to the Fenwick Note. There is in the Widener Collection in the Harvard College Library a precious little volume—outwardly a cheap household account-book, suggesting in its general physiognomy that "butcher-ledger-like book" in which the first jottings of "In Memoriam" were kept—which has written in ink on the cover: "Account of the Books lent out of the Library at Rydal Mount." The entries, with ruled columns for names and dates of withdrawal and return, are in the hands of the various members of the Wordsworth family, and show that from 1824 on, Wordsworth's books were at the service of his friends and neighbors. On November 8, 1832, "Shelvockes Voy." was lent to a "Mrs. Godwin." The volume,

*And a good south wind sprung up behind; / The Albatross did follow, /
And every day, for food or play, / Came to the mariners' hollo!*

then, was on Wordsworth's shelves as late as 1832. And it was still in his Library a dozen years later, when the Fenwick note was made, for it was among the books sold at public auction after his death.

Now the passage which Wordsworth had been reading in Captain George Shelvocke's *Voyage round the World by the Way of the Great South Sea* is of interest in more ways than one. Let us turn first to a couple of sentences a dozen pages before the important paragraph:

> From the latitude of 40 deg. to the latitude of 52 deg. 30 min. we . . . were constantly attended by Pintado birds. . . . These were accompanied by *Albitrosses, the largest sort of sea-fowls, some of them extending their wings 12 or 13 foot.*

Wordsworth's statement to Miss Fenwick is worth looking at again:

> I had been reading in Shelvocke's Voyages, a day or two before, that, while doubling Cape Horn, they frequently saw *albatrosses in that latitude, the largest sort of sea-fowl, some extending their wings twelve or thirteen feet.*

Wordsworth was seventy-three when he dictated these words, and the reading to which he referred lay forty-five years behind him. Had Shelvocke's exact phraseology stuck in his memory for almost half a century? I doubt it. The book was there in the library at Rydal Mount, and I strongly suspect that while the adoring Isabella Fenwick waited, pen in hand, her "beloved old poet" walked over to the bookcase and refreshed his memory!

However that may be, the passage in Shelvocke which set the action of *The Ancient Mariner* going is this:

> We had continual squals of sleet, snow and rain, and the heavens were perpetually hid from us by gloomy dismal clouds. In short, one would think it impossible that any thing living could subsist in so rigid a climate; and, indeed, we all observed, that we had not had the sight of one fish of any kind, since we were come to the Southward of the streights of *le Mair,* nor one sea-bird, except a disconsolate black *Albitross,* who accompanied us for several days, hovering about us as if he had lost himself, till *Hatley,* (my second Captain) observing, in one of his melancholy fits, that this bird was always hovering near us, imagin'd, from his colour, that it might be some ill omen. That which, I suppose, induced him the more to encourage his superstition, was the continued series of contrary tempestuous winds, which had oppress'd us ever since we had got into this sea. But be that as it would, he, after some fruitless attempts, at length, shot the *Albitross,* not doubting (perhaps) that we should have a fair wind after it.

That raises at once an interesting question. What was this "disconsolate black Albitross" which Captain Hatley shot? The albatross which Captain Shelvocke earlier describes, with its wingspread of twelve or thirteen feet, is clearly the great Wandering Albatross (*Diomedea exulans*) of the Southern Seas, and that is white. It is the bird which Buffon depicts across the page, and which Herman Melville rhapsodizes over in a famous passage in the chapter on "The Whiteness of the Whale." For the layman it is the albatross *par excellence,* and we have tacitly assumed that it was Coleridge's albatross. But there is another bird, the so-called "sooty albatross" (once *Diomedea fuliginosa,* now, in scientific parlance, *Phoebetria palpebrata antarctica*), which haunts the same latitudes; and this albatross, as its name in the vernacular implies, may quite properly be called black. I have never seen it living, but I have seen it dead, and I have little doubt that it was the bird which Captain Hatley shot. Whether or not it was Coleridge's albatross is quite another matter. He may or may not have known that albatrosses are not all alike. But in any case we may, I think, acquit him of one charge.

The size of the albatross, in a word, has long been a stone of stumbling to matter-of-fact souls, who protest that Coleridge has strained verisimilitude to the breaking point through his patent misconception of the albatross's size. For he has suspended about a sailor's neck a bird the sweep of whose regal wings was twice a tall man's height, and, in the poem as it originally stood, has fed the Brobdingnagian creature "biscuit worms," as if it had the tastes and the dimensions of a wren. There is little to choose, such unbending spirits will complain, between Coleridge and that paragon of cheerful faith, the visionary gardener in *Sylvie and Bruno:*

> He thought he saw an Albatross
> That fluttered round the lamp;
> He looked again, and saw it was
> A Penny-Postage-Stamp.

One may admit at once the piquant incongruity of the biscuit worms, which were promptly banished from the poem. As for the rest, Coleridge was intent upon poetic truth, not ornithological fact. But even a poet may be presumed to know that size is a matter of species and age, and the sooty albatross, which is much the smaller bird, might readily enough, as I know from experiment, have been carried suspended from a sailor's neck. And in another passage which entered into the very fabric of *The Ancient Mariner* there is warrant enough for Coleridge's impression. For the three sentences which immediately follow the well-conned account of the luminous protozoa in Captain Cook tell of "two large birds [which] settled on the water, near the ship." And one of them, which was little more than half the size of the other, "seemed to be of the *albatross* kind . . . upon the whole, *not unlike the sea-gull, though larger.*" In the use to which Coleridge puts the albatross in the poem, neither ornithological fact nor poetic truth moults a feather.

All this, however, is beside the main point. The essential matter is that the incident in Shelvocke crystallized the structural design of the poem. The earlier chapters of this book have made it clear that a vast concourse of images was hovering in the background of Coleridge's brain, waiting for the formative conception which should strike through their confusion, and marshal them into clarity and order. And among them, on Wordsworth's evidence, was the person of the Mariner himself. What Wordsworth did was to catch up Coleridge's Old Navigator out of general space, where presumably he was floating unattached, and to set him down definitely, cross-bow in hand, at the entrance to the South Sea, after the doubling of Cape Horn. But that implied the circumnavigation of the continent. And on "A Correct Map of the World Describing Capt. Shelvocke's Voyage round," prefixed to the book, runs, in a distinct dotted line from Equator to Equator around the Cape, the great curve of the voyage. I think (for reasons which I have given in the Notes) that Coleridge saw this curve; but whether he did or not, the shooting of the albatross carried in its train the ground plan of the poem. And the thronging images which that released we have already seen.

But Wordsworth's suggestion set free another host. "'Suppose,' said I, 'you represent him as having killed one of these birds on entering the South Sea, *and that the tutelary spirits of these regions take upon them to avenge the crime.'*" Precisely what Wordsworth may have had in mind, I do not know. But what sprang into life in Coleridge's memory is clear enough. For the albatross flies into a supramundane *mise en scène* which had been preparing even longer than the background of the voyage, which Wordsworth's suggestion also stirred to life. The fitness of the setting in Antarctic seas is obvious enough. But I question if ever another fowl, before or since, found itself intermeddled (as Chaucer would say) with Plotinus and Porphyry, and Platonic Constantinopolitan, Michael Psellus, and Marsilio Ficino of the Florentine Academy. The lucky bird, to be sure, is immortal as they are now; and it is so, largely by virtue of this imaginative merging of its brief career with the visions of centuries, which just then, like the ancient associations of the southern voyage, were once more stirring in men's minds.

III

One of those "wingy mysteries" which haunt the upper regions of the air, and descend to earth at intervals to captivate the thinking of a period is that elusive changeling left by Plotinus in Plato's house, and nurtured

there by Porphyry and Iamblichus and Proclus, and their followers. This is no place for an exposition of Neoplatonism, even were I a competent expositor. To call it the shimmering mist into which the cloud-capped towers and gorgeous palaces of Plato's luminous fabric had dissolved, would be, I know, to the Greeks foolishness, and anathema to spirits of sternly philosophic mould. But as Sir Thomas Browne has comfortably said, "where there is an obscurity too deep for our reason, 'tis good to sit down with a description, periphrasis, or adumbration," and that astute procedure is the better part in dealing with "airy subtleties . . . which have unhinged the brains of better heads." Nor for our purpose is rigid definition needful. It is happily not the collective profundities of the system, but a single aspect only of its occult and misty supernaturalism, with which we have to do.

To follow the strand, however, which leads to *The Ancient Mariner*, we must go back for a moment to the early Christian centuries. For through Plotinus, and Porphyry, and Iamblichus, and Proclus, and their followers, there came about a singular impregnation of Platonic philosophy with the theosophic mysticism of the Orient, and the more esoteric tenets of Judaism and Christianity. With the nebulous and grandiose conceptions which resulted, we have nothing whatever to do. The one thing which does come into our reckoning is the fact that into this metaphysical cloudland there drifted strange waifs and strays from those obscure fastnesses of the supernatural, and rites and mysteries of the ancient cults. The *mélange,* with its soaring visions and its haunted deeps, was as cosmopolitan as the crumbling empire, and in that catholic but utterly uncritical inclusiveness lay, in part, the secret of its fascination for imaginative minds. And on the roll of its adherents is a galaxy of starry names: the Emperor Julian the Apostate, who gave of late to Ibsen a high theme for tragedy; that Hypatia of Alexandria, who shines, snow-white in Kingsley's pages; her friend Synesius, "the hyperplatonic Jargonist" (I quote the Note Book), whose recondite Hymns Coleridge translated with his mother's milk (one gathers!) scarce dry upon his lips; Macrobius, whose voluminous commentary on the Dream of Scipio cast a spell upon the Middle Ages; the grave and lofty figure of Boethius, who numbered among his translators a king, a queen, and two illustrious poets—Alfred the Great, Jean de Meun, Chaucer, and Elizabeth. Even Michael Psellus, preserved for most of us in Coleridge's gloss, like some glittering but forgotten fly in amber, has come to life again, in 1921, in the *Eudocia* of Eden Philpotts! Dreamers they were, if you will, but assuredly no feeble line of mere visionary spinners of the cobwebs of the brain. And all these rich and varied minds called Plato master.

Then came, in the fulness of time, the stirring of fresh life, through the Renaissance, in the forgotten mysteries. And the Platonic Academy at Florence fell eagerly upon Plato, and no less avidly upon the Neoplatonists. Marsilio Ficino translated into Latin not only the works of the master, but also the mystical teachings of Plotinus and his followers. And as Iamblichus and Proclus had incorporated with the Platonic myths the hoary mysteries of Egypt and Mesopotamia and Tyre, so the most brilliantly gifted of the Florentine Academicians, Pico della Mirandola, sought to blend with Neoplatonic philosophy the vast, bizarre agglomeration of the Jewish Cabbala. And so reinterpreted, Neoplatonism permeated the mystical thought and fitfully glimmered through the poetry of the next two centuries. Then, at the close of the eighteenth century, history repeated itself. And that brings us back to Coleridge, and, in the end, to the immortal albatross.

One of the most pithy and memorable letters that Coleridge ever wrote was addressed to John Thelwall, before the two men met. It is dated from Bristol, November 19, 1796, and I doubt if more of Coleridge were ever packed in briefer compass. It contains an almost matchless *tour de force* of self-description—equalled only, perhaps, by that ineffable portrait of himself which the aged but still gallant Samuel Richardson penned for a lady who had never seen him—and I am reluctant to omit a line of it. But I shall, and here is the part which is pertinent:

> I am, and ever have been, a great reader, and have read almost everything—a library cormorant. I am *deep* in all out of the way books, whether of the monkish times, or of the puritanical era. I have read and digested most of the historical writers; but I do not *like* history. Metaphysics and poetry and "facts of mind," that is, accounts of all the strange phantasms that ever possessed "your philosophy"; dreamers, from Thoth the Egyptian to Taylor the English pagan, are my darling studies. In short, I seldom read except to amuse myself, and I am almost always reading. Of useful knowledge, I am a so-so chemist, and I love chemistry. All else is *blank*; but I *will* be (please God) an horticulturalist and a farmer. [That is *not* pertinent; but as quintessential comedy I leave it in] . . . Such am I. I am just going to read Dupuis' twelve octavos, which I have got from London. I shall read only one octavo a week, for I cannot *speak* French at all and I read it slowly.

Then follows a characteristic postscript, which rivals the letter in significance:

> P.S. I have enclosed a five-guinea note. The five shillings over please to lay out for me thus. In White's (of Fleet Street or the Strand, I forget which—O! the Strand I believe, but I don't know which), well, in White's catalogue are the following books:—

4674. Iamblichus, Proclus, Prophyrius, etc., one shilling and six pence, one little volume.

4686. Juliani Opera, three shillings: which two books you will be so kind as to purchase for me, and send down with the twenty-five pamphlets. But if they should unfortunately be sold, in the same catalogue are:—

2109. Juliani Opera, 12s. 6d.

676. Iamblichus de Mysteriis, 10s. 6d.

2681. Sidonius Apollinaris, 6s.

And in the catalogue of Robson, the bookseller in New Bond Street, Plotini Opera, a Ficino, £1.1.0, making altogether £2.10.0.

If you can get the two former little books, costing only four and six pence, I will rest content with them.

"Thelwall," says E. H. Coleridge, "executed his commission. The Iamblichus and the Julian were afterwards presented by Coleridge to his son Derwent. They are still in the possession of the family."

The postscript is a bead-roll of Coleridge's "dreamers." "Thoth the Egyptian" (Milton's "thrice-great Hermes") is there, concealed beneath the pregnant "etc." of the "one little volume" which heads the memorandum. "Taylor the English pagan," otherwise Thomas Taylor the Platonist, credulous, uncritical, and pedestrian in style, but fired with the ardour of a devotee, was doing for England what Marsilio Ficino, three centuries before, had done for Italy, and was at the moment busily translating everybody mentioned in Coleridge's list—Iamblichus, Proclus, Porphyrius, Julian, and Plotinus—with the sole exception of Sidonius Apollinaris. Nor was this commission to Thelwall Coleridge's first or last attempt to possess himself, by hook or crook, of his precious purveyors of strange phantasms. In a batch of memoranda of 1807, which no one who would see how Coleridge browsed, or (better) *grazed,* in bookshops can afford to overlook, he is still proposing to "hunt for Proclus." Charles Lamb wrote racily in 1796, and again in 1814, about pressing instructions from Coleridge to pick up Plutarch and Porphyry and Proclus. The famous passage in "Christ's Hospital Five-and-Thirty Years Ago" is no less in point—that description of "the young Mirandula . . . unfolding in [his] deep and sweet intonations the mysteries of Iamblichus or Plotinus." And Iamblichus and Plotinus and their followers down to Pico starred his pages to the end. The errand on which Thelwall was dubiously sent to either Fleet Street or the Strand not only exhibits one of Coleridge's inveterate preoccupations, but also epitomizes one of the strangest tendencies which marked the tumultuous exit of the century. For Neoplatonism was again in the air, and in Coleridge's postscript Bristol and London join hands, through Florence, with Alexandria, Constantinople, Athens, and Rome—the eighteenth century, through the fifteenth, with the Platonizing third, fourth and fifth.

But what of Dupuis's twelve octavos which Coleridge was painfully going through, a volume a week, in French? Well, if Thomas Taylor was the plodding British counterpart of Marsilio Ficino, the eighteenth century had also its flock of inglorious, though anything but mute, Mirandolas, and the voluminous Dupuis was one of them. The title of his work is: *Origine de tous les Cultes, ou Religion universelle,* par Dupuis, Citoyen Francois. And it was printed "L'an III. de la République, une et indivisible" (which in years of Our Lord was 1795), and on the title-page below the date stands the legend: "Liberté, Égalité, Fraternité." The treatise is, I am compelled to think (for I have sedulously turned some hundreds of its pages), a mad performance, as the flaunted banner of its title-page might lead us to suspect. I doubt whether Coleridge got anything from it beyond those unconsidered trifles which genius has the trick of filching as it goes, for conversion into jewels rich and strange. But explicit in its footnotes and implicit in its text are the ubiquitous Neoplatonists—Plotinus, Porphyry, Iamblichus, Proclus, Julian, Hermes, and Marsilio Ficino. And mingled with the testimony of the ancient witnesses is an array of observations, reported by voyagers and explorers, touching the rites and customs. The genii and dæmons and angel guardians, of primitive tribes. And excerpts from these same voyages were even then enriching with anthropological data the *Philosophical Transactions.*

Ancient cults, in a word, and primitive religions, Neoplatonic speculations, ethnology and oxygen and electricity were all seething together in men's minds. And with the new wonders of the air which science was disclosing merged the immemorial beliefs in its invisible inhabitants, whether vouched for by Iamblichus, or Hermes Trismegistus, or Captain Cook. Nobody who knows the period can dream of isolating its poetry from the ferment of its thought, or of detaching Samuel Taylor Coleridge from that ferment. And when Wordsworth suggested his "spectral persecution," all this accumulated lore, held in solution in Coleridge's brain, was precipitated in the strange vengeance which overtook in haunted seas the slayer of a solitary albatross. What the fortunate bird acquired, in fact, along with immortality, was the efficient, if belated, championship of a fully accredited Neoplatonic dæmon.

IV

For the cloud of witnesses whom we have summoned from here and there along the course of sixteen centuries were unanimous in the recognition they accorded to one powerful order in the hierarchy of being— the order of the *dæmons.* I have no intention of going into the beginnings of Greek and Roman dæmonology. That has been done to repletion in two colossally learned monographs in the *Transactions* of the Berlin and Leipzig Academies respectively, for anyone who cares to track his dæmons from the egg. But I do wish to observe that Coleridge, whatever the obliquities of slipshod editors, spells the word correctly in his gloss. For a *dæmon* and a *demon* are not one and the same thing. And it is dæmon, in its Platonic sense of a being intermediary between gods and men—not demon, with its Judæo-Christian import of an unclean, evil, or malignant spirit—that we must keep in mind. This would once have been superfluous caution, but not, alas! when Coleridge is made to mention, in school editions of the poem, "The Polar Spirit's fellow-*demons*" (that pair of dæmons of the air who are the Chorus of the poem) as if the "voice as soft as honey-dew" boasted, as appanages, horns, hoofs, and tail.

The gloss of the first stanza in which the Polar Spirit appears reads thus:

> A Spirit had followed them; one of the invisible inhabitants of this planet, neither departed souls nor angels; concerning whom the learned Jew, Josephus, and the Platonic Constantinopolitan, Michael Psellus, may be consulted. They are very numerous, and there is no climate or element without one or more.

Let us turn back, now, to that No. 4674, catalogued by White at one and sixpence, which Coleridge wanted, and Thelwall got for him. It contained, in its 543 closely printed, four-and-a-half by three inch pages, Iamblichus *De Mysteriis Ægyptorium, Chaldæorum, Assyriorum;* Proclus *In Platonicum Alcibiadem de Anima, atque Dæmone;* Porphyrius *De Divinis atque Dæmonibus;* Psellus *De Dæmonibus;* and the *Pimander* and *Asclepius* of Hermes Trismegistus—all edited by Marsilio Ficino. It is a *vade mecum* of Neoplatonic dæmonology, and a most seducing and frequently unintelligible little volume. And quite the most seductive pages in it are those which bear the heading: "Ex Michaele Psello de Dæmonibus, Interpres Marsilius Ficinus." For Michael Psellus writes of dæmons, not with the philosophic detachment of Porphyry or Proclus, but with the conviction of one who has himself hobnobbed with them on occasion. Witness, for example, his engaging tale of the dæmon who seems to have carried on a conversation in Armenian, and the nice point raised by Psellus whether dæmons employ the language of the country of which they are (as it were) "nationals," so that a Chaldæan dæmon should properly speak Chaldee, a Greek dæmon Greek—and so on for Persian, Syrian, Hebrew, and Egyptian dæmons. It is, accordingly, perfectly good form, dæmonically speaking, that in the poem the Polar Spirit's fellow-dæmons should speak English in their aërial dialogue. Apropos of Polar Spirits, moreover, one is interested to learn that the bitterest cold is nothing to dæmons (cum enim in locis *habitent profundissimis, ad summum quiden frigidis*), and that the dæmons of the water sometimes take the form of birds (*Aquatiles vero . . . se avibus . . . similes reddunt*). But the point on which Psellus lays most stress, with rich and curious detail, is the distribution of the dæmons among the elements—earth, air, fire, and water—with the subterraneous and light-shunning orders (these last a jocund company, *genus lucifugum, imperscrutabile, ac penitus tenebrosum*) for good measure. The last thing that Coleridge, who knew good dæmonology when he saw it, would be likely to forget would be that panorama of the peopled elements. And when Wordsworth, with Shelvocke's albatross in mind, suggested tutelary spirits to avenge a creature of the sea and sky, the flood-gates of Coleridge's Neoplatonic lore were opened, and the invisible inhabitants of the waters and the middle air, with Michael Psellus as their sponsor, took possession of the poem.

But Coleridge's acquaintance with Psellus was not confined to Marsilio Ficino's little book. He certainly knew the *Chaldæan Oracles,* for he jots down in the Note Book a fragment of one of the most magnificent of them . . . and any edition of the *Oracles* which he knew would include the Commentary of Michael Psellus. And in his commentary Psellus once more unfolds his doctrine of the dæmons of the elements. But Coleridge encountered the conception at every turn in the books that he was reading at the time. He took a volume of Apuleius from the Bristol Library in November, 1796—enthusiastically scrawling in the Library record, in lieu of the date, a pæan of victory: "9 Dutch ships taken, with 3000 troops Bravo"—and he speaks with admiration of the *Florida.* And the *De Deo Socratis* of Apuleius contains the most lucid and entertaining and suggestive discourse on elemental dæmons that I know. But it was not only on his Neoplatonists that Coleridge drew. Dupuis's first two volumes are a riot of genii, dæmons, angel guardians, and tutelary spirits of every feather. To the uninitiated it is bewildering balderdash, but, as Charles Lamb says of brawn, "'tis nuts to the adept." And Coleridge was nothing if not that. And now the haunts of the albatross come into the picture. The astrologers, Dupuis tells us, divide the universe into climates and regions ("there is no climate or element," says the gloss, "without one or more"), and five planets are assigned to the five zones. The south polar zone (la zône glaciale du pôle austral) falls to Mercury, but not to Mercury alone. For genii or angels are also guardians of the zones (On put en faire autant de Génies ou d'Anges tutélaires des zônes), and among them are included *Polar* Spirits. Maurice, whose bubble of ice and Chinese astronomers caught Coleridge's fancy,

tells also, in the same *History of Hindostan,* of "ancient Indian geographers," who represent "the southern hemisphere that is the region immediately under them . . . as a land of darkness and horrors, inhabited by evil dæmons." The austral seas are still the haunted *mare tenebrosum.* Finally (for even dæmons may wear out their welcome) Taylor the English pagan quotes, in his commentary on the *Phædrus,* from the Platonic Hermias: "But there are other dæmons transcending these, *who are the punishers of souls, converting them to a more perfect and elevated life.*" And Taylor was one of Coleridge's "darling studies," and that is the function of the polar dæmon in the poem.

Then straight into that huge conglomeration flew an unsuspecting bird! There was really no escape for the albatross. It was doomed to its dæmon from the first.

But what is the learned Jew, Josephus, doing in that galley? With adepts by the score to choose from, why should he, in the field of dæmonology no more than an authority of sorts, be singled out? He was, to be sure, not without standing as a witness to the phenomena of demoniacal possession. In the curious treatise, for example, of Balthazar Bekker, Doctor of Divinity, entitled *The World Bewitched,* he is drawn on for pertinent evidence, and that eminent authority on all matters dæmonological, Johannes Wierus, takes issue with him on a knotty point, when, in his edifying work on the Illusions of Dæmons (*De Præstigiis Dæmonum*), he discusses the treatment of those who are so hapless as to fall victims to the sorceries of lamias. And other names might easily be added. But without special reason, Josephus was indubitably a bird of strange feather to flock with Michael Psellus.

There is, I think, an answer to the question, and it lies in a most interesting association of ideas. There is excellent reason why Josephus was very definitely present in Coleridge's mind at just this period. It will be remembered that in the preface to **"The Wanderings of Cain"** Coleridge declared that after he and Wordsworth had made a botch of that particular essay at collaboration, "the Ancient Mariner was written instead." And in **"Aids to Reflection"** he states explicitly that **"The Wanderings of Cain,"** *The Ancient Mariner*, and "the first Book of *Christabel*" were written in the same year. Now since nobody has paid any real attention to the Note Book, it is not remarkable that nobody has observed that Coleridge was getting ready to write his "Cain" by reading Josephus. For in the Note Book stand, in the Greek, two excerpts from the second chapter of Book I of the *Antiquities,* which contains certain uncanonical information about Cain. Cain, and the "Old Navigator," and a strange and shadowy third were moving almost simultaneously towards the light, in Coleridge's brain. And with Cain was associated Josephus. But besides this large and general connection there was a closer link. Just three pages before Psellus "Concerning Dæmons" in Coleridge's little Neoplatonic Bible, stands, in Porphyry's discourse "On the Abstinence of the Ancients," a summary of Josephus's account of the Essenes. And Porphyry's summary, with the name of Josephus in its first line, centres about the doctrine of departed souls—disembodied spirits, who "possesse the empire of the aire." Three pages later, in his opening paragraph, Psellus draws a sharp distinction between angels and dæmons, in their respective natures There, in a word, within three compact pages, are Josephus, and Psellus, and departed souls, and angels, and dæmons. Turn, now, once more to Coleridge's description of his dæmon: "one of the invisible inhabitants of this planet, *neither departed souls nor angels; concerning whom the learned Jew, Josephus, and the Platonic Constantinopolitan, Michael Psellus,* may be consulted." Whether Coleridge wrote the gloss at or near the time when the poem was composed, or later, before 1817, makes little difference. To such a reader Josephus and Michael Psellus were grappled together, once for all, by hoops of steel.

V

There is a remarkable passage in Jerome Cardan, physician and philosopher of the sixteenth century, from that richly curious chapter of his work "On the Variety of Things" (*De Rerum Varietate*) which treats illuminatingly of "Dæmons and the Dead" (*Dæmones et Mortui*):

> Do not wonder, Reader, a man is no more able to know about a dæmon than a dog about a man. The dog knows that the man is, that he eats, drinks, walks, sleeps—no more. It knows also his form: so with a man in the case of dæmons. But you say, a man has a mind, a dog has not. But the mind of a dæmon differs far more in its operation from the mind of a man, than the mind of a man from the sense of a dog.

That reads amazingly like a remark of William James which stands, not without pertinence, at the head of the first chapter in Algernon Blackwood's *The Centaur:* "We may be in the Universe as dogs and cats are in our libraries, seeing the books and hearing the conversation, but having no inkling of the meaning of it all." Let me quote again:

> Every element has its own living denizens. Can the celestial ocean of ether, whose waves are light, in which the earth herself floats, not have hers, higher by as much as their element is higher, swimming without fins, flying without wings, moving, immense and tranquil, as if by a half-spiritual force through the half-spiritual sea which they inhabit, rejoicing in the exchange of luminous influence with one another, following the slightest pull of one another's attraction, and harboring, each of them, an inexhaustible inward wealth?

That is not Apuleius on the dæmons of the elements (though it might well be!), but an excerpt from an exposition of the philosophy of Gustav Fechner, who died in 1887. And more profoundly eloquent than all is Goethe's confession of faith in the Dæmonic (das Dämonische), near the opening of the last book of *Dichtung und Wahrheit.* Are there still peopled deeps which obscurely call, while the intellect claps its fingers to its ears, to strangely peopled deeps in us?

"I can easily believe," wrote Thomas Burnet in the lines from the *Archæologiæ Philosophical* which Coleridge in 1817 prefixed as a motto to **The Ancient Mariner**—"I can easily believe that there are more Invisible than Visible beings in the Universe (Facile credo, plures esse Naturas invisibiles quam visibiles in rerum universitate)." And in a moment, as Burnet goes on, the old familiar faces, passed over by Coleridge as he quotes, reappear: "The Ethnic Theologians philosophize at large about the invisible World—the World of Souls, of Genii, of Manes, of Dæmons, of Heroes, of Minds, of Powers, of Gods. As one may see in Iamblichus on the Mysteries of the Egyptians, in Psellus and Pletho on the Chaldean Oracles, and everywhere in the Platonic writers." Yet the stately prologue which ushers us into an invisibly populated world closes on another note: "But in the mean Time, we must take Care to keep to the Truth, and observe Moderation, that we may distinguish Certain from Uncertain Things, and Day from Night." "Facile credo . . . sed veritati interea invigilandum est": what, after all, *do* we readily believe, and what is the moderation that we keep, as we come under the compelling magic of the poem?

Coleridge announced, in the **Biographia Literaria,** "the critical essay on the uses of the Supernatural in poetry, and the principles that regulate its introduction: which the reader will find prefixed to the poem of The Ancient Mariner." The essay—with its counterpart "on the 'Preternatural,'" to be annexed to **Christabel**—lives only, with other phantasms, as one of the invisible inhabitants of this planet, and neither Josephus or Michael Psellus can this time lend us aid. But one pregnant sentence in the **Biographia** goes far to console us for our loss. Coleridge set out in the **Lyrical Ballads,** he tells us, to deal with "persons and characters supernatural . . . yet so as to transfer from our inward nature . . . a semblance of truth sufficient to procure for these shadows of imagination that willing suspension of disbelief for the moment, which constitutes poetic faith." And as for dæmons, the grounds of our willing suspension are clear. They belong, like spectra-barks and eternal wanderers, to that misty midregion of our racial as well as literary inheritance, towards which we harbour, when the imagination moves through haunted chambers, the primal instinctive will to believe. And as the immemorial projections of elemental human questionings and intuitions—shadows of things divined, "which having been must ever be"—they are the poet's inalienable possession.

VI

Now let us clear our minds of possible confusion. The incommunicable beauty of **The Ancient Mariner** is probably not enhanced one whit for anybody by a single line which I have written in this chapter. I am neither so ingenuous nor so pedantic as to cherish that particular illusion. The spell of beauty in the poem is sovereign in its exercise, and apt to pour on rashly proffered aid its beautiful disdain, and I have had another aim. For the ways of the spirit which creates the spell challenge the arduous effort to *understand,* by virtue of that very beauty in the thing created which exalts the faculty that gives it birth. And if that faculty be supreme, as we with one accord proclaim it is, then no attempt to fathom its workings is labour wholly lost—unless, indeed, we have recourse, as a last shift, to the miraculous, and relegate the plastic spirit of imagination to the category of the thaumaturgic and occult. If, then, I have made it clear—whether for dæmons of the elements, or water-snakes, or sun, or moon—that the rich suggestiveness of a masterpiece of the imagination springs in some measure from the fact that infinitely more than reached expression lay behind it in the shaping brain, so that every detail is saturated and irradiated with the secret influence of those thronged precincts of the unexpressed—if I have made that clear, my purpose is attained. I am not forgetting beauty. It is because the worth of beauty is transcendent that the subtle ways of the power that achieves it are transcendently worth searching out.

For **The Rime of the Ancient Mariner** is "a work of pure imagination," and Coleridge himself has so referred to it. And this study, far from undermining that declaration, is lending it confirmation at every turn. For a work of pure imagination is not something fabricated by a *tour de force* from nothing, and suspended, without anchorage in fact, in the impalpable ether of a visionary world. No conception could run more sharply counter to the truth. And I question, in the light of all that is now before us, whether any other poem in English is so closely compacted out of fact, or so steeped in the thought and instinct with the action which characterized its time. Keats, in "La belle Dame sans Merci," distilled into a single poem the quintessence of mediæval romance and balladry. And what "La belle Dame sans Merci" is to the gramarye of the Middle Ages, **The Rime of the Ancient Mariner** is to the voyaging, Neoplatonizing, naïvely scientific spirit of the closing eighteenth century. It has swept within its assimilating influence a bewildering diversity of facts in which contemporary interest was active. The facts are forgotten, and the poem stays. But the power that wrought the facts into the fabric of a vision outlasts both. And if we are rifling the urns

where the dead bones of fact have long quietly rested, it is because the unquenchable spirit which gives beauty for ashes is there not wholly past finding out.

James Stephens (1945) on the *Ancient Mariner*'s stature in English literature:

Coleridge is one of the strangest men and one of the strangest poets that ever lived. If one tried to elicit Coleridge from his prose writings one would never guess that he could write **The Ancient Mariner** or any other poem. The virtuosity of this poem is extreme, its fantasy is extreme, its knowledge of music and colour and pace is extreme. There is no poem like it in any language, but in my opinion that does not make it the best poem in the language, or even make it the best poem of Coleridge.

The best long poem in the English language is, of course, Milton's *Lycidas;* the second best is, I think, Chaucer's *Prelude;* the third and fourth best are Spenser's *Epithalamium* and his *Colin Clout;* John Donne's *Anniversary* could be thought of as the next greatest; then Wordsworth's "Intimations of Immortality"; and, as against these, the poor **Ancient Mariner** of Coleridge is just wherever you like, or is even nowhere. This poem suffers from the irremediable ill of being a fantasy of being: that is, in terms of life and in terms of poetry, it is non-nourishing and untrue. The very same unaccountable wandering from truth lies at the heart of **Christabel,** and even at the heart of the simple poem **"Love."** No miracle of talent or technique can quite redeem untruth from being initially and persistently inhuman in both life and letters.

James Stephens, in *James, Seumas & Jacques: Unpublished Writings of James Stephens,* edited by Lloyd Frankenberg, The Macmillan Company, 1964.

Irving Babbitt (essay date 1929)

SOURCE: "The Problem of the Imagination: Coleridge," in *On Being Creative and Other Essays,* Houghton Mifflin Company, 1932, pp. 97-133.

[*In the following essay, Babbitt claims that, especially in* The Rime of the Ancient Mariner, *Coleridge overemphasizes the natural self, ignoring a higher will in favor of a subrational animalistic self.*]

A striking feature of the whole modern movement has been its passion for origins. Tendencies that in other respects diverge widely agree in the assumption that, not the end as Aristotle asserts, but the beginning is 'the chief thing of all.' One may detect at least this likeness between the man of science who scoffs at the very idea of final causes and seeks to get back to electrons or chromosomes, and the primitivist who has a predilection for 'art's springbirth so dim and dewy' and sets 'the budding rose above the rose full blown.' We no longer believe in the nobility of the savage, but still hope, under the obsession of evolutionary theory, to derive our chief enlightenment regarding the human race itself from an endless prying into pre-history. Similarly, in dealing with the individual, we delve in the depths of the subliminal self and incline to interpret maturity in terms of childhood. Here again the backward glance is a bond between points of view that, at first sight, seem utterly dissimilar. At the very age, for example, when the child is hailed by Wordsworth as 'mighty prophet, seer blest,' he is most likely, according to Freud, developing an 'Œdipus complex.'

This passion for origins has been especially conspicuous for several generations past in both the creation and the critical study of art and literature. It has at last made possible a work like the recent important volume on Coleridge by Professor John Livingston Lowes [i.e., *The Road to Xanadu, A Study in the Ways of the Imagination*]. The search for sources—in this case the sources of *The Ancient Mariner* and **"Kubla Khan"**—has perhaps never been carried on more competently. In tracking Coleridge's immense and recondite reading Professor Lowes has displayed an industry little short of prodigious. He has claims to be regarded as the most accomplished of literary sleuths. He has devoted well over four hundred pages of his book to building up the background of two short poems, not to speak of a hundred and fifty pages of notes which are, in his own phrase, 'securely kenneled in the rear.' Moreover, he does not mean that his investigation should cater merely to learned curiosity. He has related it to another main preoccupation of our time—that with subliminal psychology—in the hope of thus throwing light on the mystery of the creative imagination itself.

Professor Lowes distinguishes three stages in the creative process. The first stage is conscious: the fixing of the attention on some particular field and the accumulation of material that bears upon it. In the second and, it would seem, essential stage the material thus accumulated sinks into the region of the subliminal self and there enters into new and unexpected associations. Professor Lowes seeks to show how in *The Ancient Mariner* and **"Kubla Khan"** the images that Coleridge had derived from his multifarious reading, especially of books of travel, were thus magically modified in the 'deep well of unconscious celebration.' The view of creative genius that has been popular ever since the eighteenth century has encouraged emphasis on the unconscious and the spontaneous, more or less at the expense of the purposeful. Thus Ruskin writes of Turner: 'He only did right when he ceased to reflect; was powerful only when he made no effort, and successful only when he had taken no

aim.' In much the same vein Emerson declares of the Parthenon and the Gothic cathedrals: 'These temples grew as grows the grass'(!). Even the partisan of a pure spontaneity cannot, however, if one is to believe Professor Lowes, afford to be ignorant. An ample preliminary enrichment of the mind is desirable, if only that the unconscious may have something to work upon.

The third stage of the creative process recognized by Professor Lowes is, like the first, conscious. However magically the material supplied by the unconscious may have been modified, it is still more or less inchoate. It is only by an effort, deliberate though still imaginative, that it can be fashioned into a harmonious whole. The 'shaping spirit of imagination' has thus presided over *The Ancient Mariner*, whereas it is absent from **"Kubla Khan"**. This latter poem may indeed be regarded as the most notable example in literature of creation that has not got beyond the second stage; at least if one accept the usual belief, based on Coleridge's own statements, that it came to him precisely in its present form as a fragment of an opium-dream. One may grant that Professor Lowes's account of the 'ways of the imagination' is relevant to the two poems he has studied and yet ask if he has not exaggerated its general relevancy. He says in his preface that he does not propose to consider whether *The Ancient Mariner* is classic or romantic or whether it meets the Aristotelian test of high seriousness. Actually, he has answered these very questions by implication in the body of the book when he mentions the poetical Coleridge in the same breath with Homer, Dante and Milton and uses the phrase 'supreme imaginative vision' in connection with *The Ancient Mariner*. My own endeavor will be to show that the imagination displayed in *The Ancient Mariner* is qualitatively different from that displayed in poetry that may rightly be regarded as highly serious. The whole problem has an importance transcending Coleridge and his influence, far-reaching though that influence has been. The imagination, as Pascal puts it, disposes of everything—even of religion, to an extent that Pascal himself would probably have been loath to admit. The importance of the subject is, however, equaled only by its difficulty. The chief difficulty is that 'imagination' belongs to a class of words, unhappily tending to increase, that have been used in so many meanings that they have almost ceased to have any meaning. One's first temptation is simply to banish words of this type from one's vocabulary. A saner precedure is to strive for more accurate definition, definition which, if it is to be valid, should be based first of all on a broad historical survey of what the general term under consideration actually has meant.

What one discovers in dealing in this fashion with the word imagination is that it has in the past been used primarily to describe the various impressions of sense or else a faculty that was supposed to store up these impressions. It therefore gives only appearances and not reality. Here is a main source of the persistent suspicion of the imagination that can be traced from early Greek times to the eighteenth century. When Saint Bonaventura, for example, says that the 'soul knows God without the support of the outer senses' he merely means to affirm that man is not dependent for his perception of religious truth on the imagination.

The association of imagination or phantasy with mere appearance no doubt explains why Aristotle does not employ the word at all in his *Poetics.* For poetry, he tells us, that is to be accounted highly serious, must penetrate beyond the impressions of sense to the universal. To be sure, this universal is not achieved directly, but only with the aid of 'myth' or fiction. Moreover, the art of representative fiction, as Aristotle conceives it, is intensely dramatic. To imitate the universal means practically to depict human actions not at random but with reference to some sound scale of ethical values. Centrality of vision is necessary if poetry is to have 'probability,' if, in other words, it is to disengage true unity and purpose from the welter of the actual. But though Aristotle's prime emphasis is in poetry and elsewhere on purpose, he recognizes man's almost insatiable craving for the marvelous. The more wonder the better, he seems to say, provided it does not involve an undue sacrifice of truth to the universal. Tragedy that has with the aid of representative fiction or significant illusion succeeded in portraying the universal through the particular, tends to raise the spectator to its own level and, as a result of this enlargement of spirit, to relieve him of what is merely petty and personal in his own emotions. This is the true *katharsis* that Milton has, with the intuition of a great poet, rendered so admirably at the end of *Samson Agonistes.*

I have been pointing out in my essay on Johnson that the neo-classic theorist made much of imitation and probability, but tended to divorce them from fiction in the sense of illusion; that fiction in this sense had come to be associated with certain forms of romantic extravagance; and that one of the reasons for the distrust of the imagination was its identification with a one-sided quest of wonder. Yet Voltaire himself had declared that 'illusion is the queen of the human heart.' The neo-classic inadequacy at this point was a chief factor in the rise of the romantic movement, a movement marked at its inception, as I have said, by the appearance of a new phrase, the 'creative imagination.' This creativeness was associated not with imitation but with spontaneity, which came to mean practically emotional spontaneity. Furthermore the movement speedily took on a primitivistic coloring.

The eighteenth-century theorists of originality and genius thus prepared the way for Wordsworth's def-inition of poetry as 'the spontaneous overflow of powerful feelings,' and for the closely related idea that this overflow is most likely to be found in peasants and other simple folk who are still close to 'nature.' Wordsworth, however, goes beyond the earlier primitivists by reinterpreting, largely it would seem under the influence of Coleridge, the word imagination. Imagination in the older sense of fiction, whether probable or improbable, he disparages. He himself lacked what he terms the 'human and dramatic imagination,' but felt he had something better in the 'enthusiastic and meditative imagination.' The imagination to which he accords his homage is not only 'Reason in her most exalted mood,' but the faculty that enables one, in contradistinction to the more or less arbitrary associations of mere 'fancy,' to achieve a true spiritual unity, not to be sure immediately but mediately through the objects of sense. For the Wordsworth of *Tintern Abbey,* God is, in M. Legouis's phrase, a 'gift of the senses,' a position radically opposed to that which appears in the sentence of Saint Bonaventura I have just quoted. Wordsworth has coined for his imaginative blending of himself with the landscape the phrase 'a wise passiveness.' But can one regard this imaginative blending as meditative? Genuine meditation requires effort. One may speak properly of the *act* of recollection but not of the act of revery; and it is pantheistic revery that *Tintern Abbey* plainly encourages. At all events, a striking feature of Wordsworth's poetical theory and, to no small degree, of his practice, is his dissociation of the imagination from effort or action in either the ordinary dramatic or the religious sense.

For the relationship he establishes between sight and insight and the resulting facility with which he reads a transcendental significance into the 'meanest flower that blows,' Wordsworth was, as I have said, indebted to Coleridge, who was in turn indebted to the Germans; though as to the exact extent of the indebtedness in either case it is well not to be too dogmatic. One would therefore have anticipated that Coleridge in his treatment of imagination and kindred topics in the *Biographia Literaria* would be in accord with Wordsworth. Coleridge would not, however, be the baffling figure he is if such were entirely the case. In the earlier chapters of this work he does indeed set out to define imagination in a way that would apparently have confirmed Wordsworth at essential points, but tends to get lost in what he himself terms 'the holy jungle of transcendental metaphysics.' One is reminded by all this portion of the *Literary Life* of Carlyle's inimitable account of Coleridge's conversation at Highgate: if anyone asked him a question, Carlyle reports, instead of answering it, or decidedly setting out towards an answer of it, he would 'accumulate formidable apparatus, logical swim-bladders, transcendental life-preservers and other precautionary and vehiculatory gear for setting out.' After much preparation of this kind in the *Literary Life,* he seems in chapter thirteen to be getting under way at last; but just at this point someone writes him a letter (the someone as we know now was Coleridge himself) warning him that he is getting beyond the depth of his public and advising him to reserve his more recondite considerations for his work on the Logos (which was of course never written). Where upon Coleridge turns from Schelling and the Germans to Aristotle.

The result of this escape from the 'jungle' is a sudden increase in clarity. There arises out of the transcendental haze one of 'the balmy sunny islets of the blest and the intelligible' that, according to Carlyle, also emerged at times in Coleridge's conversation. Indeed the chapters in which Coleridge deals on Aristotelian grounds with the paradoxes into which Wordsworth had been betrayed by his primitivism constitute the chief islet of this kind to be found in his prose writings. Thus (if I may be pardoned for summarizing material so familiar) Coleridge, having laid down the principle that poetry requires an 'involution of the universal in the individual' proceeds to apply this principle to *The Excursion.* Wordsworth has in this poem put sublime philosophic discourse in the mouth of a peddler. Some particular peddler may be sublime, Coleridge retorts, but peddlers as a class are not sublime. The peddler of *The Excursion* is a possible but not a probable peddler. Again, a child of six who is a 'mighty prophet' can scarcely be regarded as a representative child. Coleridge objects in like Aristotelian fashion to Wordsworth's assertion that the true language of poetry is to be found on the lips of dalesmen who enjoy the advantage of contact with the 'beautiful and permanent forms of nature.' Excellence of speech, Coleridge replies in substance, is a product of conscious culture. So far as the dalesmen possess it, it has come to them, not as an emanation of the landscape, but as a result above all of their reading of the Bible. Wordsworth was right in rejecting the 'gaudiness and inane phraseology' that had arisen from the imposition on poetry of the artificial decorum of a social class. But there is a true as well as an artificial decorum. Though the poet should eschew mere polite prejudice, he cannot afford to neglect in his choice of words their conventional associations, as Wordsworth, a recluse with a defective sense of humor, was at times too prone to do. The intrusion of words with trivial associations into serious verse will produce on readers the effect of 'sudden and unpleasant sinkings from the height to which the poet had previously lifted them.' Wordsworth is also guilty at times of a somewhat different type of indecorum—namely of using 'thoughts and images too great for the subject.' This latter type of disproportion Coleridge terms 'mental bombast.'

Though Coleridge's critique of Wordsworth is thus Aristotelian in its details, transcendentalism would seem to reappear in its conclusion; and transcendentalism is a doctrine that mixes about as well with that of Aristotle as oil with water. 'Last and preëminently,' he says, 'I challenge for this poet [i.e., Wordsworth] the gift of IMAGINATION in the highest and strictest sense of the word.' If Coleridge had been a more thoroughgoing Aristotelian, he might have found that the chief source of 'mental bombast' in Wordsworth arises from the disproportionate significance that he had been led by his transcendental philosophy to attach to natural appearances; when, for example, he exclaims, on his discovery of the small celandine, that he will 'make a stir, like a sage astronomer.' The stir would seem justified only in case it could be shown that, through imaginative communion with the small celandine, he attained a real spiritual unity. But what proof is there of the reality of a communion achieved in that way? One may perhaps best reply in the words of Coleridge:

> Oh, William, we receive but what we give
> And in our life alone does nature live.

In that case the nature with which one communes is not nature as known to the impartial observer but merely a projection of one's own mood on outer objects—in other words, a form of the pathetic fallacy. It follows, as I have remarked in a previous essay, that the unity thus achieved is not real but fanciful, so that the distinction between imagination and fancy that both Wordsworth and Coleridge strove to establish breaks down at the center.

Compared with the poetry that portrays action through the medium of fiction with reference to normal experience, communion with nature of the transcendental sort would appear to be only a new and fascinating mode of escape. The need of escape is deep-seated and universal and has been satisfied in manners manifold in the literature of the past. One would not, indeed, err greatly in choosing as epigraph for about nine tenths of this literature these lines of Emily Dickinson:

> I never hear the word 'escape'
> Without a quicker blood,
> A sudden expectation,
> A flying attitude.

The chief instrument of escape is the imagination—a certain quality of imagination. One need not quarrel with imagination of this quality when it shows itself frankly for what it is. It becomes dubious only when put at the basis of what purports to be idealism or even religion. This form of self-deception has flourished especially in connection with our modern return to nature. Thus Rousseau writes: 'My soul wanders and soars in the universe on the wings of imagination in ecstasies that surpass every other enjoyment.' The results that follow from indulging this type of imagination are scarcely of a kind to satisfy either the humanist or the man of science. The wandering and soaring, they would agree, are for the most part, not in the universe, but in the tower of ivory. Similarly the 'liberty' and 'intensest love' to which Coleridge lays claim as a result of 'shooting his being through earth, sea and air' are accomplished only in dreamland. Like the Wordsworth of *Tintern Abbey*, Coleridge is setting up in this passage of **"France: An Ode"**, pantheistic revery as a substitute for true meditation.

This is not of course the whole truth about either Wordsworth or Coleridge. Wordsworth attains at times to a truly religious elevation. In associating this elevation, however, with the 'light of setting suns' or some other aspect of outer nature, he is encouraging a confusion between spiritual and æsthetic perception. As a matter of fact, the first person who seems to have done justice æsthetically to the light of setting suns is 'the notorious ribald of Arezzo,' Aretino (letter to Titian, May, 1544).

There is, again, in Coleridge an element of genuine religious vision. He seems singularly different, however, in the total impression he produces, from the religious teachers of the past. These teachers, whether a Saint Bernard or a Buddha, are as energetic and purposeful as the head of some great industrial enterprise in our own time, though, one scarcely need add, in an entirely different way; whereas one can scarcely find in the whole annals of literature another personality so richly endowed as Coleridge and at the same time so rudderless. According to the familiar anecdote, he could not even determine which side of the garden walk would suit him best, but corkscrewed back and forth from one side to the other. There is more here than the ordinary contrast between the willingness of the spirit and the weakness of the flesh. His irresoluteness is related in at least some measure to his primitivism—above all to his notion that genius is shown primarily in a capacity for sinking 'back again into the childlike feeling of devout wonder.' It is no doubt true, as Mencius remarked long ago, that the great man is he who has not lost his child's heart; but it is also true that greatness appears in the power to impose on life a masculine purpose. It is not easy to estimate the precise proportion of primitivistic to genuinely religious elements in Coleridge himself. Regarding his major influence, it is possible to speak more confidently. This influence has, in Walter Pater's phrase, been a 'part of the long pleading of German culture for the things behind the veil.' Practically this has meant an interest in the elusive phenomena that are off the center of normal consciousness; the very phenomena, in short, to which Professor Lowes had devoted so much attention. As a result of his preoccupation with these crepuscular regions Coleridge impressed at times those who approached him as almost somnambulistic. The

picture Peacock has drawn of him in *Nightmare Abbey* with his curtains drawn at midday and sprinkling salt on the candle to make the light burn blue has at least the truth of caricature.

This interest in the abnormal was by no means confined to Coleridge. It has been said of his age in general that it 'grovelled in the ghastly and wallowed in the weird.' Such an age had in **The Ancient Mariner** its appropriate masterpiece. In its psychology and incidents and scenic setting it marks the extreme sacrifice of the verisimilar to the marvelous. It is at a far remove from the Aristotelian high seriousness, which not only requires relevancy to normal experience but a relevancy tested in terms of action. Apart from the initial shooting of an albatross the Mariner does not do anything. In the literal sense of the words he is not an agent, but a patient. The true protagonists of **The Rime of the Ancient Mariner**, Professor Lowes remarks rightly, are the elements—'Earth, Air, Fire and Water in their multiform balefulness and beauty.' As Charles Lamb puts it: 'I dislike all the miraculous part of the poem, but the feelings of the man under the operation of such scenery dragged me along like Tom Piper's magic whistle.' Between a poem like **The Ancient Mariner** in which the unifying element is feeling and a poem which has a true unity of action the difference is one of kind; between it and let us say *The Fall of the House of Usher* the difference is at most one of degree. In this and other tales Poe has, like Coleridge and indeed partly under his influence, achieved a unity of tone or impression, a technique in short, perfectly suited to the shift of the center of interest from action to emotion.

Intense emotion, especially under the stress of a unique experience, is isolating. Perhaps no work embodies more successfully than **The Ancient Mariner** the main romantic motif of solitude. ('Alone, alone, all, all alone!') Here if anywhere the soul is a state of the landscape and the landscape a state of the soul—the outer symbol of a ghastly isolation. The mood of solitude based on the sense of one's emotional uniqueness is closely interwoven, again, as every student of the modern movement knows, with the instinct of confession. Rousseau himself says of certain childhood experiences: 'I am aware that the reader does not need to know these details but I need to tell them to him.' In much the same fashion the Wedding Guest does not need to hear the Mariner's tale, but the Mariner needs to relate it to him. The psycho-analysts have, with rare effrontery, applied to the relief that results from a yielding to the confessional urge the noble term *katharsis*. It should be apparent that the term cannot be applied in its correct meaning to mere emotional overflow nor again to fiction in which wonder and strangeness prevail so completely, as in the present case, over imaginative imitation of the universal.

It follows from all that has been said that *The Ancient Mariner*, judged by the quality of the imagination that informs it, is not only romantic but ultra-romantic. One should not therefore disparage it, or in general regard as the only test of poetry its degree of conformity with the model set up by Aristotle in his *Poetics.* One must insist that in the house of art are many mansions. It does not follow that the mansions are all on the same level or of equal architectural dignity. That *The Ancient Mariner* is good in its own way—almost miraculously good—goes without saying. The reason for thinking that this way is inferior to the way envisaged by Aristotle is that it is less concerned with moral choices in their bearing on the only problem that finally matters—that of man's happiness or misery. Professor Lowes's praise will seem pitched in too high a key to anyone who accepts this or some similar scale of poetical values. He himself is not quite consistent at this point. At one moment he agrees with Coleridge that the fiction of the poem should have been openly irresponsible like that 'of the Arabian Nights' tale of the merchant's sitting down to eat dates by the side of a well, and throwing the shells aside, and lo! a genie starts up, and says he *must* kill the aforesaid merchant, *because* one of the date shells had, it seems, put out the eye of the genie's son.' In general Professor Lowes seems to dismiss the whole demand for probability as worthy only of literary philistines like Mrs. Barbauld, who complained, it will be remembered, of *The Ancient Mariner* that it was 'improbable and had no moral.'

At other moments, though recognizing the grotesque disproportion between the Mariner's initial act and its consequences, Professor Lowes seems to take the tale seriously as a treatment of the great drama of guilt and expiation. The fact is that it is impossible to extract any serious ethical purport from *The Ancient Mariner*—except perhaps a warning as to the fate of the innocent bystander; unless indeed one hold that it is fitting that, for having sympathized with the man who shot an albatross, 'four times fifty living men' should perish in torments unspeakable.

In the meanwhile, contrary to Mrs. Barbauld's assertion, *The Ancient Mariner* actually has a moral ('He prayeth best, who loveth best,' etc.). Moreover, this moral, unexceptionable in itself, turns out, when taken in its context, to be a sham moral. The mode in which the Mariner is relieved of the burden of his transgression, symbolized by the albatross hung about his neck—namely, by admiring the color of the water-snakes—is an extreme example of a confusion to which I have already alluded: he obtains subrationally and unconsciously ('I blessed them *unaware*') the equivalent of Christian charity. Like many other works in the modern movement, the poem thus lays claim to a religious seriousness that at bottom it does not possess. To this extent at least it is an example of a hybrid and ambiguous art.

By turning their attention to the wonder and magic of natural appearances Wordsworth and Coleridge and other romantics opened up an almost inexhaustible source of genuine poetry. Wonder cannot, however, in this or in any other form serve as a substitute for the virtues that imply a something in man that is set above the phenomenal order. If we are to believe the great teachers of the past, the pathway to religious wisdom does not lie through the flower in the crannied wall or the equivalent. The attempt to base religion on wonder becomes positively grotesque when Walt Whitman declares that 'a mouse is miracle enough to stagger sextillions of infidels.' The underlying confusion of values has, however, persisted in less obvious forms and is indeed the most dubious legacy to our own time from the romantic age. Thus Mrs. O. W. Campbell asserts that 'Christ was the first romantic and the greatest.' According to Mr. Middleton Murry, again, when a person does not dare to come out and attack Christ openly he vents his spleen on Rousseau.

The distinction between two entirely different orders of intuition that is being blurred or obliterated by the writers I have just been citing is closely related to the problem of the imagination. Perhaps no recent critic has spoken more wisely on the nature of this relationship than a French contemporary of Coleridge—Joubert; and that at the very time when Coleridge was insinuating that 'a Frenchman is the only animal in the human shape that by no possibility can lift itself up to religion or poetry.' Joubert not only displays the same high type of vision that appears at times in Coleridge but he has the advantage over Coleridge of not being addicted either to opium or German metaphysics. The most important distinction made by Joubert is that between an imagination that does not rise above the impressions of sense and an imagination that gives access to the supersensuous, that is, in short, an organ of insight. It is only with the aid of this latter type of imagination that one achieves the 'illusion of a higher reality'; the illusion is indeed, according to Joubert, 'an integral part of the reality.'

One cannot afford to disdain in the creative process what may be termed the spontaneities, all that seems to come as a free gift, for example, the magical combinations and permutations of images in the 'deep well.' Coleridge, however, falls into a dangerous primitivistic exaggeration when he says that 'there is in genius itself an unconscious activity; nay, that is the genius in the man of genius.' The imagination that Joubert calls the 'eye of the soul' is fully conscious and also creative, though in a different sense: it creates values. It does so by coöperating with reason in the service of a higher will. The unconscious activities must be controlled with reference to the values thus created with the help of the ethical imagination, as one may term it, if they are to have direction and purpose, in other words human significance. Technique is admittedly something that must be consciously acquired. The question of the ethical imagination is, however, plainly one that concerns not merely the technique or outer form of creative work, but its inmost essence.

Failure to make some such distinction as that I have been attempting, exposes one to the risk of confounding work that has abundant human substance with work that has little or none. Serious confusions of this kind are rife at the present time—more serious indeed than any with which Professor Lowes may be properly charged. For example Mr. E. E. Kellett writes in his recent volume *Reconsiderations*: 'There is something in the very choice of subject which marks out the *supreme* poet from his fellows. It is not an accident that Coleridge chose to write of *diablerie* and witchcraft. . . . The fact that Chaucer's subjects are in the main of the earth, earthy, is significant of the limits of his poetic genius.'

It may be maintained that Dante has a depth of religious insight that puts him definitely above Chaucer. But to accord to romantic *diablerie* the same rating as to religious insight and to dismiss Chaucer, one of the most human of poets, as 'of the earth, earthy' in comparison with the Coleridge of *The Ancient Mariner*, is surely inadmissible. Here and elsewhere in his volume, Mr. Kellett reminds one of the French partisans of 'pure poetry.' So much is eliminated by the Abbé Bremond, the chief spokesman for this group, as not being of the essence of poetry, that it is, like Jowett's idea of God, in danger of being defecated to a pure transparency. Poetry becomes a *je ne sais quoi,* an 'electricity,' an indefinable magic that is similar, the Abbé Bremond would have us believe, to the mysterious and impalpable something that is present in the attitude of prayer. The truth is that the Abbé is ready to make an abject surrender of conscious discrimination and control in favor of a pure spontaneity, with a resulting confusion of the subrational with the superrational and finally of romanticism with religion that, in so prominent a churchman, is positively disconcerting.

The sacrifice of human substance to the Moloch of spontaneity is even more manifest in the contemporary French group known as the 'superrealists' (*surréalistes*), affiliated in their point of view with the English and American writers who abandon themselves to the 'stream of consciousness.' The very name that the members of this group have assumed would indicate that they are in error as to the direction in which they are moving. What they term 'reality' is plainly not above but below the human and rational level. The upshot of the quest of creative renewal in this region would appear to be, if one may judge from some of the contributions to *transition*, the organ of the group, a sort of psychic automatism.

I am not going too far afield in speaking of the *surréalistes* apropos of Coleridge. If a poem like **"The Pains of Sleep"** anticipates Baudelaire, **"Kubla Khan,"** as I have already remarked, probably remains the best example of a spontaneity that, so far from having been disciplined to either humanistic or religious purpose, has not even undergone any technical shaping of the kind one finds in *The Ancient Mariner*. It illustrates what Coleridge himself calls the 'streamy nature of association' in revery at least as well, and far more agreeably, than, let us say, the closing pages of Joyce's *Ulysses*.

The notion that one becomes creative only by being spontaneous is closely related to the notion that one becomes original only by being unique. If we are to judge by *surréalisme* and other recent literary cults the time is approaching when each writer will, in the name of his genius conceived as self-expression, retire so completely into his own private dream that communication will become impossible. To be sure the drift of these recent cults towards sheer unintelligibility marks a violent extreme of the kind that usually comes towards the end of a movement. It is an extreme, however, that points to a one-sidedness in the movement from the start—the tendency, namely, to exalt the differences between man and man and to disparage or deny the identities. The result has been a fatal confusion between individuality and personality. True personality is not something that, like individuality, is bestowed upon a man simply because he has taken the trouble to be born. It is something that he must consciously win with reference to a standard set above his merely temperamental self; whereas there has probably never been a blade of grass, which, if it become vocal, might not say truthfully, in the language of Rousseau, that, if not better than other blades of grass, at least it was different. The notion that one may become creative simply by combining temperamental overflow with a greater or lesser degree of technical skill has resulted in work that often displays genius indeed but suffers at the same time from a taint of eccentricity; work in which, in Aristotelian parlance, the wonderful quite overtops the probable. Anatole France writes of Victor Hugo, perhaps the extreme example of genius of the eccentric type: 'One is saddened and at the same time frightened not to encounter in his enormous work, in the midst of so many monsters, a single human figure. . . . He wished to inspire wonder and long had the power to do so, but is it possible always to inspire wonder?'

The doctrine of imitation, setting up as it does some standard with reference to which a man must humanize his gift, whatever that gift may chance to be, is, in all its forms, chastening; perhaps, in some of its forms, too chastening. One remembers the prostration of the literary aspirant before the models during the neo-classic period. On the other hand, the doctrine that discredits imitation in favor of spontaneity does not put a man sufficiently on his guard against what

Buddha and other sages have declared to be the two root diseases of human nature—conceit and laziness. It would not be difficult to find modern applications of a sentence that was written by Robert Wolseley as long ago as 1685: 'Every ass that's romantic believes he's inspired.'

But to return to Coleridge: at his best, especially when he insists that great poetry must be representative, he can scarcely be charged with having encouraged the over-facile type of inspiration. One may ask however whether he has brought the doctrine of representativeness, with its inevitable corollaries of imitation and probability, into sufficiently close relation with his actual defining of the imagination and its rôle. The most famous of his critical phrases, 'that willing suspension of disbelief for the moment, which constitutes poetic faith,' does not appear to afford any adequate basis for discriminating between poetic faith and poetic credulity. The fact that a fiction of any kind is enthralling is no sure proof that it has human substance. Otherwise certain detective stories would merit a high literary rating. The phrase was actually framed with a view to justifying *The Ancient Mariner*, a tale that lacks probability, not only in Mrs. Barbauld's sense, but, as I have been trying to show, in Aristotle's as well. Nor is it enough to speak of 'the shaping spirit of imagination,' for the imagination may shape chimeras. One cannot again be wholly satisfied with the definition of 'the primary imagination' as 'a repetition in the finite mind of the eternal act of creation in the infinite I AM.' This would seem to be an invitation to the romantic to exalt himself to the level of deity before making sure of the validity of his imaginings apart from his own emotions.

We must conclude therefore that, in spite of many admirable remarks by the way, Coleridge does not succeed in disengaging his theory of the imagination sufficiently from the transcendental mist. It is to be regretted above all that he did not affirm clearly the rôle of the imagination in giving access to a supersensuous reality; an affirmation that is necessary if the doctrine of imitation and probability is to be relieved of every suspicion of formalism. Instead, he inclined to see the highest use of the imagination in Wordsworth's communing with natural appearances, and so became one of the promoters of the great pathetic fallacy that has been bewildering the human spirit ever since.

Wordsworth, who tended to read into the landscape what is not there (for example, 'unutterable love'), at the same time that he rendered, often fortunately, the wonder that is there, disparaged science. Yet probably the chief reason for the comparative eclipse of the imagination that seizes what is normal and central in human experience in favor of the imagination that yields to the lure of wonder has been the discoveries of science. These discoveries have engendered an intox-

ication with novelty for which the past offers no parallel. The modern man has been kept on the tiptoe of expectation by one marvel after another. For the moment he is thus imaginatively enthralled by the conquest of the air. He is infinitely removed from the Horatian *nil admirari*, even though he does not set out deliberately, like a certain French minor poet, to 'live in a state of bedazzlement.' As a result of the interplay and coöperation of the various forms of naturalism, the attitude of the modern man towards life has become purely exploratory—a sheer expansion of wonder and curiosity. He cannot even conceive another attitude. Yet a situation is gradually growing up that may force him to conceive it. Wonder has a large place in the scheme of things, but is after all only a sorry substitute for the law of measure of the humanist or for the religious virtues—awe, reverence and humility.

If one wishes to understand how humanism and religion have been more or less compromised by the modern movement with its 'Renascence of Wonder,' it is still helpful to go back to its earlier stages. Matthew Arnold expressed the opinion that the burst of creative activity in English literature through the first quarter of the nineteenth century had about it something premature. Whatever justification there may be for this opinion is found in the failure of the romantic leaders to deal critically enough with the idea of creation itself. The doctrine of creative spontaneity towards which they inclined, though in the case of Coleridge with reservations, suffered, as I have been trying to show, from a one-sidedness that has persisted to the present day. Unless this one-sidedness is corrected, it is to be feared that art and literature will be menaced with a more than Alexandrian decline. As a matter of fact, Joyce's *Ulysses*, which has been saluted by Miss Rebecca West, speaking for no inconsiderable portion of the younger literary set, as a work of 'majestic genius,' marks a more advanced stage of psychic disintegration than anything that has come down to us from classical antiquity. If there is to be any recovery of humanistic or religious truth, at least along critical lines, it would appear desirable to associate the creative process once more, not with spontaneity, but with imitation, imitation of the type that implies a supersensuous model imaginatively apprehended. According to the late Stuart Sherman, 'the great revolutionary task of nineteenth-century thinkers was to put man into nature. The great task of twentieth-century thinkers is to get him out again.' Superficially, the most serious danger of the primitivistic immersion of man in nature to which Sherman refers is that it leads to a denial of reason; a still graver danger, one finds on closer scrutiny, is that it leads to an obscuring of the true dualism—that between man's natural self and a higher will—or more frequently to the setting up of some subrational parody of this will such as one finds in *The Ancient Mariner*. The obscuring of the higher will has coincided practically with the decline of the doctrine of divine grace with which it has in the Christian Occident been traditionally associated. The issues involved evidently extend far beyond the boundaries of literature. But, to consider literature alone, it would seem necessary to recover in some form, perhaps in a purely psychological form, the true dualism, if creation is once more to be achieved that deserves to be accounted highly serious—creation, in other words, that is informed by the human and dramatic quality of imagination.

G. K. Chesterton   (essay date 1934)

SOURCE: "About S.T.C.," in *As I Was Saying: A Book of Essays,* Methuen & Co., Ltd., 1936, pp. 86-91.

[*In the following excerpt, Chesterton derides criticism that would overemphasize the influence of opium on Coleridge and his poetry.*]

It seems to me that the central genius of a man like Coleridge is not a thing to be dealt with by critics at all. If they really had anything worth saying about such a poet, they would write it in poetry. It is the curse upon all critics that they must write in prose. It is the specially blighting and blasting curse upon some of them, that they have to write in philosophical or psychological or generally analytical prose. I have never read a page of such criticism, however clear and clever, which brought me the most remote echo of the actual sound of the poetry or the power of poetical images, which are like magic talismans. Therefore, in writing about a man like Coleridge, we are driven back upon secondary things; upon his second best work, or upon the second- or third-rate controversies aroused by that work. In that sense, of course, there are any number of second-rate things to be said of Coleridge. It is suggested, for instance, that the abnormal or enormous enlargement of his imagination was due to a dirty habit he had of taking opium. I will confess that I am sceptical about the divinity of the drug; or the power of any drug to act like a god, and make a man other than he really is. I will merely suggest that if exactly the same quantity of opium had been given to a number of Coleridge's contemporaries—let us say to George the Third, to Mr. Bentham, to the Duke of Wellington, to Mr. Gifford, to Beau Brummel or to William Pitt himself, not to mention Mr. Perceval—I gravely doubt whether any or all of these persons together would have produced a line of **"Kubla Khan"**. It was a pity that Coleridge took opium; because it dissolved his great intellect in dreams, when he was perhaps more fitted than most men of his time to have made some structural logical system, that should have reconciled Revolution and Religion. But *Christabel* and *The Ancient Mariner* were written by Mr. Coleridge

and not by Mr. Opium. The drug may have accelerated or made easy a work which some weaknesses in his moral character might have made him avoid or delay, because they were laborious; but there is nothing creative about a narcotic. The point is perhaps worthy of remark; for nobody who knows the nineteenth-century literature can fail to notice that there was a curious effort, under the surface, to make such Asiatic drugs as normal as European drinks. It is a sort of subterranean conspiracy that ranges from the *Confessions* of De Quincey to the *Moonstone* of Wilkie Collins. Fortunately, tradition was too strong for it; and Christian men continued to prefer the grape of life to the poppy of death.

Then it would be easy to add, upon this secondary plane, that Coleridge did really suffer from other misleading influences besides opium. *The Ancient Mariner* is probably one of the most original poems that were ever written; and, like many original things, it is almost antiquarian. Like most Romantics reviving the Gothic without understanding the medieval, he carried archaism to lengths that were almost comic. I am not sure that he did not call the Mariner a Marinere. All that affects us as too reminiscent of the Olde English Tea-Shoppe. A more serious difficulty was that he turned too sharply from France to Germany. It was very natural that a Romantic should take refuge in the German forests, and still more in the German fairy-tales. It was a more unfortunate adventure that he took refuge with the German philosophers. They encouraged him, as did the drug, in a sort of misty infinity, which confused his real genius for definition and deduction. It was in every way excellent, of course, that the great German literature of the great German age, the age of Goethe and of Lessing, should be opened up to English readers; and perhaps it could have been done by Coleridge more calmly and luminously than it was afterwards done by Carlyle. But if Goethe was the great and good influence of Germany, Kant was on the whole the great and bad influence. These two great Germans offer any number of aspects to be admired or criticized; but, on the whole, Goethe made Germany a part of Europe, while Kant cut it off from Europe, following a wild light of its own, heaven knows where. Coleridge the philosopher can be criticized on various grounds; including the ground that he did not know the great philosophy of Christendom that was behind him. But Coleridge the poet cannot be criticized at all.

E. M. W. Tillyard   (essay date 1948)

SOURCE: "Coleridge: *The Rime of the Ancient Mariner,* 1798," in *Poetry and Its Background, Illustrated by Five Poems, 1470-1870,* Chatto & Windus, 1970, pp. 66-86.

[In the following excerpt, Tillyard discusses how The Rime of the Ancient Mariner *is characteristic of Romanticism generally, and particularly "of the diversity of the* Ancient Mariner, *of the multiple layers of meaning, of the different uses to which nature is put."]*

I

First let me explain that I shall not try to criticise [*The Rime of the Ancient Mariner*] in the sense of conveying something of the total effect. It is a rich and complicated poem, and to put in words the total effect issuing from this complication would be at once surpassingly difficult and unnecessary for the humbler objects I have in view. All I seek to do is to enumerate some of the layers of significance that go to make up the whole.

First, it is an exciting story, imitated from the old ballads, drawing much of its material from old books of travel, enlivened by touches of realistic natural description, yet partly appealing to that side of our natures that delights in superstitions and in the supernatural. Secondly, in spite of the supernatural happenings, of which no rational explanation is given, the main events of the story happen logically in a sequence of cause and effect. In such a sequence the moral motive naturally enters, and the question arises of what this amounts to. Late in his life Coleridge censured the presence of a motivating morality. In reply to an objection of Mrs Barbauld that the poem lacked a moral he answered that it had too much:

> It ought to have had no more moral than the Arabian Nights' tale of the merchant's sitting down to eat dates by the side of a well, and throwing the shells aside, and lo! a genie starts up, and says he *must* kill the aforesaid merchant, *because* one of the date shells had, it seems, put out the eye of the genie's son.

Probably Coleridge was stung to perversity by Mrs Barbauld's being so stupid, and did not mean what he said. In truth, the moral story, the punishment of a crime, is the core of the poem; each part ends with a reference to the crime, the killing of the albatross: remove the moral, and the poem collapses. Granted the moral, we must beware of narrowing it to the familiar modern doctrine of kindness to animals. If the albatross had been a crow or vulture or other bird of ill omen, there would have been no crime in shooting it; yet by humanitarian standards the act would have been just as bad. The reasons for not shooting the albatross were superstitious or at least primitive. By standards of superstition animals are good or bad. It is unlucky to kill the good; the bad (the toad, for instance) can be persecuted to any extent. The albatross was a good bird, and they "hailed it in God's name". It was also their guest, and in a primitive

world treachery to a guest was a terrible crime. Coleridge's gloss sums the matter up: "The ancient Mariner inhospitably killeth the pious bird of good omen." Whether the act itself apart from its consequences can be motivated is a matter of opinion. Should we simply accept it as a piece of plot-mechanism, like Lear's resolution to divide his kingdom, or should we detect a reason? Certainly there is a very simple reason to hand. The act could be interpreted as the essential act of devilment, the act of pride, of the unbridled assertion of the self. It was what Satan did when he rebelled and what Defoe made Crusoe do when he thrice rejected God's offer of a virtuous middle way of life. Whatever the answer, we are suitably impressed by the enormity of the mariner's crime and readily accept the straits into which he falls. The way he gets out of these straits is also motivated but with a richness that makes it difficult not to encroach here on other layers of the poem's meaning. One reason for his escape is the sheer fulfilment of a frightful penance: he issues out of his prison like a prisoner who has served his time, whether repentant or not. And this punitive motive corresponds well enough to the purely superstitious crime of killing a bird of good omen. But there is the further reason of his blessing the water-snakes. And this was an act of repentance, a moral reversal of his grossly self-regarding act of killing the albatross, a forgetfulness of self in recognising the beauty of something quite independent. The crime, however, is not expiated at once. One of the two voices in the air says there is more penance to do. It is the one defect in the poem's structure that this further penance hardly exists and that the final expiation in line 442 ("And now this spell was snapt . . .") comes in very casually. Having learnt to expect motivation, we are disappointed when it is lacking. Even if we assume that the penance is now really complete, we still miss a further act of repentance to correspond to the blessing of the water-snakes. Thenceforward everything is credible in its context. The crime has been such that we accept the mariner's final doom of having periodically to relive his old experience through recounting his tale.

I have spoken of the simple narrative interest and of the moral motivation together because the second helps the first along: a logical is more emphatic than a mere casual sequence. As Lowes says in his *Road to Xanadu*: "The sequence which follows the Mariner's initial act accomplishes two ends: it unifies and it 'credibilizes' the poem". But Lowes notices something more about the morality: its truth to the ordinary experience of life. He writes:

> The train of cause and consequence is more than a consolidating factor of the poem. It happens to be life, as every human being knows it. You do a foolish or an evil deed, and its results come home to you. And they are apt to fall on others too. You repent, and a load is lifted from your

soul. But you have not thereby escaped your deed. You attain forgiveness, but cause and effect work on unmoved, and life to the end may be the continued reaping of the repented deed's results.

Though this is not how we think of the poem when we read it, we do ratify Lowes's words on reflection. And they are important, for they convey a part of the meaning that is too often forgotten. And it is precisely the blend of this sheer truth to human experience with the narrative power the fantastic happenings and the brilliant pictures that makes the *Ancient Mariner* so rich and so surprising.

But the *Ancient Mariner* is more than a fascinating story with a moral. It may be that H. I'A. Fausset is right in seeing it as an allegory of Coleridge's own life: his strange mind, his terrors, his loquacity. The Mariner, repeating his tale, may well be Coleridge, "seeking relief throughout his life in endless monologues". But even if Fausset is right, he is indicating a very minor layer of the poem's meaning. What matters is not that Coleridge should be speaking for himself but that he should be speaking for many others. Miss Bodkin in her *Archetypal Patterns in Poetry* chooses the *Ancient Mariner* as one of the poems "the ground of whose appeal is most evidently the impression of the inner life", but she rightly does not confine the inner life to Coleridge's. And if, as I think we should, we take the Mariner's voyage as a mental one, it should figure the adventures not of Coleridge alone but of all mental voyagers.

Once we postulate an allegory we are beset with dangers, above all with the temptation to grow excited, to see too much, to mistake a simple picturesque detail for a complicated moral truth. I will try to keep to the more obvious and plausible significances.

The general drift of the poem in its mental action can readily be recognised by two passages from other poets: Webster,

My soul like to a ship in a black storm
Is driven I know not whither;

and Shelley,

The breath whose might I have invoked in
    song
Descends on me; my spirit's bark is driven
Far from the shore, far from the trembling
    throng
Whose sails were never to the tempest
    given;
The massy earth and sphered skies are
    riven.
I am borne darkly, fearfully, afar!

The sea-voyage, then, indicates spiritual *adventure,* as the ordinary journey or pilgrimage indicates the course of normal life. And it is not everyone who goes out of his way to seek adventure. There is a passage in Coleridge's prose that both says this and has its bearing on the *Ancient Mariner*.

> The first range of hills, that encircles the scanty vale of human life, is the horizon for the majority of its inhabitants. On *its* ridges the common sun is born and departs. From *them* the stars rise, and touching *them* they vanish. By the many, even this range, the natural limit and bulwark of the vale, is but imperfectly known. Its higher ascents are too often hidden by mists and clouds from uncultivated swamps, which few have courage or curiosity to penetrate. To the multitude below these vapours appear, now as the dark haunts of terrific agents, on which none may intrude with impunity; and now all aglow, with colours not their own, they are gazed at as the splendid palaces of happiness and power. But in all ages there have been a few, who measuring and sounding the rivers of the vale at the feet of their furthest inaccessible falls have learned, that the sources must be far higher and far inward; a few, who even in the level streams have detected elements, which neither the vale itself nor the surrounding mountains contained or could supply. . . . It is the essential mark of the true philosopher to rest satisfied with no imperfect light, as long as the impossibility of attaining a fuller knowledge has not been demonstrated.

The Ancient Mariner and his ship represent the small but persisting class of mental adventurers who are not content with the appearances surrounding them but who attempt to get behind. (It may be added that though the class is small it stands for a universal impulse which is dormant in most minds and not absent from them.) Further, and here I recognise the danger of seeing too much, it is possible that the different degrees of nearness to normality represented in the poem do correspond to the apprehension of such degrees in actual life. The harbour-town, occurring in a narrative, is less real than the wedding-guest and the wedding but more so than the realms visited in the voyage; and these degrees of reality can hardly be without their effect.

Granted that the Mariner and his voyage signify the mental adventure of an unusually inquiring spirit, the outline of that adventure becomes tolerably clear, while it would be senseless to seek more than an outline. From the social point of view these spiritual adventurers are criminals: they disturb the existing order and they imply a criticism of the accepted round of life: they are self-appointed outcasts. The shooting of the albatross in the present context was an anti-social act: something that by everyday rules would not be done. And the avenging spirit takes the Mariner into a region and a situation the utter loneliness of which is both the logical consequence and the avengement of his revolt against society. This same region is one more version of that aridity that besets all isolated mental voyagers at one stage of their voyage. Other versions are Donne's conceit of himself in *A Nocturnal upon St Lucy's Day* as the quintessence of the primeval nothingness out of which God created the world; the emptiness experienced by the poet in Shelley's *Alastor,* who, when he awakes from his dreams, sees the "garish hills" and "vacant woods", while his "wan eyes"

> Gaze on the empty scene as vacantly
> As ocean's moon looks on the moon in
>   heaven;

and the landscape in Browning's *Childe Roland.* The Mariner escapes from his isolation by the enlargement of his sympathies in the manner least expected and he is allowed to return to common life. And he does so as a changed man. He has repented of his isolation; his greatest satisfaction is to worship in company with his fellows of all ages. But he is still the marked man, the outcast, the Wandering Jew, the victim of his own thoughts. Further, although he has been judged by society, he has the reward of the courage that propels the mental adventurer: that of arresting and disturbing and teaching those who have had no such experiences. And this ambivalent criterion enriches the poem incalculably.

But there may be yet one more important layer of meaning; something so simple and fundamental that it extends beyond the rarer sphere of self-imposed mental adventure to the common inevitable workings of the human mind. Miss Bodkin sees in the *Ancient Mariner* a rendering of the pattern of rebirth, which is at once the theme of tragedy and a very law of human life: the process of renovation through destruction. This theme is certainly present. It was only through the destruction of his old state of mind that the Mariner was able to achieve the new, enlarged state of mind that could include the watersnakes in its sympathies. But the *Ancient Mariner* is unlike the most satisfying works that render the theme, for instance the *Oresteia* or *Lycidas,* in that the renovation brought about is less powerful than the thing from whose destruction it has sprung. There is nothing to correspond to the thrust of energy that ends *Lycidas* with

> To-morrow to fresh woods, and pastures
>   new.

The Ancient Mariner has been born again into a ghostly existence, not rejuvenated. And the haunting terror of the destructive experience remains the dominant theme of the poem:

> O Wedding-Guest! this soul hath been
> Alone on a wide wide sea.

So much for some of the layers of meaning. It is (may I repeat?) their co-existence and their interplay that makes the *Ancient Mariner* a poem of which one never tires. Finally, and before I go on to the ideas which Coleridge shared with his age, there is a detail in the plotting which parallels the co-existence of two layers of meaning. At one of the high points of the poem there is a discrepancy between the emotional-rhythmical plot and the asserted or factual plot. I refer to lines 257 onwards. The stanza beginning with 257 is the climax of the Mariner's suffering, and the bare factual meaning of the words that follow is that the suffering continues.

> Her beams bemocked the sultry main,
> Like April hoar-frost spread;
> Bet where the ship's huge shadow lay,
> The charméd water burnt alway
> A still and awful red.

The moonbeams are *hostile,* mocking the sultry main, while the water beneath the ship's shadow was a *horrible* red. It is only later that the mood changes and the Mariner blesses the water-snakes. But rhythmically and emotionally the change had already come in line 263 with

> The moving Moon went up the sky
> And no where did abide:
> Softly she was going up,
> And a star or two beside.

The relaxation in the rhythm is unmistakeable, and the playing off this relaxation against the contradictory assertion that the horror is still there is a wonderful poetic stroke. And this playing off is confirmed by line 287 when we learn that the Mariner blessed the water-snakes *unaware.* The rhythm of line 263 is the index of the first unconscious motion of the mind towards renewal.

II

The claims made above for a complexity of meaning in the *Ancient Mariner* have a direct bearing on the extent to which the poem reflects the contemporary world. Most people think of it as a delightful poem and typical of its age principally for arousing our sense of wonder. Fewer will think of it as exhibiting many contemporary habits of thought. Yet it exhibits them so richly and in some points contrasts so aptly with the other poems I have chosen that it embarrasses by the amount of material it offers. All I can do is to select some of the main topics.

(a)
RELIGIOUS FEELING

A very remarkable thing in the *Ancient Mariner* is the strength of the religious or at least numinous feeling. And equally remarkable is the great variety of such feeling it contains. In these matters it speaks for a part of its age. Indeed but a part; for after the Augustan Age it becomes increasingly hard to find ways of thought and feeling universally accepted in England. And along with an undoubted expansion of religious sensibility was the steady advance of the utilitarian and scientific principles.

To begin with more general matters the *Ancient Mariner* is permeated with the sense of what people now call the numinous, with the sense of impalpable spirituality. It haunts the borders of the unknown and gives hints of terrors and joys that are awaiting exploration. It is true that Coleridge's knowledge of medieval angelology and demonology gives his poem a semblance of preciseness, but in addition there is this pervading sense of the numinous, which unites it to some of the early Wordsworth, to much of Shelley, to Ruskin and much nineteenth century writing, and which separates it from any of the poems hitherto discussed. This side of the *Ancient Mariner* may be vaguely religious but it is untheological. The *Testament of Cresseid* is not primarily a religious poem, but its tragic story is conducted under a precise, though general, theology. What theology there is is schematic. Henryson is more certain and mathematically correct about his planetary powers than Coleridge is about his spirits. If Henryson had used these spirits, he would have sorted graded and labelled them. Coleridge was learned in medieval theology and he knows about the chain of being. But he uses the links in it out of their old context and in a new context of vague numinous evocation. The spirits in the *Ancient Mariner* are akin to Shelley's:

Oh! there are spirits of the air
And genii of the evening breeze,
And gentle ghosts—

and alien to the precisely ordered spiritual hierarchies of Dionysius the Areopagite. And the albatross is no part of a scheme but a detached symbol, useful to the poet in isolation.

Along with the numinous is the hint of pantheism, again uniting Coleridge with Wordsworth and Tennyson and later writers. This hint is given by the episode of blessing the water-snakes. The Mariner watches them not as a past age would have done as moral emblems or as servants of man, or as witnesses of the ingenuity of God's craftsmanship, but as creatures with a life of their own. In so doing he is eminently modern; for apart from a purely scientific interest this delight in the autonomy of animals, in their having their own proper business, is to-day the chief attraction of watching them. Such a feeling need not lead to pantheism, witness Hopkins's very orthodox poem, the *Windhover,* where with the words, "my heart in hiding stirred for a bird", the feeling comes in. It was the bird's going about its business utterly separate from and oblivious of the watcher that gave the special excitement. Nevertheless it is easy to see how such a feeling can tend to pantheism. Once you give animals a life of their own, you can easily suggest that it is just as good a life as the human. And once you do that, you tend to confound the classic divisions of existence and to make no unclosable chasm between inanimate and animate, between spiritual and non-spiritual. And with these divisions gone, it is natural to identify God and creation and to make him both all phenomena and its animating spirit,

one intellectual breeze
At once the Soul of each, and God of all,

rather than a person who has created his separate world out of nothing.

Next (and very obviously) there is the superstitious side appealing to that in human nature which dreads giving offence to a little-known and unpredictable supernatural power. In exploiting this feeling Coleridge was at one with his age. The eighteenth century as a whole had tended both to overestimate the speed with which such feelings were dwindling in the human mind and to dislike their occurrence in earlier ages. In compensation the next age paid them marked attention. The superstitions attached to the albatross have been mentioned already. The wedding-guest's fear of the Ancient Mariner is superstitious: he might have the evil as well as the compelling eye. And the Mariner himself, although self-propelled from land to land, is yet akin to the outcasts whose gift of bringing ill-luck to whatever land they inhabit makes them wanderers over the earth. Most obviously of all, the ballad form of the poem unites it with the medieval ballad and the world of the Fairy Tale. It thus represents a contemporary happening. People were tiring of the restricted anthology of Fairy Tales—mainly the selections and adaptations of Perrault—that prevailed in polite eighteenth century circles. The brothers Grimm were collecting their folklore during the Romantic period and in 1812 began to publish their *Kinder- und Hausmärchen* (first translated into English in 1823). Nor can the crudest of all contemporary exploitations of the feeling for superstition be left unmentioned, the Gothic novel, for however remote in subtlety from the *Ancient Mariner* it does present some community of substance.

The Gothic novel suggests still another side of religion, the antiquarian; for the *Ancient Mariner* is very much of an antiquarian, Neo-Gothic poem. It is so good that we tend to forget this, just as much Neo-Gothic architecture is bad enough to remind us constantly that it is pastiche. Along with the ballad form is the medieval Catholic setting. The setting is a world of mariolatry, hermits, shriving, guardian saints and angels. However different the effect, this antiquarianism is comparable with Scott's and it has its contemporary importance. George Borrow blamed Scott for the Oxford Movement; and though he may have erred in concentrating his blame on one man, there is no doubt that the very wide antiquarian interest of the early nineteenth century in medieval things prepared the ground for a large religious movement that went right beyond the antiquarian. The hearty fun of the *Ingoldsby Legends* at the expense of the Middle Ages has its relation to the **Ancient Mariner** and testifies to the interests which contributed to the Oxford Movement.

And lastly the **Ancient Mariner** is religious in a much profounder way. Like the *Testament of Cresseid* it deals not only with the dreadful experience but with the salvation of a human soul. The Mariner is a sinner, and his blessing of the water-snakes is not only a reversal of feeling but an act of repentance. Again, the religion is little schematised. Cresseid, we can clearly infer, committed two of the Seven Deadly Sins, and her repentance followed a dictated plan. If the Mariner's sin was pride, we say so only by conjecture, and his conversion and repentance are conducted not on a plan but on the suppositions of human psychology. An interesting comparison is with T. S. Eliot's *Family Reunion,* suggesting that Coleridge looks forward not back. The turning point in Harry's mind is when he decides to follow the Eumenides not to fly from them. Just so the Mariner blesses the water-snakes instead of abhorring them. Again Coleridge speaks for his age. Between him and Dryden had interposed the expansion of the old Puritanism into the Wesleyan movement with a resultant emphasis on a sense of personal sin and on conversion. But to follow up this topic would anticipate my section on individualism.

With such different religious strains present simultaneously in a poem of six hundred lines it is astonishing that we experience no discomfort or sense of incongruity in the reading. On the contrary it is only with an effort that we can distinguish and perceive separately these strains; and we are surprised to find they are so many. Coleridge had every right to call the imagination the esemplastic power after having given so perfect a demonstration of its unifying operation.

(*b*)
NATURE

Not only in religion but in nature Coleridge sees different things. Natural objects have ceased to be clearly arranged in the chain of being, but they can be numinous or terrifyingly fantastic, or purely picturesque, or correlatives of human emotion. The variety is astonishing, as the quality of descriptive power is superlatively good. For simple picturesque effect no contemporary or later poet has surpassed the description of the moonlit harbour on the return:

> The harbour-bay was clear as glass,
> So smoothly it was strewn!
> and on the bay the moonlight lay,
> and the shadow of the Moon.

> The rock shone bright, the kirk no less,
> That stands above the rock:
> The moonlight steeped in silentness
> The steady weathercock.

But the terms in which one of the Voices describes another moonlit seascape are very different indeed.

> Still as a slave before his lord,
> The ocean hath no blast;
> His great bright eye most silently
> Up to the Moon is cast—

> If he may know which way to go;
> For she guides him smooth or grim.
> See, brother, see! how graciously
> She looketh down on him!

There is little of the purely picturesque here but much that stirs our hidden and vaguely defined emotions. This utter servitude of the sea, more familiarly a symbol of unregulated violence or, considered in its vastness, of eternity, comes as a shock, and yet, with that portion of our mind that can still understand animism and magical habits of thought, we respond. It is interesting to compare Davies's lines on the same theme containing the same metaphor:

> For lo, the sea, that fleets about the land
> And like a girdle clips her solid waist,
> Music and measure both doth understand;
> For his great crystal eye is always cast
> Up to the moon and on her fixed fast;
> And as she danceth in her pallid sphere,
> So danceth he about the centre here.

There is nothing primitive in Davies's thought, but with fantastic and sophisticated ornament he decks out a fixed inherited piece of information. For the emotional use of nature, the simple "pathetic fallacy", take another lunar description:

> Her beams bemocked the sultry main,

or the single epithet of "*star-dogged* Moon".

The uses to which the nineteenth century put nature are well enough known to make it unnecessary to say more than that in his various modes of description Coleridge was the representative of his age.

(c)
ABSENCE OF POLITICS

There is a total lack of politics in the *Ancient Mariner*. Admittedly with such a subject politics are not to be looked for; yet here is a poem of six hundred lines and without the glimmering of a reference to any body politic. It was not that Coleridge was not interested in politics: on the contrary he had just written some very political poetry. In both these matters he represents his age. There was much political activity and yet how little do politics get into the best literature. Cowper's most poignant and effective verse is personal not political. Crabbe is social rather than political. Blake, according to Bronowski, is full of covert politics, but he is read for other things. Wordsworth was passionately interested in politics and spent much time in thinking on them and some time in writing on them in prose. Yet his effective verse, when it concerns man, concerns individual and unpolitical man. Shelley indeed is political, but it is not his political verse we most know him by. Keats is not political at all. This poetical shift away from politics is new. In Henryson politics and the Church were so interconnected that his orthodox theology can include the political field, not to speak of his serene acceptance of the social divisions of the Commonwealth. In *Orchestra* Elizabeth and her court have their inalienable importance in the world scheme, just as the idea of royalty and the history plays form an organic part of the complete works of Shakespeare. Even if for Shakespeare the individual may count ultimately for most, there is, even in his most purely tragic or romantic plays, a wonderfully strong counterpoise to these other motives in the powerful political values in the background. In the *Ode on Anne Killigrew* the royalism is organic. But in the most intense and serious poetry of the Romantics (Byron perhaps excepted) the body politic and organised man have dwindled in importance, while individual man with all the complexities and perplexities of his cerebration counts for so much more: a statement which leads to the next topic.

(d)
INDIVIDUALISM

The *Ancient Mariner* speaks for its age in turning from social man to individual man and in caring for his inner motivation more than for his external activities. The two trends are not the same but they spring from such similar causes that it is hard to keep them apart.

For the novelty of this individualism contrast the *Ancient Mariner* with what Dryden makes of Anne Killigrew. Dryden praises her accomplishments with an extravagance which, taken at its face value, is ridiculous. But it is so ridiculous that we cannot possibly apply what he says, to one person. Inevitably our minds turn from the individual to the class of poets and thence to general ideas about poetry and painting; they come to rest on the social and on the political. Coleridge in his way is not less extravagant than Dryden, but with how different a result. *His* extravagances do correspond to what can take place in a human brain; they spring not from decorum but from a kind of truth. Even if they make a fascinating objective narrative, they do, in suggesting a psychological or even pathological reality, direct our attention to, or rather into, the individual mind.

The *Ancient Mariner* indeed illustrates wonderfully the psychological trend of thought which, beginning with Locke, grew powerful in the early nineteenth century, and has been a dominant thing in men's lives till the present day. Whether the death of Freud marks its decline remains for a later age to perceive.

Coleridge has put his psychology in terms of the religious idea of salvation, of sin and forgiveness. It happens that Henryson dealt with the same topic; and it is instructive to compare or contrast the two poets on this point. Cresseid, however pathetic a figure, behaves according to a formulated, classic set of rules. She falls into two classic sins; she is punished condignly; she repents; she is assured of salvation. The result is that even though her story is extremely moving it does not individualise the sufferer, rather it turns her into a version of the medieval Everyman. The Mariner, on the other hand, although given a greater semblance of acting by rules than most Romantic figures, behaves primarily according to the inner motions of the human heart. He blesses the water-snakes unaware; and how remote this *unaware* from the mathematical precision of medieval motivation. Again, the Mariner takes a journey; yet how different that journey from the pilgrimage governed by the precise moral geography of the medieval allegory. Between the medieval reliance on a religion whose rules were precisely laid down and the Mariner's heart-searching interposes a large change of ways of thought. Protestantism had put the weight on the individual act of faith as against the sufficient performance of duties. Puritanism by agonising over the act of faith had opened up strange byways in the human mind. And in the eighteenth century the scientific curiosity of Locke about the human brain and the spread of Puritan habits of thought through the Wesleys combined to effect a revolution. Not to speak of the self-communings of Rousseau. Bunyan's *Pilgrim's Progress* is a wonderfully apt work of transition. In form it is highly schematised and follows the old tradition of the medieval allegory; but in effect it expresses the Puritan exaltation of faith over works, and shadows not the keeping

A spring of love gushed from my heart, / And I blessed them unaware.

of a set of rules or the fulfilment of certain obligations but the inner struggle to be saved.

In finding that the **Ancient Mariner** typifies Romantic individualism I have brought up a very obvious and familiar topic: more so than any mentioned hitherto, through its being so close to us. But it is precisely the familiar things with which I am principally concerned, and though this additional familiarity suggests brevity it must not be allowed to impose silence. I will mention at least two sides of Romantic individualism, both implied by the **Ancient Mariner**.

First, with the stress on the individual mind, it was natural that the less obvious as well as the more obvious parts of the mind should be taken into account. When a man agonises over a decision and relies on his own natural powers of choice and not on a set of religious ordinances or social conventions he will find that he makes his decision for reasons he cannot fathom or analyse. As the Mariner blessed the water-snakes unaware, so he makes his decisions not by conscious weighing in a balance but intuitively. Along with the new preciseness and rigorous discipline of the scientific movement of the nineteenth century was a shift of emphasis from the conscious to the unconscious part of the mind, from the sophisticated to the primitive, from reasoned choices to intuition. It was a shift carried to extremes in D. H. Lawrence, for instance, for whom "politics, principles, right and wrong" are a "desert void" and who pronounces that "when it comes to living, we live through our instincts and our intuitions". Further illustration is superfluous.

Second, when choices are to be made not by a preordained set of rules but by individual preference, it becomes natural that such a choice should be more highly valued if it is new and surprising than if it is repetitive; for repetition might easily become a formula and a fixed criterion. Hence, in part, the nineteenth century cult of originality. How powerful this cult is we can see at once by the instinctive welcome we give the word. A headmaster, considering the testimonial of a would-be assistant, little as he would like a man to be odd, would emit approval if he read that the man had a vein of originality. Contrariwise to say of someone that he has no originality is an unmitigatedly adverse criticism. Such a state of affairs did not exist before the nineteenth century.

Thirdly, Romantic individualism with its interest in the composition of the human mind shows itself in the trend of literary criticism in the nineteenth century. From Wordsworth with his talk of the passions to Bradley with his analysis of motives, criticism has been predominantly psychological. Poetry for Sidney was the glimpse of a state of things better than the

actualities of life after the Fall of man allow, for Rymer an exhibition of decorum; for Wordsworth and the nineteenth century it is a rendering of individual human emotion.

Lastly, the Ancient Mariner represents a form of individualism characteristic of the Romantic period rather than of the rest of the nineteenth century. In their love of the individual the Romantics had a special fondness for a type so differentiated and original that he could not fit into ordinary human society. This type was so sensitive, or so wicked, and so obsessed by his own thoughts that he could not stay still but was driven on an unending pilgrimage. He forms a part of the true mythology of the Romantic age, and the Ancient Mariner is an eminent example of him. Shelley's Alastor is another example, and his self-description in *Adonais* perhaps the classic account of the type.

> Midst others of less note, came one frail
>   Form,
> A phantom among men; companionless
> As the last cloud of an expiring storm
> Whose thunder is its knell; he, as I guess,
> Had gazed on Nature's naked loveliness,
> Actaeon-like, and now he fled astray
> With feeble steps o'er the world's
>   wilderness,
> And his own thoughts, along that rugged
>   way,
> Pursued, like raging hounds, their father and
>   their prey.

The Byronic hero, though more of a man of action than Shelley's poet in *Alastor*, is clearly one of the type. Marmaduke, in Wordsworth's *Borderers,* turns at the end into the outcast and wanderer, unfit for human society:

>   A wanderer must I go . . .
> No human ear shall ever hear me speak;
> No human dwelling ever give me food,
> Or sleep, or rest: but over waste and wild,
> In search of nothing that this earth can
>   give,
> But expiation, will I wander on.

At his worst the self-propelled wanderer expressed a kind of snobbery of pessimism: only the inferior and insensitive find repose; the best people are like Io, driven round the world by the gadfly of remorse or of hypertrophied sensibilities. But Coleridge is exempt from the accusation of any such snobbery. Whatever his weaknesses his self-pity or the sanctimoniousness of his repentances, his desire to explore strange and frightening mental regions was genuine, as were his courage and persistence in maintaining the quest.

(e)

COMPLEXITY

I spoke above of the diversity of the *Ancient Mariner,* of the multiple layers of meaning, of the different uses to which nature is put. This diversity is the true index of the vast complication of life that occurred in the Romantic period. It was as if the data for living had suddenly been multiplied. Not only were people learning more about the human mind but about human history and about the physical world. The industrial revolution was yet another complication. The situation was all the more difficult because on the whole the eighteenth century had pretended that their own rather simpler world was much simpler than it actually was. There is no need to labour the predicament of the Romantics, for we have inherited it and many added burdens of knowledge. The *Ancient Mariner* is modern in quite a special way through expressing, however subtly, this terrifying complexity.

It was an irony that the urge to put the burden of choice on the individual should have occurred when the difficulties of choosing had been incalculably increased.

C. M. Bowra (essay date 1949)

SOURCE: *"The Ancient Mariner,"* in *The Romantic Imagination,* 1949. Reprint by Oxford University Press, 1961, pp. 51-75.

[*In the following essay, Bowra contends that* The Rime of the Ancient Mariner *"creates not a negative but a positive condition, a state of faith which is complete and satisfying because it is founded on realities in the living world and in the human heart."*]

When the first signs of the Romantic spirit appeared in the eighteenth century, the time-worn theme of the supernatural took a new character and received a new prominence. The fashionable cult of strangeness turned inevitably to this alluring world of the unknown and exploited it with a reckless carelessness. The result is that ghosts and goblins crowd the Romantic poetry of Germany, and in England the spate of "Gothick" novels spent its none too abundant resources in trying to make the flesh creep with death-pale spectres and clanking chains. The result, it must be admitted, is not very impressive. Instead of creating real horror and dread, this literature tends to be factitious and a little silly. It fails because it has not mastered the lessons of the past on how the supernatural should be treated. Instead of making it a subordinate element in a wider scheme, as Homer and Shakespeare do, the writers concentrate on it to the exclusion of almost everything else, and this over-emphasis spoils a subject which is effective only when it is taken in small doses. In the second place, they do not really believe in the super-

natural as the great writers of the past did. It is not an authentic chapter of human experience, but an indulgence, an exercise or ghoulish fancy, and therefore unconvincing and dull. When the Romantic movement came to maturity, this cult was already largely discredited. There are, it is true, traces of its influence in Shelley's love for charnel-houses, and it is not entirely absent from Keats' *Lamia,* but these are no more than legacies from a past generation. It meant nothing to Blake or to Wordsworth, for whom it was at once too unreal and too foolish. But with Coleridge it was different. It appealed to him with a special power and was responsible for his finest work.

In 1797, being then twenty-five years old, Coleridge suddenly found the full scope of his genius. The outburst of creation lasted for about two years and then began to fail, but not before he had written the first part of *Christabel, The Ancient Mariner,* and **"Kubla Khan."** He had already composed good poetry, and in the long years afterwards he was to compose it again. But in 1797 and 1798 he wrote three poems which no one else could have written and which he himself was never again to equal or approach. At this time something set all his powers to work and brought to the surface all the hidden resources of his conscious and unconscious self. The dreamer was able to give a concrete form to his dreams, the omnivorous reader to fuse the heterogeneous elements of his reading into magical combinations, and the critic to satisfy his own exacting ideas of what a poem ought to be. In his later years Coleridge too often wrote with only a part of himself and was unable to speak from his full experience or to use the whole range of his powers, but into the three great poems he put all that he had. Why this happened we cannot say. We can do no more than note that here was a young man who suddenly found a voice new and strange and indisputably his own. But we can at least say what was not responsible for this. It is wrong to connect the flowering of Coleridge's genius with the formation of the opium habit; for though he had begun to take opium, it was not yet a habit, and as yet he took it only at intervals to get rest and sleep. It certainly does not explain the prodigious outburst of energy needed to create his unique poems. On the other hand, it is possible that his new acquaintance with the Wordsworths helped to unloose his hidden strength. Coleridge was always a prey to doubts and afterthoughts and rambling speculations, but Wordsworth encouraged and sustained him and kept him to his task. And though Coleridge had a remarkable sensibility to physical nature, it is abundantly clear that this was enhanced by the quiet and delicate observation of Dorothy Wordsworth. Nevertheless, the genius was Coleridge's own, and, whatever set it to work, it is the genius that counts. Coleridge's supreme contribution to poetry was the three poems, and of all English Romantic masterpieces they are the most unusual and the most romantic.

All three poems are concerned with the supernatural. "Kubla Khan," it is true, is less directly concerned than *Christabel* or *The Ancient Mariner*, but into its wild magnificence the supernatural has found its way, whether in the "woman wailing for her demon-lover" and the "ancestral voices prophesying war," or in the magical music of its close when the poet seems to break the bounds of human kind and become a wild spirit of song. In *Christabel* the whole scheme is based on the supernatural. The evil spirit who haunts the body of Geraldine and tries to ruin the innocent happiness of Christabel is in the true tradition of vampires, and Coleridge infuses a mysterious dread into her. In her we see an embodiment of evil powers from another world and realize how helpless ordinary human beings are against them. It is the last, and indeed the only, triumph of the "Gothick" taste for the phantoms bred by darkness and fear, and it succeeds because Coleridge believes so much in his subject that he relates it to life and to living experience. Both "Kubla Khan" and *Christabel* are fragments, and we can only imagine what they might have been. *The Ancient Mariner* is complete. In it Coleridge did what he set out to do and showed what his powers could be. It too deals with the supernatural, on a large scale and in a generous sense. From what divers sources it came may be read in the pages of John Livingston Lowes' *The Road to Xanadu*, which shows the strange alchemical process of its creation. To that superb work of scholarship there is nothing to add. What we have to consider is not how *The Ancient Mariner* came into existence, but what it is and what it means.

Coleridge intended to introduce *The Ancient Mariner* with an essay on the supernatural. Like so many of his projects, this was never realized, and though Coleridge seems to have lectured on the subject in 1818, we do not know what he said or what his views were. Perhaps it is as well, since when Coleridge began to theorize on literary matters, he was apt to forget his own practice or at least to make it out to be more elaborate than it was. We have therefore to deduce his theory from his practice and to look at what he actually did. His first idea came from a Mr. John Cruikshank, who, according to Wordsworth, had a dream about "a person suffering from a dire curse for the commission of some crime" and "a skeleton ship with figures in it." Coleridge spoke of this to Wordsworth, who saw that it was a subject well suited to Coleridge's genius and would fit into the part allotted to him in the plan of the *Lyrical Ballads.* Wordsworth was to take the subjects "chosen from ordinary life," and Coleridge another class in which

> the incidents and agents were to be, in part at least, supernatural; and the excellence aimed at was to consist in the interesting of the affections by the dramatic truth of such emotions, as would naturally accompany such situations, supposing them real.

On a walk in the Quantock Hills on November 20th, 1797, the plan of *The Ancient Mariner* was formed. Wordsworth contributed not only one or two phrases but the part played by the albatross and the navigation of the ship by dead men. The rest is the work of Coleridge, and on March 23rd, 1798, he brought the finished text to the Wordsworths at Alfoxden.

In taking the supernatural for his province, Coleridge must at the start have had to face a certain degree of prejudice. The subject was outmoded in the view of good judges, and any attempt to revive it might be greeted with suspicion. On the surface, *The Ancient Mariner* belonged to a class of poetry which provoked adverse comment. Even Hazlitt, who regards it as Coleridge's "most remarkable performance," adds less kindly that "it is high German, however, and in it he seems to 'conceive of poetry but as a drunken dream, reckless, careless, and heedless, of past, present, and to come.'" Charles Lamb responded with greater sympathy, but he too had his doubts about the use of the supernatural and said: "I dislike all the miraculous part of it, but the feelings of the man under the operation of such scenery dragged me along like Tom Piper's magic whistle." Coleridge set himself a difficult task. To succeed in it he must do a great deal more than reproduce the familiar thrills of horrific literature: he must produce a poetry of the supernatural which should in its own way be as human and as compelling as Wordsworth's poetry of everyday things. Coleridge saw these difficulties and faced them courageously. Though his poem has a supernatural subject, its effect is much more than a thrill of horror. He lives up to his own program and interests the affections by the dramatic truth of what he tells.

The triumph of *The Ancient Mariner* is that it presents a series of incredible events through a method of narration which makes them not only convincing and exciting but in some sense a criticism of life. No other poet of the supernatural has quite done this, at least on such a scale and with such abundance of authentic poetry. In his conquest of the unknown, Coleridge went outside the commonplace thrills of horror. Of course, he evokes these, and his opening verses, in which the Mariner stays the Wedding-Guest, suggest that at first Coleridge followed familiar precedents in appealing to a kind of horrified fear. But as he worked at his poem, he widened its scope and created something much richer and more human. To be sure, he chose his subject well. The weird adventures of his Mariner take place not in the trite Gothic setting of a medieval castle, which Coleridge used once and for all in *Christabel*, but on a boundless sea with days of pitiless sun and soft nights lit by a moon and attendant stars. Nor are his "machining persons" of the same breed as his Geraldine. They are spirits of another sort, who may have their home in some Neo-Platonic heaven, but are transformed by Coleridge into powers who watch over the good and evil actions of men and requite them with appropriate rewards and punishments. The new setting and the new persons with which Coleridge shapes the supernatural give to it a new character. Instead of confining himself to an outworn dread of spectres and phantoms, he moves over a wide range of emotions and touches equally on guilt and remorse, suffering and relief, hate and forgiveness, grief and joy. Nor has his creation the misty dimness commonly associated with the supernatural. What he imagines is indeed weird, but he sees it with so sharp a vision that it lives vividly before our eyes. At each point he anticipates the objection that his is an outmoded kind of composition, and does the opposite of what his critics expect.

The first problem for any poet of the supernatural is to relate it to familiar experience. So long as it was accepted as part of the scheme of things, there was no great difficulty in this. No doubt Homer's audience accepted the ghost of Odysseus' mother because they believed in ghosts and saw that they must be like this and behave in this way. But Coleridge could not rely on his readers' feeling at home with his unfamiliar theme. He must relate it to something which they knew and understood, something which touched their hearts and imaginations, and he did this by exploiting some of the characteristics of dream. Here was something which would appeal to them and through which they could be led to appreciate the remoter mysteries which he keeps in reserve. No doubt Coleridge did this because his first impulse to *The Ancient Mariner* came from Mr. Cruikshank's dream, but, once he saw this, he made full use of it and shaped his poem in accordance with it. Dreams can have a curiously vivid quality which is often lacking in waking impressions. In them we have one experience at a time in a very concentrated form, and, since the critical self is not at work, the effect is more powerful and more haunting than most effects when we are awake. If we remember dreams at all, we remember them very clearly, even though by rational standards they are quite absurd and have no direct relation to our waking life. They have, too, a power of stirring elementary emotions, such as fear and desire, in a very direct way, though we do not at the time ask why this happens or understand it, but accept it without question as a fact. It is enough that the images of dreams are so penetrated with emotional significance that they make a single and absorbing impression. Coleridge was much attracted by their strange power. In *Christabel* he speaks of

> such perplexity of mind
> As dreams too lively leave behind,

and *The Ancient Mariner* bears the marks of such a liveliness. On the surface it shows many qualities of dream. It moves in abrupt stages, each of which has its own single, dominating character. Its visual im-

pressions are remarkably brilliant and absorbing. Its emotional impacts change rapidly, but always come with an unusual force, as if the poet were haunted and obsessed by them. When it is all over, it clings to the memory with a peculiar tenacity, just as on waking it is difficult at first to disentangle ordinary experience from influences which still survive from sleep.

In the criticism of *The Ancient Mariner* which Wordsworth added to the edition of *Lyrical Ballads* published in 1800, he complained that "the events, having no necessary connection, do not produce each other." Now no one expects the events of dream to have the kind of necessary connection which we find in waking life, and Wordsworth's criticism is beside the mark. Indeed, he is less than fair to Coleridge, who gives to the world of his poem its own coherence and rules and logic. Things move indeed in a mysterious way, but not without some connecting relations which may reasonably be called causal. When in a fit of irritation or anger the Mariner shoots the albatross, he commits a hideous crime and is punished by the doom of "life-in-death," which means that, after being haunted by the presence of his dead comrades, he carries a gnawing memory to the end of his days. His shipmates, too, are the victims of the same laws when they are doomed to death as accomplices in his crime for saying that he was right to kill the bird. In such a system it is no less appropriate that when the Mariner feels love gushing from his heart at the sight of the water-snakes, he begins to break the first horror of his spell, and the albatross falls from his neck. Once we accept the assumption that it is wrong to kill an albatross, the rest of the action follows with an inexorable fatality. It is true that this assumption is perhaps the hardest which *The Ancient Mariner* demands of us, but of that Wordsworth was in no position to complain, since it was he who suggested the idea to Coleridge.

This imaginary world has its own rules, which are different from ours and yet touch some familiar chord in us. Nor, when we read the poem, do we really question their validity. Indeed, they are more convincing than most events in dreams, and we somehow admit that in such a world as Coleridge creates it is right that things should happen as they do. It is not too difficult to accept for the moment the ancient belief that spirits watch over human actions, and, once we do this, we see that it is right for them to interfere with men and to do extraordinary things to them. Both the figures on the skeleton ship and the spirits who guide the Mariner on his northward voyage have sufficient reality for us to feel that their actions are appropriate to their characters and circumstances. Nor is it absurd that, when the ship at last comes home, it sinks; it has passed through adventures too unearthly for it to have a place in the world of common things. It and its stricken inmate bear the marks of their ordeal, and it is no wonder that the Pilot's boy goes mad at the sight or that the only person able to withstand their influence is the holy Hermit. Coleridge makes his events so coherent and so close to much that we know in ourselves that we accept them as valid in their own world, which is not ultimately very dissimilar from ours. Because it has this inner coherence, *The Ancient Mariner* is not a phantasmagoria of unconnected events but a coherent whole which, by exploiting our acquaintance with dreams, has its own causal relations between events and lives in its own right as something intelligible and satisfying.

Coleridge knew that he must make the supernatural convincing and human. In the *Biographia Literaria,* after saying that such poetry must interest the emotions and have dramatic truth, he adds that his aim is

> to transfer from our inward nature a human interest and a semblance of truth sufficient to procure for these shadows of imagination that willing suspension of disbelief for the moment, which constitutes poetic faith.

We may connect these words with what Coleridge said in 1818 in a lecture on dreams:

> In ordinary dreams we do not judge the objects to be real;—we simply do not determine that they are unreal.

It is clear that Coleridge felt about the creations of his imagination something similar to what he felt about dreams. He assumes that while we have them we do not question their reality. *The Ancient Mariner* lives in its own world as events in dreams do, and, when we read it, we do not normally ask if its subject is real or unreal. But this is due to a consummate art. Each action, and each situation, is presented in a concrete form in which the details are selected for their appeal to common experience. Coleridge exercises an imaginative realism. However unnatural his events may be, they are formed from natural elements, and for this reason we believe in them. We may even be at home with them because their constituents are familiar and make a direct, natural appeal. Once we have entered this imaginary world, we do not feel that it is beyond our comprehension, but respond to it as we would to actual life.

In other words, though Coleridge begins by appealing to our experience of dreams, he so uses it as to present something which is more solid and more reasonable and more human than the most haunting dreams. He uses the atmosphere of dreams to accustom us to his special world, and then he proceeds to create freely within his chosen limits. At each step he takes pains to see that his eery subject is real both for the eye and for the emotions, that it has both the attraction of visible things and the significance which belongs to

actions of grave import. His natural background for instance, could have been fashioned only by a man who had learned about nature from loving observation and shared the Wordsworths' devotion to it. Amid all these strange happenings nature remains itself, and its perseverance in its own ways sometimes comes in ironical contrast to what happens on the ship, as when, at the moment when the Mariner is haunted by the look in his dead comrades' eyes, the moon continues her quiet, unchanging course:

> The moving Moon went up the sky,
> And no where did abide:
> Softly she was going up,
> And a star or two beside.

Even when nature breaks into more violent moods, it is still itself, and each touch of description makes it more real, as when Coleridge sketches a storm with something of Turner's delight in wild effects of sky and cloud:

> The upper air burst into life!
> And a hundred fire-flags sheen,
> To and fro they were hurried about!
> And to and fro, and in and out,
> The wan stars danced between.

In such scenes there is no indeterminacy of dream. Each detail comes from the known world and gives a firm background to the supernatural events which accompany it.

This realistic treatment of the setting is matched by the appeal which Coleridge makes to our emotions in handling his human persons. The Mariner and his comrades are hardly characters in any dramatic sense. They lack lineaments and personality. But perhaps this is well, since what touches us in them is the basic humanity of their sufferings. They are more types than differentiated human beings, and for this reason their agonies are simply and universally human. We feel that what happens to them might in similar circumstances happen to anyone, and we respond readily to their pathos and their misery. And these Coleridge conveys with a masterly directness. He portrays the helpless agony of thirst in the crew becalmed at sea:

> And every tongue, through utter drought,
> Was withered at the root;
> We could not speak, no more than if
> We had been choked with soot.

When at last the rain comes, and the Mariner's thirst is slaked as he sleeps, Coleridge makes no less an appeal to elementary human and physical feelings, as with a striking economy of words he shows how this happens and what a wonderful relief it is:

My lips were wet, my throat was cold,
My garments all were dank;
Sure I had drunken in my dreams,
And still my body drank.

Of course, physical sensations play a large part in dreams, but Coleridge describes them as we know them in a waking state, and the lively way in which he handles them creates a powerful emotional effect.

What is true of physical sensations in *The Ancient Mariner* is no less true of mental states. The Mariner passes through an ordeal so weird and so fearful that it might seem impossible to make it real for us. We shrink from asking what such suffering means in conditions so unfamiliar and so hideous as those in the poem. To rise to such an occasion and to give a persuasive and moving account of what the Mariner endures demands a powerful effort of the imagination. Coleridge rises to the full claim of his subject and by concentrating on elementary human emotions makes the most of them. His Mariner is indeed in a fearful plight, alone on a ship, surrounded by the dead bodies of his comrades, and Coleridge conveys the full implications of his state by drawing attention to his sense of utter helplessness and solitude:

Alone, alone, all, all alone,
Alone on a wide wide sea!
And never a saint took pity on
My soul in agony.

That is the authentic anguish of a man who feels himself abandoned both by God and man and faced with the emptiness of his guilty and tormented soul. Conversely, when the ship at last comes to land, the Mariner sees angels standing by the dead bodies and feels an infinite relief. The very silence of the celestial presences fills him with hope and joy:

This seraph-band, each waved his hand,
No voice did they impart—
No voice; but oh! the silence sank
Like music on my heart.

Coleridge understood the extremes of despair and of joy, and he distilled them into these brief moments. Because his poem moves between such extremes it has a certain spaciousness and grandeur and reflects through its variations the light and the shadow of human life.

Coleridge expects us to suppose that his situations are real, and to have some kind of human feelings about them. This is no doubt easy enough when they belong to ordinary experience, but when the supernatural takes command it demands a more unusual art. Then Coleridge makes it look as natural as possible because, however strange it may be, he forms it from elements which are in themselves familiar. The paradoxical nature of the Mariner's voyage from England to the Southern Pacific, from the known to the unknown, from the familiar to the impossible, is conveyed in a verse which begins with something delightfully friendly and then, without ado, breaks into an uncharted, spellbound world:

The fair breeze blew, the white foam flew,
The furrow followed free;
We were the first that ever burst
Into that silent sea.

There is perhaps nothing fundamentally strange in the silence of this sea, and yet after the bustle of the waves and the wind it comes with a magical surprise. When dreadful and unnatural things happen, the same art shows how they would look and what impression they would make. When the albatross first begins to be avenged, the sea changes its appearance, and horrible things are seen on it:

The very deep did rot: O Christ!
That ever this should be!
Yea, slimy things did crawl with legs
Upon the slimy sea.

Though this is seen by a man in the last agonies of thirst and has some qualities of delirious hallucination, it is poignantly real. It has the right degree of exactness for such an occasion, and it is well that the "slimy things" are not described more precisely. But when exactness is needed, Coleridge uses it with a masterly economy. When the dead men stir and begin to do again in death what they used to do in life, Coleridge epitomizes the weird situation in one highly significant action:

The body of my brother's son
Stood by me, knee to knee:
The body and I pulled at one rope,
But he said nought to me.

No more is needed than these very simple words. The habitual, perfunctory action, now conducted by a dead man and a living man together, has an extraordinary horror.

Coleridge's realism is of course much more than an art of circumstantial details. It is a special form of poetry, the reflection of his love for the sensible world and his sensitiveness to its lights and shades and colours and sounds. He possessed to a high degree that cardinal quality of poetry which he calls "the power of exciting the sympathy of the reader by a faithful adherence to the truth of nature." And he has more than "faithful adherence." He is by no means photographic or merely descriptive. His eye for nature is for its more subtle charms and less obvious appeals. In his

[*In the following essay, Boulger interprets* The Rime of the Ancient Mariner *as a reaffirmation of faith in a natural order despite apparent chaos.*]

For many years the essay of Robert Penn Warren on *The Rime of the Ancient Mariner* [i.e., "The Rime of the Ancient Mariner: a poem of pure imagination" (1946)] held wide acceptance. Warren pointed out that the two major functions of the poem were the creation of a sacramental universe by means of creative imagination and the operation within this universe of the Christian pattern of Fall and Redemption. The nature of both functions was inferred partially from outside sources, *Biographia Literaria,* **"The Friend,"** and **"Aids to Reflection,"** but also in the action of the poem itself there existed evidence for a certain kind of Imagination and for a Will which falls in a spontaneous uninitiated act. Some few inconsistencies in detail were pointed out in later criticism of Warren's analysis, but hardly enough to remove the impression that the reading was consistent, convincing and meaningful. Reopening the case seemed hardly justified. The appearance of Elliot B. Gose's essay "Coleridge and the Luminous Gloom," which, by inversion of Warren's view of the Sun:Moon symbolism, reads like a parody of Warren's essay while doing violent injustice to the poem, seemed to suggest that the case had been well enough left alone.

Edward Bostetter has recently presented a view of *The Rime of the Ancient Mariner* entirely at odds with Warren's, and not on the trivial grounds and outside sources of Gose's essay. Disregarding the evidence in outside sources pertaining to Coleridge's characteristic feelings and values attached to the moon or sun, which all critics now must allow cuts both ways, Bostetter asserts that the Fall-Redemption pattern does not hold in the poem, and with its dismissal also disappears any notion of an active vision of creative imagination sustaining a sacramental view of the Universe. Instead Bostetter sees a nightmare world of inconsequence, illogic, terror and meaningless suffering. *The Rime of the Ancient Mariner* is a voyage into the irrational, flinging terror at the real world, and not an imaginative order confirming the values of the real world.

I should like to say something in favor of Warren's overall position against that of Bostetter. It will not be a defense of the moral or symbolic minutiae of Warren's thought, which time has proven wrong, but only of the view that the Mariner's world is ultimately a religious one, as against the nightmare world insisted upon by Bostetter. It is a far different religious world than that suggested by the idea of a sacramental universe. Warren arrived at this latter view by using the process of the understanding (critical analysis) to explain the process of imagination and vision. The notion that the Mariner's world is a dream world, a world of the active imagination, is not taken seriously enough by Warren or Bostetter: one supplies us with a Christian gloss provided mainly by Coleridge's prose, the other with a gloss made up of notions taken from extreme Calvinism (as Bostetter understands it) and from Freudian doctrine. In order to take Coleridge's idea of the primary imagination seriously as the ground of the action and process of the poem, one must consider the mode of action that occurs in dreams, since *The Rime of the Ancient Mariner* is a dream vision. The soundest starting point for this view is in the now somewhat neglected seminal source for study of the poem, the final chapter of Lowes's *Road to Xanadu,* entitled "Imagination Creatrix." If Lowes's final position seems too scientifically detached today, a case history free of dogma and content, it at least is free of specific error. His hint was simply that the world of the primary imagination in the poem can be seen by analogy as having a good deal in common with what we know of dreams.

But a dream world as poem must have specific shape and source and inspiration, for which Lowes has supplied the most abundant evidence. From this evidence only a small amount will be drawn upon, by no means new; but not, thus far, considered of major importance in defining the dream quality of the poem. This is the relationship of certain passages in the sea world of the *Mariner* to ones of similar scope in various early books of the *Aeneid.* The similarities, but not the importance, were recognized by accomplished scholars like Lowes, who no doubt considered such schoolboy reminiscences in this connection inevitable. Source discussion has centered on more obscure yet more specific analogues, Purchas for instance. Two literary connections of *The Rime of the Ancient Mariner* with the *Aeneid* make the *Aeneid* important as a source.

The first is the biographical one, revealed in the *Notebooks,* that Coleridge was reading the *Aeneid* afresh in 1795, '96, '97. This reading helped shape the nature of Imagination in *The Rime of the Ancient Mariner,* and its echoes in the poem are not meaningless reminiscence. More important are the qualities Coleridge would find in the *Aeneid,* not noticed by the scholars of the early twentieth century. Coleridge's age, or at least the persons like Coleridge in it, could read epic poetry at a level hardly reached again until recent times. Witness this quotation from *Notebooks* on Milton, which surely would have startled F. R. Leavis or the early Eliot:

> A Reader of Milton must be always on his Duty: he is surrounded with sense; it rises in every line; every word is to the purpose. There are no lazy intervals: all has been considered and demands & merits observation.

If this be called obscurity, let it be remembered tis such a one as is complacent to the Reader: not that vicious obscurity, which proceeds from a muddled head &&.

One may assume, *datis dandis,* that he would notice the qualities in the *Aeneid,* especially in the books depicting the sea, which contemporary critics are again pointing out: the dreamlike quality of Virgil's vision of action, as opposed to Homer's dramatic sense, the pictorial quality of his scenes, the way in which elegy overtakes epic in places, along with a sense of detachment in the character of the main narrator, Aeneas himself, making his listeners attentive, as in the line (II, 1) *Conticuere omnes intentique ora tenebant.* The command, respect, and spellbinding quality of the respective narrators is the most obvious case in point. But there are also more subtle borrowings.

The few direct borrowings of Coleridge from the *Aeneid* were pointed out by Lowes. *Aeneid* (III, 193) *caelum undique et undique pontus,* became

"For the sky and the sea, and the sea and the sky" (250).

Aeneid (V 140-41, 150)

ferit aethera clamor
nauticus
pulsati colles clamore resultant

appears in Coleridge as

And all was still, save that the hill
Was telling of the sound (558-9).

It is not these exact analogies that are of primary importance for our purposes, although they prove a necessary point, the fact of an exact connection between the two poems. It is the dreamlike, elegiac, detached quality of Virgil's sea world which influences in an all-pervasive spirit the Mariner's voyage of the mind, which is constructed in dream-logic sequences. This vividly alive, though detached world, allows for the active presence of winds and spirits, although Coleridge also had other sources for an animated world. In Virgil, as opposed to some of these later sources, there is no strain on credulity in accepting an active, animated universe. Amid the terrors and malignancy of the elements and the sea in Books I and III of *Aeneid,* as a part of the misfortune and seeming illogicality of certain events as seen by the participants, there remains a deeply religious sense of destiny in the hero, and an almost divine sense of benignity in the elements themselves. This sense carries over into **The Rime of the Ancient Mariner**, although Coleridge's method of achieving it must be different from Virgil's. The Mariner's world is religious for the

reader, who is given the role of omniscient outsider played in the *Aeneid* by Virgil himself. The moral and intellectual confusions of the Mariner, the seeming incongruity and irrationality of his world, correspond to the view of the sea and circumstance taken by Aeneas and his tribe as they act out the destined sea scenes. But Aeneas' destiny is clear to the narrator and to the reader, while the Mariner's never becomes clear to him, and is clear in the overall structure only in a peculiar way intended by Coleridge. Both narrators of the events that have happened to them have a keen sense that the sea world is a dream world of illusion, as in the lines "a painted ship upon a painted ocean" (117-18), or *Aeneid* (III, 72) *provehimur portu terraeque urbesque recedunt.* There is an arbitrary givenness and sense of illusion about both sea worlds and about the predicaments of the narrators expressed in many ways in both poems. Coleridge's "It is an Ancient Mariner," "There was a ship," relate to Virgil's (I, 12) *Urbs antiqua fuit* and (I, 31-2) *multosque per annos errabant acti fatis maria omnia circum.* Although the ultimate benignity of Fate is asserted by both poets, the sense of fate and the acts of terror common to both poems may well seem malign to the modern reader as they pass before his eyes in a series of inscrutable acts. In both poems the narrator-subject is brought finally to an act of vision which allows him to see the ultimate positive vision of the author's world, but this final turn is arbitrary in both poems in the sense that no amount of reading in Coleridge's prose for meanings attached to Sun:Moon symbolism, or in the background of Virgil's Roman religion, is going to provide logical or theological proof of the vision. Virgil's vision is more assured than is Coleridge's, but in each case the validity of the vision is finally sanctioned only by the power of the poems themselves. This essay will not presume to analyze the methods of the Latin poet, but in Coleridge's poem it seems that the motion of the dream world itself, the special logic of the state of primary imagination, is what carries the poem along to its successful conclusion, and at the same time suggests the content of that conclusion, which in Virgil is given more directly as a fiat of fate working in the service of Roman destiny.

Dream is not nightmare, nor is it sacramental vision. Each is too easy and doctrinaire a solution to the meaning of the poem. At bottom there is mystery about **The Rime of the Ancient Mariner**, not found in *Aeneid,* or for that matter in any previous English poem. It is the mystery of dealing with a series of effects having intelligible and satisfactory shape whose causes remain unknown. Virgil could provide in a frame the pseudo-rational formulae within which occur arbitrary, illusory, and terrifying events, the causes of which remain unknown to the narrator. Aeneas' piety and belief carry him through to vision. **The Rime of the Ancient Mariner** plunges into an arbitrary framework which is incomprehensible to the narrator-Mariner and to us. He acts out an ultimately successful pattern of action which exacts a toll in experience and suffering. In *Aeneid,* and *Paradise Lost* for that matter, there is religious mystery aplenty, but not ultimate religious mystery. The authors have their reasons and explanations for what has occurred, which the reader may or may not accept. Coleridge's poem is the first modern religious poem in the sense that it asserts a mysterious religious universe but cannot give us even partial explanations of its nature. Like Blake, he had seen through the Age of Reason, but his response was of a different order.

Earlier commentators on the poem, especially Gingerich, noting Coleridge's obsession with Necessitarianism in his 1795-98 letters, tried to work out a scheme for *The Rime of the Ancient Mariner* on a necessitarian rationale. This provided an easy but erroneous explanation, ignoring both the intensity of Coleridge's religious mentality, and the subtlety of his mind as a philosopher. Coleridge's insight into the conclusions of Necessitarianism, whether of the religious or the scientific variety, was essentially that of Isaac Newton and Jonathan Edwards, namely, that necessitarianism explained nothing in the ultimate sense. It presents us with a series of related effects, ordered within themselves, the causes of which remain unknown, and the ultimate cause unknowable, in other words Kantianism by a different route (one Coleridge was also traveling at that time). As Perry Miller puts it, the Universe, whether or not God is postulated as Ultimate, is inscrutable:

> When we get behind the brilliant façade of Newtonianism, the apparently rational system, of which poets sang and which Cotton Mather embraced, we are brought more terribly face to face with the dark forces of nature than any Puritan has been while staring into the dazzling glare of pre-destination. . . . Behind the mathematical analysis . . . concealed so carefully that only the most astute might catch a glimpse of it, moved a power that could not be seen by reason's light or dispelled by science, that hid itself in matter to hold the atoms in cohesion. . . . Edwards took it [Newton's theory] to mean that cause in the realm of mechanism is merely a sequence of phenomena, with the inner connection of cause and effect still mysterious and terrifying. . . . for him the secret of nature was no longer that an efficient cause of itself works such and such an effect, but is to be defined as "that after or upon the existence of which, or the existence of it after such manner, the existence of another thing follows." All effects, therefore, have their causes, but no effect is a "result of what has gone before it."

We may take it that Coleridge was as astute in these matters as Edwards, and that his greatest response to the situation was the dream world of *The Rime of the Ancient Mariner*. His **Opus Maximum** and late **Note-books** give us other responses, those of the systematic philosopher working out of the language of Kant.

Let us see how the above assumptions work out in a rough analysis of the structure of the poem. We now assume that the cluster of moon symbols does not consistently represent the workings of imagination, nor the sun symbols the discursive reason (Coleridge's prose understanding) together with a form of alienation, but that Imagination and understanding are present in the poem in more arbitrary ways. The epistemology of the act of cognition in the poem is quite different from our everyday mode of perceiving the world, or of our usual way of reading poems, which is to give them balance and rationality. Coleridge's conceptions of the Imagination as a participation in the great I Am (and of the Understanding used alone as the faculty which partakes of death) are to be taken quite seriously as the shaping force of the poem. Its nearest contemporary prose analogue is the philosophical system of symbolic form developed by Ernst Cassirer, which holds that philosophy can only describe phenomena and must give up the attempt to understand causality of things, but neither this system nor Coleridge's own descriptions of primary imagination in early nineteenth-century philosophical terms can be our primary guide. It is better to notice how things work out in the poem itself. For instance, understanding and syllogistic logic will be inferior categories to the higher level of imaginative perception in the action of the poem, without either being explained fully. The sailors use syllogistic logic and cause and effect in the ordinary way to calculate the morality of shooting the albatross, and of course the calculations fail, because the poem deals with effects whose causes are spiritual but unknown. Ordinary reason and dualistic cosmology are clearly inoperative in the poem, intuition has higher place than discursive reason, and a sense of the world as continuum or flux is clearly stronger than our ordinary view of a dualistic world of sense perception. But to know that the intuition in the poem corresponds to the mystical "eye of reason" of Coleridge's prose does not in any way lessen the mystery of the great imaginative intuitive act, the blessing of the water snakes by the Mariner. We see the hierarchy of categories, but have no easy prose definition to explain the nature of the categories. Perhaps as Lowes said, our memories of dreams, that state in which the senses and the conscious space-time restrictions inculcated by the reasoning process weakens, allowing (if Cassirer's view has any validity) the pre-conscious state of pure imagination in us all to reassert itself, are the only sound analogy to the pre-rational sense of the world of *The Rime of the Ancient Mariner*.

The Rime of the Ancient Mariner, then, as a world of pure imagination, will have the logic of a dream, in so far as we can understand such logic. It is not an irrational world, as Bostetter claims, nor a sacramental

Nor shapes of men nor beasts we ken— / The ice was all between.

vision which implies some orderly rational way of looking at reality religiously. Nor do we have to assume any specific content or archetypal patterns *a priori* in the Mariner's world, as did Maud Bodkin in her study of the poem. It is only the form, logic, and movement of the dream that is important, for that is what Coleridge saw as giving the nearest sense of immediacy to the religious and philosophical concerns much on his mind at the time of writing the poem. By postulating the imaginative process itself as the mode of analysis here, we may perhaps understand, but not rationalize away, the general meaning of the poem. The poet wants us to play the part of the wedding guest, to be drawn into the poem unwillingly, to resist with the understanding, and finally to share his epistemological and perhaps also, for the readers who still can do so, his religious anxieties.

The difference between the outside logical world and that of the poem is brought out sharply in the first stanza, where there is a conflict between the actual order and the dream world. The wedding, its festivities, and the anxiety of the Wedding Guest all fall within the ordinary world of sense and logic. The Wedding Guest is a reasonable man, so he thinks, he wants reasons for things, but the Mariner has none to give. He also wants to participate in a function of the actual order, while the Mariner has only his dream to offer, "There was a ship." The arbitrary *givenness* of both the Mariner and his adventure has been noted above in connection with Virgil. For a short while the two worlds compete, with the orderly rational world of conventional bride and wedding gaiety gradually giving way to the phantom ship, its sudden voyage, and the living sun and moon. The Mariner's glittering eye, which might be called the eye of the higher reason which surpasses understanding, transforms the Guest until the noise and conviviality of the actual world with its logic and causality are replaced by the living world of primary imagination, by the silent white seas of the pre-rational pure imagination, in which the Mariner's voyage took place. The Wedding Guest was agonized, "I fear thee Ancient Mariner," as his world slipped out from under him.

In this world of Imagination two things are immediately noticeable: the participation of all reality, living and non-living, real and spiritual, in one organic whole assumed by the author but not necessarily perceived by the participants; and the unending series of shifts between subject and object in the phenomena of the imaginative world. The Storm Blast, the mist and snow, and the Albatross are accepted without explanation by victims and readers. Normally real objects, like the sea, are not presented in descriptions which impart the qualities of actual things as we have experienced them. Everything is alive, there are no fixities and definites in this universe. At one point the Mariner is not entirely certain of his own identity (305-8). The ordinary

ideas of causality and reason in this process are not operating, for whatever happens can be immediately accepted as a part of the unified whole perceived in a phenomenological way. Hence the killing of the bird as a gratuitous act of the will without causality is a very proper act to show the unexplainable failure in the Mariner's imaginative process to hold together all experience, and is the only proper way on this level to indicate the tension of pure imagination and rationalism. His Fall, and his Redemption, are basically psychological acts, whose ultimate cause, like that of the Universe itself, is inscrutable. For instance, before his Fall and after his Redemption the movement of winds, appearances of the sun and moon, the Polar Spirit, and the unifications between spirit and matter are accepted by the Mariner as modes of the imaginative whole which do not need explaining and cannot be explained rationally. When he does not rely upon logic to find out relationships and occurrences the answers are given to him according to the imaginative mode, that is, by spontaneous completion of related images as in dreams. He uses the ordinary modes of knowing during the time of his Fall only, to make mistakes in calculation, and to distinguish the "slimy" things of nature from himself. The alien world around him was of his own making. With the spontaneous act of blessing, as an uncaused and non-logical act, his imaginative power was restored. He simply accepted the water-snakes as a fact of experience, a mode of reality identified in some way with himself. At that point the Polar Spirit and other Spirits which had seemed malevolent were again viewed as they really were, and the continuum of all things existed again. The Sun and the Moon are important, but not overridingly so, as elements in this continuum. Everything again becomes a series of related effects, benign in appearance, whose causes remain unknown and now are wisely unsought.

After the imaginative synthesis has taken place, the Mariner no longer asks the wrong questions, but rather acts out his assigned role. Twentieth-century critics ask these wrong questions, reading the poem in the spirit of logicians. It does not really matter on the return voyage whether the Polar Spirit or the wind moved the ship, or whether the Sun-Moon patterns reoccur with systematic consistency. Critical preoccupation with such problems misses the point of the process itself. Such readings of the poem are not so far in spirit from the older moralistic ones, which made the poem appear as mere pother over a bird, in the sense that it applies too literal a significance to the phenomena, just as the early readers applied it to the moral action. Our view of the poem holds the Mariner's narration to be a vast dream-parable, understood partially by author and reader but not by Mariner or Wedding Guest. The Mariner's transgression, by gratuitous act of his Will, of the unity of the cosmos is a necessary failing common to us all, which is why he can speak to us; but the author speaks also of a world we can envision (and he as poet can create) but not return to or live in. The poetic logic of the world of ice and Albatross should not be entirely conformable to rationalistic analysis *a posteriori*. The analogy to our dream state where the primary imagination is again partially in control of our minds is the only entrance to the world of sudden, unmotivated succession of images which appear in the action of *The Rime of the Ancient Mariner*. The dream-state acts as an existential parable for the proposition that our "real" world is appearance, and the world of imagination and process "reality." This is naturally disturbing to rationalistic critics, as it was to Coleridge himself, no mean rationalist in certain moods.

Essentially then, one man, from the world of his dreams and poetic experiences, tells another, of ordinary understanding and pursuits, about his vision of the world and how it came upon him. The entire narration takes place in a dimension quite removed from the sensory and logically perceivable world of the listener, the reader, or of much poetry, for that matter. Space permits the mention of only a few details in the poem to prove this point. The world is like a painted ship upon a painted ocean. The ideal world of memory, dream and imagination has a correspondence in Virgil's verbal pictures, and in the art of painting itself. The voyages to and from the Pole take place with dreamworld vagueness and speed. All the normal distinctions in the real order, between living and non-living, natural, preternatural and supernatural, subject and object, are dissolved in this fusion and unity of the imaginative whole whose inner cause of unity is unknown. The dissolving and fusing processes in the poem are truly dreamlike, for the colors of objects, such as the red in the ocean and the shining white of the water snakes, are clearer to the percipients than the forms of the objects themselves. The objects as things are shimmery, dim, and unsubstantial. It is a world of effects interrelated in an acceptable way, but without "cause" and "substance" in the rationalistic sense, a world with antecedents in the science of Newton, the theology of Edwards, and the poetry of Virgil. The Mariner's trance, the merging of the Albatross and the Cross, and the identification of the Spirits with the sailors' bodies are a few more examples of the breakdown of ordinary reality, which reveals itself to us as contiguity and disparity of objects in the world. In the full realization of this imaginative vision, which is not without its terrors, and with the unexplainable breeze of the One Life upon him, the Mariner shouted,

> O let me be awake, my God!
> Or let me sleep alway (470-71).

In this reading of the poem the return to harbor and to land at the end is perhaps the most shocking and difficult part to accept. Yet Coleridge manages to bring it off successfully. It is no surprise that the ship, the

bodies, and all the spirits disappear on the approach of the normal order again. The Mariner's desire for ordinary Christian absolution can be understood as a reassertion of the laws of logical thinking and causality in his mind. His redemption *has* taken place in the world of symbolic action, but does not have status on land. The basic problem in this part of the poem is the possibility of successful confrontation of the Dream world with actuality. In a ghost story of the usual variety, where things are not to be taken too seriously, such as Burns's "Tam O'Shanter," one object is usually brought back to the ordinary world as a sign of "proof" that the spirit-world existed. In this poem it is the Mariner himself who is the living proof of a more serious and deeper moral order than ours, and this fact is outrageous to the normal rationalistic sensibility. The ending is supposed to leave the author, reader and Wedding Guest believing that the Mariner's voyage was a real one into the seas of the Imagination and that his haunting vision and intuitive knowledge are more valid and powerful than our everyday world. Because the world of vision does not adjust to the world of sense and understanding, either overwhelming it or frightening it away, critical rationalism must ignore this poem as an opium dream or tidy it up into being something other than it is. The life of the imagination extracts its toll, not only upon the Mariner and Wedding Guest, but upon the reader who learns that his own life, even in its most convivial and substantial forms, is a kind of alienation from deepest reality, and that the rational order of cause-effect and substance is merely a humanistic drop in an ocean of the unknown forces and causes that Newton, Edwards and Coleridge had come to intuit. The Mariner's revelations, taken seriously, are a poison cup from which one never fully recovers again into normal perception. He assaults the sensibilities of the outside world, while at the same time suffering the penance of being forced again to live in the life-in-death world of the understanding and sense realism. He is a parable of the creative poet, of course, working in the modern rationalistic world, but he is not *maudit,* but rather a necessarily suffering being, unless one is willing to grant that all creativity is an aberration.

Coleridge as poet was one of the first, with Blake, to envision this world of interrelated effects and of moral action unsupported by causes or a clear Divine cosmology. Like Blake, he did not like what he saw, but unlike him, he did not regard it as liberating the Imagination for a new humanism. As I said earlier, you might look upon the structure of *The Rime of the Ancient Mariner* as an *Aeneid* without the author's voice and epic framework to make the unknown and terrible orderly and rational. Coleridge plunges himself, his Mariner, and his readers into a seemingly arbitrary world of effects without causes, and of accidents (appearances) without substances, presented dramatically as Storms, hidden malignancy, human evils; yet finally he manages to suggest some arational, incredibly deep faith in the nature of things, analogous to that of the stumbling yet pious Aeneas. Later in life, Coleridge was to find another analogy to this condition in the post-Kantian phase of Christian philosophy and theology, which confronts a rational pious Will against a skeptical, unknowable universe. He could never bring himself to publish his speculations on this subject, and, indeed, leaves the most daring of them in Greek or Latin. Yet these speculations would provide a better gloss to the poem's meaning than the archly pious and disingenuous one he gave, which has misled commentators in various ways. Coleridge's excuse, also holding for Newton's speculations, which remain unpublished to this day, was that he was afraid of his own vision, or at least of a part of it. The world of *The Rime of the Ancient Mariner* is neither a sacramental universe nor a nightmare vision, but a parable of the uneasy Christian skepticism that has been with us since Newton and Kant.

A. E. Dyson and Julian Lovelock (essay date 1976)

SOURCE: "Uncertain Hour: The Ancient Mariner's Destiny," in *Masterful Images: English Poetry from Metaphysicals to Romantics,* Barnes & Noble Books, 1976, pp. 175-92.

[*In the following essay, Dyson and Lovelock explore the moral and epistemological questions evoked by* The Rime of the Ancient Mariner.]

> It is an ancient Mariner,
> And he stoppeth one of three.
> 'By thy long grey beard and glittering eye,
> Now wherefore stop'st thou me?'

'It is' . . . Coleridge's poem starts from the present tense, active, and, as it turns out, irresistible; the tense of absorbed narrative and compulsive confession. It is as if the whole poem is here in embryo: narrative vividness, fixed and immediate; human encounter, intense yet trancelike; questions, asked in terror or nightmare, needing answers but getting none, for whatever 'answer' there is comes obliquely. It is as if the story comes loose from time, gravitating towards that somehow eternal quality which haunts all its parts—the dramatic violence of sudden storms and appearances, sudden actions. 'By thy long grey beard and glittering eye'—strange invocation, as if feared and hypnotic qualities could be somehow besought! From the start, there is curious double vision; everything is fated and necessary, everything startling and dreadful. Whether 'it is' an ancient Mariner, or an albatross, or a ship of death or a hermit, we encounter the object and it encounters us as in a dream. Everything seems perfectly alive, perfectly unexplained, perfectly inescap-

able, terribly intense. The poem is full of elementals. Its setting, perhaps the only one possible, is the sea. Its images are calm and storm, sun and moon, life and death; its values are loyalty and betrayal, fear and hope, guilt and deliverance. Everything is extravagant—the extreme case, the ultimate possible image:

> With throats unslaked, with black lips
>   baked,
> We could not laugh nor wail;
> Through utter drought all dumb we stood!
> I bit my arm, I sucked the blood,
> And cried, A sail! a sail!

Is such poetry allegory? Certainly not, in any systematic fashion. Yet it is full of ideas. Is it a dream? Art so highly wrought must originate chiefly in the waking consciousness, radically heightened; yet it has the feel of a dream. Perhaps our best word for it is 'fantasy'—a form of literature which creates a world with its own rules and laws, depending wholly on inner consistency, yet which, at its best, continually draws strength from the 'real' world of human psychology, human intuition and spirituality, and continually feeds its own insights back into that world.

In terms of immediate influence, of course, Coleridge is directly indebted to the ballad form, which had been revived, along with much general feeling for the 'medieval', in the mid-eighteenth century, and which became a highly stylised and consciously 'literary' cult among many later romantics. The ballad is one of the most elemental and powerful forms of poetry. Like its near neighbour, the nursery rhyme, it is strongly rhythmic in form, basic and often brutal in theme, austere in diction, stark and archetypal in imagery, hypnotically repetitive in effect. Its total experience is caught up often in a refrain—some burden, grim or gay, returning with insistence, with precision, with mounting and complex irony, to intensify primitive feelings. For these reasons, the ballad is adapted to that kind of strong narrative line which demonstrates, rather than describes, human hopes, fears and sufferings, approximating to ritual re-enactment in its effect. Most of the best ballads have openings very similar to *The Ancient Mariner* in their power to arrest attention, to sketch in a situation that bypasses particulars such as names, places, dates, by drawing very immediately on the reader's own intensities:

> The twelve-month and a day being up,
> The dead began to speak:
> 'O who sits weeping on my grave,
> And will not let me sleep?

Such poetry stimulates personal echoes, personal resonances, much as the symbolists later consciously set out to do.

He was a brew gallant,
And he rid' by the ring;
And the Bonny Earl of Murray,
O he might have been a king.

Again, such poetry moves us beyond discussion and argument, as Coleridge believed creative imagination always should. In Coleridge's own categories *The Ancient Mariner* is poetry of 'Imagination', not of 'fancy'; of 'Reason', not of 'understanding'. Perhaps the function of great art is, nearly always, to probe beyond those arguments and reasonings which continually, and rightly, attend man's attempt to make sense of himself, seeking to initiate us rather, intuitively and directly, into psychic and spiritual realities of evil and good. We recognise such an achievement in Sophocles and Euripides, Shakespeare and Milton, Dickens and Dostoievsky, indeed in most literature and drama of high excellence. At a purely speculative level, we will wonder why Iago acts so (as he does himself), we will ponder Oedipus and Satan, Tulkinghorn and Raskolnikov, searching for clues. But, while motives are baffling, the truth is self-evident; no one can doubt the realism of their sufferings and deeds.

Coleridge recognised 'imagination' as the realm of revelation through recreation, the realm where beauty and goodness, and their mighty opposites, are known. Philosophers might then discuss the phenomena almost indefinitely (might so bemuse themselves, as often happens, that they become lost in words, and forget the experiences to which their words strive). But the artist, like the saint or the sinner, offers an image: a particular and tangible embodiment of complex truth. You can no more doubt Lady Macbeth, or Joe Gargery, than you can doubt Hitler, or Mother Teresa; you can no more hope to 'explain' the fictions, analytically and definitively, than you can the historical men. Coleridge recognised this great realm of 'reality' as the artist's province, just as, in his role of philosopher, he recognised it as the region of 'truth'. His poem is, therefore, in essence realistic, at this profound level, even though fantasy, not social realism, is its artistic mode.

The *Biographia Literaria* outlines the conscious plan which Coleridge and Wordsworth decided upon for *Lyrical Ballads,* and their decision to approach 'reality' in their art by two opposite paths. Since the passage is both justly famous and, by Coleridge's standards, readily accessible, it is best left to speak for itself:

> During the first year that Mr. Wordsworth and I were neighbours, our conversations turned frequently on the two cardinal points of poetry, the power of exciting the sympathy of the reader by a faithful adherence to the truth of nature, and the power of giving the interest of novelty by the modifying colours of imagination. . . .

> In this idea originated the plan of the *Lyrical Ballads*; in which it was agreed, that my endeavours should be directed to persons and characters supernatural, or at least romantic; yet so as to transfer from our inward nature a human interest and a semblance of truth sufficient to procure for these shadows of imagination that willing suspension of disbelief for the moment, which constitutes poetic faith.

> Mr. Wordsworth, on the other hand, was to propose to himself as his object, to give the charm of novelty to things of everyday, and to excite a feeling analogous to the supernatural, by awakening the loveliness and the wonders of the world before us; an inexhaustible treasure, but for which, in consequence of the film of familiarity and selfish solicitude we have eyes, yet see not, ears that hear not, and hearts that neither feel nor understand.

Of course, this begs many questions; and Coleridge's phrase 'that willing suspension of disbelief for the moment, which constitutes poetic faith' has been much discussed. For our present purpose, the important point is that Coleridge is 'to transfer from our inner nature a human interest and a semblance of truth sufficient' for his intended effect. Many times, he recognises that effects akin to those he produces in *The Ancient Mariner* are known through various 'delusions'— through dreams, drugs, or delirium for instance, none of which we finally think of as 'real'. Yet he also recognises that 'the supernatural' is not always allied to phantom experiences but, rather, that its intensities link with good and evil, joy and dereliction, wholeness and damnation, in the inner life.

What then is the best way to start reading *The Ancient Mariner*? To our minds, it is best first to release the visual imagination, allowing this to roam through the images. Everything is striking and extraordinary. The visual play suggests a near meeting of dream psychology and conscious image-making, a world close to modern imagism or modern cinema. Something like Walt Disney's *Fantasia* might suggest itself for comparison. If so, could we attempt to match the poem with appropriate music, thereby creating a *Fantasia* in reverse? An approach of this kind has the advantage of directing our attention immediately towards the archetypal image, where the poem's power surely chiefly lives: a solitary man, caught up in a drama of mortal personal guilt and divine deliverance, doomed to roam the world, telling his tale when its moment comes. The affinity is with the wandering Jew, the Flying Dutchman (a possible source for music?), with the exiled Cain even—stories linked only tangentially with religion in its orthodox forms. Perhaps we all have something of the Ancient Mariner in us (as Coleridge himself alleged of Hamlet)?—though if so, mercifully most of us keep him in check.

A legend of this kind attracts material from various sources like a powerful magnet, yet Coleridge's organisation excludes any systematic interpretation of one, definite, kind. From the literary point of view, his poem works a little like Eliot's *Waste Land*—to which, indeed, it is also spiritually akin. We are helped in our exploration if we know something of Coleridge personally, as modern scholarship has generously ensured that we may. *The Road to Xanadu* is a round-up of Coleridge's own extensive reading, looking for every possible source of his inspiration in other art. Coleridge's ideas have also been intensively studied, often by critics wishing to clarify, as well as to expound. Yet, in the end, Coleridge's poetic imagination had unusual licence, even apart from the conscious plan as he described it himself. He was familiar with opium visions, with their strange dislocation of consciousness, and their apparent heightening of consciousness in a fantasy world. The passage from ***Biographia Literaria*** already quoted includes the following puzzling words, again in connection with Coleridge's own part in the proposed scheme:

> the incidents and agents were to be, in part at least, supernatural; and the excellence aimed at was to consist in the interesting of the affections by the dramatic truths of such emotions, as would naturally accompany such situations, supposing them real. And real in *this* sense they have been to every human being who, from whatever source of delusion, has at any time believed himself under supernatural agency.

Such formulations leave the gap (the mystery?) between perception and objective reality notably yawning, and the emphasis on '*this*' (Coleridge's italics) scarcely helps to make '*this*' clear. Again, anyone reading Coleridge's poetry, and grappling (as we certainly should) with its relationship to his own powerful and influential theories of poetic imagination, cannot overlook the famous and bizarre prose introduction to **"Kubla Khan"**, strangest among all the clues that the poet has left:

> In the summer of the year 1797 [*sic*: though almost certainly he meant to write 1798: *Eds*], the Author, then in ill health, had retired to a lonely farmhouse between Porlock and Linton, on the Exmoor confines of Somerset and Devonshire. In consequence of a slight indisposition, an anodyne had been prescribed, from the effects of which he fell asleep in his chair at the moment when he was reading the following sentence, or words of the same substance, in 'Purchas's Pilgrimage': 'Here the Klan Kubla commanded a palace to be built, and a stately garden thereunto. And this ten miles of fertile ground were enclosed with a wall.' The Author continued for about three hours in a profound sleep, at least of the external senses, during which time he has the most vivid confidence, that he could not have composed less than from two to three hundred lines; if that indeed can be called composition in which all the images rose up before him as *things,* with a parallel production of the correspondent expressions, without any sensation or consciousness of effort. On awakening he appeared to himself to have a distinct recollection of the whole, and taking his pen, ink, and paper, instantly and eagerly set down the lines that are here preserved. At this moment he was unfortunately called out by a person on business from Porlock, and detained by him above an hour, and on his return to his room, found, to his no small surprise and mortification, that though he still retained some vague and dim recollection of the general purport of the vision, yet, all the rest had passed away like the images on the surface of a stream into which a stone has been cast, but, alas! without the after restoration of the latter.

If this is accepted, then it seems that Coleridge had a 'vision' (how accurately is this word intended?) in which words and images were alike 'given', in parallel form. It appears that the process of 'composition'—a word that Coleridge himself pauses over doubtfully in the context—was in fact a transcription from memory, interrupted fatally by the person from Porlock. The notion that images and words should have been equally 'given', in 'parallel production', and in a dream induced by a drug, moves us a long way from 'secondary imagination' in its official, Coleridgean form. None the less, we are also a long way from 'fancy', if that is to be defined merely as an intellectual and mechanical rearrangement of sense impressions derived from the waking world. What Coleridge appears to be saying is that he transmitted **'Kubla Khan'** rather than that he created it. But, where the transmission originated, and how far it depended upon the breaking down and recreating of 'reality' in Coleridge's unconscious rather than in his conscious mind, remains to be judged. Perhaps many people sometimes wake up with the sense of having written great poetry, composed great music, in their recent dream consciousness, but this seldom if ever with most of us gets transcribed.

If we look at Coleridge's 'the Ancient Mariner' with open minds on these questions of 'intention', certain features are, however, clear. A critic who suggests . . . that the Mariner kills the albatross chiefly to make soup, and that the spiritual punishment of himself and the crew is therefore excessive, signifies a cheerful unwillingness to take the poem seriously at all. That we are indeed faced with a drama of betrayal and damnation, grace and penitence, seems too evident to require much defence. The poem cannot be assimilated to Christian theology by any direct process, yet the religious scheme is present throughout. The phrase 'O Christ!' occurs twice, jerked out of the Mariner first in horror and revulsion, as the universe becomes hell for him:

> The very deep did rot: O Christ!
> That ever this should be!
> Yea, slimy things did crawl with legs
> Upon the slimy sea.

and later in fear and wonder, as he sees the angelic presences who have been animating the zombie crew:

> I turned my eyes upon the deck—
> Oh, Christ! what saw I there!
>
> This seraph-band, each waved his hand:
> It was a heavenly sight!
> They stood as signals to the land,
> Each one a lovely sight.

Mary is invoked twice, each time in the context of grace—first in appeal, when the ship of death becomes manifest ('Heaven's Mother send us grace!'), and later in praise, for release from torment:

> To Mary Queen the praise be given!
> She sent the gentle sleep from Heaven,
> That slid into my soul.

In other places, the religious references are more eclectic, with neo-platonism a frequent source. The Spirit who pursues the ship from the north is glossed in the poem's prose commentary in a manner referring us well outside Christian tradition for its source: 'A spirit had followed them; one of the invisible inhabitants of this planet, neither departed souls nor angels; concerning whom the learned Jew Josephus, and the Platonic Constantinopolitan, Michael Psellus, may be consulted. They are very numerous, and there is no climate or element without one or more.' And later, again in the prose commentary, there is a beautiful and quintessentially neo-platonic description of the *living* universe (though in saying this, we should never forget the great synthesis of neo-platonic and Christian ideas which took place in the early centuries of the church, so that the two traditions, while differing on certain important fundamentals, have never been very far apart): 'In his loneliness and fixedness he yearneth towards the journeying Moon, and the stars that still sojourn, yet still move onward; and every where the blue sky belongs to them, and is their appointed rest, and their native country and their natural homes, which they enter unannounced, as lords that are certainly expected and yet there is a silent joy at their arrival.'

With this in mind, we can (and must) attempt to trace the poem's central development, whether this is thought of as tentative affirmation, prophetic vision, or as a stream of suggestion flowing gently through fantasy. And here, the present critics should make clear, no doubt, that in this central development the poem is, in their view, evidently and specifically Christian. It is Christian in this sense: that it is written by a Christian; that its most characteristic ideas originate inside Christianity; and that the colour of feeling inherent in the power of the verse would not be found in any writer not profoundly influenced by Christian *experience*. We put the matter in this manner in order to safeguard certain other aspects which modify its Christianity, and defeat any attempt to read it as systematic Christian allegory, some of which have already been touched on. Again, it seems clear that Coleridge, who was not consciously allegorising, would have thought of the poem's truth as universal rather than as sectarian, and would have expected it to speak first to the imagination, and to the experience, of readers, not to their religious 'beliefs'.

Where, then, are the specific marks of Christianity? First, the albatross is welcomed as a guest, and offered friendship—which is why its betrayal cannot plausibly be glossed in terms of bird soup:

> At length did cross an Albatross,
> Through the fog it came:
> As if it had been a Christian soul,
> We hailed it in God's name.

The 'as if' suggests, of course, analogy rather than anything more definite, and it is obvious that the other mariners think of the bird merely superstitiously, hailing it as a good omen. When this view seems to be confirmed, yet the Mariner none the less kills it, they blame him not for betraying a living creature whom he has befriended, but for killing the bird that 'made the breeze to blow'. For this reason again, they praise him for killing the bird when a further reversal of weather appears now to prove the opposite:

> 'Twas right, said they, such birds to slay
> That bring the fog and mist.

No doubt this is the reason why, later, they simply die, but the Mariner himself is reserved for a different fate. This is nothing to do with a spectacular vengeance from a cruel deity (as William Empson seems to think) but is, rather, an indication of the poem's direction. We are to focus on the plight of the one man who is a moral agent, knowing good from evil, rather than upon the fate of many men excluded from spiritual insight, and so from spiritual life. The crew belongs, to use a phrase of Coleridge's already quoted, with the 'lethargy of custom'—with that majority among men who miss alike the beauty and the suffering of life, having no eyes to *see*.

The Mariner, however, who has *particularly* offered friendship to the bird, and established trust with it, commits evil in the fullest sense. The bird has come to recognise him, to receive from him, to respond when he calls to it, so the slaying is 'hellish' in the strict, Christian sense. The ancient world, Greek and

Christian alike, had accepted duty to a guest as sacred, and believed that to harm a guest or indeed to fail to protect him from evil was a wrong crying to Heaven for vengeance. Above all, duty to a friend was sacred; Dante puts Brutus and Judas Iscariot together, in hell's deepest pit.

It could be argued, of course, that this duty to guests and friends did not extend to animals, yet man's Lordship of Nature is a profoundly Christian belief. The book of *Genesis* asserts it, and Christ himself said that not a bird falls to earth without his Father's knowledge. For centuries, the church had tended to ignore this aspect of its teaching to such a degree that St Francis's close relationship with creatures seemed, in the strict sense of the word, eccentric. Perhaps this was because the assumption had grown that animals have no souls, and, therefore, that callousness towards them is permissible; certainly a divine relationship between man and the creatures lower than himself had been very generally lost.

One feature of romanticism was the radical recovery of a sense of man's kinship with all creation, and of understanding that the fruit of the Spirit, love, joy and peace, is not divisible. Blake expresses this, simply and memorably, in 'The Little Black Boy':

> Look on the rising sun! there God does live,
> And gives His light, and gives His heat
>   away;
> And flowers and trees and beasts and men
>   receive
> Comfort in morning, joy in the noon day.

In Wordsworth, the unity of creation is everywhere asserted; and, in **The Ancient Mariner**, this insight is, more than anything, the poem's coherence. Because the albatross was really befriended, it was really betrayed; and the Mariner's punishment is precisely that of Macbeth. He passes into inner torment and dereliction, which is hell brought home to him. He cannot pray (one of the traditional signs of damnation), and, like Macbeth, he cannot sleep. When he tells of the killing of the albatross he *looks* demonic (Part I, final stanza), and he knows, as the other mariners do not, that he has done a 'hellish' thing. (The irony is that while the Mariner reports the phrase 'And I had done a hellish thing' as words said to him by his fellows, he alone knows the real meaning of the words, and their for truth.) Later, during his trance, he hears the dialogue between two spirits who direct the stricken ship: and, while these appear to belong to a universe more neo-platonic than Christian in concept, they bring home the moral in a directly Christian way:

> 'Is it he?' quoth one, 'Is this the man?
> By him who died on cross,
> With his cruel bow he laid full low
> The harmless Albatross.

> 'The Spirit who bideth by himself
> In the land of mist and snow,
> He loved the bird that loved the man
> Who shot him with his bow.'

The reference to the crucifixion balances the somewhat untheological 'Spirit who bideth by himself', but the final two lines, with their image of a dance of delight and love between Creator and creatures that has been violated, are at once precise and profound. Perhaps the Christian understanding of the nature of evil has seldom been more simply and powerfully captured. There is a chain of love, including the Creator's love for the bird, and the bird's love for the man, which has been totally broken by the man. Towards the end of the poem, the community of all creation is again insisted upon, in lines which will look naïve or sentimental only to readers who wholly refuse the poem's imaged vision:

> He prayeth well, who loveth well
> Both man and bird and beast.
> He prayeth best, who loveth best
> All things both great and small;
> For the dear God who loveth us,
> He made and loveth all.

Prayer, to which we shall return, is the key concept, the word, and activity, which is the poem's key theme.

When the Mariner kills love, he commits the sin which cuts him decisively from God, and from the life of God, which *is* love, and puts himself in the self-alone, the absence of God, which is hell. Total change comes with the moment of murder, and Coleridge signifies this through a tellingly simple inversion. In Part I, we have read:

> The Sun came up upon the left,
> Out of the sea came he!
> And he shone bright, and on the right
> Went down into the sea.

This description, marvellously buoyant and compressed, of the day's ritual, returns, inverted, at the start of Part II:

> The Sun now rose upon the right:
> Out of the sea came he,
> Still hid in mist, and on the left
> Went down into the sea.

While a determinedly literal mind might deduce merely that the ship has now turned round and is going the other way, the evident force is that creation has turned round, the whole universe has turned round; and this indeed proves to be so. Arrest and fixity; dryness; horror:

The very deep did rot; O Christ!
That ever this should be!
Yea, slimy things did crawl with legs
Upon the slimy sea.

This, now, is the Mariner's 'world', and above all, he
is

Alone, alone, all, all alone,
Alone on a wide wide sea!
And never a saint took pity on
My soul in agony.

Towards the end, the Mariner yet again stresses to the
Wedding-Guest that the crowning horror of his suffering has been the absence, or the apparent absence,
of God:

O Wedding-Guest! this soul has been
Alone on a wide wide sea:
So lonely 'twas, that God himself
Scarce seemed there to be.

The universe dead and ghastly (a suicide's vision of
reality?) is the Mariner's world after his sin. It belongs
with Macbeth's world after the killing of Duncan,
with the central quality of consciousness conveyed by
T. S. Eliot in *The Waste Land,* and indeed with all
visions of loneliness and madness in literature, whether specifically Christian or not, where these sufferings
are linked, in whatever manner, with man's violation,
or loss, of love. But the poem is also about redemption. The Mariner is released from his suffering not
through anything he can do himself—above all, he
cannot pray even—but through a moment's pure grace:

O happy living things! no tongue
Their beauty might declare:
A spring of love gushed from my heart,
And I blessed them unaware:
Sure my kind saint took pity on me,
And I blessed them unaware.

'Unaware'. This word, often in the form 'unawares',
was a favourite of Wordsworth's, and any determined
student of the romantic sensibility could do worse
than spend a few hours tracking it down. Here, it is
pure grace: 'The selfsame moment I could pray.' With
prayer comes release. The albatross falls away, and he
can sleep. There's further penance to come, a strange
doom of purgation, but the Mariner is no longer in
hell. This release naturally calls to mind the moment in
Pilgrim's Progress when Christian's burden of sin rolls
away from him at the foot of the cross, since, though
Coleridge is not an allegorist like Bunyan, his imaginative effect is most closely akin.

In **The Ancient Mariner** Coleridge is moving on the
plane of Reason as he defines it; he is depicting realities of good and evil, all probing well beyond the
world of 'understanding'. The actual killing of the
albatross is no more 'explained' than is the sin of
Judas as recounted in the four New Testament accounts of it, or the sin of Eve and Adam as recounted
in *Genesis.* 'The man said, "The woman whom thou
gavest to be with me, she gave me of the tree, and I
did eat."' 'The woman said, "The serpent beguiled
me, and I did eat,"' that is all: and, though Milton, in
his dramatic presentation, tried to 'understand', tying
himself in knots along with the rest of us, *Genesis*
simply stop here. So, for Adam and Eve, there is
expulsion, and loss of Eden, as God had decreed; they
and their seed are to wander in exile for the rest of
time. The 'truth' of the story in *Genesis* is, simply,
the truth of it; men have eaten the forbidden fruit, do
wander in exile, God knows why. Coleridge leaves the
Mariner's motives likewise unexplained and mysterious; but they are met by the equally unexplained and
mysterious operations of grace. The Mariner is in hell
(as most men sometimes may be, and some men habitually) and, in human terms, he has no route back.
Yet suddenly he sees the water creatures, and they are
beautiful; in place of the rot and slime, the horror,
there is a dance of delight. Love wells up in his heart;
he praises (the moment is entirely given); above all, he
blesses them, 'unaware'. 'The self-same moment I
could pray.' The universe turns round again, and, for
the world of death, a world of life is returned. The
water creatures are still the same, in their own reality;
it is the Mariner who has changed, or been changed.

Why does human consciousness sometimes inhabit a
world of deadness and horror, where life is unbearable, sometimes rejoice in a world radiant with God?
If there is one theme that links Blake, Wordsworth
and Coleridge, it is this one, the mystery of joy, and
dereliction, in the inner soul. All three poets are driven
men, like the Mariner, with an urgent message of
healing for their fellows to hear. Yet they know they
will be dreaded and resisted, prophets unheeded; that
most men will shun the tale they have to tell.

As one would expect, the romantics are keenly aware
of different frames of reference, different interpretations, and the tension between joy and fear is at the
heart of their *thought.* If God is really there to be seen
clearly, why do many men miss him? Various traditional insights and guesses are explored. Many men
perhaps lose the visionary gifts at adolescence, preferring the 'light of common day' to the wonder of God.
Perhaps this loss is part of the harvest of sin, the
original exile from Eden; perhaps it is loss of moral
purity through deliberate sin. May it be that God pre-
ordains some men to the darkness and horror; that, in
Blake's words, 'Some are born to endless night'? Or
does God appear only when he wills, and then withdraw himself, coming and going to laws not yet revealed? In certain moods Wordsworth and Coleridge

toyed with the thought that since we 'receive but what we give' in living, then, when our exuberance and energy fail, the world must go dead. Energy, which (said Blake) is both 'eternal delight' and 'from the body', may indeed be the fuel, the vision, of the soul. Yet *this* view risks locking men in psychic solipsism, and mistaking the mechanisms of human perception for the realities perceived.

It may be that the romantic poets had to declare their strong sense of election in differing fashions, since this sense of election was also their gospel for men. But had they, by grace or purity, achieved particular insight, or were they perceiving in strange, and maybe disordered ways? Were they saner than the excluded majority, or madder, were they driven by divine, or by demonic powers? When their universe went dead, had they sinned exceptionally? Or had their mind broken; or had they merely grown old? As the nineteenth century went on, and the optimism of the early romantics receded, their successors often gravitated to bizarre and consciously perverse modes of thought. Could the heavenly light be as capricious even as the erotic, sending poor driven, infatuated men quite out of their wits? 'La belle dame sans merci', will o' the wisp glimpses of divinity; what kind of life, and destiny, were these?

The distinctive character of *The Ancient Mariner*, we are saying, is that it is Christian in its implicit understanding of such questions as these. The mystery is a Christian mystery, and to this degree accessible; while 'good' and 'evil' are not 'explained', they are held under God. The poem offers a clear polarity between a universe where men pray and celebrate and love is paramount, and a universe where blessing is absent and horror prevails. In objective fact the universe is God's, and constant; but sin removes men to a vision where God is absent; to hell. Yet the Mariner receives grace, including the supreme grace of penitence, and is led back to a living, though wounded, destiny in the world of men. In knowing he has done a hellish thing, he makes grace possible; only failure to accept guilt could lock God finally out.

What, then, is the Mariner's destiny? In one sense he seems akin to any poet or artist, or any Christian, who, healed by grace, is driven to tell his tale. Freed from hell, he remains still in Purgatory, and is an object of terror to most whom he meets. The holy hermit is aghast, the Wedding-Guest afraid and reluctant; the Pilot's boy goes mad. The Mariner's destiny is not to start the voyage of sanctity and gradually to mirror holiness, but to remain visibly touched by hell, disturbing and disturbed:

> Since then, at an uncertain hour,
> That agony returns;
> And till my ghastly tale is told,
> The heart within me burns.

The Mariner exists for this 'uncertain hour', which is also the hour of this poem; the hour chosen by God when some other man must hear the tale. The other chief aspect of the poem, which we have not so far touched on, is that its centre is really the Wedding-Guest. At the start, he is picked out by the Mariner, and himself 'arrested'; there are strong suggestions of hypnosis and trance. He fears the Mariner, tries to shake him off, but is held by him ; this is *his* moment, with no hope of escape:

> He holds him with his glittering eye—
> The Wedding-Guest stood still,
> And listens like a three years' child:
> The Mariner hath his will.
>
> The Wedding-Guest sat on a stone;
> He cannot choose but hear.

The Wedding-Guest's experience is, in this aspect, related to the Mariner's—especially at the point when, in a trance, the Mariner has heard the two spirits debate. Coleridge is dramatising the moment of encounter when, in the divine will, or the divine capriciousness, *this* man experiences the near approach of God. The encounter is unsought, it is an unwanted distraction, it is terrifying rather than comforting, but, just now, its moment has come. The Mariner's story, his destiny, is now for *this* man entirely, and everything romantic, and fantastic, will converge in its effect.

Coleridge, like Wordsworth, believed that most men are open on their God-ward side only occasionally; that normally, God's presence is ignored, or not even seen. But there are moments when a work of art springs to life, when a relationship crystallises, when something long known is *seen* suddenly—and, at such times, a response, a 'yes' or 'no' must be made. It is surely because Coleridge's poem dramatises this moment in images so bizarre, so altogether unearthly, that it can afford its moral to have the simplicity of a child's hymn. The last four stanzas of the poem, which in isolation may seem banal, rise from the poem with authentic, even with hypnotic power. The Wedding-Guest leaves the encounter not elated, but 'like one that hath been stunned / And is of sense forlorn'. None the less, he rises 'sadder and wiser'—which is certainly something; a valuable, if apparently modest role for art itself?

Lindsay Davies (essay date 1990)

SOURCE: "The Poem, the Gloss and the Critic: Discourse and Subjectivity in *The Rime of the Ancient Mariner*," in *Forum for Modern Language Studies*, Vol. XXVI, No. 3, July, 1990, pp. 259-71.

[*In the following essay, Davies claims that, contrary to the tendencies of most critics,* The Rime of the

Ancient Mariner *cannot and need not be entirely unified and unambiguous.*]

The Rime of the Ancient Mariner, which has been studied with great enthusiasm and ingenuity by many critics as a moral poem—an imaginative adventure with a moral lesson—seems actually to provide incessant problems for these critics in its refusal to finally unify to a point where all the poem's elements serve one particular reading. From the beginning the poem posed difficulties for those who strove to find in it a coherent relation of the parts to the whole. Indeed, Wordsworth himself, in his notorious criticism of the poem included in the second edition of ***Lyrical Ballads*** (1800), commented that "the events having no necessary connection do not produce each other". Yet despite the fact that, according to Wordsworth's criticism, Coleridge had failed to unify and harmonize the poem as a romantic poet should, critics nevertheless have since tried to compensate for this failure by imposing interpretations on the poem which attempt to "explain" the relation of parts to whole. Robert Penn Warren's "A Poem of Pure Imagination: An Experiment in Reading" and Edward Bostetter's "The Nightmare World of the Ancient Mariner" are good examples of such attempts to provide consistent comprehensive readings of the poem in moral terms. But, considered together, these two articles also demonstrate the impossibility of containing the poem's meaning in a single interpretation. Warren's and Bostetter's readings of ***The Ancient Mariner*** are mutually exclusive. Warren argues that the poem tells "a story of crime and punishment and repentance and reconciliation", and he focuses primarily on the theme of sacramental vision and Coleridge's concept of the "One Life". Bostetter's mariner, on the other hand, is the victim of a chaotic and irrational universe. For him the mariner's adventure results in his eternal alienation; whereas for Warren, the mariner at the end becomes "a prophet of universal charity". Each critic constructs his argument from a very careful reading of the text. But the fact that they reach such opposite conclusions demonstrates the failure of each interpretation in its unifying mission. Instead Warren and Bostetter have helped to show that the mariner is *both* the prophet of unity and order (the One Life) *and* a figure of irreconcilable alienation. Indeed this disjunction of meaning leads the way to an examination of the poem which abandons the quest to uncover an overall "meaning" for the text, and which focuses instead on the effects produced by its textual network.

Central to the desire for establishing coherent and stable meaning in this poem is the romantic desire for a smooth transmission of thought and feeling from poet to reader. But ***The Ancient Mariner*** makes even the illusion of such a process impossible, and foregrounds instead a place of competing discourses and a variety of subject positions for a reader to adopt which draw attention not simply to the difficulties of reading the poem, but also to the paradoxes of the activity of interpretation itself. A literary critic always imposes an order on the text by constructing an argument about it. But the critic's tale of order is determined by its, and thus the critic's, alienation through difference from all other readings of the text. Just as the critic produces the poem, in the sense of opening it up to view, so the poem produces the critic, as it constitutes her subjectivity through the production of yet another text—the critic's interpretation. The critic, like the mariner and his curse, is determined by her discourse. And my examination of ***The Ancient Mariner*** will focus on the contingencies of subjectivity exposed through the specular representation of critical activity that can be seen in the poem's marginal gloss.

My discussion is based on two chief assumptions: first, that poetry is a particular mode of discourse; and, second, that subjectivity not only produces discourse through the relationship between a speaker and a listener, but that it is also an effect of discourse. No "self" exists prior to language. Far from being an autonomous entity, understood as a psychologically unified and transcendental essence or "identity", subjectivity is determined by the discourses which produce it, and can come into being only by occupation of the subject positions provided within those discourses. That is, as Lacan has stressed, subjectivity only emerges in an intersubjective discourse with the Other. Moreover, even the English pronoun "I", which is used to assert autonomous identity, actually represents a split rather than a unification of subjectivity between the "I" speaking and the "I" spoken about. As Antony Easthope has put it so well [in *Poetry as Discourse*], "identity is only ever possible as misrecognition. For vision, I can only see myself in a mirror by seeing this reflection from somewhere else. For discourse, I can only identify myself in discourse by speaking about this character ('myself') from somewhere else".

Yet despite this disjunction, "self-expressive" texts, like romantic poetry or traditionally conceived autobiographical works, which foreground the pronoun "I" and suggest a unity between the subject of the text and the subject writing it, appear unproblematic because the materiality of language which disperses meaning is effaced by certain linguistic features that create the effect of a coherent stable voice within the text. That is, such texts provide a subject position easily adopted by the reader, who grasps the subject "behind" the voice as the authoritative and coherent originator of meaning, and thereby grasps her own "self" as the receiver of this meaning. As Catherine Belsey has noted [in *Critical Practice*], "expressive" texts interpellate the reader as subject:

The reader is invited to perceive and judge the "truth" of the text, the coherent, non-contradictory interpretation of the world as it is perceived by an author whose autonomy is the source and evidence of the truth of the interpretation. This model of intersubjective communication, of shared understanding of a text which re-presents the world, is the guarantee not only of the truth of the text but of the reader's existence as an autonomous and knowing subject in a world of knowing subjects.

However, the meaning and knowledge supposedly shared through this kind of transparent discourse is less stable than it seems. Language, after all, is not transparent but a material from which meanings must be produced; and thus materiality will always interpose itself between the author's intentions and the reader's reception of the text. As Easthope notes, "however much a poem claims to be the property of a speaker represented in it, the poem finally belongs to the reader producing it as a reading".

Although a romantic poem, *The Ancient Mariner* departs from romantic expressivism by overlapping three modes of discourse. The subjectivities which determine these modes are: (1) Poet/Balladeer—Reader; (2) Author of Gloss—Reader; (3) Ancient Mariner—Wedding Guest. The first two groups of these positions can be described, in Roman Jakobson's terms, as *subjects of enunciation*; that is, the speaking subject and the producer of meaning. The third group, however, are the *subjects of the enounced*, the subjects represented within the discourse. For meaning to be produced, a reader must identify herself with one of these positions, and generally will gravitate towards the one which most immediately offers intelligibility. However, *The Ancient Mariner* does not provide such an easy process of identification for the reader. Instead it offers a range of conflicting positions which disperse the reader's subjectivity across the text. Yet, interestingly, through the maze of perspectives or subject positions offered by the poem (Coleridge, the balladeer, the mariner, the wedding guest, the editor of the gloss), one can still perceive what amounts to a thematization of the romantic ideal of self-expression in the exchange between the mariner and the wedding guest; the mariner tells his story to the wedding guest, who is affected and changed through empathic identification with what he hears. Moreover, in keeping with both romantic poetry and autobiography, the mariner's narrative constitutes a confessional exposure of selfhood.

Yet while the wedding guest finally has no problem understanding the mariner's tale, this poem denies the reader any easy access to its meaning; and so the process of *constructing* meaning, of *producing the text*, is made obvious in a way that it is not in transparent discourse. Denied a place where meaning coheres and

appears obvious, the reader is forced to know herself and identify herself as a critic, or interpreter of the text. And the poem itself uncannily anticipates and complicates the reader's desire to occupy a stable position as interpreter by providing a model of just such a reader within its margins, thus reflecting back on the reader a contorted image of her very own activity.

The gloss was added to *The Ancient Mariner* for the version of the poem that appeared in *Sibylline Leaves* (1817). It was one of several changes made to the text that had been published in *Lyrical Ballads* (1798), and it was added partly in response to Wordsworth's criticism, and partly because Coleridge increasingly felt that the poem was too obscure. Accordingly today the reader is confronted with a text composed of two texts, and must either attempt to negotiate them both, or deliberately suppress one in order to appropriate the other. Generally, one would assume, the gloss is subordinated in favour of the poem. It is, after all, written as an accompaniment to the poem. But while it might be considered "natural" to focus on the poem itself, nevertheless this demands a deliberate suppression of the gloss. Indeed the gloss must be suppressed if one wishes to read the poem as unbroken narrative. However, when confronted with the puzzles of this narrative, the act of suppressing the gloss is easier said than done. Consequently, I will insist on an examination of the implications of the text as doubled text, a combination of two discontinuous texts.

If I describe the gloss and the poem as discontinuous with each other, however, it is important to define exactly the nature of this discontinuity, because presumably the gloss is added not to create more confusion but to make the poem more accessible. Lawrence Lipking, in his essay "The Marginal Gloss", devotes some time to the examination of Coleridge's gloss and is persuasive in demonstrating its role as interpreter of the poem. The gloss frequently makes explicit what the narrative of the poem only infers. For example, Lipking has shown how, in the very opening lines of the poem, the gloss begins its role as "anchorer" of meaning. The poem opens rather oddly with an "it" rather than a "he" ("It is an ancient Mariner" [1]) and the "one of three" (2) the mariner stops could be one of three of anything—the references are decidedly unstable. But the gloss accompanying the opening stanza clears up the problem by presenting the scene in a matter-of-fact and direct manner: "An ancient Mariner meeteth three Gallants bidden to a wedding feast, and detaineth one" (1-4). Moreover, the choice of the word "gallants" indicates the beginning of the gloss's role as moral judge. As Lipking points out, the gloss does not confine itself to facts, but "again and again it interprets the narrative by reading it as parable. In the world of the gloss, actions have causes and consequences, parts fit into wholes, and human motives are not arbitrary". It is the gloss, after all, that notes explicitly that the mariner's action of shooting the albatross is a "crime" (97-102). And it can be judged as such because, again, the gloss has made explicit what the poem only infers: that the albatross is a "pious bird of good omen" (79-82). The author of the gloss assumes from the start the system of universal order that the mariner, in his story, has to learn. Hence everything is interpreted accordingly; indeed, the very interpretive and explanatory agenda of the gloss corresponds with this assumption.

The gloss can not only interpret the mariner's actions but can also distinguish between the spirits, and understand man's place in both the natural and spiritual realms. Its longest entry meditates on the loneliness of the mariner by adding the perspective of the universe where the moon and stars, though constantly journeying, are nevertheless always at "home". The text of this entry reads:

> In his loneliness and fixedness he yearneth towards the journeying Moon, and the stars that still sojourn, yet still move onward; and every where the blue sky belongs to them, and is their appointed rest, and their native country and their own natural homes, which they enter unannounced, as lords that are certainly expected and yet there is a silent joy at their arrival. (263-71)

The simple stanzas these phrases are curled around do not spell out their own significance.

> The moving Moon went up the sky.
> And no where did abide:
> Softly she was going up,
> And a star or two beside—
>
> Her beams bemocked the sultry main,
> Like April hoar-frost spread:
> But where the ship's huge shadow lay,
> The charmèd water burnt alway
> A still and awful red. (263-271)

They are indeed suggestive lines; but they do not explain the mood of the mariner the way the gloss does. If anything, these stanzas express disconnection and alienation. And, instead, it is the gloss that provides the vision of universal connectedness which makes the transition to the mariner's act of blessing the water-snakes intelligible.

Indeed, the gloss plays no minor role. While convention would relegate it as a supporting text, its clarity and authority of tone, and the promise of elucidation implied by its presence, constantly draw the reader's eye away from the poem toward the margin. The gloss is always demanding attention: it attaches itself

to the poem, sometimes in short phrases, sometimes in long sentences, and constantly disrupts the narrative continuity. Moreover, it also asserts itself by having a particular voice. The gloss is no deadpan script but the delivery of a voice which can move from being "civilized" and "scholastic", to being hauntingly lyrical in its tone. Far from being subordinate to the poem, the gloss in fact is, as Lipking puts it so well, "smugly-knowing. Not in thrall to the mariner's perspective, it understands the meaning of his experiences, it understands him as he cannot understand himself". The gloss competes with the poem, and it is this tension which creates a discontinuity that supersedes the supposed continuity between the two texts.

This competition takes place on the level of form as well as through content and tone. The gloss's choppy narrative is for the most part divided up by sentences—each sentence being a separate entry. But there are several places where the entry next to a stanza is only a clause. In these places the eye is led down the margin to find the other clauses and consequently to complete the sentence. The result of this adherence to syntactic wholeness is that several of the poem's stanzas are bypassed and the reader must go back to read them. Thus the eye is led back and forth as well as from side to side (from poem to margin), and the narrative flow of both poem and gloss are destroyed. Indeed, sometimes this disruption of narrative is overtly displayed by the typographical intrusion of the gloss into the stanzaic progression of the poem: in its longer sections the gloss bleeds across the page from the margin, filling the white spaces between stanzas.

Lipking ingeniously reads the tension between gloss and poem as the actual vehicle of identification for the reader. He argues that the gloss and poem simultaneously provide the experience and the interpretation of the mariner's tale. The movement of the reader tossed between the texts, where "shocking incident" in the poem is followed by "grave reflection" in the gloss, re-enacts the fundamental movement of the mariner's experience. And Lipking asserts a final healing of the divide by noting that at the very end the gloss and poem conclude together by saying the same thing. But by positing this final unification Lipking represses the differences between the discourses which he previously had demonstrated so well. So it is on this point that I must finally part company with Lipking. There are still two distinct voices speaking at the poem's end. The text is still doubled. And it seems to me that, rather than providing the means for identification between reader and text, the coexistence of gloss and poem—two competing voices, two subject positions—divides the reader's experience, preventing identification with any one stable voice, and thus preventing identification with any one stable voice, and thus preventing the cohesion of meaning. There is no final unity achieved: the voice of the gloss provides a conflicting position of subjectivity and forces the reader to participate simultaneously in two modes of discourse. Ironically, what is designed to assist and compensate for the difficulty of the poem, actually vastly increases the complexity of any reader's experience of it. Various positions of subjectivity compete with one another and demand that the reader shift from one mode of discourse to another, reorienting herself accordingly. The reader must choose between enthralment to the tale, or knowing interpretation of it, and the coexistence of both possibilities makes neither one tenable. The choice divides the reader. The positions of the mariner and the wedding guest, which are asserted over the subject of enunciation (that is, the speaking subject as "Coleridge" or the "balladeer"), demand that the reader "suspend disbelief", be mesmerized and enthralled, both sharing the urgency of the mariner's tale and being affected, like the wedding guest, by the burden of its message. Unlike the poem, however, the gloss foregrounds the subject of enunciation as the position of intelligibility. The voice of the gloss forces the reader to adopt a position in which she must participate in distanced and knowing interpretation of the poem, where the spell is broken by "wisdom". The inconsistencies and opacity that, supposedly, a successfully mesmerized reader would not notice, must be organized and coerced into a consistent schema by the reader of the gloss. And the intrusive presence of the gloss, offering the reader elucidation and interpretive distance, prevents her from being imaginatively captivated by the poem. The imaginative capacity of all humans which, it is suggested, should enable the reader to reach the truth and meaning of the poem (the wedding guest being our model here) is belied by the presence of the gloss. And by standing in for imagination's failure to unify the poem, the gloss offers not enthralment and mesmerization but reflection and interpretive distance. Thus the text, composed of two discontinuous discourses, undermines the unity of experience that the poem thematically supports, and offers instead its own linguistic materiality. The connectedness between all things and the unifying power of the imagination become ironic concepts to a reader who, unable to pin down meaning, must know herself as a subject in process, moving from one position of intelligibility to another.

Yet in its refusal to comfortably situate the reader, *The Ancient Mariner* actually becomes a spur to the act of critical interpretation. The presence of the gloss, which has helped to split the reader in the process of reading, also stands as an example of how the reading subject can overcome this dilemma. Composed of poem and gloss, *The Ancient Mariner* is, as Roland Barthes would say, a writable text: plural and multivalent, resistant to immediate assimilation, it is a text that can only exist in terms of meaning by our rewriting of it. The critic would transform the writable text into a readable one by rewriting it in such a way that it can

be assimilated and immediately comprehended. In doing so, she both mimics the gloss and necessarily implies the failure of the gloss. But if the gloss fails to account for the poem satisfactorily, the question is raised whether another gloss can do any better. Instead of grounding meaning, the glosses only encourage further glosses. What is at stake in each interpretation of the poem, however, is not the meaning it offers but the subjectivity of the interpreter which the achievement of that meaning tentatively affirms.

In this sense, the critic writes herself, and the interpretation she produces is autobiographical in a new way. Earlier in this essay I note how autobiography, traditionally understood as "the description of a life written by the individual himself", is supposed to give direct access to the voice behind the text. The meaning of the narrative resides in the originating subject, the author who has spread the shaping of his identity before us in words. What I suggest here, however, is a reversal of this process. Instead of the author using words to "express" a self which is already given, it is the words themselves that actually constitute that self. The implications of this for autobiography are significant. Instead of affirming autonomous subjectivity, autobiography demonstrates in a heightened manner the subject in search of identity in discourse. And, in the writing of the self, it is language that has ultimate control. As Paul De Man has noted,

> We assume that life *produces* the autobiography as an act produces its consequences, but can we not suggest with equal justice, that the autobiographical project may itself produce and determine the life and that whatever the writer *does* is in fact governed by the technical demands of self-portraiture and thus determined, in all its aspects, by the resources of his medium?

Indeed, it has been posited by De Man and others that all texts are autobiographical insofar as they claim to be *by* someone, thus affirming both the subjectivity of that someone, and of the reader who knows herself in the act of reading and understanding. In the discourse of literary criticism, then, the critic can only know herself and be known as a critic by authoring a document that assumes mastery of the text in question. In writing her own text that lays bare the secrets of another text, she inevitably writes herself by substituting for own discourse for that of the other. The subjectivity of the autobiographer is constituted by the figuration in language of past "selves". But any kind of writing involves the figuration of selfhood, which is why, as Rudolphe Gasché has pointed out, autobiography can become a "paradigm for writing as such". And, insofar as her discourse determines her, the critic is also necessarily figured in her own text.

As a gesture towards the poem's themes and content which I have neglected in favour of formal and the-

"The game is done! I've won, I've won!" / Quoth she, and whistles thrice.

oretical issues, I wish now to offer a brief reading of the poem which will focus on its figuration of the subject's constitution in language. And in presenting my reading, I too enter the tradition of Coleridge studies which has for years offered elucidation of the obscurities of the poem. Moreover, I will be following the example of the gloss—mastering the poem, purporting to know more about it than it knows about itself, or than any other reader knows about it. To be part of the critical discourse, however, is only to join the proliferation of texts this poem has produced. Insofar as my reading coheres it constitutes my position as critic, but it coheres only be elision and/or repression of difference.

Nevertheless, I proceed. Given the weighty moralism of the poem's ending, it seems that it does indeed attempt to cohere at the level of Christian morality. By shooting the albatross the mariner refuses to project himself imaginatively into the concept of "One Life"—the regenerative interchange and unity between man and nature in God's universe. Instead, he demonstrates a wilful capacity for unmotivated evil that fundamentally opposes universal harmony. However, although the mariner suffers and does penance for his deed, the autonomy and assertion of individualism that it represents is sustained throughout the poem by the sheer solitariness of his position. He is consistently *apart* from community, which is represented by both the wedding and the ship's crew; and although the moral of the poem's ending strongly favours both community of mankind and the overall community of man and nature in the universe, the mariner still remains alone. It is his penance to remain so, of course. But the nature of his penance also somewhat contradictorily elevates the mariner into a prophetic figure who, by maintaining separateness from community, supposedly performs a corrective role through the perpetual retelling of his tale. Each retelling recreates the deed, reasserts his wilful autonomy, and represents his solitariness and individualism. While each retelling is a further extension of his penance, and while the mariner presents his task as a curse, the ironic fact of the matter is that this task that separates him is performed for the sake of a vision of unity. The nature of his task contradicts the moral of One Life embedded in its message. In fact, it could be argued that the task replicates his initial crime of killing the bird: the hypnotic control the mariner asserts over the listener he has accosted is the usurpation of another's life against that other's will. Furthermore, the effect of this task, as it is presented in the poem, is one that is dominated by the voice and vision of the mariner. His "role" in society not only alienates him from that society and constantly reasserts his individuality, but also actually determines his subjectivity as it is constituted through language.

The mariner tells the wedding guest that he has "strange power of speech" (587). And within the world of the poem, certainly, his speech affects his listener. The wedding guest is changed—"A sadder and a wiser man, / He rose the morrow morn" (624-25)—through empathic identification with the mariner's suffering as it is told in the tale. But given the fate of the mariner to tell his tale over and over, one might be tempted to point out that it is the strange power of speech that has him, and not the other way around. The mariner's curse figures our compulsion to narrate the events of our lives to others; which we do in order to affirm present identity, both by the ability to retain and affect a listener and by the construction of a past identity in language which is taken to be continuous with that of the present.

Geoffrey Hartman has noted that the wilfulness of the mariner's act against nature implies, at the very least, a drive on his part for self-presence. However, this act reveals not only the desire for self-presence, but also that individuation is dependent upon a dialectical awareness of self and other. As Hartman observes, "what follows [the mariner's] self-determining, self-inaugural act is, paradoxically, the presence of otherness". Throughout the tale, the mariner's "self" is constituted by differentiation. His subjectivity emerges somewhere between himself as observer and himself as observed. The most obvious example of this is the mariner's awareness of the cursing eyes of the dead crew which he imagines are fixed upon him. But more remarkable, perhaps, is the description of the sun as it appears through the mast of the skeleton ship:

> The western wave was all a-
> flame.
> The day was well nigh done!
> Almost upon the western wave
> Rested the broad bright Sun;
> When that strange shape drove
> suddenly
> Betwixt us and the Sun.

It seemeth	And straight the Sun was
him but	flecked with bars,
the ske-	(Heaven's Mother send us
leton of	grace!)
a ship.	As if through a dungeon grate
	he peered
	With broad and burning face.
	(171-80)

It is ambiguous here whether it is the sun or the mariner who is imprisoned. But what is important is that the sun stares at *him*, and not the other way around. He is central to his world; but his central position is dependent upon the existence of others external to him. Hence his "aloneness" must be accompanied by corpses whose eyes still gaze, phantoms that discuss and decide his fate, and a personified sun which stares at him. It is these things which function as otherness and thus form, through differentiation, the mariner's self. Indeed they and the wedding guest together demonstrate the dialogic structure of the self, where "I" can only be understood in relation to "non-I". But because the subjectivity of the pronoun "I" does not extend beyond the moment of a specific utterance, it must be perpetually recreated through the exercise of language—through discourse. And here a crucial contradiction emerges in the poem: insofar as the mariner's subjectivity is dependent upon his penance of perpetual discourse, his perpetual telling of himself in language, he is clearly an example of the determinate subject; yet this penance, by focusing so absolutely on the solitariness and selfhood of the mariner, at the same time continues to assert him as an autonomous individual.

The mariner's penance takes the form of transparent discourse; and for the wedding guest, who is mesmerized and drawn in, the speech is powerful. He locates "truth" in the autobiographical tale, and is affected and changed through imaginary identification and empathy with the mariner. The reader of the poem, however, is prevented from comfortably occupying the positions of either the mariner or the wedding guest, and is thus prevented from identifying with the experiences of either. As we have seen, the marginal gloss is the chief feature working against this process of imaginary identification and, under these conditions, the power of the mariner's speech is drained. Instead of being mesmerized by the "truth" of the mariner's tale, or by the "truth" of the wedding guest's experience of it, the reader is confronted with the inconsistency between the tale's moral emphasis on universal oneness that would dissolve individuality into itself, and the wilful assertion of individuality that the nature of the mariner's penance represents. This thematic contradiction, and the refusal of transparency produced by the discontinuity of poem and gloss, result in a fundamental resistance to stable meaning. And we are thus denied our place as knowing subjects unless we follow the example of gloss and write ourselves by rewriting, by interpreting the poem.

Because *The Ancient Mariner* demonstrates the powers and uses of transparent discourse within its content at the same time as it stubbornly refuses transparency in its form, it is hardly surprising that the task of fixing meaning has proved to be so difficult. But perhaps even more interesting is the self-conscious awareness the text of this poem brings to bear on the interpretive enterprise of literary criticism. The presence of the marginal gloss transforms the text into a figure of critical activity, and the discontinuity between the gloss and the poem stands as a reminder that the critical interpretive text is not a disinterested "accompaniment" to a literary work but a product of a discourse which has the specific goal of mastering the work in question and offering its own reading as the best access to meaning and truth. Just as the gloss

and the poem compete, so do literary works and criticism. Moreover, the materiality of language, which causes meaning to be dispersed, also causes the proliferation of interpretive texts. And each one, while representing the interests of its author, will finally be received and understood according to the interests of the reader. The process is endless. The activity of criticism does not stabilize meaning but actually increases its dispersal. In addition, the marginal gloss and the poem collude in an allusion to the autobiographical element of all discourse. The gloss encourages us to posit an imaginary subject "behind" it (a seventeenth-century editor), a subject we can only identify through the language of the gloss itself. And, as readers of the poem, we see in the "editor" a distorted reflection of our own activity. We are like the editor, but yet different—and our difference, our own selfhood, resides in that other (and further) gloss of the poem we must ourselves produce. The mariner's curse of speaking himself into being is also the curse of the critic.

It is obvious that my reading of *The Ancient Mariner* is determined by the self-consciousness and anxiety that poststructuralist theory has injected into literary criticism. My understanding of this poem as a text which declares its own textuality and represents the constitution of the subject through discourse could thus be regarded as the product of contemporary critical discourse as it "speaks" me, the critic. Indeed, there is no question that my interests as critic are determined largely by the current dominant discourses of my field. At this point in this century there seems no way of returning to the confidence of New Criticism and its fundamentally romantic objectives of unity and autonomy; nor can we return to the romantic concept of subjectivity as a natural, privileged and unified psychological condition. Discontinuity and the anxiety of reflexivity become preferable to illusory unity in a time when truth and meaning are understood to be only ever reached asymptotically through the systems of language and representation. And it is from this perspective that *The Ancient Mariner* seems to be a remarkably unromantic romantic text.

Camille Paglia (essay date 1990)

SOURCE: "The Daemon as Lesbian Vampire: Coleridge," in *Sexual Personae: Art and Decadence from Nefertiti to Emily Dickinson,* Yale University Press, 1990, pp. 317-46.

[*In the following essay, Paglia argues against strictly moral interpretations of* The Rime of the Ancient Mariner, *and rather insists that in the poem, "Jehovah has been obliterated by the vampire mother who rises from the slime of nature."*]

Literature's most influential male heroine is the protagonist of *The Rime of the Ancient Mariner*. Wordsworth was the first to notice the Mariner's passive suffering. In the 1800 edition of *Lyrical Ballads,* Wordsworth lists the "great defects" of the poem: "first, that the principal person has no distinct character . . . secondly, that he does not act, but is continually acted upon." Bloom speaks of the Mariner's "extraordinary passivity." Graham Hough equates the ship's motionlessness with "complete paralysis of the will." George Whalley goes further: "The Mariner's passivity is Coleridge's too." My reading of *The Ancient Mariner* makes this passivity the central psychological fact of the poem. I reject moral interpretations, typified by Robert Penn Warren's canonical essay. Edward E. Bostetter argues against Warren point by point: "The poem is the morbidly self-obsessed account of a man who through his act has become the center of universal attention." Two hundred sailors, dying, stare dolefully at the Mariner. The male heroine, by operatic self-dramatization, is a prima donna triumphing through exquisite public suffering. The eyes of the universe are fixed on him. Coleridge's ring of eyes is part paranoiac reproach, part eroticizing adoration. Eyes crucify his protagonists, pinning them in immobilized passivity, an uncanny world fear.

Sagas of the male heroine are always artistically endangered by the serpentine dynamic of self-identification. The Mariner, with his "long grey beard" and "skinny hand," recalls those Wordsworthian solitaires of "grey hairs" and "palsied hand" in whom I see a self-identification by the poet so extreme as to debilitate the text by sentimentality. Parts of *The Ancient Mariner* are ill-written to the point of Lewis Carroll parody: "'Hold off! unhand me, grey-beard loon!' / Eftsoons his hand dropt he." "The Wedding-Guest here beat his breast, / For he heard the loud bassoon." "Four times fifty living men . . . With heavy thump, a lifeless lump, / They dropped down one by one." Rhyme is merely ritualistic chiming, the darkening cloud of fate. Stanzas fall into slapstick and heedlessly sail on. *The Ancient Mariner* is one of the greatest poems in English, yet what it achieves is almost in defiance of language. Vision and execution often wildly diverge. Coleridge's sober "conversation poems" are in better taste; but they are minor works in literary history, belonging to the age of sensibility, and would never have made the poet's fame. The same disjunction of form and content afflicts Poe, Coleridge's heir. The French accused America of slighting her greatest poet in Poe, who may sound better in Baudelaire's translation than in English. Poe, like Coleridge, is a giant of imagination, and imagination has its own laws. In Poe's tales and Coleridge's mystery poems, the daemonic expresses itself nakedly. Dionysus always shakes off rules of Apollonian form.

Coleridge and Poe are seized by visions that transcend language, that belong to the dream experience beyond language. Psychoanalysis . . . overestimates the linguistic character of the unconscious. Dreaming is a pagan cinema. The wit of dreams comes from treating words as if they were objects. Coleridge and Poe have written works of cinema. Had film been available as a medium, perhaps that is the form they would have chosen, for language here is only an obstruction to vision. Evaluating the language of *The Ancient Mariner* by Renaissance or Augustan standards would be depressing. There are a few great lines in it; for example, "And ice, mast-high, came floating by, / As green as emerald." I maintain that all such wonderful moments in *The Ancient Mariner* look forward to *Christabel,* that *Christabel,* with its cold green snake, is struggling to be born throughout this poem. The rhetorical weaknesses in Coleridge and Poe have been produced by a warp of self-identification. Vision drives with such force from the unconscious that the craftsmanlike shape-making of consciousness lags behind.

The Ancient Mariner, a rhapsody of the male heroine, is filled with piercing arias: "Alone, alone, all, all alone, / Alone on a wide wide sea! / And never a saint took pity on / My soul in agony." Emotional expressionism of this kind is possible in Italian but not in English. At his maudlin fall, Shakespeare's Richard II cries, "My large kingdom for a little grave, / A little, little grave, an obscure grave" (III.iii.152-53). Intensified littleness gives you a cartoon pinpoint of dancing dwarves. Coleridge's intoning "alones" overpopulate themselves, baying like a canine chorus. Sheer velocity of identification makes him miss the infelicity of rhyming "thump" with "lump." There is too much agrarian comedy latent in our Anglo-Saxon monosyllables. The principle at work in *The Ancient Mariner,* as in **"To William Wordsworth,"** is pagan sexual exhibitionism. Self-pity in *The Ancient Mariner* is like the self-flagellation of the ancient goddess-cults. It is neither callow nor sick. It is a ritual device to facilitate daemonic vision. The Romantic male heroine is a self-emasculating devotee of chthonian nature.

Personae in *The Ancient Mariner* form a sexual allegory. The poem begins with the Mariner stopping the Wedding-Guest as he enters a marriage banquet. The scene's deep structure is exactly the same as at the opening of *Christabel*: a stranger with a "glittering eye" puts a spell on an innocent, who falls under daemonic compulsion. The Mariner detains the guest with his tale of woe, which takes up the whole poem. At the end, the guest gloomily turns away from the Bridegroom's door and departs. The merry feast goes on without him. My theory is this: Bridegroom, Wedding-Guest, and Mariner are all aspects of Coleridge. The Bridegroom is a masculine persona, the self comfortably integrated in society. This virile alter ego is always perceived longingly and at a distance, through an open door through which come bursts of happy laughter. The Wedding-Guest, "next of kin" to the Bridegroom, is an adolescent supplicant aspiring to sexual fulfillment and collective joy. To achieve this, the Wedding-Guest must merge with the Bridegroom. But he is always prevented from doing so by the appearance of a spectre self, the Mariner, the male heroine or hermaphroditic self who luxuriates in passive suffering. It's a case of always the bridesmaid and never the bride. The Wedding-Guest turns away at the end because once more the hieratically wounded self has won. The Guest will never be the Bridegroom. As many times as he attempts to pass through the door to the place of festivity, the Mariner will materialize and paralyze him with his seductive tale. This doorway is the obsessive scene of the Coleridgean sexual crux. Ostracism and casting out are the Romantic road to identity. Will that doorway ever be breached? Yes, in *Christabel*. And only by the most bizarre strategy of perversity and transsexualism.

The apparently pivotal event in the Mariner's tale is the killing of the albatross, from which follow all his sufferings. From the moment I read the poem in high school, I thought the albatross a superficial appendage, a kind of pin the tail on the donkey, and I found the stress on it by teachers and critics unconvincing and moralistic. Long afterward, I learned it was Wordsworth who suggested the idea of the albatross to Coleridge, which proves my point. This albatross is the biggest red herring in poetry. Its only significance is as a vehicle of transgression. The Mariner commits an obscure crime and becomes the focus of cosmic wrath. But he is as blameless as the shadow heroes of Kafka, who are hauled before faceless courts of law. In the world of *The Ancient Mariner*, any action is immediately punished. Masculine assertion is rebuked and humanity condemned to passive suffering.

Blake's "Crystal Cabinet" contains the same dramatic crisis: the moment the male acts, he is expelled into the wilderness. Blake's male is changed to a weeping babe in infantile dependency on a weeping woman. Coleridge's Mariner is also propelled backward to a maternal world. The ship is becalmed: "The very deep did rot: O Christ! / That ever this should be! / Yea, slimy things did crawl with legs / Upon the slimy sea." Stasis, slime. This is a vision of primal nondifferentiation, the chthonian swamp of generation. The universe has returned to one big womb, claustrophobic, airless, teeming with monstrous prehuman mud creatures. The Mariner's appeal to Christ is the opposite of what it seems. It shows that Coleridge, despite his conscious assent to Christianity, understands with the intuition of a great poet that the swamp-world of the Great Mother precedes the world of Christ and is ready at any moment to engulf it. Two remarks prove that Coleridge literally visualized a chthonian swamp: he once spoke of the "Sands and Swamps of Evil" and elsewhere of lust as "the reek of the Marsh."

The Ancient Mariner is one of Romantic poetry's great regressions to the daemonic and primeval. Every man makes a marine voyage out of the cell of archaic ocean that is the sac of womb-waters. We all emerge covered with slime and gasping for life. "The many men, so beautiful! / And they all dead did lie: / And a thousand thousand slimy things / Lived on; and so did I." All hopes for beauty and manhood lie dead. Male power can never surpass female power. We live in the slime of our bodies, which hold imagination hostage. Our mother-born bodies are unregenerate nature, beyond God's redemption. The "slimy sea" of chthonian nature nullifies the words of Christ. Coleridge is overwhelmed by a pagan vision coming to him from below and beyond his own ethics. *The Ancient Mariner* transports its Gothic tale out of the historical world of castles and abbeys into the sublime theater of a desolate nature. But expansion of space is just another cul-de-sac. Coleridge brilliantly converts the open sea into a rotting sepulchre, which I called the daemonic womb of Gothic. This is one black hole from which Christ will never rise. *The Ancient Mariner* is the source of Poe's *The Narrative of Arthur Gordon Pym,* with its disastrous voyage in a womb-tomb ship. Evolution and motion are an illusion in the dank prison space of chthonian nature. Hence the male heroine's crushing passivity. Mankind staggers under the burden of mother nature.

Language, I said, is mutilated for vision in *The Ancient Mariner*. Thus the appeal to good has a backlash effect, sparking the birth of evil. Invocation of Christ's name fails to release the Mariner from his imprisonment in ocean's nightmare womb. When a sail appears on the horizon, there is a moment of hope and joy. The Mariner attempts a new prayer: "Heaven's Mother send us grace!" But sacred language is profaned by daemonic revelation. On the ship is the grossest female apparition:

> *Her* lips were red, *her* looks were free,
> Her locks were yellow as gold:
> Her skin was as white as leprosy,
> The Night-mare Life-in-Death was she,
> Who thicks man's blood with cold.

Appeals to sky-cult are useless. As if irritated by references to her benign successor, the tender Madonna, the ur-mother makes her sensational appearance. She is the Whore of Babylon, the daemon unbound. Her lips are red with provocation and the blood of her victims. She is all health and all disease. She is a masque of the red death, a Medusa who turns men to stone but also the mother who stirs the blood pudding of her sons till their bodies congeal in her womb. To give life is to kill. This is heaven's mother, who comes when called. She is the vampire who haunts men's dreams. Aubrey Beardsley depicts a Coleridgean epiphany of the vampire Madonna in *The Ascension of St.*

Rose of Lima. Mary, lasciviously embracing St. Rose, hovers in the air like a poison black cloud. Another monstrous epiphany occurs in Ingmar Bergman's *Through a Glass Darkly* (1961), where a mad girl sees God as a sexually aggressive spider.

The Ancient Mariner surges forward on its wave of daemonic vision from Parts I through IV, but then something happens. Parts V through VII are a muddle. The poem recovers only when the Mariner's tale ceases and the narrative frame resumes, where the Mariner delays the Wedding-Guest at the Bridegroom's door. *The Ancient Mariner* drags on pointlessly for too long, and I think I know where and why it goes wrong. As Part IV ends, the Mariner sees water-snakes in the sea: "Blue, glossy green, and velvet black, / They coiled and swam; and every track / Was a flash of golden fire." This is one of the great moments in Romantic poetry. We are back at the dawn of time. Firmament has not yet separated from the waters. The sun is only a yolky yellow in the albuminous jelly of the mother-stuff. Primeval ocean swarms with slimy life. But the water is also man's body shot with veins. These serpents, writhing with Vergilian opalescence, are the chains that bind us, our physical life. Man is a Laocoön bedeviled by serpents. We all struggle in the toils of our mother-born body. Why are the sea-snakes veins? Because, as I said, all great lines in *The Ancient Mariner* look forward to *Christabel,* where the vampire has exquisite "blue-veined feet." Geraldine, the green snake who strangles the dove, is the daemon of chthonian nature, trampling man in her triumph of the will.

Coleridge has penetrated far into the daemonic realm. Too far, for there is an immediate retreat into conventional emotion. Vision fails, and the poem begins to drift. Why? What have the sea-snakes roused that Coleridge cannot face? The Mariner's response to them is embarrassingly simplistic. "A spring of love" gushes from his heart, and he blesses them. The moment he can pray, the albatross falls from his neck and into the sea. How dreadful to see our shaman-poet unmasked, cranking the bellows of afflatus like a stagehand. Coleridge is overcome by anxiety and surrenders to Wordsworth and to Christianity. Love and prayer are a ludicrously inadequate response to the chthonian horror that Coleridge has summoned from the dark heart of existence. The roiling sea-snakes are the barbaric energy of matter, the undulating spiral of birth and death. What is the proper response to this ecstatic hallucination? Coleridge is hemmed in. His protagonist, the Mariner, is insufficiently advanced as a sexual persona. The male heroine will need to be revised if daemonic vision is to be sustained. *Christabel* is a rewriting of *The Ancient Mariner* in new and more daring terms. There, as we shall see, when the protagonist meets the serpent face of nature, there will be no swerving away. The poet, disguised so that Wordsworth can no longer find him, will hurl himself into the chthonian abyss.

The problem with moral or Christian readings of *The Ancient Mariner* is that they can make no sense of the compulsive or delusional frame of the poem. If the "spring of love" felt by the Mariner were imaginatively efficacious, the poem should be able to conclude. Or at the very least, it should permit the Mariner to be redeemed. But the falling off of the albatross is followed by three more parts. And even at the end of the poem, the Mariner is still forced to wander the world, repeating his "ghastly tale" again and again. Having introduced a benevolent emotion into his daemonic poem, Coleridge is at a loss how to proceed. A new cast of characters is hustled in—seraphs, a Pilot, a Hermit. There is confused dialogue, a fuzzy twisting and turning. Here is the point: the moment the Mariner prays, the moment good rather than evil triumphs, the poem falls apart. At the end of Part IV, Coleridge is overwhelmed with fear at what he has written and vainly attempts to turn his poem in a redemptive direction. The superego acts to obscure what has come from the amoral id. Nineteen years later, Coleridge added the marginal glosses still adorning the poem. These dithery festoons are afterthoughts, revisions that often depart crucially in tone from the text they "explain." We hear in them the Christian Coleridge trying to soften the daemonic Coleridge, exactly as the older, Urizenic Wordsworth "corrected" his early nature poetry. By rationalization and moralization, Coleridge strove to put out the daemonic fires of his own imagination.

The poetic discordancies are blatant in the conclusion. The Mariner says, "O Wedding-Guest! this soul hath been / Alone on a wide wide sea: / So lonely 'twas, that God himself / Scarce seeméd there to be." This is the truth. In the cosmos of *The Ancient Mariner,* Jehovah has been obliterated by the vampire mother who rises from the slime of nature. But the Christian Coleridge keeps stitching the veil he has rent. The Mariner illogically goes on to celebrate communal churchgoing under the kind gaze of the "great Father" and ends his message: "He prayeth best, who loveth best / All things both great and small; / For the dear God who loveth us, / He made and loveth all." What a frail twig to cling to in the maelstrom of chthonian nature. This is like Blake's ironic moral tags, evasive distortions of the severity of experience depicted in his poems: "So if all do their duty, they need not fear harm"; "Then cherish pity, lest you drive an angel from your door." The Mariner's farewell stanzas are a poetic non sequitur. They contradict everything that is great in the poem. Coleridge himself seems to have sensed this, for long afterward he remarked that *The Ancient Mariner* had "too much" of a moral in it: "The only or chief fault, if I might say so, was the obtrusion of the moral sentiment so openly on the reader."

Imagination has the last word anyhow in **The Ancient Mariner**. Here are the closing lines, as the Wedding-Guest turns away from the Bridegroom's door: "He went like one that hath been stunned, / And is of sense forlorn: / A sadder and a wiser man, / He rose the morrow morn." If one accepts the Christian interpretation of the poem, how explain this peculiar reaction? The Wedding-Guest is not morally strengthened by the Mariner's exhortations. He is plunged into gloom and severed from society. The Mariner counsels Christian love, but the Wedding-Guest walks away as if the Mariner has said, "There is no God, and nature is a hell of appetite and force." But this is the secret message that the Wedding-Guest has divined, the message that has slipped past Coleridge despite his vigorous efforts to steer the poem in a morally acceptable direction. The guest arises the next day "a sadder and a wiser man," because through the smokescreen of the Christian finale has come the terrible revelation of Coleridge's daemonic dream vision.

FURTHER READING

Bibliography

Milton, Mary Lee Taylor. *The Poetry of Samuel Taylor Coleridge: An Annotated Bibliography of Criticism, 1935-1970.* New York: Garland Publishing, 1981, 251 p.

Includes an extended introduction which discusses major issues and trends in Coleridge criticism.

Raysor, Thomas M.; Schulz, Max F.; and Wellek, René. "Coleridge." In *The English Romantic Poets: A Review of Research and Criticism*, third revised edition, edited by Frank Jordan, pp. 135-258. New York: Modern Language Association of America, 1972.

Studies bibliographies and editions of Coleridge's notebooks, verse, and letters, including a section devoted to an overview of historical and literary criticism of Coleridge's poetry.

Biography

Bawer, Bruce. "Hungering for Eternity: Coleridge the Poet." *The New Criterion* 8, No. 8 (April 1990): 20-32.

Biographical essay on Coleridge's life and career.

Caine, Hall. *Life of Samuel Taylor Coleridge.* London: Walter Scott, 1887, 154 p.

Biographical study drawing on a variety of sources, including "table-talk, letters, diaries, memoirs, reminiscences, magazine articles, [and] newspaper reports."

Charpentier, John. *Coleridge: The Sublime Somnambulist,* translated by M. V. Nugent. New York: Dodd, Mead & Co., 1929, 332 p.

Extensive examination of Coleridge's life and works.

Criticism

Alcorn, Marshall W., Jr. "Coleridge's Literary Use of Narcissism." *The Wordsworth Circle* XVI, No. 1 (Winter 1985): 13-21.

Psychoanalytic study of "The Rime of the Ancient Mariner" in which Alcorn discusses and disputes various interpretations of the poem's rich symbolic meaning and Coleridge's own view of the work as theological. Alcorn suggests "that the symbology portrays original sin as an expression of narcissistic incompletion; similarly, it grasps redemption as the sublimated recovery of an original narcissism."

Austin, Frances. "Coleridge." In her *The Language of Wordsworth and Coleridge*, pp. 122-68. London: Macmillan Education, 1989.

Analyzes the verse and language of the "mystery" and "conversation" poems and compares their style and syntax to Wordsworth's poetry.

Beer, J. B. *Coleridge the Visionary.* London: Chatto & Windus, 1959, 367 p.

Studies Coleridge's political, philosophical, and religious thought, as well as literary influences on his poetry, attempting to "throw light on both the intellectual organization of the poetry and the imaginative qualities implicit in the philosophy."

Bohm, Arnd. "Text and Technology in Coleridge's *The Rime of the Ancient Mariner*." *English Studies in Canada* XV, No. 1 (March 1989): 35-47.

Hermeneutical analysis in which Bohm "historicizes" *The Rime of the Ancient Mariner*.

Findlay, L. M. "Death or Life of the Spirit: *The Rime of the Ancient Mariner*: Thalassian Poetry in the Nineteenth Century." In *Poetics of the Elements in the Human Condition: The Sea, from Elemental Stirrings to Symbolic Inspiration, Language, and Life-Significance in Literary Interpretation and Theory*, edited by Anna-Teresa Tymieniecka, pp. 23-44. Boston: D. Reidel Publishing Co., 1985.

Explains the symbolic and metaphoric function of the sea and its correlation to identity and poetry in *The Rime of the Ancient Mariner*.

Fogle, Richard Harter. "The Genre of *The Ancient Mariner*." In his *The Permanent Pleasure: Essays on Classics of Romanticism*, pp. 27-42. Athens: University of Georgia Press, 1974.

Interprets *The Ancient Mariner* according to Coleridge's own remarks regarding Romanticism.

Gravil, Richard; Newlyn, Lucy; and Roe, Nicholas, eds. *Coleridge's Imagination: Essays in Memory of Pete Laver.* Cambridge: Cambridge University Press, 1985, 277 p.

Collection of essays by Coleridge scholars such as John Beer, Thomas McFarland, J. Robert Barth, and others, offering diverse approaches to Coleridge's theories regarding the role and function of the imagination.

Grow, L. M. "*The Rime of the Ancient Mariner*: Coleridge's Scientific and Philosophic Insights." *Bucknell Review: Self, Sign, and Symbol* XXX, No. 2 (1987): 45-71.
    Discusses Coleridge's scientific writings, placing them in the context of his other works, notably *The Ancient Mariner*.

Knight, G. W. "Coleridge's Divine Comedy." In *English Romantic Poets: Modern Essays in Criticism*, edited by M. H. Abrams, pp. 158-69. New York: Oxford University Press, 1960.
    Comparison of *Christabel, The Ancient Mariner*, and "Kubla Khan" to Dante's *Divina Commedia* and the works of Shakespeare. Knight states, "These three poems . . . may be grouped as a little *Divina Commedia* exploring in turn Hell, Purgatory, and Paradise."

Magnuson, Paul. *Coleridge's Nightmare Poetry.* Charlottesville: University Press of Virginia, 1974, 133 p.
    Critical study of the major poems "that reveal an increasing awareness of [Coleridge's] failure to create the self, the resulting fear that gripped him, and the expression of that fear and guilt in dreams."

Marks, Emerson R. *Coleridge on the Language of Verse.* Princeton, N.J.: Princeton University Press, 1981, 117 p.
    Examines Coleridge's applications of his theories relative to diction, rhyme, and meter.

McFarland, Thomas. *Originality & Imagination.* Baltimore: Johns Hopkins University Press, 1985, 208 p.
    Discusses Coleridge's role in developing the Romantic concept of imagination and belief in divine intervention at the time of poetic creation.

McGann, Jerome J. "*The Ancient Mariner*: The Meaning of the Meanings." In his *The Beauty of Inflections: Literary Investigations in Historical Method and Theory*, pp. 135-72. Oxford: Clarendon Press, 1985.
    Considers the meaning of *The Rime of the Ancient Mariner* in light of modern critical theory.

McKim, A. Elizabeth. "'An Epicure in Sound': Coleridge on the Scansion of Verse." *English Studies in Canada* XVIII, No. 3 (September 1992): 289-300.
    Studies the use of rhyme and meter in Coleridge's verse.

Modiano, Raimonda. *Coleridge and the Concept of Nature.* Tallahassee: Florida State University Press, 1985, 270 p.
    Examines Coleridge's philosophical concept of nature and its manifestation in his poetical works.

Newlyn, Lucy. *Coleridge, Wordsworth, and the Language of Allusion.* Oxford: Clarendon Press, 1986, 214 p.

Explains that Coleridge and Wordsworth "mythologized their relationship" in their poetry, "presenting themselves as joint labourers, even while they were moving apart."

Ower, John. "The 'Death-Fires,' the 'Fire-Flags' and the Corposant in *The Rime of the Ancient Mariner*." *Philological Quarterly* 70, No. 2 (Spring 1991): 199-218.
    Examines metaphysical imagery in *The Ancient Mariner*.

Paley, Morton D. "Apocalypse and Millennium in the Poetry of Coleridge." *The Wordsworth Circle* XXIII, No. 1 (Winter 1992): 24-34.
    Investigates the influence of millenarian thought on Coleridge's verse.

Peterfreund, Stuart. "The Way of Immanence, Coleridge, and the Problem of Evil." *English Literary History* 55, No. 1 (Spring 1988): 125-58.
    Explicates the poetical and other writings that reveal Coleridge's theological views in relation to eighteenth-century scientific, philosophical, and religious beliefs.

Piper, H.W. *The Singing of Mount Abora: Coleridge's Use of Biblical Imagery and Natura; Symbolism in Poetry and Philosophy.* Cranbury, N.J.: Associated University Presses, 1987, 124 p.
    Analyzes the symbolism and imagery of Coleridge's verse.

Randel, Fred V. "Coleridge and the Contentiousness of Romantic Nightingales." *Studies in Romanticism* 21, No. 1 (Spring 1982): 33-55.
    Examines Coleridge's use of the nightingale as a common Romantic symbol as well as a metaphoric vehicle for his critique of John Milton's work.

Sanders, Charles Richard. "*The Ancient Mariner* and Coleridge's Theory of Poetic Art." In his *Carlyle's Friendships and Other Studies*, pp. 312-30. Durham, N.C.: Duke University Press, 1977.
    Considers *The Rime of the Ancient Mariner* as a conscious expression of Coleridge's literary theory.

Stevenson, Warren. *Nimbus of Glory: A Study of Coleridge's Three Great Poems.* Salzburg, Austria: Institut für Anglistik und Amerikanistik, Universität Salzburg, 1983, 98 p.
    Regards "Kubla Khan," *The Rime of the Ancient Mariner*, and *Christabel* as a unified grouping because of the time and place of their writing. Stevenson's study finds the impact of Wordsworth on Coleridge to be far greater than previously imagined by other scholars.

Tave, Katherine Bruner. *The Demon and the Poet: An Interpretation of 'The Rime of the Ancient Mariner' according to Coleridge's Demonological Sources.* Salzburg,

Austria: Institut für Anglistik und Amerikanistik, Universität Salzburg, 1983, 98 p.

> Traces sources Coleridge used for creating *The Rime of the Ancient Mariner*, concluding that the poem "illustrates the sometimes divergent, sometimes parallel actions of the forces of God and the forces of Evil."

Warren, Robert Penn. "A Poem of Pure Imagination: An Experiment in Reading." In his *Selected Essays*, pp. 198-272. New York: Random House, 1951.

> Extensive explication of *The Rime of the Ancient Mariner*.

Watkins, Daniel P. "History as Demon in Coleridge's *The Rime of the Ancient Mariner*." *Papers on Language & Literature* XXIV, No. 1 (Winter 1988): 23-33.

> Argues that *The Rime of the Ancient Mariner* "is a symbolic formulation of the contradictions and struggles within history."

Watson, George. *Coleridge the Poet*. London: Routledge and Kegan Paul, 1966, 147 p.

> Critical study of textual influences on Coleridge's poetry and interpretations of his most popular works.

Wheeler, K. M. *The Creative Mind in Coleridge's Poetry*. Cambridge, Mass.: Harvard University Press, 1981, 189 p.

> Investigation of the literary, political, and philosophical influences operating in Coleridge's imagery and language in several of his prominent poems.

Woodring, Carl R. *Politics in the Poetry of Coleridge*. Madison: University of Wisconsin Press, 1961, 270 p.

> Focuses on social, political, and philosophical themes in Coleridge's poetry.

The Wordsworth Circle XXII, No. 1 (Winter 1991).

> Issue devoted to Coleridge, containing eleven papers given at the Coleridge Summer Conference held in 1990 at Cannington College in Cannington, England.

Wormhoudt, Arthur. "Coleridge." In his *The Demon Lover: A Psychoanalytical Approach to Literature*, pp. 17-50. New York: Exposition Press, 1949.

> Discusses psychoanalytic themes in *Christabel* and *The Rime of the Ancient Mariner*.

Additional coverage of Coleridge's life and career is contained in the following sources published by Gale Research: *Dictionary of Literary Biography*, Vols. 93, 107; DISCovering Authors; *Nineteenth-Century Literature Criticism*, Vol. 9; *Poetry Criticism*, Vol. 11; *World Literature Criticism, 1500 to the Present*.

Carlo Collodi

1826-1890

(Pseudonym of Carlo Lorenzini) Italian author of fiction and nonfiction, journalist, children's author, critic, editor, and translator.

INTRODUCTION

Collodi created Pinocchio, hero of perhaps the best-known puppet story ever written. The subject of a two-year long centennial celebration in Italy during the early 1980s, *Le Avventure di Pinocchio* (1883; *The Adventures of Pinocchio*) has continued to fascinate children and adults with its amusing portrayal of childhood. Historically, *The Adventures of Pinocchio* marked a turning point away from overt didacticism in Italian children's literature toward the use of comedy and minimal adult intrusion. Since then, it has received a great deal of critical attention; whether seen as folklore, fantasy, or allegory, it is decidedly a classic of children's literature.

Biographical Information

Collodi was born Carlo Lorenzini in 1826 in Florence, Italy, where his father was a cook and his mother was a maid. Biographers have noted that, as a child, Collodi displayed many of the characteristics he later gave to Pinocchio: impudence, mischievousness, and curiosity. At an early age, Collodi was sent to a seminary, though at age sixteen, deciding against an ecclesiastical career, he abandoned his studies. A few years later, in the mid-1840s, he immersed himself in journalism, where he championed liberal causes and founded two journals dealing with political satire and the dramatic arts. He also wrote numerous books for adults on a variety of technical and literary subjects. After serving for a second time as a volunteer in the Italian war against Austria, he became a government official and inaugurated several educational reforms. He also continued his literary efforts, translating various French fairy tales into Italian—including several by Charles Perrault—in the late 1870s, and developing several textbooks that espoused his theory of making education entertaining. These works, together with his later stories for children, were available only in Italy, and have long since been out of print; only *Pinocchio* survives. In 1881, the editor of a new children's magazine invited Collodi, then a fifty-five-year-old bachelor, to submit a story. Collodi did so, adding a note: "I send you this childishness to do with as you see fit. But if you print it, pay me well so that I have a good reason to continue with it." The first adventure of Pinocchio met

with much success, and thereafter Collodi sent in chapters sporadically. After thirty-five episodes had appeared, *Pinocchio* was published in book form in 1883. Seven years later Collodi died suddenly in Florence, never realizing the international appeal that his story would have.

Major Works

Collodi first achieved literary recognition as a journalist, writing satires, sketches, and dramatic criticism that displayed a sharp wit and a talent for scene-writing and dialogue. In his essays he also expressed an interest in translating literary texts, and in 1876 published *I Racconti delle fate,* a collection of his translations of French fairy tales. These translations were readily received, and he followed by writing his own stories for children, many featuring the characters of "Tiny Morsel" and "Little Joe." Though these tales were popular among contemporary readers, they have largely been forgotten, overshadowed by the character of Pinocchio. The 1883 publication of *The Adventures of Pinocchio* was an immense success, selling more than one million copies in Italy. Collodi saw little wealth from the sales, however, receiving only a few thousand liras in payment. A blend of fantasy and reality that impresses upon its readers the values of school, honest work, and upright companions, *Pinocchio* is the story of a marionette who becomes a boy. Carved by Gepetto from a piece of lumber, Pinocchio comes to life—although he is still a wooden puppet— and Gepetto adopts him as his son. Though Pinocchio promises to be good, he runs away in search of adventure, escaping near-deaths by drowning, hanging, and by fire. Near the end of the story he is reunited with Gepetto and is finally transformed into a real boy. Children have continued to identify with Pinocchio's love for adventure and dislike of school, and they applaud the book's simple justice: every time the puppet lies, his nose grows longer. Without undue moralizing, Collodi succeeded in pointing out that disobedience and pleasure-seeking lead to evil and unhappiness. Though *Pinocchio* has since become an international favorite in children's literature, none of Collodi's other works has ever achieved popularity in countries other than his native one.

Critical Reception

Critics see *Pinocchio* as a story rich in imagination and symbolism. They find Collodi interweaving his classical education with peasant folklore by combining mythological, psychological, and religious elements with Tuscan speech and storytelling patterns. Other commentators, such as M. L. Rosenthal (1989), read the book as a social and political allegory, pointing out Collodi's depictions of the disparities between the poor and the wealthy, his emphasis on the working class, and his parodies of the justice system. Still other critics see the book as Collodi's attempt to recover his lost childhood, or as his portrayal of a search of children for parents or of parents for children. Pointing out the numerous adaptations of the Pinocchio story throughout the years, Richard Wunderlich (1992) in particular has concentrated on how these alterations to the original text have been shaped by cultural and social forces, including prevalent educational and child-rearing philosophies. In a negative vein, some reviewers contend that *Pinocchio* consists merely of a weak string of escapades devised by Collodi to write a winning serial and reap financial gain. Few would quarrel with the book's enduring qualities, however, and most would agree with Benedetto Croce: "The wood out of which Pinocchio is carved is humanity itself."

PRINCIPAL WORKS

Macchiette ["Odd Figures in a Landscape"]
Note Gaie ["Gay Notes"]

Occhi e Nasi ["Eyes and Noses"]
Divagazioni Critico-Umoristiche ["Satirical Digressions"]
Storie Allegre ["Light Stories"]
Giannettino (children's literature) 1876
I Racconti delle fate (translations of fairy tales) 1876
Minnuzolo: Il Viaggio per l'Italia de Giannettino (children's literature) ["Giannettino's Trip through Italy"]
La Geografica di Giannettino (children's literature) ["Giannettino's Geography"]
La Grammatica de Giannettino (children's literature) ["Giannettino's Grammar"]
Le Avventure di Pinocchio (children's literature) 1883 [*The Story of a Puppet: or, The Adventures of Pinocchio*, 1892; *The Adventures of Pinocchio*, 1925]
Beppo: or, The Little Rose-Colored Monkey (fiction) 1907

CRITICISM

The Bookman, London (review date 1892)

SOURCE: "The Story of a Puppet," in *The Bookman*, London, Vol. I, No. 1, January, 1892, p. 148.

[*The following is a positive review of the first English translation of* Pinocchio.]

Children are at once so independent and so conservative in their literary judgments, that we hesitate before recommending books to them that are not sanctified by custom and tradition. We think we might possibly be safe in this case, and if they would take our advice only for this once, they might spend even a merrier Christmas than otherwise, enlivened by the waggeries and the sprightly naughtiness of Pinocchio. But knowing the critical cast of their minds, we don't press the point. It is with their elders we have to deal, and with them we are on more certain ground. Children seeking gifts, therefore, for their sober-minded elders might do worse than choose this **Story of a Puppet**. Pinocchio is the most fascinating creature we have met with for a long time. He has a very distinct personality, and most winning manners even in his depraved moments. But his greatest charm is a certain inexhaustible vitality. With his open-mindedness, curiosity, and scorn for the prosaic round of ordinary life, of course he is bound to have many adventures. Which of them excite us most is difficult to say. Our blood curdles at the assassins' terrible chase; it is warmed by Pinocchio's noble attitude towards Harlequin, before the Fire-eater's sneeze betokens the coming on of a milder mood. We confess to have started with him in full confidence and high spirits for the Land of Boobies, and when the awful consequences of his folly were revealed to us, we instinctively put our hands to our own ears to feel if they too had grown. The Fairy with the blue hair is charming, when she is herself. She is less agreeable in her other impersonations. But here we can only hint at one or two of the incidents and vicissitudes in this remarkable career, though we must not omit a reference to what is the real attraction to us elders—the clear, straightforward, and aboveboard character of the morals. There is never any doubt about them, and in this the story is helped out by the illustrations, which are charming. The rabbits, black as ink, standing with the little bier, as a pointed warning, till the rebellious puppet swallows his medicine; the visible lengthening of the nose with the growth of a habit of untruthfulness, are admirable. We have no reservations to make about this little work. The translator's part has been skillfully carried out, and never for a moment hinders us from recognizing that the story of Pinocchio is a work of genius.

The New York Times Book Review (review date 1909)

SOURCE: "A Juvenile Classic," in *The New York Times Book Review,* April 3, 1909, p. 192.

[*In the following review, the critic examines the moral teachings of* Pinocchio.]

Among the illustrious collection of illustrated books "every child should know," the Italian juvenile classic, ***The Marvellous Adventures of Pinocchio***, by Carlo Lorenzini, is entitled to a place; if not a first place, at least one very near the top. . . .

The story of ***Pinocchio*** is an allegory, a guide to self-control, self-government, and self-determination in children. Its concise style and picture words are well calculated to hold the attention of children. A few scenes in the book, however, might be considered too gruesome for the child mind—such as the description of the young girl who died and was waiting for the hearse to come and carry her away. But the moral of the puppet who, by overcoming his evil influences and following the advice of his good fairy, changes into a "real boy," is admirable. Love and consideration for animals are taught among many other things. . . .

Carl Van Doren (essay date 1937)

SOURCE: An introduction to *Pinocchio: The Adventures of a Marionette* by C. Collodi, translated by Walter S. Cramp, The Heritage Press, 1937, pp. v-viii.

[*Van Doren is considered one of the most perceptive critics of the first half of the twentieth century. A founder of the Literary Guild and author or editor of several American literary histories, Van Doren was*

also a critically acclaimed historian and biographer. In the following essay, he claims that Pinocchio *is "a childish allegory of the moral life."*]

In the heroic ages and in the nursery all stories are anonymous. Nobody knows the name of a single bard before Homer, and I never heard of a child that asked who was the author of the story of Robinson Crusoe or Gulliver or Alice or Pinocchio. Inquiring boys and girls want to be assured that what they hear is true, but it comes like the sunrise or the wind, direct out of nature without the intervention of any story-teller. I remember perfectly how at five or six, I read about Robinson or Gulliver. The tale had not been shaped for me. The actions happened. Though I had not seen any ocean or island, and had hardly been outside a single prairie township, I shuddered and strangled with Robinson through the surf to the dry land, and lived busily alone for ages. With Gulliver I woke to find myself the captive of pygmies, and was picked up out of the grass by giants, and gradually discovered that the horses in another country I had come to were its men. I was a little older when I read about Alice's adventures. I remember being irritated by the nonsense in some of the poems and conversations, but it seemed serious and natural to follow the rabbit down his hole, to change easily from one size to another, to live on the best terms with amiable animals. If I had known Pinocchio, I am sure I should have gone with him, identified with him and at the same time his companion, in his restless experiments. But I should have been no more aware of any such person as C. Collodi than I was of Defoe or Swift or Lewis Carroll.

I still know about C. Collodi only that his real name was Carlo Lorenzini and that he was soldier, official, and editor as well as writer for children. He is said to have been what is called a bad boy, and Pinocchio is almost all bad boys in one. But he is never cruel or mean, merely an infant individualist. Consider his history. Not born a helpless baby, he has from the first the lively hands and feet of mischief. Who knows how many babies would run away from home the day they were born, if they could? Pinocchio can run, and does. Like a natural man, if there were such a person, Pinocchio acts on every impulse, and has to learn by experience which impulses are encouraged by human society, which forbidden. Here is a childish allegory of the moral life, a kind of puppet's progress. At the outset Pinocchio wants to be "eating, drinking, sleeping, playing, and wandering around from morning till night." Instinct does not tell him what is good behavior and what is bad, what is reckless and what is prudent. Hunger has to teach him, and fire, and fear and loneliness and misadventure. Reading the story of Pinocchio, any boy must recognize his own headstrong impulse to do things which he feels are natural but which he has been told are mischievous. Nature does not know what mischief is. But society does, and much of childhood is taken up with the work of cutting nature to fit society.

Of course Pinocchio is not pure nature. Very soon, sooner than his experience strictly justifies, he begins to have affections and a conscience. No child, reading the story or having it read to him, would notice anything strange in this, for such a child would already have about the same amount of affection and conscience in himself. But such a child, a rudimentary Ovid, would have dimly noticed that he could see the better and approve, and yet follow the worse. For children this is the mystery of morals, as it is for most adults, who do not understand that some things which are unsocial are not unnatural and so are followed by the natural man even while the social man disapproves of them. If at any age between, say, six and ten I had become acquainted with Pinocchio, I know I should have sympathized with him in his irresistible mischief. At the same time, I should have felt a little superior. I should have watched him learning what I should have been proud of already knowing, should have wished I could warn him now and then, and should have wanted to tell him that the outcome of his misconduct was exactly what I had expected. The constant moralizing of the story would not have troubled me at all. Adults often imagine that children object to moralizing. They seldom do, when it is, as in Pinocchio, obviously a part of the story. For children think at least as much as adults about what is good and bad. What to adults may have become an abstract luxury of speculation is to children still intensely practical, like the rules of a game, like the tricks of a trade.

The moralism in the story of Pinocchio makes it life-like. Before the puppet rushes off into fresh mischief he has moments of moral hesitation, not long enough to hold him back. After he has been punished by bad luck he is penitent for a time, until he has accumulated enough energy to be tempted again. Puppets are like men in this. The happy romantic ending does not matter. Stories of adventure must end somewhere, and one end is about as good as another. What matters is the adventures. Of those Pinocchio has as many as he could have with his size. He is an Odysseus too small and young to capture a city. Pinocchio kills a Cricket, or thinks he has done it. He sells his primer to buy a ticket for the Marionettes, and is promptly at home among them. He is duped by the Cat and the Fox. His Calypso is the benevolent, motherly Maiden with Azure Hair. He moves about in a world of serpents and watchdogs and weasels and pigeons and sharks and toys and dormice. For running away from school he is turned into a donkey. Though he can lie like Odysseus, Pinocchio's Odyssey is aimed at the nursery or the schoolroom. Any child by simple animism can think of a puppet as being alive. Suppose it did begin to talk or walk by itself. Then anything might happen—but only things the child could himself imagine. There is nothing in the story of Pinocchio beyond the reach of a child's imagination.

Major Media Adaptations of *Pinocchio*

Motion Pictures:

Pinocchio, 1940. Animated version. Disney. Director: Ben Sharpsteen. Voices: Dick Jones, Cliff Edwards, Evelyn Venable.

Pinocchio, 1976. Musical. Actors: Danny Kaye, Sandy Duncan.

Pinocchio, 1983. "Faerie Tale Theatre" adaptation. Director: Peter Medak. Actors: Pee-Wee Herman, James Coburn, Carl Reiner, Lainie Kazan.

The Adventures of Pinocchio, 1996. Live-action adaptation. Actors: Martin Landau, Jonathan Taylor Thomas.

Other Adaptations:

Pinocchio. Stage adaptation. Written for Federal Theatre Project. Director: Yasha Frank. Premiered June 1937 at Beaux Arts Theatre, Los Angeles; moved to Ritz Theatre, early 1939.

In addition, there have been innumerable other television, film, and stage, as well as book adaptations, all relying in differing degrees on Collodi's original work.

There must be many American children who are delighted with Pinocchio although they have never seen a marionette. They have only to see him as a wooden doll and the rest will follow. The Italian setting of the story need not bewilder them. Children are more cosmopolitan than adults sometimes realize. A whole stream of interracial culture seeps into the nursery in stories, maxims, rhymes. Samson, Odysseus, Aesop's talking animals, ogres, witches, fairies, gnomes and elves, Cinderella, King Alfred, Mother Goose, the Ugly Duckling, George Washington, David Copperfield, Tom Sawyer: who knows or cares precisely where they lived? They once lived in the world in which children now live, and their shadows fall charmingly or warningly across it. That rascal Pinocchio has a special place in this world. Most of the other heroes stand as examples of how children became men or women. Pinocchio is a hero who after many adventures became a child.

Giuseppe Prezzolini (essay date 1940)

SOURCE: "The Author of *Pinocchio*," in *The Saturday Review of Literature*, Vol. XXI, No. 17, February 17, 1940, pp. 14-15.

[*In the essay following, Prezzolini describes the biography of Collodi as it relates to the creation of* Pinocchio.]

The name of Pinocchio has been familiar to children the world over for the past generation; and it may be said that there isn't a grown-up who has been through school who hasn't heard the story, either told in his own language or shown on the screen, of the wooden marionette who becomes a boy. Even Soviet Russia has given us a version.

Yet no one ever asks who its author was, and few men, outside of Italy, can tell you anything about him. Even a scholar like Carl Van Doren, in the preface to a deluxe edition of *Pinocchio*—as beautiful typographically as misleading in its illustrations—confesses knowing "very little concerning its author."

Collodi is not even the real name of the author but the pseudonym which he adopted from the name of the villa where, as the son of the chef of the proprietor, he spent many years of his childhood. This villa—as it lay huddled in the arms of a valley, caressed each evening by the departing sun—was saved from eternal oblivion by the author, Carlo Lorenzini, whose fame spread the name to the four corners of the earth. As you approached the villa—which was owned by a Tuscan nobleman of the eighteenth century—on the small road surrounded by low walls, you suddenly came upon a strange architectural structure composed of foliage, a veritable theater of trees, where was evident the hand of a gardener-sculptor who had known how to mould the vegetation to his will, to have it now assume the shape of a pilaster, now of a column, now of a loggia, now of a niche, within whose branches were housed grandiose and grotesque statues, and fantastic fountains spouting up their jets to intertwine with the air in a most bizarre fashion.

Carlo Lorenzini was not born there, but in Florence, in 1826, where he later returned to complete his studies. It seems that he never went very far in them, with the result that he remained but a small-time employee of the Grand Duke. (Tuscany at the time was ruled by a good-natured but weary Austrian dynasty, whose "tyranny" consisted in keeping the Italian people in a state of enforced idleness.)

Yet in that humble employee's soul there was a spark that could not be dimmed by the monotony of those four walls of his office: there burned in him the desire to write and jest. He busied himself with dramatic criticism, he wrote sketches and satires, he even founded a small journal called *The Lamp Post*. Like all Italian writers and youths of the period, he espoused the liberal cause, and hoped some day to see a new and united Italy, free of foreign domination. In 1848 he joined the Tuscan student forces which acquitted themselves well on the battle-fields of Curtatone and Montanara in Lombardy. In 1859 he again joined the colors, this time as a member of the cavalry. Finally in 1860, with Italy free and united, he found himself transferred from the

Austrian's employ to that of his own country. He did not, however, rise in office, or change his way of life. He still remained that same perfunctory sort of employee, never really interested in his work, barely respectful toward his superiors, always dissatisfied with his salary. In all probability, he preferred writing articles or going to the theater, to recording in the archives. But even his writings, though they reveal a decided flair for dialogue and scene-making, never seem to have quite succeeded. They were later collected under the titles **"Gay Grimaces"** and **"Eyes and Noses,"** which today are scarcely ever read. In them is depicted a middle-class world with a comic moralistic touch, but without profundity or penetration.

It was by accident that he came to write for children. A modest editor of the day, a certain Felix Paggi, asked him, in 1879, to translate Perrault's *Three Fairy Tales* from the French. The book was immediately popular. Whereupon the editor invited him to send in something of his own.

Lorenzini did. There was current at the time a tradition inaugurated by one Pallavicini, an author of children's books, known as "teaching by entertaining." Its basic idea was to have pupils participate in the subject they were being taught: —map out a voyage in geography, act out the events in history. These are formulae well known to all writers of children's books, and have been the germ of a vast literature on the subject in all parts of the world. Thus came into being two of Collodi's creations, "Little Joe" and "Tiny Morsel," and with them a raft of Little Joes that went parading up and down Italy learning their reading and arithmetic, and brandishing (what was new in those days) a magic lantern.

Today "Little Joe" and "Tiny Morsel" are no longer in vogue, and are relegated to the domain of powdered wigs and carriages. No Italian child will read them now. Their editor has even tried to stream-line them, adapting them to changed social and technological conditions, but all in vain.

But Lorenzini did not stop there. Another incident occurred, purely arbitrary, which resulted in his one and only masterpiece. There had just started in Rome, in 1881, the publishing of a *Children's Journal,* with Guido Biagi, a friend of Lorenzini, as its secretary. The former relates that one day he received a batch of papers, carelessly written, together with an explanatory note from Lorenzini, whom he had invited to collaborate with him. In this note, he found the following: "I send you this bit of *Childishness,* do with it what you can, but if you publish it, *pay me well for it,* so that I'll have some incentive for following it up." This bit of childishness was called *The Adventures of a Puppet.* It became very popular. Soon Biagi began pestering him for more. He started to send in chapters every now and then, whenever it struck his fancy, without even rereading what had gone before, content to devote himself to editing and correcting the text. Thus was Pinocchio born, and thus did he grow.

From the journal he passed into book form. The editor Bemporad, who bought him, made a fortune from the book. It is estimated that in Italy alone the sale exceeded a million copies. Out of it, poor Lorenzini made but a few thousand lire. The book then passed from Italy into foreign countries, where it was translated in all languages, including the most distant and remote like Japanese and Irish.

But more interesting than its financial was its literary success. Carlo Lorenzini himself died unaware of the fact that he had written a world's best seller, one destined to become a classic in Italian literature. His contemporaries considered him just another writer of children's stories. But the trend today among the more prominent Italian critics is to see in Collodi not only the Tuscan writer of color and wit, but also the affirmation of the goodness and realistic teaching of life. Pinocchio is a hero of the soul, who, like the characters of the *Divine Comedy* and *Faust*, goes through life finally transformed by experience. It is the story of hope and fear, joy and disillusionment, death and transfiguration. From a marionette with inordinate instincts and desires, tumbling downward on the road to ruin, Pinocchio emerges from the trials and tribulations of life a real boy.

Of greater moment to the foreign reader, however, is the question of how the fame of Pinocchio and the obscurity of its author are to be reconciled; the international success of *one* of his writings and the total oblivion of all the rest. As a matter of fact, all of Lorenzini's other writings have been buried in their land of birth— not one succeeding in crossing the Alps or finding its way into the hearts of children of another day and age.

The answer usually given is that Lorenzini did not take his hero seriously; that he sat down to pen *The Adventures of a Puppet* in an indifferent state of mind, with no other end in view than that of being well-paid. By so doing, however, he unwittingly divested himself of all literary and pedagogic preoccupations. He felt himself at ease, perfectly free to roam the domains of his imagination for childhood memories and fairy tales told him by his mother in the fantastic garden of Collodi. In such a charmed state of detachment he was able to evoke and give expression to his own experiences as a boy, who perhaps used to play hookey or sneak into a puppet-show, or run from the sight of a policeman. The adventures of Pinocchio fascinated because they recalled echoes of an unknown world of childhood, recorded in accents so familiar that every child could see himself reflected in them. Had Lorenzini thought of moralizing or giving out precepts, he would have given us another Little Joe or Tiny Morsel, false artificial creations of his first period. Instead he gave us Pinocchio, a creature unhampered by intellectual and moral considerations, and who by his spontaneous display of life, has endeared himself to the hearts of every man, woman, and child the world over.

Certainly Pinocchio is Italian or, rather, Tuscan, to be more exact. (There are even Italian editions of the work with tiny glossaries of Tuscan expressions in it, to aid children from other regions). But the Italian or Tuscan atmosphere portrayed there is not the precise historical one of Little Joe and Tiny Morsel, but the vague poetical one of fairy-land. Benedetto Croce, Italy's beloved philosopher and critic, in an essay written to explain Pinocchio's great appeal to children and grown-ups alike, has said of it:

> It is a human tale which finds its way to the heart. The author intended to narrate the extravagant adventures of a marionette to amuse the curiosity and imagination of the child, and at the same time administer, by means of that interest, moral blessings and admonitions: in fact here and there are still discernible slight traces of that didactic intonation. But soon he began to take interest in the character and in his vicissitudes as in the fable of human life fraught with good and evil, error and atonement, temptation and resistance, rashness and prudence, egoistic concern and generous thought for others. The wood out of which Pinocchio is carved is humanity itself, and he who is its representative marches across the scene of life as one bent upon a perilous journey: a puppet, to be sure, but thoroughly spiritual.

Eve Merriam on *Pinocchio*'s relevance to late-1960s culture:

How will today's multimedia minis take to this old-fashioned tale? It seems so goody-goody. The naughty creature who doesn't want to go to school and do lessons turns literally into a donkey. Is it too moralistic in its don't-be-a-dropout message? Written originally in installments for a weekly children's paper, all the cliff-hanging elements are present— the puppet saved at the last possible moment from hanging, drowning, consumption by fire, death by frying pan, and escapes from the writhing green serpent and from the monstrous shark whose "tongue was so wide and so long that it looked like a country road." How pleasant to us oldsters are these touches of long-ago: country roads instead of super-lane highways, party treats of bread, an Italian detail—cups of coffee-and-milk. But will the age of Aquarius Jr. find it all too moralistic and slow-moving? Somehow I think that Pinocchio's personality will survive and that children will continue to identify with this unheroic hero who is greedy, lazy, stupid, forgetful and occasionally brave, loyal, enterprising, endearing: in short, a very human stick of wood.

Eve Merriam, in The New York Times Book Review, *November 9, 1969.*

Martha Bacon (essay date 1970)

SOURCE: "Puppet's Progress," in *The Atlantic Monthly,* Vol. 225, No. 4, April, 1970, pp. 88-91.

[In the following essay, Bacon discusses the cultural and literary impact of Pinocchio.*]*

What manner of man—or woman—sits down and deliberately writes a book for children? One would suppose that he or she would have had some firsthand experience with youngsters, coupled with a keen sense of what is suitable, pleasant, and instructive. But three of the greatest writers for children, whose contribution stands unquestioned, were all eccentric bachelors.

If we study the lives of Hans Andersen, Lewis Carroll, and Carlo Collodi, we find it impossible to picture them as fathers, or even baby-sitters. Hans Andersen was a wandering minstrel of a man, a gawky, sensitive crybaby, scarcely to be trusted to cross a street alone. Lewis Carroll was an intense neurotic, obsessed with night fears, a nervous stutterer, who had difficulty sustaining the most ordinary adult relationships. Carlo Collodi, the author of **Pinocchio,** was a school dropout, a knockabout journalist, hack playwright, odd-jobber on the fringes of literature, possibly the father of an illegitimate child but too scatterbrained apparently even to have been sure about this. At all events he eschewed marriage and legal heirs, finding fulfillment late in life in his dream child.

Yet these writers produced great symbols of their times for their own age and for generations to come. They were men who seem to have made concessions to the world, rather than an adjustment to it. They evaded everything but greatness. Andersen was scarred and shaped by Protestant Denmark in the same climate that brought forth Soren Kierkegaard in *Fear and Trembling.* The clammy fingers of Puseyism, the glow of the Victorian drawing room, and the cold wind of modern mathematics disfigured and disciplined Lewis Carroll. Collodi, a runaway seminarian, heard the call of Giuseppe Mazzini, found an obscure place in the annals of the Risorgimento, and hoped to write in the pedantic tradition of the previous century.

To write a great book for children—as opposed to an amusing, commendable, or useful book—evidently requires a volatile mixture of contradictions in the personality and a wide measure of irresponsibility. The foregoing is not to suggest that such people are not concerned with morality. But moral earnestness is skeletal to their work. They are priests in harlequinade, moralists in motley. Almost against their wills their sermons are entertainments. Collodi set out, at the urging of his publishers, to write a book for Italian children which should celebrate diligence, deplore idleness, and convey the idea that man is rationally happy only through work. He sought to caution the Italian child that pleasure-seeking leads to misery and a donkey's grave. He succeeded in writing a wry, elegant, comic, and wistful book, as universal as *Pilgrim's Progress,* which it resembles in structure, as Tuscan as a terraced vineyard and antic as the commedia dell'arte, which informs it.

Pinocchio was first published in 1880, but at the time of its appearance nothing like it had been seen in Italy, and the art of writing for children—considered as an art—was new by any standards. Although Voltaire was three years old when Perrault brought out his collection of tales in 1697 and presumably grew up with *Cinderella* and *Puss in Boots,* there was little in the Age of the Enlightenment to encourage flights of the imagination, especially in the young. The eighteenth century opened with a glimpse of fairy lands forlorn and closed with the undying fall of Blake's *Songs of Innocence,* but these peaks of joy and beauty were almost entirely surrounded by the wastes of pedagogy. The purpose of most eighteenth-century writers for children was propaganda, and to this end they harnessed meager talents to the tumbrels of solid use, discarding at a blow both fact and fancy in favor of reason and expediency.

Young people learned to be contented in the condition to which God had called them from the sublime Mrs. Hannah More. In the most appalling of all her appalling works, *The Shepherd of Salisbury Plain,* a family of heaven knows how many starving children cheerfully resign themselves to a diet of potatoes and water, while the author approves, for hundreds of pages, of both their situation and their behavior. Children learned from Maria Edgeworth to make wise choices and to prefer useful objects to gawdy ones. Young Rosamond foolishly spends her money on a beautiful purple jar instead of a pair of shoes, which she happens to need. When she arrives home with her trophy she discovers that it is not purple at all but merely seems so, having been filled with purple liquid. So poor Rosamond, a sadder, wiser girl, finds herself with no shoes and a plain glass jar. As one wanders through these wastelands one scarcely wonders that throwing eggs at grownups in pillories was a popular recreation two-hundred-odd years ago.

In fairness to these people, we must admit that for all their sanctimonious mewling, their trash served as compost. And as one century slipped into another, people of genuine talent began to find a new form of art. From Denmark came a set of tales as luminous as a display of northern lights. The authors of countless tracts and moral tales lay buried, and the Snow Queen, Alice in Wonderland, and Pinocchio danced on their graves.

Pinocchio is as firmly rooted in Italian culture as Alice is in the English. He looks back to Dante and *Orlando*

Furioso, forward to Pirandello and Federico Fellini. He is a descendant and an ancestor. He emerges from a log of wood and becomes a *"ragazzo per bene"* (a real boy). He faces death by fire, by hanging, and by drowning, and achieves at last the human condition, the unification of the flesh with the spirit. The consummation was no more than that which his author asked for his country.

Carlo Collodi was born Carlo Lorenzini in Florence in 1826, the son of a professional cook and a young woman who was lady's maid to the Marchesa Ginori Lisci. Young Carlo was bright and engaging, and the Ginori family was benevolent, and the Marchesa took pains to see that the attractive urchin should not waste his brio on the secular life. Carlo was clapped into the nearest available seminary, where by his own account he bedeviled the fathers until at the age of sixteen he went over the wall. Through this gesture the church lost a priest but the country acquired a journalist. Lorenzini remained a scribbler for the rest of his fairly long life, with intervals of soldiering in the first and second wars of independence. He wrote blood-and-thunder comedies, "mortal sins in five acts" as he called them, and served as theater censor for the provisional government of Tuscany in 1860.

Lorenzini took the name of Collodi from the Castello Collodi in Valdineme, a place which had caught his fancy. His affairs prospered in a mild way. He became an editor of the Tuscan dictionary, was rewarded for his services and made a knight of the Star of Italy. In the 1970s he came under the influence of Felice Paggi, a vigorous and imaginative man, one of the first people to see the possibilities of textbooks as an industry. He had published Italian versions of Perrault and Mme. D'Aulnoy, and he urged Collodi to turn his attention to children's books, a commodity in which Italy was notably lacking.

Collodi obliged his friend by writing the *Giannettino,* in imitation of the *Gianetto* of Paravicini. The *Giannettino* is of no more interest than its eighteenth-century prototype, and Collodi followed it with other negligible work, *Minnuzolo* and *Occhi e Nasi.*

But his work within the pedantic tradition served to show Collodi his mistakes. "The brighter the child," he observed, "the fewer adults it will question and the more it will try to find out for itself." He abandoned tedious explanations, ceased to imitate, and turned to a celebration of his Italy, its virtues and its flaws, its landscape, festivals, poverty, people, and puppets, its laws and legends.

Collodi was fifty-four when he wrote the epic of the marionette. He had fought two campaigns against the Austrian domination, his mind had been formed by his association with the makers of the Risorgimento, and

he understood completely the implications of the new industrialism which would bring the young nation abreast of the modern world. *Pinocchio* is a children's story, but it is also a political comment, an interpretation of history, a document of man's search for his soul, and a sign of the shape of things to come.

As a children's story *Pinocchio* is quite matchless. The line is true as Giotto's and the language is light as thistledown. The theme is probably the one which children most favor, the search by children for parents and by parents for children, a search which in this case ends in success and reunion. Like all good writers for children, Collodi lets his hero sin, suffer, and triumph strictly on his own recognizance and permits only minimal intrusion by the adult world. No book to be sure, was ever harmed by a wicked uncle or Satan, but any gifted writer knows that adults or Olympians must be kept in their place—in the first chapter and the last.

Collodi manages his father figure beautifully. Gepetto, nicknamed Polendina because of his yellow wig—the color of cornmeal—appears a fully rounded character, crochety, warmhearted, cynical, and selfless. He carves the puppet from a piece of wood, clothes him in scraps, and makes a little cap of bread dough for him. He embraces the marionette as a son and names him for a family of his acquaintance, Pinocchio: "Everyone in the family, Pinocchio father, Pinocchia mother, and Pinocchi all the sons and daughters: they all did well in life; the richest of them begged for a living." He pawns his jacket to buy his son an alphabet book, and the marionette, after passionate protestations of affec-

Pinocchio and Gepetto.

tion and promises of good behavior—he took to lying upon emerging from the log of wood from which he was carved—runs away in search of pleasure and excitement. He finds plenty of both, and we never encounter Gepetto again until Pinocchio discovers him inside the belly of the sea monster. By this time he has almost ceased to be a parent and is but a pathetic dotard, entirely dependent on the marionette. The reunion is partly effected now, but it is not complete until the final chapter when the magic change takes place. "Through labor and through hope" Gepetto renews his youth and finds himself the happy father, not of a puppet, but of a beautiful boy with chestnut curls and sparkling blue eyes—a boy of roses. To be a human child is to Pinocchio what the Celestial City is to Bunyan's Christian.

Like the damned as seen from heaven, the marionette lies, a discarded husk, in a corner, and the living father embraces the living son, while blessings rain upon the house. The fairy with azure hair who has watched over and disciplined Pinocchio, as Beatrice watched over and disciplined Dante, has shown herself not dead but a living presence, and in a most practical and Tuscan manner. She has paid back the forty soldi which Pinocchio earned for her during the course of his metamorphosis from puppet to person.

As a political allegory *Pinocchio* makes an unequivocal statement. Collodi believed that two imperatives must govern the mind and spirit of Italy: the republican idea and the necessity for sacrifice and work. Mazzini himself never wrote a more commanding call to republican sentiment than the opening sentences of *The Adventures of Pinocchio*:

> Once upon a time there was—
> A king! my little readers will say at once.
> No, boys and girls. You are wrong. Once
>   upon a time there was a piece of wood.

Nowhere in *Pinocchio* do we find the traditional nobility of the fairy tale. The story is about the common people of Italy, the cobblers and carpenters, the puppeteers and circus touts, the fishermen and farmers, the dogs and donkeys, the cats and crickets, the fishes of the Mediterranean, and the leaden-eyed boys who slouch at street corners to prey upon and corrupt the unwary. The book rings with the salty speech of Tuscany, and its characters live with its sardonic proverbs.

The only "personage" in the book is the fairy with azure hair, the enchanted being who has lived many thousands of years in the neighborhood of Pinocchio's adventures, and she is not a mortal maiden. Even she does not maintain at all times an exalted station in life, although she occasionally resides in a castle. She is served by a veritable zoo of queer animals, snails, jackdaws, rabbits, and she is at home in the humble guise of a peasant girl, her beautiful, blue locks neatly plaited, and once she takes the form of a little blue goat. The only official to intrude on the narrative is a judge, and he is an ape who in a fit of legal logic condemns Pinocchio to prison for having been robbed by the fox and the cat. He subsequently refuses to let the marionette out of prison on the grounds that only criminals can be released under the duke's decree of amnesty and Pinocchio is innocent of any crime.

In Collodi's book the highest level to which the human spirit may rise is humanity itself. The transcendent flaw in this spirit, as Collodi saw it, was pleasure-seeking. Pleasure is not happiness and pleasure is the business of puppets, but the business of men and of the Risorgimento was work, and it is through work alone that puppets become men.

"Open a school," cried Collodi, "and you will close a prison."

The foregoing describes the political atmosphere of Collodi's book, but if allegorical interest were its only merit it would have long been relegated to the remaindered list. *Pinocchio* is more than a puritan sermon by a conscientious patriot. It is a fragment of the commedia dell'arte. And for all that he reforms, ceases his lies and his follies, and learns wisdom and thrift, Pinocchio is Harlequin.

"Harlequin," says Professor Allardyce Nicoll, "exists in a mental world wherein concepts of morality have no being and yet despite such absence of morality, he displays no viciousness." The description fits Collodi's hero to his wooden fingertips. Harlequin haunts Italy and occurs like Buddha from time to time in one incarnation or another, and Pinocchio is one of them.

Who is Harlequin? Some say that he is the spirit of the night, Hellequin, cousin to the devil, but time has robbed him of his satanic qualities. He is one of the foremost characters to animate the commedia dell'arte. The commedia dell'arte is, we are told, dead. Even in Italy the theater is a written thing which actors study and then recite. They are no longer required to create the play which they perform, and yet it appears that the Italian theater has never quite forgotten its merry and irresponsible infancy. The titles of many of Luigi Pirandello's plays wistfully recall it: *Tonight We Improvise, Six Characters in Search of an Author, Right You Are If You Think You Are, As You Desire Me* bear witness to the influence of the theater of the cathedral square and the back alley. It is apparent also in the improvisations which occur in many recent Italian films, and the film art indeed owes some of its vocabulary to the commedia. The word scenario originally described a rough outline of the plot upon which a group of actors would improvise.

A vivid artistry was lavished on the commedia, and from records kept by individual actors we can learn something of its voice. It bears some resemblance to aria and recitative in opera, but it keeps the rhythm of common speech, the short sentence, and the quick riposte. It is with this voice that Pinocchio speaks:

> "Good morning, Master Antonio, what do you do on the floor?"
> "I am teaching the ants their alphabet."
> "Good for you."
> "What has brought you to me, Father Gepetto?"
> "My legs. You must know that I've come to ask a favor."

It pours forth without benefit of intellect and is saved by brio, by dancing, tumbling, handstands, and snatches of music. Like Harlequin, Pinocchio never thinks before he speaks. He hasn't time. The book gives the effect of improvising itself. Pinocchio is a commedia character to the end of his long nose, which grows alarmingly whenever he starts to deal in falsehoods. His nose and the indestructible cricket are his conscience, and he can never escape them.

When Collodi wrote **Pinocchio** he was determined that no mention of religion should be made in the text. He was devout, and like Lewis Carroll he had a morbid dread of anything approaching irreverence. There should be no allusion to the Deity or to the Mother of God or her Son. But how remarkable is Mary, Star of the Sea, especially in Italy? Every Italian child wakes and sleeps, plays and works under the veil of the Madonna. With her magnificent hood of azure hair she sanctifies Pinocchio in the role of the fairy. She mothers him, nurses him when he is ill, rescues him from assassins, and punishes him as a wise and just mother punishes. She teaches patience, fortitude, and resignation, and rewards him in the end with her fragrant but invisible presence in his apotheosis. She is the great lady, the Madonna Coronata in her castle and the peasant Madonna of the hill towns. She is the suffering Madonna, full of animal grief, who stands on the rock when Pinocchio is engorged by the great fish. She is the blue and worshiped Italian sky.

When Federico Fellini made his remarkable film *La Dolce Vita,* he could not, whether or not he intended to, escape Collodi's story. He preaches the same sermon and makes use of both the devices and the symbols which inform Collodi's work. The film begins with the puppet Christ carried over the rooftops of Rome and continues as a polemic delivered against idleness, lies, corruption, both sexual and spiritual, and above all pleasure for pleasure's sake. Marcello, the hero, is a Harlequin, openhanded, irresponsible, changeless, a puppet whose strings are pulled by fear and lust. He is an undutiful son, a faithless lover, a gull, the prey of any fox or cat who can catch him. He is not evil, and

he is aware of what a man ought to be but lacks the will to be one himself. We see Marcello in the final sequence of the film, about to be engulfed by the sea monster of sensation, a dead, single-eyed, and shapeless thing. Marcello sees but he cannot hear the *fanciulla*, the young girl, Paolina, who is desperately and vainly trying to recall him to her side.

It is "the sweet life," Fellini tells us, which could destroy the republic, not crime, but acedia, the deadly sin of sloth. This is the rot which besets Harlequin, Pinocchio, Marcello. In Fellini's film, Steiner, the musician, sees it and kills himself and his children rather than submit to it.

Harlequin, Child of the Sistine Chapel, Pinocchio stands at the center of Italy, "the terrible puppet of her dreams," a character forever "in search of an author."

Ester Zago (essay date 1988)

SOURCE: "Carlo Collodi as Translator: From Fairy Tale to Folk Tale," in *The Lion and the Unicorn,* Vol. 12, No. 2, December, 1988, pp. 61-73.

[*In the following essay, Zago considers the techniques Collodi used when translating the tales of Charles Perrault, Mme. d'Aulnoy, and Mme. Leprince de Beaumont.*]

There is a general consensus among critics of Collodi in acknowledging the indebtedness, on the part of the author of **Pinocchio,** toward the French fairy tales. Few have explored the topic much further, and yet it seems to me that this important influence on Collodi's work deserves closer scrutiny. Collodi's translation method appears to have been by his own training as a journalist and by the interest in folklore studies that accompanied the rise in patriotic sentiment in Italy during the nineteenth century.

My focus will be on Collodi's treatment of *Peau d'Ane* (Donkey-Skin), and shall also look at his handling of Perrault's prose tales. Finally I shall discuss Collodi's techniques in translating the six stories by Mme. d'Aulnoy and Mme. Leprince de Beaumont. First, however, it may be useful to trace a brief account of the circumstances, both personal and cultural, which led to Collodi's translation of the French fairy tales.

1. In 1875 Sandro Paggi suggested to Carlo Lorenzini, better known under the pen name of Collodi, that he translate a collection of French fairy tales which included Perrault's *Contes,* four tales by Mme. d'Aulnoy and two by Mme. Leprince de Beaumont. According to several critics, Collodi was not familiar with Perrault's fairy tales or the *Cabinet des Fées* before receiving this commission. Sandro Paggi, together with

his brother Felice, owned a bookstore in Via del Pro-consolo in Florence, as well as a publishing house. The Paggi brothers had known Collodi for a long time when they entrusted him with the translation of the French fairy tales. They became the loyal publishers of all of Collodi's work.

Collodi began his literary career in 1848. After partic-ipating as a volunteer in the first war for the indepen-dence of Italy, he came back to his native Florence, and for ten years he worked as a journalist for several Flo-rentine magazines and newspapers. This experience was probably instrumental in developing the clarity of his style, the sharpness of his wit, and his shrewd under-standing of what attracts and retains the reader's atten-tion. But Collodi was also aware of the limitations inherent in the journalist's trade. He wrote that "one is born a poet, but there is no need to be born a journal-ist. In fact, once you become a journalist, you die a journalist. . . . Journalism is like Nexus' shirt, once you have put it on, you cannot take it off."

Like many Italian writers of his time, Collodi had an excellent knowledge of the French language; more-over, he demonstrated an early interest in problems of translation. In 1854 he stated in an article entitled **"I traduttori e le traduzioni"** that a good translator must have

> . . . a thorough and perfect knowledge of the two languages he is dealing with, and not only of words and phrases, but more importantly, of the nature, the physiognomy, the temperament of each language. . . . To translate does not mean to transpose a word from one language into another. . . . This is the task of the very modest compilers of pocket dictionaries. . . . (my translation)

In the same article he went on to say that it is not sufficient to know the language: the translation of a literary text poses different problems from the trans-lation of a history text. It would seem that the trans-lation of a fairy tale poses its own unique set of problems, as Collodi was to discover some 20 years later.

When the Paggi brothers decided to publish the Italian version of the French fairy tales, they were demonstrat-ing an astute recognition of the market's demand for a literary genre which could not only please but also in-struct a public composed of children and adults. Con-cern for the imperatives of public education had consid-erably increased in Italy during the Risorgimento. Un-der the Cavour ministry, a law was passed which re-quired two years of compulsory education for all cit-izens of Piedmont and Lombardy. The law was ex-tended to Tuscany when the region was annexed to the dominions of the house of Savoy after the second war of independence.

In 1861 the first census was taken in Italy. It revealed that 78% of the population was illiterate. The mea-sures taken to curb illiteracy, together with the patri-otic fervor sweeping Italy in the wake of the Risorg-imento, gave rise to a need for books which were easy to read, but which also contained some sort of civic or moral lesson. Fairy tales and Aesopic fables were re-worked and presented with specific pedagogical pur-poses summed up in the formula "Dio, Patria e famiglia" ("God, my country and my family").

From the time of Straporola's *Piacevoli Notti,* tales of the marvelous and the fantastic had a prominent place in the Italian literary tradition. In the eighteenth centu-ry, Carlo Gozzi had been a successful writer of fairy tales. But despite their exotic charm, Gozzi's tales were not suited to Italian readers of the second half of the nineteenth century, mostly because they were just pleas-ing, and not instructive. The merit of the French fairy tales, on the other hand, lay precisely in the fact that each tale ended with a *moralité,* or moral lesson.

There were other factors which may have induced the Paggi brothers to publish the French fairy tales. Ro-mantic poets had ushered in a new wave of interest in the genre. At the same time, the study of folklore had gained momentum in Italy; just as patriots were striv-ing for the unification of the country, folklorists were seeking to demonstrate, through the study of popular traditions, the fundamental spiritual unity of the Italian people. Some of the most influential Italian political writers of the time, such as Tommaseo, Giusti, and Carducci (the Italian Victor Hugo), devoted no small portion of their time and talent to the discovery and recuperation of the traditions of those nations, such as Italy, Spain, and Greece, which were struggling for national independence. In 1855 Carducci published *The Harp of the People (L'Arpa del Popolo)*, an anthology of poetry in which he included the texts of several Tuscan folk songs and poems, together with sonnets by Dante. Tommaseo and Giusti were particularly in-terested in proverbs which, they felt, revealed "the voice of the people" and its genuine, uncorrupted wisdom. Giusti published a collection of Tuscan proverbs in 1853.

After the third war of independence in 1866, Florence became the capital of Italy. When Rome was taken in 1870, the seat of the government was moved there. In a sentence which has become proverbial, the writer Massimo d'Azzeglio declared, "Now that we have made Italy, we have to make the Italians." It was obvious to all concerned such an aim could be achieved first and foremost through education. It is in this political and cultural context that Collodi's translation of the French fairy tales should be situated.

The collection was published under the title *I Racconti delle fate.* The names of the three authors, Charles

Perrault, Mme. d'Aulnoy, and Mme. Leprince de Beaumont did not figure anywhere in the book. Only the translator's notice to the reader revealed that the fairy tales were translated from the French. The most plausible explanation for the anonymous presentation is the desire on the part of the publishers to comply with the cultural trends of the time. Without the identification of the authors of their epoch, the French fairy tales could easily be incorporated into the general revival of interest in folk culture, and in particular, in the folk tale.

It is significant, in this regard, that Collodi's book contains all of Perrault's prose tales, but that, of the three tales written in verse, only *Donkey-Skin* is included. *Griselidis* was probably eliminated because of the presence of a literary tradition which weighed heavily on the story of the Marchioness of Saluzzo, thus disqualifying it as a folk tale. As for *The Foolish Wishes,* that ancient fabliau may have been omitted because it paints the peasant class in a rather negative light. Collodi could not possibly have been ignorant of the canon of romantic poetics according to which peasants were to be lauded rather than denigrated. With the *caveat* that I am moving here into the realm of pure speculation, it is possible to identify a second reason for the omission of this tale: the fact that one of the two wishes unwarily expressed by the peasant is that his wife develop a long nose. It is not entirely implausible that Collodi preferred to store that image away for later use.

The first edition of *I Racconti delle fate* appeared in 1876; the second in 1892. Several reprints followed until 1938 when the Marzocco publishers decided to print exclusively those fairy tales which were indisputably by Perrault; the tales by Mme. d'Aulnoy and by Mme. Leprince de Beaumont were excluded. The most recent edition, published in 1976 on the occasion of the work's first centenary, is instead an exact reproduction (but not a facsimile) of the 1892 edition.

II. In the corpus of Collodi's translation, *Donkey-Skin* stands in a separate category for two main reasons. As mentioned earlier, it is the only one of Perrault's three *Contes en vers* which was included in the published collection. Secondly, it is the only tale to which Collodi brought substantial modifications, including several additional paragraphs.

According to [Paolo Paolini in "Collodi traduttore di Perrault," in AA. VV., *Studi Collodiani*, Atti del Primo Convegno Internazionale (Pescia, 5-7 ottobre 1974)], *Donkey-Skin* was the last tale translated by Collodi. It is fair to assume then that his knowledge of Perrault's style had deepened. It is also possible that, as the work progressed, Collodi's confidence in his own *écriture* grew; he felt increasingly free to manipulate the material, even to improve on it, being careful, however, to match the style of the original text. It may be significant that in the order of presentation, *Donkey-Skin* appears exactly in the middle of Perrault's tales, framed at either end by an equal number of stories. It almost seems as though Collodi had wanted to insert it in between the prose tales, so that it would be less conspicuous.

With respect to Collodi's method of translation, it should be noted first that he very carefully avoided the use of poetry. This observation is true for *Donkey-Skin* as well as for all the verse passages contained within the prose tales, including those found at the end in the form of *moralités.* We have only to go back to his early writings to understand why Collodi stayed away from poetry: "One is born a poet." He was not a poet, at least not in the literal sense, and he knew it. Furthermore, it would have been particularly difficult to transpose the refined, artfully constructed poetry of the seventeenth-century writers into the rather humble Tuscan-Italian which Collodi chose for his translation.

Collodi was a journalist and, as he himself had foreseen, he was never able to take off his journalist's shirt. He read *Donkey-Skin* with a journalist's eyes. He knew what would appeal to the reading public of his time, but he also knew which elements of a rather scandalous story should be minimized in order not to shock public opinion. *Donkey-Skin* is, after all, a story of incestuous desire; it is reasonable to suppose that the changes brought about by Collodi—changes which greatly contributed to making the story less shocking and more melodramatic—were purposeful.

Collodi did not add any psychological dimension to the characters; he simply "thickened" the plot. The dying queen is made to warn her husband that the state will put pressure on him to remarry and possibly to produce a male heir to the throne; more important, the role and influence of the high priest, barely hinted at in the original text, are greatly elaborated. These changes make the king's incestuous design upon his daughter appear far less reprehensible than in Perrault's story. Collodi also sharpened the role of the fairy—that champion of courage and virtue. He gave her a name, strengthened her speeches, and generally made her appearances more dramatic.

Ever the good journalist, Collodi also added an element of suspense to the story by moving around some circumstantial details. For example, in Perrault's text the princess sees and admires the Prince without his being aware of it. Collodi relocates the incident in the narrative, incorporating it into one of the narrator's interventions.

In *Donkey-Skin,* more than in any of the other translations, Collodi uses the formulaic language typical of folk-tale narrative techniques, thereby accentuating the presence of the narrator, and as a result, increasing the orality of the narrative. Listeners and readers alike are drawn into the text and invited to participate in the development of the events. In no other translation does Collodi insert as many proverbs and comparisons drawn from colloquial speech.

"Collodi toscaneggia" (Collodi "tuscanizes," i.e., uses Tuscan expressions), said Giovanni Arpino in ["Collodi toscaneggia," in *La Stampa*, 19 novembre 1976]. Indeed he does, but not, as has been argued, in deference to the aesthetic canons established by Alessandro Manzoni in his influential novel *The Betrothed*. Nor is his purpose simply ludic, as Paolini suggests. Rather, Collodi's use of Tuscan expressions can be read as a political rather than an aesthetic choice. He was a Florentine; he already knew how to exploit all the richness of the Tuscan idiom. But he was also a patriot, and to the Italian intelligentsia, the use of the Tuscan dialect, so close to literary Italian, represented the unity of the Italian people; it was the vernacular that Dante had chosen for his *Divine Comedy*.

If stories originally written in a foreign language were to be translated into "folk" tales, it was not enough for the translator to bend and mold his language to the exigencies of the genre in which he was working. That language had to have the rhythm of colloquial speech, and for Collodi that meant an Italian dressed in Tuscan colors. Perrault's poetry had to be tamed and domesticated in the prose rendering of *Donkey-Skin;* the fairy tale had to be transformed into a folk tale. The Tuscan touches, particularly in the form of proverbs and comparisons which Collodi wove into his translation, evoke "the voice of the people." And as a result of Collodi's efforts, that voice rings true.

III. In many respects Collodi's treatment of *Donkey-Skin* represents the high-water mark of his confidence (or perhaps arrogance) as a translator. This point of view is consistent with Paolini's suggestion that it was indeed the last story to be translated.

What has been said concerning the language in *Donkey-Skin* applies, *mutatis mutandis*, to all the other stories by Perrault which Collodi translates. However, the degree of "tuscanization" varies, depending on a number of factors. For example, Tuscan and colloquial expressions appear more frequently in a tale like *Tom Thumb,* in which the protagonists are peasants rather than kings and queens.

In order to move the French fairy tales from Versailles to Tuscany, some adjustments had to be made. Having been singled out for immigration, the tales had to be put through a process of naturalization. Certain words specifically connected with French life are changed into their Italian equivalents, such as kilometers for leagues, and "zecchini e napoleoni" (coins of the Italian monetary system) for "louis"; the famous "sauce Robert" is turned into a nondescript spicy sauce. The French word for "fairy" is translated with "fata," but more frequently with the word "comare," which has in colloquial language the meaning of "godmother." The word "infanta" is used as a synonym of princess. Mention is made of two famous Italian theaters, the "Pergola" in Florence and "La Scala" in Milan. In *Sleeping Beauty,* the enchanted palace is protected by Swiss guards; Collodi changes them into "guardaportoni," or "gate keepers," since in Italian the Swiss guards are identified only with the Pope's militia.

It has been argued, mostly by Paolini, that Collodi goes beyond this kind of obvious adaptation of geographical and cultural landmarks, and that he imposes a sort of nineteenth-century Italian *bienséances* on the seventeenth-century French tales. To some extent this is so, as already noted in the above discussion of *Donkey-Skin*. But it seems to me that Paolini often misses the mark in analyzing the particulars of this process. For example, in *Sleeping Beauty,* seven fairies are invited and each one of them bestows a gift on the baby. Collodi keeps the same number of fairies, but does not mention the gift given by the fourth one. Paolini attributes this omission to the nature of the gift: that the child "danserait parfaitement bien" (dances perfectly). He argues that this gift was left out because it was deemed inappropriate for a well brought up young lady in nineteenth-century Italian society.

Maybe so, but it should not be forgotten that Collodi put a lot of care into turning the courtly atmosphere of seventeenth-century France into a country style Italian setting. Dance was an extremely important social activity at the court of Louis XIV, and it had its place in the education of well brought up ladies and gentlemen. . . . But at the court of Versailles, dance was a subject to be studied and learned to perfection. According to theories of the "folk," on the other hand, dance was to be admired as the spontaneous manifestation of the people's exuberance. It would have been incongruous for the princess of the folk tale to dance either like a court lady or like a peasant girl; consequently, the whole question of that particular gift was simply avoided.

There are some more serious problems with Paolini's argument that Collodi was in effect censoring the texts he was working with. Paolini observes, for example, that the French word "amants" (lovers) is translated with "mariti" (husbands). This is true for the Perrault tales, but not for the other fairy tales, where the same word is translated with "amanti," the exact Italian equivalent. The reason Paolini failed to notice this difference is that his analysis is based on the 1938 Marzocco edition, from which the stories by the women writers were excluded. In several instances, his reliance on this edition led Paolini to erroneous conclusions. Consider the following example.

Paolini states that Collodi makes use of euphemistic expressions in order to attenuate all expressions related to child bearing, and cites the following examples, the first from *Riquet with the Tuft,* the second from *Sleeping Beauty:*

> 1. accoucher d'un fils = avere un figliolo (to have a son)
> 2. La Reine devint grosse et accoucha d'une fille = la Regina ebbe una bella bambina (the Queen had a beautiful baby girl).

The trouble is that these purported changes are not found in the Adelphi edition, where the same examples read as follows:

> 1. partorire un figlio.
> 2. La Regina rimase incinta e partori una bambina.

In both cases Collodi used the verb "partorire" (and not the verb "avere"), which is the direct equivalent of the French verb "accoucher." In the second example, the French word "grosse" (pregnant) is faithfully translated as "incinta." By relying on the Marzocco edition, published in 1938 under the fascist regime, Paolino winds up attributing to Collodi a censorship of the text which appears instead to have been the work of the fascists.

By far the most relevant interventions made by Collodi, aside from those in *Donkey-Skin* discussed earlier, are to be found in his rendering of the *moralités* at the end of each tale. Here again Collodi tended to avoid the use of poetry. The one exception is *The Fairies,* and one wishes he had not made that exception. Perrault drew two moral lessons from his tale, each expressed in a separate quatrain. Collodi retains the content. But with respect to form, he ventures onto treacherous ground. First, he chooses the hendecasyllable, possibly the most formal and elegant line in Italian poetry, and one whose technical demands were beyond Collodi's skills as a poet. Second, as regards diction, Collodi sounds even more didactic than Perrault, but without, unfortunately, the tone of subtle irony that makes the charm of the French texts; Collodi might very well have found the images he chose in the text of an operatic aria by Metastasio or Da Ponte. Finally, by making these stylistic choices, Collodi betrays his own chosen approach of translating the *moralités* into plain and colloquial language.

He is much more successful when, as Paolini rightly puts it, "he reduces [the *moralités*] to a benevolent, witty and prosaic dimension." For example, of the two *moralités* at the end of *Bluebeard,* Collodi keeps only the first, which contains a pedagogical message on the dangers of curiosity; he eliminates the second together with Perrault's ironic commentary on the docility of French husbands. The *moralités* of *Sleeping Beauty*

and *Tom Thumb* are condensed into popular proverbs. As a general rule, it may be said Collodi eliminates Perrault's urbane humor and replaces it with his own "folksy" gaiety and playfulness. The most telling example of this is to be found in Collodi's addition to the *moralité* of *Puss in Boots,* where he ironizes on the content of Perrault's message: "From this point of view, the story of the cat of the Marquis of Carabá is very instructive, especially for all cats and all Marquises of Carabá" (my translation).

IV. In translating the fairy tales by Mme. d'Aulnoy and Mme. Leprince de Beaumont, Collodi seems to adopt a different approach. Anyone who read Collodi's collection of French fairy tales without knowing the names of their authors would immediately sense a difference in tone between the two groups, those based on the tales by Perrault and those originally authored by Mme. d'Aulnoy and Mme. Leprince de Beaumont.

As argued earlier, Perrault's tales are subjected to a process of "tuscanization," which is also a process of "folklorization." This does not happen with the tales by the two women writers. Especially in the case of Mme. d'Aulnoy, Collodi seems to realize that he is dealing with a different artistic temperament from that of Perrault. He follows exactly the rhythm of Mme. d'Aulnoy's prose: slow and refined in the descriptions, swift and colloquial in the dialogues, particularly when it is the women who speak. In translating Perrault, Collodi intervenes in the text in several ways: he increases the frequency of the narrator's presence; he inserts traditional phrases in order to imitate the patterns of folk narrative; he expands the meaning of the verbs by adding adverbial phrases or even relative clauses. These procedures are used much less frequently in the case of the women writers. What is the basis of this difference in treatment? In order to answer this question, it is necessary, once more, to consider several factors.

First of all, when dealing with Perrault, Collodi seems to "deconstruct" (if I may be allowed to use such an anachronistic term) his language in order to expose its innermost meanings. By doing this, whether consciously or not, he arrives at his own rewriting of the tales. One almost senses a form of male solidarity between the two authors. Collodi could meet his opponent and happily beat him on his own ground, as, for example, when he turns Perrault's *moralités* upside down. In *Donkey-Skin,* he slips in a humorous touch of his own: the use of sunglasses goes back to the time when the princess wore her sun-colored dress in public. Few as these additions may be, they show that Collodi was not afraid to challenge Perrault on the terrain of irony.

With the women writers, such liberties, such variations are almost out of the question. There seems to be a different relationship between the text and the translator. Mme. d'Aulnoy and Mme. Leprince de Beaumont show in their writings a sensitivity to the psychology of their female characters, and a compassionate participation in their adventures, which are totally absent from Perrault. In other words, it was a feminine world which confronted Collodi in these stories. The common ground he shared with Perrault was missing.

As a consequence, Collodi's interventions in translating the tales from the *Cabinet des Fées* are minimal. A few details are Italianized. For example, in *The Blue Bird* the market fairs of Saint-Germain and Saint-Laurent are replaced with the fairs of Padova and Sinigaglia. Of the numerous passages in verse, Collodi translates only those in which Mme. d'Aulnoy imitates the cadence of a nursery rhyme. One intriguing intervention occurs in *The Doe in the Wood*, where the phrase "l'Ethiopienne" is rendered by Collodi as "la negra," the black girl. To seek the reason for this substitution may be a guessing game, but in homage to Collodi's playfulness, I offer two solutions: either the word "etiope" sounded too learned to the translator—(if 78% of Italians were illiterate at that time, what would they have made of such a word?)—or "the Ethiopian girl" could have evoked the heroine of *Aida*, Verdi's opera of fatal love, family duty, and patriotic sentiments, which had premiered at Cairo in 1871. The juxtaposition would have been inappropriate.

Although the tales by the women writers resisted Collodi's process of folklorization, they did not emerge completely unadulterated. The only place where he did succeed in folklorizing them was in his rendering of the *moralités* at the end of Mme. d'Aulnoy's tales (Mme. Leprince de Beaumont did not write any). He stripped them of all their rhetorical apparatus and rendered them with the country style, the modest and colloquial tone, which he used for Perrault's *moralités*. But Mme. d'Aulnoy's *moralités* do not really contain a clear moral message; they are subjective reflections on life, love, and marriage which seem to express the author's views, based on personal experience. Collodi mercilessly removes the pathetic and the sentimental. He replaces all the posturing of the original with straightforward pieces of advice. The ideas are still Mme. d'Aulnoy's but the language is unmistakably Collodian Tuscan.

As for *The Doe in the Wood,* Collodi didn't seem to know what to make of the story as a pedagogical tool, and he says so. Rather than stating the moral message as the author did, he proposed it in less dramatic terms as a piece of advice to young girls: one should never leave the parental environment too soon; the world outside is dangerous. Popular and conventional wisdom has the last word.

Conscious of the criticism that his translation of the French fairy tales might arouse, Collodi tried to protect himself with a notice which reads as follows:

In rendering these fairy tales into Italian, I did my best to remain as faithful as possible to the French texts. It would have seemed to me a crime to paraphrase them freely. At any rate, here and there I allowed myself to bring in some very slight variations as to the vocabulary, to the rhythm of the paragraph, and to the turns of certain phrases. . . . (my translation)

We have seen, albeit in a small measure, what kind of liberties and variations Collodi took with the texts he was translating. One could argue that he betrayed them by clothing them in his very own Tuscan coat. *Traduttore-traditore,* as the saying goes. And yet, as all critics have pointed out, it was through the experience of translating the French fairy tales that Collodi was introduced to the world of the magic and the fantastic. More specifically . . . the imprint of Perrault's style left its mark on Collodi's *écriture.*

The other day I opened at random Nicolas Perella's edition of **Pinocchio,** and my eyes fell on this sentence: "'Turn the key and the door will open,' said the same little voice." The words struck a familiar note; they recalled an equally familiar subtext: "'Tire la chevillette, la bobinette cherra.' Le Loup tira la chevillette, et la porte s'ouvrit." Little Red Riding Hood, Tom Thumb and all their friends came rushing in.

M. L. Rosenthal (essay date 1989)

SOURCE: "The Hidden *Pinocchio*: Tale of a Subversive Puppet," in *Literature and Revolution,* edited by David Bevan, Rodopi, 1989, pp. 49-61.

[*In the following essay, Rosenthal discusses the political views Collodi expressed in* Pinocchio.]

The Adventures of Pinocchio: Tale of a Puppet, by Carlo Lorenzini (who used his mother's birthplace, Collodi, as his pen-name), is a glorious book. Its glories have been obscured for many by Disney's syrupy treatments: his charming animated film that is nevertheless untrue to the sardonic, sometimes anarchic side of the original story; and his "book" version, a tiny, shameless bit of baby-talk.

In 1979 the late Rolando Anzilotti, that gracious man, asked me on behalf of the Collodi Foundation to try my hand at a new translation of **Pinocchio** in time for the book's 1983 centenary. He knew I had little or no Italian, but thought he saw in my poems and other writings qualities that might compensate. He even recognized that "feeling" for certain languages many of us have without really knowing them. At any rate, armed with that "feeling" and with *Cassell's Italian Dictionary* and the Palazzi *Novissimo Dizionario*—and also with the support of correspondence with Professor Anzilotti, Gaetano Prampolini, and others—I took my ignorance in hand and dived into **Pinocchio**'s delightfully clear and fast-flowing waters.

The result, for me, was buoyant discovery. I can lay no claim to authority in Italian literary or linguistic scholarship, and all I offer here is an American poet's report on some things I learned on my way through such tourist spots as the Red Crab Inn, the Field of Miracles, and the Shark's belly. Happily, it is actually easier to translate **Pinocchio** than certain modern poets such as Neruda, Rilke, Vallejo, and Foix, as I have occasionally done. In truth it is even easier, at times, than working with poets like Pound and Eliot in the original, as I have done in criticism for many years. Except for a few Tuscanisms, and a few idioms that are tricky for Anglo-American ears, **Pinocchio**—word for word and phrase by phrase—is hardly a difficult book. But that is never the real challenge of translation, which is to catch the rhythm and style of a work in a way responsive to the one language and natural to the other. If the reader will indulge me briefly, I would like to preface what I have to say about political and other dimensions of **Pinocchio**—as Carlo Lorenzini wrote it—with a comment on the challenge of catching its swift pace, its mercurial turns, and its flashes of wit.

My native speech is *American* English, but I have lived enough in England to feel I connect with British speech as well. I wanted my translation to be closer to the original in both spirit and detail than any preceding one in English; and at the same time, I hoped it would be as idiomatically modern as Lorenzini's story was in its time, and would race along with the same leaping immediacy. And so I had to deal with such facts as that American and British children are not really familiar with "polendina" or even "vetch". In instances like the latter, I simply, almost subliminally, explained the word in passing. As for "polendina", it is even less accessible to English-speaking children than "polenta". As a result, Geppetto's nickname becomes "Old Corny" because, my text explains, ". . . his big yellow wig was just the color of cornmeal mush". (I lacked the courage to change the nickname to "Bananas—because his big yellow wig looked just like a bunch of banana-skins": something every modern child would recognize.) The sounds of music had to be anglicized, and so the fifes and drums say *tweedle-dee-dee, boom-boom-boom* rather than *pì-pì-pì, zum-zum-zum.* (As all of us know, it is one of life's pleasures that musical instruments and animals speak different languages in different countries.) And I had to make one or two little adaptations for modern children in just about any Western country. In my version, for instance, Pinocchio bargains with the Fairy for *candy,* rather than *sugar,* before agreeing to take his medicine. Not only do contemporary British and American children lead lives very unlike those of nineteenth-century Italian chil-

dren, they also have no family memories or traditions that link them with the Italian past, as modern Italian children do.

I was thrown most forcibly on my own resources in this matter of phrasing, I think, in the final chapter, when Pinocchio fires his barrage of aphorisms at the Fox and the Cat:

> "Believe me, Pinocchio, we really are as poor and miserable as we look!"
> "As we look!" said the Cat.
> "Easy come, easy go!" said Pinocchio. "If you're poor, you deserve it. Remember the good old rule: 'Thou shalt not steal.' Goodbye, old crooks!"
> "Have pity on us!"
> "On us!"
> "Goodbye, old crooks! Remember the old saying: 'The Devil drives a hard bargain.'"
> "Don't abandon us!"
> "Us!" repeated the Cat.
> "Goodbye, old crooks! Remember the saying: 'Turn about is fair play.'"

This passage illustrates the point about the challenge of translation that I have suggested. A translation should be as literal as possible without betraying the spirit of the original. But you cannot render most adages literally without losing all idiomatic impact. In the familiar prevailing British translation by Murray (somewhat modernized by Tessinari), the first of the foregoing adages is translated this way: "If you are poor, you deserve it. Recollect the proverb: 'Stolen money never bears fruit.' Begone, imposters!"

This is all, incidentally, that the Murray-Tessinari version gives us of Lorenzini's witty accumulation of rejoinders. The translation by E. Harden is better, but makes the same error of depriving a proverb of its flavour by rendering it literally in another language: "He who steals his neighbour's cloak, ends his life without a shirt." Here is pure *translatorese,* native to no English-speaking region that I know of. The same thing is true of "Stolen money never bears fruit." There *is* an English aphorism that tells us that stolen fruits are sweetest, and another that makes the same claim for stolen kisses—but they would hardly do for Pinocchio's sternly righteous mood in this passage. The astringent acerbity of Lorenzini's style when he cracks a whip against those who exploit and cheat poor innocents must come through purely. The irony is Stendhalian, in the spirit of the epigraph from Danton at the start of *Le Rouge et le Noir: "La vérité, l'âpre vérité";* and it is directed especially against moral hypocrisy, both conscious and unconscious.

The affinity with Stendhal is at once subtle and striking. The character of Pinocchio, a little wooden nobody struggling to be his own wild uncontrollable self—

a tree-spirit and an artist's creation who finds his supreme moment of puppet-happiness when he is welcomed by the other marionettes—is not unlike that of Julien Sorel. Of course, there is no room for the sexual torments, conquests, and strategies of a Sorel in little Pinocchio's life. Yet perhaps we would find parallels (and I think we do) in the way the Blue Fairy comes to Pinocchio's rescue and then lets him go, but reappears at strategic times after making him grieve over her supposed death; while he, for his part, constantly betrays the very devotion toward her that is his chief inspiration. Sorel tries to find his place as a man, and Pinocchio as a human boy, and the self-transformation in both instances means death: death in the literal sense for Julien Sorel, who has betrayed his deepest needs and convictions all along the way despite his inner knowledge; and the death of the old, wayward Pinocchio as a puppet whose free spirit constantly violated the ways of the workaday world. Julien is a revolutionary spirit in an impossible reactionary period; Pinocchio is humbled into accepting the fatalistic, self-denying standards of the virtuous, hardworking poor.

Both authors share a bitter sense of the lot of the poor. In *Le Rouge et le Noir,* the issue is drawn as boldly as in Dickens. In one memorable scene, the vulgar *parvenu* Valenod, the poorhouse Director, has invited Julien to a dinner for important local personages. Valenod, in charge of what nowadays we would call welfare, has in mind only the extension of his own wealth and power:

> The collector of taxes, the chief of police, and two or three other public officials presently arrived, accompanied by their wives. These were followed by some rich Liberals. Then dinner was announced. Julien, ill-disposed for the feast, was thinking of the poor creatures on the other side of the dining-room wall who were waiting for a meal, and whose meat had perhaps been nibbled in order to provide all this coarse luxury.

> "Perhaps they are hungry at this moment," he was saying to himself. His gorge rose; it was impossible for him to eat, even to speak.

An almost parallel scene occurs in *Pinocchio,* in the town of Foolville ("Acchiappa-citrulli"):

> Pinocchio noticed at once that the streets were full of dogs whose hair had been shorn off completely and whose mouths were stretched wide open, gaping with hunger. The streets were full, too, of sheep that had also been shorn and were trembling with cold. And there were roosters whose combs and wattles had been cut away and that were begging for even one tiny grain of corn. . .

> Amid this throng of poor, disgraceful, begging creatures, elegant carriages sometimes drove through. Inside them Pinocchio could see a fox

sometimes, or a mean-eyed chattering magpie, or some nasty-looking bird of prey.

Hunger on the one hand, and the callous indifference of unscrupulous self-aggrandizers on the other, are constants in *Pinocchio.* At times, though, the prose-style breaks into a gaily baroque lyricism that all but celebrates the deprivations of honest poverty:

> Geppetto, who was very poor, lived in a tiny basement room. The only light came through a window near the stairway outside his room. His furniture was as plain as could be: an old kitchen chair, a broken-down old bed, and a wobbly old table. At one end of his room there was a fireplace, and it had a fire burning—but the fire was just painted on the wall. Above the painted fire a painted kettle boiled merrily, sending forth a cloud of painted steam that looked quite real.

To return to the interesting parallels with Stendhal: I have noted the shared preoccupation with motifs of wealth and poverty, exploitation and moral hypocrisy, and self-betrayal or self-transformation. The affective current of ironically sophisticated disillusionment common to both authors may well have nothing to do with any direct influence. It may, rather, be a reflex of nineteenth-century Europe's whole political awareness. It is suggestive that Julien and Pinocchio are co-opted in such different ways. The one is employed to further a reactionary conspiracy to undo the achievements of the Revolution—this despite his Jacobin sympathies and perfect understanding of what is going on. The other is won over to the ideals of the self-respecting workman or small craftsman: acceptance of the prevailing order of things, thrift, dutifulness, focusing on a livelihood rather than exploring the mysteries of the wide world and of the possibilities of experience. Yet there is enough satire in both works against the presumptuousness of rank and power, the absurdity of uniformed grandeur, and the anti-intellectualism rampant in all classes. However their heroes are forced to conform, the works express their sympathies symbolically in many ways; and sometimes they do so explicitly. In this respect, as in their anger and wry adjustments, they are *echt*-picaresque.

I shall suggest one more parallel: the parody in each of the workings of justice. Julien's death-sentence, although he has not actually killed Mme. de Rênal, is the result of a silent conspiracy of his philistine enemies. Lorenzini, naturally, could not let his fable turn openly tragic, although it often threatened to do so. (All but one of the supposedly dead, from the Blue Fairy to the Talking Cricket to the puppet himself, return to life after all . . .) But the imprisonment of Pinocchio makes a tale at once purely comic and truly satirical. He has come to court to bring charges against those who have robbed and swindled him:

The judge was an ape of the gorilla family. He was a respectable-looking old ape, with a nice white beard and gold-rimmed eyeglasses without lenses. He had to wear glasses all the time, since his eyes had been red and watery for so many years.

Pinocchio stood before the judge and told him the whole story, every single sad little detail, of the cruel trick the Fox and the Cat had played on him. He gave their first and last names and ended by begging for justice.

The judge listened very kindly. He took a sympathetic interest in Pinocchio's story and asked all sorts of questions. You could see how sorry he was for him. Finally, when the puppet had nothing more to say, the judge stretched out his hand and rang a bell.

At this signal two huge dogs—mastiffs—appeared, dressed in policemen's uniforms.

The judge pointed to Pinocchio and said, "This poor soul has been robbed of his four gold coins. Arrest him at once! March him right off to prison!"

The puppet was thunderstruck. He remained stock still for a moment, and then started to object. But the policemen, to prevent a pointless waste of time, clapped their paws over his mouth and dragged him off to jail.

And there he stayed four whole months—four very long months. He would have had to stay even longer, except for a great stroke of luck. You see, the young Emperor of Follyland (of which Foolville is the capital) had just won a great war against his enemies. He ordered a splendid public celebration, with colored lights and fireworks and horse races and bicycle races. And, as the most glorious thing of all, he commanded the jailers to unlock the prisons and set all the criminals free.

"If the others are leaving," said Pinocchio to his jailer, "I want to leave too."

"Oh, no," said the jailer, "not you, Pinocchio. You don't belong to the lucky ones I'm supposed to set free. You're not a criminal."

"That's an insult!" cried Pinocchio. "Excuse me, but I happen to be a criminal just like the others!"

"Oh, I beg your pardon," said the jailer. "In that case, you're certainly right." And he took off his hat, bowed respectfully, and let Pinocchio escape, too.

One hardly knows what to do when one comes upon a passage like this one, totally good-natured, or at least

straight-faced, in its tone while implicitly mordant in its ultimate bearing. It is of a piece with the debate of the doctors over whether or not Pinocchio has died, the genial tyranny of Fire-eater the puppet-master, the Rabelaisian dining scene in the Red Crab Inn, and the kindly preparations by the monstrous sea-green fisherman to fry Pinocchio and eat him. All these moments have their place in a superb child's story full of suspense and adventure but also charged with anger against the arbitrary and unfair order of the world. They are magical, with multiple resonances, yet powerfully alive in their immediate impact.

And after all, the shifting moods, the stream of the book's movement—these are what one wants to catch most of all. Translating this story was for me like watching a wonderful puppet show, an epic-comic-bouncy puppet opera full of surprises, folklore, glorious silliness, and everything dear to poets as well as to children. But I discovered, too, that it is far more than the engaging but sometimes starkly harsh, sometimes severely moralistic, and sometimes sentimental tale as I remembered it. Collodi's copious fantasy and inventiveness, his fine delight in yarn-spinning, and his unsqueamish love of the child mind, all converge in this offhand masterpiece. (There must have been marvelous storytellers in his family, from whom he absorbed the folk-tales so magically transmuted in *Pinocchio*.) From the brilliant Punch-and-Judy slapstick of the opening chapters, in which Mr Cherry and poor Geppetto have so much trouble with the demonically untamed bit of wood out of which Pinocchio will be carved, to the final moment, so startling and so touching, when the hero—now a real boy, stares at his dangling, lifeless former puppet-self and rejoices at his metamorphosis, this is a work of genius. And by the way, that famous nose: what a surprise! The first time we see its uncontrollable growth is when Geppetto carves it into existence—nothing to do with lying. The second time, it is because Pinocchio is so terribly hungry. Only twice more, actually, do we see it growing again: when Pinocchio lies to the Fairy and when he lies to the kindly old man. A forceful image, associated with wild natural disposition and then with guilt and embarrassment, its inevitable symbolism is at once earthily phallic and social—no doubt part of the buried sexual fable that also involves the Fairy's change from a girl to a woman. As with so many other elements in his tale, Collodi was content to inject these energies of combined elemental and sophisticated adult awareness into the text without pursuing them relentlessly. They float, powerful, ambiguous, unresolved, among all the other tonalities.

Pinocchio abounds with primal forces, presences out of myth, and magical elements, all of which give it a vitality beyond that of any other children's book of comparable length. The irrepressible wooden log that keeps tormenting Mr Cherry and Geppetto; the puppet-actors seen as tree-people ("*quella compagnia drammatico-vegetale*"); and the ogre Fire-eater and the Green Fisherman, both of whom step right out of ancient Greek or Celtic or even hoarier mythology—these, along with all the talking animals, some perfectly sweet and helpful, others viciously hostile, charge the zigzag progress of Pinocchio toward rebirth as a human being with both terror and delight. The tricks the Fairy plays on Pinocchio (despite her resemblance to the Virgin Mary or at least to Beatrice), and the deeply morbid pall of death and mortal illness she sometimes casts over the story, make her in part a demonic spirit herself, and give the psychic atmosphere a complex cast indeed. The book's zest, humour, and speed conceal its darker side to some extent; and the pacing—the cycles of suspense, relaxation, and unexpected renewal of suspense—makes it impossible to linger over that darker side. Yet just consider the incidents that must wring a child's heart on the way to the final triumph: the supposed death of the Talking Cricket, for instance, or the other supposed deaths—the Fairy's, Eugenio's, and even Pinocchio's; or Candleflame's actual death; or the misery of the little donkey that tries to warn Pinocchio and whose ears the terrible Little Man bites off.

Add to these truly painful elements that of Swiftian satire, and we have a tragic undertow. I have noted the author's empathy with working-class life and ideals, and his awareness of the hardships of ordinary life as opposed to privileged insensitivity. He loves gentleness, and is haunted by all the cruelty to children and animals. The Little Man's enticement of boys to donkeydoom and then his selling them into slavery is almost a Marxist parable, and their hard treatment by the masters who buy them provides other such parables. The story of the man who wants to make a drum of Pinocchio's skin adds to the litany of sadism in brutally adult terms. There is often, in fact, something in the style of certain passages of bitter narrative that reflects a deep end-of-century disillusionment; the wit itself, the implied mockery of inhuman sensibilities, has an intransigent realism anticipating a Brecht, a Kafka or a Céline. At the same time, one also feels echoes of disillusionment from the earlier, nineteenth century in the exchanges between Pinocchio and the man who buys him to make a drumskin of him—a whiff of Stendhalian complex awareness and, even more, the kind of irony we find in Balzac. There is a certain resemblance between Mme. de Rochefilde's momentarily sincere revulsion against the world as it is in Balzac's *Sarrasine*—"You have given me a disgust for life and for passions that will last a long time"—and that of Pinocchio's quondam master when he learns he will not get his drumskin after all:

> "From this moment on," said his horrified master, "I swear I'll never again put even the most delicious fish in my mouth. It would be extremely unpleasant to cut open a mullet or a fried whiting and find a donkey's tail inside."

Attilio Mussino depicts Pinocchio.

In making this tentative point I am not advancing a critical thesis about the influences acting on Lorenzini (although he was obviously a well-read man). Rather, I am reminding myself that great children's books are saturated with their authors' full consciousness. ***Pinocchio***'s chief rivals in English would certainly be Mark Twain's *The Adventures of Huckleberry Finn* and Lewis Carroll's *Alice in Wonderland*. (We should probably add *Gulliver's Travels,* not intended for children but often so treated in bowdlerized versions.) Huck and Alice and Pinocchio all move innocently through their worlds of mystery, terror, and inhumanity; all three characters are relatively humourless—although Pinocchio can be sardonic—in the midst of hilarious episodes. Freud would doubtless see in their adventures an objectification of the latent adult knowledge lurking dreamlike in them, awaiting the overwhelming moments of trauma to come. It is as if there were a conspiracy between the books and their child-readers, to suggest the most drastic truths without spelling them out as final reality. All the deaths that are not really deaths after all (like the threatened death of our puppet-hero when the rabbits arrive with a coffin to carry him away in) and the reversed mortal frailty of Geppetto, which is canceled at the story's end by his rejuvenation, are embodiments of this muffled recognition. Before the final chapter, the only death the story can afford, emotionally, is the Serpent's—and after all he dies *laughing,* like a true Nietzschean! Then, close to the miracles at the end of the book, one actual death (of Candleflame, the protagonist's alter ego) serves to present Pinocchio as perfectly transfigured by tender compassion. The comic but murderous Fox and Cat are not only typical rogue-figures such as picaresque heroes must generally encounter; they are spirits of evil who finally go too far and awaken the innocent hero into a state of worldly defensiveness and prudence and virtuous industry. This transformation would be rather depressing were it not for Lorenzini's gift for charming detail, such as Pinocchio's home-made pen and ink and the old book he gets hold of to teach himself to read.

In addition, as we have observed, there is all the implied social satire: the judge (a bestiary figure in an old allegorical tradition) who listens sympathetically to Pinocchio's account of being robbed and then sentences him to prison (an echo of Geppetto's jailing early on in the book); the learnedly idiotic doctors (more bestiary figures); the shockingly modern polecat-gangsters who have corrupted the dog Melampo and try the same game with Pinocchio—these may suffice as major examples. Much of the food for thought in the book—as in Voltaire's *Candide*—is extremely raw and gamy meat.

Against all this, of course, we have the swiftly-paced, self-renewing narrative, with its chases and sudden turns and extremes of feeling, and the never-failing comic brilliance. Suspense and laughter are magnificently combined in the episodes of the flyaway omelet, the rescue from the Green Fisherman, and the reluctant pity of Fire-eater that reprieves Pinocchio from death by burning, for instance. And the kindly, reassuring compassion and aid he gets from so many animals counteract much of the underlying grimness. Curiously enough, so does the knowledgeable but helpless sympathy the little Woodchuck gives him—a consummate touch comparable with the little donkey's hopeless attempt to warn him during the great ride to the Land of Cockaigne. In the large, *Pinocchio* is a kind of allegory, certainly,

in its waywardly appealing fashion. It counterposes two deeply human, mutually contradictory passions: the passion to remain splendidly free of social and institutional restraints, and the passion to remake ourselves into ideally considerate and responsible beings. This is after all the great unresolved contradiction that makes every self to some degree an inwardly warring self and that makes for warring theories of education. Pinocchio starts out as a purely free, independent, impersonal spirit, but is forced by the most painful kind of experience to accept responsibility. The change takes place because he sees, however sporadically, that those he cares for are suffering because of him. (The transformation of Geppetto from a comic figure scrapping with his equally comic old pal Mr Cherry to a grieving, put-upon "papa" is dazzlingly rapid—though possibly no more so than that of many a parent from care-free childlessness to careworn fatherhood or motherhood!) But mostly the change is enforced by the brutal lessons taught after the puppet becomes a donkey. Being a dutiful student, learning a decent trade, caring for aged parents: these are the world's hard lessons, absorbed through beatings, starvation, and exposure. We may be reluctant to admit it, in our quite different world from Pinocchio's rural countryside dotted with imaginary villages; but today, a century later, our concern for our children's future and safety in a dangerous world is not terribly unlike Geppetto's and the Blue Fairy's concern for Pinocchio.

Still, the genius of the book *is* largely comic and adventurous in the spirit of the egg that turns cheerfully into a little chicken and flies out the window, escaping just the way Pinocchio does from the Green Fisherman—that is, at the last minute and against the odds. And I have not mentioned the more uproarious moments . . . The glorious welcome given Pinocchio in the puppet theatre, which has the same heartwarming affection as Hamlet's greeting to the players approximately three centuries earlier is one instance. The reunion with Geppetto inside the Shark is another. And there are the extraordinary lyrical moments, such as the view of the heavens from the Shark's mouth, that add yet another aesthetic dimension:

> Now, since the shark was very old, and had a weak heart, and—as you know—suffered from asthma, he had to sleep with his mouth open. So when Pinocchio peered up through the monster's throat from inside, he could see far beyond the enormous, gaping mouth—all the way up to the starry sky and the beautiful light of the full moon.

Here whimsy, and a deliberately silly sort of pathos, and suspense, and pure imagination come together beautifully. Suddenly Lorenzini is close to the Byron of *Don Juan.* And in another, more serious dimension, he is even closer to the poet who wrote, at the close of the *Inferno*:

tanto ch' i' vidi delle cose belle
che porta 'l ciel, per un pertugio tondo;
e quindi uscimmo a riveder le stelle.

[far enough to see, through a round opening,
some of the lovely sights Heaven shows forth;
and soon we emerged and once more gazed at
   the stars.]

In retrospect, then, the variety and kinds of personalities and scenes—and of tonal effects from boisterous farce to delicate fantasy and lyricism to harsh realism or morbid grimness or sheer joy—seems amazing to me: a multitudinous orchestration. The tale's appeal has been strong enough to survive all the inaccurate, censored, and shortened treatments to which it has been subjected. It has also survived its own occasionally off-putting morality of self-righteous industriousness and thrifty practicality: echoes of an age when it was possible to live with dignity on truly meager resources (that is, to be decently poor) far more manageably than now. Be that as it may, the tale crackles with contagious vitality. When Pinocchio is desperately hungry, we start desperately "yawning with hunger" too. When he stubbornly ignores all good advice and plants gold pieces in the Field of Miracles, we are as attuned to the pity of his self-deception and the cruel fraud being practiced on him as if we were there with him. The mixture of comedy with pathos, and of realistic directness with very pure imagination, makes the book a great panorama for the child reader. There is so much to look at, to laugh at, to cry over, to fix in visual reverie, and to think about!

Obviously, I am tempted to say a great deal more . . . But I will limit myself to just one more point, having to do with Lorenzini's uncanny discovery of the dominant psychological moment, and symbol for it, that illuminates the whole work at the very end. In the largest sense, *Pinocchio* gives its miraculous, volatile, forgetful little hero every opportunity to be as naughty and unruly and greedy as a child often has to be, and yet to be loved and nourished until he (he *or* she, of course) becomes his best self of his own accord. Pinocchio may, at the end, exclaim: "How strange I was when I used to be a puppet! And how glad I am that I've become a real little boy!" But how glad the rest of us are that he *was* a puppet for all those pages, and what a twinge it gives us to read the final description of the now-abandoned puppet-form! This is the true death in the book. The new Pinocchio sees his former self as a strange object, "a large puppet leaning against a chair". All the intensity of the excitable being we have known is chillingly distanced by the language and by the figure's utter, unwonted lifelessness: ". . . its head was twisted to one side and drooping down, its arms were dangling, and its legs were so bent and crossed that it was a miracle the puppet was still upright at all."

This language is a pang of regret for the lost freedom of unselfconscious childhood. Lucky for us that Lorenzini could recover that world and bring its moods and fears and ecstasies to life again at the height of his mature powers.

Richard Wunderlich (essay date 1992)

SOURCE: "The Tribulations of *Pinocchio*: How Social Change Can Wreck a Good Story," in *Poetics Today*, Vol. 13, No. 1, Spring, 1992, pp. 197-219.

[*In the following excerpt, Wunderlich chronicles the publication history of* Pinocchio, *the many editorial changes it underwent, and its adaptations.*]

Written serially for an Italian children's weekly from 1881 to 1882, Carlo Collodi's *Pinocchio* was assembled and first released as a full-length novel in 1883. Pinocchio's tribulations, alas, did not end with the story's final chapter; a long series of quite different mishaps awaited him in North America. The first of these entailed the actual process of getting into print in the United States.

English audiences first met the puppet at Christmas time, 1891, when Fisher Unwin (London) published Mary Alice Murray's translation. The little book was decorated with Enrico Mazzanti's sketches, borrowed from the 1883 Italian edition. Murray's direct, rather literal translation of the novel was fortunate: the play it granted Collodi's ironic wit could charm English adults even if, as was likely, it went over the heads of their children.

Pinocchio's hurried trip across the Atlantic to the United States a year later, however, was less fortunate. The choice of an American distributor proved poor. Cassell (New York) had arranged to bind and market the Fisher Unwin printed sheets under its own name, and they released the novel in October 1892. Then, due to embezzlement by its president, Cassell was declared insolvent just eight months later. *Pinocchio*'s introduction to the United States, therefore, required a second debut. As befits the spirit of Collodi's adventure story and the world his puppet confronts, shady dealings entangled this second debut as well. Jordan Marsh (Boston) copyrighted and issued the novel in October 1898 with the inventive title *Pinocchio's Adventures in Wonderland*. According to the publisher, the title was created for sales appeal, intended to suggest an affinity with *Alice's Adventures in Wonderland*. However, a darker motive seems more likely, for the book had been stolen, and the new name, implying an entirely different tale, was meant to disguise the theft. Inspection of the volume shows that, except for minor modifications in format and the deletion of some illustrations, this first American printing is identical to the Fisher Unwin/Cassell sheets. Furthermore, the little book's title page is remarkable for what it omits: no credit is given to Mazzanti, Murray, *or even Collodi,* despite the fact that the printer had all of this information. . . .

Under an arrangement with Jordan Marsh, H. M. Caldwell (New York and Boston) also released three editions (i.e., separate bindings) of *Pinocchio* in 1898. (The timing raises the possibility that Caldwell might have marketed the novel even before Jordan Marsh.) As history shows, this second debut established the book, and *Pinocchio* has been printed or reprinted in the United States every year since. Jordan Marsh reprinted it once or twice after 1898, and in 1900 (or late 1899) issued a separate larger size edition with four color plates by René Quentin. Until going out of business in 1913, Caldwell released three or four distinct editions every year.

Pinocchio's greater mishaps over the course of this century, however, concerned deliberate changes in the story, its basic theme, and the very personalities Collodi had fashioned. Two such changes will be of particular interest here: the first occurred almost immediately, in the early part of this century, and the second, occurring in the middle or late 1930s, became entrenched in the 1960s and remains so to this day. Indeed, even though translations were printed almost annually and the 1980s brought a spurt of new translations, the popular image in the United States of what *Pinocchio* is all about bears little or no relation to Collodi's original.

COLLODI'S IMAGERY

In Collodi's novel, the child is portrayed realistically, although comically. He is egoistic (but not selfish), preoccupied with immediate gratification, and insensitive to (indeed, unconscious of) his impact on others: all of which traits are exacerbated by a short attention span. The child, therefore, is infuriating and frustrating to the parent. And, as in real life, Collodi's Pinocchio learns dialectically: he advances, regresses, then makes progress again. His proper purpose is to become an adult, which means to become aware of the effect he has and can have on others, to take the concerns of others into account, and, if necessary, to assume responsibility, deferring his own needs on behalf of others. Pinocchio is transformed and transforms himself when he passes three tests: (1) he puts Geppetto's needs ahead of his own and risks his life by swimming, burdened with Geppetto, out of the Shark and to land; (2) he works both day and night to support and to nurse his apparently failing parent; and (3) during this process, after having frugally saved extra money to buy clothes for himself, he turns it all over, without hesitation, to the Fairy, who is "desperately" ill. Pinocchio has now become an adult, playing the role to Geppetto and the Fairy that they had earlier played to him. . . .

As an image of the parent, Geppetto is also both realistic and comical. Clearly he loves and is concerned about Pinocchio. At the same time, however, Pinocchio angers and frustrates him, so Geppetto vacillates, as parents do, between episodes of tenderness and fury. It is also clear that Geppetto is limited in terms of what he can do to conduct the puppet to adulthood; he can offer guidance, nurturing, and himself as an anchor, yet these are all dependent on Pinocchio's response and are of no avail until the puppet accepts them. The lesson for parents here (as presented to children) is to be patient and steadfast— and to hope for a future in which the child comes to understand.

EARLY IMPACTS ON THE STORY

The first alteration of *Pinocchio* occurred in 1904, scarcely six years after the Jordan Marsh release, and was consciously dictated by educators at the primary school level. They responded to an American society that was changing precipitously, one visibly different from the Civil War period of a scant forty years earlier. Industrialization had ushered in the Gilded Age of speculation and "nation building" by manufacturers and financiers with holdings more extensive than ever before. It had also opened the country up to an unprecedented number of foreign immigrants (and the Statue of Liberty to commemorate the dream), competing with a surging native influx from country towns, to inundate cities that then expanded convulsively in size, with attendant increases in heterogeneity and congestion. Prominent in the cities were laborers and their foreign-tongued children, and child labor, the nature of which had changed with the introduction of factory machines, became an issue along with the related one of native and immigrant children's assimilation into both school and society. Well excised from latter-day history texts was the fact that this was also a period of violence, mainly initiated by manufacturers and the government against the organizing attempts of labor and the "Free Speech" movement. This was the period of national strikes and the counter-creation of the National Guard, the Haymarket Riot and the May Day demand for an eight-hour work day (both in 1886), and newspaper diatribes against anarchism, communism, and socialism. [In *Dreaming the Rational City: The Myth of American City Planning*] M. Christine Boyer summarizes well the perceived tasks of cities at that time:

> With the emergence of the vast American metropolis after the Civil War two problems arose: how to discipline and regulate the urban masses in order to eradicate the dangers of social unrest, physical degeneration, and congested contagion, which all cities seemed to breed, and how to control and arrange the spatial growth of these gigantic places so that they would support industrial production and the development of a civilization of cities.

The industrialization of America in the late nineteenth century brought with it a social reorganization and a new public sense of morality to enforce that reorganization. The new values, imposed on an often reluctant population, emphasized self-discipline, self-denial, industriousness, and respect for authority. This transitional period began much earlier in Massachusetts: it was already evident in the shoe-manufacturing town of Lynn by 1840. . . . Lynn is adjacent to Boston, where, in September 1904, the publisher Ginn released the first American translation of *Pinocchio* (by Walter S. Cramp), written to accommodate the new social order. While also intended for the trade market, it was primarily designed as a school text for national distribution. Although Cramp's translation was technically correct and had apparently been contracted for already by the school system (as well as being already in print), Lynn's school board rejected it as inappropriate. Ginn then revised almost every page of the original printing plates (changing phrases, omitting various passages and episodes, deleting half of chapter 2, adding occasional lines, even dropping two of Charles Copeland's sketches and requiring him to redraw a third). . . . Just two months after publication, Cramp's original translation was withdrawn and the revised edition substituted. The change in text was represented by a change in title: *The Adventures of Pinocchio* became *Pinocchio, the Adventures of a Marionette*. It was this later rendition, which Ginn continued to offer on the trade market until about 1919, that served classrooms through the 1950s.

CRAMP'S ALTERED TRANSLATION

The views of elementary school educators, which must have been shared by some segment of the larger population, can be deduced from what was omitted as well as from what was intentionally retained. First, some episodes of violence were removed. Most notably, the assassin's rough handling of Pinocchio was reduced to a single sentence, and Pinocchio's defense, biting off one of the attacking "hands," was deleted entirely (chapter 14); the assassins still hang Pinocchio from a tree to die, but his being hung by the neck was censored (chapter 15); also omitted were Pinocchio's provocation of the school children (chapter 27), the farmer's plan to have the captured weasels sent to town for skinning (chapter 27), and the Coachman's biting off the donkey's ears (chapter 31). Geppetto's threat to whip the puppet (chapter 3) was reduced to a threat of unspecified "punishment." What might be called social violence was also removed. When Geppetto selects a name for his puppet (chapter 3), he thinks of the Pinocchio family and reflects that "the richest of them begged." This phrase became "it was a happy family." Likewise, Copeland's illustration of the City of Stupid-Catchers, near the Field of Miracles (chapter 18), a dense scene of scrawny, miserable animals crowded on the street and sidewalk, perhaps suggestive of ur-

ban working-class living conditions, was withdrawn and a far more pleasant scene, of the smug Fox riding in an opulent carriage, was added. While the elimination of violence might have been due to an overall protective, benevolent attitude toward children, it might also have been provoked by an urgent pair of concerns facing school teachers: that is, to discourage violence among children and to maintain discipline in the classroom. In 1904 urban school children were highly aware of violence and most likely resorted to it easily themselves. With cities growing larger and more congested each year, they inevitably housed an increasingly diverse mixture of ethnic and foreign-language groups. Antipathies among the various groups, as well as conflict with the American-born population, extended to children and must have been centered in the schools, where the groups were mixed together.

A second kind of revision relates indirectly to authority: that is, the removal of scenes that disparaged adults or showed children ridiculing adults. In chapter 2, for example, all references to Geppetto's being taunted by children calling him "Corn Meal" were omitted, as was Pinocchio's use of this pejorative name (while still a block of wood) to provoke two physical scraps between Geppetto and Cherry; both fights, really the kinds of battle young children might engage in, were also omitted. When Geppetto begins carving Pinocchio (chapter 3), the puppet "sticks out its tongue." This was altered to "the features began to make grimaces." "At this insolence Geppetto looked sad and melancholy" was changed to "at this disobedience Geppetto looked very sad." When Pinocchio begs for food at night (chapter 6), the old man at the upper-story window asks him to wait, then pours "a bucket of water" on him; in the altered version the old man simply tells Pinocchio to "go away." Showing adults in a poor light or showing children mocking them was probably considered a threat to school discipline and authority.

Perhaps more revealing is not what the school board excised from Cramp's text, but what it retained and approved. Translating is not merely a matter of converting the words of one language into those of another, for words carry shades of meaning. What was more important to Cramp's translation were the shades of meaning he conveyed and their emphasis by way of repetition throughout the text. The tone of Cramp's translation reveals an attitude toward children, one that was acceptable to the school board and, hence, consonant with its views. Cramp's tone toward Pinocchio is harsh, punitive, and unsympathetic. Pinocchio, the child, is an annoyance.

To demonstrate Cramp's particular tone, his renderings can be compared with other new translations done at the time. In 1909 Joseph Walker's translation, released for the trade market, paralleled Cramp's altered translation by making similar omissions and changes, but also, more importantly, by matching his tone. Hence, its publisher, T. Y. Crowell, must have thought that there existed a section of the public which was sympathetic to such views. By contrast, also in 1909, Doubleday, Page released Augustus Caprani's translation to the trade market, one which paralleled Murray's translation in both completeness and attitude. The fourth American translation, by Carol Della Chiesa, published by Macmillan in 1925, was also a rendering closer to Murray's and different from the translations of both Cramp and Walker.

In chapter 18 the Fox and the Cat try to lure Pinocchio to the Field of Miracles a second time. The puppet debates with himself and reluctantly consents. Here is how five translators render the very same Italian sentences:

> He ended, however, by doing as all boys do who have not a grain of sense and who have no heart— he ended by giving his head a little shake, and saying to the Fox and the Cat . . . (Murray 1891)

> But after the fashion of foolish, heartless boys, he finally yielded. With a shake of his head he said to the Fox and the Cat . . . (Cramp 1904)

> But he ended by doing like all silly little boys who want to please themselves. With a nod of his head he said to the Fox and the Cat . . . (Walker 1909)

> Finally he ended by doing as all boys do who have no heart or judgment, by shaking his head and saying to the Fox and the Cat . . . (Caprani 1909)

> Then he ended by doing what all boys do, when they have no heart and little brain. He shrugged his shoulders and said to the Fox and the Cat. . . . (Della Chiesa 1925)

The renderings of Cramp and Walker are distinctly punitive. They suggest that little boys are inherently foolish and pass judgment on this characteristic. By contrast, the three other translators suggest a temporary childhood phase or a weakness to be overcome.

In a second example, Pinocchio has just arrived at the Island of Busy Bees (chapter 24). He is worn out from his many adventures and very hungry. To his dismay, he learns that everyone on the island works for a living and that he is actually expected to do something in exchange for food.

> "Ah," said that lazy Pinocchio at once, "I see that this village will never suit me! I wasn't born to work!" (Murray 1891)

> "I understand!" exclaimed that good-for-nothing Pinocchio. "This country is not for me. I was not born to work." (Cramp 1904)

> "Humph!" sniffed Pinocchio. "I'm afraid this is no place for me! I was not born to work." (Walker 1909)

> "This is not the place for me!" said that lazy little fellow, Pinocchio. "I was not born to work." (Caprani 1909)

> "I understand," said Pinocchio at once wearily, "this is no place for me! I was not born for work." (Della Chiesa 1925)

Cramp's general tone toward Pinocchio is insensitive, unsympathetic, or, at the very least, uncomplimentary. While it may not in itself stress the theme of obedience (except indirectly by continually disparaging Pinocchio's character), it is clearly supportive of such a theme. This theme becomes explicit and dominant in the two pedagogical renditions discussed below.

TWO PEDAGOGICAL RENDITIONS

Written as a play, Emily Gray's (1912) dramatic reader for first-grade use was published in early 1912 by Flanagan (Chicago). . . . This little comedy focuses on Pinocchio's sequence of misdeeds, but it does so chiefly to emphasize that he is incompetent, recalcitrant, and, ultimately, incorrigible as well. Pinocchio is demeaned and humiliated: in two rather long episodes he must recite his list of errors, one by one, having each admonished individually and acknowledging his own "stupidity." Although hammered at continually, the lessons are few: little boys should obey their parents and value the advice of their elders; Pinocchio is dull-witted and lacks sense (and, by inference, is selfish), needing to attend school in order to acquire some sense; his idleness cannot be tolerated, and so on. The play's basic theme is clear: children will come to no good end unless they heed their parents and other elders (teachers and employers?), despite their naturally contrary inclinations, since children are "stupid." One striking feature of this play is the impatient disapproval, even harshness, of the adults (Geppetto, the Fairy, Cricket), who seem to scream more often than they talk, as well as the consensus among them that Pinocchio is worthless and "stupid." Indeed, what is made clear is that, unless he or she changes, the child is a troublesome annoyance, a bother to be suffered by the child's protectors, and one they might be better off without. This image implies a threat: the child has no claim on adults, who merely condescend to assist him; if he becomes too recalcitrant and burdensome, therefore, the child might well be cut loose from all protection.

Equally remarkable is Gray's conclusion. The play does not end with Pinocchio's triumph but with his punishment: that is, with retribution for an intractable career of disobedience and poor judgment, a career pursued against the advice, warning, and care offered by adults. The play ends when Pinocchio is irreversibly changed into a donkey, then forcibly driven off-stage with a whip, to labor in the circus.

By analogy, Gray's dramatically rendered lessons about the child's future in the workplace are also clear. The most obvious lesson taught is the necessity of schooling for obtaining any job better than that of an unskilled laborer (a message coupled with a warning against the social class and distinctly negative image of people who do such unskilled labor). More important, however, are other clearly articulated messages. The child (future employee) is dull-witted, hence recalcitrant, and in need of a protector (employer). Adults (employers) know what is best and should be obeyed—and this is the well-reinforced key to future success that Gray recommends. Recalcitrant children (workers), when needlessly bothersome, run the risk of rightly losing their protectors and becoming donkeys for the rest of their lives. In 1912, this reference to labor unions and the properly different roles of blue- and white-collar workers was barely disguised. Obedience would not only protect one from "donkeyhood," but would guarantee job security and the possibility of a comfortable future.

In [*Story-Hour Favorites: Selected for Library, School, and Home*, 1918], Wilhelmina Harper anthologized a selection of short stories "for library, school, and home use," to be read aloud by adults. *Pinocchio* was among these stories: that is, Cramp's translation cut down to twenty-five pages! So radical an abridgment is necessarily even more selective and the novel thus substantially altered. It focuses entirely on Pinocchio at school: his early delinquency, his later decision to take school seriously, leading to his success in the classroom, then, alas, his succumbing to Lampwick's temptation and being finally transformed into a donkey. Harper's concluding lines read: "What happened finally to Lampwick I do not know. I know, however, that Pinocchio led a very hard and weary life." Certainly, this rendition is a cautionary tale about school and its importance. Yet due to its selectivity, it emphasizes, even more strongly than Cramp did, the destructiveness of the child's "natural" inclinations, as opposed to the adults' wisdom in attempting to mold the child—an equation adding up to the importance of obedience to adults. Such messages easily extend beyond their school setting and apply equally well to future relations in the workplace.

All the same, this industrial moralism championed by educators did not completely dominate *Pinocchio* during this period. This was a secondary, competing complex of images that, apart from the persistence in print of the Cramp and Walker translations, seemed to have disappeared by the mid-1920s. The most popular trade edition through 1919 was that of Murray's translation (which had never actually been copyrighted).

PINOCCHIO'S POPULARITY

Circulation figures for assessing *Pinocchio*'s early popularity have not survived; a count of the number of editions, reprints, and reissues, however, should enable us to gauge the book's popularity reasonably well. Between 1900 and 1919 translations were released by publishers three to four times each year on average. Further evidence of popularity is the fact that three new translations (those already noted above) were produced and two separate abridgements marketed. Moreover, three Italian sequels were translated, published, and reprinted: *Pinocchio in Africa*, published by Ginn; *Pinocchio under the Sea*, published by Macmillan; and *The Heart of Pinocchio*, published by Harper and Brothers.

Collodi's novel became increasingly popular during the 1920s (averaging seven or eight releases per year), reaching its zenith during the 1930s: twenty-six different publishers combined to average over ten releases a year. New translations, all rejecting the older moralistic slant, were published to compete with Murray's original: Carol Della Chiesa's, by Macmillan; Violet Moore Higgins's, by Albert Whitman; May M. Sweet's, by Houghton Mifflin; and Angelo Patri's, by Doubleday Doran. In addition, Maud and Miska Petersham and Edward L. Thorndike revised Murray's translation, using more contemporary language, in versions published by Garden City and Appleton-Century, respectively. Only two condensations of the novel seem to have been produced: one by Sidney G. Firman, published by John C. Winston; the other by Kathryn Heisenfelt, published by Whitman. These, along with several abridgments released by Dent/Dutton, Owen, Blue Ribbon, and Rand McNally, do suggest a change in Pinocchio's image through selective reduction. For example, Pinocchio's egoism is softened, and his mischief tends to be a series of unrelated pranks; the puppet now arouses less anger and becomes more endearing. Nonetheless, the image of *Pinocchio* in print, especially considering its diffusion through such a large number of translations, remained close to that of Collodi's novel (the exceptions being the Cramp and Walker translations, which continued to be widely available during this period).

Pinocchio's popularity during the 1930s can also be assessed by other indices. A "pop-up" book (an abridgment of Murray's translation) was produced by Blue Ribbon, and a "put-together" book (Murray's translation preceded by six cut-and-paste pages, also sold separately as "Pinocchio Stick-Up Puzzles"), by Samuel Gabriel Sons. Musical adaptations were produced, ranging from Bernard Rogers's symphonic work *Leaves from the Tale of Pinocchio* and Ernest Toch's *Pinocchio: Merry Overture*, to the *Pinocchio Fox Trot*. Four new sequels appeared during this period: *Pinocchio in America*, published by Doubleday Doran; *Puppet Parade*, published by Longmans, Green; *Hi! Ho! Pinoc-*

chio, published by Reilly and Lee; and *Smoky and Pinocchio*, published by Lippincott.

The most intense interest in *Pinocchio*'s dramatic potential to date arose during the 1930s: there were at least twenty-six new productions, including two operettas, a pantomime, a ballet, and two radio broadcasts. While much of this material has been lost, the scripts that have survived reveal a pattern: they are all faithful to Collodi's original except for a common tendency, which probably began in the early 1930s, to "soften," the puppet, that is, to make him less enraging and more amusing. All in all, then, the popular conception of Pinocchio was the same as the character portrayed by Collodi, or a somewhat milder one. This was the case until about 1937.

A CHANGE IN COLLODI'S IMAGERY

In the brief span between 1937 and 1939, three separate renditions of *Pinocchio* were rather abruptly produced, all of which markedly diverged from the original and in the same way. Collodi's puppet now becomes docile, loving, and innocent, incapable of provoking anger and more lovable precisely because of his "pranks," which have now become innocuous and cute. Geppetto becomes consistently warm and tender, and Pinocchio fulfills his desire for a son. The natural state of the family is presented as one of harmony, which may be disrupted by the cutely mischievous and inexperienced child or, unintentionally, by the innocent child or by an innocent child who is preyed on by the outside world, as in Disney's animated film. And, in the end, this new puppet is transformed into a good boy or a better boy, but not into an adult. The goal of the child is no longer to grow up, but to be a good child and to celebrate family unity and harmony.

Yasha Frank

The first of these new renditions to appear was Yasha Frank's (1939) play, written for the Federal Theatre Project. *Pinocchio* premiered in June 1937 (at the Beaux Arts Theatre, Los Angeles) and ran for more than a year with full-capacity audiences, a noticeably large proportion of which were adults and returning viewers. Over the next two years F.T.P. companies performed the show in various cities, and it ran on Broadway (at the Ritz Theatre) for the first six months of 1939. The play's run ended only when Congress shut down the entire Federal Theatre Project in June 1939. That action was presumably taken in response to a sharply negative House Un-American Activities Committee report: "A rather large number of employees . . . of the Project are either members of the Communist party or sympathizers with the Communist party." Frank's script was published commercially in April 1939.

Frank's Pinocchio is the very antithesis of Collodi's vibrant character. He is not headstrong but thoroughly docile and passive; he does not press for his own way, but trustingly allows himself to be directed like a branch in flowing water. Astoundingly, Frank's puppet makes no trouble or mischief whatsoever. He is good-natured, and mischief, rather, is thrust on him. For his own protection, therefore, this puppet must be watched over and cared for. Frank's Pinocchio is innocent and wishes harm to no one; he is incapable of being mean or ill-tempered. This puppet arouses amusement, concern, and love, but certainly not anger or frustration.

In contrast to Collodi's portrayal, Frank's Pinocchio is quiet and immobile as Geppetto puts him together. The day after being made, he and Geppetto have a quiet breakfast chat, after which Geppetto leaves to buy him a schoolbook. In his absence the pet cat discovers, frightens, and chases Pinocchio about the room, forcing him to jump to safety on top of a hot oven, where he burns his feet. Geppetto returns and realizes that he should not have left Pinocchio unattended. After repairing his feet, Geppetto sends Pinocchio off to school with good wishes and a warning not to go to Boobyland. Frank has not simply modified several episodes; rather, he has changed the very natures of the characters. This Pinocchio is sweet and gentle, quite incapable of self-assertion, much less anger or surliness. The Talking Cricket, whom Collodi's Pinocchio squashes in a hot fury for having calmly spoken the truth, is conveniently omitted altogether from the play.

Befitting its Depression-era origins, Frank's *Pinocchio* is a morality play about greed, about being concerned for and giving to those in need. And, ultimately, this is the test (giving four pennies to a blind beggar woman) that Pinocchio must pass in order to become a real, live boy. After the circus episode Pinocchio, with his four pennies, is accosted by two beggar women seeking

> Pennies for the poor . . .
> Help us buy a little food;
> Help us to endure . . .
> Surely you can spare a penny
> You are rich. You have so many.

"Greed" overcomes the puppet, but he is also intimidated by the women. He fails this first test, and they hang him up. The Fairy Queen immediately arrives to free him, explaining that the beggar women were evil spirits sent to trap him and that he must overcome his greed before he can be a living boy. In Pinocchio's final test at the play's end, of course, he does so. But we must ask just what it is that he achieves. The answer begins to suggest itself, when we see Pinocchio trapped inside the Monster Whale with Geppetto. Here it is not Pinocchio but Geppetto who discovers how to get the whale's mouth open; and it is Geppetto, not Pinocchio, who initiates and takes charge of their escape (after they get out, the scene shifts to Geppetto's cottage). Once they are at the cottage again, Pinocchio passes his final test and Geppetto arranges a birthday party (one year having elapsed since the puppet's creation) to celebrate the change that will take place. Yet what has Pinocchio achieved? He has conquered his greed and become "a living, breathing boy," which probably means a good boy, if greed or selfishness has been overcome. But he has not achieved adulthood: he is still a child, even if a good one.

At the birthday celebration, as staged by Frank, all the main characters enter to cheer Pinocchio's transformation, including the Beggar Women, the Cat and Fox, and the Jolly Coachman. Now we learn that they were instrumental agents who helped Pinocchio to become a boy and that now they are here to celebrate his success. . . . Hence, the world really is benign and not dangerous; those who had seemed menacing actually had the puppet's best interests at heart all along.

Collodi's Geppetto is a very human father caught in the natural tensions of child-rearing. He is angry and distressed when Pinocchio is disobedient and stubborn; he is loving and tender when the puppet is in need or behaves contritely. Frank's Geppetto has only one dimension: He is a gentle, loving man, capable of sorrow but not anger. No harsh word ever crosses his lips; on the contrary, he is perpetually expressing delight with Pinocchio. Therefore, the message conveyed is that parents desire their children and can only be happy with them. To further reinforce this theme, Geppetto's motive for wanting Pinocchio is made absolutely pure. Collodi's Geppetto had wanted a puppet only for use in the shows he would perform to support himself more comfortably in old age, and although he takes it reasonably well in stride, his being thrust into fatherhood comes as a shock. The dramatic adaptations of the 1930s retain Geppetto's economic concerns but then begin to add a secondary motive, his desire to have a son. Hubbard (1936) reverses these priorities: Geppetto primarily seeks a son, but he is also worried about economic security. The motive that Lillian Wade (1933) gave Geppetto in her radio script is identical to Collodi's. When she revised the script in 1938, however, she altered Geppetto's motive: economic concerns are no longer a factor; instead, Geppetto desires a puppet as a companion to travel with him and help him perform shows to "make boys and girls and grown-ups very, very happy." Curiously, in his own Depression-era play, Frank also discarded economic interests entirely: Geppetto is lonely, too old for marriage, and yearns for a son whom he can care for and bring up. Children, hence, are objects only of love and are desired for their own sakes.

Frank's play denies that fear has any legitimate place in childhood. Pinocchio, as a child, is lovable and vulnerable, precious and to be protected. The child never intentionally gives his parent or anyone else grounds for provocation. Except for errors due to innocence or inexperience, the child exists in natural harmony with his parent, who is pleased with the child and has only his best interests in mind. And when Pinocchio is transformed into a real boy, he has only become a good boy (which will surely increase the harmony between parent and child), who is still protected in a happy world orchestrated by parents. In contrast, Collodi's puppet becomes an adult, willing to take the initiative and to assume responsibility for others.

Roselle Ross

The first real book adaptation of the 1930s, a "retelling" that fundamentally altered the novel, was Roselle Ross's *Pinocchio: A Story for Children*, published in June 1939. It appears to have been created independently of Frank's play, and this reformulation was certainly not as extreme as Frank's. Rather, Ross elaborated, to the point of outright alteration, what were only tendencies and implications (due to selective omission and condensation) in prior abridged and condensed versions. In broad outline the book reflects most of Collodi's novel. The characters and episodes however, have been simplified to emphasize a single mood: happiness or merriment. Here, Pinocchio is harmlessly mischievous; his pranks are cute and make him endearing. Gone is any semblance of the puppet who causes anger or annoyance. When Collodi's Geppetto is carving Pinocchio, the puppet's eyes stare at him almost menacingly, and Geppetto is disturbed and angry. But in Ross's version, the puppet's eyes are said to "wink merrily," and Geppetto to be astonished. Whenever Pinocchio does act inappropriately, an explanation is interjected to excuse or mitigate his responsibility. His temper tantrum in the street, for example, occurred because Pinocchio "was terribly afraid of being punished" (by a Geppetto who displays no anger?). And when Pinocchio kills the Cricket, he is said to have "a very funny feeling in his stomach." This deed, which Collodi's puppet dismisses immediately, at least has the desired impact (although even this is weakened when Ross reinterprets the feeling as hunger only a sentence later). And we are reassured, "For you must know that he was really not bad at heart, and he had not meant to kill the Cricket."

Ross's Geppetto, like Frank's, is a flat character, consistently displaying only warmth and tenderness. In Collodi's novel, Geppetto gets arrested because the police are swayed by the crowd and by Pinocchio (having his temper tantrum). Released the following morning, Geppetto's anger is further intensified by his being locked out of his home and by hearing Pinocchio cry that he can't open the door (the puppet had fallen asleep while attempting to dry his drenched feet in the fireplace, after an exhausting series of adventures during Geppetto's absence). Climbing in through the window, Geppetto is furious until he sees the puppet sprawled helplessly on the floor, his feet burned off. Geppetto then becomes compassionate, comforting and feeding the puppet and, after extracting a promise from him, repairing his feet. All this is lost in Ross's account. First, Geppetto convinces the police "that he had done nothing wrong" and is released. Then he immediately "hurries home" (the same day) apparently getting in without any trouble.

> He found Pinocchio weak from hunger, and very lonely. In fact, the Marionette had had such a good lesson, he threw his arms about his Father's neck, begging to be forgiven, and promising that he would from then on be a help and a pleasure to Gepetto [sic], and that he would go to school and learn everything in the world there was to learn.

> Good-hearted Gepetto [sic] forgave him readily, for good or bad, fathers have a way of loving their sons, and they made all sorts of happy plans for the future.

So while Ross's novel does indeed follow Collodi's in outline, it is a thoroughly eviscerated replication, emphasizing a newly dominant, single dimension.

Walt Disney

The third version from the 1930s is, of course, Walt Disney's *Pinocchio*. . . . The film was not released until February 1940; nevertheless, at least seven different book-length adaptations of it were issued by various publishers between October and December, 1939, with even more to follow in 1940. However one might judge Disney's film, favorably or not, it certainly cannot be said to reflect Collodi's *Pinocchio*. Yasha Frank's play very likely influenced Disney, whose staff was instructed to attend several of the 1937 Los Angeles performances. While Frank's story line bears no resemblance to Disney's film plot, Frank's character revisions could well have offered Disney the key he needed to unlock and revamp the novel.

Unlike Collodi's egoistic, headstrong puppet, Disney's Pinocchio is the personification of childhood innocence and loving acceptance. He is the newborn infant filled with wonder, maintaining a sense of wide-eyed awe toward and joy about everything around him. He is the happy toddler who flusters Geppetto with a "why?" in response to each instruction and who eagerly accepts Jiminy Cricket's terms, then wonders what they are. This Pinocchio is sincere, and with the utmost sincerity, he wants to be liked. His honesty and simple love lead to trust; and it is this very trust, the belief that others are like himself, that brings him trouble, for which he cannot be blamed. Pinocchio is vulnerable because of his childlike, trusting innocence.

Disney's film was influenced by the experience of the Depression and the clouds of war amassing at the time. His image of the outside world, beyond the family, is a sinister and lethal one. Pinocchio's "friends," Honest John and Gideon (the Fox and Cat) kidnap him and sell him to Stromboli (Fire-Eater). Disney's film was criticized for frightening children, and not only because of Monstro the Whale. Stromboli is an enormous, physically terrifying figure whose behavior is even more terrifying. Pinocchio thinks he has become an actor employed by Stromboli, but when he tries to go home, Stromboli seizes him and locks him in a cage, claiming that he now owns him and will tour with the puppet around the world until he can no longer work, then use him for firewood. He taunts the helpless, caged puppet. The Blue Fairy gets Pinocchio out of this mess, but not for long: Honest John traps him and sells him to the Coachman almost immediately. The Coachman is even more terrifying, as is his occupation: he actively rounds up bad little children to be transformed into donkeys at Pleasure Island, and then he sells them as beasts of burden. Both Stromboli and the Coachman are engaged in kidnapping and slavery, separating children from their parents forever. And, except for Lampwick, these four characters are the *only* representatives of the world beyond the family. Moreover, none of them suffers any retribution for their deeds. Presumably, they carry on as before, since such activities are viewed as part of the natural order. No child dares to venture out alone in this world: it is a criminal one that lays in wait to harm him.

Collodi's world is not nearly so sinister, for it allows a sharp-witted puppet some room to maneuver and permits other characters to assist him along the way. But Disney's puppet, powerless to affect events, is totally at their mercy. Nor does Disney's world include any effective helpers: the supernatural Blue Fairy intervenes only once (rescuing the puppet from Stromboli), and Jiminy Cricket, except for being able to offer advice and encouragement, is impotent. The world outside the family is evil: children had best not enter it. Children, perhaps, should best not grow up.

Pinocchio does not depart entirely from Disney's usual fare of happy, wholesome films. Its various terrifying cinematic images are, after all, balanced by merry ones, in addition to the film's appropriately upbeat conclusion. The truly dark nature of the film is revealed by analyzing its characters and their roles, an analysis unlikely to be made by young children riveted by the film's imagery and fast-paced action. *Pinocchio,* however, is grim indeed. Richard Schickel, who agrees with this view, suggests that the film is largely autobiographical, projecting Disney's own isolation, his fear and distrust of an outside world that impinges on and threatens his own inner world.

Like the characterizations by Frank and Ross, Disney's Geppetto is portrayed in a single dimension: loving tenderness. He wishes on a star for Pinocchio to become a real boy. The Blue Fairy obliges by bringing the puppet to life and telling Pinocchio that, in order to become a real boy, he must prove himself brave, truthful, and unselfish, that he must learn to distinguish between right and wrong. In Disney's film, Pinocchio must pass only one test, by saving his father from Monstro, and he apparently dies when the endeavor has been completed (in the end, the limp body revives and is now human). But aside from initiating and engineering the escape and showing bravery, what else has the puppet done? Nothing! His decision to save his father, while requiring courage, was natural to the character he began life with. There is no transformation, but only a continuation at a more heroic level. And the film ends with an image of a thoroughly happy family: Pinocchio, now a real boy, is reunited with his family (Geppetto, Figaro, and Cleo), yet still as a child.

SOCIAL FORCES AND *PINOCCHIO*'S CHANGED IMAGE

The new image of Pinocchio created in the late 1930s gradually took hold and still defines *Pinocchio* in popular culture today: the public accepted it, and, if anything, began to reject Collodi's original story. While ten to eleven full translations were released annually over the 1930s, production fell to five or six in the 1940s and then to three or four per year in the 1950s. After production rose slightly to four or five new editions in the 1960s, it fell again to average only about two and a half new releases a year during both the 1970s and 1980s. Not counting the Disney versions, the number of book adaptations and dramatizations reflecting the new image and theme rose gradually, not capturing a significant portion of the market until the 1960s and not beginning to dominate the market until the 1970s and 1980s. Over the 1980s more than three times as many adaptations, excluding Disney versions, as translations were released.

Why did this change in *Pinocchio* occur, and why does it still hold sway? Neither the social sciences and history, by their natures, can identify causes with certainty: life is too complex; neither the past nor society can be objectively known, but each is always subjectively reconstructed from some particular perspective. Causes, however, can be determined with increasing degrees of probability, and part of this process mandates the rejection of untenable explanations. The change in *Pinocchio* cannot be attributed solely to the impact of "great writers" who created superior versions, for without some grounds on which to be receptive to those versions, society would probably have rejected them. Nor does the impact of the new media (nationally available radio, television, films, and audio and video cassettes) provide a sufficient explanation, for the same reason. Furthermore, one cannot argue that the new versions were specifically designed for very young

children, while Collodi's original story was not. Collodi's tale was meant to be at least read to young children, and in her introduction to Caprani's 1909 translation, Mary E. Burt explicitly recommended this (specifying the nursery context and recommending that children from the age of four use it to learn to read). Neither will it do to claim that these new versions appealed to middle-class values and that the United States had become largely middle-class: first, sociologists have now revised downward the degree to which the United States was middle-class even by the 1950s and 1960s; second, these versions of *Pinocchio* appeared toward the end of a decade-long Depression, during which the middle class had been greatly reduced, not expanded. Nor can one argue that increased schooling, coupled with the demand that children be kept in the classroom through high school and even college, encouraged such a redefinition—this was a later development which could have played a role only from the 1950s on; it was a factor in few people's minds between 1937 and 1939.

The change must have occurred and taken hold because it had some appeal for most people, and an appeal necessarily superior to that of the original. Had audiences rejected *Pinocchio*'s new image, it would not have sold but, rather, died out, as was the fate by the mid-1920s of the "industrial moralism" versions. The new versions took hold because they calmed apprehensions arising, at least initially, from the experience of the Depression. The Great Depression had traumatized people, proving how vulnerable they were to forces beyond their own control. It struck at the very foundation of family and community life: that is, at the ability of a wage earner to support his dependents. With one third of the nation unemployed, alcoholism or sheer economic ruin forced some families to split up, while others had to double up with relatives, sharing resources and crowding into already cramped living spaces. Family solidarity and cooperation became a bulwark, the ultimate defense against overwhelming economic forces—*and especially so when it was perceived to be a mere fiction*, powerless to resolve either overt conflict or strained relations among family members. Times were hard, with no end in sight.

Yet the Depression had another side. It was also a time of heightened political consciousness and social activism, as well as increased government control intended to maintain order. People organized in order to pressure local authority when it was slow to respond to their needs, and people organized against local authority when it opposed whatever action they believed to be right. This was a period of intense labor "unrest," when the unemployed were reported to have joined strikers' picket lines; a time of violence and pitched battles, when police and the National Guard, armed with clubs, "tommy" guns, and other weapons, drove out strikers in order to control unions by bringing in nonunionized labor. It was a time of heightened class consciousness. Employers, landlords, and financiers, with the law on their side, were increasingly perceived as maintaining and even adding to their wealth by squeezing workers for more, while much of the community struggled just to survive. Socialism and communism became part of public discourse, although with some circumspection. Given the pressure of the situation and an awareness of events in Europe, all factions sensed the possibility of political revolution, perhaps under the banner of fascism (Sinclair Lewis's "It Can't Happen Here" was an unusually popular Federal Theatre Project production), or of communism, or of socialism. And while the only coup known to have been attempted (in 1934) came from the Right, the government (at all levels) and the media focused only on the threat from the Left. The Depression era was not just a dismal and desperate period, but also a vibrant, dynamic one, and especially so with the sense of an impending European war in the late 1930s.

The new *Pinocchio,* then, was a means for dealing with fear and feelings of powerlessness along with the inevitable denial of such fear. Parents viewed their families as the last bastion of human security. Family harmony was therefore crucial and to be strengthened, not threatened, by the child. These new versions of *Pinocchio* project denial, especially by suppressing meaningful conflict. Hence Pinocchio must not be a burden, as indeed many children must have been during the Depression. Life within the family must be happy; it is where the child belongs and, ultimately, where he must return—as a child.

The new *Pinocchio* also espoused a political message, indeed a particularly appropriate one for calming the unrest provoked by the Depression. By analogy, *Pinocchio* portrays the government (the father) as benevolent and urges the citizen (the child) to have faith in its decisions and policies, for although it might fumble ineptly on occasion, it can be trusted to have its citizens' best interests at heart. Just as the child should be in harmony with the family, so should the citizen be in harmony with the state—for that is the natural order. Pinocchio, therefore, should obey Geppetto and thereby uphold the natural harmony.

It seems pertinent that the new *Pinocchio* became popular only in the 1960s, then becoming, in the 1970s and 1980s, the dominant version. It was during the 1960s that society became especially disrupted, when different groups coalesced to challenge various government policies, a challenge that endured at least through the mid-1970s. The 1980s brought a wave of conservatism, and the new *Pinocchio,* embodying family solidarity and obedience to authority, expressed and reinforced this conservatism. Yet the 1980s have also been marked by activism, centered on such issues as racism, unemployment, gay rights, and women's rights,

including abortion. One view of democracy holds that people participate directly in decisions—including government policy-making—that affect their own fates. But another view holds that most people are not wise enough to participate in such decisions and that, in a democracy, they delegate authority to those who are wiser. According to this latter view, democracy works best when most of the public is apathetic; this was the view expressed by Samuel Huntington when he explained the troublesome 1960s as having been caused by excessive grass-roots democracy and urged that people be taught once again to obey proper authority.

Collodi's original version, quite popular throughout the 1930s, conveys a political message quite different from that of the new renderings. To begin with, any explicit references to the state (e.g., the police, judge, prince, or jailkeeper) are negative, satirical, and cautionary. Pinocchio does, in fact, challenge authority; his adventures seem especially constructed to show that state officials are stupid at best, unjust at worst. The analogous unit, the family, Collodi portrays as conflict-ridden: Pinocchio presses his demands whether rightly or wrongly, through actions that must be responded to. He relates very actively indeed to both his parent and the outside world. Most importantly, Pinocchio is *not* expected simply to obey (in fact, the novel was originally castigated for encouraging disobedience). Rather, he is expected to assume responsibility, including carefully evaluating whatever he has been told to do. His attaining adulthood is conditional on precisely this assumption of responsibility for himself and others, as is his ability to distinguish commands that are just or in his best interests from those that are not. His adulthood is predicated on active involvement. In fact, Collodi's messages seem thoroughly consonant with participatory democracy and the notion that people should have some control over their own lives or destinies. Collodi's *Pinocchio,* therefore, is an empowering novel.

On the other hand, the new renditions accepted as *Pinocchio* today, broadcast the opposite message: children/citizens are told to have faith in their leaders, who are wiser and know what is best. Such messages are calming and foster an acquiescent citizenry; embodying the model of democracy touted by Huntington and others, they discourage political participation as inappropriate or even dangerous, especially when such participation challenges established authority.

In less than one century, the general public has lost or turned its back on a spirited novel that describes the natural difficulties of growing up, for both children and parents, a novel that describes growing up as a process of transcending egocentricity to acknowledge and respond toe the concerns of others through actively engaging in life on behalf of both oneself and others. Collodi's empowering novel has been replaced by tales that extend childhood to include the adult citizen, whose "proper role" is identical to that of the child. Social forces, as I have argued, were instrumental in effecting this transformation. Collodi's work has lost much by this change—and so have today's children and parents.

FURTHER READING

Criticism

Cambon, Glauco. "*Pinocchio* and the Problem of Children's Literature." *Children's Literature* II (1973): 50-60.

    Considers the ways in which *Pinocchio* shaped Italian culture.

Cech, John. "The Triumphant Transformations of 'Pinocchio'." In *Triumphs of the Spirit in Children's Literature*, edited by Francelia Butler and Richard Rotert, pp. 171-77. Hamden, Conn.: Library Professional Publications, 1986.

    Briefly outlines the editorial changes made in Collodi's original text, and the changing critical opinions of the character of Pinocchio.

Gannon, Susan. "A Note on Collodi and Lucian." *Children's Literature* VIII (1980): 98-102.

    Claims that Collodi drew heavily on his acquaintance with Lucian in writing *Pinocchio*.

———. "Pinocchio: The First Hundred Years." *Children's Literature Association Quarterly* VI, No. 4 (Winter 1981/1982): 1, 5-7.

    Insists that although *Pinocchio* is flawed, its main character "is surely one of the most satisfying *human* characters in all of children's literature."

Hazard, Paul. "National Traits: The Italy of Yesterday." In *Books, Children & Men*, pp. 111-44. Boston: Horn Book, 1960.

    Discusses how *Pinocchio* reflected and shaped the Italian society from which it emerged.

Heins, Paul. "A Second Look: The Adventures of Pinocchio." *The Horn Book Magazine* LVIII, No. 2 (April 1982): 200-204.

    Asserts that the key to the longevity and popularity of *Pinocchio* lies not in the moralistic turn the novel takes in its conclusion, but in the acts of "the zany, myriad-mooded puppet who constantly deceives himself but never the world, engaging our sympathy and interest, ever vibrantly alive."

Heisig, James W. "Pinocchio: Archetype of the Motherless Child." In *Children's Literature: The Great Excluded*, volume 3, edited by Francelia Butler and Bennett A. Brockman, pp. 23-35. Storrs, Conn.: MLA, 1974.

    Explores the different literary genres that intersect in *Pinocchio*'s unique blend of fantasy and reality.

Morrissey, Thomas J. "Alive and Well But Not Unscathed: A Reply to Susan R. Gannon's 'Pinocchio at 100.'" *Children's Literature Association Quarterly* VII, No. 2 (Summer 1982): 37-39.

    Confronts what Morrissey considers to be typical fallacies in literary criticism of *Pinocchio*.

Morrissey, Thomas J., and Richard Wunderlich. "Death and Rebirth in *Pinocchio*." *Children's Literature* XI (1983): 64-75.

    Contends that Pinocchio "experiences symbolic death and rebirth through both infernal descent and metamorphosis," two common epic motifs.

Perella, Nicolas J. "An Essay on *Pinocchio*." *Italica* 63, No. 1 (Spring 1986): 1-47.

    Discusses the classical motifs in *Pinocchio* and explores the text's appeal to an adult audience.

Rosenthal, M. L. "Alice, Huck, Pinocchio, and the Blue Fairy: Bodies Real and Imagined." *The Southern Review* XXIX, No. 3 (Summer 1993): 486-90.

    Examines how their fictional characters reflected the lives of Lewis Carroll, Mark Twain, and Collodi.

Street, Douglas. "*Pinocchio*—From Picaro to Pipsqueak." In *Children's Novels and the Movies*, edited by Douglas Street, pp. 47-57. New York: Frederick Ungar Publishing, 1983.

    Chronicles the transformation of *Pinocchio* in the book's screen adaptations.

Wunderlich, Richard, and Thomas J. Morrissey. "The Desecration of *Pinocchio* in the United States." *The Horn Book Magazine* LVIII, No. 2 (April 1982): 205-12.

    Claims that *Pinocchio* has been "debased and trivialized" in the United States in an attempt to reflect changing conceptions of childhood.

———. "Carlo Collodi's *The Adventures of Pinocchio*: A Classic Book of Choices." In *Touchstones: Reflections on the Best in Children's Literature*, volume 1, pp. 53-64. West Lafayette, Ind.: Children's Literature Association, 1985.

    Contends that *Pinocchio* is a "classic" of the genre, answering several criticisms levelled at the novel.

Additional coverage of Collodi's life and career is contained in the following source published by Gale Research: *Children's Literature Review*, Vol. 5.

Auguste Comte

1798-1857

(Full name Isidore Auguste Marie François Xavier Comte) French philosopher.

INTRODUCTION

Auguste Comte was best known for founding positivism, a philosophical system that acknowledges only observable, natural phenomena and that attempts to use scientific law as the basis for comprehending relationships between observable facts. Comte also is recognized as one of the originators of the science of sociology, believing that human societies are natural systems whose order and progress can be studied through scientific methodology. A deliberate and rationalistic thinker, Comte hoped to use his science of sociology to achieve spiritual and social reform and, ultimately, a new social system. He had several proponents in England and on the continent, including, most notably, John Stuart Mill (1806-1873).

Biographical Information

Born in Montpellier in January, 1798, Comte was raised in a fervently royalistic and Catholic household. His relationship with his family was strained, however, and he eventually broke ties with them, rejecting Catholicism and adopting republicanism over monarchism. In 1814 he entered the École Polytechnique in Paris, where he excelled in science and mathematics before being expelled in 1816 for leading a student revolt against the newly established royalist regime. The following year he became secretary to Henri de Saint-Simon (1760-1825), a social scientist who taught Comte the possibility of studying society and religion with scientific objectivity. Biographers have speculated that Comte may have written much of what was published under Saint-Simon's name, and in 1824 the two severed their relationship over disputed authorship. Comte then began tutoring in mathematics, as well as giving public lectures on his positive philosophy to many of the leading thinkers of his time. He was soon forced to stop due to a mental breakdown, which led to an attempt to drown himself in the Seine; he was hospitalized for mental illness periodically over the next fifteen years. In 1829 he resumed his lectures on positivism, which were later published in his six-volume *Cours de philosophie positive* (1830-42; *The Positive Philosophy of Auguste Comte,* 1853). He also took up minor teaching posts in astronomy, mathematics, and history, including a position as examiner at the École Polytechnique, but lost these due to personal misfortunes

and business and political difficulties. He continued his research with financial backing from Mill and Émile Littré (1801-1881), a French scholar, though the support dwindled as Comte increasingly appeared to take their assistance for granted. In the mid-1840s he befriended Clotilde de Vaux, for whom he developed a deep passion and who he claimed taught him to subordinate the intellect to the heart. After de Vaux's death in 1846, his writings began to emphasize the importance of a "Religion of Humanity," of which Comte was to be the high priest. In 1849 he established the Universal Church of the Religion of Humanity. He continued to write books on the subject until his death in 1857.

Major Works

As early as 1824, when he was in his mid-twenties, Comte advanced his Law of Three States, a theory conceiving of humankind's intellectual development—and thus the development of all human societies—as progressing through three periods: theological, metaphysical, and scientific (or the "positive" state). This Law of Three States remained the foundation for all his subsequent work. He further outlined his epistemology in his magnum opus, *Cours de philosophie positive,* published from 1830 to 1842, in which he laid the foundation of a new science, first called "social physics," then "sociology." Comte criticized traditional metaphysical investigations that employ baseless speculations and assumptions, and instead argued for a scientific method of organizing experience. His sociology, consisting of the dynamics of society, is based on the sciences that precede it—mathematics, astronomy, physics and chemistry, and biology. Comte believed that intellectual development was the primary cause of social change, which mirrored scientific development. He also believed that the metaphysical stage in which he lived was marked primarily by anarchy; this metaphysical stage precedes the positive era, in which scientists would engender a more spiritual, ordered society. Comte's later writings, including *Catéchisme positiviste* (1852; *The Catechism of Positive Religion,* 1858), and the four-volume *Système de politique positive* (1851-54; *The System of Positive Polity,* 1875-77), develop a positivist "Religion of Humanity" that further develops the humanism and positivism of his earlier writings.

Critical Reception

Comte's *Cours de philosophie positive* attracted many followers during his lifetime, including Mill, Littré, and

Hyppolyte Adolphe Taine (1828-1893), but he lost many of these later in his career: some could not accept his new religion of humanity, finding his views extremist; others he managed to alienate. He thus died in virtual isolation. Comte's theories and writings, though, have continued to generate criticism. Questioning his assumptions about his new social science, philosophers have pointed out that, although he possessed no observable evidence, he was convinced that the positivist stage is the last in human development. Echoing one of Mill's criticisms, other scholars have pointed out that Comte neglected to consider psychology in the formulation of his theories, leading to many unanswered questions regarding morality and ethics. Historians have also found errors of fact as well as unsupported assertions in his works. In addition, his writing style has come under attack, with several scholars finding him a poor writer who elaborated excessively and obsessed over detail. Regardless of the conceptual or stylistic censures of his work, Comte's positive philosophy and his ideas on ordering society are nevertheless recognized as greatly contributing to and influencing the course of philosophy and sociology.

PRINCIPAL WORKS

Cours de philosophie positive. 6 vols. (philosophy) 1830-42; published as *The Positive Philosophy of Auguste Comte.* 2 vols. [translated and condensed by Harriet Martineau] 1853

Calendrier positiviste (philosophy) 1849; published as *The New Calendar of Great Men* [translated by Frederic Harrison] 1892

Système de politique positive. 4 vols. (philosophy) 1851-54; published as *The System of Positive Polity.* 4 vols. [translated by J. H. Bridges, Frederic Harrison, and others] 1875-77

Catéchisme positiviste (philosophy) 1852; published as *The Catechism of Positive Religion* [translated by Richard Congreve] 1858

Testament (autobiography) 1884

Correspondence. 4 vols. (letters) 1903-4

CRITICISM

David Brewster (review date 1838)

SOURCE: Review of *Cours de philosophie positive*, in *The Edinburgh Review*, Vol. LXVII, No. CXXXVI, July, 1838, pp. 271-308.

[*In the following review, Brewster outlines a "sketch of the objects and methods of positive knowledge," focusing especially on Comte's theism and cosmology.*]

The competitors for the honours of science may be divided into several classes, actuated by very different motives, and pursuing very different objects;—those who investigate by observation and experiment the phenomena and the laws of nature; those who arrange the facts and expound the doctrines of science; those who record at different epochs the history of its progress; and those who attempt to explain the mental progresses by which discoveries have been made, and prescribe for every branch of knowledge the most appropriate methods of research.

Though the love of posthumous fame supplies these different classes with their earliest and their strongest impulse, yet this principle of action is often modified and replaced by less noble incitements, and those who have begun their career under its generous influence, have been seduced by advantages of more immediate adjudication and enjoyment.

The first of these classes of the cultivators of science, comprehends all those to whom the name of philosopher is strictly applicable. But as no sound knowledge can exist, but that which either rests immediately on facts, or is deduced from them by mathematical reasoning, this class is necessarily subdivided into two— those who observe facts, and those who reason from them—those who make experiments, and those who deduce from their results the law of phenomena, and the more general principles to which these laws may be ultimately referred.

The history of science furnishes us with many distinguished instances in which these two qualities of mind have been in a singular manner united; but the instances are doubtless more numerous where the observer and the experimentalist have confined themselves to their own sphere of labour, and where minds of a less practical and a more discursive capacity have found a more congenial exercise in the higher processes of combination and analysis. Although the last of these orders of enquirers have been generally supposed to belong to a higher rank of intelligence, yet this erroneous appreciation of mental value can be founded on no other principle than that the laws of phenomena are necessarily higher steps in the scale of knowledge than facts and observations.

The two conditions of mind by which these two classes of philosophers are characterised, are in reality incommensurable. Facts may sometimes be discovered, and observations made which demand but little attention, and involve no extraordinary exertion of the mind; but the great facts and experimental results, which form the basis of modern science, have been generally obtained from processes of reasoning at once ingenious and profound, and have called forth the highest functions of our intellectual frame. Even when the fruits of experimental philosophy are merely simple facts, their value is inestimable, and no revolution in science will ever deprive their discoverer of the honours which belong to them. But when he who discovers new facts, detects also their relation to other phenomena, and when he is so fortunate as to determine the laws which they follow, and to predict from these laws phenomena or results previously unknown, he entitles himself to a high place among the aristocracy of knowledge.

Such men are in truth the real functionaries of science. They are the hewers of its wood and the drawers of its water—the productive labourers who furnish to less industrious and more speculative minds, not only the raw material, but the embroidered fabric of intellectual luxury and splendour.

Previous to the sixteenth century the active explorers of science were few in number, and even these few had scarcely thrown off the incubus of the scholastic philosophy. Speculation unrestrained and licentious threw its blighting sirocco over the green pastures of knowledge, and prejudice and mysticism involved them in their noxious exhalations. This condition of knowledge had been long ago subverted, and in the present day the ascendancy of observation and experiment has been universally recognised. There is still, however, a body of men, insignificant in number and, with some exceptions, in talent, who, impatient of the labour of continuous research, or perhaps unfitted for its exercise, have sought to storm the temple of science, and possess themselves of its treasures. The members of this brotherhood are, generally speaking, imperfectly acquainted with the facts and laws by which modern physical science is upheld. They feel the force neither of mathematical nor of physical reasoning; and regarding the noblest doctrines of science as founded only in speculation, they are ambitious of the honour of placing them on a surer and more extended basis. Those who are thus blind to the force of physical truth, are not likely to discover the errors which their own minds create and cherish. Embarrassed by no difficulties, the stream of their speculations flows on without eddies or currents. Such a class of speculators have no position in the lists of science, and they deserve none; but in thus denouncing their labours, we must carefully distinguish them from a higher order of theorists, whose scientific acquirements are undoubted; but who, in place of employing their talents in the substantial labours of research, are ambitious of becoming the legislators of science, the adjudicators of its honours, and the arbiters of its destiny. Self-constituted and irresponsible, this legislative tribunal owed to science all the tenderness which was compatible with justice, and all the diligence and solicitude of research which perplexing

details and conflicting interests demand. To the dead it owed the gratitude which belonged to great achievements, and that respectful homage which is the birthright of exalted genius; and to the living that delicacy of criticism, and that courteous acknowledgment of their services, which to sensitive minds is the highest reward for their past, and the most powerful stimulus to their future labours.

In the history of science, and in the distribution of its honours, we must not expect to find that minute accuracy, or that nice appreciation of evidence to which we are accustomed in legal adjudications. All that is due from the historian is depth of research and honesty of purpose, and we must pronounce that judge to be righteous who holds evenly the scales of justice. The historian cannot record facts which are not within the sphere of ordinary research, and the judge is not responsible for the mathematical equipoise of his balance.

In applying these principles to those efforts of scientific legislation which are alone deserving of the name, we are confined within a very narrow range. The subject was almost exhausted by the great reformer of philosophy; and though it has been casually discussed by authors who flourished in subsequent periods, yet the only works of any distinction which are devoted to the subject are *The History of the Inductive Sciences* by Mr. Whewell, which we have examined in a previous Number, and the **Cours de Philosophie Positive** by M. Comte, which stands at the head of this article. The three volumes of Mr. Whewell's are indeed only introductory to his code of reformed philosophy; but he has indulged his readers with a foretaste of its enactments; and from the labours and decisions of the historian, we have no difficulty in anticipating the character of the lawgiver, and the temper of the judge.

The first volume of M. Comte's work was published in 1830, about seven years, and the second volume in 1835, about two years before that of Mr. Whewell; and yet no reference whatever is made by the latter to the previous labours of the French philosopher. We presume, therefore, notwithstanding several similarities of sentiment and expression, that the **Cours de Philosophie Positive** had not found its way to Cambridge, although it was well known and highly appreciated in London, before the publication of Mr. Whewell's work.

In alluding to these points of resemblance, which are, of course, merely accidental, we do not mean to convey the idea that there is any similarity between the two works in their leading and essential features. With the single exception of some just views on the value and use of hypotheses which Mr. Whewell seems to have borrowed without acknowledgment from an English work, the *History of the Inductive Sciences*, and the **Course of Positive Philosophy**, stand strongly opposed to each other; not only in the tone and temper in which they are written, and in the motives by which their authors seem to have been guided, but, to as great an extent, in the results at which they have arrived, and in the decisions which they have pronounced on the great points of scientific controversy. Such a contrariety of sentiment, while it casts a just opprobrium over the pretensions of our scientific lawgivers, has a tendency to bring science itself into disrepute; for when the Solons and the Lycurguses of philosophy are as contradictory in their enactments as the Mackenzies and Murphys of meteorology are in their predictions, men of ordinary capacity are apt to place the physical sciences on the same level with that *weather wisdom* which has been recently agitating the metropolis.

Before we proceed to a comparison of these works, and to a discussion of the subjects which they have brought into the arena of controversy, we must make our readers acquainted with the nature and object of M. Comte's researches. There is, however, a preliminary topic which forces itself upon out attention, and which, were it possible, we would pass by unnoticed. But as some of our readers might be led by this Article to study the original work, we must warn them beforehand that M. Comte avows himself an Atheist; and we think that we cannot more effectually remove this stumbling-block which he has placed in our way, and deprive it of all its danger, than by presenting his observations at once to our readers.

> To our minds unacquainted with the study of the heavenly bodies, though often otherwise well informed in other branches of natural philosophy, astronomy has still the reputation of being a science eminently religious, as if the famous verse,—*Coeli enarrant gloriam Dei* (The heavens declare the glory of God), had preserved all its force. It is, however, certain, as I have proved, that all real science stands in radical and necessary opposition to all theology; and this character is more strongly indicated in astronomy than in any other; precisely, because astronomy is, so to speak, more a science than any other, according to the comparisons already made. No science has given such terrible blows to the doctrine of final causes, generally regarded by the moderns as the indispensable basis of all religious systems, though it is in reality but the consequence of them. The knowledge of the motion of the earth ought alone to destroy the first real foundation of this doctrine—the idea of a universe subordinate to the earth, and consequently to man, as I shall more particularly show in treating of this motion. But, independent of this, the exact exploration of our solar system cannot fail to put an end essentially to that blind and boundless admiration which the general order of nature inspires, by showing in the distinctest manner, and under a great number of different aspects, that the elements of this system were certainly not arranged in the most advantageous manner, and that science allows us to conceive easily a better arrangement. In short, under another point

of view, still more important, by the development of the true celestial mechanics since the time of Newton, all theological philosophy, even the most perfect, has been henceforth deprived of its principal intellectual office; the most regular order being now conceived as necessarily established and kept up in our world, and even throughout the whole universe, by the simple mutual attraction of its different parts.

Our author then proceeds to support these feeble and innocuous arguments by a reference to the stability of the solar system; though he seems fully sensible that this doctrine of modern astronomy may be used as a powerful weapon in the hands of his opponents. 'The grand doctrine,' says he,

> when presented under a suitable aspect, may doubtless be easily made the basis of a series of eloquent declamations, having an imposing appearance of solidity. Yet, nevertheless, an arrangement so essential to the continuous existence of animal species, is a simple necessary consequence (from the mechanical laws of the world), of certain characteristic circumstances of our solar system;— the extreme smallness of the planetary masses in comparison of the central mass, the slight eccentricity of their orbits, and the moderate mutual inclination of their planes;—characters which in their turn may, with much probability, as I shall afterwards show, according to the indication of Laplace, be derived, quite naturally, from the mode of formation of the system. But besides we ought, *à priori*, to expect in general such a result from this single reflection, that *since we exist*, it follows of necessity that the system, of which we form a part, be arranged in such a manner as to permit this existence, which would be incompatible with the total absence of stability in the principal elements of our system. In order properly to appreciate this consideration, we ought to observe that this stability is by no means absolute, for it does not take place with regard to comets, whose perturbations are much greater, and may even increase almost indefinitely, from the want of those conditions of restriction which I have mentioned, and which hardly allows us to suppose them to be inhabited. The pretended final cause will therefore be reduced in the present case, as we have already seen on all analogous occasions, to this puerile remark—that there are no stars inhabited in our solar system but those which are habitable. . . . Such . . . are the immense and fundamental services which the development of astronomical theories has rendered to the emancipation of human reason.

Although we intended, in quoting these passages, to have left the refutation of them to the common sense of our readers, yet it may be proper to make a few observations on the *new* argument which our author has founded on the Cosmogony of Laplace. Admitting, as M. Comte does, that the stability of the solar system is essential to the continued existence of Animal Species, and aware of the powerful support which such an admission lends to the theological argument for design, he endeavors to show that this arrangement is the simple necessary consequence, through the operation of mechanical laws, of certain properties of the planetary orbits, and certain relations between the solar and planetary masses. Here he is again aware that such an adjustment of forms and magnitudes, is itself an extraordinary proof of design; and he strives to show that this effect may, *with much probability*, be deduced from the *mode of formation of the system*, as suggested by Laplace—one of the boldest speculations of modern fancy, but one which does not, when properly viewed, afford the smallest aid to those who are desirous of finding any substitute for the agency of an all-directing mind.

But though we consider the Cosmogony of Laplace as merely an ingenious speculation, we shall permit M. Comte to make it the basis of his argument; and we shall suppose, with its distinguished inventor, that the sun's atmosphere, expanded by heat, reached the limits of our system—that it gradually contracted in cooling, and that during the revolution of this immense system of vapour round the sun's axis, the Georgium Sidus, Saturn, Jupiter, and the other primary planets were gradually thrown off from it into their present orbits, and with the velocity of the atmosphere, of which they formed a part; that they contracted into solid globes by cooling, having previously in their turn thrown off their Satellites; and that the *characteristic* circumstances in the system thus formed, which produce stability, are the *necessary* consequences of this mode of formation. After all these admissions, the argument for design remains unshaken, and the mind still turns itself to the great first cause. Who created and planted a sun in the centre of what was to become a system of future worlds? Who supplied the due portion of heat to expand his atmosphere through that region of space in which it was to deposit the future abodes of life and intelligence? Who added the rotatory impulse, and adjusted it to that precise velocity which would throw off planets revolving in harmonious stability, in place of comets wheeling in eccentric and unstable orbits? By what power was that heat withdrawn, so as to permit the zones of the solar atmosphere to contract successively into solid planets? Who separated the 'light from the darkness' which brooded over the revolving chaos? Who gathered into the ocean's bed its liquid elements? Who decked the earth with its rich and verdant embroidery? Who conjured up the forms of animal life? And, above all, who placed over this fair empire—MAN—godlike and intellectual—breathing the divine spirit, and panting with immortal aspirations?

The Cosmogony of Laplace, even if admitted as a physical truth, would only carry us back to an earlier epoch in the history of creation, and exhibit to us the wonders of Divine power, condensed into a narrower compass, and commanding a more intense admiration.

But even if science could go infinitely farther, and trace all the forms of being to their germ in a single atom, and all the varieties of nature to its development, the human mind would still turn to its resting-point, and worship with deeper admiration before this miracle of consolidated power.

Had the opinions which we have been combating been maintained by those rash speculators who are permitted, at distant intervals, to disturb the tranquillity of the religious world, we should not have allowed them to interfere with ours. But when a work of profound science, marked with great acuteness of reasoning, and conspicuous for the highest attributes of intellectual power—when such a work records the dread sentiment that the universe displays no proofs of an all directing mind, and records it, too, as the deduction of unbiased reason, the appalling note falls upon the ear like the sounds of desolation and of death. The life-blood of the affections stands frozen in its strongest and most genial current; and reason and feeling but resume their ascendancy when they have pictured the consequences of so frightful a delusion. If man is thus an orphan at his birth, and an outcast in his destiny—if knowledge is to be his punishment and not his prize—if all his intellectual achievements are to perish with him in the dust—if the brief tenure of his being is to be renounced amid the wreck of vain desires—of blighted hopes and of bleeding affections—then, in reality as well as in metaphor, is life a dream!

Unwilling as we are to dwell upon such a subject, our readers should be informed that M. Comte is a Teacher in the Polytechnic School, and our country congratulated on possessing Institutions which prevent opinions like his from poisoning the springs of moral and religious instruction.

We are informed by M. Comte that from the time of his quitting the Polytechnic School in 1816, he was constantly occupied, during ten years, in the preparation of his '**Lectures on Positive Philosophy.**' In the spring of 1826 his course was opened to the public; but a severe malady prevented him from continuing it; and this misfortune was greatly aggravated by the circumstance, that he numbered among his auditors Baron Humboldt, M. Blainville, M. Poinsot, and other celebrated and distinguished members of the Academy of Sciences. In the winter and spring of 1829, M. Comte resumed his course before a brilliant audience; among whom were Baron Fourier, perpetual Secretary of the Academy of Sciences, M. M. Blainville, Poinsot, and Navier, members of the Academy, and Professors Broussais, Esquirol, and Binet.

The '**Course of Positive Philosophy,**' of which the two published volumes placed at the head of this Article form the principal part, comprehends *Mathematics, Astronomy, Physics,* and *Chemistry,* or the sciences of *Inorganic* Bodies; and *Physiology*, and *Social Physics*, or the sciences of *Organic* Bodies. Mathematics are subdivided into the *Calculus, Geometry*, and *Rational Mechanics*. The six lectures on the Calculus contain a general view of mathematical analysis, the Calculus of direct and indirect functions, the Calculus of variations, and that of finite differences. The five lectures on Geometry contain a general view of geometry, the geometry of the ancients, the fundamental conception of analytical geometry, and the general study of lines, and of surfaces. The four lectures on Rational Mechanics, embrace the fundamental principles of mechanics, a general view of statics and dynamics, and the general theorems of mechanics.

After some general considerations on Astronomy, he divides his subject into *Geometrical* and *Mechanical* Astronomy. Under the first division he gives a general exposition of the methods of observation; and he treats of the elementary geometrical phenomena of the heavenly bodies, of the theory of the earth's motion, and of the laws of Kepler. Under the second division, he treats of the law of universal gravitation; and after a philosophical appreciation of this law he applies it to the explanation of celestial phenomena.

The great department of Physics is divided into *Barology, Thermology, Acoustics, Optics*, and *Electrology*. Chemistry is divided into *Inorganic* and *Organic* Chemistry. Physiology embraces the structure and composition of living bodies, the classification of living bodies, vegetable physiology, animal physiology, and intellectual and *affective* physiology; and under Social Physics, our author treats of the general structure of human societies, of the fundamental natural law of the development of the human species, and of the progress of civilization. This last section is subdivided into three heads,—the theological epoch, the metaphysical epoch, and the positive epoch, the first of these epochs embracing *Fetichism, Polytheism*, and *Monotheism*.

The two volumes now before us contain only Mathematics, Astronomy, and Physics, and other two will doubtless be necessary to complete the work.

In explaining the exact meaning of the term *Positive* Philosophy, M. Comte remarks that it bears a strong analogy to the term *Natural Philosophy*, as used by English writers since the time of Newton; but as the latter includes only the sciences of observation, and excludes the subject of social physics as well as Physiology, and all the branches of natural history, he was compelled to adopt the more general though vague expression of *Positive Philosophy*. He conceives, however, that the term *positive* removes, to a certain degree, the objection which might otherwise be urged against the application of the term *philosophy* to the sciences of observation.

In studying the 'total development' of human intelligence in its various spheres of action, from its earliest and simplest effort to the present time, M. Comte believes that he has discovered a grand fundamental law to which that development is subjected by an invariable necessity; and which he conceives to be firmly established, not only by arguments furnished by the knowledge of our own organization, but by an attentive study of the history of science. 'This law,' says he,

> consists in this, that each of our principal conceptions, each branch of knowledge, passes successively through three different theoretical states—the theological or fictitious state, the metaphysical or abstract state, and the scientific or positive state; in other words, the human mind, by its nature, employs successively in each of its researches three methods of philosophizing, the character of which is essentially different, and is even radically opposite;—at first the theological method, next the metaphysical method, and lastly, the positive method. Hence we have three kinds of philosophy, or general systems of conceptions relative to phenomena, which mutually exclude each other. The *first* is the necessary point of departure of human intelligence, the *third* its fixed and definite condition, while the *second* is destined only to be a state of transition.

> In the *theological* state the human mind, directing its researches to the intimate nature of things, to the first and final causes of all the effects which we witness, in a word, to absolute knowledge, represents the phenomena as produced by the direct and continued actin of supernatural agents, whose arbitrary intervention explains all the apparent anomalies of the universe.

> In the *metaphysical* state, which is, in reality, only a simple modification of the theological one, the supernatural agents are replaced by abstract forces, real entities (personified abstractions) inherent in the different bodies of the universe, and conceived to be capable of generating by themselves all the observed phenomena; the explanation of which then consists in assigning to each a corresponding entity.

> Finally, in the *positive* state the human mind, recognising the impossibility of obtaining absolute notions, renounces the attempt of enquiring into the origin and destination of the universe, and of detecting the intimate causes of phenomena, in order to set itself only to discover, by a judicious combination of reasoning and observation, their effective laws; that is, their invariable relations of succession and similitude. The explanation of facts, then reduced to real terms, is henceforth but the connexion established between different individual phenomena and some general facts, the number of

which becomes more and more diminished in the progress of science.

> The *theological* system has reached the highest degree of perfection of which it is susceptible, when it has substituted the providential action of one being, instead of the varied agency of numerous independent divinities which had been at first imagined. In like manner the last term of the *metaphysical* system consists in conceiving, in place of different individual entities, a single great general entity, viz., *nature* viewed as the only source of all phenomena. In the same way the perfection of the *positive* system towards which it unceasingly tends, though it is very probable that it will never reach it, will be the power of representing all the different phenomena, capable of being observed as particular cases of a single general fact; such, for example, as that of gravitation.

Although M. Comte has reserved his demonstration of this fundamental law, and his discussion of the results to which it leads, for that part of his work which treats of social physics, yet we have no hesitation in admitting its general accuracy. The quaint though expressive terms in which it is announced [are] apt to prejudice an English reader against its reception; but when this prejudice is removed by the study of the early history of science, he cannot fail to recognise its truth and importance. In thus perceiving the general character of the steps by which science has been gradually attaining its more perfect and final condition, he cannot but feel that the study of its past history must indicate the general tendency of its future progress, and may probably furnish some safe, if not infallible rules of investigating truth.

Since the time of Galileo, Bacon, and Newton, every branch of knowledge has been steadily advancing towards a fixed and positive state. The precepts of Bacon, and the methods actually used by Galileo and Newton, have established it as a fundamental truth, that there can be no real knowledge but that which is founded on observation and experiment. Facts and observations, however, when standing alone and unconnected, afford no permanent satisfaction to the philosopher who has discovered them. He knows, indeed, their high value and their ultimate importance; but this conviction does not assuage the thirst of philosophy; and the mind instinctively seeks to determine the relations of the facts which it has discovered, and turns to some pole to which they appear to converge, or some general principle to which they point, and by which they may be explained. Hence it is, that in the infancy of knowledge, the mind would be compelled, were it not its natural tendency, to invent some theory by which a collection of insulated facts might be fixed in the memory, and thus presented to the judgment under a single aspect.

In the infancy of science this natural passion for generalization is easily gratified. Supernatural power offers an immediate and a complete solution of every difficulty. Metaphysical abstractions gradually replace theological agents, and in the process of time these gradually disappear, and the phenomena themselves become the principal object of our notice. In this manner the theological gradually passes into positive philosophy, the nature of which is thus described by M. Comte.

> The fundamental character of *Positive Philosophy* is to regard all phenomena as subjected to invariable natural laws, the precise discovery of which, and their reduction to the least possible number, are the object of all our researches, regarding as senseless and absolutely inaccessible the enquiry into what are called *causes*. It would be unprofitable to insist much upon a principle which has become so familiar to all who study profoundly the sciences of observation. Every one, indeed, knows that in our most perfect explanations of phenomena we never pretend to explain their *generating* causes (for this would be only driving back the difficulty), but only analyze with accuracy the circumstances of their production, and connect them by the relations of succession and similitude. Thus, in order to give the best of all examples, we say, that the general phenomena of the universe are explained as much as they can be by the Newtonian law of gravitation; because, on the one hand, this fine theory exhibits to us all the immense variety of astronomical facts as only one and the same fact seen in different points of view—the constant tendency of all the particles of matter towards one another in the direct ratio of their masses, and the inverse ratio of the squares of their distances; whilst, on the other hand, this general fact is presented to us as the simple extension of a phenomenon which is eminently familiar to us, and by it alone we consider as perfectly explained the gravity of bodies at the surface of the earth. With regard to the determination of what this attraction and that gravity are in themselves, or what are their causes, these are questions which we regard as incapable of solution—which are not within the domain of positive philosophy, and which we justly abandon to the imagination of theological speculators, or to the subtleties of metaphysicians. The most obvious proof that such solutions are impossible is, that whenever the greatest philosophers have endeavored to say anything truly rational on this subject, they have been able only to define one of these principles by the other—in saying for *attraction* that it is nothing else than *universal gravity*, and for *gravity* that it consists simply in *terrestrial attraction*.

M. Comte has given us another illustration of what he means by positive philosophy, deduced from the beautiful researches of Baron Fourier on the *Theory of Heat*, which he considers as affording a very happy verification of the preceding general remarks. 'In this work,' says he, the philosophical character of which is so eminently positive, the most important and precise laws of thermological phenomena are developed without the slightest enquiry into the intimate nature of heat, and without mentioning, for any other purpose than to point out its inutility, the long agitated controversy between the partisans of calorific matter and those that make heat consist in the vibrations of an universal Ether. And, nevertheless, the highest questions several of which have not even been previously discussed, are treated of in Baron Fourier's work—a palpable proof that the human mind without wasting its strength on unapproachable problems, and by limiting itself to researches of an absolutely positive nature, may find inexhaustible materials for the most profound activity.

Having thus indicated the general spirit and character of positive philosophy, our author proceeds to examine the degree of progress which it has made, and to ascertain the steps which are yet necessary for its establishment. The phenomena of astronomy, of terrestrial physics, of chemistry, and of physiology, he considers as reduced to positive theories; and he ascribes to the combined precepts of Bacon, the conceptions of Descartes, and the discoveries of Galileo, the first grand movement by which 'positive conceptions' were distinctly separated from the superstitious and scholastic alloy which disguised the labours of preceding philosophers. Notwithstanding, however, the great progress of the physical sciences, M. Comte admits that *Social Physics*, which forms the last division in his arrangement, has not yet acquired any positive character; and though he does not suppose that the observations which he has to offer on this subject can give to it the same degree of perfection as the older sciences, he yet hopes that they will impress upon this branch of knowledge the same positive character. When this object is once attained, he conceives that all our fundamental conceptions will become homogeneous,—that philosophy will be definitively constituted in its positive state, and, that without changing its character it will gradually develop itself by constantly increasing acquisitions which necessarily result from new facts and more profound meditations.

In proceeding to give a distinct view of the plan of his **'Course of Lectures on Positive Philosophy,'** our author warns his readers that they must not expect a series of special treatises on each of the principal branches of Natural Philosophy. Without considering the time which such an enterprise would require, M. Comte modestly states, that the task could not be accomplished by him or by any person whatever, in the present state of education. He proposes merely to give a course of *Positive Philosophy*, and not a course of *Positive Science*; and his object is only to consider each fundamental science in its relation to our whole positive system of knowledge, and to the spirit which characterizes it;—that is, under the twofold view of its essential methods and its leading results.

Having thus explained the object of his course, our author proceeds to give an account of the plan of it, or to expound his general views on what he calls the *hierarchy* of the positive sciences. The classification of the different branches of knowledge, as given by Bacon and D'Alembert, and founded on a supposed distinction of the different faculties of the mind, becomes an untenable one, from the very circumstance that such a distinction has no solid foundation; because in every mental effort all our principal faculties are simultaneously employed. With regard to other classifications, our author pronounces them to be fundamentally erroneous, from the very circumstance, that every speculator has given a new one of his own, and that all men of rightly constituted minds entertain a strong prejudice against any attempt to arrange and define the different branches of knowledge. In confirmation of these sound views, we cannot avoid referring to the singular subdivision of the sciences which so distinguished an individual as Dr. Thomas Young has adopted in his valuable work on Natural Philosophy. Even at a time when he regarded the undulatory theory of light with some distrust,—when it had not attracted that attention and acquired that importance which it now enjoys,—and when, indeed, he himself was about its only abettor, he did not scruple to make such a theory the basis of part of his classification by introducing the science of OPTICS as a branch of *Hydrodynamics*! In such a procedure the sound principles of classification were set at nought, and it remained only to divide fluids into *ponderable* and *imponderable*, and then to tack to *Hydrodynamics* the sciences of Magnetism, Electricity, Galvanism and Thermology.

Such an attempt to make a mere hypothesis the basis of a philosophical arrangement points out, in a striking manner, the necessity and the value of that severe discussion by which M. Comte has established his classification of the sciences. The general theory of classification now adopted in natural history he considers as a sure guide in the classification of the sciences,— the classification arising out of the study of the objects to be classified, and depending on the real affinities and the natural connexion which they present; so that it shall be itself the expression of the most general fact developed by an elaborate comparison of the objects which it embraces. Hence it follows that the different positive sciences must be arranged in reference to their mutual dependence, and this dependence can only be deduced from that of their corresponding phenomena. In this way our author is led, by a rigorous and philosophical survey of the different branches of knowledge, to the following arrangement of the six fundamental sciences—*Mathematics*, *Astronomy*, *Physics*, *Chemistry*, *Physiology*, and *Social Physics*—an arrangement which forms a part of the more general one to which we have already directed the attention of the reader.

In arriving at this result our author has discussed several important topics which, limited as our space is, we cannot altogether overlook. Considering all human works as bearing reference either to speculation or to action, he divides our real knowledge into *theoretical* and *practical*. The first of these departments, embracing the whole system of our fundamental conceptions on the different orders of phenomena, he conceives to be analogous to the *prima philosophia* of Bacon; and to form the basis of all that practical knowledge by which man acts upon external nature, and exercises a power over the material universe. But though in this respect *knowledge is power*, and though every branch of industry and the arts has derived from scientific theories the richest benefits, we must not suppose for a moment that the value of our enquiries can be measured by their bounty to the arts. Philosophy, while she condescends to be their landmaid, and the willing dispenser of domestic benefits, aims at a nobler and loftier object. Her insatiable spirit cherishes a paramount interest in determining the laws and detecting the causes of phenomena, even when they have no apparent application to the wants of our species; nor would that interest be at all diminished were such an application found to be impossible. The whole history of science has established the incontrovertible fact that speculations the most abstract often lead, in the course of time, to practical results of high value;—and as Condorcet has beautifully remarked, 'the sailor who has been preserved from shipwreck by an accurate observation of the longitude, owes his life to a *theory* conceived *two thousand* years before by men of genius who had in view only simple geometrical speculations.'

In pursuing the researches of science, however, we must renounce all consideration either of their immediate or contingent application; we must concentrate our undivided energies upon the subject with which we are grappling, and bequeath as a legacy to posterity any germ of usefulness which may sometimes lie hidden among our theoretical deductions.

But this view of the subject acquires new force when we consider the faculties of man as not limited in their exercise to his present sphere of activity. The capacities and cravings of our intellectual appetite are not given us merely that they might administer to our own corporeal wants, or to the vulgar necessities of our species. Is our knowledge of the heavenly bodies—of their nicely balanced actions and harmonious movements—to have no other end than to regulate a timekeeper or determine a ship's place upon the ocean? Is our study of the sun, which rules by day, and the moon, which rules by night, to have no higher aim than if they were merely to replace the pillar of cloud by day, and the pillar of fire by night? Is man to be forever a shepherd pilgrim in this lovely Oasis, treading on its green pastures and listening to the music of its quiet waters? Or is he, in the perfection of mechanism, to be forever flying over its surface with the speed of Camilla, visiting every clime, greeting every individual of his race, and compressing into the diminished span of his being all the events of an antediluvian existence? Such suppositions stand opposed to every lesson of philosophy, and to every response of revelation. Let our philosophical researches, then, be regarded as the best preparatory education for that intellectual existence, when the mind shall have burst the prison bars of its earthly durance, and received new revelations of knowledge, suited to its improved capacity and proportioned to its previous attainments.

After a preliminary lecture, entitled **'Philosophical Considerations on the General Science of Mathematics,'** M. Comte devotes nearly the whole of his first volume to an account of the Calculus, Geometry, and Rational Mechanics, following the subdivisions of those branches which we have already given. He considers mathematics as the basis of all the positive sciences; and he defines it to be the science which has for its object the indirect measure of magnitudes, and which determines one magnitude by others, by means of the precise relations which exist between them. He subdivides the general science into two great sciences, *abstract* and *concrete* mathematics. The complete solution of every mathematical question, he conceives, may be decomposed into two parts essentially distinct in their nature; namely, the *concrete* part, or that which determines the precise relations which exist between the known and unknown quantities, and the *abstract* part, or that by which the unknown quantities are determined from these relations. The *concrete* part evidently depends on the nature of the phenomena under consideration; whilst the *abstract* part is completely independent of the nature of the objects examined; and bears solely on the numerical relations which they present. The former, having for its object to discover the equations of phenomena, would seem, *a priori*, to consist of as many distinct sciences as there are really different categories among natural phenomena. But there are only two great general categories of phenomena of which we constantly know the equations, namely, geometrical and mechanical phenomena; and hence the concrete branch of mathematics must consist of geometry and rational mechanics. If, as our author remarks, all the parts of the universe are conceived to be immoveable, there could be no other phenomena but *geometrical* ones, since everything would be reduced to relations of form, magnitude, and position; but when we consider the motions which actually take place, we must take into account also the *mechanical* phenomena. Hence, in applying a philosophical conception due to M. Blainville, the universe, when seen in a *statical* point of view, presents only *geometrical* phenomena, and when seen in a *mechanical* point of view only *mechanical* phenomena. Geometry and mechanics, therefore, constitute by themselves the two fundamental natural sciences; so that all natural effects may be conceived as simple necessary results either of the laws of extent or of the laws of motion.

Again, with respect to abstract mathematics, it consists, according to our author, of what is called the *Calculus*; the object of which is to resolve all questions of number. It includes all operations, from the most simple arithmetical ones, to the most sublime combinations of transcendental analysis. This *science*, as M. Comte calls it, though more perfect than any other, is still little advanced; so that it has but rarely attained, in a completely satisfactory manner, its ultimate object of deducing the value of unknown quantities from those that are known. The following abbreviated extract will give our readers a clear idea of our author's view respecting the division of mathematical science into three branches; and the relations which these branches bear to each other and to the other sciences:—

> If we compare, on one hand, the calculus, and on the other hand geometry and mechanics, we shall verify, in relation to the two principal sections of mathematics, viz. *abstract* and *concrete*, all the essential characters of our Encyclopedic arrangement. Analytical ideas are evidently more abstract, more general, and more simple than geometrical or mechanical ideas. Though the principal conceptions of mathematical analysis, viewed historically, were formed under the influence of geometrical or mechanical considerations, with the advancement of which sciences the progress of the calculus has been closely connected, yet analysis is not the less, in a logical point of view, essentially independent of geometry and mechanics, whilst the latter, on the contrary, are necessarily founded on the first. Mathematical analysis is, therefore, the true rational basis of the whole system of our positive knowledge. It constitutes the first and the most perfect of all the fundamental sciences. The ideas with which it is conversant are the most universal, the most abstract, and the most simple which we can conceive; and were we to try to go farther under these three equivalent relations, we should inevitably fall into metaphysical reveries. This, therefore, being the proper character of mathematical analysis, we can easily explain why, when it is suitably employed, it holds out to us such powerful means, not only to give more precision to our real knowledge, but also to establish an infinitely more perfect co-ordination in the study of the phenomena to which it is applied. As a single analytical question, abstractly resolved, contains the implicit solution of a crowd of physical questions, the mind is led to perceive, with the greatest facility, the relation between phenomena which appear at first wholly insulated, and from which we can easily deduce whatever is common to them all. It is thus that in the solution of important questions in geometry and mechanics, we see springing up naturally, by the aid of analysis, the most unexpected relations between problems, which, though they present at first no apparent connexion, are often found to be identical. Who, for example, could, without the aid of analysis, perceive the least analogy between the determination of the direction of a curve at each of its points, and that of the velocity acquired at each instant of its varied motion? questions which, however different they may be, are but one in the eyes of a geometer.

After discussing the causes of the high relative perfection of mathematical analysis, and controverting the opinion of Condillac, that its supremacy is owing to the use of algebraic signs as an instrument of reasoning, he proceeds to show that it possesses by its nature a rigorous and logical universality; and he goes on to consider the great limitations by which, in consequence of our imperfect intelligence, its domain is singularly narrowed, in proportion as the phenomena become more complicated and numerous. In the leading branches of physics, it is often impracticable to reduce a question to one of numbers; so that it is only when the phenomena are of the most simple and general kind, that analysis can be successfully applied to natural philosophy. When we consider, indeed, that before such an application can be made, we must first discover precise relations between the quantities co-existing in the phenomenon which we are studying, before we can establish those equations which form the first step in our analytical enquiries, it is evident that it is only in *Inorganic Physics*, including astronomy, physics, and chemistry, that we can hope to apply the calculus with real advantage. *Organic Physics*, on the contrary, and probably some of the more complex portions of inorganic physics, are, as our author states, necessarily inaccessible to the calculus, in consequence of the extreme numerical variability of the corresponding phenomena. In the phenomena of living bodies, all idea of fixed numbers is wholly out of the question; so that any application of analysis to physiology, is an abuse of the former, and must lead to serious errors in the latter.

The case, however, is different with inorganic bodies. In all such bodies, as our author has observed, their different properties are almost invariable. Their physical properties—for example, their form, consistence, specific gravity, elasticity, &c.,—have such a remarkable numerical fixity, as to enable us to consider them in a mathematical point of view. In the chemical phenomena, however, of such bodies, the variations are more frequent, however, of such bodies, the variations are more frequent, more extensive, and consequently more irregular; and even the doctrine of definite proportions has not yet acquired such a character as to admit of the application of mathematical analysis. The science of meteorology furnishes us with phenomena nearly as complex, and as little susceptible of the application of the calculus as that of physiology. 'It cannot be doubted,' as M. Comte remarks, that 'each of the numerous agents which concur in the production of these phenomena, follow separately mathematical laws, though we are still ignorant of the greater number of them: but their multiplicity renders the observed effects as irregular in their variations, as if each cause had not been subject to any precise condition.'

But not only are we often unable to obtain fixed numerical results, even in the most special cases—the phenomena are often so complicated that, even when we shall have discovered the mathematical law, which each agent separately obeys, the corresponding problem may become absolutely insoluble, when a great number of conditions require to be combined; and hence it is that so little progress has been made in the effective study of the greater number of natural phenomena. In illustration of these views our author makes the following observations:—

We know that the very simple phenomenon of the motion of a fluid in virtue of its gravity alone, through a given orifice, has not been completely solved when we wish to take into account all the essential circumstances. The same is true of the still more simple motion of a solid projectile through a resisting medium. Why is it, then, that mathematical analysis had adapted itself with such admirable success to the profound study of the celestial phenomena? It is just because, in spite of common appearances, they are much more simple than all others. The most complicated problem which they present—that of the modification produced in the motion of two bodies tending towards each other by their mutual gravitation, by the influence of a third acting on both in the same manner, is much less complex than the simplest terrestrial problem; and yet it presents such difficulties that the solutions of it are still only approximative. It is also obvious, in examining the subject more profoundly, that the great perfection to which solar astronomy has been brought by the application of mathematics, is owing to the circumstance of our having skillfully taken advantage of all the particular, and, so to speak, accidental facilities, which the special constitution of our planetary system presents for the solution of such problems. The planets, indeed, of which it is composed, are few in number, and have their masses very unequal, and much smaller than that of the sun; their forms are most perfectly spherical, and their orbits are nearly circular, and slightly inclined to each other. Hence it results, from all these circumstances, that the perturbations are often very slight, and that in order to calculate them, it is commonly sufficient to take into account, concurrently with the action of the sun upon each, the influence of one other planet, capable, from its magnitude and proximity, of producing sensible derangements. But if, instead of such a state of things, our solar system had been composed of a greater number of planets concentrated into a smaller space, and nearly equal in mass,—if their orbits had presented very different inclinations and considerable eccentricities,—if these bodies had been of a more complicated form, very eccentric

ellipsoids, for example, it is certain that, supposing the same real law of gravitation, we should not even now have been able to submit the study of the celestial phenomena to our mathematical analysis, and probably we should not have succeeded, even at present, in establishing the principal law. These hypothetical conditions would be found accurately realized, and that too in a high degree in chemical phenomena, were we to calculate them by the theory of general gravitation.

From these admirable observations on the doctrine and application of mathematical analysis, of which we have given a very brief and imperfect notice, M. Comte proceeds to a detailed account of the history and the present state of the various branches of mathematics, following the arrangement which we have already indicated; but though we were anxious to have submitted to our readers some specimens of the fine reasoning and beautiful generalizations which distinguish this part of the work, our narrow limits force us to proceed to the more popular topics of astronomy and physics.

After defining astronomy to be the science which has for its object the discovery of the laws of the geometrical and the mechanical phenomena of the heavenly bodies, our author subdivides it into *solar* and *sidereal*; and considers the former, or that which relates to the *solar system*, as the only branch which is entitled to the name of *positive*. Our knowledge of sidereal astronomy is at present extremely limited; and though it may be considerably extended in reference to the relative motions of multiple stars which form part of the group to which our own system belongs, yet it must ever remain a comparatively imperfect branch of the science.

In estimating the rank which astronomy holds among the natural sciences, our author submits to his readers what he considers a new and very important philosophical law—namely, that in proportion as phenomena become more complex, they are at the same time susceptible, by their nature, of being explained, by more extended and varied methods, without there being an exact compensation between the increase of the difficulties, and the augmentation of the resources. Hence, he concludes, that as the phenomena of astronomy are the most simple, they ought to be those for which we have the fewest means of examination. That this is the case shows in the following manner.

Our art of observing consists, in general, of three different methods. 1. *Observation*, properly so called; that is, the direct examination of a phenomenon such as it naturally appears to us; 2. *Experiment*, or the contemplation of a phenomenon more or less modified by artificial circumstances, which we institute expressly for the purposes of examination; and, 3. *Comparison*, or the gradual comparison of a series of analogous cases, in which the phenomenon is more and more simplified. The science of organized bodies which studies phenomena of the most difficult access, is also the only one which really permits us to employ all these three methods of research. Astronomy, on the contrary, is necessarily limited to the first. Experiment is obviously impossible; and with regard to comparison, it could only exist, if we were able to observe directly several solar systems. Observation, therefore, only remains, and even it is reduced to the least possible extent; as it can be carried on solely by one of our senses. To measure angles, and to reckon time, are the only means by which our understanding can proceed to the discovery of astronomical laws. But these means are the only ones which are required for observing geometrical and mechanical phenomena—magnitudes and motions. From this, however, we ought to infer that, among all the branches of natural philosophy, astronomy is that in which direct observation, however indispensable it be, is, by itself, the least significative, and in which the reasoning part is incomparably the greatest. Nothing truly interesting is ever decided by simple inspection, contrary to what takes place in physics, chemistry, physiology, &c. We may say, indeed, without exaggeration, that the phenomena, however real they be, are for the most part essentially constructed by our understandings; for we are not able to see immediately the figure of the earth, nor the curve described by a planet, nor even the daily motion of the heavens: our mind alone can form these different notions in combining, by processes of reasoning, often very long and very complex, insulated sensations, the incoherence of which would, without this, have rendered them almost entirely insignificant.

Hence M. Comte concludes that astronomy is justly entitled to the rank which it has unanimously received of being placed at the head of the sciences, and which it owes to the perfection of its scientific character, and to the preponderating importance of the laws which it unveils. But it is not only to this preeminence that he considers it entitled. He regards the general laws of the planetary motions as the first foundation of the whole system of positive knowledge, not excepting even Social Physics, whereas astronomy itself is independent of every other science but that of mathematics.

After illustrating the fundamental axiom that *all science has for its object prediction,*—by which it is distinguished from simple erudition, which relates only to events that have been accomplished,—our author points out the advantages of astronomy in dissipating those absurd prejudices and superstitious terrors which the phenomena of eclipses and comets used to foster and inspire; but instead of confining his remarks within the limits which naturally belong to such a discussion, he digresses into those painful and groundless observations, to which we have already been obliged to refer. The stream of his eloquence, however, soon resumes its purity, and we follow him with delight through one

of the finest surveys of astronomical truth that has ever been composed.

From the methods of observation employed in this science he passes to general views respecting the elementary geometrical phenomena of the heavenly bodies. He discusses, in a general manner, the interesting problem of the earth's motion. He treats of the laws of Kepler, the finest effort of human genius, and points out their application to the geometrical study of the celestial motions. He then proceeds to give some fundamental views on the law of gravitation, and treats in successive lectures the important topics of celestial statics and dynamics; and he concludes his subject with general considerations on sidereal astronomy, and on positive cosmogony. We could have wished to place before our readers some specimens of our author's manner of treating these difficult and deeply interesting topics—of his simple, yet powerful eloquence—of his enthusiastic admiration of intellectual superiority—of his accuracy as a historian, his honesty as a judge, and of his absolute freedom from all personal and national feelings. On every subject, save that on which we have already placed a mark, the reader feels that he is conducted through the labyrinths of astronomical discovery by a safe and skilful guide, who has himself traced its windings and marked its ambiguities; and the philosopher who has grown hoary in the service of science longs for the advantage of such a historian to record his labours, and of such an arbiter to appreciate their value. Confined, however, as our limits are, we must give our readers a brief account of M. Comte's Lectures on sidereal astronomy and positive cosmogony.

Although our author has distinguished *sidereal* from *solar* astronomy as a branch of the science, respecting which we are not likely to acquire much positive knowledge, yet he has so judiciously put together its scanty materials, and so distinctly separated what is positive from what is probable, that the mind clearly apprehends not only what astronomers have achieved in this remote domain, but also all that we may expect them to achieve for centuries to come. In order that our readers may duly appreciate the talent of our author as the historian of science, we shall submit to them the whole of what Mr. Whewell has written on the very same subject, viz. the body of his section, entitled, *Discovery of the Laws of Double Stars.*

> If the stars were each insulated from the rest, as our sun appears to be from them, we should have been quite unable to answer this inquiry, Do the fixed stars obey the law of gravitation? But among the stars *there are some which are called double, and which consist of two stars,* so near to each other, that the telescope alone can separate them. The elder Herschel diligently observed and *measured such stars*; and, as has often happened in astronomical history, pursuing one object he fell in with another.

Supposing *such pairs* to be really unconnected, he wished to learn, from their phenomena, something respecting the annual parallax of the earth's orbit. But in the course of twenty years' observations he made the discovery (in 1803) *that these couples were turning round each other* with various velocities. These revolutions were, for the most part, so slow, that he was obliged to leave their complete determination as an inheritance to the next generation. His son was not careless of the bequest, and after having added an enormous mass of observations to those of his father, he applied himself to determine the laws of these revolutions. A problem so obvious and so tempting was attacked also by others, as Savary and Encke, in 1830 and 1832, with the resources of analysis. But a problem in which the data are so minute and inevitably imperfect, required the mathematician to employ much judgment as well as skill in using and combining these data; and Herschel, by employing positions only of the line joining *the pair of stars*, to the exclusion of their distances, and by inventing a method which introduced the whole body of observations, and not selected ones only, into the determination of the motion, has made his investigations by far the most satisfactory of those which have appeared. The result is, that *it has been rendered very probable that the double stars describe ellipses about each other*; and, therefore, that here also, at an immeasurable distance from our system, the law of attraction, according to the inverse square, prevails. And, according to the practice of astronomers, when a law has been established, tables have been calculated for the future motions; and we have ephemerides of the revolutions of suns round each other in a region so remote; that the whole circle of our earth's orbit, if placed there, would be imperceptible by our strongest telescopes. The permanent comparison of the observed with the predicted motions, continued for more than one revolution, is the severe and decisive test of the truth of *the theory*; and the result of this test astronomers are *now awaiting*.

The verifications of Newton's discoveries were sufficient employment for the last century; the first step in the extension of them belongs to this century. We cannot at present foresee the magnitude of this task, but every one must feel that the law of gravitation, before verified in all the particles of our own system, and *now extended to the all but infinite distance of the fixed stars, presses upon our minds with irresistible evidence as a universal law of the whole material creation.*

That the preceding view is not only barren of information, but vague in its conceptions, as well as incorrect in its statements, will be admitted by every astronomer. The reader is led to believe that the *thousands* of double stars which have been discovered are *all binary systems*, whose motions have been determined; whereas the great body of them are merely two stars lying accidentally in the same direction as seen from our system. He learns nothing respecting the phenomena

exhibited by a binary system,—the peculiar nature and delicacy of the requisite observations,—the uncertainty of the results, or the lengths of the periods of revolution which characterize each of the systems that have been really established. He is told, indeed, that Sir W. Herschel diligently observed and *measured such stars*, but unless he be an astronomer, he cannot tell what *measuring a double star* means. He learns that Savary and Encke attacked the problem analytically, but the result of the attack is withheld. He reads that Sir John Herschel invented a *method* (which is also concealed), but which renders it *very probable* that *the double stars describe ellipses round each other*, and that the law of solar attraction prevails at an immeasurable distance from our system.

Now, supposing the reader to have so little curiosity as to rest satisfied with a result deduced from phenomena and measurements and methods which have not even been named, we defy him to understand what the result actually means *that the double stars describe ellipses about each other*! We may suppose that one double star or binary system describes an ellipse round another double star, or binary system; or that, while the smaller star describes an ellipse around the greater star, the greater describes an ellipse round the smaller star; but he will never find out, unless by appealing to an elementary work, that the smaller describes an ellipse round the greater star supposed to be at rest in one of the foci of that ellipse.

Having at last reached the truth, and admired the deduction from it that the law of terrestrial gravity extends to such double stars, he becomes anxious to appreciate the evidence for a conclusion so pregnant with interest. Mr. Whewell at first tells him that the elliptical motion on which it rests is *very probable*. He then describes the conclusion as a *theory*, the proof of which astronomers are *now awaiting*; and finally, he reaches the climax of certainty by declaring that every one must feel that the law of gravitation, *now extended to the fixed stars, 'presses upon our minds with irresistible evidence* as a universal law of the *whole material* creation.'

From these flying commentaries on sidereal astronomy we shall proceed to the learned and philosophical discussion of the subject by M. Comte. After mentioning that out of more than 3000 multiple stars, almost all of which are double, there are only a few whose relative motions, as the elements of a binary system, are irrefragably established, he points out the probability that the great body of what are called double stars do not form binary systems; and concludes that the only study really positive which we can recognise in sidereal astronomy, 'is that of the well established relative motions of certain double stars, whose number does not exceed *seven* or *eight*.' But even with respect to the orbits of these stars, our knowledge can never be compared with that which we possess of the orbits of our own planets; because the apparent *radii vectores* are so small, that an error in such delicate measures may perhaps amount in general to a *fourth* or even to a *third* of their total value. The same observation applies to the periodic times when they have not been directly observed, which hitherto has always been the case. 'It is hence,' says our author, 'very difficult to conceive how these studies can ever acquire that exactness which will furnish a base sufficiently solid for dynamical conclusions that are truly *irresistible*; so as to demonstrate, for example, the effective extension of the theory of gravitation to the mutual action of the two elements of a double star, which would besides *be very far from establishing the rigorous universality of that theory*.' From these general remarks our author proceeds to sum up the amount of our positive knowledge in sidereal astronomy. 'The seven orbits,' says he,

of double stars hitherto established, and the first of which is due to the labours of M. Savary, present in general very considerable eccentricities, the least of which is almost *double* and the *greatest, quadruple* of the greatest eccentricity of our planetary orbits. With regard to their periodic times the shortest exceeds a little *forty years*, and the longest *six hundred years*. Besides, the eccentricity and the duration of the revolution do not appear to have any fixed relation to each other; and neither the one nor the other seems otherwise to depend on the angular distance of the two elements of the corresponding couples.... While the linear distances of these stars from the earth, and consequently from each other, are unknown, the preceding notions cannot have any great importance, nor perhaps even sufficient solidity. If these distances, however, should yet become known, we might easily obtain a value of the masses of the corresponding couples on the supposition that the law of gravity was legitimately applicable to them.... The quantity thus determined by which the secondary star would tend to fall in a given time towards the principal one, being compared with the fall of bodies at the surface of the earth, previously reduced to the same distance according to the ordinary law, would immediately give us the value of the ratio between the mass of the couple and that of the earth. But the repartition of this total mass between its two elements would evidently be still uncertain; since it is very possible that it may be effected in a manner much less unequal than between our planets and their satellites. This last consideration throws over the whole of the subject a new degree of uncertainty. For if the masses of the two elements of each stellar couple differ so little compared to their distance and their magnitude, that the centre of gravity of the system deviates sensibly from the principal star, *it is to this unknown centre that we must necessarily refer the observed motions;* and then *what accurate dynamical conclusion could we draw from elliptic orbits round the larger star as their focus, even if they were rigorously determined?*

Our author then proceeds to explain the ingenious method conceived by M. Savary for determining within certain limits the distances of some of the double stars from our earth or sun,—a method which he regards as constituting the only scientific conception in sidereal astronomy; being independent of every hypothesis respecting the exact form of the orbits of double stars, and the extension of the theory of gravity. It is necessary only to admit that the orbits are symmetrical relative to their longest diameter; and that the lesser star moves with the same velocity at two points equidistant from the greater star. Like the general theory of aberration, this method is founded on the fact that the velocity of light is accurately known, with this difference only, that in the case of aberration we are occupied with an error of place, whereas here we consider an error of time. 'Let us conceive,' says M. Comte,

a stellar orbit whose smaller axis is situated perpendicularly to the visual ray drawn from the sun or the earth, which may here be confounded. If the same were true of the greater axis, and, consequently, of the plane of the orbit, the two halves of the revolution which the lesser star really performs in times exactly equal, would obviously still appear of equal duration, however slow the propagation of light might be at each position. But this would no longer be the case when the plane of the orbit is greatly inclined to the visual ray; unless when the ray lay in that plane, in which case the fundamental observation becomes impossible. In this case, the duration of the semi-revolution corresponding to the half of the curve where the star moves towards us, ought to appear less than it is in reality; and that relative to the half when the star moves farther and farther from us will appear, on the contrary, to be augmented, in consequence of the difference of the times that light ought to employ in reaching us from the two points of the orbit which are most unequally distant from the earth. Hence though the total periodic time ought not to be changed, the two halves of the revolution will not have exactly the same apparent duration; and if their inequality could be well observed, it would enable us immediately to determine, from the real velocity of light, the true difference between the distances of the earth from the two extreme points of the orbit. Consequently, this difference will evidently become a sufficient geometrical base for estimating, with a corresponding approximation, the linear dimensions of the orbit, and its true distance from the earth; its inclination and its true angular extent being otherwise previously given. Every thing is then reduced to the determination of an appreciable inequality between the duration of two semi-revolutions; but it is indispensable that this appreciation be made from the effective observation of an entire revolution, so that its accuracy may not depend on any hypothesis respecting the geometrical nature of the stellar orbit, or the law relative to the velocity with which the star describes it.... Until experience has determined it, we cannot say whether or not the radii of the stellar orbits have such a relation to their distances that we can perceive a sensible difference between the two halves of their periodic times. . . . Every second of error in the periodic time, which probably can never be determined within several days, tends to introduce an error of at least 32,000 myriametres in the value of the distance required; so that the method, as its inventor has stated, is only capable of determining a *maximum* and a *minimum*, probably very remote from each other. But in spite of its necessary imperfection, it possesses the deep interest of holding out the hope of obtaining, some time or other, a certain approximation with regard to several of those distances which have a coarse inferior limit common to the innumerable stars which the heavens present to us.

From these interesting views of sidereal astronomy, our author proceeds to give an account of the cosmogony of Laplace,—a portion of modern theory omitted by Mr. Whewell,—but which, when restricted to our own planetary system, M. Comte regards not only as the most plausible which has ever been proposed, but as susceptible of a mathematical verification which its illustrious author had not ventured to anticipate. The object of this ingenious hypothesis, to which we have already had occasion to refer, is to explain, by the agency of heat and gravity, the general circumstances which characterise, the constitution of our solar system; namely, the identity in the direction of all the annual and diurnal motions of the planets and their satellites from west to east; the small eccentricity of all their orbits, and the slight deviation of their planes compared with that of the solar equator. 'The cosmogony of Laplace,' says our author,

consists in forming the planets by the gradual condensation of the solar atmosphere, supposed to have been primitively extended by the action of extreme heat to the limits of our system, and to have been successively contracted by cooling. It rests on two incontestable mathematical considerations. The first concerns the necessary relation which exists, in conformity with the fundamental theory of rotations, and especially the general theorem of areas, between the successive dilatations or contractions of any body (including in this its atmosphere, which is inseparable from it), and the duration of its rotation, which ought to be accelerated when the dimensions diminish, or become slower when they increase, so that the angular and linear variations, which the sum of the areas tend to experience, may be exactly compensated. The second consideration relates to the connexion, no less evident, between the angular velocity of the sun's rotation and the possible extent of his atmosphere; the mathematical limit of which is inevitably at the distance where the centrifugal force due to that rotation becomes equal to the corresponding gravity; so that if by any cause whatever a part of this atmosphere should come to be placed beyond such a limit, it would soon even

cease to belong to the sun, though it ought to continue to revolve round him with a velocity corresponding to the moment of separation, but without participating any more in the ulterior modifications which will take place in the solar rotation by the progress of cooling.

Hence we may easily conceive how the mathematical limit of the sun's atmosphere ought to diminish without ceasing, for the parts situated in the solar equator, in proportion as the cooling has made the rotation more rapid. This atmosphere, therefore, must successively abandon in the plane of this equator different gaseous zones situated a little beyond the corresponding limits, which will constitute the first state of our planets. The same mode of formation will evidently apply to the different satellites, by means of the atmospheres of their respective planets. Our stars being thus once detached from the solar mass, may afterwards become fluid, and finally solid, by the continued progress of their own proper cooling, without being affected with the new changes which the atmosphere and rotation of the sun may have experienced. But the irregularity of this cooling, and the unequal density of the different parts of each planet, ought naturally, during these transformations, to change almost always the primitive annular form which would not subsist without alteration, but in the solitary case of the singular satellites with which Saturn is immediately surrounded. Most frequently the preponderance of a portion of the gaseous zone ought to reunite gradually, by the way of absorption round this nucleus, the entire mass of the ring; and the star ought thus to assume a spheroidal figure, with a motion of rotation, in the same direction as the translation on account of the excess of the necessary velocity of the superior molecules with respect to the inferior ones.

This ingenious hypothesis, while it affords a rational explanation of all the general phenomena exhibited in the solar system, assigns a plausible origin to that primitive impulse belonging to each planet, which has hitherto embarrassed the fundamental conception of the celestial motions; and as our author has for the first time remarked, it follows from the hypothesis, that the creation of the different parts of the solar system has been necessarily successive; those planets being the most ancient which are farthest from the sun, and the same law being observed in each of them with respect to their different satellites,—all of which are more modern than their corresponding primaries.

After making the just remark, that we may yet be able to perfect this chronological arrangement, in so far at least as to assign within certain limits the number of centuries which have elapsed since each formation, our author proceeds to the bold attempt to give a real mathematical consistency to the cosmogony which we have now described. In order to do this, he tried to discover an aspect in which it would admit of some *numerical verification*,—an indispensable criterion, as he remarks, of every hypothesis relative to astronomical phenomena; and in discovering a class of numerical elements which should harmonize with the necessary results of the theory, he found it requisite to limit himself, at least in the first instance, to the consideration of the motions of translation, which are much more susceptible of an exact analysis than the rotations of the planets, of which we know so little.

The fundamental principle of this verification consists, as our author remarks, in this, that the periodic time of each star that is formed must necessarily be equal to that of the star from which it is formed, at the time when its atmosphere extended to that point of space. Hence the problem to be solved is this—What was the duration of the rotation of the sun when the mathematical limit of his atmosphere extended to the different planets. By combining Huygen's theorems for central forces with the law of gravitation, our author established a simple fundamental equation between the duration of the rotations of the producing star, and the distance of the star produced; the constants of this equation being the radius of the central star, and the intensity of gravity at its surface, which is a direct consequence of its mass. 'This equation,' our author observes,

> leads immediately to the third great law of Kepler, which, independent of its dynamical interpretation, thus becomes susceptible of being conceived *a priori* in a cosmogonical point of view. At the same time, the fundamental harmony of different revolutions seems to be thus completed; for though the law of Kepler clearly explained why, when the periodic time and mean distance of one star were given, another star should revolve in a period corresponding to its distance, it did not establish any necessary relation between the position and the velocity of each body considered by itself. Our principle, however, tends to establish a general law between the different initial velocities, which, in celestial mechanics, have been hitherto treated as essentially arbitrary.

The first application which M. Comte made of his equation, and with the result of which he was much struck, was to the moon, whose actual periodic time agrees within less than the tenth of a day with the duration which the revolution of the earth ought to have had at the time when the lunar distance formed the limit of our atmosphere. The coincidence he found to be less accurate, though still very striking in every other case. In the case of the planets he obtained, from the duration of the corresponding solar rotations, a value always a little less than their real periodic times. It is remarkable, as he observes, that this duration, though increasing as the planet is more distant, preserves, nevertheless, very nearly the same relation to the corresponding periodic time, of which it commonly forms

the *forty-fifth* part. This *defect* changes to an *excess* in the different systems of the satellites, where it is proportionately greater than in the planets, and unequal in different systems. From the whole of the comparisons of his formula with the periods of the primary and secondary planets, our author deduces the following general result:—*Supposing the mathematical limit of the solar atmosphere successively extended to the regions where the different planets are now found, the duration of the sun's rotation was, at each of these epochs, sensibly equal to that of the actual sidereal revolution of the corresponding planet; and the same is true, for each planetary atmosphere in relation to the different satellites.*

Although this correspondence between the hypothesis and the present state of the solar system is extremely remarkable, yet our author by no means regards it as a demonstration of Laplace's cosmogony. He looks forward, however, to the possibility of deriving from it the diurnal rotations of the different planets, which have no apparent relation to each other, notwithstanding the probability that some law actually connects them. The slight deviations between the periodic times of the planets and those indicated by our author's principle, he ingeniously employs as a base for determining, with a certain degree of approximation, the epochs when the different planets were formed. If the periodic times had coincided, and the primitive ones suffered no change, no such attempt could have been made. The increase of eight days, for example, which, according to this cosmogony, our sidereal year must have experienced since the separation of the earth, will allow us to fix, within limits more or less remote, the date of that event, if the influence of the disturbing causes which produced that change should ever be sufficiently known; and this consideration becomes more rational, as the deviation increases in the planets that are more remote and more ancient.

By the same general views our author is led to the conclusion, that our world is now as complete as it can be; because the effective extent of each atmosphere is actually below the mathematical limit which results from the corresponding rotation, so that any new formation is absolutely impossible. Hence, he concludes that our system is now as stable, in a cosmogonical point of view, as it is in a mechanical one. But, notwithstanding this coincidence, neither of these kinds of stability can be regarded as absolute. By the continued resistance of the general medium with which space is occupied, our globe must inevitably return to the solar atmosphere from which it emanated; till, by a new dilatation of the central mass, it is again thrown off, to pass through the same career of change which it had previously undergone.

These views of the origin and destiny of the various systems of worlds which fill the immensity of space, break upon the mind with all the interest of novelty, and all the brightness of truth. Appealing to our imagination by their grandeur, and to our reason by the severe principles of science on which they rest, the mind feels as if a revelation had been vouchsafed to it of the past and future history of the universe. In regarding every planet of every system as necessarily thrown off from a central sun, and again deposited on its burning nucleus, we recognise the probable cause of many sidereal phenomena, which have hitherto been objects of perplexity and wonder. The consolidation of luminous matter into brilliant centres;—the changes which take place in nebulae and clusters of stars; the sudden appearance of brilliant stars, and the equally sudden extinction of others,—are all epochs in the ever-changing cycles of the universe. Nor do these speculations at all interfere with those more cherished opinions which rest on the convictions of reason and conscience, and which faith and hope have combined to consecrate. The loftiest doctrines of natural theology appeal to us with more irresistible force when science carries us back to the Great First Cause, and points out to us, in the atmosphere of the sun, all the elements of planetary worlds so mysteriously commingled. In considering our own globe as having its origin in a gaseous zone, thrown off by the rapidity of the solar rotation, and as consolidated by cooling from the chaos of its elements, we confirm rather than oppose the Mosaic cosmogony, whether allegorical or literally interpreted. The succession of geological changes, too, which modern science has established, and the continued refrigeration of our globe from a state of incandescence, are equally consistent with the cosmogony which we have explained; and when we read in Holy Writ, that the heavens shall be dissolved and the elements shall melt in fervent heat, we anticipate the conclusion of that mighty cycle, when our planet shall be reunited with the sun, and engulfed in its devouring furnace.

In the grandeur and universality of these views, we forget the insignificant beings which occupy and disturb the planetary domains. Life in all its forms, in all its restlessness, and in all its pageantry, disappears in the magnitude and remoteness of the perspective. The excited mind sees only the gorgeous fabric of the universe, recognises only its Divine architect, and ponders but on its cycles of glory and desolation. If the pride of man is ever to be mocked, or his vanity mortified, or his selfishness rebuked, it is under the influence of these studies that he will learn humility, and meekness, and charity.

Before proceeding to the separate examination of the physical sciences, our author details in his twenty-eighth Lecture, of nearly eighty pages, his general views, under the title of **Philosophical Considerations on the Physical Sciences**. After stating that this *second* fundamental branch of Natural Philosophy did not begin to assume a positive character, by disengaging itself from

Metaphysics, till Galileo had made his splendid discoveries respecting the fall of heavy bodies, he endeavours to draw a distinct line of demarcation between *Physics* and *Chemistry*. Regarding these divisions of science as having for their united object the *knowledge of the general laws of the inorganic world*, he distinguishes them by *three* general considerations, each of which is perhaps insufficient when taken singly. The *first* of these is the *necessary generality of physical, and the necessary specialty of chemical researches.* The *second*, which he considers as less important than the first, is that *the phenomena are always related to masses in physics, and to molecules in Chemistry.* The *third*, which he regards as the most definite, is that in *physical phenomena the constitution of the body, or the mode of arrangement of its particles, may be changed, though most frequently it is essentially untouched; but its nature, that is, the composition of its molecules, remains constantly unalterable; while in chemical phenomena there is not only always a change of state with respect to one of the bodies, but the mutual actions of these bodies necessarily change their nature,* and it is indeed this change which constitutes the phenomenon. This last consideration is so well founded, as M. Comte observes, that it would still preserve its distinctive character, even if all chemical phenomena should be found to depend on physical agencies. For it would still be necessarily true, that in a chemical fact there would always be something more than in a physical one, namely, the characteristic change in the molecular composition of the body, and consequently in all its properties. Hence he defines physics as that science in which *we study the laws which govern the general properties of bodies, generally viewed in the mass, and constantly placed in circumstances susceptible of preserving untouched the composition of their molecules, and even most commonly the state of their aggregation.* And in order to complete the definition, he adds, that the ultimate object of physical theories is to *predict, as exactly as possible, all the phenomena which a body will present when placed in any given circumstances.*

From these general views, it would be natural to conclude that the physical sciences in which bodies are accessible to all our senses, must be more complicated, and in a less advanced state than astronomy, where the bodies can be viewed only under two very simple aspects, namely, their forms and their motions. But as this increased complication may be compensated by increased means of investigation, this consideration leads our author to the application of his philosophical law, *that in proportion as phenomena become more complicated, they are capable of being examined under a greater number of relations.*

In astronomy, our art of observing is limited to the use of the single sense of sight; but in physics, all our senses may be employed to discover and compare the properties of bodies. Even with these powerful auxiliaries, however, we should make but little progress in physical research, if we did not possess another powerful instrument of investigation. This instrument is *experiment*, by means of which we observe bodies out of their natural state; by placing them, in artificial aspects and conditions contrived for the purpose of exhibiting to us, under the most favourable circumstances, their phenomena and their properties.

After pointing out the relative power of experimental inquiry in physiology, chemistry, and physics, our author makes the following admirable observations on the use of mathematical analysis in physical researches.

> After the rational use of experimental methods, the principal basis for the improvement of physics arises from the more or less complete application of mathematical analysis. It is here that the actual domain of this analysis in natural philosophy terminates; and we shall see how chimerical it would be to expect that its empire should ever extend farther with any real efficacy, even if we limit it to chemical phenomena. The fixity and simplicity of physical phenomena, ought naturally to permit an extensive application of the mathematical instrument; though it is much less adapted to them than to. astronomical studies. This application may be either direct or indirect. The first takes place when the immediate consideration of phenomena allows us to recognise in them a fundamental numerical law which becomes the basis of a series more or less prolonged, of analytical deductions; as has been so distinctly seen when the celebrated Fourier created his fine mathematical theory of the repartition of heat, founded wholly on the principle of thermological action between two bodies proportional to the difference of their temperatures. On the other hand, however, mathematical analysis introduces itself only indirectly, that is, after the phenomena have been first brought, by an experimental inquiry, more or less difficult, to some geometrical or mechanical laws, and then it is not properly to physics that analysis applies itself, but to geometry or mechanics. Among other examples, in a geometrical point of view, we may mention the theories of reflection and refraction, and in a mechanical point of view, the study of gravity and that of part of acoustics.

> But whether the introduction of analysis be mediate or immediate, it is of essential consequence that it be employed with extreme circumspection, after having severely scrutinized the reality of the first step, which can alone establish the solidity of the deduction; and that the genuine spirit of physics shall unceasingly direct this powerful instrument. It must be admitted that these conditions have been rarely fulfilled in an adequate manner by geometers, who most frequently mistaking the means for the end, have embarrassed physics with a multitude of analytical labours, founded on hypotheses very hazardous, or in conceptions entirely chimerical; and

> in which sound minds can see only mathematical exercises of great abstract value, but in no way calculated to advance the progress of physics. The unjust contempt which the predominance of analysis has too frequently called down upon studies purely experimental, has a tendency to displace physics from its indispensable foundations; and to drive it back to a state of uncertainty and obscurity very little removed from its former metaphysical state. Natural philosophers have therefore no other remedy for these evils than to become themselves good enough geometers to direct the use of the analytical instrument, as they do that of the other apparatus which they employ; instead of abandoning the application of it to minds which have commonly no distinct and profound idea of the phenomena, to the investigation of which they apply it.

Notwithstanding these observations, our author pays a willing homage to the great services which mathematics have conferred on physics, but he most properly recommends a change in the preliminary education of experimental philosophers; and as he regards the art of intimately uniting analysis and experiment without making the one predominate over the other, as one almost wholly unknown, he considers it as the last fundamental step of the method which is necessary for the profound study of physics.

After determining the place which *physics* should occupy in the scale of the fundamental sciences, and pointing out its great value as a general instrument of intellectual education, he proceeds to treat of *the rational formation and the true use of hypotheses,*—a task in which he is aware that he must array himself against the opinions, and run counter to the preconceptions of the great body of natural philosophers.

Our readers may remember that we, some time ago, ventured to open the trenches in this war of innovation; and it is with much satisfaction that we hail the assistance of so powerful an auxiliary as M. Comte. Under the head of the *Fundamental Theory of Hypotheses*, he states that there are only two general methods of developing, in a direct and rational manner, the real law of any phenomenon, or its exact and immediate relation to some more general law previously established—namely *induction* and *deduction*. But even in the case of the most simple phenomena, these methods would prove insufficient were we not often to anticipate the results by making some *provisional supposition*, at first essentially conjectural, with respect to some of the notions which constitute the final object of research. Hence, says our author, *the introduction of hypotheses into natural philosophy is strictly indispensable*. But in employing this artifice such hypotheses only are to be admitted as relate to the laws of phenomena, and are susceptible by their nature of a positive verification. Hence he excludes, as utterly chimerical and inadmissible, all those hypotheses which assume the existence of calorific or luminiferous ethers; or of those invisible, intangible, and imponderable fluids by which the phenomena of light, heat, magnetism, electricity, and galvanism have been explained; and he pronounces *those hypotheses only to be scientific which bear exclusively on the laws of phenomena; and never on their modes of production*—a decision which we cannot admit without great modifications. The luminiferous ethers and the electric fluids he places on the same level with the elementary spirits of Paracelsus; he expresses his surprise that their abettors do not believe in genii and guardian angels; and in mentioning the idea of a *sonorous fluid*, proposed by the illustrious Lamarck, he observes, that it has no other fault than that of having been proposed after acoustics had been fully constituted, and that if it had been created in the infancy of the science, it might probably have had the same good fortune as the hypotheses respecting heat, light, and electricity.

After arranging the physical sciences in the following order, *Barology, Thermology, Acoustics, Optics*, and *Electrology*, our author proceeds, in separate Lectures, to give a general view of each of these sciences. These Lectures are marked with the same sagacity which characterises every portion of his work, and contain many valuable discussions, and much interesting information. We must confess, however, that we have not perused with any degree of satisfaction our author's Lecture on optics. It is a meagre abstract both of the early and the recent history of the science; and passes over in a superficial notice, and without any adequate praise, the splendid discoveries of his own distinguished countrymen. Although many just and sagacious observations are scattered through this Lecture, yet we are strongly impressed with the conviction that our author is but imperfectly acquainted with the recent acquisitions which the science has made; and this opinion is confirmed by his repeated denunciations of the undulatory theory as an assumption utterly fantastical, and calculated only to check the progress of legitimate discovery.

This grave error, which we should not have expected from so sound a reasoner, appears to originate from two causes—from his excluding all hypotheses as unscientific which bear on 'the mode of production of phenomena,' and from his not being aware of the actual power of the undulatory theory in *predicting* as well as in explaining phenomena. The hypotheses which our author condemns may be arranged in three classes—those which serve no other purpose than that of all artificial memory to group and recall insulated facts; those which afford an explanation of facts otherwise unintelligible without making any assumption incompatible with our positive knowledge; and those which to this condition unite the still more important one of being able to *predict* new facts, and extend by real discoveries the bounds of our positive knowledge.

The first of these classes of hypotheses is a very humble one; but even in its simply *mnemonic* character we are not disposed to reject its aid. Though it can neither *explain* nor *predict* phenomena, it may direct the enquirer, and even lead to discovery. If in beating the bush which has no foliage we occasionally start the noblest game—the very act of putting the most unpromising speculation to the ordeal of experiment may sometimes confound error, or elicit truth:—By pursuing even the track of the mole we may discover the mine which is to be sprung beneath our feet. The same observations are applicable *a fortiori* to the *second* class of hypotheses, and still more emphatically to the *third*, which claims the transcendent merit of predicting new phenomena.

Now, though the undulatory theory does assume an *ether*, invisible, intangible, imponderable, inseparable from all bodies, and extending from our own eye to the remotest verge of the starry heavens; yet, as the expounder of phenomena the most complex, and otherwise inexplicable; and as the predicter of highly important facts, it must contain among its assumptions (though, as a physical theory, it may still be false) some principle which is inherent in, and inseparable from, the real producing cause of the phenomena of light, and to this extent it is worthy of our adoption as a valuable instrument of discovery, and of our admiration as an ingenious and fertile philosophical conception.

The hostility and strong feeling of contempt with which M. Comte delights to speak of this theory, and contrast it with the thermological researches of Baron Fourier, may have been excited by those extreme eulogies, which have been pronounced upon it in this country. When a philosopher of the Cambridge school not only announces the undulatory theory as a reality, and capable of explaining all the varied phenomena of light, but calls upon us to praise God for having created the luminiferous ether, it is scarcely to be wondered at that men more cautious in their judgments should be driven into the opposite extreme by such ludicrous extravagances.

In such scientific collisions, however, the direct interests of truth are too often sacrificed to the impulses of ambition and vanity. He who regards the labyrinth of science as already traced, will not be disposed to follow out its windings; and he who thinks that it will lead to nothing will not enter cheerfully its most inviting paths. It was scarcely to have been expected that, in the era of positive knowledge, conflicting heresies like these should have sprung up amongst the physical sciences. In lamenting their existence, we must lament still more the unbecoming spirit in which they have been propagated. If they do not shake the Temple of Science, they cannot fail to disquiet its sanctuary. It is, however, some consolation that the leading combatants are not men who have added much to positive discovery; and that those who are destined to maintain the vestal fire on its altar are not likely to disturb the flame which has been fanned by themselves.

In the preceding sketch of the objects and methods of positive knowledge, we have viewed from a distance almost infinite the vast panorama of creation—in the foreground the worlds of the solar system—in the middle distance the binary creations of remote suns—and on the farthest verge of space the embryo systems of uncompleted worlds. In this survey of the universe the mind is alone occupied with the grand ideas of magnitude and distance. Unconscious even of its own being, everything that thinks and breathes is excluded from its contemplation. Nature appears only in the lonely grandeur of her dumb and inanimate creations; and no voice is heard save that which proclaims the power and glory of her King. Retiring within our own system, we feel ourselves at home amidst primary and secondary worlds. Our own planet and its humble attendant break upon our view. Its everlasting hills—its wide-spreading ocean—its empires—rise successively to the eye. The flood and field, the hill and valley of our youth—the habitations of man—life and all its glories—home and all its endearments—intrench us again in the mysterious position from which our reason and our imagination had transported us. Overwhelmed with a painful sense of its own littleness, and learning in the very width of their range the weakness of its faculties, the Mind pants after new powers of thought and of action, and longs for the development of that mighty plan which we 'know but in part, and see but in part.'

John Stuart Mill (essay date 1841)

SOURCE: A letter to Auguste Comte on November 8, 1841, in *The Correspondence of John Stuart Mill and Auguste Comte,* edited and translated by Oscar A. Haac, Transaction Publishers, 1995, pp. 35-6.

[*In the following letter to Comte, Mill discusses his intellectual indebtedness to Comte and his system.*]

I don't know, Sir, whether someone completely unknown to you may take a few moments of time as precious as yours, to tell you about himself and the great intellectual debt he owes you; but with the encouragement of my friend, Mr. Marrast, and believing that, in the midst of your great philosophical enterprises, you would perhaps not be entirely displeased to receive an expression of sympathy and support from abroad, I dare hope that you will not judge my present letter inappropriate.

It was in the year 1828, dear Sir, that I read your short essay on Positive Polity for the first time, and this reading gave my ideas a strong jolt which, along with other causes but much more than they, was responsible for my definitive leaving the Bentham section of the revolutionary school in which I grew up; I can almost say in which was born. Although Benthamism has doubtless remained very far from the true spirit of the positive method, this doctrine appears to me even today the best preparation for true positivity, applied to social doctrines: be it on account of its tight logic and the care it always takes to understand itself, be it above all because it categorically refuses all attempts to explain any kind of phenomenon by ridiculous metaphysical entities, the essential worthlessness of which it taught me to feel from earliest youth.

I believe that I can say that ever since the time when I learned of the first sketch of your ideas on sociology, the seeds sown by this small volume did not stay fruitless in my mind. However, it was only in 1837 that I came to know the first volumes of your *Course.* Fortunately I was rather well-prepared to appreciate its importance, since none of the basic sciences were entirely foreign to me. I had, incidentally, always concentrated on the methodology that they might provide. Since the happy moment when I came to know these two volumes, I am always looking forward to each additional volume with keen impatience; I read it and reread it with true intellectual passion. I can say that I was already embarked in a direction rather akin to yours; but I still had to learn from you many matters of the utmost importance, and I hope to give you new proof in the near future that I have learned them well. There remain some questions of secondary rank, where my opinions do not agree with yours; one day this disagreement may well disappear. At least I believe that I do not flatter myself excessively when I say: I hold no ill-founded opinion so deeply rooted as to resist thorough discussion, such as it would encounter if you do not mind my submitting my ideas to you periodically and asking for explanations of yours.

You know, dear Sir, that religion has so far had deeper roots in our country than in the rest of Europe, even though it has lost, here as elsewhere, its traditional cultural value, and I consider it regrettable that the revolutionary philosophy, which a dozen or so years ago still was in full swing, today has fallen into neglect before completing its task. It is all the more urgent that we replace it by embarking on the path of positive philosophy: and it is with great pleasure that I can tell you that, in spite of the openly antireligious spirit of your work, this great monument of the truly modern philosophy begins to make headway here, less however among political theorists than among various kinds of scientists. Incidentally, we now come to notice for the first time, among those who cultivate the physical sciences, a rather pronounced tendency toward scientific generalities, which appears as a good omen to me and leads me to believe that we can expect more of these scientists than of political thinkers, be they theorists or men of action. Indeed, the latter have fallen as low as those in France since 1830, and everyone understands that we can undertake new things only with a new doctrine; only, most of them do not as yet believe in the advent of such a new doctrine, and consequently remain in their skepticism, which becomes ever more enervating and discouraging.

Please excuse this somewhat presumptuous attempt, dear Sir, of entering directly into intellectual communication with the one great mind of our time, whom I respect and admire most. And please believe that the realization of this wish would be for me of immense value.

G. H. Lewes (essay date 1853)

SOURCE: "The Future," in *Comte's Philosophy of the Sciences: Being an Exposition of the Principles of the Cours de philosophie positive of Auguste Comte,* 1853. Reprint by George Bell and Sons, 1878, pp. 327-38.

[*In the following essay, Lewes considers Comte's Law of Three States and his class system.*]

Guided by his logical principles of the general extension of the Positive Method to the rational study of social phenomena, Comte has gradually applied to the whole of the past his fundamental law of the evolution at once mental and social, consisting in the passage of humanity through three successive states: the preparatory Theological state, the transitory Metaphysical state, and the final Positive state. By the aid of this single law he has explained all the great historical phases, considered as the principal consecutive phases of development, so as rightly to appreciate the true character proper to each of them, with the natural emanation of one phase from the preceding, and its tendency towards the following phase: whence results the conception of a homogeneous and continuous connection in the whole series of anterior ages, from the first manifestation of sociality, to the most advanced condition of mankind.

A law which has sufficed to fulfil adequately these conditions is no mere philosophical fancy, but must contain an abstract expression of the reality. It can be employed with rational security in connecting the future with the past. The foremost portion of mankind, after having exhausted the successive phases of Theological life, and even the different degrees of metaphysical transition, is now approaching the completely positive state, the principal elements of which have already sufficiently received their partial elaboration, and now only await their general co-ordination to constitute a new social system.

This co-ordination must be first intellectual, then moral, and lastly, political. Every attempt rising from any other logical source would be utterly powerless against the present state of disorder which is essentially mental. As long as this disorder remains, no durable institution can be possible, for want of a solid basis; and our social condition will admit of only provisionary political measures, destined for the most part to guarantee the maintenance of a degree of material Order against ambitions everywhere excited by the gradual diffusion and extension of spiritual anarchy. To fulfil this office, all governments, whatever be their form, will continue necessarily to count as they do upon nothing but a vast system of corruption, assisted, on occasions of necessity, by a repressive force.

Nothing of what is at present classed is capable of being directly incorporated in the final system, all the elements of which must previously undergo an entire intellectual and moral regeneration: thus the future spiritual power, the first basis of a genuine reorganization, will reside in an entirely new class, having no analogy with any of those now existing, and originally composed of members issuing indifferently, according to their peculiar individual vocation, from all ranks of society; the gradual arrival at this salutary incorporation will be also essentially spontaneous, since its social ascendancy can result only from the voluntary assents of all intelligences to the new doctrines successively worked out: so that by its nature such an authority could neither be decreed nor interdicted.

As we have recognized in principle that the evolution of mankind is characterized by a perpetually increasing *influence* of the speculative over the active life, although the latter will always preserve the *actual* ascendancy, it would be contradictory to suppose that the contemplative part of man will remain for ever deprived of proper cultivation and distinct direction in a social state in which intelligence will have the most habitual exercise, even among the lowest classes.

At a time when all thinking minds admit the necessity of a permanent division between theory and practice for the simultaneous perfecting of both, in the least important subjects to which our efforts are directed, can we hesitate to extend this healthy principle to the most difficult and most important operations, when such a progress has become sufficiently realizable? Now, under the purely mental aspect, the separation of the two powers, spiritual and temporal, is in fact the mere exterior manifestation of the same distinction between science and art, transferred to social ideas, and made systematic.

While spiritual reorganization is the most urgent, it is also, in spite of the great difficulties attending it, the best prepared amongst the most advanced minds. On one hand, existing governments renouncing the task of directing such an operation, tend thereby to confer this high office upon that philosophical system which shall prove worthy of presiding over it. On the other hand, the populations radically freed from metaphysical illusions by the teaching of half a century of decisive experiments, begin to understand that all the social progress compatible with current doctrines has been accomplished, and that no important political institution can now arise which is not based upon an entirely new philosophy.

The general principle which determines the separation between the respective attributes of spiritual and temporal power consists in considering the spiritual authority *as decisive* in all that concerns education, whether special or general, and merely *deliberative* in all that concerns action, whether private or public, its habitual interference being only to recall in every case the rules of conduct previously established. The temporal authority, on the contrary, entirely absolute as far as regards action, to the extent of being able, under responsibility as to results, to follow a line of conduct opposed to the corresponding authority, cannot exercise more than a simple *deliberative* influence over education, being limited to solicit the revision or partial modification of the precepts apparently condemned by practice.

It is principally as a general basis to such a system that the Positive Philosophy must be previously coordinated and established, destined as it is to furnish henceforward to the human mind a resting-place, by means of a homogeneous and hierarchical series of positive ideas, at once logical and scientific, upon all orders of phenomena, from the lowest to the most eminent moral and social phenomena.

Positive education will be principally characterized by the final systematization of human ethics, which, freed from all theological conceptions, will rest on positive philosophy. The indefinite dispersion of religious creeds left to individuals will prevent anything being established on such insecure foundations. What philosophical inconsistency can be compared to that of our deists, whose dream is now the consecration of morality, by a religion without a revelation, without a worship, and without a clergy?

Humanity must be looked upon as still in a state of infancy, as long as its principal rules of conduct, instead of being drawn from a just appreciation of its own nature, shall continue to rest upon extraneous fictions. Such is the general aim, nature, and character of the spiritual reorganization which must necessarily commence and direct the entire regeneration, towards which we have seen the permanent course of all the different social movements, since the middle ages, more or less directly converge.

As to the temporal reorganization, we will confine ourselves to the general principle of the elementary coordination of modern society.

In proceeding to do this, we must set aside the distinction between the two sorts of functions, *public* and *private*. In every truly constituted social body, each member may, and ought to be, considered as a public functionary, inasmuch as his particular activity concurs with the general economy.

The dignity which still animates the most obscure soldier in the exercise of his humblest duties, is certainly not peculiar to the military order; it belongs equally to everything that is systematic; it will one day ennoble the simplest profession, when Positive Education, causing a just general notion of modern sociality to prevail everywhere, shall have made it sufficiently understood by all, that each partial activity has a continuous participation in the common economy. Thus the general cessation of the division now existing between private and public professions, depends necessarily upon the universal regeneration of modern ideas and manners.

Although this final elevation of private professions to the dignity of public functions will certainly make no essential change in the existing mode of exercising them, it will entirely transform their general spirit, and probably have a considerable effect upon their usual conditions. Whilst on the one hand such a normal appreciation will develop in all classes a noble personal feeling of their social value, it will on the other hand make evident the permanent necessity of a certain systematic discipline, tending to guarantee the preliminary and continuous obligations proper to every career. In one word, this simple change will constitute spontaneously an universal symptom of regeneration.

In every society, whatever be its nature and destination, each different partial activity becomes classed according to the degree of generality which distinguishes its habitual character. Consequently the real philosophical difficulty in this matter consists in the true appreciation of the different degrees of generality inherent in the different functions of the positive organism.

Now this has already been almost entirely accomplished, although with another intention. Social progress, in fact, first presented itself to us as a sort of necessary prolongation of the animal series, in which beings are the more elevated the nearer they approach to the human type; whilst, on the other hand, the human evolution is especially characterized by its constant tendency to make those essential attributes predominant which distinguish man from the animal. Such is the first basis which positive philosophy will naturally furnish to social classification.

The first application of this hierarchical theory to the new social economy leads us to conceive the *speculative* class as superior to the *active* class, since the first affords a wider field for the exercise of the faculties of generalization and abstraction which form the great distinction of human nature. For this purpose, however, it is first necessary that the members of this speculative class should be sufficiently freed from that *speciality* in their studies and ideas, which we have seen to be a decided obstacle to the elaboration of a Philosophy, although originally indispensable an a division of labour.

The speculative class separates itself into two distinct parts, according to the two very different directions taken by the contemplative spirit, sometimes philosophical or scientific, sometimes aesthetic or poetical. Whatever the social importance of the Fine Arts, it is unquestionable that the aesthetic point of view is less abstract and less general than the philosophical or aesthetic. The latter has immediate relation to the fundamental conceptions destined to direct the universal exercise of human reason, whereas the other merely relates to the faculty of expression, which can never occupy the first rank in our mental system.

The active or practical class, which necessarily embraces an immense majority in its more distinct and complete development, has already made its essential divisions appreciable: so that with respect to them the hierarchical theory has only to systematize the distinctions hitherto consecrated by use. To this end we must consider first the principal division of industrial activity into *production*, properly so called, and the *transmission of products*. The second is evidently superior to the first, as regards the abstract nature of its operations, and the generality of its relations.

After dividing the active or practical class into two principal categories, one of which confines itself to production, while the other employs itself in the transmission of products, Comte again subdivides each of these into two according as the production is that of *simple materials,* or their *direct employment,* and as the transmission refers to the *products themselves* or merely to their *representative signs.* It is plain that of these two divisions the last has a more general and abstract character than the preceding one, conformably to our established rule of classification. These two divisions constitute the real industrial hierarchy: placing in the highest rank the Bankers, by reason of the superior generality and abstract nature of their operations; next the Merchants, then the Manufacturers, and lastly the Agriculturists, whose labours are necessarily more concrete, and whose relations are more restricted than those of the other three practical classes.

By an easy combination of the preceding indications every one may form a conception of the positive econ-omy. The normal classification resulting from it will be naturally consolidated by its homogeneity: since in this hierarchy no class can refuse to recognize the superior dignity of the preceding one, except by immediately altering his own position towards the one following, the uniformity of the principle of co-ordination being constant. The same hierarchical principle extended to domestic life, comprises the true law of the subordination of the sexes.

By imposing moral obligations, more extensive and more strict in proportion as social influences become more general, the fundamental education will directly tend also to the abuses inherent in these necessary inequalities. It is clear, too, that these different elementary tendencies of the new economy cannot obtain their social efficacy until a system of universal education shall have sufficiently developed the attributes and manners which must distinguish these different classes, and of which we can form no idea in the present confused state of things.

Considered with regard to the degrees of material preponderance, henceforward measurable principally by wealth, our statical series presents necessarily opposite results according as we examine the speculative or the active class: for in the former the preponderance diminishes, while in the latter it augments, as we ascend in the hierarchy. If, for example, the first cooperation, seen in a purely industrial point of view, of the grand astronomical discoveries which have brought material arts to their present perfection, could be duly appreciated in every expedition, it is evident that no existing fortune could give any idea of the monstrous accumulation of riches which would thus have been realized by the temporal heirs of a Kepler, a Newton, &c., even if their partial remuneration were fixed at the lowest rate. Nothing can serve better than such hypotheses to demonstrate the absurdity of the pretended principle relative to an uniformly pecuniary remuneration for all real services; proving as they do that the most extensive usefulness, inasmuch as it is too distant and too much diffused in consequence of its superior generality, can never find its just recompense except in the higher social consideration it enjoys.

From these remarks it is clear that the principal pecuniary ascendancy will reside in about the middle of the entire hierarchy, in the class of bankers, naturally placed at the head of the industrial movement, and whose ordinary operations have precisely the degree of generality most proper for the accumulation of capital. Here it is that we shall find the principal ultimate seat of temporal power, properly so called. We must remark also, on this subject, that this class will always be by its nature the least numerous of the industrial classes; for in general the positive hierarchy will necessarily present an increasing numerical extension in proportion as its labours becoming more special and more urgent, admit and require at once more multifarious agents.

After this sociological summary it would surely be superfluous to add any direct explanation of the necessarily mobile composition of the various classes making up the positive hierarchy. Universal education is eminently fitted in this respect, without exciting any disturbing ambitions, to place every one in the situation most suitable to his principal aptitudes, in whatever rank he may have been born. This happy influence, far more dependent by its nature upon public opinion than upon political institutions, demands two opposite conditions both equally indispensable, the fulfillment of which will in no wise assail the essential basis of the general economy. On the one hand it is necessary that the access to every social career should remain constantly open to just individual pretensions, and that nevertheless, on the other hand, the exclusion of the unworthy should be always practicable according to the common appreciation of the normal guarantees, both intellectual and moral, which the fundamental education will have prescribed for every important case.

Doubtless after the present existing confusion shall have terminated in some primary regular classification, such changes, although always possible, will become essentially exceptional, being considerably neutralized by the natural tendency to hereditary professions: for the greater number of men have in reality no special vocation, and at the same time the greater number of the social functions require none; which will naturally leave a great habitual efficacy to imitation, except in the very rare cases of a real predisposition.

It would besides be evidently chimerical to dread the ultimate transformation of classes into castes, in an economy entirely free from the theological principle: for it is clear that castes could never have any solid existence without a religious consecration. Puerile terror on this score must not be made the occasion or pretext for an indefinite opposition to every true social classification, when the preponderance of the positive spirit, always in its nature accessible to a wide discussion, will be able to dissipate the anxieties raised by the vague and absolute character of theologico-metaphysical conceptions.

Let us now consider the great spiritual reorganization of modern society, pointing out its intimate connection with the just social reclamations of the lower classes. Every spiritual power should be essentially popular, since its most extended sphere of duty relates to the constant protection of the most numerous classes, habitually the most exposed to oppression, and with which the education common to all leads it into daily contact. In the final state the spiritual class will be connected with the popular mass by common sympathies, consequent upon a certain similitude of situation, and parallel habits of material improvidence, as well as by analogous interests with regard to the temporal chiefs, necessarily possessors of the principal wealth.

But we must especially remark the extreme popular efficacy of speculative authority, whether by reason of its office of universal education, or because of the regular interference which, according to our previous indications, it will always exercise in the different conflicts of society: thereby developing suitably the mediatory influence habitually attendant on the elevation of its views, and the generosity of its inclinations. Narrow views and malignant passions will in vain attempt to institute legally laborious hindrances against the accumulation of capital, at the risk of paralyzing directly all real social activity. It is clear that these tyrannical proceedings will have much less real efficacy than the universal reprobation applied by the positive ethics to any utterly selfish use of the wealth possessed.

When the new speculative class shall have arisen, the great practical collisions continually becoming more numerous in the total absence of any industrial systematization, will doubtless constitute the principal occasions of its social development, by making apparent to all classes the increasing utility of its active moral intervention, alone capable of sufficiently tempering material antagonism, and of habitually modifying the opposing sentiments of envy and disdain inspired on either hand. The classes most disposed at present to recognize the real ascendancy which wealth enjoys, will then be led by decisive and probably melancholy experience to implore the necessary protection of that very spiritual power which they now look upon as essentially chimerical.

It is in this manner that a power which by its nature can rest on no other foundation than that of its universal free recognition, will be gradually established on the ground of the services rendered by it. The popular point of view is henceforward the only one which can spontaneously offer at once sufficient grandeur and distinctness to be able to place the minds of men in a truly organic direction.

The unavailing changes of individuals, ministerial or even royal, which appear of so much importance to the various present factions, will naturally become quite indifferent to the people, whose own social interests can in no wise be affected thereby.

The assurance of education and work to every one will always constitute the sole essential object of popular policy properly so called: now this great end, perfectly separated from constitutional discussions and combinations, can never be adequately attained but by a real reorganization; first and foremost spiritual; afterwards necessarily temporal.

Such is the connection which the entire situation of modern society institutes between popular necessities and philosophical tendencies, and according to which the true social point of view will gradually prevail in proportion as the active intervention of the People, speaking in their name, begins to characterize more and more the grand political problem.

Emile Durkheim (essay date 1895)

SOURCE: "Sociology and the Social Sciences (1903)," in *The Rules of Sociological Method, and Selected Texts on Sociology and Its Method,* edited by Steven Lukes, translated by W. D. Halls, The Macmillan Press Ltd, 1982, pp. 175-208.

[In the following essay, originally written in 1895, Durkheim discusses Comte's conception of sociology.]

Engendered within a philosophy, sheer necessity obliged sociology from the beginning to display the distinctive character of any philosophical discipline: a leaning towards general, overall views and, in contrast, a certain indifference to factual details and specialist investigations. Consequently it was natural for it to develop untrammelled by any special techniques, as an autonomous mode of speculation, capable of being self-sufficient. This stance was moreover justified by the state in which the sciences then were and by the spirit which infused them, one which on these essential points was radically opposed to that on which the new science proceeded. Not without reason does Comte reproach political economy in his day with not being a truly positivist science, but with still being shot through with metaphysical philosophy, lingering over sterile discussions on the elementary notions of value, utility and production. Such discussions, he declares, recall 'the strange debates of the medieval Schoolmen about the basic attributes of their pure, metaphysical entities'. Moreover, the general admission by economists of 'the necessary isolation of their so-called science in relation to social philosophy in general' justifiably appeared to him to constitute 'an involuntary recognition, decisive though indirect, of the scientific uselessness of that theory. . . . For, by the very nature of the subject, in social studies as in all those relating to living objects, by force of necessity the various general aspects are solidly linked to one another and are rationally inseparable, to the point where they can only be clearly elucidated by reference to one another'. In fact [it] is certain that the notion of natural law as understood by Comte was unknown to economic science. Undoubtedly the economists freely used the word 'law', but on their lips it possessed none of the meaning that it had in the sciences of nature. It did not connote relationships between facts, objectively observable among things, but purely logical connexions between concepts formed in entirely ideological fashion.

For the economist the task was not to discover what occurs in reality or investigate how stated effects derive from causes that are likewise stated, but mentally to combine purely formal notions such as value, utility, scarcity, supply and demand. The same charge could be levelled against the most current theories concerning law and morality—that of Montesquieu no less than of Kant.

For such diverse reasons, therefore, sociology could only achieve a consciousness of itself within the framework of philosophical thinking, remote from special disciplines and their influence. Indeed this characteristic sprang from causes too deep-seated to be entirely abandoned from the moment when the science began to be organised. Thus it is in no way surprising to discover that it recurs with Spencer, Comte's immediate successor. It is abundantly plain that Spencer worked on sociology as a philosopher, because he did not set out to study social facts in themselves and for their own sake, but in order to demonstrate how the hypothesis of evolution is verified in the social realm. But in so doing he was able to complement and correct in important respects the general conceptions of Comtean sociology. Although Comte had definitively integrated societies with nature, the excessive intellectualism which marked his doctrine was not easily reconcilable with that fundamental axiom of all sociology. If scientific evolution determines political, economic, moral and aesthetic evolution, a wide gulf separates sociological explanations from those employed in the other sciences of nature, so that it is difficult to avoid relapsing into ideology. By showing that under different forms the same law governs the social and the physical worlds, Spencer narrowed the gap between societies and the rest of the universe. He gave us a sense that, beneath the facts produced on the surface of the collective consciousness—facts which are interpreted as being the fruits of reflective thinking—obscure forces are at work which do not move men to act out of that sheer logical necessity which links together the successive phases of scientific development. On the other hand Comte did not admit that a large number of social types existed. According to him, only one society existed, the association of mankind in its totality; the various states represented only different moments in the history of that one society. Sociology was therefore placed in a peculiar position among all the sciences, since the object of study was an entity of a unique kind. Spencer disposed of this anomaly by showing that societies, like organisms, can be classified into genera and species and, whatever the merits of the classification he proposed, the principle at least was worthy of retention and has in fact survived. Although elaborated in philosophical terms, these two reforms thus represented invaluable gains for the science.

Yet if this way of understanding and developing sociology has at a given moment in time certainly been necessary and useful, that necessity and usefulness proved only temporary. To build itself up and even take its first steps forward, sociology needed to rely upon a philosophy. But to become truly itself, it was indispensable for it to assume a different character.

The very example of Comte can serve to prove this point, for because of its philosophical character, the sociology he constructed was in no position to satisfy any of the conditions which he himself demanded for any positivist science.

In fact, of the two divisions that he distinguished in sociology, the static and the dynamic, he really treated only the latter. From his viewpoint this was moreover the more important, for if, according to him, social facts exist distinct from purely individual phenomena, this is chiefly because a progressive evolution of humanity occurs. It is because the work of each generation survives it and is aggregated to that of succeeding generations. Progress is the paramount social fact. Thus social dynamism, as he expounded it, in no way presents 'that continuity and that fecundity' which, as Comte himself observed, constitute 'the least equivocal symptoms of all truly scientific conceptions', for he himself considered that he had finally explained social dynamism in broad terms. In fact, it is contained wholly in the law of the three stages. Once this law had been discovered it was impossible to see how it could be added to or extended, and even less so, how different laws might be discovered. The science was already complete before it had hardly been founded. In fact those disciples of Comte who adhered closely to the substance of his doctrine could do no more than reproduce the propositions of their master, sometimes illustrating them with new examples, but without such purely formal variants ever constituting truly new discoveries. This explains the full stop to the development of the strictly Comtean school after Comte's death; the same formulae were religiously repeated without any progress being realised. This is because a science cannot live and develop when it is reduced to one single problem on which, at an ever-increasing distance in time, a great mind has placed its seal. For progress to be accomplished, the science must resolve itself into an increasingly large number of specific questions, so as to render possible co-operation between different minds and between successive generations. Only upon this condition will it have the collective, impersonal character without which there is no scientific research. But the philosophical and unitary conception which Comte imposed upon sociology ran counter to this division of labour. Thus his social dynamics are in the end only a philosophy of history, remarkable for its profundity and novel character, but constructed on the model of earlier philosophies. The task is to discern the law which controls 'the necessary and continuous movement of humanity', which alone will allow insertion into the succession of historical

events the unity and continuity which they lack. But Bossuet set himself no other task. The method varies, as does the solution, but the investigation is no different in kind.

Yet, despite the lesson that could have been learnt from the failure of such an attempt, sociology has remained for most of our contemporaries approximately what it was for Comte, as essentially philosophical speculation. Over the last twenty years we have seen a veritable flowering of sociological literature. Its production, once intermittent and sparse, has become continuous; new systems have been constructed and others are being constructed every day. But they are always, or almost always, systems in which the entire science is more or less undisguisedly reduced to a single problem. As with Comte and Spencer, the task is to discover the law which governs social evolution as a whole. For some it is the law of imitation, for others it is the law of adaptation, or the struggle for survival and, more particularly, the struggle between races. For yet another it is the influence of the physical environment, etc. Really, as we survey all these seekers after the supreme law, the cause which dominates all causes, the 'key which opens all locks', we cannot help thinking of the alchemists of former days in their search for the philosopher's stone.

Far from there having been any progress, rather has there been regression. For Comte, at least sociology was the complete science of social facts, encompassing the multifarious aspects of collective life. No category of phenomena was systematically excluded from it. If Comte refused to regard political economy as a sociological science, it is because in his day it was treated in a thoroughly unscientific spirit and because it mistook the true nature of social reality. But in no way did he intend to place economic facts beyond the pale of sociology. Consequently the way remained open for a further division of labour, for an increasing specialisation in problems, as the domain of the science was extended and its complexity more fully grasped. The very opposite has occurred. The latest sociologists have gradually developed the idea that sociology is distinct from the social sciences, that there is a general social science which contrasts with these special disciplines, one with its own subject matter, its own special method, to which is reserved the name of sociology. Starting from the fact that the social sciences have been constituted outside the great philosophical syntheses which gave rise to the word sociology, it has been concluded from this that there must exist two kinds of investigations clearly different in kind, and efforts have been made to differentiate between them. Whilst each science specialises in a determinate category of social phenomena, it has been stated that sociology has as its subject collective life in general. It is by virtue of this designation as being a *general* social science that it constitutes a distinct and individual entity.

L. Levy-Bruhl (essay date 1900)

SOURCE: "Conclusion," in *The Philosophy of August Comte,* Swan Sonnenschein & Co. Lim., 1903, pp. 343-63.

[In the following essay, Levy-Bruhl contrasts Comte's philosophy with the metaphysics that preceded it.]

At the end of the **Cours de philosophie positive** Comte has himself summed up the results which he believed himself to have established. In the first place it is, from the intellectual point of view (which at first takes precedence of all others, although, in the positive state, the mind must be subject to the heart), a "perfect mental coherence which, as yet, has never been able to exist in a like degree," not even in the primitive period when man explained the phenomena of nature by the action of wills. For already, in this period, although imperceptibly, the positive spirit was making itself felt, while, in the positive period, nothing will subsist of the theological and metaphysical mode of thought. From the moral point of view, which comes next, the agreement of minds upon speculative problems, and in particular upon the relations between man and humanity, will allow of a common education, which will bring about ardent moral conviction in all. Powerful "public prejudices" will develop, and with them, such irresistible fullness of conviction, according to Comte, that Humanity will be able to realise what our penal system is incapable of achieving: to prevent instead of punishing, at least in the majority of cases. From the political point of view, the two spiritual and temporal powers will be duly separated, and a lasting organisation will at once insure order and progress. Finally, from the aesthetic point of view, a new art will appear. No longer an aristocratic and learned art like the one which has been with us since the Renaissance, but an art closely connected with the convictions and the life of all, which will be accessible and familiar to all, as was the case with the art of the Middle Ages. The positive conception of man and of the world, will become an "inexhaustible spring" of poetical beauty.

All these results will be ordered, protected and sanctified by the positive religion, or religion of Humanity, of which Auguste Comte, in his "second career," established the dogma, the worship and the *régime.*

Without entering into the details of this religious construction we see that, like the ethics and the politics, it depends upon the "perfect mental coherence" founded, in the first place, by positive philosophy. In its turn, this perfect mental coherence, reduces itself to the unity of the understanding, whose necessary and sufficient conditions are "homogeneity of doctrine and unity of method." Now, when Comte began to write, this homogeneity and this unity already existed for all the categories of natural phenomena. The moral and social phenomena alone were still an exception. In conclusion everything was reduced to this question: "can moral and social facts be studied in the same way as the other natural phenomena?" If not, we must be resigned to the indefinite duration of the disorder of minds, and consequently of the disorder of customs and institutions. But, if the contrary is true, then the human understanding reaches the unity to which it aspires. Is sociology impossible? then we have no politics and no religion. Is sociology founded? then all the rest is based upon it.

Thus, the creation of social science is the decisive moment in Comte's philosophy. Everything starts from it and comes back to it. As in Platonism, all paths lead to the theory of ideas, so, from all the avenues of positivism we see sociology. Here, as in a common centre, are joined the sciences, the theory of knowledge, the philosophy of history, psychology, ethics, politics and religion. Here, in a word, is realised the unity of system, a unity which, in Comte's eyes, is the best proof of its truth.

If, in sociology, we chiefly consider the end which Comte proposes to attain by its means, it is true that this doctrine is principally a political one, and the very title of Comte's second great work bears this out. But, considered in itself, it is essentially a speculative effort, and the principle of a philosophy in the proper sense of the term. What Kant called a totality of experience is made possible by the creation of social science.

Before Comte, this totality had been attempted many times. But those who attempted it started from this postulate that philosophy is specifically distinct from scientific knowledge proper. Whether philosophy were dogmatic or critical, whether it had bearings upon the essence of things or rather upon the laws of the mind, it none the less presented characteristics of its own, which seemed to separate it from positive science, and even allowed it to dominate over this science, and to "explain" its principles. Comte rejects this postulate. He is going to endeavour to see if, by taking the contrary postulate as his foundation, he will not succeed better than his predecessors.

In order to reject the postulate admitted by philosophers before him, he appeals at the same time to arguments founded on facts and demonstration; but we must notice that, in his doctrine, these two orders of arguments logically reduce themselves to one another. Indeed he says, up to the present time no philosophy which commands acceptance by all minds has been established. Idealisms, materialisms, pantheisms from all sources and in every shape have never done more than ruin the doctrines opposed to them, without becoming finally established themselves. Those systems claimed to give a rational knowledge of that which by nature is beyond the reach of science. They prided themselves upon explaining the essence, the cause, the end and the order of the phenomena of the universe. Thus they could only build up temporary conceptions which were undoubtedly indispensable at the time but which were doomed to die. Metaphysics is never anything but a rationalized theology which is weakened by this very fact, and deprived of what constituted its strength during the period when it was an object of belief.

But in the name of what principle can Comte discern what is and what is not "beyond the reach of science?" In order to justify a distinction of this kind should he not before everything begin by a criticism of the human mind, that is to say by a theory of knowledge similar to that proposed by Kant in his "Criticism of Pure Reason"? M. Renouvier endeavours to show that, through the absence of this preliminary criticism, with which Comte dispensed, his philosophy remains superficial. Mr. Max Muller expressly says that there is no need to take into account a philosophical doctrine which proceeds as if the "Criticism of Pure Reason" had not been written.

On the whole the objection reduces itself to reproaching Comte with not having attempted to do what he considered to be impracticable: namely, not to have determined the intellectual laws by the analysis of the mind reflecting upon itself. But, it is said, by what right does he affirm that this is impossible? Because, like all the others, these laws can only be discovered by means of the observation of facts, and because the only method which is suitable for the discovery of intellectual facts is the sociological method: the nature of these facts being such that, especially from the dynamic point of view, they can only be grasped in the evolution of humanity. The theory of knowledge demanded by M. Renouvier and Mr. Max Muller is not wanted in positive philosophy. It is not seen in this philosophy, because it is not presented in its traditional form. It is there none the less; but, instead of consisting in an analysis *a priori* of thought, as a preliminary to philosophy, it is not separated from the philosophy itself. It is one of the many aspects of sociology.

In the positive doctrine, as in all the others, there are dialectics—dialectics which are no longer abstract and logical, but real and historical. They do not seek to see the laws of the human mind through an effort at reflection in which the mind, beneath the phenomena, apprehends its very essence. They endeavour to discover these laws in the necessary sequence of periods which constitute the progress of the human mind. They, in their turn, study the "universal subject" whose forms, categories and principles have been determined by Kant *a priori*. But this universal subject is no longer reason grasping itself, so to speak, outside and above the conditions of time and of experience: it is the human mind becoming conscious of the laws of its activity

through the study of its own past. Instead of the "absolute ego" of "impersonal reason," or of the "conscience of the understanding," positive philosophy analyses the intellectual history of humanity. It has then neither ignored nor neglected the problem. It has put it in new terms, and has been obliged to deal with it by a new method.

The critic is free to point out the defects of this method and the insufficiency of these terms. But, to reproach positive philosophy with not having dealt with the problem in the usual form in which it is taken by metaphysicians, and, for this reason, to put it aside unexamined, is to commit a kind of "petitio principii." If Comte abstains from attempting an abstract theory of knowledge, he gives philosophical reasons for his refusal to do so. Before condemning him, it is but right to examine them. Had he done what M. Renouvier and Mr. Max Muller reproach him with having omitted, he would have contradicted himself. There would have been no reason for the existence of his system. He claimed to have reformed the very conception of philosophy: can we reproach him with the fact that his conception does not coincide with the view preferred by his adversaries? Briefly that which, according to Comte, characterises positive philosophy, is that it no longer requires for its constitution what in the judgment of M. Renouvier and Mr. Max Muller on the contrary, is indispensable. Are they or is he in the right? The question cannot evidently be solved by the mere affirmation of those interested. The examination of the doctrines themselves is necessary.

II

The position taken by Comte may be briefly defined in a few words. Seeing that philosophy, such at least as it had been conceived until the XIX. century, could not assume the characteristics of science, he asks himself whether one would not succeed better by endeavouring to give the characteristics of science to philosophy. Like Kant, he might have compared the revolution he was attempting to that accomplished by Copernicus in astronomy, had he not preferred to present it as prepared and gradually brought about by the very "progress" of science and philosophy.

According to his own expression then he endeavours "to transform science into philosophy." But on what conditions will the transformation be effected? If science were to lose in it its characteristics of positiveness, of reality, and of relativity, to assume those of a metaphysical doctrine, this change would be neither desirable nor possible. The transformation will simply consist in giving to science the philosophical character which it does not yet possess, namely universality. While thus acquiring a new property, positive science should lose none of those which it already possesses, and which constitute its value.

Thus, in the "transformation of science into philosophy," what is transformed at bottom is not science which remains itself while becoming general from being special: it is philosophy rather which is transformed. The latter will henceforth undoubtedly be conceived as the highest and most comprehensive form of positive knowledge, but as constituting a part of that knowledge. It has been said that Comte does away with philosophy, by reducing it to being merely the "generalisation of the highest results of the sciences." This is not a proper interpretation of his thought. Up to the present time the duties performed by the philosophical doctrines have been indispensable. Comte intends that his system shall fulfil them in future. Beside science properly so-called, which is always special, philosophy which represents the "point of view of the whole" must arise. On this condition alone can the government of minds and the "perfect logical coherence" become possible.

Philosophy will then not merely be a "generalisation of the highest results of the sciences." The synthesis of the sciences must be brought about according to a principle to which they will be all related. It must really be a "summing up of experience." But if this philosophy thus coalesces with science it must also be *real* like it, and all real knowledge is necessarily positive and relative. In short, the distinction between science and philosophy implies no specific difference between these two kinds of speculation. On the contrary, there exists between them homogeneity of doctrine and unity of method.

Therein lies the novelty of Comte's system. The question was, without leaving the scientific point of view, to discover a single universal conception of the whole of Reality as we find it in experience. The solution of this problem was found on the day when Comte created social science. For indeed, in the first place, sociology makes the positive method universal by extending it to the highest order of natural phenomena accessible to us. Moreover, once it is established as a special science, *ipso facto* it assumes the character of a universal science, and consequently of a philosophy. Under a certain aspect, sociology is the sixth and last of the fundamental sciences. Under another aspect it is the only science, since the other sciences may be regarded as great sociological facts, and since the whole of what is given to us is subordinated to the supreme idea of humanity.

Such is the way in which the transformation of science into philosophy takes place. If it dates from the foundation of sociology, it is because, once this last positive science has been created, nothing remains in nature of which we conceive the possibility of obtaining an absolute knowledge. "The relative character of scientific conception is necessarily inseparable from the true notion of natural laws, in the same way as the

chimerical tendency to absolute knowledge spontaneously accompanies whatever use we make of the logical fictions or of metaphysical entities."

Considered as a whole, the object of positive science, according to Comte, necessarily coincides with that of philosophy. For both of them it is the whole of the reality given to us. The human mind cannot exert itself in a vacuum. What it might draw from itself, without the help of experience, (if such a conception be not absurd), is purely fictitious, and has no objective value. If then the human mind remains attached to a metaphysical philosophy, this can only be in so far as the mind still conceives the whole or a part of reality from the absolute point of view, that is to say in so far as it still fails to understand that the laws of phenomena alone are within its reach, and persists in seeking the essence and the first or final cause for some among them. There was a time when the whole of reality was so understood. The conception of the world was then entirely metaphysical or partly theological. But the human mind has gradually constituted the positive science, first of the more simple and more general phenomena, and then of the more complicated ones. Finally the most complex of all, that is to say, the moral and social phenomena alone remained untouched by the scientific form. Let us suppose that this last order of facts is conquered by the positive method: the metaphysical mode of thought being no longer possessed of real objects, *ipso facto* disappears. At the same time the positive mode of thought becomes universal, and positive philosophy is founded.

In this way two great connected facts which occupy a considerable place in the philosophical history of our century are explained. We understand: 1. that the fate of metaphysics appears to be closely bound up with that of psychology, of ethics of the philosophy of history and of the moral sciences in general, while the connection between physics, for instance, and metaphysics seems to be very weak; 2. that the foundation of sociology determines that of positive philosophy. So long as psychology speculates upon the nature of the soul and upon the laws of thought; ethics, upon the final cause of man; the philosophy of history, upon the final cause of humanity; metaphysics remains standing. Indeed it seems better able than positive knowledge to lead the human mind to a conception of the whole of the real. It appears to be all the more appropriate for doing this in that the point of view of the Absolute can be easily made to harmonise with the point of view of the Universal, in the same way as the conception of substance, whatever it may be, leads without any difficulty to the conception of the unity of substance. But, from the day when we no longer should seek anything but the laws of psychical, moral and social facts, refraining from any hypothesis as to causes and essences, (a method already made use of for all the other categories of phenomena), three results would be obtained at a single blow: metaphysical philosophy would disappear, social science would be created, and positive philosophy would be founded.

According to the essential law of social dynamics, the metaphysical stage is never anything but a transitory one between the theological and the positive stages. The human intellect could not pass immediately from the former to the latter. The metaphysical stage which can assume an endless number of forms and of degrees, insensibly leads it from one to the other. Metaphysical philosophy partakes of the theological in so far as it claims to "explain" the totality of the Real by means of a first principle, and of the positive, in so far as it endeavours to demonstrate its "explanations," and to bring them into accordance with the real knowledge already acquired. It originates in theology and it ends in science. But, however near it may come to positive knowledge, its original theological brand is never effaced. Were they compelled to choose between the theological and the positive doctrines, metaphysicians would certainly adopt the former. The essence of metaphysical philosophy is to tend towards the absolute, whilst positive philosophy only seeks the relative. In favouring the progress of positive science, metaphysical philosophy was working to make itself useless.

To those then who reproach him with not leaving any function proper to philosophy, Comte would answer that, in his doctrine, philosophy is on the contrary better defined and more fully constituted than in any other. Indeed metaphysical philosophy has never been anything but a compromise, destined to satisfy more or less, the needs of theological explanation and of rational science. But positive philosophy is pure and unalloyed with heterogenous elements. It gives to the whole of experience all the intelligibility which we can hope for, through the discovery of laws, and, in particular, of the encyclopedic laws. By making humanity the supreme end at once of our speculation and of our activity, it furnishes morality and politics with a definite basis, and gives religion an object. In this way, according to Comte, positive philosophy is more truly a philosophy than metaphysics, since it secures the homogeneity of knowledge and the "perfect mental coherence," and it is also more truly religious since, as its final conclusion, it shows that the end of the intellect itself lies in devotion to humanity.

III

Every new philosophical doctrine is in general guided by a double tendency. At the same time it seeks to establish its originality and to find out its antecedents. In order to reach the former result, it criticises preceding and contemporary doctrines, and shows that, better than any of the others, it succeeds in "summing up experience." But, at the same time, it discovers a pedigree for itself in history which is never very difficult to establish.

Like the others, positive philosophy fulfills this twofold requirement, in such measure, however, as its particular nature and the definition of its object reasonably allow. Properly speaking, it does not undertake to refute the metaphysical systems which it deems itself destined to replace. Those systems in refuting positive philosophy, are faithful to their principle; and positive philosophy is faithful to its own principle in not following their example. It suffices for it to "locate" them in the general evolution of the human mind, and to show, according to this law of evolution, how the very necessity which brought them into being is also the cause of their disappearance. Their office is fulfilled, their part is ended. It matters little that they should seek to prolong an ebbing existence; cases of survival may slacken the rate of progress, but they are powerless to arrest it. And so positive philosophy is the only one which can be perfectly just towards its adversaries. "It ceases," says Comte, "being critical in regard to the whole of the past." In order to be established, it does not require to combat and to supplant the philosophies which have preceded it. With itself, it places all doctrines in history. It substitutes the historical genesis to abstract dialectics.

Undoubtedly Comte recognises a long series of his precursors properly so-called, in the double line of philosophers and scientific men who have contributed to the progress of the positive spirit from Aristotle and Archimedes to Condorcet and Gall. But positive philosophy, none the less, looks upon itself as heir to all the philosophies, even to those which are most opposed to its principle. For they, like the others, have been necessary moments in the progress which was to end in the positive system.

Thus considered in its relation to the metaphysical speculation which preceded it, this system does not refute it, for it is neither necessary nor even possible for it to do so. Neither does it incorporate it within itself, for it could not do so without a formal contradiction. Still, according to Comte's own confession, it proceeds from metaphysics as much as from science properly so-called. In what then does this relation consist, if positive philosophy neither opposes nor adopts previous doctrines?—It *transposes* them. What its predecessors had studied from the absolute point of view, it projects upon the relative plane.

As we proceeded we have noted more than one of these *transpositions*. It may perhaps not be useless to make a recapitulation of them here, without, however, claiming for it perfect completeness.

Metaphysical Philosophy.	*Positive Transpositions.*
I. Distinction between potentiality and reality.	I. Distinction between the statistical and the dynamical points of view, or between order and progress.
II. Principle of finality.	II. Principle of the conditions of existence.
III. Theory of innateness.	III. Definition of human nature as immutable, evolution creating nothing, but bringing out the latent potentialities in that nature.
IV. The idea of the universe.	IV. The idea of the world.
V. All the phenomena of the universe are related to one another.	V. The idea of humanity is the only really universal conception, because the conditions of existence of human societies are in a necessary relation, not only with the laws of our organisation, but also with all the physical and chemical laws of our planet, and the mechanical laws of the solar system.
VI. The Aristotelian theory of science, (knowledge through causes, *a priori*), and Cartesian theory, (deductive knowledge starting from the simple).	VI. Science consists in substituting rational prevision to the empirical establishment of facts.
VII. The principles of mathematics are synthetical *a priori* propositions. (Kant).	VII. Geometry and mechanics are natural sciences, and pure analysis can never establish their principles.
VIII. The order of the universe is the basis of moral order: (Stoics, Spinoza, Leibnitz).	VIII. The conduct of man is regulated externally by the whole of the laws of the world in which he lives.
IX. The history of humanity is directed by a providential wisdom.	IX. The evolution of humanity is accomplished according to a law.
X. The notion of a natural law does not necessarily imply a mechanism.	X. The various orders of natural phenomena are irreducible and nevertheless convergent, the real becoming richer at each new degree.
XI. Theory of the immortality of the soul.	XI. Theory of the "subjective existence," or of survival in the consciousness of others.
XII. Rational theology.	XII. The positive science of Humanity.

This list might easily be prolonged. Once again it shows us that, in the history of philosophy as in history in general, the result of the most apparently radical revolutions is not so much to abolish as to transform. Thus, Kant's philosophy might seem to be entirely opposed to that of Leibnitz. Yet we see that the metaphysics of Leibnitz is to be found almost in its entirety in Kant. Of this dogmatic philosophy Kant has preserved the doctrine. He only rejected its dogmatism; which, as a matter of fact, was of capital importance. In the same way, positive philosophy has often been presented as the formal negation of the philosophy which preceded it When we verify this, we nearly always find them both concerned with the same problems, and often reaching analogous solutions. Here again it is only a question of transposition; an extremely serious one it is true, on account of all that it implies.

Errors of interpretation are very often due to a lack of historical perspective. Once they have been formulated and adopted by current opinion they are difficult to rectify. Time is needed in order that beneath superficial differences, deep seated resemblances may appear. During many years Kant was in all sincerity looked upon as a sceptic in France. Those who criticised him could not conceive how any one could give up metaphysical dogmatism, without at the some time abandoning the doctrines which had been cast in the metaphysical form before Kant. In the same way, in the eyes of most of his adversaries, Comte's system must have appeared as the very negation of philosophy, because the terms "philosophy" and "relative" seemed incompatible to them. But this system, which is an effort to realise, from the point of view of positive science, the unity of the understanding, and the "perfect logical coherence," in reality ends by putting the traditional problems of philosophy in a form suitable to the spirit of our age.

IV

If the relationship between Comte's philosophy and the doctrines which preceded it is sufficiently evident, it does not follow that this philosophy has brought with it nothing new. On the contrary, the "transposition" of problems and the constant effort to substitute the relative to the absolute point of view, entails serious consequences with very far reaching effects. Some of these were at once apparent, and first served to characterise positive philosophy in the eyes of the public. Others, more remote, but no less important, appeared more slowly.

The negative consequences almost alone attracted attention at first. The chief characteristic of the new philosophy seemed to be the denial of the legitimacy and even of the possibility of metaphysics in all its forms: rational psychology, the philosophical theory of matter and of life, rational theology, etc. It seemed also to deny the possibility of introspective psychology, of ethics in its traditional form, as well as of logic. In a word, one after another, it excluded all the parts of what constituted a "course of philosophy." No wonder, then, if this doctrine which took the name of "positive" appeared to be chiefly negative.

However, in reality, the negation only affected the so-called "rational" or "philosophical sciences." . . . Stringently applying the principle of the relativity of knowledge, he refused to admit anything absolute. He was therefore perfectly true to himself in rejecting doctrines founded upon metaphysical principles. But this entirely negative aspect of his philosophy is very far from being the one according to which we can best understand it. Truly speaking, it is only preparatory, and historians have often committed the mistake of allowing people to believe that it is essential. *"We only destroy what we replace,"* said Comte.

The question was not to ruin but to transform the psychological, moral and social sciences. As we have seen, positive philosophy does not deny the possibility of a psychology.

On the contrary, it establishes that psychical phenomena like the others, are subject to laws, and that these laws must be looked for by the positive method. It only rejects the psychology of the ideologists as abstract, and that of Cousin as metaphysical. It claims that, in presence of the phenomena which he is studying, the psychologist should assume the same attitude as the biologist or the physicist, that any search after cause or essence should be carefully avoided, that any metaphysical or ethical after-thought should be set aside. Then a science of physical phenomena will be established; still it will only be able to study the highest mental functions in the "universal subject," in humanity. If we wish to do so, we may continue to call it by its traditional name, although it is to the old psychology only what the chemistry of our day is to alchemy.

A similar transformation gives rise to social science. Here again, the indispensable condition for the scientific knowledge of facts and of laws is a new attitude of mind in presence of these facts. We must set aside what interests us subjectively in them, and consider what is "specifically social" in them just as the physiologist studies what is "specifically biological" in the phenomena of the organism. M. Durkheim, as a real heir of Auguste Comte, reasonably maintains that this is a condition *sine qua non* of positive sociology. This only exists as a science if there are facts which are properly social subject to special laws, besides the more general laws of nature which rule them also, and if these facts, by constant objective characteristics, are sufficiently distinct from the phenomena called psychological.

Positive psychology is now already constituted. Positive sociology is being formed. The science of language, the science of religions, the history of art are also assuming a positive form. The movement which has begun, and of which we only see the beginnings, will probably extend much further than we think. It supposes at least a provisional separation between the scientific interest and the political, moral and religious interests. Being already constituted for a considerable part of our knowledge, this separation for the remainder is still distasteful to the traditional habits of the majority of minds We are accustomed to speculate upon physical or chemical nature with perfect disinterestedness as to the metaphysical consequences of the results which we may obtain. For we are convinced that the laws of these phenomena do not necessarily imply any consequences of this kind, or that they can be almost indifferently brought into accord with any form of metaphysics we may be pleased to adopt. What do physics, chemistry, natural philosophy *prove,* as to the destiny of man or the supreme cause of the universe? Nothing, and it does not occur to us to be surprised at it. We consider that these sciences are in accordance with their definition if they give us a knowledge of the laws of phenomena, and if this knowledge enables us within certain limits to exercise a rational and efficacious action upon nature.

Are we in the same position in what concerns psychology and the moral and social sciences? This is doubtful. The very name of "moral sciences" is significant enough on this point. We cannot refrain from thinking that these sciences "prove" something outside themselves. For several of the schools of this century, psychology is still the path that leads to metaphysics. Spirituality and the immortality of the soul seem to have a direct interest in it. In a more or less conscious manner orthodox political economy has found itself "proving" the legitimacy of the modern capitalist *régime*, and has represented it as being in conformity with the immutable laws of nature. The historical materialism of Marx "proves" the necessity of collectivism. History too often serves national interests, or political parties.

Comte's most interesting and fertile leading idea is that the sciences conceived in this way are still in their infancy and do not deserve their name. Those who take them up should, in the first place, convince themselves of the fact that they prove no more in favour of spiritualism or materialism, of protection or of free exchange, than physics or chemistry prove in favour of the unity or the plurality of substances in the universe. In the school of the more advanced sciences men may be taught to distinguish between the objects of positive research and the metaphysical or practical questions. They will see also that the human mind did not begin by making this distinction in the case of inorganic and of living nature. For a long time it could only think of physical phenomena religiously. Without the admirable effort of the Greek men of science and philosophers, we might yet find ourselves in this period, and positive philosophy might still be awaiting the hour of its birth. To-day this philosophy has come into being. In order to prove finally established, it requires that individual and social human nature should become the object of a science as distinterested as physics and biology have already become. From that day alone will the "Social sciences" be definitely constituted.

It is true that since in a certain way the object of these sciences is ourselves, it seems paradoxical to look upon them in the same way as if it were a question of salts or of crystals. We persist in believing that any knowledge of this order, as soon as it is acquired, admits of immediate applications to our condition or conduct. But this is an illusion. Is not the importance of the "*milieu*" in which we find ourselves, and of the forces which affect us from without for our welfare and even for our preservation which depends upon them at every moment, a simple matter of evidence? Nevertheless, we seek a purely abstract, scientific knowledge of the laws of phenomena, because we know that our effective power upon natural forces is subordinate to science. In the same way we separate physiology from therapeutics and medicine, and from physiology. So in the same way, paedagogy, rational economy, politics, and in general all the social arts in the future will be subordinated to the theoretical science of the individual and social nature of man, when this science has been constituted by means of a purely positive method, and is no longer expected to "prove" anything but its laws.

This may perhaps be the work of centuries. We are only witnessing its early beginnings. We still have only a vague idea of a polity founded upon science; and we do not yet know what individual and social psychology will yield as a positive science. Comte anticipated results which could not be immediate. This is yet another feature which he has in common with Descartes, to whom we have so often had occasion to compare him. Having conceived a certain mathematical ideal of physical science, Descartes pictured the problems of nature, and especially of living nature, as being infinitely less complex than they are. Our scientific men to-day no longer venture to put to themselves the biological questions whose solution appeared to Descartes to be comparatively easy. In the same way, Auguste Comte, having recognised that moral and social phenomena should be objects of science, just as those of inorganic and living nature, believed this new science to be far more advanced by his own labours than it was in reality.

It is easy to understand his mistake. He was anxious to proceed to the "social reorganisation," in view of which he was constructing his philosophy. Then, given the conception he had formed of social science, he was bound to think that the discovery of the great dynamic law of the three States was sufficient to finally constitute it. In his eyes "the hardest part of the work was done." Sociologists at present believe that almost everything remains to be done. But, here again, we may renew the comparison between Descartes and Comte. In the work of both, without much difficulty, we can distinguish what is done by the scientific man properly so-called and what is done by the philosopher. It is the same with Comte the sociologist as with Descartes the physicist. Their hypotheses have met with the fate common to scientific labours, of which Comte himself has so well set forth the necessary transitoriness. The other portion of their work, more general in character, is possessed of more enduring qualities. In this sense, and setting aside his political and religious views, which belong to another order, the speculative philosophy of Comte is living still, and pursues its evolution even within the minds of those who are engaged in opposing it.

Jane M. Style (essay date 1928)

SOURCE: "After Days," in *Auguste Comte: Thinker and Lover,* Kegan Paul, Trench Trubner & Co., Ltd., 1928, pp. 196-205.

[*In the following essay, Style discusses the legacy of Comte's religion of Humanity.*]

Before Comte died he felt that the religion of Humanity had been proclaimed to the world, and believed that fervent disciples would be found to preach and perfect it. How has his prophecy been fulfilled in the years since his death? As to the date of its systematic acceptance it has certainly failed, but the ablest seaman, while he can tell the date at which a ship should reach its destination, cannot tell what tempests, head winds, undercurrents or other causes may delay the voyage. Had Comte himself lived longer he might have influenced the rapidity of the change, for his voice was beginning to be heard in many lands, the last work he had planned, his volume on Industry, would have appealed to leading practical men, and his followers would have profited by his direct guidance, for Comte was the truly modern man, the embodiment of the new age in which the social outlook is consciously attained and dominates the whole of life. He was the modern man while we grope and stumble towards modernity, our mental make-up resembling that of a snake whose parched and dried skin has parted strewing a little of the beauty and promise of the future while all the rest is dim, dusty and outworn. France seems to have sold her birthright and abandoned any attempt at religious construction, probably the disturbance which led to the Franco-Prussian war and the bitter resentment which was its consequence, delayed her development though

Gambetta was Comte's follower, and the cultured Parisian, who may be of any class and is frequently a workman, has still the most central outlook among the sons of Humanity. Faithful apostles in many lands have not been lacking. As Comte foresaw, the most devoted have been found in the Portuguese and Spanish settlements in South America. In Brazil the Republic was peacefully established under the leadership of Benjamin Constant, an avowed Positivist, the motto "Order and Progress" being chosen for the national flag, while in public affairs the positivists have exercised a marked influence. They have instituted the public celebration of many historic types and the last act of Senhor Mendes, their revered leader, was connected with the statue of St. Francis of Assisi to be erected in Rio. In the older civilisations their voices have been more drowned but in England they have faithfully proclaimed the doctrine with regard to Gibraltar, India, Egypt, Ireland, China, Trades Unions and other matters, while much of the improvement in Poor Law administration, sanitation and the general care of health is due to the strenuous labours of Dr. Bridges, one of Comte's followers who "renounced private practice to devote himself to public work". In Liverpool a Temple of Humanity has been erected of which the beauty and dignified simplicity is recognised across the Atlantic.

Small indeed have been the conscious and systematic results compared with what might have been, but only seventy years have elapsed since the premature death of Comte, and, it must be remembered, he continually emphasised the fact that there are two ways in which the religion of Humanity may come. The one, the conscious and systematic of which we have spoken, that is, by the acceptance of the doctrine and the attempt to put it into practice, the other, the spontaneous and unconscious, by the gradual dissolving of the old and formation of the new order. "All men are", he says, "especially in the present day, spontaneous positivists at different stages of evolution which only need completeness".

To those who have had the privilege of observing society for over half a century, with the enlightening help of the doctrine of Humanity, the change in this respect has been very marked in all spheres of thought and activity: Much careful scientific observation has been carried on, notably in anthropology. Royalty is everywhere passing away, hereditary titles are losing their glamour, dictators tend to arise, and in the country which Comte thought would be second in the acceptance of the religion of Humanity a dictator has arisen from the people who has tried to introduce order into a disorganised society and to foster habits of discipline and devotion to work, unfortunately he has not fulfilled the indispensable condition of allowing spiritual liberty and freedom of speech, and rather resembles a dictator of the past than of the future a position which must inevitably lead to reaction. Turning to our own country, although the ruling classes have not risen, as Comte hoped, to the realisation of the grandeur of the work of accomplishing re-organisation without revolution and have lately, e.g. in the struggle over miners' wages, been engaged in delaying the incorporation of all workmen into society, still, much has been gained. Beautiful parks with costly and rare flowers are secured and tended for the enjoyment of the poorest citizens. Public playgrounds with appliances, far better than those provided for the wealthy fifty years ago, are ready for the little ones. Games, dancing and the arts which teach control and grace of body are doing away with the class consciousness so evident a short time ago, the wives and daughters of the workmen can scarcely be distinguished in the streets from their wealthier sisters. Suffering enough remains, but the dissolving process has begun, class distinction is passing away and the one Humanity is being realised. Cruel and revolting doctrines are preached and forgotten such as "the destruction of the old and diseased", compulsory birth control, and through it all devoted doctors are striving with all their skill to save and succour the diseased, and nurses are sacrificing their health and their careers to keep those alive who have lost all but life. Miners instead of securing their own safety are going into the burning pit to lose their lives in the effort to save their fellows. Everywhere men and women are realising that improvement depends on self control and on the gradual advance of the whole, that acts of cruelty and tyranny defeat themselves by lowering the general standard of feeling. Consideration for animals has increased as shown by the Bird Sanctuaries, and such institutions as the Horse processions are a foretaste of the "Festival of the Animals", when the lesser brethren will be honoured in the Temple of Humanity. The improvement in Poor Law Infirmaries, which now compare favourably with the best, the care of children brought up by the State, old age pensions, the humane treatment of prisoners, the diminution of the desire for vengeance by punishment, all point to the growth of social feeling and recognition of social duty. Such a saying as "A man may do what he likes with his own", prevalent fifty years ago, would hardly be asserted now even by the men who still act upon it. Such a saying as "My country right or wrong", once considered rather fine, and certainly a necessity for the soldier in the execution of his duty, is now discredited, and one of the most significant signs of the times is, that, whenever a country is acting tyrannically to a weaker, or exploiting a less advanced race, champions of the oppressed are sure to arise in the oppressing country, who, shewing themselves true patriots oppose her wrong-doing and dishonour. International feeling has grown among the mass of the people in all countries. Men are beginning to realise that as no family can work worthily or gain honour save in the service of city or country so no country can find its fulfillment save as a part of the one whole to which all belong. The League of Nations is one sign of this change and the Assembly of the League is an attempt at an advising or spiritual power resembling in some respects the International Council proposed by Comte.

An extraordinary change has taken place in the doctrines of theology, little acknowledged but none the less vital. The popular novelists have scarcely a rag of theological belief left, yet people who consider themselves orthodox read, admire and applaud. It sometimes seems as if we needed the little child to say, as in the fairy tale of the King's beautiful garment: "Why he has nothing on." The very dignitaries of the Church have long given up belief in doctrines such as that of the resurrection of the body, still included in the services and creeds. Quite recently a bishop had the courage to acknowledge that the belief in hell was past, though when he put forward the positive doctrine that the fear of injuring others should be a sufficient deterrent from sin, he did not add that the belief in heaven must also pass away for if the bad did not need punishment surely the good would not need reward. One curious anomaly is seen in the religious teaching of the day. Many preachers have thrown aside the magnificent conception of supreme sacrifice in Christ Jesus, who left the glories of Heaven to suffer for man on earth, but have attempted to retain in the individual man Jesus all the qualities which have grown up around the ideal type through the Christian era. Even the finest individual type is not enough. It may suffice for private worship, for here the worshipper is nearly always of the opposite sex and the heart of the worshipper becomes a combination of masculine and feminine attributes, but in the public worship the symbol must combine the virtues, thoughts and powers of all mankind. The energy and wisdom of man, the tenderness and wisdom of woman, the widely differing forms of excellence of both exhibited in every relation and accident of life can be found in no individual man or woman. To imagine them in one must result in the unreality which it is the aim of the modern man to avoid. In the God ideal this mixture was more permissible but the tendency was to monstrosity. This was largely overcome in the Christian dogma by the conception of the Trinity but its inadequacy was felt by Saint Bernard who added the Madonna to introduce the more strictly feminine element. In 'Humanity' all types are of necessity combined. Goodwill is growing everywhere but with confused thought. Phrases are used without attention to the meaning of words or, at any rate, of their implication. The phrase "Science and Religion are reconciled", a truth which Comte's life and work have triumphantly proved to the extent that religion can only embrace the whole of life when it is firmly founded on science carried into the highest regions, this phrase, loosely used, makes the ordinary hearer believe that there has been some discovery proving the existence of God, or, in other words, that Science and Theology are reconciled, a very different proposition and totally untrue. They are different ways of accounting for things and can only be reconciled as different phases in the history of Humanity. As in Comte's day, the mental plan is not clear, men have but a confused idea that the industrial era is the ideal of the future while they constantly turn back to the military ideal of the past. We have a vision of the promised land of peace and industry founded on human truth and love but, like the Israelites in the old legend, many turn back to the golden calf of superstition, militarism or of hereditary privilege. While the superstitious belief in science as an end in itself, which was so marked in the 19th century, has passed away few have recognised that the solution is found in science taking service under love while many have returned to more primitive superstitions. Men like Sir James Mackenzie have striven to free the people from the medical tyranny which results from applying the general rule to the particular case using the deductive method in an art which especially calls for careful observation; everywhere men of exceptional insight are adopting the positive method in isolated cases but the mental chaos remains. This mental attitude is, in default of the complete acceptance of the new order, a matter of congratulation as under it the dissolving process is carried on. The new Liverpool Cathedral, situate on a hill not much more than a stone's throw from the Temple for the conscious worship of Humanity, is a place for spontaneous human worship, the noble lives of humble women are recorded in the windows, its bishop strives to draw into one fellowship the different sects of theology, and, by special services for railwaymen and others, begins the festivals of the transition.

The ground of confidence lies in the law of human progress "Man ever grows more religious," discovered by Comte. This is difficult to see because the meaning of religious is not understood. Men compare the modern world with the theocracies and with the Middle Age and think that religion is dying out, and even comparing the present with a generation or two ago, the discipline of life and recognition of religious duty seems passing away. But religion as Comte defines it, consists of harmony within and without, peace in the mind and union with our fellows. Harmony is the result of the increase of social, and the greater control of personal, feelings. This results from living together. Modern industry depends in a constantly increasing degree on mutual trust, there is less room for suspicion and resentment. As men from different classes and lands associate together and find in all the same kindly feelings, the same aspirations, a sense of security and confidence grows up. As in a happy family the atmosphere is one of fearlessness, wit, humour, joyousness and all the sweet flowers of human intercourse grow apace, so, as the same confidence finds its place in the larger life, as each one feels that his fellows will stand by him in misfortune and share with him in need, joyousness will be the mark of the religious man. It is worthy of notice that the two most widely beloved saints in the Catholic Church, St. Francis and St. Catherine, were distinguished by their gaiety of heart. This gaiety is not that of mere exhuberance of youth, which may be accompanied by much selfishness and lead to a sombre and discontented age, it is the supreme joy of life which results when duty and happiness are one. It is a harmony of heart and this can only be fully attained when there is also a harmony of mind, when feeling, thought and action all tend to one centre. The spontaneous growth of religion can be clearly seen around us and the day is not distant when men will see in whom they have believed and will delight to render honour where honour is due. When that time shall come, as one of our novelists has said, the name of Auguste Comte must arise into prominence. And when the light of Comte's memory rises on the human horizon it will be accompanied by that of the mother who first "by her love his love awoke," by that of the fair and delicate spirit who by one short year of companionship glorified the whole of his after life and by that of the simple noble hearted woman who loved and tended him to the end.

Etienne Gilson (essay date 1937)

SOURCE: "The Sociology of A. Comte," in *The Unity of Philosophical Experience,* Charles Scribner's Sons, 1937, pp. 248-70.

[*In the following essay, Gilson considers Comte's sociologism to be "one of the most striking philosophical experiments recorded by history."*]

On the third day of the month of Dante in the sixty-sixth year of the Great Western Crisis, the French philosopher Auguste Comte was completing the list of the one hundred fifty volumes that make up his "Positivist Library." In the **Positivist Calendar,** the third day of the month of Dante is the feast of Rabelais. Yet the "Positivist Library" was not a joke; it was a catalogue of the books which it is necessary and sufficient to read in order to acquire all the knowledge required by our social needs. Thirty volumes of poetry, thirty volumes of science, sixty volumes of history, and thirty volumes of what Comte called synthesis, make one hundred fifty volumes. The philosophical works in that library are listed among the thirty volumes of *Synthesis,* and do not comprise more than four or five volumes. Plato is not represented; nor are Leibniz, Spinoza, Locke, Kant; but one volume is reserved for the *Politics* and *Ethics* of Aristotle, a second volume for Descartes' *Discourse on Method,* preceded by Bacon's *Novum Organum* and followed by Diderot's *Interpretation of Nature:* Pascal's *Thoughts,* followed by those of Vauvenargues, and the *Counsels of a Mother* by Mme. de Lambert make up a third volume; the main works of Auguste Comte himself provide the matter for a fourth volume, and Hume's *Philosophical Essays*

form an essential part of the last. At the origins of Comte, as at the origins of Kant, stands Hume.

Born in 1798, educated at the college of Montpellier, then a pupil at the Polytechnic School, whence he was expelled because of subversive political opinions, Comte had been confronted, from early youth, with the social consequences of the eighteenth-century philosophy. His starting point was not only the breakdown of classical metaphysics, as it had been with Kant, but also the breakdown of the very social structure which, for several centuries, had both sheltered that form of Philosophy and been sheltered by it. Destroyed by the Revolution, the France of the Kings had gone; but the Revolution itself had failed to establish a new order of political life, and after the glorious and tragic episode of Napoleon's Empire, the country seemed to be headed for a return to the past. The Kings were coming back, and were pretending to rule France as though nothing had happened since 1789. Comte's whole career was to be dominated by the settled conviction that after the Revolution a restoration was indeed necessary, but that at the same time the past was irrevocably dead. Comte's thought is wholly contained in his adverbs; "irrevocably" means that the death sentence which was passed upon the old social régime could not possibly be revoked by men, because it expressed a historic and objective fatality.

This being the case, a restoration had to be a reorganization; that is, the building of a new type of social order according to new principles. Comte was not the only one to feel concerned with the problem: De Bonald and de Maistre, Fourier, and Saint-Simon had already suggested various remedies for the political anarchy of the times; but Comte approached the situation as a born philosopher for whom the whole problem was essentially a problem of ideas, solution of which must necessarily be a philosophical solution. To him social and political anarchy was but the outward manifestation of the state of mental anarchy that had been prevailing ever since the old ways of thinking had become obsolete. Although those old ways were gone, no new way had come to take their place, or to play, in a new social order, the part which metaphysics had played in the old. That was why no new social order could arise. When men do not know what to think, they cannot know how to live. Comte would show men how to live by teaching them what to think. This was, no doubt, a high ambition, but one from which Comte never shrank, and which he ultimately felt had been wholly fulfilled. From 1830 to 1810 the new reformer had published the six volumes of his **System of Positive Philosophy**; now he could inscribe the words of the French poet, Alfred de Vigny, as a motto for his **System of Positive Politics:** "What is a great life? A thought of youth fulfilled in maturity." Yet Comte's great life was but one more great dream, for an evil genius had attended the birth of his philosophy;

and once again it was a dazzling scientific idea: not mathematics, or physics, but sociology. Comte's philosophy was to be a Sociologism.

The choice of a new standard science can not be considered as an entirely arbitrary decision in this case any more than it can in that of Abailard, Descartes or Kant. Taken at any one moment of its evolution, a society is always defined by three fundamental elements whose mutual relations are unchangeable, and which Comte described as follows. First of all, lying at the very root of each social group there is a definite state of intellectual knowledge. It is an obvious fact that a society in which fetichism reigns supreme is wholly different, in every element of its internal structure, from a society in which monotheism prevails; and that such a society, in its turn, must needs be different from another in which a monotheistic theology has been superseded by scientific knowledge. A social group is essentially constituted of families united by the same intellectual conception of the world. In connection with and determined by, this factor of knowledge, there always appears a second factor, which is a definite form of political government. It flows from the first; for government is but the natural reaction of the whole upon its parts, and since the whole is the common intellectual outlook which ties together the members of the community, any political regime is bound to express the belief from which it springs. Finally there is the third element, which also flows from the first two: a specific literary, artistic, commercial and industrial civilization, born of both the ruling belief and the political regime of that society. An easy way to remember this part of Comte's doctrine is to reverse it. In that case we have Marxism, with a definite industrial situation at the root of the system, whence springs a political regime, which is, in turn, attended by its religious, artistic and philosophical justifications. Reverse it again, and we are back to Comtism, with a definite state of knowledge at the root of the system, an equally definite industrial situation at the top, and, in between, a specific form of art. In short, just as Marxism is an historical materialism, Comtism was an historical idealism, in which the whole structure of a given society, at a given time, is strictly determined by the communion of beliefs on which it is founded. The ideological cohesion of these beliefs is one and the same with the social cohesion.

Such being the static structure of all social groups, let us now consider the dynamic law of their development. Given the position adopted by Comte, the development of human societies had to be conceived necessarily as that of a certain idea or, rather, of a certain spirit. In point of fact, Comte conceived it as the slow but almost regular process by which what he calls "the positive spirit" has reached the complete awareness of its own nature. What we call political or social history, together with the history of art, literature, or philosophy, tells us of mere episodes incidental to the great central epic of the positive spirit. For this spirit existed from the very beginning when the human mind was still explaining all phenomena by the wills of deities. That was the so-called "theological state"; but the proof that the positive spirit was already there lies in the fact that, even during that primitive state, there was a progressive rationalization of theological beliefs, from fetichism to polytheism, and from polytheism to monotheism. This is so true that the transition from monotheism to the second state was almost imperceptible. This second is the "metaphysical state," in which abstract causes are substituted for gods, or for God, as an ultimate explanation of the world. In point of fact, says Comte, metaphysics is but the ghost of dead theologies. Yet it is a necessary interlude during which positive science reaches its complete maturity. Now the positive spirit is essentially the spirit of positive science, which feels no interest in gods, or in causes, because it is never concerned with the "why," but only with the "how." Laws, not causes, are the only valid explanations for all knowable facts. Such is the third and last of the three stages through which all human conceptions, and therefore all human societies, have to pass necessarily in the course of their development. The famous "law of the three states" was completely formulated by Comte as early as 1822, and was to remain the basis of his whole system: every branch of human knowledge successively passes through the theological or fictitious state, the metaphysical or abstract state, and the scientific or positive state.

The discovery of that universal law was not only the foundation of Comte's sociology, but it also offered him the complete explanation of the social crisis in which he was living, and a safe means of bringing it to a close. Supposing a society in which theology reigns supreme, a corresponding social order is not only possible but necessary. The Middle Ages, for which Comte always entertained a romantic admiration, were a clear proof of the fact. A revealed truth taught by theology and received through faith was bound to bring about a theocracy in which the popes ruled the priests, and the priests the kings, and the kings the lords, and so on, in accordance with the laws of the feudal system. To this were added a Christian art and a Christian literature, so that the whole structure of medieval society was permeated, quickened from within, and kept together by the same theological spirit. Not so in Europe at the beginning of the nineteenth century. Owing to the necessary growth of the positive spirit, medieval theology had become a thing of the past. In due time it had given way to the metaphysical state, whose rise had been attended by the absolute monarchies of the seventeenth century, their art and their literatures. But the positive spirit marches on; its advance must bring about the disruption of the metaphysico-monarchical order, and this had, in fact, been the effect of the French Revolution. Metaphysics had now become obsolete, even as theology before it. Hume and the critical spirit of the eighteenth century had revealed its complete vanity to the world. The difficulty, however, was that the positive spirit had failed so far to produce a completely rounded interpretation of the world, whose general acceptance would become the common bond of a new social order. Who was to do for the positive state in the nineteenth century what St. Thomas Aquinas had done for the theological state in the Middle Ages, and what Descartes had done for the metaphysical state in the seventeenth century? The world was waiting for a prophet whose mission it would be to usher in the last and final age in which humanity was to live forever. Of course, you know the name of the prophet—Auguste Comte. But how was he to do it?

Gifted as he was with an immense power for abstract speculation, Comte began by showing why positive science had failed to provide mankind with a systematic view of the world. True, there were already many positive sciences, but there still remained one order of facts whose interpretation was purely metaphysical: the order of social and political facts. In a time when no one would have dreamt of dealing with matter without resorting to physics, chemistry, or biology, it was still the general belief that social facts obey no laws and that, consequently, any man can make any society to be what he wants it to be, provided only he has the power to do so. Hence the illusions of the belated conservatives, or of the reckless revolutionists, who draw plans for ideal and dreamlike cities without asking what the laws of social life actually are. Therefore the first task of our reformer was necessarily to extend the spirit of positive science to social facts; that is, to create the still missing science, sociology. By doing so, Comte hoped to achieve a twofold result. First, by taking politics out of its metaphysical and chaotic state and turning it into a positive science, he would initiate an era of social and political engineering. We can act upon matter because we know its laws; when we know social laws, it will be at least as easy to act upon societies. Next, having thus extended the positive spirit to the only class of facts still outside of its jurisdiction, Comte could proceed to build up a perfectly consistent system of human knowledge and to procure the scientific dogma required for the new social order. By driving metaphysics out of its last position, Comte had ensured the perfect uniformity of the whole of human knowledge; all ideas, all laws, being equally positive, could henceforth be reduced to a homogeneous system, whose ideological cohesion would be the social cohesion of humanity.

All well and good. Even realizing how delusive it is, I cannot withhold my sympathy for the pure enthusiasm of these young philosophers. There is nothing on earth more beautiful than the birth of an idea when, in its pristine novelty, it throws a new light on our old world. Whereas everything was out of joint, now everything has found its place, because logic revealed itself to Abailard, mathematics to Descartes, physics to Kant, or because the young Comte now discovers the science of social facts. But why should each one of them be so certain that he has at the same time discovered philosophy itself? We are now, I hope, much nearer to the answer of that important question than we were at the beginning of our inquiry, but before giving it we must pursue the sociological experiment of Comte and his successors to its bitter end.

There was nothing wrong in discovering sociology. A new science is always welcome, and though this science is not the most secure, it may in time become a very decent branch of knowledge, especially if it takes into account the fact that not animal groups, but human societies, are its object. The only trouble with Comte was that, after having conceived the possibility of such a science, he thought that he could achieve it all alone; and that, having more or less achieved it, he asked it to solve all philosophical problems. First of all, he asked it to make philosophy itself possible by reorganizing all human knowledge from within.

There is nothing arbitrary in the ventures of a philosopher, even when he is mistaken. Comte was in quest of a scientific dogma whose common acceptance would bring forth a new social order. At first glance, the whole body of scientific knowledge now completed by the discovery of sociology seemed to be in itself a sufficient answer to the question. Science was replacing metaphysics in human reason; the only thing to do was to wait patiently for the inevitable day when, the old ideas having completely vanished, all men would spontaneously adopt the same scientific outlook on the world. Then would the new social order naturally arise as a necessary offspring of the new mental unity.

This was a very tempting solution because it was so simple; but Comte never accepted it, and for a very profound reason. Science, whereby he meant the body of all positive sciences from mathematics to biology and sociology, is an objective representation of what the world actually is; but if we look at it from the point of view of science, the world has no unity of its own. Every scientist naturally has the temper and the tastes of a specialist; he first specializes in his own science; then he begins to specialize in a special part of that same science, and he goes on restricting his outlook on the world until, at last, turning his back on all the other sciences and their results, he finds himself engaged in the exhaustive investigation of some microscopic detail which has now become the whole of reality—so far as he is concerned. This is the reason why, already in Comte's time, the teaching of the sciences in universities was absolutely chaotic, no one science being related to any other, and each professor holding his own bit of the world, as a dog his bone, with an unfriendly look at those who would touch it. In short, the natural tendency of science is not towards unity, but towards an ever more complete disintegration. Such facts point to an intrinsic heterogeneity of the world. True enough, everything is strictly determined, but the sum total of all those determinations does not make up a whole. Now, even though the physical world, as expressed by positive science, is not a coherent system of things, yet a society, to be a real society, must be a coherent system of men; this is impossible, however, unless its fundamental outlook on the world has some sort of unity. A primitive tribe is a whole because of its fetich; a theological civilization is one because of its god; a metaphysical society is swayed by the Author of Nature; but if it has nothing to live by except science and its disconnected laws, society will inevitably find itself condemned to a state of a complete disintegration; in fact, it will not be a society at all.

This train of thought led Comte to the conclusion that, although all the material of the future dogma had to be borrowed from science, science alone could never produce the dogma itself. What was needed now, above and beyond positive science, was a positive philosophy—a strictly unified system of thoughts, each of which would be a scientifically demonstrated truth, and all of which taken together, would constitute a completely rounded explanation of reality. All the data of the problem with which we have been dealing from the beginning of this book are here before our eyes, numbered and defined by Comte with an amazing lucidity. Men no longer believe in theology; they also know that metaphysics is a thing of the past; yet they need a philosophy; but the only thing that remains for them is not philosophy, but science; hence the problem: how will science give us a philosophy? That which makes Comte's case highly significant is the fact that, having thus asked the question, he was clear-sighted enough to give it the right answer: science alone will not and cannot give us a philosophy. Unless we look at science from a non-scientific point of view, our positive knowledge will never be reduced to unity. Now if we do not look at things from the point of view of things, as science does, the only alternative is to look at them from the point of view of man. To express the same idea in Comte's own terminology, let us say that since no "objective synthesis" is attainable, the only possible synthesis is a "subjective synthesis." Consequently, philosophy has to be the subjective synthesis of positive knowledge from the point of view of man and his social needs.

Being compelled to take that fatal leap, Comte did it as scientifically as possible. First he pointed out the fact that the youngest of all positive sciences, sociology, was the science of man. Nor was it by chance that the science of man had been the last to be discovered; for the positive knowledge of societies, which are the most complex of all facts, presupposes the positive knowledge of all other facts, and hence all the other

sciences had to be discovered before sociology. But then, and for the same reason, human social life is the only fact from which we can view all the others with the certainty of not overlooking any that is fundamental. Thus science itself invites us to unify positive knowledge from the point of view of humanity. The consequences of this subjective interpretation of science in Comte's doctrine are simply amazing. In order to draw a subjective synthesis from positive knowledge, Comte had first to reduce it to what he calls the theoretical and abstract sciences: mathematics, astronomy, physics, chemistry, biology, and sociology. Such sciences deal with laws, not with things; should we take into account such concrete sciences as mineralogy, botany or zoology, we would again lose ourselves in the heterogeneous character of reality. Let us therefore stick to the abstract sciences and eliminate all the rest as unfit for a philosophical synthesis. From the point of view of science itself this was, of course, an arbitrary move. In his book, *The Classification of the Sciences* (1864), H. Spencer raised a strong protest against the "anthropocentric" character of Comte's classification. Spencer was right; how could one, in the name of science, eliminate half the sciences for the benefit of the other half? But Comte was not wrong: if you do nothing to science, how are you to turn it into a philosophy?

Having proceeded to this drastic reduction in the number of the sciences, Comte found himself confronted with the still more difficult task of reducing those that remain to a synthetic unity. To ask sciences themselves to restrict their activities to what furthers the social needs of man would have been a waste of time. Science cares not for man, but for things, and to the pure scientist it is just as important to know one thing as it is to know another, provided only that it falls within the scope of his own science. The consequence was that every one of the fundamental sciences themselves had to be reorganized from within to suit the needs of the philosopher. Comte called this operation the "regeneration" of a science, by which he meant: to cause the spiritual rebirth of science by infusing into it a proper dose of subjective spirit. Unfortunately the subjectively regenerated sciences looked so queer that the scientists failed to recognize them in their new positive garb. Astronomy, for example, was reduced to the study of the solar system, because this is the system in which man happens to live; as to so-called sidereal astronomy, Comte branded it as a "grave scientific aberration." Later on he submitted astronomy to a still more drastic reduction by restricting it to the study of the earth and of the other celestial bodies in their relation to the earth. For the earth is *our* planet, the *human* planet, and therefore our astronomical studies should be concentrated around it. In the same way chemistry should be simplified: first, by supposing that all composite bodies are made up of two simple bodies, or of any number of other complex bodies, which may in turn be resolved into two simpler ones; next, by casting off the study of practically all those innumerable chemical bodies which are unworthy of our attention.

When a science had gone through this process of regeneration, what little of it was left had still to face the last, and by far the most dangerous, of its trials: its actual incorporation into the subjective synthesis. As Comte had said at the end of his *System of Positive Philosophy*: "The essentially philosophical point of view finally assigns no other end to the study of natural laws than that of providing us with such a representation of the external world as will meet the essential requirements of our intelligence, insofar as is consistent with the degree of accuracy required by the whole of our practical needs." As soon as he set about to build up his subjective synthesis, it became apparent that practical needs would not tolerate much intellectual accuracy. After all, Comte had now reached a point at which reason had nothing more to say. Were a scientist to say to him: "Since you are so fond of the spirit of science, which you call the positive spirit, why does not positivism let science alone? As a scientist, I strongly object to any one tampering with science on any ground whatsoever, even in the highest interests of man. You do not want science to be the handmaid of theology; I do not want it to be the handmaid of humanity, for the result will be the same in either case, science will be destroyed." What rational arguments could Comte have opposed to such an attitude? Absolutely none. The ultimate reason why science should be regenerated to suit the social needs of humanity cannot possibly be found within science itself; the less you interfere with science, the better it feels; and the more you love science, the less you feel like sacrificing it to anything else. The only justification for such a venture could be not a reason, but a feeling; in point of fact, it could be no other feeling than love for humanity. By thus making love the ultimate foundation of positivism, Comte was repeating, in his own way, and for reasons that were entirely his own, Kant's famous move decreeing the primacy of practical reason. Obviously Comte owed nothing to Kant, but, left as he was with the task of contriving a philosophy without metaphysics, he had no choice other than some sort of moralism. Comte's moralism was to be the sentimentalism which asserts itself at the beginning of his *Discours sur l'ensemble du Positivisme*: "The necessity of assigning with exact truth the place occupied by the intellect and by the heart in the organization of human nature and of society leads to the decision that affection must be the central point of the synthesis." And again: "The foundation of social science bears out the statement made at the beginning of this work, that the intellect under Positivism accepts its proper position of subordination to the heart. The recognition of this, which is the subjective principle of Positivism, renders the construction of a complete system of human life possible." The initial condemnation of metaphysics in the name of science, posited by such philosophies as the only type of rational knowledge, invariably culminates in the capitulation of science itself to some irrational element. This is a necessary law, inferable from philosophical experience, and wholly confirmed by what is often called Comte's second career.

The popular explanation of his sentimental subjectivism is, of course, quite different. When, after going through the six volumes of the *System of Positive Philosophy*, the render stumbles upon the motto of *A General View of Positivism*: "We tire of thinking and even of acting; we never tire of loving," he cannot help wondering what lies behind it? The obvious answer is: a woman; and, in fact, there was one. In Comte's case, *cherchez la femme* is a perfectly superfluous piece of advice, for the problem is not to find her, but to get rid of her and of what he calls "her angelic influence." As Comte says in his inimitable manner: "My career had been that of Aristotle—I should have wanted energy for that of St. Paul, but for her." One should never quarrel with prophets about the source of their inspiration. Comte tells us that Clotilde de Vaux was to him a "new Beatrice." It is a rather good comparison, for it reminds us that though Beatrices are plentiful, very few find their Dante; and so long as there is no Dante, there is no *Divine Comedy*: Clotilde never inspired Comte except with his own ideas. Let us therefore pay due homage to the new Beatrice, without forgetting that the second part of Comte's career flows, not from Clotilde de Vaux, but from the first part of his career, and that with an organic necessity.

As early as 1826, that is eighteen years before he met Clotilde, Comte had laid down the principles of his social and religious reformation in his *Considerations on Spiritual Power*. Anticipating the time when the new positive dogma would have been formulated, he could already foresee the necessity of organizing a new clergy, whose proper function it would be to teach the new truth and to facilitate the rise of a positive social order. As soon as his *System of Positive Philosophy* and his *Positive Politics* were completed, the next move obviously was for Comte to establish a positive spiritual power and, of course, to assume its direction. From that time on, instead of being simply the central principle of his subjective synthesis, humanity became for Comte an object of worship, the positive god, or Great Being, of the new religion whose self-appointed pope he was. The science of sociology thus gave rise to sociolatry, with love as the principle, order as the basis, and progress as the end. As he grew older, Comte felt more and more convinced of the holiness of his religious mission. On Sunday, October 19, 1831, he concluded his third course of philosophical lectures on the General History of Humanity with what he modestly calls "a summary of five hours." The memorable conclusion of that summary was this uncompromising announcement: "In the name of the Past and of the Future, the servants of Humanity—both its philosophical and practical servants—come forward to claim as their due the general direction of this world. Their object is to constitute at length a real Providence in all departments—moral, intellectual, and material. Consequently they exclude, once and for all, from political supremacy all the different servants of God—Catholic, Protestant, or Deist—as being at once outdated and a cause of disturbance."

Having thus excommunicated all the other religions, the High Priest of Humanity set about organizing the new cult. His first thought was for his immortal predecessors, the great men of the eighteenth century, whose destructive work had been carried on so consistently, both in religion and in politics, that, after them, a total and direct reorganization of society had become an absolute necessity. It was not for Voltaire, or Rousseau, whose vague metaphysical deism had given rise to "superficial and immoral sects" wholly alien to the positive spirit, but rather for the great and immortal school of Diderot and Hume. "Hume," says Comte, "is my principal precursor in philosophy," and now we know why his *Essays* are among the few philosophical books listed in the catalogue of the "Positivist Library." But the most important point lies not there, but in the necessary connection which Comte perceived between Hume's complete destruction of metaphysics and religion, and his own reconstruction of religion and politics on the basis of a new philosophy. As compared with Hume, Kant, whose "fundamental conception had never really been systematized and developed except by Positivism," was merely an accessory to Comte. Comte, not Kant, had brought the great Western crisis to a close, since, starting from the universal and absolute negation of Hume, he had at last reached what he calls "the noble object of his wishes, a religion resting on demonstration."

In contrast to Kant, Comte had been both his own Fichte and his own Hegel. This notable fact accounts not only for his lack of enthusiasm for Kant's work, but also for the fact that the two schools broke down in two opposite ways. Kant had to cut loose from Fichte, because he refused to be dragged from positive knowledge to metaphysics and from metaphysics to religion. John Stuart Mill and Littré had to cut loose from Comte, because they refused to be dragged by him from positive philosophy to a new theology and a new religion. The disciples of Kant had travelled too fast and too far for him, Comte was travelling too fast and too far for his early followers. Hence the endless controversy in which Mill and Littré were obliged to oppose Comte on the same point, though not for the same reasons.

Mill had been an independent, but very close, follower of Comte during the first part of the latter's career. He

was very much in favour of a positive philosophy, whereby he meant a complete reliance on scientific knowledge coupled with a decided agnosticism in metaphysics as well as in religion; but as soon as he heard of the subjective synthesis, Mill accused Comte of yielding to an inordinate passion for abstract unity. He then withdrew from the school on the ground that Comte's positive politics and positive religion had really nothing to do with his positive philosophy. Comte, Mill concluded, was at least as great as Descartes and Leibniz, who, of all great scientific thinkers, "were the most consistent, and for that reason the most Absurd, because they shrank from no consequences, however contrary, to common sense, to which their premises appeared to lead." Yes, Comte was as great as they, and hardly more extravagant; only, writing in an age "less tolerant of palpable absurdities," those which he committed, though not in themselves greater, at least appeared more ridiculous.

Littré also wanted a philosophy based upon science and nothing else, but he took exception to the comparison drawn by Mill between Comte and the old metaphysicians. According to Littré, Descartes and Leibniz were wrong because, having laid down wrong principles, they had consistently pursued them to their last consequences; whereas, said Littré, Comte had laid down true philosophical principles, but had failed to follow them in a consistent way: "In the case of both Descartes and Leibniz, the principle was responsible for the consequences; in the case of Mr. Comte, the consequences were arbitrary, but the principle itself remained safe." Littré concluded accordingly that true positivism must be exclusively restricted to Comte's scientific philosophy without any admixture of subjective religion.

Mill and Littré were good men, but they were no match for Comte. Naturally, he was deeply hurt, but that at which he marvelled above all was their shortsightedness. They wanted a positive philosophy free from all subjectivism; in other words, they wanted an "objective synthesis." But *that* was a "palpable absurdity"! Were we to remove from his positivism all its subjective elements, the positive politics and the positive religion would, of course, go, but the positive philosophy itself would also have to go. Comte knew his own doctrine from the inside, and he could not forget how he had made it. Remove the subjective purpose of reorganizing the sciences to suit the social needs of humanity, and nothing will remain but disconnected scientific knowledge, a chaos of unrelated sciences, most of them useless, and the few useful ones themselves encumbered with irrelevant speculation. In short, science would be left, not philosophy. If you reject positive politics and positive religion because of their subjectivity, you must also reject positive philosophy, and for the same reason; if, on the contrary, you accept positive philosophy in spite of its subjectivity, what right have you to condemn positive politics and positive religion? Philosophy is a synthesis; all synthesis is subjective; positive philosophy is a subjective synthesis of objective facts, and this is why it is a philosophy; therefore, you must either take the whole as it is, or leave it.

Comte's sociologism is one of the most striking philosophical experiments recorded by history. Reduced to its simplest expression, it means that if you give up metaphysics as incompletely rational, there remains no other choice but to "regenerate" science on a non-scientific basis, which entails the loss of science; or strictly to maintain the complete objectivity of scientific knowledge, which entails the loss of philosophy. Mill and Littré were right in refusing to tamper with the absolute objectivity of science, for the very existence of science was at stake; but Comte also was right in replying that, having identified rational knowledge with objective scientific knowledge, Mill and Littré could not reject all subjectivity and still have a philosophy. Such being the case, men naturally chose to lose philosophy, thus opening the age of intellectual disorder and social anarchy in which we ourselves are now groping our way.

Eric Voegelin (essay date 1950?)

SOURCE: "The Apocalypse of Man: Comte," in *From Enlightenment to Revolution,* edited by John H. Hallowell, Duke University Press, 1975, pp. 136-59.

[*In the following essay, Voegelin contends that Comte's political philosophy is an apocalyptic vision that establishes Comte as an authoritarian figure.*]

After a century of misunderstanding we are approaching today, on the basis of more recent experiences, a more adequate understanding of Comte both in his quality as an astute philosopher of history and in his more sinister quality as a spiritual dictator of mankind. The history of the misunderstanding of Comte and of the gradual dissolution of these misunderstandings is, at the same time, the history of our growing insight into the Western crisis. Auguste Comte (1798-1857) was well aware of the fact that Western civilization faced a crisis and while he misjudged the duration of the crisis he neither misjudged its scale nor its nature. While his attempt at a solution was as abortive as the contemporary ones, at least one important cause of the failure was the close relationship between Comte's ideas and the totalitarian practice of our times. We might say that our historical understanding is catching up today with the insight of Comte and our political practice with his projected solution.

The split in the life of Comte

If we set aside for a moment the important monographic studies on Comte which have been published in recent years, we may say that the picture of Comte is still determined by the incision in his life that was deep enough to make Comte himself speak of his "first" and "second" life. The crowning achievement of the "first" life is the **Cours de Philosophie Positive** (6 vols., 1830); in his "second" life Comte institutes the Religion of Humanity through his **Système de Politique Positive, ou Traité de Sociologie instituant la Religion de l'Humanité** (4 vols., 1851-54). Between the two periods lies the "incomparable year" of his relation with Clotilde de Vaux in 1845. In the first period he was the theorist of Positivism and the founder of the science to which he gave the name, sociology; in the second period he was the *Fondateur* and *Grand-Prêtre* of the new religion. Until quite recently, this articulation of Comte's life and work has remained the guiding principle for the critical interpretation of the thinker. Comte the positivist and founder of sociology was accepted while Comte the founder of the Religion of Humanity was rejected. For England in particular this pattern was set by John Stuart Mill's study on Comte, first published in the *Westminster Review.* Part I of this study deals with the **Cours** and, within the limits of Mill's abilities, gives a fair, critical appreciation of the work; Part II deals with "The Later Speculations of M. Comte" and gives a somewhat indignant account of the curiosities that are to be found in this later work and which, we agree, do not make sense to common sense. Mill concludes his account with the sentence: "Others may laugh, but we would far rather weep at this melancholy decadence of a great intellect."

Mill's concluding sentence conveys two implications. First, it implies that there was a deep incision in the life and thought of Comte and that Comte's "two lives" self-interpretation should be accepted as correct; second, it implies that the incision has the nature of a "decadence," of something like a mental disturbance. Let us consider this second point first, for this assumption of a mental disturbance and decadence has been for more than one critic the reason which justified his rejection of the "second" Comte. The assumption of the mental disturbance originated in 1851 when Comte greeted with satisfaction the *coup d'état* of Louis Napoleon as a step toward the establishment of the Occidental Republic in which the Positivists would function as the *pouvoir spirituel.* A note, entitled **Essor empirique du républicanisme français** and dated June 17, 1852, gives a fairly clear idea of Comte's political conception at this time; it outlines the phases of development toward the final Republic:

(1) The French Government should be republican and not monarchial. (Crisis of February 1848).

(2) The French republic should be social and not political. (Crisis of June 1848).

(3) The social republic should be dictatorial and not parliamentary. (Crisis of December 1851).

(4) The dictatorial republic should be temporal and not spiritual, in the sense of a complete freedom of exposition, and even of discussion.

(5) Decisive arrival of the systematic triumvirate, characterizing the temporal dictatorship which Positivism has announced since 1847, as the preparatory government that will facilitate the organic transition.

This conception of the *coup d'état* as the step that would lead to the dictatorial "systematic" republic, which in its turn would prepare the final Occidental Republic of all Europe with Positivism as its state religion and with Comte and his successors as the new High Priests—all that was too much for the liberals among Comte's followers. From this time dates the distinction between the unconditional Positivists and the others whom Comte styled the "intellectual Positivists." Among the liberals who left the *Société Positiviste* in December, 1851 was Emile Littré. It seems that to him is due more than to others the new attitude of loyally accepting the first part of Comte's work and of justifying the rejection of the second part by the charge of mental derangement. In his biography of Comte, Littré undertook to "split" his subject, and in a later work he suggested that "the absurdities (in Comte's late work) are more pathological than philosophical.'" In support of the thesis, he recalled Comte's "*crise cérébrale*" of 1826, which incapacitated him for two years, and the charge received publicity when Mme. Comte demanded the annulment of the testament of the *Grand-Prêtre* "because of insanity of mind."

As a matter of fact, Comte was about as sane as anybody. The famous "*crise cérébrale*" of 1826, as far as one can determine on the basis of insufficient reports, seems to have been what today we would call a "nervous breakdown," caused by the unfortunate coincidence of ruthless overwork and domestic troubles; the recovery seems to have been complete. The seceding liberals did not find any insanity in Comte before the "incomparable year." Considering this situation, it will be worthwhile to examine the diagnosis and to see at precisely what point a man becomes insane in the eyes of a liberal, intellectual Positivist. We find the answer to this question in Littré's biography of Comte, in the chapter on "*Retour à l'état théologique.*" Littré first describes the "normal" state of mind which is the "positive" state. In this state the human mind conceives of phenomena as governed by immanent laws. There is no sense in addressing prayers to them or in adoring them. Man must approach them by intelligence; he must get acquainted with them and submit to them in order

to achieve by these means an increasing dominion over nature and over himself, "*ce qui est le tout de la civilization.*" This state of mind is the essential, mature state which is reached historically after the mind has passed through the nonessential, transitory, theological and metaphysical states. In his first period, Comte has developed this theory of the mind and Littré accepts it fully. In his second phase, however, Comte reverts to the theological type; he creates new divinities and, what is worse, he creates a trinity of supreme gods. This leads us to suspect the Catholic influences of his early youth, and we know that such influences, however quiescent they seem to have become, "sometimes will reawaken, not without force, at the decline of life." Moreover, this relapse into theology, as into a kind of second childhood, is not an inconsequential weakness. The return to the theological state is a matter of principle for Comte. When the mind has reached the height of its evolution, when its attitude toward phenomena has become positive, then on Comte's view it must return to its fetishistic beginnings and superimpose on the universe of laws a world of "fictions" which give free expression to the affective and volitional part of the human soul. This part of Comte's philosophy is for the liberal Littré the great fall. The order of the mind can be preserved only if the affective part is under the guidance of reason, for the "heart" and "love" can generate heat but no light. And if it is accepted that the mind cannot do without the belief in divine entities, endowed with will and sentiments, then the whole system of positive philosophy comes crashing down. Positivism rests on the assumption that the theological and metaphysical phases of the mind are transitory and not necessary. If, however, the return to the theological state is considered the end of evolution and progress, if the mind is necessarily theological, then the struggle against this necessity would be as foolish as the struggle against the laws which govern the phenomena of the external world. If the end is the return to the theological state, then we might as well stay in the theological state in which we were before the advent of Positivism. Moreover, if that is the end, how can such dry fictions as those of Comte enter into competition "with the theology which emanates from the depth of history and is enhanced by the grandeur of its institutions and rituals?"

The criterion of integral sanity is the acceptance of Positivism in its first stage. The criteria of decadence or decline are (1) a faith in transcendental reality, whether it expresses itself in the Christian form or in that of a substitute religion, (2) the assumption that all human faculties have a legitimate urge for public expression in a civilization, and (3) the assumption that love can be a legitimate guiding principle of action, taking precedence before reason. This diagnosis of mental deficiency is of an importance which can hardly be exaggerated. It is not the isolated diagnosis of Littré; it is rather the typical attitude toward the values of Western civilization which has continued among "intellectual positivists" from the time of Mill and Littré down to the neo-Positivistic schools of the Viennese type. Moreover, it has not remained confined to the schools but has found popular acceptance to such a degree that this variant of Positivism is today one of the most important mass movements. It is impossible to understand the graveness of the Western crisis unless we realize that the cultivation of values beyond Littré's formula of civilization as the dominion of man over nature and himself by means of science is considered by broad sectors of Western society to be a kind of mental deficiency.

As far as the interpretation of Comte is concerned, it took a considerable time until the fable of his mental derangement was overcome outside the restricted circle of Comtean sectarians. The decisive publication is the monograph by George Dumas on the *Psychologie de Deux Messies* [1905]. Dumas does not burden himself with the problem of the two lives of Comte; Saint-Simon has only one, but in this one life he is quite capable of developing the same messianic characteristics as Comte. Dumas, furthermore, dispels the atmosphere of strangeness, which disturbed Littré and Mill, by placing the two prophets into the spiritual situation of their time. The critique of the eighteenth century had ruined the prestige of Catholicism and monarchy; the Revolution had marked the end of a religious as well as of a political régime. The contemporaries were too near to the catastrophe to see how much was left standing of the old civilization in spite of the general destruction. They believed that nothing survived, that the future had to be made anew, and enthusiasts in great numbers felt the call to preach the moral and political gospel for the new age. Saint-Simon was only the first of them, through his *Lettres d'un habitant de Genève* of 1803, but he was soon followed by Fourier, Comte, d'Enfantin, Bazard and a host of minor Saint-Simonians. "They took themselves seriously for men of destiny, marked by a fatal sign on their forehead." Saint-Simon entitles himself the scientific pope of humanity and vicar of God on earth; he acts as the successor to Moses, Socrates and Christ and he admonishes the princes to listen to the voice of God that speaks through his mouth. Enfantin divinizes Saint-Simon and sees himself in the role of the new Isaac, new Jesus and new Gregory VII. In a letter to Duveyrier he writes: "When you believe to speak to Moses, Jesus and Saint-Simon, Bazard and I shall receive your words. Have you well considered that Bazard and I have nobody above ourselves except Him who is always tranquil because He is eternal love." Comte released in 1851 the "decisive" Proclamation by which he "took over" the leadership of the Western world: "in the name of the past and the future, the theoretical servants and the practical servants of Humanity assume befittingly the general leadership of the affairs of the earth in order to construct, at last, the true provi-

dence, moral, intellectual and material; they irrevocably exclude from political supremacy all the various slaves of God, Catholics, Protestants, or Deists, since they are retrogrades as well as perturbators." Dumas, finally, draws attention to the great model of the messianic figures on the historical scene as well as in contemporary literature, that is to Napoleon. His influence is visible, in various degrees, in most of the historical and literary figures of this type, and it is visible in particular in Comte. Not that Comte was his follower; on the contrary, he execrated him as the "retrograde genius." But Napoleon was nevertheless for Comte the concretization of the messiah, though of a rival messiah. The sentiment of rivalry was so intense that Comte considered it one of the foremost symbolic acts of the coming Occidental Republic to destroy the monument on the Place Vendôme and to replace it by a monument for the true founder of the Occident whose work Comte wanted to continue, that is of Charlemagne. Saint-Simon and Comte, thus, were no more extravagant or strange than any number of their contemporaries. [In the words of Dumas, they] were two instances of a species "that was rather widespread between 1800 and 1848 and of which one cannot say that it ever disappears completely, although in the great social revolutions it will without doubt find the occasion and the special reasons for its development."

The work of Dumas has disposed of Comte's mental derangement. The disposal leads us back to the problem of Littré. If there was no decline in Comte's later years, if as a messiah he was a typical figure, one of many in his age, the question arises: What actually did happen? Did anything happen at all? Or did not perhaps the "second" life, in spite of the "incomparable year," quite intelligibly continue the "first" one? And is not the great break perhaps an invention of Littré's? We shall have to deal with the problem of continuity in Comte's life presently but for the moment we shall anticipate the result and state that there was no break in continuity. The messianism of Comte is not a second phase in his life; it is present from the beginning, that is from approximately 1820. The idea of the new *pouvoir spirituel* of which he will be the founder is fully developed by 1822. If anything is characteristic of Comte's life it is the peculiar "plan" which it follows from the mid-twenties to his death in 1857. Moreover, this "plan," as we shall see, was no secret, since several times in the course of its gradual realization it was published in print for everybody to read. The great theoretical work, the **Cours**, was never intended as anything but the basis for the later religious work, and anyone who cared to inform himself could know it.

If we realize this situation clearly, the withdrawal of Littré, as well as the indignation of Mill, appear in a new light. For the interpretation of this phenomenon, Dumas has given the clue. The contemporaries of the great revolutionary upheaval were too near to the catastrophe to see how much of the old structure of sentiments and institutions was left standing. Hence the crowding of the prophets and messiahs of the new age. By the middle of the century, in spite of unpleasant reminders that all might not be well (such as the revolutions of 1830 and 1848 and the *coup d'état* of Louis Napoleon), the structure of the liberal bourgeois society begins to emerge with the appearance of stability. Comte is a late comer. His messianism reaches in its origins into the unsettlement of the Revolution and it comes to its full flowering precisely at the opening of the temporary stabilization of the Western crisis in the second half of the nineteenth century. That part of Comte's theoretical work that serves the destruction of the *ancien régime,* that attacks Christianity and establishes the scientist creed, is acceptable to the generation of the mid-century; the part that serves the foundation of the new religion and the institutionalization of a new society is unacceptable to the liberals who feel comfortable precisely in the fragmentary civilization which Littré has so succinctly formulated as to its substance and which he calls *"le tout de la civilization."* We have heard, furthermore, Littré's heart-felt complaint: for what purpose have we destroyed the unreasonable, nonpragmatic values of Western civilization, if now we must cultivate the same type of values again in a not so glorious imitation?

A diagnosis of Littre's liberalism

In this conflict between Comte and Littré, we can lay our finger on the principal structural problem of the Western crisis. Its structure is that of a gradual decomposition of civilizational values, consummated historically by repeated upheavals which destroy, or intend to destroy, the social bearers of the condemned values. Between the upheavals we find periods of stabilization at the respective levels of destruction. The attitudes toward this structure of the crisis may differ. In the case of Comte we see the great, intramundane eschatologist who underestimates the length of time which such a process of destruction needs, who anticipates its end, and who "plans" the new age. On the other side we see the liberal Littré who is satisfied by the amount of destruction worked up to this point and who is ready to settle down in the ruins. The two types are brothers under the skin though the virtues and vices are variously distributed among them. The Comtean type is vitiated by the megalomania that an individual man can grasp and "plan" the course of history and impose his "plan" on mankind. He is distinguished, however, from the other type by his profound insight into the nature and dimensions of the crisis. He knows that destruction is not an end in itself but the prelude to regeneration, and when he attacks the spiritual authority of the Church he does it in order to replace it by the church that lives by his own spiritual authority. Littré's type represents the peculiar mixture of destruc-

tiveness and conservatism that is an important component in the complex of sentiments and ideas which we call "liberal." He is willing to participate in revolution until civilization is destroyed to the point which corresponds to his own fragmentary personality. He is not literate enough to understand that Christianity is one thing, and the corruption of a Church quite another; hence, he is ready to eliminate Christianity from history because, quite understandably, he does not like the state of the Church. He is not intelligent enough to understand the problem of the institutionalization of the spirit. Since he lives in the illusion that one can ruin the prestige of a Church or abolish it, and that then matters will be settled, he is greatly surprised and frightened when a new variant of the spirit raises its head, one that he likes even less than Christianity, and clamors for institutionalization in place of the Church of which he has just got rid. He cannot understand these problems, because as a man he has not substance enough to be sensitive to spiritual problems and to cope with them adequately. On the other hand, he is only a mild megalomaniac; he certainly believes that this is the best of all worlds when it is ruined enough to correspond to his limitations, but at least he does not believe that he is a demiurge who can form men in his image. On the contrary, there is left in him from the Christian and humanistic periods a certain self-respect and respect for the personality of others, a sturdy sense of independence which distinguishes French republicanism in its good period, before it was finally broken by the mob hysterics during the Dreyfus affair. By virtue of these qualities, the liberal of this type is highly sensitive to movements which are apt to endanger his independence economically or politically. Since the process of decomposition does not stop, he is pressed more and more into a conservative position, until, in our time, the few surviving specimens of the genus are labelled as reactionary. The break of Littré with Comte is due to his fright in face of the dictatorial spectre, though he was blind to the inner logic of Comte's movement from "intellectual Positivism" to its religious form. In spite of our weighing of virtues and vices there is not much to choose between them. The liberal Positivist reduces the meaning of humanity to the dominion, by science, over nature and man, and thereby deprives man of his spiritual life and freedom; the dictatorial eschatologist collects the castrates and grafts his own spirit on them. The one plays into the hands of the other and through their interplay the crisis goes its accelerating course.

We have stressed that Comte never made a secret of his plan. If a contemporary did not have enough imagination to visualize the end toward which theoretical Positivism must lead, he could inform himself about the continuity of Comte's intention and about the aim toward which it was moving from the ample expositions of Comte himself. The enigmatic element in this situation receives some light from a passage in [Henri]

Gouhier's treatise on Comte, where the author deals with the strange blindness. As Gouhier points out: "It is easy for the independent historian to believe in the unity of Comte's thought; that does not oblige him to anything. He must place himself, however, in the position of Littré and Professor Ch. Robin, before he says that they have not understood or, as certain positivists have suggested, that they were not interested to understand. For them, let us not forget, it was a question of conceding to a high priest the right to marry them and to baptize their infants; they ran the risk of being appointed triumvirs and, on occasion of their funeral, to be judged in public with an outspokenness of which the unfortunate Blainville had experienced the severity, though he was associated with Lamarck in the new calendar. That the 'intellectual positivists,' as Comte said, have mutilated the authentic doctrine, is certain; our historical reconstruction of the system, however correct it may be, does not authorize us, however, to neglect the fact that, beginning from a certain moment, eminent and sincere men have no longer recognized the philosophy which study and their life had rendered them familiar." Gouhier has touched the decisive point: the "eminent and sincere men" are willing to accept Positivism as long as it is an irresponsible intellectual attitude but they no longer recognize it when the necessity for order in their lives obliges them to practice its principles in every day life. Gouhier's book was published in 1933. A few years later, he might have recognized in the "eminent and sincere men" the forerunners of the good Germans who got emotionally drunk on the harangues of the savior as long as their intellectual stupor did not oblige them to anything, and who shrank back in horror when the program, about which they were perfectly well informed, was translated into political action. Littré and his contemporaries had the good fortune to live at a time when they could withdraw when the crucial moment came; their modern successors could barely murmur "*so haben wir es nicht gemeint*" before they were caught and silenced by the machinery of the new Golden Age.

The continuity in the life of Comte

The question of continuity in Comte's ideas, thus, has dissolved into the question of the split between integral Positivists and intellectual Positivists. A generation later, when the animosities among the living had died, agreement on the continuity is achieved. The work of Lévy-Bruhl on Comte is representative of the new atmosphere. Nevertheless, with this agreement we have not reached the end of the affair. We remember that the seceding intellectuals could support their charges by Comte's own insistence on the great incision of 1845. Hence the love for Clotilde de Vaux and the bearing which it had on the development of Comte needs some clarification. Moreover, the word "continuity" raises a question rather than answering one. As a matter of fact, the question of what precisely the

continuous element in the various phases of Comte's work consists turns out to be rather thorny. In endeavoring to answer this question we receive considerable help from the studies on Comte by Gouhier and Ducassé, but even these studies, masterful as they are, can hardly be the last word, for they are inclined to neglect what is most important, that is, the character of Comte as an intramundane eschatologist.

We shall approach the problem through the intellectual autobiography which Comte has given, under the title *Préface Personnelle*, in the last volume of the *Cours*. The story is somewhat stylised but substantially correct. Comte came from a family of southern France, strongly Catholic and monarchical. He received his first education in one of the *lycées* which Napoleon had created for the restoration of the old "theologico-metaphysical" educational régime. At the age of fourteen he had already gone through the essential phases of the revolutionary spirit and had experienced the need for a "universal regeneration" that would be both philosophical and political. The later education at the *École Polytechnique* made him see the only intellectual path that would lead to this "great renovation": the methods of science which are used in mathematics and physics must be applied not only to inorganic phenomena but to organic and social phenomena as well. During the period in which he acquired a knowledge of biology and history, the idea of the true "encyclopedic hierarchy" of the sciences began to develop. And at the same time there was growing in him the instinct of a "final harmony" between his intellectual and political tendencies. These beginnings, which were influenced by Condorcet, were thrown into some confusion, on leaving the *École,* through his association with Saint-Simon. The older man had also understood the need for a "social regeneration" based on a "mental renovation" and this coincidence had a disturbing influence because it interrupted the philosophical work of Comte and turned his interests toward a regeneration through "futile attempts at direct political action." By 1822, however, he had recovered his equilibrium, and at the age of twenty-four he made the fundamental discovery of the law of the three phases which produced in him the "true mental and even social unity." Such a "philosophical harmony," however, could not be truly "constituted" before the actual elaboration of the new positive philosophy. In 1842, this task is finished and the reader now has in his hands the "final systematization" of this philosophy that had been in formation since Descartes and Bacon.

In the closing pages of the *Préface Personnelle,* Comte reveals some details of the technique which he employed in the conscious "operation" of producing his own "unity." He reflects that the philosophers of antiquity were in a more favorable position than the moderns because their "meditation" was not disturbed by reading vast quantities of literature; permanent irritation through reading affects the "originality" of a meditation as well as its "homogeneity." Comte protected himself against this disturbance in the following manner. In his early youth he amassed the materials which seemed to him necessary for his great plan of founding the final positive philosophy and "for the last twenty years" (this date would carry us back to the great discovery of 1822) he had imposed on himself a *hygiène cérébrale*. In order not to confuse the "*esprit fondamental*" of his work, he denied himself the reading of any literature which had a bearing on the subject-matter on which he was working. When he approached the second part of the *Cours,* that is the volumes on sociology, he went further and stopped reading any philosophical and political periodicals, dailies or monthlies. With regard to the sociological volumes, moreover, he reduced his preparatory reading and he prides himself on never having read Vico, Kant, Herder or Hegel in any language, though he is willing now to learn German in order to compare his "new mental unity" with the German systematic efforts. To this *hygiène* he attributes the "precision, energy and consistency" of his conceptions.

At the end of volume 6 of the *Cours,* finally, Comte views in retrospect what has happened during the "operation" of writing the six volumes. The *Cours* resumes "the philosophical impulse of Bacon and Descartes." This impulse was exhausted with the preliminaries of creating the inorganic sciences in the spirit of "rational positivity." Through the Revolution, the human mind was compelled to face the problem of "final renovation" in this spirit. At first this problem was only seen in a confused manner but now we know that a "situation without precedent" required "philosophical intervention" in order to dispel imminent anarchy and to transform the revolutionary agitation into organic activity. The *Cours* is this philosophic intervention in the troubles of the age. It is not, however, "direct action" in the Saint-Simonian sense; rather, it is the concrete process in which a man's intelligence reproduces "personally" the principal successive phases of modern mental evolution. As a consequence, the intelligence of Comte has disengaged itself at the end of this work completely from metaphysics and theology and arrived at the "full positive state." And by virtue of this substantial transformation it will now hopefully exert such a fascination on all energetic thinkers as will induce them to collaborate with him in the *systématisation finale de la raison moderne.* The "spontaneous reproduction," in the sense of Descartes, of modern evolution in the *Cours* which has elevated the reader and himself to the "positive state," must now be followed by the detailed elaboration of the various sciences in the spirit of the "new philosophical unity." This explanation is followed by the enumeration of the works through which he will participate in the systematization. The most important of these works will be the *Philosophie Politique,* projected as a treatise of

four volumes. Since the present *Cours* has culminated in the "universal mental preponderance" of the social point of view, conceived logically and scientifically, one cannot cooperate better toward the "final installation" of the new philosophy than by elaborating the "normal state" of the corresponding political science.

The phases in Comte's work

The self-interpretation of 1842 can be corroborated by later utterances of Comte; we shall confine ourselves, however, to the present summary as the basis for further discussion because the autobiography of the *Cours* lies before the critical year 1845 and hence cannot be suspected of hindsight with regard to the problem of continuity. The foregoing passages cast light on several aspects of this problem. We shall consider them successively. The first will be the sequence of the phases of Comte's work that emerges from his own account.

The first phase is the period of the initial intuition, centering in the "great discovery" of 1822. The works of this period which in the opinion of Comte merited permanent attention were republished by him as the *Appendice Général* of Volume 4 of the *Système.* Besides two minor works, this appendix contains the *Plan de travaux scientifiques nécessaires pour reorganiser la société.* This is the work of 1822 in which Comte developed the law of the three phases. It was republished in 1824 under the title *Système de politique positive.* Comte appropriated this title later for his second main work, and assigned to the minor work the new title in the appendix. The *Plan* is followed by the *Considérations philosophiques sur les sciences et les savants* (1825) and the *Considérations sur le pouvoir spirituel* (1826). These three works together contain, indeed, as Comte maintained, the substance of his later elaboration. The second phase is the period in which Comte elaborates his positive theory, first orally, then in literary form. The result is the *Cours de Philosophie Positive,* published 1830-42. The third phase is that of the Occidental Republic and the writings which institute its religion and its spiritual power. The main work is the *Système de Politique Positive,* 1851-54. Other writings which are of specific importance for the history of political ideas are the *Discours sur l'ensemble du positivisme* (1848), later incorporated as *Discours Préliminaire* in Volume 1 of the *Système;* the *Appel au public occidental* (1848); the manifesto for the Positivist Society (1848): *Le Fondateur de la Société positiviste, a quiconque désire s'y incorporer;* the *Calendrier positiviste* of 1849; the *Catéchisme Positiviste, ou Sommaire exposition de la religion universelle en onze entretiens systématiques entre une femme et un prêtre de l'Humanité* (1852); and, finally, the *Appel aux conservateurs* (1855), destined to fulfill for the Occidental statesmen the function which the *Cathéchisme* fulfills for "proletarians and women." The fourth and last phase we may call that of the Global Republic. The main work of this period is the *Synthèse Subjective, ou Système universel des conceptions propres a l'état normal de l'Humanité*. Of this work only the first volume, *Système de Logique Positive, ou Traité de philosophie mathématique* (1856), was published. In 1857 Comte died. This last work is written already within the new age and it is destined for use by the educational authorities of the new republic. The work was planned in three parts. The first part, the only one published, contains the philosophy of mathematics, the second part was to contain the *Système de Morale Positive,* the last part was to be the *Système d'Industrie Positive*. We have designated this last phase as that of the Global Republic because in the 1850's Comte's imagination began to range beyond the Occidental Republic and to include the non-Western civilizations into his great plan. The documents for this final development are the letter *A Sa Majesté le tzar Nicolas* (December 20, 1852) and the letter *A Son Excellence Reschid-Pascha, ancien grand vizir de l'Empire Ottoman* (February 4, 1853), which must be considered as diplomatic approaches for a federation of Russia and the Islamic world with the Occidental Republic. In the *Synthèse,* finally, we find indications that the religious system of the Republic was to be enlarged in such a manner that it could absorb African and Chinese forms of religiousness.

Meditation and personal renovation

The phases of Comte's work are no more than the skeleton of his mental development. Even the brief characterization of this skeleton, however, confirms the interpretation which Comte himself has put on the process of his meditation. Let us turn now to this process itself. The works of Comte are not simply a series of treatises on various subject matters. They are connected with each other as the "elaboration" of an initial "intuition." Moreover, elaboration is not the systematic amplification of a "good idea," or the carrying out of a "project." While the term "elaboration" certainly contains the element of conscious direction or of a "plan," this "operation" is conceived as the "renovation" of a person, as its substantial transformation to the point where it has reached the state of "positive rationality." The initial intuition is the visionary anticipation of this final state and the meditative process (which precipitates in the literary work) is the means by which this state is reached. The insight into the character of the work as a precipitate of a meditation is the first requirement for understanding Comte's peculiar *modus operandi*. The encyclopedic survey of the sciences from mathematics to sociology in the *Cours* is not meant as an introduction to these sciences. It is meant, first, as the disengagement of the positive method from the actual state of the sciences in which it was previously employed, secondly, as the extension of this method to the science of man in society (which for this purpose had to be created) and thirdly, by means of this extension to clarify the true place of man in society in such a manner that in the thinker who has engaged in this meditation there will be created the disposition toward "a way of life" in conformity with this insight. Since the meditation is a spiritual practice, and not at all primarily a scientific exploration of the world, the question whether Comte's *Cours* renders faithfully the actual state of science, or the question of obsolescence, cannot legitimately be raised. Comte defends himself in the *Préface Personnelle* against criticisms of this kind precisely by the argument that the changing state of science has no bearing on the spirit which characterizes the positive method. The famous *hygiène cérébrale,* which aroused Mill is therefore entirely appropriate to Comte's "operation": once the initial orientation and vision are given, the accumulation of new materials and the opinions of others can only disturb a process of which the end is known at the beginning.

Intervention and social regeneration

Thus far we have considered the meditative process only in the solitary existence of the thinker. The Comtean operation, however, gains a further dimension through the relation between personal "renovation" and social "regeneration." We have seen that Comte characterized the state which the "great discovery" produced in him as a state of "mental and even social unity." The personal intuition has the consequence of integrating the thinker into society because the law of the three phases is a law of personal evolution as well as of social evolution. If we use a later biological terminology, we may say that the law is valid for the ontogenesis as well as for the phytogenesis. Comte passes from the early Catholicism of his home, through the revolutionary spirit of eighteenth century metaphysics, to the positive intuition, and correspondingly mankind passes from the theological, through the metaphysical, to the positivistic stage. The convergence of the two evolutions, however, is not automatic. Mankind does not pass from contemporary anarchy to the positive order without a personal effort. The social regeneration requires an active, personal intervention. A man of vision must come and realize the meaning of the critical epoch. He must produce in himself the transition to the positive state and through the fascination of his personal renovation inspire the regeneration of mankind. Correspondingly, his spiritual authority in this social operation will derive from the fact that the transformation which he produces in himself personally is the very transformation which it is the destiny of mankind to undergo at this crucial hour of its history. The man who initiates the social regeneration through his personal renovation thus becomes the chosen instrument by means of which the *esprit humain* operates its own progress to the new and final level of positive order.

The interlocking of the personal and the social processes in the one historical movement of mankind sometimes assumes curious forms in the routine of daily life. In the **Préface Personnelle,** Comte explains the reasons why volume 2 of the **Cours** appeared only in 1834, that is four years after the publication of the first volume, though it had been projected for a much earlier date. The reason was the upheaval of 1830 which compelled Comte to find a new publisher. The point is that the delay was not due to the fact that a finished manuscript could not go to press but that Comte would not even start to write the second volume before he had the guarantee that it would be printed as soon as he had finished the last sentence. "My nature and my habits," he tells us, made it impossible ever to write a book "unless it is written in view of immediate publication." The personal meditative process has to stream over immediately into the social process of regeneration. This is not an accidental trait in Comte's character; it is a fundamental trait in his style of communication. It accounts for the interminable length of sentences, paragraphs, chapters and volumes which is not necessitated by the requirement of clear presentation of the subject matter, but by the desire for relentless communication of every intellectual shade of the precious meditation. It accounts in particular for the monomanic use of adjectives and adverbs which characterize and qualify nothing but incessantly convey the sense of fatality of the urgent operation in which the author is engaged and in which the reader through his perusal is supposed to participate. These are *"les adverbes, les innombrables, les assonnants adverbes"* such as *assurément, radicalement, décisivement, spontanément, pleinement, directement, suffisament, necessairement, irrévocablement, certainement, exclusivement, principalement, irresistiblement,* and so forth. These adverbs (of which we have given the crop of two pages), a corresponding series of adjectives, and the deadly host of adverbial appositions, swamp the nucleus of meaning so effectively that only with a continuous effort can it be disengaged from the steady stream of words. This does not mean that Comte's writing is confused; on the contrary, the construction of the sentences is logically and grammatically impeccable, and the organization of the subject matter is superbly clear. Comte's style is a phenomenon *sui generis* for which Ducassé has found the formula of a complete explicitation of the meditative existence of the thinker. Nothing remains unsaid; every nook and corner of Comte's thought, every swerve and every side path of this priceless operation must be communicated to the public.

Comte seems to have been a man without privacy. His style is only one symptom of the conscious and radical transformation of his personal life into a part of the public, historical life of mankind. Nothing is too intimate to escape this monumentalization. The details of his relation with Clotilde de Vaux, the most intimate movements of his soul, have been spread before the public in a manner that could not be called anything but tactless and repulsive, unless this publicity is understood as the eternal embodiment into the memory of mankind of a spiritual event that is of greater importance than the birth of Christ. The principle of *"Vivre au grand jour"* does not respect even the dignity of death. Those who have entered into the body of positive mankind live in it forever "subjectively" in commemoration. This memory of mankind must be both public and just; hence it is incumbent on the High Priest of Humanity to fix the just image of the deceased forever, and what occasion could be more fit for fixing this image than a speech at the grave? In fulfillment of this obligation, Comte delivered a most insulting appreciation of Blainville on the occasion of his funeral. He was not in the least abashed by the scandal which he created. He reprinted the speech in the appendix to volume 1 of the **Systéme** and he even added a postscript in which he reports how various public dignitaries left the ceremony when Comte disturbed it by his outrageous performance: "In order to understand this discourse better, one must note that its opening determined the brusque departure of all the official representatives of the various decadent classes, both theological and academic. That the field was left in this manner to the *esprits positifs* indicates sufficiently where the reputation of Blainville will find its permanent home."

Let us, finally, record the monumentalization of troubles and trivialities of his personal life. A man of this character, as one can imagine does not fit too well into social institutions and public functions. The professorship which he expected as his due never materialized and he was finally discharged even of his secondary functions. The details of this struggle with the educational authorities again were communicated to the public in long hagiographic accounts. And when Comte was ultimately without an income, he solved the problem by public subscriptions from Positivists sectarians. He issued annual "budget messages" to the subscribers in which he formulated his requirements for the coming year and accounted for the expenditures of the revenue received during the last year. These *Circulaires* were also communicated in print because they were public documents in which the High Priest, besides the budget of the sacerdotal power, also reported the progress which the Church had made in the spreading of membership and administration of sacraments during the past year as well as the projects for the future. The monumentalizing, hagiographic obsession goes to such extremes that we are informed about the relation between the meditative progress of Comte and his consumption of stimulants. On the occasion of the crisis of 1826 he gave up tobacco, on the occasion of a minor crisis in 1838 he gave up coffee, and on the occasion of Clotilde de Vaux he gave up wine—a sacrifice which reduced materially his personal expenditures, as he assured the subscribers in the *Circu-*

laires. If he had survived his death, he certainly would have informed mankind that now he had given up everything. As a matter of fact, even in death he did not give up everything for through his **Testament** he took care at least of his "subjective" survival. His apartment (10, rue Monsieur-le-Prince) will be the Holy See of the Religion of Humanity. It will belong to the successor in the pontificate on the same conditions as it belonged to Comte: that its content, and everything that will be added to it, will belong to the future pontiffs in the succession. Only one exception is made. The successor must respect all the reliques of Clotilde de Vaux as belonging to the sacred treasure of the universal Church. Particular veneration is due to "the red chair, enveloped in a green cover, and marked on its front board with my initials in red wax." This is the chair on which Clotilde de Vaux has sat during her sacred visits on Wednesdays. "I have erected it, even during her life-time, and still more so after her death, into a domestic altar; I have never sat on it except for religious ceremonies." It must serve no other function so long as it lasts.

The divinization of woman

What influence did the relation with Clotilde de Vaux have on the development of Comte's ideas? While the relationship did not influence the theoretical content of Comte's philosophy it strongly affected Comte's *vie sentimentale.* The daily prayers which Comte offered to Clotilde are illustrative. In the **Prière du Matin** we find Comte saying: "It is only you, my saint Clotilde, to whom I am obliged that I do not leave this life without having experienced the best emotions of human nature. An incomparable year made spontaneously surge up the only love, pure and profound, that was destined for me. The excellence of the adored being allows me in my maturity, more favored than my youth, to glimpse in all its fullness true human felicity. *Vivre pour autrui.*" In the **Commémoration Générale**, which comprises a *Revue Chronologique de tous nos souvenirs essentials d'après les passages correspondants de nos lettres,* we find, under the heading *Union définitive,* the quotation: "In order to become a perfect philosopher I needed a passion, profound and pure, that would make me appreciate the affective part of human nature." The letter from which this passage is taken continues: "Its explicit consideration, no more than implied in my first great work, will now dominate my second one. This final evolution, even more indispensable for me today than eight or ten years ago, was the decisive upsurge of my aesthetic tastes." The **Prière du Soir** continues this reflection: "By virtue of your powerful invocation, the most painful crisis of my intimate life has finally improved me in every respect, for I was able, though I was alone, to develop the sacred seeds of which the belated but decisive evolution I owe to you. The age of private passions had terminated for me. . . . From then on I surrendered myself exclusively to the eminent passion which, since my adolescence, has consecrated my life to the fundamental service of Humanity. . . . The systematic preponderance of universal love, gradually emanating from my philosophy, would not have become sufficiently familiar to me without you, in spite of the happy preparation which resulted from the spontaneous upsurge of my aesthetic tastes." "Under your various images, in spite of the catastrophe, you will always recall to me that my final situation surpasses everything I could have hoped for, or even dreamt of, before you. The more this harmony without example between my private and my public life develops (which I owe to you), the more you incorporate yourself, in the eyes of my true disciples, into every mode of my existence."

Without the transformation of the affective life of Comte through Clotilde there would have been a positive political theory which would have even postulated the preponderance of sentiment over intellect, but the faith would have lacked its existential concreteness. The religiousness of Comte that was released through the experience of 1845 has certain characteristics which merit attention. The concrete unity of Comte's existence is reached through the incorporation of Clotilde "into every mode of his existence." Comte's love, for which he has invented the term *altruism,* is not an *amor Dei* that would orient the soul toward transcendental reality. The place of God has been taken by social entities (by family, country and mankind) and more particularly by woman as the integrating, harmonizing principle. Woman in general and Clotilde concretely as the representative of the principle has become the unifying power for the soul of man; hence the cult of Clotilde is an essential part of the Comtean religious foundation. In the **Prières** we find a section *A genoux devant l'autel recouvert* (that is, the famous red chair), with the following litany:

(A mon éternelle compagne)
Amem te plus quam me, nec me nisi propter
  te!
(A l'Humanité dans son temple, devant son
  grand autel)
Amem te plus quam me, nec me nisi propter
  te!

(A ma noble patronne, comme personnifiant
  l'Humanité)
Vergine-madre, Figlia del tuo figlio,
Amem te plus quam me, nec me nisi propter
  te!

Tre dolci nome ha' in te raccolti
Sposa, madre, e figliuola!

                                   (Petrarca)

To the new *vergine-madre* is transferred the Christian *Amem te plus quam me, nec me nisi propter te!*

The historicity of the mind

The pages of the **Discours Préliminaire** reveal Comte's conception of the historicity of the mind. The mind has a constant intellectual-affective structure. The possibility and necessity of historical evolution enters this structure because the two component factors can stand in various relations to each other. The history of the mind begins with an excessive preponderance of the affective and volitional life. This preponderant experience is projected into the environment and the events in nature are interpreted as actions which emanate from entities endowed with a will and affects. The evolution of the intellect is secondary. It has an "insurrectional" aspect because its function is to dissolve the false interpretation of the world that has been created by the affective component. Nevertheless, the volitional and affective interpretation is not altogether false. Once the domain of the intellect has been extended far enough to bring the order of the universe, and the place of man in it, into full view, the "insurrectional" function of the intellect must come to an end. The terminal point for the expansion of the intellect is reached when all sciences of the world content, that is the inorganic, organic and social sciences, are fully developed. The laws which govern this world are all that man can know and ought to know. Once he has become acquainted with this order, he must submit to it. He must fit his life into it and embrace it with affection. The advancement of science abolishes the excesses of the theological state but it does not abolish religiousness and the affective life. On the contrary, without the guidance of the affections the work of intellect would be aimless. The supreme affection of altruism must be the guiding principle of social life, providing the aims; the function of science can only be the increasing knowledge of the means by which the aims can be realized. Ducassé remarks rightly: "We must completely reverse the pejorative appreciation that is sometimes extended to the utilitarianism of Comte. If we charge the word 'utility' with its true affective, spiritualist and charitable intentions, we must say: Precisely because of the immediate connection which it institutes between the experience of mathematical invention and the exigencies of charity (that is of the desire of spiritual utility among men), is the Comtean form of inspiration new and superior." Comte has compressed these principles of the constitution of the mind in the formula: "*L'Amour pour principe et l'Ordre pour base, le Progrès pour but.*" In his last work, the **Synthèse**, he expresses the subordination of the intellect to the heart in the Christian formula: "*Omnis ratio, et naturalis investigatio fidem sequi debet, non precedere, nec infringere.*"

Nevertheless, the Christian assonances, the magic of such words as "charity," "love," "spirituality" and "faith" must not deceive us. When Ducassé stresses the spirituality of Comte's utilitarianism, he certainly is right; but such spirituality is not at all reassuring. A consistent utilitarian who believes that the problems of life are solved when the standard of living is rising is a comparatively innocuous fellow. A spiritual utilitarian is a much more dangerous person for he speaks with the authority of spirit and for this reason his claims may gain a semblance of legitimacy. He does not merely insist that you make yourself "useful" (which would be bad enough in itself), he demands that you conform your personality to his faith—and the nature of his faith may not be to your liking. That there is such a thing as an evil spirit has never occurred to Comte, nor does it seem to have occurred to Ducassé, who is a convinced Comtean sectarian. Once such terms as "love" or "faith" can be used at all, no further problems of the spirit seem to exist. We also must beware of such formulations as Thomas Huxley's that Positivism is "Catholicism minus Christianity." The formula is brilliant but senseless. That the Comtean Religion of Humanity is not Christian, we may agree. That Comte has been inspired in his dogmatic formulations as well as in his ecclesiastical projects by Catholic forms, we may also agree. What Huxley's formula does not convey is the positive substance of Comte's religiousness which has to be expressed in such terms as the apocalypse of man, as intramundane eschatology, as divinization of world-immanent entities.

Hence Littré's complaint about Comte's *rétour à l'état théologique* must be taken with a grain of salt. Comte returns, indeed, to the *état théologique* of his conception but he does not return to the religiousness of Christianity as it has existed, and still does exist, historically. And he cannot return to a Christian religiousness because he never had an adequate conception of it in the first place. Comte's conception of the mental constitution of man is monadic. To be sure, the mind evolves historically; but the historical evolution of the mind is immanent to its constitution; the component factors of the mind are the only forces which determine this evolution. The mind is a monad with an immanent history; at no point can this prison be broken. Religiousness, for Comte, is not a participation in transcendental reality, a communication in which the spirituality of man is constituted as the autonomous, organizing center of his personality; rather, religiousness is a movement of the *vie sentimentale* which results in a more or less true interpretation of the world. The fallacy of Comte's position can be put in one sentence; Religion is theology, and theology is an interpretation of the world in competition with science. This demonic closure of the monad is the basis of Comte's speculation. The historical world of Comte does not begin with an *état théologique*; it begins with Comte's "intuition." Insofar as this intuition has absorbed a certain amount of historical knowledge, this knowledge can be projected on a time scale and be called the evolution of the *esprit humain,* and since Comte's historical knowledge was considerable, the projection will even have a certain degree of empirical adequacy. Nevertheless, an adequate philosophy of history can never result from an "intuition" which is itself nothing but an event in history, for the problem of human history is precisely the tension between the historical existence of man and his transcendental destination. The speculation of Comte begins with a compact "intuition" and is followed by its "explication," "elaboration," and "concretization" quite legitimately supported by the *hygiène cérébrale.* The elaboration, therefore, can follow a "plan" and it can be directed from the beginning to the foreknown end. We should pay attention in particular to Comte's favorite word for this process, namely, the word "operation." The word awakens the association of the alchemystic *opus operatum,* of the successful liberation of the spirit from matter through a human agency.

The personal "renovation" of Comte merges with social "regeneration" into the one process of progressing mankind. The life of the *Grand Être,* of Divine Humanity, streams through the life of Comte. Every phase of this life is a divine manifestation since in this life is revealed the new, positivist phase of the *Grand Être.* This revelation is not a personal event but the public, historical coming of the new age, overflowing from the focal point of the revelation into ever-widening circles of humanity. The life of Comte is a true apocalypse in the religious sense of the word. Only if we recognize the apocalyptic character of Comte can we understand his actions in the political phase after 1845. The Third Realm of the positive spirit has come, its spiritual power institutionalized in the Pontifex Maximus who functions and administers sacraments. The Occidental Republic is founded in substance and in a few years it will have created institutions devised by the man who signs himself as *Fondateur de la Religion de l'Humanité.* By his authority as the High Priest of the Occidental Republic he sends diplomatic notes to the non-Western powers. And finally he sends an ambassador to the General of the Jesuit Order suggesting that he associate himself with Comte in a demand to the Pope that the ecclesiastic budgets be abolished. The abolition of state support for the Catholic Church would advance the free coming of the new spirituality, while the old spiritual power "would gain the independence and morality that is necessary for its positive transformation or its dignified extinction."

In the present state of the crisis, we cannot know whether Comte is a forerunner of the apocalyptic founders of new realms whom we have witnessed in our time and of more formidable ones who will appear in the future, or whether the contemporary apocalyptic figures are the last ones of a breed of which Comte is by intellect and personal style the most grandiose specimen. Whatever the answer of the future will be, there can be no doubt even now that Comte belongs, with Marx, Lenin, and Hitler, to the series of men who would save mankind and themselves by divinizing their particular existence and imposing its law as the new order of society. The satanic Apocalypse of Man begins with Comte and has become the signature of the Western crisis.

Arline Reilein Standley (essay date 1981)

SOURCE: "Conclusion," in *Auguste Comte,* Twayne Publishers, 1981, pp. 154-58.

[*In the following essay, Standley discusses the paradoxical legacy of Comte and his philosophy.*]

The space of more than a century between us and Comte has done little to clarify his image. Now, the paradoxes of his own nature are overlaid with the multiple reflections, compounded of everything from firmly delineated parts to free-floating myth. We are challenged to define the impact on society of a man whose characteristics could be so negatively summed up as they are by Sir Isaiah Berlin: "His grotesque pedantry, the unreadable dullness of his writing, his vanity, his eccentricity, his solemnity, the pathos of his private life, his insane dogmatism, his authoritarianism, his philosophical fallacies. . . . [his] naïve craving for unity and symmetry at the expense of experience," his "bureaucratic fantasies. . . . with his fanatically tidy world of human beings joyfully engaged in fulfilling their functions, each within his own rigorously defined province, in the rationally ordered, totally unalterable hierarchy of the perfect society." As Simon observes, the fact that Comte's system had any diffusion at all is not something to be taken for granted. Given the weaknesses of his doctrines and the unattractiveness of his style, literary and personal, the critic cannot but wonder how Comte found any following at all. "That such a system so presented should have enlisted hundreds of full-fledged disciples and attracted partial assent from hundreds of others, including names both famous and unknown, is a matter that calls for explanation." And the explanation has to encompass, too, the view that Comte might be regarded "as the central figure of his century—of the century whose special problem was the reconciling of destruction with reconstruction, negation with affirmation, science with religion, the head with the heart, the past with the present, order with progress." Out of these multiple images how can we find the truest of all possible Comtes? Is the essential Comte the comprehensive systematizer of knowledge, the self-proclaimed Messiah of the Religion of Humanity, the organizer of the new sociocracy, or the Blakean angel—the visionary creator who tries to project his dream on us?

For many, the main contribution of Comte was his vast synthesis of all knowledge. Comte's comprehensiveness of view and vigor of mind represented to them the dawn of a new era—an era in which science and technology could be seen in proper perspective and put into integral relationship with the life of mankind. Whether we view this synthesis as a philosophy, as a history of science, or as a philosophy of science, we see the same strengths—and the flaws that go with them. As systematizer, he could not rest until his system was complete—and rigid; every detail had to be made to fit into that closed structure. Nevertheless, Comte's history of science, his classification of the sciences, and his development of sociology all represent significant contributions to Western thought.

In his moral and religious concepts, Comte was no less creative. On the one hand, his cultural relativism and his belief in moral progress attracted those who needed reassurance that mankind could develop spiritual values, even without the assistance of divine wisdom. Meliorism and creative evolution had strong roots here. On the other hand, Comte's Religion of Humanity appealed to those who needed an organized church. Unfortunately, that organization hardened into the same rigidity as his intellectual system; and, as Voegelin points out, the dangers implicit in Comte's spiritual dictatorship are not ones we can safely ignore. Though we recoil from his authoritarianism, it was precisely this attempt to forge a new religion "that makes it possible," says Basil Willey, "to regard Comte as the central figure of his century. . . ." It was here that he addressed himself to some of the most troubling issues of his day and their source in the all too general spiritual disorientation.

Comte's moral and religious ideas were closely linked to his plans for the new sociocracy, and the main link between the two was education. Though Comte's specific course of instruction was not adopted, his work encouraged interest in education for all. The educational program he devised was progressive in its emphasis on the general principles of science and the broad outlines of history though it was, perhaps, too oriented to science, too uniform, and too little encouraging to the free play of mind. Despite its scientific base, however, Comte's program bared the fact that education is in reality, moral and social in nature; he clearly designed his educational system to manipulate public opinion.

As for the social structure that this public opinion was to recreate, it had its anomalies, too. Though Comte was on the side of the social planners, he at first expected the new society he envisioned to come about by a natural process of evolution. Ultimately, he simply awaited the arrival of the dictator who would imprint it on the world. Comte seems naive in his belief that a spiritual force would develop that would be strong enough to control either human greed or the increasingly threatening power of modern technology; he was sanguine enough to think that altruism could be effec-

tively cultivated in a society built on competition (capitalism). Indeed, the morality that Comte enjoined taught submission to the powers that be and encouraged a passivity that would simply justify the status quo. The Brazilian novelist Machado de Assis neatly satirized this aspect of Comte's ideas in his portrait of Quincas Borba, the mad philosopher of Humanitism, whose motto is: To the winner the potatoes!

With Machado de Assis's challenging of the Comtean vision, we are reminded again of Blake's turning on the Angel who has almost imposed his vision of Hell on him. What strikes us most of all with Comte is the tenacious strength and unitary nature of his vision. Such intensity of vision tends to impose itself on others. The force of Comte's imagination seems to have made its impression, as we have seen, whether extolling the virtues of objectivity (or scientism), of utopianism, or of the subjective empire of Love.

George Eliot pictured just that intensity of vision in her portrait of Mordecai in *Daniel Deronda*—no matter that her "real model" was Emmanuel Deutsch. Mordecai, poor and scorned, lives with an adoptive family; learned, he lives in and for a dream—a vision of the Jews restored to their land and reunited as a nation. This enthusiast feeds himself on visions, for, he says, "visions are the creators and feeders of the world. I see, I measure the world as it is, which the vision will create anew."

So, too, was Comte absorbed by his vision of unification. His real life was marred by poverty, mental illness, and difficulties with family, wife, colleagues, and the establishment; but his system, he convinced himself, would make all into harmonious oneness. His dogged search for this unity—his idealization of relationships (his mother, Clotilde, Sophie)—his own almost-immaculate conception of the final synthesis (he did need some help from Clotilde)—these are Comte's steps into the world of vision. It is surely ironic that this man, whose name is for many synonymous with scientism, is at heart so thorough-going a Romantic.

The inevitable effect of such vision is, as Eliot says of Mordecai, the belief that this dream must have a farther destiny, fulfillment in reality. "An insane exaggeration of his own value, even if his ideas had been as true and precious as those of Columbus or Newton, many would have counted this yearning, taking it as the sublimer part for a man to say, 'If not I, then another,' and to hold cheap the meaning of his own life. But the fuller nature desires to be an agent to create, and not merely to look on. . . . And while there is warmth enough in the sun to feed an energetic life, there will still be men to feel, 'I am lord of this moment's change, and will charge it with my soul.'"

So, too, Comte sought to fulfill his destiny. Anointing himself High Priest of Humanity—as Napoleon had crowned himself Emperor—Comte saw himself as the spiritual leader not only of France but of the Republic of the West.

But Mordecai is not just a visionary, he is also a dying man. Aware that he himself will never fulfill his dream, he searches for the heir to whom he can entrust this sacred vision. The young man who has taken him into his family is too preoccupied with business; this young man's small son, though he loves Mordecai, only plays contentedly with a bright farthing while Mordecai is trying to plant in his young mind a sense of the spiritual richness of the Hebrew past and to fire this young heart with his own glowing hopes for the future. Finally, Mordecai meets Daniel Deronda and sees in him the one he has been seeking. Though sympathetic, Daniel can only respond to Mordecai's vision of him as the reincarnation of himself: But I am not of your race. Eventually, however, Daniel discovers that he is a Jew. In finding his roots and his heritage (his blood, and the ancient manuscripts left him by his father), Daniel finds himself—and he accepts the dead hand of the Past, the present task, and the vision of Mordecai. "It is," Daniel says, "through your inspiration that I have discerned what may be my life's task. . . . Since I began to read and to know, I have always longed for some ideal task, in which I might feel myself the heart and brain of a multitude—some social captainship, which would come to me as a duty, and not be striven for as a personal prize." And Daniel makes the pledge of his life with "sacred solemnity."

Mordecai's dream of the Jewish nation as the spiritual heart of mankind and of the restored Jewish nation as the unifier of East and West has lost some of its glow for us in the twentieth century. This heart seems as corrupt and divided as the rest of the world's body, and unification seems more beyond our capabilities than ever. History has an unpleasant way, as Voegelin points out, of turning dream into nightmare.

Comte found no son and heir, no High Priest he could anoint as his successor. For all that, there were those who accepted the heritage, the task, and the vision of Humanity's High Priest, and through that found the transmutation of the self that they, like Daniel, had yearned for. Comte's vision—whether it was that of Devil or Angel—was, indeed, a Memorable Fancy.

Mary Pickering (essay date 1993)

SOURCE: "*Cours de philosophie positive*: Positivism and the Natural Sciences," in *Auguste Comte: An Intellectual Biography,* Volume I, Cambridge University Press, 1993, pp. 561-604.

[*In the following essay, Pickering outlines Comte's positive philosophy, mathematics, astronomy, physics, chemistry, and biology.*]

> Let us not forget that in almost all minds, even the most elevated, ideas usually remain connected following the order of their first acquisition and that it is, consequently, a failing, which is most often irremediable, not to have begun by the beginning. Each century allows only a very small number of capable thinkers at the time of their maturity, like Bacon, Descartes, and Leibniz, to make a true tabula rasa in order to reconstruct from top to bottom the entire system of their acquired ideas.
>
> Comte, 1830

AN INTRODUCTION TO POSITIVE PHILOSOPHY

Comte dedicated the *Cours* to Joseph Fourier and Blainville, both of whom had been a source of personal encouragement and exemplified the positive spirit in the inorganic and organic sciences respectively. In Comte's view, Fourier's mathematical theory of heat was the most valuable scientific contribution since Newton's law of gravity. Blainville's work was admirable for its synthetic and systematic character and use of classification and hierarchy. His theory that every living being should be studied from two points of view—the static (its conditions) and the dynamic (its actions)—was used throughout the *Cours,* for Comte believed it could be applied to *all* phenomena "without exception." Although he would later harshly criticize the Academy of Sciences, Comte now sought to enhance the validity and respectability of his project by claiming Blainville, a member of the Academy of Sciences, and Fourier, its permanent secretary, as his "illustrious friends."

In the two introductory lessons to volume I, Comte outlined his main ideas clearly and systematically. The first lesson discussed the importance of "positive philosophy." Without mentioning that he took his definition from Saint-Simon, Comte explained that the term "positive" meant "this special manner of philosophizing that consists of envisaging the theories in any order of ideas as having for their object the coordination of observed facts." Positive philosophy thus represented a way of reasoning that could be applied to all subjects. Comte did not explain what he meant by "observation" or by "fact," although these terms were crucial to his definition.

Instead, he took a historicist approach to his own philosophy, using the past to justify it. Because, to him, no conception whatsoever could be understood without grasping its history, he explained positive philosophy by means of the law of three stages, which showed its development. He had propounded this theory in his fundamental opuscule of 1824, and here he elaborated it further, explaining that the theological, metaphysical, and positive stages represented different methods of philosophizing and thus different ways of looking at the world. The existence of each stage could be verified by considering not only the historical epochs of the human species but the different phases of individual development. In a famous passage, chiefly reflecting his own experience, Comte wrote, "Now each one of us, in contemplating his own history, does he not remember that he has been successively, in terms of his most important notions, a *theologian* in his childhood, a *metaphysician* in his youth, and a *natural philosopher* [*physicien*] in his virility?"

Each stage in the evolution of knowledge was characterized by a drive for perfection because human understanding was systematic by nature; it always sought to consolidate its methods and make its doctrines homogeneous. The apogee of the theological system was monotheism, in which one God replaced numerous independent supernatural agents. The metaphysical system reached its height when it considered nature, instead of numerous different forces, to be the source of all phenomena. The positive philosophy's quest for perfection consisted of connecting all phenomena by relations of succession and resemblance and subjecting them to a decreasing number of invariable natural laws. Rejecting other philosophers' search for a "vague and absurd unity," Comte insisted that a single explanatory law would remain impossible to attain. As the last and definitive stage of human intellectual development, the positive era would seek unity not in one entity, principle, or law, but in one method. In espousing a revolution based on a new method, Comte was following the example set by Bacon and Descartes.

He further explained the diversity of these three stages by referring to the problems encountered by the human mind in understanding the world. The human mind was always torn between the "necessity of observing to form real theories and the necessity, not any less imperious, of creating some theories in order to devote oneself to coherent observations." The nature of human understanding had compelled primitive man to begin with the theological system, for he could escape the vicious circle between fact and theory only by creating hypotheses, that is, myths, to explain the universe. The theological system stimulated social activity and development by giving him the illusion that the universe was made for him and that he had some control over it. The positive system grew out of this provisional system and reflected man's humbling realization that the causes and nature of phenomena and the origin and purpose of the universe were mysteries beyond his reach. But man's reason was now sufficiently mature for him to be stimulated solely by his intellectual desire to understand the laws of phenomena. Because the positive outlook was so radically opposed to the theological, Comte claimed that the

metaphysical state had acted as a necessary transition between the two and partook of enough of their respective characteristics to ensure some degree of continuity in mankind's development.

Though he described three distinct stages, Comte maintained that history was a gradual development; elements of each stage had been growing since the beginning of civilization. For example, although the positive "revolution" had begun in the seventeenth century with the work of Bacon, Descartes, and Galileo, positive philosophy had, in reality, existed since Aristotle. Again, Comte's approach was paradoxical. He wished to justify the future by looking toward the past. To satisfy conservatives afraid of risk, he sought to make his enterprise legitimate by appealing to tradition, but at the same time he hoped to appease those on the Left by giving the past a revolutionary cast. He took his approach from biology, where germs and embryos were preexisting objects that developed in time.

The first and "special" aim of the *Cours* was to establish social physics, which would extend the positive method to the last group of phenomena still under the theological and metaphysical regimes. The creation of this last science was, according to Comte, the "greatest and most pressing need of our intelligence." By finally making all our conceptions homogeneous, he would realize the positive revolution.

Yet Comte had already fallen into an intellectual trap. As Lévy-Bruhl pointed out, Comte began the *Cours* with the law of three stages to demonstrate that the coming of social physics was inevitable. However, the law proved at the same time that the science of society *already* existed because this was the main law of sociology. In using universal sociological laws to verify sociology, Comte was making sociology legitimize itself—a questionable procedure.

Comte's second and "general" aim was pedagogical: to give a course in positive philosophy as a whole. Since social physics now was completing the system of natural sciences, it was possible and necessary to review the positive state of scientific knowledge in its entirety. Not aimed at specialists, the *Cours* would examine each of the five fundamental positive sciences—astronomy, physics, chemistry, physiology, and social physics—in terms of its relation to the whole positive system, especially to see how it developed the logical procedures of the positive method, which could not be understood apart from its application. This review of the individual sciences was important not only for revealing the method and tendencies of the new philosophy, but also for laying the groundwork for social physics, which required a firm grasp of the various scientific methods as well as the laws of the more simple phenomena that influenced society. Therefore, Comte's two aims in writing the *Cours* were inseparable.

Finally, this overview of the sciences was necessary to combat specialization, one of the main characteristics of the positive age. Comte believed that increased specialization was a crucial component of progress, but he condemned this tendency to become isolated and lost in detail as the great weakness of positive philosophy. To diminish its impact, Comte urged the formation of a class of learned men, the positive philosophers, who would specialize in the "study of scientific generalities." Other scientists would study the work of these generalists so that their own specialties would profit from the knowledge of the whole. In this way, positive philosophy would ensure the unity of human knowledge.

Comte believed his course on positive philosophy had four advantages. The first was that, because scientific theories were products of man's intellectual faculties and showed the mind in action, studying these theories would lead to a firm grasp of the logical laws of the human mind. One of the main themes of the *Cours,* whose importance was recognized by Mill, was that the logical and scientific points of view were indivisible because logical education coincided with scientific education. The way to understand logic was to study the history of science. Like Hegel, Comte was concerned with studying the mind in action, that is, the way it manifested itself throughout history and in society. Rejecting abstract, static studies of logic and of the individual, he sought to substitute positive philosophy for psychology, which he called the "last transformation of theology." Unlike the members of Cousin's school, who disagreed among themselves due to the looseness of their speculations about the mind's observation of itself, positive philosophers would agree on how the mind functioned and could lay the basis of social consensus.

The second main advantage of the establishment of positive philosophy would be the reorganization of the educational system to make it more responsive to the "needs of modern civilization." Objecting to the confused curriculum of traditional schools and to premature specialization, Comte felt that positive philosophy—the study of the spirit, results, and method of every science—must not be a monopoly of the scientists but had to become the basis of the education of even the "popular masses." After all, science's "true point of departure" always consisted of ideas held by the common people about the "subjects under consideration." Comte's animus against the scientific elite and the populist strain in his thought, which had been apparent in his earliest writings, could not have been clearer.

The third advantage of the positive philosophy would be the reform of the sciences. Arguing that the divisions among the sciences were ultimately artificial, he hoped he could encourage a more interdisciplinary approach to the solution of problems, which would lead to more rapid progress.

The fourth advantage of this new philosophy would be the most important: the reorganization of the social system, which would end the state of crisis that had existed since the French Revolution. Although Comte was frequently accused of materialism, he believed that "ideas govern and overturn the world, or in other words, that the entire social mechanism rests ultimately on opinions." The "intellectual anarchy" that was at the root of the present social disorder was caused by the simultaneous use of theological, metaphysical, and positive ways of thinking. With the inevitable extension of the positive method to social phenomena, human knowledge would become homogeneous, and there would emerge the intellectual consensus necessary for society to return to "normal." Thus in his first "lesson" of the *Cours,* Comte made it clear that he was advocating a "general revolution of the human mind" and that its ultimate object was practical and political: the completion of the social revolution. Although not directly involved in politics, he aimed in an indirect and profound fashion to shape the world of action.

The first lesson summed up the important results of Comte's lifework. It did not introduce any new material or reflect any radical changes in his opinions since his fundamental opuscule. Most of the significant themes of positivism were developed in a concise and austere manner: the importance of ending the revolutionary crisis by a philosophy of the sciences, the law of three stages, the theory of hypotheses, the necessity of raising politics to a positive science, the reorganization of the educational system, the interdisciplinary approach to intellectual problems, and the condemnation of psychology, reductionism (in terms of both reducing one science to another and reducing scientific knowledge to one law), and excessive specialization.

Lesson 2, the complement of lesson 1, dealt with the classification of the sciences. He argued that this classification was possible only at the current time because social physics, which ensured the uniformity of our knowledge, was becoming a positive science. Moreover, botanists and zoologists had only recently provided a model of classification based on observation. Comte made it clear that he was not seeking to classify and unify *all* of human knowledge as the Encyclopedists endeavored to do, for this was impossible. The *Cours* was concerned only with theoretical knowledge, above all, the laws of nature, which led to action. Even he admitted that his classification of this knowledge was ultimately "arbitrary" and "artificial."

One of Comte's favorite aphorisms was *"from science comes prediction; from prediction comes action."* The aim of each science was therefore prediction. Prediction to Comte meant going not only from the present to the future, but from the known to the unknown. "Scientific prevision . . . consists . . . in knowing a fact independently of its direct exploration in virtue of its relations with others already given." Larry Laudan [in an article in *Philosophy of Science,* March 1971] has pointed out that Comte departed in a significant way from traditional criteria of what made knowledge scientific. Up to this point, scientists insisted on the certainty and infallibility of their knowledge. But with his relativism, which outlawed appeals to truth, Comte declared that knowledge was scientific if it displayed predictive power. He thus could avoid the problem of dictating one means of scientific investigation. According to Laudan, Comte was influential in the philosophy of science because he believed that "a statement is scientific so long as it makes *general* claims about how nature behaves, which are capable of being put to experimental test." Scientific propositions were thus different from nonscientific ones if they were general and capable of being tested.

In lesson 28, Comte clarified this novel and important methodological approach in his famous theory of hypotheses, to which he had previously alluded in the third and fourth opuscules and the first lesson of the **Cours**. He agreed with Bacon that knowledge must rest on facts, but rejecting his empiricism, he maintained that facts could not even be perceived or retained without the guidance of an a priori theory. At the beginning of the scientific investigation of a subject, a "provisional supposition"—a hypothesis—was "indispensable" for aiding the discovery of natural laws. The scientist was not a passive, mechanical observer as the empiricists believed; he first had to use his imagination and come up with an explanatory theory simply to be able to make an observation:

> If, in contemplating phenomena, we did not immediately attach them to some principles, not only would it be impossible for us to connect these isolated observations, and, consequently, to draw something from them, but also we would even be entirely incapable of remembering them; and facts would most often remain imperceptible before our very eyes.

Although geometers had devised the artifice of a theory, Comte asserted that no one had yet discussed the fundamental condition that legitimized its usage:

> This condition . . . consists of imagining only hypotheses [that are] susceptible . . . of a positive verification, more or less in the future, but always clearly inevitable, and whose degree of precision is exactly in harmony with that which the study of the corresponding phenomena comprises. In other words, truly philosophical hypotheses must constantly present the character of simple anticipations of that which experiment and reason would have revealed immediately, if the

circumstances of the problem had been more favorable.

Once a hypothesis that was in harmony with already determined data was conceived, the science could freely develop and would explore new consequences that would confirm or negate the conjecture. Hypotheses could not be considered scientific theories until they were verified by induction ("the immediate analysis" of the movement of a phenomenon) and deduction (the analysis of the relation of a phenomenon to a previously established law). Thus one reason Comte insisted upon prediction as a criterion of scientific knowledge was that he wished to avoid having to base this knowledge solely on induction, as empiricists did. Scientific investigation rested on the use of both induction and deduction. His predilection is revealed in a comment he later made to a disciple:

> I consider Descartes and even Leibniz infinitely superior to Bacon. The latter, who wrote so much on deduction, never made a single inductive discovery of any value, . . . while Descartes, who . . . philosophically appreciated only deduction, made important advances in mathematics and elsewhere by means of induction.

In volume 3, Comte also introduced the "art" of "scientific fictions," which he acknowledged derived from the "poetic imagination." Whereas the art of hypothesis related fictions to the solution of a problem, this other art applied them to the problem itself by inventing a series of purely hypothetical cases. One example of the possible use of this new method in biology would be to place "purely fictive organisms," which one hoped to discover later, between already known organisms in order to make the biological series more homogeneous, continuous, and regular.

Like his theory of hypothesis, this art of scientific fiction showed that Comte was not a slave to his belief in the supreme importance of observation. Despite the criticism of the Saint-Simonians, he always gave a large role to imagination in the scientific process. And to avoid giving reason too much importance in scientific research, he deliberately refused to offer elaborate, ahistorical rules of scientific procedure and proof.

Comte's attitude toward the use of hypotheses and "scientific fictions" resembled his view of the manipulation of mathematical principles because they all offered man the ability to do scientific exploration in an indirect manner whenever direct investigation was impossible. In proclaiming the utility and advantages of such conjectures and fictions, which were not exact representations of reality, Comte was stressing the relativity of knowledge while trying to save man from total skepticism or empiricism.

At the same time, he carefully limited the range of this indirect means of investigation. Hypotheses, for example, could pertain only to the laws of phenomena, that is, to their "constant relations of succession or of similitude." They could not be used to solve problems concerning the causes or nature of phenomena, which were beyond our means of observation and reasoning and thus "necessarily insoluble." Thus, as Warren Schmaus has pointed out [in an article in *Studies in History and Philosophy of Science,* March 1985], Comte did not insist that hypotheses be formulated in the "language of observation." They could use theoretical terms as long as they did not refer to "unobservable *entities, especially causal entities.*" The molecule was, for example, a theoretical term whose use Comte permitted, although he did not think this "artifice" pertained to "reality." But theories about God, for example, could never be affirmed or refuted. And isolated facts were not scientific either because they had no predictive capability.

The majority of early-nineteenth-century methodologists still believed that scientific theories could be constructed simply on the basis of induction or analogy, without recourse to conjectures. Although Comte did not spell out the rules of verification, his explanation of hypotheses as useful, convenient, and respectable devices that served a crucial function in scientific discovery was a novel theory, one that became very influential. It foreshadowed the later work of Hans Vaihinger and Henri Poincaré and may have also influenced Claude Bernard, Marcelin Berthelot, Paul Janet, Ernst Mach, Wilhelm Ostwald, and Pierre Duhem. The logical positivists took up a similar approach to the problems of ascertaining meaningfulness, distinguishing scientific from nonscientific knowledge, and using verifiability to criticize metaphysicians.

To Comte, prediction was important in itself as a way of demarcating scientific knowledge, but it was also crucial because it enabled man to act more effectively. Despite the determinism of the law of three stages and his stress on the limitations of human knowledge and operations, Comte retained an activist conception of man. Like Marx, he believed man must use his intellect to discover scientific laws enabling him to modify the universe "to his advantage . . . despite the obstacles of his condition." Comte never lost sight of the practical goal of his *Cours*. His scientific exposition was always subordinated to his social goal; philosophy had to be realized in politics.

While emphasizing that theoretical knowledge had a utilitarian end, he argued, nevertheless, that it had to be pursued in a separate domain without regard to its practical application. He rejected the new, materialistic trend to make the sciences the handmaidens of industry, for to him, they had a "more elevated destination, that of satisfying the fundamental need felt by

our intelligence to know the laws of phenomena." This innate desire to put facts into order and to arrive at simple, general conceptions was more important than practical needs in stimulating scientific research and thus intellectual progress.

Comte upheld a philosophical, historicist approach to the sciences. Influenced by Blainville, he maintained that the philosophy of a science could not be studied apart from the "intellectual history" of that science and vice versa. (This consideration of a science in terms of either its ideas or its history corresponded to the dichotomy between statics and dynamics, i.e., order and progress.) As Johan Heilbron has suggested [in an article in *Sociological Theory,* Fall 1990], Comte's epistemology rejected the traditional approach of grounding the sciences on universal principles and showed that scientific knowledge itself had to be considered a historical process.

This process was complex. According to Comte, the history of a particular science could not be studied in isolation because the progress of each science was connected to the simultaneous development of the other sciences, to the arts (practical applications), and to society as a whole. In other words, one could not understand how the ideas and theories of a single science changed without studying the entire history of humanity. Comte was thus one of the first thinkers to point out that the history of science was the "most important" and "neglected" part of the development of humanity and, moreover, had to be interdisciplinary in scope. His analysis later had a large impact in France, where scholars such as Bachelard and Canguilhem sought to approach the formation of concepts and theories from a historical, instead of a logical, perspective.

Comte's basic rules for classifying the sciences elaborated on the principles that he had announced in his fundamental opuscule. The sciences devoted to the most simple and thus the most general phenomena came first in the hierarchy. Influencing all other phenomena without in turn being influenced by them, these simple, abstract phenomena were also the most independent and the farthest away from man. The later, more complicated sciences studied phenomena that were increasingly complex, particular (specialized), and concrete. These phenomena were closer to man and more dependent on the phenomena studied by the previous sciences in the hierarchy. In sum, because the classification of the sciences reflected the dependence that existed among their corresponding natural phenomena, each science was founded on the knowledge of the principal laws of the preceding one and became, in turn, the foundation of the one that came after it. Therefore, each science depended on its antecedents but had its own peculiarities that prevented it from being reduced to the science preceding it. Likewise, each science could influence only the sciences that followed it in the hierarchy.

According to Heilbron, Comte's important "differential theory of science" reflected his profound grasp of the new kind of disciplinary battles raging in the age of specialization. At this time, the spokesmen for the mathematico-mechanical disciplines were fighting the representatives of the life sciences; each group claimed universal validity for its models and methods. Comte's theory was effective in destroying the illusions of such monism.

Concerned with differentiating the sciences in terms of their history and ideas, Comte argued that the organic sciences were more complex and more particular than the inorganic ones and thus came after them in the hierarchy. The inorganic sciences were divided into those dealing with celestial phenomena—astronomy—and those dealing with terrestrial phenomena—physics and chemistry. The organic sciences were divided into the science of the individual physiology—and that of the species—social physics. The most difficult science of all, social physics, dealt with the most particular, complex, and concrete phenomena—those closest to man. It depended on all of the other sciences but could not influence them. Beside these five sciences, natural philosophy included a sixth—mathematics—which was its "true fundamental basis." Mathematics was more significant to Comte as a method, that is, as a "means of investigation in the study of other natural phenomena," than as a doctrine. It constituted the "most powerful instrument that the human mind can use in the search for the laws of natural phenomena." It was the most perfect science as well as the oldest, and because it served as the foundation of the other five sciences, it came first in his classification. Comte was making the science that was his own specialty the "head of positive philosophy." At the opposite end of the hierarchy, he placed the other science to which he was most attached—social physics. It too represented the point of departure and the head of positive philosophy but in a different sense that would become clearer later on.

Comte declared that his classification of the sciences not only reflected the divisions that had grown up spontaneously among them but also accorded with their development in history. His classification verified the law of the three stages by showing why the diverse branches of our knowledge were often at different stages of development. Because the simplest sciences were studied first and thus matured quickly, they were the first to reach the positive state. The more complex sciences took longer to reach that stage, for they depended on the knowledge of the simpler sciences and could not make any real progress until the preceding sciences did.

Moreover, the classification marked the "relative perfection" of the diverse sciences. Throughout the *Cours* Comte defined perfection in terms of unity, abstraction, simplicity, universality, precision, and coordination of facts, which made predictions more exact. Yet at the same time, he stressed the limitations of knowledge—as he had done when he prohibited man from trying to uncover first causes and the destiny of the universe and when he showed the necessity of using hypotheses because of the feebleness of the mind. Now he declared that whereas astronomy was fairly precise and tightly organized, the sciences of organic phenomena (especially social phenomena) could never be very exact or systematic. However, although physiology and social physics might even be extremely imprecise, Comte maintained somewhat dogmatically that they were as certain as the other sciences, for "everything that is positive, that is, founded on well-observed facts, is certain." He did not revel in the torments of doubt.

The most important property of the classification of the sciences was that it presented the general outlines of a rational scientific education. To learn what constituted a scientific law, a positive conception, or a valid observation, one first needed to study the simpler sciences, which were easiest to understand. Otherwise, one would not be able to comprehend the more complex sciences. Moreover, the simpler sciences should be studied first because their greater distance from man meant they did not generate passions and prejudices. (This distance and objectivity also helped make them more precise than the science of society, whose phenomena were so close to man and defied exactitude.) Comte insisted, furthermore, that this order of study was important for both the scientist and layperson. He was thinking not only of Guizot and other brilliant men who had disappointed him because they lacked scientific knowledge, but also of scientists themselves, who had neglected to start "at the beginning" and thus lacked a "rational education." Most of all, he was worried that without a grasp of all the sciences, people undertaking the study of society would not know how to relate society to natural phenomena or apply the positive method to social phenomena.

Composed of these two lessons, the "Exposition" of the *Cours* was a remarkably clear discussion of most of the main points of Comte's doctrine. It has, in fact, become a classic text of nineteenth century French philosophy. Arguing his points well, he anticipated criticisms and added numerous nuances, which made the tone of his discourse much less dogmatic than many of his other writings. His theory of hypotheses showed that he did not believe that scientific discoveries could proceed by the observation of facts alone. His concern with the practical side of the sciences was balanced by his warning that considerations of pure utility would stifle the sciences. His attraction to the law of gravity as one unifying principle was offset by his realization that the sciences were too complex to be reduced in this fashion. His classification of the sciences according to their ideas was modified by his assertion that this classification was consistent with their historical development. Although he repeatedly emphasized the necessity of establishing a science of society, he did not attempt to hide the fact that its findings would not always be as precise as one would like. In brief, despite his many peremptory statements and his often gross assumptions, Comte revealed himself to be a complex thinker.

The "Exposition" is perhaps most striking by what it left out. The passion of his earlier opuscules was replaced by a cool, dry, "objective" tone suitable to a scientific treatise. Absent from the lessons is any reference to the separation of powers, especially to the new spiritual power controlling the educational system and advising the government. Such questions were reserved for the last volumes. Comte may have decided to keep his vehemently anticlerical and anti-Catholic opinions temporarily to himself so as not to estrange his readers before they read even a hundred pages.

He was also being true to the decision that he had made just before his mental breakdown of 1826, when he suddenly recognized the necessity of establishing positive philosophy before positive politics. Realizing that intellectual supremacy had to precede political dominion, Comte believed that only positive philosophy could give validity and authority to positive politics, which completed it. He felt that what distinguished him from reactionaries, revolutionaries, and liberals was his creation of a philosophy supplying the *scientific* basis of the reorganization of society. His first volumes did initially appear "scientistic" and "materialistic" for he did nothing but discuss the sciences. But as he explained later to Mill, he was trying to systematize ideas without which social regeneration would fall "into a sort of more or less vague mysticism." Emphasizing the threat of mysticism, which would come from basing a reorganization first on feelings, he continued:

> This is why my fundamental work [the *Cours*] had to address itself almost exclusively to the intellect: this had to be a work of research and even incidentally of discussion, destined to discover and constitute true universal principles by climbing by hierarchical degrees from the most simple scientific questions to the highest social speculations.

Only when these "highest social speculations" came up at the end of the *Cours* could Comte logically develop his ideas of a spiritual power and spiritual doctrine. Once these views of spiritual reorganization were established at the end of the *Cours*, he could then turn his attention to systematizing the feelings. Broaching these subjects at the beginning would have ruined the

scientific impressions of his enterprise, which were initially most important to impart to his readers.

MATHEMATICS

Except for the two introductory lessons, volume I was devoted to mathematics. It developed ideas that had first appeared in Comte's incomplete essays of 1818 to 1820. Whereas at that time he had not been sure about the proper way to begin intellectual reform, he now decided it must start with mathematics. In fact, he inserted a long critique of French mathematical education, whose defects he blamed on the "extreme inferiority" of the majority of teachers. They did not fully appreciate Descartes's "fundamental revolution," lacked a grasp of the whole of their subject, and failed especially to give their students a solid understanding of geometry, which was important for showing the relationship between the abstract and the concrete. Comte's disparagement of his fellow professors and of the Ecole Polytechnique would not win him many friends in the future and was undiplomatic considering his current attempts to find a position. But it shows that he had a poor opinion of these scientists even before they created problems for him. His later difficulties merely confirmed what he had already thought and dared to write.

In these lessons, Comte's highest praises went to Descartes, Leibniz, Newton, and Lagrange. Greatly inspired by Lagrange, a former professor at the Ecole Polytechnique, Comte relied heavily on several of his books, going so far as to paraphrase whole sections of them. Much of the text of the *Cours* is plainly derivative.

As he would do with the other five sciences, Comte first treated mathematics as a whole. He considered its aim, subject matter, composition, theories, discoveries, methods, relationships with the other sciences, limitations, and possibilities for future development. He then broke the science down into different divisions, which he further subdivided and characterized, revealing his passion for classifications and definitions. Dividing and labeling in this fashion gave him a feeling of power, a feeling that he was in control of his subject. Disregarding his criticism of scientists for creating specialized languages, he also often tried to imprint an original character on his reflections by simply giving a new name of his own to old terms.

Throughout the *Cours*, Comte aimed to show how each science incorporated the positive method and contributed to the positive system. He believed mathematics represented the origin of positive philosophy. Only by studying this quintessential science could one arrive at a "correct and deep idea" of what a science was in general. One learned that positive laws must show relationships between independent and even apparently isolated phenomena, which enabled the scientist to make predictions. Indifferent to the search for causes or substances, mathematics was, in short, the science of invariable relationships and best demonstrated the positive method.

Thanks especially to the work of Descartes in geometry, mathematics exhibited the interrelationship of the abstract and concrete realms. Comte argued that intellectual development was synonymous with the growth of abstraction; the consideration of increasingly abstract ideas allowed people to solve more concrete problems. As the most abstract science, mathematics first stimulated this intellectual development. Thus its translation of concrete facts into abstract ideas was necessary for scientific advancement.

Deeply influenced by Descartes, Comte asserted that the range of mathematics could be extended indefinitely; its deductive logic was universal. In fact, he hoped to replace formal logic, which was too abstract and ontological, with mathematics, which would then become the "normal basis of all healthy logical education." Ideally, each science would be one day as rigorously deductive and rational as mathematics:

> One can even say generally that *science* is essentially destined to dispense with all direct observation—as much as the diverse phenomena allow—by making it possible to deduce from the smallest possible number of immediate data the greatest possible number of results.

Comte was thus no simple inductivist. He believed science must aim at constructing laws and theories that would do away with the tedious task of observing facts and enable one to go beyond direct evidence.

Yet although very loyal to Descartes and deduction, Comte distrusted pure abstraction. Trained in the synthetic or realist school of geometry of Monge, he maintained that positive theories had to be ultimately founded on the observation of a real, concrete body. To prevent an "abuse of pure reasoning" that would lead to "sterile" works, even the most rational science had to remember its experiential roots, for there was no a priori knowledge.

Comte rejected Descartes's effort to make mathematics the universal science by reducing every problem in natural philosophy to a question of numbers. He argued that the human mind could represent mathematically only the least complicated and most general inorganic phenomena, those whose properties were fairly fixed. Complex inorganic phenomena and all organic phenomena would always remain closed to mathematical analysis because they exhibited "extreme numerical variability" and were affected by so many factors that no two cases were alike. This criticism of the abuse of statistics, particularly in biology and the sci-

ence of society, reflected Comte's effort to preserve the autonomy and individuality of each science.

In sum, although Comte praised mathematics for being the most universal and most applicable of all the sciences, he warned his contemporaries not to continue to exaggerate its power. Mathematicians, who were dominant in early-nineteenth-century France, could not, in his eyes, continue to pretend to monopolize the scientific realm. A certain realism about the range of the human mind and consequently a certain humility characterized Comte's approach to the science that occupied his daily life. Indeed, one of the main principles of the ***Cours*** was the deficiency of our knowledge even in the limited realm of what was understandable. Comte insisted that

> it was necessary to recognize that by an indisputable law of human nature, our means for conceiving new questions . . . [are] much more powerful than our resources for solving them, or in other words the human mind . . . [is] far more capable of imagining than of reasoning.

Although one could not determine with precision the boundaries of the power of the mind, their existence was undeniable. Comte reveled in the fruitfulness of the sciences, but he never declared them to be all-powerful. His arguments were far more complex than those who accused him of scientism admit.

ASTRONOMY

The first part of the second volume was devoted to astronomy, which Comte considered to be the first "direct" natural science and a model for the "true study of nature." It best demonstrated that a science consisted of laws, not isolated facts, and predictions. Newton's law of gravity brought astronomy to the "highest philosophical perfection" that any science could hope to achieve. This theory proved the importance not only of reducing phenomena to a single law but also of using hypotheses to advance one's understanding, especially when concrete, observed facts were missing. Pointing out that even this model of a positive explanation could conceivably be superseded one day by another hypothesis, Comte did not fail to stress the relativity of knowledge even in the most precise and certain science.

He also placed astronomy at the head of the natural sciences because its laws represented the foundation of our whole system of knowledge. Astronomical phenomena influenced physical, chemical, physiological, and social phenomena but could not be influenced by them in turn. Subsequent research, however, proved him wrong.

One of Comte's scientific laws was that "as the phenomena to be studied become more complex, they are at the same time susceptible . . . of more extensive and varied means of exploration." Since astronomical phenomena were the simplest, astronomy had only one means of exploration, observation, which it introduced into the positive system. Here Comte explained that the art of observation consisted of three methods: the direct observation of concrete objects (which led to induction), experimentation, and comparison. He thus restricted astronomical research to "simple visual observations." Again, later developments regarding dark stars and black holes would invalidate his position. Furthermore, he unwisely limited the range of astronomy to the solar system. His rejection of sidereal astronomy was based on his assumption that it was impossible to arrive at a true conception of the universe of stars. Moreover, he believed man did not need to know about this universe, which did not affect him. To Comte, man should always ask what he needed to know, not what he could know.

This optimistic assumption that a basic harmony existed between man's needs and the scope of his knowledge would run throughout the *Cours*. Instead of being frustrated by the restrictions of knowledge, Comte simply dismissed them as irrelevant. His engineering mindset was evident in the supposition that science could solve the practical problems of man's existence. Although worried about the enslavement of theory to practice, he was not always in favor of scientific curiosity for its own sake and sometimes adopted a more utilitarian approach.

Astronomy was also an important science because it showed the importance of combining induction and deduction. Given that astral bodies were distant and hard to observe, astronomy had to make recourse to mathematics, which it used to represent its simple objects and make deductions. Comte considered astronomy the most perfect science and a model for all the others precisely because its method was primarily mathematical and abstract and consequently the most free of theological and metaphysical influences.

However, once again, he condemned the calculus of probabilities. He believed the notion of "evaluated probability" could never regulate human conduct. Often contradicting common sense, it would lead people to "absurd consequences," such as rejecting "as numerically unlikely events that are, nevertheless, going to happen." Comte therefore denied a place for probabilities in any of the sciences—especially the science of society, where he felt that its repercussions could be especially damaging. Here again, Comte proved to be conservative about scientific innovations. Despite his faith in the predictive power of scientific thought and his law of three stages, his projections about the future direction of scientific development often missed the mark.

Comte argued that the two extremes of natural philosophy—astronomy and physiology—had the most beneficial impact on intellectual progress because questions concerning the world and man had always attracted the most attention. As the most scientific of all the sciences, astronomy was the most opposed to theology. It had not only freed the human mind of its "absurd prejudices" and "superstitious terrors," but also hurt the doctrine of final causes, the keystone of the theological system. The heliocentric theory humiliated man, who had thought he was the center of the universe, and it stripped providential action of any intelligible aim. Challenging the theological argument by design and arguing that man was more intelligent than nature, Comte maintained, moreover, that the elements of the solar system were not arranged in the best manner as theologians liked to imagine; science could "easily" conceive of a better one. Inspired by Laplace, he argued that astronomers presented a much more ordered universe than did theologians, who believed all things were governed by the will of one or several supreme beings and were thus irregular. To Comte, order was "necessary and spontaneous" and not dependent on outside agents."

In these chapters on astronomy, he repeatedly stressed the harmony, regularity, and stability of the solar system, which were reflected in the precision, rationality, and invariability of astronomical laws. Although he wrote in a cold, dry style, he could hardly contain his passion for the order incarnated in the solar system and in the science that explored it. It is evident that he found more certainty, consistency, and reassurance in a world explained by the sciences than in a world ruled by a god. This love of stability, which would pervade the remaining lessons of the *Cours*, seemed discordant with his activist image of human nature.

PHYSICS

After considering the laws of the heavens, Comte turned his attention in volume 2 to the laws of the earth, studied by physics and chemistry. As the second natural science, dealing with more complex phenomena, physics was more backward than astronomy. Whereas astronomy had been positive (at least in its geometrical aspect) ever since the foundation of the School of Alexandria, physics had reached this stage only with Galileo. Instead of the "perfect mathematical harmony" that characterized astronomy, physics was, moreover, marked by disunity; it was composed of numerous branches that had little relation to each other, and its theories were not well coordinated.

Physics demonstrated Comte's law that as one ascended the scale of the sciences, prediction became more imperfect and the power of man to modify phenomena increased. There was therefore an inverse relation between prediction and human intervention. In physics, where prediction was not as wide-ranging or exact as it was in astronomy, natural phenomena began for the first time to be modified by human intervention. Comte argued that this ability to modify phenomena proved that phenomena were not under the control of the gods.

Because of its imperfections, physics was still pervaded by metaphysical habits, which were absent in astronomy. It was in the context of contrasting astronomy with physics that Comte appeared to use the term "positivism" for the first time:

> In astronomy the discussion [among people supporting the positive spirit and those maintaining metaphysics] was less marked, and positivism triumphed almost spontaneously, except on the subject of the earth's movement.

Up to this point, Comte had usually referred to his system as the "positive philosophy." Occasionally, he had used the word "positivity." In general, he was very careful about the fabrication of new terms, which he thought often served to "hide the real emptiness of ideas." Nevertheless, he liked to use neologisms, such as "positivity," and conscientiously explained their background. Because this time he did not claim to have invented the term "positivism," it seems probable that Comte adopted it from someone else, perhaps from Bazard, who had used the word during the summer of 1829. Comte later made a virtue of having "spontaneously" chosen this word, pointing out that his philosophy, unlike all others, such as Christianity and Fourierism, was the "only one" that had a name different from that of its author.

Comte believed that the complicated nature of physical phenomena meant that physics would never be as perfect as astronomy, but this complexity gave it more methods of exploration. Physics introduced and fully developed the art of experimentation—the second method of observation—thanks to the possibility of modifying physical bodies almost without restriction. The emphasis on experimentation meant that induction was more important in physics than in astronomy and that deduction was no longer dominant. Yet once again, Comte argued for the simultaneous use of deduction and induction, lamenting that the "art of closely combining analysis and experimentation, without subordinating one to the other, is still almost unknown."

Although he urged that mathematical analysis be used to a greater extent in physics, where it could connect isolated facts and make experiments more rational, he warned against its misapplication, which would lead to "useless hypotheses" and "entirely chimerical conceptions." Therefore, mathematicians, who despised experimentation and liked excessive abstraction, should not be allowed to dominate in physics. But this fear of the possible abuse of mathematics led Comte to make

imprudent statements. For example, his assertion that physics, not chemistry, was the last field where purely mathematical analysis was effective showed his ignorance of stoichiometry, which covers the quantitative expressions of chemical reactions.

Comte used his doctrine of hypotheses to warn physicists not to resort to the metaphysical theories of universal ethers and imaginary fluids that were popular in his era as a means of explaining the phenomena of heat, light, electricity, and magnetism. These ethers and fluids, he said, were like angels and genies: their existence could be neither negated nor affirmed, and they explained nothing. He also unwisely treated all questions of light in the same manner. To him, both the corpuscular and undulatory theories of light were "antiscientific" because they simply piled one mystery on top of another. They also connected optics too closely with mechanics and acoustics.

It seems clear that Comte's goals were occasionally problematical. On the one hand, he was eager to unify the sciences as much as possible through the discovery of their interrelationships. On the other hand, he wished to keep each science (or branch of science) distinct by avoiding the temptation of reducing one to another. Yet he carried his antireductionist tendencies too far when he wrote "Despite all arbitrary assumptions, luminous phenomena will always constitute one sui generis category necessarily irreducible to any other: a light will be eternally heterogeneous to a movement or to a sound." Such an absolutist position went against scientific progress.

CHEMISTRY

The subject of the first half of the third volume was chemistry, a science that had been developing rapidly since the late eighteenth and early nineteenth centuries. Based to a large extent on the works of Claude-Louis Berthollet, a former professor at the Ecole Polytechnique, Comte's exposition centered on what prevented chemistry from becoming a true science consisting of uniform laws. Instead of urging chemists to find new facts, Comte encouraged them to systematize the knowledge they already had in order to make one homogeneous doctrine. They should particularly take advantage of the comparative method, the third scientific means of observation, which chemistry introduced into the positive system for it would at least allow them to classify chemical phenomena according to their natural families.

Comte's objective in the lessons on chemistry was to stress its distinctiveness as a science, for he saw many threats to the validity of its findings and to its independence. For example, he strongly criticized Lorenz Oken, the leader of German *Naturphilosophen*, for trying to reduce all substances to four elements. Oken, according to Comte, had carried the search for simplification to such an extreme that he had disregarded the "reality" of natural phenomena. When Comte turned to the relationship of chemistry to physics and physiology, which was one of the leading questions of the day, he concluded that chemistry had an ambiguous but nevertheless independent position between these two sciences. He insisted that the separate identities of all three sciences should be preserved and that scientists should not completely take over the work of a less developed science. Condemning reductionism, he warned physicists not to include chemical phenomena in their science. He also reprimanded chemists for trying to deal with organic phenomena, because he said they lacked an understanding of the whole of physiology. In fact, he argued against the existence of organic chemistry as a separate science. Precluded from dealing with the phenomena of life, all of chemistry should be inorganic. Despite his stress on the need to preserve a place for chemistry in the positive hierarchy, Comte seemed most interested in saving physiology from its encroachments. His restrictions on the realm of direct chemical investigation would be unacceptable today.

Comte argued that verification of the results of chemical research could occur by the double process of analysis and synthesis, terms that he suggested had been abused by the Saint-Simonians and other metaphysicians. Properly confined to chemistry, analysis pertained to decomposition, and synthesis to composition. To verify a chemical demonstration, a substance that was decomposed should be able to be recomposed exactly. Comte criticized chemists for using their analytical faculties far more than their synthetic ones. Just as he encouraged both induction and deduction, he was arguing for the use of both analysis and synthesis in scientific investigation in order to maximize possibilities in research.

Comte claimed that chemistry had an important impact on intellectual development, especially on humanity's liberation from theology and metaphysics. The ability to transform chemical phenomena improved the "human condition" and represented the "principal source" of people's power to effect change in general. The "positive notions of decomposition and recomposition" and the "necessarily indefinite perpetuity of all matter" replaced the theological dogma of "absolute destructions and creations." Also, by showing that transformations in living bodies obeyed the laws of chemical phenomena, chemistry put an end to the theological dogma that organic matter was radically different from inorganic matter.

In sum, Comte's five lessons on chemistry are remarkable for their reformist spirit. Although the rapid changes in chemistry caused most of his specific suggestions for improvement to become outdated, his demand for homogeneity, systematization, predictive laws, and

clearer hypotheses remained valid and encouraged the science to develop to a higher stage of "positivity."

EVALUATION OF COMTE'S LESSONS ON THE INORGANIC SCIENCES

The last lesson on chemistry marked the end of Comte's discussion of the inorganic sciences. Many scientists and philosophers from Comte's time to the present have judged these thirty-nine lessons in an unfavorable light. As mentioned previously, Comte's rigid approach to the classification of the sciences— particularly his infatuation with the vague term "complexity of phenomena"—often led him to make untenable, if not absurd, predictions about their development. At times, he also appears to have made errors in discussing certain laws or discoveries. Comte's contemporary Joseph Bertrand even accused him of making significant errors in his discussion of mathematics, the very subject he taught. In a recent article [in *Studies in History and Philosophy of Science,* June 1990], Craig Fraser points out that Comte's personal animosity toward Cauchy and Poisson prevented him from taking seriously their important work, which showed the weaknesses of Lagrange's mathematics.

The renowned philosopher Michel Serres [in his notes to the 1982 edition of the *Cours*] has also demonstrated that Comte's knowledge of purely mathematical developments was remarkably poor. Serres goes so far as to say that Comte's mathematical knowledge stopped with Lagrange, who died in 1813, and that he consequently neglected the "great mathematical revolution of his time"—the rebirth of formalism and abstraction that was occurring in the early nineteenth century with Gauss, Abel, and Jacobi. Comte was therefore partly responsible for the backwardness of French mathematical instruction in the nineteenth and twentieth centuries. Although Serres praises Comte's explanation of astronomy as "clear" and "definitive" for his time, he suggests that his Cartesian conception of this science was likewise turned toward the past and totally missed the trends toward thermodynamics and astrophysics. Serres caustically calls the entire *Cours* a "monument" of the times:

> His encyclopedia of the exact sciences was . . . dead the first day of its birth. Let us not speak of the errors, which are especially notable in mathematics. It was dead for two reasons, two praises: because it *recapitulates,* and the exhaustive knowledge of the author is rarely in the wrong: whence the best general survey of a present and its past: because it *prohibits* what, for us, became its future, and the wisdom of the author is unsurpassable: he perceives in a dazzling manner what will be, only to cross it out immediately.

Presenting its own static "decisive model of the universe," the *Cours* thus ironically tried to prevent the development of the modern scientific spirit, which was occurring at the very moment Comte was writing.

Paul Tannery, a famous historian of the sciences who was Comte's disciple, claimed that at the very least the *Cours* was a historical document that faithfully reflected the state of the sciences in the early nineteenth century. Yet he had to admit that Comte was not at all informed about the new developments in the mathematical and physical sciences. As a result, scientists even of Comte's time did not take him seriously. It seems, then, that in his knowledge of the sciences, Comte had not gone much beyond what he had learned as an adolescent at the Ecole Polytechnique.

Pierre Arnaud points out that these criticisms of Comte's knowledge of mathematics and the other sciences are irrelevant because he was not a specialist and was not trying to write on the sciences per se but on philosophy. Yet most of the lessons in the *Cours* deal with specific scientific questions. Comte spoke with confidence and authority, even proposing reforms and fruitful areas of research to scientific specialists. His lack of credibility on some of these issues—especially in the first volume on mathematics and astronomy may have hindered the reception of the positive philosophy. His audience was probably less sympathetic to these problems, given the fact that the science of society, which would put all the other sciences in perspective philosophically, was merely a distant prospect. The general reader, who had great difficulty wading through the long volumes on the sciences with no relief in sight, was no happier than the scientist, who was offended by Comte's scientific errors and criticisms.

Comte was repeatedly advised to discuss at the beginning the main principles of social science, but he angrily rejected this counsel as illogical. Discussing social science first would have "ruined in advance the fundamental principles of the scientific hierarchy," which "best" characterized his philosophy. After all, one of the points of the *Cours* was that the education of each individual had to start at the beginning and go through the whole history of knowledge. And this history ended with the science of society. Moreover, by following such advice, Comte would have deprived himself of the scientific foundation necessary for the establishment of a social theory. The *Cours* was a learning process not only for his readers but, more important, for himself.

COMTE'S STYLE

Besides finding it difficult to follow a work published in pieces over a period of twelve years, both the layperson and the scientist had one other hurdle to face: Comte's poor writing. Comte's method of composing

the *Cours* had a significant effect on the work. He always had to think first about his subject matter for a very long time in order to formulate a complete outline in his mind. Without taking a single note, he ordered the main ideas, the secondary points, and then the mass of supporting details. Before he was ready to write, the chapter had to be already composed in his head. Then it almost poured forth onto the page as he scribbled away at a furious pace. Comte was so pressed for time to finish the *Cours* and to realize his many projects and so confident that he had not forgotten anything in what he had just written that he immediately gave the finished pages to his publisher. The manuscript of the *Cours* shows that he indeed made very few corrections. He crossed out on average only three to seven words a page. As a result, the *Cours* is basically a rapidly executed first draft, one that Comte never even reread.

His method of composition is reflected in his atrocious style. Valat had attacked him for his use of a dry scientific language in 1824, and many other readers criticized him throughout the years as well. But in defending his mode of discourse, Comte suggested that he sought precisely to avoid literary and rhetorical devices that would have made reading his works more pleasant, because he sought to differentiate himself from the *littérateurs,* or metaphysicians, who spoke in dangerous abstractions. To mark the uniqueness of his approach, he chose another style, a difficult "scientific style" that made his study of society seem scientific and objective and thus more worthy of respect. Boasting about the direct, spontaneous nature of his writing, one not marred by artistic conventions, he added:

> I write under the inspiration of my thought and . . . I have the profound conviction that it would be absolutely impossible for me to write in any other manner than that which the moment dictates to me. . . . [S]*tyle* is the man himself, and the one cannot be remade any more than the other.

Very much an individualist when questions of his own development arose, Comte viewed his style as a means of self-expression—a position in keeping with the romantic age in which he lived. Yet he sought to disprove the romantic writers' conviction that scientists could not be creative. Refusing to be manipulated by the marketplace, with its demands for pleasure, Comte wished to display his originality and maintain his purity.

The result, however, is that the *Cours* is almost unreadable. Its sentences are far too long and convoluted, littered with too many adjectives, adverbs, and parenthetical phrases. The reader's attention span is further taxed by Comte's repetitions, digressions, and numerous empty formulas, such as the "nature of things." One professor wrote to Littré in despair:

You told me that reading it [the *Cours*] once cannot suffice. In fact, from reading it once, I retained almost nothing. . . . Reading Comte's book is tiring. The sentences are so long that one has trouble remembering the beginning when one gets to the end. Now one must remember in order to understand, and one must understand in order to remember. It is a vicious circle. The essence and the form are, for the reader, two causes of serious difficulties.

Especially in France, where style is highly prized, Comte's graceless, heavy prose undoubtedly worked against him and was another factor reinforcing his isolation.

BIOLOGY

Although Comte's review of the inorganic sciences was open to criticism, there was one natural science that he covered in an extraordinarily insightful manner: biology. Having studied this science since 1816, when he enrolled in the famous Ecole de Médecine in Montpellier, he recognized that it was in an important and exciting period of development. By classifying biology as one of the five major sciences, instead of a division of terrestrial physics as Lamarck and others did, Comte ensured its new significance.

Although the medical school in Montpellier had taught Comte much about biology, especially about the popular theories of vitalism, it was Blainville who most influenced his views and made him a strong opponent of mechanism. From 1829 through 1832, Comte had followed Blainville's lectures on general and comparative physiology at the Faculty of Sciences. He considered this course to be the "most perfect example of the most advanced state of present biology." Therefore, thanks to Blainville, Comte knew the latest ideas in this nascent science far better than those in the other sciences. Moreover, because biology was the "immediate point of departure" for the science of society and had to be established first, he exercised greater care in discussing it. His efforts to unify and systematize biology's new theories and to make it an independent science would have a decisive impact on its development.

What first strikes the reader of these lessons in volume 3 is Comte's use of the term "biology" rather than the usual word, "physiology." He adopted the expression "biology" from Blainville, whom he wrongly credited with inventing it. (Lamarck actually introduced the term "biology" into France in 1802 to denote theories relating to the vegetal and animal series.) Comte adopted Blainville's idea that to understand all the phenomena of life, biology had to cover the study of man as an individual (physiology) as well as that of animals and plants. Comte's influence in this instance was such that henceforth people referred to the study of the phenomena of life as "biology" instead of "physiology."

Comte was convinced that only the positive philosophy could establish biology on a solid basis. Because theology and metaphysics studied man, then nature, they tended to explain all phenomena from man's standpoint, attributed an arbitrary will to these phenomena, and thus ultimately neglected nature. Positivism used the inverse method. It subordinated the conception of man to that of the external world, made the concept of "natural laws" of primary importance, and opened up the possibility of extending such laws to man and society.

On the basis of this difference in methodology, Comte criticized vitalism. He rejected such notions as the "soul" of Stahl, the "vital principle" of Barthez, and the "vital forces" of the "great Bichat himself." He felt all three vitalists were metaphysicians because there was no evidence for their theory of an independent life force, which resembled a first cause. He disapproved of their studying man in isolation from nature and their neglect of general laws, especially those of chemistry. They did not see that the study of man had to rest on the inorganic sciences. Above all, Comte was preoccupied with linking the two great subjects of philosophical speculation—man and the universe.

Besides vitalism, the other great enemy of biology was, in Comte's eyes, the mechanism of Boerhaave, which was particularly strong in the medical school in Paris. Although Boerhaave had introduced the "fundamental link between inorganic philosophy and biological philosophy," making all of natural philosophy "one homogeneous and continuous system," he had gone too far. Whereas vitalism exaggerated the independence of vital phenomena, mechanism denied it altogether by reducing biology to physics.

Comte argued that the true nature of biology lay somewhere between the two extremes of vitalism and materialism, whose disputes he blamed for making the science eclectic and disorderly. Although he appreciated the fact that Boerhaave had demonstrated the importance of physico-chemical phenomena, Comte was also favorable, if not more so, to the vitalists, because he continually defended the idea of the distinctiveness of life and said that they at least recognized physiology as a separate science. His views were influenced by Jacques Lordat, a renowned expert on Barthez and one of the professors at the Montpellier Ecole de Médecine who had befriended him. Thanks to Lordat, Barthez, along with Bichat, had a large impact on Comte.

Comte also wanted to free biology from medicine. Now that it was becoming a science in its own right, biology required speculative freedom to develop and thus had to separate itself from its corresponding practical science of application, that is, medicine. It needed scientists exclusively devoted to it and a place in formal scientific bodies, such as academies. Comte recognized that the proper organization of the scientific division of labor was a necessary element in the progress of science itself.

In discussing the nature of biology, Comte objected to the widely held definition of life originally proposed by Bichat. To combat mechanism and to separate organic from inorganic phenomena, Bichat had defined life as the totality of functions opposed to death. But having learned from Cabanis, Lamarck, and especially Blainville of the environment's strong influence on the living organism, Comte argued there could be no such absolute antagonism between "living nature" and "dead nature"; living bodies were so fragile that they could not exist if their surroundings tended to destroy them. Thus life depended on matter, and the fundamental condition of life was a "harmony between the living being and the corresponding milieu." Comte expanded the definition of the word "milieu" to include the "total ensemble of all types of external circumstances that are necessary for the existence of each determined organism." In this way, he encouraged interest in the relationship between man and his environment, which was already being stimulated by the industrial revolution. Inspired by Blainville and German *Naturphilosophen,* Comte also urged biologists to create a special general theory clarifying the influence of milieus on organisms. In a sense, he was promoting the importance of ecology.

In searching for the correct definition of life, Comte criticized contemporary German philosophy (*Naturphilosophie*) for equating life with spontaneous activity. He argued that this definition failed to relate the idea of life to inorganic laws and made life lose all significance because all natural bodies were active. Instead, he adopted Blainville's definition of life as the "double internal movement, both general and continuous, of composition and decomposition." Comte was therefore close to the mechanists in arguing that organic life was characterized by chemical and physical activity. In fact, according to Paul Tannery, Comte's conception of the chemical foundation of life had a significant impact on nineteenth-century biological research. But Comte also reproached Blainville for not having emphasized in his definition that the organism had to exist in a proper milieu. A biological phenomenon could be understood only in relation to other phenomena in the living body and to the outside world. Life was, in effect, this dualism between the milieu and the organism.

Thanks to Blainville, Comte also maintained that one of the key differences between the organic and the

inorganic was that only the former was characterized by organization. Without organization, there was no life. Therefore, biology could not be reduced to chemistry because vital phenomena were influenced not only by laws of composition and decomposition but by their organization, that is, their anatomical structure. The chemical transformations in living organisms were different from those in inorganic bodies in that they were continuous and dependent on the anatomical organization of the living bodies in question. Comte did not endeavor to define the essence of life but insisted that it could not be summed up in chemical reactions.

Influenced again by Blainville, Comte criticized biologists for separating the static state (the anatomical point of view) and the dynamic state (the physiological point of view). He argued that this division would disappear only when the whole biological system derived from his principle that the concept of life was inseparable from that of organization. Biologists would then see that there could be no organ without a function and no function without an organ. (Function designated the "action" of the organism when influenced by the milieu.) They would accept the principle that when an organism was "placed in a given system of external circumstances," it must act in a "determined manner." Such determinism was necessary for biology to fulfill the primary aim of all positive sciences, that of prediction. By insisting on determinism, Comte opposed the vitalists and made a significant contribution to the development of biology in the nineteenth century. Thanks to Claude Bernard, determinism became one of the leading principles of this new science.

Comte's theory of organization and milieu was one of the most important and original points of the entire *Cours*. It enabled him to create a theory of life totally distinct from that of death. On the one hand, in proclaiming the originality and autonomy of life and the specificity of biology, he avoided taking a purely empirical or materialistic position. His stress on organization as one of the conditions of life allowed him to avoid the reductionism of the physico-chemical school. On the other hand, his insistence that the second condition of life was a suitable milieu eliminated the mystical or vitalist notion that life was universally diffused throughout nature and could be produced spontaneously. Thanks to the efforts of the Société de Biologie, founded by his disciples, Comte's theory of milieu had an enormous impact on French biology. The term "milieu" would later be applied to historical circumstances by the historian Hippolyte Taine.

In discussing methodology, Comte declared, as he had in 1824, that in contrast to the inorganic sciences, the study of life should begin with the best known phenomena, which were the most particular and complex (i.e., human beings), and proceed gradually to the least known phenomena, which were the most general and simplest. Since life was characterized above all by solidarity and consensus, the whole had to be grasped before the details could be comprehended. Epistemologically, biology was, therefore, a synthetic science.

Because it dealt with more complex phenomena than the sciences that preceded it, its means of investigation were greater. Direct observations made by the natural senses could be improved by artificial apparatuses, such as the microscope. However, reflecting the fears of Bichat and Blainville, Comte had some reservations about its use, because he feared it could lead to illusions.

Like Cuvier and Blainville, he was also wary of experimentation, the second means of investigation. Since each organism was very complex, depended on many interconnected external and internal influences, and formed an indivisible system, it was impossible to isolate phenomena sufficiently to make experimentation as effective as it was in the inorganic sciences. Comte particularly protested against the increasing use of vivisection, for he believed it disturbed the organism too much and led to a "deplorable levity" and "habits of cruelty," which were intellectually and morally detrimental to the scientist. The only experimentation that Comte endorsed was the introduction of disturbances into the milieu—a much less "violent" procedure than vivisection. He also believed the study of disease was like experimentation in that the biologist learned about normal physiological conditions by investigating a variation of the normal state. Comte credited Broussais with this idea and unwisely attacked the "incompetent judges" at the Academy of Sciences for rejecting his candidacy.

Impressed by Blainville's use of the comparative method in anatomy, Comte declared that this third general mode of investigation would blossom in biology because of the fundamental resemblance of organic phenomena. Relying on classification for organizing distinct but analogous beings, the comparative method was the most important means of investigating living bodies. His recommendation of a wide use of this method in physiology was one of the original points of the *Cours*.

Comte believed that biology was the most intellectually demanding natural science because it depended on a preliminary mastery of the methods and laws of all the other sciences preceding it in the hierarchy. Though critical of Bichat's vitalism, Comte did agree with his prohibition of the excessive use of mathematics in biology. Like chemical phenomena, biological phenomena were too complicated, varied, and diverse to permit numerical calculations. Comte's views on this subject were shortsighted.

Comte claimed that biology had a strong impact on the "emancipation of human reason." By proving that the organic world was regulated by natural laws and that organisms and the environment could be modified by human intervention, it actively combated "theological fictions" and "metaphysical entities." In terms of method or logic, biology contributed to the positive system of knowledge by developing two of man's most basic powers, those of comparison and classification. Biology had taught Comte himself that he could unify the sciences by classifying them in a hierarchy and that subordination was one of the characteristics of order.

Comte expressed reservations about several recent developments in biology. He rejected nascent cell theory because he felt cells were an absurd and incomprehensible imitation of molecules and tissue theory already established anatomy on a solid scientific base. Microscopic research, which supported the "metaphysical" cellular theory, was in his eyes much too vague and unreliable. Comte's views on cell theory, microscopic research, and vivisection meant that he failed to put himself in the forefront of biological research, and they proved embarrassing to some of his disciples.

Following Blainville's lead, Comte also took a conservative approach in rejecting Lamarck's new theories of evolution. It is clear that Comte greatly admired Lamarck's linear approach to the chain of being, his investigations into the influence of the milieu on the organism, his concept of the heredity of acquired characteristics, and his theory of habit, whereby habit was "one of the principal bases of the gradual perfectibility of animals and especially of man." Yet he considered Lamarck's concept of the variation of the species to be a farfetched exaggeration. Repeating Cuvier's argument, Comte maintained that observation could not verify Lamarck's theory that needs created organs. Moreover, if, as Lamarck asserted, different species could transform themselves into others owing to external influences, the idea of "species" would be deprived of meaning, classification would become almost impossible, and the science of biology itself would become muddled. Lamarck's suggestion that the organism was completely determined by its milieu threatened the unity and distinctiveness of the living organism. Whereas earlier in these lessons on biology Comte seemed closer to Lamarck in insisting on the effect of the milieu on the organism, he now stressed that the influence of the milieu on the species was limited to nonessential changes, and he seemed to increase the power of the organism to modify its environment.

Instead of Lamarck's transformism, Comte maintained the old doctrine of the fixity of the species. Just as he admired the stability of the celestial world, he insisted upon the unchanging order of the world of vital phenomena. Although he referred to the adaptation of the organism to its milieu and even to the "perfectibility" of the animal and human species, his conception of biology neglected the significance of time and was ultimately more static than dynamic. Comte's position is paradoxical, considering that he is regarded as the philosopher of progress. He apparently wished to empower individuals so that they could transform their world in an advantageous manner, but reflecting the strains of the postrevolutionary era, he seemed basically more concerned about the disruptive consequences of change.

The last chapter of volume 3 was devoted to the biological study of cerebral phenomena. By extending the positive method to these phenomena, Comte claimed to complete the scientific revolution begun by Descartes. Comte believed that Descartes had erred when he separated the study of man from that of the animals, thereby giving new life to the theological and metaphysical philosophies. But thanks to the work of Gall, intellectual and moral phenomena, which represented the last stronghold of the theological and metaphysical philosophies, now could be made a subject of scientific investigations. In denying the separation of matter and spirit, phrenology thus strengthened Comte's stance against Cartesian dualism.

Much of Comte's discussion was motivated by his dislike of metaphysical theories of psychology, which he divided into three schools. First there was the Scottish school, which he most admired. Then there was the French school of the Idéologues and their predecessors, the sensationalists Condillac and Helvétius, which he felt was the clearest and most systematic. Finally there was the German school, which included the French eclectics, such as the "famous sophist" Cousin, whom he accused of inspiring in French youth the "deplorable psychological mania." These three schools based their theories on the unscientific notion of "interior observation." Because the mind could not be studied apart from nature, as the psychologists claimed, the study of the mind, according to Comte, had to be a physical science based on the other, more simple sciences.

Psychologists, fond of referring to "purely nominal entities," such as the soul, the will, and the ego, also neglected the fact that every function had an organ and vice versa. "Phrenological physiology" was superior to psychology because it determined intellectual and affective functions by considering the organs on which they depended in the brain. Phrenology showed that intellectual and moral phenomena depended in a *concrete* fashion on organization, that is, on anatomical structure.

At this point, Comte added another criticism of the psychologists and Idéologues, which sheds light on his concept of human nature. In his private letters, he had often mentioned that he had strong emotional needs that directed the way he lived. Now backed by Gall, he criticized psychology and Idéologie for neglecting the

affections and wrongly subordinating them to the intellect. As if directing his attack against Hegel and Cousin, Comte denounced the exclusive attention given to the "mind" (*l'esprit*). "Daily experience" shows that "the affections, penchants, [and] passions constitute the principal motives of human action." Arising spontaneously and independently from the intellect, they stimulate the "first awakening and the continuous development of the different intellectual faculties" because they give them a "permanent goal," without which these faculties would remain "dull." Comte added, "It is even only too certain that the least noble and the most animalistic penchants are habitually the most energetic, and consequently, the most influential." Because the psychologists and Idéologues vaguely attached the affections to some unifying principle, such as sympathy or egoism, which was supposedly directed by the intellect, they portrayed man "against all evidence as an essentially reasoning being, executing continually, without his knowledge, a multitude of imperceptible calculations with almost no spontaneity of action, even from the most tender age of childhood." Attacking one of the bases of Enlightenment and liberal theory, Comte insisted, furthermore, that it was wrong to argue that man could be changed and improved by his intelligence. Stressing the limits of rationalism, Comte was not only responding to the criticisms that the Saint-Simonians had made of him but contributing in his own fashion to the cult of the emotions that was having an impact on literature and the arts at the time.

Comte was convinced that the psychologists' unified ego represented a "purely fictive state," one designed to preserve artificially the separation between men and animals and to maintain the theological idea of a unified soul. In reality, human nature was "essentially multiple, that is, prompted almost always by several very distinct and fully independent powers, between which equilibrium is established very painfully." Influenced by Barthez and Broussais, Comte argued that the only real unity was physical; it was the "fundamental unity of the animal organism," which resulted from an "exact harmony among [its] diverse principal functions," that is, from the association of the animal's different organs. This primarily physical sense of equilibrium among the faculties constituted health and determined the "general feeling of the self [*le moi*]." Moreover, the sentiment of personal harmony was extremely unstable and complex and could not be the basis of a philosophy, despite Cousin's assertions to the contrary. As Lévy-Bruhl indicates, Comte was here speaking as a successor of Hume and Cabanis. In sum, by stating that the ego was merely the "universal consensus of the whole of the organism," Comte was arguing, in contrast to the psychologists, that both men and animals had a feeling of the ego because this feeling was mainly physical. He was, in effect, placing man and the animals on the same level, reaffirming the unity of living beings and attacking theologians and metaphysicians for painting a more noble picture of man than was scientifically admissible.

To combat Descartes's original, fatal distinction between intelligence and instinct that was used by the psychologists and Idéologues to separate human from animal nature, Comte praised Gall's view that instinct and intelligence were not opposites. Instinct was not confined to animals any more than intelligence was to humans. Instinct, defined as "any spontaneous impulse toward a determined direction," could be applied to any faculty, including intelligence. One could have an instinct for mathematics or music, and people had at least as many instincts as animals. Furthermore, since intelligence was the "aptitude for modifying one's conduct in conformity to the circumstances of each case," animals, like people, were obviously intelligent because they could transform their behavior if necessary. The usual theological and metaphysical definition of man as a "rational animal" was, therefore, "nonsense," for animals themselves had to act in a reasonable manner in order to survive. People were different from animals only because they developed the intellectual and affective faculties more fully. This difference was one of degree, not of kind. Comte's stress on the affective and intellectual attributes of animals helps explain his antivivisectionism. Denying once again that man was the center of the universe, Comte found theologians' and metaphysicians' worries about degrading human nature a barrier to scientific progress. Although he himself opposed theories of evolution, his predilection for placing animals and humans on the same continuum pointed the way toward Darwinism.

Comte's purely "naturalistic" approach to man made him vulnerable to accusations of materialism. Yet he distanced himself from the sensationalists, such as Locke, Condillac, and Helvétius, who were considered the leading exponents of materialism, for he believed that they grossly exaggerated the power of intellectual faculties and the environment's influence on man. He particularly criticized Helvétius for suggesting not only that all men had similar senses and were equal intellectually but also that "egoism" should be the sole moral principle. These dangerous ideas led to the "most absurd exaggerations about the unlimited power of education" to make improvements. They also reduced social relations to "ignoble coalitions of private interests." Again, Comte was criticizing Enlightenment and liberal philosophy, which he held partly responsible for the destructive political movements since the French Revolution.

Comte praised German philosophy (German idealism) for trying to refute the errors of the French school, but he felt that it was hindered by the "vague Absolute of its unintelligible doctrines." Thinking probably of Fichte's ego, Comte argued that because the German phi-

losophers claimed the ego to be characterized by "vagabond liberty," they made it "essentially ungovernable" and free from all laws. This approach ran counter to Comte's basic principle that all phenomena were subject to natural laws. Kant's and Fichte's notions of the categorical imperative seemed equally false. Condemning the Germans' tendency toward "universal mystification," Comte criticized their idea of allowing "each individual to direct exclusively his conduct according to the abstract idea of duty." Acting in the name of an abstract metaphysical entity "would lead ultimately to the exploitation of the species by a small number of clever charlatans." Thus the errors of German philosophy had social and political consequences as dangerous as the French school's.

The school of psychology that Comte found the "least absurd of all" was the Scottish. Although their doctrines suffered from a lack of clarity, unity, and widespread influence, Hume, Smith, and Ferguson offered the best metaphysical rebuttal to the philosophy of sensationalism because they recognized that sympathy was at least as powerful a force in man as egoism.

Despite Comte's admiration for the Scots, he was still most enthusiastic about Gall's doctrine, which he believed was the clearest and most scientific refutation of metaphysical theories, especially sensationalism. Although Comte claimed to be a relativist, he argued that two of Gall's principles of human nature would remain forever unchanged. Indeed, since they provided Comte with the basis for his social and political philosophy, his own system would fall if they one day proved false.

The first principle was the innateness of fundamental intellectual and emotional dispositions. Because it asserted that people were born with different characteristics, this principle put an end to the sensationalists' insistence on equality and their optimistic approach to the effects of environment.

The second principle involved the plurality of distinct, independent faculties. Far from being one organ, the brain was an apparatus composed of different organs that corresponded to these faculties or dispositions. Comte rejected Gall's view that each action was linked to a faculty and that there were "organs" of theft, murder, music, poetry, and so forth. He preferred Spurzheim's theory that action depended on the *association* of certain faculties (or "organs") and the corresponding circumstances, especially because he believed this theory could be verified anatomically and applied to both human beings and animals. Comte commended both Gall and Spurzheim for having eliminated the sensationalist and metaphysical theory that sensation, memory, imagination, and judgment were fundamental, separate faculties of abstraction, invariable in all human beings. Instead, these abilities were related to each phrenological function and varied from one person (and animal) to the next, according to how much they were exercised. Eliminating the idea that everyone had a similar intellectual makeup, this second principle also showed the absurdity of the notion of human equality.

Most important, Gall's principles provided scientific confirmation for the Scottish philosophers' theory that sympathy was an innate disposition in man. Arguing in favor of the predominance of the affective faculties in human and animal nature, Gall placed the affective faculties in the back and middle part of the brain and the intellectual faculties in the front part, where they constituted merely a quarter or a sixth of the encephalic mass. This anatomical discovery destroyed the basis of psychology and Idéologie, which insisted on the preeminence of man's intellect. By placing the affections directly in the brain, Gall disproved Cabanis's and Bichat's theories that the brain was one organ composed solely of the intellect and that the passions were located in other organs such as the heart or the liver. Comte was delighted to have this "proof" of the human being's inherent sociability because it demonstrated man's natural tendency to form a group without resorting to the old theories of the social contract and utility, which were ultimately based on individualism.

Comte admitted that Gall's and Spurzheim's efforts to localize the diverse cerebral functions were full of errors. So far, there was no conclusive theory about the "type, number, range, and reciprocal influence of the organs" that could be assigned to the intellectual and affective functions. Nevertheless, Comte did accept phrenology's main subdivisions. What were traditionally called the heart, character, and mind could be found respectively in the back, middle, and front parts of the brain. Comte denied that this schematic presentation of the brain meant that all human action was predetermined. Since moral and intellectual phenomena were more complex than other phenomena, they could be modified more easily. Also the faculties could be exercised and strengthened. In particular, the intellectual faculties, which affected an animal's or a person's behavior, could significantly alter the influence of all the other faculties. Yet although Comte claimed that Gall upheld human freedom and responsibility, what appealed most to him was clearly Gall's principle of the innateness of certain dispositions, which challenged not only the German philosophers' insistence on the unlimited power of the ego to transform one's moral nature, but also the French philosophers' belief in the unlimited ability of institutions to change the individual.

Comte maintained that Gall's theories demonstrated that people could not be improved through education unless they had the requisite predispositions. He fully accepted the phrenological principle that people, for the most part, were "essentially mediocre" both intellectually and emotionally. Each person possessed all the penchants, sentiments, and elementary aptitudes, but usually none of these faculties dominated the others. Although education could improve people, it would never allow them to overcome their essential mediocrity, which in fact was necessary for "good social harmony." It seems that Comte's years of teaching had discouraged him and left him with a certain bitterness that was strikingly different from the enthusiasm of his youth. But even in his youth he had once said to Valat that a friend of theirs had disappointed him by displaying an "odious trait":

> I thought I could consider that man one of the people who came to virtue through instruction, and I see that I must erase him from my list. In truth, I am beginning to discover that the more one examines men, the less one finds within their interior anything that gains in being seen.

Nevertheless, Comte's views on the limitations of instruction seem incongruous considering that the purpose of the *Cours* was to effect an educational revolution leading to the regeneration of humanity.

Despite his enthusiasm for Gall and Spurzheim, Comte criticized them and other phrenologists for their arbitrary localizations, their superficial grasp of the association of the different faculties, and their excessive multiplication of "organs" and functions. (Gall claimed there were twenty-seven faculties, and Spurzheim, thirty-five.) He insisted that phrenology's analysis of the brain had to be "entirely" redone, especially with the help of anatomical studies, in order to avoid the base charlatanism that was now endangering its credibility. Once corrected, this new science would be useful politically and socially because it would improve the "difficult art of judging men according to incontestable signs."

Like many other of his scientific forecasts, Comte's prediction that cerebral physiology would become one of the most important scientific developments of the nineteenth century proved erroneous. Nevertheless, his criticism of the vagueness and limited views of the psychological schools of his day as well as his insistence that psychology be considered a part of biology instead of epistemology proved valid. Lévy-Bruhl pointed out that Comte's dislike of "psychology" referred mainly to the "science of the soul obtained by the introspective method," a method that would be unacceptable to many modern psychologists. He avoided the use of the term "psychology" to denote the study of cerebral phenomena because he did not want to be confused with Cousin's metaphysical school. Lévy-Bruhl was right to insist that "it is inexact to say that there is no psychology in Comte." Comte's animosity toward scholars who speculated in an a priori manner about the nature of the mind foreshadowed the position of twentieth-century behaviorists. B. F. Skinner and other behavioral psychologists still contend that one cannot directly observe the processes of the mind itself and challenge the Freudian interest in the unconscious. Furthermore, Comte's vision of man as an emotional being not entirely governed by reason and his insistence that human equilibrium was very fragile would not be denied by later psychologists. Like him, they have stressed the importance of studying animal behavior, insanity, and more respectable forms of "cerebral localization" as a means of deepening one's understanding of human nature. In recent years, there seems to have been a revival of Comte's ideas that there are physiological bases for mental illness, that parts of the brain control certain actions, and that the brain has "functions." Thus, although Comte's enthusiasm for phrenology seems singularly unscientific, at least some of his views remain worthy of attention.

Angèle Kremer-Marietti (essay date 1995)

SOURCE: "Introduction: Comte and Mill: The Philosophical Encounter," in *The Correspondence of John Stuart Mill and Auguste Comte,* edited and translated by Oscar A. Haac, Transaction Publishers, 1995, pp. 1-23.

[*In the following essay, Kremer-Marietti chronicles the relationship between Comte and Mill, documenting possible mutual influences.*]

On November 8, 1841, when John Stuart Mill (1806-1872) first wrote to Auguste Comte (1798-1857), he introduced himself as a devoted disciple with such humility, that Comte replied: "Your scrupulous modesty had led you, Sir, to overemphasize the influence of my work on your philosophical development." A close friendship and sincere affection rapidly grew between the two. Then issues arose that affected their relations, and in 1847 they terminated their correspondence. But evidence of how close their relations had been is apparent when Comte laments in 1857, the year of his death, that he had been unable to win John Stuart Mill's approval of his "Religion of Humanity."

MILL AND POSITIVISM

Mill received a rigorous intellectual education from his father, James Mill (1773-1836), a Scottish philosopher who wrote for the *Edinburgh Review* between 1808 and 1813. In 1819 James Mill authored an important work entitled *History of India.* He was also an economist and a friend and associate of Jeremy Bentham (1748-1832). Bentham's brother invited John Stuart Mill to spend a year in France when he was fourteen, which included six months in Montpellier in the winter of 1820-21. John Mill learned French rap-

idly and developed a keen interest in French thought. (Comte's acquaintance, Dr. Roméo Pouzin, knew Mill when he was quite young and recognized his superior intelligence.)

At fourteen, John Stuart Mill had already read Jeremy Bentham's works and felt "transformed" by them. They corresponded and, in 1825, Mill edited Bentham's *Rationale of Judicial Evidence.* Not long after, Mill became aware of Auguste Comte and Positivism. He met Comte's disciple, Gustave d'Eichthal, who sent him the short *Système de politique positive.* Mill read it in 1828 and, by 1837, the first two volumes of the *Cours.* He discovered that he shared numerous ideas with Comte: they were both opposed to metaphysics and theology; they both sought to organize human knowledge by creating a systematic philosophy; and they hoped to reform society.

Thus, when Mill addressed his first letter to Comte, he could speak of his great philosophic debt and of his enthusiasm for the first volumes of the *Cours* where he found, "the essential doctrine for modern times." He salutes Positivism as a bulwark against skepticism and as the philosophy which will carry on the great traditions of the past, those of the medieval church, of the absolute state of the seventeenth century and of the French Revolution. Mill welcomes Positivism as the legitimate heir to the great philosophic movements of the past, a faith for the present and an inspiration for the future. Just as Rationalism had replaced religious beliefs that had become dated and meaningless, so Positivism was to take over from the "negative" and "critical" spirit of the Enlightenment.

Mill could identify with Positivism all the more easily as he had grown up without any Christian commitment. He felt that here was the doctrine for the new age. He foresaw its success especially among scientists, a group broadly conceived to include philosophers like Comte and himself, but not among contemporary politicians for whom he held little hope. Both men believed in religious tolerance but hailed Positivism as the path to intellectual and philosophical renewal.

WHILE MILL AND COMTE AGREED

The publication of the sixth and last volume of the *Cours* in 1842 is an important event in the correspondence between the two men. Comte was now ready to create the "Positive Committee of Western Nations," to coordinate the efforts of scientists, "establish . . . spiritual power" separate from temporal power and prepare for the "positive" renewal of the leading nations toward *unity, continuity* and *solidarity*—a plan Comte had envisioned as early as 1826.

Volume six completed twelve years of intensive work; it was a comprehensive survey of human knowledge.

It was the culmination of Comte's first philosophic endeavor; the second was to center on *Positive Polity* and the Religion of Humanity. In the **Cours**, Comte had formulated his grand law of social evolution by defining the three ages of humankind: the theological, the metaphysical (critical) and the positive (scientific). To the basic sciences he had surveyed—mathematics, astronomy, physics, chemistry, and biology—the last volume of the **Cours** had added a sixth, the supreme science of sociology, the crown of human knowledge. Comte proclaimed the epistemological need for sociology as a social, historical and political science. He considered his own historical and systematic classification of "positive sciences" to be far superior in defining a hierarchy of human knowledge to earlier attempts made by Francis Bacon (1561-1626) and d'Alembert (1717-1783), which had centered around human faculties such as memory, reason and imagination.

Thus, in 1842, the mutual agreement between Mill and Comte was broad enough for Mill to honestly say, even before reading volume six, that he was ready to join Comte's Positive Committee of Western Nations. Mill stood ready to support the philosophic rebirth envisaged by Comte, an association of social elites that would sponsor a new morality and stand ready to stem what they considered the decline of the West, caused by the rule of negative, metaphysical (critical) philosophy. The group of "positive" nations was called upon to combat such "subversive utopias."

Comte and Mill were warning Western Europe of great perils when they adopted the spirit of the motto Comte was to publicize in 1847: "Order and Progress." The great nations of the West were to initiate a new European revolution which would be quite unlike the disruption of 1789 or 1793. Comte saw the *philosophes* of the Enlightenment as critics of church and religion whose "critical metaphysics" brought about the French Revolution. Their "negative" role, though necessary, was destructive. Positivism, by contrast, was to be reconstructive. Mill and Comte were looking forward to the "positive" period of reorganization, to the salutary and much needed substitution of Positivism for theology and metaphysics. Positive science, based on observation and applied by pragmatic methods, would enable positivist philosophers to anticipate the needs of society; better still, the positive science of sociology gave philosophers the right and the duty to act in the political sphere. Indeed, they were obliged to intervene in European affairs so that moral and social renewal, guided by Positivism and inspired by sociology, could create the "scientific" philosophy of the future. In solidarity, England and France were to join in a radical reorganization of Europe.

To Mill, this was close to an apocalyptic vision, heralding the impending triumph of Positivism. He was willing to go along with Comte, sincerely convinced that a true, social philosophy was the solid foundation for moral regeneration. The motto, "a Revolution in Western Europe," looks forward to the radical transformation Comte and Mill were trying to accomplish. Meanwhile, Mill was convinced that the concept of God would yield to the idea of Humanity (Letter 21).

For a time, both men expected that their philosophic sympathies would cause their views to coincide, first on basic issues and later on secondary questions. They believed that the expanding harmony of the French and the English spirit would propel the hoped-for reorganization of Europe. Both men looked forward to an active commitment. It was in such expectation of agreement that Comte, in his "thinker's solitude," lonely also because his wife had left him, welcomed the bond with Mill. He was looking forward to sharing ideas in fraternal solidarity. They felt like fellow citizens of Western Europe. Their philosophic steps were to take precedence over political considerations, for these were to be solved *after* spiritual reorganization, which in turn required further temporal measures.

At this "epistemological point of agreement" Comte and Mill found that their accord depended more on "method" than on "doctrine;" in other words, it depended more on philosophical principle than on any body of data in particular sciences. For Comte, general principles of method mattered more than scientific data of doctrine, though the two were inseparable. Mill agreed and, in his *Logic,* emphasized inductive demonstration. Both believed that positive philosophy could not be separate from the body of observations to which it applied.

Comte was a generalist. As he considered his social and intellectual surroundings, he focused on principles equally applicable to astronomy, physics, chemistry, biology, sociology and moral speculation. He looked on anthropology, the basic science of society, as the ultimate product of "western history," as stated in his **Discours sur l'esprit positif** of 1844. Mill, meanwhile, had published *A System of Logic, Ratiocinative and Inductive* (1843), which placed the emphasis on the study of human nature (psychology) and character (ethology).

Thus both Mill and Comte looked upon social anthropology (sociology) as the principal achievement of the scientific traditions of England, France, Germany, Italy, and the smaller neighboring nations; for positive science depended above all on the cooperative effort of "the West," on common endeavors and reforms along essential lines. These are defined by Comte to include:

1. a synthesis of knowledge serving a common purpose, to relate man to the world, subject to object;
2. a common body of positive knowledge, the

sciences being viewed from a social perspective; altruism replaces egoism, as individuals serve other individuals, not society as such;

3. the realization that history is a continuum and solidarity a social fact; nation states must unite in the common goal of positive polity, conceived so as to improve modern society.

These ideals stem in part from the Scottish school of philosophy discussed by Comte (Letters 24, 58); both he and Mill owed it a significant debt. Comte had taken much from David Hume (1711-1776), Adam Smith (1723-1790) and Adam Ferguson (1723-1816). In lesson 45 of the **Cours**, these philosophers are said to stand very close to Positivism; they are empiricists who adopt the ideal of sympathy which links man's "interest" to "altruism" and establishes an essential social bond.

Comte's idea of society has much in common with Ferguson's, for Ferguson was interested in the history of civil society and, contrary to Rousseau, saw self-interest as the basis of our social conscience. This theory can be found in his *Institutes of Moral Philosophy* (1772). In Comte as in Ferguson, altruism does not spring spontaneously from human nature; it may, in fact, derive from self-interest. Comte speaks of *egoism* as opposed to *altruism* but also as a preparation for it. This is the way in which Comte felt that the Scottish school, including Ferguson, had made their great contribution, Descartes's *cogito* seeming all too individualistic to serve as the starting point for modern philosophy. It may be astonishing to find Comte calling Descartes "irrational" for not being oriented toward society, but for Comte, rationalism must be neither theological nor metaphysical in the traditional sense. Ferguson, on the other hand, and his Scottish colleagues, had better understood man's "supposed egoism" and subordinated it to the essential social reality. The Scottish philosophers, Comte felt, had grasped the import of society as such, and this conception was also at the root of John Stuart Mill's theory of general happiness. In short, Comte believed, as did Ferguson, that individual (self-)interest merges with the interest of the group.

As for Hume, Comte read especially his *History of England* (1754) and was as suspicious of causality in nature as Hume was himself. However, he did not share Hume's skepticism and preferred a kind of "scientific legalism." In Comte's epistemology the notion of law replaces the notion of cause.

Scottish philosophy did bring Comte and Mill together, although Comte seems to seek out the Scottish philosophers of a more distant past. One exception to this was Adam Smith, whose ideas separated Mill from Comte rather than bringing them together. Comte cited Smith's early *Philosophical Essays*, especially the *Considerations Concerning the First Formation of Languages* on the age of theology. He also mentions Smith's *History of Astronomy* on fetishes in his own **Considérations philosophiques sur les sciences et les savants** (1825), but he neglected Smith's economic theory presented in the famous *Inquiry into the Nature and Causes of the Wealth of Nations* (1776). Comte read it and retained the idea of the division of labor. He applied it not to industry, but to intellectual enterprises as a way of deriving theory from practice and of separating them. Indeed, he was not speaking about the advantages of specialization: he was opposed to undue specialization in intellectual activities. Mill, on the contrary, used the *Wealth of Nations* as the model for his *Principles of Political Economy*.

THE CORRESPONDENCE EVOLVES

As we read the letters of Comte and Mill, we see their harmony giving way to a number of fundamental disagreements in the areas of psychology, economics and, above all, in the appraisal of the social role of women. In each case Comte expected his young colleague to accept his views as those of his elder, the voice of experience, while Mill questioned Comte's analysis, not only on the basis of his personal convictions but on those of his fiancée, Harriet Taylor. Gradually their exchanges became less forthright, even hostile; we find Mill's ambivalence in the portrait he draws in *Auguste Comte and Positivism* (1865).

Psychology

Although they did not stand far from each other, psychology found Mill and Comte divided; both were searching for a positive view based on the latest findings of biology and physiology, but their reactions differed. Comte had been strongly attracted by Gall (1758-1828) and his phrenology, and for a while, considered Gall to be the founder of psychophysiology. In Lesson 45 of the **Cours**, he describes Gall as the "creator" of a new science, while in the first volume of Comte's **Politique positive**, Gall is reduced to the status of a "precursor" of Comte's own Brain Chart.

Actually Comte had never fully agreed with Gall; he called Gall's analysis "irrational" since it studied the individual without reference to his milieu and to the influence of society. Among other determinants, Gall had studied the dominant influence of the organism on the brain, but he had left out the social environment, ignoring the influence of education, the social context. Gall had limited his study of the brain to anatomy and physiology, outside of the concerns of sociology, whereas Comte was convinced that sociology must "regenerate" biology. In the **Discourse on the positive spirit,** Comte spelled out this requirement. Comte's new "rationalism" had to be "social" or "sociological." "Sociality" is said to be the precondition of the scientific state. Mill, on the other hand, rejected Gall almost entirely (Letters 9 and 11). Mill gave him credit only for the idea that animal instincts and mental functions were related to specific areas of the brain. Mill's reaction was negative, while Comte's friends, Broussais (1772-1838) and Blainville (1777-1850), held Gall in the highest esteem.

Comte derived his psycho-physiology from Gall's phrenology, without, however, going as far as Broussais, who adopted it with enthusiasm and taught it in his courses at the medical school. Comte's famous *Brain Chart* describes the psycho-physiological base of sense experience, of man's affective and intellectual aptitudes. The Chart becomes the necessary base for analyzing social statics. With ethics as the seventh in his hierarchy of sciences, Comte provides the "universal synthesis," which enables man to understand how the *individual* reacts to social and biological factors.

As Comte explains in Lessons 1 and 45 of the *Cours*, he rejects the kind of introspection or "interior observation" dear to Mill. In Lesson 1 he is arguing against the metaphysical method. According to the criteria of positive science, interior observation is of no scientific value. Then in Lesson 45, directing himself once more against the metaphysicians and against German philosophy in particular, he explains that the unity of the self is a false concept. He is searching for a science of the mind relating psychic phenomena to the brain and to the nervous system.

In 1841, Mill writes to Comte that, like him, he is looking for a "positivist psychology which would certainly be neither that of Condillac, nor that of Cousin, nor even that of the Scottish school" (Letter 3). Later on Mill, thinking of the argument Comte proposed in Lesson 1, that is of the impossibility of observing the observer, Mill contradicts Comte: Mill believes that by means of "interior observation" we do have direct knowledge of the mind. For him, psychology leads to ethology. Mill argues that "there is a direct connection between Comte's sexist misuse of anatomy and physiology and his rejection of psychology." Such will still be their arguments when they come to discuss the status of women.

Let us conclude that Mill's appraisal of Gall is more reserved, more negative than that of Comte, whose major critique appears when he proposes to integrate the physical sciences into sociology. Mill, on the other hand, insists that a full appreciation of psychology is called for. Mill considers psychology a science, while for Comte it does not deserve to be included among the positive sciences, either as an independent or as a basic one.

Economics

We now turn to another major issue that caused Mill to abandon Comte. The analysis of political economy was as important for Mill as it had been for his father, while Comte, though not entirely opposed, did not rank it as a positive science. He did discuss political economy in his *Considérations sur le pouvoir spirituel* (1826), later in lesson 47 of the *Cours*, and in *Positive Polity*, volume II, ch. 2, which includes "positive economics." However, Comte disliked the limited principles of contemporary economists. Their research did not concern society as a whole and was too particularized; so he called them "metaphysical" and "irrational," not yet scientific. In Comte's eyes, economics was still based *a priori* on absolute principles, rather than on the observation of interrelated social phenomena that would lead to a realistic view of society. He felt justified, therefore, in omitting economics from his list of basic, positive sciences.

Mill's orientation was very different. He shared Comte's reservations concerning current practice; like Comte, he regretted that the historical method was little used and that metaphysical assumptions precluded "positive" results. Economics seemed to Comte insufficient and transient in nature, while Mill was deeply interested in the field and planned to write several studies of it. The first of these, *Principles of Political Economy* (1848), was composed while he was corresponding with Comte, and was written directly after *A System of Logic* (1843).

The two philosophers debated one epistemological issue in particular: "scientific prediction." Mill believed future developments could be anticipated, that economic forecasting could yield accurate results based on practical skill and careful observation. Comte denied this, though he conceded that forecasts would succeed once they fitted the "positive" conceptions: the symmetry of explanation and prediction. As he put it: "From science comes foresight, from foresight action" (*science, d'où prévoyance; prévoyance, d'où action*).

Actually their differences in opinion produced constructive results: Comte made Mill aware of the transitory nature of the data currently available. Mill was willing to proceed and made every effort to apply positive methods to economic matter. As his model in economics, he chose Adam Smith, *The Wealth of Nations*, whereas Comte was basically indebted to Jean-Baptiste Say, although Comte came to criticize him also.

On April 3, 1844, (Letter 46) Mill explains how the general principle of production differs from what he calls "principles of exchange and wealth." None of these explanations alter Comte's negative stance (Letter 49). He insists that Mill's data apply insufficiently to the overall structure of society, to the social order in social statics, and to historical and social progress in social dynamics. As their debate unfolds, it becomes apparent that neither the technique of "prediction" nor the "principles" on which it is based mean exactly the same thing to both men.

Comte cites his motto from the *Cours*: "Progress is the extension of Order," to indicate that social dynamics depends on statics and that, therefore, the principles of economics must simultaneously inform on both. Comte wants economics to be an exact social science and finds that it does not meet this requirement. For Comte there exists no true positive science of economics; he is thereby rejecting research that is very important to Mill.

The Status of Women: Social Statics Threatens Their Synergy

In their debates on psychology and economics, there remained points of contact between Comte and Mill, but as they turned to the social position of women even their common estimate, that the insufficiency of social statics stood in their way, was of little avail. The subject arose at a moment of heartfelt friendship. Comte and Mill were satisfied with the favorable course of their correspondence. Mill was busy composing *A System of Logic* and was eager to receive the last volume of the *Cours*. In October, 1842, when he finally read it, he enthusiastically expressed the great interest it aroused (Letter 19). Mill even liked the **"Personal Preface,"** which, he had feared, might be offensive for being too frank (it was!), but he was pleased to find it written in the same tone as the remainder of the work. In December of the same year, after a second and more attentive reading, Mill was astounded that the positive spirit had been so fully realized (Letter 21). When he learned that Comte was not reappointed as an examiner at the Ecole Polytechnique and that he had lost a good part of his income, Mill offered to use every penny at his disposal to come to his aid (Letter 20 of 15 June 1843).

At this high point of their solidarity, the argument concerning the status of women intervened, for in that same letter Mill emphasized several points of divergence concerning marriage and property. He argued that social evolution would bring appreciable changes. He had raised the problem of divorce once before (Letter 17 of 10 September 1842), saying that he could not understand why one sex should be subordinate to the other. Comte countered that marriage was "indissoluble" and later even added his theory of "eternal widowhood." Mill vigorously rejected them both. Still, they remained optimistic about their relationship. They prized their philosophic "synergy"; expected it to overcome disagreements and eventually to extend to all essential concepts, as it already had on some issues (such as the separation of spiritual power from the temporal). Yet, on the intellectual and social capacities of women they could not agree at all.

Why, then, their debate on social statics? Because it considered not only the structure of society but also the anatomical and physiological make-up of men and women while for Mill, social dynamics suggested that opportunities of education and training could affect women's social position. Though Comte granted the importance of the milieu, he was convinced that women could not transcend their natural limitations, anatomically and physiologically determined. Social dynamics studied changes in history but these, Comte believed, could not greatly affect the "natural" constitution of men and women, each with their own innate capacities; he assumed that historical changes occur only along lines of their given, natural and permanent constitution. The two sides to the debate were clear: Comte believed that women could not acquire capacities equal to those of men, while Mill must be regarded as a leading feminist: to Harriet Taylor's essay, "The Enfranchisement of Women" (1851), Mill added *The Subjection of Women* (1861, 1869) and he campaigned for women's suffrage as a member of Parliament in 1867.

Comte derived his definitions of social statics and dynamics in good part from the zoologist, Blainville, considered to be a worthy successor of Jean-Baptiste Lamarck (1744-1829). Blainville had introduced into biology the concept of a dynamic state—that is the "dynamic" activity of the organism as distinguished from its "static" structure. Comte found a parallel distinction in the work of the mathematician Lagrange (1736-1813), who used "dynamics" to designate motion in mechanics and "statics" for states of equilibrium. Comte admitted that he first considered developing statics without biological implications. He added them later by viewing biology anew through sociology.

The problem was that Comte was defining a constitutional (static) inferiority of women, not subject to education or historical (dynamic) change, quite unaware that he was hurting Mill's deeply held convictions. He simply invoked biological determinants to justify the social subordination of women and expected his younger colleague to recognize his view.

The Debate Concerning Women Intensifies

Mill objected that Comte's principles were insufficiently established to be "positive"; affection between men and women was in no way furthered by a master-slave relationship; true love and reciprocal sympathy could not thrive under inequality! Mill clearly espoused the modern position. He suggested interviews with the women themselves, especially those who were living in a state of open rebellion. Comte replied by referring back to "the natural hierarchy of sexes" (Letter 33). This time, Mill did not answer. Comte had to write a second letter, more than a month after the previous exchange.

Upon receiving this letter, Mill took up the discussion where they had left off, reasoning along lines of common sense and empirical observation: Even suppose, he replied, that women were closer to childhood than were men—how do we know that children are inferior to men solely because their brain is insufficiently developed, and not by their lack of training? For Mill, even if the brain of women were smaller than the brain of men and, therefore, according to certain physiologists, less suited for scientific study, the fact remained that women had never received the proper education to pursue advanced studies. In addition, their household chores neither prepared them for quiet meditation, nor gave them time to meditate. Even men who lacked the necessary education, available only to persons in the upper strata of society, could not make up for what they missed in childhood.

Mill mentioned that women possessed general capacities while men knew only the specialty for which they were being trained. Above all, he questioned that the "affections" were typically feminine and in women replaced what Comte and others called "male intelligence." Mill saw weaknesses in both sexes. Egoism in its pure form, he said, was most common in men.

All the while Mill pleaded a lack of exact knowledge in these matters; his affected tone of humility is the opposite of Comte's determined affirmations. Mill admitted that he was arguing from everyday observation, but pursuing the inductive reasoning he knew well. His strength was a healthy skepticism. He rightly emphasized the neglect of women's education. Above all, he noted that women were human beings and cleverly emphasized the milieu, which Comte otherwise considered so important. In fact, did Comte not speak of the harmony between the organism and the milieu as a *determining aspect* of life? In Comte's thought, the concordance (*l'harmonie*) between milieu and organism found its parallel in the *consensus* of the organs within the organism.

This is why Mill introduced Ethology, "the science of the formation of character," into his *System of Logic.* Ethology was to study the variations in the universal human type, called forth by different living conditions; nationality and femininity were Mill's examples of these variations. Unfortunately, Comte did not recognize that Ethology fitted perfectly into his notion of organism and milieu. They were approaching no consensus.

In his letter of early October, 1843, Comte finally noted "a serious difference of opinion" between them (Letter 36). It was all a matter of biology as much as of sociology. He therefore returned to his comparison between women and children, calling women ill-formed children, and added that his conception of domestic life was "definitive," empirically drawn from an experience of over twenty years. He became blunt, spoke of women's "inborn inferiority," of their being unfit for abstraction and intellectual concentration; he ac-

cused them of being unable to overcome passion, of yielding to feelings. Personal observations, he claimed, had brought him to notice in women "a very insufficient ability to generalize relationships, to make consistent deductions, also to give reason precedence over passion" (Letter 36). This is what we might call the "tacit general theory of anti-feminism of all times."

Comte concluded that education and training cannot alter the basic inferiority of women or lead to a change in their social status and capacities. Comte refused to even discuss the merits or potential of an appropriate education; he also refused to consider the influence of the milieu. This is an astounding stance to take for "the creator of sociology."

For Comte, the primary function of women remained what it had been traditionally: that of motherhood, of bringing up the children in the family. Nevertheless, he assigned them what he considered an important social mission, a role complementary to the masculine in the "domestic order": they are the auxiliaries of the (masculine) spiritual forces and intervene (in male action) as (feminine) forces of moderation. There is a fundamental contradiction in the fact that those who tend to be carried along by passion (women), are to restrain the passion of those (men) who reason better than they! Comte added that the position of women as auxiliaries made them the guardians of universal morality. In judging men and women, he considered social functions, not rights.

Here Comte is in perfect agreement with Aristotle. In *Politics,* men are first in the family and in society, for women are unable to direct and command. Therefore, Comte demanded that they be protected and "nourished." Comte, indeed, supported his wife from whom he had separated for his entire life and even beyond (by his written will)—all this to escape anarchy!

Mill compared the subservience of women to that of the slaves and serfs. He found significant parallels between the subjection of women and the institution of slavery. He even tried to explain why the emancipation of women occurred so long after that of the serfs. Arguing like Aristotle in book I of his *Politics,* Comte simply rejected Mill's comparison between women and slaves.

In his anti-feminism, Comte was not alone: the avowed successors of Aristotle, the medical anthropologists of his day and the physiologists (including Gall) all approved of male dominance, while the zoologists showed that female supremacy among animals was limited to ants and bees. Comte adduced from the superb colors of the male peacock and the subdued grey of the female, that a rigid hierarchy was natural for living beings and that man must rule the family as well as society.

Mill did not concede the argument. He felt that Comte based his points on indeterminate experiences of daily life and on insufficient data, carelessly selected (Letter 40). He accused Comte of affirming with great assurance, conclusions based on data that were far from verified. Further, Mill disliked being treated as one ignorant of animal life and of the physiology of the brain (Letter 83). Did Comte not accept Gall's conclusions, knowing full well that they were most doubtful? How could Gall's localized functions of the brain serve to prove that women were inferior? Mill suggested that women be allowed to follow their vocations and not be subject to a theoretical judgment of their aptitudes (Letter 40): the whole "problem of women," he felt, must be studied anew in all of its complexity.

The correspondence breaks off in 1847. In his *Autobiography* Mill describes how he first slowed the rate of his letters and of how Comte refused to answer his last of May 17, 1847. He did so with good reason, for Mill had sent a sarcastic account of the unemployed in Ireland. He was thinking back to Comte's request for financial support from his wealthy friends, implying that he should have returned to private tutoring, just as the Irish were asking for support when they should be seeking employment. This comparison with recipients of public welfare must have hurt Comte deeply. He was a proud man. Not long before he had told Mill that one must not beg for relief in the face of injustice; one must conquer it! At times Comte spoke as the heir of the French Revolution.

THE CORRESPONDENCE BREAKS OFF; THE CONTROVERSY CONTINUES

In later writings, such as Comte's *Positive Polity* (1851-54) and Mill's *Auguste Comte and Positivism* (1865), also in his posthumous *Autobiography,* we find the sequel of the issues debated in the correspondence. Their arguments center on Comte's theory of the affections, on social statics, especially with respect to the status of women, and on positive religion.

The Affections and Comte's Brain Chart

The essential new element in *Positive Polity* is the theory of the affections, which is to balance the emphasis on scientific thought in the *Cours*. The affections are the philosophical ground of Comte's new Religion of Humanity. We can appreciate their importance in the Brain Chart in volume one.

Comte sketched the psychosociological functions as early as July, 1839, in his "preliminary considerations on social statics," of Lesson 50 of the *Cours*. Sociability is described as the "mortar" of social conditions. Comte's love for Clotilde de Vaux and her premature death on April 5, 1846, confirmed this position. The Brain Chart was conceived in 1847 and further elabo-

rated for *Positive Polity* I (1851). The Brain Chart concerns social statics and the individual but also the collectivity; this is why it implies social dynamics. Human industry reconciles opposing directions and progresses beyond them—beyond military ambition for conquest, characteristic of the theological age, and beyond the defensive military maneuvers of the metaphysical age. The Brain Chart deals with the essence of the particular stages of human development.

A few comments are in order:

> 1. Some of Comte's terms become clear if we compare them with note "O" or XV of Rousseau's *Discourse on the Origin of Inequality:* the instinct for self preservation is like Rousseau's love of self *(amour de soi);* the perfecting instinct and ambition equal Rousseau's self-esteem *(amour-propre);* egoism includes all of these.

> 2. The listings under "altruism" are based on Comte's conviction that egoism is transmuted into altruism by the social instinct.

> 3. The emphasis on the affections reflects Comte's new appreciation of the feminine forces of humankind, but they are in no way restricted to women; this is evident in the listings of "military aspects" or "goodness." The appearance of "motherhood" without reference to "fatherhood" reflects his conception of domestic life which remains essentially unchanged. The distinctions between "veneration" and "attachment" places Comte's love for Clotilde de Vaux in a category by itself, beyond the scope of ordinary love. Clotilde is the patron saint of his Religion of Humanity.

> 4. There is, above all, a balance between intellect and affections, between the male and the female principle.

[See Brain Chart on page 242.]

All along Mill recognizes the originality of Comte in social dynamics; he likes his explanation of the rise of civilization from the theological (fetishism, polytheism, monotheism) to the metaphysical and finally to the modern positive and scientific state, which brings about the era of modern science and industry; but Mill criticizes his social statics. For Comte it is the basis of social order, the element that "harmonizes" the changes in history, the fundamental conditions of life. It reflects human nature, in the face of historical change, for instance, after the military conquests of the theological age give way to the defensive tactics of absolute governments in the metaphysical age, these in turn are forced to yield to the modern industrial age. Comte's illustration stems from Saint-Simon, but he adds important arguments in support.

Brain Chart

HUMANITY: TO LIVE FOR OTHERS

Principles

Ten Affective Forces

Egoism: Seven Personal Affective Functions:
Five functions of interest:

Instinct of self-preservation	(1) The need for nutrition.
	(2) Sexual desire.
	(3) Motherhood.
Perfecting instinct, destructive	(4) Military instinct.
constructive	(5) Industry instinct.

Two functions of ambition:

| Pride | (6) The need to dominate. |
| Vanity | (7) The need for approval. |

Altruism: Three Social Affective Functions:

Individual	(8) Attachment.
	(9) Veneration.
Generalized	(10) Goodness.

Means

Five Intellectual Functions

Conception, passive:	(11) Concrete or synthetic thought.
	(12) Abstract or analytic thought.
Conception, active:	(13) Inductive or generalizing thought.
	(14) Deductive or systematic thought.
Expression:	(15) Mimicry, oral or written: communication.

Results

Three Practical Qualities

Activity:	(16) Courage.
	(17) Prudence.
Determination:	(18) Perseverance.

Social Statics

Mill rejects the idea of a permanent make-up of humankind, the basis of Comte's definition of the limited capacities of women; he finds it unfounded and overly restrictive, even fatalistic. It is characteristic that Comte counters the objections by asking Mill to read *Positive Polity,* where he will develop his system and make it convincingly clear. Developed it was but, as was to be expected, Comte's explanations will not convince Mill; probably Mill did not read *Positive Polity* very carefully. By justifying "the subjection of women" (Mill) within the framework of his systematic philosophy, Comte compounded Mill's objections.

Social statics, the theory of social existence, as described in volume II of *Positive Polity,* includes an essential code of ethics, just as social dynamics, set forth in volume III, includes the laws governing politics. By analogy, ethics and politics serve as cornerstones of Comte's Religion of Humanity. It is important to note that he conceives of women as the guardians of morality (ethics), one more aspect of the fundamental if "auxiliary" role women play in *Positive Polity.*

In volume II . . . , Auguste Comte analyzes the influence of the social milieu, first on the individual, then on the family, finally on society as a whole. It represents a fundamental reorientation, also a reply to Mill's complaint that too little attention was paid to the social milieu and to its influence.

Critics have not always realized that Comte's study of society begins with the individual and self-interest. Like Ferguson, Comte makes the general interest flow from individual interest, just as the social instinct channels individual interests to support altruism. Social concern shapes the attitudes of the individual and guides his intellectual activities. Thus egoism, which is ultimately transformed into altruism, need not be suppressed. The individual will overcome his social insufficiency by aiding others. Love and affection will rule. Comte's optimism flows from an immense faith in social progress.

The Social Status of Women

Auguste Comte assumes that, within this natural framework, men and women take up their separate and distinct social functions. It is true that their efforts are inter-dependent, like all aspects of social statics and dynamics, but they will depend on their biological and psychological constitution, which Comte viewed as a permanent make-up, part of "the order of humanity" which determines what women can and will do, for social statics spills over into social dynamics and historical development. As stated, Comte assumes that human development surmounts breaks and finds a harmony in successive movements and opposing tendencies, a harmony based on the lasting qualities in men and women. The basic "harmony" reconciles order (statics) and progress (dynamics), for Comte history is a continuum, an aspect of the fundamental nature of men and women.

Mill on the other hand resists Comte's universal and natural hierarchy. Comte's "order" seems as objectionable to him as it will appear to the modern reader, who would certainly take contention with the beliefs that women are capable of managing the household only under male supervision or that male dominance rules city and State. Comte believes that the household is a microcosm that foreshadows loftier levels of action and authority. All the essentials of political constitutions are already contained in the constitution of the household. In the positivist polity, women might appear as a kind of proletariat, but Comte makes a clear distinction between women and proletarians.

In terms of the affections, he sees their role as brilliant, for they incarnate love as a social principle. They live for others (*Vivre pour autrui,* 1849) according to Comte's general motto.

Everywhere he assigns them an educational role: in the family, in the State and in the nation. His veneration for Clotilde de Vaux leads Comte to identify the feminine ideal with the affections in social relations. He considers them even more important than reason, that is to say, than male intelligence: the heart must lead the head!

The identification of inborn capacities, biologically determined, in men and in women was a characteristic nineteenth century phenomenon. The problem was that, once such definitions were accepted, the qualities assigned to them were then discovered, in varying proportions, in everyone. Each man and woman had partly male, partly female characteristics and both intellect and affections. Mill, even while arguing sharply against Comte, did not arrive at a clear statement of this fact. He argues that if women stand closer to children than do men, nothing proves that children are less intelligent; they are merely less experienced. Both philosophers compare the capacities of the sexes but vary widely in their conclusions: Mill wants to raise women to a status equal to that of men; Comte, on the contrary, finds that, in the area of the affections, men must ultimately imitate women and develop qualities of heart. As a matter of fact, both philosophers seem to imply that men and women can develop qualities of either gender.

Mill's critique must have prompted Comte to redefine social statics and to study the "milieux subjectifs" as he calls the realms in which we operate, such as religion, property, family and language in domestic, civil and religious society. None of these considerations settled the differences between them, for their arguments were not so much due to varying or insufficient concepts of social statics—though both claimed this—but to basic attitudes that would not yield to evidence.

Comte loved to illustrate problems by diagrams and mottos. Here are his essential formulations concerning men and women, applicable to matters of heart. The *Brain Chart* defines their life with the motto, "*vivre pour autrui*" [to live for others]; a second slogan reads: "To act out of affection and to think in order to act." His "definitive" formulation is the following: "*L'Amour pour principe, et l'Ordre pour base; le Progrès pour but!*" [The principle: love; the base: order; the objective: progress].

Comte's Positive Religion

The institution of a positive religion in no way represents a return to revealed religion, for the Religion of Humanity is "demonstrated." If Comte links it to a higher principle, it is one inherent in the world; it includes all men, dead and living. He will have it supported by a hierarchy of "positivist" priests who counsel the government.

This call for a religious establishment produces the most violent reactions from Mill. In the name of liberty, he protests against this dictatorial enterprise, worthy of Ignatius of Loyola. Like Comte, Mill upholds the ideal of Humanity, but wants no part of Clotilde as a patron saint, adored in positivist chapels.

It is paradoxical to see Comte's religion of love, conceived to compensate for an excessive emphasis on the intellect in his earlier philosophy, become the focus of the most vigorous attacks. Mill abhorred Comte's hierarchy of priests as a threat to liberty and his proposed ritual as a "residue" of Catholicism. Mill's non-sectarian background makes him resist ecclesiastic authority, especially of the Catholic stripe.

Even so, their orientations were surprisingly similar. Comte would have found no quarrel with Mill's opening address (1867) as Rector of the University of Saint-Andrews, a call to the study of the life sciences (including psychology and sociology) in the spirit of Positivism. Mill's utilitarianism is tempered by a "higher" dimension which brings him close to Comte and distinguishes between the *useful* and the *expedient,* one directed toward general happiness, the other aimed at personal gain. He considers virtue and justice to be, not just a way to happiness, but a finality in itself, a way to the truth. Mill is sincere in his devotion to Positivism and community oriented like Comte. Both men envisage a transcendent ideal, but in the case of Comte, it takes the form of a powerful institution, a "demonstrated religion" whose "time had come." This is where Mill withdraws in horror. In *Auguste Comte and Positivism* he uses strong words of condemnation. He prefers the ideal in education, the faith in science and "moral utilitarianism," which we find in his latest work, *Nature, the Utility of Religion, Theism, Being Three Essays on Religion* (1874). Like Comte, Mill underlines the ideal of Humanity, but not as the base of a new religion, an "unacceptable residue of Catholicism." In his *History of English Literature,* Hippolyte Taine, a shrewd observer, writes something which applies to John Stuart Mill: "In England, the religious and the positive spirit live side by side and separately."

Mill considers Comte's positive religion to be "a deviation" from Positivism, while Comte takes Mill to be an incomplete Positivist, who rejects the affective (religious) element. Yet, to the end, Mill recalls (in the

Autobiography) how much he gained from Comte, how avidly he read the ***Cours de philosophie positive,*** how he welcomed Comte's method.

As they drift apart, Mill admits a particular debt for two of Comte's ideas: the separation of the spiritual and temporal powers since the Middle Ages, and his comparative ("inverse deductive") method. He knew how important these factors were in his *Logic* (1843) and how he made use of Comte's historical analysis in the *Principles of Political Economy* (1848), as he compared different coexisting states of society and formulated his theory of production.

THE IMPORTANCE OF THE COMTE-MILL RELATIONSHIP

The letters portray the high point of a sincere friendship of two major philosophers of the nineteenth century. They inform us of significant developments throughout Europe. After the Saint-Simoniens, especially Gustave d'Eichthal, introduced Mill to Positivism and Auguste Comte (around 1828), Mill became an enthusiastic supporter of positive philosophy. It alone, he believed at the time, could renew modern philosophy. Long before he wrote his first letter in 1841, he recognized the originality with which Comte analyzed philosophical problems, his "positive method."

Mill approved of Comte's philosophy of history (or social dynamics); he accepted the law of three ages, the theological, metaphysical and the positive, also Comte's classification of basic sciences. Above all, Mill, recognized that Comte had made a precious inventory of the "methods of investigation," in other words, he had developed what we call an epistemology.

Then differences arose. In 1865, Mill criticized Comte for not having analyzed the methods of verification and established criteria for truth; he regretted that Comte did not include psychology and economics in his list of basic sciences, if they could only be brought to the level of positive sciences.

Mill greatly appreciated the ***Cours de philosophie positive.*** He justly emphasized that, after the masterful *Cours,* Comte's success was greater in England than in France. Alexander Bain (1818-1903), who is frequently mentioned in the correspondence and founded the journal, *Mind* (1876), adhered if not directly to Comte's philosophy, at least to the English positivist school. Like Comte, Bain tied his psychology to the spontaneous action of the brain.

In the ***Cours,*** Comte was the first to define social statics and social dynamics. The distinction was used later by sociologists everywhere and more recently by Lévi-Straus. Herbert Spencer (1820-1903) carried on the discipline of social statics, although he insists that there are vast differences between his own conception and that of Comte. In *Social Statics* (1851) Spencer expresses a pronounced measure of individualism, but he does take up Comte's principal themes, such as social evolution. He rejects his philosophy but does apply positive doctrine. The English Positivist, Frederic Harrison (1832-1923), founder of *The Positive Review* (1893) and the author of another *Social Statics* (1875), embarked on a polemic with Spencer, to force him to admit that he shared many ideas with Comte. Spencer declined; he would only recognize that he owed Comte the notion of social *consensus.*

Mill emphasized the difference between Comte's first and second philosophy: one ending with the publication of the ***Cours,*** the other centered around ***Positive Polity*** and the institution of positive religion. Indeed, the future of Positivism was greatly affected, for it was "positivist intellectuals" like Mill and Littré, who refused to follow Comte to the "applied Positivism" of the later period. They did not adopt its religious, moral and political applications.

One can find a fundamental unity in Comte's thought, as he did himself and also Dr. J. H. Bridges, when he replied to Mill's book, *Auguste Comte and Positivism,* but Comte realized that he had neglected the affections in the ***Cours*** and that the *Système* with its emphasis on positive religion introduced fundamental changes.

The great difference between Comte and Mill lies in the way their philosophy evolves: Mill reformulates his view step by step. This is how the *Autobiography* describes his process of constant review: "I found the fabric of my old and taught opinions giving way in many fresh places, and I never allowed it to fall to pieces, but was constantly occupied in weaving it anew" (*Collected Works* 1:163-64). This method, pictured for 1829, applies throughout. Comte also developed concepts regularly from the beginning, but he experienced an ecstatic love for Clotilde de Vaux. Mill's letters show how foreign this was to him; he refused to publish even one fragment written for her.

Mill turns increasingly to "moral" utilitarianism as he emphasizes first principles, especially liberty and justice. His two essays on Bentham and Coleridge (1838, 1840) initiate this trend. Mill's positions, often at variance and not always pertaining to distinct periods, reveal a radical as well as a liberal Mill, even a more conservative Mill. This is what his letters illustrate so well. His defense of liberty is individualistic; he is anxious to safeguard his independence, in the face of the prior experience, in the face also of his original admiration for Comte and of his early tendency to defer to him. Mill's final "lesson" for Comte: how to handle the Irish unemployed, his ideal of self-reliance is the very opposite of Comte's claim that society owes a debt to men of genius and must support them so they can fulfill their task. Often their arguments run counter to their early agreement that radical changes were needed to justify power and privilege: their conclusions clash. They come to life in the correspondence.

Mill is perfectly aware of what sociology in the Comtian perspective did offer: a link between "universal history" and the philosophical concept of progress, applied to history; social statics, the coexistence of social phenomena, along with social dynamics which observes their succession (*A System of Logic,* VI. 10). Mill expresses in Comtian terms that social statics is the theory of the *consensus* between the different aspects of social organization; he even uses Comte's analogy between the biological organism and society. Mill is assimilating Comte's principles when he defines social unity to mean: (1) recognizing a government, (2) feeling allegiance for it, (3) realizing the inter-dependence of the members of society. By combining the static and dynamic point of view, they acknowledge the interplay of "spontaneous" states of society and their "simultaneous" changes. From this analysis they draw a "scientific" law of history. Among the agents of social progress, they stress the influence of human intelligence on society. They differ in character and temperament, but it is remarkable to what extent the correspondence reveals their similarities: they share the essentials of positivist doctrine and draw on the sciences of social statics and dynamics to elucidate social, political and intellectual progress. The correspondence is live testimony of their speculations, the essential commentary of two important philosophers on their times, a wide-ranging panorama of nineteenth century thought.

FURTHER READING

Criticism

Kent, Christopher A. "Higher Journalism and the Promotion of Comtism." *Victorian Periodicals Review* XXV, No. 2 (Summer 1992): 51-56.

> Claims that "Comte's English disciples became a force largely through the practice of journalism."

Martí, Oscar R. "August Comte and the Positivist Utopia." In *The Utopian Vision: Seven Essays on the Quincentennial of Sir Thomas More,* edited by E. D. S. Sullivan, pp. 93-114. San Diego State University Press, 1983.

> Examines Comte's philosophy as it prescribes a positivist utopia, focusing on its legacy abroad and critiquing its philosophical assumptions.

Pickering, Mary. "New Evidence of the Link Between Comte and German Philosophy." *Journal of the History of Ideas* L, No. 3 (July-Sept. 1989): 443-63.

> Explores the influence of German philosophers, especially Johann Gottfried Herder, on the philosophy of Comte.

Whittaker, Thomas. *Comte and Mill.* New York: Dodge Publishing Company, 1908, 91 p.

> Discusses the ideas of Comte and Mill, and how the two influenced each other throughout their careers.

James Fenimore Cooper

1789-1851

American novelist, essayist, historian, travel writer, and satirist.

For additional information about Cooper's life and career, see *NCLC*, Volume 1; for discussion of Cooper's Leatherstocking novels, see *NCLC*, Volume 27.

INTRODUCTION

Cooper, who created a uniquely American myth of the pioneer with his historical romances, is considered the first major American novelist and is often credited with establishing the United States as a major force in world literature. Most American critics concur with regards to the historical importance of his works, although some scholars still dismiss him as an artist because of his crude style. However, praise from such writers as D. H. Lawrence, combined with a recent increase in Cooper scholarship, has brought his achievements to light as one of the first American novelists to undertake the creation of a distinct national literature, appropriating his country's history as the central theme of his work.

Biographical Information

Born in Burlington, New Jersey, Cooper moved with his family in 1790 to Cooperstown, New York, an upstate town founded and governed by his father and which later served as a model for the frontier communities of Cooper's fiction. Cooper was sent to Yale at age thirteen, though he was eventually expelled for misconduct. In 1805 he entered the Navy, serving for six years and later drawing on his experiences to write such factually accurate sea tales as *The Pilot* (1824) and *The Red Rover* (1828). An inheritance from his father enabled him to leave the Navy in 1811, marry, and lead a leisured existence for about a decade, during which time he fell deeply in debt. In 1826, Cooper left the United States for Europe, where he both defended American democracy and developed sympathy for the aristocratic point of view; he returned to the United States in 1833. By 1850 he had fallen ill, and, returning to Cooperstown, he died the following year, leaving behind a vast and varied body of work.

Major Works

In response to a declaration to his wife that he could write a better novel than the one they were reading, Cooper began his literary career with *Precaution* (1820), a weak imitation of Jane Austen. Although

this novel was largely ignored, his next, *The Spy* (1821), met with astounding success and established Cooper as the most prominent American writer of his time. Two years later he published *The Pioneers* (1823), the first of his "Leatherstocking Tales," a series of five novels that also includes *The Last of the Mohicans* (1826), *The Prairie* (1827), *The Pathfinder* (1840), and *The Deerslayer* (1841). Presenting a fictional rendering of United States history, the Leatherstocking Tales established a number of cultural archetypes, including that of the noble native American as well as the savage and treacherous counterpart of this figure. The Leatherstocking novels also feature Cooper's most enduring character, the backwoodsman Natty Bumppo, who has become a national legend and representation of a fictional paradigm of the American character. For *The Pioneers*, Cooper took as his model the historical romance made popular by Sir Walter Scott, telling a story of the American frontier in a form that had traditionally depended on the cultural background of European history. The uniquely American characters, settings, and themes of *The Pioneers* engaged the nation's nostalgia for an appealing and historically rich period of the recent past, and Cooper developed the frontier romance and the central character of Leatherstocking further in *The Last of the Mohicans* and *The Prairie*. For more than a decade thereafter, Cooper espoused republican social and political convictions in fiction and nonfiction which criticized European forms of government and condemned American reliance on foreign culture. These works were not well received: the readers and critics who extolled Cooper as America's first historical romancer did not accept him in the role of social and political critic. After writing several politically-oriented travel books, Cooper returned to fiction, completing the Leatherstocking Tales with *The Pathfinder* and *The Deerslayer*, often considered his finest works. While there are indications that he had intended to conclude the series with *The Prairie*—which depicts Leatherstocking's death and the retreat of the westward vanguard of settlers—some commentators suggest that he returned to the Leatherstocking saga primarily to recoup the critical and popular regard that had attended the earlier novels in the series. In 1845, Cooper began the "Littlepage Trilogy," a defense of landed aristocracy which sprang from the "Anti-Rent" conflict and pitted the landowners of New York against rebellious squatters. In his last few novels, particularly *The Crater* (1847) and *The Ways of the Hour* (1850), Cooper turned to more religious and aristocratic themes, defending his notion that democracy could survive only if privileges were granted to the gentry.

Critical Reception

Critics have often noted the influence of the wilderness on Cooper throughout his writing career, praising his depictions of the American landscape. However, some scholars have asserted that his detailed natural descriptions overshadow his plots and characters. Throughout the latter part of the nineteenth century and in the first part of the twentieth, literary historians generally acknowledged Cooper as a leading figure in the development of American literary nationalism, but considered his actual achievement of little importance. Beginning in the 1960s, Cooper's works have undergone a revaluation, focusing for the most part on the Leatherstocking novels. Individual studies have examined Cooper's use of historical sources; his treatment of women and native American characters; his facility with landscape description, an aspect of Cooper's literary art that is almost universally commended; and the explication of the hierarchy of class distinctions that is a salient feature of the series. Many commentators have also suggested that Cooper has been undervalued, contending that as America's first popularly successful man of letters, his contribution to the literary and cultural life of his country was considerable. Current study of Cooper has concentrated on his social and political views, noting that the conflict between his democratic and aristocratic sympathies, which he

tried to reconcile in his writing, contributed to the decline of his reputation both at home and abroad.

PRINCIPAL WORKS

Precaution (novel) 1820

The Spy (novel) 1821

*The Pioneers; or, The Sources of the Susquehanna (novel) 1823

The Pilot (novel) 1824

Lionel Lincoln; or, The Leagues of Boston (novel) 1825

The Last of the Mohicans (novel) 1826

The Prairie (novel) 1827

Notions of the Americans (travel essay) 1828

The Red Rover (novel) 1828

The Wept of Wish-ton-Wish (novel) 1829; published in England as *The Borderers; or, The Wept of Wish-ton-Wish*

The Water-Witch; or, The Skimmer of the Seas (novel) 1830

The Bravo (novel) 1831

A Letter to His Countrymen (essay) 1834

The Monikins (satire) 1835

Sketches of Switzerland (travel essays) 1836; published in England as *Excursions in Switzerland*

Sketches of Switzerland: Part Second (travel essays) 1836; published in England as *A Residence in France: With an Excursion up the Rhine, and a Second Visit to Switzerland*

Gleanings in Europe (travel essays) 1837; published in England as *Recollections of Europe*

Gleanings in Europe: England (travel essays) 1837; published in England as *England: With Sketches of Society in the Metropolis*

The American Democrat; or, Hints on the Social and Civic Relations of the United States of America (essay) 1838

Gleanings in Europe: Italy (travel essays) 1838; published in England as *Excursions in Italy*

Home as Found (novel) 1838

Homeward Bound; or, The Chase (novel) 1838

History of the Navy of the United States of America (history) 1839

Mercedes of Castile; or, The Voyage to Cathay (novel) 1840

The Pathfinder; or, The Inland Sea (novel) 1840; published in England as *Lake Ontario*

The Deerslayer; or, The First War Path (novel) 1841

The Two Admirals (novel) 1842

The Wing-and-Wing; or, Le Feu-Follet (novel) 1842

Wyandotté: or, The Hutted Knoll (novel) 1843

Afloat and Ashore; or, The Adventures of Miles Wallingford (novel) 1844; published in England as *Lucy Harding*; also published as *Miles Wallingford*

The Chainbearer; or, The Littlepage Manuscripts (novel) 1845

Satanstoe; or, The Littlepage Manuscripts (novel) 1845

The Redskins; or, Indian and Injin: Being the Conclusion of the Littlepage Manuscripts (novel) 1846

The Crater; or, Vulcan's Peak (novel) 1847; published in England as *Mark's Peak; or, The Crater*

Jack Tier; or, The Florida Reefs (novel) 1848; published in England as *Captain Spike; or, The Islets of the Gulf*

The Oak Openings; or, The Bee Hunter (novel) 1848; published in England as *The Bee Hunter; or, The Oak Openings*

The Sea Lions; or, The Lost Sealers (novel) 1849

The Ways of the Hour (novel) 1850

---

*Although Cooper claims that this novel was published in 1822, all bibliographic sources consulted give 1823 as the date of publication.

CRITICISM

James Fenimore Cooper (essay date 1849)

SOURCE: An introduction to *The Spy*, Grosset & Dunlap Publishers, 1849, pp. iii-vii.

[*In the following introduction to* The Spy, *Cooper discusses the basis of the novel and the state of the union since the Revolutionary War.*]

The author has often been asked if there were any foundation in real life for the delineation of the principal character in this book. He can give no clearer answer to the question than by laying before his readers a simple statement of the facts connected with its original publication.

Many years since, the writer of this volume was at the residence of an illustrious man, who had been employed in various situations of high trust during the darkest days of the American Revolution. The discourse turned upon the effects which great political excitement produces on character, and the purifying consequences of a love of country, when that sentiment is powerfully and generally awakened in a people. He who, from his years, his services, and his knowledge of men, was best qualified to take the lead in such a conversation, was the principal speaker. After dwelling on the marked manner in which the great struggle of the nation, during the war of 1775, had given a new and honorable direction to the thoughts and practices of multitudes whose time had formerly been engrossed by the most vulgar concerns of life, he illustrated his opinions by relating an anecdote, the truth of which he could attest as a personal witness.

The dispute between England and the United States of America, though not strictly a family quarrel, had many of the features of a civil war. The people of the latter were never properly and constitutionally subject to the people of the former, but the inhabitants of both countries owed allegiance to a common king. The Americans as a nation, disavowed this allegiance, and the English choosing to support their sovereign in the attempt to regain his power, most of the feelings of an internal struggle were involved in the conflict. A large proportion of the emigrants from Europe, then established in the colonies, took part with the crown; and there were many districts in which their influence, united to that of the Americans who refused to lay aside their allegiance, gave a decided preponderance to the royal cause. America was then too young, and too much in need of every heart and hand, to regard these partial divisions, small as they were in actual amount, with indifference. The evil was greatly increased by the activity of the English in profiting by these internal dissensions; and it became doubly serious when it was found that attempts were made to raise various corps of provincial troops, who were to be banded with those from Europe, to reduce the young republic to subjection. Congress named an especial and a secret committee, therefore, for the express purpose of defeating this object. Of this committee Mr. —, the narrator of the anecdote, was chairman.

In the discharge of the novel duties which now devolved on him, Mr. — had occasion to employ an agent whose services differed but little from those of a common spy. This man, as will easily be understood, belonged to a condition in life which rendered him the least reluctant to appear in so equivocal a character. He was poor, ignorant, so far as the usual instruction was concerned; but cool, shrewd, and fearless by nature. It was his office to learn in what part of the country the agents of the crown were making their efforts to embody men, to repair to the place, enlist, appear zealous in the cause he affected to serve, and otherwise to get possession of as many of the secrets of the enemy as possible. The last he of course communicated to his employers, who took all the means in their power to counteract the plans of the English, and frequently with success.

It will readily be conceived that a service like this was attended with great personal hazard. In addition to the danger of discovery, there was the daily risk of falling into the hands of the Americans themselves, who invariably visited sins of this nature more severely on the natives of the country than on the Europeans who fell into their hands. In fact, the agent of Mr. — was several times arrested by the local authorities; and, in one instance, he was actually condemned by his exasperated countrymen to the gallows. Speedy and private orders to the jailer alone saved him from an ignominious death. He was permitted to escape; and this seeming and indeed actual peril was of great aid in supporting his assumed character among the English. By the Americans, in his little sphere, he was denounced as a bold and inveterate Tory. In this manner he continued to serve his country in secret during the early years of the struggle, hourly environed by danger, and the constant subject of unmerited opprobrium.

In the year —, Mr. — was named to a high and honorable employment at a European court. Before vacating his seat in Congress, he reported to that body an outline of the circumstances related, necessarily suppressing the name of his agent, and demanding an appropriation in behalf of a man who had been of so much use, at so great risk. A suitable sum was voted; and its delivery was confided to the chairman of the secret committee.

Mr. — took the necessary means to summon his agent to a personal interview. They met in a wood at midnight. Here Mr. — complimented his companion on his fidelity and adroitness; explained the necessity of their communications being closed; and finally tendered the money. The other drew back, and declined receiving it. "The country had need of all its means," he said; "as for myself, I can work, or gain a livelihood in various ways." Persuasion was useless, for patriotism was uppermost in the heart of this remarkable individual; and Mr. — departed, bearing with him the gold he had brought, and a deep respect for the man who had so long hazarded his life, unrequited, for the cause they served in common.

The writer is under an impression that, at a later day, the agent of Mr. — consented to receive a remuneration for what he had done; but it was not until his country was entirely in a condition to bestow it.

It is scarcely necessary to add, that an anecdote like this, simply but forcibly told by one of its principal actors, made a deep impression on all who heard it. Many years later, circumstances, which it is unnecessary to relate, and of an entirely adventitious nature, induced the writer to publish a novel, which proved to be, what he little foresaw at the time, the first of a tolerably long series. The same adventitious causes which gave birth to the book determined its scene and its general character. The former was laid in a foreign country; and the latter embraced a crude effort to describe foreign manners. When this tale was published, it became matter of reproach among the author's friends, that he, an American in heart as in birth, should give to the world a work which aided perhaps, in some slight degree, to feed the imaginations of the young and unpracticed among his own countrymen, by pictures drawn from a state of society so different from that to which he belonged. The writer, while he knew how much of what he had done was purely accidental, felt the reproach to be one that, in a measure, was just.

As the only atonement in his power, he determined to inflict a second book, whose subject should admit of no cavil, not only on the world, but on himself. He chose patriotism for his theme; and to those who read this introduction and the book itself, it is scarcely necessary to add, that he took the hero of the anecdote just related as the best illustration of his subject.

Since the original publication of *The Spy,* there have appeared several accounts of different persons who are supposed to have been in the author's mind while writing the book. As Mr. — did not mention the name of his agent, the writer never knew any more of his identity with this or that individual, than has been here explained. Both Washington and Sir Henry Clinton had an unusual number of secret emissaries; in a war that partook so much of a domestic character, and in which the contending parties were people of the same blood and language, it could scarcely be otherwise.

The style of the book has been revised by the author in this edition. In this respect, he has endeavored to make it more worthy of the favor with which it has been received; though he is compelled to admit there are faults so interwoven with the structure of the tale that, as in the case of a decayed edifice, it would cost perhaps less to reconstruct than to repair. Five-and-twenty years have been as ages with most things connected with America. Among other advantages, that of her literature has not been the least. So little was expected from the publication of an original work of this description, at the time it was written, that the first volume of *The Spy* was actually printed several months, before the author felt a sufficient inducement to write a line of the second. The efforts expended on a hopeless task are rarely worthy of him who makes them, however low it may be necessary to rate the standard of his general merit.

One other anecdote connected with the history of this book may give the reader some idea of the hopes of an American author, in the first quarter of the present century. As the second volume was slowly printing, from manuscript that was barely dry when it went into the compositor's hands, the publisher intimated that the work might grow to a length that would consume the profits. To set his mind at rest, the last chapter was actually written, printed, and paged, several weeks before the chapters which precede it were even thought of. This circumstance, while it cannot excuse, may serve to explain the manner in which the actors are hurried off the scene.

A great change has come over the country since this book was originally written. The nation is passing from the gristle into the bone, and the common mind is beginning to keep even pace with the growth of the body politic. The march from Vera Cruz to Mexico was made under the orders of that gallant soldier who, a quarter of a century before, was mentioned with honor, in the last chapter of this very book. Glorious as was that march, and brilliant as were its results in a military point of view, a stride was then made by the nation, in a moral sense, that has hastened it by an age, in its progress toward real independence and high political influence. The guns that filled the valley of the Aztecs with their thunder, have been heard in echoes on the other side of the Atlantic, producing equally hope or apprehension.

There is now no enemy to fear, but the one that resides within. By accustoming ourselves to regard even the people as erring beings, and by using the restraints that wisdom had adduced from experience, there is much reason to hope that the same Providence which has so well aided us in our infancy, may continue to smile on our manhood.

William Cullen Bryant (lecture date 1852)

SOURCE: "Discourse on the Life, Genius, and Writings of J. Fenimore Cooper," in *Precaution: A Novel* by J. Fenimore Cooper, D. Appleton and Company, 1881, pp. v-xli.

[*In the excerpt below, from the text of a lecture delivered in 1852 at a Public Memorial Meeting in honor of Cooper, Bryant surveys Cooper's career and assesses its significance.*]

It is now somewhat more than a year since the friends of JAMES FENIMORE COOPER, in this city, were planning to give a public dinner in his honor. It was intended as an expression both of the regard they bore him personally, and of the pride they took in the glory his writings had reflected on the American name. We thought of what we should say in his hearing; in what terms, worthy of him and of us, we should speak of the esteem in which we held him, and of the interest we felt in a fame which had already penetrated to the remotest nook of the earth inhabited by civilized man.

To-day we assemble for a sadder purpose: to pay to the dead some part of the honors then intended for the living. We bring our offering, but he is not here who should receive it; in his stead are vacancy and silence; there is no eye to brighten at our words, and no voice to answer. "It is an empty office that we perform," said Virgil, in his melodious verses, when commemorating the virtues of the young Marcellus, and bidding flowers be strewn, with full hands, over his early grave. We might apply the expression to the present occasion, but it would be true in part only. We can no longer do any thing for him who is departed, but we may do what will not be without fruit to those who remain. It is good to occupy our thoughts with the example of great talents in conjunction with great virtues. His genius has passed away with him; but we

may learn, from the history of his life, to employ the faculties we possess with useful activity and noble aims; we may copy his magnanimous frankness, his disdain of everything that wears the faintest semblance of deceit, his refusal to comply with current abuses, and the courage with which, on all occasions, he asserted what he deemed truth, and combated what he thought error.

The circumstances of Cooper's early life were remarkably suited to confirm the natural hardihood and manliness of his character, and to call forth and exercise that extraordinary power of observation, which accumulated the materials afterward wielded and shaped by his genius. His father, while an inhabitant of Burlington, in New Jersey, on the pleasant banks of the Delaware, was the owner of large possessions on the borders of the Otsego Lake, in our own State, and here, in the newly cleared fields, he built in 1786, the first house in Cooperstown. To this home, Cooper, who was born in Burlington, in the year 1789, was conveyed in his infancy; and here, as he informs us in his preface to the **Pioneers,** his first impressions of the external world were obtained. Here he passed his childhood, with the vast forest around him, stretching up the mountains that overlook the lake, and far beyond, in a region where the Indian yet roamed, and the white hunter, half Indian in his dress and mode of life, sought his game,—a region in which the bear and the wolf were yet hunted, and the panther, more formidable than either, lurked in the thickets, and tales of wanderings in the wilderness, and encounters with these fierce animals, beguiled the length of the winter nights. Of this place, Cooper, although early removed from it to pursue his studies, was an occasional resident throughout his life, and here his last years were wholly passed.

At the age of thirteen he was sent to Yale College, where, notwithstanding his extreme youth—for, with the exception of the poet, Hillhouse, he was the youngest of his class, and Hillhouse was afterward withdrawn—his progress in his studies is said to have been honorable to his talents. He left the college, after a residence of three years, and became a midshipman in the United States navy. Six years he followed the sea, and there yet wanders, among those who are fond of literary anecdote, a story of the young sailor who, in the streets of one of the English ports, attracted the curiosity of the crowd, by explaining to his companions a Latin motto in some public place. That during this period he made himself master of the knowledge and the imagery which he afterward employed to so much advantage in his romances of the sea, the finest ever written, is a common and obvious remark; but it has not been, so far as I know, observed that from the discipline of a seaman's life he may have derived much of his readiness and fertility of invention, much of his skill in surrounding the personages of his novels with imaginary perils, and rescuing them by probable expedients. Of all pursuits, the life of a sailor is that which familiarizes men to danger in its most fearful shapes, most cultivates presence of mind, and most effectually calls forth the resources of prompt and fearless dexterity by which imminent evil is avoided.

In 1811, Cooper, having resigned his post as midshipman, began the year by marrying Miss Delancey, sister of the present bishop of the diocese of Western New York, and entered upon a domestic life happily passed to its close. He went to live at Scarsdale, in the county of Westchester, where he occupied himself with the improvement of a farm, and occasionally with landscape gardening, then an art little practiced in this country, and while here he wrote and published the first of his novels, entitled **Precaution**. Concerning the occasion of writing this work, it is related, that once, as he was reading an English novel to Mrs. Cooper, who has within a short time past been laid in the grave beside her illustrious husband, and of whom we may now say, that her goodness was no less eminent than his genius, he suddenly laid down the book, and said, "I believe I could write a better myself." Almost immediately he composed a chapter of a projected work of fiction, and read it to the same friendly judge, who encouraged him to finish it, and when it was completed, suggested its publication. Of this he had at the time no intention, but he was at length induced to submit the manuscript to the examination of the late Charles Wilkes, of this city, in whose literary opinions he had great confidence. Mr. Wilkes advised that it should be published, and to these circumstances we owe it that Cooper became an author.

I confess I have merely dipped into this work. The experiment was made with the first edition, deformed by a strange punctuation—a profusion of commas, and other pauses, which puzzled and repelled me. Its author, many years afterward, revised and republished it, correcting this fault, and some faults of style also, so that to a casual inspection it appeared almost another work. It was a professed delineation of English manners, though the author had then seen nothing of English society. It had, however, the honor of being adopted by the country whose manners it described, and being early republished in Great Britain passed from the first for an English novel. I am not unwilling to believe what is said of it, that it contained a promise of the powers which its author afterward put forth.

Thirty years ago, in the year 1821, and in the thirty-second of his life, Cooper published the first of the works by which he will be known to posterity, the **Spy**. It took the reading world by a kind of surprise; its merit was acknowledged by a rapid sale; the public read with eagerness and the critics wondered. Many withheld their commendations on account of defects in the plot or blemishes in the composition, arising from want of practice, and some waited till they could hear

the judgement of European readers. Yet there were not wanting critics in this country, of whose good opinion any author in any part of the world might be proud, who spoke of it in the terms it deserved. "Are you not delighted," wrote a literary friend to me, who has since risen to high distinction as a writer, both in verse and in prose, "are you not delighted with the **Spy**, as a work of infinite spirit and genius?" In that word genius lay the explanation of the hold which the work had taken on the minds of men. What it had of excellence was peculiar and unborrowed; its pictures of life, whether in repose or activity, were drawn with broad lights and shadows, immediately from living originals in nature or in his own imagination. To him, whatever he described was true; it was made a reality to him by the strength with which he conceived it. His power in the delineation of character was shown in the principal personage of his story, Harvey Birch, on whom, though he has chosen to employ him in the ignoble office of a spy, and endowed him with the qualities necessary to his profession,—extreme circumspection, fertility in stratagem, and the art of concealing his real character,—qualities which, in conjunction with selfishness and greediness, make the scoundrel, he has bestowed the virtues of generosity, magnanimity, an intense love of country, a fidelity not to be corrupted, and a disinterestedness beyond temptation. Out of this combination of qualities he has wrought a character which is a favorite in all nations and with all classes of mankind. The introduction of General Washington as one of the personages of the story, was a blemish in the work which Cooper, in later years, regretted to such a degree that he spoke of writing the **Spy** over again.

It is said that if you cast a pebble into the ocean, at the mouth of our harbor, the vibration made in the water passes gradually on till it strikes the icy barriers of the deep at the south pole. The spread of Cooper's reputation is not confined within narrower limits. The **Spy** is read in all the written dialects of Europe, and in some of those of Asia. The French, immediately after its first appearance, gave it to the multitudes who read their far-diffused language, and placed it among the first works of its class. It was rendered into Castilian, and passed into the hands of those who dwell under the beams of the Southern Cross. At length it crossed the eastern frontier of Europe, and the latest record I have seen of its progress toward absolute universality, is contained in a statement of the *International Magazine*, derived, I presume from its author, that in 1847 it was published in a Persian translation at Ispahan. Before this time, I doubt not, they are reading it in some of the languages of Hindostan, and, if the Chinese ever translated any thing, it would be in the hands of the many millions who inhabit the far Cathay.

I have spoken of the hesitation which American critics felt in admitting the merits of the **Spy**, on account of crudities in the plot or the composition, some of which no doubt really existed. An exception must be made in favor of the *Port Folio*, which, in a notice written by Mrs. Sarah Hall, mother of the editor of that periodical, and author of *Conversations on the Bible*, gave the work a cordial welcome; and Cooper, as I am informed, never forgot this act of timely and ready kindness.

It was perhaps favorable to the immediate success of the *Spy*, that Cooper had few American authors to divide with him the public attention. That crowd of clever men and women who now write for the magazines, who send out volumes of essays, sketches, and poems, and who supply the press with novels, biographies, and historical works, were then, for the most part, either stammering their lessons in the schools, or yet unborn. Yet it is worthy of note, that just about the time that the *Spy* made its appearance, the dawn of what we now call our literature was just breaking. The concluding number of Dana's *Idle Man*, a work neglected at first, but now numbered among the best things of the kind of our language, was issued in the same month. The *Sketch Book* was then just completed; the world was admiring it, and its author was meditating *Bracebridge Hall*. Miss Sedgwick, about the same time, made her first essay in that charming series of novels of domestic life in New England, which have gained her so high a reputation. Percival, now unhappily silent, had just put to press a volume of poems. I have a copy of an edition of Halleck's *Fanny*, published in the same year; the poem of *Yamoyden*, by Eastburn and Sands, appeared almost simultaneously with it. Livingston was putting the finishing hand to his *Report on the Penal Code of Louisiana*, a work written with such grave, persuasive eloquence, that it belongs as much to our literature as to our jurisprudence. Other contemporaneous American works there were, now less read. Paul Allen's poem of *Noah* was just laid on the counters of the booksellers. Arden published at the same time, in this city, a translation of Ovid's *Tristia*, in heroic verse, in which the complaints of the effeminate Roman poet were rendered with great fidelity to the original, and sometimes not without beauty. If I may speak of myself, it was in that year that I timidly entrusted to the winds and waves of public opinion a small cargo of my own—a poem entitled *The Ages*, and half a dozen shorter ones, in a thin duodecimo volume, printed at Cambridge.

We had, at the same time, works of elegant literature, fresh from the press of Great Britain, which are still read and admired. Barry Cornwall, then a young suitor for fame, published in the same year his *Marcia Colonna*; Byron, in the full strength and fertility of his genius, gave the readers of English his tragedy of *Marino Faliero*, and was in the midst of his spirited controversy with Bowles concerning the poetry of Pope. The *Spy* had to sustain a comparison with Scott's *Antiquary*, published simultaneously with it, and with Lockhart's *Valerius*, which seems to me one of the most remarkable works of fiction ever composed.

In 1823, and in his thirty-fourth year, Cooper brought out his novel of the *Pioneers*, the scene of which was laid on the borders of his own beautiful lake. In a recent survey of Mr. Cooper's works, by one of his admirers, it is intimated that the reputation of this work may have been in some degree factitious. I cannot think so; I cannot see how such a work could fail of becoming, sooner or later, a favorite. It was several years after its first appearance that I read the *Pioneers*, and I read it with a delighted astonishment. Here, said I to myself, is the poet of rural life in this country—our Hesiod, our Theocritus, except that he writes without the restraint of numbers, and is a greater poet than they. In the *Pioneers*, as in a moving picture, are made to pass before us the hardy occupations and spirited amusements of a prosperous settlement, in a fertile region, encompassed for leagues around with the primeval wilderness of woods. The seasons in their different aspects, bringing with them their different employments; forests falling before the axe; the cheerful population, with the first mild day of spring, engaged in the sugar-orchards; the chase of the deer through the deep woods, and into the lake; turkey-shootings, during the Christmas holidays, in which the Indian marksman vied for the prize of skill with the white man; swift sleigh-rides under the bright winter sun, and perilous encounters with wild animals in the forests; these, and other scenes of rural life, drawn, as Cooper knew how to draw them, in the bright and healthful coloring of which he was master, are interwoven with a regular narrative of human fortunes, not unskillfully constructed; and how could such a work be otherwise than popular?

In the *Pioneers*, Leatherstocking is first introduced—a philosopher of the woods, ignorant of books, but instructed in all that nature, without the aid of science, could reveal to the man of quick senses and inquiring intellect, whose life has been passed under the open sky, and in companionship with a race whose animal perceptions are the acutest and most cultivated of which there is any example. But Leatherstocking has higher qualities; in him there is a genial blending of the gentlest virtues of the civilized man with the better nature of the aboriginal tribes; all that in them is noble, generous, and ideal, is adopted into his own kindly character, and all that is evil is rejected. But why should I attempt to analyze a character so familiar? Leatherstocking is acknowledged, on all hands, to be one of the noblest, as well as most striking and original creations of fiction. In some of his subsequent novels, Cooper—for he had not yet attained to the full maturity of his powers—heightened and ennobled his first conception of the character, but in the *Pioneers* it dazzled the world with the splendor of novelty.

His next work was the *Pilot*, in which he showed how, from the vicissitudes of a life at sea, its perils and escapes, from the beauty and terrors of the great deep,

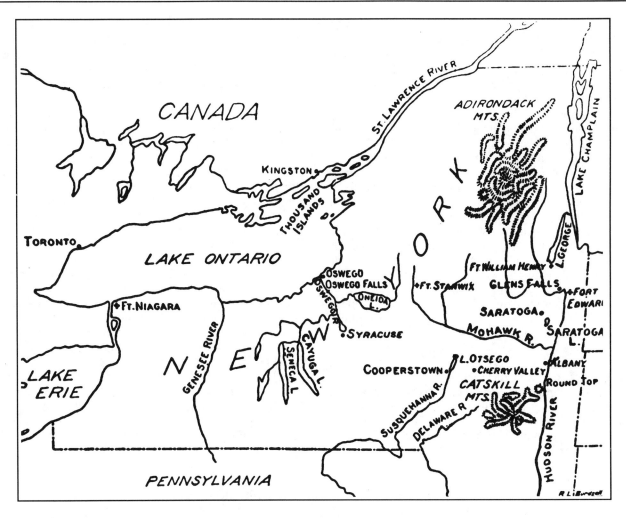

A map showing the scenes of the Leatherstocking Tales.

from the working of a vessel on a long voyage, and from the frank, brave, and generous, but peculiar character of the seaman, may be drawn materials of romance by which the minds of men may be as deeply moved as by any thing in the power of romance to present. In this walk, Cooper has had many disciples, but no rival. All who have since written romances of the sea have been but travellers in a country of which he was the great discoverer, and none of them all seemed to have loved a ship as Cooper loved it, nor have been able so strongly to interest all classes of readers in its fortunes. Among other personages drawn with great strength in the *Pilot*, is the general favorite, Tom Coffin, the thorough seaman, with all the virtues, and one or two of the infirmities of his profession, superstitious, as seamen are apt to be, yet whose superstitions strike us as but an irregular growth of his devout recognition of the Power who holds the ocean in the hollow of his hand; true-hearted, gentle, full of resources, collected in danger, and at last calmly perishing at the post of duty, with the vessel he has long guided, by what I may call a great and magnanimous

death. His rougher and coarser companion, Boltrope, is drawn with scarcely less skill, and with a no less vigorous hand.

The *Pioneers* is not Cooper's best tale of the American forest, nor the *Pilot*, perhaps, in all respects, his best tale of the sea; yet, if he had ceased to write here, the measure of his fame would, possibly, have been scarcely less ample than it now is. Neither of them is far below the best of his productions, and in them appear the two most remarkable creations of his imagination—two of the most remarkable characters in all fiction.

It was about this time that my acquaintance with Cooper began, an acquaintance of more than a quarter of a century, in which his deportment toward me was that of unvaried kindness. He then resided a considerable part of the year in this city, and here he had founded a weekly club, to which many of the most distinguished men of the place belonged. Of the members who have since passed away, were Chancellor

Kent, the jurist; Wiley, the intelligent and liberal book-seller; Henry D. Sedgwick, always active in schemes of benevolence; Jarvis, the painter, a man of infinite humor, whose jests awoke inextinguishable laughter; De Kay, the naturalist; Sands, the poet; Jacob Harvey, whose genial memory is cherished by many friends. Of those who are yet living was Morse, the inventor of the electric telegraph; Durand, then one of the first of engravers, and now no less illustrious as a painter; Henry James Anderson, whose acquirements might awaken the envy of the ripest scholars of the old world; Halleck, the poet and wit; Verplanck, who has given the world the best edition of Shakespeare for general readers; Dr. King, now at the head of Columbia College, and his two immediate predecessors in that office. I might enlarge the list with many other names of no less distinction. The army and navy contributed their proportion of members, whose names are on record in our national history. Cooper when in town was always present, and I remember being struck with the inexhaustible vivacity of his conversation and the minuteness of his knowledge in every thing which depended upon acuteness of observation and exactness of recollection. I remember, too, being somewhat startled, coming as I did from the seclusion of a country life, with a certain emphatic frankness in his manner, which, however, I came at last to like and to admire. The club met in the hotel called Washington Hall, the site of which is now occupied by part of the circuit of Stewart's marble building.

Lionel Lincoln, which cannot be ranked among the successful productions of Cooper, was published in 1825; and in the year following appeared the *Last of the Mohicans*, which more than recovered the ground lost by its predecessor. In this work the construction of the narrative has signal defects, but it is one of the triumphs of the author's genius that he makes us unconscious of them while we read. It is only when we have had time to awake from the intense interest in which he has held us by the vivid reality of his narrative, and have begun to search for faults in cold blood, that we are able to find them. In the *Last of the Mohicans* we have a bolder portraiture of Leatherstocking than in the *Pioneers*.

This work was published in 1826, and in the same year Cooper sailed with his family for Europe. He left New York as one of the vessels of war, described in his romances of the sea, goes out of port amid the thunder of a parting salute from the big guns on the batteries. A dinner was given him just before his departure, attended by most of the distinguished men of the city, at which Peter A. Jay presided, and Dr. King addressed him in terms which some then thought too glowing, but which would now seem sufficiently temperate, expressing the good wishes of his friends, and dwelling on the satisfaction they promised themselves in possessing so illustrious a representative of American

literature in the old world. Cooper was scarcely in France when he remembered his friends of the weekly club, and sent frequent missives to be read at its meetings; but the club missed its founder, went into a decline, and not long afterward quietly expired.

The first of Cooper's novels published after leaving America was the *Prairie*, which appeared early in 1827, a work with the admirers of which I wholly agree. I read it with a certain awe, an undefined sense of sublimity, such as one experiences on entering for the first time upon these immense grassy deserts from which the work takes its name. The squatter and his family—that brawny old man and his large-limbed sons, living in a sort of primitive and patriarchal barbarism, sluggish on ordinary occasions but terrible when roused, like the hurricane that sweeps the grand but monotonous wilderness in which they dwell—seem a natural growth of those ancient fields of the West. Leatherstocking, a hunter in the *Pioneers*, a warrior in the *Last of the Mohicans*, and now, in his extreme old age, a trapper on the prairie, declined in strength but undecayed in intellect, and looking to the near close of his life and a grave under the long grass as calmly as the laborer at sunset looks to his evening slumber, is no less in harmony with the silent desert in which he wanders. Equally so are the Indians, still his companions, copies of the American savage somewhat idealized, but not the less a part of the wild nature in which they have their haunts.

Before the year closed Cooper had given the world another nautical tale, the *Red Rover*, which with many is a greater favorite then the *Pilot*, and with reason, perhaps, if we consider principally the incidents, which are conducted and described with a greater mastery over the springs of pity and terror.

It happened to Cooper while he was abroad, as it not unfrequently happens to our countrymen, to hear the United States disadvantageously compared with Europe. He had himself been a close observer of things, both here and in the old world, and was conscious of being able to refute the detractors of his country in regard to many points. He published in 1828, after he had been two years in Europe, a series of letters, entitled *Notions of the Americans, by a Travelling Bachelor*, in which he gave a favorable account of the working of our institutions, and vindicated his country from various flippant and ill-natured misrepresentations of foreigners. It is rather too measured in style, but is written from a mind full of the subject, and from a memory wonderfully stored with particulars. Although twenty-four years have elapsed since its publication, but little of the vindication has become obsolete.

Cooper loved his country and was proud of her history and her institutions, but it puzzles many that he should have appeared, at different times, as her eulogist and her censor. My friends, she is worthy both of praise and of blame, and Cooper was not the man to shrink from bestowing either, at what seemed to him the proper time. He defended her from detractors abroad; he sought to save her from flatterers at home. I will not say that he was in as good humor with his country when he wrote **Home as Found**, as when he wrote his **Notions of the Americans**, but this I will say, that whether he commended or censured, he did it in the sincerity of his heart as a true American, and in the belief that it would do good. His **Notions of the Americans** were more likely to lessen than to increase his popularity in Europe, inasmuch as they were put forth without the slightest regard to European prejudices.

In 1829 he brought out the novel entitled the **Wept of Wish-ton-Wish**, one of the few of his works which we now rarely hear mentioned. He was engaged in the composition of a third nautical tale, which he afterward published under the name of the **Water-Witch**, when the memorable revolution of the Three Days of July broke out. He saw a government ruling by fear and in defiance of public opinion, overthrown in a few hours with little bloodshed; he saw the French nation, far from being intoxicated with their new liberty, peacefully addressing themselves to the discussion of the institutions under which they were to live. A work which Cooper afterward published, his **Residence in Europe**, gives the outline of a plan of government for France, furnished by him at that time to La Fayette, with whom he was then on habits of close and daily intimacy. It was his idea to give permanence to the new order of things by associating two strong parties in its support, the friends of legitimacy and the republicans. He suggested that Henry V. should be called to the hereditary throne of France, a youth yet to be educated as the head of a free people, that the peerage should be abolished, and a legislature of two chambers established, with a constituency of at least a million and a half of electors; the senate to be chosen by the general vote as the representatives of the entire nation, and the members of the other house to be chosen by districts as the representatives of the local interests. To the middle ground of politics so ostentatiously occupied by Louis Philippe at the beginning of his reign, he predicted a brief duration, believing that it would speedily be merged in despotism or supplanted by the popular rule. His prophecy has been fulfilled more amply than he could have imagined—fulfilled in both its alternatives.

In one of the controversies of that time Cooper bore a distinguished part. The *Révue Britannique*, a periodical published in Paris, boldly affirmed the government of the United States to be one of the most expensive in the world, and its people among the most heavily taxed of mankind. This assertion was supported with a certain show of proof, and the writer affected to have established the conclusion that a republic must necessarily be more expensive than a monarchy. The partisans of the court were delighted with the reasoning of the article, and claimed a triumph over our ancient friend La Fayette, who, during forty years, had not ceased to hold up the government of the United States as the cheapest in the world. At the suggestion of La Fayette Cooper replied to this attack upon his country, in a letter which was translated into French, and together with another from General Bertrand, for many years a resident in America, was laid before the people of France.

These two letters provoked a shower of rejoinders, in which, according to Cooper, misstatements were mingled with scurrility. He began a series of letters on the question in dispute, which were published in the *National,* a daily sheet, and gave the first evidence of that extraordinary acuteness of controversy, which was no less characteristic of his mind than the vigor of his imagination. The enemies of La Fayette pressed into their service Mr. Leavitt Harris, of New Jersey, afterward our *chargé d'affaires* at the court of France, but Cooper replied to Mr. Harris in the *National* of May 2d, 1832, closing a discussion in which he had effectually silenced those who objected to our institutions on the score of economy. Of these letters, which would form an important chapter in political science, no entire copy, I have been told, is to be found in this country.

One of the consequences of earnest controversy is almost invariably personal ill-will. Cooper was told by one who held an official station under the French government, that the part he had taken in this dispute concerning taxation, would neither be forgotten nor forgiven. The dislike he had incurred in that quarter was strengthened by his novel of the **Bravo**, published in the year 1831, while he was in the midst of his quarrel with the aristocratic party. In that work, of which he has himself justly said, that it was thoroughly American in all that belonged to it, his object was to show how institutions professedly created to prevent violence and wrong become, when perverted from their original design, the instruments of injustice, and how, in every system which makes power the exclusive property of the strong, the weak are sure to be oppressed. The work is written with all the vigor and spirit of his best novels: the magnificent city of Venice, in which the scene of the story is laid, stands continually before the imagination, and from time to time the gorgeous ceremonies of the Venetian republic pass under our eyes, such as the marriage of the Doge with the Adriatic, and the contest of the gondolas for the prize of speed. The Bravo himself and several of the other characters are strongly conceived and distinguished, but the most remarkable of them all is the spirited and generous-hearted daughter of the jailer.

It has been said by some critics, who judge of Cooper by his failures, that he had no skill in drawing female characters. By the same process it might, I suppose, be shown that Raphael was but an ordinary painter. It must be admitted that when Cooper drew a lady of high breeding, he was apt to pay too much attention to the formal part of her character, and to make her a mere bundle of cold proprieties. But when he places his heroines in some situation in life which leaves him nothing to do but to make them natural and true, I know of nothing finer, nothing more attractive or more individual than the portraitures he has given us.

Figaro, the wittiest of the French periodicals, and at that time on the liberal side, commended the *Bravo*; the journals on the side of the government censured it. *Figaro* afterward passed into the hands of the aristocratic party, and Cooper became the object of its attacks. He was not, however, a man to be driven from any purpose which he had formed, either by flattery of abuse, and both were tried with equal ill success. In 1832 he published his *Heidenmauer*, and in 1833 his *Headsman of Berne*, both with a political design similar to that of the *Bravo*, though neither of them takes the same high rank among his works.

In 1833, after a residence of seven years in different parts of Europe, but mostly in France, Cooper returned to his native country. The welcome which met him here was somewhat chilled by the effect of the attacks made upon him in France, and remembering with what zeal, and at what sacrifice of the universal acceptance which his works would otherwise have met, he had maintained the cause of his country against the wits and orators of the court party in France, we cannot wonder that he should have felt this coldness as undeserved. He published, shortly after his arrival in this country, *A Letter to his Countrymen*, in which he complained of the censures cast upon him in the American newspapers, gave a history of the part he had taken in exposing the misstatements of the *Révue Britannique*, and warned his countrymen against the too common error of resorting, with a blind deference, to foreign authorities, often swayed by national or political prejudices, for our opinions of American authors. Going beyond this topic, he examined and reprehended the habit of applying to the interpretation of our own constitution maxims derived from the practice of other governments, particularly that of Great Britain. The importance of construing that instrument by its own principles he illustrated by considering several points in dispute between the parties of the day, on which he gave very decided opinions.

The principal effect of this pamphlet, as it seemed to me, was to awaken in certain quarters a kind of resentment that a successful writer of fiction should presume to give lessons in politics. I meddle not here with the conclusions to which he arrived, though I must be allowed to say that they were stated and argued with great ability. In 1835 Cooper published the *Monikins*, a satirical work, partly with a political aim, and in the same year appeared his *American Democrat*, a view of the civil and social relations of the United States, discussing more gravely various topics touched upon in the former work, and pointing out in what respects he deemed the American people in their practice to have fallen short, as they undoubtedly have, of the excellence of their institutions.

He found time, however, for a more genial task, that of giving to the world his observations on foreign countries. In 1836 appeared his *Sketches of Switzerland*, a series of letters in four volumes, the second part published about two months after the first, a delightful work, written in a more fluent and flexible style than his *Notions of the Americans*. The first part of *Gleanings in Europe*, giving an account of his residence in France, followed in the same year, and the second part of the same work containing his observations on England, was published in April, 1837. In these works, forming a series of eight volumes, he relates and describes with much of the same distinctness as in his novels; and his remarks on the manners and institutions of the different countries, often sagacious and always peculiarly his own, derive, from their frequent reference to contemporary events, an historical interest.

In 1838 appeared *Homeward Bound*, and *Home as Found*, two satirical novels, in which Cooper held up to ridicule a certain class of conductors of the newspaper press in America. These works had not the good fortune to become popular. Cooper did not, and, because he was too deeply in earnest, perhaps would not, infuse into his satirical works that gayety without which satire becomes wearisome. I believe, however, that if they had been written by anybody else they would have met with more favor; but the world knew that Cooper was able to give them something better, and would not be satisfied with any thing short of his best. Some childishly imagined that because, in the two works I have just mentioned, a newspaper editor is introduced, in whose character almost every possible vice of his profession is made to find a place, Cooper intended an indiscriminate attack upon the whole body of writers for the newspaper press, forgetting that such a portraiture was a satire only on those to whom it bore a likeness. We have become less sensitive and more reasonable of late, and the monthly periodicals make sport for their readers of the follies and ignorance of the newspaper editors, without awakening the slightest resentment; but Cooper led the way in this sort of discipline, and I remember some instances of towering indignation at his audacity expressed in the journals of that time.

The next year Cooper made his appearance before the public in a new department of writing; his *Naval History of the United States* was brought out in two octavo volumes at Philadelphia, by Carey & Lea. In writing his stories of the sea, his attention had been much turned to this subject, and his mind filled with striking incidents from expeditions and battles in which our naval commanders had been engaged. This made his task the lighter, but he gathered his materials with great industry and with a conscientious attention to exactness, for he was not a man to take a fact for granted or allow imagination to usurp the place of inquiry. He digested our naval annals into a narrative, written with spirit it is true, but with that air of sincere dealing which the reader willingly takes as a pledge of its authenticity.

An abridgment of the work was afterward prepared and published by the author. The *Edinburgh Review*, in an article professing to examine the statements both of Cooper's work and of the *History of the English Navy*, written by Mr. James, a surgeon by profession, made a violent attack upon the American historian. Unfortunately it took James' narrative as its sole guide, and followed it implicitly. Cooper replied in the *Democratic Review* for January, 1840, and by a masterly analysis of his statements, convicting James of self-contradiction in almost every particular in which he differed from himself, refuted both James and the reviewer. It was a refutation which admitted of no rejoinder.

Scarce any thing in Cooper's life was so remarkable or so strikingly illustrated his character, as his contest with the newspaper press. He engaged in it after provocations, many and long endured, and prosecuted it through years with great energy, perseverance, and practical dexterity, till he was left master of the field. In what I am about to say of it I hope I shall not give offence to any one, as I shall speak without the slightest malevolence toward those with whom he waged this controversy. Over some of them, as over their renowned adversary, the grave has now closed. Yet where shall the truth be spoken if not beside the grave?

I have already alluded to the principal causes which provoked the newspaper attacks upon Cooper. If he had never meddled with questions of government on either side of the Atlantic, and never satirized the newspaper press, I have little doubt that he would have been spared these attacks. I cannot, however, ascribe them all, or even the greater part of them, either to party or to personal malignity. One journal followed the example of another, with little reflection, I think, in most cases, till it became a sort of fashion, not merely to decry his works, but to arraign his motives.

It is related that in 1832, while he was at Paris, an article was shown him in an American newspaper, purporting to be a criticism on one of his works, but reflecting with much asperity on his personal character. "I care nothing," he is reported to have said, "for the criticism, but I am not indifferent to the slander. If these attacks on my character should be kept up five years after my return to America, I shall resort to the New York courts for protection." He gave the newspaper press of this state the full period of forbearance on which he had fixed, but finding that forbearance seemed to encourage assault he sought redress in the courts of law.

When these litigations were first begun I recollect it seemed to be that Cooper had taken a step which would give him a great deal of trouble, and effect but little good. I said to myself—

"Alas! Leviathan is not so tamed!"

As he proceeded, however, I saw that he had understood the matter better than I. He put a hook into the nose of this huge monster, wallowing in his inky pool and bespattering the passers-by; he dragged him to the land and made him tractable. One suit followed another; one editor was sued, I think, half a dozen times; some of them found themselves under a second indictment before the first was tried. In vindicating himself to his readers against the charge of publishing one libel, the angry journalist often floundered into another. The occasions of these prosecutions seem to have been always carefully considered, for Cooper was almost uniformly successful in obtaining verdicts. In a letter of his written in February, 1843, about five years, I think, from the commencement of the first prosecutions, he says "I have beaten every man I have sued who has not retracted his libels."

In one of these suits, commenced against the late William L. Stone of the *Commercial Advertiser*, and referred to the arbitration of three distinguished lawyers, he argued, himself, the question of the authenticity of his account of the battle of Lake Erie, which was the matter in dispute. I listened to his opening; it was clear, skillful, and persuasive, but his closing argument was said to be splendidly eloquent. "I have heard nothing like it," said a barrister to me, "since the days of Emmet."

Cooper behaved liberally toward his antagonists, so far as pecuniary damages were concerned, though some of them wholly escaped their payment by bankruptcy. After, I believe, about six years of litigation, the newspaper press gradually subsided into a pacific disposition toward its adversary, and the contest closed with the account of pecuniary profit and loss, so far as he was concerned, nearly balanced. The occasion of these suits was far from honorable to those who provoked them, but the result was, I had almost said, creditable to all parties; to him as the courageous prosecutor, to the administration of justice in this country, and to the docility of the newspaper press which he had disciplined into good manners.

It was while he was in the midst of these litigations that he published, in 1840, the *Pathfinder*. People had begun to think of him as a controversialist, acute, keen, and persevering, occupied with his personal wrongs and schemes of attack and defense. They were startled from this estimate of his character by the moral beauty of that glorious work—I must so call it; by the vividness and force of its delineations, by the unspoiled love of nature apparent in every page, and by the fresh and warm emotions which everywhere gave life to the narrative and the dialogue. Cooper was now in his fifty-first year, but nothing which he had produced in the earlier part of his literary life was written with so much of what might seem the generous fervor of youth, or showed the faculty of invention in higher vigor. I recollect that near the time of its appearance I was informed of an observation made upon it by one highly distinguished in the literature of our country and of the age, between whom and the author an unhappy coolness had for some years existed. As he finished the reading of the *Pathfinder* he exclaimed, "They may say what they will of Cooper; the man who wrote this book is not only a great man but a good man."

The readers of the *Pathfinder* were quickly reconciled to the fourth appearance of Leatherstocking, when they saw him made to act a different part from any which the author had hitherto assigned him—when they saw him shown as a lover, and placed in the midst of associations which invested his character with a higher and more affecting heroism. In this work are two female characters portrayed in a masterly manner, the corporal's daughter, Mabel Dunham, generous, resolute, yet womanly, and the young Indian woman, called by her tribe the Dew of June, a personification of female truth, affection, and sympathy, with a strong aboriginal cast, yet a product of nature as bright and pure as that from which she is named.

Mercedes of Castile, published near the close of the same year, has none of the stronger characteristics of Cooper's genius, but in the *Deerslayer*, which appeared in 1841, another of his Leatherstocking tales, he gave us a work rivaling the *Pathfinder*. Leatherstocking is brought before us in his early youth, in the first exercise of that keen sagacity which is blended so harmoniously with a simple and ingenuous goodness. The two daughters of the retired freebooter dwelling on the Otsego lake, inspire scarcely less interest than the principal personage; Judith in the pride of her beauty and intellect, her good impulses contending with a fatal love of admiration, holding us fascinated with a constant interest in her fate, which with consummate skill, we are permitted rather to conjecture than to know; and Hetty, scarcely less beautiful in person, weak-minded, but wise in the midst of that weakness beyond the wisdom of the loftiest intellect, through the power of conscience and religion. The character of Hetty would have been a hazardous experiment in feebler hands, but in his it was admirably successful.

The *Two Admirals* and *Wing-and-Wing* were given to the public in 1842, both of them taking a high rank among Cooper's sea tales. The first of these is a sort of naval epic in prose; the flight and chase of armed vessels hold us in breathless suspense, and the sea-fights are described with a terrible power. In the later sea tales of Cooper, it seems to me that the mastery with which he makes his grand processions of events pass before the mind's eye is even greater than in his earlier. The next year he published the *Wyandotte or Hutted Knoll*, one of his beautiful romances of the woods, and in 1844 two more of his sea stories, *Afloat and Ashore* and *Miles Wallingford* its sequel. The long series of his nautical tales was closed by *Jack Tier, or the Florida Reef*, published in 1848, when Cooper was in his sixtieth year, and it is as full of spirit, energy, invention, life-like presentation of objects and events—

The vision and the faculty divine—

as any thing he had written.

Let me pause here to say that Cooper, though not a manufacturer of verse, was in the highest sense of the word a poet; his imagination wrought nobly and grandly, and imposed its creations on the mind of the reader for realities. With him there was no withering, or decline, or disuse of the poetic faculty; as he stepped downward from the zenith of life no shadow or chill came over it; it was like the year of some genial climates, a perpetual season of verdure, bloom, and fruitfulness. As these works came out I was rejoiced to see that he was unspoiled by the controversies in which he had allowed himself to become engaged, that they had not given to these better expressions of his genius any tinge of misanthropy, or appearance of contracting and closing sympathies, any trace of an interest in his fellow-beings less large and free than in his earlier works.

Before the appearance of his *Jack Tier*, Cooper published, in 1845 and the following year, a series of novels relating to the Anti-rent question, in which he took great interest. He thought that the disposition manifested in certain quarters to make concessions to what he deemed a denial of the rights of property, was a first step in a most dangerous path. To discourage this disposition he wrote *Satanstoe*, the *Chainbearer*, and the *Redskins*. They are didactic in their design, and want the freedom of invention which belongs to Cooper's best novels; but if they had been written by anybody but Cooper—by a member of Congress, for example, or an eminent politician of any class—they would have made his reputation. It was said, I am told, by a distinguished jurist of our state, that they entitled the author to as high a place in law as his other works had won for him in literature.

In 1848 Cooper published his novel entitled *Oak Openings, or the Bee-Hunter*. This work bears many traces of the author's fondness for discussion. He often pauses in his narrative briefly to reprehend some prevailing error, to refute some groundless boast of his countrymen or some attack made upon them by foreigners; to settle some point of theology, or even to set his readers right on some question of orthoëpy or of the use of language. The scene is laid in the park-like groves of Michigan, where a Pennsylvanian, whose occupation is that of a bee-hunter, has fixed his solitary summer residence, and astonishes the savages who occasionally visit him by the exhibition of his craft. The bee-hunter has many qualities that interest us; he is brave and generous by nature, wary by experience, calm in danger, full of resources, and the gentlest and best-mannered man that ever followed his solitary calling. A personage performing an equally important part in the story, and marked by still stronger characteristics, is the Indian who has acquired the surname of Scalping Peter, a powerfully drawn impersonation of the art and dissimulation ascribed to the American savage. Toward the close of the narrative Peter is won over to Christianity by the moral beauty of a prayer made by a simple-hearted Methodist missionary, who, at the very moment that they are about to take his life, fervently implores the mercy of God for his remorseless enemies. The various expedients of a bee-hunter's life, the dangers of the wilderness full of lurking savages bent on hostile designs, the stealthy flight of a small party of white people, and the equally stealthy pursuit of a small party of white people, and the equally stealthy pursuit of the aborigines, furnish matter for a narrative of almost painful interest. There is great art shown in complicating the difficulties which beset the hero of the story, in prolonging the pauses of suspense, and in devising the means by which he is extricated. The other characters of the novel are well distinguished from each other, and among them Margery is one of Cooper's better class of female portraits—full of gentleness, sweetness, and native dignity.

I had thought, in meditating the plan of this discourse, to mention all the works of Mr. Cooper, but the length to which I have found it extending has induced me to pass over several written in the last ten years of his life, and to confine myself to those which best illustrate his literary character. The last of his novels was the *Ways of the Hour*, a work in which the objections he entertained to the trial by jury in civil causes were stated in the form of a narrative.

It is a voluminous catalogue—that of Cooper's published works—but it comprises not all he wrote. He committed to the fire, without remorse, many of the fruits of his literary industry. It was understood some years since, that he had a work ready for the press on the *Middle States of the Union*, principally illustrative of their social history; but it has not been found among his manuscripts, and the presumption is that he must have destroyed it. He had planned a work on the *Towns of Manhattan*, for the publication of which he made arrangements with Mr. Putnam of this city, and a part of which, already written, was in press at the time of his death. The printed part has since been destroyed by fire, but a portion of the manuscript was recovered. The work, I learn, will be completed by one of the family, who, within a few years past, has earned an honorable name among the authors of our country. Great as was the number of his works, and great as was the favor with which they were received, the pecuniary rewards of his success were far less than has been generally supposed— scarcely, as I am informed, a tenth part of what the common rumor made them. His fame was infinitely the largest acknowledgment which this most successful of American authors received for his labors.

The *Ways of the Hour* appeared in 1850. At this time his personal appearance was remarkable. He seemed in perfect health and in the highest energy and activity of his faculties. I have scarcely seen any man at that period of life on whom his years sat more lightly. His conversation had lost none of its liveliness, though it seemed somewhat more gentle and forbearing in tone, and his spirits none of their elasticity. He was contemplating, I have since been told, another Leatherstocking tale, deeming that he had not yet exhausted the character, and those who consider what new resources it yielded him in the *Pathfinder* and the *Deerslayer*, will readily conclude that he was not mistaken.

The disease, however, by which he was removed was even then impending over him, and not long afterward his friends here were grieved to learn that his health was declining. He came to New York so changed that they looked at him with sorrow, and after a stay of some weeks, partly for the benefit of medical advice, returned to Cooperstown, to leave it no more. His complaint gradually gained strength, subdued a constitution originally robust, and finally passed into a confirmed dropsy. In August, 1851, he was visited by his excellent and learned friend, Dr. Francis, a member of the weekly club which he had founded in the early part of his literary career. He found him bearing the sufferings of his disease with manly firmness, gave him such medical counsels as the malady appeared to require, prepared him delicately for its fatal termination, and returned to New York with the most melancholy anticipations. In a few days afterward Cooper expired, amid the deep affliction of his family, on the 14th of September, the day before that on which he should have completed his sixty-second year. He died apparently without pain, in peace and religious hope. The relations of man to his Maker and to that state of being for which the present is but a preparation, had occupied much of his thoughts during his whole lifetime, and he crossed, with a serene composure, the mysterious boundary which divides this life from the next.

The departure of such a man in the full strength of his faculties—on whom the country had for thirty years looked as one of the permanent ornaments of its literature, and whose name had been so often associated with praise, with renown, with controversy, with blame, but never with death—diffused a universal awe. It was as if an earthquake had shaken the ground on which we stood, and showed the grave opening by our path. In the general grief for his loss, his virtues only were remembered, and his failings forgotten.

Of his failings I have said little; such as he had were obvious to all the world; they lay on the surface of his character; those who knew him least made the most account of them. With a character so made up of positive qualities—a character so independent and uncompromising, and with a sensitiveness far more acute than he was willing to acknowledge, it is not surprising that occasions frequently arose to bring him into friendly collision and sometimes into graver disagreements and misunderstandings with his fellow-men. For his infirmities his friends found an ample counterpoise in the generous sincerity of his nature. He never thought of disguising his opinions, and he abhorred all disguise in others; he did not even deign to use that show of regard toward those of whom he did not think well, which the world tolerates and almost demands. A manly expression of opinion, however different from his own, commanded his respect. Of his own works he spoke with the same freedom as of the works of others; and never hesitated to express his judgement of a book for the reason that it was written by himself; yet he could bear with gentleness any dissent from the estimate he placed on his own writings. His character was like the bark of the cinnamon, a rough and astringent rind without and an intense sweetness within. Those who penetrated below the surface found a genial temper, warm affections, and a heart with ample place for his friends, their pursuits, their good name, their welfare. They found him a philanthropist, though not precisely after the fashion of the day; a religious man, most devout where devotion is most apt to be a feeling rather than a custom, in the household circle; hospitable, and to the extent of his means, liberal-handed in acts of charity. They found, also, that though in general he would as soon have thought of giving up an old friend as of giving up an opinion, he was not proof against testimony, and could part with a mistaken opinion as one parts with an old friend who has been proved faithless and unworthy. In short, Cooper was one of those who, to be loved, must be intimately known.

Of his literary character I have spoken largely in the narrative of his life, but there are yet one or two remarks which must be made to do it justice. In that way of writing in which he excelled, it seems to me that he united, in a pre-eminent degree, those qualities which enabled him to interest the largest number of readers. He wrote not for the fastidious, the over-refined, the morbidly delicate; for these find in his genius something too robust for their liking—something by which their sensibilities are too rudely shaken; but he wrote for mankind at large—for men and women in the ordinary healthful state of feeling—and in their admiration he found his reward. It is for this class that public libraries are obliged to provide themselves with an extraordinary number of copies of his works; the number in the Mercantile Library, in this city, I am told, is forty. Hence it is that he has earned a fame wider, I think, than any author of modern times—wider, certainly, than any author of any age ever enjoyed in his lifetime. All his excellencies are translatable—they pass readily into languages the least allied in their genius to that in which he wrote, and in them he touches the heart and kindles the imagination with the same power as in the original English.

Cooper was not wholly without humor; it is sometimes found lurking in the dialogue of Harvey Birch, and of Leatherstocking; but it forms no considerable element in his works; and if it did, it would have stood in the way of his universal popularity, since, of all qualities, it is the most difficult to transfuse into a foreign language. Nor did the effect he produced upon the reader depend on any grace of style which would escape a translator of ordinary skill. With his style, it is true, he took great pains, and in his earlier works, I am told, sometimes altered the proofs sent from the printer so largely that they might be said to be written over. Yet he attained no special felicity, variety, or compass of expression. His style, however, answered his purpose; it has defects, but it is manly and clear, and stamps on the mind of the reader the impression he desired to convey. I am not sure that some of the very defects of Cooper's novels do not add, by a certain force of contrast, to their power over the mind. He is long in getting at the interest of his narrative. The progress of the plot, at first, is like that of one of his own vessels of war, slowly, heavily, and even awkwardly working out of a harbor. We are impatient and weary, but when the vessel is once in the open sea, and feels the free breath of heaven in her full sheets, our delight and admiration are all the greater at the grace, the majesty, and power with which she divides and bears down the waves, and pursues her course, at will, over the great waste of waters.

Such are the works so widely read, and so universally admired in all the zones of the globe, and by men of every kindred and every tongue; works which have made, of those who dwell in remote latitudes, wanderers in our forests and observers of our manners, and have inspired them with an interest in our history. A gentleman who had returned from Europe just before the death of Cooper, was asked what he found the people of the Continent doing. "They are all reading Cooper," he answered; "in the little kingdom of Holland, with its three millions of inhabitants, I looked into four different translations of Cooper in the language of the country." A traveller, who has seen much of the middle classes of Italy, lately said to me, "I found that all they knew of America, and that was not little, they had learned from Cooper's novels; from him they had learned the story of American liberty, and through him they had been introduced to our Washington; they had read his works till the shores of the Hudson and the valleys of Westchester, and the banks of Otsego lake had become to them familiar ground."

Over all the countries into whose speech this great man's works have been rendered by the labors of their scholars, the sorrow of that loss which we deplore is now diffusing itself. Here we lament the ornament of our country, there they mourn the death of him who delighted the human race. Even now while I speak, the pulse of grief which is passing through the nations has haply just reached some remote neighborhood; the news of his death has been brought to some dwelling on the slopes of the Andes, or amid the snowy wastes of the North, and the dark-eyed damsel of Chile or the fair-haired maid of Norway is sad to think that he whose stories of heroism and true love have so often kept her for hours from her pillow, lives no more.

He is gone! but the creations of his genius, fixed in living words, survive the frail material organs by which the words were first traced. They partake of a middle nature, between the deathless mind and the decaying body of which they are the common offspring, and are, therefore, destined to a duration, if not eternal yet indefinite. The examples he has given in his glorious fictions, of heroism, honor, and truth; of large sympathies between man and man, of all that is good, great, and excellent, embodied in personages marked with so strong an individuality that we place them among our friends and favorites; his frank and generous men, his gentle and noble women, shall live through centuries to come, and only perish with our language. I have said with our language; but who shall say when it may be the fate of the English language to be numbered with the extinct forms of human speech? Who shall declare which of the present tongues of the civilized world will survive its fellows? It may be that some one of them, more fortunate than the rest, will long outlast them, in some undisturbed quarter of the globe, and in the midst of a new civilization. The creations of Cooper's genius, even now transferred to that language, may remain to be the delight of the nations through another great cycle of centuries, beginning after the English language and its contemporaneous form of civilization shall have passed away.

Thomas R. Lounsbury (essay date 1883)

SOURCE: "1850-1851," in *James Fenimore Cooper,* Houghton Mifflin and Company, 1883, pp. 265-89.

[*In the following excerpt, Lounsbury assesses the p itive and negative characteristics of Cooper's writing.*]

More than sixty years have gone by since Cooper began to write; more than thirty since he ceased to live. If his reputation has not advanced during the period that has passed since his death, it has certainly not receded. Nor does it seem likely to undergo much change in the future. The world has pretty well made up its mind as to the value of his work. The estimate in which it is held will not be materially raised or lowered by anything which criticism can now utter. This will itself be criticised for being too obvious; for it can do little but repeat, with variation of phrase, what has been constantly said and often better said before. There is, however, now a chance of its meeting with fairer consideration. The cloud of depreciation which seems to settle upon the achievement of every man of letters soon after death, it was Cooper's fortune to encounter during life. This was partly due to the literary reaction which had taken place against the form of fiction he adopted, but far more to the personal animosities he aroused. We are now far enough removed from the prejudices and passions of his time to take an impartial view of the man, and to state, without bias for or against him, the conclusions to which the world has very generally come as to his merits and defects as a writer.

At the outset it is to be said that Cooper is one of the people's novelists as opposed to the novelists of highly-cultivated men. This does not imply that he has not been, and is not still, a favorite with many of the latter. The names of those, indeed, who have expressed excessive admiration for his writings far surpass in reputation and even critical ability those who have spoken of him depreciatingly. Still the general statement is true that it is with the masses he has found favor chiefly. The sale of his works has known no abatement since his death. It goes on constantly to an extent that will surprise any one who has not made an examination of this particular point. His tales continue to be read or rather devoured by the uncultivated many. They are often contemptuously criticised by the cultivated few, who sometimes affect to look upon any admiration they may have once had for them as belonging exclusively to the undisciplined taste of childhood.

This state of things may be thought decisive against the permanent reputation of the novelist. The opinion of the cultivated few, it is said, must prevail over that of the uncultivated many. True as this is in certain cases, it is just as untrue in others. It is, in fact, often absurdly false when the general reading public represents the uncultivated many. On matters which come legitimately within the scope of their judgment the verdict of the great mass of men is infinitely more trustworthy than that of any small body of men, no matter how cultivated. Of plenty of that narrow judgment of select circles which mistakes the cackle of its little coterie for the voice of the world, Cooper was made the subject, and sometimes the victim, during his lifetime. There were any number of writers, now never heard of, who were going to outlive him, according to literary prophecies then current, which had everything oracular in their utterance except ambiguity. Especially is this true of the notices of his stories of the sea. As I have turned over the pages of defunct criticism, I have come across the names of several authors whose tales descriptive of ocean life were, according to many contemporary estimates, immensely superior to anything of the kind Cooper had produced or could produce. Some of these writers enjoyed for a time high reputation. Most of them are now as utterly forgotten as the men who celebrated their praises.

But however unfair as a whole may be the estimate of cultivated men in any particular case, their adverse opinion is pretty certain to have a foundation of justice in its details. This is unquestionably true in the present instance. Characteristics there are of Cooper's writings which would and do repel many. Defects exist both in manner and matter. Part of the unfavorable judgment he has received is due to the prevalence of minor faults, disagreeable rather than positively bad. These, in many cases, sprang from the quantity of what he did and the rapidity with which he did it. The amount that Cooper wrote is something that in fairness must always be taken into consideration. He who has crowded into a single volume the experience of a life must concede that he stands at great advantage as regards matters of detail, and especially as regards perfection of form, with him who has manifested incessant literary activity in countless ways. It was the immense quantity that Cooper wrote and the haste and inevitable carelessness which wait upon great production, that are responsible for many of his minor faults. Incongruities in the conception of his tales, as well as in their execution, often make their appearance. Singular blunders can be found which escaped even his own notice in the final revision he gave his works. In *Mercedes of Castile,* for instance, the heroine presents her lover on his outward passage with a cross framed of sapphire stones. These, she tells him, are emblems of fidelity. When she comes to inquire about them after his return she speaks of them as turquoise. Again, in *The Deerslayer* three castles of a curious set of chessmen are given in one part of the story to the Indians. Later on, two other castles of the same set make their appearance. This is a singular mistake for Cooper to overlook, for chess was a game of which he was very fond.

In the matter of language this rapidity and carelessness often degenerated into downright slovenliness. It was bad enough to resort to the same expedients and to repeat the same scenes. Still from this charge few prolific novelists can be freed. But in Cooper there were often words and phrases which he worked to death. In *The Wept of Wish-ton-Wish* there is so perpetual a

reference to the quiet way in which the younger Heathcote talks and acts that it has finally anything but a quieting effect upon the reader's feelings. In *The Headsman of Berne,* "warm" in the sense of "well-to-do," a disagreeable usage at best, occurs again and again, until the feeling of disagreeableness it inspires at first becomes at last positive disgust. This trick of repetition reaches the climax of meaninglessness in *The Ways of the Hour.* During the trial scene the judge repeats on every pretext and as a part of almost every speech, the sentence "time is precious;" and it is about the only point on which he is represented as taking a clear and decided stand.

There were other faults in the matter of language that to some will seem far worse. I confess to feeling little admiration for that grammar-school training which consists in teaching the pupil how much more he knows about our tongue than the great masters who have moulded it; which practically sets up the claim that the only men who are able to write English properly are the men who have never shown any capacity to write it at all; and which seeks, in a feeble way, to cramp usage by setting up distinctions that never existed, and laying down rules which it requires uncommon ignorance of the language to make or to heed. Still there are lengths to which the most strenuous stickler for freedom of speech does not venture to go. There are prejudices in favor of the exclusive legitimacy of certain constructions that he feels bound to respect. He recognizes, as a general rule, for instance, that when the subject is in the singular it is desirable that the verb should be in the same number. For conventionalities of syntax of this kind Cooper was very apt to exhibit disregard, not to say disdain. He too often passed the bounds that divide liberty from license. It scarcely needs to be asserted that in most of these cases the violation of idiom arose from haste or carelessness. But there were some blunders which can only be imputed to pure unadulterated ignorance. He occasionally used words in senses unknown to past or present use. He sometimes employed grammatical forms that belong to no period in the history of the English language. A curious illustration of a word combining in itself both these errors is *wists,* a verb, in the third person, singular. If this be anything it should be *wist,* the preterite of *wot,* and should have accordingly the meaning "knew." Cooper uses it in fact as a present with the sense of "wishes." Far worse than occasional errors in the use of words are errors of construction. His sentences are sometimes involved in the most hopeless way, and the efforts of grammar to untie the knot by any means known to it serve only to make conspicuous its own helplessness.

All this is, in itself, of slight importance when set off against positive merits. But it is constantly forced upon the reader's attention by the fact that Cooper himself was exceedingly critical on points of speech. He was perpetually going out of his way to impart bits of information about words and their uses, and it is rare that he blunders into correct statement or right inference. He often, indeed, in these matters carried ignorance of what he was talking about, and confidence in his own knowledge of it to the extremest verge of the possible. He sometimes mistook dialectic or antiquated English for classical, and laboriously corrected the latter by putting the former in parentheses by its side. In orthography and pronunciation he had never got beyond that puerile conception which fancies it a most creditable feature in a word that its sound shall not be suggested by anything in its spelling. In the case of proper names this was more than creditable; it was aristocratic. So in *The Crater* great care is taken to tell us that the hero's name, though written Woolston, was pronounced Wooster; and that he so continued to sound it in spite of a miserable Yankee pedagogue who tried hard to persuade him to follow the spelling. So, again, in *The Ways of the Hour* we are sedulously informed that Wilmeter is to be pronounced Wilmington. But absurdities like these belonged not so much to Cooper as to the good old times of gentlemanly ignorance in which he lived. In his etymological vagaries, however, he sometimes left his age far behind. In *The Oak Openings* he enters upon the discussion of the word "shanty." He finds the best explanation of its origin is to suppose it a corruption of *chiènté*, a word which he again supposed might exist in Canadian French, and provided it existed there, he further supposed that in that dialect it might mean "dog-kennel." The student of language, much hardened to this sort of work on the part of men of letters, can read with resignation "this plausible derivation," as it is styled. Cooper, however, not content with the simple glory of originating it, actually uses throughout the whole work *chiènté* instead of "shanty." This rivals, if it does not outdo, the linguistic excesses of the sixteenth and seventeenth centuries.

There are imperfections far more serious than these mistakes in language. He rarely attained to beauty of style. The rapidity with which he wrote forbids the idea that he ever strove earnestly for it. Even the essential but minor grace of clearness is sometimes denied him. He had not, in truth, the instincts of the born literary artist. Satisfied with producing the main effect, he was apt to be careless in the consistent working out of details. Plot, in any genuine sense of the word "plot," is to be found in very few of his stories. He seems rarely to have planned all the events beforehand; or, if he did, anything was likely to divert him from his original intention. The incidents often appear to have been suggested as the tale was in process of composition. Hence the constant presence of incongruities with the frequent result of bringing about a bungling and incomplete development. The introduction of certain characters is sometimes so heralded as to lead us to expect from them far more than they actually perform.

Thus, in *The Two Admirals,* Mr. Thomas Wychecombe is brought in with a fullness of description that justifies the reader in entertaining a rational expectation of finding in him a satisfactory scoundrel, capable, desperate, full of resources, needing the highest display of energy and ability to be overcome. This reasonable anticipation is disappointed. At the very moment when respectable determined villainy is in request, he fades away into a poltroon of the most insignificant type who is not able to hold his own against an ordinary house-steward.

The prolixity of Cooper's introductions is a fault so obvious to every one that it needs here reference merely and not discussion. A similar remark may be made as to his moralizing, which was apt to be cheap and commonplace. He was much disposed to waste his own time and to exhaust the patience of his reader by establishing with great fullness of demonstration and great positiveness of assertion the truth of principles which most of the human race are humbly content to regard as axioms. A greater because even a more constantly recurring fault is the gross improbability to be found in the details of his stories. There is too much fiction in his fiction. We are continually exasperated by the inadequacy of the motive assigned; we are irritated by the unnatural if not ridiculous conduct of the characters. These are perpetually doing unreasonable things, or doing reasonable things at unsuitable times. They take the very path that must lead them into the danger they are seeking to shun. They engage in making love when they ought to be flying for their lives. His heroes, in particular, exhibit a capacity for going to sleep in critical situations, which may not transcend extraordinary human experience, but does ordinary human belief. Nor is improbability always confined to details. It pervades sometimes the central idea of the story. In *The Bravo,* for instance, the hero is the most pious of sons, the most faithful of friends, the most devoted of lovers. The part he has to play in the tale is to appear to be a cutthroat of the worst type, without doing a single thing to merit his reputation. It is asking too much of human credulity to believe that a really good man could long sustain the character of a remorseless desperado by merely making faces. This improbability, moreover, is most marked in the tales which are designed to teach a lesson. A double disadvantage is the result. The story is spoiled for the sake of the moral; and the moral is lost by the grossly improbable nature of the story. In the last novel Cooper wrote this is strikingly seen. He who can credit the possibility of the events occurring that are told in *The Ways of the Hour* must give up at the same time his belief in the maxim that truth is stranger than fiction.

It has now become a conventional criticism of Cooper that his characters are conventional. Such a charge can be admitted without seriously disparaging the value of his work. In the kind of fiction to which his writings belong, the persons are necessarily so subordinate to the events that nearly all novelists of this class have been subjected to this same criticism. So regularly is it made, indeed, that Scott when he wrote a review of some of his own tales for the *Quarterly* felt obliged to adopt it in speaking of himself. He describes his heroes as amiable, insipid young men, the sort of pattern people that nobody cares a farthing about. Untrue as this is of many of Scott's creations, it is unquestionably true of the higher characters that Cooper introduces. They are often described in the most laudatory terms; but it is little they do that makes them worthy of the epithets with which they are honored. Their talk is often of a kind not known to human society. One peculiarity is especially noticeable. A stiffness, not to say an appearance of affectation is often given to the conversation by the use of *thou* and *thee*. This was probably a survival in Cooper of the Quakerism of his ancestors; for he sometimes used it in his private letters. But since the action of his stories was in nearly all cases laid in a period in which the second person singular had become obsolete in ordinary speech, an unnatural character is given to the dialogue, which removes it still farther from the language of real life.

His failure in characterization was undoubtedly greatest in the women he drew. Cooper's ardent admirers have always resented this charge. Each one of them points to some single heroine that fulfills the highest requirements that criticism could demand. It seems to me that close study of his writings must confirm the opinion generally entertained. All his utterances show that the theoretical view he had of the rights, the duties, and the abilities of women, were of the most narrow and conventional type. Unhappily it was a limitation of his nature that he could not invest with charm characters with whom he was not in moral and intellectual sympathy. There was, in his eyes, but one praiseworthy type of womanly excellence. It did not lie in his power to represent any other; on one occasion he unconsciously satirized his inability even to conceive of any other. In *Mercedes of Castile* the heroine is thus described by her aunt: "Her very nature," she says, "is made up of religion and female decorum." It is evident that the author fancied that in this commendation he was exhausting praise. These are the sentiments of a man with whom devoutness and deportment have become the culminating conception of the possibilities that lie in the female character. His heroines naturally conformed to his belief. They are usually spoken of as spotless beings. They are made up of retiring sweetness, artlessness, and simplicity. They are timid, shrinking, helpless. They shudder with terror on any decent pretext. But if they fail in higher qualities, they embody in themselves all conceivable combinations of the proprieties and minor morals. They always give utterance to the most unexceptionable sentiments. They always do the extremely correct thing. The dead perfection of their virtues has not the alloy of a single

redeeming fault. The reader naturally wearies of these uninterestingly discreet and admirable creatures in fiction as he would in real life. He feels that they would be a good deal more attractive if they were a good deal less angelic. With all their faultlessness, moreover, they do not attain an ideal which is constantly realized by their living, but faulty sisters. They do not show the faith, the devotion, the self-forgetfulness, and self-sacrifice which women exhibit daily without being conscious that they have done anything especially creditable. They experience, so far as their own words and acts furnish evidence of their feelings, a sort of lukewarm emotion which they dignify with the name of love. But they not merely suspect without the slightest provocation, they give up the men to whom they have pledged the devotion of their lives, for reasons for which no one would think of abandoning an ordinary acquaintance. In *The Spy* the heroine distrusts her lover's integrity because another woman does not conceal her fondness for him. In *The Heidenmauer* one of the female characters resigns the man she loves because on one occasion, when heated by wine and maddened by passion, he had done violence to the sacred elements. There was never a woman in real life, whose heart and brain were sound, that conformed her conduct to a model so contemptible. It is just to say of Cooper that as he advanced in years he improved upon this feeble conception. The female characters of his earlier tales are never able to do anything successfully but to faint. In his later ones they are given more strength of mind as well as nobility of character. But at best, the height they reach is little loftier than that of the pattern woman of the regular religious novel. The reader cannot help picturing for all of them the same dreary and rather inane future. He is as sure, as if their career had been actually unrolled before his eyes, of the part they will perform in life. They will all become leading members of Dorcas societies; they will find perpetual delight in carrying to the poor bundles of tracts and packages of tea; they will scour the highways and by-ways for dirty, ragged, listless, shoeless, and godless children, whom they will hale into the Sunday-school; they will shine with unsurpassed skill in the manufacture of slippers for the rector; they will exhibit a fiery enthusiasm in the decoration and adornment of the church at Christmas and Easter festivals. Far be the thought that would deny praise to the mild raptures and delicate aspirations of gentle natures such as Cooper drew. But in novels, at least, one longs for a ruddier life than flows in the veins of these pale, bleached-out personifications of the proprieties. Women like them may be far more useful members of society than the stormier characters of fiction that are dear to the carnal-minded. They may very possibly be far more agreeable to live with; but they are not usually the women for whom men are willing or anxious to die.

These are imperfections that have led to the undue depreciation of Cooper among many highly cultivated men. Taken by themselves they might seem enough to ruin his reputation beyond redemption. It is a proof of his real greatness that he triumphs over defects which would utterly destroy the fame of a writer of inferior power. It is with novels as with men. There are those with great faults which please us and impress us far more than those in which the component parts are better balanced. Whatever its other demerits, Cooper's best work never sins against the first law of fictitious composition, that the story shall be full of sustained interest. It has power, and power always fascinates, even though accompanied with much that would naturally excite repulsion or dislike. Moreover, poorly as he sometimes told his story, he had a story to tell. The permanence and universality of his reputation are largely due to this fact. In many modern creations full of subtle charm and beauty, the narrative, the material framework of the fiction, has been made so subordinate to the delineation of character and motive, that the reader ceases to feel much interest in what men do in the study which is furnished him of why they do it. In this highly-rarefied air of philosophic analysis, incident and event wither and die. Work of this kind is apt to have within its sphere an unbounded popularity; but its sphere is limited, and can never include a tithe of that vast public for which Cooper wrote and which has always cherished and kept alive his memory, while that of men of perhaps far finer mould has quite faded away.

It is only fair, also, to judge him by his successes and not by his failures; by the work he did best, and not by what he did moderately well. His strength lies in the description of scenes, in the narration of events. In the best of these he has had no superior, and very few equals. The reader will look in vain for the revelation of sentiment, or for the exhibition of passion. The love story is rarely well done; but the love-story plays a subordinate part in the composition. The moment his imagination is set on fire with the conception of adventure, vividness and power come unbidden to his pen. The pictures he then draws are as real to the mind as if they were actually seen by the eye. It is doubtless due to the fact that these fits of inspiration came to him only in certain kinds of composition, that the excellence of many of his stories lies largely in detached scenes. Still his best works are a moving panorama, in which the mind is no sooner sated with one picture than its place is taken by another equally fitted to fix the attention and to stir the heart. The genuineness of his power, in such cases, is shown by the perfect simplicity of the agencies employed. There is no pomp of words; there is an entire lack of even the attempt at meretricious adornment; there is not the slightest appearance of effort to impress the reader. In his portrayal of these scenes Cooper is like nature, in that he accomplishes his greatest effects with the fewest means. If, as we are sometimes told, these things are easily done, the pertinent question always remains, why are they not done.

Moreover, while in his higher characters he has almost absolutely failed, he has succeeded in drawing a whole group of strongly-marked lower ones. Birch, in *The Spy,* Long Tom Coffin and Boltrope in *The Pilot,* the squatter in *The Prairie,* Cap in *The Pathfinder,* and several others there are, any one of which would be enough of itself to furnish a respectable reputation to many a novelist who fancies himself far superior to Cooper as a delineator of character. He had neither the skill nor power to draw the varied figures with which Scott, with all the reckless prodigality of genius, crowded his canvas. Yet in the gorgeous gallery of the great master of romantic fiction, alive with men and women of every rank in life and of every variety of nature, there is, perhaps, no one person who so profoundly impresses the imagination as Cooper's crowning creation, the man of the forests. It is not that Scott could not have done what his follower did, had he so chosen; only that as a matter of fact he did not. Leather-Stocking is one of the few original characters, perhaps the only great original character, that American fiction has added to the literature of the world.

The more uniform excellence of Cooper, however, lies in the pictures he gives of the life of nature. Forest, ocean, and stream are the things for which he really cares; and men and women are the accessories, inconvenient and often uncomfortable, that must be endured. Of the former he speaks with a loving particularity that lets nothing escape the attention. Yet minute as are often his descriptions, he did not fall into that too easily besetting sin of the novelist, of overloading his picture with details. To advance the greater he sacrificed the less. Cooper looked at nature with the eye of a painter and not of a photographer. He fills the imagination even more than he does the sight. Hence the permanence of the impression which he leaves upon the mind. His descriptions, too, produce a greater effect at the time and cling longer to the memory because they fall naturally into the narrative, and form a real part in the development of the story; they are not merely dragged in to let the reader know what the writer can do. "If Cooper," said Balzac, "had succeeded in the painting of character to the same extent that he did in the painting of the phenomena of nature, he would have uttered the last word of our art." This author I have quoted several times, because far better even than George Sand, or indeed any who have criticised the American novelist, he seems to me to have seen clearly wherein the latter succeeded and wherein he failed.

To this it is just to add one word which Cooper himself would have regarded as the highest tribute that could be paid to what he did. Whatever else we may say of his writings, their influence is always a healthy influence. Narrow and prejudiced he sometimes was in his opinions; but he hated whatever was mean and low in character. It is with beautiful things and with noble things that he teaches us to sympathize. Here are no incitements to passion, no prurient suggestions of sensual delights. The air which breathes through all his fictions is as pure as that which sweeps the streets of his mountain home. It is as healthy as nature itself. To read one of his best works after many of the novels of the day, is like passing from the heated and stifling atmosphere of crowded rooms to the purity, the freedom, and the boundlessness of the forest.

In these foregoing pages I have attempted to portray an author, who in any community would have been a marked man had he never written a word. I have not sought to hide his foibles and his faults, his intolerance and his dogmatism, the irascibility of his temperament, the pugnacity of his nature, the illiberality and injustice of many of his opinions, the unreasonableness as well as the imprudence of the course he often pursued. To his friends and admirers these points will seem to have been insisted upon too strongly. Their feelings may, to a certain extent, be just. Cooper is, indeed, a striking instance of how much more a man loses in the estimation of the world by the exhibition of foibles, than he will by that of vices. In this work one side of the life he lived—the side he presented to the public— is the only one that, owing to circumstances, could be depicted. It does not present the most attractive features of his character. That exclusiveness of temperament which made him misjudged by the many, endeared him only the more to the few who were in a position to see how different he was from what he seemed. In nothing is the essential sweetness of Cooper's nature more clearly shown than in the intense affection he inspired in the immediate circle which surrounded him or that was dependent upon him. He could not fail to feel keenly at times how utterly his character and motives were misapprehended and belied. "As for myself," says the hero of **Miles Wallingford,** "I can safely say that in scarce a circumstance of my life, that has brought me the least under the cognizance of the public, have I ever been judged justly. In various instances have I been praised for acts that were either totally without any merit, or at least the particular merit imputed to them; while I have been even persecuted for deeds that deserved praise."

His faults, in fact, were faults of temper rather than of character. Like the defects of his writings, too, they lay upon the surface, and were seen and read of all men. But granting everything that can be urged against him, impartial consideration must award him an ample excess of the higher virtues. His failings were the failings of a man who possessed in the fullest measure vigor of mind, intensity of conviction, and capability of passion. Disagree with him one could hardly help; one could never fail to respect him. Many of the common charges against him are due to pure ignorance. Of these, perhaps, the most common and the most absolutely baseless is the one which imputes to him excessive literary vanity. Pride, even up to the point of arrogance, he had; but even this was only in a small degree connected with his reputation as an author. In the nearly one hundred volumes he wrote, not a single line can be found which implies that he had an undue opinion of his own powers. On the contrary, there are many that would lead to the conclusion that his appreciation of himself and of his achievement was far lower than even the coldest estimate would form. The prevalent misconception on this point was in part due to his excessive sensitiveness to criticism and his resentment of it when hostile. It was partly due, also, to a certain outspokenness of nature which led him to talk of himself as freely as he would talk of a stranger. But his whole conduct showed the falseness of any such impression. From all the petty tricks to which literary vanity resorts, he was absolutely free. He utterly disdained anything that savored of manoeuvring for reputation. He indulged in no devices to revive the decaying attention of the public. He sought no favors from those who were in a position to confer the notoriety which so many mistake for fame. He went, in fact, to the other extreme, and refused an aid that he might with perfect propriety have received. In the early period of his literary career he wrote a good deal for the *New York Patriot,* a newspaper edited by his intimate friend, Colonel Gardiner. He objected to the publication in it of a favorable notice, which had been prepared of **The Pioneers,** because by the fact of being an occasional contributor he was indirectly connected with the journal. Accordingly the criticism was not inserted. It would not have been possible for him to offer to review his own works, as Scott both offered to do and did of the *Tales of My Landlord,* in the *Quarterly.* Nor would he have acceded to a request to furnish a review of any production of his own, as Irving did, in the same periodical, of his *Conquest of Granada.* No publisher who knew him, even slightly, would have ventured to make him a proposition of the kind. I am expressing no opinion as to the propriety of these particular acts; only that Cooper, constituted as he was, could not for a moment have entertained the thought of doing them.

The fearlessness and the truthfulness of his nature are conspicuous in almost every incident of his career. He fought for a principle as desperately as other men fight for life. The storm of detraction through which he went never once shook the almost haughty independence of his conduct, or swerved him in the slightest from the course he had chosen. The only thing to which he unquestioningly submitted was the truth. His loyalty to that was of a kind almost Quixotic. He was in later years dissatisfied with himself, because, in his novel of **The Pilot,** he had put the character of Paul Jones too high. He thought that the hero had been credited in that work with loftier motives than those by which he was actually animated. Feelings such as these formed the groundwork of his character, and made him intolerant of the devious ways of many who were satisfied with conforming to a lower code of morality. There was a royalty in his nature that disdained even the semblance of deceit. With other authors one feels that the man is inferior to his work. With him it is the very reverse. High qualities, such as these, so different from the easy-going virtues of common men, are more than an offset to infirmities of temper, to unfairness of judgment, or to unwisdom of conduct. His life was the best answer to many of the charges brought against his country and his countrymen; for whatever he may have fancied, the hostility he encountered was due far less to the matter of his criticisms than to their manner. Against the common cant, that in republican governments the tyranny of public sentiment will always bring conduct to the same monotonous level, and opinion to the same subservient uniformity, Democracy can point to this dauntless son who never flinched from any course because it brought odium, who never flattered popular prejudices, and who never buckled to a popular cry. America has had among her representatives of the irritable race of writers many who have shown far more ability to get on pleasantly with their fellows than Cooper. She has had several gifted with higher spiritual insight than he, with broader and juster views of life, with finer ideals of literary art, and, above all, with far greater delicacy of taste. But she counts on the scanty roll of her men of letters the name of no one who acted from purer patriotism or loftier principle. She finds among them all no manlier nature, and no more heroic soul.

Mark Twain (essay date 1895)

SOURCE: "Fenimore Cooper's Further Literary Offenses," in *The New England Quarterly,* Vol. XIX, No. 3, September, 1946, pp. 291-301.

[*In the following essay, originally composed in 1895, Twain criticizes Cooper for his inflexible style and verbosity.*]

Young Gentlemen: In studying Cooper you still find it profitable to study him in detail—word by word, sentence by sentence. For every sentence of his is interesting. Interesting because of its make-up, its peculiar make-up, its original make-up. Let us examine a sentence or two, and see. Here is a passage from Chapter XI of *The Last of the Mohicans* one of the most famous and most admired of Cooper's books:

> Notwithstanding the swiftness of their flight, one of the Indians had found an opportunity to strike a straggling fawn with an arrow, and had borne the more preferable fragments of the victim, patiently on his shoulders, to the stopping-place. Without any aid from the science of cookery, he was immediately employed, in common with his fellows, in gorging himself with this digestible sustenance. Magua alone sat apart, without participating in the revolting meal, and apparently buried in the deepest thought.

This little paragraph is full of matter for reflection and inquiry. The remark about the swiftness of the flight was unnecessary, as it was merely put in to forestall the possible objection of some over-particular reader that the Indian couldn't have found the needed "opportunity" while fleeing swiftly. The reader would not have made that objection. He would care nothing about having that small matter explained and justified. But that is Cooper's way; frequently he will explain and justify little things that do not need it and then make up for this by as frequently failing to explain important ones that do need it. For instance he allowed that astute and cautious person, Deerslayer-Hawkeye, to throw his rifle heedlessly down and leave it lying on the ground where some hostile Indians would presently be sure to find it—a rifle prized by that person above all things else in the earth—and the reader gets no word of explanation of that strange act. There was a reason, but it wouldn't bear exposure. Cooper meant to get a fine dramatic effect out of the finding of the rifle by the Indians, and he accomplished this at the happy time; but all the same, Hawkeye could have hidden the rifle in a quarter of a minute where the Indians could not have found it. Cooper couldn't think of any way to explain why Hawkeye didn't do that, so he just shirked the difficulty and did not explain at all. In another place Cooper allowed Heyward to shoot at an Indian with a pistol that wasn't loaded—and grants us not a word of explanation as to how the man did it.

No, the remark about the swiftness of their flight was not necessary; neither was the one which said that the Indian found an opportunity; neither was the one which said he *struck* the fawn; neither was the one which explained that it was a "straggling" fawn; neither was the one which said the striking was done with an arrow; neither was the one which said the Indian bore the "fragments"; nor the remark that they were preferable fragments; nor the remark that they were *more* preferable fragments; nor the explanation that they were fragments of the "victim," nor the over-particular explanation that specifies the Indian's "shoulders" as the part of him that supported the fragments; nor the statement that the Indian bore the fragments patiently. None of those details has any value. We don't care what the Indian struck the fawn with; we don't care whether it was a straggling fawn or an unstraggling one; we don't care which fragments the Indian saved; we don't care why he saved the "more" preferable ones when the merely preferable ones would have amounted to just the same thing and couldn't have been told from the more preferable ones by anybody, dead or alive; we don't care whether the Indian carried them on his shoulders or in his handkerchief; and finally, we don't care whether he carried them patiently or struck for higher pay and shorter hours. We are indifferent to that Indian and all his affairs.

There was only one fact in that long sentence that was worth stating, and it could have been squeezed into these few words—and with advantage to the narrative, too:

"During the flight one of the Indians had killed a fawn, and he brought it into camp." You will notice that "During the flight one of the Indians had killed a fawn and he brought it into camp," is more straightforward and businesslike, and less mincing and smirky, than it is to say "Notwithstanding the swiftness of their flight, one of the Indians had found an opportunity to strike a straggling fawn with an arrow, and had borne the more preferable fragments of the victim, patiently on his shoulders, to the stopping-place." You will notice that the form "During the flight one of the Indians had killed a fawn and he brought it into camp" holds up its chin and moves to the front with the steady stride of a grenadier, whereas the form "Notwithstanding the swiftness of their flight, one of the Indians had found an opportunity to strike a straggling fawn with an arrow, and had borne the more preferable fragments of the victim, patiently on his shoulders, to the stopping-place," simpers along with an airy, complacent, monkey-with-a-parasol gait which is not suited to the transportation of raw meat.

I beg to remind you that an author's way of setting forth a matter is called his Style, and that an author's style is a main part of his equipment for business. The style of some authors has variety in it, but Cooper's style is remarkable for the absence of this feature. Cooper's style is always grand and stately and noble. Style may be likened to an army, the author to its general, the book to the campaign. Some authors proportion an attacking force to the strength or weakness, the importance or unimportance, of the object to be attacked; but Cooper doesn't. It doesn't make any difference to Cooper whether the object of attack is a hundred thousand men or a cow; he hurls his entire force against it. He comes thundering down with all his battalions at his back, cavalry in the van, artillery on the flanks, infantry massed in the middle, forty bands braying, a thousand banners streaming in the wind; and whether the object be an army or a cow you will see him come marching sublimely in, at the end of the engagement, bearing the more preferable fragments of the victim patiently on his shoulders, to the stopping-place. Cooper's style is grand, awful, beautiful; but it is sacred to Cooper, it is his very own, and no student of the Veterinary College of Arizona will be allowed to filch it from him.

In one of his chapters Cooper throws an ungentle slur at one Gamut because he is not exact enough in his choice of words. But Cooper has that failing himself. . . . If the Indian had "struck" the fawn with a brick, or with a club, or with his fist, no one could find fault with the word used. And one cannot find much fault when he

strikes it with an arrow; still it sounds affected, and it might have been a little better to lean to simplicity and say he shot it with an arrow.

"Fragments" is well enough, perhaps, when one is speaking of the parts of a dismembered deer, yet it hasn't just exactly the right sound—and sound is something; in fact sound is a good deal. It makes the difference between good music and poor music, and it can sometimes make the difference between good literature and indifferent literature. "Fragments" sounds all right when we are talking about the wreckage of a breakable thing that has been smashed; it also sounds all right when applied to cat's-meat; but when we use it to describe large hunks and chunks like the fore- and hind-quarters of a fawn, it grates upon the fastidious ear.

"Without any aid from the science of cookery, he was immediately employed, in common with his fellows, in gorging himself with this digestible sustenance."

This was a mere statistic; just a mere cold, colorless statistic; yet you see Cooper has made a chromo out of it. To use another figure, he has clothed a humble statistic in flowing, voluminous and costly raiment, whereas both good taste and economy suggest that he ought to have saved these splendors for a king, and dressed the humble statistic in a simple breech-clout. Cooper spent twenty-four words here on a thing not really worth more than eight. We will reduce the statistic to its proper proportions and state it in this way:

"He and the others ate the meat raw."

"Digestible sustenance" is a handsome phrase, but it was out of place there, because we do not know these Indians or care for them; and so it cannot interest us to know whether the meat was going to agree with them or not. Details which do not assist a story are better left out.

"Magua alone sat apart, without participating in the revolting meal," is a statement which we understand, but that is our merit, not Cooper's. Cooper is not clear. He does not say who it is that is revolted by the meal. It is really Cooper himself, but there is nothing in the statement to indicate that it isn't Magua. Magua is an Indian and likes raw meat.

The word "alone" could have been left out and space saved. It has no value where it is.

I must come back with some frequency . . . to the matter of Cooper's inaccuracy as an Observer. In this way I shall hope to persuade you that it is well to look at a thing carefully before you try to describe it; but I shall rest you between times with other matters and thus try to avoid over-fatiguing you with that detail of our theme. In *The Last of the Mohicans* Cooper gets up a stirring "situation" on an island flanked by great cataracts—a lofty island with steep sides—a sort of tongue which projects downstream from the midst of the divided waterfall. There are caverns in this mass of rock, and a party of Cooper people hide themselves in one of these to get away from some hostile Indians. There is a small exit at each end of this cavern. These exits are closed with blankets and the light excluded. The exploring hostiles back themselves up against the blankets and rave and rage in a blood-curdling way, but they are Cooper Indians and of course fail to discover the blankets; so they presently go away baffled and disappointed. Alice, in her gratitude for this deliverance, flings herself on her knees to return thanks. The darkness in there must have been pretty solid; yet if we may believe Cooper, it is as a darkness which could not have been told from daylight; for here are some nice details which were visible in it:

> Both Heyward and the more tempered Cora witnessed the act of involuntary emotion with powerful sympathy, the former secretly believing that piety had never worn a form so lovely as it had now assumed in the youthful person of Alice. Her eyes were radiant with the glow of grateful feelings; the flush of her beauty was again seated on her cheeks, and her whole soul seemed ready and anxious to pour out its thanksgivings, through the medium of her eloquent features. But when her lips moved, the words they should have uttered appeared frozen by some new and sudden chill. Her bloom gave place to the paleness of death; her soft and melting eyes grew hard, and seemed contracting with horror; while those hands which she had raised, clasped in each other, towards heaven, dropped in horizontal lines before her, the fingers pointed forward in convulsed motion.

It is a case of strikingly inexact observation. Heyward and the more tempered Cora could not have seen the half of it in the dark that way.

I must call your attention to certain details of this work of art which invite particular examination. "Involuntary" is surplusage, and violates Rule 14. [*Note:* "Rule 14: 'Eschew surplusage.' In the published essay, Twain wrote: 'There are nineteen rules governing literary art in the domain of romantic fiction—some say twenty-two. In *Deerslayer* Cooper violated eighteen of them.'"] All emotion is involuntary when genuine, and then the qualifying term is not needed; a qualifying term is needed only when the emotion is pumped up and ungenuine. "Secretly" is surplusage, too; because Heyward was not believing out loud, but all to himself; and a person cannot believe a thing all to himself without doing it privately. I do not approve of the word "seated," to describe the process of locating a flush. No one can seat a flush. A flush is not a deposit on an exterior surface, it is a something which squashes out from within.

I cannot approve of the word "new." If Alice had had an old chill, formerly, it would be all right to distinguish this one from that one by calling this one the new chill; but she had not had any old chill, this one was the only chill she had had, up till now, and so the tacit reference to an old anterior chill is unwarranted and misleading. And I do not altogether like the phrase "while those hands which she had raised." It seems to imply that she had some other hands—some other ones which she had put on the shelf a minute so as to give her a better chance to raise those ones; but it is not true; she had only the one pair. The phrase is in the last degree misleading. But I like to see her extend these ones in front of her and work the fingers. I think that that is a very good effect. And it would have almost doubled the effect if the more tempered Cora had done it some, too.

A Cooper Indian who has been washed is a poor thing, and commonplace; it is the Cooper Indian in his paint that thrills. Cooper's extra words are Cooper's paint—his paint, his feathers, his tomahawk, his warwhoop.

In the two-thirds of a page elsewhere referred to, wherein Cooper scored 114 literary transgressions out of a possible 115, he appears before us with all his things on. As follows, the italics are mine—they indicate violations of Rule 14:

> In a minute he was once more fastened to the tree, *a helpless object of any insult or wrong that might be offered. So eagerly did every one now act, that nothing was said.* The fire was immediately lighted *in the pile, and the end of all was anxiously expected.*

> It was not the intention of the Hurons *absolutely* to destroy *the life* of their victim by *means* of fire. They designed merely to put his *physical fortitude* to the severest proofs it could endure, short of that extremity. In the end, they fully intended to carry his scalp into their village, but it was their wish first to break down his resolution, and to reduce him to *the level* of a complaining sufferer. With this view, the pile of brush *and branches* had been placed at a *proper* distance, *or one* at which it was thought the heat would soon become intolerable, though *it might* not *be* immediately dangerous. *As often happened, however, on these occasions,* this distance had been miscalculated, and the flames *began to wave their forked tongues in a proximity, to the face of the victim that* would have proved fatal in another instant had not Hetty rushed through the crowd, armed with a stick, and scattered the blazing pile *in a dozen directions.* More than one hand was raised to strike the *presumptuous* intruder to the earth; but the chiefs prevented the blows by reminding their *irritated* followers of the state of her mind. Hetty, herself, was insensible to the risk she ran; but, *as soon as she had performed this bold act, she* stood looking about her in frowning resentment, as if to rebuke the *crowd of attentive* savages *for their cruelty.*

'God bless you, dear*est sister*, for that brave and ready act,' murmured Judith, *herself unnerved so much as to be incapable of exertion*; 'Heaven itself has sent you on its holy errand.'

Number of words, 320; necessary ones, 220; words wasted by the generous spendthrift, 100.

In our day those 100 unnecessary words would have to come out. We will take them out presently and make the episode approximate the modern requirement in the matter of compression.

If we may consider each unnecessary word in Cooper's report of that barbecue a separate and individual violation of Rule 14, then that rule is violated 100 times in that report. Other rules are violated in it. Rule 12 ["*Say* what he is proposing to say, not merely come near it"], two instances; Rule 13 ["Use the right word, not its second cousin"], three instances; Rule 15 ["Not omit necessary details"], one instance; Rule 16 ["Avoid slovenliness of form"], two instances; Rule 17 ["Use good grammar"], one or two little instances; the Report in its entirety is an offense against Rule 18 ["Employ a simple and straightforward style"]—also against Rule 16. Total score, about 114 violations of the laws of literary art out of a possible 115.

Let us now bring forward the Report again, with the most of the unnecessary words knocked out. By departing from Cooper's style and manner, all the facts could be put into 150 words, and the effects heightened at the same time—this is manifest, of course—but that would not be desirable. We must stick to Cooper's language as closely as we can:

> In a minute he was once more fastened to the tree. The fire was immediately lighted. It was not the intention of the Hurons to destroy Deerslayer's life by fire; they designed merely to put his fortitude to the severest proofs it could endure short of that extremity. In the end, they fully intended to take his life, but it was their wish first to break down his resolution and reduce him to a complaining sufferer. With this view the pile of brush had been placed at a distance at which it was thought the heat would soon become intolerable, without being immediately dangerous. But this distance had been miscalculated; the fire was so close to the victim that he would have been fatally burned in another instant if Hetty had not rushed through the crowd and scattered the brands with a stick. More than one Indian raised his hand to strike her down but the chiefs saved her by reminding them of the state of her mind. Hetty herself was insensible to the risk she ran; she stood looking about her in frowning resentment, as if to rebuke the savages for their cruelty.
>
> 'God bless you, dear!' cried Judith, 'for that brave and ready act. Heaven itself has sent you on its holy errand, and you shall have a chromo.'

Number of words, 220—and the facts are all in.

C. Hartley Grattan (essay date 1925)

SOURCE: "A Note on Fenimore Cooper," in *The Double Dealer*, Vol. 7, No. 45, July, 1925, pp. 219-22.

[*In the following essay, Grattan considers Cooper to be an overrated writer who is remembered today mostly for his personality rather than his writings.*]

Among all the figures in American literature who have lately been under critical fire, Cooper has suffered as little as any. A curious chapter indeed could be written on the antics critics have gone through in swallowing him. Such a situation is not astonishing in the light of a knowledge of the dominant critics but it is astonishing to find so keen a man as Van Wyck Brooks concluding "the characters of Cooper lighted up a little fringe of the black uncut forest; they linked the wilderness with our own immemorial world," when he has dealt so caustically with figures of vastly greater literary importance. Part of this may be explained perhaps through reference to selective forgetting. A great many people formerly read Cooper in childhood, and in after years he assumed a place in the delirious haze that spread over those years, taking a place with tops, marbles, and the multiplicity of games. But today I doubt that it is so. The urge that he satisfied is catered to by the motion pictures and in spite of the fact that his books are still issued in elaborate illustrated editions I doubt that he is popular. The boy of immediate yesterday read Horatio Alger and the boy of today reads with greatest zest about the utilizers of some at the moment bizarre fashion in mechanical invention, or gives his allegiance, not to the idealized primitives of Cooper, but to the conquering hero of business. Cooper will always no doubt retain a hold upon children, but I doubt that he ever again can conquer the adult intelligence. In this respect his case resembles Dickens. And it seems right and logical to take him from his high place in American literary history and consider him as an interesting fossil.

The older critics have not been reluctant to make objections to Cooper, as may be discovered by reading Lounsbury's "Life" and Brownell's essay, but by some unknown mechanism they have in concluding dismissed the objections with a gesture and repeated the formula of his greatness, which seems both absurd and unnecessary. Their objections have tended to fall into a definite pattern however. They have been chiefly objections to form, where Cooper is obviously vulnerable, and not to substance, where he is presumed to be invulnerable. At this point it seems to me they fail.

Cooper, beyond everything else, was a frontier man. As a boy he was taken to western New York by his father. He was notoriously without interest in intellectual concerns, and his ideals were colored by two fundamentals: to be a gentleman, and to be a man of action. The society he was brought up in emphasized the virtues of action rather than thought. Cooper was, in psychological parlance, an extrovert. His letters and journals reveal, not a thinking, but an active man. I do not know of a figure who is held in such high regard whose letters are so barren of substance. Henry James complained of the tenuosity of Hawthorne's journals, but what would he have made of the fragments of Cooper's that we have? He would, of course, have put them aside in pain, for they are an amazing revelation of a total lack of intellectual interests. Lounsbury remarked Cooper's distressingly narrow religious and social opinions, but he did not accuse Cooper of intellectual vacuity, as he should have. For days and days Cooper's reading consisted of a few chapters from the Bible, and the occasional non-religious books that come in for mention are never analyzed beyond the point of being denominated interesting or dull. A typical journal entry is this:

> 10 Monday. Began the Acts. Last night was severely cold, as has been today. Thermometer in cold places below zero all day. Went with wife to Chalet, but were nearly frozen. Caught a turkey and killed it myself, and bought a keg of oysters on my way back. Sleighing tolerable, but not as good as we are accustomed to at this season. Paul returned. Chess with wife, she beating outrageously. No more ice.

And so it goes on. It is customary in exculpating Cooper for his literary crimes to refer to his ignorance of literature historically. His culture was that of a gentleman of the day and may be rather accurately measured by running through the quoted chapter headings of a few of his books. He quotes regularly from Shakespeare, Thompson, Campbell, Scott, Byron, Pope, Burns, Gray, Freneau, Bryant and Halleck. The only novelist he read with any thoroughness was Scott. He regarded all New Englanders, literary and otherwise, with suspicion. Culturally there is little to be said for Cooper, that cannot equally be said of any rural gentleman of his social position in that day. The frontier society that he knew cared nothing for culture and neither did he. His ideals were of the frontier pattern. It is well remembered that he gave up a life of action to satisfy his wife, and that he came to writing purely by accident. There is probably no particular merit in a man deliberately turning to writing but it seems obvious that the major artists always have a deep seated drive in that direction. Cooper certainly did not.

His writing reminds one forcibly of the writing that occasionally comes to us from men of action today. Barring certain astonishing encumbrances of style, adequately exposed by Mark Twain, it is strait forward narrative unencumbered by subtleties. It tells without adornment, a story. The characters are excessively simplified. The action is based upon pursuit. It is apt to lack an adequately motivated beginning and an inexplicable ending. Who knows why the girls have chosen to join their father in times of peril in *The Last of the Mohicans*? Or why the hostile Indians are hostile? Motives were outside of Cooper's interests. His novels go—that is all. Cooper's ability to realize a succession of scenes, usually accounted one of his merits, and his reliance upon mere succession, or pursuit, for plot are essentially the same as the bases of the cheaper motion pictures, and those who are swiftest to defend Cooper are just as swift to condemn this class of movies. What gives an abiding and satisfying interest in the terse narratives of heroic action is the authentic experience that rings through them. You feel it all, you experience it vicariously. But in Cooper it is not so. His single appeal is that of melodrama, which is not, I believe an authentic utilization of emotional appeal, but either a pandering to it or vulgarization of it.

But Cooper is excused on the grounds that his literary milieu supplied no correctives. This is entirely sophistical. The uncompromising truth is that Cooper lacked intellectual force in the field of aesthetics, for it should be realized that Poe and Hawthorne were his contemporaries and that they wrestled successfully with the very problems that Cooper so egregiously muffed. Poe with his critical-mathematical intelligence hammered out certain rigid and altogether astonishing, in the light of his surroundings, canons of form. Hawthorne investigated with amazing subtlety human motives and concentrated on "internal drama." Cooper did neither. He achieved neither form nor style, nor psychological subtlety. Cooper did not even realize the legitimate limitations of the novelist's art, but used many of his fictions to teach didactically his irritated opinions on contemporary problems and concerns. And he was as careless of form as he was of province. There is, of course, no transcendental merit in tight construction. That is recognized today if never before, for the perfection of Flaubert has fallen before the onslaughts of the Russians and such writers as James Joyce. But whatever the form, to be meritorious a novel must have inner justification, and, Cooper's never do. Style, however, seems indispensable, and so is a modicum of attention to the obscure inner urges that control men. Cooper's characters are cardboard characters, or clockwork ones. Natty Bumppo comes nearest to being a subtle creation, but the only distinction between Le Gros Serpent and Le Renard Subtil is simply the distinction between good Indian, that is favorably enclined toward the whites, and bad Indian.

Did Cooper, in spite of all this, write high romance? If he was a primitive in his method, where are the mature examples of the genre? It is significant to note that the romantic appeal he made to the French consisted of two parts: the appeal of scenery, and the appeal of the Indians. Balzac remarked: "If Cooper had succeeded in the painting of character as well as he did in the painting of the phenomena of nature he would have uttered the last word of our art." Neither appeal that he did make had any necessary literary basis. Both were based on the appeal of the strange, unknown and far away. The post-war interest in the South Seas was on the same basis and Herman Melville rode into fame, fortuitously, on that basis. So slim a support cannot keep Melville up, and what he has, as contrasted to Cooper, is vastly significant. Melville has an emotional intensity which grips up, and carries the reader beyond any mere reaction to a barren parade of distant and ill-apprehended facts. You always feel a vital mind behind the words. A fiction writer is not valued for the strangeness of his material so much as for the quality of the experience he communicates and his success in communicating it. Conrad undoubtedly had that in mind when he asked with some irritation why it was that he was called a novelist of the sea when Thomas Hardy was never called a novelist of the land. Cooper is decidedly not an early member of the romantic tradition of Melville and Conrad. He belongs with Robert Louis Stevenson, and Stevenson, Frank Swinnerton has with excellent reasons assured us, killed romance. In Cooper's way of romance is death, not literary vitality.

From a primitive it is not pertinent to demand the highest development of possibilities, nor even that he follow the trends he starts to logical conclusions. Cezanne did not develop cubism, but Picasso did. Of a primitive we may demand intrinsic interest, and we may legitimately look for the developments of the genre. But where are the literary descendants of Cooper? And of what intrinsic interest are Cooper's books? The latest important essay on Cooper concentrates upon his personality. And really the great interest he still has for students of American literature is as a personality who solved the problem of the literary life in the frontier community. Broadly speaking there are two ways to do that: a writer may resolutely attack the problem of portraying, or being concerned with, his immediate surroundings, or he may turn to older, more fixed cultures and immerse himself in them. In either case limitations of circumstance are imposed on the writer. Cooper by and large did the former, while Washington Irving did the latter. Irving, naturally and inevitably attained to a more "literary" achievement. But Cooper never became literary in an admirable or derogatory sense. He remained a frontier man to the end. He remained an extrovert to the end, with a mind uncomplicated by much culture. But perhaps because he imagined rather than personally experienced his stories they lack the merits sometimes found in the writings of minds of his type. And he lacked the qualities of a genuine literary artist. Because the intellectual values in Cooper are so slight they do not buoy up his work today. His books may continue for a long time interesting to children and as a personality he will always be an interesting type in our early literary history. But why blink the fact that he is no longer of high literary significance and try to make of a fossil a living man?

Van Wyck Brooks (essay date 1944)

SOURCE: "Cooper: The First Phase," in *The World of Washington Irving,* E. P. Dutton & Company, Inc., 1944, pp. 167-82.

[In the following essay, Brooks discusses the influence of the sea on Cooper's early fiction.]

While Irving was exploring England, another New Yorker, six years younger, who had served for a while in the navy after going to Yale, had married and settled in Westchester county, where he lived as a country gentleman without so much as a thought of writing a book. In 1819, James Fenimore Cooper was thirty years old, and he was looking forward to a farmer's life, planting trees at Angevine, the house he had built at Scarsdale, grading his lawns, building fences, grouping the shrubs and draining the swamps.

Cooper had inherited from the founder of Cooperstown, his father, a sufficiently ample fortune and twenty-three farms, and his wife was one of the De Lanceys, the old New York Huguenot family, who had connections in New Rochelle, near by. He had spent some years at sea, his youth had been adventurous, he had acted, like Irving, as a colonel on the governor's staff, and he was thoroughly enjoying a leisurely existence, visiting his neighbours, riding and reading to his wife. He knew Shakespeare well enough to find in him appropriate mottoes for hundreds of the chapters that he wrote later, but, while he kept up with the Waverley novels and liked Jane Austen and Mrs. Opie, he preferred books on history and military matters. He had the air of a sailor or a man of affairs,—he was frank, robust, active, blunt and fearless. With his wind-blown look and bright grey eyes, he was an out-of-doors man, sometimes boisterous, often brusque and always sure of his opinions. His feelings were occasionally violent and he had a way of expressing them with the vehemence of a naval officer in a battle in a storm.

As the son of a great landowner in the semi-feudal state of New York, Cooper had spent his childhood in Federalist circles, and he had been sent to a school at Albany, kept by a Tory parson, where the other boys were Van Rensselaers, Livingstons and Jays. His father's house was the Federalist citadel of the western part of the state, and Judge Cooper had preached the doctrine that government was for gentlemen and that simple folk should vote as they were told. Cooper had been confirmed at school in his preference for the Episcopal church and his contempt for New Englanders, Puritans and traders, and throughout his life he regarded merchants, mercantile interests and business men with the scorn of a country proprietor of the old regime. Where Irving had grown up with merchants and always felt at home with them, Cooper was their natural adversary, and for this reason, in days to come, he drew away from Federalism, which was dominated more and more by the interests of trade. He also reacted against the Federalists in their attachment to English things, which he had shared instinctively when he was a child; and yet, becoming a Democrat and even a supporter of Andrew Jackson, he never lost many of his inborn Federalist traits. He loved the conservative old-time ways, the grave manners and stately style, the simple good taste and decorum of the older gentry, and he had a passion for the land that was shared by his father's friends Chancellor Kent and the former Chief Justice John Jay, who was living at Bedford. From Cooper's farm at Scarsdale, it was an easy drive to Bedford, over the winding roads of the Westchester hills, and there the old patriot and sage, who had played a large role in American history, was passing the evening of his days. A devout Episcopalian, Jay, who was partly of Huguenot blood, lived in respectable comfort in his half-stone farmhouse, studying the science of the soil from Columella down and developing new varieties of melons. Like Jefferson, he carried on a voluminous correspondence, and Wilberforce consulted him about reforms in England, while to Cooper he was a sort of uncle, for the sagacious old man was an ancient friend of the De Lanceys as well as of the Coopers. He smoked a long church-warden pipe, and Cooper delightedly listened while Jay related stories of the Revolution, for he had been chairman of a committee that was appointed by Congress to gather news about the British plans. He had employed a secret agent whom he described to Cooper and who appeared soon afterward, under the name of Harvey Birch, in a novel that Cooper wrote and called *The Spy*. For Cooper suddenly took up novel-writing, and his book was a prodigious success at once. It had been preceded by a novel called *Precaution*, which Cooper had read aloud to the household of the Jays. He had written it on a sort of wager that he could produce a better book than some of the fashionable novels he was reading to his wife, and he and Mrs. Cooper and their daughter Susan had driven over in a gig to the Bedford farmhouse. *Precaution* purported to be written by an Englishman. It was a story of county society in England, and Cooper even went out of his way to compliment King George the Third and air the views of duchesses, countesses and earls. The novel reflected not only his reading but also the Anglophile atmosphere in which he had lived as a boy and continued to live, for the De Lanceys were notable Tories and the old-established Westchester families admired and resembled similar families in England. He had scarcely begun to think for himself, and, regarding the book as a trifle, he mirrored this Anglophile atmosphere in perfect good faith, although for the rest of his life he so bitterly resented these "craven and dependent feelings" towards England and the English. These feelings, however, oddly enough, were compatible with patriotism, even of the stoutest kind, such as old John Jay's, and the retired Chief Justice approved of the story. It was then that Cooper wrote *The Spy*, influenced no doubt by Scott, to retrieve the heroic past and the beauty of his country.

For Cooper, a patriot first, last and all the time, was ardently and eagerly interested in the history of the country and especially of his own beloved state of New York. When it came to historical stories, he was all ears, and he had spent many an evening at Scarsdale with an old Westchester farmer who remembered the days of the Hessians, the skinners and the cowboys. This region had been the "neutral ground" between the English in New York and the American forces to the northward, in the Highlands, the scenes that Cooper pictured in *The Spy*, and Westchester still abounded in hale old men, and this farmer, whom he entertained with cider and hickory nuts, had a vivid recollection also of the battle of White Plains. Cooper's mind overflowed with images of history, and he knew much of the state of New York by heart, for he had lived all over it, at Cooperstown, in Albany and now in this Westchester village with a view of the Sound. He knew Long Island also, for he bought a whaler at Sag Harbor and occasionally spent weeks in the town when she was in port, and he had been up and down the Hudson at least a hundred times. He was familiar with all its promontories, the cheerful, spacious villages that lined the stream, the country-seats, the windings and the islands. He recollected the old Dutch inns that once existed along the Mohawk, and the days when Albany was almost wholly Dutch. Most of the houses had crow-stepped gables at the time when he was a schoolboy there, while there were pews in St. Peter's church with canopies and coats-of-arms, like the Stuyvesant pew in St. Mark's-in-the-Bonwerie in New York. He knew the lovely New York lakes, Champlain, Cayuga, Oneida, Seneca, not to mention Scroon Lake, supposedly named by some old French scout in honour of Madame de Maintenon, the wife of Paul Scarron; and he might well have been at Ogdensburg when Thomas Moore wrote the *Canadian Boatsong* there. The town of Malone had come into being at about the same time as Cooperstown and was named for Edmund Malone, the Shakespearean scholar. As a young midshipman, Cooper had visited Lake Ontario, walking all the way through the forest, and he had wandered among the Thousand Islands, observing the wild life of the frontier. Game had been so common there that the innkeepers apologized for it, ashamed when they could not offer a traveller pork; for even stringy turnips and half-cooked cabbage were a joy after weeks of trout, pigeons, venison, salmon and ducks.

Well Cooper knew the "pleasure in the pathless woods," and well he knew the "rapture on the lonely shore," and everywhere he found traces of history,—he had even known one Hendrik Frey, a long-surviving friend of Sir William Johnson. He might have picked up other tales from a prosaic old hunter named Shipman, who wore leather stockings, at Cooperstown. There still stood near Albany one of the Van Rensselaer houses with loop-holes constructed for defence against the crafty redmen, and Cooper had often found the remains of blockhouses and scaling-ladders,—near the ruins of Fort Owego, for instance,—in the woods. He had visited the remains of Fort William Henry, with its bastion, moat and glacis, planted with corn, together with the road that ran straight through it, and he knew Fort George, which was fairly well preserved, and the relics of the batteries on French Mountain. When the water was still and the sunlight strong one saw on the bottom of Lake George the wrecks of Abercrombie's vessels lying, and then there was Ticonderoga, with its cluster of grey ruined walls, some of them sixty feet high, a great chateau. It was impressive on its promontory, but neighbouring farmers had carried away many tons of the cut stone to use in their own walls and houses.

The "old French war" was a vivid fact to Cooper, although he was too late himself to see very much of the Indians. As a boy he had met a few Oneidas, camping in the woods, where they made baskets and brooms to sell in the village, but they were dirty and degraded, as he recalled them. Later, on Long Island, he had visited a chief, a descendant of the ancient sachems, in his primitive wigwam, but he too had the sullen air that betrayed the disposition without the boldness of the savage. One had to travel beyond the Mississippi to see the fine traits of the Indians in their natural state, although deputations of the Western tribes occasionally visited the Eastern cities, Washington, Boston and New York. Cooper, in 1826, followed one of these parties to Washington,—it was composed of Pawnees and Sioux,—and he talked through an interpreter with a Pawnee chief who well deserved the name of a hero of the desert. Twenty-six or seven years old, this Peterlasharroo had gained renown as a warrior and a master in council, and Cooper was deeply impressed by his loftiness of bearing, his gravity and courtesy and the steadiness and boldness of his glance. With the view, as he said, of propitiating so powerful a chief, Cooper presented him with some peacock feathers, which he had arranged to produce the greatest effect, and he was pleased when the young man received them with a quiet smile, well as he knew the value of the gift. For the Pawnee purchased thirty horses with them. This young chief appeared in *The Prairie* as Hard-Heart, but Cooper had shown from the first how much he knew of the Indians, their endurance and their dignity as well as their cruelty and cunning. Those who knew the Indians best, Schoolcraft and Catlin, for instance, shared Cooper's admiration of their noble traits,— and men of imagination are the most realistic: Sam Houston admired the Indians too, and so did David Crockett and the Arkansas lawyer and poet Albert Pike.

Cooper was familiar with the "old French war," and he might have lived through the Revolution. He had learned as a boy to love Lafayette, whose intimate friend he became years later in Paris; and he remembered then the tale of the old soldier's torments, locked away in his Austrian prison at Olmütz. The schoolmaster at Cooperstown had fought under Lafayette himself, and the children had listened to his tales with reverence and awe. Lafayette had seized a place in American affections such as no man perhaps had ever possessed in a foreign land before. His devotion to the American cause was not only first in time but first as well in all its moral features, for he was impelled by the highest and most generous intentions, and where others had sought emoluments and rank he had sought only the field of battle. Cooper, like numberless other Americans, exulted in Lafayette's later successes and mourned over his reverses and his defeats, while, as for himself, he always felt very close to the Revolution and retained the political enthusiasm of those great days. Not at all a politician, he was politically minded almost more than he was a man of letters.

He knew the ocean, meanwhile, as well as the woods. For Cooper had spent three years in the navy and had previously served in the merchant marine, the usual way of acquiring naval training. His father had sent him off to sea soon after he was expelled from Yale,— supposedly for roping a donkey in the chair of his tutor,—and he had sailed at fifteen on the "Sterling" of Wiscasset for the most adventurous year of all his life. It left more traces than any other in his novels later, memories of the Spanish coast, Gibraltar and the Mediterranean as well as Falmouth, London and the Isle of Wight. The ship was stopped by a pirate felucca off the coast of Portugal, and English searching-parties impressed some of the seamen, incidents that might well have explained Cooper's lifelong dislike of the English, whose arrogant ways at sea he could never forgive. The captain relished his high spirits and taught him the arts of knotting and splicing, and Cooper saved from drowning a shipmate who fell overboard, with whom he roamed through the London streets and saw the Monument and St. Paul's. This was Ned Myers, who turned up thirty-five years later and visited his old comrade at Cooperstown, where day after day he related the story of his life. He was living at the time in Sailors' Snug Harbor, and Cooper later retold the story, a more or less literal narrative, *Ned Myers*, one of his happiest tales of the sea. It gave one a good idea of the life of a typical American sailor, for Ned, a Wiscasset boy, had sailed in more than seventy vessels, fought with pirates, fought in the navy and served on a South Sea whaler. He had smuggled tobacco on the Irish coast and opium in China and visited Morocco, Batavia, Rio and Malta, Limerick, Japan, the Spanish Main and Canton. Cooper, on their voyage together, had passed four times through the Straits of Dover in 1806 and 1807, and he knew all about them when he wrote *The Pilot*, which was based upon John Paul Jones's cruise in the "Ranger."

Then Cooper was a midshipman on Captain Lawrence's sloop, the "Wasp," and he also served on the "Chesapeake" with Lawrence, whose birthplace adjoined his in Burlington, New Jersey. He was sent to Lake Ontario with a detachment to supervise the building of a brig of war, and he joined an expedition that was dispatched to Niagara with his friend Lieutenant Melanchthon Woolsey. All his adventures in the service antedated 1812, and the war in which the navy won most of the battles, but they confirmed the pride that he felt in his country; for the brief history of the navy bristled with exploits that delighted the hearts of Americans and Cooper among them. The names of John Paul Jones, Decatur, Lawrence, Bainbridge and Perry were almost as famous as those of the national statesmen, and their manly bearing and frank demeanour charmed the American imagination as much as the tales of their heroism and their youth. Bainbridge had quelled a mutiny when he was eighteen years old, and Cooper liked to remember too that in the year 1800 the navy had carried the flag to Constantinople. America had scarcely been heard of in Turkey before. Because of their wide-ranging travels the American naval officers were unusually cultivated men, and Washington Irving shared the pride that led Cooper in later years to write a standard history of the navy. Irving wrote brief biographies of Lawrence, Burrows, Perry and Porter, while he was himself a friend of Decatur and Bainbridge, and he was happy when he thought of the War of 1812 because it had taught the country to know its own value. Cooper wrote another series of short lives of officers, some of whom gave him data for his history of the navy, and among his lifelong friends were Woolsey and Shubrick, to whom he dedicated two of his novels. He deplored the indifference of Americans to their navy and the small chance that existed for rising in it, for he saw it as a means of developing the mental independence of the country and bringing the states together in a common pride.

During these years of active service, Cooper amassed a prodigious knowledge of ships and the "sea dialect" and sailors, for although his first and deepest love was the wild frontier and the life of the woods he had a feeling for the sea that was lasting and profound. He really invented the sea-novel, for *The Pilot* was the first long story that pictured in detail the movement and handling of vessels, and he wrote at one time or another a dozen sea-tales, some of which were certainly among his best. *The Sea Lions* and *The Red Rover* were capital stories. Meanwhile, to keep his own hand in, he sailed his whaler at Sag Harbor,—up the Sound to Newport on one occasion,—as a few years later in New York he kept a sloop that was called the "Van Tromp" anchored near his house by a wharf on the river. He had his own felucca in Italy, and afterwards,

when he returned from Europe, he rigged a skiff with a lug-sail on Lake Otsego. Cooper, besides, had many of the traits of a sailor, a seadog of the old-fashioned kind for whom everything was black or white and who defended flogging at sea and whipping-posts at home. He had much in common with Captain Truck, the master of the ship "Montauk," decided, daring by nature, self-reliant, who was never more bent on following his own opinions than when everybody grumbled and opposed him. Cooper was like Captain Truck in his feeling that most men were fools, in his sangfroid and his scorn of what "folks would say," and he created superb sea-characters in the captain and in Long Tom Coffin, the freshwater sailor Jasper and Moses Marble. Their language, as he gave it, was inimitably racy, with its pungent nautical images and homely good sense, and he liked to bring their characters out in those wonderful talks at cross purposes in which, in several stories, he followed Shakespeare. Such was the talk, in *Home as Found*, between the two stubborn old mariners, the grave, ceremonious commodore and the dignified captain, who discussed philosophy as they fished and the laws of salt-water and fresh-water sailing, yet never came within hail of each other's real thoughts. Cooper delighted in these blind and ambiguous conversations that revealed the simplicity and integrity of worthies he admired. He felt that, however coarse a true sailor might be, there was never any vulgarity about him.

In Cooper's novels, from first to last, the sea was to rival the forest, and one might have said that Cooper's solution for all the problems of fiction was to take his readers on a voyage. At least, he did so frequently when he found himself in a tight place, just as he usually provided a beautiful girl and placed her in a position to be rescued. He had spent at sea the most susceptible years of his youth, and many of his young heroes followed the sea,—Mark Woolston and Miles Wallingford, for instance,—and he was almost always ready to oblige when his friends called for "more ship." He knew the terrors of the sea, yet it gladdened his heart, and the sailors' toast "sweethearts and wives" resounded in the novels in which he recorded his joy in everything that floated. One of his ships was "as tight as a bottle," another was "as neat as a mariner's musket," and he liked to dwell even on the cabins of the yacht-like packet-ships that plied between the hemispheres in increasing numbers. These cabins were lined with satinwood and bird's-eye maple, and little marble columns separated the rows of glittering panels of polished wood, and Cooper recalled the fine carpets that covered the floors, the sofas, the mirrors, the tables, even the piano. He loved to describe a ship with her sails loosened and her ensign streaming in the breeze or a chase on a bright day when everyone felt the pleasure of motion as the steady vessel raced with the combing seas. He was always ready with a reason for a chase, perhaps with a revenue-cutter or a sloop-of-war that pursued a packet over half the ocean, and these were the days when anything might happen on Captain Truck's "great prairie." There was nothing unusual in the fate of the ship "Montauk" in *Homeward Bound* that was plundered by the Bedouins on the African coast when the gale blew its masts off and drove it a thousand miles out of its course and it safely reached New York in spite of all. Cooper enjoyed describing, too, one of those fine, free, leisurely voyages, perhaps of a year or so, around the world, voyages that made men out of boys and abounded in shipwrecks and perilous adventures, such as Henry Mulford's race with the shark in the story called *Jack Tier*. Now, as in *Afloat and Ashore*, the voyagers discovered and christened an island, now they were cast away on a coral reef, or they put a volcano to good use and raised a garden in it, the feat of Mark Woolston in *The Crater*. There was nothing in these tales that might not have been as true as anything in the voyages of Captain Cook, while Cooper delighted in the homely details of the toilet of the sailors on the sabbath, for instance, drawing out of bags and chests their razors, soap and scissors. With his marked feeling for the sublime, he rose moreover now and then to moments of the noblest and most eloquent prose. Such were the descriptions of the icefields in *The Sea Lions*,—a tale of American sealers in antarctic waters,—the vast mass of floating mountains, generally of a spectral white, through which the mariners moved in an unknown sea. The walls, like ridges of the Alps, bowed and rocked and ground one another, stirred by the restless ocean, with a rushing sound, and sometimes a prodigious plunge as of a planet falling tossed the water over the heaving ramparts. The cliffs, half a league in length, with their arches and pinnacles and towers and columns, suggested the streets of some fantastic city that was floating in the sunlight in the sea, black here and there in certain lights and orange on the summits, throwing out gleams and hues of emerald and gold. There were many of these moving passages in the novels of Cooper, especially in the Leather-Stocking tales, although he could never have been called a master-craftsman. He was a rough-and-ready writer, hasty, frequently clumsy or pompous and "remarkably and especially inaccurate," as Poe observed, and yet, despite his "inattention to the minor morals of the Muse," his style, as a rule, was direct, energetic and effective. This was the case, at least, whenever his theme possessed him fully, when his interest, his feelings, his devotion were engaged and aroused.

On lakes and streams, as well as on the ocean, Cooper rejoiced in ships and boats. The motion of a canoe enchanted him as it passed like a feather over the foam of rapids. He had seen one that was thirty feet long safely descend Oswego Falls in the wilderness which he loved even more than the sea, that other world where men "breathed freely;" for Cooper, after all, was a

F. O. C. Darley illustration for Afloat and Ashore.

child of the forest and the frontier and the earliest of his impressions were his deepest and dearest. Before he established himself at Scarsdale, he had taken his wife to Cooperstown, driving in a gig through the forest on the corduroy roads, and there for three years the family lived in a house that he built near Otsego Hall beside the sylvan lake that glittered in the sun. Cooper, in his childhood, had heard wolves and panthers wailing and howling on winter nights as they ventured over the ice of the lake, and the footpaths round this "Glimmerglass" and the Fairy Spring and the Speaking Rocks were all compact of magical memories for him. In the lake stood the Otsego Rock where the tribes had resorted for council in order to make their treaties and bury their hatchets, and there one saw the shoal marked by rushes, where Floating Tom Hutter in *The Deerslayer* built his "castle." Near by rose the Silent Pine with its trunk branchless for a hundred feet before the foliage appeared in dark-green masses, clinging round the stem like wreaths of smoke. Cooper liked to think of the hunters who had lingered in these woods long years before his family had first appeared there. Even now at any moment one might see a majestic buck emerging from a thicket with stately step and pausing to quench its thirst in the clear water. In its repose and solitude, the lake, as it placidly mirrored the sky, with its dark setting of woods and the trees overhanging, was a haunting symbol for Cooper of the grandeur of the forest, sublime in the light of the moon, lovely by day. One heard the owl moaning there and the mourning notes of the whippoorwill, while at night the quavering call of the loon rose among the shadows and the fantastic forms of the surrounding hills. Cooper could never remember a time when he had not imagined there the former inhabitants of the woods, the Indians and the scouts, who had also listened to the rippling of the water, the sighing of the wind in the pines and the creaking of the branches on the trunks, the oaks and the pines and the creaking of the branches on the trunks.

The region of the Leather-Stocking tales was the southwestward facing angle that was formed by the junction of the Mohawk river and the Hudson, stretching as far as Lake Ontario, together with Lake George to the north, and Lake Otsego was the centre of this region for Cooper, although he knew most of its mountains and valleys by heart. He recalled the times of **The Pioneers**, when the settlement was new, the sugar-making and the sleighing in winter, the turkey-shoots at Christmas, and his fancy went back to the days of *Wyandotte* and the bustle of the building of the town. The settlers had drained the lake and planted their corn. They had made their own tools, constructed sleds and bridges, laid out their roads through the forest and built a sawmill, as in thousands of other hamlets on all the frontiers. Then Cooper evoked a still earlier day when the dark and interminable forest had scarcely as yet been disturbed by the struggles of men, when the youthful Natty Bumppo first beheld the Glimmerglass and met his friend Chingachgook at the rock. There Natty found the dwelling of the Hutters and the ark with the tamarack spar and the sail that had once been the topsail of an Albany sloop, and the "brilliant and singular beauty" of Judith appeared through the opening of the leaves with a smile for the Deerslayer in his canoe.

Cooper was possessed by the image of the tall, gaunt hunter, with his foxskin cap and shirt of forest green, with the knife in his girdle of wampum and his buckskin leggings, and a cycle of stories rose in his mind of which Natty was always the central figure, as the lake-strewn forest was the scene of the Deerslayer's exploits. The Deerslayer, the Pathfinder and Leather-Stocking were one and the same, and sometimes Natty also appeared as Hawkeye, the poet of the wilderness who loved to speak in favour of a friend and who never clung too eagerly and fondly to life. Wholly indifferent to any distinctions save those that were based on personal merit, with a natural faith that knew no subtleties of doctrine, he was the inseparable comrade of the Delaware chief, with whom he had lived so happily among the streams. Since they were boys the two had consorted together, fighting in company on Lake George, the Mohawk and Ontario, when Natty was a scout for the English in their battles with the French, and together they had marched on the flanks of the enemy, hunting for the army, providing it with beavers' tails, bears' hams, venison and trout. The swallows were not more certain to be on the wing than

they to be afoot when it was light, and no whine of the panther could cheat them, no whistle of the catbird, nor any other invention of the devilish Mingos. For no one was prompter or wiser with the cunning of the woods.

Now Cooper, in the course of thirty years, was to write thirty-three novels, as well as many books of other kinds. These novels were of all types, simple romances, tales of adventure, historical stories, satires, pictures of manners, and they varied in their degrees of merit as in the range of their characters and settings, which in the end proved to be very wide. Disregarding his tales of Europe, Cooper's scope was national,—as Charles Brockden Brown's had also been,—he was by no means a regional or sectional writer,—and he was successful, on the whole, in his portrayal of local types and the characteristic scenes of many regions. Captain Jack Lawton in **The Spy** was an admirably drawn Virginian, as the frank, manly Paul Hover was a Kentuckian to the life, while the Bush family from Tennessee savoured as strongly of their native world as the odious Deacon Pratt, the Long Island Yankee. One could even feel Louisiana in Inez in **The Prairie**, as one felt the Delaware valley in the past of Mark Woolston, and as one felt and saw Key West in the story of *Jack Tier* and Moravian Pennsylvania in the life of Ben Boden. All this,—for whatever the point might be worth,—was an indication of the range of Cooper's all-American imagination, as the character of Natty Bumppo was also all-American and might have been observed as well in the South or the West. For his "forest gifts" and frontier ways suggested equally Daniel Boone and Kennedy's Horse Shoe Robinson of South Carolina. Cooper was a multifarious author, but he was undoubtedly right in feeling that his Leather-Stocking tales would outlive the rest, although they shared with many another the pleasure in bravery, gallantry and courage,—"the ardent tones of generous youth,"—that was always Cooper's note. He delighted in the chivalrous rivalry of the captains in **The Sea Lions**, in the high courtesy and fortitude of his Indian braves, in the true freedom of the American borderer, honourable and fearless, in the valour of ingenious men contending with the sea. A noble nature shone through Cooper's novels, and, roughly written as most of them were, full of improbabilities, as rudely built as cabins of the pioneers, they lived very largely by virtue of this and the wonderful eye for the forest and the sea that made Cooper, as Balzac said, the master of literary landscape-painters. Like the sea-tales, these frontier romances were mostly stories of flight and pursuit, and they struck some deep ancestral chord in the hearts of men of the northern races who remembered as it were the primordial struggle of their forbears in the solitude and silence of the woods. Cooper deeply understood the passion for a solitary life that went with a feeling for the vastness and freshness of the forest and that sometimes bred elevated characters, steady as the pines, humble and grand at once, with head erect. Natty Bumppo was destined to remain the symbol of a moment of civilization, the dawn of the new American soul in a scene in which the European contended with savages, animals and primitive nature. Masculine, stoical, earnest and simple, ardent, loyal, just and a veritable American woodsman, in his habit, as he lived, Natty, leaning on his long rifle, was a type whom everyone recalled and a proof that an American could also be a sage and a saint.

James Grossman (essay date 1950)

SOURCE: "Chapter IX," in *James Fenimore Cooper*, Methuen & Co. Ltd., 1950, pp. 221-64.

[In the following essay, Grossman discusses Cooper's political views and the influence of European values on his writings.]

Cooper's literary career, beginning haphazardly without conscious preparation or plan and advancing rapidly to world fame, in its apparently eccentric course from the time of the European experience onward touches on almost every situation that can confront the American writer or that criticism insists on confronting him with. The questions so often argued since are thoroughly argued in Cooper's work and in contemporary criticism of it: whether an American writer expatriates himself and loses touch with his own country by living abroad; whether it is dangerous for his development to write on "foreign" subjects; the extent to which he should be influenced by popular opinion and, conversely, should try to influence it; his role in American civilization, and his duty both to represent and to create it.

Stated bluntly the questions seem unprofitable and unreal, but they have a historical reality. They are as old as American literature, and in fact largely preceded it. Before there was a national literature a critical attitude toward it, an anxious parental expectation of what it was to achieve, had been developed. The questions are significant not for the answers that we may give them now but for what they reveal about the demands that the nation was making of the American writer, and the strained relation that in consequence of these demands was to exist between him and his country.

In Cooper's day and for long afterward every question about American culture involved Europe, and it was the European trip that made Cooper self-consciously aware of the great American questions. The length of the trip itself presented a problem. Jefferson had said that an American could safely live abroad only five years. Cooper meant to stay away for no more than the allotted period but overstayed his leave. He returned out of step with his country; he doubted, however, that

he had fallen behind, as Jefferson said an American would, and suggested brashly that he had gone too far ahead alone. This may be a way of admitting that Europe had unfitted him for life in America, but he never regretted his European adventure. To the end of his life he defended the American artist's right of access to Europe as part of his heritage. It was a "provincial absurdity" for Americans to say that Thomas Cole's painting or even Washington Irving's writing had lost in originality after their European years. He insisted always that his own *Bravo*, which had analyzed European aristocracy, was in spirit the most American book he ever wrote.

Europe had made Cooper feel the need to write about the American democratic ideal and to adopt new forms for this purpose—the treatise, the pamphlet, the propaganda novel with the direct and often intrusive exposition of ideas. Cooper's theme in Europe, the superiority of American principles, became, after his return, the inferiority of American life. His countrymen failed to live up to the high standards which he had proclaimed were theirs. In defense of the ideal he denounced the actual as a fraud. The newspapers, largely under the control of the Bank of the United States, the self-appointed leaders of small-town life calling and manipulating "public" meetings, the provincial rich in the cities, were not the real America. He attacked them as usurpers who spoke in the country's name; but the usurpation was so broad that he frequently sounded as if he were attacking all American opinion and ultimately came close to doing so. The manufacture of public opinion by the few was no less undemocratic merely because it succeeded and brought the many around to their views; success only made the tyranny of opinion more complete. The liberalism of the 1830's during which he asserted the soundness of the great mass of the people gave way in his conservative last years to a struggle for democracy carried on against the people. According to Cooper, it was the masses and not he who had abandoned the democratic faith.

Cooper saw as a fundamental problem of democracy his own right to be different and on his own terms. It is hard to describe his position with any exactness, for in its defeat the very word that would most accurately define the difference that he asserted, "gentleman," has been erased from the language as a meaningful term. American democracy has at times gone about solving the problems of the various kinds of difference by glossing over them. In Cooper's own day, as he gleefully noted, such frank terms as "master" and "servant" were disappearing and their place was being taken by "boss" (the Dutch word for master) and "help" (surely a euphemistic understatement of the amount of work expected from the worker). The right of a gentleman to be different has been denied by denying the existence of gentlemen as a special class, just as, by much the same device, the rights of racial and religious minor-ities have been defended chiefly by denying that they are really different from the rest of the community.

Cooper was writing about American class manners and attitudes in the very period in which they were undergoing a profound change. The traditional rights of social position were being reduced to mere perquisites that might be gracefully offered to a man but which it was unbecoming for him to demand. The political revolution of Jacksonian democracy had brought about a revolution in social tone, more thoroughgoing in politics than elsewhere. The discovery was made—but not by the Jacksonians—that in the era of the common man it was politically astute for his leaders to appear to be common men. At almost the same time that Whig editors were attacking Cooper as an aristocrat who aped the style of an English lord and looked down on his fellow townsmen as peasants, the Whig party was inveighing against Martin Van Buren as the little aristocrat who drank champagne and used finger cups amid the royal splendor of the President's palace; its own candidate, William Henry Harrison, who it was hoped would restore the Bank of the United States, was presented successfully in 1840 as a simple man, happy in a log cabin with a barrel of hard cider. This triumph of "democratic" manners was for Cooper the triumph of the worst elements of the commercial classes. The honest observance of class distinctions and the honest description of social classes might help preserve political sanity and the distinction between true democracy and the bastard democracy of the demagogue. In the Anti-Rent novels Cooper seems nearly as indignant at the inaccurate description of the landlords as feudal aristocrats as he does at the attempt to take away their property. He was not a large landholder himself, but both he and they were victims of the same loose rhetoric. In his hatred, if not in his love, he was still guided by what he had always thought the standards of the true democrat.

The Whig myth of Fenimore Cooper—Dorothy Waples' happy phrase for the editors' composite picture of their adversary as a morbidly sensitive, embittered failure—is, as Miss Waples insisted, a gross distortion. Yet, normal though it was for Cooper to resent the attacks on him, there is something disconcerting in the elaborate publicness of his resentment, in his going so thoroughly into the minutiae of his quarrels, as if bent on immortalizing each moment of his anger. The genteel and the democratic tradition both agree—the one in the name of dignity, the other in that of good fellowship—that a man attacked, stoutly though he may defend himself, must pretend not to mind too much or too long.

Cooper was too obviously really hurt. He was a literal patriot, and beneath the excellent formal logic of the political philosopher and novelist of ideas there is always the illogic of love. Half a dozen Whig editors

were not the country—this is his political point—but his personal one is that his country, speaking through them, has rejected him. While he is discoursing on his country's faults and on the distance to be kept between himself and his countrymen, his aggrieved tone reveals his need for their affection.

There is nothing remarkable in the fact that the writer who denounces demands admiration. It was bound, however, to be denied Cooper for reasons which he himself had indicated: Americans of his day were accustomed to flattery from their fellow-Americans; and in a society that strove so hard to seem homogeneous, there was no place for an opposition from within—it was not the recognized function of a democrat to harry democracy.

Because his right to speak out was questioned, he insisted not only on the substance but on the appearance of opposition. He became as absorbed in the denunciatory role as in denunciation, but too frequently is not frank enough about it; only as Miles Wallingford does he generously give himself away and admit his honest pleasure as a self-appointed censor. The role which he typically assumed, often to the disadvantage of his modulated thought, may be described as that of the plain dealer, that blunt foe of hypocritical cant and friend of disagreeable truths. It is not too far from the editors' myth by which the warm, eager, social, hopelessly domestic Fenimore Cooper of private life, fond of his friends and good talk, had been transformed, for his contemporaries, into the legendary isolated misanthrope. Misanthropy and plain dealing are close to each other and can be taken as rough equivalents (as we can see by the fact that Molière's *Misanthrope* became *The Plain Dealer* on its adaptation into English by Wycherley). And at times Cooper seems to be almost cooperating with the editors in myth-making, to show that their version of his role is accurate. In refusing to join the Copyright Club, although believing in its objective, international copyright, he wrote to the club's secretary that he desired to do nothing for his country beyond his inescapable duty, paying his taxes.

Cooper was not withdrawing from American life in actuality; the letter to the Copyright Club may represent a moment of churlishness, and his true adherence is demonstrated by his continuing to write. But the subject of his writing was more and more his withdrawal in his imagination, his estrangement from the world he knows and in which he feels increasingly insecure. When, in his last wholly successful novel, *Satanstoe*, he imagines a hero secure in all of his relations to the world and certain of its affection, he has made him not an American like himself struggling between two worlds but a dependent colonial for whom there is but one. Cooper has not in his old age become the conventional conservative loving the past for its own sake as inevitably superior to the present. He has moved Corny back in time to escape not only the American present but America itself. In terms of national existence, past and present are remarkably alike. A grey disenchantment hangs over the beginnings of the nation in **Wyandotté** and **The Chainbearer**; if Cooper has become too disillusioned to see Utopia in the American future, he refuses with equal steadfastness to see it in the purely American past.

The instability and impermanence of American life, which Cooper in the last half of his career sees as endangering the gentleman's right to his rational enjoyments, the landowner's right to his property, and finally, in his last novel, the literal right to life itself, had been one of his themes in the years of his untroubled beginnings. His first worth-while novel, **The Spy**, is about a revolution, and his next, **The Pioneers**, is about the destruction of an older way of life by the coming of civilization. Even in his early works Cooper's finest awareness is of the victims of change and of the cruelty of the process. But he is not yet committed to seeing as evil the irresistible forces that make for change, and it is this uncommitted insight, which sees no more than the mere inevitability of life, that makes the persecuted and exiled Natty so great. With his most famous class of the dispossessed, his good Indians, Cooper succeeds not by sympathetic identification but by a pathetic fallacy which endows them with his own ability to accept their dispossession philosophically; and it is this capacity for acceptance that gives them their haunting improbable charm.

Cooper's untroubled detachment—so remarkable because he was himself one of the victims of American instability and his writing career was begun just after, perhaps because of, the loss of the family fortune which left him burdened with family debts—gives way to personal involvement only when he feels himself unjustly victimized. He may have been wrong in his feeling, may in fact have created the conspiracy against himself which he discovered and which soon by his efforts took on an objective reality. He was not, however, turning aside from his work. His creative energy burst forth amid his fiercest quarrels with the press. For all of its nagging byways, small folly is his own road, at once difficult and self-indulgent, to inaccessible truths. The sense of betrayal, so unbecoming in him personally, enriches the meaning of his work. It gives him, while he seems perversely bent on taking his stand against time itself, his sudden tragic glimpses that every present moment of living is in some form a treachery to the past.

He never found a wholly adequate symbol in which to concentrate his tragic vision, perhaps because in the depths of his nature his heart was cheerful, and the bitterness was on the surface, for all the world to see, in his mind. The vision remains scattered and fragmentary, distributed not quite impartially, among his

best and his poorest works, for his best, the Leather-Stocking Tales by which he was content to be remembered, do not have their full share. But to know his best well and to enjoy it fully, his other work, his very failures, must also be taken into the reckoning; for the gusto and enjoyment of life of which the best are so full are all the finer for a knowledge of their bitter price.

John P. McWilliams (essay date 1985)

SOURCE: "Red Satan: Cooper and the American Indian Epic," in *James Fenimore Cooper: New Critical Essays,* edited by Robert Clark, Vision and Barnes & Noble, 1985, pp. 143-61.

[*In the following essay, McWilliams contends that Cooper failed to employ the epic and romantic imagery that his contemporaries used to describe American Indians.*]

Americans who first conceived of heroic historical romance about the American Indian may have lacked facts about the red man, but they were familiar with conflicting preconceptions of him. Cooper, Bird, and Simms had all read historical sources which portrayed Indians as Homeric warriors living on in the American forest. They were also drawn in varying degrees to the Enlightenment belief that the red man had been Nature's noble savage, Man in all his unspoiled virtue. To a generation raised on Homer and Milton, yet exposed to the continuing demand for an American epic in verse or prose, these conflicting images suggested usable literary parallels. To imagine the Indian as hard, solitary, unyielding, aging and doomed (Hector, Achilles, Turnus, Satan) would prompt romancers and historians to create the Big Serpent, Magua, Mahtoree, Sanutee and Pontiac. To imagine the Indian as graceful, generous, pliable, young and equally doomed (Apollo, Patroclus, Achates, Chactas) would lead the same writers to create Uncas, Hard Heart and Occonestoga. Although these two models of Indian heroism were often to appear as separate characters within one work, the way in which the romancer shaped them became a crucial measure of his attitude, not only toward the American Indian, but toward the nature of heroism in the New World.

Cadwallader Colden's 'Introduction' to his widely read *History of The Five Indian Nations* (1727) is clear testimony to the power of the Homeric lens. Familiar with the red man at treaty signings, but not in the forest, Colden writes of councils of chieftains, feasts, war songs, rites of hospitality, games and ceremonial burials. Again and again he likens Indians who practice these customs to the peoples of heroic poetry. The red man's willingness to die for his nation exalts him to heroic stature: 'None of the greatest Roman Heroes have discovered a greater love to their Country or a greater Contempt for Death, than these people called Barbarians have done.' Indian ceremonies of convening prompt Colden to assert that 'all their extraordinary visits are accompanied with giving and receiving Presents of some Value; as we learn likewise from Homer was the practice in Old times.' The most telling sign of Colden's inability to perceive Indians apart from *The Iliad* is his discussion of the Indian oratory heard in war councils. Although Colden admits he is 'ignorant of their language,' he praises the eloquence of Indian speech by asserting 'the same was practised by Homer's Heroes.'

By the 1780s the notion of noble savagery had blurred Colden's rather one-dimensional view. The five-month journey Chateaubriand made through America in 1791 was motivated, he later insisted, by a desire to gather materials for his epic on American Indians, *Les Natchez:* 'J'etois encore très jeune lorsque je conçus l'idée de faire *l'epopée de l'homme de la nature*, ou de peindre les moeurs des sauvages.' The enormously popular prose poems which resulted from this trip, *Atala* (1802) and *Renée* (1803), portray heroic Indians as gentle, disaffected philosophers of the simple way, who almost never seem to have to engage in killing.

The rapidity with which this view of the red man was welcomed in America is apparent as early as Sarah Wentworth Morton's four-canto poem, *Ouabi: or the Virtues of Nature* (1790). Mrs. Morton's title hero at first seems a gentle man of Nature, loving to his wife and protective of his tribe, a figure 'form'd by Nature's hand divine / Whose naked limbs the sculptor's art defied'. As soon as Ouabi appears on the battlefield, however, he hardens into the requisite Homeric stature:

> Thus before Illion's heav'n-defended towers
> Her godlike Hector rais'd his crimson'd arm;
> Thus great *Atrides* led the Grecian powers,
> And stern Achilles bid the battle storm.

Mrs. Morton, who calls herself, 'Philenia, a lady of Boston,' evidently remained discomfited by her red Achillean hero. At the poem's end, she arranges for Ouabi to die nobly in battle, relinquishing his gentle wife to an adopted white tribesman, and thereby enabling the softer red virtues to live on into the future.

Despite his calculated bonhomie, Washington Irving was similarly troubled by the issue of Indian heroism. His two essays, 'Traits of Indian Character' and 'Philip of Pokanoket' describe New England's oppressed seventeenth-century Indians as 'a band of untaught native heroes . . . worthy of an age of poetry'; 'No hero of ancient or modern days can surpass the Indian in his lofty contempt of death.' When these essays were as-

similated into *The Sketch Book,* their firm accusatory tone, their sense of a lost heroic world, jarred tellingly amid the pretentious modesty of that genial sketchist, Geoffrey Crayon. And yet, Irving was not prepared to embrace the red values he seemed to be condoning. Regretting that the Indian's primitive virtues are still unsung, Irving seems to call for an American Scott to write a *Lay of the Last Minstrel* about our fast-disappearing Indians. Almost immediately, however, Irving compromises the value of courageous resistance by castigating primitivist poets and romancers as sentimental idealists: 'Thus artificially excited, courage has arisen to an extraordinary and factitious degree heroism'.

The more the Indian resembled a Homeric warrior, the more clearly American writers could be sure that their land had known an heroic age. The price of having had an heroic culture, however, was accepting the dignity of the Indian's presumably barbarous values. In 1824 Harvard Professor Edward Everett, who had long been anticipating an heroic American literature, developed 'a comparison of the heroic fathers of Greece with the natives of our woods'. Intent upon proving the Homeric stature of the red man, Everett offered the following evidence:

> The ascendancy acquired by personal prowess independent of any official rank, the nature of the authority of the chief, the priestly character, the style of hospitality in which the hero slays the animal and cooks the food, the delicacy with which the stranger is feasted before his errand is inquired for, the honor in which thieving is held, and numerous other points will suggest themselves to the curious inquirer, in which the heroic life reappears in our western forests.

The single word 'thieving' here taints our impression of epic heroism by its inference of savage immorality. Everett's only hope for extricating himself from this tonal inconsistency is to claim that 'barbarism, like civilization, has its degrees'.

Everett's comparison ends with a sentence which, for a Professor of Greek who revered *The Iliad*, is a bizarre testimony to his culture's divided images of savage identity:

> Nations who must be called barbarous, like the Mexicans, have carried some human improvements to a point unknown in civilized countries; and yet the peasant in civilized countries possesses some points of superiority over any hero of the Iliad, or Inca of Peru. Though we think, therefore, the heroic life of Greece will bear a comparison with the life of our Northern American savages, inasmuch as both fall under the class of *barbarous;* yet the Agamemnons and Hectors are certainly before the Redjackets and Tecumsehs; whether they are before the Logans would bear an argument.

Although Logan might even be as great a hero as Hector, Everett would have us believe that both are somehow inferior to the civilized peasant who, in other equally unspecified ways. does not participate in the improvements of barbarous cultures!

In spite of his shaky logic, Everett is attempting to resolve the problem of assessing the savage hero by the same device used in imaginative literature—the gradation of barbarous qualities among a range of Indian characters. The Indian as noble savage would prove to be especially useful because he humanized the harshly stoic grandeur of the fighting chieftain. Celario outlives Ouabi, Yamoyden's gentleness balances King Philip's rage. the memory of Uncas seems to outlive the memory of Magua. Matiwan's humanity relieves Sanutee's intransigence, and so forth. Although the Roman chief usually remains the dominant model of the heroic Indian, the doubling of his image with the noble savage heightens elegiac regret while it conveniently assuages the reader's fear.

The activating call for an American heroic literature about the Indian occurred in consecutive articles in the 1815 issue of the *North American Review*. During the journal's ardently nationalistic first year, editor William Tudor solicited from Walter Channing an essay which would have the blunt title 'Reflections on the Literary Delinquency of America'. Joel Barlow's would-be epic poem *The Columbiad* (1807) had evidently convinced Channing that the great American work could not now be written about so recent and so familiar a topic as the American Revolution:

> In the most elevated walk of the muses, the Epick, we cannot hope much distinction [*sic*]. . . . We live in the same age; we are too well acquainted with what has been, and is, among us, to trust to the imagination. It would be an 'old story' to our criticks, for the events transpired yesterday, and some of our oldest heroes are not yet dead.

Convinced that epic literature can only concern the distant past, Channing calls for a complete, celebratory history of American peoples, a work so comprehensive that it vaguely anticipates the heroic histories of Bancroft, Prescott and Parkman.

The renewed hope of Channing's article suited Tudor's purpose exactly. In his Harvard Phi Beta Kappa address of 1815, Tudor had recently reached the same conclusion about the failure of American epic literature, though he had proposed a markedly different solution. Offering his own address as the lead article in the November 1815 issue, Tudor placed Channing's essay after his in a complementary but subordinate position. Like Channing, Tudor begins by attacking the cliché that America must have a verse epic on the founding fathers:

> The American Revolution may some centuries hence become a fit and fruitful subject for an heroick poem; when ages will have consecrated its principles, and all remembrance of party feuds and passions, shall have been obliterated; when the inferiour actors and events will have been levelled by time, and a few memorable actions and immortal names shall remain.

Tudor, however, has no interest either in the gradual winnowing of the true Revolutionary hero, or in trying to prove that Washington could be convincingly decked out in Virgilian clothing Preferring the remote past, Tudor insists that the wars between the Five Nations and the Algonquins, together with the wars between the French and the English, constitute the heroic subject now pertinent and possible for American writers. It is the Indian, not the Revolutionary gentleman, who 'possessed so many traits in common with some of the nations of antiquity, that they perhaps exhibit the counterpart of what the Greeks were in the heroick ages'.

Tudor draws up a kind of literary prospectus specifying the traits common to Greeks and Indians: martial codes of honour, solitary and exalted heroes, feasts and games, eloquence in tribal council, a pantheon of nature deities, and the virtues of 'hospitality, reverence to age, unalterable constancy in friendship'. An American writer would be historically accurate if he conceived of Indian eloquence according to the Homeric pattern:

> The speeches given by Homer to the Characters in the Iliad and Odyssey form some of the finest passages in those poems. The speeches of the Indians only want similar embellishment, to excite admiration.

Responding to the romantic affinity for the Natural Sublime, Tudor proclaims that the American Indian epic should contain word paintings of our unspoiled grandeur—particularly 'the numerous waterfalls, and 'the enchanting beauty of Lake George'. Episodic adventures similar to the tenth Iliad and the ninth Aeneid should be developed in order to enliven the narrative pace ('These episodes are two of the finest in these immortal Epicks, yet it is only to the genius of Homer and Virgil, that they are indebted for more than may be found in several Indian adventures'). Although Walter Scott is not mentioned by name, his heroic verse romances surely prompted Tudor to assert that 'the actions of these people in war had a strong character of wildness and romance; their preparations for it, and celebrations of triumph, were highly picturesque'.

Although Tudor avoids specific consideration of genre, he seems to be conceiving of an historical romance in verse which would recount the deeds of the French and Indian War around Lake George, and end with a 'prophetick vision' of the Indian's demise. Tudor's

H. M. Brock illustration for The Last of the Mohicans.

refusal to restrict the medium to poetry was timely and prescient, because the delivery of his address shortly followed the publication of *Waverley.* Whether Tudor privately had any firm conception of genre or not, his address provides a crucial transition in American literary history. Without the model of heroic literature he somewhat ingenuously offered, the Indian romances of Cooper and Simms would perhaps have developed both later and differently.

'Funeral Fires'

The author of **The Last of the Mohicans** was clearly never deterred by the possibility that an heroic romance about the American Indian should be written in verse by any aged minstrel, red or white. In his tetchy review of Lockhart's *Life of Sir Walter Scott,* Cooper was to contend that Scott's great achievement as a writer had been that 'he raised the novel, as near as might be, to the dignity of the epic.' The epic might remain the highest of forms, but the novel was the only genre through which contemporaries could approximate it. Nor was Cooper disposed to be timid in suggesting that America's one trace of an heroic culture might have passed away with the last warriors of a red tribe. As early as **The Pioneers** (1823), Cooper's

approving view of America's expanding settlements had been qualified by condescension toward the gaucheries of middle class progress. In **The Redskins** (1846), Cooper's gentlemanly narrator, Hugh Littlepage, offers a passing slight upon the pretensions of old Albany's new rival, Troy:

I wonder the Trojan who first thought of playing this travestie on Homer, did not think of calling the place Troyville or Troyborough! That would have been semi-American, at least, whereas the present appellation is so purely classical! It is impossible to walk through the streets of this neat and flourishing town, which already counts its twenty thousand souls, and not have the images of Achilles and Hector, and Priam, and Hecuba, pressing on the imagination a little uncomfortably. Had the place been called Try, the name might have been a sensible one.

Like Fisher Ames and James Russell Lowell, Cooper was sufficiently appreciative of the inner spirit of *The Iliad* to realize how ill-suited it was to a commercial, middle-class democracy. When the children of the Templeton Academy botch their scansion of Virgil, their ineptitude nicely complements a passage from Cooper's letter to his onetime Yale professor, Benjamin Silliman. After jokingly admitting that he had 'never studied but *one* regular [i.e. Greek] lesson in Homer', Cooper promptly added that he had studied *The Iliad* in 'the latin translation which I read as easily as English'. The probable exaggeration in this statement is not as important as Cooper's desire to have it believed.

If American society truly were as impoverished in ancestral legend and human variety as Cooper claimed in **Notions of the Americans,** then the dying Indian tribes of the eighteenth century could provide the colour and figurative language of poetry. Poetry, in turn, was the *sine qua non* of romantic fiction. In his 1831 Preface to **The Last of the Mohicans,** Cooper asserts 'the business of a writer of fiction is to approach, as nearly as his powers will allow, to poetry.' When Cooper wrote the 1850 preface to the Leatherstocking series, he ended with a paragraph that suggests how the conjunction of these two ideas had led him to attempt (with apologies to Henry Fielding) a tragic-epic-poem in prose:

It is the privilege of all writers of fiction, more particularly when their works aspire to the elevation of romances, to present the beau-ideal of their characters to the reader. This it is which constitutes poetry, and to suppose the red man is to be represented only in the squalid misery or in the degraded moral state that certainly more or less belongs to his condition, is, we apprehend, taking a very narrow view of an author's privileges. Such criticism would have deprived the world of even Homer.

Throughout the 1850 Preface, the phrase 'elevation of romance' is linked with characterizations of the Indians and of the heroic Leatherstocking, who in many ways resembles them. Homer, the only author named in the preface, provides its closing word.

As soon as Hawkeye appears in *The Last of the Mohicans,* Cooper endows him with the knowledge that the days of oral transmission of heroic legend are fading fast:

> I am willing to own that my people have many ways of which, as an honest man, I can't approve. It is one of their customs to write in books what they have done and seen, instead of telling them in their villages, where the lie can be given to the face of a cowardly boaster, and the brave soldier can call on his friends to witness for the truth of his words. In consequence of his bad fashion, a man who is too conscientious to misspend his days among the women, in learning the names of black marks, may never hear of the deeds of his fathers, nor feel a pride in striving to outdo them.

Cooper's own 'black marks' are, of course, the only means by which Hawkeye's complaint against written language can be preserved. Everything that troubles Hawkeye about the removal of white legends from cultural currency becomes many times aggravated when applied to the tribal histories of the Indians, whose oral legends, even if extant in 1757, let alone 1826, have been distorted in translation. Throughout the novel, Hawkeye tells only two oral lays, which concern white soldiers' battle exploits around the Bloody Pond and the blockhouse. From Heckewelder's *Account,* if nowhere else, Cooper had become familiar with the general nature of Indian oral heroic legends, yet he never allows his Indians to tell or invent one. Instead, the void in oral epic legend is filled with the matter of medieval romance. Around the councils and battle scenes which comprise the epic substance of *The Last of the Mohicans,* Cooper fashions escape and pursuit adventures in which the chivalry of rescuing distressed maidens serves as the unifying motif. By thus adapting the captivity narrative for purposes of historical romance, Cooper found a workable, highly popular compromise which avoids patent fakery of Indian legends (Chateaubriand) at the risk of trivializing the stature of his heroes.

The problems of generic adaptation seem to have troubled Cooper less than the dilemma of approving a practicable heroic code. The antebellum American romancer who would find an epic history in the Indian had to ascribe heroic qualities to a race then being dispossessed and killed by the very people who would read his book. To depict the Indian as an inhuman savage lusting to scalp white maidens would be historically indefensible and would ultimately diminish the achievement of conquest—as the hopefully 'epic' po-

ems of Daniel Bryan and James K. Paulding had sadly shown. But to depict the Indian as an aged stoic hero or a noble savage would implicitly deny the justice of the continuing March of Civilization. Throughout the *Leatherstocking Tales,* Cooper would pursue this problem as an issue of daily conduct, as well as of historical displacement. How far could an enlightened author, bent on the *beau idéal* of romance, excuse the 'virtues' of retaliatory justice (scalping, killing in cold blood) and of stoic endurance (sadomasochistic torture scenes) on the relativistic grounds that these were the norms of courage for an heroic people defending their own lands?

The extraordinarily complex and intricate narrative of *The Last of the Mohicans* rests upon a simple symmetrical arrangement of sections:

(1) Exposition (chapters 1-4).
(2) Battle around Glenn's Falls (5-9).
(3) Cora and Alice captured by Magua: Captivity Narrative (10-14).
(4) Fall of Fort William Henry (15-17). End of Volume I.
(5) Cora and Alice recaptured by Magua; Captivity Narrative (18-22).
(6) Rescues of Alice, Uncas and Cora (23-30).
(7) Battles between Delawares and Hurons, Uncas and Magua (31-32).
(8) Denouement, funeral ceremonies for Uncas (33). End of Volume II.

After the escape and pursuit sequences, the narrative of each volume is resolved in a climactic military action. At the end of the first volume, the fall of Fort William Henry, prefaced with epigraphs from Gray's 'The Bard', reveals white principles of military honour through a panoramic rendering of an historical event. At the end of the second volume, the victory of the Delawares over the Hurons, prefaced with epigraphs from Pope's *Iliad,* demonstrates red war codes as they are practiced in a wholly imagined combat. Only by comparing the two battles do the full complexities of deciding upon a code that is both heroic and morally honourable clearly emerge.

In his first paragraph, Cooper emphasizes that his subject is anything but a celebration of the founding of a western empire. The French and the English, 'in quest of an opportunity to exhibit their courage', have learned to make an 'inroad' upon any 'lovely' and 'secret place' in the forest. In the context of international politics, such intrusions serve only to 'uphold the cold and selfish policy of the distant monarchs of Europe'. Over the entire narrative Cooper casts a perspective of historical futility by remarking

> the incidents we shall attempt to relate occurred during the third year of the war which England and

France last waged for the possession of a country that neither was destined to retain.

Only within this controlling sense of overall historical doom, so like *The Iliad,* are we allowed to appreciate the momentary heroics shown on battlefields or during forest rescues.

Throughout the antebellum era, the presumably humanitarian if not Christian conduct of the white man remained the crucial justification for dispossession of the red man. Nostalgia for the demise of Indian virtues could readily be indulged so long as the white man illustrated his ethical superiority. Unfortunately, none of Cooper's European military commanders conducts himself with the needed combination of integrity and success. General Webb's refusal to send reinforcements is a self-protective cowardice far worse than the flight from battle of the Huron named Reed-That-Bends, who welcomes his own death after he has been ostracized from his tribe. Duncan Heyward may marry Cooper's fair heroine, but he proves so incompetent in the woods that Hawkeye finally tells him that he could best assist by remaining silent in the rear. Although the commanding British officer who is present, Colonel Munro, has the requisite integrity and courage for heroic stature, he proves to be so victimized by chance disadvantages, by the disloyalty of Webb, and by the treacheries of his environs, that he withdraws from the wilderness a beaten, half-senile man.

The hypocrisy of white pretension to ethical superiority is the controlling theme of Cooper's rendering of the fall of Fort William Henry. After introducing the Marquis de Montcalm as the epitome of refined European gentility, Cooper pictures him offering Munro terms for bloodless surrender which are honourable according to white, but not red, war codes. Because Montcalm then stands apathetically by while his 2,000 Huron mercenaries slaughter every English person they can reach, including women and children, Montcalm's deceit seems the most dishonourable form of barbarism. Intending to qualify the popular memory of Montcalm as a man who 'died like a hero on the plains of Abraham', Cooper asserts that Montcalm was 'deficient in that moral courage without which no man can be truly great'. By selecting Chapter 17's epigraph from 'The Bard' ('Weave we the woof. The thread is spun / The Web is wove. The work is done') Cooper likens the fall of the fort to the atrocities through which Christian King Edward I conquered the people of Wales. An analogy less flattering to civilization's march might be difficult to find.

Indian heroic codes prove to be no more commendable than white. However often Hawkeye may excuse Indian scalping and Indian tortures because they are red 'gifts', Cooper always describes them with fascinated disgust. The principle of retaliatory justice may moti-vate Magua, Chingachgook and Uncas to perform remarkable feats of tracking and endurance, but the principle itself leads only to ever-increasing carnage. Montcalm's cowardice causes the slaughter at Fort William Henry, but the most graphic brutalities, from the dashing of a baby's head against a rock, to the scalping of the wounded, are committed by red men. Inflamed by the sight of blood, Cooper's Hurons far outdo Achilles in their berserk butchery; we are told that 'many of them even kneeled to the earth and drank freely, exultingly, hellishly, of the crimson tide'.

The climactic battle of the second volume proves to be the most hollow of triumphs. Because both the Hurons and the Delawares are being used as pawns in an inter-imperial struggle, their fighting against one another, as Magua knows, can only hasten their destruction while it underscores their ignorance. Although the Delawares may have routed the Hurons, the fighting in the woods is confused, desultory, historically insignificant and little like the hand-to-hand confrontations at the end of *The Iliad* and *The Aeneid.* Cora is stabbed, for little apparent purpose, by one of Magua's followers; Magua stabs Uncas in the back because of the frustration of losing his captive; Hawkeye shoots Magua when Magua is immobile and exposed. Like both Achilles and Aeneas, Uncas, Magua and Hawkeye attack their worst enemy to avenge a fallen friend, but all three men attack in a manner that avoids the risk of equal combat. The irony of the Delawares' triumph is emphasized by the epigraph Cooper chooses from Kalchas's prophecy in book one of *The Iliad*:

> But plague shall spread, and funeral fires increase
> Till the great King, without a ransom paid,
> To her own Chrysa send the black-eyed maid.

Lest the reader forget the cost of the Delawares' victory, Cooper thus darkens their triumph by a reminder of the many deaths caused by the demeaning abducting and ransoming of women (Briseis by Agamemnon, Cora by Magua).

The contrast Cooper establishes between his gentle noble savage (Uncas) and his brutal Satanic villain (Magua) proves not to be so total as it first appears. Deprived of their due status as tribal leaders, both Uncas and Magua regain command before the climactic battle. Magua's eloquent accusations of white greed and white deceit merely confirm, in far more inflammatory language, the conclusions reached by Chingachgook, Hawkeye and a tellingly silent Uncas in Chapter 2. Whereas Milton's Satan had sought vengeance against God because of his limit-defying pride, Cooper's Magua ('the Prince of Darkness') seeks vengeance against the white race because of the tangible injustice done him by Colonel Munro. Uncas and Magua, both of them wronged, and both pursuing vengeance, must be killed together at the tale's conclusion. The red devil who would turn inter-tribal war into genocidal war cannot remain a continuing forest force. But the noble Apollonian hero whose fine feelings 'elevated him far above the intelligence, and advanced him probably centuries before the practices of his nation' cannot be allowed to survive either. Whereas Magua would pose a threat to white conquest through force and cunning, Uncas would challenge white superiority through simple human example.

The determining differences between Magua and Uncas have little to do with their tribal loyalties, their prowess or their courage. Unlike Magua, Uncas has no personal motive for feeling vengeance toward the white man. Uncas's silent acceptance of white authority has its counterpart in his deference to white women. Whereas Uncas even outdoes Duncan Heyward in his chivalrous regard for Alice and Cora, Magua is endowed with the presumably red trait of treating women as serviceable beasts. In spite of the taboo against miscegenation, Uncas proves capable of genuinely loving Cora. Magua's consummate villainy (a villainy which determines the plot) is his decision to abduct Cora three separate times, not primarily to exact vengeance upon Munro, but to satisfy his own conveniently unexplained lust. The protective reverence which the white man and the exceptional 'white' Indian pay to white women thus serves as Cooper's only sure means of upholding the presumed moral superiority of his own 'civilized' and conquering race.

The concluding scene of *The Last of the Mohicans*, surely the finest chapter of fiction any American had yet written, was clearly influenced by the twenty-fourth book of *The Iliad*. The lamentations of Andromache, Hecuba and Helen over the body of Hector, like the Delaware maidens' lamentations over the body of Uncas, precede the climactic short laments of those aged father-kings, Chingachgook and Priam, who know that their nation's demise is one with their son's death. The images of fire with which *The Iliad* closes, a fire that envelops Greek and Trojan, Achilles as well as Hector, conveys the same sense of impending conflagration we find in Tamenund's words: 'It is enough. Go, children of the Lenape, the anger of the Manitou is not done'. Just as Cooper was the first American clearly to recognize that prose was the genre for a national heroic literature, so he was the first to recognize that the death of brave men and the end of an heroic age, rather than any panegyric of republican empire, are the true measure of the epic art.

However similar these endings may be in deed and in spirit, the characters of the two mourned heroes differ markedly. Uncas never boasts of his search for personal battle glory, nor does Hector often display Uncas's gentleness and grace. Neither Chingachgook nor Magua can serve as the Indian for whom white readers could

mourn. Wholly committed to red values, these two older chieftains deeply resent the red man's dispossession. Political enemies though they may be, Magua and the Big Serpent are similar in their racial ethos; when they are joined in single combat, Cooper even remarks that 'the swift evolutions of the combatants seemed to incorporate their bodies into one'. The warrior to be elegized must rather be the younger red man who most closely approximates, and defers to, the white man's supposed moral sensitivity. Through Uncas's death, the best of Indian qualities can thus be mourned and removed, allowing his less flexible father to remain, a figure of real but lesser challenge to the injustice of dispossession.

Because neither the red man nor the white man practices a code that is both moral and heroic, the closing paragraphs of the novel offer us an alternative that combines yet supersedes them both. The bond between the Big Serpent and Hawkeye, formed over the body of Uncas and beyond the incursions of civilization, is based upon absolute honesty, a mastery of forest skills, and a wordless sense for the divinity of nature. Their heroic life can only be maintained, not by leading either of their peoples, but by separating themselves from any culture whatsoever. The most admirable men of America's heroic age are thus held forth, not as examples for backwoodsmen and Indians to imitate, but as exceptions who represent a promise never fulfilled. The Big Serpent and Hawkeye, like many a semi-divine pair in epic poetry (Gilgamesh and Enkidu, Achilles and Patroclus, Beowulf and Wiglaf, Roland and Oliver) seem to have the ability to perform anything except to escape suffering and mortality. Unlike every one of these pairs of heroes, however, Hawkeye and the Big Serpent represent no community, lead no men, and defend no civilization. Embodying the unrealized potential of two passing cultures, they are nothing more, but nothing less, than the last of their several kinds. In the oldest of extant epics, Gilgamesh forms his abiding bond with Enkidu (a dark skinned 'hunter' from the wilderness) and they undertake adventurous tasks together. Whereas Gilgamesh finally returns to the city of Uruk to guard the walls he has built, Leatherstocking's heroism has been forever defined by his departure from the compromised civilization of Templeton.

By the time Cooper had completed all five tales, the importance of the red man's Greek-like heroism had receded, the bond between the Big Serpent and Hawkeye had become increasingly central, and Leatherstocking had finally become the acknowledged 'hero' of the entire series. At no time, however, did Cooper suggest that Leatherstocking had solved the problem of how to be a Christian hero in the wilderness. In *The Last of the Mohicans*, Cooper twice refers to the Roman worship of household gods in order to convey the acuity of the dilemma. When Magua urges his Hurons to kill Uncas in order to fulfil a tribal custom 'to sacrifice a victim to the *manes* of their countrymen', Cooper admits that Magua is factually correct, but then condemns him for having 'lost every vestige of humanity in a wish for revenge'. Shortly thereafter, the psalmodist David Gamut, convinced that unresisting death is better than 'the damnable principle of revenge', tells Hawkeye 'Should I fall, . . . seek no victims to my *manes,* but rather forgive my destroyers'. Caught between Christian principle and forest necessity, Hawkeye replies with the fullest account he ever gives of his forest code:

> There is a principle in that . . . different from the law of the woods; and yet it is fair and noble to reflect upon. . . . It is what I would wish to practice myself, as one without a cross of blood, though it is not always easy to deal with an Indian as you would with a fellow Christian. God bless you, friend; I do believe your scent is not greatly wrong, when the matter is duly considered, and keeping eternity before the eyes, though much depends on the natural gifts and the force of temptation.

Hawkeye's statement begins confidently, but soon breaks down into hesitant qualifications and appeals both to 'gifts' and to human weaknesses. Although he may denounce revenge and bloodshed, Hawkeye knows that he must always be ready to fire first in self-protection. The heroism of Cooper's 'magnificent moral hermaphrodite' clearly depends on trying to remain Christian in principle, while surviving by un-Christian, if not Indian, displays of deadly prowess.

The few demurrers from the praise with which reviewers greeted **The Last of the Mohicans** reflect a failure to concede that fiction might incorporate the romance and the epic. Acute though W. H. Gardiner had been in assessing **The Spy**, he objected to the presumably breathless pace of Cooper's adventure sequences because even a frontier novel should contain 'a little quiet domestic life'. Lewis Cass's accusation that Cooper's Indians were 'of the school of Heckewelder and not of the school of nature' was based upon the constricting premise that no author should imagine red men as they might have been during their irrecoverable forest lives. Two years later, Grenville Mellon sharpened the terms of Cass's attack into a critical absurdity:

> The Indian chieftain is the first character upon the canvass or the carpet; in active scene or still one, he is the nucleus of the whole affair; and in almost every case is singularly blessed in some dark-eyed child, whose complexion is made sufficiently white for the lightest hero. This bronze noble of nature, is then made to talk like Ossian for whole pages, and measure out hexameters, as though he had been practicing for a poetic prize.

Mellon's probably deliberate conflation of Homer's metric with Macpherson's prose, like his misleading

inferences about Cora and Uncas, are of small importance. His blinding error was his refusal to admit either that Indian life might have shared the spirit of the heroic age, or that prose fiction could absorb the spirit of heroic poetry. **The Last of the Mohicans** had already brought both possibilities to convincing realization.

Russell Kirk (essay date 1987)

SOURCE: "Liberal Conservatives: Macaulay, Cooper, Tocqueville," in *The Conservative Mind: From Burke to Eliot,* revised edition, Regnery Books, 1987, pp. 185-204.

[*In the following excerpt, Kirk discusses Cooper's political views, especially how his aristocratic sympathies shaped his views on democracy.*]

> In Democracies there is a besetting disposition to make publick opinion stronger than the law. This is the particular form in which tyranny exhibits itself in a popular government; for wherever there is power, there will be found a disposition to abuse it. Whoever opposes the interests, or wishes of the publick, however right in principle, or justifiable by circumstances, finds little sympathy; for, in a democracy, resisting the wishes of the many, is resisting the sovereign, in his caprices. Every good citizen is bound to separate this influence of his private feelings from his publick duties, and to take heed that, while pretending to be struggling for liberty, because contending for the advantage of the greatest number, he is not helping despotism. The most insinuating and dangerous form in which oppression can overshadow a community is that of popular sway.
>
> —Cooper, *The American Democrat*

Anyone who endeavors to trace the parallel development of ideas in Europe and in America must feel sometimes that he is treating of superficial resemblances; that the American mind was hardly more than the mirror of unique social circumstances; and that the pale ghost of European civilization was as powerless to alter the course of thought in America as the chorus was impotent to arrest the action in a Sophoclean drama. But Ortega y Gasset, that urbane and acute defender of European culture, would remark (in *The Revolt of the Masses*) that even today civilization could not endure in America, were civilization dead in Europe. In the first half of the nineteenth century, when America was rawer, the importance of European ideas was correspondingly greater. They filtered into the United States, often against the protest of an arrogant American public; and the Americans who tempered democratic overconfidence with old-world prudence ought to receive in our generation the thanks denied in their own time. The boldest thinker of this description was Fenimore

Cooper, belligerently American, unsparingly critical of Americanism.

Cooper was a democrat; but he was the son of a great landed proprietor of conservative opinions, and himself the champion of the Hudson River patrons. This indefatigable controversialist and novelist did his utmost to steer a course between capitalistic consolidation and Southern separatism. He tried quite as hard to reconcile the spirit of a gentleman with political equality. Stubborn as Cato of Utica, and as honest, he never yielded an inch to public delusion nor endured the least infringement of his private rights; and so presently he made himself bitterly detested by popular opinion, in the very democratic society he both defended and chastised with imprudent forthrightness. Unbending rectitude of this sort, however vexatious in its hour, becomes lovable in retrospect. Cooper believed in progress, freedom, property, and gentility. He provides a link between the liberalism of Macaulay and the liberalism of Tocqueville.

Cooper knew American democracy must be purged of its ignorance and roughness if it was to endure. The lawlessness of American agrarian avarice he depicts in old Thousandacres and his brood, in *The Chainbearer;* the brutal individualism of the pioneering spirit, in Ishmael Bush of *The Prairie;* the vulgarity of the American self-made man, in Aristabulus Bragg of *Home as Found;* the ubiquitous professional democrat, in Steadfast Dodge of *Homeward Bound.* And through many of his books runs a pervading distrust of America's anarchic temper, her appetite which respects no prescription, her intolerance that scowls from behind a bombastic affirmation of absolute liberty. Cooper was conservative in every fibre, quite as concerned for tradition, constitutions, and property as were his great legal contemporaries Chancellor Kent and Justice Story. But he saw that no kind of conservatism is possible in America unless political democracy first is made secure and just. America had no political alternative: she could choose only between democracy defecated of popular delusion and democracy corrupted by passion. The regular aim of his literary endeavors was to demonstrate how any society, if it would be civilized, must submit to moral discipline, permanent institutions, and the beneficent claims of property. This general subjection of appetite to reason is possible only if a society consents to be led by gentlemen. Very English, this idea; but of greater importance in the United States, perhaps, than our age tends to think.

When abroad, Cooper was as aggressively proud of his country as he was critical of America when at home. He was abroad a good many years, and during that time he wrote three historical novels of a political turn, intended as warnings to Americans of how venerable establishments may be corrupted: *The Bravo, The Heidenmauer,* and *The Headsman.* He feared privi-

lege, consolidation, and constitutional tinkering quite as much as did Randolph and the Old Republicans. In *The Heidenmauer,* so wearisomely didactic as a romance, so interesting as a political exercise, is this vigorous passage:

> However pure may be a social system, or a religion, in the commencement of its power, the possession of an undisputed ascendancy lures all alike into excesses fatal to consistency, to justice, and to truth. This is a consequence of the independent exercise of human volition, that seems nearly inseparable from human frailty. We gradually come to substitute inclination and interest for right, until the moral foundations of the mind are sapped by indulgence, and what was once regarded with the aversion that wrong excites in the innocent, gets to be not only familiar, but justifiable by expediency and use. There is no more certain symptom of the decay of the principles requisite to maintain even our imperfect standard of virtue, than when the plea of necessity is urged in vindication of any departure from its mandate, since it is calling in the aid of ingenuity to assist the passions, a coalition that rarely fails to lay prostrate the feeble defenses of a tottering morality.

America was not exempt from this general truth. Her size, indeed, was some protection against corruption; for, Montesquieu and Aristotle notwithstanding, republics are better on a large than on a small scale, "since the danger of all popular governments is from popular mistakes; and a people of diversified interests and extended territorial possessions are much less likely to be the subjects of sinister passion than the inhabitants of a single town or country." Because centralization would reduce the United States to the condition of a unitary republic, exposed to the appetites of mobs and the manipulations of privilege, Cooper remained a consistent state-powers advocate.

Late in 1833, Cooper and his family returned to America from an extended Grand Tour; and less than four years later, he found himself deeply involved in the first of two distressing controversies which blasted his popularity and injured his prosperity. Both were the result of popular egalitarian assumptions that Cooper could not accept. The first affair, trifling in its inception, was an altercation with the people of his community, Cooperstown, who without permission had used as a public park—and badly scarred—a bit of land Cooper owned. He expelled the public; for this he was fantastically reviled by local newspaper editors of the sort Mark Twain later damned to immortal fame; he sued these persons for libel, and eventually won, but at the cost of a soured temper and much litigation. While these suits were in progress, Cooper published *The American Democrat,* a book full of perspicuity and courage, cogent and dignified. Perhaps it is well this little treatise was written before the prolongation of his struggle against the editors, and later the Anti-Rent War, had exacerbated Cooper.

Cooper's home, Otsego Hall, in Cooperstown, New York.

The American Democrat is an endeavor to strengthen democracy by marking out its natural bounds. In much, the book anticipates Tocqueville's analysis of American society. Democracies tend to press against their proper limits, to convert political equality into economic levelling, to insist that equal opportunity become mediocrity, to invade every personal right and privacy; they set themselves above the law; they substitute mass opinion for justice. But there are compensations for these vices—or tendencies toward vice. Democracy elevates the character of the people; it reduces military establishments; it advances the national prosperity; it encourages a realization of natural justice; it tends to serve the whole community, rather than a minority; it is the cheapest form of government; it is little subject to popular tumults, the vote replacing the musket; unless excited, it pays more respect to abstract justice than do aristocracy and monarchy. We cherish democracy, therefore; but we do not cherish democracy unlimited and lawless.

"It ought to be impressed on every man's mind, in letters of brass, *'That, in a democracy, the publick has no power that is not expressly conceded by the institutions, and that this power, moreover, is only to be used under the forms prescribed by the constitution. All beyond this, is oppression, when it takes the character of acts, and not infrequently when it is confined to opinion.'*" How can the public be persuaded of the necessity for these limitations? By exposure of the popular delusions concerning equality and government, and by the influence of gentlemen upon democratic society. "In America, it is indispensable that every well wisher of true liberty should understand that acts of tyranny can only proceed from the publick. The publick, then, is to be watched. . . . Although the political liberty of this country is greater than that of nearly every other civilized nation, its personal liberty is said to be less."

Cooper undertakes to analyze those popular misconceptions which endanger private liberty. Equality is not absolute; the Declaration of Independence is not to be understood literally, not even in a moral sense; the very existence of government infers inequality. And "liberty, like equality, is a word more used than understood. Perfect and absolute liberty is as incompatible with the existence of society, as equality of condition." We adopt the popular polity not because it is perfect, but because it is less liable to disturb society than is any other. Liberty properly is subordinate to natural justice, and must be restrained within limits. False theories of representation, reducing representatives to mere delegates, are a peril to American liberty; so is consolidation, in a system intended, as ours is, for diffusion. A venal and virulent press threatens decent life: "If newspapers are useful in overthrowing tyrants, it is only to establish a tyranny of their own." The inclination of democratic peoples to invade the securities of private life is a shocking perversion of liberal democracy, for "individuality is the aim of political liberty": happiness and depth of character are dependent upon it. With these and similar arguments, often employed by conservatives but expressed here with a force and precision rarely attained, Cooper attempted to awaken the American public to consciousness of its own vices. He trod on many toes, and made himself detested, and never got his book read as it deserves to be.

Together with the need for awakening the people to the necessity for restraint in exercising their powers, Cooper believed the hope for democracy lay in the survival of gentlemen, leaders of their communities, superior to vulgar impulses, able to withstand most forms of legislative or extra-legal intimidation. "Social station is that which one possesses in the ordinary associations, and is dependent on birth, education, personal qualities, property, tastes, habits, and, in some instances, on caprice, or fashion." Social station is a consequence of property, and so cannot be eliminated in a civilized society; so long as civilization exists, property is its support. Our endeavor should be so to arrange matters that the possessors of superior social station are endowed with a sense of duty. One man is *not* as good as another, even in the grand moral system of Providence. "This social inequality of America is an unavoidable result of the institutions, though nowhere proclaimed in them, the different constitutions maintaining a profound silence on the subject, they who framed them probably knowing that it is as much a consequence of civilized society, as breathing is a vital function of animal life." Station has its duties, private and public. We ought to see that those duties are fulfilled by gentlemen.

"All that democracy means, is as equal a participation in rights as is practicable; and to pretend that social equality is a condition of popular institutions, is to assume that the latter are destructive of civilization, for, as nothing is more self-evident than the impossibility of raising all men to the highest standard of tastes and refinement, the alternative would be to reduce the entire community to the lowest." The existence of gentlemen is not inconsistent with democracy, for "aristocracy" does not mean the same thing as "gentlemen." "The word 'gentleman' has a positive and limited signification. It means one elevated above the mass of society by his birth, manners, attainments, character, and social condition. As no civilized society can exist without these social differences, nothing is gained by denying the use of the term." Liberal attainments distinguish the gentleman from other people; simple gentlemanlike instincts are not enough. Money, however, is no criterion of gentility. If the gentleman and the lady vanish from a society, they take with them polite learning, the civilizing force of manners, the example of elevated conduct, and that high sense of station which lifts private and public duty above mere salary earning. If they go, eventually civilization will follow them.

In the book which someone ought to write on the idea of a gentleman, Cooper's remarks deserve an honorable place. Yet they exerted no wide influence. Gentlemen are not altogether extirpated in America, but the social and economic conditions requisite for their survival have always been unfavorable, and are becoming precarious. Only two years after *The American Democrat* was published, the Anti-Rent War in New York, which excited Cooper nearly to frenzy, disclosed how difficult was the position of gentlemen in the United States. For the existence of the gentleman has been founded upon the inherited possession of land; and the radicals of the anti-rent movement were determined that the landed proprietors of central New York should give way to farmers and squatters; no prescription, no title in law, should operate against the demand of the majority for ownership of their fields. In the long run, the farmers and squatters won, through intimidation of the landowners and timidity of the courts before popular enthusiasm. The great proprietors of the Hudson vanished from history. This violation of the rights of property, and the means by which it was accomplished, dismayed Cooper immeasurably. If democratic society were bent upon eradicating the class of gentlemen, how would it provide for its own leadership, how would it retain a high tone? That question never has been answered satisfactorily in the United States; and a marked hostility toward large property in land seems embedded in American character. "Land reform" was one of the first American enactments in conquered Japan, dispossessing a conservative and moderate element in Japanese society; and the United States urged upon Italy and El Salvador "agrarian reform," and for a long while smiled upon those "agrarian reformers" the Chinese Communists. With the same sort of hostility the Manchesterians felt toward the English landed proprietors, American industrial society has resented the survival of landed estates.

"The instability and impermanence of American life," writes Cooper's best critic, "which Cooper in the last half of his career sees as endangering the gentleman's right to his property, and finally, in his last novel, the literal right to life itself, had been one of his themes in the years of his untroubled beginnings. . . . He never found a wholly adequate symbol in which to concentrate his tragic vision, perhaps because in the depths of his nature his heart was cheerful, and the bitterness was on the surface, for all the world to see, in his mind." A staunch optimism never altogether deserted Fenimore Cooper, from whom so many of the best American qualities bristled defiantly. But he lost his fight for a democracy studded with men of good birth and high principle. Most reflective Americans must fall now and then into sober considerations upon the extent of this deficiency. Perhaps the lack of the gentleman in America is most conspicuous in rural regions and small towns and the great empty states of the West, but even in the older cities, society often seems declining into an ennui formerly characteristic only of senescent peoples, for lack of leadership and tone. Perhaps without gentlemen, society bores itself to death. In such a people is no leaven of diversity. "The effect of boredom on a large scale in history is underestimated," writes Dean Inge. Today it seems a force that must be reckoned with. . . .

Charles Hansford Adams (essay date 1990)

SOURCE: "'A Parental Affection': Law and Identity in Cooper's America," in *"The Guardian of the Law": Authority and Identity in James Fenimore Cooper,* The Pennsylvania State University Press, 1990, pp. 1-24.

[*In the following essay, Adams contends that Cooper was ambivalent toward the law in America because he "was impelled to believe—emotionally and intellectually—in the law's ability to achieve both social and individual integrity by the same set of historical and psychological conditions that encouraged him to reject the law as divisive."*]

I

Early in *The Prairie*, deep in the long night that opens the novel, Natty Bumppo and Ishmael Bush have a conversation about one of Cooper's persistent concerns—property law. The squatter has just been robbed of his horses by the Tetons, so Natty's innocent observation that the Indians consider themselves owners of the plains, and thus entitled to all it holds, draws from Bush a predictably angry response:

"Owners!" echoed the squatter. "I am as rightful an owner of the land I stand on, as any governor in the States! Can you tell me, stranger, where the law or reason, is to be found, which says that one man

shall have . . . perhaps a county, to his use, and another have to beg for 'arth to make his grave in. This is not natur and I deny that it is law. That is, your legal law."

Natty, in responding, is in an awkward position. He cannot agree with the squatter. Bush is a criminal, a thief and a murderer whose exile on the plains indicates the menace he poses to his fellow man. Moreover, Bush's lawlessness signifies an anarchic egotism at odds with Natty's innate sense of order. Bush's thoughtless appropriation of nature's riches and his contempt for the rights of others mark him as the herald of the "wasty ways" of those from whom Leatherstocking fled in *The Pioneers*. Yet Natty cannot quite bring himself to defend the law. The cruelty of Templeton's civil justice has driven him to spend his last years far from the beautiful forests of his native New York. His strongest memory of the legal system is his public humiliation at Judge Temple's hands. Virtually the last words he speaks to the Effinghams on leaving Templeton condemn Temple's law to eschatological irrelevance: "I pray that the Lord will keep you in mind . . . from this time, till the great day when the whites shall meet the red-skins in judgment, and justice shall be the law, and not power". The law Bush condemns is for Natty an evil with which he cannot compromise, since it asks him to sacrifice an individual integrity rooted in divine order to the false standard of social harmony.

In the end, the trapper equivocates.

"I cannot say that you are wrong . . . and I have often thought and said as much, when and where I have believed my voice could be heard. But your beasts were stolen by them who claim to be masters of all they find in these deserts."

While he "cannot say" that Bush is wrong, he will not say he is right, either. Law may be, as in Templeton, arbitrary and unjust, but some sort of legal order seems necessary unless "desert" justice is to become precisely the struggle of the "powerful" that Natty abhors. Ownership may entail arrogance, but some "claims" of property rights at least must be considered in order to check the despotism of grab. As Natty has already said to Ellen Wade, "The law—'Tis bad to have it, but, I sometimes think it is worse to be entirely without it. . . . Yes—yes, the law is needed, when such as have not the gifts of strength and wisdom are to be taken care of".

Leatherstocking is here caught in what Perry Miller [in *The Life of the Mind in America from the Revolution to the Civil War*] calls "the American dilemma" of the ante-bellum era. Between the Revolution and the Civil War, the perennial debate in the national consciousness between the claims of self and community was focused on the practical question of government. The effort to give form to the new country's various ideals and prejudices sparked a national interest in the relations between institutions and the rights of the citizen, whether singly or in private associations. The tension informing Natty's response electrified many American political conversations more momentous than that on the prairie. Echoes of the trapper's "yes, but . . ." come to us from Madison's *Notes on the Constitutional Convention,* from *The Federalist Papers,* from the Dartmouth College case, from Calhoun's *Disquisition on Government,* and from numerous other documents which debate the place of institutions in the personal and social life of the nation.

Yet, as both contemporary records and the work of recent scholars show, the great "dilemma" of America's formative years most frequently resolved into a national conversation about the law. As the most visible and consequential institution in the new nation, the law provided a natural focus for the struggle to shape America's political identity. Miller's analysis in *The Life of the Mind in America* emphasizes the intensity of discussions among the legal scholars and professors of moral philosophy, but concern with law pervaded virtually every level of American society. While the technicians argued about the specific content of legal structures, the lay mind asked more searching questions. Who is to determine the law? On what moral grounds does its legitimacy rest? Shall it serve any social purpose beyond the simple resolution of conflict? The young nation examined the law with a vitality that suggests that the issue mattered in ways that went beyond the business of establishing a coherent system of justice. For writers from the Federal period through the age of Jackson, the law was intimately connected with the very idea of the nation; the institution provided the lexicon by which to articulate a coherent American political character in the face of the regional diversity inherited from the colonial era. From a more modern perspective, our reading of contemporary comments on the law reveals its importance for establishing and maintaining the early republic's identity as a culture. Americans of the time were, to an extent that can astonish a modern reader, conscious of the way the institutional life of the developing country both mirrored and molded the national character. In the deliberations over what sort of country this new land would be, the nature of "legal law" was perceived as crucial.

The best foreign observer of the American scene in the 1830s, Alexis de Tocqueville, saw clearly the importance of law in the national consciousness. Tocqueville's aristocratic background, his legal training, and the nature of his mission to this country—he came to study the American penal system for the French government—combined to give him a unique perspective on the role of law in a democracy. Several of the most penetrating chapters in *Democracy in America* describe how a democratic society fosters the political power of the bar, and indeed relies on lawyers for stability. Like the aristocracy whose role they assume in a democracy, lawyers form "the most powerful, if not the only, counterpoise to the democratic element." As a class, attorneys work to "neutralize the vices inherent in popular government" by opposing "their superstitious attachment to what is old" to the "passion" and "impetuosity" of the people.

Even so, Tocqueville recognized that, if lawyers enjoy a privileged political status in America, their manifest power is sustained by the mass's tacit acceptance of law as a legitimate principle of order. The lawyers' strength, he claims, issues from the popular mind's profound respect for law, and this respect derives in turn from the fact that law lies close to the heart of the American social consciousness. Everyday relations, Tocqueville tells his readers repeatedly and with mild surprise, are saturated with the spirit of the law:

> Scarcely any question arises in the United States which is not resolved, sooner or later, into a judicial question. Hence all parties are obliged to borrow, in their daily controversies, the ideas, and even the language, peculiar to judicial proceedings. . . . The language of the law thus becomes, in some measure, a vulgar tongue; the spirit of the law, which is produced in the schools and the courts of justice, penetrates beyond their walls into the bosom of society, where it descends to the lowest classes, so that at last the whole people contract the habits and the tastes of the magistrate.

Tocqueville's assessment has been echoed by more recent students of the period. Lawrence Friedman, in his landmark *History of Law in America,* affirms that "one basic central fact of nineteenth-century law was that the official legal system began to penetrate deeper into society. . . . American law was popular, in a profound sense." To adopt a metaphor from Tocqueville's analysis, law in Cooper's time was the *lingua franca* of social relations. As legal language permeated the deep structure of the nation's social grammar, the law's symbol system emerged as the most accurate description of the texture of American society.

In this sense, law is indispensable for defining the republic's social identity in this era. In a nation of strangers, as one historian calls early American society, the law furnished a primary medium of social communion. The disparate cultural elements composing the young nation had abandoned the authority structures that gave cohesiveness to their social relations in the Old World. In the swarm of ethnic and religious groups and subgroups, law provided an established framework for social intercourse. The law, with its precise description of the obligations of each to each, and its formidable array of rituals designed to enforce those bonds, reduced social friction in a world characterized by competing codes of behavior.

Yet in describing the conditions of social consolidation, the law also helped define the individual in the new land. The law, as an articulation of personal rights and restrictions, facilitated an understanding of the boundaries of self and furnished the individual with a language through which he could achieve self-consciousness. Tocqueville, for one, is quite explicit about the relationship among self, social identity, and law. He attributes the prominence of law in American life to the fact that "in the United States everyone is personally interested in the law." The average American feels this way "not only because it [the law] is the work of the majority, but because it is his own, and he regards it as a contract to which he is a party." Tocqueville argues that every individual in a democracy sees the law as an extension of his will, as somehow an expression of himself. And, "because it is his own," the character of the law is felt, consciously or not, as an influence in the creation of personal character. Thus the language of the law moves outward from individual identity to permeate social relations, while coincidentally penetrating the individual's self-perception from the social network in which he lives. . . .

This close tie between law and American identity should not be surprising. After all, the country was from the first a creature of law. Its birth was a legal act; the Declaration dissolved an old contract, and the Constitution created a new one. America had been born *ex nihilo*, with a host of lawyers for midwives. As Robert Ferguson has recently pointed out [in *Law and Letters in American Culture*], the dissolution of the tie with Britain was justified by an appeal to British law.

> The rhetoric of revolution had been . . . patently legalistic. The inalienable rights of rebellion could be and were derived from right reason and natural law, but American vehemence depended on the particular expression of these rights in the common law of England, the statutory enactments of Parliament, and the various royal charters pertaining to colonial government. Participation in the central Revolutionary debates over parliamentary jurisdiction in the colonies required a detailed knowledge of the same legal, historical sources.

After the Revolution, the effort to construct a government for the new nation similarly took place in an intellectual environment defined by the English legal tradition, even as that tradition was being transformed by peculiarly American needs and desires. The ideological assumptions informing the drafting of the Constitution were, as Ferguson reminds us, those of eighteenth-century European legal humanism. The common law tradition "enabled Anglo-American intellectuals to *assume* a visible link between the observance of natural law and the attainment of civic happiness":

the "fortuitous conjunction" of the creation of the American republic with the "high phase" of European legal thought meant that the Founding Fathers saw their task as nation-makers as a matter of crafting the legal code that would most closely imitate the natural order. Their intellectual commitment was quickened and given an emotional immediacy by the circumstances of the new nation. The wilderness—the vast, unspoiled land whose immensity and historical potency were already pressing on the American imagination—presented to the Founders an image of that natural order they were striving to realize in their laws. The continent offered them an unprecedented chance to create a nation whose man-made order might shape the human history of the land to conform with the order of nature.

[In *Justice Without Law?*] Jerold Auerbach has suggested that, since the beginning of the Republic, law has been our "national religion," lawyers our "priesthood," and the courtroom our "national cathedral." With the Revolution, the law assumed in American culture the role reserved in less secular societies for the spiritual institutions around which the life of the nation revolves. It has never surrendered that station. Especially in Cooper's America, the law gave shape to a nation in search of a center. As Robert Ferguson convincingly argues, perhaps the law's greatest contribution to the early Republic was aesthetic; the law's persistent assumption of "the harmony of nature, the efficacy of reason, the importance of hierarchy and decorum, and the inherent structure of all knowledge" were especially useful in a culture in which imaginative "order and control" were indispensable for a sense of national solidarity. Out of the cultural, economic, and religious diversity of colonial America, the law's commitment to finding unity in multiplicity gave it a unique power to forge national coherence. The law's neoclassical vision provided a "thematic perspective" which, whether on the Constitutional level or through its profound influence on the daily life of the Republic, insisted on the "careful understanding and placement of things in a totality."

From this dependency on law for the resolution of American diversity into unity developed, in Ferguson's words, a "mystic identification of law and country" that would persist in the national rhetoric, and which would find its way into the literature of ante-bellum America. As we shall discover, this "mystic identification" plays a vital role in Cooper's novels, and lies near the center of his effort to define his own identity as an American author. The shape of Cooper's imagination depends heavily on the neoclassical perspective, and the need to define a harmonizing "totality" fuels his lifelong fascination with the law. The law's aesthetic appeal informs his persistent tendency to articulate in legalistic language the conditions of personal and national identity.

The law's neoclassicism was best expressed, of course, in the structure of the common law. When Cooper looked in 1845 for a conception of law that would most effectively combat the forces of disintegration he believed to be at work in American society, he naturally shaped his polemical Littlepage Trilogy around the tenets of the Anglo-American common law. By the time Cooper wrote his Anti-Rent books, the common law's authority had been severely compromised by the growth of black-letter law—the democratic, statutory law that Cooper named as one of the culprits in the upstate agitations—but the common law's very existence in America had been the subject of powerful debate in the half-century after the Revolution. Indeed, the controversy in the formative period over the extent to which the common law should influence the legal system of the new country provides perhaps the clearest illustration of the close relationship between the law and America's identity in the ante-bellum era.

In the minds of the Founding Fathers, and most importantly in the mind of John Marshall, the common law transcended its nationalist origins. It represented instead the clearest articulation of the law of nature. While the common law may have developed erratically—through the slow accretion of particular and often conflicting cases—its accumulated principles were seen as statements of universal truth. In its long history, it had grown to encompass all of human experience, resolving the world's apparent chaos into a firm constellation of moral verities. The age willingly embraced the paradox that, by persisting through time, the common law had acquired a sort of timelessness. For post-Revolutionary America, the common law was not "an artificial invention of man, but wholly 'natural.'" As Lawrence Friedman says [in *History of Law*], "one rhetorical pillar of the men of 1776 was that the common law embodied fundamental norms of natural law." Or, in the more inspired rhetoric of a contemporary writer, whoever rejects the common law "sets up his own weak reason against the instincts of society; instincts as unerring as those which guide the wild fowls in their annual migrations."

Thus many of America's leaders looked at the common law as a great piece of wisdom inherited from an otherwise repugnant parent. Because its lesson contained the deepest truths of nature, the child could accept the gift without fear of inheriting any of the donor's peculiarities. The common law, stripped of its feudal and royalist elements, could "legitimately be transplanted to the American landscape and be permitted to grow according to its inherent disposition amid flora of the new world" [Miller]. Indeed, the common law was seen as the only form of law capable of providing the sort of social coherence described by Tocqueville. Justice Joseph Story saw the common law as indispensable for maintaining the nation as an intelligible political entity. In a speech entitled "The Progress of Jurisprudence" (1821), Story cautioned against the modern tendency to repudiate our legal heritage:

> And what, let me ask, with becoming solemnity, would be the consequence if these attempts [at repudiation] should succeed? What but subject it [the law] to the independent and uncontrollable interpretation of twenty-four sovereign states and drive us back to . . . the old practices under the confederation, when the national power died away in recommendations. . . .

He concludes the address by claiming that proscription of the common law would lead to nothing short of national disintegration:

> It will add another, and probably the last, to the long list of experiments to establish a free government, which have alternately illuminated and darkened the annals of other nations, as renowned in arts and arms, as they were for their advancement in literature and jurisprudence.

James Kent, the "American Blackstone" and a good friend of Cooper's, took Story's argument one step further. While pointing out that critical areas of American law are heavily dependent on the common law for meaning—including the Federal and several state constitutions, as well as numerous less conspicuous but crucial enabling laws—Kent emphasized the connection between the nation's legal identity and its social life. He argued that the common law was so inextricably woven into the fabric of American law, and thus into the fabric of American social life, that removing it would threaten the integrity of the nation. The common law, despite its origins, was seen to constitute "the very life of the nation"—it was the "only hope" for the country to "maintain identity." In language reminiscent of Tocqueville's, Kent equates the common law and the nation's being:

> We meet it [the common law] when we wake and when we lay down to sleep, when we travel and when we stay at home; it is interwoven with every idiom that we speak; and we cannot learn another system of law, without learning, at the same time, another language.

To reject the common law simply because it is British would deprive every American of an essential part of himself. It would deprive him not merely of his rightful place in the order of nature. It would equally deny him the identity he derives from the social order in which he lives.

Perhaps Tocqueville provides the most appropriate metaphor to explain not only the rhetorical energy of the jurists' defense of the common law, but the intimate association generally between law and the national experience in Cooper's America. "In the United States," Tocqueville writes in the section of *Democracy* entitled "Respect for the Law in the United States,"

> that numerous and turbulent multitude does not exist who, regarding the law as their natural enemy, look upon it with fear and distrust. It is impossible, on the contrary, not to perceive that all classes display the utmost reliance upon the legislation of their country and are attached to it by a kind of parental affection.

The law's "parental" role was especially important in this period of America's youth. As several commentators have noted—most recently, and most powerfully, Jay Fliegelman in *Prodigals and Pilgrims* (1982)—the American mind in the years surrounding the Revolution was marked by a search for legitimate "parental" authorities. The nation's rejection of the king, and the consequently uncertain status of the English cultural inheritance, created a need for new and more appropriate political and social authority. The law provided just such a "parent" for the Republic. The law, and particularly a common law purged of monarchism, was a structure of authority that offered continuity without oppression, and coherence without cruelty. The law offered a plastic authority—one which was organized around a commitment to ordered change, one which could respond flexibly to a rapidly developing social environment while providing a firm core of premises touching the rights and obligations of the individual in a liberal society. It provided, to borrow Fliegelman's lexicon, a *nurturing* parental authority; Americans could look to the law with the same "affection" they accorded George Washington, since both man and institution lent the Republic the stability it required to grow toward a fulfilled national adulthood.

Of course, we can see now that Tocqueville's and Kent's analyses of the significance of law for America may have been right, but only half right. Indeed Tocqueville's identification of the "parental" element in the relationship between law and the national consciousness may have been wiser than he knew. For, like most rebellious children, America had deeply ambivalent feelings about its institutional "parent." If the nation looked to the law for an image of itself, it paradoxically insisted that its identity could be maintained only by rejecting the institution. Essentially, the antilegal position saw the law as undemocratic, thus un-American. In a land supposedly founded on the ability of every man to discover self-evident truths, the law insisted on authority and tradition in the search for justice. Instead of instinctive or intuitive notions of right, the law relied on reason and collective judgment. As an intellectual discipline which presumed to govern the natural right of each man to pursue happiness his own way, the law was considered by many early Americans as an "artificial imposition on [the] native intelligence."

One important manifestation of this anti legalism was a strenuous effort to discard the common-law tradition. If Kent and Story argued that America's rejection of its legal inheritance would compromise its identity, others, now forgotten but no less talented, felt differently. For these latter, America could only establish her own identity by casting off from the "old Blackstone moorings" and charting her own legal destiny. Probably the leading spokesman for this faction was Robert Rantoul (1805-52), the leading member of the Massachusetts bar, and easily the intellectual match of Story or Kent. In an oration at Scituate in 1836, Rantoul succinctly presented the case for American judicial independence. "The common law sprang from the dark ages," Rantoul declared. It is riddled with "folly, barbarism, [and] feudality." The common law is the "work of judges who held their places during the good pleasure of the king, and of course decided the law so as to suit the pleasure of the king." To "transplant" it is "subversive of the fundamental principles of a free government." The fact that Rantoul's address was delivered the same year as Emerson published "Nature" is significant—Rantoul's call for legal independence images Emerson's demand that America at last set herself free from European intellectual models.

Indeed, Rantoul provides merely the most scholarly expression of a broad anti-common-law sentiment at work in the young nation. Lawrence Friedman says that "the first generation seriously argued the question" of the common law's annulment:

> The common law had been badly tarnished; so was the reputation of lawyers, many of whom had been Tories. It seemed to some men that new democratic states needed new democratic institutions, from top to bottom, including fresh nonmonarchical law.

Abrogation of the common law was increasingly a favorite theme of the Democrats in the first four decades of the century, spurred by anti-common-law promptings from revolutionary heroes like Jefferson and Paine. Paine, writing in 1805, complained that "the courts still hobble along by the stilts and crutches of English and antiquated precedents." These represent the vestiges of "tyranny" in the heart of the newborn democracy. Benjamin Austin, a prominent Massachusetts politician, asked in 1819 whether "the monarchical and aristocratical institutions of England be consistent with . . . republican principles," and answered with a firm negative: it is "melancholy" to see the "numerous volumes" of English law "brought into our courts, arranged in formidable order, as the grand artillery to batter down every plain, rational principle of law." A new land, in short, requires new laws. Legislation, written by the people's representatives in response to the people's needs, was the logical foundation of a truly American law. Until the creaky precepts of the common law had been replaced with republican

Pages 99 and 213 of the manuscript of The Pathfinder.

codes, America would remain enslaved to a dying civilization.

But the fight against the common law was only one aspect of an antilegalism that found expression in diverse works published in Cooper's America. It emerges in its richest intellectual form in Ralph Waldo Emerson's metaphysics of radical individualism. In "Politics" (1844), the essay in which Emerson addresses the law's status most directly, he recognizes that law, as an expression of man's spirit, must be taken seriously: "We must trust infinitely to the beneficent necessity which shines through all laws. Human nature expresses itself in them as characteristically as in statues, or songs, or railroads; and an abstract of the codes of nations would be a transcript of the common conscience." But while the Higher Law may more or less "shine through" the work of legislators, the moral light cast by society's rules is negligible compared to the radiance of Character, the individual expression of universal Being. By imposing the collective will on the self, laws violate the individual's divine preroga-

tive to dictate his own rules of conduct. In America, the land in which the power of character is destined to be realized, the law is one of the darkest of the "sepulchres" of tradition and prejudice that threaten to bury Adam in his new paradise.

In a passage that, by echoing Jefferson's most famous political *dictum,* links the fulfillment of America's promise with the demise of law, Emerson affirms the incompatibility of true character and the legal mind.

> Hence the less government we have the better—the fewer laws, and the less confided power. The antidote to this abuse of formal government is the influence of private character, the growth of the Individual . . . of whom the existing government is, it must be owned, a shabby imitation. . . . The appearance of character makes the State unnecessary. The wise man is the state.

If America is to consummate its destiny as the land of apotheosis, where the individual consciousness, free of external restraints, can achieve the sublime integrity of

Reason, the "shabby" expedient of law must disappear.

Emerson's antilegal metaphysic is reiterated throughout the ante-bellum era—indeed, antilegal rhetoric is so pervasive and well documented that I need only suggest its depth and range here. Thoreau's "Civil Disobedience" (1849) comes to mind immediately. In Thoreau's life and work, Emerson found the best answer to his call at the end of "Politics" for "a single human being who has steadily denied the authority of the laws, on the simple ground of his own moral nature." The best fiction of the period—from Brackenridge's *Modern Chivalry* (1792-1805) and Brown's *Wieland* (1798), to Irving's fanciful *History of New York* (1809) and Cooper's **The Pioneers** (1823), to Hawthorne's *House of the Seven Gables* (1851) and Melville's "Bartleby, the Scrivener" (1853)—offers a wide variety of perspectives on the law's moral limitations. Less memorable works, too, gave voice to this democratic antilegalism. John Neal's *Rachel Dyer* (1828), a widely read tale of the injustice committed by the Salem courts during the witch trials, is clearly an attack on legal rationalism. Neal, a practicing attorney most of his life, provides a stern critique of the law's epistemology from a utilitarian perspective—the author's dramatization of the law's moral myopia, and his gothic portrayal of the suffering caused by the institution's endemic inability to know the human heart, lend his narrative substantial emotional power despite its aesthetic failures.

As Miller argues,

> There can be no worse falsification of American history than to suppose that the antilegalism of the early nineteenth century was merely "Jacksonian," merely the expression of party. . . . Instead . . . the mood was something more pervasive than either of the parties could control, something deep, atavistic, pervasive in the community.

It represented a popular insistence—given intellectual depth by the sanction of writers like Emerson and Thoreau—on the principles which, for many, defined the new country. Of course, antilegalism was not an American invention—from Shakespeare's *The Merchant of Venice* to Dickens' *Bleak House,* the English literary tradition provided Cooper's America with many antilegal models, and the agitation for legal reform in the direction of greater popular expression increased throughout Europe in the wake of the American and French Revolutions. But the rhetoric of the American experiment—the tremendous emotional energy generated in the ante-bellum imagination by the ideals of democracy and individual freedom—gave the antilegal impulse in America a special resonance. In their hatred of the law as antidemocratic and anti-individualist, the law's opponents saw themselves as arguing for an America more nearly in harmony with its true identity. Without the oppressive structure of the law, America could be more nearly itself.

From our perspective, the outcome of the debate among these various observers of the law was never really in doubt. The common law, tempered by Rantoul's legislation, is still the centerpiece of American law: as Friedman puts it, "in hindsight, the common law was as little threatened as the English language." And if in Cooper's time the law was lodged in the "bosom of society," its place today is if anything more visceral. The law is firmly embedded in the American character—we turn to it, for moral guidance and the resolution of conflict, more often than any other people. We turn to it, in essence, for a sense of who we are. The law's influence in shaping our perceptions of our powers and obligations as individuals—of the nature of self in a complex society—is as subtle as instinct.

But the law's legitimacy is rarely discussed in the tone of the dialogue of the 1820s and 1830s. Then the matter seemed much more one of choice. The law, perceived as the central organizing principle of American reality, demanded of its subjects important decisions. If the young country were to be articulated correctly, the law and its place had to be carefully defined. This task of articulation had, as Tocqueville suggests, a personal meaning for Americans. In this formative time, every American identified himself with the country's political existence. One's identity as an American was self-consciously a significant element of one's identity as a person. So, by a key cultural syllogism, shaping the law was in effect shaping the self: defining the law meant defining the nation, and defining the nation meant defining the individual citizen. One who felt that being an American meant being free of external constraints could seriously propose abolishing law and lawyers. Another, like James Kent, who saw American-ness as the opportunity to realize a community free of Old World blunders yet founded on unalterable natural principles, could argue that law must form the moral and spiritual backbone of the land.

II

For a friend and political ally of Kent's in New York, James Cooper of Cooperstown, the law meant all this and much more. Cooper's understanding both of the relationship of law and identity, and of the ambivalent feelings the law produced in the American mind, was deepened and complicated by an unusually intense response to legal questions. For if Tocqueville's figure of the law as "parent" was meant metaphorically, to Cooper it was all too powerfully real.

To say that Judge William Cooper was a strong personality is rather an understatement. He was one of those frontier characters of whom local legends are made. His shrewdness and ambition, if they did not enable him to "tame the wilderness" like Judge Temple, at least secured him the right to sell other men the opportunity to do so. While James Cooper was growing up, William Cooper *was* Otsego—he was the regional landlord, he held the local judgeship, and he represented the area twice in Congress. His distinctive blend of physical force and what James Grossman calls "shrewd kindness" enabled him to rule the county with an authority that rested equally on personal and legal foundations. This sort of power was manifested in his willingness to use his position as judge to effect personal ends. As chief of the Otsego Federalist party, and its occasional representative in Washington, he did not hesitate to threaten his indebted tenants with the full legal sanctions if they did not vote correctly, and on at least one infamous occasion actually imprisoned a man for, essentially, inciting Cooper's tenants to question their landlord's politics. In the judge, the line between personal and legal authority was thoroughly blurred; his reign in Otsego synthesized civil power and the vitality of character.

To the boy James Cooper, the judge must have seemed like a god. But growing up with a god typically prompts a deep and lasting psychic conflict; the father is established as the central figure in the child's consciousness, so that whether worshipping the icon or abusing it, the son's identity is largely defined by the father's. As Freud and others have pointed out, such psychic conflicts are not resolved in adulthood—they persist to influence all of the child's later behavior. For the judge's youngest son, the result was, in Stephen Railton's words, an "ambivalent attitude toward the figure of his father."

> . . . Cooper never freed himself psychically from William Cooper. His attitude toward his father was complex and ambivalent: in the course of his life Cooper felt compelled variously to reconcile himself with his father and to struggle against him.

As Railton points out, these simultaneous desires to please and deny his father colored every aspect of his "relationship with the rest of the world." In particular, they influenced his attitude toward all forms of external authority. Railton suggests that both Cooper's adolescent rebellion against authority, which culminated in his expulsion from Yale for setting fire to a dormitory door, and his fervent embrace of the established social order after his return from Europe, are explicable in terms of his unresolved psychic relationship with his father. As Daniel Peck puts it in *A World By Itself,* "the primary conflict of his imagination, the struggle between authority and freedom," is, "at the deepest level," a struggle "between the claims of the father and the rights of the son."

In his fiction, Cooper's lifelong struggle with authority most often appears as a deep concern with the law.

Considering the Judge's identity as a man of law, it is not surprising that Cooper's emotional engagement with authority should focus on this institution. But I want to emphasize, here and throughout this study, that if Cooper's interest in the law reflects his father's abiding presence in his life, it more profoundly reveals his historical circumstances. His psychological relationship with his father only deepens and makes more resonant a conflict whose essential form and content were shaped by living in a land struggling to define itself. His identity as Judge Cooper's son "colors," as Railton puts it, a set of impulses and opinions regarding the law derived from his identity as a particularly sensitive citizen in the age of Kent, Rantoul, and Emerson. If his own personal struggle with law allowed him to see the ways in which everyone wrestles with authority in order to achieve self-definition, the public debates about law gave that awareness political and historical meaning. Most importantly, the cultural conversation about the law furnished Cooper with a language through which to explore the theme in his art.

The public and private contexts of Cooper's contact with the law are thus linked by the theme of identity. It provides the central moral value in his fictional explorations of the law, and his concern with its implications determines the orientation of his lifelong criticism of the institution. . . . I should pause long enough here to make some preliminary observations and distinctions. The term perhaps carries, for modern readers, a psychological or existential significance that clearly is foreign to Cooper. He uses the term—as well as others, like "individuality" and "character"—to refer to a condition involving the relations of the self with external structures of authority, rather than the sort of self-integration more modern ears may hear in the word. The difficulty for criticism is that Cooper uses the word throughout his fiction to refer to two very different types of integration with objective structures. One, of which Leatherstocking is the most conspicuous example, concerns the individual's place in a transcendental order: Natty's identity is, as every reader knows, inconceivable apart from the laws of "nater" that shape his acts. The other, of which virtually any of Cooper's conventional heroes provides an instance, concerns the integration of public and private selves—the integration of an individual's motives with his historical, social, and political roles. This integration is, as we shall see, typically expressed by the individual's assumption of an identity defined by legal authority. Cooper's celebration throughout his canon of both transcendental and secular versions of legal identity means, of course, that he is rarely able to create a consistent perspective on law, self, or their proper relationship.

Focusing on the relationship between law and identity helps to bridge the traditional distinction in Cooper studies between Cooper's ideas and his concerns as a novelist. The best studies that address Cooper's interest in the law—John McWilliams's *Political Justice in a Republic* (1972) and Brook Thomas's more recent work, for instance—principally focus on the law as an object of concern for Cooper the social critic. That is, Cooper's analysis of its social, political, and historical elements are the central interest. But a look at the way the law in Cooper's novels determines identity, and the way identity conditions the law, furthers our understanding of the relationship in his fiction between ideas and character. A focus on identity allows insight into, among other things, the connection between Cooper's social thought and his handling of character development, and the relationship between character and the fictional forms that permit both the articulation of social problems and attempts at their resolution. Indeed, one of my purposes in this study is to argue against a tendency to isolate Cooper's ideas—many of which are more or less related to his abiding interest in the role of law in society—from his art, and to suggest that the disjunction between the two felt by many readers is made less evident by focusing on the way that this theme of identity shapes both.

This is not, of course, to say that Cooper's artistic failures can be justified by this approach. The novelistic faults for which he has been amply criticized—among them, his awkward conclusions and clumsy plot contrivances—cannot be explained away. But attention to the ways in which Cooper's shifting conceptions of the relationship between law and self determine his novelistic choices can help make sense of some of his "literary offenses." For instance, his affirmation within a single work of both the transcendental and secular versions of legal identity described above is often to blame for conspicuous aesthetic failures. The conclusion of *Lionel Lincoln* (1825), to take just one example, has been justly criticized because the logic of Cooper's plot forces the hero of this Revolutionary War romance to assert his sympathy with the American cause by returning to his ancestral home in England. But . . . the root of this jarring finale is less novelistic sloppiness than the author's ambivalence about the proper relationship between law and the American self—or even what sort of self and what sort of law he is principally interested in affirming.

Central to Cooper's investigations of the legitimacy of law is his conviction that the law is always essentially an interpretation of human nature, and that the abiding standard for judging its interpretation at a given historical moment is the extent to which it provides a coherent picture of man, and functions as a means of promoting cohesiveness in society. When the law divides man unnaturally into warring legal and nonlegal selves, or when it facilitates the disruption of social bonds by individuals willing to manipulate legal forms and rhetoric for personal ends, the law loses its legitimacy. On the other hand, when it provides what Cooper considers a coherent interpretation of human identity, and

establishes a firm framework for social relations, threats to its authority are treated as the worst form of villainy. Cooper's novelistic problems often arise from his inability to impose dramatic unity on contradictory combinations of the elements of this formula. The legal conditions that promote personal identity may work against social harmony, or vice versa; *The Spy* (1821), for instance, contains both possibilities. Here, and in other novels containing similar ambivalences, Cooper's overriding concern with creating in his books a world of order typically leads him to fabricate conclusions that paper over, unconvincingly, these contradictions.

A brief look at one of Cooper's most powerfully imagined trial scenes will perhaps help define and illustrate some of these preliminary points. Near the end of *The Last of the Mohicans* (1826), the Delaware nation is assembled before the "seat of judgment" occupied by the great Tamenund, the "Judge" and "father" of his people. Various petitioners approach the patriarch, pleading for their respective rights. Magua, the evil Huron, has come before his nation's traditional enemies to legitimize his malevolent designs; he asks Tamenund to return to him the beautiful Cora Munro, and to appease the French authorities by burning Hawkeye and Uncas at the stake. Cora and Alice sue for protection from Magua, and for the safety of their captive defenders. But the most significant brief brought before the "Judge" belongs to Uncas. Uncas' presence invites Tamenund and his people to address the central issue of the trial—whether or not the Delaware nation will, in the twilight of its existence, finally do justice to itself. Once the young brave reveals himself to the Delawares as "Uncas, the child of Uncas," "a son of the great Unamis," the trial becomes a matter of tribal identity. Magua's suit is all but forgotten as Uncas calls on Tamenund to recognize his authority to lead the tribe, and thus heal the national rupture caused by the squabbling of two European monarchs. Uncas' suit is brought in the name of his race—he argues that if the council condemns the heir of the Delawares' most illustrious family, the nation will deserve the doom it knows is inevitable. He urges the tribe at least to meet its death with dignity, with self-knowledge, and with pride in the integrity of its culture.

Tamenund hears the plea of the Serpent's son, and rejects the cultural amnesia encouraged by Magua's suit. Tamenund's language as he acknowledges the restoration to power of the Children of the Turtle suggests the nation's consolidation in a cathartic compression of past and present: "Does Tamenund dream [he asks himself] . . . ? What voice is at his ear! Have the winters gone backward! Will summer come again to the children of the Lenape!" The trial is thus a realization of identity on two levels. A divided nation discovers, by asserting the integrity of its traditions, its true "voice." Closely associated with the remembrance of tribal self is the redemption of personal identity. Uncas' command of the climactic pursuit of the devilish Huron symbolizes the young chief's self-realization in his suit before the "seat of judgement."

Tamenund's law is the temporal complement of Natty Bumppo's higher law of nature, the transcendental standard of justice by which all social arrangements are measured in the Tales. Leatherstocking's "nater" guarantees personal identity by locating its source in an ahistorical, eternally abstract law. The law promulgated in the Delaware camp provides a historical expression of that same perfect coherence between law and self. Delaware justice confirms civil and personal integrity with regard, not to a static order, but to social relations and cultural traditions. As the organizing principle of the civilization, the law Uncas advocates creates roles and hierarchies and inheritances that give the individual and collective life meaning. It firmly orients every member of the tribe toward his particular place in its present structure, and his personal relation to its mythic and historical past. This seamless bond between personal identity, social integrity, legal order, and ontic coherence is the ideal informing Cooper's social criticism.

Of course, Delaware law is inherently tragic. The national and personal self-realizations achieved in the trial represent at once a fulfillment of pre-European history and its apocalypse. The reunion of past and present celebrated by Tamenund excludes the future; it is the end of time for his people. Indeed, the irony of this scene is that, while it presents an ideal relation between law and identity, it really has little to do with Indians. It functions principally as a metaphor for the configuration of law and identity that Cooper wants for white America. Tamenund's law is, significantly, "without a cross"; Cooper never brings his Indians into any serious relation with white law except as, figuratively speaking, wards of the court.

In general, Cooper's treatment of the Indians in his legal fiction suggests a connection between the aboriginals and American law much like that described in the landmark decisions handed down by Justice John Marshall throughout the first phase of Cooper's career. As Marshall put it in *Johnson and Graham's Lessee v. McIntosh* (1823), the Indians' right to "complete sovereignty, as independent nations," was denied by "the original fundamental principle that discovery gave exclusive title to those who made it." They are, in effect, children: "dependents," as Marshall would put it in *The Cherokee Nation v. The State of Georgia* (1831). Like the concept of the "noble savage," the realization of Indian identity through law had no meaning for Cooper, or his America— except, to use his phrase from the 1850 Preface to the Leather-Stocking Tales, as *beau idéal*.

I should add that the exclusion of Indians from the law in Cooper's fiction parallels his exclusion of women. The relationship between law and identity I am describing in this study concerns almost exclusively white males. On the issue of women's legal rights, as on many social issues, Cooper's attitude is reactionary. The law of Cooper's day treated women much more respectfully than Indians, but the two groups were significantly alike in being judged by the law as somewhat less than full individuals. [In *Women and the Law of Property in Early America*, legal] historian Marylynn Salmon says that women were in a position of "enforced dependence" on white males in antebellum America. Cooper was very much a man of his time in this regard. In *The American Democrat* (1838) he makes a comment about women and the law that provides a gloss on his treatment of the matter in his fiction. In the section "On Equality," Cooper approvingly explains the reason for denying women full political rights:

> The interests of women being thought to be so identified with those of their male relatives as to become, in a great degree, inseparable, females are, almost generally, excluded from the possession of political rights. There can be no doubt that society is greatly the gainer, by thus excluding one half its members, and the half that is best adapted to give a tone to its domestic happiness, from the strife of parties, and the fierce struggle of political controversies.

There is for Cooper nothing unfortunate about this inequality. Indeed, if there is an injustice, it is toward men: because of the woman's childlike state of "dependence" on the man, "the wife, usually, can neither sue nor be sued, while the husband . . . is made liable to all legal claims on account of the wife."

The law in Cooper's novels offers women no context for the sort of transcendent or secular integration by which he measures his male characters. Interestingly, when women do play a significant role in the legal novels, they do so as spokespersons for an anti-legal position. In *The Spy,* for instance, Frances Wharton speaks passionately against the law's injustice to her brother; her emotional plea for sympathy and mercy is naturally thrown out of court as being legally inadmissible. Cooper's clear identification with Frances' position in this early novel is in striking contrast to his portrayal at the end of his career of a woman whose entanglement with the law offers Cooper's most considered dramatization of the relationship between women and the law. Mary Monson, in *The Ways of the Hour* (1850), is described as insane precisely because she opposes her legal status of "enforced dependence" on her husband. Her mental recovery is made possible by her acceptance of the law's wisdom in making her something less than a person. . . .

Cooper's virtual exclusion of Indians and women from the circle defined by the twin themes of law and identity poses a serious and persistent challenge to his efforts to persuasively close the circle. Considering that he sometimes, as in *The Pioneers* or *Lionel Lincoln*, clearly intends to offer a vision of personal and social coherence made possible by the law as an interpretation of the meaning of the national experience, his silence on the subjects of women and Indians represents a fatal flaw in his efforts to give fictional shape to American culture. But . . . he often leaves a great deal out of the resolutions of his novels about law and identity in the interest of his deepest imaginative and psychic need—order. At the center of Cooper's moral vision is a desire for order, a need to believe that there is a law pervading and binding all levels of life. As Henry Nash Smith says in *Virgin Land,* underneath all of the "genuine ambivalence" of Cooper's thought, "his strongest commitment is to the forces of order." That social and natural creation rests on law is the intellectual faith, emotional conviction, and psychic demand on which depends much of what he tried to do in fiction.

But, clearly, Cooper's narratives, and especially the Leatherstocking Tales, are far from sanguine about man's efforts to create order through law. [In *The American Vision: Actual and Ideal Society in Nineteenth-Century Fiction*] A. N. Kaul speaks for many readers when he identifies "the basic tension" in Cooper's social criticism as that between a vision of perfect harmony and a disastrous reality.

> If actual social development defines one side of this [basic] tension, the other is provided, not by an alternative historical possibility, but by an archetype of what a new society should be. . . . The Leatherstocking Tales attempt to recreate the myth which history was supposed to validate but which in reality it violated from the outset.

If on the deepest level Cooper is committed to order, on another, perhaps equally unconscious level, he is strongly ambivalent about the law's ability to achieve it. If he is driven to establish throughout his fiction a firm link between law and the conditions of personal and social identity, he is equally driven to question the ability of civil power—the law of Templeton in *The Pioneers,* or of the British in *Mohicans*—to create the sort of private or public integrity provided by Natty's "nater" or the ideal society of Tamenund's court.

His ambivalence stems, undoubtedly, from the cultural and personal circumstances that I described earlier in this [essay]. Cooper was impelled to believe—emotionally and intellectually—in the law's ability to achieve both social and individual integrity by the same set of historical and psychological conditions that encouraged him to reject the law as divisive. The several

elements of Cooper's explorations in fiction of the legitimacy of law often make neat generalizations difficult. Yet the reader's effort to hold in suspension the possibilities Cooper explores—his conflicting images and contradictory insights—is a small price to pay for the moral energy generated by his ambivalences.

FURTHER READING

Biography

Grossman, James. *James Fenimore Cooper.* New York: William Sloane Associates, 1949, 286 p.
    Biographical and critical study that includes discussion of the Leatherstocking novels.

Quinn, Arthur Hobson. "James Fenimore Cooper." In *American Fiction: An Historical and Critical Survey*, pp. 53-76. New York: Appleton-Century-Crofts, 1936.
    Survey of Cooper's career, naming the Leatherstocking novels as his best works.

Criticism

Baym, Nina. "The Women of Cooper's Leatherstocking Tales." *American Quarterly* XXIII, No. 5 (December 1971): 696-709.
    Examines the role of women in the Leatherstocking novels.

Beers, Henry A. "James Fenimore Cooper, 1789-1889." *The Critic* 15, No. 298 (14 September 1889): 125-26.
    Pronounces the Leatherstocking novels to be Cooper's "surest claim to immortality."

Bier, Jesse. "Lapsarians on *The Prairie*: Cooper's Novel." *Texas Studies in Literature and Language* IV, No. 1 (Spring 1962): 49-57.
    Contends that a mythic Christian pattern of a fall from grace underlies the action of *The Prairie*.

Blakemore, Steven. "Language and World in *The Pathfinder.*" *Modern Language Studies* XVI, No. 3 (Summer 1986): 237-46.
    Considers ways that facility with language affects the perception of reality on the part of characters in *The Pathfinder*.

Clark, Robert, ed. *James Fenimore Cooper: New Critical Essays.* London: Vision Press Ltd., 1985, 208 p.
    Includes essays on the Leatherstocking novels by Eric Cheyfitz, Charles Swann, Richard Godden, John P. McWilliams, and Gordon Brotherston.

Clavel, Marcel. *Fenimore Cooper and His Critics: American, British and French Criticisms of the Novelist's Early Work.* Aix-en-Provence: Imprimerie Universitaire de Provence, 1938, 418 p.

A study of critics' early attitudes toward Cooper, generally using excerpts from the criticism itself, arranged and annotated by Clavel.

Darnell, Donald. *"The Deerslayer*: Cooper's Tragedy of Manners." *Studies in the Novel* XI, No. 4 (Winter 1979): 406-15.

Considers issues of social hierarchy central to the plot of *The Deerslayer* and terms the novel a tragedy of frustrated social ambition patterned after the novel of manners.

Dekker, George. *James Fenimore Cooper the Novelist.* London: Routledge & Kegan Paul, 1967, 265 p.

A systematic critical study of Cooper's novels, placing them in their biographical and historical background.

Franklin, Wayne. *The New World of James Fenimore Cooper.* Chicago: University of Chicago Press, 1982, 275 p.

Offers commentary on Cooper's frontier novels, suggesting that in choosing to write fiction about the expanding American frontier, Cooper "found an opportunity and left a tradition."

Gladsky, Thomas S. "The Beau Ideal and Cooper's *The Pioneers.*" *Studies in the Novel* XX, No. 1 (Spring 1988): 43-54.

Suggests that Cooper's genteel male protagonists, beginning with the character of Oliver Effingham in *The Pioneers*, were offered as desirable models of behavior to his American readers.

Haberly, David T. "Women and Indians: *The Last of the Mohicans* and the Captivity Tradition." *American Quarterly* XXVIII, No. 4 (Fall 1976): 431-43.

Considers the impact of American captivity narratives on *The Last of the Mohicans.*

Hale, Edward Everett Jr. "American Scenery in Cooper's Novels." *The Sewanee Review* XVIII, No. 3 (July 1910): 317-32.

Explores Cooper's treatment of the American landscape, and how his attitudes changed during the course of his career.

House, Kay Seymour. *Cooper's Americans.* Columbus: Ohio State University Press, 1965, 350 p.

Examines Cooper's pioneering portrayal of uniquely American characters and situations in his novels. Individual chapters discuss his fictional treatment of women, native Americans, ethnic groups, and social classes. A concluding chapter is devoted to the character of Natty Bumppo.

Kaul, A. N. "James Fenimore Cooper: The History and Myth of American Civilization." In *The American Vision: Actual and Ideal Society in Nineteenth-Century Fiction*, pp. 84-138. New Haven: Yale University Press, 1963.

Includes discussion of the Leatherstocking novels as "the clearest statement in literature of the archetypal American experience."

Lawrence, D. H. "Fenimore Cooper's Anglo-American Novels." In *The Symbolic Meaning: The Uncollected Versions of "Studies in Classic American Literature,"* pp. 73-87. Fontwell, England: Centaur Press, 1962, 264 p.

Analyzes, between stream-of-consciousness philosophical dialogues, Cooper's treatment of American and English social values.

Överland, Orm. *The Making and Meaning of an American Classic: James Fenimore Cooper's "The Prairie."* Oslo: Universitetsforlaget, 1973, 205 p.

Provides a detailed record of Cooper's life when he wrote *The Prairie*, an examination of Cooper's literary theories, and discussion of the setting, characters, plot, and historical context of *The Prairie.*

Owen, William. "In War as in Love: The Significance of Analogous Plots in Cooper's *The Pathfinder.*" *English Studies in Canada* X, No. 3 (September 1984): 289-98.

Draws analogies between the romantic plot and the military action that are jointly presented in *The Pathfinder.*

Pearce, Roy Harvey. "The Metaphysics of Indian-Hating: Leatherstocking Unmasked." In *Historicism Once More: Problems and Occasions for the American Scholar.* Princeton: Princeton University Press, 1969, 357 p.

Considers ways that the Leatherstocking novels depict the historical process, examining in particular the role of Natty Bumppo in facilitating the encroachment of civilization—a process that would ultimately render both himself and the aboriginal inhabitants of the continent obsolete.

Peck, H. Daniel. *A World by Itself: The Pastoral Moment in Cooper's Fiction.* New Haven: Yale University Press, 1977, 213 p.

Studies Cooper's pictorialism, focusing on the symbolic use of landscape in the major novels.

Philbrick, Thomas. "Cooper's *The Pioneers*: Origins and Structure." *PMLA* LXXIX, No. 5 (December 1964): 579-93.

Considers Cooper's authorial intent in writing *The Pioneers* by examining his life at the time of its composition, and offers commentary on the settings, plot, and characters of the novel.

Rose, Marilyn Gaddis. "Time Discrepancy in *Last of the Mohicans.*" *American Notes and Queries* VIII, No. 5 (January 1970): 72-73.

Notes that the plot of *The Last of the Mohicans* deviates from the historical sequence of events on which the action of the novel is based.

Scheckter, John. "History, Possibility, and Romance in *The Pioneers*." *Essays in Literature* VIII, No. 1 (Spring 1981): 33-44.

> Contends that *The Pioneers* incorporates moral and philosophical dialogue about developing American traditions in a plot modeled on the traditional historical romance.

Slotkin, Richard. "Man without a Cross: The Leatherstocking Myth (1823-1841)." In *Regeneration Through Violence: The Mythology of the American Frontier, 1600-1860*, pp. 466-516. Middletown, Conn.: Wesleyan University Press, 1973.

> Discusses the mythic nature of the Leatherstocking novels and the character of Natty Bumppo.

Walker, Warren S. "The Tragic Wilderness." In *James Fenimore Cooper: An Introduction and An Interpretation*, pp. 30-63. New York: Barnes & Noble, 1962.

> Discusses the importance of the Leatherstocking novels in shaping American conceptions of early United States history.

Zoellner, Robert H. "Conceptual Ambivalence in Cooper's Leatherstocking." *American Literature* 31, No. 4 (January 1960): 397-420.

> Contends that Natty Bumppo must be seen neither as a hero nor as an Adamic figure, but rather as a reflection of contradictory social views in Cooper himself.

Additional coverage of Cooper's life and career is contained in the following sources published by Gale Research: *Concise Dictionary of American Literary Biography, 1640-1865; Dictionary of LIterary Biography,* **Vol. 3:** *Antebellum Writers in New York and the South; Something about the Author,* **Vol. 19; and** *Nineteenth-Century Literature Criticism,* **Vols. 1 and 27.**

Heinrich Heine

1797-1856

(Born Harry Heine) German poet, essayist, critic, journalist, editor, dramatist, novella and travel writer.

For additional information about Heine's life and career, see *NCLC,* Volume 4.

INTRODUCTION

Heine is one of the outstanding literary figures of nineteenth-century Europe. He is best known for his *Buch der Lieder* (1827; *Heinrich Heine's Book of Songs*), a collection of love lyrics which were, in time, set to music by Franz Schubert, Robert Schumann, and other composers. He was the first major poet of his era to adopt a humorous, ironic tone, which pervades his poetry, prose, and commentaries on politics, art, literature, and society.

Biographical Information

Heine was born in Düsseldorf into a Jewish household, the poor relations of a larger, wealthy family. His early years were greatly influenced by his uncle, Salomon Heine, a successful and influential banker who financed Heine's university education. In 1819, Heine was sent to study law at the University of Bonn, where he showed a growing interest in literature and history and studied under the famous critic August Wilhelm Schlegel, who introduced him to the ideas of the German Romantic school. He completed his studies at the University of Göttingen and received his law degree in 1825. In that same year he changed his name from Harry to Heinrich and converted to Protestantism, a practical measure necessary for any career because of anti-Semitic laws in nineteenth-century Germany. In 1831 Heine emigrated to Paris, where he remained in self-imposed exile for most of his life. From the mid-1830s through the rest of his life, he suffered with increasing illness from venereal disease, and in the spring of 1848 he became completely paralyzed and partially blind. Confined to what he called his "mattress-grave," Heine lived in constant pain, yet was intellectually alert until his death in 1856.

Major Works

Heine began his literary career while still a student. His first book of poetry, *Gedichte* (1822; *Poems*), was considered promising, though his next published work, *Tragödien nebst einem lyrischen Intermezzo* (1823), which contained his only attempts at drama, was considered unimportant and was largely ignored. Heine

had far more success with his next work, a fictional account of a walking tour he had taken through the Harz Mountains. This work, *Die Harzreise,* was the first of a four-volume set titled *Reisebilder* (1826-31; *Pictures of Travel*). This work contains sketches of Heine's travels to England, Italy, and Nordenay on the North Sea, but it is also a record of his personal journey and a successful combination of autobiography with descriptions of scenery and social criticism.

With the publication of his next work, *Book of Songs*, Heine became the most popular German poet of his day. The work established his preeminence as a lyric poet, and has long remained the basis of his international reputation. This early poetry reflects the influence of Romanticism in its emphasis on love and despair, as well as its pervasive tone of reverie. Yet *Book of Songs* encompasses much more. The book abounds with realism, skepticism, wit, and irony. Heine did not share the positive world view of such German Romantics as Johann Wolfgang von Goethe and Friedrich Schiller, and he lacked their faith in the ability of modern poetry to overcome the alienation and anxiety of modern life. *Book of Songs* represents Heine's rejection of the German Romantic tradition and marks the beginning of the post-Romantic movement in German literature.

The compositions that followed his emigration to Paris, unlike his early and late poetry, are primarily concerned with politics, religion, society, art, and philosophy. These include essays that were collected in *Französische Zustände* (1833; *French Affairs: Letters from Paris*), *Lutezia* (1854; *Lutetia*), and *De l'Allemagne* (1835; *Germany*). With these works he hoped to encourage understanding between his adopted nation of France and his homeland, Germany; his efforts were enhanced by his ability to write in both French and German. His presentation of the human side of historical figures and his skillful evocation of the mood of the period give his essays their lasting value. Heine's *Heinrich Heine über Ludwig Börne* (1840; *Ludwig Börne: Recollections of a Revolutionist*), a biographical work including criticism and fictional letters, is an attempt by Heine to defend his views against those of Börne, a recently deceased leader of the exiled German radicals in Paris. The biting satire for which Heine had become known also pervades his long political poems, *Deutschland: Ein Wintermärchen* (1844; *Germany: A Winter's Tale*) and *Atta Troll: Ein Sommernachtstraum* (1847; *Atta Troll*). These two poems are a mixture of history and political and literary satire, and defy generic classification. His most powerful and compelling poetry, including that in *Romanzero* (1851; *Romancero*) and *Letzte Gedichte und Gedanken* (1869), dates from late in his career. In these works, Heine frequently returns to the lyrical form of his earliest poetry. They vividly describe a man preparing for death, which he alternately fears and welcomes as a refuge. With their self-mocking, ironic tone, these poems capture the full range of Heine's tenderness and delicacy as well as his pain and terror, and are considered the fullest expression of his poetic genius.

Critical Reception

Although Heine was one of the most influential and popular poets of the nineteenth-century, critical response has varied widely over the years. His works have met with both admiration and disapproval in his native land, where his ruthless satires and radical pronouncements made him appear unpatriotic and subversive to his contemporaries. His religion consistently worked against him: he was ostracized as a Jew among Germans, but when he converted to Protestantism, both Jews and Christians assailed him as an opportunist. All of Heine's works were banned in 1835 and he was at one time forbidden to return to Germany. During the 1930s and 1940s, the Nazis tried to erase Heine's name from German history. They destroyed his grave, banned his works, and when they found that they could not eliminate his famous poem "Die Lorelei"

from the memory of the German people, they attributed it to an unknown author. Heine's reputation has fared better outside Germany, but while his poetry is widely praised, his ironic and satiric writings have only recently met with critical acclaim. The complexity and variety of his views have often made him an outcast, for those who appreciate the politically militant poet of the 1840s in some cases resent the older, more conservative poet. The only part of Heine's work to be accepted by all critical factions is the *Book of Songs*.

PRINCIPAL WORKS

Gedichte (poetry) 1822
  [*Poems* published in *The Poems of Heine, Complete*, 1878]
Tragödien nebst einem lyrischen Intermezzo (drama and poetry) 1823
Reisebilder. 4 vols. (travel sketches) 1826-31
  [*Pictures of Travel*, 1855]
Buch der Lieder (poetry) 1827
  [*Heinrich Heine's Book of Songs*, 1856]
Französische Zustände (essays) 1833
  [*French Affairs: Letters from Paris*, 1893]
Zur Geschichte der neuern schönen Literatur in Deutschland (essay) 1833; also published as *État actuel de la littérature en Allemagne* in journal *L'Europe littéraire*, 1833; and *Die romantische Schule*, 1836
  [*Letters Auxiliary to the History of Modern Polite Literature in Germany*, 1836; also published as *The Romantic School*, 1882]
Der Salon. 4 vols. (criticism, poetry, unfinished novels, essays, and letters) 1834-40
  [*The Salon; or, Letters on Art, Music, Popular Life and Politics*, 1893]
De l'Allemagne (essays) 1835
  [*Germany.* 2 vols. 1892]
Zur Geschichte der Religion und Philosophie in Deutschland (essay) 1835; published in *Der Salon, Vol. 2*; also published as *De l'Allemagne depuis Luther* in journal *Revue des deux mondes*, 1834
  [*Religion and Philosophy in Germany* (partial translation), 1882]
Shakespeares Mädchen und Frauen (criticism) 1839
  [*Heine on Shakespeare: A Translation of His Notes on Shakespeare's Heroines*, 1895]
Heinrich Heine über Ludwig Börne (criticism and fictional letters) 1840
  [*Ludwig Börne: Recollections of a Revolutionist* (abridged edition), 1881]
Deutschland: Ein Wintermärchen (essay and poetry) 1844
  [*Germany: A Winter's Tale*, 1944]
Neue Gedichte (poetry) 1844
  [*New Poems*, 1904]
Atta Troll: Ein Sommernachtstraum (poetry) 1847
  [*Atta Troll* published in *Atta Troll and Other Poems*, 1876]

*Der Doktor Faust: Ein Tanzpoem, nebst kurosien Ber-
   ichten über Teufel, Hexen und Dichkunst* (ballet
   scenario) 1851
      [*Doktor Faust: A Dance Poem, Together with
      Some Rare Accounts of Witches, Devils and
      the Ancient Art of Sorcery*, 1952]
Romanzero (poetry) 1851
      [*Romancero* published in *The Works of Hein-
      rich Heine.* Vols. XI and XII, 1892]
Die Verbannten Götter (novella) 1853; also published as *Les
   dieux en exil* in journal *Revue des deux mondes*, 1853; and
   Die Götter im Exil in *Vermischte Schriften*, 1854
      [*Gods in Exile*, 1962]
Vermischte Schriften. 3 vols. (poetry, novella, ballet
   scenario, and essays) 1854
Letzte Gedichte und Gedanken (poetry) 1869
The Poems of Heine, Complete (poetry) 1878
Heinrich Heines sämtliche Werke. 12 vols. (poetry,
   essays, ballet scenario, criticism, novella, unfinished
   novels, travel sketches, and memoirs) 1887-90
Heinrich Heines Familienleben (letters) 1892
      [*The Family Life of Heinrich Heine*, 1893]
The Works of Heinrich Heine. 12 vols. (poetry, un-
   finished novels, essays, criticism, travel sketches,
   and letters) 1892-1905
Briefe. 6 vols. (letters) 1950-51
Last Poems (poetry) 1954

CRITICISM

Jocelyne Kolb (essay date 1981)

SOURCE: "Heine's Amusical Muse," in *Monatshefte*,
Vol. 73, No. 4, Winter, 1981, pp. 392-404.

[*In the following essay, Kolb evaluates Heine's criticism of music, claiming that the poet was inexperienced and fairly uninterested in music itself, and that
he used music, rather, as a touchstone to discuss the
feelings it evokes and the creative process.*]

> Whenever a novelist writes two words
> about music, one of them is wrong.
> —Aaron Copland

In his book on Heine's music criticism, Michael Mann
calls the poet a "musical nihilist." The phrase is a felicitous
one, for it conveys both Heine's antagonism towards the
"most romantic of the arts" and his ignorance of it. There
were probably physiological reasons for Heine's malevolence or, at least, indifference towards music: his brother
tells us that he was always hypersensitive to noise and
found it increasingly painful as his illness progressed, and
his secretary reports that he could not tolerate the slightest
sound. But Heine's feelings about music and knowledge of
the art need not concern the reader of his so-called musical
writings; a case study of these texts reveals little if any

connection between what Heine claims to be hearing and
an actual acoustic impression.

Caroline Jaubert is one of the few contemporaries of
Heine's to have realized that he was not actually writing about music he had heard. In the precious yet witty
way characteristic of the century and city in which she
lived, the *grande dame* remarked of Heine that

> Il prétendait n'aimer que la grande musique. Ce
> qu'il entendait par là serait difficile à préciser, fuyant
> également l'Opéra, les Italiens et le Conservatoire.
> Peut-être ne goûtait-il que les symphonies qu'il
> entendait en rêve.

As early as the **Briefe aus Berlin** (1822), Heine himself speaks, not of his indifference towards music but
his ignorance of the art:

> Ich bin zu sehr Laye im Gebiete der Tonkunst, als
> daß ich mein eignes Urtheil über den Werth der
> Spontinischen Kompositionen aussprechen dürfte,
> und alles, was ich hier sage, sind bloß fremde
> Stimmen, die im Gewoge des Tagesgesprächs
> besonders hörbar sind.

Such a comment gives Heine full license; he does not
have to be careful of the things he writes about music
because he can always plead ignorance, either his own
or that of his source. But it is unlikely that he would
choose to write about something he ignored; either he
knew more than he claimed (which I doubt), or this
confession of inadequacy is an admission that he was
not writing about that which he said he was.

A century after Jaubert had expressed her scepticism, an
American critic tried to readjust Heine's reputation as a
musical ignoramus by claiming that the poet was the
undeserving victim of a biographer's harsh judgement.
But the disparaging opinions of Heine's musical proclivities were not limited to one biographer. The question of
his musical knowledge may be a red herring, but it raises
an important issue, for it is based on the false assumption
that his texts treat their ostensible subject. In order to
dispel the confusion and indignation Heine's music criticism has caused, it seems proper to review that critical
response to these texts, in particular that of such contemporaries as Ludwig Börne and Hector Berlioz.

Much of the criticism of Heine's ignorance is unreliable because it merely masks a writer's wish to express his own grievances. Mann goes so far as to claim
that Heine was judged as a credible or incompetent
critic depending on whether he praised or condemned
a work. Certainly we must be wary of Börne's rabid
criticism; his animosity towards Heine is notorious,
and he doubtless exaggerated Heine's antagonism towards music because of his own antagonism towards
the poet. Börne attended a concert with Heine and

wrote of his shock at the latter's lack of familiarity with musical customs:

> Heine saß in Hillers Konzert neben mir. Der ist so unwissend in Musik, daß er die 4 Teile der großen Symphonie für ganz verschiedene Stücke hielt und ihnen die Nummern des Konzertzettels beilegte, wie sie da aufeinander folgen. So nahm er den 2ten Teil der Symphonie für das angekündigte Alt-Solo, den 3ten Teil für ein Violoncello-Solo und den 4ten für die Ouvertüre zum Faust! Da er sich sehr langweilte, war er sehr froh, daß alles so schnell ging und ward wie vom Blitz gerührt, als er von mir erfuhr, daß erst Nr. 1 vorbei sei, wo er dachte, schon 4 Nummern wären ausgestanden.

Heine wrote a review of the same concert that sounds remarkably competent despite what Börne says. While it reflects his gift for mimicry and his receptivity to the comments of others (perhaps even Börne's own) rather than his own musical sensitivity, it does contain some of the typical features of his musical pronouncements, such as his belief in the aesthetic superiority of poetry.

The idiom in this review is unmistakably Heine's, but the text differs from his other on the subject of music because of the connection he makes between words and a musical experience. Heine evokes specific instruments, and he neither seeks a musical refuge in anecdotes about Hiller's person nor indulges in his phony, imitative synaesthesia. His distaste for music is nevertheless evident from the word "unheimlich":

> . . . wilder unheimlicher Jubel hebt an und breitet sich abenteuerlich aus; mitten durch das Geräusch und den begeisterten Aufschwung kriegerisch eintretender Blechinstrumente tönt ein Gesang einsamer Klage, vor welcher das helle Getümmel, zwar nicht teilnahmlos, aber doch unerbittlich vorüber [in] die Weite zieht.

This is not a dry description but a poetic one; Heine uses adverbial embellishments such as "abenteuerlich," "kriegerisch," "teilnahmlos," and "unerbittlich" and leads the reader from musical sounds to the images awakened in his fantasy by them. What is unusual is the fact that he mentions the acoustic experience before transposing it into a literary one—though here too, he is plainly less interested in the music than in the images it brings to mind. Poetry takes the upper hand, as for instance in the following sentence:

> Gern vertieft sich der Zuhörer in die Poesie solcher Darstellung und ruft durch zahlreiche Stellen interessante Bild ins Gedächtnis zurück.

Music means poetry, and images are more important than sound. This is particularly evident in the most spirited part of the review, Heine's criticism of Hiller's overture to *Faust,* where he voices his offense at the idea that one can reduce a literary work to music:

> Man findet in der Hillerschen Komposition, was im "Fauste" der Musik zugänglich ist, die Liebe, den Zauber, das Geheimnisvolle, Rätselhafte, mehr oder minder glücklich aufgefaßt; man erkennt ihre Bedeutung, aber man sieht Absicht und man wird verstimmt [*sic*].

In his own review, of course, Heine has no qualms about gleefully and willfully reducing musical sound to poetic images.

Another trademark of Heine's in this text is the preterition with which it opens and through which the poet reminds the reader of politics. When he says that the current obsession with politics has not managed to obliterate the public's taste for music, he is not dismissing the subject of politics but rather bringing it to the reader's attention: "Trotz der Politik, die alle Geister befangen hält, vermag die Musik sich dennoch hier diesen Winter ganz besonders geltend zu machen." Mann says that we hear in this line "etwas . . . wie nicht ganz freiwilliges Aufatmen von politischem Treiben," and he believes that Heine is disdainful of music because of its inability to communicate political thought.

Anton Schindler is another contemporary of Heine's whose derision of the poets' musical tastes is unreliable. Schindler (1795-1864) was the man of whom Heine made fun as "l'ami de Beethoven." He was Beethoven's friend and first biographer, a violinist and conductor whose many qualities, alas, did not include a sense of humor. His main claim to fame rests indeed upon the fact that he was Beethoven's friend, and this parasitic occupation made him as interesting a target for Heine as the Shakespeare scholar who is ridiculed in *Atta Troll*, Franz Horn. When Heine says that Schindler identified himself on calling cards as "l'ami de Beethoven," he exaggerates in order to increase his repertory of bons mots. Schindler's response, however, is far more exaggerated for "l'ami de Beethoven" seeks to vindicate himself with a retort that lacks wit and bears no resemblance to Heine's own examples of *ad hominem* argumentation. Schindler says the poet is completely ignorant of music, and he bases his assertion on the testimony of—*mirabile dictu*—Börne! But Schindler is less interested in deriding Heine's musical tastes than in rehabilitating his own reputation, and his article (called "Erwiderung") is so obviously petulant and self-serving that his rage and rhetoric are simply embarrassing. Had he cited Heine's criticism of Beethoven's music in the *Lutezia* article of April 1841 (the very article in which Schindler's august person is attacked), then one might take him seriously; but he cites only Börne as his source. He opens his retort by referring to Heine's immoral fall from immortality:

> Diese einstens geistige Größe, Heine, ohne moralischen Unterbau leider sehr früh zur Ruine geworden, leidet nun häufig an übler Laune.

It is painfully evident that Heine's "ruin" dates from the moment he ridiculed Schindler and wrote what the latter calls "schamlose Folgerungen und Verleumdungen wie aus der Feder des ordinairsten Scriblers." Even more painful is Schindler's list of his own successes and talents, which he closes with the modest statement that he need not have mentioned these glories; they are, he says, well known to all but Heine.

Such personal attacks, veiled as music criticism, were not uncommon at the time. Equally common was a penchant for using musical images in literary works. E. T. A. Hoffmann called music the most romantic art because it "expresses the inexpressible," and his veneration for it is echoed throughout the 19th century by writers who imitate the famous essay on Beethoven's instrumental music that Hoffmann wrote in 1809. Musical imagery is omnipresent in romantic poetry, and the figure of the musician is even more prominent after the appearance of Hoffmann's eccentric musical genius, Johannes Kreisler. Yet the admiration of poets for the independence of music coincides with the interest of musicians in program music; paradoxically, the art prized for its lack of referentiality is reduced to a mimetic one. In 1806, Beethoven wrote the *Pastoral Symphony,* a composition with descriptive titles, and in 1830, at the height of the romantic movement in France, Berlioz wrote a literary text explaining the dramatic action of his *Fantastic Symphony.* Two of Schumann's works for piano bear the same title as literary works by Hoffmann, *Kreisleriana* and *Nachtstücke,* and many of Schumann's other works are programmatic as well, such as the *Carnaval* or the *Davidsbündlertänze.* The musician's use of literary texts and titles and the poet's interest in the non-verbal nature of music are paradigmatic of a kind of aesthetic synaesthesia that mirrors the synaesthetic imagery in much writing of the romantic period. The connection of music and text also reflects the growth of commercialism during the 19th century: narratives and titles make music seem less alien to the untrained ear and thus increase the size of concert audiences.

Ever contradictory, Heine was unimpressed by the mysterious and religious qualities of music that enchanted his literary colleagues, but he took advantage of the new musical narratives. At times his writings sound like Hoffmann's, even though the music to which he refers is inaudible. Far from envying the musician, Heine believes that the musician should envy the poet instead; in his works, music is a metaphor for something else, usually for poetry and sometimes for politics, and he scorns the composer's inability to express political concerns through his art. But music is not only a popular subject, it is also a safe one because—as in the Hiller review—it is considered to have no connection with politics. Music as a non-referential art gives the poet more freedom than an art like painting would, and its apparent remoteness from political and social questions paradoxically makes it an appropriate vehicle for the utterance of political, though more often poetical thoughts. It is an attractively vague, but also a voguish, metaphor.

It was not unusual in Heine's time for writers to translate musical experiences into visual ones. Schumann, who like many other romantic composers was also a writer, mentions two ways of writing about music, either "in a poetic fashion by reproducing the various images it evokes in me, or in a dissection of the mechanics of the work." Musicians who write about their art generally combine impressionistic remarks with analytical observations, a trait that differentiates their musical texts from those of non-musicians. For instance, Schumann begins his famous review of Berlioz's *Fantastic Symphony* in the voice of the emotional Florestan, the *persona* he created to express his rhapsodic utterances, but he soberly continues in the voice of Eusebius, the rational *persona* who is more technical in tone and ridicules the sentimentality of Florestan's words. The self-consciousness of this change in perspective is symptomatic of the difficulty inherent in writing about music, and Schumann elsewhere in the review deplores the inability of words to convey musical impressions. Berlioz himself, another composer who was a talented writer, speaks not of "picturing" music but of "understanding" and "conceiving" it. When he writes about music, in however flowery a style, he, too, combines technical and poetic language. His repetition of the imperative "écoutez" when describing Beethoven's *Pastoral Symphony* underlines his attempt to evoke auditory impressions.

There is not a trace of an "écoutez" in those writings of Heine that appear to treat music. Heine could ignore musical sounds altogether by relying on literary texts connected with music, or he could adopt the opinions of friends who knew more than he did. He need not know about his ostensible subject—there would be no way of checking either—for he was an incomparable mimic who could profit from the model of a knowledgeable writer like Hoffmann. But he is as original in his use of the music critic's idiom as he is in his adoption of the lied form in his ***Buch der Lieder.***

Heine could have written about Berlioz's *Fantastic Symphony* without having heard it merely by relying on the composer's program. In the passage about the latter's work, contained in the 10th of his ***Briefe über die Französische Bühne*** (1837), he dissociates words from a musical impression and pays no more than occasional rhetorical homage to the convention of translating acoustic impressions into visual ones. Instead he writes about the people in the concert hall, and it is only by accident that the people on stage happen to be musicians. I do not understand how anyone could take literally Heine's amusing story about the composer and his symphony. The description of Berlioz's "antediluvian" hair and of his impassioned attacks on the drum in response to a glance from Harriet Smithson bears no relation to his meticulous orchestration of his works or to the care with which he oversaw performances of them; it is a delightful tale and no more. Anyone familiar with Heine knows how imprudent it would be to derive historical evidence from such an account; it would be no more prudent to draw musical conclusions from it. Heine's utterances about music are either speculative pronouncements concerning aesthetics or they mask his discussion of another subject.

When describing a performance in a literary work, as for example in the Paganini passage of *Florentinische Nächte,* Heine enters into a poetic daydream. The musical performance is an excuse for him to think poetic thoughts or to write about the creative process. He does not want to be distracted by the music yet is invariably awakened from his daydream, not by the end of the music but by the audience's applause or a philistine's comments. For Heine, music should not shock the listener with its sudden shifts from the sublime to the ridiculous—the poetic equivalent to what Berlioz calls the "contrastes et oppositions" of his musical compositions. Heine's notion of the way to listen to music is that of a self-centered poet, and it explains his aversion to the music of Beethoven, Berlioz, and Wagner; what he likes is that which Berlioz derisively calls "la musique qui berce."

The description of Paganini is preceded by a description of Maximilian's (and Heine's) friend, the bizarre painter Johann Peter Lyser. Lyser was an opera critic in Hamburg, but also happened to be deaf, and not just tone deaf. Heine's interest in a man like Lyser reflects his own non-aural understanding of music; his emphasis on Beethoven's deafness and "extrasensory" music also signals the incompatibility for him of music with sound. In *Lutezia,* he calls music a spiritual art, and the word "spiritual"—given his opposition of sensuality to spirituality—can be translated as "non-sensual." He also says that Beethoven's music is not real (which necessarily makes it inaudible) because it is "eine Vernichtung der Natur"; furthermore, "seine Töne waren nur Erinnerungen eines Tones, Gespenster verschollener Klänge." Heine does not refer to sound yet, paradoxically, is horrified by Beethoven's music since it demands the listener's attention and diverges from his conservative musical expectations. The listener is forced to concentrate on the music and cannot indulge in poetic visions:

> Namentlich Beethoven treibt die spiritualistische Kunst bis zu jener tönenden Agonie der Erscheinungswelt, bis zu jener Vernichtung der Natur, die mich mit einem Grauen erfüllt, das ich nicht verhehlen mag, obgleich meine Freunde darüber den Kopf schütteln. Für mich ist es ein sehr bedeutungsvoller Umstand, daß Beethoven am Ende seiner Tage taub ward und sogar die

> unsichtbare Tonwelt keine klingende Realität mehr für ihn hatte. Seine Töne waren nur noch Erinnerungen eines Tones, Gespenster verschollener Klänge, und seine letzten Produktionen tragen an der Stirne ein unheimliches Totenmal.

Heine expresses what he perceives as the extrasensory nature of Beethoven's music with the synaesthetic phrase "tönende Agonie der Erscheinungswelt," but the dominant sense in it is not, as one would expect, the sense of hearing; it is the sense of sight. The word "tönend" is the least important and serves merely to embellish the visual noun, "Erscheinungswelt," which is more descriptive of poetry than music.

> Il juge de la musique
> comme tous les poètes, c'est-
> à-dire que le sens de cet art
> *lui manque complètement.*
>
> —Hector Berlioz

The most reliable contemporary judge of Heine's competence as a music critic was Berlioz. He is credible because he was the poet's artistic equal and because, besides being his friend, he was a writer as well as a musician. If Berlioz had belittled Heine's musical tastes, we could hardly blame him, for his music was no safer from the satirist's attacks than that of Beethoven or Wagner. Yet it seems he better understood that his contemporaries (and some more recent critics) that whatever Heine said about him had little to do with his person and even less with his music. Berlioz did not respond vengefully to his friend's caricature of him; he was amused by it because he recognized Heine's artistic distortion of fact. His response to the poet's notorious account of the *Fantastic Symphony* is contained in a letter to Liszt, dated 8 February, 1838—a letter remarkable not only because of the composer's leniency towards Heine, but also because of his magnanimity towards Chopin:

> Notre ami Heine a parlé de nous deux dans la *Gazette Musicale* [of February 4] avec autant d'esprit que d'irrévérence, mais sans méchanceté aucune toutefois; il a, en revanche, tressé pour Chopin une couronne qu'il mérite depuis longtemps.

Heine's irreverent and witty text bears quoting, at least in part, so that the reader can be his own judge of Heine's wickedness, on the one hand, and of Berlioz's understanding, on the other:

> Man erwartet Außerordentliches, da dieser Komponist schon Außerordentliches geleistet. Seine Geistesrichtung ist das Phantastische, nicht verbunden mit Gemüt, sondern mit Sentimentalität: er hat große Ähnlichkeit mit Callot, Gozzi und Hoffmann. Schon seine äußere Erscheinung deutet darauf hin. Es ist schade, daß er seine ungeheure, antediluvianische Frisur, diese aufsträubenden Haare,

die über seine Stirne wie ein Wald über eine schroffe Felswand sich erhoben, abschneiden lassen; so sah ich ihn zum erstenmale vor sechs Jahren, und so wird er immer in meinem Gedächtnisse stehen. Es war im Conservatoire de Musique, und man gab eine große Symphonie von ihm, ein bizarres Nachtstück, das nur zuweilen erhellt wird von einer sentimentalweißen Weiberrobe, die darin hin- und herflattert, oder von einem schwefelgelben Blitz der Ironie. Das Beste darin ist ein Hexensabbat, wo der Teufel Messe liest und die katholische Kirchenmusik mit der schauerlichsten, blutigsten Possenhaftigkeit parodiert wird. Es ist eine Farce, wobei alle geheimen Schlangen, die wir im Herzen tragen, freudig emporzischen. Mein Logennachbar, ein redseliger junger Mann, zeigte mir den Komponisten, welcher sich am äußersten Ende des Saales in einem Winkel des Orchesters befand und die Pauke schlug. Denn die Pauke ist sein Instrument. 'Sehen Sie in der Avant-scene,' sagte mein Nachbar, 'jene dicke Engländerin? Das ist Miß Smithson; in diese Dame ist Herr Berlioz seit drei Jahren sterbens verliebt, und dieser Leidenschaft verdanken wir die wilde Symphonie, die Sie heute hören.' In der That, in der Avant-scene-Loge saß die berühmte Schauspielerin von Conventgarden; Berlioz sah immer unverwandt nach ihr hin, und jedesmal, wenn sein Blick dem ibrigen begegnete, schlug er los auf seine Pauke wie wütend. Miß Smithson ist seitdem Madame Berlioz geworden, und ihr Gatte hat sich seitdem auch die Haare abschneiden lassen. Als ich diesen Winter im Conservatoire wieder seine Symphonie hörte, saß er wieder als Paukenschläger im Hintergrunde des Orchesters, die dicke Engländerin saß wieder in der Avant-scene, ihre Blicke begegneten sich wieder . . . aber er schlug nicht mehr so wütend auf die Pauke.

The French version Berlioz read is different. For instance, Harriet Smithson is not called a "dicke Engländerin" but rather a "belle Anglaise que les actrices françaises ont tant imitée," a change that is gallant rather than substantive. Besides, the reference to her talent and fame would have been out of place in the German version. A more important change is Heine's addition of a note after the sentence, "aber er schlug nicht so wütend auf die Pauke":

Cette lettre a été écrite au commencement de l'année 1837. Il s'est opéré depuis une transformation dans la musique de Berlioz, et nous en avons la preuve dans sa deuxième symphonie, d'un caractère plus *mélodique* et plus doux, ainsi que dans sa deuxième composition: le *Requiem,* en l'honneur des morts de Constantine, dont le style diffère essentiellement de celui de ses précédentes oeuvres, et qui a eu un retentissement si général en Europe (Note de l'auteur).

Berlioz's compositions were often criticized for a lack of melody, and these words must certainly have pleased

him. They could even have quelled an ill humored response. But his charitable reaction was not exceptional: he was greatly amused by a parody of his monodrama *Lélio* (the second symphony of which Heine speaks) and did not take ill to the caricatures of him in the satirical journal *Charivari.* Of the *Lélio* parody he said that:

pour moi, qui en ai ri du meilleur de mon coeur, je ne puis que souhaiter sincèrement de pouvoir écrire et faire exécuter *avant* l'année prochaine une autre composition *semblable* pour servir de texte aux lazzis des bouffons de l'opéra.

Berlioz had a keen sense of humor and was willing to submit to mockery when it came from a man whom he recognized to be his artistic equal. Nevertheless, I believe there are still other reasons besides magnanimity and the changes in Heine's French text for Berlioz to have been amused rather than infuriated by his friend's description.

The striking thing about Heine's narration is not that it lacks verisimilitude, but that it is, literally, amusical. He mentions the sound of the drum, but it is the only sound he mentions, and he is not interested in the acoustic properties of the instrument, only in Berlioz's vigor and subsequent lack of vigor when beating on it. The music is not even described affectively; there is no attempt to recreate its effect on the listener's emotions, as is usually the case in what Steven Scher has termed "verbal music." The concert merely provides a setting for the poet's narrative and satirical talents; is itself not the subject of the article, and Berlioz apparently recognized the lack of a connection between his music and Heine's text.

The vocabulary Heine uses is entirely literary, as for example when he calls the *Fantastic Symphony* "ein bizarres Nachtstück, das nur zuweilen erhellt wird . . . von einem schwefelgelben Blitz der Ironie." "Nachtstück" immediately recalls Hoffmann, whom Heine mentions a few lines earlier and the word "irony" can only be applied to music with difficulty, in the uneasy way the word "musical" is applied to literature. The sentence that follows appears to have a direct relation to the music and, furthermore, to explain the use of "irony" as descriptive of the parody of religious music; but this, too, is deceptive, for the word "parody" is taken from Berlioz's own program for the *Fantastic Symphony* (in its 1832 version). Thus Heine's recognition of musical parody is not, as it might appear, an indication of his musical sophistication. Since Berlioz speaks of "une parodie burlesque du dies irae," Heine's words are little more than a translation, as "Possenhaftigkeit" is a good rendering of "burlesque." Berlioz would have liked to hear the word "irony" applied to his music, even though it is vague; likewise, he could hardly object to what he must have recognized as the similarity between Heine's words and his own.

The French composer was not jealous of his dignity, but he was very serious about his art, which is obvious from many passages in his *Memoirs* and from his reaction to the *Lélio* parody. Berlioz considered himself one of an artistic élite; he had little patience with philistines, and his intolerance of the musical ignorance of those professing to be musicians could make him as vicious as Heine. He was not offended by Heine's ridicule, because the latter was an artist of genius and no musician; but he did not accept the ridicule passively and, in turn, mocked his friend's musical inferiority. Léon Guichard is right when he remarks that Berlioz understood Heine better than Heine tried to understand Berlioz. Yet this is only to be expected, since Heine was unreceptive to music whereas Berlioz was himself a writer.

Berlioz addressed to Heine one of the letters in which he recorded the details of his first concert tour in Germany. It probably is the best document for an assessment of knowledge of music, because Berlioz kept his supposed correspondent clearly in mind even when discussing musical matters in some detail. Guichard says that Berlioz, in writing these letters, which, later on, were included in his *Memoirs* as "Premier Voyage en Allemagne,"

> s'est appliqué à donner à chacune d'elles un ton, un tour particuliers, en rapport avec la personnalité de celui ou celle à qui il s'adressait.

But I do not agree, even though the other recipients, with the exception of Liszt, are less well-known than Heine, which makes it hard to know exactly what the "proper" tone would be, Berlioz does not address them as often as he does Heine; one can read the other letters for pages without being reminded of a supposed correspondent.

The letter to Heine opens with a bantering tone; Berlioz calls his friend a "chat-tigre" and alludes both to Heine's talent as a poet and, in much less flattering terms, to his "musicianship." With a detachment and self-irony not uncommon to Berlioz, but here, in addition, reflecting an attempt to imitate the poet's style, the composer notes the absurdity of discussing musical matters with a non-musician. Mockingly, he states: "Je vous parle de tous ces détails pour vous faire une réputation de musicien." At the end of the letter, when citing a musical example, Berlioz says in parenthesis: "J'en suis fâché, mon cher poëte, mais vous voilà compromis comme musicien." Berlioz thus exposes both his friend's ignorance and the fiction that this was a real letter to Heine; he also shows himself aware of the illogicality of addressing to a musical nihilist so many technical remarks. His letter is of interest because it gives more evidence of his self-irony and shows his receptivity to fictionalizations presented as facts. Further it offers what is, in all likelihood, the most sober

view of Heine's musical limitations while at the same time, putting them into their proper perspective: Berlioz's mockery of Heine's musical gifts is rendered insignificant by his admiration of the German's poetical and satirical talents.

In an article from 1855, Berlioz again refers to Heine and music, this time bestowing on him a back-handed compliment. Namely, he claims that all poets write badly about music, but that Heine writes less nonsense than most:

> Aujourd'hui tout le monde s'occupe peu ou prou de ce pauvre bel art. . . . Voyez ce que vient d'écrire sur les musiciens modernes cet infatigable mourant, d'un si cruel et charmant esprit, Henri Heine. . . . Je répéterai seulement ici que Heine parlant de musique ne déraisonne pas plus, qu'il déraisonne même beaucoup moins que la plupart des poètes. Il a évidemment le sens de la grandeur de cet art, sinon de ses finesses; il a une idée des qualités qui constituent le style musical; il ne prend pas des taupinières pour des Alpes.

Berlioz's mistrust of poets who write about music is echoed by Heine's distaste for program music—the contemptuous poet's answer to the scornful musician's scepticism. It is not surprising that Berlioz, who often makes use of the word "poetic" when writing about music does refer to poetry no more than does Heine to music when he uses the words "Lied" or "Gesang." Each writer applies to his own art the vocabulary of the other, but in a metaphorical sense. It is a mistake to take them literally.

What Berlioz says about Heine in his critical yet not vituperative remarks gives us an idea of the latter's—at the best, sketchy—knowledge of music. Heine's writings on the subject do not tell us much about the art he claims to be discussing, but this is the result less of his ignorance than of his wish to make original use of a common image and to treat topics that interest him. It seems to me that instead of maligning Heine's musical sense, like Schindler, or defending it, like Graf, one should recognize that the references to music in his works, especially his fiction, are not to be read as evocation of music. The comments about music attributed to Heine by Alexander Weill illustrate the necessity to understand the poet's musical pronouncements figuratively. Weill quotes Heine as saying what to a musician sounds mostly like gibberish:

> On m'a dit—je crois que c'est Berlioz, car Meyerbeer me boude,—que deux dissonances produisent toujours une harmonie et que l'accord parfait est composé d'une tierce, d'une quinte et d'une octave, mystère que les cabalistes ont appliqué à l'amour. On m'a même assuré qu'il existait une gamme de couleurs. Bref, tout ce qui dure, tout ce qui fait plaisir est un composé de contrastes.

It would not have bothered Heine that this makes little musical sense; what would have interested him is the notion that two dissonances always produce something pleasant, and that whatever lasts is composed of contrasts. For his own aesthetic is based on these very assumptions. The translation of musical terms into poetical ones so that they apply only to poetry, though not a very precise use of metaphor, exists in all of Heine's writings on music. Heine was not envious of the musician's mysterious language; he exploited the mysterious subject to create a secret language of his own.

S. S. Prawer (essay date 1983)

SOURCE: "Prologue: A Comet Lights the Diaspora," in *Heine's Jewish Comedy: A Study of His Portraits of Jews and Judaism,* Oxford at the Clarendon Press, 1983, pp. 1-43.

[*In the following excerpt, Prawer discusses Heine's life, especially his relationship with Eduard Gans, focusing on his changing attitudes toward Judaism.*]

Heine's work is full of verbal snapshots, portraits, and caricatures of Jews actual and imagined, historical and contemporary, famous and obscure, single and in groups, ex-Jews, and Jews who remained within the community to which their fathers had belonged. . . . The gallery . . . depicts peddlers, old clothes men, pawnbrokers, corn-cutters, shopkeepers, brokers, speculators of various kinds, bankers, scholars, rabbis, synagogue cantors and beadles, university students, poets, musicians, painters, impresarios, journalists, society hostesses, and Jews in many other walks of life—all seen from the perspective of a nineteenth-century German poet who was born a Jew but who thought it necessary to pay the price of baptism for his entry into the wider cultural community of the West. 'Modern poetry', Heine said in one of his works, echoing Hegel but speaking very much out of his own experience, 'is no longer objective, epic, and naive; it is subjective, lyrical and reflective'. The portraits are therefore coloured by the poet's mood, by his own changing problems and purposes; they are often parabolic, exaggerating aspects of an individual's outer appearance in order to portray what Heine called the 'signature' of his inner being, or using his name and aspects of his personality in order to characterize a whole group. He frequently invents incidents in order to bring out what he considers essential traits, and uses dream and fantasy as readily as realistically described action in pursuit of this same purpose. 'History', he wrote in 1828, in defence of his method, 'is not falsified by the poets. They faithfully convey its meaning even when they invent figures and incidents'. For Heine, every true historian must have something of the poet in him; but he must also have something of the philosopher. The

highest compliment he could pay to a historian he admired was to say that he combined the talents and insights of a philosopher with those of a great artist (letter to Jules Michelet, 20 January 1834).

While Heine was ever anxious to champion the imaginative writer's approach against that of professional historians, to urge the claims of Sir Walter Scott against those of David Hume and his own against those of Leopold von Ranke, he was also perfectly well aware of temperamental quirks and weaknesses which impaired the clarity of his own view of men and events.

> It is part of my character, or rather my sickness, that in moments of ill humour I do not spare even my best friends, going so far as to mock and maltreat them in the most hurtful way. (Letter to Joseph Lehmann, 26 June 1823)

Heine's utterances have to be seen in their particular context (at whom are they directed? what purpose is the poet pursuing? what provocation has he had? what censorship does he seek to circumvent?); and they have to be held and weighed against other evidence. Nevertheless, he does convey certain aspects of nineteenth-century experience more powerfully than any other writer—and among these aspects the Jewish experience looms large, not in spite of but just because of the feeling, expressed in a letter to Rudolf Christiani dated 7 March 1824, that what water was to the fish, Germanness was to him. He just could not live outside the element of the German language and German culture. Heine was a poet truly alive in his own time and place, sensitive to social and intellectual currents, aware of the historical forces which had made Europe what it was and were transforming it into what it was yet to become. And being a poet meant that he was not only sensitive and aware, but also able to express himself more fully than others, able to use words 'to sharpen his awareness of his ways of feeling, so making these communicable.' These qualities are well to the fore in his depiction of what [Prawer] calls [Heine's] 'Jewish Comedy'.

The choice of this title should serve to remind the reader that Dante was one of Heine's literary heroes—he often glanced towards him for confirmation of his own personality and art, assenting to his description of the miseries and humiliations of exile, and calling the author of the *Inferno* 'the public prosecutor among the poets.' In the final stanzas of **Germany. A Winter's Tale (Deutschland. Ein Wintermärchen)** he compares his own work with the *Inferno*: whoever has once been consigned to these "melodious flames" is doomed to stay there for eternity—no saint and no saviour can release him for as long as there are men to read and respond to the poet's words. And if the wealth of sharply etched figures in Heine's writings does indeed recall the *Divine Comedy,* from which they differ in so many other fundamental respects, then the recurrence of many of these figures in one work after another recalls the technique of the *Human Comedy* of Balzac, whom Heine knew personally and who dedicated one of his stories to him. The 'Jewish Comedy' of my title should therefore recall aspects of both Dante and Balzac. It should also remind us of the sharp and often cruel eye for the *comic* which Heine demonstrated in his depiction of other men, including the many Jews who appear in his pages; but his 'Comedy' can no more be restricted to the merely comic than can those of his great predecessor and contemporary.

> What a tragic story is the history of the Jews in modern times! And if one tried to write about this tragic element, one would be laughed at for one's pains. That is the most tragic thing of all.

This inextricable intertwining of the comic and the tragic gives his Jewish Comedy its sharply distinctive flavour, and helps to make it an important part of that *comédie intellectuelle,* that drama of the human mind, which Paul Valéry saw in all literature.

Among the famous who appear in these pages are the Rothschilds, Meyerbeer and his family, Ludwig Börne, the Mendelssohns, Achille Fould, and many others; they are intermingled with fictional characters like the corn-cutter Hirsch-Hyazinth, and little Samson, the champion of a God who works no miracles through him. Biblical characters and characters from Jewish history are presented in a new light by a poet deeply concerned with the problems of his own time; and we find depictions of the Jews as a people, a kinship group, a religious-social community, and a cultural subgroup, which place the individual portraits into a wider, developing context. From his own existential vantage point, of which this book tries at all times to keep the reader aware, Heine looked out at other men and women, including many of Jewish origin, and created out of what he saw a fascinating portrait gallery. . . .

When one speaks of 'portraits' in this context one is, of course, applying a metaphor from the visual to the verbal arts. Heine himself constantly sought such metaphoric illumination, and in the course of his life he described his own writings in terms of at least four distinct visual forms. One of these is the early photograph, the daguerreotype, whose development Heine viewed with fascination though also with some misgivings: in one of his last works he speaks of the scenes from Parisian life which he first published in the 1840s and then radically revised in the 1850s as 'honest daguerreotypes' significantly arranged by the artist. The second of the visual forms for which Heine saw analogies in his own writings is that of painting in general and realistic painting in particular—an art which, however faithfully it seeks to match the superficies of life, is of necessity more selective, and more expressive of the artist as well as the ostensible subject, than a photograph. We shall find him presenting himself to his readers, more than once, as a guide through a picture-gallery. Thirdly, perhaps most important of all, Heine not infrequently speaks of some of the contemporaries whom he introduces into his writings as *Fratzen* or *Karikaturen*. The second of these terms reminds us that his later works were composed in a Paris that saw an unprecedented flowering of the art of caricature in the cartoons and lampoons of Charles Philipon, in Grandville's scenes from 'animal' life, and above all in the superb drawings and lithographs of Honoré Daumier. When Heine introduces a thumb-nail sketch of an obscure mustachioed contemporary into one of his letters from Paris, or when he merges Meyerbeer's activities as an orchestral conductor with his alleged activities as an orchestrator and conductor of his own fame, then we cannot but recall the cartoons and caricatures that were so prominent features of French life, entertainment, and social comment in the mid-nineteenth century: an age in which no Parisian could look at Louis Philippe's head without being at once reminded of Philipon's pear. Most of Heine's portraits could be ranged along a scale whose end-points are suggested by Fielding in his Preface to *Joseph Andrews*: the scale, let us say, between Hogarth at one end and Gillray at the other. One is constantly reminded of the *portrait-charge* or loaded likeness which dominated French caricature from Philipon to André Gill, and of Daumier's caricature maquettes: little clay busts which depicted in the round the lawyers and politicians that people his lithographs. Heine in fact uses the image of the portrait statue—*ein ikonisches Standbild*—when he talks of his depiction of Ludwig Börne: an attempt, surely, to counteract the two-dimensional suggestions adhering to his other images from the visual arts, and to suggest a greater multiplicity of possible angles of vision from which the same portrait might be seen.

One must not, however, think of the literary portrait, as it is found in Heine's works, too exclusively in terms of the visual arts. The historical portraits he found in the works of historians he read—particularly such French contemporaries as Thiers, Mignet, Michelet, and Thierry—were a powerful influence; here he could find confirmation of his own penchant for subordinating visual to intellectual and moral elements, for characterizing by description and evocation of activities, thoughts, and verbal expressions, rather than those of peculiar features of face and body. Nor is it only *contemporary* historians, in Germany as well as France, who are assimilated in this way. There is an illuminating remark in Theodor Creizenach's recollections of a conversation he had with Heine when he visited him in 1846. Creizenach found the poet reading J. M. Jost's history of the Jews; and he tells us that Heine said to him: 'If I were certain of another ten years of life, then I too would write Jewish histories. As preparation, however, it would be necessary to read no book but Herodotus for a whole year.' Herodotus's cosmopolitan interest in states and individuals beyond his own Dorian front door; his scepticism, again and again overwhelmed by delight in Arabian Nights' and travellers' tales; his powerful sense of the mythic; his love of digressions to embellish his central themes, and his deliberate intermingling of the great and the small; his handling of the Ionian language, so easy and fluent, yet at the same time so consummately polished—all these features may be found again, *mutatis mutandis,* in Heine's verbal portraits, sketches, and cartoons of historical and contemporary figures. Above all, Herodotus would seem to have offered him what he also saw in the work of writers like Michelet and Thierry: a combination of curiosity about life with an artist's command of language, a union, in short, of poetry and history. But Heine had not been a pupil of Hegel's for nothing; poetry and history had also to be informed, in his view, by philosophy. The letter to Jules Michelet of 20 January 1834 to which I have already referred, is particularly illuminating in this respect; for it shows clearly what he missed in Herodotus as well as what he found there.

> You are the true historian, because you are at the same time a philosopher and a great artist. You are a Herodotus who is not credulous, you are a Tacitus who does not despair. . . . You believe in progress and in providence. In that belief we are at one.

Heine ends his letter with an admiring reference to Michelet's style, which he dare not comment on further because of what he feels to be his own imperfect command of the French language.

Throughout his life, Heine read and assimilated a great deal of literature, and literary traditions, actual and nascent, play a powerful part in all his works. He saw himself in many ways as the heir of Aristophanes: in both authors vigorously characterized personages become symbols or indices of social, political, and aesthetic forces and conditions. The 'character' tradition too, running from Theophrastus via La Bruyère into many European literatures, Menippean satire, the 'characterizations' of Friedrich Schlegel, and the European novel, from his beloved *Don Quixote* to the writings of Scott and the young Dickens, all helped to shape his way of seeing and his manner of expression, as did the pen-portraits of contemporaries which he found in the journals he so avidly read until paralysis made it impossible to frequent Parisian *cabinets de lecture.* For all his assimilation of such varied elements he retains his distinctive voice—a voice never drowned by the voices of his predecessors and contemporaries whose echoes are still audible as we listen, with our inner ear, to what Heine has to tell us.

Heine more than once deplored the use of documents a poet had not himself intended for publication; and

the stress in this book will be on works that first appeared before the general reading public in a form the poet himself sanctioned. We would lose a great deal, however, if we disregarded other material that became public property after his death—his letters, jottings, and conversations with others. Such material will therefore be considered in the 'Intermezzi' which follow each of the four main parts into which the present book is divided. Heine's portraits and caricatures of Jews and Judaism will be brought before the reader in chronological sections, and in the context of his development as a man and as a poet; this Prologue, however, will introduce the material and methods to be used by following one such depiction all the way through his work and then through all the letters and conversations that have been preserved.

The extent and the (severe) limitations of Heine's knowledge of Torah and Talmud, of Jewish ritual and folklore, of the Hebrew language and contemporary Yiddish, have been exhaustively documented and examined—most recently by Ruth L. Jacobi in her book on Heine's Jewish heritage (*Heines jüdisches Erbe,* 1978) and by Jeffrey L. Sammons in *Heinrich Heine. A Modern Biography* (1979). Professor Sammons describes very well how Jewishness became and remained a significant part of the poet's cultural consciousness. At the age of six, he tells us, Heine

> was placed in a communal Hebrew school run by a distant relative of the family named Rintelsohn. It is not easy to say how much he learned in this school. One of the deepest students of his Jewish environment thinks it probably was not much and that the time would have been taken up largely by relating Midrashic legends, which would have suited young Heine perfectly. In the greatest of his late 'Hebrew Melodies' he ascribes to the poet Jehuda ha-Levi a youthful preference for the homiletic and parabolic narratives of the Talmud to its legal disputation, which very likely reflects his own boyhood inclination. It is doubtful that he ever learned to read Hebrew with any facility. He knew some words and phrases, naturally; he could remember part of a verb paradigm, which he built into a joke in *The Book of LeGrand,* and he could write the cursive script, which he employs very occasionally for a word or two in his letters. But his transliterations of Hebrew phrases are often wildly faulty and, when he needed a translation of sections from the Passover service, he had to ask a friend to do it for him.

This raises, for Professor Sammons and for us, the question of the quality of Jewish life in Heine's paternal home. His mother had become hostile to orthodox Judaism after early clashes with the Jewish community in Düsseldorf, though she never formally abandoned the faith into which she had been born. Her son soon found himself, to quote Professor Sammons yet again, 'on one side of a rather rapid generational transition'.

His father appears to have been conventionally if sincerely pious, though at the end of his memoir-fragment Heine tells us that his father advised him against the appearance of atheism because it would be bad for business; furthermore, Samson Heine was apparently a Freemason, which he certainly could not have been if this orthodoxy had still been intact. Uncle Salomon was certainly strongly committed to the Jewish community, which he supported generously and to which he left a variety of significant legacies in his will. But in that same document he excused his son from all memorial rituals, including the 'kaddish' which, of course, he had no right in Jewish law to do. The ambitious social climbing of the family naturally presupposed conversion to Christianity by all hands, and Salomon must have regarded this circumstance with equanimity, though in fact his own son resisted it. There are anecdotes indicating that Heine was raised to keep the Sabbath, and his evident familiarity with the Passover 'seder', so effectively described in *The Rabbi of Bacherach,* suggests the probability that it was celebrated in his home. Heine remarked there that even renegade Jews are moved in their hearts when they hear the melody of the Passover ritual; very likely he was thinking of himself. There is no other evidence that the family was observant. Heine nowhere mentions celebrating any holy days and there is no indication that he ever had a bar mitzvah or was even exposed to the rites and customs of the observant Jew. In fact he makes errors in simple Jewish matters of a kind that would not be usual for one with a traditional upbringing. During his student days he undertook an extensive study of Jewish history and tradition, and it is likely that most of what he knew derived from that experience rather than from his boyhood. It is true that he was very firm in the Bible—in Luther's translation, of course—and that his interest in it increased as the years went by. But Luther's Bible has always been a fundamental resource for German writers, and Heine differs from the usual pattern perhaps only by a somewhat greater emphasis on the Old Testament. . . .

But one important caveat must now be entered. Into Heine's many and varied writings portraits of Jews intrude surprisingly often—as contemporary friends and enemies were quick to notice. Nevertheless, they form only one strand in a most varied tapestry; and though I shall try, throughout, to place the portraits I isolate into their full context, the very fact of focusing on just one set of details is bound to lend these a prominence that is not theirs in the original design. For every single portrait of a recognizably Jewish figure there are many portraits or sketches of Germans and Frenchmen, Englishmen and Italians, men and women of past and present, which have no overt connection with Jews or Judaism. We also find, of course, many portraits of those whose connection with Judaism was that they were implacably hostile to it and to all those who professed it. Historians who want to trace the development of Jew—hatred from primitive xenophobia and religious intolerance to modern racial

anti-Semitism can find many relevant pages in Heine's works—some of these, indeed, seem to anticipate the holocaust of the present century. This context too I shall try to keep before the reader. Nevertheless, as I have said, isolation of a single group of portraits is bound to lend that group a prominence which the author did not intend. I am encouraged, however, by my experience with some volumes issued many years ago by the curators of the British National Gallery under the title: *100 Details from Pictures in the National Gallery* and *More Details from Pictures in the National Gallery.* These treasured volumes have helped me, over the years, to appreciate the National Gallery collection more fully than I would have done without their help. Need I say that I hope the reader of the present book will have the same experience when he returns to Heine's own works and reintegrates into their original context the passages I have transferred into mine?

Heine's attitudes developed and changed, and the portraiture this book discusses developed and changed with them. Moreover, his portraits of individuals usually occur in contrasting or supportive groups—as when Mendelssohn-Bartholdy and Meyerbeer are compared and contrasted with Rossini, when Ludwig Börne is shown in the midst of his admirers and disciples, when James de Rothschild is held against the Foulds or the Péreires. The same holds good of fictional portraits: Gumpelino and Hirsch-Hyazinth need one another like Don Quixote and Sancho Panza, and by the time Heine begins to write the third chapter of the incomplete *Rabbi von Bacherach* the pious Ashkenazic rabbi has come to need a worldly, Sephardic foil and complement. . . . Before launching into a chronological discussion of such portraits and portrait groupings I would like to look in some detail at just one developing portrait: that of Eduard Gans (1797-1839), a pupil and editor of Hegel who became a professor of law in the University of Berlin.

Heine first met Gans in the early 1820s. They came together in Berlin, where Gans had helped to found a Society for the Culture and Science of the Jews (*Verein für Cultur und Wissenschaft der Juden*), which Heine himself joined on 4 August 1822. The *Wissenschaft* of this title denoted an ideal of scholarly discipline which sought to apply carefully thought-out critical-philological methods to the source materials that speak to us of the past, without the need to pronounce 'superior' value-judgements on the ages and cultures whose 'essence' was to be disengaged. The genitive construction *Wissenschaft der Juden* implied that this discipline was to be *applied to* the products of Jewish culture and to be *spread among* the Jews. One of the suborganizations of this Society was an institute for the scholarly, *wissenschaftlich* study of Judaism, whose results were to be published in a journal: the term used to describe both institute and journal, *Wissenschaft des Judentums,* was to have a great future in Jewish scholarship. There was also an education section in which Heine lectured on German history and institutions to young Jews from the Polish provinces. Since most of the younger members of the Society had come under the influence of Hegel, their conception of science and scholarship tended to have a Hegelian slant; but among the older members there was at least one confirmed Kantian, Lazarus Bendavid. It is also worth noting that the fullest statement of the Society's aims and philosophy, formulated by I. Wohlwill with help from the others, alluded to Leibniz's monadology in one of its key sentences—an allusion Heine seems to have found highly amusing.

Gans was born in the same year as Heine; like Heine he received his secondary education in a Gentile *Gymnasium;* like Heine again, he refused to consider a business career (traditional in both their fathers' families) and studied law at the universities of Göttingen and Berlin; like Heine he hoped to take advantage of the more tolerant attitudes that seemed to be developing in Germany in order to obtain a professorship at a German university. What drew the two men together into the Society for the Culture and Science of the Jews was a feeling that the Jewish communities of Germany were failing to realize their full cultural potential; that scientific (*wissenschaftlich*) study of all the manifestations of Jewish life (*Kultur* in the all-embracing sense) was necessary in order to show actualities and possibilities—to make Jews aware of what they had been, what they were, and what they could be in nineteenth-century German society. It was also hoped that 'scientific' study of Jewish culture would dispel prejudices among Germans and would lead, through the absorption of Jewish energies in matters other than trade and money transactions, to a better integration of Jews into German society. The Society's aim, therefore, was threefold:

> (i) to spread modern science and scholarship, a spirit of *Wissenschaft* whose chief philosophical repre-sentative was thought to be Hegel, among German Jews, in order to enable them to take their proper place in German society once full civil rights had been granted them;
>
> (ii) to study, in a scholarly, 'scientific' way, Jewish cultural achievement in all fields, in order to disengage—in Hegelian fashion—the 'essence' of Judaism; this would help to define the nature of the contribution Jews had made throughout the ages to religion, philosophy, history, law, literature, and civic affairs;
>
> (iii) to inform Jews and Gentiles alike of the results of these studies, by means of scholarly publications and lectures, in order to acquaint the Jewish world with its own inner essence and the Gentile word with the valuable contributions Jews had made, and could continue to make, to the sum total of human culture.

The Society did not find wide support, and was disbanded after a few years for lack of money and membership; but through the scholarly labours of Leopold Zunz it exerted a powerful influence on Jewish scholarship and Jewish self-definition in Germany long after it had ceased to exist.

Gans and Heine met outside the framework of the Society too; but there were some temperamental clashes, and each therefore tended to visit circles in which they were both received only at times when he knew that the other would not be there. Both Heine and Gans accepted baptism for the sake of their careers rather than out of conviction that Christianity was the only true faith. 'If the state is so stupid', Gans is reported to have said to Felix Eberty, 'as to forbid me to serve it in a capacity which suits my particular talents unless I profess something I do not believe—and something which the responsible minister *knows* I do not believe: all right then, it shall have its wish.'

The reader of Heine's works meets Gans first in a series of *Letters from Berlin* (*Briefe aus Berlin*) in which the young poet sought to convey his experience of city life to the readers of a provincial newspaper. The writer of these *Letters* encounters Gans in the street, and at once asks him for news—'petty news of the town', *armselige Stadtneuigkeiten,* such as provincial readers will lap up. But Gans is not in a mood for gossip: 'He shakes his grey reverent head and shrugs his shoulders.' The questioner therefore deserts him abruptly and collars another informant, a musician who 'always has a pocketful of news' and who, once he starts unpacking these, goes on without stopping, like a mill-wheel.

This brief first glimpse of Gans (in the context of many other figures or institutions) suggests that he is known as a gossip, but that he is also moody; that despite his youth (he was just twenty-five years old at the time) he can give the impression of being an old man; that the shrug is a gesture characteristic of him. The young-old man shrugging his shoulders: a Jewish caricature is in the making.

Gans next surfaces, for a moment, in one of the fictional dreams that are so important a structural feature of *The Hartz Journey* (*Die Harzreise,* 1826). Having climbed the 'Brocken' mountain, famed for its association with witches and devil-worship, the narrator finds himself troubled by 'chaotic, frightening, fantastic visions'—'Dante's *Inferno* arranged for the piano'—which culminate in the performance of a dream opera entitled *Falcidia.* That opera, the narrator tells us, had a legal text by Gans, something to do with the laws of inheritance, and music by Berlin's most fashionable Italian composer, Gasparo Spontini. *Erbrechtlicher Text von Gans*: here *The Hartz Journey* adds three further items to the developing portrait-caricature. First, a piece of information: the subject which Gans had made his special study was the Law of Inheritance, of which the Roman *lex Falcidia* was an important component. Secondly, a pun: *érbrechtlich* means 'pertaining to inheritance'; but if the stress is slightly shifted (*erbréchtlich*) it looks as though the word were an absurd Yiddishism, cognate with *sich erbrechen* ('to be sick') and meant 'sick-making'. We know from other evidence that Heine did not think highly of the style in which Gans's early works were written. Lastly, an atmosphere: is there not something theatrical, bombastic, Italian opera-like about Gans?

A later 'travel picture', ***Ideas. The Book of LeGrand*** (***Ideen. Das Buch LeGrand,*** 1827) introduces Gans yet again in a brief but significant passage. Heine mocks the pedantic habit of excessive quotation to which German scholars are particularly prone and he illustrates this with the case of the man who in early editions is simply designated as 'my friend G. in Berlin'.

> My friend G. in Berlin is, so to speak, a little Rothschild in the matter of quotations. He'll be glad to lend me a few million, and if he happens not to have that many in store, he can easily get them together for me with the help of a few cosmopolitan bankers of the spirit [*bei einigen kosmopolitischen Geistesbankiers.*]

Here, for the first time, we have a public hint that Gans is of Jewish origin—through the juxtaposition with Rothschild in a sentence whose speech rhythms (*ist so zu sagen ein kleiner Rothschild*) resemble those Heine will employ later when characterizing the speech of Jewish figures like Hirsch-Hyazinth (***The Baths of Lucca,*** 1830). The mention of Rothschild alongside Gans fulfils, once again, at least three purposes. It suggests, first of all, that men of Jewish origin now play a significant part in the intellectual as well as in the financial life of Europe. Secondly, the juxtaposition serves to convey that even though Gans may now be baptized, he is still categorized with his former coreligionists by friend and foe. Thirdly, the mention of Rothschild leads to the notion of 'cosmopolitan bankers of the spirit'—a notion which suggests, among other things, that excessive quoting is connected with a commercialization and mechanization of the intellectual and spiritual life. The word here translated as spirit, *Geist*, was of course a keyword in Hegelian philosophy, and serves to remind us that Gans, whose father was a court Jew well known for his banking transactions, had become one of Hegel's most eminent disciples.

What neither Gans nor the contemporary reading public could know, was that Heine had written a poem, after hearing of Gans's baptism, which gave bitter expression to his sense that the President of the Society for the Culture and Science of the Jews had deserted his post in an irresponsible manner. Gans is

not named, but later documents make it quite clear that he is meant.

> O des heil'gen Jugendmutes!
> Oh, wie schnell bist du gebändigt!
> Und du hast dicta, kühlern Blutes,
> Mit den lieben Herrn verständigt.
>
> Und du bist zu Kreuz gekrochen,
> Zu dem Kreuz, das du verachtest,
> Das du noch nor wenig Wochen
> In den Staub zu treten dachtest!
>
> Oh, das tut das viele Lesen
> Jener Schlegel, Haller, Burke—
> Gestern noch ein Held gewesen,
> Ist man heute schon ein Schurke.
>
> [O for youth's sacred courage!
> How speedily you are tamed!
> Now your blood has cooled somewhat, you have
> come to an arrangement with the gracious lords.
>
> You have humbled yourself before the cross
> the very cross that you despised,
> that only a few short weeks ago
> you sought to tread into the dust!
>
> That's what comes of all that reading
> Of people like Schlegel, Haller, and Burke—
> the man who but yesterday was still a hero
> has turned into a knave today.]

Heine never published this poem, but he did not destroy it either—he must, therefore, have reckoned with its ultimate appearance, even if only posthumously, in his collected works. It alludes, prominently, to its protagonist's assumption of Christianity; but what it really deplores (as Klaus Briegleb has well said) is a decay of the fighting spirit, a decay of strength. The reading of conservative philosophers has led, the poet tells us, to an unprincipled abandonment of the fight for emancipation—emancipation from the tutelage of those who used the religion of the cross to rule over others. The poem characterizes its protagonist as a man who seemed courageous but crumbled into cowardly submission when the test came; it never names Gans, however, as it moves inexorably towards that impersonal construction of the final line which gives it a wider application and an especially bitter note. One remembers, suddenly, that Heine's own baptism, his own 'crawl to the cross', had *preceded* Gans's by several months. In venting his rage against Gans he is raging against himself. The portrait of Gans is becoming more than just the portrait of an individual: it is the portrait of a generation to which Heine also belonged, a generation of young Jews who had abandoned the ways of their rabbinically trained forefathers (who would have deplored not only the reading of Friedrich Schlegel, Haller, and Burke, but that of Hegel too!) and had lost the strength and authenticity single-minded adherence to Jewish traditions might have lent them. Emancipation from the tyranny of the rabbis—one of the planks in the platform of the Society for the Culture and Science of the Jews!—had led to submission to another kind of tyranny.

The bitter mood of this poem is absent from a bibulous section of *The North Sea* (*Die Nordsee* II) which, for the first time in Heine's work, brings Gans into proximity with Hegel, the great teacher to whom Gans owed the philosophical framework within which he thought and wrote. The speaker of the poem, who is refreshing himself at an inn after an arduous sea voyage, looks into his glass of wine and sees all history there:

> Alles erblick ich im Glas,
> Alte und neue Völkergeschichte,
> Türken und Griechen, Hegel und Gans,
> Zitronenwälder und Wachtparaden,
> Berlin und Schilda und Tunis und Hamburg . . .
>
> [In my glass I see everything:
> ancient and modern history,
> Turks and Greeks, Hegel and Gans,
> lemon groves and military parades,
> Berlin and Gotham and Tunis and Hamburg . . .]

The great and the little, the admirable and the contemptible, are as inextricably commingled in the drinker's mind as they are in life; and the reader is deliberately left in doubt whether the relationship between Hegel and Gans is analogous to that between Turkey and Greece, or that between poetic Italian landscapes and prosaic Prussian parade-grounds . . . or any of the other relationships suggested by the parallel pairs. Unlike the unpublished 'renegade' poem, this *North Sea* poem is content to suggest an intellectual and spiritual relationship and to leave judgement on it in abeyance. We may be quite sure, however, that in the context of Heine's developing work an affinity with Hegel is more respectable than an affinity with Schlegel, Haller, and Burke.

Heine's portrayal of Gans's philosophical affinities, and his place within the constellation of German intellectual life, is carried on by a fantastic passage in *The Baths of Lucca* (1830) in which an Italian professor of law is credited with some very strange notions. The Italian had heard of F. K. von Savigny, the leader of the conservative 'historical school of law' (*historische Rechtsschule*) in Prussia, and of Heine's own equally conservative teacher, the Göttingen professor Gustav Hugo. He has also heard of their more liberal opponent in Heidelberg, A.F.J. Thibaut, and Thibaut's protégé and

pupil Eduard Gans. Somehow, however, he has transmogrified their relationship into that between participants in a ball—a ball at which Gans had asked Savigny to be his partner, but had been refused and had then become Savigny's enemy. Many of Heine's contemporary readers would here have recognized an allusion to the anti-Jewish Savigny's unswerving opposition to Gans's appointment at the University of Berlin, where Savigny himself occupied a chair of law. In that sense Savigny had indeed refused to become Gans's partner. The narrator of *The Baths of Lucca* then recounts how he tried to disabuse the Italian professor of his error.

> 'Your information, sir, is incorrect . . . Signor Gans does not dance, he loves mankind too much for that—for if he did dance, there might be an earthquake. The invitation to a dance of which you have told me is probably a misunderstood allegory. The historical and the philosophical schools of law are presented as dancers; and in this allegorical sense a quadrille of Hugo, Thibaut, Gans, and Savigny may be conceived. And in this same sense it may perhaps be said that Signor Ugone [= Hugo], although he is the *diable boiteux* of jurisprudence, dances as daintily as Lemiere, while Signor Gans has recently attempted some high leaps that have made him the Hoguet of the philosophical school.'

The quadrille Heine describes in this transparent allegory had begun to interest the German public in 1814. In that year Thibaut had published his pamphlet *On the Necessity of a Common Civil Law for Germany* (*Über die Notwendigkeit eines allgemeinen bürgerlichen Rechts für Deutschland*), which was favourable to the spirit that had produced the Declaration of the Rights of Man and the Code Napoléon. Savigny had countered in the same year with *The Vocation of Our Time for Legislation and Jurisprudence* (*Vom Beruf unserer Zeit für Gesetzgebung und Rechtswissenschaft*), arguing for a law that was not rationally constructed according to general principles but had grown up historically within a given people. In the spirit of Romanticism, Savigny and his school 'rejected the idea of a universal source of law and justice and a universal sanction for laws—i.e. natural law—and claimed the national spirit and the unique national history to be the source of all laws, and the idea of justice prevailing in any nation.' By partnering Gans with Thibaut in the 'philosophical' school and opposing him to such formidable 'historicals' as Savigny and Gustav Hugo, Heine not only defines Gans's position on the politico-intellectual map of Germany but also leaves no doubt of Gans's importance. Identification with M. F. Hoguet, one of the most celebrated dancers and choreographers of the day, whose leaps and turns he had already converted into political allegory in *The Hartz Journey,* again suggests the outstanding position Gans had now gained in the intellectual world. At the same time, however, portrait is once again passing over into caricature.

Gans's physical clumsiness and lack of grace is suggested by the remark that if he were to dance in a literal rather than an allegorical sense, he would cause an earthquake; and the observation that Gans had tried some high leaps in recent times ('daß Signor Gans in der neuesten Zeit einige große Sprünge versucht') alludes obliquely to Gans's notorious desire to shine, to be the centre of attention, in any company in which he found himself. This last suggestion is strengthened by the reaction of the Italian professor after his error had been dispelled: he takes up his guitar and sings of the loud trumpetings, the 'Tarar', with which Gans's name resounds through the world.

> Es ist wahr, sein teurer Name
> Ist die Wonne aller Herzen.
> Stürmen laut des Meeres Wogen,
> Droht der Himmel schwarz umzogen,
> Hört man stets Tarar nur rufen,
> Gleich als beugten Erd und Himmel
> Vor des Helden Namen sich.

> [It is true, his well-loved name
> is the joy of every bosom.
> Though the ocean waves be stormy,
> though heaven threatens with black clouds,
> all we hear is a trumpeted 'Tarar',
> as though heaven and earth bowed down
> before the mighty hero's name.]

The 'Tarar' that outroars wind and waves represents at once the trumpetings of fame and Gans's own booming voice. The passage thus mingles, characteristically, admiration of Gans's achievements, approval of his intellectual position, with irritation at his fame, his maladroitness, and his lack of reticence and tact.

In the 'travel picture' which followed **The Baths of Lucca**, entitled **The Town of Lucca** (1831), Gans's name is not mentioned; but his figure nevertheless appears in one of those allegories which we can recognize by now as an integral part of Heine's literary portraiture. The narrator tells us of a conversation he purports to have had with some grey lizards he encountered in the Apennine mountains, and he comments:

> Nature has her history too—one that differs from the 'natural history' taught in schools. It would be good to appoint one of the grey lizards that have been living in the clefts of the Apennine rocks for thousands of years to an extraordinary associate professorship [als ganz außerordentliche Professorin] at one of our universities—then we would hear extraordinary things. But this would offend the pride of some gentlemen of the faculty of law, who would protest against such an appointment. One of them is already secretly jealous of poor *Fido savant* and is afraid that he might one day supplant him as a fetcher and carrier of learning at his masters' command [im gelehrten Apportieren].

Mathilde Heine.

Heine's allusion to the unwillingness of German professors to accept members of a thousands-of-years-old species as colleagues at their universities is an unmistakable allegorization of their attitude to the Jews; and his reference to the faculty of law makes it obvious that he is attempting to call up in his readers' minds the *cause célèbre* of Eduard Gans, who had invoked the tolerant Prussian edict of 1812 in vain, had seen the edict modified in the Jews' disfavour, and had received his associate professorship, his *Extraordinariat,* only after submitting to baptism. This initial submission, Heine suggests, may lead Gans on to become a *Fido savant*—just another academic retriever ready to obey his Prussian master's voice. And it is precisely this, Heine tells us, which has roused the deepest apprehensions of other academic retrievers in ordinary: what they are afraid of now is not that their new colleague would introduce alien and subversive notions into university life, but that he would become too good at what they themselves were doing and would thus threaten their cherished monopoly. The sound-link between 'Fido savant' and 'Savigny' is surely not fortuitous; it seems well calculated to make subliminal connections.

In one respect Heine's caricature is well on target. Gans did exhibit some *Fido savant* tendencies after obtaining his long-desired professorship. His opposition to Savigny lessened (though Savigny would never have anything to do with him) and he declared himself against allowing Jews unlimited freedom to take law degrees at German universities. Nevertheless Gans remained, for his own part, an adherent of the Hegelian Left, a thorn in the conservatives' side, and an opponent of political reaction. He was never an advocate of Friedrich Schlegel, Karl Ludwig Haller, or Edmund Burke. When he died, however, at the early age of forty-two, the successor chosen to replace him was none other than Friedrich Julius Stahl—a convert from Judaism who had become one of the principal theoreticians and apologists of Prussian conservatism. Stahl was precisely the sort of person whom Heine (borrowing the voice of irritated competitors) had caricatured as *Fido savant*; precisely the sort of person, too, who would support his political and social views by appealing to the authority of Haller and Burke. Yet by a final irony we can find Heine himself, when he sketched out a preface for a new edition of *Pictures of Travel* IV in 1834, quoting Stahl with approval:

> O what fools they are who allow their vanity to impel them to become leaders in revolutionary times! 'Do you know what the leader of a party is?' Friedrich von Stahl has asked; 'He is a man who stands at the very edge of an abyss while his followers constantly push him forwards from behind.'

Always torn between his suspicion of revolutionaries and his desire for social amelioration, the poet had more sympathies with Stahl's views than were ever shown by Eduard Gans. It is equally characteristic of his attitudes in the 1830s that he penned the passage just quoted and that he forbore to make it public.

In 1831 Heine moved to Paris; he was never again to set eyes on Gans, but he did not dismiss him from his mind or his work. He learnt that Gans had been giving very successful lectures on modern history, whose positive evaluation of the French Revolution of the previous century had filled the Prussian authorities with suspicion and alarm. This information the poet used in his reworking of the Tannhäuser legend, in which Tannhäuser is made to traverse Germany on his way from Rome back to his Parisian Venusberg.

> Zu Potsdam vernahm ich ein lautes Geschrei—
> 'Was gibt es?' rief ich verwundert.
> 'Das ist der Gans in Berlin, der liest
> Dort über das letzte Jahrhundert.'

> [At Potsdam I heard loud yelling—
> 'What is it?' I asked, with astonishment.
> 'It's Gans in Berlin—he is lecturing there
> on the history of the last hundred years.']

This stanza unites, in Heine's best manner, the physical and the spiritual, the literal and the metaphoric. Gans's loud voice was notorious among his acquaintances; but he had now acquired a voice that carried—*eine weithin hallende Stimme*, as Heine once proudly said of himself—in another sense. The reverberations of his lectures were heard in the traditional stronghold of Prussianism, Frederick the Great's Potsdam, and the *großes Geschrei* Tannhäuser purports to have heard, may well be the cries of consternation among Prussian conservatives swelling the noise made by Gans's pronouncements. Gans himself, it should be remembered, took this passage in good part as a caricature of his own loud voice: 'Dear Heine,' he wrote on 7 June 1838, 'we have not heard from one another since you recognized me by those loud yells at Potsdam . . . Let me hear from you again, dear friend; and if vocal chords are capable of perfection, I might soon be audible as far as Paris.'

For some five years after his early death, Eduard Gans appears only peripherally and anonymously in Heine's works. One of the comic bear's tirades in *Atta Troll*, for instance, first published in 1843, seems to contain an allusion to Gans's last published treatise—a refutation of Savigny's views on property rights (*Das Recht des Besitzes*, 1803) entitled *Über die Grundlage des Besitzes. Eine Duplik* (1839)—along with an allusion to the slogan 'La propriété est le vol' from Proudhon's *Qu'est-ce que la propriété?* of 1840.

> "Ja, das Erbe der Gesamtheit
> Wird dem Einzelnen zur Beute,
> Und von Rechten des Besitzes
> Spricht er dann, von Eigentum!
>
> "Eigentum! Recht des Besitzes!
> O des Diebstahls! O der Lüge! . . ."

> ["The community's heritage
> becomes the prey of an individual
> who then speaks of the right of possession,
> of property.
>
> Property! Right of possession!
> Shame on such theft and on such lies!"]

In 1844, however, Gans surfaces with a vengeance, when the poet took the death of Ludwig Marcus, who like Gans and like Heine himself had been a prominent member of the Society for the Culture and Science of the Jews, as his opportunity to look back on his friends and associates in the hopeful years he had spent in Berlin.

The first thing we hear of Gans in *Ludwig Marcus* (later revised and entitled *Ludwig Marcus. Words in his Memory*) is loud laughter. The naïve savant Marcus, a man of tiny physical stature, had written a work on the history of Abyssinia which touched on the subject of female circumcision. Heine tells us:

> How heartily the late Eduard Gans laughed when he showed me the sentence in Marcus's essay in which the author expressed the wish that someone better up to it than he was himself might devote his labours to this subject [*es möchte jemand diesen Gegenstand bearbeiten, der demselben besser gewachsen sei*].

An appreciation of linguistic *doubles ententes*, especially those which involved sexual allusions, was something Gans clearly shared with Heine. The possible double meanings Gans is made to point out in Marcus's innocent sentence centre on the words *bearbeiten* and *besser gewachsen*; the humorous implications perceived in this last word, derived from *wachsen* ('to grow'), refer not only to a presumed sexual inadequacy, but also to little Marcus's stunted growth. It is a joke which Heine will turn against Gans later in this same obituary.

The turn comes very soon, in fact. Having made Gans ostentatiously demonstrate his undoubted superiority in intelligence, knowledge of the world, and physical stature over poor little Marcus, Heine proceeds to characterize the Society for the Culture and Science of the Jews to which all three of them belonged, and comments:

> The obituary of the late Ludwig Marcus has insensibly led me to an obituary of the Society of which he was a most honourable member and as whose president Eduard Gans, whom I have already mentioned and who has also departed this world, made his influence felt. This highly gifted man is the last person one could praise for his modest self-sacrifice and anonymous martyrdom. Though his soul opened itself readily to all questions concerning the welfare and the salvation of mankind, enthusiasm never intoxicated him to the point of leaving his own immediate interest out of account. A witty lady with whom Gans often took his tea in the evenings rightly observed that even in the most heated discussion and despite his great absent-mindedness Gans always managed, when he reached for the plate that held the sandwiches, to get hold of those which had fresh salmon on them rather than those with ordinary cheese.

With the help of Rahel Varnhagen—for she, surely, is the 'witty lady' referred to in the last sentence I have just quoted—Heine here brings together once again the physical and the moral, the apparently random detail and the essence of a character. He evokes the complexity of Gans—his combination of self-seeking and altruism, professorial absent-mindedness and expert gourmandise, great gifts and petty habits, idealism and an eye for the main chance with a completeness that surpasses all his previous portrayals.

The dualism of presentation now analysed continues in the passage that follows.

> How much German scholarship owes to the late Eduard Gans is widely known. He was one of the most active apostles of the Hegelian philosophy, and he vulgarized Hegel's writings in an elegant way—in so far as he understood them himself.

Heine believed, as we know from his *Towards a History of Religion and Philosophy in Germany*, that he had understood better than Hegel's more orthodox pupils certain elements of the movement in German philosophy which culminated in the Hegelian system—but that except for Hegel and God, no one had ever fully understood the Hegelian system and its implications. As for 'vulgarizing'—he himself had often been accused of that; but it was a charge he saw as a compliment rather than an insult. He took pride, in fact, in what he thought to be his ability to disengage the kernel of a doctrine from its shell or husk and to make his insights generally accessible in a style as unlike as possible to the ponderous periods of German academics. If Gans could 'vulgarize' in this positive way, he must have transcended that clumsiness of style, lightened that impenetrability of utterance, which Heine had once laid to his charge. The epithet 'elegant', with which Heine here dignifies Gans's 'vulgarizations', would have seemed to him wholly inappropriate as a description of Gans's early writings. The later Gans, it would seem, had come nearer to Heine's own mode of excellence; and it is significant that he now praises his dead comrade in arms for making Hegel's thought fruitful in German jurisprudence in a way that Heine believed unequivocally beneficial.

> In jurisprudence he fought and annihilated those lackeys of Roman law who, having no inkling of the spirit that animated the law-givers of the ancient world, busied themselves with brushing the dust out of the garments they had left behind, freeing them from moths, or even patching them up for use in modern times. Gans scourged such servility even when it wore the most elegant livery . . .

In 1854, when *Ludwig Marcus* was reissued, Heine added a sentence which made his meaning crystal clear:

> How the poor soul of Herr von Savigny whimpers as it feels Gans's kicks!

So Gans did not, after all, become a mere *Fido savant*. On the contrary: even in his professorial capacity he remained a fighter against obscurantism and blind worship of the past. That showed itself in his lectures even more than in his writings.

> More even by his words than by his writings Gans furthered the development of the German

idea of liberty and the desire for it [*des deutschen Freiheitssinnes*]. He unshackled the most carefully fettered thoughts and tore the mask from the face of liars. He was a nimble, fiery spirit; the sparks of his wit kindled splendid fires or—at the very least—spread glorious illumination all around.

Wit; furthering the conception of liberty and the desire for it; unmasking hypocrisy; saying what the authorities did not want to be said—the virtues Heine here detects in Gans's lectures are precisely those which he himself strove to realize in the poetry of the 1840s. As so often, the lineaments of a self-portrait shine through the portrait Heine is painting of his contemporary and early associate.

This is true also of the negative accentuation that marks the next stage of his description of Gans. Taking his cue from a 'gloomy saying' in Goethe's *Faust, Part II*, Heine contemplates the relationship between genius and virtue, *Genialität* and *Tugend*, in a way which must irresistibly remind readers of Börne's charges against Heine himself—charges which we shall see the poet attempt to counter and refute in *Ludwig Börne. A Memorial* and in *Atta Troll*. Genius and virtue, he now declares, with regard to Eduard Gans,

> live in perpetual enmity and sometimes turn their backs on each other. I grieve to report that in respect of the Society for the Culture and Science of Judaism [*sic*] . . . Gans did not behave virtuously at all; that he was, in fact, guilty of the most unforgivable felony. His defection was all the more revolting because he had played the agitator and had taken on specific duties as president of the Society. Traditionally it is the duty of the captain to be the last to leave his floundering ship—but Gans saved himself first. When it comes to moral stature, surely, little Marcus towered above the great Gans, and he in turn might have regretted that Gans was not more up to his task.

And so we have come full circle. Once again the great President of the Society for the Culture and Science of the Jews confronts its tiniest member, but the proportions are inverted in this moral context: Marcus is the great and Gans is the little one. Heine himself, whose baptism had after all *preceded* that of Gans, is invisibly present at this moral measuring: 'I had not taken on any presidential duties, I had not helped to found the Society, I was not the captain', we seem to hear him say; nevertheless it is only too plain that, on the moral scale here set up, the poet himself stands much nearer to the negative pole of Gans than to the positive one of Ludwig Marcus.

This brings us to the ultimate paradox and the real point of the comparison. Marcus is morally far superior to Gans—but Gans has been more useful to the world. Where Marcus's researches have not led to

anything Heine thinks permanently valuable, Gans has advanced the cause of truth, and the emancipation not just of Jews but of Gentile Germans too, through his championship of the 'philosophical' against the 'historical' school of law, his exposition and development of Hegel's doctrines in a liberal sense, his research into the historical basis and social significance of the laws of inheritance, his unstuffy views on the history of Germany, and his fight for more adequate conceptions of freedom and progress.

It has of late become clear that Heine's work is all of a piece, that the procedures of his poetry are not abandoned in his prose *Pictures of Travel*, his attempts at narrative fiction, and his journalistic reports. The mosaic portrait our investigations have so far constructed confirms this; its materials have been gathered from all these sources, and have fitted together perfectly. There is also, as one might expect, a good deal of continuity between Heine's published work on the one hand and his letters and recorded conversations on the other, a continuity which will enable us to gather further significant fragments for our mosaic. In these letters and conversations Heine speaks to a more limited public, of course, than in his writings for publication; but except in a few letters to his immediate family Heine is as careful in his formulations, as conscious of the need to project a persona, as he is when addressing the public at large.

On 1 September 1833 we find Heine writing to a Potsdam lawyer, E. C. A. Keller, in order to persuade him to support a new legal journal which Gans and Heine were attempting to establish. Since this project had to be made as attractive as possible to Keller, Heine emphasizes the qualities which fitted Gans for the post of editor.

> A few weeks before leaving Berlin I made the acquaintance of Dr. Gans, and found in him an honourable and energetic young man, who deserves my respect in every way and who is, I am sure, worth more than any of the gentlemen who display their Christian charity by maligning him because of his Mosaic affiliation [*die ihn, den Mosaisten, gehörig anfeinden*]. I value his stalwart, virtuous disposition; his learning is not in the common mould, if my judgement of human knowledge can be trusted; for Dr. Gans has complete command of his materials, penetrates science and scholarship with the sharp eye of a man who thinks for himself, and constantly promotes new and striking views of the things he discusses.

In emphasizing the qualities that make Gans an ideal journalist as well as a scholar to be taken seriously—his sharp and quick penetration, his promotion of new and striking ideas based on sound knowledge of the facts—Heine is at pains to counteract unfavourable aspects of the Jewish stereotype which might prejudice the non-Jew Keller against Gans. Hence the stress on his 'stalwart, virtuous disposition', on that *Tüchtigkeit in der Gesinnung* which German Gentiles so often assumed to be present in themselves but absent in their Jewish fellow citizens. The very terms *Jude* and *jüdisch* had come to denote unadmirable qualities in popular usage. Heine's letter therefore follows, for once, the practice of many of his contemporaries in avoiding these terms; his choice of *Mosaist* (rather than *Israelit*) was perhaps influenced by the thought that a Christian lawyer might be presumed to have some respect for Moses the Lawgiver. At the same time his dig at what Christian charity had come to mean in practice reminds the Gentile world, in the person of the recipient of the letter, that it might do better to look to its own faults instead of projecting them all on to the Jews.

When he writes to his Jewish friends in Berlin, Heine does not, of course, have to adopt these particular strategies. There he engages in good-humoured banter about Gans's scholarly habit of quoting authorities and sources for his slightest remarks, praises his work on the laws of inheritance from which Heine himself has derived many important insights, and describes a dream in which Gans knocks at the window while his fellow Hegelians are trying to reduce the poet himself to a Hegelian *Idee*.

> But I leapt about the room in my rage and called out: 'I am not an Idea, I know nothing of an Idea, all my life long I have never had an Idea'—it was a horrible dream, I remember how Gans yelled even louder than I; little Marcus sat on his shoulder and shouted the relevant quotations with an uncanny hoarse voice, smiling the while with such ghastly friendliness that I awoke with terror. (to Moses Moser, 23 May 1823)

This dream-vision caricatures Gans and Marcus in ways we have already observed in Heine's published work—but the element of the grotesque is strengthened when the little man is put on the bigger man's shoulder like an organ-grinder's monkey and made to supply, in a shout toned down by hoarseness, the quotations Gans could never do without. The passage also suggests, for the first time in Heine's writings, that he felt an element of the demonic in Hegel's generalizations and abstractions. This may help to explain why towards the end of his life, when he tried the experiment of 're-turning' to the God he had once declared dead, he made Hegel rather than the Saint-Simonians responsible for the hubris of his earlier years.

Another aspect which Heine omitted from his public portrayals of Gans is the interest both Gans and Heine took, during their brief collaboration, in Jewish emigration from Germany to a homeland of their own. This interest was kindled by a project for settling Jews on Grand Island in the State of New York put forward by M. M. Noah in the early 1820s. The idea was soon abandoned; but in Heine's mind the Grand Island project became so firmly identified with Gans that he could imagine no name but 'Ganstown' for the capital of the hoped-for settlement.

> When, one day, Ganstown will be built and a happier generation than ours blesses its palm branches and chews its unleavened bread [*Lulef benscht und Matzes kaut*] by the Mississippi—the mercantile and Stock Exchange expressions we use today will become part of poetic language . . . (to Moser, 23 May 1823)

With self-torturing humour Heine here adopts the Gentile stereotype of what a Jewish poet would be like—he had earlier used a metaphor taken from financial transactions and asked his Jewish correspondent Moser: 'Does this image not make you appreciate that I am a Jewish poet?' (Ibid.) In another letter to Moser he describes his vision of a Jewish exodus from Berlin not to the new American colony, but to Jerusalem: 'It was a great Jewish army, and Gans ran from one man to the next in order to bring some order into it.' (20 July 1824.) What is highlighted here, besides the discontent with life in Germany which could lead to a Jerusalem nostalgia of which Gans himself showed no sign, is Gans's energy and organizing talent.

Other letters of the 1820s dwell mainly on Gans's faults: his indiscreet love of gossip:

> If I had anything to say to him, I might just as well publish it in the *Berlin Advertiser* . . . (to Joseph Lehmann, 26 June 1823);

his excessive love of quotations; his desire to hear himself talked about:

> How is Gans? Does he still consult his servant-girl Molly when he considers, each morning, whom he should quote in the course of the day—and does he still take stock of his fame each evening? (to Moser, 25 October 1824);

and the rebarbative style of his earlier writings. After reading an issue of the journal put out by the Society for the Culture and Science of the Jews, Heine writes to Leopold Zunz:

> I have studied all kinds of German: Saxon, Swabian, Franconian—but our Journal-German I find the most difficult of all. If I did not happen to know what Ludwig Marcus and Dr. Gans want to say, I would not understand a word of what they have written.

There are other complaints of this kind: but one day after the letter just quoted Heine writes to tell Moser of his joy at hearing that the King of Prussia had granted Gans a stipend which would enable the latter to devote himself to his studies for two years. The joy was not unconfined, however, for the stipend was only a consolation prize for the professorship Gans had been denied because he was a Jew. We have already seen that in later days Heine would distinguish sharply between Gans's style and Marcus's, and would acknowledge that the former was far more effective—beneficially effective—than the latter.

The next glimpse we have of Gans in Heine's letters is, however, the most disenchanted yet. It occurs in the course of an epistle in which Heine laments that the Jews of Hamburg, most of whom he dislikes, should think Gans a mere clown:

> Gans is considered a fool in Hamburg, and I am not surprised . . . I deeply regret that Gans's silly behaviour, his gossiping with friend and enemy, could have put me off my stroke for even a minute. It serves him right if the Jews abuse him and make him responsible for every ill; why does he talk so much about what he is going to do, why must he always make promises and arouse expectations? I also intend to do things, perhaps I am doing something significant merely by being the man I am; but in future I shall take what steps I can to protect myself from the kind of publicity Gans doles out—one that is wholly incompatible with my activities. (to Moser, 23 August 1823)

Gans here acts as a warning example while also constituting a danger to Heine's own reputation in Germany. Nevertheless, the poet adds, his strictures on Gans do not arise from motives of personal spite or pique; they are due, rather, to 'love for our good cause', the cause of those emancipatory struggles to which the subject of these strictures was as devoted as the writer and recipient of the letter in which they were made. His love, therefore, extended also to Gans, to whom he won't write directly 'for fear he could tell too many of his dearest friends, in strict confidence of course, what I candidly tell him'.

> In the future you will always see how dear he is to my heart, how highly I esteem his generous nature, and how much I count on him.

And why does he still harbour such affection for Gans? 'Not', Heine says to Moser on 30 September 1823, 'because of the fat books he writes, not even because of the nobility of his actions—but only because of the funny way in which he used to pull me about when he was telling me something, and because of the good-natured childlike expression that came over his face when he encountered hostility or when something bad happened to him.' I hope most of my readers will agree that Heine has here made a significant contribution to our understanding of the way in which sympathy may arise between human beings, and has made Gans's gestures and expressions vividly present to posterity.

On 20 July 1824 a huffy note may be heard again: Gans, it appears, had shown his displeasure with Heine by failing to transmit greetings to him when such greetings might have been expected. Might Gans not be poisoning the poet's relations with other friends? Has Gans's prattle, perhaps—Heine asks Moser, who was famous for a cloak that made him resemble Schiller's Marquis Posa—'managed to make a hole in your beautiful Posa cloak?' The image of malicious gossip rending the cloak of magnanimous friendship is at once allegoric and surrealistic—an earnest of what Heine could do in conversation too when he improvised symbolic anecdotes about Gans's odd behaviour.

> When, one evening, he and Gans came from the *Tiergarten* [a large park in Berlin] to Mendelssohn-Bartholdy's house, he told the company there, among other things: 'We bought some pinks on the way; I plucked mine to pieces and threw them into the water, and Gans'—he continued in a weary, melancholy tone—'has *eaten* his!' This recitation, perfect and rounded in itself like a little poem, so expressive of Gans's bad habits, worked like magic: everybody at that gathering was beside himself with delight.

Gans was not slow to rib Heine in return—no wonder that the two of them avoided meeting each other in public whenever they could! 'Is it not annoying', Heine asks Moser on 25 June 1824, in a letter in which respect far outweighs contempt,

> that one of the greatest thinkers of our time gives so little thought to himself and what he looks like to others? It is wrong of me to pull his leg, I know, although I never hurt him, and although he unconsciously provokes such leg-pulling; it would be better if I had told him the strict truth every time he made a public exhibition of his weaknesses and caused them to be talked about by all the world. His friends should always do this. Just the other day I was told some typical anecdotes about Gans which are fit only for the ears of those who appreciate his intelligence, and those who know how lovable he is in reality. But all the world sees of this comet is his trailing tail.

The image of the comet, which Heine uses in that passage, has been plausibly linked with Jean Paul; but it also has its place in a series of 'light' metaphors which Heine used in respect of Gans and of himself: 'I am a pale will o' the wisp; but Gans is a light, a light of exile.' (To Moser, 28 November 1823.) 'Light of Exile', or 'Light of the Diaspora'—*Meor ha-Golah*—was, we must remember, a traditional Jewish title; it had been most notably applied to Rabbi Gershom ben Yehuda of Mainz, who lived from c. 965 to 1028.

When he applies Rabbi Gershom's title to his eminent contemporary, Heine places the latter's career in an unmistakably Jewish context—the context of Jewish history in the Diaspora; and when he next takes up the 'comet' image again, as he does in an important letter to Moser dated 8 October 1825, he places it in the context of Gans's baptism, which had been preceded (we must again remember) by the poet's own. Now that Eduard Gans has officially divested himself of the Jewish equivalent of his first name, 'Eli', Heine plays on it in a passage dominated by the Hebrew-Yiddish terms *Goim*—often transliterated '*Goyim*'—and *Roshoim*. The first of these means 'non-Jews' and the second 'evil-doers' (or simply anti-Semites).

> I await Gans's return with great suspense. I believe he will return with new Eli-gance. I also believe that although according to the way Zunz classified the Society's library the first part of his *Law of Inheritance* qualifies fully as a source of Jewish history, that part of the work which will appear after his return from Paris will no more be a source for Jewish history than the writings of Savigny and other *Goyim und Reschoim* [sic]. In short— Gans will return from Paris as a Christian, in the most watery sense of that term. Sugar-Cohn, I fear, will become his Carl Sand.

The Hamburg sugar broker, Gustav Gerson Cohn, who favoured the reform of Jewish modes of worship but detested apostasy from Judaism, is here likened to Carl Sand, whose disapproval of August von Kotzebue's political activities led him to assassinate the object of his detestation. Works which Gans—and, as the poet often reminded Jewish correspondents, Heine himself too—would write after the apostasy that drew the wrath of more faithful Jews on his head, could no longer count as unsullied 'sources' of Jewish history. How deeply Gans's baptism stirred up remorse about his own appears clearly in one of the bitterest letters Heine ever wrote. It is addressed, once again, to his friend and confidant Moses Moser.

> I don't know what to say; Cohn tells me Gans is preaching Christianity and seeking to convert the children of Israel. If he does this out of conviction, he is a fool; if he does it out of hypocrisy, he is a blackguard. I won't ever stop loving Gans, but I must confess that I would have been happier if instead of the above news I had been told that Gans had stolen silver spoons.
>
> I just cannot believe, dear Moser, that you should be of the same opinion as Gans, although Cohn assures me that this is so and that he has it from your own mouth. I would be particularly sorry if you should see my own baptism in a favourable light. I assure you that if the laws had allowed the stealing of silver spoons, I would not have had myself baptized. I'll tell you more when I see you. (19 December 1825)

Nowhere else does Heine make it so clear that the betrayal of the fighting, oppositional spirit, which was all he could see in Gans's acceptance of the religion of the Cross, was but the mirror image of his own apostasy. 'We spoke of Gans,' he adds a little later in this same letter; 'Can one speak of anything else in this world nowadays? Everyone sees him, everyone hears him. Hallelujah.' The appointment to an associate professorship of law in the University of Berlin, with which Prussia rewarded Gans's conversion, increased his fame and ensured (as Heine says in another letter) that posterity would have a chance to understand Gans's style better than Heine himself felt able to do in the third decade of the nineteenth century (to Moser, 24 February 1826).

In this same year of 1826 Heine dates a letter to Moser 'Hamburg, the 23rd of the month Gans', immediately adding the following ironic disclaimer:

> But, you changeable, inconsistent month of April, pardon me the wrong I did you when I juxtaposed you with Dr. Gans. That you have not deserved! (I am speaking of the month.) It is a manly, consistent month, a decent, orderly month . . .

In calling April an *ordentlicher Monat* Heine is not only suggesting that baptism had brought disorder into Gans's life, but he is also punning on the *Extraordinariat* or *außerordentliche Professur*, the associate professorship, which he received in payment. The next paragraph of the letter to Moser which I have here begun to cite again refers to this *Extraordinariat*:

> Give my regards to our 'extraordinary' friend and tell him that I love him. I say this in all seriousness— it comes from my soul. His image is still dear to me, though it is not the image of a saint, an image one can worship and expect to perform miracles.

Now comes an especially revealing sentence:

> I often think of him, because I do not want to think of myself;

after which Heine continues:

> This night I thought: what kind of a face would Gans make if he came to stand before *Moshe Rabbenu*, supposing the latter appeared again on earth? And Moses, surely, is the greatest jurist that ever lived—the laws he gave have endured until our present day.

It is not only Professor Gans, then, but also Dr. Heine, who has to confront the greatest practitioner of the subject in which both won their academic laurels: the prophet who proclaimed the Jewish God from Mount Sinai and first welded the Israelites into a people. The use of the Hebrew phrase for 'Our Teacher

Moses', which Heine actually writes out in Hebrew letters, underscores the poet's sense that he, and Gans too, cannot simply wash away his past allegiances, his early history, in the water of the baptismal font. And as so often, the emotional turmoil into which thoughts of Gans now threw Heine gives birth to a dream-picture in which Gans appears in familiar surroundings but uncharacteristic silence. The scene is Strahlau, a place near Berlin famous for its fishing and scenic beauty, a favourite spot for excursions, at which some anti-Jewish riots had recently occurred.

> I . . . dreamt that Gans and Mordecai Noah came together in Strahlau and Gans was—*mirabile dictu*—silent as a fish. Zunz stood by, smiling sarcastically, and said to his wife: 'Now do you see, little mouse?'

Noah had appointed Gans his representative in Germany, not knowing that the man he wished to help him establish a Jewish settlement in America had abjured Judaism. Zunz and his wife (the *Mäuschen* endearment at the end is characteristic of their affectionate relationship) are introduced as a kind of chorus. They had remained Jews, though even Zunz had at one time considered baptism; and Zunz can now smile sarcastically at the absurd human spectacle the confrontation of Gans and Noah offers. Later Heine introduces another as yet unbaptized member of the (now defunct) Society for the Culture and Science of the Jews into his dream-vision—the writer and editor Joseph Lehmann, who is made to mouth slogans of the Enlightenment and of Hegelian philosophy, which provide the background against which Gans's, and Heine's, abandonment of Judaism must be seen. That Gans remains uncharacteristically silent may be regarded, not just as caricature *e contrario,* but also as a sign of guilt or of doubt.

The imagined confrontation of Gans with Moses, with Mordecai Noah, and with Leopold Zunz is capped, in Heine's letter to Moser of 14 October 1826, by a confrontation with the spirit of Judaism itself. Moser had compared the Jewish people to Christ crucified, and Heine borrows this image as he punningly connects Gans's Hebrew name 'Eli' with the words from the Cross attributed to Christ in Matthew 27:46.

> Give my regards to Gans too. I do hope that Gans, who is still a freshman in Christianity, is not already beginning to talk in pious Christian accents. No, Clumsy Cohen has surely lied to me about that. But if ever Gans should do so, then the Judaism you have presented as the crucified Saviour of the World would call out to him, full of grief: 'Dr. Eli! Dr. Eli! lama sabachthani!'

Heine adds to this his usual protestation that he still loves Gans and that he will always remain his friend.

The only letter to Gans himself which editors of Heine have ever been able to unearth belongs to this period. It was written in May 1826 and accompanied the first volume of Heine's *Pictures of Travel.* The poet begins by distancing himself from any theological views Gans's baptism might have entailed.

> Dear Gans! Valued Colleague!
>
> The word 'colleague' refers to jurisprudence and not to theology. The word dear, however, refers to my heart, which still loves you dearly, loves you heartily—*quand même*—perhaps I would not write to you at all if there were no *quand même.* You don't understand me; what I want to suggest is that it offends me to the depths of my soul to think that our books are no longer *sources*; that because of this I am angry with you and angry with myself; and that because of this anger, I feel I must say to you that *I* love you just the same, that I love you *quand même.*

Heine then proceeds to belittle the book he is sending to Gans, and draws attention to the dedication of one of its sections to Rahel Varnhagen.

> This name, which is dear to me, I have nailed to the doorpost of my book, and this had made it more homely [*wöhnlich*] and more safe for me. Books too must have their *mezuzzah.* Farewell, and love me still, me
>
> Your friend
> H. Heine

H.G. Reissner, to whom we owe the fullest account so far of Gans's life and work, has perceptively remarked on the 'height of irony' reached by the passage just quoted. Here we find the Christian convert Heine explaining to the Christian convert Gans, by means of an image taken from Jewish ceremonial, why he dedicated the poems of *The Homecoming* (*Die Heimkehr*) to the Christian convert Rahel Varnhagen! Notwithstanding his baptism, Gans could still be expected to respond to the symbolism of the *mezuzzah,* the ritual capsule containing a Hebrew prayer which is affixed to the right-hand doorpost of a house inhabited by Jews. Such a capsule, Heine confesses, makes a house more *wöhnlich* for him—an unusual term which forms part of Heine's poetic vocabulary and denotes the sensation of being safely at home, of feeling at ease in one's surroundings. The water of baptism, the poet here reminds Gans, cannot wash away one's Jewish feelings and one's Jewish history.

The *quand même* which Heine sounds in this revealing letter to Gans was often heard in this period. Originally one of the battle cries of the Restoration—being for king and royalty *quand même,* despite everything that had happened—it was frequently converted to other uses by men who could not be said to belong to the conservative camp. The note struck by this *quand même* continues to resound through Heine's letters when he speaks of Gans. We find him constantly reiterating that he is annoyed by something or other that Gans has done but that at the bottom of his heart he loves him very much (for example, to Joseph Lehmann, 26 May 1826). In the autumn of 1826 he seems to have reread some of Gans's writings and felt confirmed in his liking; he now calls him the *Oberhegelianer*, Chief of the Hegelians, and on 9 June 1827 he sends him greetings, via Moser, in unusually warm terms. A few months later another letter to Moser speaks of Heine's plans for a journal he will edit in Munich, entitled *New Political Annals* (*Neue politische Annalen*). He asks him not to say anything about this to Gans, because 'apostates are unsuitable'—presumably unsuitable to further the cause of Jewish emancipation which Heine intends to champion. He then strikes out the remark about the unsuitability of apostates, reflecting, perhaps, that it did not come well from himself; but he never did ask Gans to contribute to his journal.

An especially revealing passage is to be found in a letter to Moser, date 9 June 1827, in which the poet describes the popularity he now believes himself to have attained in Germany.

> I now have a voice that sounds far into the land [*eine weitschallende Stimme*]. In years to come you will often hear it thunder against the policing of men's thoughts and the suppression of their fundamental rights. I shall obtain a quite extraordinary professorship in the university of the intellectual and spiritual élite [*in der Universitas hoher Geister*].

The metaphors Heine here uses to portray his own literary achievements and aspirations are clearly derived from his portrait of Eduard Gans. Moser could not possibly have missed the significance of his references to a voice that carries far into the distance, and to that *Extraordinat* at a prestigious university which Gans had finally attained but which was forever to elude Heine himself—at least in the literal sense.

Soon there came a time in which he felt dire need of the support which the now 'established' Gans might give him by wielding his pen. In *The Baths of Lucca* Heine had savagely attacked a fellow poet who had reviled him for being a Jew; and he felt that by doing this, by making August von Platen an example, he had performed a valuable service for other men and women of Jewish origin. Few of the latter agreed with him; the upwardly mobile members of his own family were shocked and incensed; but from Gans Heine hoped for understanding and support. A last brush-stroke is now added to his developing portrait.

> [Ludwig] Robert, Gans, Michael Beer, and others have all shown Christian patience when they were attacked as I was. They chose to keep wisely silent— I am different, and that is a good thing. It is good if the wicked find the right man for once, the man who will ruthlessly and unsparingly take revenge for himself and others. (to Varnhagen von Ense, 4 January 1830)

Since the revenge he had taken was on Gans's behalf as well as his own, he thought Gans morally obliged to champion his cause.

> It is Gans's most sacred duty to do battle on my behalf; please ask him to do so, in my name. He must now fulfil his promise to have my book immediately reviewed in the *Yearbooks for Scientific Criticism*; if not, I'll cut off his ears and thus inflict what is for him the ultimate punishment: he won't be able to hear himself talk any more. But whatever he elects to do, he must do soon. (Ibid.)

Nothing happened, of course: neither now nor when Heine appealed for help against attacks in French journals would Gans allow himself to be drawn into the polemics stirred up by the poet's attacks on Count Platen in ***The Baths of Lucca***. He still tried to keep up friendly relations with him however; in 1838 he sent him a note, brought to Heine by that very Gasparo Spontini whose name the poet had linked with Gans's in ***The Hartz Journey***, expressing the hope that they would meet again. They never did; but Gans's name crops up occasionally in Heine's conversations in Paris; and whenever he enumerates interesting acquaintances whom he intends to portray in his memoirs, Gans figures in the list.

> Lichtenberg says very justly that we may not only love ourselves but also hate ourselves in other people. And so I quarrelled recently with our friend Gans. If you see him, tell him what I said and give him my most friendly greetings. I love him very much and I thought of him when I wrote the opening of the Göttingen chapter of my ***Hartz Journey***. (to Varnhagen von Ense, 14 May 1826)

Here Heine, with the help of Lichtenberg, says it himself: his portrait of Gans is really a double portrait; the love-hate it exhibits is directed towards the portrayer as well as the portrayed. Heine too, like Gans, had believed for a time that Judaism could be lightly abandoned; but what he has to say about Gans's baptism and his conduct afterwards shows clearly that he soon learnt to think differently. A characteristic letter to Moser shows the poet looking back nostalgically to the heyday of the Society for the Culture and Science of the Jews.

> That was a much warmer time. If I am not mistaken, Gans was not yet baptized then and wrote long

speeches for the Society, and sported the device: *Victrix causa diis placuit, sed victa Catoni*—the conquering cause was pleasing to the gods, but the conquered one to Cato . . .

Heine tells Moser to speak freely about the baseness of Jews who have themselves baptized to gain some material advantage. He need not spare either Gans or Heine himself:

> As Solon said that no one should be called happy before his death, one could also say that no one should be called an honest man before his death. (23 April 1826)

The quotation at the head of this paragraph also shows how deeply hidden Heine's references to contemporaries may be—for without his hint, who would have suspected the presence of Gans in the opening section of *The Hartz Journey*? It may parody, once again, Gans's fondness for quotations, or embody reminiscences of Gans's own student days recalled when Heine met him in Göttingen in July 1825. Or might Heine be referring to the *Falcidia* dream? There are bound to be hidden references which later readers can no longer catch.

Nor is this the only way in which the portrait of Gans that I have tried to reconstitute from Heine's writings will seem incomplete. We miss descriptions of his appearance, of the kind we find in the reminiscences of Friederike von Hohenhausen, for instance:

> Eduard Gans, whose strikingly handsome head with its fresh colouring, its proudly arched eyebrows over dark eyes, recalled a spiritual Antinous;

or Laube's more sober portrait of Professor Gans at a somewhat later time:

> This man of medium height, fleshy, ruddy and healthy-looking with protuberant blue eyes and curly black hair receding from his high forehead . . .

> This man who went about his business, most of the time, in a formal dark coat, who bowed calmly and confidently, who came over to you slowly and with self-assurance . . .

or Laube again, recalling Gans just before his premature death:

> He was portly and overweight, and this caused the blood to rise to his head. His face was very red, his eyes were protuberant. 'Apoplectic', said those who knew about such things . . .

We learn from Heine that he was in the habit of ribbing Gans in company; but he tells us nothing of the 'biting sarcasm', the jokes about the poet's 'vanity and lechery', with which, according to I. H. von Fichte, Gans used to regale Heine in return. None the less we do get, from Heine's writings, a clear if complex picture of the man whom Fanny Hensel once called a cross between a man, a child, and a savage. We see and hear Gans with his shoulder-shrugging, his precociousness, his good-natured expression, his habit of pulling his partner about when he was telling him something, his loud voice, his hearty laughter, his jokes, his effective lecturing technique, his organizing talent strangely yoked with lack of tact and discretion, the sometimes clumsy style of his early writing, his Hegelizing, his effective opposition to the historical school of law, his self-regard and inordinate desire for fame, and his happily never fully-realized potential for metamorphosing from a rebel sympathetic to the aspirations of 'Young Germany' into a *Fido savant,* a poodle of the establishment. A man stands before us, with all his contradictions, in a difficult historical situation: a German and a Jew, at once Light of the Diaspora and swiftly vanishing Comet, a renegade from Judaism who, for all his baptism and his subsequent refusal to engage himself in Jewish causes, nevertheless remained a Jew in the eyes of his friends and foes. And Heine conveys all this now in realistic, now in almost surrealistic scenes; now in exhortations and direct statement, now in humorous or uncanny dream-visions which convey in subtle and nuanced ways the impression Gans had made on a poet whose own fate was bound up with his in so many ways. The letters and conversations complete and round out in important ways the double portrait which emerges from Heine's published works and which is surely of interest, not only to the literary critic, but to all who concern themselves with the troubled social history of countries in which Jews and Gentiles try to live together.

As we saw in the case of *The Hartz Journey*, Gans may be implicitly present even where Heine does not explicitly mention him. When the poet speaks of the obstacles the Prussian State put into the path of its Jewish intellectuals; when he glances at the ideological function of Roman law and, especially, the 'historical school of law' in German life and German thought; when he speaks of the comfort German liberals could derive from penetrating to the essence of Hegel's political and social philosophy; when he analyses the legal implications of the story told in *The Merchant of Venice;* when he has one of his characters remark that no democratic victory can be of use unless it leads to reforms of *Erbrecht,* laws of inheritance—in all these cases and many more he voices opinions which contacts with Gans, and reflections on Gans's career, had helped to shape. In that way he could present his influential contemporary not only as a reflection of himself and his own problems as a Jew born on German soil, but also as a fellow worker and fellow fighter in the cause of man's emancipation from outworn laws, inhumane conventions or restrictions, and noxious privilege. In the same way Leopold Zunz may be present, by implication, when the poet dwells on the cultural achievements of the Jewish past, or Uncle Salomon Heine when he speaks of Jewish bankers and plutocrats, or Giacomo Meyerbeer when he satirizes the manipulation of fame made possible by a venal press. By their very nature such presences are often intangible—yet we must remain conscious of them if we want to assess the full extent to which Heine's experience of Jews and conception of Judaism affected his work.

Having recognized such presences, we must, however, beware of over-simplification. Certainly Gans (and Moses Moser) helped Heine to interpret Hegel—but Heine attended Hegel's own lectures on the philosophy of world history throughout the summer semester of 1823, and probably sampled those on the philosophy of history and the philosophy of law in 1821-2. He also encountered many other Hegelians on his life's way. It would therefore be absurd to see only Gans's influence when we look at Heine's belief in the importance of world-historical individuals; his faith in ideas which must precede and inform actions if these are to further true progress; his search for the 'spirit' of individual peoples and his long-held conviction that the 'spirit' of Judaism was one of abstraction and denial of sensuality; or, indeed, his fascination with 'dying' or 'exiled' or 'degraded' gods which has clear connections with Hegel's views on the necessary rise and decline of religions. Certainly Gans helped Heine to see the reactionary dangers inherent in the 'historical' school of law, and Gans's career helped Heine to see the hostility to Jewish aspirations inherent in Savigny's social attitudes—but Heine had had a close look at representatives of the 'historical' school as a law student in Göttingen and had been taught opposition to them in the University of Bonn before he had ever heard of Gans. Certainly Gans helped Heine to see the necessity for tearing down the cultural wall that divided Jew from Christian, the Jewish world from the non-Jewish world, without abolishing totally the substance of Judaism (*aufgehen,* Gans said like a true Hegelian, does not mean *untergehen*)— but that was a conclusion at which he could well have arrived without Gans's help, in opposition, perhaps, to the liberal Professor Georg Sartorius whom he had come to admire in Göttingen but who opined that once Jews had been educated to German citizenship they should accept baptism as a preliminary to losing their Jewish identity altogether. Certainly Gans helped him to appreciate the importance of *Erbrecht* the law of inheritance, in the affairs of men—but he could easily have gathered this from his own law studies or from his later contacts with the Saint-Simonians, who popularized the device: 'Plus d'héritage'. . . .

Robert C. Holub (essay date 1988)

SOURCE: "Heine and Utopia," in *Heine-Jahrbuch,* Vol. 27, 1988, pp. 86-112.

[*In the following essay, Holub claims that utopian concerns are not central to Heine's writings, despite claims to the contrary by many contemporary critics of Heine, and that Heine instead expresses a realistic political agenda.*]

> So pflegen immer große Poeten zu verfahren:
> sie begründen zugleich etwas Neues, indem sie das Alte
> zerstören; sie negieren nie, ohne etwas zu bejahen.
>
> (Heine: **Einleitung zu *Don Quixote***)

It is almost certain that Heine would have protested against the application of the label, "utopian" to his thought or works. For in his day the word had largely pejorative connotations. No longer associated solely with Thomas More's epoch-making work, "utopia" was nonetheless still clearly identified with models of better states or societies. Even by the middle of the eighteenth century, however, the term seems to have been reserved principally for those models which were logically impossible, fantastic, or completely divorced from reality. Utopias were ideal alternatives that had no possibility of realization in this world; anyone promoting a utopia was either eccentric or mad. This seems to be the way Heine understood the word as well. In his *Memoiren,* where we find one of the only occurrences of the term in his oeuvre, he makes the following comment about his great uncle: "er war halb Schwärmer, der für kosmopolitische, weltbeglückende Utopien Propaganda machte". Although Heine exhibits a great degree of sympathy for his relative here, the association of "Schwärmer" with utopias clearly indicates the sense which this word carried. The way Heine and the nineteenth century use the term thus sets up an implicit opposition between utopia and Realpolitik; the latter deals with the art of the possible, the former with the dreams of the impossible.

It was precisely this sort of dichotomy that returned to haunt Heine—or at least Heine criticism—during the past fifteen years. Just as this much maligned writer was beginning to recover from over a century of defamation as a frivolous, Francophilic, unpatriotic, journalistic, Jewish pretender to German literature; just as his reputation as a political writer, in the wake of the student movement, was beginning to be rehabilitated, he was suddenly, albeit predictably labeled a utopian. This counter-offensive against the political interpretation of Heine seeks to undermine his practical significance for present concerns. If his views are merely "utopian," then they cannot be taken seriously as guidelines for political practice. Heine's works may be aesthetically and historically interesting, but from this perspective they are ultimately useless for effecting changes in the social sphere. In Germany the loudest voice of this ilk belongs to Dolf Sternberger, who deals explicitly with Heine as a utopian in his *Heinrich Heine und die Abschaffung der Sünde.* In subsuming Heine's thought about the future under the rubric of religion, Sternberger endeavors to preserve a narrow, superannuated category of the political from which apparently all but statesmen and political scientists are excluded. In England Nigel Reeve's book *Poetry and Politics* accomplishes a similar task with slightly different means. Although the British author appears to give more room to the political elements in Heine's works, it is evident that he considers the utopian—again in the sense of "unrealistic"—to be the driving force behind Heine's criticism of the present and his vision of the future. The number of enthusiastic reviews these books received, precisely because they opposed the "political" trend in Heine criticism, shows that Sternberger and Reeves are not alone in their opinions.

But while there seems to be a large contingent of Heine scholars prepared to call him utopian, the same cannot be said for those who most frequently discuss utopian elements in literature. In recent anthologies on this topic Heine's name scarcely appears. As far as I can tell, it is totally absent from the collection *Literatur ist Utopie.* In the three-volume interdisciplinary study entitled *Utopie-Forschung* Heine is mentioned only once in passing. And in *Literarische Utopie-Entwürfe* we find a contribution by Walter Jens in which Heine and Lessing converse, but there is nothing particularly utopian about their discussion except that it is taking place at all. This neglect of Heine on the part of critics dealing with utopian themes is understandable, though. For unlike Goethe in *Faust II* or Schiller in his *Ästhetische Erziehung,* for example, Heine avoids portraying schemes for the benefit of humankind and composing long treatises on the future perfectability of the individual and the state. His work is characterized throughout by a concentration on the here and now. The early love poetry, with its ironic reflections on the motifs and manners of his predecessors, amounts to a compendium of the emotions of the bourgeois youth of his era. His **Reisebilder** likewise focus on the contemporaneous by critically illuminating the political, social, and aesthetic values of the early Restoration. The long essays and correspondence articles written during the first decade and a half of his self-imposed Parisian exile have a similar function. Indeed, the very fact that, in volume, the largest part of his work from 1831-1845 consists of contributions to various German periodicals on actual occurrences in France indicates that Heine's major concerns during this period were current events rather than literary pipe dreams. In his final years one can note a definite waning in this preoccupation with contemporary happenings, but the depression and disillusionment accompanying the onset of his illness coupled with the defeat of the progressive forces in Europe were hardly conducive to utopian propositions. In the so-called *Matratzengruft,* as in earlier times of more robust health, utopian thoughts play a relatively small role. It would be foolish, of course, to deny the occurrence of various kinds of prophesies, predictions, and futuristic visions throughout his career, and we will have occasion shortly to examine some of these in more detail. But quantitatively such passages occupy only a tiny fraction of Heine's writings. In no work and at no time—with two possible exceptions—does the utopian stand at the center of his concerns.

"Bimini" is Heine's only work in which a utopia of sorts predominates thematically. Composed presumably at some time during the 1850s, this fragmentary epic relates Ponce de Leon's futile attempt to find the fountain of youth. While governing Cuba—the real Ponce was governor of Puerto Rico—the aging conquistador hears about Bimini from the old Indian woman Kaka. Rocking him to sleep in his hammock, she sings the lullabye about the fantastic island. After referring to the melodies of the larks, the lavish vegetation, and the ideal climate, she turns to the item which catches the slumbering Ponce's attention:

> Auf der Insel Bimini
> Quillt die allerliebste Quelle;
> Aus dem teuren Wunderborn
> Fließt das Wasser der Verjüngung.
> [. . .]
> Trinkt ein Greis von jenem Wasser,
> Wird er wieder jung; das Alter
> Wirft er von sich, wie ein Käfer
> Abstreift seine Raupenhülle.

Although from this depiction Bimini seems more magical than utopian, there are several elements which connect it with the utopian tradition. The first is the lack of a definite location; as Kaka presents it, Bimini is a fantasy of the mythological mind, a place which does not exist in the real world, and thus literally "nowhere." Furthermore, the fact that Bimini is described as an island, that ist, as a place geographically separate from the known world, echoes earlier utopias, from More's island state to the flood of "Robinsonade" in the early eighteenth century. We also find the suggestion that Bimini, like earlier utopias, is a hermetic society; once outsiders drink from the miraculous waters, they remain and fail to return to their native lands:

> Mancher Graukopf, der zum blonden
> Jüngling sich getrunken hatte,
> Schämte sich zurückzukehren
> Als Gelbschnabel in die Heimat—
>
> Manches Mütterchen insgleichen,
> Die sich wieder jung geschlückert,

Wollte nicht nach Hause gehen
Als ein junges Ding von Dirnlein—

Und die guten Leutchen blieben
Immerdar in Bimini;
Glück und Lenz hielt sie gefesselt
In dem ewgen Jugendlande . . .

Although there is no talk of a perfect constitution or even of how this society functions, the closed, remote, and ideal character of this island community brings it into the proximity of a familiar literary heritage. In Heine's oeuvre, though, Bimini, as the radically other, stands alone.

This unique occurrence of a place—utopia—as opposed to a temporal utopia in Heine's work has usually been seen as evidence for the repudiation of his earlier poetic vision. It is evident that Bimini does not and cannot exist. Ponce's naive belief that he can attain eternal youth turns out to be a self-deception. The narrator—and hence the reader—knows that the old woman is telling a fairy tale; Ponce unfortunately finds out the hard way. Instead of cures for his illnesses, he encounters further sickness and disease:

Ach, anstatt von altem Siechtum
Zu genesen, ward der Ärmste
Heimgesucht von vielen neuen
Leibesübeln und Gebresten.

He does not become young, but rather grows older and more decrepit:

Während er die Jugend suchte,
Ward er täglich noch viel älter
Und verrunzelt, abgemergelt
Kam er endlich in das Land,
[. . .]

And in lieu of Bimini's fountain of youth, he tastes the bitter waters of the Lethe:

Lethe heißt das gute Wasser!
Trink daraus, und du vergißt
All dein Leiden—ja, vergessen
Wirst du was du je gelitten—

Gutes Wasser! gutes Land!
Wer dort angelangt, verläßt es
Nimmermehr—denn dieses Land
Ist das wahre Bimini.

That these instances of disillusionment are not unrelated to Heine's personal situation is rather obvious. But the identification between Heine, or at least the Heine-persona as narrator, and the conquistador is emphasized in another way as well. In an elaborate extended metaphor in the **"Prolog"** the narrator compares the

ship which Ponce builds for his voyage to the poem he has constructed. Both have the same ultimate destination: the utopia, that is, the nowhere that Bimini turns out to be. His journey has likewise revealed itself as a "Narrenfahrt" on a "Narrenschiff" with "Narrenpassagiere". He too longs for his youth when he thinks of Bimini; it awakens in him "die verstorbenen Jugendträume" as well. The only difference between Ponce and the narrator is that the latter knows that the trip is futile and foolish from the outset; Ponce will only learn this in the course of his voyage. Nonetheless, this emphasis on the similarity between the narrator and the fictional Ponce makes it rather easy to interpret this poem as a renunciation on Heine's part of all those dreams and visions he had harbored in his youth, as a melancholy rejection of the ideal of human divinity, as an unequivocal and poignant **"Abschied von der Utopie."**

This conclusion, however, is too easy to be totally accurate. Certainly **"Bimini"** presents an unflattering picture of utopian thinking, and there surely seems to be a similarity between Heine and his aging and ill conquistador; but the nature of the rejected utopia, the context and content of the island paradise make the formula of an "Abschied von der Utopie" questionable. In the first place we should note that Heine repeatedly emphasizes the anachronistic quality of Ponce's undertaking from the perspective of the nineteenth century. In doing so, he is following closely the presumed source for the poem, Washington Irving's *Voyages and Discoveries of the Companions of Columbus*. Both Heine and Irving call the reader's attention to Ponce's naiveté in believing the tales about the fountain of youth. For Heine this credulity is accounted for by the era in which Ponce lived:

Wunderglaubenszeit! Ein Wunder
War sie selbst. So viele Wunder
Gab es damals, daß der Mensch
Sich nicht mehr darob verwundert.

If the belief in miracles is the norm, then doubt becomes a sign of foolishness. The roles of reason and madness are thus reversed:

Nur der Tor war damals Zweifler,
Die verständgen Leute glaubten:
Vor den Tageswundern beugte
Gläubig tief sein Haupt der Weise.

Here Heine is taking up a theme familiar to his readers from chapter XV of **Buch Le Grand**. In the earlier work it is evident that the reasonable represent the more progressive force in society; the fools are associated with the hegemonic elements during the Restoration. In **"Bimini,"** with the total confusion of roles, it is unclear which party should be identified with progress, or if such an identification is possible or necessary at all. What is clear, however, is that this age of miracles belongs to a distant past. The initial line of the poem suggests a connection with romanticism ["Wunderglaube! blaue Blume, / Die verschollen jetzt"], and it seems likely that Heine is situating Ponce where he was historically, at the close of the Catholic Middle Ages, from which romanticism, according to Heine, drew its inspiration. When we read:

> Juan Ponce de Leon wahrlich
> War kein Tor, kein Faselante,
> Als er unternahm die Irrfahrt
> Nach der Insel Bimini.

we should understand this as the narrator's concession to the "Wunderglaubenszeit," not as a further sign of identification with Heine. In the Restoration period in which Heine first articulated his hopes for the future, Ponce's anachronistic belief in utopia would have perforce relegated him to the party of the fools.

There is another aspect of **"Bimini"** that makes it anachronistic for Heine's age, however. The very fact that it is a place and that this place is located in the "new world" shows that this island with the enchanted waters is an obsolete mode of utopia for the nineteenth century. By the end of the eighteenth century the globe had been circumnavigated. With the closing of this last earthly frontier, there were literally no more places left to discover. It is no coincidence therefore, that utopian literature at just about the same time shifts its focus from the unknown place to the unknown time, that utopias increasingly become projections into the future rather than exotic islands on uncharted maps. That Heine here resorts to this antiquated utopian tradition only demonstrates again how dissimilar Bimini is to his earlier visions. A similar argument can also be made concerning the Caribbean as the location for the utopia. In earlier centuries the fascination with the newly discovered continents was connected with spices, precious metals, and the new species of plant and animal life found there. Taking the sometimes exaggerated reports of explorers and adding a little imagination, the European mind had no trouble conceiving of a paradise on earth located in some unexplored corner of the Americas. But again, by the nineteenth century these hopes had been totally dashed. Although some were still attracted to the political ideals of the former English colonies or allured by the vast and largely uninhabited (by Europeans) expanses of land, by 1800 there were no illusions concerning American utopias. When **"Bimini"** was written, it must have been patently clear that the Americas held little enchantment for the European fantasy, even if they continued to promise food and land for the European worker.

In this context a letter Heine received from Georg Weerth, at just about the time of **"Bimini"**'s composition, is significant. Weerth was in South America on a business venture for his firm, and he writes to Heine from along the Orinoco River, the same river at whose source Columbus suspected an earthly paradise. After extolling the virtues of European civilization, Weerth comments on the mundane and mercantile nature of contemporary visitors to the new world. While a half-century earlier there were still areas to explore—even if the idea of a utopia was no longer alive—in 1853 even this spirit of adventure is missing:

> heut zu Tage dringen unsre Kaufleute ohne viel Geräusch bis in das Herz der Kontinente und vielleicht habe ich gestern noch Tigerfelle von denselben Indianern gekauft, deren Väter einst Herrn von Humboldt und Herrn Bonpland durch die Katarakte von Atures Maypures ruderten.

Concerning an expedition to the "paradise" at the source of the Orinoco, which is supposedly guarded by the local Indian tribes, Weerth has the following sarcastic and significant remark:

> Nach meinen Erfahrungen würde die Expedition am besten mit einer Ladung Nürnberger Spielwaren gelingen, mit jenen Produkten deutscher Gemüthlichkeit welche schon auf so viele Nationen ihren welterobernden Einfluß ausübten. Meine Indianer [. . .] sind ebenfalls dieser Ansicht.

For the nineteenth century, then, the formerly exotic and potentially utopian "new world" means commerce and capitalism, not the magical waters of eternal youth. By thus locating Bimini in this obsolete utopian landscape, Heine implicitly distances it from his own earlier temporal "utopias."

But even if Heine had not made Ponce's dream-island an anachronism for the nineteenth-century European, his notion of paradise in Bimini would still be quite far from the visions of his earlier years. For Bimini is only a utopia for the aged. There is no mention of splendor, riches, eroticism, or divine pleasure on the island. Nor does Ponce seem to crave youth in order to enjoy these things. This is particularly significant since Heine here deviates from his source; Irving stresses that Ponce wanted youth so that he could accomplish great exploits and amass new riches. Heine's Ponce, by contrast, is willing to forfeit all possessions if he can only live on:

> Nehmt mir Reichtum, Ruhm und Würden,
> Nennt mich nicht mehr Excellenza,
> Nennt mich lieber junger Maulaff,
> Junger Gimpel, Bengel, Rotznas!

Ponce's single request is an extension of his life; he does not seem interested in the pleasures youth offers. His utopia is thus disclosed as one of contentment and renunciation, and we can easily imagine him sighing, as Heine does in the final poem of **"Zum Lazarus"**: "O laß mich froh / Hinleben noch viel schöne Tage / Bei meiner Frau im statu quo!" The identification of Ponce with his creator may be strengthened by this correspondence in world view, but the association of Heine's earlier vision with the conquistador's meager dream of youth would seem to become more tenuous. Heine may well have given up his "utopia" by the time he composed this fragmentary epic, but the poem itself does not document that renunciation. If there is an "Abschied" in **Bimini,"** then it is more like a farewell to the poet's last hopes of life and health; it is the melancholy recognition that the modest "utopia" of a sick and dying man is unattainable.

Biographically Heine seems to have shied away from membership or participation in any single party or movement. At no point in his life, therefore, do we even suspect an involvement in groups propagating utopian schemes. The exception to this general rule, of course, is Saint-Simonism. Dubbed a "utopian socialist" movement in retrospect largely because of Engels' influential work *Die Entwicklung des Sozialismus von der Utopie zur Wissenschaft* (1882), Saint-Simonism seems to have been something of a vogue when Heine arrived in Paris in 1831. Especially among intellectuals and artists, in short, in exactly those circles which Heine was likely to frequent, the doctrine of Saint-Simon as interpreted by his loyal and sometimes fanatic disciples found, for a brief period at least, a number of celebrated fellow-travelers. The degree to which Heine was one of these and the duration of his active interest are still disputed issues in scholarship despite the wealth of studies and speculation surrounding the Saint-Simonian connection. The reason these questions remain unresolved is ultimately due to Heine's own statements and silence on the matter. Although in several passages in published works he labels the Saint-Simonists the most advanced group in French society, in other places he pokes fun at them for their eccentricities. While he obviously adopted significant parts of their terminology, he never calls himself a Saint-Simonist and rarely gives this movement credit for the ideas he is promoting—and later renounces. Perhaps the strangest feature of Heine's Saint-Simonian association, however, is the infrequency with which it is mentioned in his correspondence and in reports by others about him. In over 1000 pages of the *Begegnungen mit Heine,* for example, Saint-Simonism crops up only a handful of times. From the entries of Karl Grün and Eduard von Fichte, Heine seems to have displayed an immediate interest in this movement after his arrival in Paris and it may well be true, if von Fichte is accurate and Heine was candid with him, that he found the French utopians a welcome antidote to republicanism. But the only other mention of Saint-Simonism that has any substance at all occurs in the memoirs of Heinrich Laube, who indicates that Heine hardly took these people

seriously. He reportedly ridiculed their odd dress and mockingly commented that Mathilde had thought of submitting herself for the "Mère-Examen." Heine, of course, was perfectly capable of deriding something one minute and lauding it the next, but the sheer absence of references to Saint-Simonism where one might expect it to be mentioned and the off-hand manner in which it is treated when it does appear are certainly troublesome for those seeking a more substantial link.

On the basis of this evidence most commentators have concluded that Heine was intellectually fascinated by, but never seriously involved with the Saint-Simonists. There was a happy overlap between Heine's views and those propagated by these French friends, and this explains why Heine could so easily appropriate key phrases and catch-words, and why he occasionally depicts Saint-Simonism in the theoretical vanguard. Except for those studies in which Heine's Saint-Simonism has been the main theme, it was rarely devoted more than a chapter. A little more than a decade ago, however, Dolf Sternberger, in his aforementioned book, made significantly greater claims for the impact of Saint-Simonism on Heine's life and works. For Sternberger the encounter with this French school of thought was the central intellectual experience in Heine's development. According to this view Heine not only appropriated a large portion of its social and "religious" doctrine, but also prided himself in being the outstanding German apostle of the new church. In a series of detailed arguments Sternberger relates how Heine was exposed to these French utopians, what he adopted from their texts, where this reappears in his oeuvre, and how Heine acted at times in accord with Enfantin's wishes. This image of "Heine unter den Priestern" has some rather drastic consequences for our picture of his intellectual development and "utopian" vision. Of greatest significance is the relatively minor role thereby accorded to the German tradition— especially to Hegel and the left Hegelians. In fact, if one had to summarize Sternberger's thesis in one thought, it would be that Heine was a Saint-Simonian utopian and not a left Hegelian. As Sternberger himself writes: "in Sachen der Utopie hat Heine auf Enfantin und die Seinen gehört."

Since the Saint-Simonists are the only utopian group with which Heine purportedly had any prolonged contact, it is advisable to examine more closely some of the evidence Sternberger presents for Heine's adherence to the movement. In terms of personal involvement, as we have seen already, there is an astounding scarcity of documents. Sternberger, therefore, has to make the most of what is available. And what is available is the rather prolix and confusing letter Enfantin addressed to Heine from Egypt after reading *De l'Allemagne,* which the author had sent and dedicated to him. There is no necessity to delve very deeply into the strange content of this missive, which criticizes Heine for various violations of *le doctrine,* lauds Bavaria and Austria, and recommends that Heine in the future sing the praises of the "sinnigen, fleißigen, sparsamen, biederen, aufgeklärten" German people. Even Sternberger concedes that the letter bears witness to the gap which existed between Heine's views and those of Le Père. What is at issue, rather, is Heine's use of the letter. In Sternberger's narrative of events the promulgation of the letter in early 1836 is part of Heine's endeavor to clear himself with the Bundestag, which had recommended proscription of his writings in December of 1835. In contrast to the standard view, which sees the publication of the letter as an act of defiance, Sternberger finds it a perfect supplement to the claims of innocence and unjustified persecution found in Heine's petition "An die Hohe Bundesversammlung." Since the letter advises moderation rather than revolution, since it praises Austria—the dominant force in the Bundestag—and since the postscript indicates that Heine's recent French preface to the Reisebilder is in accord with current Saint-Simonian dogma, Sternberger reasons that Heine wanted it printed to help demonstrate his religious and moral integrity. Furthermore, on 30 January 1836 Heine forwarded a copy of his petition to the *Augsburger Allgemeine Zeitung;* on the same day he sent copies of Enfantin's letter to Campe with the request that he promulgate it. This coincidence in timing prompts the following interpretation:

> Wenn er buchstäblich an einem und demselben Tag das Schreiben 'an die Hohe Bundesversammlung' zur Veröffentlichung nach Deutschland schickt und den "Wunsch" nach Hamburg gehen läßt, man möge für die Verbreitung von Enfantins Brief sorgen, so muß man—angesichts der Lage, in der er sich befand—vermuten, daß die Motive und die Zwecke der beiden Handlungen in seinem Kopf miteinander verknüpft waren.

The logic of this argument is obviously shaky; from other letters Heine wrote at about the same time we see that he was not so disturbed that he was incapable of performing two separate actions in the course of one day. Nonetheless, Sternberger is probably correct in seeing a connection between the attempt to publish the two documents, but Heine's motives have nothing to do with clearing his name through the epistolary testimony of Enfantin. In the letter to Campe the reason for wanting the public to read Enfantin's comments is stated clearly enough: "Ich schicke Ihnen diese Tage auch Exemplare des Briefes von Enfantin, und wünsche daß Sie denselben so verbreiten, daß sie im Publikum etwas Aufsehen erregen." It is very likely that the endeavor to publish the almost comically obsequious petition to the Bundestag was prompted by the same sort of reasoning, namely, to create publicity. Furthermore, it is difficult to understand how a letter from Enfantin could have made Heine appear less threatening to the religious and moral underpin-

nings of the state, nor why Heine would have presumed that this would have been the effect. It was well known, after all, that the Saint-Simonists had been persecuted even in liberal France. Certainly Heine, as well as the rest of the German intelligentsia of the 1830s, was aware that the Young German connection with the French utopian movement was hardly an asset in conservative circles. In fact, in newspaper articles preceding and surrounding the ban placed on the Young Germans, their role as propagators of Saint-Simonism is seen as particularly offensive. Heine would have had to have been completely out of touch with the polemics launched against him and the Young Germans to think that he could improve his standing with the ruling powers through a letter from Le Père himself. Here Campe's view of the ideological landscape proves to be much clearer than Sternberger's. In a letter to his star author on 16 February 1836 he explains why he chose not to publish the Enfantin letter himself: "Alle Welt wird sagen 'sehet ihr wol, das junge Deutschland steckt mit den St Simonisten unter einer Decke!'" In short, Campe feared that in publishing the letter he would help to substantiate the charges against "die junge Literatur." But Campe also understood the value of publicity. He, like Heine, knows that Enfantin's name will attract attention, and thus he makes sure that his letter is made public. He informs Heine that he gave copies to "sogenannte Stadttrompeter" and remarks further: "Mir macht es Spaß, die Dummheiten noch mehr zu verwirren, damit die Bursche am Ende lächerlich in Deutschland werden, was doch das Ende vom Liede bleibt." From this statement it appears that Heine's publisher does not have a very high opinion of these French utopians. Moreover, there is not the least suggestion that Enfantin's letter could be used for the purpose Sternberger ascribes to it. It is clear, then, that for Campe the promulgation of this letter is a gimmick, a joke, something that will cause a stir in the public.

The final point that should be rectified in this affair of the Enfantin letter concerns Heine's attitude towards the authorities. Sternberger claims that it is something less than "kämpferisch" based on the petition, his interpretation of the Egyptian missive, and a number of statements found in Heine's letters concerning future quietism. But Heine's immediate reaction to the decree of the Bundestag was clearly one of solidarity with the Young German cause, even though he had no reason to consider himself part of any literary conspiracy. At the end of December 1835, thus *after* the decree, Heine wrote to Gustav Kolb in Augsburg that he had not distanced himself from the Young Germans' plans for the journal *Deutsche Revue.* In a letter to Campe on 12 January 1836, in which he indicates that the entire affair with the Bundestag seems like a tempest in a teapot to him, he reiterates this sentiment:

> [ich] werde [. . .] nicht so feige seyn die jungen Leute, die politisch unschuldig sind, zu

desavouiren, und ich habe im Gegentheil gleich eine Erklärung nach der *Allgemeinen* Zeitung geschickt [. . .] worin ich erkläre daß ich gar keinen Anstand genommen hätte an der Deutschen Revüe mitzuarbeiten.

The sentence which immediately follows makes it clear that this declaration was an oppositional gesture on his part: "Spaßhaft genug ist es, daß ohne die letzten Vorfälle, ich mir nie in den Sinn kommen lassen an irgend einer solchen Zeitschrift zu arbeiten." Indeed, in the next months Heine repeatedly implores Campe to challenge the government by not submitting his *Salon III* for pre-censorship, a request that Campe, much to Heine's outrage, disobeys. In this context the publication of Enfantin's letter can be seen in its true double role. It is not a sign of cowardice, compromise, and conciliation, as Sternberger would have it, but rather both an act of open defiance and an effective piece of publicity.

Sternberger's final attempt to bind Heine more firmly to these early French utopians and, in the process, to cast his actions in a dubious light politically is similarly based on questionable philological assumptions and convoluted speculation. At issue are two letters, one Heine purportedly addressed to Metternich in June of 1836 and the other sent to Campe on 23 January 1837. We have no copy of the former letter; only the report of Graf Maltzan, the Prussian ambassador in Vienna, testifies to its existence. From this report the content has been reconstructed as follows: "*Heine bitter den Fürsten, so großmütig zu sein, wie es dem Sieger zukommt—denn das von Österreich verteidigte politische System triumphiert—, ihn zu empfangen und so aus der Misere zu ziehen.*" The relevant passage from the letter to Campe refers to Heine's standing among the powerful in government, and in this context Metternich is again mentioned:

> Die wichtigsten Männer in Preußen interessiren sich in diesem Augenblick für meine Rückkehr ins Vaterland, woran ich freylich nicht denke, welche Verwendung aber jedenfalls mich vor litterarischer Schererey künftig schützt. In Oestreich ist mir der Fürst Metternich geneigt und mißbilligt die Unbill, die mir widerfahren. Ohne daß ich servil werde, gewinne ich das Zutrauen der Staatsmänner, die wohl einsehen, daß mein Revoluzionsgeist sich nicht an die Thätigkeit der rohen Menge wendet, sondern an die Bekehrung der Höchstgestellten.

Sternberger connects these two letters with Enfantin's praise of Austria in his Egyptian letter and with his attempt to persuade his German disciple to initiate change by actively converting the kings: "Prophète, que votre voix parvienne à l'oreille des rois, si vous voulez affranchir les peuples." According to Sternberger, "Heine hat den Gedanken, den Wink, den Apell verstanden." With true missionary zeal this devout convert to the Saint-Simonian church obeyed the commandment from on high. He wrote to Metternich, asking him for an audience so that he might act as the modern Constantine for his faith. His letter to Campe simply confirms his adherence to Enfantin's switch from favoring an "apostolat populaire" to an "apostolat royal."

Now this is a very nice story. It has the potential for high drama and secret diplomacy. One could imagine Schiller writing a play about it. Moreover, if it were true, one would certainly have to grant that Heine was more thoroughly under the spell of the Saint-Simonian wand then anyone has hitherto suspected. But unfortunately there are some rather large gaps in Sternberger's account, for example, the half-year between Enfantin's missive, which Heine allegedly understood so well, and the apostle's carrying out of his Holyness's order. Why did Heine hesitate so long in contacting Metternich? If Heine actually did write the sort of letter Sternberger suggests—assuming, of course, that there was a letter at all—if he really took Enfantin's suggestion so seriously, then why was June a more propitious month for missionary work than January? And why did Heine choose to ignore the other suggestions he received? In the following years he does not revise his opinions on Schelling or Bavaria, for example, despite Enfantin's favorable remarks on both; nor does he sing the praises of the "simple, patriarchical customs" of the German people from the Kaiser to the peasant. Furthermore, why was Metternich singled out for conversion and no other German ruler? It is true, of course, as Sternberger points out, that Heine criticizes Metternich less than almost any other German in power. At some point the rumor that reached Heine concerning the Austrian statesman's appreciation of ***Das Buch der Lieder*** may have affected this charitable behavior. But Heine's apparent restraint with respect to Metternich and Austria is evidenced well before he was ever acquainted with Saint-Simonism. Indeed, several elements in Enfantin's praise of Austria crop up somewhere in Heine's writings—often mixed with a good deal of irony—before he received the letter from Egypt. There is thus no reason to suspect that Heine altered his attitude toward Austria because of Enfantin's remarks, nor that his own letter to Metternich had anything to do with Saint-Simonian evangelism.

Finally, Heine's comments to Campe, as strange as they may be and as mistaken as they were, also have in all likelihood no connection with Enfantin's letter, which, after all, he had received over one year before. The same sentiments occur in the Menzel polemic, except that here neither Metternich nor the "Floskel" about conversion is specifically mentioned: "wie ich aus den sichersten Quellen erfahren, haben viele der höchsten Staatsmänner den exzeptionellen Zustand, worin man mich versetzt, mit würdiger Teilnahme bedauert und baldigste Abhülfe versprochen". It is impossible to know exactly whom Heine means either here or in his correspondence with Campe, but a letter he received on 5 January 1837—the Menzel polemic is dated 24 January, the letter to Campe 23 January—contains no doubt the sort of remarks which led him astray. Eugen von Vaerst, after requesting a contribution from Heine for the *Neue Breslauer Zeitung*, urges him to utilize his friend Varnhagen von Ense for a reconciliation with Prussia. He adds that he has influential friends in Berlin and states further. "Auch die gute Meinung des Herrn von Werther würde Ihnen nützlich sein." Now Werther, whom Heine had visited in 1832 when he was the Prussian ambassador in Paris—a position he held until 1837—was certainly what one would call an "important man." His mention in the context of a reconciliation with Prussia, as well as the other remarks in this letter, could have easily given Heine the erroneous impression that "the highest statesmen" were taking an interest in his affairs. Or he could have picked up similar gossip from misinformed connections in Paris. We should recall, for example, that about a year later, when Werther had become Außenminister, Heine appears to believe that Prussia can be convinced not to prohibit a journal he is planning to bring out. He was wrong about this and wrong to think that high officials would intervene on his behalf. But even if he deluded himself in evaluating his standing among the influential in government, there is still no reason to think that Enfantin had any influence whatsoever on this delusion. Metternich's appreciation of good poetry, a casual acquaintance with Wilhelm von Werther, the usual antipathy for the republican rabble, and a few rumors and misconceptions may not make as good a story as Sternberger's. But these elements do have more of the "authentische Wahrscheinlichkeit" Sternberger values than the farfetched notion that Heine acted as a Saint-Simonian missionary.

Unfortunately, the method Sternberger applies to establish Heine's intellectual reliance on the Saint-Simonian vision is just as unsatisfactory as his method for connecting him personally with these utopian thinkers. The most unnerving feature of his approach is the almost fetishistic dependence on textual comparisons. For Sternberger this technique is evidently a secure manner of establishing impact: "eben auf die Sprache, auf die Worte, ja die Wörter kommt alles an, wenn ein geistiger Zusammenhang aufgedeckt werden soll." Thus the central evidence used for determining Saint-Simonian influence consists of the various words and phrases Heine lifted from the French sources There can be no doubt that such borrowing did in fact occur. The appearance of "Synthese," "Doktrin," "Rehabilitation des Fleisches" ("der Materie"), "Sensualismus," and "Spiritualismus" can all be traced to a Saint-Simonian source. Heine's criticism of the present as well as his vision of the future, however, are formulated in slightly different terms well before his acquaintance with the French utopians. A cosmopolitanism is evidenced as early as the *Briefe aus Berlin* and *Über Polen*. The idea of a third testament, so important for Seraphine

VII, is anticipated in the "Bergidylle" of *Die Harzreise*. Here Heine was most likely adopting Lessing's speculation in the *Erziehung des Menschengeschlechts* (1780), a work, incidently, which the Saint-Simonians translated and included as an appendix to the *Réligion saint-simonienne*. In this third stage of the religious development of humankind, which is misleadingly associated with the Holy Spirit, we encounter the "Abschaffung der Sünde," the "Rehabilitation des Fleisches," before its Saint-Simonian formulation:

> Er [der heilige Geist] verscheucht die bösen Nebel,
> Und das dunkle Hirngespinst,
> Das uns Lieb und Lust verleidet,
> Tag und Nacht uns angegrinst.

We also find signs of the "Vergöttlichung des Menschen" in the *Reisebilder,* for example, in "Die Götter Griechenlands," where the narrator recognizes an "ambrosiches Recht", or, more clearly, at the beginning of *Nordsee III*. In opposition to the Middle Ages, we can now anticipate a different and higher form of future happiness:

> wir wissen auch daß ein Glück, das wir der Lüge verdanken, kein wahres Glück ist, und daß wir, in den einzelnen zerrissenen Momenten eines gottgleicheren Zustandes, einer höheren Geisteswürde, mehr Glück empfinden können, als in den lang hinvegetierten Jahren eines dumpfen Köhlerglaubens.

Indeed, in Sternberger's "Nachtrag 1975," which appears in the Suhrkamp edition of his book, he is forced to admit that most of the motifs he had associated with Heine's Saint-Simonian utopia appear in *Die Reise von München nach Genua*, written in 1829—before Heine could have been exposed to the exposition of Enfantin & Co. But the verbal gesture we find here concerning a new race with free thoughts and feelings can be traced back even earlier in Heine's works. Although it is not nearly as sensual as later versions, in *Buch Le Grand* (1826) we already find a sort of "utopian" projection that serves as a model for later occurrences, from the outbursts in *Religion und Philosophie in Deutschland* to the Weill preface in 1847: "ein neues Geschlecht ist hervorgeblüht mit neuen Wünschen und neuen Gedanken, voller Verwunderung höre ich neue Namen und neue Lieder". In light of this evidence it is difficult to accept Sternberger's contention that Heine's "utopia" is derived from Saint-Simonism. He certainly listened carefully to the language of Enfantin and his cohorts, and evidently found the catchy phrasing and the imaginative idiom much to his liking. The major notions identified with Saint-Simonism, however, can all be found in his writings before his exposure to *le doctrine*. He may have derived his "utopianism" from Hegel or, as I would contend, from the German Grecophilic tradition, but it is evident that Saint-Simonism provides only the outer garments for what was already a well-formed body of thought.

In his introduction to Cervantes' *Don Quixote,* written in early 1837, Heine locates the comic nature of the hero in his attempt to bring the past to life. In a personal aside that follows he then notes what he has learned:

> daß es eine eben so undankbare Tollheit ist, wenn man die Zukunft allzu frühzeitig in die Gegenwart einführen will und bei solchem Ankampf gegen die schweren Interessen des Tages nur einen sehr mageren Klepper, eine sehr morsche Rüstung und einen eben so gebrechlichen Körper besitzt!

This anti-utopian sentiment accords well with what we can find in the rest of Heine's works. He was not fond of the "geträumten Mondschein der Zukunft", a phrase he applied to the thought of the Saint-Simonist Leroux; as our glance at **"Bimini"** and his French utopian connection suggest, he does not adhere to chimeras of a new Eden; nor does he fancy an ideal society, which, without mediation, is assigned the task of remedying present abuses. In spite of these considerations, however, one could still apply the term "utopian" to his thought, but only if this word is understood without the pejorative overtones usually associated with it. If we instead conceive of a utopia in a more Blochian fashion, as something which anticipates or pre-views the future, then the word describes rather well a good part of Heine's vision. In this case Heine would not be a starry-eyed dreamer gazing into a poetic crystal ball, but rather a perceptive observer of current trends and past behavior projecting possibilities into the future. He would not be a Don Quixote trying to salvage an obsolete past, a Ponce de Leon longing for an eternal paradise, or even a Leroux fantasizing about an ideal industrial community, but a committed writer who sensitively registers currents and tendencies of contemporary life. He would be utopian, then, in the sense that Jost Hermand defines it in *Orte. Irgendwo*: as a model for progressive thinking who rejects stasus as well as romantic escapism, as someone who points to the real possibilities for a more satisfying life on earth.

For the most outstanding feature of Heine's future vision is that it is thoroughly this-worldly. Permeated with the reality in which it originates, his utopia is based on what one could call "materialism," provided this term is understood in a non-Marxist sense. The frequency with which good food, fine clothing, and sensual enjoyment appear in Heine's optimistic projections of future life is difficult to overlook. It is no coincidence, therefore, that Heine introduces perhaps his most celebrated utopian outburst—in *Religion und Philosophie in Deutschland*—with the materialist sentiment attributed to Saint-Just: "le pain est le droit du peuple." Nor is it a coincidence that this maxim follows Heine's demand for a rehabilitation of the material side of existence:

> Wir befördern das Wohlsein der Materie, das materielle Glück der Völker, nicht well wir gleich den Materialisten den Geist mißachten, sondern well wir wissen, daß die Göttlichkeit des Menschen sich auch in seiner leiblichen Erscheinung kund gibt, und das Elend den Leib, das Bild Gottes, zerstört oder aviliert, und der Geist dadurch ebenfalls zu Grunde geht.

At the very basis of this vision lies a pantheistic, philosophical materialism; but in Heine's text it is inextricably entwined with the concern for the fulfillment of the most elementary needs of the population. This is the prerequisite for his non-fantastic utopia, and despite Heine's disclaimers concerning the economic side of Saint-Simonism, it may well be partially derived from exactly this source. What he seems to have learned from the writings of these French utopians is not primarily the thought of eroticism and luxury, but the much simpler fact that the basic needs of all humans—and here Heine, like Saint-Simon himself, seems to be thinking only of Western Europe and the United States—are able to be satisfied with our present productive capacities. In order for this to happen, however, some structural changes in the process of production will have to occur as well. Chief among these is the elimination of "l'exploitation de l'homme par l'homme," an insight Heine explicitly credits to his French friends in May of 1834. At just about the same time, in *Die Romantische Schule*, this idea of non-exploitation is brought into a definite utopian context:

> Wir haben die Lande gemessen, die Naturkräfte gewogen, die Mittel der Industrie berechnet, und siehe, wir haben ausgefunden: daß diese Erde groß genug ist; daß sie jedem hinlänglichen Raum bietet, die Hütte seines Glückes darauf zu bauen; daß diese Erde uns alle anständig ernähren kann, wenn wir alle arbeiten und nicht einer auf Kosten des anderen leben will; und daß wir nicht nötig haben die größere und ärmere Klasse an den Himmel zu verweisen.

And in one of the most famous passages in the *Wintermärchen* this association between earthly happiness, the end of exploitation, and "le pain" is again repeated:

> Wir wollen auf Erden glücklich sein,
> Wir wollen nicht mehr darben;
> Verschlemmen soll nicht der faule Bauch
> Was fleißige Hände erwarben.
>
> Es wächst hienieden Brot genug
> Für alle Menschenkinder, [. . .]

What we find, then, prefacing, as it were, Heine's utopian vision is the concern with the satisfaction of rudimentary needs—symbolized by the image of bread—coupled with the cessation of exploitation.

On this foundation of the productive capacities of the earth and its peoples Heine builds his utopian structures. A future with only bread, with only simple and meager pleasures, would hardly be something to celebrate. Thus Heine transforms the symbolic bread from a basic need to a divine right: "le pain est le droit divine de l'homme" becomes his utopian battle cry. This slight alteration has some rather drastic political implications, of course. The divine right, usually associated with kings, is now usurped by the commoners. There is no longer one monarch or a single social class which enjoys the luxury the earth has to offer; the treasures of this world are to be opened up to the populace at large. In terms of politics equality will reign: "wir stiften eine Demokratie gleichherrlicher, gleichheiliger, gleichbeseligter Götter." The pleasures these earthly gods will enjoy are accordingly things traditionally identified with royalty and divinity: "wir [. . .] verlangen Nektar und Ambrosia, Purpurmäntel, kostbare Wohlgerüche, Wollust und Pracht, lachenden Nymphentanz, Musik und Komödien". A similar technique is employed in the **Wintermarchen**. From the simple bread which satisfies basic needs, Heine moves to finer, more luxurious items when he completes the stanza cited above:

> Auch Rosen und Myrten, Schönheit und Lust,
> Und Zuckererbsen nicht minder.

The critique of spiritualist religion is not enough; Heine postulates a materialistically tinged "Religion der Freude". The end of exploitation is also not a sufficient goal; Heine's utopia must contain an abundance of pleasures and delicacies. And mere equality in the political realm is a demand which is far too modest; Heine envisions the more revolutionary "Gleichheit der Genüsse". The third testament, the last word, the millennium—this eschatological vocabulary in Heine's writings proclaims not just the coming of an anti-spiritualist epoch, nor merely the end of want and poverty, but, more importantly, the establishment of the "Reich der ewigen Freude".

The movement from bread to ambrosia, from the end of exploitation to the introduction of universal enjoyment, from sustenance to surfeit, serves to anchor Heine's utopian projections in the world around him. But there is another, more formal technique he uses to emphasize the connection, as well as the disparity, between utopia and reality. It should be obvious to most readers that Heine rarely delineates the positive features of his utopia even in those passages in which it is a theme. The precise contours of the new society remain vague and general; what Heine means by his symbolic empire of eternal joy with its overtones of eroticism and abundance is left unspecified, perhaps

Deathmask of Heine.

with intention. Much more often the reader encounters instead in these passages the presumed thoughts of future, happier, more god-like generations about their unfortunate ancestors. Heine thus presents us with a future that negates the past, especially those elements most restrictive to the full development of the human personality. Out of the total negation of certain features of Heine's contemporary society, one can begin to construct the outlines of the new and better world of our grandchildren, but this task is left to the imagination of the reader; it is not accomplished already by the author. Thus this constant referring to the present, this technique of utopia through negation, is a multifunctional devise in Heine's texts. The vision of the utopian society serves as a critique of the present, a hope or guide to the future, and a stimulation to the reader's activity. By seeing the present through the eyes of a future generation, readers are forced to consider critically the mores and manners of their own world.

The preface Heine wrote to Weill's *Sittengemälden* provides a perfect illustration of this sort of technique, although, as we have seen above, it appears as early as 1826 in **Buch Le Grand**. In the Weill preface Heine first situates himself firmly in the malaise of the old world. His inability to escape from tradition, the "sickness" or "romanticism" he often refers to, is a topos which runs through his works from the *Reisebilder* to the last poems:

> Ach! ich bin ja noch ein Kind der Vergangenheit, ich bin noch nicht geheilt von jener knechtischen Demut, jener knirschenden Selbstverachtung, woran das Menschengeschlecht seit anderthalb Jahrtausenden siechte, und die wir mit der abergläubischen Muttermilch eingesogen . . .

That his preface is dated on Good Friday 1847 is only a further sign of his entrapment in the old order with its mythology of death and suffering. But even though Heine cannot himself transcend his heritage, he is able to glimpse some thing different. As a great poet, he can see "the gods of the future"; he can envisage a society in which the spiritual and material enslavement he has experienced no longer exist. What the future will bring, however, and how it will differ from the past, are left typically hazy. We read the coming generations will be more healthy, and that they will contemplate and assert their divinity in the most joyful calm. And later we are also introduced to "eine freudige Götterversammlung" which sits around an altar in "Tempelpalästen" where stories about the history of humankind are told amid the burning of incense. But aside from these generalizations cloaked in highly rhetorical phrases and quasi-religious vocabulary, there is little that we can say about these healthier and happier human divinities. In a manner characteristic of Heine we encounter in two full paragraphs of utopian vision more references to Europe in the nineteenth century than to the qualities of the regained paradise. In short, textually Heine's vision amounts to what we might term a utopia of retrospection.

The contents of the utopian retrospection are twofold: a critique of spiritualism and a debunking of Christian myths, both presented in the guise of fairy tales from the perspective of the euphoric future. What is reality for the nineteenth century will seem like an incredulous flight of fantasy for the inhabitants of Heine's utopia:

> Es wird ihnen wie ein Märchen klingen, wenn sie hören, daß weiland die Menschen sich alle Genüsse dieser Erde versagten, ihren Leib kasteiten und ihren Geist verdumpften, Mädchenblüten und Jünglingsstolz abschlachteten, beständig logen und greinten, das abgeschmackteste Elend duldeten . . .

Here the anti-materialist, anti-sensual, and anti-sensuous prejudices of Heine's Europe are examined critically through the magnifying glass of the future. Presented in this fashion, of course, the actions of humankind seem preposterous. We can understand why (and hope that) our descendants will consider such behavior a fairy-tale. The critique of Christianity is then accomplished in a similar manner. Heine introduces a motif familiar to his readers from *Buch Le Grand*. One of

the surviving old men, someone who can still recall the distant past, consents to relate a few stories about those strange beliefs from long ago. Again we find that the customs and conventions of contemporary society, when seen in utopian retrospection, appear as unbelievable legends:

> dann erzählt vielleicht einer der Greise, daß es ein Zeitalter gab, in welchem ein Toter als Gott angebetet und durch ein schauerliches Leichenmahl gefeiert ward, wo man sich einbildete, das Brot, welches man esse, sei sein Fleisch, und der Wein, den man trinke, sei sein Blut.

From this feigned perspective of the future, Christian mythology seems as fantastic as Nordic or Greek mythology in the nineteenth century. "In der Tat, unsere Enkel werden ein Ammenmärchen zu vernehmen meinen, wenn man ihnen erzählt, was wir geglaubt und gelitten!". By thus relativizing the eternal truths of orthodox religion, Heine negates its validity. Unburdened by an ethics of abstinence and a religion of purely symbolic pleasures, the "schönen Enkel" will presumably be able to enjoy all the riches the earth and its people have to offer. The negation of the renunciatory, spiritualistic present necessarily brings about an image of a fulfilling, sensualist future.

There is a final aspect of Heine's vision which locates it among non-fantastic, reality-bound utopias. Often when Heine has finished writing about the thoughts of coming generations and their community of pleasure, he abruptly questions his own optimism about the future with the sobering thought of stagnation or decline. The closing paragraphs of *Französische Maler* illustrate this sort of textual strategy for the particular case of the art of the future. Here Heine first predicts a new age and a new art which will not borrow its symbolism from the past. He even describes the transition phase to this renaissance as one of "selbsttrunkenste Subjektivität, weltentzügelte Individualität, die gottfreie Persönlichkeit mit all ihrer Lebenslust". But the very next passage casts a dark shadow on this optimistic forecast:

> Oder hat es überhaupt mit der Kunst und mit der Welt selbst ein trübseliges Ende? Jene überwiegende Geistigkeit, die sich jetzt in der europäischen Literatur zeigt, ist sie vielleicht ein Zeichen von nahem Absterben, wie bei Menschen, die in der Todesstunde plötzlich hellsehend werden und mit verbleichenden Lippen die übersinnlichsten Geheimnisse aussprechen?

This sort of questioning does not cancel the original vision, but rather marks it as one of several possibilities. By tempering utopia with the cold shower of reality, Heine elicits reflection on the part of the reader. Confronted with the alternatives of death or rebirth, we are compelled to find our own answer to Heine's apparently rhetorical queries.

But in Heine's oeuvre the *locus classicus* for this textual strategy occurs in the first book of *Religion und Philosophie in Deutschland*. Using the imagery of sickness and health for Christianity and the coming utopian faith respectively, Heine first cites most of the elements we have come to associate with his most optimistic vision. We read about our happier and more beautiful descendants, the harmony of body and mind, the demise of the debilitating, spiritualistic, Christian religion, and the introduction of an erotic religion of joy. We even encounter the familiar technique of future retrospection:

> Die glücklichern und schöneren Generationen [. . .] werden wehmütig lächeln über ihre armen Vorfahren, die sich aller Genüsse dieser schönen Erde trübsinnig enthielten, und, durch Abtötung der warmen farbigen Sinnlichkeit, fast zu kalten Gespenstern verblichen sind!

Then Heine affirms his optimism about the future in a manner seldom evidenced in his other utopian outbursts: "Ja, ich sage es bestimmt, unsere Nachkommen werden schöner und glücklicher sein als wir." The reason for Heine's confidence is his unshakable faith in the progress of the human species: "Denn ich glaube an den Fortschritt, ich glaube, die Menschheit ist zur Glückseligkeit bestimmt." And he continues his utopian reflection with a thought that would later receive prominence in the *Wintermärchen*, namely, the realization of happiness on earth as opposed to the deferred blessedness in the afterlife: "Schon hier auf Erden möchte ich, durch die Segnungen freier politischer und industrieller Institutionen, jene Seligkeit etablieren, die, nach der Meinung der Frommen, erst am jüngsten Tage, im Himmel, stattfinden soll." Already in this sentence, however, Heine has begun to waver ever so slightly from his earlier conviction. The words "ich möchte" subjectivize the vision, making the thought of a more beautiful and happier posterity a wish rather than a certitude. But the following sentence, which closes the paragraph, suddenly and unexpectedly calls the entire utopia into question: "Jenes ist vielleicht eben so wie dieses eine törigte Hoffnung, und es gibt keine Auferstehung der Menschheit, weder im politisch moralischen, noch im apostolisch katholischen Sinne." And the next short paragraph raises further doubts about the earlier vision by summarizing what the consequences would be if the progress Heine so vehemently affirmed is really an illusion:

> Die Menschheit ist vielleicht zu ewigem Elend bestimmt, die Völker sind vielleicht auf ewig verdammt von Despoten zertreten, von den Spießgesellen derselben exploitiert, und von den Lakaien verhöhnt zu werden.

In the course of a few sentences, then, absolute certainty has ceded to the most dismal doubts. Again, though, the effect of this apparent turnabout is not necessarily the renunciation of the utopian impulse.

Rather, this technique provokes the reader to protest against the continuation of present practices; it goads him/her to deny the misery of spiritualist hegemony and to affirm, with Heine, the arrival of a more beautiful, more fulfilling world. Certainly the introduction of this sort of skepticism is not just a trick to induce reader response; it undoubtedly bears witness to Heine's own misgivings about his most favorable forecasts. But on a textural level it has the effect of focusing attention once again on the reality from which any utopia must depart. It reinforces the link to this world by showing us what has to be combatted and what humankind will suffer if the status quo is maintained.

Here too, then, the most salient aspect of Heine's vision consists in its unusual and complex relationship to reality. Throughout his work, therefore, utopia is not characterized by an unmediated leap into a paradisiacal state. Much more often, upon closer examination, it turns out to be a polemical denunciation of the ideological and moral fetters which keep humans in both physical and intellectual bondage. It is both critique and hope, condemnation and prediction. Like most literary utopias, Heine's is formed and informed throughout by a dialectic of present and future, but in contrast to other visions, his is permeated in a unique fashion by this dialectic. As we have seen above, both the form and the content of Heine's text constantly force the reader back to a consideration of the present. Not only do the utopian passages in Heine's works frequently originate in reflections on the possibility for society to satisfy material needs, but we also find a series of textural devices whose function is to focus attention on the deleterious aspects of Restoration Europe. His utopia should thus be considered "realistic," not because it contains a blueprint for a perfect society or even a concrete series of actions which must be undertaken to change the world; but rather, first, because it is developed and laid out in a dynamic interplay with the real world and, more importantly, because the fundamental aims it promotes are well within the grasp of humanity. In this latter sense especially Heine's vision is eminently political as well, and we would thus have to disagree with Nigel Reeve's contention: If politics is "the art of the possible, then Heine's goal is hardly political at all." For once Heine's rhetoric is stripped of its metaphorical flourishes and quasi-religious imagery, we are confronted with the rather simple hope that the riches of the earth will someday be shared by all its inhabitants in a more just fashion, that each of us will have an equal opportunity for a happy, fulfilling, and joyous existence. This vision is so powerfully political precisely because it lies within the realm of human possibility. Those who would depoliticize this goal and relegate it to some idealist dust-bin deny, therefore, what is perhaps Heine's most important lesson for us—the future generation that has, unfortunately, still not attained the "health" and happiness he foresaw. What we need now is not the smug dismissal of Heine's utopian thought, but its full rehabilitation. For we would serve ourselves—and him—much better if we refused to view him as an impractical or "religious" visionary, and instead affirmed his utopia by incorporating it into a wider and ultimately more emancipatory notion of political action.

Russell A. Berman (essay date 1988)

SOURCE: "Poetry for the Republic: Heine and Whitman," in *Heinrich Heine and the Occident: Multiple Identities, Multiple Receptions,* edited by Peter Uwe Hohendahl and Sander L. Gilman, University of Nebraska Press, 1991, pp. 199-223.

[*In the following essay, first presented at a symposium in 1988, Berman compares the poetry and political agendas of Heine and the American poet Walt Whitman.*]

It was a tricky situation in which Thomas Mann found himself in October 1922. Addressing a conservative audience hostile to the young Weimar Republic, the renowned author, whose wartime support for the German Empire against the Western democracies had won him acclaim in nationalist circles now undertook the onerous task of convincing his listeners of the worthiness of democracy. Avoiding the easy path of pragmatic realism—democracy as the result of the military defeat of the empire in 1918 or as an ideological demand of the emergent American hegemony—he attempted instead to demonstrate the compatibility of democratic principles with fundamental aspects of German culture in order to defend the counterintuitive proposition that the notion of a German republic was not itself a contradiction in terms.

The literary formula that Mann selected to make his case was Novalis plus Walt Whitman, that is, the presumed affinity of the cipher of German aesthetic culture with the representative poet of American democracy. With a series of quotations he suggests that German culture at its most Romantic—and for the public that meant at its most German moment—was not at all hostile to the political thought of enlightened modernity. Thus, glossing a Novalis citation on international law, Mann comments, "That is political enlightenment; it is indisputably democracy—from the mouth of a knight of the blue flower who was moreover a born junker from whom one would expect a medieval sense of battle or a love of honor in a suit of mail rather than these modernisms." The clincher then follows with the link to Whitman. For if Junker and Yankee are at one in their enthusiasm for democracy, the conservative *Bildungsbürgertum* would do best to follow Novalis's lead by rallying around the new republic, German to its core and not—as the anti-republican right claimed—a foreign form dictated by the victors at Versailles and imposed on an essentially undemocratic German *Volk*.

So far, so good, at least as far as Mann's intentions go, and this speech, "Von deutscher Republik" [The German Republik], can be treated as a literary counterpart to the Weimar constitution, two of the founding documents of republican culture in Germany. That is, however, a very ambivalent praise, implying that Mann's speech and its formula, Novalis plus Whitman, may have been as flawed as the republic and its constitution. For scrutinizing the text, one cannot but wonder if Mann has not conceded too much to his opponents or if the attempt to make the republic palatable has not already eviscerated it. In fact, it seems as if Mann's efforts to assert the identity of a German republic keep running aground on the resilience of the oxymoron he is trying to repress. Does the text, then, in current parlance, subvert itself?

One might note, for example, that the very project of a German republic—Mann stresses the adjective—is not without a nationalist ring, for it is distinguished emphatically from alternative, more radical versions: the individualism of what be calls nefariously "a certain West," and the "political mysticism" of, even more ominously *Slawentum*, the slavic East; hence a sort of two-front war in the competition of political forms. In addition, the articulation of the republic as a Romantic (and therefore acceptable) possibility is achieved only at the price of adopting the Romantic critique of the Enlightenment state, that is, Novalis's attack on Frederician Prussia. Yet that critique is directed not at all against the authoritarian substance of enlightened despotism but only at its putatively mechanical character, which, according to Novalis, might be overcome with more religion, more enthusiasm, and, particularly trenchant, more uniforms.

Mann's rhetorical strategy may be working backward: instead of persuading conservatives to support the republic, the author may be transforming democracy into a program acceptable to conservatives because it has been robbed of its radical substance, a democracy without a democratic revolution, so to speak. This reading of "The German Republic" as a covertly anti-democratic program despite the author's intentions might be confirmed by an examination of the introduction, a *laudatio* to Gerhart Hauptmann on his sixtieth birthday. Assiduously avoiding any of the likely images of republicanism—popular sovereignty or civic virtue or heroic rebellion—Mann opts instead for a prescription that could hardly offend his recalcitrant public: royal legitimacy and patriarchal authority, whereby it is now the playwright Hauptmann who plays the role of a glorious *Volkskönig*, while the *Reichspräsident* is endearingly invoked as an irresistible Mr. Niceguy, good old *Vater Ebert*. The cast of characters chosen by Mann clearly suggests a political orientation toward a centrist support for the new regime; Hauptmann's social dramas of the 1890s are invoked piously, and in any case Mann affirms his loyalty to the Social Democratic head of state. Nevertheless, the organization of this state of affairs is one in which traditional structures of authority have been retained with only a minor shuffling of the players. Royalty and paternity are the terms that pervade the opening passages of the speech; the logic of power has clearly not been interrupted, the state has not been refashioned by a revolutionary process, and it is therefore only consistent for Mann, the self-described conservative, to suggest that conservatives would do themselves a better service by participating in the political processes of the Weimar Republic rather than opposing it from without.

If the really-existing Weimar Republic was indeed represented by the pair Hauptmann plus Friedrich Ebert (1871-1925), themselves representing the rather unrepublican constellation of king plus father, then something is evidently amiss with the democratic claims of "The German Republic," and the error may well lie in Mann's formula for democracy. Is Novalis plus Whitman a literary Article 48 of the cultural constitution of the Weimar Republic? Should Whitmanesque democracy ever threaten to go too far, conservatives might count on Novalis for a Romantic tradition to preserve law and order—faith and love instead of parliament and popular suffrage.

My point here is to suggest not that Romantic political philosophy is necessarily conservative but that Mann, for obviously tactical reasons, makes this equation to mount the following argument: Novalis is a conservative; Novalis is a democrat; therefore, conservatives may be democrats, and democracy may be conservative. The weakness of that model—a weakness congenital to the Weimar Republic—is that it could quickly transmute Hauptmann and Ebert into Ebert and Noske, and this derives from Mann's definition of the republic as thoroughly inoffensive to the anti-republican right. The response of right-wing political theory such as that of Carl Schmitt, would be to claim that "the crisis of parliamentary democracy" is inescapable, that mass democracies are always logically impossible, and that, to the extent that a state asserts its sovereignty, it will eventually take the form of a dictatorship, despite the illusions of a bourgeois liberalism ignorant of the exigencies of power. Less cynically and with an eye to the possibility of a democratic culture, one must ask if the problem is inherent not in the emancipation project but rather in its specific formulation and historical manifestation, that is, the inadequacy of the German Republic at its inception. If Novalis plus Whitman was not enough, was an alternative definition imaginable?

One can answer this question without unrolling the political history of the early twenties. It suffices to

ravel the speech, because an alternative formula to Novalis plus Whitman is inscribed in this founding text of the republic itself. While Mann's liberal undertaking undermines itself the more it attempts to sublate the self-marginalization of the conservatives by incorporating them into the republican body politic, the text is simultaneously marked by a second vector that locates an outside to the same conservatism Mann is attempting to recuperate. To exhort his audience to participate in the democratic process, he must also scare them by suggesting the consequences of their continued boycott, that is, a more radical republic. Thus the republic may well remain substantively German, a vessel for all the blue-flowered values represented by the reassuring figure of Novalis, but only if the Romantic conservatives take hold of it and do not surrender it to threatening antagonists, whose generic name is revealed in Mann's anxious plea: "I beseech you again: don't be shy. There is no reason in the world to regard the republic as a matter for smart Jewboys [scharfe Judenjungen]. Don't leave it to them! As the popular political phrase goes, take 'the wind out of their sails'—the republican wind!"

That is surely a difficult passage. For the moment, Mann is evidently adopting the anti-Semitic rhetoric of the conservative right: in the semantic value of the pejorative designation *Judenjunge,* in the adjective, and in the exclusionary politics of the exhortation. Yet later in the speech, when the same *Judenjungen* make a second cameo appearance, Mann suggests that they too are an integral part of the German tradition. Nevertheless, even that moderating gloss, bordering on apologetics, pales when one grasps that the phrase presumably refers to Foreign Minister Walter Rathenau (1867-1922), victim of a recent right-wing assassination. Mann in this same speech notes bitterly that the assassins, despite their opposition to the republic, have de facto recognized the actuality of republican culture: As he puts it, "shooting ministers is a superbly republican mode of action," for it implies the priority of public and political virtue over a solely private sphere of aesthetic culture.

Of course, Mann's intention is neither to advocate political violence nor to foster anti-Semitism, but that initial imperative, the plea to seize the republic from the smart Jewboys, is a crucial moment in the text and ought not be dissolved too quickly into the dialectic of the full argument or the vicissitudes of Mann's subsequent career. My concern here is, after all, not Thomas Mann's intentions, and my goal is even less a harmonious reconciliation of the material in a conservative hermeneutic circle. The point is rather that the cultural formula for the republic that would fail—Novalis plus Whitman—is itself hopelessly flawed because of a repression that comes to the fore in the exclusionary admonition. Yet the very articulation of that repression leaves symptomatic traces of the alternative, the road not taken, a more radical republic not dependent on the marginalization of the Jewboys, smart or otherwise. Translated into literary-historical terms, that would have implied a revision of the cultural formula: instead of Novalis, might Mann have proposed Heine plus Whitman? What more appropriate symbol of a German democratic tradition than Heine? Still, one might object that this imaginary proposal is absurd, and not only because of the irrelevance of retrospective wishful thinking. For a century, Heine's reception had been marked by vitriolic opposition from conservatives—from the initial persecution and censorship of the pre-1848 period through the battles regarding a monument at the turn of the century. Heine was an overdetermined figure, representing all that the right wing rejected: political radical, Left Hegelian, Jew, Parisian exile, sensualist, materialist, internationalist, and so on—hardly a figure to inspire confidence among conservatives in the desirability of the republic, obviously an impossible choice. That, however, is precisely the point. Opting for Novalis, Mann opted for a conservative constitution of the republic: Heine's absence in "The German Republic" is ultimately another chapter in his repression, a negative reception history. Heine appears only as the unnamed object of negation, and it is that exclusion built into the 1922 formula of the republic which cripples the enterprise from the start. Even Mann must have come to a similar recognition less than a decade later when he recast the political project with a more radical formula—Friedrich Hölderlin and Karl Marx—but by then his topic was, instead of a German republic, itself considerably more radical: culture and Socialism.

To identify the smart Jewboy as Heine is an intentional misreading that flushes out the limits of liberal culture at the outset of the Weimar Republic by measuring it against its repressed doppelgänger, the democratic potential of a forgotten nineteenth-century legacy. Now I want to direct some closer consideration to the odd couple Mann could not name, Heine and Whitman, and their significance for a poetry for a republic. At stake is not a positivistic documentation of literary influences or borrowings. The first edition of *Leaves of Grass* appeared in 1855, the year before Heine's death, and it is not likely that Heine's verse contributed significantly to the formulation of Whitman's lyric project. The closest intellectual-historical connection that might be argued is the shared indebtedness to German idealist philosophy of the two Hegelian cousins: Heine's relationship to Hegel is rich and well known, whereas Whitman's familiarity was presumably only secondhand, part of the extensive mid-century American reception of idealism. The connection is interesting but ultimately somewhat beside the point, since Heine's work—like that of Marx—is better understood as a critical break with G. W. F. Hegel than as a continuation, and for Whitman, in any case, other

experiences and endeavors had a considerably more formative impact than the watered-down philosophical lineage. So although a comparison of Heine and Whitman as post-Hegelian poets would not be without some historicist value, the connection would be a strained one. Moreover, it would miss the much more profound similarity, of which the shared idealism was no doubt a noteworthy characteristic, namely, the pivotal role of the two poets in their respective literary traditions. Both were deeply engaged in the construction of a democratic culture, and both were committed to the transformation of the prevailing institution of lyric verse in such a way so as to explore the possibility of a genuine poetry for the republic. Not that their solutions look very much alike on paper: nothing in Heine resembles Whitman's long lines, and little in Whitman approaches Heine's irony. Perhaps, however, Whitman's expansive verse and Heine's ironic demolition of Romanticism represent homologous innovations in the tentative construction of a new culture. The success of their experiments and the failures that they encounter at their limits can tell us something about the social-historical substance embedded in nineteenth-century verse as well as the utopian challenge of a democratic literature. I want to pursue these matters through parallel readings of Heine and Whitman with regard to three issues in particular: (1) the public voice of poetry, (2) tradition and revolution, and (3) the critique of modernity.

To speak of the "pivotal role" of Heine and Whitman is somewhat of an overstatement, since it suggests the successful establishment of a literary legacy that their respective poetic traditions in fact withheld (although certainly more for Heine than for Whitman). Nevertheless, the pivoting each undertook amounted to the same effort to transform the institutionalized character of lyric verse and to replace with a language adequate to a democratic modernity. Both attempted to dismantle aspects of what can be coarsely labeled as a bourgeois-aristocratic culture, characterized by aesthetic autonomy, social elitism, and a strictly vertical hierarchy of cultural organization. For Whitman, this approach necessitated a painful critique of Emerson, to whom he was in fact deeply indebted, and for Heine a parallel distancing from Goethe. In both cases a new literary language had to be constructed that would incorporate aspects of everyday life and politics, public concerns mediated, again in both cases, by influential experiences in journalism.

Despite the surfeit of landscape imagery in Whitman's verse and his constant self-identification with the American topography, his "usual diction is," as F. O. Matthiessen noted in *American Renaissance*, "clearly not that of a countryman but of what called himself, 'a jour printer,'" that is, a journalist. This point is crucial for Matthiessen, since he has to counteract a simplistic reception, common among the first generations of Whitman's admirers, to accept the poet's self-equation with the geography of the New World. "His speech did not spring primarily from contact with the soil, for though his father was a descendant of Long Island farmers, he was also a citizen of the age of reason, an acquaintance and admirer of Tom Paine. . . . [Whitman] was attracted by the wider sweep of the city, and though his language is a natural product, it is the natural product of a Brooklyn journalist in the eighteen-forties who had previously been a country school-teacher and a carpenter's helper, and who had finally felt an irresistible impulse to be a poet."

Yet Matthiessen's insistence on the journalistic and not agrarian derivation of Whitman's language is more than a reaction against naturalistic reductions of the poet. This emphasis on the journalist Whitman is hardly a matter of praise. On the contrary, the critic proceeds to review Tocqueville's account of the corruption of language in democracy as an adequate sociology of Whitman's faulted diction. Whitman's introduction of journalistic experience into literary language is consequently, in Matthiessen's eyes, implicitly a falling off from the intellectual heights of Emerson's "cold intellectuality," to which the mere journalist, carpenter, and country schoolteacher could never be adequate:

> In its curious amalgamation of homely and simple usage with half-remembered terms he read once somewhere, and with casual inventions of the moment, he often gives the impression of using a language not quite his own. In his determination to strike up for a new world, he deliberately rid himself of foreign models. But, so far as his speech was concerned, this was only very partially possible, and consequently Whitman reveals the peculiarly American combination of a childish freshness with a mechanical and desiccated repetition of book terms that had significance for the more complex civilization in which they had had their roots and growth. The freshness has come, as it did to Huck Finn, through instinctive rejection of the authority of those terms, in Whitman's reaction against what he called Emerson's cold intellectuality: "Suppose his books becoming absorb'd, the permanent chyle of American general and particular character—what a well-wash'd and grammatical, but bloodless and helpless race we should turn out!"

Hearing Matthiessen's judgment on the plebeian journalist Whitman, one cannot help but recall similarly derogatory accounts of Heine. Indeed, Karl Kraus (1874-1936) plays out Heine against Goethe in an identical manner to Matthiessen's measuring of Whitman against Emerson and, more broadly, American democracy against "more complex civilizations." Moreover, Theodor Adorn, drawing on Kraus, accounts for the inadequacy of Heine's language by suggesting that he came from a background not quite at home in German— "Heines Mutter, die er liebte, war des Deutschen nicht ganz mächtig" ["His mother, whom Heine loved, did not have a firm grasp of German"]—not far from

Matthiessen's "impression of [Whitman's] using a language not quite his own." Yet this cultural conservatism (in the case of Adorno, certainly, a conservatism of the canon that stands at odds with his negative dialectics) mistakes for a failure the social practice of the texts, the effort to articulate a public language less exclusionary than Emerson's or Goethe's, a democratic alternative to the bourgeois-aristocratic culture of criticism and literature in the early nineteenth century. Whitman's distance from Emerson is a direct corollary to the sentiment expressed in Heine's poem *An einen ehemaligen Goetheaner* [**To a Former Goethe Disciple**]:

> Hast du wirklich dich erhoben
> Aus dem müßig kalten Dunstkreis,
> Womit einst der kluge Kunstgreis
> Dich von Weimar aus umwoben?
>
> [Have you really gotten free
> From the chilly, vapory cage
> In which once the Weimar sage
> Had you cooped unwittingly?]

The rejection of Goethean classicism and Emerson's "cold intellectuality" might have plausibly led to versions of Romantic irony, a hypostatization of the impossibility of any communicative language as a superficially radical critique of the established language of the cultural elite. Heine definitively closes off that option with his judgment on *Die romantische Schule* [**The Romantic School**]; for the younger Whitman, it was never quite as strong a temptation. His poetic attitude stood, as Matthiessen put it, "in strong contrast to much European romanticism, to the pattern of qualities that Madame de Staël had seen in the emerging new literatures, 'the sorrowful sentiment of the incompleteness of human destiny, melancholy, reverie, mysticism, the sense of the enigma of life.'" This distance from the Romantic option is evident especially in his evaluation of Edgar Allan Poe, whom Whitman ultimately found "almost without the first sign of moral principle, or of the concrete or its heroisms, or the simpler affections of the heart." Despite his appreciation for Poe's "intense faculty for technical and abstract beauty," Whitman concludes by ranking him "among the electric lights of imaginative literature, brilliant and dazzling but with no heat." Poe's brilliance with no heat, Emerson's cold intellectuality, the "kalter Dunstkreis" of the "kluger Kunstgreis," the Romantics with all their magic warts— the counterprograms of Heine and Whitman are parallel in their efforts to expand the participation in cultural life, to give away the esoteric secrets (*ausplaudern*), to strip away the restrictive aura of established art and to develop a secular and nonauthoritarian literary language. Emerson viewed *Leaves of Grass* as a mixture of the *Bhagavad Gita* and the *New York Tribune*.

That secularization was certainly never complete or thoroughly consistent; Whitman could write that "the priest departs, the divine literatus comes." Yet the tendency remains one of deauraticization, the social-historical substance that links the two poetic projects in the search for a public voice. The subsequent reaction against this loss of aura, be it in *l'art pour l'art* or Stefan George's symbolism or some of the early Anglo-American modernism, indicates the resistance the modernization of culture encountered. In *Democratic Vistas* Whitman describes this resistance and its social base—he calls it feudalism:

> with the priceless value of our political institutions, general suffrage, . . . I say that, far deeper than these, what finally and only is to make our Western world a nationality superior to any hither known, and outtopping the past, must be vigorous, yet unsuspected Literatures, perfect personalities and sociologies, original, transcendental, and expressing (what, in the highest sense, are not yet expressed at all) democracy and the modern. . . . For feudalism, caste, the ecclesiastic traditions, though palpably retreating from political institutions, still hold essentially, by their spirit, even in this country, entire possession of the more important fields, indeed the very subsoil, of education, and of social standards and literature.

For Whitman, the cultural revolution was still in the making; beyond the rejection of the models represented by Emerson and Poe, it demanded the positive development of new literary forms. As with Heine, this literary project was grounded in the struggle against "feudalism, caste, the ecclesiastic tradition," and it unfolds within a structural feature of the *longue durée* of modernity: the unresolved tension between cultural elitism and what might be termed an emancipation project of a vernacular liberalism. At important points in the oeuvre of the two writers, each explores the problematic of a public language in an exemplary poem: *Beat! Beat! Drums!* from the *Drum-Taps* section of *Leaves of Grass* of 1861, and **Doktrin [Doctrine]**, the first of the **Zeitgedichte [Poems for the Times]** in the **Neue Gedichte [New Poems]** of 1844. Despite the seventeen years that separate them, the poems are in a substantive sense contemporary, since each is deeply imbued with the political urgency of the moment: the outbreak of the American Civil War and the rapid radicalization on the eve of the 1848 Revolution. That shared political urgency explains why these two programmatic poems both commence with nearly identical imperatives of military and acoustic force: "Beat! Beat! Drums!—blow! bugles! blow!" and "Schlage die Trommel und fürchte dich nicht" ["Beat on the drum and don't be afraid"].

In each case the text grounds the possibility of a new poetic language by insisting on the demise of an earlier social order. All established relationships break down and are swept into a whirlwind of radical reorganization:

> . . . burst like a ruthless force
> Into the solemn church, and scatter the
>   congregation,
> Into the school where the scholar is studying;
> Leave not the bridegroom quiet—no happiness
>   must
> he have now with his bride,
>
> Nor the peaceful farmer any peace, ploughing
>   his
> field or gathering his grain

Heine's account is tighter but fundamentally compatible: "Trommle die Leute aus dem Schlaf" ["Go drum the people up from sleep"]. A new poetry is imagined that can participate in the dismantling of an enervated past, sleepy, private, and above all quiet. The new poetry, in contrast, is loud and decidedly public, a vehicle of mass mobilization. Yet the programmatic exhortation is, despite the sense of emergency, never linked to a particular political crisis. Whitman eschews any reference to slavery or secession, and Heine, who otherwise delights in the inclusion of contextual allusions, mentions no new abuse in Berlin or Munich. These are, therefore, not political poems or protest poems in the manner of a *Tendenzgedicht* [tendentious poem]. On the contrary, they are explorations of the possibility of an innovative poetic language geared to a democratic public sphere, a new literary institution described as an acoustic realm of collective activity and counterposed to the muffled inferiorities of Whitman's "school" and "solemn church" and to the indolence of Heine's sleepy readers.

Whitman suggests that this new public sphere will undermine established notions of acquisitive individualism and the market economy: "No bargainers' bargains by day—no brokers or speculators—would they continue?" Moreover, if established social structures and business as usual have grown obsolete, so have established forms of speech and culture:

> Would the talkers be talking? would the singer
>   attempt to sing?
> Would the lawyer rise in the court to state his
>   case before the judge?
> Then rattle quicker, heavier drums—you
>   bugles wilder blow.

In this new public organization of sound, even the familiar figure of the singer, the traditional poet, becomes an anachronism. In the high speed of modernity, where all that is solid melts into air, hegemonic culture is stripped of its aura, and a new postauratic culture presumably becomes possible.

Heine provides the corollary to the end of Whitman's singer, insofar as **Doktrin** asserts that the new activism is the consequence and genuine content and therefore the conclusion of idealist philosophy, which has only interpreted the world.

> Das ist die Hegelsche Philosophie,
> Das ist der Bücher tiefster Sinn.

> [That's Hegel's philosophy in short,
> That's the deepest wisdom books bestow!]

These lines are not merely a left-wing interpretation of Hegel; they clearly also indicate a supersession, since the dimension of books and scholarship is displaced, as much as is Whitman's singer, by the fearless beating of the drum. That is, both Whitman and Heine indicate the termination of a worn-out organization of culture, in the place of which a postauratic culture model, still unnamed, is taking shape.

Yet when Whitman silences his singer, one cannot but hear a deep sense of anxiety and ambivalence. He is not yet the new poet—if he were, the imperatives would be out of place; has he discovered the possibility of his own demise? Both poems modify their programmatic exuberance with some considerable doubts and fears regarding the possible consequences of the democratic poetry that they nevertheless invoke. At the end of the first stanza Whitman's drums are fierce and the bugles shrill, but the third stanza concludes the poem on an ominous note. This work is not an unbroken paean to cultural modernization:

> Mind not the old man beseeching the young
>   man,
> Let not the child's voice be heard, nor the
>   mother's entreaties,
> Make even the trestles to shake the dead
>   where they lie awaiting the hearses,
> So strong you thump O terrible drums—so
>   loud you bugles blow.

This is the violence of modernity: what begins with the obliteration of moribund cultural forms, the "solemn church" as a cipher of "feudalism," ends with the uncanny silencing of all human relations. The dialectic of enlightenment entails a dialectic of political poetry, in which the galvanizing acoustics of the *levée en masse* turns into the cacophany of "terrible drums," breaking all social bonds. It is the same ambiguity with which **Doktrin** concludes, although Heine expresses it in the less overwhelming register of his characteristic irony:

> Das ist die Hegelsche Philosophie
> Das ist der Bücher tiefster Sinn!
> Ich hab sie begriffen, weil ich gescheit
> Und weil ich ein guter Tambour bin.

> [That's Hegel's philosophy in short,
> That's the deepest wisdom books bestow!
> I understand it, because I'm smart,
> I'm a good drummer boy myself; I know.]

It was Ludwig Börne (1786-1837) who labeled Heine the drum major of liberalism, and Heine himself elsewhere seems to feel comfortable with such political-military self-identification: he liked to say that he was a brave soldier in liberation wars of humanity. Nevertheless, the concluding point of **Doktrin** indicates a dissatisfaction with a potential reduction of poetry to a mere instrument of political tendency. That sort of reduction might be labeled, in the language of critical theory, a false sublation of life and art, the bad outcome of the process of deauraticization. Heine is as aware of it as Whitman. The two programmatic poems for a democratic literature understand that, after "feudalism," the vicissitudes of cultural modernity are by no means certain—hence the ambivalence inscribed in the text, symptomatic of the liminal status of the modern poet, poised between auratic seclusiveness and public discourse.

If that liminality is a consequence of the historical setting of the poetic projects—both poets stand, so to speak, with one foot still in the past of the ancien régime, and both, moreover, understand the foreboding future of aesthetic modernization—historicity is not only a matter of external contexts. On the contrary, inscribed in the poetic projects themselves is an imagined past that traps the necessarily belated writing in a present of neurotic repetition. In other words, the melancholic recollection of a traumatic event located at some distance in the past but to which the writer has not yet achieved full critical distance both determines the possibility of writing and sets a limit to the potential innovation. Poetic secularization cannot proceed untroubled along a linear path of progressive optimism. The tests are haunted by an unmastered past; their content is an incomplete *Durcharbeiten* [working through].

My point now is not to psychoanalyze Heine and Whitman but to explore the internal temporality of their verse with the help of psychoanalysis properly understood as a theory of history. For in their two perhaps best-known poems the original deed that casts its shadow on subsequent writing is recognized as a death, the texts betray a distorted experience of guilt, and the prominent ambivalence turns out to be a matter of remorse. If "O Captain! My Captain!" records the death of Lincoln, it also locates the poet in a complicitous proximity to the oedipal murder, catching him red-handed. Privy to the knowledge of death, he is consequently set apart from "the swaying mass, their eager faces turning," awaiting the victorious leader. While public life goes on elsewhere, the isolated poet is condemned to a repetitive cadence, serving the same sentence he is writing:

Exult O shores and ring O bells!
But I with mournful tread,
Walk the deck my Captain lies,
Fallen cold and dead.

Passing over water toward the erotic object on shore, the Captain is killed; the same primal scene structures the *Lore-Ley,* and the poet flaunts or feigns his mourning for the anonymous sailor early: "daß ich so traurig bin" ["that / I am so sadly inclined"]. Yet if the accusation in the final finger-pointing lines—"Und das hat mit ihrem Singen / Die Lorelei getan" ["And this is the fate that follows / The song of the Lorelei"]—is supposed to solve the crime and answer the initial question of significa-tion—"was soll es bedeuten" ["I do not know what it means"]—the text is equally a hopelessly incriminating confession. For if it was singing that killed cock robin, the poet stands condemned. As long as blame is pro-jected onto the imaginary figure, that is, as long as the poet does not come to grips with his past, his past grips him, progressive history is prohibited, and an adequate cognition of the present is prevented by per-manent ideology: "Ein Märchen aus alten Zeiten / Das kommt mir nicht aus dem Sinn" ["There is an old tale and its scenes that / Will not depart from my mind"].

The parricide in the wake of which poetry takes place is the radical revolution that necessarily entails the murder of the leader. It is not an empirical revolution that matters here—certainly not the American Revolu-tion or the absent German revolution—but the imag-ined revolutions, the violent breaks with a prior order in which Heine and Whitman both take part vicarious-ly. Yet no matter how fictional, the affective valence of the murderous wish is as great as that of any fanta-sized trauma of imaginary seduction, "die wahre Ge-walt" [true violence]. The identification with the rev-olution implies a complicity in death:

Did we think victory great?
So it is—but now it seems to me, when it
   cannot be help'd, that defeat is great,
And that death and dismay are great.

Thus Whitman closes the 1856 *To a Foil'd European Revolutionaire;* within less than a decade the experi-ence of death takes on an American character: the Civil War and Lincoln's assassination. Whitman's represen-tative mourning for Lincoln is homologous to Heine's commemorations of Napoleon and his fantasies of rev-olution and regicide in *Karl I, Maria Antoinette,* or the guillotine passage in the *Wintermärchen* [Winter's Tale]. The primal murder liberates and burdens simul-taneously: the king is dead, long live the king.

If this poetry is always in the wake of a revolution or, better, of a revolutionary wish, the theme of death, even in its most Romantic guises, is always the trace of political violence for which the guilty poet does

penance. In both cases an anterior act of violence is a condition of possibility of verse. Yet here a crucial distinction must be made that may account for the al-ternative institutionalizations of poetry in the two cul-tures. In the seventh section of the *Wintermärchen* the poet walks with death, his writing is a bloody scrawl, and it is the gesture of the poet that unleashes the regicidal force:

Da sah ich furchtbar blinken
Des stummen Begleiters furchtbares Beil—
Und er verstand mein Winken.

[The fearsome ax shining brightly I saw
In my mute companion's fearsome hands—
And he read my signals rightly.]

Yet the death of the king is, so the text implies, also the poet's death—"Blutströme schossen aus meiner Brust" ["And spurts of blood shot from my breast"]. The revolutionary poet is still deeply implicated in the old order, and presumably, revolutionary poetry has not broken cleanly with the categories of hegemonic culture. Whitman, too, sets death at the origin of poet-ry in the crucial *When Lilacs Last in the Dooryard Bloom'd.* Yet whereas Heine stages the struggle within the oppressive and lugubrious confines of a feudal-ecclesiastic interior, Whitman has Lincoln's coffin pass through the expanse of the American landscape, re-plete with imagery of vibrant nature and vigorous so-ciety. The poet can survive the murdered leader with-out an onerous legacy or an internalized guilt, and an effective public voice is achieved, as the deceased is lain to rest:

Passing I leave thee lilac with heart-shaped
   leaves,
I leave thee there in the door-yard, blooming,
   resuming with the spring.

Heine never reaches a similar reconciliation, and a similarly consoling leave-taking is withheld. For the melancholic Heine, the dead are not yet buried; Whit-man can mourn and describe the funeral procession. In the terms of literary history, Whitman takes leave of the literary past more effectively than Heine; the desire for the death of the leader, as both a political and a literary revolution, induces a guilt that impedes the secularization of German poetry. After Heine, and despite Heine, the power of tradition and autonomy aesthetics remains considerably greater than was the case in the wake of Whitman—hence the *Sonderweg* of German lyric verse in which a subversive counter-tradition, say from Heine to Brecht, has always re-mained secondary to the authoritative canon from Goet-he to George.

If the death of the father, in literature and politics, burdens the two writers, they can equally appropriate it as part of their project for a public poetry by redirecting it into a vehicle for public criticism. The remorse for the radical rupture makes the poetry all the more sensitive to the failures of the revolution and a bad modernity: was the break with tradition in vain? was all the violence for nought? The vision of death marching arrogantly through their poetry constitutes a radical critique of a developing bourgeois society that denies identity only a split second after promising its fulfillment: everyday life is capital punishment. This vision is not the aestheticist cult of death that Mann ascribed to a Whitman read beside Novalis, death as some weird source of creativity. On the contrary, it is a precise naming of the fatal character of the modern social condition, a night of the living dead, and it simultaneously expresses a challenge and a utopian hope: better dead than reduced to this reality. Hence the death wish at the end of the third of the *Heimkehr* [Homecoming] poems:

> Mein Herz, mein Herz ist traurig,
> Doch lustig leuchtet der Mai;
> Ich stehe, gelehnt an der Linde,
> Hoch auf der alten Bastei.
>
> Da drunten fließt der blaue
> Stadtgraben in stiller Ruh;
> Ein Knabe fährt im Kahne
> Und angelt und pfeift dazu.
>
> Jenseits erheben sich freundlich,
> In winziger, bunter Gestalt,
> Lusthäuser und Gärten und Menschen,
> Und Ochsen und Wiesen und Wald.
>
> Die Mägde bleichen Wäsche
> Und springen im Gras herum:
> Das Mählrad stäubt Diamanten,
> Ich höre sein fernes Gesumm.
>
> Am alten grauen Turme
> Ein Schilderhäuschen steht;
> Ein rotgeröckter Bursche
> Dort auf und nieder geht.
>
> Er spielt mit seiner Flinte,
> Die Funkelt im Sonnenrot,
> Er präsentiert und schultert—
> Ich wollt, er schösse mich tot.
>
> [My heart, my heart is heavy,
> Though May shines bright on all;
> I stand and lean on the linden
> High on the bastion wall.
>
> Below me the moat is flowing
> In the still afternoon;
> A boy is rowing a boat and
> Fishing and whistling a tune.

> Beyond in colored patches
> So tiny below, one sees
> Villas and gardens and people
> And oxen and meadows and trees.
>
> The girls bleach clothes on the meadow
> And merrily go and come;
> The mill wheel scatters diamonds—
> I hear its distant hum.
>
> On top of the old grey tower
> A sentry looks over the town;
> A young red-coated lad there
> Is marching up and down.
>
> He handles his shining rifle,
> It gleams in the sunlight's red;
> He shoulders arms, presents arms—
> I wish he would shoot me dead.]

"Ich wollt, er schösse mich tot" ["I wish he would shoot me dead"]. The pastoral idyll of a cheerful springtime, the fisherboy, the healthy servant girls, and the glistening mill wheel—a postcard picture of Old Germany that turns out to be a nightmare, always about to flip over into the brutality that lurks in the heart of *Gemütlichkeit.* The poet invokes the catastrophe; he calls for the shooting to begin, to unmask the structural horror and, as victim, to escape. Heine's contemporary Eichendorff could also invoke violence and destruction in his verse, but it appeared as a Romantic sublime counterposed to a beautiful bourgeois order, therefore presenting a conservative apologetics for the order. Heine's text indicates that it is the order itself that is always the site of catastrophe: there's no place like home.

This concern, early in the *Buch der Lieder* [Book of Songs], antedates by two decades the *Zeitgedichte;* for Whitman, the insistence on the presence of death as a critique of a bad life can be traced in the *Calamus* poems, before the Civil War. That is to say that for both, the social-critical substance of the theme is established before any explicit politicization of the verse. Nevertheless, it is again in *Lilacs* that Whitman comes closest to Heine in articulating the morbidity of the social order:

> Then with the knowledge of death as walking
>> one side of me,
> And the thought of death close-walking the
>> other side of me,
> And I in the middle with companions, and
>> as holding the hands of companions,
> I fled forth to the hiding receiving night
>> that talks not.

There he discovers the possibility of an appropriate incantation, "the carol of the bird," and then "with my comrades there in the night," he has an apocalyptic battlefield vision of the war:

> I saw battle-corpses, myriads of them,
> And the white skeletons of young men, I saw
> them,
> I saw the debris and debris of all the slain
> soldiers of the war.

Yet even more poignant than the discovery of poetry or the recognition of the carnage of the war is the very constitution of the seeing subject through "the knowledge of death": a universal negativity that is the substance of the social contract among *soi-disant* "companions." The poet can comprehend the sorrow and bereavement dictated by history only by understanding that bereavement has become the principle of social organization of the failed community. The pseudo identity of the most intimate relations is susceptible to destruction in the context of total reification; unproblematic self-identity is relegated to a distant and mythic past: Whitman's *Manhatta* or Heine's *Hammonia*. For the present, however, not even the radical poem can achieve that sovereign freedom: Heine's free thought rarely approaches free verse, and Whitman's open lines are condemned to a syntactic eternal return and a repetitive periodic structure. The limits of social emancipation are enfigured in the limits of formal innovation; the emancipation of poetry is blocked by the failure of the revolution that has engendered a failed modernity.

What links Heine and Whitman, then, is the attempt to secularize poetry and to transform it into a public medium; the insight into the dialectics of engaged literature; the exploration of the revolution against tradition and its consequences for democratic culture; the critique of modernity inherent in the thematics of death. It is a shared project, deeply interwoven with the democratic culture of the nineteenth century and presumably too radical for Mann in his 1922 address. The failure of the German republic is a measure of the repression of Heine and of a Whitman understood differently.

The name of the failure of the republic was fascism. Heine and Whitman play an important role in the formation of fascist aesthetics, as objects of negation. The two poets are not merely repressed and marginalized; rather, their insistence on the publicity of poetry is simultaneously denounced and appropriated from the standpoint of a self-described superior poetics: the aestheticization of politics. Adolph Bartels (1862-1945) rants and raves against Heine the political radical to formulate the program for a reactionary literature, devoted to the extremely political project of an illusory national regeneration. Knut Hamsun's early denunciation of Whitman's crudity is still an aestheticist gesture, colored by his lifelong hostility to democracy. Ezra Pound's reception of Whitman is more to the point: Pound is eager to take on the mantle of the great American poet but insists on subjecting Whitman's backwoods boorishness to the imperatives of modernist rigor. The democratic public, Whitman's subject, turns into the national community, subject to imperatives. The acoustic revolution of the beating drums, addressed by Whitman, gives way to the authorial counterrevolution of Pound, addressing American troops on Italian radio: the poetic history of the structural transformation of the public sphere.

I have only briefly outlined an inquiry into the negativity of Heine and Whitman within the construction of a fascist aesthetics. A project of more immediate concern, however, is a consideration, from the standpoint of republican poetry, of the repercussions of fascism in the 1980s and 1990s, and the relevance of a poetry suppressed by fascism to our most self-assuredly post-fascist criticism. In this context what is most germane is the discourse on fascism and literary criticism which has developed in the wake of the discovery of the early writings of Paul de Man. There is little reason to spend time demonstrating the self-evident incompatibility of the democratic lyric project of Heine and Whitman with the texts de Man published in the collaborationist press of occupied Belgium. Those texts, usually confused and often egregious, do not provide a conclusive answer to the *Gretchenfrage* of deconstructive criticism: Wie steht es mit der Politik? [Where do things stand politically?]. The answer can be sought instead, ironically enough, in the prose that has been mobilized in de Man's defense, a vigorously political prose that simultaneously denounces his critics for pursuing a political agenda:

> Ich weiß, sie tranken heimlich Wein
> Und predigten öffentlich Wasser.
>
> [I know how in secret they guzzle wine
> and in public preach water-drinking.]

This sort of paradox and the corollary contempt for a public culture indicate the continuity of a hierarchical structure of institutionalized culture which Whitman lambasted in *Democratic Vistas*:

> Literature, strictly considered, has never recognized the People, and whatever may be said, does not today. . . . It seems as if, so far, there were some natural repugnance between a literary and professional life, and the rude rank spirit of the democracies. . . . I know nothing more rare, even in this country, than a fit scientific estimation and reverent appreciation of the People, . . . their entire reliability in emergencies, and a certain breadth of historic grandeur, of peace or war, far surpassing all the vaunted samples of book-heroes, or any *haut ton* coteries, in all the records of the world.

Precisely this conflict between the *haut ton* and a "rude rank spirit" is the backdrop to the effort of

Heine and Whitman to develop a democratic literature in which belletristic and journalistic languages are mixed to construct a postauratic public voice. This conflict is also the backdrop for de Man's apologists, who denounce the rude journalistic intervention into a sphere of high literary theory allegedly inappropriate for public scrutiny, according to the coterie's motto: close the border, stop the gap. Thus in a letter published in a prestigious literary journal in April 1988, one could read the following comment from a well-respected critic: "When [de Man] resumed writing about literature [after the war], as a graduate student at Harvard, it was to initiate the critique of organicist and narrative figures through which he had sought to master literature for journalistic purposes." Note that according to this account the young de Man had no political and certainly no fascist purposes, but only journalistic ones, as if the error of the 1940s was only a generic peccadillo, his willingness to engage in journalism at all, and not the substance or the location of that particular journalism. How fortunate then—this is the apparent suggestion of the letter's author, a professor of literature—that de Man renounced journalism and chose to pursue a graduate study of literature, at Harvard no less. Whether de Man himself shared this contempt for public discourse, including journalism, is, to say the least, doubtful, and one may eventually be forced to defend de Man against his defenders, at least on this score.

The public voice of literature was, for Heine and Whitman, a key aspect in the demolition of tradition, the radical break with inherited forms in art and politics. In other words, the project of republican poetry and the democratization of culture is not thinkable without a revolutionary gesture, even when, as I have tried to show, the authors are well aware of the dangerous risks inherent in the project. Despite these risks, the project retains a plausibility because of the utopian hopes it awakens, and its failure is not treated as an inescapable fate—because political action is deemed not only urgent, it is also imaginably successful.

How different, then, how much more responsible and sober, is the argument that atones for de Man's political juvenalia by lauding the mature de Man's putative admonition against all politics? Whether this sort of reading of de Man's trajectory is adequate can remain open; more important is the intervention of another critic, writing in the *New Republic,* in order to teach the lesson that politics slides into messianic revolutions that are always likely to end in fascism: "The political culture he championed in the *Le Soir* articles, a culture that claimed to be modern and revolutionary, was based on such a hope," that is, a "messianic" hope in the possibility of "new beginnings." Revolutions of the left, like those of the right, democratic or antidemocratic, are, by implication, always totalitarian. The dialectic of enlightenment,

inscribed in the ambiguity of republican poetry, turns out to be no dialectic at all but rather blind fate heading necessarily to catastrophe. For this good citizen, then, "the only activity that escapes the immediate ideological pressure is art itself," an analysis that clearly falls behind the level of **Doktrin** and *Drums.* Art, already superior to journalism, is now declared superior to bad politics or, rather, to politics, which is always bad.

But if politics is always bad, so is the public voice of a postauratic poetry, and so is any radical critique of modernity. Not in de Man's own texts but in the anxious prose of his defenders one finds the sophisticated version of the hegemonic cultural conservatism of the 1980s and 1990s lodged in a solely ad hoc theory of fascism. It is a conservatism that has as little room for the terms of republican poetry and democratic culture as did Thomas Mann's formula of 1922. In the light of this double repression in the course of the century, Heine, Whitman, and the cultural alternative they represent might seem to fade into the recesses of an irretrievable past, thoroughly irrelevant to contemporary criticism. Yet it is exactly the shrillness of that repression that indicates the continued viability of the emancipation project, in politics and literature and in their potential congruence. Heine and Whitman investigate this potential and chart a terrain that is ours to rediscover or ours to repress. Their challenge stands in either case: to replace the hegemonic culture of conservative criticism with a culture that is critical of the conservative hegemony.

FURTHER READING

Bibliography

Arnold, Armin. *Heine in England and America: A Bibliographical Check-List.* London: Linden Press, 1959, 80 p.

A thorough research guide to translations and criticism of Heine's work.

Biography

Bieber, Hugo, ed. *Heinrich Heine: A Biographical Anthology.* Philadelphia: Jewish Publication Society of America, 1956, 452 p.

A well-annotated collection of excerpts from Heine's poetry, prose, and letters which attempts to present Heine's own interpretation of his life.

Brod, Max. *Heinrich Heine: The Artist in Revolt.* Translated by Joseph Witriol. New York: New York University Press, 1957, 355 p.

A comprehensive biography which approaches Heine's life and work through an awareness of his German-Jewish background.

Butler, E. M. *Heinrich Heine: A Biography*. New York: Philosophical Library, 1957, 291 p.

A critical biography. Butler believes that a purely aesthetic approach to Heine is inadequate because his works "are all fragments of a great confession, and, passionately personal in nature throughout, they are frequently autobiographical in content."

Marcuse, Ludwig. *Heine: A Life between Love and Hate*. Translated by Louise M. Sievelking and Ian F. D. Morrow. New York: Farrar & Rinehart, 1933, 345 p.

An important biographical study. Marcuse portrays Heine as a representative of a divided society.

Monahan, Michael. *Heinrich Heine: Romance and Tragedy of the Poet's Life*. New York: Nicholas L. Brown, 1924, 199 p.

A biographical tribute to Heine as a poet and patriot.

Sammons, Jeffrey L. *Heinrich Heine: A Modern Biography*. Princeton University Press, 1979, 425 p.

A thorough and objective biography.

Selden, Camille. *The Last Days of Heinrich Heine*. Translated by Clare Brune. London: Remington & Co., 1884, 118 p.

A personal remembrance of Heine by his companion during his final years in his "mattress-grave." Selden includes not only her reminiscences of Heine, but also his love letters to her.

Untermeyer, Louis. *Heinrich Heine, Paradox and Poet: The Life*. New York: Harcourt, Brace and Co., 1937, 403 p.

Biography that accurately recounts Heine's life and also captures his artistic temperament. A second, companion volume contains Untermeyer's translations of Heine's poetry, considered by many to be the best rendering of Heine's work in English.

Walter, H. *Heinrich Heine: A Critical Examination of the Poet and His Works*. New York: E. P. Dutton & Co., 1930, 322 p.

A biographical and critical study of Heine and his poetic achievements.

Winegarten, Renee. "Revolutionary Desires and Fears: Heine." In *Writers and Revolutions: The Fatal Lure of Action*, pp. 113-26. New York: New Viewpoints, 1974.

A sympathetic portrait of Heine as a prominent figure in an era of great social unrest.

Criticism

Atkins, H. G. "The Revaluation." In *German Literature Through Nazi Eyes*, pp. 25-81. London: Methuen & Co, 1941.

A brief survey of Nazi opinion of Heine.

Atkins, Stuart. "The Evaluation of Heine's *Neue Gedichte*." In *Wächter und Hüter: Festscrift für Hermann J. Weigand zum 17 November 1957*, edited by Curt von Faber du

Faur, Konstantin Reichardt, and Heinz Bluhm, pp. 99-107. New Haven: Department of Germanic Languages, Yale University, 1957.

Examines the controversy surrounding Heine's poetic achievement through a survey of critical evaluations of *New Poems*.

Atkinson, Ross. "Irony and Commitment in Heine's *Deutschland: Ein Wintermärchen*." *Germanic Review* L, No. 3 (May 1975): 184-202.

Closely analyzes the use of irony in *Germany: A Winter's Tale* and concludes that the work was not intended as a political manifesto.

Butler, E. M. *The Saint-Simonian Religion in Germany: A Study of the Young German Movement*. New York: Howard Fertig, 1968, 446 p.

Includes a lengthy analysis of Heine's dealings with the Saint-Simonians and the influence of their doctrine on his thought and work.

Fairley, Barker. *Heinrich Heine: An Interpretation*. Oxford: Clarendon Press, 1954, 176 p.

An important study of Heine's imagery.

Feise, Ernst. "Heinrich Heine: Political Poet and Publicist." *Monatshefte* XL, No. 4 (April 1948): 211-20.

Evaluates Heine's political and religious beliefs.

Hannah, Richard W. "The Broken Heart and the Accusing Flame." *Colloquia Germanica* XIV, No. 4 (1981): 289-312.

Discusses Heine's conflicting political sentiments in *Deutschland: ein Wintermärchen*.

Holub, Robert C. "Heine and the New World." *Colloquia Germanica* XXII, No. 2 (1989): 101-15.

Outlines Heine's critical reception in the United States and gives a Marxist interpretation of Heine's poetry against a capitalistic background.

Kolb, Jocelyne. "The Sublime, the Ridiculous, and the Apple Tarts in Heine's *Ideen. Das Buch Le Grand*." *The German Quarterly* LVI, No. 1 (January 1983): 28-38.

Details how Heine describes his own satirical style in *Das Buch le Grand*.

Komar, Kathleen L. "The Structure of Heine's 'Harzreise': Should We Take the Narrator at His Word?" *Colloquia Germanica* XVII, No. 1 (1984): 14-59.

Discusses the structure and unreliable narrative voice of "Harzreise."

Marcuse, Ludwig. "Heine and Marx: A History and a Legend." *Germanic Review* XXX, No. 2 (April 1955): 110-24.

A thorough explication of Heine's relationship with the early communists. Marcuse denies the widespread view that Heine and Karl Marx shared a personal and political alliance.

Peters, George F. "Heine and the Myth of Passion." In *Erkennen und Deuten: Essays zur Literatur und Literaturtheorie, Edgar Lohner in memoriam*, edited by Martha Woodmansee and Walter F.W. Lohnes, pp. 127-42. Berlin: Erich Schmidt Verlag, 1983.

Examines the biographical and historical events that may have formed Heine's theories about love as developed in his poetry, especially *Buch der Lieder*.

Prawer, S. S. *Heine: "Buch der Lieder."* London: Edward Arnold, 1960, 64 p.

Attempts to assess Heine's poetic achievement in *Book of Songs*, considering themes such as escape and return, nature, and the divided self.

Rose, William. *Heinrich Heine: Two Studies of His Thought and Feeling*. Oxford: Clarendon Press, 1956, 163 p.

A scholarly and historical consideration of Heine's political, social, and religious views.

————. *The Early Love Poetry of Heinrich Heine: An Inquiry into Poetic Inspiration*. Oxford: Clarendon Press, 1962, 89 p.

Disputes the popular view that Heine's love for his cousins Amalie and Therese provided the inspiration for the *Book of Songs*.

Sammons, Jeffrey L. "Problems of Heine Reception: Some Considerations." *Monatshefte* LXXIII, No. 4 (Winter 1981): 383-91.

Briefly discusses Heine's critical reception and contends that he serves as "an especially apt test case of the validity and usefulness of reception history and hermeneutics."

————. "Mortification of the Emancipated Flesh: The Case of Heine." In *Hypatia: Essays in Classics, Comparative Literature, and Philosophy Presented to Hazel E. Barnes on Her Seventieth Birthday*, edited by William M. Calder III, Ulrich K. Goldsmith, and Phyllis B. Kenevan, pp. 187-98. Boulder: Colorado Associated University Press, 1985.

Analyzes the shift in Heine's poetic themes following the onset of his illness, claiming that "he needed to find a way to integrate the experience of extreme illness into his imagination and into the role he had shaped for himself as poet, revolutionary, and visionary."

Sandor, A. I. *The Exile of Gods: Interpretation of a Theme, a Theory and a Technique in the Work of Heinrich Heine*. The Hague, Paris: Mouton, 1967, 192 p.

Detailed thematic study in which Sandor endeavors "to trace the theme of gods in exile in [Heine's] work, to restate the underlying concept or theory, and to show to what type of attitudes and actions, both social and artistic, he was led by it."

Tabak, Israel. *Judaic Lore in Heine: The Heritage of a Poet*. Baltimore: Johns Hopkins Press, 1948, 338 p.

A detailed study of the Judaic elements in Heine's work.

Wikoff, Jerold. *Heinrich Heine: A Study of "Neue Gedichte."* Bern: Herbert Lang, 1975, 90 p.

Argues that *New Poems* is a "varied yet single and cohesive poetic cycle."

Wood, Frank Higley, Jr. *Heine As a Critic of His Own Works*. N.p., 1934, 182 p.

Attempts to develop a composite portrait of Heine's view of his own work, which the critic considers "the most interesting aspect of Heine's critical genius."

Wormley, Stanton Lawrence. *Heine in England*. Chapel Hill: University of North Carolina Press, 1943, 310 p.

A comprehensive survey of Heine's significance and literary reputation in England. The work provides a complete record of Heine in English translation, and in works of criticism, letters, diaries, and poetry.

Additional coverage of Heine's life and career is contained in the following resources published by Gale Research: *Dictionary of Literary Biography*, **Vol. 90;** *Nineteenth-Century Literature Criticism*, **Vol. 4.**

Taras Shevchenko

1814-1861

(Also transliterated as Ševčenko) Ukrainian poet.

INTRODUCTION

Considered the national poet of Ukraine, Shevchenko virtually created a Ukrainian literary language by resisting Russian political and cultural impositions. His first collection of poetry, *Kobzar* (*The Minstrel*, 1840), earned him the nickname "the Ukrainian Pushkin." Active in the Ukrainian nationalist movement for independence from tsarist Russia, Shevchenko remained a symbol of resistance for Ukrainian nationalists even after his death. In addition to his importance for Ukrainian literature, he also influenced Russian literature through contemporary translations of his poetry into Russian. In 1964, during the sesquicentennial of his birth, Shevchenko was honored both by anti-communist Ukrainian nationalists, for his resistance to Russian dominance, and by the Soviet government, for his political resistance to the tsar.

Biographical Information

Born a serf in a province of Kiev and orphaned at a very young age, Shevchenko endured a childhood of deprivation and abuse. After an apprenticeship as an icon-maker, he was taken into the service of a landowner named Engelhardt to work as an interior decorator. In 1832 he was sold to a painting contractor in St. Petersburg as an indentured servant. Six years later, his freedom was purchased by the painter Bryullov and the poet Zhukovsky, who recognized Shevchenko's poetic and artistic talents. He entered the Academy of Art in St. Petersburg, where he studied painting with great success and also began writing the poems that would appear in his first published collection two years later. He returned to the Ukraine in 1843, painting an album of life in that area. After completing his studies at the Academy in St. Petersburg, he again went to the Ukraine as the commissioned artist of an archeological team studying Ukrainian relics. Shevchenko voiced his protests against Russian oppression in strongly nationalist poems, which he circulated in manuscript form. In 1847, when he was about to be appointed to Kiev University, he was arrested for his unpublished anti-tsarist poetry and for membership in the secret "Brotherhood of Saints Cyril and Methodius," an outlawed society that advocated Slavic union based on independence from Russia. Shevchenko was exiled to penal army service in central Asia and prohibited from writing or painting, although sympa-

thetic superiors often overlooked the prohibition; it was during the period of his exile that Shevchenko wrote his nine novellas in Russian. He was pardoned and released in 1857, but his health was broken and he was never free from police surveillance. Shevchenko returned to the St. Petersburg Academy in 1858, where he edited his army memoirs and continued to paint. After a year in the Ukraine he went back to St. Petersburg in 1860, and was helping to establish a periodical on Ukrainian affairs when he died in 1861.

Major Works

Although Shevchenko wrote two long poems, two plays, and nine novellas in Russian, they are considered of a lesser quality than his Ukrainian works, especially his first published collection of poems, *Kobzar* (*The Minstrel*), which appeared in 1840. Other poems, such as *Haidamaki* (*Free Cossacks,* 1841), and dramas, such as *Nikita Haidai,* were published in journals, but the majority of his poems were circulated privately in manuscript form. Most of his political poems remained unpublished until after the Revolution of 1905, and although he wrote most of his work in Ukrainian, none of his poetry was published in that language until the publication of his collected works beginning in 1939.

Critical Reception

Shevchenko's *The Minstrel* found a mixed reception in Russia. While praising his poetic talents, critics felt he would have done better to exercise them in Russian rather than in his native Ukrainian. Some Russian intellectuals, including the noted critic N. A. Dobrolyubov, supported his resistance to Russian repression. Shevchenko's principal detractor was V. G. Belinsky, who faulted the poet for trying to develop a specifically Ukrainian literature; Belinsky thought that Ukrainians should write in Russian to be appreciated by a wider audience. While most Russian intellectuals resisted Ukrainian separatism and considered Ukrainian romanticism representative of a lesser literature, Shevchenko endorsed a nationalistic development of Ukrainian literature on the same scale critics such as Belinsky advocated for Russian literature. The question of the relationship of Shevchenko's work to Russian literature has been clouded by the official Soviet interpretation of literary history, which insisted on the primacy of Russian literature over the other national literatures of the USSR.

PRINCIPAL WORKS

Kobzar (poetry) 1840
 [*The Minstrel*, 1964]
Haidamaki (poetry) 1841
Nikita Haidai (drama) 1841
Nazar Stodolja (drama) 1843
Zivopisnaja Ukraina (etchings) 1844
 [*The Pictorial Ukraine*]
Xudoznik (novel) 1887*
 [*The Artist* published in *Taras Schevchenko Selected Works*, 1961(?)]
Povne zibrannya tvoriv 10 vols. (poetry and paintings) 1939-64
Taras Shevchenko: Tvory (poetry and prose) 1959-62
Poems; Poésies; Gedichte (poetry) 1961
Taras Schevchenko Selected Works (poetry and prose) 1961(?)
Selected Works; Poetry and Prose (poetry and prose) 1963
Povne zibrannya tvoriv 6 vols. (poetry) 1963-64
The Poetical Works of Taras Shevchenko (poetry) 1964
Selected Works (poetry and prose) 1964

*Written in 1856

CRITICISM

Panteleimon Kulish (essay date 1861)

SOURCE: "Why Shevchenko Is a Poet of Our People," in *Shevchenko and the Critics: 1861-1980,* edited by George S. N. Luckyj, translated by Dolly Ferguson and Sophia Yurkevich, University of Toronto Press, 1980, pp. 57-63.

[*In the following essay, Kulish mourns Shevchenko's death, citing his great impact on Ukrainian culture.*]

News of the death of Taras Shevchenko has reached even those of us who live in the country. It is a grievous misfortune that this great poet is no longer with us, and every tear that fell on his grave is blessed in the eyes of God: our accumulated tears have established the worth of this champion of our native word, which alone constitutes our strength as a people, our glory as a people, and alone gives us the right to a separate place among other nations. As long as Shevchenko was with us, we gave him the reverence due a great poet and turned a blind eye to all the mistakes and lapses along his lonely, arduous path; how great was the deed that he performed for us as Ukrainians and what we would be without Shevchenko has only now been fully revealed to us.

Literate townspeople have long neglected the illiterate villagers and their unprinted language; intellectually they embraced strangers, those who, in the vast community of the uneducated, keep together in a small group and, like an assembly of Jewish elders, understand only each other and do not care at all that they have left far behind them countless thousands of the illiterate. Our writers, too, have trailed behind these townspeople and with them written academic books and given themselves airs because they have managed to cast a net over human souls from sea unto sea with a single, bookish, academic language. These great writers and creators of the written word did not care that because of this net all our ordinary people appeared tongue-tied. They did not care that for these simple people there was no path to literature other than renunciation of the simple and easily understood native word. When our country people put their children in Russian schools, it was the same as sending them to the Russian army for because of this illusory education the numbers of those who speak as we do, look at God's world as we do, and live among the peasantry as we do grew smaller.

The townspeople were muddying our common sense and unsullied taste with their books and then, behold, there came into our simple cottage a little man, dressed in our fashion, seemingly sharing our customs and our language, who slowly spelled out the words of who knows what kind of verses about some Aeneas. It looked as if we should rejoice! The man is writing verses in our language! But hardly! God save us from versification like that! Soon some of us realized what sort of wonder that was. 'Just look at this man closely,' they began to say. 'He is a little gentleman from town dressed up like us. Look: he has the bearing of a gentleman and his character is entirely that of a gentleman. He simply imitates us with his words and holds us up to ridicule. He is making fun of our customs, of our native land, of our simplicity in not having genteel tastes—imagine that!—not having genteel whims and spurning genteel bonbons. Look: his Aeneas says such things about his own mother in public that it makes you want to run out of the house; listen to the way he derides our customs, how he mangles our Ukrainian language. The gentlefolk have presented us with the kind of mirror that, when a simple man looks into it, he cannot even recognize himself.'

This was the judgment handed down by our wise people on these verses and every clear-thinking soul turned away from this Aeneas dishevelled in God only knows what fashion. But then Kvitka's 'Marusia' dropped in on us for a visit. Dear heart, how lovely and dignified you seemed to us after that Trojan gypsy! It was our soul nestled against God's breast speaking in our language. It was the first book to breathe the same spirit as the word of our blessed Teacher. Kvitka cast upon us simple folk the same gaze as that great lover of man. We were amazed at how brightly our image as a people shone forth, even though a plowman's sweat had settled upon it like a thick layer of dust. We gazed deeply with Kvitka into the soul of our simple folk and wondered where its inexpressible depth came from.

We were pondering this when suddenly Shevchenko called out loudly all over Ukraine. It was as if all the folk songs and all human tears had spoken in unison. He raised our silent memory from the grave, summoned up our silent antiquity to judge, and set before it the Ukrainian as he is now, as he has been moulded by history. Who could not make an effort to understand, or feel in his soul that, having bathed in their own blood and endured devastation and conflagration numberless times, our forefathers must have drawn into their souls much from ancient times. Whether he described himself in his meditative poems, or old Perebendia, Kateryna's mother and father, or even Kateryna herself with her sincere feelings of love and her immense torment, Shevchenko immediately demonstrated a unique way of painting portraits in words, for both his own spiritual portrait and this entire family of kindred spirits were all children of our history. He took the sound and structure of his masterful language from those songs and *dumy* (historical songs) which only we in the country still listened to and understood in our hearts; the soul of our unwritten folk poetry became his muse's soul. His far-reaching embrace

encompassed Ukraine with its bloody burial mounds and awesome glory and in his hands the language of the folk songs was transformed into images of what was and is in Ukraine. Our whole people sang of their fate with his lips: his words reverberated wherever our blood had flowed, wherever our bones lay; every heart was awakened by his song.

Kvitka was the first to understand that the poetry of our folk customs was that of a blessed and truly human family. Shevchenko presented us with the poetry of our life as a people. Kvitka surprised us all by revealing the noble, heroic soul of the quiet, meek plowman, of simple village life. Shevchenko allowed us to plumb its mysterious depths, recalled to us our forgotten Ukrainian history, and showed that this meek soul had existed in misery not for days or hours but for centuries and had not become contemptible, did not crouch timidly, had not become the servant of evil, but had retreated deep into itself and, standing among evil people with lowered gaze, silently bided its time, and awaited its fate. Thus, when Shevchenko's fiery poetry illuminated Kvitka's native works, then we realized that Naum Drot is that same folk hero Samiilo Kishka for, living in foreign parts, he endured a test no less demanding than Samiilo's and, suffering through century after century, did not bend, did not allow his steadfast and noble spirit to be diminished in stature.

Shevchenko is our poet and our first historian. He was the first to inquire of our silent burial mounds what they were and to him alone they gave an answer as clear as God's word. Shevchenko was the first to understand where the glory of our history lay and the reasons why future generations would curse it. Just as the folk song set the tone for his masterful language, so he gave us all the true tone upon which to tune our word. High above us, Shevchenko raised his poetic light, and everywhere in Ukraine the direction in which each of us must proceed became clear. In this light everyone came to understand how truly glorious and great in its simplicity is the village world from which Kvitka had selected his Marusia and her poetic family. In this light, everyone could see that our folk customs are one with the history of our spirit, our folk songs, and the folk *duma,* but only to the more lofty poetic gaze is their beauty and dignity revealed. Everyone with any claim to wisdom understood that in our letters we were not to follow in any footsteps other than those of our folk genius, which is silent in the chronicles of our gentry and monks but lives secretly in our customs and speaks loudly only in the folk song and *duma.*

There was Konysky who, with his *Istoriia Rusov* (A History of the Russes), obscured our history with an ornate curtain until Shevchenko rent that curtain, tore it apart. Immediately after him came Kotliarevsky who, in his *Eneida,* made our simple life and wise customs seem like the refuse heap outside the gentry's doors. Both our poets turned away from this refuse heap and showed us different Ukrainians with their Ukrainian women in 'Marusia,' 'Serdeshnia Oksana' (Poor Oksana), 'Kozyr-Divka' (A Lively Wench), 'Kateryna,' 'Naimychka' (The Servant Girl), and other genuinely poetic works.

Kvitka was the first to draw tears from Ukrainians by using the Ukrainian language and in doing so showed us that we have not yet been reduced to numbers; there really are things to be told in our language, things over which to shed tears. And perhaps our simple folk in their homespun peasant cloaks are worthy of greatness if, joining this family, the wisest and most educated among us regards it as his own—if the strongest and most celebrated among us, the noblest and purest in spirit, does not refuse to call Marusia his own sister, her mother—his mother and her father his father. These are the poor, meek people whom Kvitka praised before the entire world; is their equal anywhere on this vast earth?

We crowded around Kvitka, however many of us there were then of like mind and sharing the same faith. We were few, because some had been blighted by the false learning of the towns and others necessarily tethered to the land; but all the same Shevchenko found us ready to listen to his mournful meditations and began to summon into our small circle our countrymen from all over the world.

They responded to our *kobzar* with cordial greetings in the Caucasus, in Siberia, from beyond Bendery, and the Sluch and Danube rivers. Ukrainians throughout the world were aroused, pricked up their ears, and accepted the good tidings of their *narodnist* (identity as a people). Shevchenko was like a lofty banner among a people scattered over thousands of miles and since then we have divided into the living and the dead and will long continue to do so. His life-giving word became the kernel of a new force never dreamed of by the wisest among our countrymen before Kotliarevsky and that new force is *narodnist*. It made kinsmen of us, united us, and affirmed our Ukrainian being for all time. With this great feat in the realm of letters, Shevchenko completed the deed that our hetmans, with their impure hearts, had attempted. Having raised our resonant Ukrainian language out of its decline, Shevchenko marked out generous boundaries for our national spirit. No longer is our right to be a people carved by the sword on enemy fortresses; not only by old documents and seals is it secured against human subterfuge; it lies protected in thousands of faithful Ukrainian souls and is sealed by recollections a thousand years old.

Only our native word restored us to a respected position among nations and laid a new foundation for our existence as a historical entity. For Shevchenko took his language with its miraculous power not from the large towns, not from the self-acclaimed academies, not from the midst of the luminaries and the powerful; he passed them all by, disregarded, and forsook them. The language of the country and the village alone served his purposes; only in the villages, in simple cottages, did he search out people for his poems, people noble in spirit, pure of heart, dignified, of high repute. Through these people, through their poetic and righteous souls, the mystery of our past was revealed to him; these people, forgotten by the gentry, gave him the strength to open ancient graves and from our blood-stained land, as though from parchment, to read the sacred truth. Through their independent spirit he was able to rise to those great works which, without benefit of a printer, circulate throughout the world and in fiery letters are imprinted upon all sincere Ukrainian hearts. They gave him the wings to rise above the earth like an exalted, other-worldly phantom and survey from the heights all human souls and mourn them. Our living history and our renowned chronicles also placed before him Prometheus, whose bloodied heart dies each hour and each hour revives. Their eternal souls taught him to speak both to the dead and to the unborn.

Taking our history as viewed by the simple, sound mind of the people, Shevchenko gave it a new image—not the one found in Konysky—taking our people through their history, he reveals them to be other than they are in Kotliarevsky. He cleansed our history of all deception by means of the righteous and noble spirit of the folk, and gave it dignity in the eyes of the wise through his memories of the old world. After that time Ukraine entered upon a new life and whoever undertook to work on behalf of the community and was not dim-sighted knew very well where to set to work and where to go. Our popular efforts made great advances, if not in the name of all those who lived in Ukraine, then in the name of all loyal Ukrainian souls. It was as if under Shevchenko's banner we had returned to our sacred hearth from foreign lands and our native literature had become the servant of God's truth. After Shevchenko's majestic and sacred word, Kotliarevsky and his followers seemed an affront to all that we hold most sacred, and only those who were not afraid of disturbing the prayer of our *narod* with their pitiful clamour continued to babble the frivolous little verses of our sterile flowers, like children. Our literature fell silent for some time, listening attentively to the solemnly joyous proclamation of Taras's poetry, and the silence in which the poet presented us with the new canons for the Ukrainian word was life-giving. He performed no small feat with this joyous proclamation; he summoned the forgotten into the family, into the midst of those whom we justly exalt. That word was a test for the forgotten, a test of whether they were worthy of such company, of whether they would rise from that sleep which had lasted for tens and even hundreds of years. That word was their eternal right to have dominion over that which no one can either confer or destroy. Through the word a new fraternal union, a new Ukrainian family, was affirmed.

This was Shevchenko's feat! This was Taras's place in our life as a people. Making the majestic soul of the *narod* the supreme model for his creativity, he designated a simple path, a path chosen without others' advice. Only now will the efforts of those who lead our great national community, who know its spiritual needs, share its pure tastes, and look upon the world with its righteous gaze not be insignificant. For this reason only those from the country and villages know best and feel in their hearts the true value of Shevchenko. He led them, like another Israel, out of their bondage to that bookishness from which the literate townsfolk obtained all their instruction. He cast off the ignominy for which they were known the world over, that they were a good-for-nothing people. He extolled their spiritual image and offered it as an example to the civilized world: behold, enlightened lands and states, this indigent people can trace its existence to a thousand years ago and for a thousand years it submitted in its darkness and need to the representatives of authority. It did not bow down before those who sought to rise above it and distinguish themselves by putting on lordly airs; it spat them out like bad blood; only the community was extolled as 'the great one.' This great and just word, which will remain unblemished for all time, I proclaimed to the poor and simple and they understood it, showered and sanctified it with their burning tears and for them this word of mine will become an unconquerable power. No earthly force will lessen its power and, as long as the sun continues to rise, it will not be forgotten. Some day the celebrated deeds and triumphs of the great townsmen, who from time to time look down at you, my poor orphans, from their lofty heights, will pass into oblivion but through my word your spiritual image will never be forgotten. Through my word I created for you an eternal memory and from you fashioned eternal remembrance among the living.

Thus does Taras's spirit speak to our sorrowing souls. His death gave his poetry fresh force and here in the country and in villages it is being read again. All his words are now illuminated by a new light and it seems strange to us that only a short time ago such a poet lived in our midst. A small volume of his writings will appear and a volume tenfold larger can be written about it. Let others abler than we take up this task; as for us, it is enough that we wrote in our simple way what we thought about Taras and what we felt in our hearts. Renown will be yours, Taras, as long as there is one young lass in Ukraine to sing our native songs, as long as there is one mother to fondle her child in our way, as long as there is one father to tell his son about our ancient burial mounds in words not foreign to our ears.

W. R. Morfill   (essay date 1886)

SOURCE: "A Cossack Poet," in *Macmillan's Magazine,* Vol. LIII, No. 318, April, 1886, pp. 458-464.

[*In the following essay, Morfill introduces Shevchenko to a western European audience, focusing on his life, his political views, and the idyllic character of his poetry.*]

I propose in the following pages to introduce to the notice of my readers a poet whose name has hardly been heard in the western parts of Europe. This is the Cossack Taras Shevchenko, whose funeral in 1861 was followed by so many thousands of his countrymen, and whose grave—a tumulus surmounted by a large iron cross, near Kaniov on the Dnieper—has been called the Mecca of the South Russian revolutionists. Shevchenko has become the national poet of the Malo-Russians, a large division of the Slavonic family amounting to ten millions, and speaking what has been called a Russian dialect, but is more justly styled by Micklosich and other eminent Slavists an independent language. The object of my little sketch is not philological, so that I shall only dwell upon such points so far as to enable my readers to form a correct idea what the Malo-Russian language is, and where it is spoken. I shall give a notion of its area if I say that drawing a straight line from Sandech, near Cracow, to the Asiatic frontier of Russia, we shall find this language the dominant tongue of Galicia and all the southern parts of Russia, till we come to the Caucasus. It is even spoken in a thin strip of territory in the north of Hungary. It has a rich collection of legendary poems, tales and folk-songs, but its written and artificial literature only dates from the end of last century. When we look at the part of Europe where the language is spoken, we might reasonably expect to find in the surroundings a great deal to stimulate a national poet. These broad steppes form one of the cockpits of Europe. Here Turk, Russian, Pole, Tartar, and Rouman have met in many a deadly contest. On the islands of the Dnieper were the settlements of the strange Cossack Republic, the *Setch,* which cost Peter the Great and Catherine the Second so much trouble to break up; here were the battle-grounds of the celebrated Bogdan Khmelnitzki in his long struggles against the Polish *pans.* Over these steppes the Tartars used to drive their numerous herds of prisoners of all ages and both sexes to the slave-markets. Such a country is sure not to want its *vates sacer;* but if he will sing of it as a real son of his country, he will not tell of delicate-handed dealings; he will talk more of the shedding of blood than the sprinkling of rose-water. Shevchenko has left us an autobiography, though but a meagre one; and it is from this, which is included in the editions of his works published at Lemberg and Prague, that I shall chiefly take my sketch. To the two handsome volumes which appeared at Prague in 1876 is prefixed the portrait of the poet, with his Cossack cap. It is a manly, expressive face, though somewhat rough, and with care deeply stamped upon it; but we shall not be surprised at this when we make a closer acquaintance with his fortunes. Tourgueniev tells us that he had a heavy look till he became animated; and one of his friends humorously styled him "a wild boar with a lark in his throat."

Shevchenko was born on the ninth of March, 1814, in the village of Mornitza, near Kerelivka, in the government of Kiev. His parents were serfs on the estate of a Russian nobleman of German extraction named Engelhardt. His troubles began in earliest childhood. In 1823 he lost his mother, and on his father's marrying again he was doomed to experience the cruelties of a stepmother. Tarras wandered about the village, a neglected bare-footed urchin, with his little sister Irene for his sole companion. The elder Shevchenko only survived his second marriage two years, and then the orphan was sent to be instructed by a drunken priest named Buhorski, who treated him with great brutality. "This was the first despot I ever had to deal with," says Taras in his autobiography, "and he instilled in me for the rest of my life a loathing for every act of oppression which one man can commit against another." He has tales to tell us about two other preceptors of the same sort, from whom he also learned something of the art of painting; for, in addition to the instruction of children both of his masters were engaged in the trade of preparing sacred *icons,* or representations of saints for churches. Thus an inclination for art was produced in him besides his inborn propensity for poetry.

In this way Shevchenko spent a considerable part of his early youth; but in 1829 his master Engelhardt died, and his son-and-heir took the youngster as a page. This new post, although it seemed at first to abridge his liberty, was in the end advantageous to him. His duty was to remain in his master's ante-chamber and answer his call. He began to amuse himself by copying the pictures hanging on the walls, a practice, however, which on one occasion led to very unpleasant results. He had accompanied his master to Vilna, on the occasion of a festival in honour of the Tzar. A grand ball was given at which most of the Engelhardt family were present. While the rest of the household slept, the young artist rose secretly, lit a candle, and began copying a portrait of Platov, the well-known hetman of the Cossacks, who visited England with the Allied Sovereigns in 1814. Shevchenko became so engrossed in this occupation that he did not perceive the return of his master, till he was rudely awakened from his artistic studies by having his ears pulled by the angry nobleman, who reminded his careless serf that by sitting with a candle among the papers he had almost set the house on fire. He received a beating at the time, and on the following day a severer castigation by his masters' orders.

Better days, however, were in store for him. M. Engelhardt, seeing in what direction his talents lay, resolved to send him to a house-painter and decorator, with a view to employing him in those capacities on his own estate. To a painter of this sort he was accordingly sent, and luckily found a kind-hearted man, who, seeing how superior his apprentice was to such work, recommended his master to put him under a certain Lampi, at that time a portrait-painter of some reputation at Warsaw. Consent was given to this step, but the youth remained unhappy and restless, and, according to one of his biographers, was on the point of committing suicide. In the year 1832 the Engelhardts removed permanently to St. Petersburg, and the poet followed with the rest of the servants. He was now eighteen years of age, and at his earnest request was put under the care of another painter, who was, however, little better than a house-decorator. But his mind developed in the capital. On holidays he used to visit the picture galleries, and a longing seized him to imitate the great masters whose works he saw exhibited there. By good luck he made the acquaintance of the artist Soshenko, who felt especial sympathy with him, as being a native of the same part of Russia. By the advice of his new friend he began to work in water-colours. His success in this branch of art was so great that his master used to employ him to paint the portraits of his friends, and rewarded him for so doing. Soshenko assisted him in his work, and laboured also for his moral and intellectual progress, introducing him to the Malo-Russian novelist Grebenka. These worthy men between them succeeded in purchasing the freedom of the poor artist. The celebrated Broulov painted a portrait of the poet Zhoukovski, then one of the most popular men in Russia. The picture was sold for twenty-five hundred roubles at a lottery and for this sum his master Engelhardt gave him his freedom.

This was in April, 1838, and Shevchenko at once became a member of the Academy of Arts. A successful career seemed now to lie open before him. A fondness for poetry had developed itself in him as early as his love of art. His surviving friends still speak of his enthusiasm for the songs of his country, and the tenderness and pathos with which he was in the habit of singing them. In 1840 appeared his **'Kobzar,'** containing a collection of lyrical pieces in the Little or Malo-Russian language. In the following year were published the **'Haidamaks'** and **'Hamalia.'** These poems were received with great enthusiasm by the South Russians, and made the name of the poet deservedly celebrated among his countrymen. The Ukraine and the surrounding lands have always been the most poetic region of Russia, and have been celebrated not only by the authors who have used the national language, but also by the so-called Ukraine school of Polish poets, including Zaleski, Malczewski, Goszcrynski, Padura, Slowacki, and others. Soon after the poet visited his native province, and there made the acquaintance of Koulish and

Kostomarov. The former of these writers was well known throughout Russia for his sympathies with the language and literature of the Ukraine. He is the author of some excellent works on the subject, but from a recent publication his opinions seem to have undergone a great change. Kostomarov died in the earlier part of the present year, having left a considerable reputation as a worker in the field of history and the author of many valuable monographs on Russian celebrities. But these friendships led to some serious troubles. The three men were of advanced political opinions, and were so indiscreet as to give utterance to them. At some meetings in the house of Artemovski Goulak, a Malo-Russian author, their unguarded utterances were heard by a student of the University of Kiev, who undertook the degrading office of an informer. This, we must remember, occurred under the iron rule of the Emperor Nicholas; but there is also a story that the poet composed some biting epigrams on members of the Imperial family.

The companions of his indiscretion were hurried off to imprisonment and exile in separate places. Shevchenko was sentenced to serve as a common soldier, at Orenburg on the Asiatic frontier of the empire. This banishment he endured for ten years, from 1847 to 1857. He has told us of his sufferings in many of his lyrical pieces. From Orenburg he was removed to Siberia, and afterwards to the Fort of Novopetrovsk on the Asiatic coast of the Caspian Sea. His punishment was rendered more severe because he was forbidden to draw or paint. He continued, however, to secrete materials for the exercise of his favourite art, even carrying a pencil in his shoe; and the good-natured officer in command winked at these breaches of discipline. The following story is told by Tourgueniev in the interesting recollections which he has furnished to the Prague edition of the poet's works:

> One general, an out-an-out martinet, having heard that Shevchenko, in spite of the prohibition, had made two or three sketches, thought it his duty to report the matter to Perovski (the commander-in-chief of the district) on one of his days of reception; but the latter, looking sternly on the overzealous informer, said in a marked tone, 'General, I am deaf in this ear; be so good as to repeat to me on the other side what you have said.' The general took the hint, and going to the other ear told him something which in no way concerned Shevchenko.

The poor poet lamented his captivity in many pathetic poems. In one, addressed to his friend Kozachovski, he speaks of "often bedewing his couch with tears of blood." But a day of deliverance was at hand. In 1855 the Emperor Nicholas died. Up to that time the only alleviation of Shevchenko's treatment had been when he was allowed to accompany as draftsman through part of Siberia the expedition under Lieutenant Boutakov. A year or so before the end of his captivity his

treatment became more gentle; and at last came his release, owing to the efforts of Count Feodore Tolstoi and his wife, whom Shevchenko ever afterwards reckoned among his greatest benefactors. There was some delay, however, before he received his freedom. He was detained several months at Nizhni-Novgorod, and sold a few drawings there for his maintenance. He did not return to St. Petersburg till April, 1858. In the summer of 1859 he paid a visit to the Ukraine, and saw his sister Irene in his native village; but he was so poor that he was only able to give her a rouble. At that time all the surviving members of his family were serfs; but in 1860 they received their freedom to the number of eleven souls, owing to the efforts of a society established to assist poor authors and their families. The emancipation of the serfs throughout Russia by the *oukaze* of Alexander the Second was to follow in the next year. The poverty of Shevchenko, indeed, continued till the end of his days, but in truth he was, as is popularly supposed to be the way of poets, remarkably careless of his money. We are told that when he had taken lodgings with a friend he would frequently hand over his purse to him, leaving him to make all arrangements for their common wants. Taras had now a fixed plan of settling in the Ukraine. He wished to purchase a cottage and a little piece of land within sight of the Dnieper, but he was not destined to have his wishes fulfilled. Towards the middle of July he again made his appearance at St. Petersburg, and a new edition of his '**Kobzar**' was published, which was very favourably received. At this time he had chambers in the Academy buildings, and occupied himself with engraving. He now resolved to marry, and his choice fell upon a peasant girl, in spite of the remonstrances of his friends, who reminded him that he was a man of talent and culture. His answer was characteristic: "In body and in soul I am a son and brother of our despised common people. How, then, can I unite myself to one of aristocratic blood? And what would a proud, luxurious lady do in my humble cottage?" In pursuance of this plan he successively endeavoured to gain the affections of two women in humble life, named Charita and Glukeria, but in neither case was he successful: preparations were indeed made for his marriage with the latter, but the girl herself broke off the engagement. According to the testimony of his friends, Shevchenko rarely visited the houses of those who were in a social station superior to his own. He had a natural dread of being patronised, and conducted himself in a reserved and haughty manner. In the appreciative circles of a few private friends he appeared in his native strength, told amusing anecdotes, and sang some of the songs of the Ukraine in a pathetic and impressive manner.

After the failure of his second attempt at marriage, he became more than ever anxious to get away from his lonely life in St. Petersburg, and purchased a piece of land on the right bank of the Dnieper near Kaniov. His health, once so vigorous, now began to show signs of breaking up, owing to his long sufferings both in early youth and in his Siberian exile, and, it must also be added, to an unfortunate habit of drinking. But even in the last days of his life he was labouring for his country, being busy in writing books to assist popular education in the Little-Russian language; of these, one, a grammar, was published during his life; the others, works on arithmetic, geography, and history, were never finished. In January, 1861, Shevchenko wrote to his brother Bartholomew: "I have begun this year very badly; for two weeks I have not stirred out of the house. I feel debilitated and cough continually." A fortnight afterwards he said: "I feel so ill that I can hardly hold the pen in my hand." On his birthday, although very weak, he was cheered by telegrams from his countrymen in the Ukraine, who regarded him with enthusiastic affection. He received their messages on the ninth of March, and encouraged by their warm expressions of sympathy he talked cheerfully with his companions, and expressed a hope that he might get to the south, where he felt sure that his health would be restored. On the following day, March the tenth, he rose at five o'clock in the morning and went to his studio, but suddenly fell down and in about an hour breathed his last. Two days afterwards he was buried in the Smolensk cemetery at St. Petersburg, where every Sunday his grave was visited by the Southern Russians residing in that city. But this was only to be the temporary resting-place of the poet. In one of his poems he had expressed a wish to be buried in the Ukraine—

> When I am dead
> Bury me in a grave,
> Amidst the broad steppe
> In my beloved Ukraine!
> That I may see the wide-extending meadows
> And the Dnieper and its bank,
> And hear the roaring river
> As it eddies onward.

This wish was to be granted. His body was disinterred and conveyed south. It was received everywhere with all possible honour and, carried through the city of Kiev by the students of the university, was laid at last in a picturesque spot on the banks of the Dnieper in the presence of a great concourse of people. A vast mound of earth was piled on the grave, surmounted by an iron cross. In a recent number of the Russian magazine, 'Historical Messenger,' an account is given of the present condition of the "Hill of Taras" (*Tarasova Gora*) as it is called. The grave has been inclosed with iron railings; at the basement of the cross is a medallion of the poet, with his name and the date of his birth and death.

Shevchenko is pre-eminently the national poet of the Southern Russians, a title he has well earned by his intense national feeling. I can only hope in a short sketch like the present to give a general idea of the characteristics of his genius. His verse loses much of its native simplicity in translation, and if a version be attempted it ought to be made in Lowland Scotch. He loves to describe the wild lives of the Cossacks in their old independent days, before the *setch* had been gradually reduced to insignificance by Peter the Great and Catherine; and in the stirring poem known as '**The Haidamaks,**' their revolt in 1768 under Gonta and Zelezniak against their Polish masters is described at length.

Another fine poem, too, is that devoted to the celebrated hetman Ivan Podkova, or in the Malo-Russian form *pidkova*, lit., a horseshoe—a name which this redoubtable chief is said to have gained from his skill in crumpling up a horseshoe by a mere twist of the hand. Having broken out into rebellion he was executed by order of Stephen Batory. But it is not only in these longer pieces, devoted to deeds of the Cossack heroes, that Shevchenko shines. He has many short lyrical pieces of great pathos and elegance which almost defy translation. It would be merely *du clair du lune empaillé*, as, quoting the words of Gérald de Nerval, M. Durand says in his valuable article on the poet contributed to the 'Revue des deux Mondes' (1876, vol. iii. p. 919). This, by the way, and a longer sketch in German published by Obrist at Czernowitz, are the only attempts which have been hitherto made to introduce this interesting poet to Western readers.

Shevchenko has, in a clever way, interwoven with his poems the popular superstitions and customs of his countrymen; and this probably explains the great charm which they have for all Southern Russians, by whom his memory is regarded with idolatry. Moreover no poet was ever more autobiographical; he is always giving us details of his sad but interesting life. He writes for the most part in short unrhymed metres; the well-marked accent of the Little-Russian language amply supplying the place of rhyme, which, however, he sometimes employs, though more frequently contenting himself with a mere assonance. There is a wonderful spontaneity in his verse; and despite his careless, unfettered style, there is always the truest agreement between the language and meaning, while in the most graphic passages the lines seem to rush on headlong. Sometimes we have the strangest and most powerful onomatopoeia, as in the poem '**Outoplena**' (the drowned woman), where we seem to hear the wind howling among the reeds, and asking, as it were, what melancholy figure sits upon the bank. In the '**Night of Taras**' (*Tarasova Nich*) the poet sings a fine elegy on the past glories of his country.

He has perfectly caught the spirit of the little Russian folk-songs, and reproduces them as faithfully as Burns did the Scottish. Their superstitions about birds, water-nymphs, magic herbs, and other weird beliefs, are freely introduced. Thus ravens, as in Serbian poetry, bring intelligence of a disaster; the falcon is the favourite bird with which a young man is compared; and the cuckoo is a prophet. It is not a little curious to find tales of magic handkerchiefs, such as that which Othello gave to Desdemona—

> . . . there's magic in the web of it;
> A sibyl, that had numbered in the world
> The sun to course two hundred compasses,
> In her prophetic fury sew'd the work.

It has sometimes occurred to me that the superstition might have got into the Italian story upon which Shakespeare based his noble play from Slavonic sources. Close to Venice is the Dalmatian littoral, with its Slavonic population and traditions of Ragusa and the Ragusan school, which produced some of the most celebrated poets of the South Slavonic peoples.

The belief also is widely spread that human beings are changed into trees. In one lay the poet tells us a tale of two poplars, which were once sisters and enchantresses (*sestri-charivnitzi*), who both fell in love with the same person, a certain Ivan. There is also a belief in the existence of the evil eyes and of love potions. The favourite plant of the Little-Russians is the elder tree, which has a thousand magic virtues. The following little poem is so pathetic that, even in a prose version, it may perhaps give some idea of Shevchenko's manner in the minor pieces:—

> Here three broad ways cross, and here three brothers of the Ukraine parted on their several journeys. They left their aged mother. This one quitted a wife, the other a sister, and the third, the youngest, a sweetheart. The aged mother planted three ashes in a field, and the wife planted a tall poplar; the sister three maples in the dell, and the betrothed maiden a red elder tree. The three ashes throve not, the poplar withered; withered also the maples, and the elder faded. Never more came the brothers. The old mother is weeping, and the wife, with the children, wails in the cheerless cottage. The sister mourns and goes to seek her brothers in the far-away lands; the young maiden is laid in her grave. The brothers come not back: they are wandering over the world, and the three pathways, they are overgrown with thorns.

Or let us take this pretty little idyl, which loses, perhaps, even more by translation:—

> There is a garden of cherry-trees round the cottage, and the insects are humming near them. It is the time when the labourers are coming in with their ploughs, the maidens sing as they enter, and the mothers await them all for supper. The family take their meal about the cottage, the evening glow arises in the sky, the daughter gives the meal to each, and the mother would fain be advising her, but the nightingale hinders it by her singing. The mother

has laid her little children to sleep in the cottage, and herself rests by them. All is hushed—only the maiden and the nightingale do not sleep.

And these opening stanzas of the lament of a lonely girl have not a little of the manner of Burns in them:

> Alas I am solitary, solitary like a patch of weeds in a field: God has given me neither happiness nor good fortune. He has only given me beauty and brown eyes, and these I have nearly wept out in my desolate maidenhood.

National poetry, such as proceeds from the hearts of the people and lives in their mouths, is now, thanks to the spread of civilisation and cosmopolitanism, fast disappearing. The conditions of its existence are every day becoming more impossible. Had Shevchenko lived a hundred years ago, his lyrics would not have been committed to the printer, but would have been handed on from singer to singer, as was the case with the Scottish ballads 'Sir Patrick Spens,' 'Lord Randal,' and many others, which are now read with astonishment and delight, but whose authors are unknown. In these days of excessive curiosity the popular minstrel is dragged from his rural solitudes, where he sang only to an audience of the surrounding villages, is brought to the great capitals and becomes an object of wonderment. The people of the Ukraine, like the modern Serbs, are not sufficiently near the great centres of Western culture to have exchanged their folk-songs for operatic airs and the conventional lyrics of the music-hall. One of the last genuine minstrels of that interesting part of Russia was Taras Shevchenko.

Valerian Revutsky (essay date 1962)

SOURCE: "Ševčenko and the Theatre," in *Taras Ševčenko, 1814-1861: A Symposium,* edited by Volodymyr Mijakovs'kyj and George Y. Shevelov, Mouton & Co., 1962, pp. 136-52.

[*In the following essay, Revutsky discusses Shevchenko's experiences with the opera, his acquaintances in the theater, his drama criticism, and the influence of these experiences on his dramatic writings.*]

This subject has been frequently discussed. Almost a century after the birth of the poet V. Bocjanovs'kyj wrote a study "Ševčenko and the Ukrainian Theatre" (1912); in 1925 Petro Rulin devoted an article to this topic; in the symposium entitled Ševčenko *ta joho doba* he also gave a detailed analysis of Ševčenko's dramatic criticism. The problem of the relations between Ševčenko and the prominent Russian actor M. Ščepkin has been analyzed by a number of students such as N. Storoženko, A. Jarcev, M. Močul's'kyj, V. Hajevs'kyj, M. Josypenko, O. Borščahivs'kyj, and others. Ševčenko's connection with music and the stage was dealt with by M. Hrinčenko, D. Revuc'kyj, P.

Kozyc'kyj and others. This article therefore does not offer new research but aims at a summary of past studies.

Chronologically Ševčenko's connection with the theatre falls into two periods, one from 1838 to 1845, that is, from the year of his liberation from serfdom to his return to the Ukraine, and the second, from 1857 to his death (with brief interruptions). In the first period Ševčenko came to know the theatre of St. Petersburg and the Ukraine; in the second period he attended, in addition, the theatre in Nižnij Novgorod and, during a brief visit, in Moscow. The earlier period saw his dramatic activity and the beginning of acquaintance with various outstanding theatrical personalities, while in the latter we observe his attempts as a dramatic critic.

I. ŠEVČENKO AND THE CONTEMPORARY OPERATIC AND DRAMATIC REPERTOIRE

Toward the end of the 1830's, when Ševčenko found himself in St. Petersburg, the city was distinguished by its lively theatrical life. In addition to the Great Opera Theatre, which had existed since the eighteenth century, there was the Alexandrinskij Theatre for drama, founded in 1832. In 1833 the Mixajlovskij Theatre was opened, where the French troupe presented its performances. From 1827 performances were given continuously during the summer by the Kamennoostrovskij Theatre as well as by the Theatre-Circus, which functioned up to 1840 and afterwards was called "The New Theatre Near the Semenovskij Bridge".

The prevalent genres were Western European, mostly French or Italian opera, ballet, melodrama and vaudeville. However, in the mid-thirties these began to alternate with the national Russian repertory. In 1834 the historical melodrama *The Hand of the Almighty Has Spared the Fatherland* (Ruka Vsevyšnego otečestvo spasla) by N. Kukol'nik created a great sensation; in 1835 *Askold's Mound* (Askol'dova mogila) was staged, while in 1836 the premiere performance of Glinka's first opera *A Life for the Tsar* (Žizn' za carja) took place. Ševčenko was able to attend many performances. From the poet's diary and his stories it is possible to make a list of the operatic works seen by Ševčenko in St. Petersburg. Of works by German composers he mentioned Weber's *Preciosa* and *Der Freischütz*, and Mozart's *Don Giovanni*; by Italian composers, Donizetti's *La Figlia del reggimento* and *Linda de Chamouni*, Bellini's *Norma* and *I Puritani*, and Rossini's *William Tell* (he was not acquainted with Verdi on the stage); by the French composers Meyerbeer's *Robert le diable* and *Les Huguenots*, and Auber's *Le cheval de bronze* and *La Muette de Portici*; by the Russian composers Verstovskij's *Askol'd's Mound*, Glinka's *A Life for the Tsar* and *Ruslan and Ljudmila* and Dargomyžkij's *Rusalka*. Probably Ševčenko could have listened to such current operas as Mozart's *The Abduction from the Seraglio*, Weber's *Fra Diavolo*, Rossini's *The Barber of Seville*, and others. From among all these operas Ševčenko most warmly praised *Don Giovanni, William Tell*, and the operas of Meyerbeer and Glinka.

While in Nižnij Novgorod Ševčenko noted in his diary: ". . . During the intervals small orchestra played beautifully several pieces from Mozart's *Don Giovanni*, perhaps because it is difficult not to play this enchanting creation beautifully . . ." We also learn that "he greatly admired Rossini's *William Tell* and was completely carried away by Tamberlink's and de Bassini's singing," being in the habit of exclaiming in Little Russian: "May the deuce take his mother, how splendid!" The melody and the mighty dramatic temperament of Meyerbeer could not but have influenced Ševčenko. He called the overture to *Robert le Diable* "A beauty of a melody" and in a letter to M. Ščepkin he wrote: "Be so kind as to snatch somehow from that K-v those 100 roubles and send me fast the score of *Les Huguenots*—I cannot afford to go to it; such a misery!" While in Nižnij Novgorod Ševčenko related with enthusiasm that the pianist Tatarinov "played several pieces from Meyerbeer's *Le Prophète* and *Les Huguenots* and has elevated me to seventh heaven." *Les Huguenots* are also mentioned in Ševčenko's ***The Artist***.

Both Glinka operas evoked Ševčenko's complete approbation. M. Mikešin notes in his reminiscences that "Ševčenko idolized Glinka." About the opera *A Life for the Tsar* Ševčenko wrote: "A work of genius! Immortal Glinka!" About Glinka's second opera *Ruslan and Ljudmila* in a letter of January 25, 1843, to H. S. Tarnavs'kyj, he wrote: "And what an opera, indeed! And especially when Artemovs'kyj sings as Ruslan, it fairly takes one's breath away—indeed, it's quite true!"

Three aspects of Ševčenko's favorite operas engaged his interest. The first was the melodies, some of which he knew by heart. The second aspect was their effective and colorful pageantry. The high style of the performances, in settings by the famous Viennese designer Andrew Roller (1805-1891), who began his career in St. Petersburg opera in 1834, made a great impression on Ševčenko. Finally, Ševčenko was very sensitive to the heroic and patriotic aspects of performances such as *William Tell, A Life for the Tsar, Les Huguenots,* and others.

Ševčenko was indifferent to comic opera, which abundantly figured in the repertories of the St. Petersburg theatres. Similarly the contemporary ballet repertory received scant attention in his writings. The exception to this was an incident connected with the arrival of Maria Taglioni who, literally, created a revolution in the conservative ballet performances in St. Petersburg in the 1830's. In the story ***The Artist*** he notes that after the completion of his painting duties in the *Great*

Opera Theatre "the theatre has opened and the enchanting Taglioni began her bewitching performance". In the same story he describes his visit to Taglioni with K. Brjullov during her performance of *Gitana,* which was one of the most remarkable items of her repertory. The reason for Ševčenko's enthusiasm for Taglioni must be sought in the romanticism of her style. F. Koni wrote about her that ". . . in all her movements, hoverings, gestures and dances—there is no effort nor artifice visible. . . The ground is for her only a point of support, her real element is air."

Ševčenko never saw the works of Victor Hugo, the founder of the romantic drama. Hugo's plays could not be staged in Russia, except for the German melodramatic adaptation of his novel *Notre Dame de Paris,* produced under the title *Esmeral'da* in St. Petersburg by V. Karatygin. In 1838 Karatygin freely translated Shakespeare's *King Lear* and in 1841 *Coriolanus.* Because of the strict Russian censorship Schiller's romantic dramas were not staged either. A dominant position in the dramatic theatre was maintained by French melodrama in the original (performed by the French troupe in the Mixajlovskij Theatre) and in translations and reworkings by V. Karatygin, R. Zotov, M. Obodovskij, young N. Nekrasov and others. Along with Guibert Pixérécourt, known as *le père du mélodrame,* and A. Dumas (*père*) there appeared such dramatists as F. Pyat, V. Du Cange, Ph. Dennery, A. Anicet-Bourgeois, a German dramatist J. Auffenberg and others, authors of melodramas bearing such poignant titles as *Thirty Years, or the Life of a Gambler; Salvator-Chieftain of Invisible Brothers; Kean, or Genius and Frustration; A Living Dead Woman; Sixteen Years of the Arsonists;* and *The Haunted House.* Ševčenko was not attracted by the melodrama *Thirty Years, or the Life of a Gambler* which he agreed with K. Brjullov in terming "an oversalted drama". He was still more critical of the dramas of N. Kukol'nik and N. Polevoj. In the story **Kapitanša** (The Captain's Wife) he wrote ironically about the authors who can "construct on nothing an entire dramatic fantasy of no less mediocre style than that of the respected N. Kukol'nik, who has distinguished himself in this fantastic genre". It is not known whether Ševčenko saw the drama *The Spanish Mother* by another tendentious writer, N. Polevoj, in 1842 in St. Petersburg, but later in Nižnij Novgorod he saw it and made the following remark: "And in general *The Spanish Mother* is an ordinary drama."

Finally, as far as melodrama is concerned, there is an interesting remark which Ševčenko made in his diary for 1857 after seeing for the first time the play *The Son of Love* by A. Kotzebue. In that year the play was an absolute anachronism. Hearing himself called by a German lady he spoke with, "a coarse barbarian, incapable of sympathizing with anything beautiful and moral", he still delicately remarked . . . "I . . . also liked it in a sense, but not exactly."

Ševčenko had an opportunity to see vaudeville many times at the end of the 1830's and the beginning of the 1840's (for example *Mish-mash* [Plutanina] by P. Fedorov), but vaudeville in general occupies an insignificant part in his writings. Even one of the most outstanding vaudeville writers of that time, D. Lenskij (1805-1860), attracted Ševčenko merely as a translator of Béranger: Ševčenko failed to mention Lenskij's vaudeville *Plain and Fancy* (Prostuška i vospitannaja) which he saw. In this genre, the only lasting impression which Ševčenko gained was from his countryman M. Ščepkin in the vaudeville *The Soldier-Magician* (Moskal' čarivnyk) by I. Kotljarevs'kyj. Ševčenko also had an opportunity to see in the role of Čuprun his other distinguished countrymen K. Solenyk (1811-1851) and S. Artemovs'kyj (1813-1874).

The dramatic repertory in St. Petersburg changed radically during Ševčenko's years of exile. In the final years of the 1850's there appeared realistic comedies, the beginnings of Ostrovskij's and Suxovo-Kobylin's theatre. Ševčenko did not let this change go unremarked. As early as 1850, while still in exile in Novopetrovskoe, he read Ostrovskij's first comedy *It's All in the Family* (Svoi ljudi sočtemsja) and noted later: "It appears to me that for our time and our half-literate middle class satire is indispensable, but it must be intelligent, noble satire, such as for example in Fedotov's *The Bridegroom* (Ženix), Ostrovskij's *It's All in the Family,* and Gogol's *The Inspector General.*" But he did not like two other plays by Ostrovskij with which he was acquainted, *A Lucrative Position* (Doxodnoe mesto) and *A Holiday Nap* (Prazdničnyj son do obeda). In the latter he found . . . "repetitiousness and dull repetitiousness". With respect to the former play P. Rulin was probably correct in stating that "Ševčenko accepted deviations from naturalness in romanticism, but he was too genuine to be able to hear the preaching of copy-book morality". In general Ševčenko remained more in sympathy with the theatre of the 1840's. Acknowledging the achievements of the new epoch, he still felt that to affect the spectators' emotions was the main purpose of every theatrical performance—drama or opera.

II. ŠEVČENKO'S THEATRICAL ACQUAINTANCES

Most of Ševčenko's theatrical acquaintances made St. Petersburg their headquarters. Ševčenko was personally associated with many actors for a long time, including Ščepkin, the opera singers Semen Hulak-Artemovs'kyj and Iosif Petrov and their wives (Aleksandra Artemovs'ka and the renowned opera singer Anna Petrova-Vorob'eva). Other personalities in the theatre field were met by Ševčenko only sporadically, but some of them left traces in his works. Mention is to be made first of all of the world renowned artists—the tragic actor Ira Aldridge and the ballerina Maria Taglioni, as well as of a group of Nižnij-Novgorod actors, headed by C. Piunova (Klimovskij, Vladimirov, Vasil'eva, Trusova), the Moscow actors I. Samarin and S. Šumskij and others.

Ševčenko met Ščepkin (1788-1863) in Moscow in 1843. In 1844 he dedicated to Ščepkin his poems **"Čyhyryn"** and **"Pustka"**. In the same year he met Ščepkin in St. Petersburg when the latter stayed there for a month and a half. Among the new roles which Ščepkin brought with him was that of Čuprun in Kotljarevs'kyj's *The Soldier-Magician*. On his way to the Ukraine in 1845, Ševčenko again met Ščepkin. The next well-known meeting was in Nižnij Novgorod, where Ščepkin came to see Ševčenko on the latter's return from exile. The poet referred to it as the "holiday of holidays and the celebration of celebrations . . . six days filled with joyous, triumphant life". Later, Ševčenko was Ščepkin's guest in Moscow.

Ščepkin, since he was considerably older, had a strong psychological influence on Ševčenko. When Ščepkin brought to Nižnij Novgorod *The Soldier-Magician,* in which he performed Ševčenko's favorite part, it was because he wanted to bolster Ševčenko's morale after his banishment. Nor was it by chance that in Nižnij Novgorod his repertory included such plays as Gogol's *Inspector General* and the vaudeville by T. M. Sauvage and Deslaurier's *The Sailor* (Matros). While playing the part of Ljubim Torcov in Ostrovskij's *Poverty Is No Crime,* Ščepkin acquainted Ševčenko with the most recent developments in drama.

After *The Soldier-Magician* the greatest impression Ščepkin made on Ševčenko while in Nižnij Novgorod was in the vaudeville *The Sailor.* This role was one of the best in the romantic actor's repertory, and the aria

> Otčizna dorogaja,
> tebja ja vižu vnov'!
> Vse ta že žizn' prostaja,
> te ž laski i ljubov'!

(Oh my beloved homeland, / I see you again! / There is the same simple way of life, / the same tenderness and love) which he sang must have had an enormous impact on Ševčenko, who had hoped to return to his native Ukraine again.

There is no doubt that Ševčenko had a considerable influence on Ščepkin, too. Močul's'kyj states that *Kobzar* dispelled Ščepkin's doubts about the vitality of the Ukrainian language and had made him an ardent apologist for Ukrainian.

The second close friend of Ševčenko in the theatrical field was his fellow countryman, the well-known opera singer Semen Hulak-Artemovs'kyj (1813-1874). The son of a priest, he was born in the town of Horodyšče, in the Čerkasy district of the province of Kiev.

In 1838 the composer Glinka took him from the Ukraine and after a year sent him to study singing in Italy, where in two years he made successful appearances in Florence. In 1842 he joined the opera of St. Petersburg. He distinguished himself in the role of Čuprun in *The Soldier-Magician*, Karas' in his own opera *A Cossack Beyond the Danube* (Zaporožec' za Dunajem), and as a Zaporozhian Cossack and the elder, respectively, in his own plays *Ukrainian Wedding* (Ukrajinskaja svad'ba) (1851) and *St. John's Eve* (Noč' nakanune Ivanova dnja) (1852). The actual subject of *A Cossack Beyond the Danube* reflects the love and deep nostalgia for the Ukraine which were common to both Artemovs'kyj and Ševčenko. Both became acquainted some time before 1842 and from that time their friendship grew steadily until Ševčenko's death. When Ševčenko was permitted to correspond from his confinement in Novopetrovskoe, Artemovs'kyj helped him financially. In a letter of June 30, 1856, Ševčenko again speaks of Artemovs'kyj's help. On the second day after his return to St. Petersburg Ševčenko visited Artemovs'kyj and felt "as if in one's own house. We reminisced and talked over many things, but still did not manage to recall or discuss them all thoroughly."

Artemovs'kyj's operatic repertory consisted of 32 roles. Ševčenko greatly admired *Ruslan and Ljudmila, Don Giovanni, Le Cheval de bronze* and *William Tell* and there was undoubtedly a sentimental attachment to "my friend Semen" who sang the leading roles in them (the role of Don Giovanni was regarded as his best). As for the role of Čuprun, Kuliš wrote that "this is a thorough personification of a Little Russian common man, who is simple, happy and completely contented with his lot. It is not a fool whom you see before you, at whom you are laughing . . ." These words testify quite vividly as to what exactly could have attracted Ševčenko in Čuprun as performed by Artemovs'kyj ("the enchanting Semen"). It was the portrayal of national and personal dignity.

Similarly Ševčenko maintained a close relationship with another singer, Iosif Petrov (1807-1878). Petrov also came from the Ukraine. He was born in Jelysavethrad. In 1826 he joined the company of the well-known Ukrainian entrepreneur Danylo Žuraxovs'kyj, where he appeared with Ščepkin. Four years later, in 1830, he entered the St. Petersburg opera company, made his debut as Sarastro in *The Magic Flute* and remained with them until his death, performing about 130 most varied roles. It was for his excellent voice (bass with baritone high notes) that Glinka wrote the parts of Susanin and Ruslan, and S. Dargomyžskij that of the miller. Petrov revealed his dramatic talent with particular power and strength in the role of Bertram in Meyerbeer's opera *Robert le diable.* Ševčenko greatly admired this romantic opera with Petrov participating in it. The Russian writer Ivan Lažečnikov wrote of Petrov's performance as Bertram: ". . . that glare from the fascination of which your soul cannot free itself and that saffron face distorted with devilish passion, and that thick crop of hair from which, it seems, a whole nest of snakes is ready to come out at any moment . . ." Ševčenko mentioned a similar role performed by Petrov—that of Caspar in *Der Freischütz*.

During the first period of St. Petersburg life up to his banishment Ševčenko expressed enthusiasm for Petrov's wife, Anna Petrova-Vorob'eva (1816-1901). He noted later that ". . . Petrov in the role of Susanin is as good as before, and Leonova in the role of Vanja is also good, but she is much below the excellence of Petrova, whom I heard in 1845". Glinka, attracted by her charming contralto, wrote that part for her as well as the part of Ratmir (*Ruslan and Ljudmila*). At the end of the 1850's Ševčenko was unable to hear her, because she had left the stage, after her voice had broken in the baritone part of Richard Forth (*I Puritani*).

Among the theatrical personalities whom Ševčenko met occasionally, in the dawn of his enthusiasm for the theatre, sporadic meetings with M. Taglioni opened before him "a still unheard of fabulous world . . .", a world of exalted theatrical romanticism. Another event which took place in St. Petersburg at the end of 1858 and which affected his whole being was the arrival in St. Petersburg of the Negro tragedian, Ira Aldridge (1805-1867). The Russian actor Sosnickij said that he ". . . has never seen in his lifetime such a talent [as Aldridge's] and never imagined what height talent may attain". The performance of this actor made an unusual impression on Ševčenko. The sculptor M. Mikešin relates how he saw Aldridge in his dressing room after the performance: ". . . in a wide chair, reclining in fatigue, King Lear was lying, and on him, literally on him, was to be found Taras Hryhorovyč; tears poured down from his eyes; incoherent, passionate words of swearing and tenderness drowned by a loud whisper were heard from him as he covered with kisses the great actor's oily face, hands and shoulders . . ." A student of Ševčenko, B. Suxanov-Podkolzin, states that Ševčenko and his friend Starov "reacted so intensely to Aldridge's performance that the public protested".

Ševčenko met Aldridge in the family of Count F. Tolstoj, where the daughter of the Count K. Junge acted as interpreter for them. "I recall how both of them were deeply moved one evening, when I told Aldridge Ševčenko's story and translated for Ševčenko the tragic actor's account of his life. The warm friendship continued during the meetings at which Ševčenko painted Aldridge's portrait . . ."

Ševčenko's theatrical acquaintances bespeak his artistic inclinations and tendencies. He was usually fascinated by romantic actors—actors of soul, and not of mere technique. Thus we can explain his reaction to the performances of Aldridge and Taglioni. To this

type of actor, in the main, his talented countrymen Ščepkin, Artemovs'kyj and Petrov belonged.

III. ŠEVČENKO AS A DRAMA CRITIC

Ševčenko wrote only one drama review: of the performance of Catherine Piunova and other actors of the theatre in Nižnij Novgorod; but his critical evaluations of the actors of his time are abundantly scattered in his diary, letters and writings, especially in **The Artist**. Ševčenko had a broad knowledge of theatrical repertory; his acquaintance with theatre personalities gave him an opportunity to obtain an insight into the inner life of the theatre. Kuliš mentions an amateur performance of **Nazar Stodolja** at Christmas in 1844 in St. Petersburg; during the period of Ševčenko's banishment to the Novopetrovskoe fortress, according to the memoirs of the company commander Kosarev, Ševčenko took an active part as an actor and designer in the presentation of *It's All in the Family*. He played the role of Rispoloženskij. Even if we were to reject this story, as the poet's first biographer Konys'kyj does, there still remains the indisputable fact that Ševčenko knew how to produce a play. Ševčenko himself was a playwright. Finally, he was interested in the general theory of art. It is well known, for example, that he read very carefully and critically K. Libelt's *Estetyka*.

And yet, Ševčenko's only dramatic review was evoked by a personal incident in his life, his affection for the young actress C. Piunova (1843-1909) during his stay in Nižnij Novgorod. By writing his review he wanted to do her a favor. In his diary Ševčenko noted: "A benefit performance by the pretty Piunova. The theatre is filled to the brim with spectators and the performer was charming—a wonderful topic for a newspaper article. Why not try it? Shall I try it? Let's try at random . . ." Thus, there appeared in *Nižegorodskie Gubernskie Vedomosti* Ševčenko's review, which obviously roused interest since it was reprinted in *Moskovskie Vedomosti* No. 18, 1858. The review gives a brief analysis of performances by four Nižnij Novgorod actors (Vladimirov, Klimovskij, Vasil'eva, Trusova) and the benefit performer C. Piunova in a romantic melodrama *The Ragpicker of Paris* by F. Piat, and in the French vaudeville *The Smart Grandmother* in Fedorov's version.

Ševčenko, since he was in love with Piunova, could easily have become subjective, but he did not. Acknowledging at the beginning the abilities of Piunova and her prospects for the future, Ševčenko realized that she was at her best in the roles of young girls. "There is no doubt" he wrote "that these are her better roles, but she should not forget that in these there is a hidden monotony and facility which can harm her talent." The advice follows that "she can boldly expand her repertory; there will be more work and she will have to ponder her roles more carefully." With regard to her performance in the role of Antoinette in *The Rag-picker of Paris* Ševčenko writes: "Madam Piunova performed Antoinette's role quite conscientiously, but it is evident that she had no sympathy for the character."

Thus Ševčenko correctly analyzed Piunova's stagecraft. During her early years she was successful because of her youth, but she was rather indifferent to her work and this with the lack of training made her later merely an average actress. P. Rulin in his study "T. Ševčenko i K. Piunova" quotes an interesting remark by a well known drama critic B. Varneke, who saw her in her later years in the Ostrovskij's play *The Storm*: "She played the role of Kabanixa rather superficially."

In the first period of Ševčenko's stay in St. Petersburg the most celebrated tragic actor was Vasilij Karatygin (1802-1851). He excelled in melodrama. Reviewers emphasized his exceptional technique. These characteristics did not escape Ševčenko's attention. Ševčenko commented on one of his best roles, in the melodrama *Thirty Years, or a Gambler's Life*: ". . . Between the second and third [act] he [K. Brjullov] went backstage and dressed Karatygin for the role of a beggar. The public raved, not knowing why. What does the costume mean to a good actor!"

There is not the least doubt that Karatygin's best monologues, especially in his historical roles, performed in a highly rhetorical style, impressed Ševčenko greatly. Karatygin's skill as an actor was responsible for Ševčenko's high opinion of a melodrama by a little known dramatist, J. von Auffenberg.

Although Ščepkin remained for Ševčenko the ideal actor, on one occasion at least he preferred Karpo Solenyk "the first Ukrainian professional actor", whom Ševčenko saw in the Ukraine in 1845 in Romny during the famous Illins'kyj fair: "There I saw for the first time the actor of genius Solenyk in the role of Čuprun (*The Soldier-Magician*). He appeared to me natural and more graceful than the inimitable Ščepkin". Solenyk was then appearing with the Kharkiv group of actors. N. Myz'ko, comparing his performance of Ukrainian roles with that of other actors, wrote: " . . . in their performance there was more or less expression of the national character; but in Solenyk's performance all these features were united, came into focus, and formed the complete and finished type of a real Ukrainian . . ."

The best evidence that these remarks of Ševčenko about Solenyk were objective is Ščepkin's own statement. Ščepkin referred to Solenyk as "a man of enormous talent", and his daughter relates that he was sufficiently impartial to acknowledge that Solenyk played Ukrainian roles better than he himself did.

Finally, in order to evaluate Ševčenko as a theatre critic, it is worth while to examine one more note in his

diary: "Samojlov," writes Ševčenko, "is inferior to Sadovskij . . ." It is said that Sadovskij (1818-1872) was a master of realistic folk character, while V. Samojlov (1812-1887) was an exceptionally talented actor in the characterization of types. In Ševčenko's time there was no clear distinction between art as imitation and art as psychological identification. Samojlov personified the former, Sadovskij the latter. Ševčenko sensed in Sadovskij more "soul" and thus appreciated him more highly. The contrast Ševčenko felt between the two actors was a contrast in two types of theatre. The preference for Sadovskij conveys what Ševčenko expected and demanded from the theatre.

IV. ŠEVČENKO AS A PLAYWRIGHT

Ševčenko's activity as a dramatist falls in the same first period of his St. Petersburg life during which he made the acquaintance of the theatre personages of that time. D. Antonovyč in his article "Ševčenko as a Dramatist" assumes that it was the critic Alexander Elkan who could have prompted Ševčenko to write plays, "promising that, thanks to his contacts, they would be presented on the stage of the Aleksandrinskij Theatre". Chronologically, Ševčenko's activities as a playwright began in 1841.

Ševčenko's attempts at playwriting cannot be understood if we fail to consider that they appeared during the popularity of French melodrama. "Pixérécourt was not distinguished from Hugo, merging with him into one current of *romantic drama*." The rhetoric of the elevated, emphatic style of the romantics fused with the adventurous, pageant-like elements of the boulevard melodrama of Pixérécourt. These peculiarities were also transplanted into the Russian theatre. Ševčenko, in all probability, saw the historical melodramas of N. Kukol'nik (1851) and the plays of his follower, N. Polevoj, such as *A Russian Never Forgets a Good Deed* (Russkij čelovek dobro pomnit) (1839) and *Paraša from Siberia* (Paraša Sibirjačka) (1840), along with those of other writers like V. Zotov, A. Viskovatov, and I. Skobelev. Nekrasov wrote about this genre of Russian melodrama that in these works there is an obligatory ". . . admixture of several scenes of madness, love of a poor man for a rich daughter, prison, a military march and music, paintings and so on". But the most important element was a conflict between patriotism and love.

Ukrainian historical drama originated primarily in the interest in national past, which marked the Ukrainian romantics, but the period of melodrama left a deep imprint on it.

Kostomarov's historical dramas *Sava Čalyj* and *The Night at Perejaslav* (Perejaslavs'ka nič) were written in 1838 and 1840. Ševčenko was acquainted with them. However, the immediate impetus for Ševčenko's playwriting was his friendship with Ja. Kuxarenko (1798-1862), the author of the play *Life of the Black Sea Cossacks* (Čornomors'kyj pobyt). P. Zajcev notes that the discussions which were conducted in Ševčenko's circle during Kuxarenko's stay in St. Petersburg resulted in the writing by Ševčenko of the three-act play ***Danylo Reva***.

Ševčenko's first sketches of drama known to us bear the traces of romantic influences in general, and Ukrainian historical romanticism in particular. While writing his poem ***Hajdamaky*** he inserts in it a prose dialogue with an element of folk speech ("Svjato v Čyhyryni"). Dated the same year (1841) is a fragment of the play ***Mykyta Hajdaj***, in Russian, adapted by Ševčenko from the melodrama *The Bride* (Narečena). Judging from the excerpt, we may conclude that this was a historical melodrama from the times of Xmel'nyc'kyj, like Kostomarov's *The Night at Perejaslav*. A close resemblance can also be perceived in the names of the heroines of Ševčenko's and Kostomarov's dramas (in Ševčenko—Marjana, in Kostomarov—Maryna). *The Night at Perejaslav* was written in 1840, the year the melodrama by N. Polevoj *Paraša from Siberia* opened. Kostomarov's play was to a certain extent a Ukrainian parallel to *Paraša from Siberia*. Like Polevoj's play it revolves around a conflict of love and patriotism, shifting this conflict to the Cossack period of Ukrainian history. However, *The Night at Perejaslav* proved to be a drama for reading and never reached the stage.

Ševčenko decided to try to create his own drama *The Bride* with the plot from the same Xmel'nyc'kyj epoch. How far he advanced in its writing and exactly when it changed into ***Mykyta Hajday***, is difficult to ascertain. With regard to style the extant fragment of it is, judging by its intensity, elevated language and rhetorical features, closely related to Victor Hugo. The fragment has an aura of mystery about it, so typical of the melodramatic genre, for example in the episode where the charter is sewed into a fur cap before it is sent to the Polish king and the sejm. The setting: ("Evening, The interior of the house is dimly lighted by a smoking candle . . .") preserves a typical romantic, "Rembrandt-like" color. The gloom and mystery are enhanced by the guard's song describing [a] young wife's unfaithfulness to an old and jealous *voivode* who has gone to war. There are also in the excerpt from ***Mykyta Hajdaj*** indications of the national Ukrainian and Pan-Slavic idea, typical of the period of the Brotherhood of Saints Cyril and Methodius.

After ***Mykyta Hajdaj*** Ševčenko planned another drama *The Blind Beauty* (Slepaja krasavica). In a letter of December 8, 1841, to H. Kvitka-Osnovjanenko Ševčenko wrote: "I am working on another drama—it will be called *The Blind Beauty*. I don't know what will happen to it . . ." There is every reason to think that this drama did not get beyond the planning stage; nine months later,

on September 30, 1842, in a letter to Kuxarenko, Ševčenko mentioned the poem **"The Blind One"** (*Slepaja*) in Russian, a poem which has been preserved. Apparently, the versified form of drama in Russian proved difficult for Ševčenko and consequently he abandoned these attempts and undertook the prose form.

M. Novyc'kyj establishes the date of writing of ***Nazar Stodolja*** as some time before 1843 and there are cogent reasons for assuming that it is a reworking of Ševčenko's previous drama ***Danylo Reva***. This drama was under the definite influence of Kuxarenko's play *Life of the Black Sea Cossacks,* which Ševčenko himself passed on to the censor, hoping to see it on the stage. Kuxarenko's drama "describes a series of interestingly written sketches of life among the Black Sea Cossacks during the time (1794-96) when the customs and traditions of the Zaporozhian *Sič* were still alive among them . . .". Ševčenko was also well acquainted with other Ukrainian dramas, primarily with the works of I. Kotljarevs'kyj and H. Kvitka-Osnovjanenko. In all probability, he knew such plays as *Little Russian Life* (Byt Malorossii v pervuju polovinu XVIII st) (1831), *Čary* (Sorcery) by K. Topolja (1837), *St. John's Eve* (Kupala na Ivana) by St. Šereperja (1839), but all these plays, including the most outstanding, Kotljarevs'kyj's *Natalka from Poltava* (Natalka Poltavka), did not affect Ševčenko's writings. Ševčenko decidedly opposed the great accumulation of detail describing the mode of life and the sentimentality of the heroes typical of these plays.

Nazar Stodolja, as has been stated, appeared in 1843. In a letter to Kuxarenko Ševčenko wrote ". . . I have composed in addition a short poem ***Hamalija*** which is being printed in Warsaw. Once it is printed, I shall send it to you. Also ***Nazar Stodolja***, a three-act play—in Russian. It will be performed in the theatre after Easter."

Hence we get a clear impression that Ševčenko was preparing his play in the Russian language for performance in the Aleksandrinskij Theatre. This is confirmed by the conjectures of D. Antonovyč that . . . "Nazar's role itself seems to be adapted to the stage technique of V. Karatygin, and that of Hnat to Brjanskij, who in his youth had played a role in the Ukrainian language in *The Cossack-Poet* (Kozak-stixotvorec) by Prince Šaxovskoj; the part of Xoma was destined for Tolčanov (father), who distinguished himself in villains' roles . . ."

There is no doubt that the strict Russian censorship was responsible for the delay in its performance; perhaps major alterations were demanded. Kuliš indicated later that, for example, the heroine in the earlier (probably in the first) version was called Lukija and not Halja. The censorship procedures in all likelihood dragged on for a long time and in the end permission was not granted. It was not the Imperial Theatre but an amateur group of the Medical Academy which performed *Nazar Stodolja* at Christmas of 1844. This was a second version, a Ukrainian one, which has come down to us and into which Ševčenko included additional scenes describing Ukrainian Christmas customs.

O. Kysil' described *Nazar Stodolja* as a melodrama with four basic characters typical of this genre: a noble hero in love (Nazar), a virtuous heroine (Halja), a villain (Xoma), a kindhearted comedian-simpleton (Stexa). The play depicts the universal conflict of good and evil (Nazar and Hnat vs. Xoma) where virtue ought to triumph over evil. The conflict centers neither on social nor religious grounds. Both Xoma and Nazar are officers in the Cossack army; but Nazar is a bearer of loyalty, Xoma of treachery. The ideal yearnings of Nazar are in conflict with Xoma's materialist proclivities. The simplicity and open-mindedness of Nazar are contrasted with Xoma's duplicity. Xoma's callousness is in conflict with Nazar's generosity. Xoma sees himself as a human being, but in the eyes of Hnat he is "such a villain that he is not worth even mentioning".

The play is constructed as a series of contrasting situations, abrupt transitions from threats to supplications, from pride and self-assurance to self-humiliation. Thus, on entering, Nazar says that he "will not let himself be a laughing stock even to the hetman himself", then he prostrates himself before Xoma, begging for mercy. This contrast is underlined by Hnat's words: ". . . Whom are you begging for? To whom are you bowing? Before whom are you prostrating yourself?", and then again suddenly the scene changes to the former setting: ". . . Do you want fire? There will be plenty of fire! For you I shall call forth all hell" . . . Xoma is called by Nazar a "liar", in contrast he becomes a "kind person", and then again an "executioner". The same method of rapid switches was employed by Ševčenko in a scene with Nazar and Hnat. In the estimation of Nazar, Hnat at the beginning was a "scoundrel", then a "good friend", later a "stone", and finally a "reliable friend". Xoma's anger is replaced by terror, then by self-assurance and finally by trepidation . . .

The plot of *Nazar Stodolja* is activated, as is typical of melodrama, by fortuitous and unexpected incidents. In the first act the sudden appearance of Nazar is a surprise, in the second act the main line of action undergoes an abrupt change with Hnat's suggestion that Halja be kidnapped, in the third act the appearance of Xoma interrupts the solemnly triumphal scene of the lovers; the last surprise is Xoma's repentance at the end of the play.

Like an opera, *Nazar Stodolja* contains numerous scenes effective theatrically but not necessary for the evolving of the plot: the household servants in the first act, girls and boys in the inn, Jewish entertainers, ser-

vants in the third act; the play also encompasses ritual elements: a matchmaking, a singing and story-telling *kobzar*, dances, pantomimes, etc. Light and darkness alternate in a contrasting manner without any transitional modulations (the first act—darkness, the second—light, the third—darkness); there predominates an atmosphere of mystery and horror (Christmas eve, a snowstorm, the howling of wolves, a ruined inn where a Cossack officer and Jews were murdered, where a corpse of Tymofij, the son of Xmel'nyc'kyj, is lying, the brightness of the moon's reflection, etc.). The ritual and the moments pertaining to the mode of life are utilized primarily as exotic ornamentation. In the composition of *Nazar Stodolja* the three unities are absent. The action is transferred from Xoma's living room to a peasant's house and then to an inn and so on. The atmosphere of place and time is achieved in a condensed but successful manner by employing historical details rather than a broad historical setting. With respect to historicity, *Nazar Stodolja* is superior to the historical melodramas of Ševčenko's contemporaries like Kukol'nik or Polevoj.

Ševčenko's dramatic writings cannot be compared with his poetry. Ševčenko was not a playwright by vocation. But in the history of the Ukrainian theatre his *Nazar Stodolja* initiated a new genre—the historical melodrama, which was partially continued by M. Staryc'kyj and I. Tobilevyč. The novelty introduced by Ševčenko consisted in a departure from the overburdening of dramas with features of everyday life. The former Ukrainian dramaturgy (especially I. Kotljarevs'kyj and H. Kvitka-Osnovjanenko) portrayed a moral hero. Nazar still has some traits of this hero, although he is endowed with romantic qualities, too. Unfortunately, after Ševčenko, heroic character on the Ukrainian stage was again lost in the imitation of everyday life.

Nazar Stodolja was the apex of Ševčenko's art as a dramatist. Besides this play, Ševčenko also wrote in dialogue form the mystery **"Velykyj Ljox"** (1845), fragments from **"Vid'ma"** (1847), **"Moskaleva Krynycja"** (1848), and **"Sotnyk"** (1849). But they were not destined for the theatre and their dialogue constitutes only a device in Ševčenko's poetry.

George S. N. Luckyj (essay date 1971)

SOURCE: "Ševčenko," in *Between Gogol' and Ševčenko: Polarity in the Literary Ukraine: 1798-1845,* Wilhelm Fink Verlag, 1971, pp. 128-61.

[*In the following essay, Luckyj overviews Shevchenko's life and evaluates his writing and historical importance, claiming that "Ševčenko's role in Ukrainian literature can hardly be overstressed."*]

The appearance of Ševčenko must be seen not only in contrast to Gogol' but also to the Ukrainian intellectual milieu of the day. The existence of such a milieu, small as it was, was in itself of cardinal importance. In the 1820's and 1830's a series of issues, centered around the Ukraine, came into the open and there crystallized a certain definite attitude, shared by Ukrainian writers, historians and folklorists as to the need for a distinctly Ukrainian culture and literature. Linguistic efforts were made to form a separate Ukrainian literature. Gogol's decision not to participate in these efforts does not exclude him from the intellectual debate of the time. On the contrary, his attitude was shared by many Ukrainians. On the other hand, Ševčenko's intellectual origins owe much to the milieu described in chapters I and II of this study. It is impossible to imagine him without his predecessors. Yet great as was his debt to them the pace at which he surpassed them was much greater. There is, indeed, a great leap in the Ukraine between the 1830's and the 1840's. That it was accomplished almost entirely single handedly is a testimony to the great power of poetry. For it was through the miracle of the poetic word that Ševčenko galvanized the country which was not yet sure of its course. The impact of Ševčenko on the Ukraine was in intensity such as Gogol' in his wildest dreams about the Cossack elan could not imagine. The story of Ševčenko's life holds the key to the understanding of this influence.

Childhood and Youth

Taras Ševčenko was born on March 9, 1814, in the village of Morynci, in the province of Kiev. His father, Hryhorij and his mother Kateryna, nee Bojko, were serfs. Morynci, the village in which Taras' mother was also born, was one of the many possessions of Vasilij Engel'hardt, a Russian magnate and retired general. Taras' father came from the neighbouring village of Kyrylivka to which the whole family moved in 1815. There, in a large family consisting of grandfather Ivan, his parents, two brothers and four sisters, Taras spent his childhood. In his novel ***Knjaginja* (Princess)** Ševčenko recalled those times.

> And there before me stands our poor, old, white house with a dark thatched roof and black chimney, and near the house, on one side, an appletree with red apples, and around the appletree a flowerbed, the darling of my unforgettable sister, my patient and gentle nurse. A ramous willow withered at the top stands at the gate and behind the willow is a barn, surrounded by stacks of rye, wheat and all sorts of crops, and beyond the barn on a slope of the hill an orchard spreads itself. And what an orchard! Thick, dark and quiet . . . Beyond the orchard there is a meadow and beyond the meadow a valley and in the valley—a silent, barely rippling stream shaded by willows and guelder rose and smothered by wide-leaved dark green burdocks.

All this provided some refuge from the dark realities of serfdom. Not that the little Taras was a shy introvert

spending most of his time amid the burdocks. In his wanderings he ventured out beyond the boundaries of the village, attracted mainly by the itinerary of the salt-vendors (*čumac'kyj šljax*) who bypassed the neighbourhood. Once he went out determined to find "the columns which support the sky" and was lost until night, when *čumaky* brought him back. With great affection he remembered his elder sister, Catherine, who looked after him when he was small. When he was nine Catherine got married and moved to a neighbouring village.

Taras' father was an exception among the serfs in that he could read. On Sundays he would usually spend some time reading to his family the lives of the saints. He must have valued his literacy because young Taras was sent to the local deacon (*djak*) to learn reading too. Taras preferred the stories which his grandfather could relate rather than formal schooling which was often accompanied by beatings. Old Ivan Ševčenko as a young man was a participant in the bloody rebellion of the Ukrainian peasants against the Polish landowners in 1786 (the so-called *Kolijivščyna*). His accounts of those stirring times were later used by Taras in his poem ***Hajdamaky***.

His mother died when Taras was nine years old and two years later, in 1825, his father, who had married again, also died. Before dying Hryhorij Ševčenko said: "My son Taras has no need to inherit any of my property. He will not be an ordinary man; either something very good or no good at all, and for him my inheritance will either mean nothing or be of no help." As an orphan Taras faced his most trying time. His stepmother beat him and he protested by running away from home and hiding. Often he was no longer living at home but with the deacon Bohors'kyj whose underling he became. Life there was not any easier. One night Taras decided to run away from his tyrannical master. Before he did, "finding him completely drunk," he "used against him his own weapon—the birch rod and as much as his childish strength permitted, repaid him for all his cruelties."

Eventually Ševčenko returned to Kyrylivka where at the age of thirteen he became a shepherd. At that age he first fell in love, for there is no other way to describe his deep attachment to Oksana Kovalenko. She was remembered later in several of his poems. His first attempts to write poetry probably began at that period too. Apart from ecclesiastical literature there was ever present another source of poetic inspiration—the folk songs. Ševčenko himself said that as a small boy he liked to copy and sing verses by Skovoroda. It is also likely that at quite an early age Ševčenko read Kotljarevs'kyj's *Enejida*.

His artistic ability showed itself in another direction. As a small child Taras showed a great desire to draw and to paint. "Whenever possible," writes an early biographer of Ševčenko, "on walls, doors, gates, Ševčenko constantly drew with charcoal or chalk. In school where he could get paper and pencil this passion developed even more strongly in him." During his shiftless teenage existence Ševčenko made several efforts to become apprenticed to a painter. For this he, as a serf, needed permission from his master. While trying to obtain it at Vilšana, the residence of the Engel'gardts, he was involuntarily enrolled in his master's domestic staff.

In 1828 the old master Vasilij Engel'gardt died and the Vilšana and neighbouring estates passed to his illegitimate son, Pavel, a lieutenant of the guards and aide-de-camp to the Vilno governor-general Rimskij-Korsakov. The new master liked the appearance of Ševčenko and the "tattered wandering schoolboy was straightaway given a twill jacket and pants to match and ultimately ended up as a pageboy (*kozačok*)." Sometime in the fall of 1829 he travelled in his new capacity to join his master in Vilno. He was not to return to the Ukraine for several years. Ševčenko's new duties were not onerous but rather dull. He had to wait on his master, bring him a new pipe and be on hand. There were compensations too. Taras spent his time in the residence of his master, and could browse through the books and look at pictures. The temptation to copy the latter led to the following incident, described later by Ševčenko in his autobiographical letter.

> One day, when we were in Vilno, on December 6, 1829, my master and his wife had gone to a ball to celebrate the name day of His Majesty . . . I lit a candle in my solitary room . . . and started to copy with real zeal. The time passed . . . [Suddenly] the door opened and my master and his wife, coming back from the ball, entered. Enraged he took me by the ears and slapped my face because I could have set on fire not only the house but the whole town. Next day the master ordered coachman Sidorka to give me a good beating which was carried out with special zeal.

Engel'gardt realized that the boy had talent and decided to apprentice him to a painter. Some scholars believe Ševčenko became a pupil of the well-known Jan Rustem in Vilno. Other hold that his teacher was Franciszek Lampi, who lived in Warsaw. The evidence that Ševčenko lived in Warsaw is not very convincing. Two incidents from days in Vilno are of importance. Both incidents represented Ševčenko's first contacts with Poland which later had an important influence on his ideas. First, Ševčenko formed a friendship with a Polish girl, Dziunia Husikowska. They talked in Polish, a language which Ševčenko knew fairly well. The Right-Bank Ukraine from which he came had become a part of Russia late in the eighteenth century and therefore retained Polish traditions and language. When he first met Dziunia, who was not a serf, Ševčenko is said to

have remarked: "For the first time it occurred to me: why aren't we, the wretched serfs, the same people as those in other social classes?"

The second episode was more important. Either in Warsaw or in Vilno one day late in November, 1830, Ševčenko was a witness of the Polish uprising against the Russians. For a few days the revolutionaries held the upper hand. Engel'gardt left in a hurry for St. Petersburg and Taras was left behind, but not for long. He had orders to rejoin his master and made his way in a group of servants through a country full of insurgents openly fighting the Russian troops. There is little doubt that witnessing this anti-Russian revolution left a deep impression on the Ukrainian serf.

In St. Petersburg

Once in the capital Ševčenko reverted to his role of pageboy. Not until 1832 did his master agree to apprentice him to a painter, Širjaev, a well-known St. Petersburg decorator. Širjaev's friend I. Zajcev has recorded in his memoirs that when he recited Puškin and Žukovskij at Širjaev's he could see Ševčenko listening to these verses through an open door. It was also at Širjaev's that Ševčenko must have learned to speak Russian properly for up to that time his knowledge of the language was still imperfect. The lack of formal secondary education could, in Ševčenko's case, be regarded as a blessing in disguise for the schools were the media of Russification.

It was a chance meeting which proved so fateful for Ševčenko's further career. In his free moments he often went to the Summer Gardens to copy some statues. On one of these outings, during a St. Petersburg "white night", he was approached by a stranger, admiring his drawings. It turned out that the stranger was a fellow Ukrainian, Ivan Sošenko, himself a student at the Academy of Fine Arts, a native of Bohuslav, only about 20 miles away from Ševčenko's birthplace. The two young men struck up a firm friendship. At first Sošenko supplied Ševčenko with books and told him all about his life as an art student. Then, realizing Ševčenko's great talent and his plight at Širjaev's, he went out of his way to find influential friends who could help Ševčenko's lot. Among those to whom he introduced Ševčenko were Jevhen Hrebinka, a well-known Ukrainian writer and Vasyl' Hryhorovyč, the secretary of the Academy of Fine Arts. The latter was also of Ukrainian origin.

Although Ševčenko's first friends in St. Petersburg were Ukrainians it would not be true to say that they were the only ones interested in his future. The fate of a gifted artist who was a serf and therefore could not study at the Academy, struck a responsive chord in many Russian hearts. Among these the most powerful were the famous painter Brjullov and the well-known poet Žukovskij. It was finally decided to buy Ševčenko his freedom by offering a sum of money to Engel'hardt. "V. A. Žukovskij," wrote Ševčenko in his autobiographical letter, "having first of all learnt the price from the landowner asked Brjullov to paint his, [Žukovskij's] portrait for the Imperial family with a view of offering it for sale in a lottery within the tsar's family. The great Brjullov willingly agreed. The portrait was painted. Žukovskij, with the help of Count Vel'gorskij, arranged a lottery to the amount of 2,500 rubles and with this sum the freedom of T. Ševčenko was purchased on April 22, 1838."

At first Ševčenko was elated. He was a free man, a student at the Imperial Academy of Fine Arts and a holder of a scholarship. What more could he desire? For a while he was drawn to the social and artistic world from which he had been barred. He went out in the evenings, bought new clothes and thereby annoyed his new roommate Sošenko. But gradually the hard work at the Academy absorbed all his energies. He became a devoted and conscientious student eagerly filling the gaps in his almost non-existent education. During the next six years he received at the Academy a thorough liberal education. Among the subjects studied were aesthetics, history, anatomy and art history. Above all, he became the favourite pupil of Brjullov, whose house he frequently visited even staying for weeks and months.

Brjullov was at the zenith of his fame. Having returned to Russia after living for many years in Italy he was worshipped by the Russian *cognoscenti* as the greatest Romantic painter. His huge canvas "The Last Days of Pompei" was admired by all, among them Puškin and Gogol'. Gogol' even wrote an essay about it, full of adulation for Brjullov. It was Brjullov who not only opened the doors to the highest artistic circle in St. Petersburg for Ševčenko, but who also introduced him to the world of Romantic literature and art. During readings at Brjullov's house Ševčenko heard the latest Western European poetry and prose. In his autobiographical novel ***Xudožnik* (The Artist)** Ševčenko recreated the atmosphere of his student days, particularly his devotion to the "divine Brjullov" and his friendship with the painter Šternberg. It was also at Brjullov's that Ševčenko became aware of another urge which for some time had been stirring in him. It was in the year he gained freedom that we hear for the first time of Ševčenko as a poet. Later, in his diary, he gave the following account of his first literary attempts.

> I lived in his [Brjullov's] apartment, or I should say, in his studio. And what did I do? What did I work at in this holy of holies? It is strange even to recollect . . . I wrote Ukrainian verses, which later fell like a terrible burden upon my poor soul. Before his [Brjullov's] bewitching canvas I fell into reveries and evoked in my heart my blind *kobzar* and the bloodthirsty *hajdamaks*. In the twilight of his

luxurious studio, as if on torrid and wild steppes along the Dnieper, before me passed the martyred shadows of our hapless Hetmans. The steppe spread out before me, dotted with high mounds. My beautiful, my unfortunate Ukraine preened herself before me in all her immaculate and melancholy beauty . . . And so I grew more pensive and I could not take my spiritual eyes off that native and enchanting beauty. This was nothing less than my destiny.

Actually, Ševčenko started writing at least a year earlier. His ballad **"Pryčynna" (Bewitched)** was composed in 1837. In 1838 he wrote four *dumky* (meditations) as well as **"Na vičnu pamjat' Kotljarevs'komu" (To the Eternal Memory of Kotljarevs'kyj)**, **"Kateryna" (Catherine)** and **"Tarasova nič" (The Night of Taras)**. On November 18, 1838, Hrebinka wrote to Kvitka: "There is also here a countryman of ours, Ševčenko, who is very anxious to write verses. Whatever he writes you can only smack your lips and clap your hands in admiration. He gave me several beautiful poems for my collection." The collection in question did not materialize until 1841. However, these facts indicate that no sooner did Ševčenko become a free man than he started thinking of publishing his poems. What were the reasons for this development?

Undoubtedly the St. Petersburg milieu had much to do with this. Many of Ševčenko's new friends were men of letters and literary critics. Among them the most influential was Hrebinka. It was probably through him that Ševčenko heard in greater detail about the Ukrainian writers of the day. Although little was published, still there existed not only collections of Ukrainian folk songs and historical materials but also the original works of poets and prosewriters. Some of them Ševčenko met personally; with others (Kvitka) he started to correspond. In the winter of 1839 he probably met Mykola Markevyč who came to St. Petersburg after failing to have his *Istorija Malorossii* printed in Moscow. By that time Ševčenko had also read *Istorija Rusov* which circulated in several copies. In a sense, the St. Petersburg atmosphere was charged with Ukrainian themes and interests in which Gogol's early works held a prominent place. There were, therefore, many models which Ševčenko could have followed. Indeed, the first known poem by Ševčenko, the ballad **"Bewitched"** which probably dates from 1837, shows traces of many influences (Metlyns'kyj, Borovykovs'kyj). Yet **"Bewitched"** remains an original work of great poetic power. It is striking how right at the beginning of his poetic career Ševčenko showed the markings of genius. The musicality of his language was extraordinary. The beginning of the ballad, set to music, has become a popular folk song. Ševčenko's language vibrated with colour and richness, his imagery evoked the mood perfectly. Some qualities of this poem are not entirely lost in translation. While Ševčenko was imitating folk-song motifs he rose above them so much that the finished product was perfect in a form and structure which were his own creations. His alone were the metric patterns, the rhythms and rich rhymes. More characteristic for Ševčenko than a ballad was the short lyric meditation (*dumka*), a brief song, with personal reflections. Among the earliest is **"Teče voda v synje more" (Water Flows into the Blue Sea**, 1838).

> The waters flow down to the sea
> And never more return;
> A cossack goes to seek his fortune,
> —Fortune there is none.
> The Cossack journeys far away
> Where dance the dark blue waves,
> —Like them the Cossack's heart is dancing,
> But thought speaks and says:
> "Where do you journey without asking?
> To whose care abandoned
> Father, and your dear old mother.
> And a fair young maiden?
> And hard to live indeed
> Among them;—none to share your tears,
> No one with whom to speak."
> The Cossack sits there on the further
> Shore—the blue waves dance.
> He dreamed that he would find good fortune:
> Sorrow crossed his path.
> And now the cranes fly in long skeins'
> Towards the further shore.
> The Cossack weeps—the beaten tracks
> Are overgrown with thorns.

The directness and simplicity of Ševčenko's language may be seen in all the early poems written in 1838. Not one of them can be rejected as weak. The appeal they had to Ukrainian listeners was instant. As Panaev recalled in his memoirs:

> I saw Ševčenko for the first time twenty-four years ago [in 1837] at a soiree at Grebenka's. At that time they were still talking about buying out the poet . . . Ševčenko was 23 years old. He was full of life; thoughts of near freedom and hope of a better future enlivened him. He had already written some poems, but they, it seems, were not included in the *Kobzar.* His Little Russian friends even then spoke of him with enthusiasm and said that Ševčenko showed promise of poetic genius.

Apart from purely lyrical verse Ševčenko wrote three longer poems in 1838 which showed his other interests. One of them was **"To the Eternal Memory of Kotljarevs'kyj"** written after Kotljarevs'kyj's death in 1838. Its panegyrical tone was in sharp contrast to Ševčenko's later opinion of Kotljarevs'kyj. In the poem Ševčenko was full of reverence for the "father" of Ukrainian literature. He praised him for depicting the "Cossack glory" and for reminding the Ukrainians of their ancient history. It is significant that Ševčenko revealed in that poem his sense of the continuity of

modern Ukrainian literature. In his desire to listen to the "nightingale-like" language of Kotljarevs'kyj there was clear willingness to continue the process of Ukrainian letters. No contemporary of Ševčenko was filled with exactly these emotions.

The sense of continuous literary tradition, of which the Romantics became aware, was awakened in them by historical rather than aesthetic considerations. The new feeling of national identity led them to a discovery of their past which in turn reinforced the national awareness. As artists, however, they found in the past written literature little that attracted them. The medieval and Baroque era on the whole repelled them because of its Church Slavonic language and ecclesiastical outlook. Classicism was also of little help since it used popular language for comic effect and therefore, in the eyes of some Romantics, debased it. Ševčenko, who struggled hard to refine the language, was remarkable in his restraint and in the respect he showed towards older writers who were hardly his predecessors.

Ševčenko's first historical poem was **"The Night of Taras"** (1838). For the first time he turned for inspiration to the history of the Ukrainian Cossacks and found it relevant to his own times. Ševčenko's discovery of the clue to Ukrainian history was presented in simple terms: at one time Ukrainians had a glorious history, now they had lost this glory and could only recall it in songs. The past is remembered with sharp poignancy.

> Once there was the Hetmanate—
> It passed beyond recall;
> Once, it was, we ruled ourselves,
> But we shall rule no more . . .
> Yet we never shall forget
> The Cossack fame of yore!

In the poem Ševčenko recalled one incident from Cossack history—the victory of the Cossacks, led by Taras Trjasylo, over the Poles in 1630. Ševčenko's main sources were *Istorija Rusov* and the history of the Ukraine by Bantyš-Kamens'kyj. As described by Ševčenko, conditions in the Ukraine before Trjasylo's rebellion were those of severe national and social oppression. Yet despite ruthless domination by the Poles the Ukrainians were able to rise and fight. Now, the reader must surely conclude, conditions are equally bad but there is no sign of rebellion. That such a contemporary allusion could be drawn from the poem may be seen from the tsarist censors who, before the poem was printed in the *Kobzar,* deleted such passages as the one quoted above. Even in its censored version the poem was quite revolutionary in the eyes of General Dubel't, chief of the Third Section, who in 1847 condemned it as "being written with the clear purpose of comparing historical conditions with the present ones."

The last work to be written in 1838 was a long poem, **"Catherine"**, dedicated to Žukovskij. It is Ševčenko's first real masterpiece. This long poem of 750 lines relates the story of a Ukrainian peasant girl who is seduced by a Russian officer who then abandons her. Disgraced, she is expelled, with a small child, by her parents and vainly searches for her Ivan. When finally she finds him he refuses to acknowledge her and drives her away. Catherine ends her life by drowning. This Karamzinian theme is given a fresh treatment in which no trace is left of sentimentality. Ševčenko's poem, while in places reminiscent of Kvitka's short story "Serdešna Oksana", is a moving tragedy. It consists of Catherine's transgression of the accepted family order. In Shlemkevych's words, it is the "clash between emotion and the wisdom of the kin, between eros and logos." Ševčenko depicts this conflict not in national or social but in universal human terms and evokes deep sympathy for the suffering woman. An exploration of the human condition, especially of the suffering caused by the conflict of the general good versus personal will, becomes, with **"Catherine"**, the central preoccupation of his better works. The archetypal theme of the mother dominates much of his later poetry. While enjoying his newly won freedom in St. Petersburg, Ševčenko did not forget his family in Kyrylivka. On November 15, 1839, he wrote a letter to his brother, Mykyta, sending him at the same time some money. "As you see," he wrote, "I live, study, don't bow to anybody and I am not afraid of anyone except God; it is a great happiness to be a free man, you can do what you like and nobody can stop you." He added this characteristic remark, repeating it twice: "Please write to me as I write to you, not in Russian, but in our language."

At the same time Ševčenko was eager to broaden the horizon of his education. He studied French, taking lessons from a Polish friend, L. Demski. From him he obtained Polish literature, some of it like the works of Lelewel, forbidden in Russia. His progress at the Academy was moderate. In May 1839 he was awarded a silver medal for his drawings. This meant that he could not be awarded a travelling scholarship which might have taken him to Italy. His attention was more and more devoted to literature and he was ready when an opportunity presented itself to publish his first collection of poems.

The Publication of the *Kobzar*

Three men with three different approaches to Ukrainian literature were instrumental in the publication of Ševčenko's first work. They were Hrebinka, Ševčenko's friend who himself wrote in Ukrainian; P. Martos, a wealthy Ukrainian landowner, who financed the project; and P. Korsakov, the censor, who passed the book for printing. On February 12, 1840, preliminary permission was issued for the printing of *Kobzar* (The Minstrel).

The book appeared on sale in the second half of April. It was 114 pages long and contained eight poems— **"Dumy moji, dumy moji"** (O My Thoughts, My Thoughts), **"Perebendja"**, **"Kateryna"**, **"Topolja"** (The Poplar), **"Dumka"** (A Song), **"Do Osnovjanenka"** (To Osnovjanenko), **"Ivan Pidkova"** and **"Tarasova nič"** (The Night of Taras). The volume was adorned by Šternberg's frontispiece drawing of a blind minstrel.

The appearance of the *Kobzar* is the single most important event in Ukrainian literature. It heralded a new and bold beginning, an attempt to express what was still thought by many to be impossible—a wide range of feelings and ideas in Ukrainian of the highest artistic form. Ševčenko's language was not based on a particular dialect; nor was it simply a reproduction of popular speech. It grew out of an amalgam of three dialects (southeastern, northern and southwestern) as well as of Church Slavicisms, colloquialisms and elements of earlier writings by different authors. The linguistic synthesis achieved by Ševčenko was a great success. The secret of it lay in "simplicity, not as the opposite of complexity, but as limpid and crystallized complexity."

In the first poem **"Dumy moji, dumy moji,"** which is a kind of invocation to the Muse, Ševčenko is full of anguish about his poetic efforts. Although ultimately he sends his poems to his native land in the hope that they may find response there, his sorrows and questionings do not leave him. Ševčenko became even more conscious of the difficulties which a Ukrainian poet faced in the second poem in the collection entitled **"Perebendja"**. The name itself is given here to a blind old minstrel who is exceptionally garrulous and ready to sing all kinds of songs to those who will listen to him. However, behind the superficial facade of gaiety and popularity there is in him another self—that of a poet struggling with himself and his art. On the surface, Ševčenko implies, his songs may appear entertaining, but deep in his heart he wants to do more for his reader. True, even then he will sing about the Ukraine, not to amuse and divert, but to stir and evoke the deepest emotions and thoughts. It is this "inner Ukraine", a part of suffering humanity, that Ševčenko turns to in his poem. There is, therefore, a contrast between the minstrel and the poet. What only a decade earlier was considered by Ukrainian intellectuals to be the prerogative of folk poetry in which the blind *kobzar* was the "father of poetry", became in Ševčenko's poem a new form—the minstrel turned into an archetypal figure of wise man and teacher.

The minstrel's chief claim to fame lies in his evocations of the past glory of the Ukraine. Here, indeed, is the main contribution of Ševčenko's collection. With unparalleled skill he depicts Ukrainian history in the poems **"To Osnovjanenko," "Ivan Pidkova,"** and the

"Night of Taras". Their value is not so much in the external richness of poetic description as in the internal, philosophical undercurrent which makes history alive and relevant to his readers. Ševčenko contrasts the past with the present and asks, by implication, what are the causes of the decline and decay of his country. Thereby he arouses feelings not only of patriotism but also of nationalism. Patriotism or the love of one's country was an old and universally known sentiment, but nationalism, a transformation of what was after all an ethnic community into a politically conscious nation, was a new idea in the Ukraine. The logic of Ševčenko's argument was based on the premises of *narodnost'* and Romanticism, applied to the situation in the Ukraine. If the Ukraine possessed in the sixteenth century a large measure of independence and enjoyed periods of home rule (the Het'man state) then Ševčenko's contemporaries had an historical heritage—a basic requirement for the creation of a nation. The old liberties, destroyed after the absorption of the Het'man Ukraine by Russia were worthy of revival, especially as the present conditions in the Ukraine were unsatisfactory. Readers of Ševčenko's historical poems must have made this comparison between the past and the present. The blame for the extinction of Ukrainian independence and for the conditions of serfdom introduced in the Ukraine by Catherine II were placed squarely on Russia.

By creating an adequate linguistic and literary medium in the *Kobzar* Ševčenko was in fact laying the foundation for modern Ukrainian literature which from now on could be defended and developed by Ukrainian writers and intellectuals. It was to them that in a few years' time Ševčenko would be directing his appeals. In 1840 he hoped that some of the leading Ukrainian writers would take upon themselves the task of defining the goals of Ukrainian nationhood. Therefore, very inappropriately, he turned to Kvitka, who, in October, 1839, had published in the *Notes of the Fatherland* an account of the Cossack leader Antin Holovatyj. In **"To Osnovjanenko"** Ševčenko gratefully acknowledged Kvitka's contribution and encouraged him to write more on historical themes. His appeal fell on deaf ears because the conservative sentimentalist Kvitka was not prepared to share Ševčenko's ideas for a Ukrainian national rebirth. What Ševčenko hoped Kvitka might do he did later himself ("and see Ukraine revive again in accents deep and strong").

At this "singing of the olden times" Ševčenko was the greatest master. **"Ivan Pidkova"** in particular may be regarded as a poetic *tour de force* in which little attention is paid to historical accuracy but everything is concentrated on the heroic image of the Cossack leader during a rough sea voyage. Ševčenko admires him for his leadership and recalls nostalgically how

There was a time in our Ukraine
When cannon roared with glee
A time when Zaporožian men
Excelled in mastery.

"The Night of Taras" as was pointed out earlier is a similar work. The other poems in the *Kobzar* provide a balance for the historical works. Among them are **"Catherine,"** the ballad **"Poplar"** and a song **"What Use Are Black Brows to Me?"** They confirm that Ševčenko was not a narrow nationalist but a poet of a wide range of interests and moods.

Seven reviews of the *Kobzar* were published in the Russian press. Five of them appeared in the journals—*Son of the Fatherland, Library for Reading, The Contemporary, Notes of the Fatherland* and *The Lighthouse,* and two in the newspapers—*The Literary Gazette* and the *Northern Bee.* Although there were many important differences between them, they all agreed on several main points. All the reviewers acknowledged the high poetic talent of the author. All but one of them also were disappointed that he wrote in Ukrainian, which most of them regarded as a dying dialect, and not in Russian. The one exception was in the *Notes of the Fatherland.* Some Soviet scholars, particularly V. Spiridonov and F. Pryjma, attribute this unsigned review to Belinskij who at that time was the review editor of the journal. They do this in an attempt to show that Belinskij, who later became very hostile to Ševčenko and to Ukrainian literature in general, did write a favourable review of Ševčenko's first work. The whole crux of the matter, however, is that this review is not, in fact, favourable. At first reading it may sound like a defense of Ševčenko. "Here," declared the Russian critic, "are the poetic *dumy,* the historical legends and fascination of abandoned love and the artless story of Katerina's love, in a word, all the elements of the folk poetry of the south of our fatherland." Why should he not write in Ukrainian, asked the reviewer, "if Mr. Ševčenko grew up in Little Russia, if destiny placed him in such relations to the language in which we write and communicate—i. e. Russian—that he cannot express in it his feelings? If from his youth his impressions assumed the forms of the southern dialect, should he therefore bury his talent in the earth? Must the sacred sounds be silenced in his soul only because some gentlemen in stylish tailcoats do not understand these sounds, do not or will not understand the native echoes of the Slavic tongue, the echoes fleeting from the south, from the cradle of glory and religion of Russia . . . Moreover, books written in Little Russian such as . . . Ševčenko's Katerina will undoubtedly be of great benefit to the South Russian general reader." The allusion to the poet's inability to write in Russian could hardly be regarded as a compliment. Even less flattering was the relegation of Ševčenko's work to the province of folk poetry. In publishing the *Kobzar* Ševčenko had a different aim in mind than to contribute to the treasure trove of the "folk poetry of the south of our fatherland" or to amuse or educate simple Ukrainian readers by writing verse in their "dialect".

Most other Russian reviewers misunderstood Ševčenko's intention by regretting that he did not write in Russian. The whole point of the *Kobzar* was that it was in Ukrainian. It had no ambition to be what the critics chided it with failing in—to become a part of the mainstream of Russian literature; rather it claimed a status of its own. It is interesting and rather ironic that the only review which showed great sympathy for Ševčenko's point of view was that in the *Lighthouse*. Hidden behind its initials P. K. its author was Pëtr Korsakov, the censor of the *Kobzar*. For rather special reasons, some of which were not necessarily ulterior, he favoured Ševčenko's writings and prepared a niche for them in the arch-conservative journal. Like the other reviewers he was totally unaware of their revolutionary significance. As so often in literary history, the work outpaced its critics.

The Maturing Artist

Among Ševčenko's friends in St. Petersburg the appearance of the *Kobzar* caused quite a stir. The Russians tried to belittle its importance and the Ukrainians greeted it with enthusiasm. Markevyč noted in his diary for April 23, 1840, that in the company of Čižov, Strugovščikov, Korsakov, count F. Tolstoj and Bulgarin, Kukol'nik a popular dramatist and the classmate of Gogol' from Nižyn "attacked Martos [and] criticized Ševčenko, maintaining that the tendency of his *Kobzar* was harmful and dangerous. Martos fell into despair. Nestor [Kukol'nik] added that it was now imperative to prohibit the languages: Polish, Little Russian and German in the sea coast provinces." On the other hand, in the Ukraine the triumph of the book was almost unchallenged. Kvitka waxed sentimental over it. Writing to Ševčenko on October 23, 1840, he described how he pressed the book to his heart "because I respect very much you and your thoughts. And **'Kateryna'** . . . Beautiful . . . I cannot say more. That is exactly how the *moskal'* soldiers deceive our girls." The Ukrainian writers Afanas'-ev-Čužbyns'kyj and Metlyns'kyj expressed their delight at the appearance of the *Kobzar*. The reaction of Kostomarov, recorded by Korsun, was quite striking. "Once we were walking with Nikolaj Ivanovič [Kostomarov] to the cathedral for high mass when we dropped in at Aparin's bookstore. We asked if he had any new books and Aparin showed us a thin book—*Kobzar*. We sat down on a bench and sat there right through the lunch hour. We read the entire book . . . This was something quite special, new and original. *Kobzar* has stunned us!"

The welcome he received from his countrymen and the reserved Russian criticism must have had a great effect on Ševčenko. Not that it turned him against the Russian critics. No young poet could afford to ignore them and in a few years' time Ševčenko would try for the time being to follow their advice and to write in Russian. But the reception of the *Kobzar* undoubtedly strengthened this feeling of national identity and made him more aware of his mission as a Ukrainian poet. From then on his dedication to Ukrainian literature superseded his love of painting. Unlike Gogol' he did not think of making a literary career in Russia, but of kindling the small spark of national regeneration in the Ukraine. In 1841-42 he conducted correspondence with the Ukrainian writers Kvitka, Afanas'-ev-Čužbyns'kyj, Korsun and discussed with them his literary plans. In their exchanges they mutually encouraged each other but Ševčenko was the most active of them. He was full of new ideas, eager to co-operate with others. The result of his endeavours was the publication of the literary almanac *Swallow* (1841) edited by Hrebinka. It is almost certain that Ševčenko acted as co-editor, since Hrebinka himself wrote to Kvitka on January 13, 1839, "I have a wonderful assistant Ševčenko, a marvellous fellow." The almanac was long in coming out; when it finally appeared after a year's delay, it contained 42 contributions by 13 authors. Ševčenko had four poems in it—**"Vitre bujnyj" (Wild Wind), "Pryčynna" (Bewitched)**, the ode on the death of Kotljarevs'kyj and the first chapter of his long poem *Hajdamaky*.

. . . Hrebinka's almanac was bitterly attacked by Belinskij who saw no value in a literature in modern Ukrainian. His scathing review was very likely read by Hrebinka (who knew Kraevskij well) before publication and its content communicated to Ševčenko. Deeply aroused, he decided to add a postscript in his invocation to the poem *Hajdamaky* which he was then publishing. In it he refuted Belinskij's criticism as well as that of other Russian critics who advised him against writing in Ukrainian. Ševčenko wrote:

> You've given me a sheepskin coat;
> Alas, it does not fit.
> The garment of your own wise speech
> Is lined with falsehood's wit.

The poem *Hajdamaky* was published in St. Petersburg at Ševčenko's own expense in December, 1841. The censor agreed to pass it only after Ševčenko assured him that there was nothing revolutionary in the poem. Ostensibly this was so for the poem narrated in great detail the peasant rebellion, the so-called *Kolijivščyna*, against the Poles in 1768. But as in his other historical poems Ševčenko often made contemporary allusions. This poem, Ševčenko's longest (2569 lines), is based mostly on folk legends about the *hajdamaks*, some of them heard by the author from his grandfather, although it also owes something to published sources, especially the Polish novel *Wernyhora* by Michal Czajkowski. It is a work of great originality and poetic power, quite

Byronic in its conception. Its opening invocation, written with philosophic sweep, sets the perspective for the violent events which follow.

> All things must ever flow and pass away . . .
> Whence did they come and whither have they
> vanished?
> Nor fool nor sage an answer can convey.
> Things come by life, by dying they are
> banished.
> For one thing blooms; one withers now
> forever,
> Its yellowed leaves are scattered by the blast.
> Suns will still rise, nor cease their vast
> endeavour,
> The bright-red stars flow on as in the past;
> And you, o silver moon, with visage shining,
> Will rise and wander in the azure sky,
> Peering in troughs and wells with eye
> designing,
> Painting the sea with glory from on high.

What follows is the love story of Jarema, the poor servant and Oksana, a story which is gradually overshadowed by the activities of the *hajdamak* rebels whom Jarema joins. A large part of the poem deals with the rebellion itself. It depicts many cruel incidents committed by both the Poles and the rebels and portrays two historical characters, the *hajdamak* leaders Zaliznjak and Honta. The latter, in a fashion reminiscent of Taras Bul'ba, kills his own sons whose only fault was that they were Catholics. Ševčenko is also conscious in the poem of the social problem: the oppressed peasants battle against the landlords, not only Ukrainians against Poles.

There is a curious ambivalence about the latter part of the poem. On the one hand, some of the best passages describe glowingly the revenge wreaked by the rebels on their oppressors. The rebels are regarded by Ševčenko as direct descendants of the Cossacks and share with them his full admiration. Yet towards the end a note of alarm is sounded at all the unnecessary carnage between the Ukrainians and the Poles and only the Polish Jesuits are condemned for their schemings. In the preface which Ševčenko appended to the poem he wrote "thank God, it [the fighting] is all over, moreover when you recall that we are children of one mother, that we are all Slavs. My heart aches yet I must tell it all: let the sons and grandsons see that their fathers were wrong; let them be brothers with their enemies. Let the Slavic land, covered with wheat like gold, be undivided, for ever from sea to sea." This is the first indication that Ševčenko had lent his ear to Pan-Slav ideas and deplored the internecine strife among the Slavs.

The Russian critics received *Hajdamaky* with reserve. *Literaturnaja gazeta* on April 12, 1842, praised Ševčenko as a poet but deplored his use of Ukrainian. The sharpest attack came from Belinskij. "The readers of the *Notes of the Fatherland*," he wrote, "are familiar with our opinion about works of so-called Little Russian literature. We shall not repeat it here and will only say that the new attempt, songs by Mr. Ševčenko, this privileged it seems Little Russian poet, convinces us more than ever that works of such a type are published for the pleasure and edification of their authors only; there seems to be no other public for it." The poem itself was dismissed by Belinskij with scorn and ridicule. Although the Ukrainian reading public was delighted with the poem, Russian criticism was not without effect and to defy it completely was impossible. Ševčenko, therefore, tried to write in Russian "so that the Russians don't say that I don't know their language." The results were disappointing. Ševčenko commented in a letter to Kuxarenko, on September 30, 1842: "I have copied [in Russian] my **"Blind Girl"** and now I cry over it—what devil made me do it and for what sins do I confess to the Russians (*Kacapam*) in a stale Russian (*kacaps'kym*) language . . . Here, my countrymen and those who are not my countrymen call me a fool, but what can I do—is it my fault that I wasn't born a Russian (*kacapom*) or a Frenchman?" A few months later Ševčenko returned to this topic. In a letter to Tarnovs'kyj on January 25, 1843, he wrote ". . . Here the Russians call me an enthusiast, that is, a fool. God forgive them; let me be even a peasant poet, so long as I am a poet, I don't need anything more." The last remark shows that Ševčenko disliked the label "peasant poet" but was willing to put up with it if people recognized his talent.

In 1842 Ševčenko was tired of the "cursed" St. Petersburg. For a time he still hoped that the Academy would send him to Italy where his friend Šternberg had gone earlier. The lively literary circles in which Ševčenko spent much of his free time fascinated him no longer. From the memoirs of various literary figures of the 1840's we know that among those Ševčenko met infrequently were the Vice-President of the Academy, Count Fedor Tolstoj, the composer Glinka and the literati N. Polevoj, N. Kukol'nik, S. Sobolevskij, I. Sosnickij, F. Bulgarin, Prince Odoevsky, A. Nikitenko, A. Strugovščikov and even, once, Belinskij himself. Ševčenko and Gogol' never met and later, in exile, Ševčenko deplored this as a great loss.

Occasionally Ševčenko gravitated to more purely Ukrainian gatherings. This was already so in the circles of Hrebinka and Markevyč. In the summer of 1842 Ševčenko found very close friends in two Ukrainian visitors to St. Petersburg, Jakiv Kuxarenko, a minor writer and a "Black Sea Cossack chieftain" and the opera singer Semen Hulak-Artemovs'kyj. The trio did actually sing many Ukrainian songs.

In October, 1842, Ševčenko embarked on a sea voyage to Denmark and Sweden. He fell ill on the way and had to abandon his plans in Revel from where he returned to St. Petersburg. It was on this trip that he wrote **"Hamalija,"** a short masterpiece describing sea voyages of the Zaporožian Cossacks to Constantinople. Early in 1843 he wrote to Kuxarenko "In March I am going abroad and I shall not go to Little Russia. To heck with it. There, apart from crying, I shall not hear anything." The last remark betrays Ševčenko's first critical attitude to his countrymen. The Ukraine of his poems was after all in reality a Little Russia full of sentimental landowners and unhappy peasants. This mood was only momentary. In the end Ševčenko did not go abroad, but returned on a prolonged visit to his native Ukraine which he missed so much.

First Ukrainian Journey

In response to an invitation Ševčenko visited first the rich Ukrainian landowner Hryhory Tarnovs'kyj in his estate in Kačanivka near Borzna. Tarnovs'kyj's residence was a virtual palace, built according to the plan of Rastrelli, containing a large picture gallery and surrounded by a huge park. Tarnovs'kyj himself was ambitious to be a patron of the arts, a role he played *ad nauseam*. Conscious of his host's opulence and arrogance Ševčenko remained on friendly yet reserved terms with him. At different times Kačanivka was visited by many writers; Gogol', Maksymovyč and Markevyč were among them. The composer Glinka wrote his opera *Ruslan and Ljudmila* there. Sometimes Ševčenko wandered in the park and talked to the peasants. He did not avoid social life, making many new friends, among them the Ukrainian poet Viktor Zabila, and visiting places of interest in the neighbourhood. From Kačanivka Ševčenko went to Kiev. There he met Pantelejmon Kuliš, a writer and an enthusiast for everything Ukrainian whose friendship meant so much to Ševčenko. Their first meeting was recorded by Kuliš in his memoirs.

> When I was sitting behind the easel, lost in the play of lines, tones and colours, before me appeared the still unfamiliar figure of Ševčenko in a loose canvas coat and a cap pushed back like Cossack headgear.
>
> —"And guess who?"—These were Taras' first words pronounced in the captivating gay voice which endeared him to women and children.
>
> —"Don't you want to offer me a drink?" This was the second sentence I heard from Ševčenko.
>
> This question astonished me a little.

Their first meeting at once marked the contrast between Ševčenko and Kuliš. Ševčenko's cocky, bohemian manner clashed with Kuliš's studious seriousness. The difference between the two personalities was best described by Kuliš in his autobiography.

> Kuliš did not quite like Ševčenko for his cynicism; he put up with his eccentricities for the sake of his talent. Ševčenko, on the other hand, did not like Kuliš's aristocratism . . . Kuliš loved cleanliness around his tidy person, he loved order in things and time; his ear was like that of a maiden, nobody ever heard him use foul language. It would be possible to say that this was a meeting between the lowland Cossack from the Sič and a rich city Cossack. Indeed they were representatives of both parts of Cossackdom. Ševčenko represented the Right-Bank Cossacks who after the treaty of Andrusovo were left without leadership and finding themselves under Polish domination, fled to the Sič and from there returned to their landlords' estates as rebellious *hajdamaks* . . . anxious to smash the landlords completely. Kuliš was a descendant of the Cossacks who sat in council with the tsar's boyars, formed for Tsar Peter the Little Russian Collegium, helped Tsarina Catherine to write her Code and introduce schools in place of old seminaries.

Together with Kuliš, Ševčenko visited many places of historical interest around Kiev, among them the burnt out ruins of the famous monastery Mežyhirs'kyj Spas, patronized in the seventeenth century by the Zaporožian Cossacks. In Kuliš Ševčenko met for the first time a Ukrainian intellectual. They found many common interests and ideas, but occasionally they would not agree.

From Kiev Ševčenko went to visit his friend Hrebinka in his *xutir* near Pyrjatyn. From there both of them travelled to the estate called Mojsivka, owned by the rich Tetjana Volxovs'ka. She entertained the neighbouring Ukrainian society on a grand scale and Ševčenko found himself the centre of attention of the numerous gentry. Yet by far the most important place to which Ševčenko travelled with Aleksej Kapnist was Jahotyn, the estate of Prince Repnin. The former governor general of the provinces of Poltava and Černihiv resided here with his family. The actual mistress of the house was his daughter, Princess Barbara. Six years older than Ševčenko she was strongly attracted to him from the first and in the fall of the same year, when he again visited Jahotyn, she fell in love with him. Of her true feelings for Ševčenko she left two records: her letters to Charles Einard in Geneva and, less transparently, her novel *Devočka* (A Girl). In one of her letters to Einard written on January 27, 1844, Princess Barbara confessed that "if I saw love from his [Ševčenko's] side, I would, perhaps, answer with passion." The reasons why Ševčenko did not respond to her love were several. No doubt he felt the gap between himself, a former serf, and a princess. Perhaps he also resented a little Barbara's overprotective solicitude. But most of all he remained reserved because at the same time he was deeply in love with someone else.

In the neighbouring village, Berezovi Rudky, Ševčenko met the Zakrevs'kyj family. At first he was attracted to Viktor Zakrevs'kyj who was the eccentric brother in the family and who organized the "society of wet mugs" (*obsčestvo močemordija*), a kind of drinking club to which Ševčenko for a time belonged. There is good reason to believe that Zakrevs'kyj's circle was dedicated to other things apart from drinking. A few years later, in 1848, a denunciation was made against it in which it was claimed that at one of their gatherings toasts were raised to the French Republic. According to one source, an officer present added "Long live the Ukrainian Republic." The whole matter merited an investigation by the tsarist police. It was against Ševčenko's association with the Zakrevs'kyj's that Repnina protested so much. She had good reason. For Ševčenko, an even greater attraction in Berezovi Rudky was Hanna Zakrevs'ka, the wife of Viktor's brother, Platon. The discovery of the deep affection which Ševčenko felt for this young married woman belongs to Marietta Šaginjan. In her study of Ševčenko she proved beyond any doubt that Ševčenko was deeply in love with Hanna Zakrevs'ka to whom he later dedicated some of his best love poems. In his relationship to women, which was warm and responsive, Ševčenko was the very opposite of Gogol'.

Sometime in July and August Ševčenko gave up visiting the Ukrainian gentry who were so anxious to see him and made a longer journey, probably on the Dnieper, to the very heart of Cossack history—the island of Xortycja, the former seat of the Zaporožian Sič. He also visited the historic towns of Čyhyryn and Subotiv, sketching on the way many old monuments. In his later works Ševčenko would return many times to the memories of this journey through the desolate steppes and past the ruins of Cossack glory. Ruins, that favourite theme of most Romantics, for him assumed a national significance.

At the end of August Ševčenko visited a Ukrainian scholar Platon Lukaševyč in the villate of Berezan'. From him he obtained news of the literary stirrings in Galicia. Respect for scholarship did not blind Ševčenko to Lukaševyč's cruel treatment of the peasants. In September Ševčenko finally reached his home village of Kyrylivka. The contrast between his life and the life of his family must have been very painful. He was determined to alleviate their lot and to help them out financially. In free moments he sketched his old house and drew a portrait of his grandfather Ivan who was still very much alive. Returning early in October to Berezan' he resumed writing, completing the poem **"Rozryta mohyla" (The Ransacked Grave)**. Its opening lines best express Ševčenko's mood:

> O gentle region, fair Ukraine,
> Dear beyond every other!
> Why are you plundered and despoiled,
> Why do you perish, mother?

From late October, 1843, to February, 1844, Ševčenko lived in Repnin's palace in Jahotyn, only occasionally travelling to neighbouring villages. He was commissioned to paint copies of Repnin's portrait by the Swiss artist Hornung. He spent his free time talking to Princess Barbara whom he called his "sister" in his poems, reading, reciting some poetry to enthusiastic guests, or just enjoying the hospitality of the gracious prince. The liberal atmosphere of Repnin's home was very congenial. It was no doubt then that Ševčenko became more closely acquainted with the ideas of the Decembrists. The house he stayed at harboured many memories of Sergej Volkonskij and his wife. Added to this was the Ukrainophilism of the old prince himself.

Another insight into what was going on at Jahotyn was provided by the Ukrainian landowner Selec'kyj, who was to compose an opera for which Ševčenko was to write a libretto. The subject on which all at first agreed was Mazepa, but soon the composer and the poet came to disagree when the former branded Mazepa as a "traitor." Ševčenko, apparently, insisted that Mazepa be represented as a fighter for liberty: besides he wanted to write the libretto in Ukrainian. No wonder that the project collapsed before it began.

When the time came to leave the Ukraine, Ševčenko was sorry to say goodbye to his new friends. During the eight months spent in his homeland, where he had been so warmly received, he had changed a great deal. Above all he was struck by the contrast between the comfortable life of the gentry and that of the serfs. The Ukraine he had dreamt about in St. Petersburg became real, too real. The rich and beautiful land was plundered by both Russian and Ukrainian exploiters. Several months later he wrote to Kuxarenko: "Last year I was in the Ukraine. I was at the Mežyhirs'kyj Spas [monastery]. I was on Xortycja; I went everywhere and cried all the time. Our Ukraine has been plundered by the goddam Germans and Russians, confound them."

On the other hand, Ševčenko met with an unusually friendly response and this convinced him that his poetry had admirers not only among the common people but among the gentry and the intellectuals. He was now preparing to speak to them more directly.

Back in St. Petersburg

On his way from the Ukraine to St. Petersburg Ševčenko stopped for a few days in Moscow. Here he met Ščepkin, the famous actor, who, like Ševčenko, was at one time a serf. Ševčenko and Ščepkin remained friends for life. Ševčenko also met the young Ukrainian historian, Osyp Bodjans'kyj and perhaps through him some leading Russian Slavophiles. But in his thoughts Ševčenko was preoccupied with the Ukraine, still under the fresh impact of the journey. It was in Moscow that he wrote the poem "Čyhyryne, Čyhyryne" (Čyhyryn, O Čyhyryn) dedicating it to Ščepkin. For the first time the poet's despair at the unhappy state of his country was drowned in an outburst of defiance.

> Do not rend, thoughts, do not burn!
> I shall bring back, may be,
> My truth, all fortuneless, my words
> Spoken quietly;
> Perhaps, indeed, I yet may forge
> A new blade from it, make a
> Keen new share for the old plough,
> And, sweating out the acres,
> Maybe I'll plow that fallow land
> And on the fallow, there
> I shall scatter all my tears
> Sow my heartfelt tears.
> Maybe they will shoot and grow
> Into two-edged blades
> That will cleave the evil, rotten
> Sickly heart, will drain
> From it all the poisoned blood,
> And in its place will pour
> Into it living Cossack blood
> Holy, clean and pure!

Back in St. Petersburg Ševčenko returned to the Academy from which he was anxious to graduate. He became sidetracked by the idea of publishing a series of etchings **"Živopisnaja Ukraina" (Pictorial Ukraine)** and from its sale getting enough money to purchase freedom for his brothers and sisters. Princess Barbara Repnina actively supported this plan which took up a great deal of Ševčenko's time and energy. At first he envisaged brief literary commentaries to accompany the etchings. He was going to ask Kuliš to write them. Later his plans changed and yet he persevered with them and in November, 1844, **"The Pictorial Ukraine"** was published. There is a strong historical emphasis in these etchings. The best known of them is the etching "The Gifts in Čyhyryn in 1649" depicting foreign envoys bringing presents to Bohdan Xmel'nyc'kyj when he was still a powerful leader of the "strong and free" Ukrainian people. Explanatory notes to the illustrations were in Russian and French. A second volume of the series was planned but never appeared. Ševčenko attached the greatest importance to this publication. In a letter to Certelev he wrote "If God will help me to complete what I have begun I would fold my hands and be ready for the coffin. I would have achieved enough; the Ukraine would not forget me."

The year 1844 saw the republication of the *Kobzar* and *Hajdamaky* (*Čigirinskij Kobzar' i Gaydamaki*) and the separate appearance of two poems written earlier, **"Hamalija"** and **"Tryzna" (Funeral Feast)**. The latter, strongly influenced by Ryleev, was dedicated to Barbara Repnina and therefore written in Russian. From the new poems written in that year in St. Petersburg,

one stands out prominently. It was entitled **"Son" (Dream)** and was not meant for publication.

"The Dream" is a political poem set in the complex form of a vision. Its purpose was to unmask and expose the workings of the Russian state system in the Ukraine. Ševčenko does this very skillfully by alternating lyrical passages with the most vehement satire of Russia and especially Nicholas I. The effect of this venomous ridicule is greater than anything Saltykov-Ščedrin and other later satirists of tsardom ever produced. Ševčenko's pen is like a merciless sword not sparing anything. **"The Dream"** is one of the most violent and effective attacks on tyranny. Here the rebellious peasant minces no words about the despotic tsar and his bureaucrats—his robust and straightforward expostulation is in the finest tradition of Romantic protest. Ultimately, the poem succeeds not so much because of its down-to-earth critical view of tsarism, but because of its overall design of exposing human unawareness of evil and the poet's concern with truth and justice. The social and political degradation of the country is made even darker by the contrast with its natural beauty. The poem which is called "a comedy" begins by retelling a dream in which the poet flies over the Ukraine.

> We fly . . . I look: the dawn is glimmering,
> The skyline is ablaze
> In a dark grove a nightingale
> Greets the sun with praise.
> A gentle breeze bows quietly
> The steppes, the cornfields glimmer,
> Among ravines, by lakes there gleams
> The green blush of the willows;
> Orchards bow down, richly laden,
> Poplars, standing straight
> Like sentinels, in the open land
> Are speaking with the plain.
> And all around me the whole country,
> Mantled round in beauty
> Shimmers green and bathes herself
> In the morning dew,
> From the dawn of time, she bathes
> Herself and greets the sun,
> There is nowhere a beginning
> Ending there is none.

All the more striking is the contrast when the poet turns aside to describe the life and conditions of the people. He finds that human rights are abused everywhere, "a poor widow is crucified for poll-tax" while her son is "handcuffed and put in the army." Somewhere, "under the fence a child, starved and swollen, is dying of hunger." Over there "a ruined girl limps footsore with her bastard." Even worse is the indifference with which these injustices and sufferings are accepted. In his Dante-like wanderings the poet then flies to the capital of the Empire. St. Petersburg, which inspired Gogol' to start a new literary theme in Russia—that of the nightmare city—is for Ševčenko without any charm or mystery. It is simply a "city on a bog, enveloped by a black cloud of heavy mist," a centre of Russia's power over the Ukraine. Puškin's bronze horseman is to Ševčenko "the one who crucified our Ukraine." The poet discovers that there are hundreds of Ukrainians in the city, all serving obediently their Russian masters. Then with bitter mockery he portrays the tsar and tsarina and their entourage "like fattened boars, big-mugged and bloated." Not only the present tsar is assailed and ridiculed, but so are his predecessors, in particular Peter the First and Catherine the Second, both responsible for the destruction of Ukrainian autonomy. The following lines are addressed to Peter:

> Accursed tsar, insatiate,
> Perfidious serpent, what
> Have you done, then, with the Cossacks?
> You have filled the swamps
> With their noble bones! And then
> Built the capital
> On their tortured corpses, and
> In a dark dungeon cell
> You slew me too, me a free Hetman,
> In chains, with hunger martyred! . . .

From there the poet returns to berate his fellow countrymen in Russia's service blaming them for the sufferings of the "childless widow Ukraine." His anger is that of a biblical prophet castigating sinners. The total effect of the poem, which ends abruptly like a dream, is very powerful. Never before had a Ukrainian raised his voice so loudly against Russia. Never before had this voice been of such poetic power. **"The Dream"** enjoyed clandestine circulation in hand-written copies and by word of mouth. It was found at the time of Ševčenko's arrest and contributed heavily to the harsh sentence meted out to the poet.

It was probably in 1844 that Ševčenko met some Russian revolutionaries (N. Mombelli, R. Štrandman), future members of the "Petraševskij circle." It is idle to speculate on the influence these men might have had on Ševčenko. Quite naturally he was attracted by kindred spirits, especially by the *Petraševcy* with their Fourierism and federalism, but as later, in his relation to Černyševskij, Ševčenko was rarely on the receiving end of revolutionary theories. He developed his convictions independently and was often in advance of people who supposedly influenced him. Not insensitive to the currents of the age, Ševčenko built his radicalism privately, with a very definite orientation which the Russian revolutionaries did not share. His concern with the Ukraine was unique in the intellectual history of the time and he was an almost Blake-like figure in his solitariness and vehemence. Ševčenko's art also bears a resemblance to Blake's. Both writers have a

visionary and prophetic quality, both represent man's existence as tragedy and find release in apocalyptic visions; both are mythopoeic poets.

Ševčenko's moods of dejection, in which he lamented his inability to reach the Ukrainian reader and to awaken him spiritually led him to write, in December, 1844, a poem in the form of an epistle to Gogol'. Although the message was never received, and the poem was first published in 1859, it reveals Ševčenko's attitude to Gogol'.

To Hohol'

> Thought follows thought, off in a swarm each
>   flits:
> One mauls the soul, one tears it all to bits,
> A third weeps gently, softly, deep concealed:
> Perhaps to God Himself it's not revealed.
>   To whom shall I unfold it?
>   By whom will it be heard—
>   This speech of mine, who will divine
>   The import of my Word?
>   All deaf and all indifferent,
>   In chains our people bend! . . .
>   You laugh full deep while I must weep,
>   My great and mighty friend!
>   What harvest yields my weeping?
>   Weeds it perchance may be.
>   No cannon roar now in Ukraine
>   With voice of liberty;
>   Nor will the father slay his son,
>   His own dear child with pain,
>   For honour, glory, brotherhood,
>   The freedom of Ukraine.
>   He'll rather rear him up to sell
>   To Moscow's slaughterhouse . . .
>   This is our tribute to "the throne"
>   (Our honour though they dowse),
>   Our offering to "the fatherland,"
>   A gift that Germans reap . . .
>   So let it be, my friend, while we
>   Still fiercely laugh and weep.

Why did Ševčenko write this poem dedicating it to Gogol'? The immediate stimulus might have come from watching Gogol's plays on the stage of the Alexandrinsky theatre in the fall of 1844. There is little doubt that Ševčenko did go to see them, even if it were just to admire the performance of his friend Ščepkin. Beyond that there is really no direct explanation as to why he suddenly thought of Gogol'. Obviously, rightly or wrongly Ševčenko considered him as a Ukrainian, concerned with the fate of his country. He wanted to emphasize the contrast between Gogol''s art and his own. Gogol' was to him in the first place a satirist and a humourist, while his own works he considered tragic lamentations ("You laugh . . . while I must weep"). One of Gogol''s works to which a direct reference is made in this poem is *Taras Bul'ba*. Ševčenko compares it to his own *Hajdamaky* whose hero killed his own sons, as Taras killed Andrej, for renouncing the Ukraine. Apart from this similarity the paths of the two writers had diverged. In Gogol''s laughter Ševčenko saw a criticism of Russia and therefore welcomed his countryman's "immortal" work. At the same time he was also letting him know of his own sorrows and lamentations which he poured out in his poetry. Therefore, in Ševčenko's view, the view of a Ukrainian writer, their aspirations were separate but complementary.

The only time on record when Ševčenko disapproved of Gogol' was in a passage in the *Artist* which tells of Gogol' sitting in Rome's Cafe Greco and "telling over his lunch the most obscene Little Russian anecdotes." In after years Ševčenko showed great admiration for Gogol''s works. While he saw a great deal of social satire in them (once he compared Gogol' to Saltykov-Ščedrin), he also sensed their universality. Writing to Barbara Repnina in 1850 from exile and recalling pleasanter days in Jahotyn, he declared: "I admire your present view of Gogol' and his immortal work. I am delighted that you have understood his truly Christian purpose. One should venerate Gogol as a man endowed with the profoundest mind and the most tender love for men . . . Our Gogol' is a true diviner of the human heart!"

Ševčenko's spirits rose considerably in January, 1845, when permission was obtained to put several Ukrainian plays on the stage of the Ukrainian amateur theater, manned by the students of the Medical and Surgical Academy. Among the plays was one by Ševčenko—*Nazar Stodolja*. In March Ševčenko completed his studies at the Imperial Academy of Fine Arts, having received the title of "artist." On March 25,1845, he obtained permission to travel to the Ukraine "for artistic pursuits." He left St. Petersburg and after a few days in Moscow, travelled south to the Ukraine.

Second Ukrainian Journey

This time Ševčenko's itinerary was dictated by commissions received from various landowners to paint portraits. This brought him once again into contact with the Ukrainian gentry among whom he found many admirers. At the same time he could not help noticing the cruel conditions of serfdom. After all, Ševčenko, unlike most of the intelligentsia, was not merely observing these conditions; he had had direct experience of them from childhood. Occasionally he would visit old friends, such as Barbara Repnina in Jahotyn who was then mourning her father's death. In June he visited Kiev briefly and obtained a position on the Temporary Commission for the Study of Antiquities, which authorized him to travel across the Ukraine and sketch historical monuments. For the time being this was an ideal occupation. The entire summer was taken up by travelling and sketching through the districts of Zvenyhorod, Pryluky, Romny, Myrhorod, Lubny and Perejaslav. In September he again visited his home village Kyrylivka. There he proposed to the daughter of the neighbouring priest, Košyc', for whom he used to work as a little boy. The girl liked Ševčenko but her parents would not agree to a marriage. In October Ševčenko stayed for a longer time at the village of Marjans'ke with the landowner Lukjanovyč. There he wrote a poem **"Jeretyk" (The Heretic)** dedicating it to the great Czech scholar of Slovak origin Pavel Šafařik.

"The Heretic" is Ševčenko's first major poem on a non-Ukrainian topic. The idea for it came from his conversations with Bodjans'kyj who at that time was the foremost authority on Bohemia in Russia. Bodjans'kyj had written a study *O narodnoj poezii slovjanskix plemen* (On Folk Poetry of Slavic Races, 1837) in which he dwelt on the Hussite wars, and had also translated Šafařik's works into Russian. Bodjans'kyj's student, Palauzov, wrote a separate study of John Huss and his successors (1845). The heretic in Ševčenko's poem is John Huss, the Czech reformer who under Wycliffe's influence rebelled against Papal authority and was subsequently burnt at the stake. In the poem, as in history, the account of Huss's struggle against the Papacy merges with Czech strivings for national liberation from the Germans. Once again for Ševčenko the cause of national liberation was seen in the wider framework of a struggle for human rights.

In the introduction dedicated to Šafařik Ševčenko stresses the Pan-Slavic ideals which were then very much in vogue. However, Ševčenko emphasizes the equality of all Slavs and directly challenges the dream of those Russians who took for granted that the answer to Puškin's question "will Slavic streams flow into a Russian sea?" was yes. For Ševčenko this sea is clearly "Slavic and new," not Russian. There is some evidence that Ševčenko later sent a copy of his poem to Šafařik who was very moved by it. Ševčenko liked to dedicate his poems to his friends or to those to whom he owed a debt of gratitude. It is interesting that in selecting a mentor he turned to a Czech.

Very soon after writing **"The Heretic"** Ševčenko turned once more to his favourite topic—Ukrainian history. His view had undergone considerable change since the earliest poems which glorified the Cossacks. After two visits to the Ukraine he became convinced that the Cossack leadership was in part to blame for the loss of independence. He then dedicated himself to a searching and critical exploration of Ukrainian history and came up with new and startling discoveries. This reconsideration of the Ukrainian past was carried out independently. Very often Ševčenko went against the popular views expressed by some of his historian friends.

In the allegorical poem **"Velykyj l'ox" (The Great Vault)** which after the medieval drama genre he called a "mystery," Ševčenko examined several turning points of Ukrainian history and gave his interpretation of their consequences. He did this in a strikingly original poetic form, reminiscent of his earlier poem **"The Dream,"** by using symbolic imagery and the distortion of reality. In the first part of the poem three souls are barred from heaven because of their sins. The first soul suffers because she crossed the path of Xmel'nyc'kyj with full pails of water (thus bringing him luck) when he was riding to Perejaslav to make an alliance with Russia. The second soul is barred from heaven because she watered the Russian tsar's horse when he ruined Mazepa's stronghold at Baturyn. The third soul's sin is that she smiled on Tsarina Catherine when she sailed down the Dnieper. The meaning of this allegory is quite clear. Ševčenko blamed the Ukrainians for supporting Xmel'nyc'kyj's alliance with Russia, he deplored the lack of support to Mazepa and, finally, he considered the reign of Catherine the Second as another tragic event in the Ukraine. There follows the exchange between three crows, one Ukrainian, one Polish and one Russian. They represent the evil forces in these nationalities. The Ukrainian crow symbolizes those Ukrainians who in the course of history helped the enemies of the Ukraine. The last part depicts three minstrels. It is generally agreed that they represent the impotent and spineless Ukrainian intellectuals, unable to protect the best interests of their country. The ending is optimistic. The Ukrainian vault which Moscow tried to uncover remains untouched. It keeps the vital energies of the people which will one day come into the open and restore freedom for the Ukraine. This optimism is even more clearly evident in the short poem **"Stojit' v seli Subotovi" (There Stands in the Village of Subotiv)** written soon after **"The Great Vault"** and representing a kind of epilogue to it.

> That church beneath the skies
> May crumble down, but from its vaults
> A new Ukraine will rise
> To end the night of slavery;
> Injustice will be gone;
> Our serf-born sons' orisons
> Will greet sweet Freedom's dawn.

Soviet critics of Ševčenko had a great deal of trouble in interpreting **"The Great Vault."** Nowadays they grudgingly admit that Ševčenko lacked the "correct" understanding of the Russian-Ukrainian union, but console themselves that he was opposed to tsarism and not to the Russian people. The figure of Bohdan Xmel'nyc'kyj, the chief architect of Ukrainian-Russian understanding remains odious to Ševčenko till the end. He regarded him as a "rebel of genius," but could never forgive him the treaty of Perejaslav. On the other hand, Ševčenko sympathised with the anti-Russian

het'mans Mazepa and Dorošenko. Politically, Ševčenko was clearly on the side of Ukrainian independence from Russia.

This in itself represented a revolution in Ukrainian thought. The eighteenth century notions of the inseparability of Great and Little Russia and of loyalty to the Russian tsar as the supreme duty of Ukrainians were discarded. Instead, Ševčenko called the tsar a tyrant and pointed to the right of his people to form their own national destiny. It is not without some significance for this particular study that Ševčenko wrote **"The Great Vault"** in Myrhorod, a town which ten years earlier (1835) served as the title for Gogol's stories about the Ukraine, poetic, idyllic and decaying but never nationally self-conscious (not even in *Taras Bul'ba*). The contrast between Gogol"s and Ševčenko's Ukraine could not be greater.

Ševčenko's continued concern with the meaning and direction of Ukrainian history was a severe limitation to his universality. National freedom was to him the basis of universal freedom. Today this assumption is no longer of direct relevance to most countries in the Western World. In Ševčenko's own time as well as in ours in the "underdeveloped countries" of the world this was and still is a vital problem. If Ševčenko's patriotism did not go beyond the defense of Ukrainian independence he could rightly be classed as a nationalist and his concept of freedom as parochial. However, combined with this fierce patriotism was a profound and everpresent concern for justice and charity among men. The fight for the future of his country could be won, he believed, only in a bigger battle between good and evil in the soul of man. Ševčenko's nationalism belongs, historically, to the first stages of that movement, when it was motivated by liberal and universalist ideals and had nothing in common with the later bigoted variety.

In his travels Ševčenko went through much of Gogol's country. On October 23, 1845, he wrote to a friend from Myrhorod:

> Since I arrived in Mirgorod I have not once left my room and to crown everything there is nothing to read. If it weren't for the Bible I would go mad. I caught a bad chill coming from Xorol and believe it or not famous Mirgorod has no doctor or pharmacy. The city hospital is located on the main street. As far as Mirgorod is concerned Gogol' is quite right, but it is strange that his observant eye has not noticed one very interesting detail. The officials, having finished their daily duties in the rural and district courts, journey in a group for about ten versts to a free sale of vodka and having drunk eight times return to their homes to dinner. Quite original, isn't it?

From Myrhorod Ševčenko visited Gogol's Vasylivka and there painted a watercolour of the local church.

Later he went to see his old friend Viktor Zakrevs'kyj and at the end of October, feeling quite ill, stopped at the house of another friend, Kozačkovs'kyj, in Perejaslav. Here he stayed for two months and wrote the poems **"Najmyčka" (The Servant Girl)** and **"Kavkaz" (The Caucasus)**. He dedicated the latter to Jakiv de Bal'men, a Ukrainian landowner of French origin, a good friend and admirer of the poet. Earlier that year de Bal'men was killed while a member of a Russian military expedition to the Caucasus. His death in the hated cause of Russian conquest of the free peoples of the Caucasus prompted Ševčenko to write the poem. It contains some of the strongest declarations of self-determination of nations Ševčenko ever wrote. Characteristically, Prometheus becomes the symbol of oppressed peoples who in the Russian Empire "from the Moldavians to the Finns are silent in every tongue." Russian imperialism is ridiculed with extreme sarcasm.

> We are the enlightened! Now
> We bring the radiant sun,
> Reveal the blessed light of truth
> To sightless little ones.
> Come to us, and all you ought
> To know will be made plain:
> Prison buildings will be taught,
> How to forge your chains,
> How to wear then, how the knout
> Is plaited—we'll explain
> All our science. Only yield
> Your dark-blue mountains, please—
> They alone defy us now,
> We hold the plains and seas!

A copy of the poem Ševčenko sent through a friend to Adam Mickiewicz in Paris. Ševčenko was familiar with Mickiewicz's works and was influenced by his *Dziady* (The Ancestors). A contemporary of Ševčenko recorded that the Ukrainian poet "felt a special affection for Mickiewicz." There is some artistic kinship between the two poets which shows itself especially strongly in the prophetic tone of their works. The influence of Polish political and patriotic literature emanating from the circle of Lelewel was even greater. Ščurat has conclusively demonstrated Ševčenko's great debt to these Polish sources. Several of Ševčenko's Polish friends were members of revolutionary societies in St. Petersburg.

Ševčenko's greatest prophecy is contained in the poem **"I mertvym, i žyvym, i nenarodženym zemljakam mojim v Ukrajini i ne v Ukrajini moje družnjeje poslanije" (To My Fellow Countrymen, in the Ukraine and Not in the Ukraine, Living, Dead and as yet Unborn My Friendly Epistle)**, written on December 14, 1845. For a change the poet turns his back on the past and looks at the present and the future. He speaks directly to his contemporaries and implores them to be human or else to suffer the terrible

consequences of their wickedness. His prime target is the Ukrainian landowning gentry whom he mercilessly satirizes. In his two journeys through the Ukraine he had met many of these liberals who cared little about the lot of their serfs and whose only ambition was to serve Moscow well. In the poem he lashes out against social injustice and against the intellectual hypocrisy of the gentry. Their chief error was that they had forsaken the Ukraine and had accepted a foreign (Russian) culture. Therefore, even the fine ideas of Westernism or Slavophilism are empty in the mouths of Russified Ukrainians who do not know the value of their native culture. Uncritical glorification of Ukrainian history is meaningless, for only objective historical research can clarify the issues for the future. Above all, Ševčenko was concerned with the gap between the Ukrainian people (peasantry) on the one hand, and the gentry and the intellectuals on the other. He calls on them to unite and to embrace each other in love and mutual respect. The alternative is terrible to contemplate. If the present social divisions continue there will break out a revolution which will destroy everything. Ševčenko hopes that the popular uprising can be averted, that the different classes of Ukrainian society may yet find harmony. For this, however, it is necessary to see reality as it is and make immediate and drastic changes. The form of this "epistle" is very striking. The style of Biblical exhortation ideally fits the content of the poem.

The end of 1845 was an unusually productive period in Ševčenko's life. He was writing a new poem practically every week. Immersed in creative work he was approaching an exalted mood in which his innermost thoughts came to be expressed with unusual clarity and ease. These thoughts concerned the Ukraine, but they were generated by an outlook on life that knew no national boundaries. Despite and perhaps because of his anti-clerical sallies Ševčenko's outlook was deeply religious. Ševčenko's most inspired lines almost always relate to the meaning of Christian fraternity (*bratoljubije*), the betrayal of the true God and the unconquerable power of love—*caritas*. All these are present in his adaptations of the Psalms of David (**"Psalmy Davydovi"**) completed on December 19, 1845. They lent themselves ideally to expressing Ševčenko's sombre mood of rebellion and evangelism. The Hebrew idea of God revealing himself as a moral force in history was successfully adapted by the poet to his native conditions. Ševčenko's predisposition towards religious sentiments was noticed by his contemporaries. Vasyl'Bilozers'kyj in a letter to Mykola Hulak, on May 6, 1846, wrote:

> Yesterday Ivan Posjada was here and told me that Ševčenko had written a new poem—**"John Huss"**. I could not help thinking what a man of genius we have in Taras Grigorievič. Only a genius, through deep sympathy, can guess the needs of the people

and of the whole age, which will not be revealed by science without poetic and religious fire. How much I hope that the translation of the Psalms will contain evidence of a truly happy spiritual mood in our Minstrel. Our literature then would be refreshed by a new sense of life and confirmed on true foundations.

A week after completing **"The Psalms of David"** Ševčenko was taken seriously ill and in fear of the approaching end he wrote the stirring stanzas of his **"Zapovit" (Testament).** In spite of the fact that this poem has become something like a national anthem of the Ukraine, it has great artistic merit and is the crowning achievement of the "three year" cycle, begun in 1843, where it occupies the last place.

> When I die, then make my grave
> High on an ancient mound
> In my own beloved Ukraine,
> In steppeland without bound;
> Whence one may see wide-skirted wheatland,
> Dnipro's steep-cliffed shore,
> There whence one may hear the blustering
> River wildly roar.
>
> Till from Ukraine to the blue sea
> It bears in fierce endeavour
> The blood of foemen—then I'll leave
> Wheatland and hills forever:
> Leave all behind, soar up until
> Before the throne of God
> I'll make my prayer. But till that hour
> I shall know naught of God.
>
> Make my grave there—and arise,
> Sundering your chains,
> Bless your freedom with the blood
> Of foemen's evil veins!
> Then in that great family,
> A family new and free
> Do not forget, with good intent
> Speak quietly of me.

Ševčenko's role in Ukrainian literature can hardly be overstressed. He was its true founder, because for the first time in his work the Ukrainian language achieved literary excellence. His place in Ukrainian intellectual history is even more striking. It marks a clear watershed in the development of ideas. Ševčenko's poems expressed boldly the national self-awareness in terms never used before. "The whole subsequent development of Ukrainian nationalism," writes an English historian, "derives from Ševčenko's poetry." If by nationalism is meant an assertion of basic human rights (social, national, cultural and linguistic) then by that definition Ševčenko was a nationalist. His demands for social justice and national self-expression amounted to a declaration of independence. His call to "sunder the chains" was revolutionary. But side by side with revolution Ševčenko advocates regeneration which in his later works was to gain ascendancy.

All this was new and startling. At first it found response only in a small circle of Ševčenko's friends, for the simple reason that his political poems remained in manuscript. To a wider public he was known primarily through his published works as an author of ballads, lyrics and historical poems. His political poems were copied by hand and remained unpublished till the 1860's (in some cases the first complete texts did not appear in print until after the 1905 revolution). Yet their influence was profound. They became the credo of the Ukrainian intelligentsia and found, as Ševčenko had hoped, "an open heart" among the people. For the time being Ševčenko's influence grew stronger as his ideas spread. They encountered opposition from those of his countrymen who found him too radical and refused to accept his belief that Ukrainian readers should demand Ukrainian literature. This appeared to some to be a deliberate narrowing of cultural horizons, a form of parochialism. No doubt the spirit of the ghetto was also aroused. It remained to be seen in what direction the Ukrainian movement would grow. It could remain defensive and narrow, but it could also unfold and mellow.

George G. Grabowicz (essay date 1980)

SOURCE: "A Study of the Deep Structures in Shevchenko's Works," in *Shevchenko and the Critics: 1861-1980,* edited by George S. N. Luckyj, translated by Dolly Ferguson and Sophia Yurkevich, University of Toronto Press, 1980, pp. 481-94.

[*In the following essay, Grabowicz claims that the duality in Shevchenko's poetry, which has led to contrary interpretations, stems from his attempts to mediate between the Ukrainian past and future.*]

Beginning with the first ambivalent reactions in the Russian press to the first edition of the **Kobzar** of 1840, and shortly thereafter with the more analytical studies of Kulish and Kostomarov, the critical genre now known as *Shevchenkoznavstvo* came to occupy an ever more prominent role in Ukrainian life. The critical, scholarly, panegyrical, ideological, and polemical attention devoted to Shevchenko and his writings has been immense—and immensely diverse. Some considerable results have been achieved, particularly in textual studies (including, of course, publication of the entire canon of Shevchenko's works and many facsimile editions), in historical and biographical documentation, in matters of prosody, poetic language, and some formal analyses. On the other hand, the meaning and the broader social, historical (and, need one add, political) implications of Shevchenko's work, specifically his poetry, have been and remain the source of intense

and acrimonious differences. The ideologically polarized interpretations of the present day, with each side
accusing the other of 'falsifying Shevchenko,' not only
reflect the peculiarity of the Ukrainian political situation but in fact are also a logical culmination of the
entire critical legacy. In a deeper sense, however, these
divergences stem from the very nature of Shevchenko's poetry.

It is a poetry that touched the innermost core of the
Ukrainian experience. In the words of Mykola Kostomarov, 'Shevchenko's muse sundered the veil
of national life. It was terrifying and sweet and
painful and fascinating to peer inside.' Panteleimon Kulish, himself a tragic and fascinating individual, who was at once a continuator and exegete,
rival and opponent of Shevchenko, put it even more
directly in his eloquent funeral oration in St Petersburg. 'None of us is worthy,' he said, 'to speak our
native Ukrainian word over the grave of Shevchenko: all the power and all the beauty of our language were revealed only to him alone. And yet it
is through him that we have the great and precious
right to proclaim the native Ukrainian word in
this distant land.' It was Kulish who said that
'Shevchenko is our great poet and our first historian. It was Shevchenko who was the first to ask our
mute burial mounds what they are, and it was only
to him that they gave their answer, clear as God's
word. Before all others Shevchenko realized what
the glory of our antiquity is and what it will be
cursed for by coming generations.' As eloquent and
true as these statements were, their implicit thesis—swelled in time by various less profound commentaries—soon gave rise to a mass of misconceptions. In a word, because of its unprecedented emotional directness and immediacy Shevchenko's poetry, his 'message,' was seen as essentially straightforward, indeed simple. Hand in hand with the growing cult of Shevchenko, his poetic *oeuvre* came to
be viewed as a convenient repository of handy bits
of sentiment:

> Selo! i sertse odpochyne.
> Sela na nashii Ukraini—
> Nenache pysanka selo . . .

> A village! and the heart will rest / A village in our
> Ukraine / A village like an Easter egg . . .

or of pious pedagogic injunctions:

> Uchites, chytaite,
> I chuzhomu nauchaites,
> I svoho ne tsuraites . . .

> Study, read, / Learn foreign subjects / But do not
> deny your own . . .

or of political prescriptions:

> . . . Koly
> My dizhdemosia Vashingtona
> Z novym i pravednym zakonom?

> When / Shall we see a Washington / With a new
> and just law?

or:

> V svoii khati svoia i pravda,
> I syla, i volia . . .

> In one's own house—one's own truth / And power
> and freedom . . .

or finally of revolutionary calls to arms:

> Pokhovaite ta vstavaite,
> Kaidany porvite
> I vrazhoiu zloiu kroviu
> Voliu okropite.

> Bury me and rise, / Break your chains / And with
> the enemy's evil blood / Sprinkle your freedom.

Most significantly, the practice of rifling the poetry for
the appropriate *sententia* was not confined to propagan-
dists, journalists, or school teachers—it also became the
methodology for much of what passed as scholarship. By
far the worst offenders were the engagé ideologues whose
only method of discussing, for example, Shevchenko's
alleged atheism or conversely his religiosity and piety,
was simply the culling of citations to be interpreted by
free association. In the absence of any rigorous and comprehensive method for dealing with the levels of meaning
and symbolism in Shevchenko's works, the study of
Shevchenko's writings became increasingly moribund—
both in the Soviet Union and in the West. In fact, it was
only the rare and outstanding scholar who ventured to
remind his colleagues that the fundamental issues had
still not been confronted. Such, for example, was the
dean of Soviet Ukrainian literary scholars, Oleksander
Biletsky, who at the ninth Shevchenko Conference held
in 1960 in Leningrad, in a period of relative thaw, attempted to curb various endemic forms of vulgarization
and inanity—and redirect the efforts of Soviet *Shevchenkoznavstvo*. In the West, specifically in the emigration,
the opportunity for free intellectual inquiry did not galva-
nize Ukrainian scholarship, and the Shevchenko scholarship that was undertaken was in its literary-critical conceptions and methods essentially parallel to, if not imitative of, what was being done in the Soviet Union; sadly,
no new approaches were forthcoming. Perhaps the single
exception was the *Symposium* published in 1962 under
the editorship of Miiakovsky and Shevelov, which contained a number of fine articles. From our perspective
the most provocative was the one by the late Mykola

Shlemkevych which proposed to deal with 'The Substratum of Shevchenko's View of Life' through a kind of Jungian depth psychology. The various insights presented here, however, were made rather on the basis of intuition than on scholarly method or mode of analysis; indeed—very revealingly—he doubted whether such investigations could readily be made the stuff of scholarship.

To sum up this brief summary, it is clear that there exists in modern Shevchenko scholarship (albeit still in a limited way) the understanding that Shevchenko's imaginative universe is highly symbolic and coded, and that beneath the surface structures—which I take to encompass not only such matters as ideology and in general the whole sphere of rational elaborations, programs, and so on, but also such things as conventions, that is literary romantic conventions—there are much more important deep structures. However, the deep structures and the symbolic code in which they are couched, have not been investigated at all. And it is to this that I wish to address myself.

The first issue to which we come, which is at the same time the most basic structure in Shevchenko's creativity, concerns the context, or rather the *placing in context* of the various forms and modes of his expression. It flows from the fundamental holistic premise that systematic analysis must deal with the whole of the phenomenon. Shevchenko, as everyone knows, *is* what he is by virtue of his poetic production, his Ukrainian poetry; but what many (including scholars) tend to gloss over, and many more probably indeed do not know, is that this is a segment—in quantitative terms a smaller segment—of his whole self-expression. In addition to the Ukrainian poetry, with which he is so often exclusively identified, Shevchenko also wrote some Russian poetry (two long poems), a considerable body of prose in Russian (by his own account about twenty novellas, of which nine have survived), a diary written in Russian that covers a crucial year of his life, a sizeable epistolary legacy in Ukrainian and Russian, a few prose fragments in Ukrainian, three or four dramas in Russian (of which two have survived, one in prose, in a Ukrainian translation probably made by Kulish, and an unfinished one in verse), and a large body of pictorial art—paintings, drawings, and etchings, which while certainly pertinent to the overall question, will not concern us here.

One need not be a scholar and a specialist but only an informed and sensitive reader to see that there is a profound difference between the Ukrainian poetry on the one hand, and on the other all the other forms of expression. Let us provisionally call these the two basic categories in question. Leaving aside for the moment the obviously different mode of nonbelletristic writings (letters, etc.) one could simply say that the difference between the two categories hinges on aesthetic and artistic quality—and the lack of it: where the Ukrainian poetry

is powerful and moving and very often great, the other writings are often only good and frequently mediocre. While true, this does not suffice as an answer. For the task now is not to evaluate the works or categories in question but to determine their essential differences, their mode of existence, as it were. Ultimately, the aesthetic and artistic values are based on these differences.

One possible immediate answer is that the difference here is one of poetry and prose. Closer analysis, however, shows that while there is considerable consistency, this is not the basis for the fundamental divergences in question. One could show, for example, that various pieces of Shevchenko's Ukrainian prose, such as his postscript to the *Haidamaky,* or the preface to the unpublished second *Kobzar,* or fragments of various letters, are much closer to the spirit of his Ukrainian poetry than is the Russian poem *Trizna* (**The Wake**). This, of course, leads us to the most obvious and most frequently noted basis of differentiation, namely language. There is a whole critical legacy, going back to Kulish and still favoured by the rationalistically minded, that sees between Shevchenko's Ukrainian- and Russian-language works the basic division in his entire canon; it is, of course, explicitly evaluative (not to say biased), and, taking its cue from a statement made by Shevchenko himself in one of his letters where he castigated himself for confessing to the Russians in stale Russian ('spovidaiusia katsapam cherstvym katsapskym slovom . . .'), it sees all of Shevchenko's Russian writings as inherently flawed (if not a betrayal of his Muse) by the very choice of linguistic medium. Even more than the opposition of poetry and prose, this language criterion has validity: the Ukrainian works are strikingly different from, and as a rule greatly superior to the Russian ones. But this criterion as well does not provide the solution, for two reasons. One is the exceptions that undercut the whole equation: the Russian poem **'Slepaia'** (**The Blind Woman**) or the fragments of **'Nikita Gaidai'** are much closer to the spirit of the Ukrainian poetry than some of the Ukrainian letters. Similarly, we have the problem posed by the *Diary*—a work that is manifestly excellent and intimate—but is written in Russian. The other and much more important reason, however, is that merely stating (and then evaluating) the existence of these two classes of works leaves the entire question open: we are left no wiser as to what is and what can be said in the given medium, as to what is the structure of the respective contents of these two categories. This is precisely the task at hand.

Before turning to it I should like to adduce the following to illustrate my argument. As everyone who reads him knows, Shevchenko's poetry is highly personal, intimate, and autobiographical; if one deciphers the code of the narrative and 'political' poems, then, as we shall see, the autobiographical element appears to be virtually ever-present. But if we look at what is actually portrayed or alluded to, a most fascinating picture develops, for we see that whole segments of Shevchenko's life, indeed most of his mature life, remain outside the range of his poetry. There is, for example, no reference at all to his life in St Petersburg and the Academy of Arts (which as we know from his own novel *Khudozhnik* (**The Artist**) were so important to him), no reference to the time spent in Ukraine and his many contacts with the Ukrainians, especially the Brotherhood of Saints Cyril and Methodius, in fact no reference even to the momentous event of being freed from serfdom. The only apparent exceptions to this are the first years of exile and the last months of his life; on closer analysis, however, the exile poems are not an exception, and the very late poetry is also quite ambivalent in this regard. The issue is not even so much one of chronology, of time gaps, as of subject matter, of content. We know from Shevchenko's own writings—the autobiographical novels, the *Diary,* the letters—and from numerous other sources, such as the memoirs and letters of friends and acquaintances—of the kind of life he lived, not only in St Petersburg, in Kiev, in his travels in Ukraine, but indeed (and *mutatis mutandis*) at times even in exile, that is, in the first two years in Orenburg. It was the active, intense, and full life of a young artist and littérateur; it was full of social and intellectual contacts, of literary salons, theatres, and the opera. It was the life of an attractive young man accepted in the highest society, esteemed and in fact lionized by both Russians and Ukrainians. Given Shevchenko's origins this was, in a word, a remarkable success story. And yet literally none of this is reflected in his poetry. The only thing more remarkable than this massive 'blind spot' of his poetic creativity is the blindness of generations of Shevchenko scholars to this crucial situation.

Now, I believe, we *can* define the basic duality in Shevchenko's creativity. It is a duality, an opposition, that rests on two very different creative stances, different self-perceptions and self-definitions, and entirely different intellectual and emotional modes of expression. In fact, one should not speak here of different stances, or styles, but of different personalities. Although I shall briefly refer to the psychoanalytic dimension in Shevchenko's creativity, I do not want this structure to be reduced solely to the psychoanalytic level, to an ego-split, or dissociation. For one, there is considerable interplay, in terms of common themes and values, as in *Nai-mychka* (**The Servant Girl**), the poem and the novella, or '**Kniazhna**' (**The Princess**), and *Kniaginia* (**The Princess**); for another there are elements involved other than the purely psychological. The two entities are not hermetic, but they *are* radically different.

What are these two personalities? One, which is represented by the Russian prose, the *Diary,* the letters, and so on is what I would call the adjusted. Even

while speaking out most forcefully against the inequities of the social order, above all the unspeakable outrage of serfdom, it manifestly sees itself as part of the imperial reality, and shares many of the civilized, progressive values of this society. The basic defining features of this mode are a sense of intellectual distance (for example, with respect to Ukrainian history), a sense of perspective on the role of Ukraine vis-à-vis the Russian Empire, and on the role and efficacy of the artist (for example, in the novels *Khudozhnik,* or *Muzykant* [**The Musician**]), a rational and basically measured perception of human behaviour, and, not least, the point of view of the mature self.

The other, represented primarily by the poetry, is what I would call, for want of a better term, the non-adjusted self. Shevchenko himself felt full well the power of this side of his ego, which in his *Diary* he saw as being animated by a 'strange and restless calling,' but he made no attempt to analyse it. We, however, can do so. This personality is marked above all by an intense emotionality, and of the emotional perception of reality, which in consequence becomes totally or almost totally polarized into the sacred and the profane. In its sharpest form the world, mankind, is often divided into absolute good and absolute evil. But the poet himself is so polarized: he or his persona is either the victim, one of the lowly and despised—the bastard, the blind, vagabond minstrel, the fallen woman (the *pokrytka*)—or even the moral reprobate (see, for example, the poem 'chy to nedolia ta nevolia . . .' / 'Is it ill fate and captivity . . .'), or he is the martyr and the prophet, the last hope of his nation. Significantly, there is hardly any middle ground: there is, rather, the apotheosis, again of the sacred and the profane. In contrast to the adjusted and the rational, this mode refuses to accept and abide by the truths and wisdoms of this world; it conjures up and revives the past that for everyone else is dead. But he wills it alive, as he says in the opening lines of '**Chernets**' (**The Monk**):

> U Kyievi na Podoli
> Bulo kolys . . . i nikoly
> Ne vernetsia, shcho diialos
> Ne vernetsia spodivane
> Ne vernetsia . . . A ia, brate,
> Taky budu spodivatys,
> Taky budu vyhliadaty,
> Zhaliu sertsiu zavdavaty . . .

> In Kiev, in the Podil / There once was . . . and what occurred / Will never return / What was hoped for will not return / Will not return . . . and yet, brother, / I will continue to hope, / I will continue to expect, / To inflict sorrow on my heart . . .

It is a mode that relies on visions to convey the past and the future, and when it turns to the present it does not present [reality], but rather the depths of the whole collective soul, as he says,

. . . nevchene oko
Zahliane . . . v samu dushu
Hlyboko! hlyboko!

. . . the untutored eye / Will look deep, deep into
the very soul!

From the chronological or biographical point of view
there is also a radical difference, for in contrast to the
mature, man-of-the-world narrator and authorial ego
of the novels, for example, the perspective of the authorial ego here is moulded—not equivalent to but
moulded—by the child and the old man. Indeed, he at
times explicitly conflates the two, as in the wonderful
exile lyric 'A numo znovu virshuvat . . .'/ 'So let us
versify again . . .' where he conjures up the grey-
whiskered child:

. . . bach, shcho [dolia] narobyla:
Kynula maloho
Na rozputti, ta i baiduzhe,
A vono ubohe,
Molodeie, syvouse,—
Zvychaine, dytyna—
I podybalo tykhenko
Popid chuzhym tynom
Azh za Ural. Opynylos
V pustyni, v nevoli . . .

. . . see what [fate] has done: / She abandoned the
little one / At the crossroads, and she doesn't care,
/ And it is poor, / Young, grey-whiskered,—/ Just
a child—/ And quietly it dragged itself / Along
someone's fence / Beyond the Urals. It arrived / In
the desert, in captivity . . .

In the sense that the world of the poetry is moulded
primarily by the experiences and emotions of childhood (cf. for example, *Haidamaky*) (a childhood moreover that contains the principal narrative model of the
minstrel-kobzar) we can speak of it—descriptively, not
evaluatively—as regressed. This regression, however,
is the source of the poetry's imaginative power and the
foundation of its symbolic code. Again it is the power
of this unadjusted, rebelling personality that must be
stressed, for its effects are clearly visible to this day.
For in contravention of the real state of affairs, and the
large body of evidence that buttresses it, the picture
now in the minds of millions of his countrymen, and
indeed of many scholars, is that projected by Shevchenko's poetry: of Shevchenko the martyr and prophet
living only in and for his *narod*. This has become the
real Shevchenko. As the Parisian structuralists would
say, he has become the product of his own myth.

My awareness of the fundamental dichotomy in
Shevchenko's writings allows me to posit, perhaps for
the first time with some rigour, a frame work for dealing with the symbolic code of his poetry. Two basic
lines of inquiry are possible, corresponding to the two
basic levels of the code. One is the psychoanalytic,
which deals above all with the author's symbolic autobiography. One can hardly offer conclusions or sum-
maries without reconstructing a rather complex analysis, and for this reason I shall leave this for another
occasion. Instead I propose to turn to the other level of
the code, that of mythical structures. It must be stressed
that the parallel existence of a psychoanalytic, that is,
a personal—symbolically autobiographical—and a
mythical, collective system of coding constitutes the
second basic deep structure, which we now see as
contained in the poetry itself.

Let me now summarize what I mean by mythical thinking, by the mythical organization of thought and experience. It is a mode that moves from structures to events:
one starts with a structure, which in the case of Shevchenko is a sense, an understanding, a deeply felt 'truth' of,
say, the nature of Ukrainian existence, and from this
one creates or adapts various events or figures, for example an archetypal Cossack, or a purported historical
event. Mythical thought is the opposite of rational, analytical, historical thought, which takes a discrete body
of data, that is, events, and by analysis and deduction
sees a pattern or meaning or structure in them. (Mythical and rational thought can co-exist, however, in the
thinking of the individual and the group.) Moving as it
does from structure to event, myth can generate any
number of narratives, all of which convey the same basic
structure or 'truth.' What in Shevchenko has traditionally been called history is in fact myth—the portrayal of
the Ukrainian past—but with almost no regard for chronology, or dates, or concrete events or figures. Above
all in myth, things are telescoped; we see this highlighted in a number of poems, in *Velykyi lokh* (**The Great
Vault**), in *Chyhryne, Chyhryne,* and perhaps most strikingly in the poem *Slipyi (Nevolnyk)* (**The Blind Man
[The Captive]**) which apparently in the lifetime of the
title character encompasses the whole history of Cos-
sackdom, from the sea raids against Turkey in the sixteenth century, to the destruction of the Sich and the
creation of the Zadunaiska Sich in the late eighteenth
century. A different kind of telescoping occurs in *Haidamaky,* where in contravention of historical fact, but
because of the requirement of the structure, the haidamaks, the peasant rebels, are identified with Cossacks,
which is a very different kind of thing.

Myth, and Shevchenko's is a quintessential example,
operates on the emotional level; it is this which allows
it to be understood by the mass of the audience—for
it is geared to them, not the thoughtful or learned individual. Here is the very core of the difference between Shevchenko and Kulish, for the latter, in his
novel *Chorna rada* (The Black Council), intended to
present history rationally and even analytically; and it
is not surprising that Kulish's work did not have even
a fraction of the resonance of Shevchenko's so-called
historical poems.

Shevchenko's poetry may be classified according to three different formal modes of presentation: (1) the tribunitial and prophetic poems, for example, **'Poslaniie' (I mertvym i zhyvym . . .) (Epistle [To the Dead and the Living])**, **'Kavkaz' (The Caucasus)**, **'Prorok' (The Prophet)**, the paraphrases of the Old Testament Prophets, and so on; (2) the intimate or 'purely lyrical' short poems, many written during exile, and (3) the longer narrative poems. The latter group, including such poems as **'Kateryna,' 'Haidamaky,' 'Vidma' (The Witch), 'Kniazhna' (The Princess), 'Slipyi' (The Blind Man), 'Moskaleva krynytsia' (The Soldier's Well)** (both versions), **'Tytarivna' (The Sexton's Daughter), 'Mariia,'** and others, is by far more complex and in one sense more interesting, but, significantly, the least attention has been paid to it. Yet it is precisely here, with the almost obsessive repetition of motifs and patterns of movement and character, that we see the nature of Shevchenko's imaginative world at its best. For as in true myth (that is, primitive or classical), the essential unit is a narrative; and having established by comparison and superimposition the underlying structures in these 'versions' we can decode the whole. The redundancy, in fact, the repetition of patterns, the 'excess of information' (to which Shevchenko himself sometimes ironically refers: 'duzhe vzhe i meni samomu / Obrydly tii muzhyky, / Ta panychi, ta pokrytky' / 'I myself am very fed up / with these peasants, / and lordlings, and seduced girls'), is a sign of the mythical mode. The only means of 'defence' that myth has against deformation and against failure of memory is not the accuracy of the account—it is precisely the details that are first deformed and forgotten—but repetition through different versions. Ultimately, however, the first two categories as well, that is, the non-narrative poems, also express the same myth, though they tend to focus on one aspect of it.

At its most basic, Shevchenko's myth of Ukraine, like that of his countryman, Gogol, shows a world divided against itself; in more technical language, a situation of permanent asymmetry, with no hope of mediation. As in Gogol, one side is the male, the Cossack, the mobile or nomadic, and the other the female, the peasant, and the settled world. (The similarity is to be fully expected, since both writers are expressing a common collective experience; on the other hand there will also be some significant differences.) The unresolved conflict between the two sides, their inability to develop and reproduce, is the curse of this world. Significantly (again as in Gogol), this is shown from both perspectives. From the perspective of the woman's world it is conveyed by the pattern of love (or sex), followed by desertion and then by transformation, either by death (**'Kateryna'**) or transformation into the non-human, into nature, for example, in **'Topolia' (The Poplar)**. As part of nature this side survives, but neither is it capable of true, human life. The most revealing work in this category is **'Utoplena' (The Drowned Girl)**, which in the murder of the daughter by the mother to frustrate her union or symbolic marriage with the fisherman shows the working of the curse at its starkest. In the present, all that remains of Ukraine is a suspended, helpless feminine world—the world of serfs tied to the land but with no memory of their glorious past, with no sense of identity, of descendants of Cossacks now willing slaves to tsarist despotism. It is a world of fallen women and illegitimate children; its cursed victimized state of being is stressed by the recurring motifs of incest and rape.

Once there was a golden age, not only of glory but also of harmonious existence; this is more alluded to than described, however. The great number of poems written from the male, Cossack perspective also show the workings of the curse—the impossibility of marrying, of vagabond wandering, and above all, insistently, of death. The image of the Cossack is invariably linked with the image of the grave, the burial mound, as in **'Ivan Pidkova'**:

> Bulo kolys—zaporozhtsi
> Vmily panuvaty.
> Panuvaly, dobuvaly
> I slavu i voliu,—
> Mynulosia: ostalysia
> Mohyly po poliu.

> There was a time when the Zaporozhians / Knew how to rule. / They ruled and captured / Glory and freedom. / It has passed: there remain / Burial mounds in the fields.

The structure conveyed here, however, is not only that the Cossacks are now dead and in the past, but even more that they were precisely carriers of death, and they brought death to their people, the brother-peasants. And for this, as we see so vividly in **'Za bairakom bairak' (Beyond the Ravine, Another Ravine)**, in the words of the Cossack's song, they are cursed by a living death, by their descendants forgetting their memory, by the very earth refusing to accept them:

> —Nanosyly zemli
> Ta i dodomu pishly,
> I nikhto ne zhadaie.
> Nas tut trysta, iak sklo,
> Tovarystva liahlo!
> I zemlia ne pryimaie.
> Iak zaprodav hetman
> U iarmo khrystyian
> Nas poslav pohaniaty.
> Po svoii po zemli
> Svoiu krov rozlyly
> I zarizaly brata.
> Krovy brata vpylys
> I otut poliahly
> U mohyli zakliatii.

They heaped up the earth / And went home, / And no one remembers. / Three hundred of us comrades, pure as glass, / Have perished here! / And the earth does not receive us. / When the hetman sold / The Christians into slavery / He sent us to drive them along. / On our soil / We shed our blood / And butchered our brothers. / Having drunk our brothers' blood / We have fallen here / In this cursed burial mound.

The most drastic instance of the destructiveness of the Cossack world comes in **Haidamaky** as Honta kills his children; as in its feminine counterpart, **'Utoplena,'** this is also a symbolic killing of the mediating element, of any hope for reconciling opposites. And although it is given an 'ideological' elaboration, that is, that this is a form of holy vengeance against the Poles, the deep structure is unaffected by it.

There is also a third perspective. Where Gogol saw the Ukrainian curse as unresolved and unresolvable and fled to a different reality, Shevchenko does provide a resolution. It is a ritual mediation made by himself as the myth-carrier. The only resolution—and he is the only one to provide it—is to retell the past, to resurrect memory and identity, to open the eyes and ears of his debased countrymen to the great ruin that Ukraine has become. He does this in two ways: in the overt mode of the political poems where his impassioned appeals and invocations give a rational elaboration to what he had already presented in the structure of myth, and also on a more symbolic level where he becomes the martyr whose expiation will signal a new beginning. The images used to convey this are grandiose indeed: he is the martyr Hus and Prometheus, the holy tree (in **'U Boha za dvermy lezhala sokyra' / 'An Axe Lay behind God's Door'**) and the oak that represents Ukraine (in **'Buvaly voiny . . .' / 'There had been wars . . .'**); he not only speaks *with* God as the sole representative of his people (**'Zapovit'** [Testament]) but in the very voice *of* God, in his paraphrase of *Hosea* Chap. 14. Yet this is precisely the domain of the myth-carrier, the shaman, to mediate for his people between the earth and the sky, the past and the future, to provide for their most fundamental spiritual needs. Shevchenko's claim to this role seems to have been substantiated by later history.

Ray LaPica   (essay date 1981)

SOURCE: "Shevchenko's Nine Russian 'Novels'," in *The Ukrainian Quarterly*, Vol. XXXVII, No. 1, Spring, 1981, pp. 25-41.

[*In the following essay, LaPica analyzes and evaluates the novels that Shevchenko wrote in Russian, summarizing their plots and explaining their significance in his oeuvre.*]

I. INTRODUCTION

Shevchenko's nine Russian "novels" are a literary curiosity of interest to everyone who loves his poetry. The nine works are really long short stories or novelettes rather than novels, and were written during his 10 years in exile in the Caspian Sea region. They were never published during his lifetime. Only one, *The Artist*, has been translated into English. All have been translated from the Russian, which Shevchenko wrote, into Ukrainian. The time has come when all should now be translated into English—directly from Shevchenko's Russian.

(This article is based on the reading of the Ukrainian translations of all nine novels and both the Ukrainian and English translations of *The Artist* since the writer does not know Russian).

II. PRELIMINARY COMMENTS

A few preliminary comments about the novels are in order before we summarize them. *The Musician* was the first novel to be published, in 1881, in the Kiev newspaper *Trud*. *The Unfortunate* appeared the same year in *Ystorychesky Vestnyk*. *The Princess* was published in 1884 in the *Kievska staryna*. It then published the rest of Shevchenko's Russian prose from 1886 to 1887 and then published it in a single volume in 1888. All were in Ukrainian translation.

Shevchenko wrote his Russian novels in exile during the period of 1853 to 1857 when his morale was at its lowest ebb. He wrote nothing in Ukrainian during this period. He was convinced that he had "deteriorated, grown numb in bondage." That the inspired spark within him had been extinguished. That he needed desperately for someone or something to light "the sacred flame" again so that his heart "would weep." He wrote in Russian as an outlet for his depressed spirit. In fact he wrote ceaselessly without a let-up—eight Russian novels poured from his pen between 1853 and 1856, and the last one, which he began in 1857, he completed in 1858 while en route from exile. He wrote "in an effort to save his soul."

As soon as he was freed (in 1857) he cast the Russian works aside and began to write his illimitable Ukrainian poetry again. **"The Neophytes"**—a thinly disguised but stinging attack on Tsarism—was his first and one of his greatest works written immediately after he departed from Fort Novopetrovsk and was waiting in Nizhni-Novgorod for permission to return to St. Petersburg.

Eight of the stories were never rewritten, edited or polished and appear to be a first draft only. Shevchenko made some effort to get Russian editors to publish them in their periodicals but failed. He seems to have lost interest in them upon his return from exile to St. Petersburg in 1858, and one hears nothing further about them from him.

The novels were not well received either by Ukrainians like Panteleimon Kulish (1819-1897) or Russian writers like Sergey Aksakov (1791-1859).

When Shevchenko asked Kulish what he should do with his Russian works, Kulish wrote back, after reading *The Princess* and *The Sailor* (**Matros**) later renamed *Wandering—with Pleasure but Not without Morals*:

> "If I had the money, I would buy them all—and burn them."

The Russian writer advised him against publishing *Wandering* and said, "It is not equal to your great poetical talent." Shevchenko wrote back thanking him for his sincerity. "You told me what I've already thought for a long time . . ." The Ukrainian writer Y. Tukhovksy caps the criticism with the comment that Shevchenko's Russian works were "fit for one thing—food for mice."

Modern critics agree as to the style but not the content. Pavlo Zaytzev, who edited the complete works of Shevchenko republished in a massive 14-volume edition by the Mykola Denysiuk Publishing Company, appears to agree with Sergey Efremov, who examined the original manuscripts in Kiev after World War I and concluded that they were rough drafts only and not ready for publication. Zaytsev says Shevchenko did not know Russian very well, that "at times it just seems to him (Shevchenko) that he was writing in Russian, but in fact it was the Ukrainian language."

But the Russian "novels" remain creative works written by the greatest master of the Ukrainian language, the Shakespeare of Ukraine, who not only literally created the literary Ukrainian language but influenced more human beings with his poetry than any other poet who ever lived. Therefore anything he wrote, in any language, is bound to fascinate us.

Shevchenko wrote the novels under the pseudonym "Kobzar Darmohray" or "Darmogray." He had to use a pseudonym because the Tsar (Nicholas I) himself had sentenced him to lifelong silence upon Shevchenko's conviction for what amounted to treason or sedition in 1847. He wrote in Russian because there was a complete ban on Ukrainian literature from 1847 to 1855 after the members of the Brotherhood of Saints Cyril and Methodius had been tried and convicted with Shevchenko in St. Petersburg. (Russian writers were also persecuted during this period. Dostoyevsky, for example, was condemned to death in 1848 but escaped

with his life. Of interest is the fact that Dostoyevsky, a great admirer with Turgenev of Shevchenko's poetry, attended Shevchenko's funeral in St. Petersburg in 1861.)

Even the publication of the Bible in the Ukrainian language was prohibited by the Russian Orthodox Synod. By 1862 Ukrainian schools were closed. In 1863 the Minister of Home Affairs, Valuev, prohibited the printing of Ukrainian books, declaring: "The Ukrainian language does not exist, has never existed and must not exist."

In 1876 Tsar Alexander II signed a secret ukase in Ems decreeing the absolute prohibition of all Ukrainian books, Ukrainian music and the Ukrainian theater. Ukraine was "muzzled."

As an aside, Shevchenko wrote 11 Russian prose works, as well as some Russian poetry but two works disappeared from Kostomarov's collection when their publication began: **"Povisty o besrodnom Petrush"** (**Stories of the Orphan Petrush**) and a fragment from an untitled drama. Shevchenko wrote at least two poems in Russian (in the 1840's) as well as his Russian novels, his diary of one year and most of his correspondence, all in Russian. The poems are **"Slepaya"** (**A Blind Woman**) (1842) and **"Tryzna"** (**Ancient Feast**) renamed **"Beztalanny"** (**The Unfortunate**) (1843) written in honor of the Decembrists of 1825. He also wrote a play in Russian: *Nikita Hayday* (of which only the third act was published). Shevchenko wrote another play in 1843: the popular and still produced *Nazar Stodolia* (1843) about old Cossack days. There is much evidence that this play was actually written in Ukrainian.

What is the value of Shevchenko's Russian prose? For the first time in Russian literature themes appeared from Ukrainian life dealing with Ukrainian peasantry. The stories give the first description of the Ukrainian peasant as a human being in the Western mould. We learn far more of Ukrainian life from Shevchenko's novels than we can from his poetry. Manners, customs, habits and fascinating relationships pour from his pen. He describes Ukrainian life in the 1820's to 1840's in a manner no other Ukrainian author approached.

To paraphrase the perceptive comments of the fine editor Pavlo Zaytsev in his article *"Prozova tvorchist Shevchenka"* in *Tvory,* Volume VI:

> Shevchenko was unable to continue writing in Ukrainian during the seven-year "dry period" of his life from 1850 to 1857 in exile because (1) he was not allowed to write; (2) his work would not have been published anyway. So he wrote in Russian under a pseudonym hoping to serve Ukraine in that manner and also like all true authors to be read.

Out of 10 novels and short stories which we know of (one was lost), eight are written entirely on Ukrainian themes. All are sprinkled with passionate Ukrainian patriotism. Yakim Herlo in *The Servant* cannot even bear to hear the word "Moscow." The girl Katria does not understand the Russian language. The unfortunate hero in *The Convict* in far-off exile furnishes his cottage so that everything in it "reminds one of Ukraine." He takes a Ukrainian woman for a servant, mourns for his "beautiful Ukraine." Vatia Sokera, seeing a Ukrainian village in the Ural region, cries with happiness because for the first time since he left his native land he can speak in Ukrainian (*The Twins*). The poet points up the fact that one of his main characters speaks in Ukrainian (Maria Yakimivna in *The Musician*). Ukrainian poems are the finest, the epos being better than Homer (*Wandering*). Ukraine is a country far different than Russia (*The Captain's Mistress*). Shevchenko draws sympathetic portraits of people who live in the national tradition (the elderly Sokeras in *The Twins*). He loves to recall examples of Ukrainian national culture. He speaks fondly of the enemies of Moscow—Hetmans Mazepa and Doroshenko. He criticizes even Skovoroda, the great Ukrainian philosopher, for not writing in Ukrainian (in *The Twins*) and complains that in the schools "they teach everything but our dear native language" (*Wandering*).

Shevchenko's problem was that his style was old-fashioned, even for the 1850's. He read everything he could lay hands on in St. Petersburg as he matured, but there wasn't that much. The Russians in the 19th century were still translating Europe's 17th and 18th century authors. So Shevchenko read Voltaire, Rousseau, Montesquieu, Goldsmith, Burns and Shakespeare among the older writers, and Dickens, Scott, George Sand and Washington Irving among the 19th century authors. He also knew church Slavonic well. This contributed to his archaisms.

The Russian style then was what Shevchenko used in his prose: forewords, epilogues, deliberate obscurity, odd meetings, a mixture of localities and author's reflections and asides. His Russian prose reflects the elements common to European literature of the late 18th and early 19th centuries; pseudo-classicism, sentimentality, romanticism and sentimental naturalism and realism.

Shevchenko once wrote to Aksakov: "It is hard for me to master the Russian language . . . It is like paint on a palette which I mix without order."

Nevertheless, Shevchenko wrote in Russian with artistry, especially his descriptions. Those of a storm in *Wandering,* a rural country scene near Sula in *The Servant* and Ukrainian and Kirghiz steppes in *The Twins* and many others are prose poems of great beauty. Shevchenko painted with words as well as he could

paint with oil (and readers might recall that before he died Russian critics had begun to refer to Shevchenko as "the Russian Rembrandt.")

Shevchenko could characterize well, having been exposed to the whole pageantry of life in Ukraine and Russia, from the lowliest self's hovel to the mansions of counts, generals and princesses. He was especially good at village types: Yakim and Lukiya in *The Servant* and Tuman in *The Captain's Mistress,* for example. The St. Petersburg characters like Pasha and her aunt in *The Artist* and Kulia Karlivna, who runs a house of prostitution in *The Unfortunate,* are true to life. He does well with the rural intelligentsia in *Wandering*—the Prekhtels, in *The Twins*—the Sokeras, in *The Musician*—Anton Karlovich and Maria Yakimivna. His Russian seducers, officers and *pany* are probably his weakest characters because they are all of one piece, and he obviously dislikes them: Zosha Sokera (who Russified his name to Sokirin) in *The Twins,* Kornet in *The Servant,* Count Boleslav in *The Convict,* Prince Mordaty in *The Princess* and Kurnatovsky in *Wandering*.

Shevchenko's Russian novels belong with his letters and diary (which he kept for only one year but it is priceless) in completing the portrait of the great artist-poet as an author.

III. THE NINE RUSSIAN "NOVELS"

What then are these Russian "novels" all about? Here is a brief summary (but only a careful reading will bring out their full flavor and beauty):

1. The Servant (Naymychka)

> (Written in 1853 at Fort Novopetrovsk, translated by V. Sapitsky, 86 pp., first published in *Kievskaya staryna* 1886).

Shevchenko signed the story "February 25, 1844, Periaslav"—he was free at the time—to confuse the censors and avoid the Tsar's prohibition that he was never to write or paint. The story describes the love of a young unmarried mother for the child she gives up to an elderly couple and then proceeds to raise while working for the family as a servant without ever revealing her relationship.

This is apparently Shevchenko's first Russian "novel" and possibly as a result over-sentimentalized. It definitely was not revised, edited or polished, and shows it. The Russian officer-seducer, Kornet, is the most interesting character and disappears long before the end. The girl mother is Lukia, and Yakim and Marta, to whom she entrusts her son, Mark, are well-to-do landowners rather than serfs. So this is not so much an attack on serfdom, but rather a double-edged condemnation of the morals of the "Moskali" as Russian offic-ers and therefore the Russian army in which Shevchen-ko served 10 bitter years, and on the social practice of the villages (and parents) in condemning a young woman who put love above "honor." The style seems to bear out Editor Zaytsev's comment that Shevchenko did not have the time nor interest to rewrite or revise any of his Russian "novels" (except **Wandering**). But it is fascinating nevertheless. Note that Shevchenko wrote a poem of the same name in 1845 with an al-most identical theme.

At least one Ukrainian critic disagrees as to the social importance of work. Biletsky says in his review: "The main theme of the story is to show the dark side of the serf order in the dvoriansky empire. Its rotten morals are contrasted with the healthy life of a village fam-ily . . ."

Biletsky sees the novel as portraying the hatred of the Ukrainian village for everything Russian as foreign. The Russian "Don Juan," Biletsky says, symbolizes the curse of the Russian occupation of Ukraine

Incidentally Ivan Franko, the great Western Ukrainian writer, rated the story at a higher level than the poem of the same name.

2. The Convict (Varnak)

(Written in 1853 at Fort Novapetrovsk, translated by D. Doroshenko, 37 pp., first published in *Kievskaya staryna* 1886.)

Shevchenko dated this story "1845 in Kiev" also to confuse the censor and avoid the Tsar's writing prohi-bition. It is a grim and bloody story of crime and punishment growing out of the Ukrainian serf's hatred for his landlords. The motif is the moral rehabilitation of a human being driven into crime by the fury of his hatred and revenge. The profligate rich man's son, Count Boleslav, seduces Kirilo's stepdaughter, Mare-sia (Marusia). Kirilo is a kindly peace-loving and ed-ucated serf. This changes his character completely, and he proceeds to burn his own cottage and become a bandit. As he is being captured, he kills the Count. While under arrest, he is rescued by his bandit horde, who proceed to slaughter the Countess's friends and burn her manor. Kirilo says goodby to his beloved benefactress and tutor, Magdalena, and his stepdaugh-ter, Maresia, and surrenders himself to the Governor who sentences him to Siberia for life.

Shevchenko met people like this during his exile, and this is the story of one of them. Kirilo is a Robin Hood character who robs the rich and gives to the poor dur-ing his two years as a bandit. Shevchenko had read Scott and was doubtless familiar with the Robin Hood story popularized in Scott's *Ivanhoe*. He also saw

Schiller's play *The Prisoners* on the stage and had read Vulpius' novel about the noble robber Rinaldo Rinaldini.

One of the absorbing by-products of Shevchenko's Russian novels is the occasional insight he gives into his own life. For example, here is Kirilo describing how he buried his mother as a boy (literally a page out of the boyhood of Shevchenko, whose mother died when he was nine):

> I do not remember my father (Shevchenko's father died when Taras was 11, and he of course remembered him very well), but I see my mother as in a dream; I see them place her in a coffin and carry her to the cemetery. I remember the priest reading a prayer over her body, a prayer printed on white paper with red and black letters, and having read the prayer, covering her face with it. Then they nailed shut the coffin and lowered it into the grave. The priest blessed the grave with the cross and told me to throw a handful of soil on my mother's coffin . . . I threw it, and followed the people back to the village.

What is **The Convict** worth? Oddly, Shevchenko thought so little of it that he wanted it destroyed by a friend to whom he had sent it. Fortunately it was not. The author Doroshenko calls it "a document of un-compromising hatred by the poet of everything de-cayed, of oppression, and of subjugation." He adds:

> This is a most beautiful example of Shevchenko's 'Rousseauism'—the poet's deep belief in the incorruptibility and nobility of the human spirit.

Here too Shevchenko wrote an earlier poem, **"Var-nak"** (1848), but in it the "hero"—in revenge for the seduction of his beloved—turns into a bandit leader and massacres and robs the landowners without mercy before he is rehabilitated at the end.

3. The Princess (Kniahynia)

(Written in 1853 at Fort Novapetrovsk, translated by V. Sapitsky, 36 pp., first published in full in *Kievskaya staryna* 1884.)

This story is a strange tale of a mother's ambition to make her daughter a princess. It is more tightly written than most of the other Russian stories. The narrator is the grandmother Mikitivna. Katerina is the mother who succeeds in marrying her daughter, Katrusha, to Prince Mordaty, a Russian dragoon. The Prince is utterly without redeeming features: cruel, drunken, heartless. His princess goes mad at the end. The story is another attack on the Russian-imposed serfdom in Ukraine, with such events as a famine that is followed by the burning of the village, the villagers justifiedly attributing both events to the Prince. The Russians are portrayed as villains throughout, perhaps another reason for the fact that the story was not published until long after Shevchenko's death.

The editor Zaytsev calls *The Princess* Shevchenko's strongest denunciation of serfdom. He says Shevchenko tried for three years to get someone in St. Petersburg to publish it, but the Russian editors refused, either from fear of the censor, or the obvious manifestations of pro-Ukrainianism or because of Shevchenko's old-fashioned style—a first person narrative inside a first-person narrative inside a first-person narrative. (Incidentally Shevchenko used the first-person technique in all his Russian prose works.)

Shevchenko was heartsick over the hard life of his fellow Ukrainians as serfs under Russian rule. He wrote three earlier poems on this subject which can and do serve as a prelude to *The Princess*: The poem **"Kniazhna" ("The Princess"** or more literally **"The Prince's Daughter")** in 1847, **"I vyris ya na chyzhyni" ("I Grew Up in a Foreign Land"** (1848) and **"Yak by vy znaly, panychi . . ." (If You Only Knew, Lords . . .)** (1850).

The value of this story lies in Shevchenko's revelations of a serf's life in Ukraine in the first half of the 19th century. As Editor Zaytsev says:

> . . . No one before Shevchenko wrote with such daring and expression about the most brutal events of the landowners' wantonness. Describing the sad life of the serfs, Turgenev did not touch on such themes. Only the American Harriet Beecher Stowe, in her *'Khattsi diad'ka toma'* (Uncle Tom's Cabin) (1852) dared to use the utmost naturalism in writing of the violence of the American slave owners, but Shevchenko had not read her work at that time.

Of special interest are the first seven pages of *The Princess* which are completely autobiographical and tell of Shevchenko's boyhood in his beautiful village whose grounds he compares with Peterhof, the palatial gardens of St. Petersburg. One paragraph to illustrate his early life deserves quotation:

> From then on (after the new schoolmaster arrived) began the saddest and most unhappy of my memories. Soon my mother died. My father married a young widow and took her three children with her instead of a dowry. (Shevchenko had two brothers and three sisters). Who saw even from afar the stepmother and the so-called stepchildren saw hell at its worst. Not an hour passed without tears and fighting among us children, and not an hour passed without arguments and cursing between my father and the stepmother; the stepmother detested me, perhaps because I often struck her whining Stepan. That year in the fall my father took a trip to Kiev, fell ill on the road and, returning home, soon died.

Shevchenko concludes his autobiographical introduction to the novel with the words:

My later memories are even sadder. Far far from my poor beloved country

Without love, without joy
My youth passed away!

In truth it did not pass away but crept away, in misery, in ignorance, in insult. And all this dragged on for 20 long years . . .

4. *The Musician (Muzyka)*

(Begun November 28, 1854, completed January 15, 1855, at Fort Novopetrovsk, translated by V. Yakybovsky, 95 pp., first published in *Trud* 1882.)

This is a fine romance although it begins slowly (the main character does not appear until the 12th page). It deals with a gifted serf musician, Taras Federovich, and his love, Natasha. It moves with numerous dramatic touches to a happy ending. It is Shevchenko's only story dealing with an "urban" serf. The theme is to show the usual fate of talented serfs under the feudal system of 19th-century Russia. They must, first and always, serve their masters to the detriment of their talent.

The musician Taras becomes a free man at the end. But the subplot tells of a girl, Maria Tarasevich, who, to become an actress, has to submit to *Pan* Klenovsky. She bears his child and ultimately dies. Some dramatic events are sprung suddenly on the reader without sufficient characterization, such as Lisa's hard-to-believe marriage to Klenovsky. But Shevchenko's technique of moving the story forward over two decades through letters is quite effective.

Of interest is Shevchenko's love for and knowledge of music as shown throughout the novel. For example, Mendelssohn's "Storm," Weber's "Preciosa," Chopin's mazurkas, Beethoven's sonatas, Mozart's "Requiem," Liszt's etudes, Haydn's "Creation," Schubert's "Serenade" and many other famous compositions are mentioned.

The musician Taras in the story is a violoncellist. Shevchenko shows his love for the cello through these words of his hero:

> Only a human soul can weep and rejoice like this magnificent instrument as it sings and cries. The master who created it was no other than Prometheus himself. I lie down to sleep and place it beside me. It is my sweetheart, my life, my I. If I were twice a serf, for this instrument I would sell myself a third time.

Why no immediate publication of *The Musician*? Perhaps because of lines like this one where Shevchenko exclaims in an aside as he views a beautiful Ukrainian farm sown with wheat and rye:

Dear God, for whom is this field ripening?

(The tillers of the soil were Ukrainian serfs; the landowners were mostly Poles and Russians.)

5. The Unfortunate (Neschasny)

(Written January 24–February 20, 1855, at Fort Novopetrovsk, translated by S. Siropolko, 56 pp., first published in *Ystorychesky vestnyk* 1881)

This is Shevchenko's most consistent story in point of chronology. At least it has very few digressions. The stepmother, Maria Fedorivna; "one of the most satirical figures in Shevchenko's Russian prose," tries to get rid of two stepchildren, Kolya and Lisa, and steal their inheritance for her own wastrel son, Ipolit Khliupin, after their father dies. She is outwitted by a hustling "madam" in St. Petersburg, Yulia Karlivna. The disappointed stepmother catches her son stealing and signs him over to the army to serve at hard labor. Her crime of placing Lisa in a house of prostitution under a false name in St. Petersburg is uncovered, and she is sent to a nunnery. The ending is pat. Lisa, the heroine, is happily married to her lover and is reunited with her blind brother.

"The Unfortunate" is the youth Ipolit, whom the narrator, presumably Shevchenko, meets at Fort Orsk in the Caspian Sea region, where Shevchenko served for 11 months in 1847-48 and spent six months in the stockade in 1850. (It was Shevchenko's second arrest for writing poetry). Shevchenko was intrigued by the fact that the youth had been signed into the army by his mother. The story underlines the immoral upbringing of the children of the well-to-do and contrasts it with the morality of the poor. It is an attack on the Russian custom of permitting landlords and parents to consign their disobedient serfs and sons to the army.

Of interest is how a village fights a smallpox epidemic.

Editor Zaytsev says *The Unfortunate* is Shevchenko's best-composed work in Russian. He compares it with the best of Gogol and Dickens and says: "Had this novel been published during Shevchenko's life in a more revised style, it would have left not a little impression on literature."

6. The Captain's Mistress (Kapitansha)

(Written March 15 to June, 1885 at Fort Novopetrovsk, translated by S. Siropolko, 74 pp., first published in *Kievskaya staryna* 1887)

This is the story of a Ukrainian veteran of the War of 1812 in Russia. He is a musician (drummer) who brings up an orphan girl and then marries her to save her from shame after she is seduced by a Russian captain. Again a rambling story with many asides and with several interesting characters, especially Victor, the narrator of the subplot; Tuman, the hero, and the seduced heroine, Varochka. The story contrasts the morals of the Russian officers with those of the ordinary people of Ukraine and excoriates the practice of Russian civil servants in cheating the illiterate peasantry.

The fascination of the story is two-fold: First, the quiet courage of the soldier-servant Tuman in devoting a good portion of his life to helping the orphan Varochka, whom he later marries and, second, the sympathetic portrait Shevchenko paints of the narrator, Victor, a Ukrainian officer in the Russian army and a veteran of the War of 1812. Shevchenko knew many veterans of that war and must have drawn much of his material from the stories they told him.

Shevchenko's tremendous fund of knowledge of Russian and Ukrainian history is never more evident than in this work. He mentions the Prussian field marshal Bluecher, who helped defeat Napoleon at Waterloo; talks of Beatrice Cenci, who was executed in 1599 for killing her father because he attempted to rape her; denounces the "Little Russian Collegium" which the Russians established to control Ukraine in the 18th century; talks of Homer, Rembrandt, Donizetti (and his opera "Daughter of the Regiment"), Metternich, Rousseau, Socrates and numerous other historical, mythical and fictional characters.

Shevchenko's description of the beautiful Olesha, daughter of Varochka, is poetical:

> Olesha sat before me with her mother, and only now did I observe her with devoted attention. She was truly a freshly blossoming beauty; thick dark chestnut hair braided into two tresses and bound with blue and yellow periwinkles and ribbons gave a touch of freshness to her lovely head; a sheer white blouse with white embroidery on the wide sleeves covered her shoulders and breast with such folds that not even Skopas or Phide (ancient Greek sculptors) ever dreamed of—in a word there sat before me a goddess beautiful and immaculate.

One trait developed in the novels and not evident in Shevchenko's poetry is his sense of humor. For example, here is how a father berates his wife when she suggests that their son be sent to the Art Academy:

> What . . . an artist? A painter? . . . You must have drunk too much and not slept it off! An artist! Hah, hah, hah! . . . An artist . . . Think, wise head: Is that a vocation for a nobleman—daubing paint? To the Academy? . . . Together with serfs? What a fine career you picked out for your son. Beautiful! Nothing more need be said!

Taking the boy in his arms, the father says: "No, my dear Sashko, you are going to be a true genuine soldier!" (The boy is in military school within a year.)

7. *The Twins (Blyzniata)*

(Written June 10–July 10, 1855, at Fort Novopetrovsk, translated by V. Prokopovych, 146 pp., first published in *Kievskaya staryna* 1886)

The Twins is a slow-moving but dramatic study of the education of twin boys whose adult paths separate. One becomes a Russian army officer and a wastrel, the other a doctor. Shevchenko paints a fine picture of the different types of education a youth could receive if he were lucky in those days—one militaristic, which Shevchenko believed with much justification ruined a person for life, and the other that of a humanist, who devoted his life to helping his fellow man.

The characters are the twins Zosha and Vatia (Savaty) Sokera. Their mother, having been seduced by a Russian cavalryman, leaves them where the elderly Sokeras can find them and then drowns herself. The stepparents, Nechepir Federovich and Paraskovia Tarasivna Sokera, proceed to raise the children in opposite ways. The stepfather wants one son to be a "seminarian"—a student; the stepmother wants one boy to become an officer. So they draw lots and Zosha is designated for the army and Savaty for the "gymnasium" or high school. The problems begin immediately. The military begins to "corrupt" the boy; the other grows in learning and wisdom in school. Zosha graduates as an officer and Russifies his name to "Sokirin." Savaty becomes a doctor. Zosha begins to gamble heavily and borrow money from his stepmother. Tragedy strikes as it does in most of Shevchenko's novels. Zosha is sent to Fort Orsk (where Shevchenko himself was exiled for a time), jailed for his gambling and finally returns home. At home he drives his mother out and drinks himself to death. Savaty marries a Ukrainian girl.

The story is a study of the influence of environment and permits Shevchenko to pillory the Russian military, its morals and its degradation of the human spirit. The Fort Orsk incident gives him the opportunity of painting a fine picture of his own expedition to the Aral Sea (1848-49).

The novel is filled with historical references to Ukrainian culture, Ukrainian historical figures, the religious life and clergy, Ukrainian literature, the then existing theater and the old Ukrainian school. Its significance lies in the fact that it was the first serious attempt at a realistic historical novel of Ukrainian life. Ukraine was asleep between 1820 and 1840. Shevchenko, who traveled up and down Ukraine in the 40's during his two visits there and while at work for the Archeological Commission sketching ancient churches and monuments, recreates the period beautifully. In doing so he could have helped to reawaken his people to their magnificent past, as he did so successfully with his poetry. Unfortunately this masterful novel was never published until long after his death.

Zaytsev calls *The Twins* "the most colorful of Shevchenko's novels from the national outlook." "It is all alive and sweet. It awakens in the imagination of the reader a live portrait of this misty yet dazzling epoch as imagined by Shevchenko."

It is that indeed.

8. *The Artist (Khudozhnyk)*

(Written January 25–October 4, 1856, in Fort Novopetrovsk, Russian version translated into Ukrainian by L. Biletsky in Denysiuk edition, 132 pp., English translation by John Weir, *Taras Shevchenko Selected Works,* Progress Publishers, Moscow, undated but probably 1961. First published in *Kievskaya staryna* 1887.)

This is the writer's favorite. It is the most exciting of all of Shevchenko's Russian works because it is almost entirely autobiographical. It deals with his last years as an apprenticed serf-painter to the theater decorator Shirayev and his emancipation from serfdom. Shevchenko later called the post-emancipation period in St. Petersburg his "golden years."

Shevchenko's opening paragraph has to be one of the most astounding in the history of fiction: he mentions 14 historical artistic and religious figures, ranging from Thorvaldsen, Rubens and Van Dyke to Wycliffe, Huss, Luther, Leo X and Julius XI. The first narrator is Ivan Soshenko, the Ukrainian artist who befriended Shevchenko as he painted in the summer Gardens of St. Petersburg. We meet Karl Briulov, the celebrated Russian painter of "The Last Days of Pompeii," who painted the portrait of Vassily Zhukovsky, the poet and tutor to the Tsarevich Alexander, which was later sold for 2500 rubles to the royal family and used to buy Shevchenko out of serfdom. Dozens of artists and their works, Russian and West European, are mentioned. Numerous literary works are cited, from Ozerov's *Oedipus in Athens* to Dickens's novel *Nicholas Nickleby.*

For all its brilliance, the novel has an odd and melodramatic ending. The hero marries an ignoramus when his art program or projected work is not accepted at the Academy. He becomes a drunkard, goes insane and dies after painting a beautiful but unfinished portrait entitled "The Madonna." There is no similarity between the ending and Shevchenko's own life, of course. But one interpretation of it is that it reflects Shevchenko's own treason trial and sentence to a lifetime exile with the presumed extinction of his creative talents. He wrote *The Artist* in his ninth year of exile, probably when he thought it would last forever. But it was the year after Tsar Nicholas I died, so he must have felt that he had a chance of being released by the new tsar, Alexander II. (This happened in 1857.)

Another oddity is Shevchenko's criticism of beautiful women as the bane of artists in the closing portion of the novel. This might have been a reflection on the souring of his platonic romance with the lovely Agatha Uskova, wife of the commandant Major Irakly Uskov, at Fort Novopetrovsk a short time before.

The Artist deserves immediate re-translation by a competent Ukrainian-American into English so that it can become more widely disseminated in the free world as the most detailed account of a critical period of Shevchenko's life that we have.

9. Wandering—With Pleasure But Not Without Morals (Mandrivka z pryemnistiu ta y ne bez morali)

> (First draft completed November 30, 1856 at Fort Novopetrovsk, second draft April 22, 1857, same place; third draft completed February 16, 1858, in Nizhni Novgorod en route from exile to St. Petersburg, translated by D. Doroshenko, 162 pp.; Shevchenko's longest novel, first excerpts published in *Trud* December 1881, first complete publication in *Kievskaya staryna* 1887.)

This is Shevchenko's most fascinating picture of Ukraine in the 1840's. It tells of the wanderings or meanderings of the narrator through his native land as an artist looking for objects to paint. The narrator of course is Shevchenko and he exploits his personal experiences while painting for the Kiev Archeological Commission in the mid-1840's to the fullest.

Wandering was inspired by an incident which illustrates Shevchenko's deep humanity; a young Ukrainian sailor lost both arms in the Crimean War. Asked in the hospital what he wanted most as his reward, he answered—his serf sister's freedom. Shevchenko read about this incident in a military newspaper and based his novel on it, at least as a starting point. It of course was of poignant interest to Shevchenko, for he still had two brothers and a sister in serfdom at that time. Two other sisters had died.

Osip Federovich Oboromenko is the sailor in the novel. It is Shevchenko's last Russian prose work, and he worked harder on it than any of the others and tried harder to get it published, but failed. Shevchenko first mentions the novel in a letter to Michael Lazarevsky December 8, 1856. He originally called it "Etude," then "Metros" (The Sailor) and finally "Prohulka" in Russian. Kulish read the first part of *Wandering* and also *The Princess*. His advice to Shevchenko that he would burn the poet's Russian works was based on [these] two readings. Kulish obviously wanted Shevchenko to write only in Ukrainian.

The Russian writer Aksakov ended Shevchenko's dream of having *Wandering* published when he wrote the poet:

> I do not advise you to publish this novel. It is not equal to your great poetical talent . . . You are—a lyricist, an elegist; your humor is humorless, and the joking not always amusing. It is true that when you deal with nature, it is beautiful, but that is not enough to redeem the faults of the whole narration.

Shevchenko thanked him for his frankness. "You told me what I have long thought but—why, I don't know—I dared not say. I am triply grateful for your sincere and frank word; it has lighted the path which I had been following gropingly."

What Shevchenko meant was that he would drop his efforts to become a "Russian" novelist like Gogol and return to his beautiful Ukrainian poetry, which he did. His first post-exile poem, **"The Neophytes,"** was perhaps his greatest. He wrote it at Nizhni-Novgorod on the way home from 10 years of exile. It is a savage attack on the Tsar, on Tsarism and on the whole rotten Russian system of oppression, brutality, dishonor, and serfdom. Thinly disguised as an elegy of the Christian martyrs under Nero of Rome, it was obvious to all of Shevchenko's friends who read it that Nero was the Tsar, Rome was Russia and the martyrs were the Ukrainian people. Shevchenko was indeed fortunate that this work never fell into the hands of the hated Third Viddil (Department) which had convicted him in 1847, or he would have been promptly returned to Fort Novopetrovsk or worse.

Doroshenko and Zaytsev conclude their article on the novel with these perceptive words:

> . . . in his Russian novels Shevchenko remained true to himself; a great Ukrainian patriot and a true son of his people for whom he thought and suffered even unto his soul in bondage in far-off exile.

Wandering, Shevchenko's most diffuse Russian work and his last, deserves attention because he worked hardest on it—and it gives us an insight into the deepening humanity with which he came out of ten years of exile—an exile which had broken his health and almost silenced his creative soul.

IV. CONCLUSION

Shevchenko's Russian works, coming from the pen of one of the most creative writers in the history of literature, deserve immediate translation and widespread dissemination. They show a Ukraine that no other writer wrote about during the first half of the 19th century. They are illuminating as to Shevchenko's own life, such as the autobiographic details in *The Artist, The Princess* and *Wandering*, among others. They are even more illuminating as to his thought processes, his idealism, his philosophy of life and his hopes for a better future for his country.

These books, or rather their writing, sustained him during the most difficult and hopeless period of his life. They should become through translation part of the heritage that is Shevchenko—truly a genius whose life has enriched all humanity.

FURTHER READING

Criticism

Dobriansky, Lev E. "The Shevchenko Affair." *The Ukrainian Quarterly* XX, No. 1 (Spring 1964): 108-17.
> Defends the erection of the Shevchenko statue in Washington, D.C., against a disparaging editorial in *The Washington Post.*

Gitin, Vladimir. "The Reality of the Narrator: Typological Features of Ševčenko's Prose." *Harvard Ukrainian Studies* IX, Nos. 1/2 (June 1985): 85-117.
> Reevaluates Shevchenko's prose pieces in light of their seemingly autobiographical elements.

Grabowicz, George G. "The Nexus of the Wake: Ševčenko's *Trizna.*" *Harvard Ukrainian Studies* III/IV, Pt. 1 (1979-80): 320-47.
> Insists that Shevchenko's Russian poem *Trizna* represents a phase in his development between his Ukrainian idealism and his recognition of official Russian repression.

House of Representatives. *Europe's Freedom Fighter.* Washington, D.C.: Government Printing Office, 1960, 45 p.
> Collects a number of essays on Shevchenko by various authors, discussing the author's life, influence, and religion. The book also includes a short bibliography.

LaPica, Larry. "Taras Shevchenko: Bard of the Ukraine." *The Ukrainian Quarterly* XXVIII, No. 2 (Summer 1972): 146-65.

> Describes Shevchenko's life and historical context, describing his influence and his political views.

Panchuk, John. *Shevchenko's Testament: Annotated Commentaries.* Jersey City: Svoboda Press, 1965, 146 p.
> Discusses Shevchenko's poetry, his influences, and the history of Ukraine during the nineteenth century. The book focuses on his *Testament* and contains a list of selected translations.

Rozumnyj, Jaroslav. "Byzantinism and Idealism in the Aesthetic Views of Taras Shevchenko." *Canadian Slavonic Papers* XIX, No. 2 (June 1977): 193-206.
> Details the aesthetic theory that lies behind Shevchenko's innovative poetry.

Rubchak, Bohdan. "Taras Shevchenko as an Émigré Poet." *Journal of Ukrainian Studies* XIV, Nos. 1 and 2 (Summer/Winter 1989): 21-56.
> Claims that Shevchenko's writing develops an idealized Ukraine in response to his life under Russian oppression.

Rylsky, Maxim. "Taras Shevchenko, Poet, the Innovator." *Soviet Literature* III, No. 432 (1984): 143-52.
> Examines the influences on Shevchenko's poetic development.

Schneider, Lisa E. "An Examination of Shevchenko's Romanticism." *Journal of Ukrainian Graduate Studies* III, No. 1 (Spring 1978): 5-28.
> Distinguishes Shevchenko's romanticism from Western European romanticism.

Shabliovsky, Yevhen. *The Humanism of Shevchenko and Our Time.* Translated by Mary Skrypnyk. n.p., n.d., 327 p.
> Discusses Shevchenko's humanism and his role in the development of Ukrainian socialism.

Sloane, David A. "The Author's Digressions in Ševčenko's 'Hajdamaky': Their Nature and Function." *Harvard Ukrainian* II, No. 3 (September 1978): 310-33.
> Discusses the "lyrical digressions" in "Hajdamaky."

Smal-Stocki, Roman. *Shevchenko Meets America.* Milwaukee: Marquette University, 1964, 71 p.
> Explores the influence of George Washington and the ideas expressed in the Declaration of Independence on Shevchenko and on the development of political ideas in Eastern Europe.

Nineteenth-Century
Literature Criticism

Cumulative Indexes
Volumes 1-54

How to Use This Index

The main references

Calvino, Italo
1923-1985.....CLC 5, 8, 11, 22, 33, 39,
73; SSC 3

list all author entries in the following Gale Literary Criticism series:

BLC = Black Literature Criticism
CLC = Contemporary Literary Criticism
CLR = Children's Literature Review
*CMLC = Classical and Medieval Literature
    Criticism*
DA = DISCovering Authors
DAB = DISCovering Authors: British
DAC = DISCovering Authors: Canadian
DAM = DISCovering Authors Modules
   DRAM: Dramatists module
   MST: Most-studied authors module
   MULT: Multicultural authors module
   NOV: Novelists module
   POET: Poets module
   POP: Popular/genre writers module

DC = Drama Criticism
HLC = Hispanic Literature Criticism
LC = Literature Criticism from 1400 to 1800
NCLC = Nineteenth-Century Literature Criticism
PC = Poetry Criticism
SSC = Short Story Criticism
TCLC = Twentieth-Century Literary Criticism
*WLC = World Literature Criticism, 1500 to the
    Present*

The cross-references

See also CANR 23; CA 85-88;
   obituary CA 116

list all author entries in the following Gale biographical and literary sources:

AAYA = Authors & Artists for Young Adults
AITN = Authors in the News
BEST = Bestsellers
BW = Black Writers
CA = Contemporary Authors
*CAAS = Contemporary Authors
    Autobiography Series*
*CABS = Contemporary Authors
    Bibliographical Series*
*CANR = Contemporary Authors New
    Revision Series*
*CAP = Contemporary Authors Permanent
    Series*
*CDALB = Concise Dictionary of American
    Literary Biography*
*CDBLB = Concise Dictionary of British
    Literary Biography*

DLB = Dictionary of Literary Biography
*DLBD = Dictionary of Literary Biography
    Documentary Series*
DLBY = Dictionary of Literary Biography Yearbook
HW = Hispanic Writers
JRDA = Junior DISCovering Authors
*MAICYA = Major Authors and Illustrators for
    Children and Young Adults*
MTCW = Major 20th-Century Writers
NNAL = Native North American Literature
*SAAS = Something about the Author Autobiography
    Series*
SATA = Something about the Author
YABC = Yesterday's Authors of Books for Children

Literary Criticism Series
Cumulative Author Index

A. E. . . . . TCLC 3, 10
See also Russell, George William

Abasiyanik, Sait Faik 1906-1954
See Sait Faik
See also CA 123

Abbey, Edward 1927-1989 . . . . . . CLC 36, 59
See also CA 45-48; 128; CANR 2, 41

Abbott, Lee K(ittredge) 1947- . . . . . . CLC 48
See also CA 124; CANR 51; DLB 130

Abe, Kobo 1924-1993 . . . . . CLC 8, 22, 53, 81
See also CA 65-68; 140; CANR 24;
DAM NOV; MTCW

Abelard, Peter c. 1079-c. 1142 . . . CMLC 11
See also DLB 115

Abell, Kjeld 1901-1961 . . . . CLC 15
See also CA 111

Abish, Walter 1931- . . . . CLC 22
See also CA 101; CANR 37; DLB 130

Abrahams, Peter (Henry) 1919- . . . . . CLC 4
See also BW 1; CA 57-60; CANR 26;
DLB 117; MTCW

Abrams, M(eyer) H(oward) 1912- . . . CLC 24
See also CA 57-60; CANR 13, 33; DLB 67

Abse, Dannie 1923- . . . . CLC 7, 29; DAB
See also CA 53-56; CAAS 1; CANR 4, 46;
DAM POET; DLB 27

Achebe, (Albert) Chinua(lumogu)
1930- . . . . . CLC 1, 3, 5, 7, 11, 26, 51, 75;
BLC; DA; DAB; DAC; WLC
See also AAYA 15; BW 2; CA 1-4R;
CANR 6, 26, 47; CLR 20; DAM MST,
MULT, NOV; DLB 117; MAICYA;
MTCW; SATA 40; SATA-Brief 38

Acker, Kathy 1948- . . . . CLC 45
See also CA 117; 122

Ackroyd, Peter 1949- . . . . CLC 34, 52
See also CA 123; 127; CANR 51; DLB 155;
INT 127

Acorn, Milton 1923- . . . . CLC 15; DAC
See also CA 103; DLB 53; INT 103

Adamov, Arthur 1908-1970 . . . . . . CLC 4, 25
See also CA 17-18; 25-28R; CAP 2;
DAM DRAM; MTCW

Adams, Alice (Boyd) 1926- . . . CLC 6, 13, 46
See also CA 81-84; CANR 26; DLBY 86;
INT CANR-26; MTCW

Adams, Andy 1859-1935 . . . . TCLC 56
See also YABC 1

Adams, Douglas (Noel) 1952- . . . CLC 27, 60
See also AAYA 4; BEST 89:3; CA 106;
CANR 34; DAM POP; DLBY 83; JRDA

Adams, Francis 1862-1893 . . . . NCLC 33

Adams, Henry (Brooks)
1838-1918 . . . . . . TCLC 4, 52; DA; DAB;
DAC
See also CA 104; 133; DAM MST; DLB 12,
47

Adams, Richard (George)
1920- . . . . CLC 4, 5, 18
See also AAYA 16; AITN 1, 2; CA 49-52;
CANR 3, 35; CLR 20; DAM NOV;
JRDA; MAICYA; MTCW; SATA 7, 69

Adamson, Joy(-Friederike Victoria)
1910-1980 . . . . CLC 17
See also CA 69-72; 93-96; CANR 22;
MTCW; SATA 11; SATA-Obit 22

Adcock, Fleur 1934- . . . . CLC 41
See also CA 25-28R; CAAS 23; CANR 11,
34; DLB 40

Addams, Charles (Samuel)
1912-1988 . . . . CLC 30
See also CA 61-64; 126; CANR 12

Addison, Joseph 1672-1719 . . . . LC 18
See also CDBLB 1660-1789; DLB 101

Adler, Alfred (F.) 1870-1937 . . . . . . TCLC 61
See also CA 119

Adler, C(arole) S(chwerdtfeger)
1932- . . . . CLC 35
See also AAYA 4; CA 89-92; CANR 19,
40; JRDA; MAICYA; SAAS 15;
SATA 26, 63

Adler, Renata 1938- . . . . CLC 8, 31
See also CA 49-52; CANR 5, 22; MTCW

Ady, Endre 1877-1919 . . . . TCLC 11
See also CA 107

Aeschylus
525B.C.-456B.C. . . . . CMLC 11; DA;
DAB; DAC
See also DAM DRAM, MST

Afton, Effie
See Harper, Frances Ellen Watkins

Agapida, Fray Antonio
See Irving, Washington

Agee, James (Rufus)
1909-1955 . . . . TCLC 1, 19
See also AITN 1; CA 108; 148;
CDALB 1941-1968; DAM NOV; DLB 2,
26, 152

Aghill, Gordon
See Silverberg, Robert

Agnon, S(hmuel) Y(osef Halevi)
1888-1970 . . . . CLC 4, 8, 14
See also CA 17-18; 25-28R; CAP 2; MTCW

Agrippa von Nettesheim, Henry Cornelius
1486-1535 . . . . LC 27

Aherne, Owen
See Cassill, R(onald) V(erlin)

Ai 1947- . . . . CLC 4, 14, 69
See also CA 85-88; CAAS 13; DLB 120

Aickman, Robert (Fordyce)
1914-1981 . . . . CLC 57
See also CA 5-8R; CANR 3

Aiken, Conrad (Potter)
1889-1973 . . . CLC 1, 3, 5, 10, 52; SSC 9
See also CA 5-8R; 45-48; CANR 4;
CDALB 1929-1941; DAM NOV, POET;
DLB 9, 45, 102; MTCW; SATA 3, 30

Aiken, Joan (Delano) 1924- . . . . CLC 35
See also AAYA 1; CA 9-12R; CANR 4, 23,
34; CLR 1, 19; DLB 161; JRDA;
MAICYA; MTCW; SAAS 1; SATA 2,
30, 73

Ainsworth, William Harrison
1805-1882 . . . . NCLC 13
See also DLB 21; SATA 24

Aitmatov, Chingiz (Torekulovich)
1928- . . . . CLC 71
See also CA 103; CANR 38; MTCW;
SATA 56

Akers, Floyd
See Baum, L(yman) Frank

Akhmadulina, Bella Akhatovna
1937- . . . . CLC 53
See also CA 65-68; DAM POET

Akhmatova, Anna
1888-1966 . . . . CLC 11, 25, 64; PC 2
See also CA 19-20; 25-28R; CANR 35;
CAP 1; DAM POET; MTCW

Aksakov, Sergei Timofeyvich
1791-1859 . . . . NCLC 2

Aksenov, Vassily
See Aksyonov, Vassily (Pavlovich)

Aksyonov, Vassily (Pavlovich)
1932- . . . . CLC 22, 37
See also CA 53-56; CANR 12, 48

Akutagawa Ryunosuke
1892-1927 . . . . TCLC 16
See also CA 117

Alain 1868-1951 . . . . TCLC 41

Alain-Fournier . . . . TCLC 6
See also Fournier, Henri Alban
See also DLB 65

Alarcon, Pedro Antonio de
1833-1891 . . . . NCLC 1

Alas (y Urena), Leopoldo (Enrique Garcia)
1852-1901 . . . . TCLC 29
See also CA 113; 131; HW

Albee, Edward (Franklin III)
1928- . . . . . . CLC 1, 2, 3, 5, 9, 11, 13, 25,
53, 86; DA; DAB; DAC; WLC
See also AITN 1; CA 5-8R; CABS 3;
CANR 8; CDALB 1941-1968;
DAM DRAM, MST; DLB 7;
INT CANR-8; MTCW

Alberti, Rafael 1902- . . . . CLC 7
See also CA 85-88; DLB 108

Albert the Great 1200(?)-1280 . . . . CMLC 16
See also DLB 115

Alcala-Galiano, Juan Valera y
See Valera y Alcala-Galiano, Juan

Andrews, Elton V.
See Pohl, Frederik

Andreyev, Leonid (Nikolaevich)
1871-1919 .... TCLC 3
See also CA 104

Andric, Ivo 1892-1975 .... CLC 8
See also CA 81-84; 57-60; CANR 43;
DLB 147; MTCW

Angelique, Pierre
See Bataille, Georges

Angell, Roger 1920- .... CLC 26
See also CA 57-60; CANR 13, 44

Angelou, Maya
1928- .... CLC 12, 35, 64, 77; BLC; DA;
DAB; DAC
See also AAYA 7; BW 2; CA 65-68;
CANR 19, 42; DAM MST, MULT,
POET, POP; DLB 38; MTCW; SATA 49

Annensky, Innokenty Fyodorovich
1856-1909 .... TCLC 14
See also CA 110

Anon, Charles Robert
See Pessoa, Fernando (Antonio Nogueira)

Anouilh, Jean (Marie Lucien Pierre)
1910-1987 ...... CLC 1, 3, 8, 13, 40, 50
See also CA 17-20R; 123; CANR 32;
DAM DRAM; MTCW

Anthony, Florence
See Ai

Anthony, John
See Ciardi, John (Anthony)

Anthony, Peter
See Shaffer, Anthony (Joshua); Shaffer,
Peter (Levin)

Anthony, Piers 1934- .... CLC 35
See also AAYA 11; CA 21-24R; CANR 28;
DAM POP; DLB 8; MTCW; SAAS 22;
SATA 84

Antoine, Marc
See Proust, (Valentin-Louis-George-Eugene-)
Marcel

Antoninus, Brother
See Everson, William (Oliver)

Antonioni, Michelangelo 1912- ..... CLC 20
See also CA 73-76; CANR 45

Antschel, Paul 1920-1970
See Celan, Paul
See also CA 85-88; CANR 33; MTCW

Anwar, Chairil 1922-1949 .... TCLC 22
See also CA 121

Apollinaire, Guillaume .. TCLC 3, 8, 51; PC 7
See also Kostrowitzki, Wilhelm Apollinaris
de
See also DAM POET

Appelfeld, Aharon 1932- .... CLC 23, 47
See also CA 112; 133

Apple, Max (Isaac) 1941- .... CLC 9, 33
See also CA 81-84; CANR 19; DLB 130

Appleman, Philip (Dean) 1926- ..... CLC 51
See also CA 13-16R; CAAS 18; CANR 6,
29

Appleton, Lawrence
See Lovecraft, H(oward) P(hillips)

Apteryx
See Eliot, T(homas) S(tearns)

Apuleius, (Lucius Madaurensis)
125(?)-175(?) .... CMLC 1

Aquin, Hubert 1929-1977 .... CLC 15
See also CA 105; DLB 53

Aragon, Louis 1897-1982 .... CLC 3, 22
See also CA 69-72; 108; CANR 28;
DAM NOV, POET; DLB 72; MTCW

Arany, Janos 1817-1882 .... NCLC 34

Arbuthnot, John 1667-1735 .... LC 1
See also DLB 101

Archer, Herbert Winslow
See Mencken, H(enry) L(ouis)

Archer, Jeffrey (Howard) 1940- .... CLC 28
See also AAYA 16; BEST 89:3; CA 77-80;
CANR 22; DAM POP; INT CANR-22

Archer, Jules 1915- .... CLC 12
See also CA 9-12R; CANR 6; SAAS 5;
SATA 4, 85

Archer, Lee
See Ellison, Harlan (Jay)

Arden, John 1930- .... CLC 6, 13, 15
See also CA 13-16R; CAAS 4; CANR 31;
DAM DRAM; DLB 13; MTCW

Arenas, Reinaldo
1943-1990 .... CLC 41; HLC
See also CA 124; 128; 133; DAM MULT;
DLB 145; HW

Arendt, Hannah 1906-1975 .... CLC 66
See also CA 17-20R; 61-64; CANR 26;
MTCW

Aretino, Pietro 1492-1556 .... LC 12

Arghezi, Tudor .... CLC 80
See also Theodorescu, Ion N.

Arguedas, Jose Maria
1911-1969 .... CLC 10, 18
See also CA 89-92; DLB 113; HW

Argueta, Manlio 1936- .... CLC 31
See also CA 131; DLB 145; HW

Ariosto, Ludovico 1474-1533 .... LC 6

Aristides
See Epstein, Joseph

Aristophanes
450B.C.-385B.C. .... CMLC 4; DA;
DAB; DAC; DC 2
See also DAM DRAM, MST

Arlt, Roberto (Godofredo Christophersen)
1900-1942 .... TCLC 29; HLC
See also CA 123; 131; DAM MULT; HW

Armah, Ayi Kwei 1939- .... CLC 5, 33; BLC
See also BW 1; CA 61-64; CANR 21;
DAM MULT, POET; DLB 117; MTCW

Armatrading, Joan 1950- .... CLC 17
See also CA 114

Arnette, Robert
See Silverberg, Robert

Arnim, Achim von (Ludwig Joachim von
Arnim) 1781-1831 .... NCLC 5
See also DLB 90

Arnim, Bettina von 1785-1859.... NCLC 38
See also DLB 90

Arnold, Matthew
1822-1888 ..... NCLC 6, 29; DA; DAB;
DAC; PC 5; WLC
See also CDBLB 1832-1890; DAM MST,
POET; DLB 32, 57

Arnold, Thomas 1795-1842 ...... NCLC 18
See also DLB 55

Arnow, Harriette (Louisa) Simpson
1908-1986 .... CLC 2, 7, 18
See also CA 9-12R; 118; CANR 14; DLB 6;
MTCW; SATA 42; SATA-Obit 47

Arp, Hans
See Arp, Jean

Arp, Jean 1887-1966............... CLC 5
See also CA 81-84; 25-28R; CANR 42

Arrabal
See Arrabal, Fernando

Arrabal, Fernando 1932- ... CLC 2, 9, 18, 58
See also CA 9-12R; CANR 15

Arrick, Fran..................... CLC 30
See also Gaberman, Judie Angell

Artaud, Antonin (Marie Joseph)
1896-1948 .... TCLC 3, 36
See also CA 104; 149; DAM DRAM

Arthur, Ruth M(abel) 1905-1979.... CLC 12
See also CA 9-12R; 85-88; CANR 4;
SATA 7, 26

Artsybashev, Mikhail (Petrovich)
1878-1927 .... TCLC 31

Arundel, Honor (Morfydd)
1919-1973 .... CLC 17
See also CA 21-22; 41-44R; CAP 2;
CLR 35; SATA 4; SATA-Obit 24

Asch, Sholem 1880-1957 .... TCLC 3
See also CA 105

Ash, Shalom
See Asch, Sholem

Ashbery, John (Lawrence)
1927- ...... CLC 2, 3, 4, 6, 9, 13, 15, 25,
41, 77
See also CA 5-8R; CANR 9, 37;
DAM POET; DLB 5; DLBY 81;
INT CANR-9; MTCW

Ashdown, Clifford
See Freeman, R(ichard) Austin

Ashe, Gordon
See Creasey, John

Ashton-Warner, Sylvia (Constance)
1908-1984 .... CLC 19
See also CA 69-72; 112; CANR 29; MTCW

Asimov, Isaac
1920-1992 ... CLC 1, 3, 9, 19, 26, 76, 92
See also AAYA 13; BEST 90:2; CA 1-4R;
137; CANR 2, 19, 36; CLR 12;
DAM POP; DLB 8; DLBY 92;
INT CANR-19; JRDA; MAICYA;
MTCW; SATA 1, 26, 74

Astley, Thea (Beatrice May)
1925- .... CLC 41
See also CA 65-68; CANR 11, 43

Aston, James
See White, T(erence) H(anbury)

Balzac, Honore de
1799-1850 . . . . NCLC 5, 35, 53; DA;
DAB; DAC; SSC 5; WLC
See also DAM MST, NOV; DLB 119

Bambara, Toni Cade
1939-1995 . . . . . . CLC 19, 88; BLC; DA;
DAC
See also AAYA 5; BW 2; CA 29-32R; 150;
CANR 24, 49; DAM MST, MULT;
DLB 38; MTCW

Bamdad, A.
See Shamlu, Ahmad

Banat, D. R.
See Bradbury, Ray (Douglas)

Bancroft, Laura
See Baum, L(yman) Frank

Banim, John 1798-1842 . . . . NCLC 13
See also DLB 116, 158, 159

Banim, Michael 1796-1874 . . . . . . NCLC 13
See also DLB 158, 159

Banks, Iain
See Banks, Iain M(enzies)

Banks, Iain M(enzies) 1954- . . . . CLC 34
See also CA 123; 128; INT 128

Banks, Lynne Reid . . . . CLC 23
See also Reid Banks, Lynne
See also AAYA 6

Banks, Russell 1940- . . . . CLC 37, 72
See also CA 65-68; CAAS 15; CANR 19;
DLB 130

Banville, John 1945- . . . . CLC 46
See also CA 117; 128; DLB 14; INT 128

Banville, Theodore (Faullain) de
1832-1891 . . . . NCLC 9

Baraka, Amiri
1934- . . . . CLC 1, 2, 3, 5, 10, 14, 33;
BLC; DA; DAC; DC 6; PC 4
See also Jones, LeRoi
See also BW 2; CA 21-24R; CABS 3;
CANR 27, 38; CDALB 1941-1968;
DAM MST, MULT, POET, POP;
DLB 5, 7, 16, 38; DLBD 8; MTCW

Barbauld, Anna Laetitia
1743-1825 . . . . NCLC 50
See also DLB 107, 109, 142, 158

Barbellion, W. N. P. . . . . TCLC 24
See also Cummings, Bruce F(rederick)

Barbera, Jack (Vincent) 1945- . . . . . CLC 44
See also CA 110; CANR 45

Barbey d'Aurevilly, Jules Amedee
1808-1889 . . . . NCLC 1; SSC 17
See also DLB 119

Barbusse, Henri 1873-1935 . . . . TCLC 5
See also CA 105; DLB 65

Barclay, Bill
See Moorcock, Michael (John)

Barclay, William Ewert
See Moorcock, Michael (John)

Barea, Arturo 1897-1957 . . . . TCLC 14
See also CA 111

Barfoot, Joan 1946- . . . . CLC 18
See also CA 105

Baring, Maurice 1874-1945 . . . . TCLC 8
See also CA 105; DLB 34

Barker, Clive 1952- . . . . CLC 52
See also AAYA 10; BEST 90:3; CA 121;
129; DAM POP; INT 129; MTCW

Barker, George Granville
1913-1991 . . . . CLC 8, 48
See also CA 9-12R; 135; CANR 7, 38;
DAM POET; DLB 20; MTCW

Barker, Harley Granville
See Granville-Barker, Harley
See also DLB 10

Barker, Howard 1946- . . . . CLC 37
See also CA 102; DLB 13

Barker, Pat(ricia) 1943- . . . . CLC 32, 91
See also CA 117; 122; CANR 50; INT 122

Barlow, Joel 1754-1812 . . . . NCLC 23
See also DLB 37

Barnard, Mary (Ethel) 1909- . . . . . . CLC 48
See also CA 21-22; CAP 2

Barnes, Djuna
1892-1982 . . . CLC 3, 4, 8, 11, 29; SSC 3
See also CA 9-12R; 107; CANR 16; DLB 4,
9, 45; MTCW

Barnes, Julian 1946- . . . . CLC 42; DAB
See also CA 102; CANR 19; DLBY 93

Barnes, Peter 1931- . . . . CLC 5, 56
See also CA 65-68; CAAS 12; CANR 33,
34; DLB 13; MTCW

Baroja (y Nessi), Pio
1872-1956 . . . . TCLC 8; HLC
See also CA 104

Baron, David
See Pinter, Harold

Baron Corvo
See Rolfe, Frederick (William Serafino
Austin Lewis Mary)

Barondess, Sue K(aufman)
1926-1977 . . . . CLC 8
See also Kaufman, Sue
See also CA 1-4R; 69-72; CANR 1

Baron de Teive
See Pessoa, Fernando (Antonio Nogueira)

Barres, Maurice 1862-1923 . . . . . . TCLC 47
See also DLB 123

Barreto, Afonso Henrique de Lima
See Lima Barreto, Afonso Henrique de

Barrett, (Roger) Syd 1946- . . . . CLC 35

Barrett, William (Christopher)
1913-1992 . . . . CLC 27
See also CA 13-16R; 139; CANR 11;
INT CANR-11

Barrie, J(ames) M(atthew)
1860-1937 . . . . TCLC 2; DAB
See also CA 104; 136; CDBLB 1890-1914;
CLR 16; DAM DRAM; DLB 10, 141,
156; MAICYA; YABC 1

Barrington, Michael
See Moorcock, Michael (John)

Barrol, Grady
See Bograd, Larry

Barry, Mike
See Malzberg, Barry N(athaniel)

Barry, Philip 1896-1949 . . . . TCLC 11
See also CA 109; DLB 7

Bart, Andre Schwarz
See Schwarz-Bart, Andre

Barth, John (Simmons)
1930- . . . . . . CLC 1, 2, 3, 5, 7, 9, 10, 14,
27, 51, 89; SSC 10
See also AITN 1, 2; CA 1-4R; CABS 1;
CANR 5, 23, 49; DAM NOV; DLB 2;
MTCW

Barthelme, Donald
1931-1989 . . . . . . CLC 1, 2, 3, 5, 6, 8, 13,
23, 46, 59; SSC 2
See also CA 21-24R; 129; CANR 20;
DAM NOV; DLB 2; DLBY 80, 89;
MTCW; SATA 7; SATA-Obit 62

Barthelme, Frederick 1943- . . . . CLC 36
See also CA 114; 122; DLBY 85; INT 122

Barthes, Roland (Gerard)
1915-1980 . . . . CLC 24, 83
See also CA 130; 97-100; MTCW

Barzun, Jacques (Martin) 1907- . . . . CLC 51
See also CA 61-64; CANR 22

Bashevis, Isaac
See Singer, Isaac Bashevis

Bashkirtseff, Marie 1859-1884 . . . NCLC 27

Basho
See Matsuo Basho

Bass, Kingsley B., Jr.
See Bullins, Ed

Bass, Rick 1958- . . . . CLC 79
See also CA 126

Bassani, Giorgio 1916- . . . . CLC 9
See also CA 65-68; CANR 33; DLB 128;
MTCW

Bastos, Augusto (Antonio) Roa
See Roa Bastos, Augusto (Antonio)

Bataille, Georges 1897-1962 . . . . CLC 29
See also CA 101; 89-92

Bates, H(erbert) E(rnest)
1905-1974 . . . . . . CLC 46; DAB; SSC 10
See also CA 93-96; 45-48; CANR 34;
DAM POP; DLB 162; MTCW

Bauchart
See Camus, Albert

Baudelaire, Charles
1821-1867 . . . . NCLC 6, 29, 55; DA;
DAB; DAC; PC 1; SSC 18; WLC
See also DAM MST, POET

Baudrillard, Jean 1929- . . . . CLC 60

Baum, L(yman) Frank 1856-1919 . . . TCLC 7
See also CA 108; 133; CLR 15; DLB 22;
JRDA; MAICYA; MTCW; SATA 18

Baum, Louis F.
See Baum, L(yman) Frank

Baumbach, Jonathan 1933- . . . . . . CLC 6, 23
See also CA 13-16R; CAAS 5; CANR 12;
DLBY 80; INT CANR-12; MTCW

Bausch, Richard (Carl) 1945- . . . . . . CLC 51
See also CA 101; CAAS 14; CANR 43;
DLB 130

Baxter, Charles 1947- . . . . CLC 45, 78
See also CA 57-60; CANR 40; DAM POP;
DLB 130

Baxter, George Owen
See Faust, Frederick (Schiller)

Bottoms, David 1949-............. **CLC 53**
See also CA 105; CANR 22; DLB 120;
DLBY 83

Boucicault, Dion 1820-1890...... **NCLC 41**

Boucolon, Maryse 1937-
See Conde, Maryse
See also CA 110; CANR 30

Bourget, Paul (Charles Joseph)
1852-1935 .... **TCLC 12**
See also CA 107; DLB 123

Bourjaily, Vance (Nye) 1922-.... **CLC 8, 62**
See also CA 1-4R; CAAS 1; CANR 2;
DLB 2, 143

Bourne, Randolph S(illiman)
1886-1918 .... **TCLC 16**
See also CA 117; DLB 63

Bova, Ben(jamin William) 1932-.... **CLC 45**
See also AAYA 16; CA 5-8R; CAAS 18;
CANR 11; CLR 3; DLBY 81;
INT CANR-11; MAICYA; MTCW;
SATA 6, 68

Bowen, Elizabeth (Dorothea Cole)
1899-1973 ...... **CLC 1, 3, 6, 11, 15, 22;**
SSC 3
See also CA 17-18; 41-44R; CANR 35;
CAP 2; CDBLB 1945-1960; DAM NOV;
DLB 15, 162; MTCW

Bowering, George 1935-........ **CLC 15, 47**
See also CA 21-24R; CAAS 16; CANR 10;
DLB 53

Bowering, Marilyn R(uthe) 1949-... **CLC 32**
See also CA 101; CANR 49

Bowers, Edgar 1924- .... **CLC 9**
See also CA 5-8R; CANR 24; DLB 5

Bowie, David .... **CLC 17**
See also Jones, David Robert

Bowles, Jane (Sydney)
1917-1973 .... **CLC 3, 68**
See also CA 19-20; 41-44R; CAP 2

Bowles, Paul (Frederick)
1910- .... **CLC 1, 2, 19, 53; SSC 3**
See also CA 1-4R; CAAS 1; CANR 1, 19,
50; DLB 5, 6; MTCW

Box, Edgar
See Vidal, Gore

Boyd, Nancy
See Millay, Edna St. Vincent

Boyd, William 1952-........ **CLC 28, 53, 70**
See also CA 114; 120; CANR 51

Boyle, Kay
1902-1992 ..... **CLC 1, 5, 19, 58; SSC 5**
See also CA 13-16R; 140; CAAS 1;
CANR 29; DLB 4, 9, 48, 86; DLBY 93;
MTCW

Boyle, Mark
See Kienzle, William X(avier)

Boyle, Patrick 1905-1982......... **CLC 19**
See also CA 127

Boyle, T. C. 1948-
See Boyle, T(homas) Coraghessan

Boyle, T(homas) Coraghessan
1948- .... **CLC 36, 55, 90; SSC 16**
See also BEST 90:4; CA 120; CANR 44;
DAM POP; DLBY 86

Boz
See Dickens, Charles (John Huffam)

Brackenridge, Hugh Henry
1748-1816 .... **NCLC 7**
See also DLB 11, 37

Bradbury, Edward P.
See Moorcock, Michael (John)

Bradbury, Malcolm (Stanley)
1932- .... **CLC 32, 61**
See also CA 1-4R; CANR 1, 33;
DAM NOV; DLB 14; MTCW

Bradbury, Ray (Douglas)
1920- .... **CLC 1, 3, 10, 15, 42; DA;**
DAB; DAC; WLC
See also AAYA 15; AITN 1, 2; CA 1-4R;
CANR 2, 30; CDALB 1968-1988;
DAM MST, NOV, POP; DLB 2, 8;
INT CANR-30; MTCW; SATA 11, 64

Bradford, Gamaliel 1863-1932..... **TCLC 36**
See also DLB 17

Bradley, David (Henry, Jr.)
1950- .... **CLC 23; BLC**
See also BW 1; CA 104; CANR 26;
DAM MULT; DLB 33

Bradley, John Ed(mund, Jr.)
1958- .... **CLC 55**
See also CA 139

Bradley, Marion Zimmer 1930-..... **CLC 30**
See also AAYA 9; CA 57-60; CAAS 10;
CANR 7, 31, 51; DAM POP; DLB 8;
MTCW

Bradstreet, Anne
1612(?)-1672 ...... **LC 4, 30; DA; DAC;**
PC 10
See also CDALB 1640-1865; DAM MST,
POET; DLB 24

Brady, Joan 1939- .... **CLC 86**
See also CA 141

Bragg, Melvyn 1939- .... **CLC 10**
See also BEST 89:3; CA 57-60; CANR 10,
48; DLB 14

Braine, John (Gerard)
1922-1986 .... **CLC 1, 3, 41**
See also CA 1-4R; 120; CANR 1, 33;
CDBLB 1945-1960; DLB 15; DLBY 86;
MTCW

Brammer, William 1930(?)-1978 .... **CLC 31**
See also CA 77-80

Brancati, Vitaliano 1907-1954..... **TCLC 12**
See also CA 109

Brancato, Robin F(idler) 1936-..... **CLC 35**
See also AAYA 9; CA 69-72; CANR 11,
45; CLR 32; JRDA; SAAS 9; SATA 23

Brand, Max
See Faust, Frederick (Schiller)

Brand, Millen 1906-1980.......... **CLC 7**
See also CA 21-24R; 97-100

Branden, Barbara .... **CLC 44**
See also CA 148

Brandes, Georg (Morris Cohen)
1842-1927 .... **TCLC 10**
See also CA 105

Brandys, Kazimierz 1916-......... **CLC 62**

Branley, Franklyn M(ansfield)
1915- .... **CLC 21**
See also CA 33-36R; CANR 14, 39;
CLR 13; MAICYA; SAAS 16; SATA 4,
68

Brathwaite, Edward Kamau 1930-... **CLC 11**
See also BW 2; CA 25-28R; CANR 11, 26,
47; DAM POET; DLB 125

Brautigan, Richard (Gary)
1935-1984 ... **CLC 1, 3, 5, 9, 12, 34, 42**
See also CA 53-56; 113; CANR 34;
DAM NOV; DLB 2, 5; DLBY 80, 84;
MTCW; SATA 56

Braverman, Kate 1950- .... **CLC 67**
See also CA 89-92

Brecht, Bertolt
1898-1956 ...... **TCLC 1, 6, 13, 35; DA;**
DAB; DAC; DC 3; WLC
See also CA 104; 133; DAM DRAM, MST;
DLB 56, 124; MTCW

Brecht, Eugen Berthold Friedrich
See Brecht, Bertolt

Bremer, Fredrika 1801-1865 ..... **NCLC 11**

Brennan, Christopher John
1870-1932 .... **TCLC 17**
See also CA 117

Brennan, Maeve 1917-............ **CLC 5**
See also CA 81-84

Brentano, Clemens (Maria)
1778-1842 .... **NCLC 1**
See also DLB 90

Brent of Bin Bin
See Franklin, (Stella Maraia Sarah) Miles

Brenton, Howard 1942- .... **CLC 31**
See also CA 69-72; CANR 33; DLB 13;
MTCW

Breslin, James 1930-
See Breslin, Jimmy
See also CA 73-76; CANR 31; DAM NOV;
MTCW

Breslin, Jimmy .... **CLC 4, 43**
See also Breslin, James
See also AITN 1

Bresson, Robert 1901- .... **CLC 16**
See also CA 110; CANR 49

Breton, Andre
1896-1966 ..... **CLC 2, 9, 15, 54; PC 15**
See also CA 19-20; 25-28R; CANR 40;
CAP 2; DLB 65; MTCW

Breytenbach, Breyten 1939(?)- .. **CLC 23, 37**
See also CA 113; 129; DAM POET

Bridgers, Sue Ellen 1942- .... **CLC 26**
See also AAYA 8; CA 65-68; CANR 11,
36; CLR 18; DLB 52; JRDA; MAICYA;
SAAS 1; SATA 22

Bridges, Robert (Seymour)
1844-1930 .... **TCLC 1**
See also CA 104; CDBLB 1890-1914;
DAM POET; DLB 19, 98

Bridie, James .... **TCLC 3**
See also Mavor, Osborne Henry
See also DLB 10

Brin, David 1950-............... **CLC 34**
See also CA 102; CANR 24;
INT CANR-24; SATA 65

Cage, John (Milton, Jr.) 1912- ..... **CLC 41**
See also CA 13-16R; CANR 9;
INT CANR-9

Cain, G.
See Cabrera Infante, G(uillermo)

Cain, Guillermo
See Cabrera Infante, G(uillermo)

Cain, James M(allahan)
1892-1977 .... **CLC 3, 11, 28**
See also AITN 1; CA 17-20R; 73-76;
CANR 8, 34; MTCW

Caine, Mark
See Raphael, Frederic (Michael)

Calasso, Roberto 1941- .... **CLC 81**
See also CA 143

Calderon de la Barca, Pedro
1600-1681 .... **LC 23; DC 3**

Caldwell, Erskine (Preston)
1903-1987 .... **CLC 1, 8, 14, 50, 60;
SSC 19**
See also AITN 1; CA 1-4R; 121; CAAS 1;
CANR 2, 33; DAM NOV; DLB 9, 86;
MTCW

Caldwell, (Janet Miriam) Taylor (Holland)
1900-1985 .... **CLC 2, 28, 39**
See also CA 5-8R; 116; CANR 5;
DAM NOV, POP

Calhoun, John Caldwell
1782-1850 .... **NCLC 15**
See also DLB 3

Calisher, Hortense
1911- .... **CLC 2, 4, 8, 38; SSC 15**
See also CA 1-4R; CANR 1, 22;
DAM NOV; DLB 2; INT CANR-22;
MTCW

Callaghan, Morley Edward
1903-1990 ..... **CLC 3, 14, 41, 65; DAC**
See also CA 9-12R; 132; CANR 33;
DAM MST; DLB 68; MTCW

Calvino, Italo
1923-1985 ..... **CLC 5, 8, 11, 22, 33, 39,
73; SSC 3**
See also CA 85-88; 116; CANR 23;
DAM NOV; MTCW

Cameron, Carey 1952- .... **CLC 59**
See also CA 135

Cameron, Peter 1959- .... **CLC 44**
See also CA 125; CANR 50

Campana, Dino 1885-1932 .... **TCLC 20**
See also CA 117; DLB 114

Campanella, Tommaso 1568-1639 .... **LC 32**

Campbell, John W(ood, Jr.)
1910-1971 .... **CLC 32**
See also CA 21-22; 29-32R; CANR 34;
CAP 2; DLB 8; MTCW

Campbell, Joseph 1904-1987 .... **CLC 69**
See also AAYA 3; BEST 89:2; CA 1-4R;
124; CANR 3, 28; MTCW

Campbell, Maria 1940- .... **CLC 85; DAC**
See also CA 102; NNAL

Campbell, (John) Ramsey
1946- .... **CLC 42; SSC 19**
See also CA 57-60; CANR 7; INT CANR-7

Campbell, (Ignatius) Roy (Dunnachie)
1901-1957 .... **TCLC 5**
See also CA 104; DLB 20

Campbell, Thomas 1777-1844 .... **NCLC 19**
See also DLB 93; 144

Campbell, Wilfred .... **TCLC 9**
See also Campbell, William

Campbell, William 1858(?)-1918
See Campbell, Wilfred
See also CA 106; DLB 92

Campos, Alvaro de
See Pessoa, Fernando (Antonio Nogueira)

Camus, Albert
1913-1960 .... **CLC 1, 2, 4, 9, 11, 14, 32,
63, 69; DA; DAB; DAC; DC 2; SSC 9;
WLC**
See also CA 89-92; DAM DRAM, MST,
NOV; DLB 72; MTCW

Canby, Vincent 1924- .... **CLC 13**
See also CA 81-84

Cancale
See Desnos, Robert

Canetti, Elias
1905-1994 .... **CLC 3, 14, 25, 75, 86**
See also CA 21-24R; 146; CANR 23;
DLB 85, 124; MTCW

Canin, Ethan 1960- .... **CLC 55**
See also CA 131; 135

Cannon, Curt
See Hunter, Evan

Cape, Judith
See Page, P(atricia) K(athleen)

Capek, Karel
1890-1938 ...... **TCLC 6, 37; DA; DAB;
DAC; DC 1; WLC**
See also CA 104; 140; DAM DRAM, MST,
NOV

Capote, Truman
1924-1984 ...... **CLC 1, 3, 8, 13, 19, 34,
38, 58; DA; DAB; DAC; SSC 2; WLC**
See also CA 5-8R; 113; CANR 18;
CDALB 1941-1968; DAM MST, NOV,
POP; DLB 2; DLBY 80, 84; MTCW

Capra, Frank 1897-1991 .... **CLC 16**
See also CA 61-64; 135

Caputo, Philip 1941- .... **CLC 32**
See also CA 73-76; CANR 40

Card, Orson Scott 1951- .... **CLC 44, 47, 50**
See also AAYA 11; CA 102; CANR 27, 47;
DAM POP; INT CANR-27; MTCW;
SATA 83

Cardenal (Martinez), Ernesto
1925- .... **CLC 31; HLC**
See also CA 49-52; CANR 2, 32;
DAM MULT, POET; HW; MTCW

Carducci, Giosue 1835-1907 ...... **TCLC 32**

Carew, Thomas 1595(?)-1640 .... **LC 13**
See also DLB 126

Carey, Ernestine Gilbreth 1908- .... **CLC 17**
See also CA 5-8R; SATA 2

Carey, Peter 1943- .... **CLC 40, 55**
See also CA 123; 127; INT 127; MTCW

Carleton, William 1794-1869 ...... **NCLC 3**
See also DLB 159

Carlisle, Henry (Coffin) 1926- ...... **CLC 33**
See also CA 13-16R; CANR 15

Carlsen, Chris
See Holdstock, Robert P.

Carlson, Ron(ald F.) 1947- .... **CLC 54**
See also CA 105; CANR 27

Carlyle, Thomas
1795-1881 .. **NCLC 22; DA; DAB; DAC**
See also CDBLB 1789-1832; DAM MST;
DLB 55; 144

Carman, (William) Bliss
1861-1929 .... **TCLC 7; DAC**
See also CA 104; DLB 92

Carnegie, Dale 1888-1955 .... **TCLC 53**

Carossa, Hans 1878-1956......... **TCLC 48**
See also DLB 66

Carpenter, Don(ald Richard)
1931-1995 .... **CLC 41**
See also CA 45-48; 149; CANR 1

Carpentier (y Valmont), Alejo
1904-1980 .... **CLC 8, 11, 38; HLC**
See also CA 65-68; 97-100; CANR 11;
DAM MULT; DLB 113; HW

Carr, Caleb 1955(?)- .... **CLC 86**
See also CA 147

Carr, Emily 1871-1945........... **TCLC 32**
See also DLB 68

Carr, John Dickson 1906-1977 ...... **CLC 3**
See also CA 49-52; 69-72; CANR 3, 33;
MTCW

Carr, Philippa
See Hibbert, Eleanor Alice Burford

Carr, Virginia Spencer 1929- .... **CLC 34**
See also CA 61-64; DLB 111

Carrere, Emmanuel 1957- .... **CLC 89**

Carrier, Roch 1937- ..... **CLC 13, 78; DAC**
See also CA 130; DAM MST; DLB 53

Carroll, James P. 1943(?)- .... **CLC 38**
See also CA 81-84

Carroll, Jim 1951- .... **CLC 35**
See also AAYA 17; CA 45-48; CANR 42

Carroll, Lewis .... **NCLC 2, 53; WLC**
See also Dodgson, Charles Lutwidge
See also CDBLB 1832-1890; CLR 2, 18;
DLB 18, 163; JRDA

Carroll, Paul Vincent 1900-1968.... **CLC 10**
See also CA 9-12R; 25-28R; DLB 10

Carruth, Hayden
1921- ...... **CLC 4, 7, 10, 18, 84; PC 10**
See also CA 9-12R; CANR 4, 38; DLB 5;
INT CANR-4; MTCW; SATA 47

Carson, Rachel Louise 1907-1964 ... **CLC 71**
See also CA 77-80; CANR 35; DAM POP;
MTCW; SATA 23

Carter, Angela (Olive)
1940-1992 ...... **CLC 5, 41, 76; SSC 13**
See also CA 53-56; 136; CANR 12, 36;
DLB 14; MTCW; SATA 66;
SATA-Obit 70

Carter, Nick
See Smith, Martin Cruz

Carver, Raymond
    1938-1988 . . . **CLC 22, 36, 53, 55; SSC 8**
    See also CA 33-36R; 126; CANR 17, 34;
    DAM NOV; DLB 130; DLBY 84, 88;
    MTCW

Cary, Elizabeth, Lady Falkland
    1585-1639 . . . . **LC 30**

Cary, (Arthur) Joyce (Lunel)
    1888-1957 . . . . **TCLC 1, 29**
    See also CA 104; CDBLB 1914-1945;
    DLB 15, 100

Casanova de Seingalt, Giovanni Jacopo
    1725-1798 . . . . **LC 13**

Casares, Adolfo Bioy
    See Bioy Casares, Adolfo

Casely-Hayford, J(oseph) E(phraim)
    1866-1930 . . . . **TCLC 24; BLC**
    See also BW 2; CA 123; DAM MULT

Casey, John (Dudley) 1939- . . . . **CLC 59**
    See also BEST 90:2; CA 69-72; CANR 23

Casey, Michael 1947- . . . . **CLC 2**
    See also CA 65-68; DLB 5

Casey, Patrick
    See Thurman, Wallace (Henry)

Casey, Warren (Peter) 1935-1988 . . . **CLC 12**
    See also CA 101; 127; INT 101

Casona, Alejandro . . . . **CLC 49**
    See also Alvarez, Alejandro Rodriguez

Cassavetes, John 1929-1989 . . . . **CLC 20**
    See also CA 85-88; 127

Cassill, R(onald) V(erlin) 1919- . . . **CLC 4, 23**
    See also CA 9-12R; CAAS 1; CANR 7, 45;
    DLB 6

Cassirer, Ernst 1874-1945 . . . . **TCLC 61**

Cassity, (Allen) Turner 1929- . . . . **CLC 6, 42**
    See also CA 17-20R; CAAS 8; CANR 11;
    DLB 105

Castaneda, Carlos 1931(?)- . . . . **CLC 12**
    See also CA 25-28R; CANR 32; HW;
    MTCW

Castedo, Elena 1937- . . . . **CLC 65**
    See also CA 132

Castedo-Ellerman, Elena
    See Castedo, Elena

Castellanos, Rosario
    1925-1974 . . . . **CLC 66; HLC**
    See also CA 131; 53-56; DAM MULT;
    DLB 113; HW

Castelvetro, Lodovico 1505-1571 . . . . . **LC 12**

Castiglione, Baldassare 1478-1529 . . . **LC 12**

Castle, Robert
    See Hamilton, Edmond

Castro, Guillen de 1569-1631 . . . . **LC 19**

Castro, Rosalia de 1837-1885 . . . . . **NCLC 3**
    See also DAM MULT

Cather, Willa
    See Cather, Willa Sibert

Cather, Willa Sibert
    1873-1947 . . . . **TCLC 1, 11, 31; DA;**
             DAB; DAC; SSC 2; WLC
    See also CA 104; 128; CDALB 1865-1917;
    DAM MST, NOV; DLB 9, 54, 78;
    DLBD 1; MTCW; SATA 30

Catton, (Charles) Bruce
    1899-1978 . . . . **CLC 35**
    See also AITN 1; CA 5-8R; 81-84;
    CANR 7; DLB 17; SATA 2;
    SATA-Obit 24

Cauldwell, Frank
    See King, Francis (Henry)

Caunitz, William J. 1933- . . . . **CLC 34**
    See also BEST 89:3; CA 125; 130; INT 130

Causley, Charles (Stanley) 1917- . . . . . **CLC 7**
    See also CA 9-12R; CANR 5, 35; CLR 30;
    DLB 27; MTCW; SATA 3, 66

Caute, David 1936- . . . . **CLC 29**
    See also CA 1-4R; CAAS 4; CANR 1, 33;
    DAM NOV; DLB 14

Cavafy, C(onstantine) P(eter)
    1863-1933 . . . . **TCLC 2, 7**
    See also Kavafis, Konstantinos Petrou
    See also CA 148; DAM POET

Cavallo, Evelyn
    See Spark, Muriel (Sarah)

Cavanna, Betty . . . . **CLC 12**
    See also Harrison, Elizabeth Cavanna
    See also JRDA; MAICYA; SAAS 4;
    SATA 1, 30

Cavendish, Margaret Lucas
    1623-1673 . . . . **LC 30**
    See also DLB 131

Caxton, William 1421(?)-1491(?) . . . . . **LC 17**

Cayrol, Jean 1911- . . . . **CLC 11**
    See also CA 89-92; DLB 83

Cela, Camilo Jose
    1916- . . . . **CLC 4, 13, 59; HLC**
    See also BEST 90:2; CA 21-24R; CAAS 10;
    CANR 21, 32; DAM MULT; DLBY 89;
    HW; MTCW

Celan, Paul . . . . . . **CLC 10, 19, 53, 82; PC 10**
    See also Antschel, Paul
    See also DLB 69

Celine, Louis-Ferdinand
    . . . . **CLC 1, 3, 4, 7, 9, 15, 47**
    See also Destouches, Louis-Ferdinand
    See also DLB 72

Cellini, Benvenuto 1500-1571 . . . . **LC 7**

Cendrars, Blaise . . . . **CLC 18**
    See also Sauser-Hall, Frederic

Cernuda (y Bidon), Luis
    1902-1963 . . . . **CLC 54**
    See also CA 131; 89-92; DAM POET;
    DLB 134; HW

Cervantes (Saavedra), Miguel de
    1547-1616 . . . . **LC 6, 23; DA; DAB;**
                 DAC; SSC 12; WLC
    See also DAM MST, NOV

Cesaire, Aime (Fernand)
    1913- . . . . **CLC 19, 32; BLC**
    See also BW 2; CA 65-68; CANR 24, 43;
    DAM MULT, POET; MTCW

Chabon, Michael 1965(?)- . . . . **CLC 55**
    See also CA 139

Chabrol, Claude 1930- . . . . **CLC 16**
    See also CA 110

Challans, Mary 1905-1983
    See Renault, Mary
    See also CA 81-84; 111; SATA 23;
    SATA-Obit 36

Challis, George
    See Faust, Frederick (Schiller)

Chambers, Aidan 1934- . . . . **CLC 35**
    See also CA 25-28R; CANR 12, 31; JRDA;
    MAICYA; SAAS 12; SATA 1, 69

Chambers, James 1948-
    See Cliff, Jimmy
    See also CA 124

Chambers, Jessie
    See Lawrence, D(avid) H(erbert Richards)

Chambers, Robert W. 1865-1933 . . . **TCLC 41**

Chandler, Raymond (Thornton)
    1888-1959 . . . . **TCLC 1, 7**
    See also CA 104; 129; CDALB 1929-1941;
    DLBD 6; MTCW

Chang, Jung 1952- . . . . **CLC 71**
    See also CA 142

Channing, William Ellery
    1780-1842 . . . . **NCLC 17**
    See also DLB 1, 59

Chaplin, Charles Spencer
    1889-1977 . . . . **CLC 16**
    See also Chaplin, Charlie
    See also CA 81-84; 73-76

Chaplin, Charlie
    See Chaplin, Charles Spencer
    See also DLB 44

Chapman, George 1559(?)-1634 . . . . . . **LC 22**
    See also DAM DRAM; DLB 62, 121

Chapman, Graham 1941-1989 . . . . . . **CLC 21**
    See also Monty Python
    See also CA 116; 129; CANR 35

Chapman, John Jay 1862-1933 . . . . . **TCLC 7**
    See also CA 104

Chapman, Walker
    See Silverberg, Robert

Chappell, Fred (Davis) 1936- . . . . **CLC 40, 78**
    See also CA 5-8R; CAAS 4; CANR 8, 33;
    DLB 6, 105

Char, Rene(-Emile)
    1907-1988 . . . . **CLC 9, 11, 14, 55**
    See also CA 13-16R; 124; CANR 32;
    DAM POET; MTCW

Charby, Jay
    See Ellison, Harlan (Jay)

Chardin, Pierre Teilhard de
    See Teilhard de Chardin, (Marie Joseph)
    Pierre

Charles I 1600-1649 . . . . **LC 13**

Charyn, Jerome 1937- . . . . **CLC 5, 8, 18**
    See also CA 5-8R; CAAS 1; CANR 7;
    DLBY 83; MTCW

Chase, Mary (Coyle) 1907-1981 . . . . . . **DC 1**
    See also CA 77-80; 105; SATA 17;
    SATA-Obit 29

Chase, Mary Ellen 1887-1973 . . . . **CLC 2**
    See also CA 13-16; 41-44R; CAP 1;
    SATA 10

Chase, Nicholas
    See Hyde, Anthony

Clarke, Arthur C(harles)
    1917- . . . . . . CLC 1, 4, 13, 18, 35; SSC 3
    See also AAYA 4; CA 1-4R; CANR 2, 28;
    DAM POP; JRDA; MAICYA; MTCW;
    SATA 13, 70

Clarke, Austin 1896-1974. . . . . CLC 6, 9
    See also CA 29-32; 49-52; CAP 2;
    DAM POET; DLB 10, 20

Clarke, Austin C(hesterfield)
    1934- . . . . CLC 8, 53; BLC; DAC
    See also BW 1; CA 25-28R; CAAS 16;
    CANR 14, 32; DAM MULT; DLB 53,
    125

Clarke, Gillian 1937- . . . . CLC 61
    See also CA 106; DLB 40

Clarke, Marcus (Andrew Hislop)
    1846-1881 . . . . NCLC 19

Clarke, Shirley 1925- . . . . CLC 16

Clash, The
    See Headon, (Nicky) Topper; Jones, Mick;
    Simonon, Paul; Strummer, Joe

Claudel, Paul (Louis Charles Marie)
    1868-1955 . . . . TCLC 2, 10
    See also CA 104

Clavell, James (duMaresq)
    1925-1994 . . . . CLC 6, 25, 87
    See also CA 25-28R; 146; CANR 26, 48;
    DAM NOV, POP; MTCW

Cleaver, (Leroy) Eldridge
    1935- . . . . CLC 30; BLC
    See also BW 1; CA 21-24R; CANR 16;
    DAM MULT

Cleese, John (Marwood) 1939- . . . . . CLC 21
    See also Monty Python
    See also CA 112; 116; CANR 35; MTCW

Cleishbotham, Jebediah
    See Scott, Walter

Cleland, John 1710-1789 . . . . LC 2
    See also DLB 39

Clemens, Samuel Langhorne 1835-1910
    See Twain, Mark
    See also CA 104; 135; CDALB 1865-1917;
    DA; DAB; DAC; DAM MST, NOV;
    DLB 11, 12, 23, 64, 74; JRDA;
    MAICYA; YABC 2

Cleophil
    See Congreve, William

Clerihew, E.
    See Bentley, E(dmund) C(lerihew)

Clerk, N. W.
    See Lewis, C(live) S(taples)

Cliff, Jimmy . . . . CLC 21
    See also Chambers, James

Clifton, (Thelma) Lucille
    1936- . . . . CLC 19, 66; BLC
    See also BW 2; CA 49-52; CANR 2, 24, 42;
    CLR 5; DAM MULT, POET; DLB 5, 41;
    MAICYA; MTCW; SATA 20, 69

Clinton, Dirk
    See Silverberg, Robert

Clough, Arthur Hugh 1819-1861 . . NCLC 27
    See also DLB 32

Clutha, Janet Paterson Frame 1924-
    See Frame, Janet
    See also CA 1-4R; CANR 2, 36; MTCW

Clyne, Terence
    See Blatty, William Peter

Cobalt, Martin
    See Mayne, William (James Carter)

Cobbett, William 1763-1835 . . . . . NCLC 49
    See also DLB 43, 107, 158

Coburn, D(onald) L(ee) 1938- . . . . . . CLC 10
    See also CA 89-92

Cocteau, Jean (Maurice Eugene Clement)
    1889-1963 . . . . CLC 1, 8, 15, 16, 43; DA;
                                    DAB; DAC; WLC
    See also CA 25-28; CANR 40; CAP 2;
    DAM DRAM, MST, NOV; DLB 65;
    MTCW

Codrescu, Andrei 1946- . . . . CLC 46
    See also CA 33-36R; CAAS 19; CANR 13,
    34; DAM POET

Coe, Max
    See Bourne, Randolph S(illiman)

Coe, Tucker
    See Westlake, Donald E(dwin)

Coetzee, J(ohn) M(ichael)
    1940- . . . . CLC 23, 33, 66
    See also CA 77-80; CANR 41; DAM NOV;
    MTCW

Coffey, Brian
    See Koontz, Dean R(ay)

Cohan, George M. 1878-1942 . . . . . TCLC 60

Cohen, Arthur A(llen)
    1928-1986 . . . . CLC 7, 31
    See also CA 1-4R; 120; CANR 1, 17, 42;
    DLB 28

Cohen, Leonard (Norman)
    1934- . . . . CLC 3, 38; DAC
    See also CA 21-24R; CANR 14;
    DAM MST; DLB 53; MTCW

Cohen, Matt 1942- . . . . CLC 19; DAC
    See also CA 61-64; CAAS 18; CANR 40;
    DLB 53

Cohen-Solal, Annie 19(?)- . . . . CLC 50

Colegate, Isabel 1931- . . . . CLC 36
    See also CA 17-20R; CANR 8, 22; DLB 14;
    INT CANR-22; MTCW

Coleman, Emmett
    See Reed, Ishmael

Coleridge, Samuel Taylor
    1772-1834 . . . . . NCLC 9, 54; DA; DAB;
                                DAC; PC 11; WLC
    See also CDBLB 1789-1832; DAM MST,
    POET; DLB 93, 107

Coleridge, Sara 1802-1852 . . . . NCLC 31

Coles, Don 1928- . . . . CLC 46
    See also CA 115; CANR 38

Colette, (Sidonie-Gabrielle)
    1873-1954 . . . . . . TCLC 1, 5, 16; SSC 10
    See also CA 104; 131; DAM NOV; DLB 65;
    MTCW

Collett, (Jacobine) Camilla (Wergeland)
    1813-1895 . . . . NCLC 22

Collier, Christopher 1930- . . . . CLC 30
    See also AAYA 13; CA 33-36R; CANR 13,
    33; JRDA; MAICYA; SATA 16, 70

Collier, James L(incoln) 1928- . . . . . CLC 30
    See also AAYA 13; CA 9-12R; CANR 4,
    33; CLR 3; DAM POP; JRDA;
    MAICYA; SAAS 21; SATA 8, 70

Collier, Jeremy 1650-1726 . . . . LC 6

Collier, John 1901-1980 . . . . SSC 19
    See also CA 65-68; 97-100; CANR 10;
    DLB 77

Collins, Hunt
    See Hunter, Evan

Collins, Linda 1931- . . . . CLC 44
    See also CA 125

Collins, (William) Wilkie
    1824-1889 . . . . NCLC 1, 18
    See also CDBLB 1832-1890; DLB 18, 70,
    159

Collins, William 1721-1759 . . . . LC 4
    See also DAM POET; DLB 109

Collodi, Carlo 1826-1890 . . . . NCLC 54
    See also Lorenzini, Carlo
    See also CLR 5

Colman, George
    See Glassco, John

Colt, Winchester Remington
    See Hubbard, L(afayette) Ron(ald)

Colter, Cyrus 1910- . . . . CLC 58
    See also BW 1; CA 65-68; CANR 10;
    DLB 33

Colton, James
    See Hansen, Joseph

Colum, Padraic 1881-1972 . . . . CLC 28
    See also CA 73-76; 33-36R; CANR 35;
    CLR 36; MAICYA; MTCW; SATA 15

Colvin, James
    See Moorcock, Michael (John)

Colwin, Laurie (E.)
    1944-1992 . . . . CLC 5, 13, 23, 84
    See also CA 89-92; 139; CANR 20, 46;
    DLBY 80; MTCW

Comfort, Alex(ander) 1920- . . . . CLC 7
    See also CA 1-4R; CANR 1, 45; DAM POP

Comfort, Montgomery
    See Campbell, (John) Ramsey

Compton-Burnett, I(vy)
    1884(?)-1969 . . . . . . CLC 1, 3, 10, 15, 34
    See also CA 1-4R; 25-28R; CANR 4;
    DAM NOV; DLB 36; MTCW

Comstock, Anthony 1844-1915 . . . . TCLC 13
    See also CA 110

Comte, Auguste 1798-1857 . . . . NCLC 54

Conan Doyle, Arthur
    See Doyle, Arthur Conan

Conde, Maryse 1937- . . . . CLC 52, 92
    See also Boucolon, Maryse
    See also BW 2; DAM MULT

Condillac, Etienne Bonnot de
    1714-1780 . . . . LC 26

Condon, Richard (Thomas)
    1915- . . . . CLC 4, 6, 8, 10, 45
    See also BEST 90:3; CA 1-4R; CAAS 1;
    CANR 2, 23; DAM NOV;
    INT CANR-23; MTCW

Crane, Stephen (Townley)
1871-1900 . . . . **TCLC 11, 17, 32; DA;
DAB; DAC; SSC 7; WLC**
See also CA 109; 140; CDALB 1865-1917;
DAM MST, NOV, POET; DLB 12, 54,
78; YABC 2

Crase, Douglas 1944- . . . . **CLC 58**
See also CA 106

Crashaw, Richard 1612(?)-1649 . . . . . **LC 24**
See also DLB 126

Craven, Margaret
1901-1980 . . . . **CLC 17; DAC**
See also CA 103

Crawford, F(rancis) Marion
1854-1909 . . . . **TCLC 10**
See also CA 107; DLB 71

Crawford, Isabella Valancy
1850-1887 . . . . **NCLC 12**
See also DLB 92

Crayon, Geoffrey
See Irving, Washington

Creasey, John 1908-1973 . . . . **CLC 11**
See also CA 5-8R; 41-44R; CANR 8;
DLB 77; MTCW

Crebillon, Claude Prosper Jolyot de (fils)
1707-1777 . . . . **LC 28**

Credo
See Creasey, John

Creeley, Robert (White)
1926- . . . . . **CLC 1, 2, 4, 8, 11, 15, 36, 78**
See also CA 1-4R; CAAS 10; CANR 23, 43;
DAM POET; DLB 5, 16; MTCW

Crews, Harry (Eugene)
1935- . . . . **CLC 6, 23, 49**
See also AITN 1; CA 25-28R; CANR 20;
DLB 6, 143; MTCW

Crichton, (John) Michael
1942- . . . . **CLC 2, 6, 54, 90**
See also AAYA 10; AITN 2; CA 25-28R;
CANR 13, 40; DAM NOV, POP;
DLBY 81; INT CANR-13; JRDA;
MTCW; SATA 9

Crispin, Edmund . . . . **CLC 22**
See also Montgomery, (Robert) Bruce
See also DLB 87

Cristofer, Michael 1945(?)- . . . . **CLC 28**
See also CA 110; DAM DRAM; DLB 7

Croce, Benedetto 1866-1952 . . . . . **TCLC 37**
See also CA 120

Crockett, David 1786-1836 . . . . **NCLC 8**
See also DLB 3, 11

Crockett, Davy
See Crockett, David

Crofts, Freeman Wills
1879-1957 . . . . **TCLC 55**
See also CA 115; DLB 77

Croker, John Wilson 1780-1857 . . **NCLC 10**
See also DLB 110

Crommelynck, Fernand 1885-1970 . . **CLC 75**
See also CA 89-92

Cronin, A(rchibald) J(oseph)
1896-1981 . . . . **CLC 32**
See also CA 1-4R; 102; CANR 5; SATA 47;
SATA-Obit 25

Cross, Amanda
See Heilbrun, Carolyn G(old)

Crothers, Rachel 1878(?)-1958 . . . . . **TCLC 19**
See also CA 113; DLB 7

Croves, Hal
See Traven, B.

Crowfield, Christopher
See Stowe, Harriet (Elizabeth) Beecher

Crowley, Aleister . . . . **TCLC 7**
See also Crowley, Edward Alexander

Crowley, Edward Alexander 1875-1947
See Crowley, Aleister
See also CA 104

Crowley, John 1942- . . . . **CLC 57**
See also CA 61-64; CANR 43; DLBY 82;
SATA 65

Crud
See Crumb, R(obert)

Crumarums
See Crumb, R(obert)

Crumb, R(obert) 1943- . . . . **CLC 17**
See also CA 106

Crumbum
See Crumb, R(obert)

Crumski
See Crumb, R(obert)

Crum the Bum
See Crumb, R(obert)

Crunk
See Crumb, R(obert)

Crustt
See Crumb, R(obert)

Cryer, Gretchen (Kiger) 1935- . . . . . . **CLC 21**
See also CA 114; 123

Csath, Geza 1887-1919 . . . . **TCLC 13**
See also CA 111

Cudlip, David 1933- . . . . **CLC 34**

Cullen, Countee
1903-1946 . . . . . . **TCLC 4, 37; BLC; DA;
DAC**
See also BW 1; CA 108; 124;
CDALB 1917-1929; DAM MST, MULT,
POET; DLB 4, 48, 51; MTCW; SATA 18

Cum, R.
See Crumb, R(obert)

Cummings, Bruce F(rederick) 1889-1919
See Barbellion, W. N. P.
See also CA 123

Cummings, E(dward) E(stlin)
1894-1962 . . . . . . **CLC 1, 3, 8, 12, 15, 68;
DA; DAB; DAC; PC 5; WLC 2**
See also CA 73-76; CANR 31;
CDALB 1929-1941; DAM MST, POET;
DLB 4, 48; MTCW

Cunha, Euclides (Rodrigues Pimenta) da
1866-1909 . . . . **TCLC 24**
See also CA 123

Cunningham, E. V.
See Fast, Howard (Melvin)

Cunningham, J(ames) V(incent)
1911-1985 . . . . **CLC 3, 31**
See also CA 1-4R; 115; CANR 1; DLB 5

Cunningham, Julia (Woolfolk)
1916- . . . . **CLC 12**
See also CA 9-12R; CANR 4, 19, 36;
JRDA; MAICYA; SAAS 2; SATA 1, 26

Cunningham, Michael 1952- . . . . **CLC 34**
See also CA 136

Cunninghame Graham, R(obert) B(ontine)
1852-1936 . . . . **TCLC 19**
See also Graham, R(obert) B(ontine)
Cunninghame
See also CA 119; DLB 98

Currie, Ellen 19(?)- . . . . **CLC 44**

Curtin, Philip
See Lowndes, Marie Adelaide (Belloc)

Curtis, Price
See Ellison, Harlan (Jay)

Cutrate, Joe
See Spiegelman, Art

Czaczkes, Shmuel Yosef
See Agnon, S(hmuel) Y(osef Halevi)

Dabrowska, Maria (Szumska)
1889-1965 . . . . **CLC 15**
See also CA 106

Dabydeen, David 1955- . . . . **CLC 34**
See also BW 1; CA 125

Dacey, Philip 1939- . . . . **CLC 51**
See also CA 37-40R; CAAS 17; CANR 14,
32; DLB 105

Dagerman, Stig (Halvard)
1923-1954 . . . . **TCLC 17**
See also CA 117

Dahl, Roald
1916-1990 . . . . . . **CLC 1, 6, 18, 79; DAB;
DAC**
See also AAYA 15; CA 1-4R; 133;
CANR 6, 32, 37; CLR 1, 7; DAM MST,
NOV, POP; DLB 139; JRDA; MAICYA;
MTCW; SATA 1, 26, 73; SATA-Obit 65

Dahlberg, Edward 1900-1977 . . . **CLC 1, 7, 14**
See also CA 9-12R; 69-72; CANR 31;
DLB 48; MTCW

Dale, Colin . . . . **TCLC 18**
See also Lawrence, T(homas) E(dward)

Dale, George E.
See Asimov, Isaac

Daly, Elizabeth 1878-1967 . . . . **CLC 52**
See also CA 23-24; 25-28R; CAP 2

Daly, Maureen 1921- . . . . **CLC 17**
See also AAYA 5; CANR 37; JRDA;
MAICYA; SAAS 1; SATA 2

Damas, Leon-Gontran 1912-1978 . . . **CLC 84**
See also BW 1; CA 125; 73-76

Dana, Richard Henry Sr.
1787-1879 . . . . **NCLC 53**

Daniel, Samuel 1562(?)-1619 . . . . **LC 24**
See also DLB 62

Daniels, Brett
See Adler, Renata

Dannay, Frederic 1905-1982 . . . . **CLC 11**
See also Queen, Ellery
See also CA 1-4R; 107; CANR 1, 39;
DAM POP; DLB 137; MTCW

D'Annunzio, Gabriele
1863-1938 . . . . **TCLC 6, 40**
See also CA 104

Delibes Setien, Miguel 1920-
    See Delibes, Miguel
    See also CA 45-48; CANR 1, 32; HW;
    MTCW

DeLillo, Don
    1936- ..... **CLC 8, 10, 13, 27, 39, 54, 76**
    See also BEST 89:1; CA 81-84; CANR 21;
    DAM NOV, POP; DLB 6; MTCW

de Lisser, H. G.
    See De Lisser, Herbert George
    See also DLB 117

De Lisser, Herbert George
    1878-1944 .... **TCLC 12**
    See also de Lisser, H. G.
    See also BW 2; CA 109

Deloria, Vine (Victor), Jr. 1933- .... **CLC 21**
    See also CA 53-56; CANR 5, 20, 48;
    DAM MULT; MTCW; NNAL; SATA 21

Del Vecchio, John M(ichael)
    1947- .... **CLC 29**
    See also CA 110; DLBD 9

de Man, Paul (Adolph Michel)
    1919-1983 .... **CLC 55**
    See also CA 128; 111; DLB 67; MTCW

De Marinis, Rick 1934- .... **CLC 54**
    See also CA 57-60; CANR 9, 25, 50

Demby, William 1922- ...... **CLC 53; BLC**
    See also BW 1; CA 81-84; DAM MULT;
    DLB 33

Demijohn, Thom
    See Disch, Thomas M(ichael)

de Montherlant, Henry (Milon)
    See Montherlant, Henry (Milon) de

Demosthenes 384B.C.-322B.C. .... **CMLC 13**

de Natale, Francine
    See Malzberg, Barry N(athaniel)

Denby, Edwin (Orr) 1903-1983 ..... **CLC 48**
    See also CA 138; 110

Denis, Julio
    See Cortazar, Julio

Denmark, Harrison
    See Zelazny, Roger (Joseph)

Dennis, John 1658-1734 .... **LC 11**
    See also DLB 101

Dennis, Nigel (Forbes) 1912-1989 .... **CLC 8**
    See also CA 25-28R; 129; DLB 13, 15;
    MTCW

De Palma, Brian (Russell) 1940- .... **CLC 20**
    See also CA 109

De Quincey, Thomas 1785-1859 ... **NCLC 4**
    See also CDBLB 1789-1832; DLB 110; 144

Deren, Eleanora 1908(?)-1961
    See Deren, Maya
    See also CA 111

Deren, Maya .... **CLC 16**
    See also Deren, Eleanora

Derleth, August (William)
    1909-1971 .... **CLC 31**
    See also CA 1-4R; 29-32R; CANR 4;
    DLB 9; SATA 5

Der Nister 1884-1950 .... **TCLC 56**

de Routisie, Albert
    See Aragon, Louis

Derrida, Jacques 1930- .... **CLC 24, 87**
    See also CA 124; 127

Derry Down Derry
    See Lear, Edward

Dersonnes, Jacques
    See Simenon, Georges (Jacques Christian)

Desai, Anita 1937- ...... **CLC 19, 37; DAB**
    See also CA 81-84; CANR 33; DAM NOV;
    MTCW; SATA 63

de Saint-Luc, Jean
    See Glassco, John

de Saint Roman, Arnaud
    See Aragon, Louis

Descartes, Rene 1596-1650 .... **LC 20**

De Sica, Vittorio 1901(?)-1974 ..... **CLC 20**
    See also CA 117

Desnos, Robert 1900-1945 .... **TCLC 22**
    See also CA 121

Destouches, Louis-Ferdinand
    1894-1961 .... **CLC 9, 15**
    See also Celine, Louis-Ferdinand
    See also CA 85-88; CANR 28; MTCW

Deutsch, Babette 1895-1982 .... **CLC 18**
    See also CA 1-4R; 108; CANR 4; DLB 45;
    SATA 1; SATA-Obit 33

Devenant, William 1606-1649 ...... **LC 13**

Devkota, Laxmiprasad
    1909-1959 .... **TCLC 23**
    See also CA 123

De Voto, Bernard (Augustine)
    1897-1955 .... **TCLC 29**
    See also CA 113; DLB 9

De Vries, Peter
    1910-1993 .... **CLC 1, 2, 3, 7, 10, 28, 46**
    See also CA 17-20R; 142; CANR 41;
    DAM NOV; DLB 6; DLBY 82; MTCW

Dexter, Martin
    See Faust, Frederick (Schiller)

Dexter, Pete 1943- .... **CLC 34, 55**
    See also BEST 89:2; CA 127; 131;
    DAM POP; INT 131; MTCW

Diamano, Silmang
    See Senghor, Leopold Sedar

Diamond, Neil 1941- .... **CLC 30**
    See also CA 108

Diaz del Castillo, Bernal 1496-1584 .. **LC 31**

di Bassetto, Corno
    See Shaw, George Bernard

Dick, Philip K(indred)
    1928-1982 .... **CLC 10, 30, 72**
    See also CA 49-52; 106; CANR 2, 16;
    DAM NOV, POP; DLB 8; MTCW

Dickens, Charles (John Huffam)
    1812-1870 ...... **NCLC 3, 8, 18, 26, 37,**
        50; DA; DAB; DAC; SSC 17; WLC
    See also CDBLB 1832-1890; DAM MST,
    NOV; DLB 21, 55, 70, 159; JRDA;
    MAICYA; SATA 15

Dickey, James (Lafayette)
    1923- .... **CLC 1, 2, 4, 7, 10, 15, 47**
    See also AITN 1, 2; CA 9-12R; CABS 2;
    CANR 10, 48; CDALB 1968-1988;
    DAM NOV, POET, POP; DLB 5;
    DLBD 7; DLBY 82, 93; INT CANR-10;
    MTCW

Dickey, William 1928-1994 ...... **CLC 3, 28**
    See also CA 9-12R; 145; CANR 24; DLB 5

Dickinson, Charles 1951- .... **CLC 49**
    See also CA 128

Dickinson, Emily (Elizabeth)
    1830-1886 .... **NCLC 21; DA; DAB;**
        DAC; PC 1; WLC
    See also CDALB 1865-1917; DAM MST,
    POET; DLB 1; SATA 29

Dickinson, Peter (Malcolm)
    1927- .... **CLC 12, 35**
    See also AAYA 9; CA 41-44R; CANR 31;
    CLR 29; DLB 87, 161; JRDA; MAICYA;
    SATA 5, 62

Dickson, Carr
    See Carr, John Dickson

Dickson, Carter
    See Carr, John Dickson

Diderot, Denis 1713-1784 .... **LC 26**

Didion, Joan 1934- ..... **CLC 1, 3, 8, 14, 32**
    See also AITN 1; CA 5-8R; CANR 14;
    CDALB 1968-1988; DAM NOV; DLB 2;
    DLBY 81, 86; MTCW

Dietrich, Robert
    See Hunt, E(verette) Howard, (Jr.)

Dillard, Annie 1945- .... **CLC 9, 60**
    See also AAYA 6; CA 49-52; CANR 3, 43;
    DAM NOV; DLBY 80; MTCW;
    SATA 10

Dillard, R(ichard) H(enry) W(ilde)
    1937- .... **CLC 5**
    See also CA 21-24R; CAAS 7; CANR 10;
    DLB 5

Dillon, Eilis 1920-1994 .... **CLC 17**
    See also CA 9-12R; 147; CAAS 3; CANR 4,
    38; CLR 26; MAICYA; SATA 2, 74;
    SATA-Obit 83

Dimont, Penelope
    See Mortimer, Penelope (Ruth)

Dinesen, Isak .... **CLC 10, 29; SSC 7**
    See also Blixen, Karen (Christentze
    Dinesen)

Ding Ling .... **CLC 68**
    See also Chiang Pin-chin

Disch, Thomas M(ichael) 1940- ... **CLC 7, 36**
    See also AAYA 17; CA 21-24R; CAAS 4;
    CANR 17, 36; CLR 18; DLB 8;
    MAICYA; MTCW; SAAS 15; SATA 54

Disch, Tom
    See Disch, Thomas M(ichael)

d'Isly, Georges
    See Simenon, Georges (Jacques Christian)

Disraeli, Benjamin 1804-1881 .. **NCLC 2, 39**
    See also DLB 21, 55

Ditcum, Steve
    See Crumb, R(obert)

Dixon, Paige
    See Corcoran, Barbara

Dixon, Stephen 1936- ..... **CLC 52; SSC 16**
    See also CA 89-92; CANR 17, 40; DLB 130

Dobell, Sydney Thompson
    1824-1874 .... **NCLC 43**
    See also DLB 32

Doblin, Alfred .... **TCLC 13**
    See also Doeblin, Alfred

Dobrolyubov, Nikolai Alexandrovich
1836-1861 . . . . NCLC 5

Dobyns, Stephen 1941-. . . . . CLC 37
See also CA 45-48; CANR 2, 18

Doctorow, E(dgar) L(aurence)
1931- . . . . . CLC 6, 11, 15, 18, 37, 44, 65
See also AITN 2; BEST 89:3; CA 45-48;
CANR 2, 33, 51; CDALB 1968-1988;
DAM NOV, POP; DLB 2, 28; DLBY 80;
MTCW

Dodgson, Charles Lutwidge 1832-1898
See Carroll, Lewis
See also CLR 2; DA; DAB; DAC;
DAM MST, NOV, POET; MAICYA;
YABC 2

Dodson, Owen (Vincent)
1914-1983 . . . . CLC 79; BLC
See also BW 1; CA 65-68; 110; CANR 24;
DAM MULT; DLB 76

Doeblin, Alfred 1878-1957. . . . . . . TCLC 13
See also Doblin, Alfred
See also CA 110; 141; DLB 66

Doerr, Harriet 1910- . . . . CLC 34
See also CA 117; 122; CANR 47; INT 122

Domecq, H(onorio) Bustos
See Bioy Casares, Adolfo; Borges, Jorge
Luis

Domini, Rey
See Lorde, Audre (Geraldine)

Dominique
See Proust, (Valentin-Louis-George-Eugene-)
Marcel

Don, A
See Stephen, Leslie

Donaldson, Stephen R. 1947-. . . . . . . CLC 46
See also CA 89-92; CANR 13; DAM POP;
INT CANR-13

Donleavy, J(ames) P(atrick)
1926- . . . . CLC 1, 4, 6, 10, 45
See also AITN 2; CA 9-12R; CANR 24, 49;
DLB 6; INT CANR-24; MTCW

Donne, John
1572-1631 . . . . LC 10, 24; DA; DAB;
DAC; PC 1
See also CDBLB Before 1660; DAM MST,
POET; DLB 121, 151

Donnell, David 1939(?)-. . . . . CLC 34

Donoghue, P. S.
See Hunt, E(verette) Howard, (Jr.)

Donoso (Yanez), Jose
1924- . . . . CLC 4, 8, 11, 32; HLC
See also CA 81-84; CANR 32;
DAM MULT; DLB 113; HW; MTCW

Donovan, John 1928-1992 . . . . CLC 35
See also CA 97-100; 137; CLR 3;
MAICYA; SATA 72; SATA-Brief 29

Don Roberto
See Cunninghame Graham, R(obert)
B(ontine)

Doolittle, Hilda
1886-1961 . . . . . CLC 3, 8, 14, 31, 34, 73;
DA; DAC; PC 5; WLC
See also H. D.
See also CA 97-100; CANR 35; DAM MST,
POET; DLB 4, 45; MTCW

Dorfman, Ariel 1942-. . . . CLC 48, 77; HLC
See also CA 124; 130; DAM MULT; HW;
INT 130

Dorn, Edward (Merton) 1929-. . . CLC 10, 18
See also CA 93-96; CANR 42; DLB 5;
INT 93-96

Dorsan, Luc
See Simenon, Georges (Jacques Christian)

Dorsange, Jean
See Simenon, Georges (Jacques Christian)

Dos Passos, John (Roderigo)
1896-1970 . . . . . . CLC 1, 4, 8, 11, 15, 25,
34, 82; DA; DAB; DAC; WLC
See also CA 1-4R; 29-32R; CANR 3;
CDALB 1929-1941; DAM MST, NOV;
DLB 4, 9; DLBD 1; MTCW

Dossage, Jean
See Simenon, Georges (Jacques Christian)

Dostoevsky, Fedor Mikhailovich
1821-1881 . . . . . NCLC 2, 7, 21, 33, 43;
DA; DAB; DAC; SSC 2; WLC
See also DAM MST, NOV

Doughty, Charles M(ontagu)
1843-1926 . . . . TCLC 27
See also CA 115; DLB 19, 57

Douglas, Ellen . . . . CLC 73
See also Haxton, Josephine Ayres;
Williamson, Ellen Douglas

Douglas, Gavin 1475(?)-1522. . . . . . . LC 20

Douglas, Keith 1920-1944 . . . . TCLC 40
See also DLB 27

Douglas, Leonard
See Bradbury, Ray (Douglas)

Douglas, Michael
See Crichton, (John) Michael

Douglass, Frederick
1817(?)-1895 . . . . NCLC 7, 55; BLC; DA;
DAC; WLC
See also CDALB 1640-1865; DAM MST,
MULT; DLB 1, 43, 50, 79; SATA 29

Dourado, (Waldomiro Freitas) Autran
1926- . . . . CLC 23, 60
See also CA 25-28R; CANR 34

Dourado, Waldomiro Autran
See Dourado, (Waldomiro Freitas) Autran

Dove, Rita (Frances)
1952- . . . . CLC 50, 81; PC 6
See also BW 2; CA 109; CAAS 19;
CANR 27, 42; DAM MULT, POET;
DLB 120

Dowell, Coleman 1925-1985. . . . . . . CLC 60
See also CA 25-28R; 117; CANR 10;
DLB 130

Dowson, Ernest (Christopher)
1867-1900 . . . . TCLC 4
See also CA 105; 150; DLB 19, 135

Doyle, A. Conan
See Doyle, Arthur Conan

Doyle, Arthur Conan
1859-1930 . . . . TCLC 7; DA; DAB;
DAC; SSC 12; WLC
See also AAYA 14; CA 104; 122;
CDBLB 1890-1914; DAM MST, NOV;
DLB 18, 70, 156; MTCW; SATA 24

Doyle, Conan
See Doyle, Arthur Conan

Doyle, John
See Graves, Robert (von Ranke)

Doyle, Roddy 1958(?)-. . . . . CLC 81
See also AAYA 14; CA 143

Doyle, Sir A. Conan
See Doyle, Arthur Conan

Doyle, Sir Arthur Conan
See Doyle, Arthur Conan

Dr. A
See Asimov, Isaac; Silverstein, Alvin

Drabble, Margaret
1939-. . . . . CLC 2, 3, 5, 8, 10, 22, 53;
DAB; DAC
See also CA 13-16R; CANR 18, 35;
CDBLB 1960 to Present; DAM MST,
NOV, POP; DLB 14, 155; MTCW;
SATA 48

Drapier, M. B.
See Swift, Jonathan

Drayham, James
See Mencken, H(enry) L(ouis)

Drayton, Michael 1563-1631. . . . . LC 8

Dreadstone, Carl
See Campbell, (John) Ramsey

Dreiser, Theodore (Herman Albert)
1871-1945 . . . . TCLC 10, 18, 35; DA;
DAC; WLC
See also CA 106; 132; CDALB 1865-1917;
DAM MST, NOV; DLB 9, 12, 102, 137;
DLBD 1; MTCW

Drexler, Rosalyn 1926- . . . . CLC 2, 6
See also CA 81-84

Dreyer, Carl Theodor 1889-1968. . . . CLC 16
See also CA 116

Drieu la Rochelle, Pierre(-Eugene)
1893-1945 . . . . TCLC 21
See also CA 117; DLB 72

Drinkwater, John 1882-1937 . . . . . . TCLC 57
See also CA 109; 149; DLB 10, 19, 149

Drop Shot
See Cable, George Washington

Droste-Hulshoff, Annette Freiin von
1797-1848 . . . . NCLC 3
See also DLB 133

Drummond, Walter
See Silverberg, Robert

Drummond, William Henry
1854-1907 . . . . TCLC 25
See also DLB 92

Drummond de Andrade, Carlos
1902-1987 . . . . CLC 18
See also Andrade, Carlos Drummond de
See also CA 132; 123

Drury, Allen (Stuart) 1918-. . . . . CLC 37
See also CA 57-60; CANR 18;
INT CANR-18

Dryden, John
1631-1700 . . . . LC 3, 21; DA; DAB;
DAC; DC 3; WLC
See also CDBLB 1660-1789; DAM DRAM,
MST, POET; DLB 80, 101, 131

Duberman, Martin 1930-. . . . . CLC 8
See also CA 1-4R; CANR 2

Dubie, Norman (Evans) 1945- ...... **CLC 36**
See also CA 69-72; CANR 12; DLB 120

Du Bois, W(illiam) E(dward) B(urghardt)
1868-1963 ...... **CLC 1, 2, 13, 64; BLC;**
                          DA; DAC; WLC
See also BW 1; CA 85-88; CANR 34;
   CDALB 1865-1917; DAM MST, MULT,
   NOV; DLB 47, 50, 91; MTCW; SATA 42

Dubus, Andre 1936- ... **CLC 13, 36; SSC 15**
See also CA 21-24R; CANR 17; DLB 130;
   INT CANR-17

Duca Minimo
See D'Annunzio, Gabriele

Ducharme, Rejean 1941- .... **CLC 74**
See also DLB 60

Duclos, Charles Pinot 1704-1772 ..... **LC 1**

Dudek, Louis 1918- .... **CLC 11, 19**
See also CA 45-48; CAAS 14; CANR 1;
   DLB 88

Duerrenmatt, Friedrich
1921-1990 ...... **CLC 1, 4, 8, 11, 15, 43**
See also CA 17-20R; CANR 33;
   DAM DRAM; DLB 69, 124; MTCW

Duffy, Bruce (?)- .... **CLC 50**

Duffy, Maureen 1933- .... **CLC 37**
See also CA 25-28R; CANR 33; DLB 14;
   MTCW

Dugan, Alan 1923- .... **CLC 2, 6**
See also CA 81-84; DLB 5

du Gard, Roger Martin
See Martin du Gard, Roger

Duhamel, Georges 1884-1966 .... **CLC 8**
See also CA 81-84; 25-28R; CANR 35;
   DLB 65; MTCW

Dujardin, Edouard (Emile Louis)
1861-1949 .... **TCLC 13**
See also CA 109; DLB 123

Dumas, Alexandre (Davy de la Pailleterie)
1802-1870 .... **NCLC 11; DA; DAB;**
                         DAC; WLC
See also DAM MST, NOV; DLB 119;
   SATA 18

Dumas, Alexandre
1824-1895 .... **NCLC 9; DC 1**

Dumas, Claudine
See Malzberg, Barry N(athaniel)

Dumas, Henry L. 1934-1968 ..... **CLC 6, 62**
See also BW 1; CA 85-88; DLB 41

du Maurier, Daphne
1907-1989 .... **CLC 6, 11, 59; DAB;**
                       DAC; SSC 18
See also CA 5-8R; 128; CANR 6;
   DAM MST, POP; MTCW; SATA 27;
   SATA-Obit 60

Dunbar, Paul Laurence
1872-1906 ...... **TCLC 2, 12; BLC; DA;**
            DAC; PC 5; SSC 8; WLC
See also BW 1; CA 104; 124;
   CDALB 1865-1917; DAM MST, MULT,
   POET; DLB 50, 54, 78; SATA 34

Dunbar, William 1460(?)-1530(?) .... **LC 20**
See also DLB 132, 146

Duncan, Lois 1934- .... **CLC 26**
See also AAYA 4; CA 1-4R; CANR 2, 23,
   36; CLR 29; JRDA; MAICYA; SAAS 2;
   SATA 1, 36, 75

Duncan, Robert (Edward)
1919-1988 .... **CLC 1, 2, 4, 7, 15, 41, 55;**
                          PC 2
See also CA 9-12R; 124; CANR 28;
   DAM POET; DLB 5, 16; MTCW

Duncan, Sara Jeannette
1861-1922 .... **TCLC 60**
See also DLB 92

Dunlap, William 1766-1839 .... **NCLC 2**
See also DLB 30, 37, 59

Dunn, Douglas (Eaglesham)
1942- .... **CLC 6, 40**
See also CA 45-48; CANR 2, 33; DLB 40;
   MTCW

Dunn, Katherine (Karen) 1945- ..... **CLC 71**
See also CA 33-36R

Dunn, Stephen 1939- .... **CLC 36**
See also CA 33-36R; CANR 12, 48;
   DLB 105

Dunne, Finley Peter 1867-1936.... **TCLC 28**
See also CA 108; DLB 11, 23

Dunne, John Gregory 1932-........ **CLC 28**
See also CA 25-28R; CANR 14, 50;
   DLBY 80

Dunsany, Edward John Moreton Drax
   Plunkett 1878-1957
See Dunsany, Lord
See also CA 104; 148; DLB 10

Dunsany, Lord .... **TCLC 2, 59**
See also Dunsany, Edward John Moreton
   Drax Plunkett
See also DLB 77, 153, 156

du Perry, Jean
See Simenon, Georges (Jacques Christian)

Durang, Christopher (Ferdinand)
1949- .... **CLC 27, 38**
See also CA 105; CANR 50

Duras, Marguerite
1914- ...... **CLC 3, 6, 11, 20, 34, 40, 68**
See also CA 25-28R; CANR 50; DLB 83;
   MTCW

Durban, (Rosa) Pam 1947-........ **CLC 39**
See also CA 123

Durcan, Paul 1944-............ **CLC 43, 70**
See also CA 134; DAM POET

Durkheim, Emile 1858-1917 ...... **TCLC 55**

Durrell, Lawrence (George)
1912-1990 ... **CLC 1, 4, 6, 8, 13, 27, 41**
See also CA 9-12R; 132; CANR 40;
   CDBLB 1945-1960; DAM NOV; DLB 15,
   27; DLBY 90; MTCW

Durrenmatt, Friedrich
See Duerrenmatt, Friedrich

Dutt, Toru 1856-1877.......... **NCLC 29**

Dwight, Timothy 1752-1817...... **NCLC 13**
See also DLB 37

Dworkin, Andrea 1946- .... **CLC 43**
See also CA 77-80; CAAS 21; CANR 16,
   39; INT CANR-16; MTCW

Dwyer, Deanna
See Koontz, Dean R(ay)

Dwyer, K. R.
See Koontz, Dean R(ay)

Dylan, Bob 1941- ...... **CLC 3, 4, 6, 12, 77**
See also CA 41-44R; DLB 16

Eagleton, Terence (Francis) 1943-
See Eagleton, Terry
See also CA 57-60; CANR 7, 23; MTCW

Eagleton, Terry .... **CLC 63**
See also Eagleton, Terence (Francis)

Early, Jack
See Scoppettone, Sandra

East, Michael
See West, Morris L(anglo)

Eastaway, Edward
See Thomas, (Philip) Edward

Eastlake, William (Derry) 1917-..... **CLC 8**
See also CA 5-8R; CAAS 1; CANR 5;
   DLB 6; INT CANR-5

Eastman, Charles A(lexander)
1858-1939 .... **TCLC 55**
See also DAM MULT; NNAL; YABC 1

Eberhart, Richard (Ghormley)
1904- .... **CLC 3, 11, 19, 56**
See also CA 1-4R; CANR 2;
   CDALB 1941-1968; DAM POET;
   DLB 48; MTCW

Eberstadt, Fernanda 1960-........ **CLC 39**
See also CA 136

Echegaray (y Eizaguirre), Jose (Maria Waldo)
1832-1916 .... **TCLC 4**
See also CA 104; CANR 32; HW; MTCW

Echeverria, (Jose) Esteban (Antonino)
1805-1851 .... **NCLC 18**

Echo
See Proust, (Valentin-Louis-George-Eugene-)
   Marcel

Eckert, Allan W. 1931- .... **CLC 17**
See also CA 13-16R; CANR 14, 45;
   INT CANR-14; SAAS 21; SATA 29;
   SATA-Brief 27

Eckhart, Meister 1260(?)-1328(?) .. **CMLC 9**
See also DLB 115

Eckmar, F. R.
See de Hartog, Jan

Eco, Umberto 1932-.......... **CLC 28, 60**
See also BEST 90:1; CA 77-80; CANR 12,
   33; DAM NOV, POP; MTCW

Eddison, E(ric) R(ucker)
1882-1945 .... **TCLC 15**
See also CA 109

Edel, (Joseph) Leon 1907-...... **CLC 29, 34**
See also CA 1-4R; CANR 1, 22; DLB 103;
   INT CANR-22

Eden, Emily 1797-1869 .... **NCLC 10**

Edgar, David 1948-.............. **CLC 42**
See also CA 57-60; CANR 12;
   DAM DRAM; DLB 13; MTCW

Edgerton, Clyde (Carlyle) 1944- .... **CLC 39**
See also AAYA 17; CA 118; 134; INT 134

Edgeworth, Maria 1768-1849... **NCLC 1, 51**
See also DLB 116, 159, 163; SATA 21

Edmonds, Paul
See Kuttner, Henry

Edmonds, Walter D(umaux) 1903- . . **CLC 35**
See also CA 5-8R; CANR 2; DLB 9;
MAICYA; SAAS 4; SATA 1, 27

Edmondson, Wallace
See Ellison, Harlan (Jay)

Edson, Russell . . . . **CLC 13**
See also CA 33-36R

Edwards, Bronwen Elizabeth
See Rose, Wendy

Edwards, G(erald) B(asil)
1899-1976 . . . . **CLC 25**
See also CA 110

Edwards, Gus 1939- . . . . **CLC 43**
See also CA 108; INT 108

Edwards, Jonathan
1703-1758 . . . . **LC 7; DA; DAC**
See also DAM MST; DLB 24

Efron, Marina Ivanovna Tsvetaeva
See Tsvetaeva (Efron), Marina (Ivanovna)

Ehle, John (Marsden, Jr.) 1925- . . . . **CLC 27**
See also CA 9-12R

Ehrenbourg, Ilya (Grigoryevich)
See Ehrenburg, Ilya (Grigoryevich)

Ehrenburg, Ilya (Grigoryevich)
1891-1967 . . . . **CLC 18, 34, 62**
See also CA 102; 25-28R

Ehrenburg, Ilyo (Grigoryevich)
See Ehrenburg, Ilya (Grigoryevich)

Eich, Guenter 1907-1972 . . . . **CLC 15**
See also CA 111; 93-96; DLB 69, 124

Eichendorff, Joseph Freiherr von
1788-1857 . . . . **NCLC 8**
See also DLB 90

Eigner, Larry . . . . **CLC 9**
See also Eigner, Laurence (Joel)
See also CAAS 23; DLB 5

Eigner, Laurence (Joel) 1927-1996
See Eigner, Larry
See also CA 9-12R; CANR 6

Eiseley, Loren Corey 1907-1977 . . . . . **CLC 7**
See also AAYA 5; CA 1-4R; 73-76;
CANR 6

Eisenstadt, Jill 1963- . . . . **CLC 50**
See also CA 140

Eisenstein, Sergei (Mikhailovich)
1898-1948 . . . . **TCLC 57**
See also CA 114; 149

Eisner, Simon
See Kornbluth, C(yril) M.

Ekeloef, (Bengt) Gunnar
1907-1968 . . . . **CLC 27**
See also CA 123; 25-28R; DAM POET

Ekelof, (Bengt) Gunnar
See Ekeloef, (Bengt) Gunnar

Ekwensi, C. O. D.
See Ekwensi, Cyprian (Odiatu Duaka)

Ekwensi, Cyprian (Odiatu Duaka)
1921- . . . . **CLC 4; BLC**
See also BW 2; CA 29-32R; CANR 18, 42;
DAM MULT; DLB 117; MTCW;
SATA 66

Elaine . . . . **TCLC 18**
See also Leverson, Ada

El Crummo
See Crumb, R(obert)

Elia
See Lamb, Charles

Eliade, Mircea 1907-1986 . . . . **CLC 19**
See also CA 65-68; 119; CANR 30; MTCW

Eliot, A. D.
See Jewett, (Theodora) Sarah Orne

Eliot, Alice
See Jewett, (Theodora) Sarah Orne

Eliot, Dan
See Silverberg, Robert

Eliot, George
1819-1880 . . . . . **NCLC 4, 13, 23, 41, 49;
DA; DAB; DAC; WLC**
See also CDBLB 1832-1890; DAM MST,
NOV; DLB 21, 35, 55

Eliot, John 1604-1690 . . . . **LC 5**
See also DLB 24

Eliot, T(homas) S(tearns)
1888-1965 . . . . . **CLC 1, 2, 3, 6, 9, 10, 13,
15, 24, 34, 41, 55, 57; DA; DAB; DAC;
PC 5; WLC 2**
See also CA 5-8R; 25-28R; CANR 41;
CDALB 1929-1941; DAM DRAM, MST,
POET; DLB 7, 10, 45, 63; DLBY 88;
MTCW

Elizabeth 1866-1941 . . . . **TCLC 41**

Elkin, Stanley L(awrence)
1930-1995 . . . . . . **CLC 4, 6, 9, 14, 27, 51,
91; SSC 12**
See also CA 9-12R; 148; CANR 8, 46;
DAM NOV, POP; DLB 2, 28; DLBY 80;
INT CANR-8; MTCW

Elledge, Scott . . . . **CLC 34**

Elliott, Don
See Silverberg, Robert

Elliott, George P(aul) 1918-1980 . . . . . **CLC 2**
See also CA 1-4R; 97-100; CANR 2

Elliott, Janice 1931- . . . . **CLC 47**
See also CA 13-16R; CANR 8, 29; DLB 14

Elliott, Sumner Locke 1917-1991 . . . **CLC 38**
See also CA 5-8R; 134; CANR 2, 21

Elliott, William
See Bradbury, Ray (Douglas)

Ellis, A. E. . . . . **CLC 7**

Ellis, Alice Thomas . . . . **CLC 40**
See also Haycraft, Anna

Ellis, Bret Easton 1964- . . . . **CLC 39, 71**
See also AAYA 2; CA 118; 123; CANR 51;
DAM POP; INT 123

Ellis, (Henry) Havelock
1859-1939 . . . . **TCLC 14**
See also CA 109

Ellis, Landon
See Ellison, Harlan (Jay)

Ellis, Trey 1962- . . . . **CLC 55**
See also CA 146

Ellison, Harlan (Jay)
1934- . . . . **CLC 1, 13, 42; SSC 14**
See also CA 5-8R; CANR 5, 46;
DAM POP; DLB 8; INT CANR-5;
MTCW

Ellison, Ralph (Waldo)
1914-1994 . . . . **CLC 1, 3, 11, 54, 86;
BLC; DA; DAB; DAC; WLC**
See also BW 1; CA 9-12R; 145; CANR 24;
CDALB 1941-1968; DAM MST, MULT,
NOV; DLB 2, 76; DLBY 94; MTCW

Ellmann, Lucy (Elizabeth) 1956- . . . . **CLC 61**
See also CA 128

Ellmann, Richard (David)
1918-1987 . . . . **CLC 50**
See also BEST 89:2; CA 1-4R; 122;
CANR 2, 28; DLB 103; DLBY 87;
MTCW

Elman, Richard 1934- . . . . **CLC 19**
See also CA 17-20R; CAAS 3; CANR 47

Elron
See Hubbard, L(afayette) Ron(ald)

Eluard, Paul . . . . **TCLC 7, 41**
See also Grindel, Eugene

Elyot, Sir Thomas 1490(?)-1546 . . . . . **LC 11**

Elytis, Odysseus 1911- . . . . **CLC 15, 49**
See also CA 102; DAM POET; MTCW

Emecheta, (Florence Onye) Buchi
1944- . . . . **CLC 14, 48; BLC**
See also BW 2; CA 81-84; CANR 27;
DAM MULT; DLB 117; MTCW;
SATA 66

Emerson, Ralph Waldo
1803-1882 . . . . . **NCLC 1, 38; DA; DAB;
DAC; WLC**
See also CDALB 1640-1865; DAM MST,
POET; DLB 1, 59, 73

Eminescu, Mihail 1850-1889 . . . . . **NCLC 33**

Empson, William
1906-1984 . . . . **CLC 3, 8, 19, 33, 34**
See also CA 17-20R; 112; CANR 31;
DLB 20; MTCW

Enchi Fumiko (Ueda) 1905-1986 . . . . **CLC 31**
See also CA 129; 121

Ende, Michael (Andreas Helmuth)
1929-1995 . . . . **CLC 31**
See also CA 118; 124; 149; CANR 36;
CLR 14; DLB 75; MAICYA; SATA 61;
SATA-Brief 42; SATA-Obit 86

Endo, Shusaku 1923- . . . . . **CLC 7, 14, 19, 54**
See also CA 29-32R; CANR 21;
DAM NOV; MTCW

Engel, Marian 1933-1985 . . . . **CLC 36**
See also CA 25-28R; CANR 12; DLB 53;
INT CANR-12

Engelhardt, Frederick
See Hubbard, L(afayette) Ron(ald)

Enright, D(ennis) J(oseph)
1920- . . . . **CLC 4, 8, 31**
See also CA 1-4R; CANR 1, 42; DLB 27;
SATA 25

Enzensberger, Hans Magnus
1929- . . . . **CLC 43**
See also CA 116; 119

Ephron, Nora 1941- . . . . **CLC 17, 31**
See also AITN 2; CA 65-68; CANR 12, 39

Epsilon
See Betjeman, John

Epstein, Daniel Mark 1948- . . . . **CLC 7**
See also CA 49-52; CANR 2

Epstein, Jacob 1956- .... **CLC 19**
See also CA 114

Epstein, Joseph 1937-............. **CLC 39**
See also CA 112; 119; CANR 50

Epstein, Leslie 1938- .... **CLC 27**
See also CA 73-76; CAAS 12; CANR 23

Equiano, Olaudah
1745(?)-1797 .... **LC 16; BLC**
See also DAM MULT; DLB 37, 50

Erasmus, Desiderius 1469(?)-1536.... **LC 16**

Erdman, Paul E(mil) 1932- .... **CLC 25**
See also AITN 1; CA 61-64; CANR 13, 43

Erdrich, Louise 1954-......... **CLC 39, 54**
See also AAYA 10; BEST 89:1; CA 114;
CANR 41; DAM MULT, NOV, POP;
DLB 152; MTCW; NNAL

Erenburg, Ilya (Grigoryevich)
See Ehrenburg, Ilya (Grigoryevich)

Erickson, Stephen Michael 1950-
See Erickson, Steve
See also CA 129

Erickson, Steve .... **CLC 64**
See also Erickson, Stephen Michael

Ericson, Walter
See Fast, Howard (Melvin)

Eriksson, Buntel
See Bergman, (Ernst) Ingmar

Ernaux, Annie 1940- .... **CLC 88**
See also CA 147

Eschenbach, Wolfram von
See Wolfram von Eschenbach

Eseki, Bruno
See Mphahlele, Ezekiel

Esenin, Sergei (Alexandrovich)
1895-1925 .... **TCLC 4**
See also CA 104

Eshleman, Clayton 1935-.......... **CLC 7**
See also CA 33-36R; CAAS 6; DLB 5

Espriella, Don Manuel Alvarez
See Southey, Robert

Espriu, Salvador 1913-1985........ **CLC 9**
See also CA 115; DLB 134

Espronceda, Jose de 1808-1842... **NCLC 39**

Esse, James
See Stephens, James

Esterbrook, Tom
See Hubbard, L(afayette) Ron(ald)

Estleman, Loren D. 1952- .... **CLC 48**
See also CA 85-88; CANR 27; DAM NOV,
POP; INT CANR-27; MTCW

Eugenides, Jeffrey 1960(?)- .... **CLC 81**
See also CA 144

Euripides c. 485B.C.-406B.C. .... **DC 4**
See also DA; DAB; DAC; DAM DRAM,
MST

Evan, Evin
See Faust, Frederick (Schiller)

Evans, Evan
See Faust, Frederick (Schiller)

Evans, Marian
See Eliot, George

Evans, Mary Ann
See Eliot, George

Evarts, Esther
See Benson, Sally

Everett, Percival L. 1956-........ **CLC 57**
See also BW 2; CA 129

Everson, R(onald) G(ilmour)
1903- .... **CLC 27**
See also CA 17-20R; DLB 88

Everson, William (Oliver)
1912-1994 .... **CLC 1, 5, 14**
See also CA 9-12R; 145; CANR 20; DLB 5,
16; MTCW

Evtushenko, Evgenii Aleksandrovich
See Yevtushenko, Yevgeny (Alexandrovich)

Ewart, Gavin (Buchanan)
1916-1995 .... **CLC 13, 46**
See also CA 89-92; 150; CANR 17, 46;
DLB 40; MTCW

Ewers, Hanns Heinz 1871-1943 ... **TCLC 12**
See also CA 109; 149

Ewing, Frederick R.
See Sturgeon, Theodore (Hamilton)

Exley, Frederick (Earl)
1929-1992 .... **CLC 6, 11**
See also AITN 2; CA 81-84; 138; DLB 143;
DLBY 81

Eynhardt, Guillermo
See Quiroga, Horacio (Sylvestre)

Ezekiel, Nissim 1924-............. **CLC 61**
See also CA 61-64

Ezekiel, Tish O'Dowd 1943-....... **CLC 34**
See also CA 129

Fadeyev, A.
See Bulgya, Alexander Alexandrovich

Fadeyev, Alexander.............. **TCLC 53**
See also Bulgya, Alexander Alexandrovich

Fagen, Donald 1948-............. **CLC 26**

Fainzilberg, Ilya Arnoldovich 1897-1937
See Ilf, Ilya
See also CA 120

Fair, Ronald L. 1932-............. **CLC 18**
See also BW 1; CA 69-72; CANR 25;
DLB 33

Fairbairns, Zoe (Ann) 1948- .... **CLC 32**
See also CA 103; CANR 21

Falco, Gian
See Papini, Giovanni

Falconer, James
See Kirkup, James

Falconer, Kenneth
See Kornbluth, C(yril) M.

Falkland, Samuel
See Heijermans, Herman

Fallaci, Oriana 1930-............. **CLC 11**
See also CA 77-80; CANR 15; MTCW

Faludy, George 1913-............. **CLC 42**
See also CA 21-24R

Faludy, Gyoergy
See Faludy, George

Fanon, Frantz 1925-1961..... **CLC 74; BLC**
See also BW 1; CA 116; 89-92;
DAM MULT

Fanshawe, Ann 1625-1680 .... **LC 11**

Fante, John (Thomas) 1911-1983 ... **CLC 60**
See also CA 69-72; 109; CANR 23;
DLB 130; DLBY 83

Farah, Nuruddin 1945-....... **CLC 53; BLC**
See also BW 2; CA 106; DAM MULT;
DLB 125

Fargue, Leon-Paul 1876(?)-1947 ... **TCLC 11**
See also CA 109

Farigoule, Louis
See Romains, Jules

Farina, Richard 1936(?)-1966 .... **CLC 9**
See also CA 81-84; 25-28R

Farley, Walter (Lorimer)
1915-1989 .... **CLC 17**
See also CA 17-20R; CANR 8, 29; DLB 22;
JRDA; MAICYA; SATA 2, 43

Farmer, Philip Jose 1918-....... **CLC 1, 19**
See also CA 1-4R; CANR 4, 35; DLB 8;
MTCW

Farquhar, George 1677-1707........ **LC 21**
See also DAM DRAM; DLB 84

Farrell, J(ames) G(ordon)
1935-1979 .... **CLC 6**
See also CA 73-76; 89-92; CANR 36;
DLB 14; MTCW

Farrell, James T(homas)
1904-1979 .... **CLC 1, 4, 8, 11, 66**
See also CA 5-8R; 89-92; CANR 9; DLB 4,
9, 86; DLBD 2; MTCW

Farren, Richard J.
See Betjeman, John

Farren, Richard M.
See Betjeman, John

Fassbinder, Rainer Werner
1946-1982 .... **CLC 20**
See also CA 93-96; 106; CANR 31

Fast, Howard (Melvin) 1914- ...... **CLC 23**
See also AAYA 16; CA 1-4R; CAAS 18;
CANR 1, 33; DAM NOV; DLB 9;
INT CANR-33; SATA 7

Faulcon, Robert
See Holdstock, Robert P.

Faulkner, William (Cuthbert)
1897-1962 ..... CLC 1, 3, 6, 8, 9, 11, 14,
18, 28, 52, 68; DA; DAB; DAC; SSC 1;
WLC
See also AAYA 7; CA 81-84; CANR 33;
CDALB 1929-1941; DAM MST, NOV;
DLB 9, 11, 44, 102; DLBD 2; DLBY 86;
MTCW

Fauset, Jessie Redmon
1884(?)-1961 .... **CLC 19, 54; BLC**
See also BW 1; CA 109; DAM MULT;
DLB 51

Faust, Frederick (Schiller)
1892-1944(?)................ **TCLC 49**
See also CA 108; DAM POP

Faust, Irvin 1924-................. **CLC 8**
See also CA 33-36R; CANR 28; DLB 2, 28;
DLBY 80

Fawkes, Guy
See Benchley, Robert (Charles)

Fearing, Kenneth (Flexner)
1902-1961 .... **CLC 51**
See also CA 93-96; DLB 9

Foote, Shelby 1916- . . . . **CLC 75**
See also CA 5-8R; CANR 3, 45;
DAM NOV, POP; DLB 2, 17

Forbes, Esther 1891-1967. . . . . **CLC 12**
See also AAYA 17; CA 13-14; 25-28R;
CAP 1; CLR 27; DLB 22; JRDA;
MAICYA; SATA 2

Forche, Carolyn (Louise)
1950- . . . . **CLC 25, 83, 86; PC 10**
See also CA 109; 117; CANR 50;
DAM POET; DLB 5; INT 117

Ford, Elbur
See Hibbert, Eleanor Alice Burford

Ford, Ford Madox
1873-1939 . . . . **TCLC 1, 15, 39, 57**
See also CA 104; 132; CDBLB 1914-1945;
DAM NOV; DLB 162; MTCW

Ford, John 1895-1973. . . . . **CLC 16**
See also CA 45-48

Ford, Richard 1944- . . . . **CLC 46**
See also CA 69-72; CANR 11, 47

Ford, Webster
See Masters, Edgar Lee

Foreman, Richard 1937- . . . . **CLC 50**
See also CA 65-68; CANR 32

Forester, C(ecil) S(cott)
1899-1966 . . . . **CLC 35**
See also CA 73-76; 25-28R; SATA 13

Forez
See Mauriac, Francois (Charles)

Forman, James Douglas 1932- . . . . . **CLC 21**
See also AAYA 17; CA 9-12R; CANR 4,
19, 42; JRDA; MAICYA; SATA 8, 70

Fornes, Maria Irene 1930- . . . . . **CLC 39, 61**
See also CA 25-28R; CANR 28; DLB 7;
HW; INT CANR-28; MTCW

Forrest, Leon 1937- . . . . **CLC 4**
See also BW 2; CA 89-92; CAAS 7;
CANR 25; DLB 33

Forster, E(dward) M(organ)
1879-1970 . . . . . **CLC 1, 2, 3, 4, 9, 10, 13,
15, 22, 45, 77; DA; DAB; DAC; WLC**
See also AAYA 2; CA 13-14; 25-28R;
CANR 45; CAP 1; CDBLB 1914-1945;
DAM MST, NOV; DLB 34, 98, 162;
DLBD 10; MTCW; SATA 57

Forster, John 1812-1876 . . . . **NCLC 11**
See also DLB 144

Forsyth, Frederick 1938- . . . . . **CLC 2, 5, 36**
See also BEST 89:4; CA 85-88; CANR 38;
DAM NOV, POP; DLB 87; MTCW

Forten, Charlotte L. . . . . **TCLC 16; BLC**
See also Grimke, Charlotte L(ottie) Forten
See also DLB 50

Foscolo, Ugo 1778-1827. . . . . **NCLC 8**

Fosse, Bob . . . . **CLC 20**
See also Fosse, Robert Louis

Fosse, Robert Louis 1927-1987
See Fosse, Bob
See also CA 110; 123

Foster, Stephen Collins
1826-1864 . . . . **NCLC 26**

Foucault, Michel
1926-1984 . . . . **CLC 31, 34, 69**
See also CA 105; 113; CANR 34; MTCW

Fouque, Friedrich (Heinrich Karl) de la Motte
1777-1843 . . . . **NCLC 2**
See also DLB 90

Fourier, Charles 1772-1837 . . . . . . **NCLC 51**

Fournier, Henri Alban 1886-1914
See Alain-Fournier
See also CA 104

Fournier, Pierre 1916- . . . . **CLC 11**
See also Gascar, Pierre
See also CA 89-92; CANR 16, 40

Fowles, John
1926- . . . . . . **CLC 1, 2, 3, 4, 6, 9, 10, 15,
33, 87; DAB; DAC**
See also CA 5-8R; CANR 25; CDBLB 1960
to Present; DAM MST; DLB 14, 139;
MTCW; SATA 22

Fox, Paula 1923-. . . . . **CLC 2, 8**
See also AAYA 3; CA 73-76; CANR 20,
36; CLR 1; DLB 52; JRDA; MAICYA;
MTCW; SATA 17, 60

Fox, William Price (Jr.) 1926- . . . . . **CLC 22**
See also CA 17-20R; CAAS 19; CANR 11;
DLB 2; DLBY 81

Foxe, John 1516(?)-1587 . . . . **LC 14**

Frame, Janet . . . . **CLC 2, 3, 6, 22, 66**
See also Clutha, Janet Paterson Frame

France, Anatole . . . . **TCLC 9**
See also Thibault, Jacques Anatole Francois
See also DLB 123

Francis, Claude 19(?)- . . . . **CLC 50**

Francis, Dick 1920- . . . . **CLC 2, 22, 42**
See also AAYA 5; BEST 89:3; CA 5-8R;
CANR 9, 42; CDBLB 1960 to Present;
DAM POP; DLB 87; INT CANR-9;
MTCW

Francis, Robert (Churchill)
1901-1987 . . . . **CLC 15**
See also CA 1-4R; 123; CANR 1

Frank, Anne(lies Marie)
1929-1945 . . . . **TCLC 17; DA; DAB;
DAC; WLC**
See also AAYA 12; CA 113; 133;
DAM MST; MTCW; SATA 87;
SATA-Brief 42

Frank, Elizabeth 1945- . . . . **CLC 39**
See also CA 121; 126; INT 126

Franklin, Benjamin
See Hasek, Jaroslav (Matej Frantisek)

Franklin, Benjamin
1706-1790 . . . . . **LC 25; DA; DAB; DAC**
See also CDALB 1640-1865; DAM MST;
DLB 24, 43, 73

Franklin, (Stella Maraia Sarah) Miles
1879-1954 . . . . **TCLC 7**
See also CA 104

Fraser, (Lady) Antonia (Pakenham)
1932- . . . . **CLC 32**
See also CA 85-88; CANR 44; MTCW;
SATA-Brief 32

Fraser, George MacDonald 1925- . . . . **CLC 7**
See also CA 45-48; CANR 2, 48

Fraser, Sylvia 1935- . . . . **CLC 64**
See also CA 45-48; CANR 1, 16

Frayn, Michael 1933- . . . . . . **CLC 3, 7, 31, 47**
See also CA 5-8R; CANR 30;
DAM DRAM, NOV; DLB 13, 14;
MTCW

Fraze, Candida (Merrill) 1945- . . . . . **CLC 50**
See also CA 126

Frazer, J(ames) G(eorge)
1854-1941 . . . . **TCLC 32**
See also CA 118

Frazer, Robert Caine
See Creasey, John

Frazer, Sir James George
See Frazer, J(ames) G(eorge)

Frazier, Ian 1951- . . . . **CLC 46**
See also CA 130

Frederic, Harold 1856-1898 . . . . . . **NCLC 10**
See also DLB 12, 23; DLBD 13

Frederick, John
See Faust, Frederick (Schiller)

Frederick the Great 1712-1786 . . . . . . **LC 14**

Fredro, Aleksander 1793-1876 . . . . . **NCLC 8**

Freeling, Nicolas 1927- . . . . **CLC 38**
See also CA 49-52; CAAS 12; CANR 1, 17,
50; DLB 87

Freeman, Douglas Southall
1886-1953 . . . . **TCLC 11**
See also CA 109; DLB 17

Freeman, Judith 1946- . . . . **CLC 55**
See also CA 148

Freeman, Mary Eleanor Wilkins
1852-1930 . . . . **TCLC 9; SSC 1**
See also CA 106; DLB 12, 78

Freeman, R(ichard) Austin
1862-1943 . . . . **TCLC 21**
See also CA 113; DLB 70

French, Albert 1943- . . . . **CLC 86**

French, Marilyn 1929- . . . . . . **CLC 10, 18, 60**
See also CA 69-72; CANR 3, 31;
DAM DRAM, NOV, POP;
INT CANR-31; MTCW

French, Paul
See Asimov, Isaac

Freneau, Philip Morin 1752-1832 . . **NCLC 1**
See also DLB 37, 43

Freud, Sigmund 1856-1939 . . . . **TCLC 52**
See also CA 115; 133; MTCW

Friedan, Betty (Naomi) 1921- . . . . . . **CLC 74**
See also CA 65-68; CANR 18, 45; MTCW

Friedlaender, Saul 1932- . . . . **CLC 90**
See also CA 117; 130

Friedman, B(ernard) H(arper)
1926- . . . . **CLC 7**
See also CA 1-4R; CANR 3, 48

Friedman, Bruce Jay 1930- . . . . **CLC 3, 5, 56**
See also CA 9-12R; CANR 25; DLB 2, 28;
INT CANR-25

Friel, Brian 1929- . . . . **CLC 5, 42, 59**
See also CA 21-24R; CANR 33; DLB 13;
MTCW

Friis-Baastad, Babbis Ellinor
1921-1970 . . . . **CLC 12**
See also CA 17-20R; 134; SATA 7

Garrigue, Jean 1914-1972 . . . . **CLC 2, 8**
  See also CA 5-8R; 37-40R; CANR 20

Garrison, Frederick
  See Sinclair, Upton (Beall)

Garth, Will
  See Hamilton, Edmond; Kuttner, Henry

Garvey, Marcus (Moziah, Jr.)
  1887-1940 . . . . **TCLC 41; BLC**
  See also BW 1; CA 120; 124; DAM MULT

Gary, Romain . . . . **CLC 25**
  See also Kacew, Romain
  See also DLB 83

Gascar, Pierre . . . . **CLC 11**
  See also Fournier, Pierre

Gascoyne, David (Emery) 1916- . . . . **CLC 45**
  See also CA 65-68; CANR 10, 28; DLB 20;
  MTCW

Gaskell, Elizabeth Cleghorn
  1810-1865 . . . . **NCLC 5; DAB**
  See also CDBLB 1832-1890; DAM MST;
  DLB 21, 144, 159

Gass, William H(oward)
  1924- . . . **CLC 1, 2, 8, 11, 15, 39; SSC 12**
  See also CA 17-20R; CANR 30; DLB 2;
  MTCW

Gasset, Jose Ortega y
  See Ortega y Gasset, Jose

Gates, Henry Louis, Jr. 1950- . . . . . . **CLC 65**
  See also BW 2; CA 109; CANR 25;
  DAM MULT; DLB 67

Gautier, Theophile
  1811-1872 . . . . **NCLC 1; SSC 20**
  See also DAM POET; DLB 119

Gawsworth, John
  See Bates, H(erbert) E(rnest)

Gay, Oliver
  See Gogarty, Oliver St. John

Gaye, Marvin (Penze) 1939-1984 . . . **CLC 26**
  See also CA 112

Gebler, Carlo (Ernest) 1954- . . . . **CLC 39**
  See also CA 119; 133

Gee, Maggie (Mary) 1948- . . . . **CLC 57**
  See also CA 130

Gee, Maurice (Gough) 1931- . . . . **CLC 29**
  See also CA 97-100; SATA 46

Gelbart, Larry (Simon) 1923- . . . **CLC 21, 61**
  See also CA 73-76; CANR 45

Gelber, Jack 1932- . . . . **CLC 1, 6, 14, 79**
  See also CA 1-4R; CANR 2; DLB 7

Gellhorn, Martha (Ellis) 1908- . . **CLC 14, 60**
  See also CA 77-80; CANR 44; DLBY 82

Genet, Jean
  1910-1986 . . . **CLC 1, 2, 5, 10, 14, 44, 46**
  See also CA 13-16R; CANR 18;
  DAM DRAM; DLB 72; DLBY 86;
  MTCW

Gent, Peter 1942- . . . . **CLC 29**
  See also AITN 1; CA 89-92; DLBY 82

Gentlewoman in New England, A
  See Bradstreet, Anne

Gentlewoman in Those Parts, A
  See Bradstreet, Anne

George, Jean Craighead 1919- . . . . . . **CLC 35**
  See also AAYA 8; CA 5-8R; CANR 25;
  CLR 1; DLB 52; JRDA; MAICYA;
  SATA 2, 68

George, Stefan (Anton)
  1868-1933 . . . . **TCLC 2, 14**
  See also CA 104

Georges, Georges Martin
  See Simenon, Georges (Jacques Christian)

Gerhardi, William Alexander
  See Gerhardie, William Alexander

Gerhardie, William Alexander
  1895-1977 . . . . **CLC 5**
  See also CA 25-28R; 73-76; CANR 18;
  DLB 36

Gerstler, Amy 1956- . . . . **CLC 70**
  See also CA 146

Gertler, T. . . . . **CLC 34**
  See also CA 116; 121; INT 121

Ghalib . . . . **NCLC 39**
  See also Ghalib, Hsadullah Khan

Ghalib, Hsadullah Khan 1797-1869
  See Ghalib
  See also DAM POET

Ghelderode, Michel de
  1898-1962 . . . . **CLC 6, 11**
  See also CA 85-88; CANR 40;
  DAM DRAM

Ghiselin, Brewster 1903- . . . . **CLC 23**
  See also CA 13-16R; CAAS 10; CANR 13

Ghose, Zulfikar 1935- . . . . **CLC 42**
  See also CA 65-68

Ghosh, Amitav 1956- . . . . **CLC 44**
  See also CA 147

Giacosa, Giuseppe 1847-1906 . . . . . . **TCLC 7**
  See also CA 104

Gibb, Lee
  See Waterhouse, Keith (Spencer)

Gibbon, Lewis Grassic . . . . **TCLC 4**
  See also Mitchell, James Leslie

Gibbons, Kaye 1960- . . . . **CLC 50, 88**
  See also DAM POP

Gibran, Kahlil
  1883-1931 . . . . **TCLC 1, 9; PC 9**
  See also CA 104; 150; DAM POET, POP

Gibran, Khalil
  See Gibran, Kahlil

Gibson, William
  1914- . . . . **CLC 23; DA; DAB; DAC**
  See also CA 9-12R; CANR 9, 42;
  DAM DRAM, MST; DLB 7; SATA 66

Gibson, William (Ford) 1948- . . . **CLC 39, 63**
  See also AAYA 12; CA 126; 133;
  DAM POP

Gide, Andre (Paul Guillaume)
  1869-1951 . . . . **TCLC 5, 12, 36; DA;**
                        DAB; DAC; SSC 13; WLC
  See also CA 104; 124; DAM MST, NOV;
  DLB 65; MTCW

Gifford, Barry (Colby) 1946- . . . . **CLC 34**
  See also CA 65-68; CANR 9, 30, 40

Gilbert, W(illiam) S(chwenck)
  1836-1911 . . . . **TCLC 3**
  See also CA 104; DAM DRAM, POET;
  SATA 36

Gilbreth, Frank B., Jr. 1911- . . . . **CLC 17**
  See also CA 9-12R; SATA 2

Gilchrist, Ellen 1935- . . **CLC 34, 48; SSC 14**
  See also CA 113; 116; CANR 41;
  DAM POP; DLB 130; MTCW

Giles, Molly 1942- . . . . **CLC 39**
  See also CA 126

Gill, Patrick
  See Creasey, John

Gilliam, Terry (Vance) 1940- . . . . **CLC 21**
  See also Monty Python
  See also CA 108; 113; CANR 35; INT 113

Gillian, Jerry
  See Gilliam, Terry (Vance)

Gilliatt, Penelope (Ann Douglass)
  1932-1993 . . . . **CLC 2, 10, 13, 53**
  See also AITN 2; CA 13-16R; 141;
  CANR 49; DLB 14

Gilman, Charlotte (Anna) Perkins (Stetson)
  1860-1935 . . . . **TCLC 9, 37; SSC 13**
  See also CA 106; 150

Gilmour, David 1949- . . . . **CLC 35**
  See also CA 138, 147

Gilpin, William 1724-1804 . . . . **NCLC 30**

Gilray, J. D.
  See Mencken, H(enry) L(ouis)

Gilroy, Frank D(aniel) 1925- . . . . **CLC 2**
  See also CA 81-84; CANR 32; DLB 7

Ginsberg, Allen
  1926- . . . . . . **CLC 1, 2, 3, 4, 6, 13, 36, 69;**
                  DA; DAB; DAC; PC 4; WLC 3
  See also AITN 1; CA 1-4R; CANR 2, 41;
  CDALB 1941-1968; DAM MST, POET;
  DLB 5, 16; MTCW

Ginzburg, Natalia
  1916-1991 . . . . **CLC 5, 11, 54, 70**
  See also CA 85-88; 135; CANR 33; MTCW

Giono, Jean 1895-1970 . . . . **CLC 4, 11**
  See also CA 45-48; 29-32R; CANR 2, 35;
  DLB 72; MTCW

Giovanni, Nikki
  1943- . . . . . . **CLC 2, 4, 19, 64; BLC; DA;**
                  DAB; DAC
  See also AITN 1; BW 2; CA 29-32R;
  CAAS 6; CANR 18, 41; CLR 6;
  DAM MST, MULT, POET; DLB 5, 41;
  INT CANR-18; MAICYA; MTCW;
  SATA 24

Giovene, Andrea 1904- . . . . **CLC 7**
  See also CA 85-88

Gippius, Zinaida (Nikolayevna) 1869-1945
  See Hippius, Zinaida
  See also CA 106

Giraudoux, (Hippolyte) Jean
  1882-1944 . . . . **TCLC 2, 7**
  See also CA 104; DAM DRAM; DLB 65

Gironella, Jose Maria 1917- . . . . **CLC 11**
  See also CA 101

Gissing, George (Robert)
  1857-1903 . . . . **TCLC 3, 24, 47**
  See also CA 105; DLB 18, 135

Giurlani, Aldo
  See Palazzeschi, Aldo

Gladkov, Fyodor (Vasilyevich)
  1883-1958 . . . . **TCLC 27**

Glanville, Brian (Lester) 1931- ...... **CLC 6**
See also CA 5-8R; CAAS 9; CANR 3;
DLB 15, 139; SATA 42

Glasgow, Ellen (Anderson Gholson)
1873(?)-1945 .... **TCLC 2, 7**
See also CA 104; DLB 9, 12

Glaspell, Susan (Keating)
1882(?)-1948 .... **TCLC 55**
See also CA 110; DLB 7, 9, 78; YABC 2

Glassco, John 1909-1981 .... **CLC 9**
See also CA 13-16R; 102; CANR 15;
DLB 68

Glasscock, Amnesia
See Steinbeck, John (Ernst)

Glasser, Ronald J. 1940(?)- .... **CLC 37**

Glassman, Joyce
See Johnson, Joyce

Glendinning, Victoria 1937- .... **CLC 50**
See also CA 120; 127; DLB 155

Glissant, Edouard 1928- .... **CLC 10, 68**
See also DAM MULT

Gloag, Julian 1930- .... **CLC 40**
See also AITN 1; CA 65-68; CANR 10

Glowacki, Aleksander
See Prus, Boleslaw

Glueck, Louise (Elisabeth)
1943- .... **CLC 7, 22, 44, 81**
See also CA 33-36R; CANR 40;
DAM POET; DLB 5

Gobineau, Joseph Arthur (Comte) de
1816-1882 .... **NCLC 17**
See also DLB 123

Godard, Jean-Luc 1930- .... **CLC 20**
See also CA 93-96

Godden, (Margaret) Rumer 1907- ... **CLC 53**
See also AAYA 6; CA 5-8R; CANR 4, 27,
36; CLR 20; DLB 161; MAICYA;
SAAS 12; SATA 3, 36

Godoy Alcayaga, Lucila 1889-1957
See Mistral, Gabriela
See also BW 2; CA 104; 131; DAM MULT;
HW; MTCW

Godwin, Gail (Kathleen)
1937- .... **CLC 5, 8, 22, 31, 69**
See also CA 29-32R; CANR 15, 43;
DAM POP; DLB 6; INT CANR-15;
MTCW

Godwin, William 1756-1836 ...... **NCLC 14**
See also CDBLB 1789-1832; DLB 39, 104,
142, 158, 163

Goethe, Johann Wolfgang von
1749-1832 .... **NCLC 4, 22, 34; DA;
DAB; DAC; PC 5; WLC 3**
See also DAM DRAM, MST, POET;
DLB 94

Gogarty, Oliver St. John
1878-1957 .... **TCLC 15**
See also CA 109; 150; DLB 15, 19

Gogol, Nikolai (Vasilyevich)
1809-1852 .... **NCLC 5, 15, 31; DA;
DAB; DAC; DC 1; SSC 4; WLC**
See also DAM DRAM, MST

Goines, Donald
1937(?)-1974 .... **CLC 80; BLC**
See also AITN 1; BW 1; CA 124; 114;
DAM MULT, POP; DLB 33

Gold, Herbert 1924- .... **CLC 4, 7, 14, 42**
See also CA 9-12R; CANR 17, 45; DLB 2;
DLBY 81

Goldbarth, Albert 1948- .... **CLC 5, 38**
See also CA 53-56; CANR 6, 40; DLB 120

Goldberg, Anatol 1910-1982 .... **CLC 34**
See also CA 131; 117

Goldemberg, Isaac 1945- .... **CLC 52**
See also CA 69-72; CAAS 12; CANR 11,
32; HW

Golding, William (Gerald)
1911-1993 .... **CLC 1, 2, 3, 8, 10, 17, 27,
58, 81; DA; DAB; DAC; WLC**
See also AAYA 5; CA 5-8R; 141;
CANR 13, 33; CDBLB 1945-1960;
DAM MST, NOV; DLB 15, 100; MTCW

Goldman, Emma 1869-1940 ...... **TCLC 13**
See also CA 110; 150

Goldman, Francisco 1955- .... **CLC 76**

Goldman, William (W.) 1931- .... **CLC 1, 48**
See also CA 9-12R; CANR 29; DLB 44

Goldmann, Lucien 1913-1970 ...... **CLC 24**
See also CA 25-28; CAP 2

Goldoni, Carlo 1707-1793 .... **LC 4**
See also DAM DRAM

Goldsberry, Steven 1949- .... **CLC 34**
See also CA 131

Goldsmith, Oliver
1728-1774 ...... **LC 2; DA; DAB; DAC;
WLC**
See also CDBLB 1660-1789; DAM DRAM,
MST, NOV, POET; DLB 39, 89, 104,
109, 142; SATA 26

Goldsmith, Peter
See Priestley, J(ohn) B(oynton)

Gombrowicz, Witold
1904-1969 .... **CLC 4, 7, 11, 49**
See also CA 19-20; 25-28R; CAP 2;
DAM DRAM

Gomez de la Serna, Ramon
1888-1963 .... **CLC 9**
See also CA 116; HW

Goncharov, Ivan Alexandrovich
1812-1891 .... **NCLC 1**

Goncourt, Edmond (Louis Antoine Huot) de
1822-1896 .... **NCLC 7**
See also DLB 123

Goncourt, Jules (Alfred Huot) de
1830-1870 .... **NCLC 7**
See also DLB 123

Gontier, Fernande 19(?)- .... **CLC 50**

Goodman, Paul 1911-1972 .... **CLC 1, 2, 4, 7**
See also CA 19-20; 37-40R; CANR 34;
CAP 2; DLB 130; MTCW

Gordimer, Nadine
1923- .... **CLC 3, 5, 7, 10, 18, 33, 51, 70;
DA; DAB; DAC; SSC 17**
See also CA 5-8R; CANR 3, 28;
DAM MST, NOV; INT CANR-28;
MTCW

Gordon, Adam Lindsay
1833-1870 .... **NCLC 21**

Gordon, Caroline
1895-1981 ... **CLC 6, 13, 29, 83; SSC 15**
See also CA 11-12; 103; CANR 36; CAP 1;
DLB 4, 9, 102; DLBY 81; MTCW

Gordon, Charles William 1860-1937
See Connor, Ralph
See also CA 109

Gordon, Mary (Catherine)
1949- .... **CLC 13, 22**
See also CA 102; CANR 44; DLB 6;
DLBY 81; INT 102; MTCW

Gordon, Sol 1923- .... **CLC 26**
See also CA 53-56; CANR 4; SATA 11

Gordone, Charles 1925-1995 ...... **CLC 1, 4**
See also BW 1; CA 93-96; 150;
DAM DRAM; DLB 7; INT 93-96;
MTCW

Gorenko, Anna Andreevna
See Akhmatova, Anna

Gorky, Maxim .... **TCLC 8; DAB; WLC**
See also Peshkov, Alexei Maximovich

Goryan, Sirak
See Saroyan, William

Gosse, Edmund (William)
1849-1928 .... **TCLC 28**
See also CA 117; DLB 57, 144

Gotlieb, Phyllis Fay (Bloom)
1926- .... **CLC 18**
See also CA 13-16R; CANR 7; DLB 88

Gottesman, S. D.
See Kornbluth, C(yril) M.; Pohl, Frederik

Gottfried von Strassburg
fl. c. 1210- .... **CMLC 10**
See also DLB 138

Gould, Lois .... **CLC 4, 10**
See also CA 77-80; CANR 29; MTCW

Gourmont, Remy (-Marie-Charles) de
1858-1915 .... **TCLC 17**
See also CA 109; 150

Govier, Katherine 1948- .... **CLC 51**
See also CA 101; CANR 18, 40

Goyen, (Charles) William
1915-1983 .... **CLC 5, 8, 14, 40**
See also AITN 2; CA 5-8R; 110; CANR 6;
DLB 2; DLBY 83; INT CANR-6

Goytisolo, Juan
1931- .... **CLC 5, 10, 23; HLC**
See also CA 85-88; CANR 32;
DAM MULT; HW; MTCW

Gozzano, Guido 1883-1916 .... **PC 10**
See also DLB 114

Gozzi, (Conte) Carlo 1720-1806 .. **NCLC 23**

Grabbe, Christian Dietrich
1801-1836 .... **NCLC 2**
See also DLB 133

Grace, Patricia 1937- .... **CLC 56**

Gracian y Morales, Baltasar
1601-1658 .... **LC 15**

Gracq, Julien .... **CLC 11, 48**
See also Poirier, Louis
See also DLB 83

Grade, Chaim 1910-1982 . . . . **CLC 10**
See also CA 93-96; 107

Graduate of Oxford, A
See Ruskin, John

Graham, John
See Phillips, David Graham

Graham, Jorie 1951- . . . . **CLC 48**
See also CA 111; DLB 120

Graham, R(obert) B(ontine) Cunninghame
See Cunninghame Graham, R(obert)
B(ontine)
See also DLB 98, 135

Graham, Robert
See Haldeman, Joe (William)

Graham, Tom
See Lewis, (Harry) Sinclair

Graham, W(illiam) S(ydney)
1918-1986 . . . . **CLC 29**
See also CA 73-76; 118; DLB 20

Graham, Winston (Mawdsley)
1910- . . . . **CLC 23**
See also CA 49-52; CANR 2, 22, 45;
DLB 77

Grant, Skeeter
See Spiegelman, Art

Granville-Barker, Harley
1877-1946 . . . . **TCLC 2**
See also Barker, Harley Granville
See also CA 104; DAM DRAM

Grass, Guenter (Wilhelm)
1927- . . . . . **CLC 1, 2, 4, 6, 11, 15, 22, 32,
49, 88; DA; DAB; DAC; WLC**
See also CA 13-16R; CANR 20;
DAM MST, NOV; DLB 75, 124; MTCW

Gratton, Thomas
See Hulme, T(homas) E(rnest)

Grau, Shirley Ann
1929- . . . . **CLC 4, 9; SSC 15**
See also CA 89-92; CANR 22; DLB 2;
INT CANR-22; MTCW

Gravel, Fern
See Hall, James Norman

Graver, Elizabeth 1964- . . . . **CLC 70**
See also CA 135

Graves, Richard Perceval 1945- . . . . **CLC 44**
See also CA 65-68; CANR 9, 26, 51

Graves, Robert (von Ranke)
1895-1985 . . . . . . **CLC 1, 2, 6, 11, 39, 44,
45; DAB; DAC; PC 6**
See also CA 5-8R; 117; CANR 5, 36;
CDBLB 1914-1945; DAM MST, POET;
DLB 20, 100; DLBY 85; MTCW;
SATA 45

Gray, Alasdair (James) 1934- . . . . . . **CLC 41**
See also CA 126; CANR 47; INT 126;
MTCW

Gray, Amlin 1946- . . . . **CLC 29**
See also CA 138

Gray, Francine du Plessix 1930- . . . . **CLC 22**
See also BEST 90:3; CA 61-64; CAAS 2;
CANR 11, 33; DAM NOV;
INT CANR-11; MTCW

Gray, John (Henry) 1866-1934 . . . . **TCLC 19**
See also CA 119

Gray, Simon (James Holliday)
1936- . . . . **CLC 9, 14, 36**
See also AITN 1; CA 21-24R; CAAS 3;
CANR 32; DLB 13; MTCW

Gray, Spalding 1941- . . . . **CLC 49**
See also CA 128; DAM POP

Gray, Thomas
1716-1771 . . . . . . **LC 4; DA; DAB; DAC;
PC 2; WLC**
See also CDBLB 1660-1789; DAM MST;
DLB 109

Grayson, David
See Baker, Ray Stannard

Grayson, Richard (A.) 1951- . . . . **CLC 38**
See also CA 85-88; CANR 14, 31

Greeley, Andrew M(oran) 1928- . . . . **CLC 28**
See also CA 5-8R; CAAS 7; CANR 7, 43;
DAM POP; MTCW

Green, Anna Katharine
1846-1935 . . . . **TCLC 63**
See also CA 112

Green, Brian
See Card, Orson Scott

Green, Hannah
See Greenberg, Joanne (Goldenberg)

Green, Hannah . . . . **CLC 3**
See also CA 73-76

Green, Henry . . . . **CLC 2, 13**
See also Yorke, Henry Vincent
See also DLB 15

Green, Julian (Hartridge) 1900-
See Green, Julien
See also CA 21-24R; CANR 33; DLB 4, 72;
MTCW

Green, Julien . . . . **CLC 3, 11, 77**
See also Green, Julian (Hartridge)

Green, Paul (Eliot) 1894-1981 . . . . . . **CLC 25**
See also AITN 1; CA 5-8R; 103; CANR 3;
DAM DRAM; DLB 7, 9; DLBY 81

Greenberg, Ivan 1908-1973
See Rahv, Philip
See also CA 85-88

Greenberg, Joanne (Goldenberg)
1932- . . . . **CLC 7, 30**
See also AAYA 12; CA 5-8R; CANR 14,
32; SATA 25

Greenberg, Richard 1959(?)- . . . . **CLC 57**
See also CA 138

Greene, Bette 1934- . . . . **CLC 30**
See also AAYA 7; CA 53-56; CANR 4;
CLR 2; JRDA; MAICYA; SAAS 16;
SATA 8

Greene, Gael . . . . **CLC 8**
See also CA 13-16R; CANR 10

Greene, Graham
1904-1991 . . . . **CLC 1, 3, 6, 9, 14, 18, 27,
37, 70, 72; DA; DAB; DAC; WLC**
See also AITN 2; CA 13-16R; 133;
CANR 35; CDBLB 1945-1960;
DAM MST, NOV; DLB 13, 15, 77, 100,
162; DLBY 91; MTCW; SATA 20

Greer, Richard
See Silverberg, Robert

Gregor, Arthur 1923- . . . . **CLC 9**
See also CA 25-28R; CAAS 10; CANR 11;
SATA 36

Gregor, Lee
See Pohl, Frederik

Gregory, Isabella Augusta (Persse)
1852-1932 . . . . **TCLC 1**
See also CA 104; DLB 10

Gregory, J. Dennis
See Williams, John A(lfred)

Grendon, Stephen
See Derleth, August (William)

Grenville, Kate 1950- . . . . **CLC 61**
See also CA 118

Grenville, Pelham
See Wodehouse, P(elham) G(renville)

Greve, Felix Paul (Berthold Friedrich)
1879-1948
See Grove, Frederick Philip
See also CA 104; 141; DAC; DAM MST

Grey, Zane 1872-1939 . . . . **TCLC 6**
See also CA 104; 132; DAM POP; DLB 9;
MTCW

Grieg, (Johan) Nordahl (Brun)
1902-1943 . . . . **TCLC 10**
See also CA 107

Grieve, C(hristopher) M(urray)
1892-1978 . . . . **CLC 11, 19**
See also MacDiarmid, Hugh; Pteleon
See also CA 5-8R; 85-88; CANR 33;
DAM POET; MTCW

Griffin, Gerald 1803-1840 . . . . **NCLC 7**
See also DLB 159

Griffin, John Howard 1920-1980 . . . . **CLC 68**
See also AITN 1; CA 1-4R; 101; CANR 2

Griffin, Peter 1942- . . . . **CLC 39**
See also CA 136

Griffiths, Trevor 1935- . . . . **CLC 13, 52**
See also CA 97-100; CANR 45; DLB 13

Grigson, Geoffrey (Edward Harvey)
1905-1985 . . . . **CLC 7, 39**
See also CA 25-28R; 118; CANR 20, 33;
DLB 27; MTCW

Grillparzer, Franz 1791-1872 . . . . . . **NCLC 1**
See also DLB 133

Grimble, Reverend Charles James
See Eliot, T(homas) S(tearns)

Grimke, Charlotte L(ottie) Forten
1837(?)-1914
See Forten, Charlotte L.
See also BW 1; CA 117; 124; DAM MULT,
POET

Grimm, Jacob Ludwig Karl
1785-1863 . . . . **NCLC 3**
See also DLB 90; MAICYA; SATA 22

Grimm, Wilhelm Karl 1786-1859 . . **NCLC 3**
See also DLB 90; MAICYA; SATA 22

Grimmelshausen, Johann Jakob Christoffel
von 1621-1676 . . . . **LC 6**

Grindel, Eugene 1895-1952
See Eluard, Paul
See also CA 104

Grisham, John 1955- . . . . **CLC 84**
See also AAYA 14; CA 138; CANR 47;
DAM POP

Grossman, David 1954- .... **CLC 67**
See also CA 138

Grossman, Vasily (Semenovich)
1905-1964 .... **CLC 41**
See also CA 124; 130; MTCW

Grove, Frederick Philip .... **TCLC 4**
See also Greve, Felix Paul (Berthold
Friedrich)
See also DLB 92

Grubb
See Crumb, R(obert)

Grumbach, Doris (Isaac)
1918- .... **CLC 13, 22, 64**
See also CA 5-8R; CAAS 2; CANR 9, 42;
INT CANR-9

Grundtvig, Nicolai Frederik Severin
1783-1872 .... **NCLC 1**

Grunge
See Crumb, R(obert)

Grunwald, Lisa 1959- .... **CLC 44**
See also CA 120

Guare, John 1938- .... **CLC 8, 14, 29, 67**
See also CA 73-76; CANR 21;
DAM DRAM; DLB 7; MTCW

Gudjonsson, Halldor Kiljan 1902-
See Laxness, Halldor
See also CA 103

Guenter, Erich
See Eich, Guenter

Guest, Barbara 1920- .... **CLC 34**
See also CA 25-28R; CANR 11, 44; DLB 5

Guest, Judith (Ann) 1936- .... **CLC 8, 30**
See also AAYA 7; CA 77-80; CANR 15;
DAM NOV, POP; INT CANR-15;
MTCW

Guevara, Che .... **CLC 87; HLC**
See also Guevara (Serna), Ernesto

Guevara (Serna), Ernesto 1928-1967
See Guevara, Che
See also CA 127; 111; DAM MULT; HW

Guild, Nicholas M. 1944- .... **CLC 33**
See also CA 93-96

Guillemin, Jacques
See Sartre, Jean-Paul

Guillen, Jorge 1893-1984 .... **CLC 11**
See also CA 89-92; 112; DAM MULT,
POET; DLB 108; HW

Guillen (y Batista), Nicolas (Cristobal)
1902-1989 ..... **CLC 48, 79; BLC; HLC**
See also BW 2; CA 116; 125; 129;
DAM MST, MULT, POET; HW

Guillevic, (Eugene) 1907- .... **CLC 33**
See also CA 93-96

Guillois
See Desnos, Robert

Guiney, Louise Imogen
1861-1920 .... **TCLC 41**
See also DLB 54

Guiraldes, Ricardo (Guillermo)
1886-1927 .... **TCLC 39**
See also CA 131; HW; MTCW

Gumilev, Nikolai Stephanovich
1886-1921 .... **TCLC 60**

Gunesekera, Romesh .... **CLC 91**

Gunn, Bill .... **CLC 5**
See also Gunn, William Harrison
See also DLB 38

Gunn, Thom(son William)
1929- .... **CLC 3, 6, 18, 32, 81**
See also CA 17-20R; CANR 9, 33;
CDBLB 1960 to Present; DAM POET;
DLB 27; INT CANR-33; MTCW

Gunn, William Harrison 1934(?)-1989
See Gunn, Bill
See also AITN 1; BW 1; CA 13-16R; 128;
CANR 12, 25

Gunnars, Kristjana 1948- .... **CLC 69**
See also CA 113; DLB 60

Gurganus, Allan 1947- .... **CLC 70**
See also BEST 90:1; CA 135; DAM POP

Gurney, A(lbert) R(amsdell), Jr.
1930- .... **CLC 32, 50, 54**
See also CA 77-80; CANR 32;
DAM DRAM

Gurney, Ivor (Bertie) 1890-1937 ... **TCLC 33**

Gurney, Peter
See Gurney, A(lbert) R(amsdell), Jr.

Guro, Elena 1877-1913 .... **TCLC 56**

Gustafson, Ralph (Barker) 1909- .... **CLC 36**
See also CA 21-24R; CANR 8, 45; DLB 88

Gut, Gom
See Simenon, Georges (Jacques Christian)

Guterson, David 1956- .... **CLC 91**
See also CA 132

Guthrie, A(lfred) B(ertram), Jr.
1901-1991 .... **CLC 23**
See also CA 57-60; 134; CANR 24; DLB 6;
SATA 62; SATA-Obit 67

Guthrie, Isobel
See Grieve, C(hristopher) M(urray)

Guthrie, Woodrow Wilson 1912-1967
See Guthrie, Woody
See also CA 113; 93-96

Guthrie, Woody .... **CLC 35**
See also Guthrie, Woodrow Wilson

Guy, Rosa (Cuthbert) 1928- .... **CLC 26**
See also AAYA 4; BW 2; CA 17-20R;
CANR 14, 34; CLR 13; DLB 33; JRDA;
MAICYA; SATA 14, 62

Gwendolyn
See Bennett, (Enoch) Arnold

H. D. .... **CLC 3, 8, 14, 31, 34, 73; PC 5**
See also Doolittle, Hilda

H. de V.
See Buchan, John

Haavikko, Paavo Juhani
1931- .... **CLC 18, 34**
See also CA 106

Habbema, Koos
See Heijermans, Herman

Hacker, Marilyn
1942- .... **CLC 5, 9, 23, 72, 91**
See also CA 77-80; DAM POET; DLB 120

Haggard, H(enry) Rider
1856-1925 .... **TCLC 11**
See also CA 108; 148; DLB 70, 156;
SATA 16

Hagiwara Sakutaro 1886-1942 .... **TCLC 60**

Haig, Fenil
See Ford, Ford Madox

Haig-Brown, Roderick (Langmere)
1908-1976 .... **CLC 21**
See also CA 5-8R; 69-72; CANR 4, 38;
CLR 31; DLB 88; MAICYA; SATA 12

Hailey, Arthur 1920- .... **CLC 5**
See also AITN 2; BEST 90:3; CA 1-4R;
CANR 2, 36; DAM NOV, POP; DLB 88;
DLBY 82; MTCW

Hailey, Elizabeth Forsythe 1938-... **CLC 40**
See also CA 93-96; CAAS 1; CANR 15, 48;
INT CANR-15

Haines, John (Meade) 1924- .... **CLC 58**
See also CA 17-20R; CANR 13, 34; DLB 5

Hakluyt, Richard 1552-1616 .... **LC 31**

Haldeman, Joe (William) 1943-..... **CLC 61**
See also CA 53-56; CANR 6; DLB 8;
INT CANR-6

Haley, Alex(ander Murray Palmer)
1921-1992 .... **CLC 8, 12, 76; BLC; DA;**
DAB; DAC
See also BW 2; CA 77-80; 136; DAM MST,
MULT, POP; DLB 38; MTCW

Haliburton, Thomas Chandler
1796-1865 .... **NCLC 15**
See also DLB 11, 99

Hall, Donald (Andrew, Jr.)
1928- .... **CLC 1, 13, 37, 59**
See also CA 5-8R; CAAS 7; CANR 2, 44;
DAM POET; DLB 5; SATA 23

Hall, Frederic Sauser
See Sauser-Hall, Frederic

Hall, James
See Kuttner, Henry

Hall, James Norman 1887-1951 ... **TCLC 23**
See also CA 123; SATA 21

Hall, (Marguerite) Radclyffe
1886-1943 .... **TCLC 12**
See also CA 110; 150

Hall, Rodney 1935- .... **CLC 51**
See also CA 109

Halleck, Fitz-Greene 1790-1867 .. **NCLC 47**
See also DLB 3

Halliday, Michael
See Creasey, John

Halpern, Daniel 1945- .... **CLC 14**
See also CA 33-36R

Hamburger, Michael (Peter Leopold)
1924- .... **CLC 5, 14**
See also CA 5-8R; CAAS 4; CANR 2, 47;
DLB 27

Hamill, Pete 1935- .... **CLC 10**
See also CA 25-28R; CANR 18

Hamilton, Alexander
1755(?)-1804 .... **NCLC 49**
See also DLB 37

Hamilton, Clive
See Lewis, C(live) S(taples)

Hamilton, Edmond 1904-1977....... **CLC 1**
See also CA 1-4R; CANR 3; DLB 8

Hamilton, Eugene (Jacob) Lee
See Lee-Hamilton, Eugene (Jacob)

Herbert, Zbigniew 1924- .... **CLC 9, 43**
See also CA 89-92; CANR 36;
DAM POET; MTCW

Herbst, Josephine (Frey)
1897-1969 .... **CLC 34**
See also CA 5-8R; 25-28R; DLB 9

Hergesheimer, Joseph
1880-1954 .... **TCLC 11**
See also CA 109; DLB 102, 9

Herlihy, James Leo 1927-1993 ..... **CLC 6**
See also CA 1-4R; 143; CANR 2

Hermogenes fl. c. 175- .... **CMLC 6**

Hernandez, Jose 1834-1886 ...... **NCLC 17**

Herodotus c. 484B.C.-429B.C..... **CMLC 17**

Herrick, Robert
1591-1674 ..... **LC 13; DA; DAB; DAC;**
PC 9
See also DAM MST, POP; DLB 126

Herring, Guilles
See Somerville, Edith

Herriot, James 1916-1995 .... **CLC 12**
See also Wight, James Alfred
See also AAYA 1; CA 148; CANR 40;
DAM POP; SATA 86

Herrmann, Dorothy 1941- .... **CLC 44**
See also CA 107

Herrmann, Taffy
See Herrmann, Dorothy

Hersey, John (Richard)
1914-1993 .... **CLC 1, 2, 7, 9, 40, 81**
See also CA 17-20R; 140; CANR 33;
DAM POP; DLB 6; MTCW; SATA 25;
SATA-Obit 76

Herzen, Aleksandr Ivanovich
1812-1870 .... **NCLC 10**

Herzl, Theodor 1860-1904 .... **TCLC 36**

Herzog, Werner 1942- .... **CLC 16**
See also CA 89-92

Hesiod c. 8th cent. B.C.- .... **CMLC 5**

Hesse, Hermann
1877-1962 .... **CLC 1, 2, 3, 6, 11, 17, 25,**
69; DA; DAB; DAC; SSC 9; WLC
See also CA 17-18; CAP 2; DAM MST,
NOV; DLB 66; MTCW; SATA 50

Hewes, Cady
See De Voto, Bernard (Augustine)

Heyen, William 1940- .... **CLC 13, 18**
See also CA 33-36R; CAAS 9; DLB 5

Heyerdahl, Thor 1914- .... **CLC 26**
See also CA 5-8R; CANR 5, 22; MTCW;
SATA 2, 52

Heym, Georg (Theodor Franz Arthur)
1887-1912 .... **TCLC 9**
See also CA 106

Heym, Stefan 1913- .... **CLC 41**
See also CA 9-12R; CANR 4; DLB 69

Heyse, Paul (Johann Ludwig von)
1830-1914 .... **TCLC 8**
See also CA 104; DLB 129

Heyward, (Edwin) DuBose
1885-1940 .... **TCLC 59**
See also CA 108; DLB 7, 9, 45; SATA 21

Hibbert, Eleanor Alice Burford
1906-1993 .... **CLC 7**
See also BEST 90:4; CA 17-20R; 140;
CANR 9, 28; DAM POP; SATA 2;
SATA-Obit 74

Higgins, George V(incent)
1939- .... **CLC 4, 7, 10, 18**
See also CA 77-80; CAAS 5; CANR 17, 51;
DLB 2; DLBY 81; INT CANR-17;
MTCW

Higginson, Thomas Wentworth
1823-1911 .... **TCLC 36**
See also DLB 1, 64

Highet, Helen
See MacInnes, Helen (Clark)

Highsmith, (Mary) Patricia
1921-1995 .... **CLC 2, 4, 14, 42**
See also CA 1-4R; 147; CANR 1, 20, 48;
DAM NOV, POP; MTCW

Highwater, Jamake (Mamake)
1942(?)- .... **CLC 12**
See also AAYA 7; CA 65-68; CAAS 7;
CANR 10, 34; CLR 17; DLB 52;
DLBY 85; JRDA; MAICYA; SATA 32,
69; SATA-Brief 30

Highway, Tomson 1951- ...... **CLC 92; DAC**
See also DAM MULT; NNAL

Higuchi, Ichiyo 1872-1896 .... **NCLC 49**

Hijuelos, Oscar 1951- ...... **CLC 65; HLC**
See also BEST 90:1; CA 123; CANR 50;
DAM MULT, POP; DLB 145; HW

Hikmet, Nazim 1902(?)-1963 ...... **CLC 40**
See also CA 141; 93-96

Hildesheimer, Wolfgang
1916-1991 .... **CLC 49**
See also CA 101; 135; DLB 69, 124

Hill, Geoffrey (William)
1932- .... **CLC 5, 8, 18, 45**
See also CA 81-84; CANR 21;
CDBLB 1960 to Present; DAM POET;
DLB 40; MTCW

Hill, George Roy 1921- .... **CLC 26**
See also CA 110; 122

Hill, John
See Koontz, Dean R(ay)

Hill, Susan (Elizabeth)
1942- .... **CLC 4; DAB**
See also CA 33-36R; CANR 29;
DAM MST, NOV; DLB 14, 139; MTCW

Hillerman, Tony 1925- .... **CLC 62**
See also AAYA 6; BEST 89:1; CA 29-32R;
CANR 21, 42; DAM POP; SATA 6

Hillesum, Etty 1914-1943 .... **TCLC 49**
See also CA 137

Hilliard, Noel (Harvey) 1929- ...... **CLC 15**
See also CA 9-12R; CANR 7

Hillis, Rick 1956- .... **CLC 66**
See also CA 134

Hilton, James 1900-1954 .... **TCLC 21**
See also CA 108; DLB 34, 77; SATA 34

Himes, Chester (Bomar)
1909-1984 .... **CLC 2, 4, 7, 18, 58; BLC**
See also BW 2; CA 25-28R; 114; CANR 22;
DAM MULT; DLB 2, 76, 143; MTCW

Hinde, Thomas .... **CLC 6, 11**
See also Chitty, Thomas Willes

Hindin, Nathan
See Bloch, Robert (Albert)

Hine, (William) Daryl 1936- .... **CLC 15**
See also CA 1-4R; CAAS 15; CANR 1, 20;
DLB 60

Hinkson, Katharine Tynan
See Tynan, Katharine

Hinton, S(usan) E(loise)
1950- .... **CLC 30; DA; DAB; DAC**
See also AAYA 2; CA 81-84; CANR 32;
CLR 3, 23; DAM MST, NOV; JRDA;
MAICYA; MTCW; SATA 19, 58

Hippius, Zinaida .... **TCLC 9**
See also Gippius, Zinaida (Nikolayevna)

Hiraoka, Kimitake 1925-1970
See Mishima, Yukio
See also CA 97-100; 29-32R; DAM DRAM;
MTCW

Hirsch, E(ric) D(onald), Jr. 1928-... **CLC 79**
See also CA 25-28R; CANR 27, 51;
DLB 67; INT CANR-27; MTCW

Hirsch, Edward 1950- .... **CLC 31, 50**
See also CA 104; CANR 20, 42; DLB 120

Hitchcock, Alfred (Joseph)
1899-1980 .... **CLC 16**
See also CA 97-100; SATA 27;
SATA-Obit 24

Hitler, Adolf 1889-1945 .... **TCLC 53**
See also CA 117; 147

Hoagland, Edward 1932- .... **CLC 28**
See also CA 1-4R; CANR 2, 31; DLB 6;
SATA 51

Hoban, Russell (Conwell) 1925- .. **CLC 7, 25**
See also CA 5-8R; CANR 23, 37; CLR 3;
DAM NOV; DLB 52; MAICYA;
MTCW; SATA 1, 40, 78

Hobbs, Perry
See Blackmur, R(ichard) P(almer)

Hobson, Laura Z(ametkin)
1900-1986 .... **CLC 7, 25**
See also CA 17-20R; 118; DLB 28;
SATA 52

Hochhuth, Rolf 1931- .... **CLC 4, 11, 18**
See also CA 5-8R; CANR 33;
DAM DRAM; DLB 124; MTCW

Hochman, Sandra 1936- .... **CLC 3, 8**
See also CA 5-8R; DLB 5

Hochwaelder, Fritz 1911-1986 ...... **CLC 36**
See also CA 29-32R; 120; CANR 42;
DAM DRAM; MTCW

Hochwalder, Fritz
See Hochwaelder, Fritz

Hocking, Mary (Eunice) 1921- ..... **CLC 13**
See also CA 101; CANR 18, 40

Hodgins, Jack 1938- .... **CLC 23**
See also CA 93-96; DLB 60

Hodgson, William Hope
1877(?)-1918 .... **TCLC 13**
See also CA 111; DLB 70, 153, 156

Hoffman, Alice 1952- .... **CLC 51**
See also CA 77-80; CANR 34; DAM NOV;
MTCW

Jewsbury, Geraldine (Endsor)
1812-1880 .... **NCLC 22**
See also DLB 21

Jhabvala, Ruth Prawer
1927- .... **CLC 4, 8, 29; DAB**
See also CA 1-4R; CANR 2, 29, 51;
DAM NOV; DLB 139; INT CANR-29;
MTCW

Jibran, Kahlil
See Gibran, Kahlil

Jibran, Khalil
See Gibran, Kahlil

Jiles, Paulette 1943- .... **CLC 13, 58**
See also CA 101

Jimenez (Mantecon), Juan Ramon
1881-1958 .... **TCLC 4; HLC; PC 7**
See also CA 104; 131; DAM MULT,
POET; DLB 134; HW; MTCW

Jimenez, Ramon
See Jimenez (Mantecon), Juan Ramon

Jimenez Mantecon, Juan
See Jimenez (Mantecon), Juan Ramon

Joel, Billy .... **CLC 26**
See also Joel, William Martin

Joel, William Martin 1949-
See Joel, Billy
See also CA 108

John of the Cross, St. 1542-1591 .... **LC 18**

Johnson, B(ryan) S(tanley William)
1933-1973 .... **CLC 6, 9**
See also CA 9-12R; 53-56; CANR 9;
DLB 14, 40

Johnson, Benj. F. of Boo
See Riley, James Whitcomb

Johnson, Benjamin F. of Boo
See Riley, James Whitcomb

Johnson, Charles (Richard)
1948- .... **CLC 7, 51, 65; BLC**
See also BW 2; CA 116; CAAS 18;
CANR 42; DAM MULT; DLB 33

Johnson, Denis 1949- .... **CLC 52**
See also CA 117; 121; DLB 120

Johnson, Diane 1934- .... **CLC 5, 13, 48**
See also CA 41-44R; CANR 17, 40;
DLBY 80; INT CANR-17; MTCW

Johnson, Eyvind (Olof Verner)
1900-1976 .... **CLC 14**
See also CA 73-76; 69-72; CANR 34

Johnson, J. R.
See James, C(yril) L(ionel) R(obert)

Johnson, James Weldon
1871-1938 .... **TCLC 3, 19; BLC**
See also BW 1; CA 104; 125;
CDALB 1917-1929; CLR 32;
DAM MULT, POET; DLB 51; MTCW;
SATA 31

Johnson, Joyce 1935- .... **CLC 58**
See also CA 125; 129

Johnson, Lionel (Pigot)
1867-1902 .... **TCLC 19**
See also CA 117; DLB 19

Johnson, Mel
See Malzberg, Barry N(athaniel)

Johnson, Pamela Hansford
1912-1981 .... **CLC 1, 7, 27**
See also CA 1-4R; 104; CANR 2, 28;
DLB 15; MTCW

Johnson, Samuel
1709-1784 ..... **LC 15; DA; DAB; DAC;
WLC**
See also CDBLB 1660-1789; DAM MST;
DLB 39, 95, 104, 142

Johnson, Uwe
1934-1984 .... **CLC 5, 10, 15, 40**
See also CA 1-4R; 112; CANR 1, 39;
DLB 75; MTCW

Johnston, George (Benson) 1913- ... **CLC 51**
See also CA 1-4R; CANR 5, 20; DLB 88

Johnston, Jennifer 1930- .... **CLC 7**
See also CA 85-88; DLB 14

Jolley, (Monica) Elizabeth
1923- .... **CLC 46; SSC 19**
See also CA 127; CAAS 13

Jones, Arthur Llewellyn 1863-1947
See Machen, Arthur
See also CA 104

Jones, D(ouglas) G(ordon) 1929- .... **CLC 10**
See also CA 29-32R; CANR 13; DLB 53

Jones, David (Michael)
1895-1974 .... **CLC 2, 4, 7, 13, 42**
See also CA 9-12R; 53-56; CANR 28;
CDBLB 1945-1960; DLB 20, 100; MTCW

Jones, David Robert 1947-
See Bowie, David
See also CA 103

Jones, Diana Wynne 1934- .... **CLC 26**
See also AAYA 12; CA 49-52; CANR 4,
26; CLR 23; DLB 161; JRDA; MAICYA;
SAAS 7; SATA 9, 70

Jones, Edward P. 1950- .... **CLC 76**
See also BW 2; CA 142

Jones, Gayl 1949- .... **CLC 6, 9; BLC**
See also BW 2; CA 77-80; CANR 27;
DAM MULT; DLB 33; MTCW

Jones, James 1921-1977.... **CLC 1, 3, 10, 39**
See also AITN 1, 2; CA 1-4R; 69-72;
CANR 6; DLB 2, 143; MTCW

Jones, John J.
See Lovecraft, H(oward) P(hillips)

Jones, LeRoi .... **CLC 1, 2, 3, 5, 10, 14**
See also Baraka, Amiri

Jones, Louis B. .... **CLC 65**
See also CA 141

Jones, Madison (Percy, Jr.) 1925- ... **CLC 4**
See also CA 13-16R; CAAS 11; CANR 7;
DLB 152

Jones, Mervyn 1922- .... **CLC 10, 52**
See also CA 45-48; CAAS 5; CANR 1;
MTCW

Jones, Mick 1956(?)- .... **CLC 30**

Jones, Nettie (Pearl) 1941- .... **CLC 34**
See also BW 2; CA 137; CAAS 20

Jones, Preston 1936-1979 .... **CLC 10**
See also CA 73-76; 89-92; DLB 7

Jones, Robert F(rancis) 1934- ...... **CLC 7**
See also CA 49-52; CANR 2

Jones, Rod 1953- .... **CLC 50**
See also CA 128

Jones, Terence Graham Parry
1942- .... **CLC 21**
See also Jones, Terry; Monty Python
See also CA 112; 116; CANR 35; INT 116

Jones, Terry
See Jones, Terence Graham Parry
See also SATA 67; SATA-Brief 51

Jones, Thom 1945(?)- .... **CLC 81**

Jong, Erica 1942- ...... **CLC 4, 6, 8, 18, 83**
See also AITN 1; BEST 90:2; CA 73-76;
CANR 26; DAM NOV, POP; DLB 2, 5,
28, 152; INT CANR-26; MTCW

Jonson, Ben(jamin)
1572(?)-1637 .... **LC 6; DA; DAB; DAC;
DC 4; WLC**
See also CDBLB Before 1660;
DAM DRAM, MST, POET; DLB 62,
121

Jordan, June 1936- .... **CLC 5, 11, 23**
See also AAYA 2; BW 2; CA 33-36R;
CANR 25; CLR 10; DAM MULT,
POET; DLB 38; MAICYA; MTCW;
SATA 4

Jordan, Pat(rick M.) 1941- .... **CLC 37**
See also CA 33-36R

Jorgensen, Ivar
See Ellison, Harlan (Jay)

Jorgenson, Ivar
See Silverberg, Robert

Josephus, Flavius c. 37-100 ...... **CMLC 13**

Josipovici, Gabriel 1940- .... **CLC 6, 43**
See also CA 37-40R; CAAS 8; CANR 47;
DLB 14

Joubert, Joseph 1754-1824 .... **NCLC 9**

Jouve, Pierre Jean 1887-1976 ...... **CLC 47**
See also CA 65-68

Joyce, James (Augustine Aloysius)
1882-1941 .... **TCLC 3, 8, 16, 35, 52;
DA; DAB; DAC; SSC 3; WLC**
See also CA 104; 126; CDBLB 1914-1945;
DAM MST, NOV, POET; DLB 10, 19,
36, 162; MTCW

Jozsef, Attila 1905-1937.......... **TCLC 22**
See also CA 116

Juana Ines de la Cruz 1651(?)-1695 ... **LC 5**

Judd, Cyril
See Kornbluth, C(yril) M.; Pohl, Frederik

Julian of Norwich 1342(?)-1416(?) .... **LC 6**
See also DLB 146

Juniper, Alex
See Hospital, Janette Turner

Junius
See Luxemburg, Rosa

Just, Ward (Swift) 1935- .... **CLC 4, 27**
See also CA 25-28R; CANR 32;
INT CANR-32

Justice, Donald (Rodney) 1925- .. **CLC 6, 19**
See also CA 5-8R; CANR 26; DAM POET;
DLBY 83; INT CANR-26

Juvenal c. 55-c. 127 .... **CMLC 8**

Juvenis
See Bourne, Randolph S(illiman)

Kenyon, Robert O.
See Kuttner, Henry

Kerouac, Jack ..... **CLC 1, 2, 3, 5, 14, 29, 61**
See also Kerouac, Jean-Louis Lebris de
See also CDALB 1941-1968; DLB 2, 16;
DLBD 3

Kerouac, Jean-Louis Lebris de 1922-1969
See Kerouac, Jack
See also AITN 1; CA 5-8R; 25-28R;
CANR 26; DA; DAB; DAC; DAM MST,
NOV, POET, POP; MTCW; WLC

Kerr, Jean 1923- .... **CLC 22**
See also CA 5-8R; CANR 7; INT CANR-7

Kerr, M. E. .... **CLC 12, 35**
See also Meaker, Marijane (Agnes)
See also AAYA 2; CLR 29; SAAS 1

Kerr, Robert .... **CLC 55**

Kerrigan, (Thomas) Anthony
1918- .... **CLC 4, 6**
See also CA 49-52; CAAS 11; CANR 4

Kerry, Lois
See Duncan, Lois

Kesey, Ken (Elton)
1935- ...... **CLC 1, 3, 6, 11, 46, 64; DA;
DAB; DAC; WLC**
See also CA 1-4R; CANR 22, 38;
CDALB 1968-1988; DAM MST, NOV,
POP; DLB 2, 16; MTCW; SATA 66

Kesselring, Joseph (Otto)
1902-1967 .... **CLC 45**
See also CA 150; DAM DRAM, MST

Kessler, Jascha (Frederick) 1929- .... **CLC 4**
See also CA 17-20R; CANR 8, 48

Kettelkamp, Larry (Dale) 1933- .... **CLC 12**
See also CA 29-32R; CANR 16; SAAS 3;
SATA 2

Keyber, Conny
See Fielding, Henry

Keyes, Daniel 1927- .... **CLC 80; DA; DAC**
See also CA 17-20R; CANR 10, 26;
DAM MST, NOV; SATA 37

Khanshendel, Chiron
See Rose, Wendy

Khayyam, Omar
1048-1131 .... **CMLC 11; PC 8**
See also DAM POET

Kherdian, David 1931- .... **CLC 6, 9**
See also CA 21-24R; CAAS 2; CANR 39;
CLR 24; JRDA; MAICYA; SATA 16, 74

Khlebnikov, Velimir .... **TCLC 20**
See also Khlebnikov, Viktor Vladimirovich

Khlebnikov, Viktor Vladimirovich 1885-1922
See Khlebnikov, Velimir
See also CA 117

Khodasevich, Vladislav (Felitsianovich)
1886-1939 .... **TCLC 15**
See also CA 115

Kielland, Alexander Lange
1849-1906 .... **TCLC 5**
See also CA 104

Kiely, Benedict 1919- .... **CLC 23, 43**
See also CA 1-4R; CANR 2; DLB 15

Kienzle, William X(avier) 1928- .... **CLC 25**
See also CA 93-96; CAAS 1; CANR 9, 31;
DAM POP; INT CANR-31; MTCW

Kierkegaard, Soren 1813-1855.... **NCLC 34**

Killens, John Oliver 1916-1987..... **CLC 10**
See also BW 2; CA 77-80; 123; CAAS 2;
CANR 26; DLB 33

Killigrew, Anne 1660-1685.......... **LC 4**
See also DLB 131

Kim
See Simenon, Georges (Jacques Christian)

Kincaid, Jamaica 1949- ... **CLC 43, 68; BLC**
See also AAYA 13; BW 2; CA 125;
CANR 47; DAM MULT, NOV;
DLB 157

King, Francis (Henry) 1923- ..... **CLC 8, 53**
See also CA 1-4R; CANR 1, 33;
DAM NOV; DLB 15, 139; MTCW

King, Martin Luther, Jr.
1929-1968 .... **CLC 83; BLC; DA; DAB;
DAC**
See also BW 2; CA 25-28; CANR 27, 44;
CAP 2; DAM MST, MULT; MTCW;
SATA 14

King, Stephen (Edwin)
1947- ...... **CLC 12, 26, 37, 61; SSC 17**
See also AAYA 1, 17; BEST 90:1;
CA 61-64; CANR 1, 30; DAM NOV,
POP; DLB 143; DLBY 80; JRDA;
MTCW; SATA 9, 55

King, Steve
See King, Stephen (Edwin)

King, Thomas 1943- .... **CLC 89; DAC**
See also CA 144; DAM MULT; NNAL

Kingman, Lee .... **CLC 17**
See also Natti, (Mary) Lee
See also SAAS 3; SATA 1, 67

Kingsley, Charles 1819-1875 ..... **NCLC 35**
See also DLB 21, 32, 163; YABC 2

Kingsley, Sidney 1906-1995....... **CLC 44**
See also CA 85-88; 147; DLB 7

Kingsolver, Barbara 1955- ...... **CLC 55, 81**
See also AAYA 15; CA 129; 134;
DAM POP; INT 134

Kingston, Maxine (Ting Ting) Hong
1940- .... **CLC 12, 19, 58**
See also AAYA 8; CA 69-72; CANR 13,
38; DAM MULT, NOV; DLBY 80;
INT CANR-13; MTCW; SATA 53

Kinnell, Galway
1927- .... **CLC 1, 2, 3, 5, 13, 29**
See also CA 9-12R; CANR 10, 34; DLB 5;
DLBY 87; INT CANR-34; MTCW

Kinsella, Thomas 1928- .... **CLC 4, 19**
See also CA 17-20R; CANR 15; DLB 27;
MTCW

Kinsella, W(illiam) P(atrick)
1935- .... **CLC 27, 43; DAC**
See also AAYA 7; CA 97-100; CAAS 7;
CANR 21, 35; DAM NOV, POP;
INT CANR-21; MTCW

Kipling, (Joseph) Rudyard
1865-1936 ...... **TCLC 8, 17; DA; DAB;
DAC; PC 3; SSC 5; WLC**
See also CA 105; 120; CANR 33;
CDBLB 1890-1914; CLR 39; DAM MST,
POET; DLB 19, 34, 141, 156; MAICYA;
MTCW; YABC 2

Kirkup, James 1918- .... **CLC 1**
See also CA 1-4R; CAAS 4; CANR 2;
DLB 27; SATA 12

Kirkwood, James 1930(?)-1989 ...... **CLC 9**
See also AITN 2; CA 1-4R; 128; CANR 6,
40

Kirshner, Sidney
See Kingsley, Sidney

Kis, Danilo 1935-1989 .... **CLC 57**
See also CA 109; 118; 129; MTCW

Kivi, Aleksis 1834-1872 .... **NCLC 30**

Kizer, Carolyn (Ashley)
1925- .... **CLC 15, 39, 80**
See also CA 65-68; CAAS 5; CANR 24;
DAM POET; DLB 5

Klabund 1890-1928.............. **TCLC 44**
See also DLB 66

Klappert, Peter 1942-............. **CLC 57**
See also CA 33-36R; DLB 5

Klein, A(braham) M(oses)
1909-1972 .... **CLC 19; DAB; DAC**
See also CA 101; 37-40R; DAM MST;
DLB 68

Klein, Norma 1938-1989 .... **CLC 30**
See also AAYA 2; CA 41-44R; 128;
CANR 15, 37; CLR 2, 19;
INT CANR-15; JRDA; MAICYA;
SAAS 1; SATA 7, 57

Klein, T(heodore) E(ibon) D(onald)
1947- .... **CLC 34**
See also CA 119; CANR 44

Kleist, Heinrich von
1777-1811 .... **NCLC 2, 37**
See also DAM DRAM; DLB 90

Klima, Ivan 1931-............... **CLC 56**
See also CA 25-28R; CANR 17, 50;
DAM NOV

Klimentov, Andrei Platonovich 1899-1951
See Platonov, Andrei
See also CA 108

Klinger, Friedrich Maximilian von
1752-1831 .... **NCLC 1**
See also DLB 94

Klopstock, Friedrich Gottlieb
1724-1803 .... **NCLC 11**
See also DLB 97

Knebel, Fletcher 1911-1993........ **CLC 14**
See also AITN 1; CA 1-4R; 140; CAAS 3;
CANR 1, 36; SATA 36; SATA-Obit 75

Knickerbocker, Diedrich
See Irving, Washington

Knight, Etheridge
1931-1991 .... **CLC 40; BLC; PC 14**
See also BW 1; CA 21-24R; 133; CANR 23;
DAM POET; DLB 41

Knight, Sarah Kemble 1666-1727 ..... **LC 7**
See also DLB 24

Knister, Raymond 1899-1932...... **TCLC 56**
See also DLB 68

Knowles, John
1926- ...... **CLC 1, 4, 10, 26; DA; DAC**
See also AAYA 10; CA 17-20R; CANR 40;
CDALB 1968-1988; DAM MST, NOV;
DLB 6; MTCW; SATA 8

Lafayette, Rene
See Hubbard, L(afayette) Ron(ald)

Laforgue, Jules
1860-1887 . . . . **NCLC 5, 53; PC 14;
SSC 20**

Lagerkvist, Paer (Fabian)
1891-1974 . . . . **CLC 7, 10, 13, 54**
See also Lagerkvist, Par
See also CA 85-88; 49-52; DAM DRAM,
NOV; MTCW

Lagerkvist, Par . . . . **SSC 12**
See also Lagerkvist, Paer (Fabian)

Lagerloef, Selma (Ottiliana Lovisa)
1858-1940 . . . . **TCLC 4, 36**
See also Lagerlof, Selma (Ottiliana Lovisa)
See also CA 108; SATA 15

Lagerlof, Selma (Ottiliana Lovisa)
See Lagerloef, Selma (Ottiliana Lovisa)
See also CLR 7; SATA 15

La Guma, (Justin) Alex(ander)
1925-1985 . . . . **CLC 19**
See also BW 1; CA 49-52; 118; CANR 25;
DAM NOV; DLB 117; MTCW

Laidlaw, A. K.
See Grieve, C(hristopher) M(urray)

Lainez, Manuel Mujica
See Mujica Lainez, Manuel
See also HW

Lamartine, Alphonse (Marie Louis Prat) de
1790-1869 . . . . **NCLC 11; PC 15**
See also DAM POET

Lamb, Charles
1775-1834 . . . . **NCLC 10; DA; DAB;
DAC; WLC**
See also CDBLB 1789-1832; DAM MST;
DLB 93, 107, 163; SATA 17

Lamb, Lady Caroline 1785-1828 . . **NCLC 38**
See also DLB 116

Lamming, George (William)
1927- . . . . **CLC 2, 4, 66; BLC**
See also BW 2; CA 85-88; CANR 26;
DAM MULT; DLB 125; MTCW

L'Amour, Louis (Dearborn)
1908-1988 . . . . **CLC 25, 55**
See also AAYA 16; AITN 2; BEST 89:2;
CA 1-4R; 125; CANR 3, 25, 40;
DAM NOV, POP; DLBY 80; MTCW

Lampedusa, Giuseppe (Tomasi) di . . . **TCLC 13**
See also Tomasi di Lampedusa, Giuseppe

Lampman, Archibald 1861-1899 . . **NCLC 25**
See also DLB 92

Lancaster, Bruce 1896-1963 . . . . **CLC 36**
See also CA 9-10; CAP 1; SATA 9

Landau, Mark Alexandrovich
See Aldanov, Mark (Alexandrovich)

Landau-Aldanov, Mark Alexandrovich
See Aldanov, Mark (Alexandrovich)

Landis, John 1950- . . . . **CLC 26**
See also CA 112; 122

Landolfi, Tommaso 1908-1979 . . . **CLC 11, 49**
See also CA 127; 117

Landon, Letitia Elizabeth
1802-1838 . . . . **NCLC 15**
See also DLB 96

Landor, Walter Savage
1775-1864 . . . . **NCLC 14**
See also DLB 93, 107

Landwirth, Heinz 1927-
See Lind, Jakov
See also CA 9-12R; CANR 7

Lane, Patrick 1939- . . . . **CLC 25**
See also CA 97-100; DAM POET; DLB 53;
INT 97-100

Lang, Andrew 1844-1912 . . . . **TCLC 16**
See also CA 114; 137; DLB 98, 141;
MAICYA; SATA 16

Lang, Fritz 1890-1976 . . . . **CLC 20**
See also CA 77-80; 69-72; CANR 30

Lange, John
See Crichton, (John) Michael

Langer, Elinor 1939- . . . . **CLC 34**
See also CA 121

Langland, William
1330(?)-1400(?) . . . . . . **LC 19; DA; DAB;
DAC**
See also DAM MST, POET; DLB 146

Langstaff, Launcelot
See Irving, Washington

Lanier, Sidney 1842-1881 . . . . **NCLC 6**
See also DAM POET; DLB 64; DLBD 13;
MAICYA; SATA 18

Lanyer, Aemilia 1569-1645 . . . . . . **LC 10, 30**
See also DLB 121

Lao Tzu . . . . **CMLC 7**

Lapine, James (Elliot) 1949- . . . . **CLC 39**
See also CA 123; 130; INT 130

Larbaud, Valery (Nicolas)
1881-1957 . . . . **TCLC 9**
See also CA 106

Lardner, Ring
See Lardner, Ring(gold) W(ilmer)

Lardner, Ring W., Jr.
See Lardner, Ring(gold) W(ilmer)

Lardner, Ring(gold) W(ilmer)
1885-1933 . . . . **TCLC 2, 14**
See also CA 104; 131; CDALB 1917-1929;
DLB 11, 25, 86; MTCW

Laredo, Betty
See Codrescu, Andrei

Larkin, Maia
See Wojciechowska, Maia (Teresa)

Larkin, Philip (Arthur)
1922-1985 . . . . **CLC 3, 5, 8, 9, 13, 18, 33,
39, 64; DAB**
See also CA 5-8R; 117; CANR 24;
CDBLB 1960 to Present; DAM MST,
POET; DLB 27; MTCW

Larra (y Sanchez de Castro), Mariano Jose de
1809-1837 . . . . **NCLC 17**

Larsen, Eric 1941- . . . . **CLC 55**
See also CA 132

Larsen, Nella 1891-1964 . . . . . **CLC 37; BLC**
See also BW 1; CA 125; DAM MULT;
DLB 51

Larson, Charles R(aymond) 1938- . . **CLC 31**
See also CA 53-56; CANR 4

Las Casas, Bartolome de 1474-1566 . . **LC 31**

Lasker-Schueler, Else 1869-1945 . . **TCLC 57**
See also DLB 66, 124

Latham, Jean Lee 1902- . . . . **CLC 12**
See also AITN 1; CA 5-8R; CANR 7;
MAICYA; SATA 2, 68

Latham, Mavis
See Clark, Mavis Thorpe

Lathen, Emma . . . . **CLC 2**
See also Hennissart, Martha; Latsis, Mary
J(ane)

Lathrop, Francis
See Leiber, Fritz (Reuter, Jr.)

Latsis, Mary J(ane)
See Lathen, Emma
See also CA 85-88

Lattimore, Richmond (Alexander)
1906-1984 . . . . **CLC 3**
See also CA 1-4R; 112; CANR 1

Laughlin, James 1914- . . . . **CLC 49**
See also CA 21-24R; CAAS 22; CANR 9,
47; DLB 48

Laurence, (Jean) Margaret (Wemyss)
1926-1987 . . . . **CLC 3, 6, 13, 50, 62;
DAC; SSC 7**
See also CA 5-8R; 121; CANR 33;
DAM MST; DLB 53; MTCW;
SATA-Obit 50

Laurent, Antoine 1952- . . . . **CLC 50**

Lauscher, Hermann
See Hesse, Hermann

Lautreamont, Comte de
1846-1870 . . . . **NCLC 12; SSC 14**

Laverty, Donald
See Blish, James (Benjamin)

Lavin, Mary 1912- . . . . . . **CLC 4, 18; SSC 4**
See also CA 9-12R; CANR 33; DLB 15;
MTCW

Lavond, Paul Dennis
See Kornbluth, C(yril) M.; Pohl, Frederik

Lawler, Raymond Evenor 1922- . . . . **CLC 58**
See also CA 103

Lawrence, D(avid) H(erbert Richards)
1885-1930 . . . . **TCLC 2, 9, 16, 33, 48, 61;
DA; DAB; DAC; SSC 4, 19; WLC**
See also CA 104; 121; CDBLB 1914-1945;
DAM MST, NOV, POET; DLB 10, 19,
36, 98, 162; MTCW

Lawrence, T(homas) E(dward)
1888-1935 . . . . **TCLC 18**
See also Dale, Colin
See also CA 115

Lawrence of Arabia
See Lawrence, T(homas) E(dward)

Lawson, Henry (Archibald Hertzberg)
1867-1922 . . . . **TCLC 27; SSC 18**
See also CA 120

Lawton, Dennis
See Faust, Frederick (Schiller)

Laxness, Halldor . . . . **CLC 25**
See also Gudjonsson, Halldor Kiljan

Layamon fl. c. 1200- . . . . **CMLC 10**
See also DLB 146

Laye, Camara 1928-1980 . . . **CLC 4, 38; BLC**
See also BW 1; CA 85-88; 97-100;
CANR 25; DAM MULT; MTCW

Lermontov, Mikhail Yuryevich
1814-1841 . . . . **NCLC 47**

Leroux, Gaston 1868-1927. . . . . . . **TCLC 25**
See also CA 108; 136; SATA 65

Lesage, Alain-Rene 1668-1747. . . . . . **LC 28**

Leskov, Nikolai (Semyonovich)
1831-1895 . . . . **NCLC 25**

Lessing, Doris (May)
1919- . . . . . **CLC 1, 2, 3, 6, 10, 15, 22, 40,**
91; DA; DAB; DAC; SSC 6
See also CA 9-12R; CAAS 14; CANR 33;
CDBLB 1960 to Present; DAM MST,
NOV; DLB 15, 139; DLBY 85; MTCW

Lessing, Gotthold Ephraim
1729-1781 . . . . **LC 8**
See also DLB 97

Lester, Richard 1932- . . . . **CLC 20**

Lever, Charles (James)
1806-1872 . . . . **NCLC 23**
See also DLB 21

Leverson, Ada 1865(?)-1936(?) . . . . **TCLC 18**
See also Elaine
See also CA 117; DLB 153

Levertov, Denise
1923- . . . . . . **CLC 1, 2, 3, 5, 8, 15, 28, 66;**
PC 11
See also CA 1-4R; CAAS 19; CANR 3, 29,
50; DAM POET; DLB 5; INT CANR-29;
MTCW

Levi, Jonathan . . . . **CLC 76**

Levi, Peter (Chad Tigar) 1931- . . . . . **CLC 41**
See also CA 5-8R; CANR 34; DLB 40

Levi, Primo
1919-1987 . . . . **CLC 37, 50; SSC 12**
See also CA 13-16R; 122; CANR 12, 33;
MTCW

Levin, Ira 1929- . . . . **CLC 3, 6**
See also CA 21-24R; CANR 17, 44;
DAM POP; MTCW; SATA 66

Levin, Meyer 1905-1981 . . . . **CLC 7**
See also AITN 1; CA 9-12R; 104;
CANR 15; DAM POP; DLB 9, 28;
DLBY 81; SATA 21; SATA-Obit 27

Levine, Norman 1924- . . . . **CLC 54**
See also CA 73-76; CAAS 23; CANR 14;
DLB 88

Levine, Philip 1928-. . **CLC 2, 4, 5, 9, 14, 33**
See also CA 9-12R; CANR 9, 37;
DAM POET; DLB 5

Levinson, Deirdre 1931- . . . . **CLC 49**
See also CA 73-76

Levi-Strauss, Claude 1908- . . . . **CLC 38**
See also CA 1-4R; CANR 6, 32; MTCW

Levitin, Sonia (Wolff) 1934- . . . . . . **CLC 17**
See also AAYA 13; CA 29-32R; CANR 14,
32; JRDA; MAICYA; SAAS 2; SATA 4,
68

Levon, O. U.
See Kesey, Ken (Elton)

Lewes, George Henry
1817-1878 . . . . **NCLC 25**
See also DLB 55, 144

Lewis, Alun 1915-1944. . . . . **TCLC 3**
See also CA 104; DLB 20, 162

Lewis, C. Day
See Day Lewis, C(ecil)

Lewis, C(live) S(taples)
1898-1963 . . . . . **CLC 1, 3, 6, 14, 27; DA;**
DAB; DAC; WLC
See also AAYA 3; CA 81-84; CANR 33;
CDBLB 1945-1960; CLR 3, 27;
DAM MST, NOV, POP; DLB 15, 100,
160; JRDA; MAICYA; MTCW;
SATA 13

Lewis, Janet 1899- . . . . **CLC 41**
See also Winters, Janet Lewis
See also CA 9-12R; CANR 29; CAP 1;
DLBY 87

Lewis, Matthew Gregory
1775-1818 . . . . **NCLC 11**
See also DLB 39, 158

Lewis, (Harry) Sinclair
1885-1951 . . . . . **TCLC 4, 13, 23, 39; DA;**
DAB; DAC; WLC
See also CA 104; 133; CDALB 1917-1929;
DAM MST, NOV; DLB 9, 102; DLBD 1;
MTCW

Lewis, (Percy) Wyndham
1884(?)-1957 . . . . **TCLC 2, 9**
See also CA 104; DLB 15

Lewisohn, Ludwig 1883-1955. . . . . . **TCLC 19**
See also CA 107; DLB 4, 9, 28, 102

Leyner, Mark 1956- . . . . **CLC 92**
See also CA 110; CANR 28

Lezama Lima, Jose 1910-1976 . . . **CLC 4, 10**
See also CA 77-80; DAM MULT;
DLB 113; HW

L'Heureux, John (Clarke) 1934- . . . . **CLC 52**
See also CA 13-16R; CANR 23, 45

Liddell, C. H.
See Kuttner, Henry

Lie, Jonas (Lauritz Idemil)
1833-1908(?) . . . . **TCLC 5**
See also CA 115

Lieber, Joel 1937-1971. . . . . **CLC 6**
See also CA 73-76; 29-32R

Lieber, Stanley Martin
See Lee, Stan

Lieberman, Laurence (James)
1935- . . . . **CLC 4, 36**
See also CA 17-20R; CANR 8, 36

Lieksman, Anders
See Haavikko, Paavo Juhani

Li Fei-kan 1904-
See Pa Chin
See also CA 105

Lifton, Robert Jay 1926- . . . . **CLC 67**
See also CA 17-20R; CANR 27;
INT CANR-27; SATA 66

Lightfoot, Gordon 1938- . . . . **CLC 26**
See also CA 109

Lightman, Alan P. 1948- . . . . **CLC 81**
See also CA 141

Ligotti, Thomas (Robert)
1953- . . . . **CLC 44; SSC 16**
See also CA 123; CANR 49

Li Ho 791-817. . . . . **PC 13**

Liliencron, (Friedrich Adolf Axel) Detlev von
1844-1909 . . . . **TCLC 18**
See also CA 117

Lilly, William 1602-1681 . . . . **LC 27**

Lima, Jose Lezama
See Lezama Lima, Jose

Lima Barreto, Afonso Henrique de
1881-1922 . . . . **TCLC 23**
See also CA 117

Limonov, Edward 1944- . . . . **CLC 67**
See also CA 137

Lin, Frank
See Atherton, Gertrude (Franklin Horn)

Lincoln, Abraham 1809-1865. . . . . **NCLC 18**

Lind, Jakov . . . . **CLC 1, 2, 4, 27, 82**
See also Landwirth, Heinz
See also CAAS 4

Lindbergh, Anne (Spencer) Morrow
1906- . . . . **CLC 82**
See also CA 17-20R; CANR 16;
DAM NOV; MTCW; SATA 33

Lindsay, David 1878-1945 . . . . **TCLC 15**
See also CA 113

Lindsay, (Nicholas) Vachel
1879-1931 . . . **TCLC 17; DA; DAC; WLC**
See also CA 114; 135; CDALB 1865-1917;
DAM MST, POET; DLB 54; SATA 40

Linke-Poot
See Doeblin, Alfred

Linney, Romulus 1930- . . . . **CLC 51**
See also CA 1-4R; CANR 40, 44

Linton, Eliza Lynn 1822-1898. . . . **NCLC 41**
See also DLB 18

Li Po 701-763 . . . . **CMLC 2**

Lipsius, Justus 1547-1606 . . . . **LC 16**

Lipsyte, Robert (Michael)
1938- . . . . **CLC 21; DA; DAC**
See also AAYA 7; CA 17-20R; CANR 8;
CLR 23; DAM MST, NOV; JRDA;
MAICYA; SATA 5, 68

Lish, Gordon (Jay) 1934-. . **CLC 45; SSC 18**
See also CA 113; 117; DLB 130; INT 117

Lispector, Clarice 1925-1977. . . . . . . **CLC 43**
See also CA 139; 116; DLB 113

Littell, Robert 1935(?)- . . . . **CLC 42**
See also CA 109; 112

Little, Malcolm 1925-1965
See Malcolm X
See also BW 1; CA 125; 111; DA; DAB;
DAC; DAM MST, MULT; MTCW

Littlewit, Humphrey Gent.
See Lovecraft, H(oward) P(hillips)

Litwos
See Sienkiewicz, Henryk (Adam Alexander
Pius)

Liu E 1857-1909 . . . . **TCLC 15**
See also CA 115

Lively, Penelope (Margaret)
1933- . . . . **CLC 32, 50**
See also CA 41-44R; CANR 29; CLR 7;
DAM NOV; DLB 14, 161; JRDA;
MAICYA; MTCW; SATA 7, 60

Luzi, Mario 1914-............... **CLC 13**
See also CA 61-64; CANR 9; DLB 128

L'Ymagier
See Gourmont, Remy (-Marie-Charles) de

Lynch, B. Suarez
See Bioy Casares, Adolfo; Borges, Jorge
Luis

Lynch, David (K.) 1946-........... **CLC 66**
See also CA 124; 129

Lynch, James
See Andreyev, Leonid (Nikolaevich)

Lynch Davis, B.
See Bioy Casares, Adolfo; Borges, Jorge
Luis

Lyndsay, Sir David 1490-1555 ...... **LC 20**

Lynn, Kenneth S(chuyler) 1923-.... **CLC 50**
See also CA 1-4R; CANR 3, 27

Lynx
See West, Rebecca

Lyons, Marcus
See Blish, James (Benjamin)

Lyre, Pinchbeck
See Sassoon, Siegfried (Lorraine)

Lytle, Andrew (Nelson) 1902-1995 .. **CLC 22**
See also CA 9-12R; 150; DLB 6

Lyttelton, George 1709-1773........ **LC 10**

Maas, Peter 1929- .... **CLC 29**
See also CA 93-96; INT 93-96

Macaulay, Rose 1881-1958 ..... **TCLC 7, 44**
See also CA 104; DLB 36

Macaulay, Thomas Babington
1800-1859 .... **NCLC 42**
See also CDBLB 1832-1890; DLB 32, 55

MacBeth, George (Mann)
1932-1992 .... **CLC 2, 5, 9**
See also CA 25-28R; 136; DLB 40; MTCW;
SATA 4; SATA-Obit 70

MacCaig, Norman (Alexander)
1910- .... **CLC 36; DAB**
See also CA 9-12R; CANR 3, 34;
DAM POET; DLB 27

MacCarthy, (Sir Charles Otto) Desmond
1877-1952 .... **TCLC 36**

MacDiarmid, Hugh
.... **CLC 2, 4, 11, 19, 63; PC 9**
See also Grieve, C(hristopher) M(urray)
See also CDBLB 1945-1960; DLB 20

MacDonald, Anson
See Heinlein, Robert A(nson)

Macdonald, Cynthia 1928-...... **CLC 13, 19**
See also CA 49-52; CANR 4, 44; DLB 105

MacDonald, George 1824-1905..... **TCLC 9**
See also CA 106; 137; DLB 18, 163;
MAICYA; SATA 33

Macdonald, John
See Millar, Kenneth

MacDonald, John D(ann)
1916-1986 .... **CLC 3, 27, 44**
See also CA 1-4R; 121; CANR 1, 19;
DAM NOV, POP; DLB 8; DLBY 86;
MTCW

Macdonald, John Ross
See Millar, Kenneth

Macdonald, Ross..... **CLC 1, 2, 3, 14, 34, 41**
See also Millar, Kenneth
See also DLBD 6

MacDougal, John
See Blish, James (Benjamin)

MacEwen, Gwendolyn (Margaret)
1941-1987 .... **CLC 13, 55**
See also CA 9-12R; 124; CANR 7, 22;
DLB 53; SATA 50; SATA-Obit 55

Macha, Karel Hynek 1810-1846 .. **NCLC 46**

Machado (y Ruiz), Antonio
1875-1939 .... **TCLC 3**
See also CA 104; DLB 108

Machado de Assis, Joaquim Maria
1839-1908 .... **TCLC 10; BLC**
See also CA 107

Machen, Arthur.......... TCLC 4; SSC 20
See also Jones, Arthur Llewellyn
See also DLB 36, 156

Machiavelli, Niccolo
1469-1527 ...... **LC 8; DA; DAB; DAC**
See also DAM MST

MacInnes, Colin 1914-1976...... **CLC 4, 23**
See also CA 69-72; 65-68; CANR 21;
DLB 14; MTCW

MacInnes, Helen (Clark)
1907-1985 .... **CLC 27, 39**
See also CA 1-4R; 117; CANR 1, 28;
DAM POP; DLB 87; MTCW; SATA 22;
SATA-Obit 44

Mackay, Mary 1855-1924
See Corelli, Marie
See also CA 118

Mackenzie, Compton (Edward Montague)
1883-1972 .... **CLC 18**
See also CA 21-22; 37-40R; CAP 2;
DLB 34, 100

Mackenzie, Henry 1745-1831 .... **NCLC 41**
See also DLB 39

Mackintosh, Elizabeth 1896(?)-1952
See Tey, Josephine
See also CA 110

MacLaren, James
See Grieve, C(hristopher) M(urray)

Mac Laverty, Bernard 1942-....... **CLC 31**
See also CA 116; 118; CANR 43; INT 118

MacLean, Alistair (Stuart)
1922-1987 .... **CLC 3, 13, 50, 63**
See also CA 57-60; 121; CANR 28;
DAM POP; MTCW; SATA 23;
SATA-Obit 50

Maclean, Norman (Fitzroy)
1902-1990 .... **CLC 78; SSC 13**
See also CA 102; 132; CANR 49;
DAM POP

MacLeish, Archibald
1892-1982 .... **CLC 3, 8, 14, 68**
See also CA 9-12R; 106; CANR 33;
DAM POET; DLB 4, 7, 45; DLBY 82;
MTCW

MacLennan, (John) Hugh
1907-1990 .... **CLC 2, 14, 92; DAC**
See also CA 5-8R; 142; CANR 33;
DAM MST; DLB 68; MTCW

MacLeod, Alistair 1936- ..... **CLC 56; DAC**
See also CA 123; DAM MST; DLB 60

MacNeice, (Frederick) Louis
1907-1963 ...... **CLC 1, 4, 10, 53; DAB**
See also CA 85-88; DAM POET; DLB 10,
20; MTCW

MacNeill, Dand
See Fraser, George MacDonald

Macpherson, James 1736-1796 ...... **LC 29**
See also DLB 109

Macpherson, (Jean) Jay 1931-..... **CLC 14**
See also CA 5-8R; DLB 53

MacShane, Frank 1927-........... **CLC 39**
See also CA 9-12R; CANR 3, 33; DLB 111

Macumber, Mari
See Sandoz, Mari(e Susette)

Madach, Imre 1823-1864........ **NCLC 19**

Madden, (Jerry) David 1933- .... **CLC 5, 15**
See also CA 1-4R; CAAS 3; CANR 4, 45;
DLB 6; MTCW

Maddern, Al(an)
See Ellison, Harlan (Jay)

Madhubuti, Haki R.
1942-.......... **CLC 6, 73; BLC; PC 5**
See also Lee, Don L.
See also BW 2; CA 73-76; CANR 24, 51;
DAM MULT, POET; DLB 5, 41;
DLBD 8

Maepenn, Hugh
See Kuttner, Henry

Maepenn, K. H.
See Kuttner, Henry

Maeterlinck, Maurice 1862-1949 ... **TCLC 3**
See also CA 104; 136; DAM DRAM;
SATA 66

Maginn, William 1794-1842...... **NCLC 8**
See also DLB 110, 159

Mahapatra, Jayanta 1928-........ **CLC 33**
See also CA 73-76; CAAS 9; CANR 15, 33;
DAM MULT

Mahfouz, Naguib (Abdel Aziz Al-Sabilgi)
1911(?)-
See Mahfuz, Najib
See also BEST 89:2; CA 128; DAM NOV;
MTCW

Mahfuz, Najib................ CLC 52, 55
See also Mahfouz, Naguib (Abdel Aziz
Al-Sabilgi)
See also DLBY 88

Mahon, Derek 1941-.............. **CLC 27**
See also CA 113; 128; DLB 40

Mailer, Norman
1923- ...... **CLC 1, 2, 3, 4, 5, 8, 11, 14,
28, 39, 74; DA; DAB; DAC**
See also AITN 2; CA 9-12R; CABS 1;
CANR 28; CDALB 1968-1988;
DAM MST, NOV, POP; DLB 2, 16, 28;
DLBD 3; DLBY 80, 83; MTCW

Maillet, Antonine 1929-...... **CLC 54; DAC**
See also CA 115; 120; CANR 46; DLB 60;
INT 120

Mais, Roger 1905-1955 .... **TCLC 8**
See also BW 1; CA 105; 124; DLB 125;
MTCW

Maistre, Joseph de 1753-1821.... **NCLC 37**

Maitland, Sara (Louise) 1950-...... **CLC 49**
See also CA 69-72; CANR 13

Major, Clarence
1936- . . . . **CLC 3, 19, 48; BLC**
See also BW 2; CA 21-24R; CAAS 6;
CANR 13, 25; DAM MULT; DLB 33

Major, Kevin (Gerald)
1949- . . . . **CLC 26; DAC**
See also AAYA 16; CA 97-100; CANR 21,
38; CLR 11; DLB 60; INT CANR-21;
JRDA; MAICYA; SATA 32, 82

Maki, James
See Ozu, Yasujiro

Malabaila, Damiano
See Levi, Primo

Malamud, Bernard
1914-1986 . . . . . . **CLC 1, 2, 3, 5, 8, 9, 11,**
18, 27, 44, 78, 85; DA; DAB; DAC;
SSC 15; WLC
See also AAYA 16; CA 5-8R; 118; CABS 1;
CANR 28; CDALB 1941-1968;
DAM MST, NOV, POP; DLB 2, 28, 152;
DLBY 80, 86; MTCW

Malaparte, Curzio 1898-1957 . . . . . **TCLC 52**

Malcolm, Dan
See Silverberg, Robert

Malcolm X . . . . **CLC 82; BLC**
See also Little, Malcolm

Malherbe, Francois de 1555-1628 . . . . . **LC 5**

Mallarme, Stephane
1842-1898 . . . . **NCLC 4, 41; PC 4**
See also DAM POET

Mallet-Joris, Francoise 1930- . . . . . . **CLC 11**
See also CA 65-68; CANR 17; DLB 83

Malley, Ern
See McAuley, James Phillip

Mallowan, Agatha Christie
See Christie, Agatha (Mary Clarissa)

Maloff, Saul 1922- . . . . **CLC 5**
See also CA 33-36R

Malone, Louis
See MacNeice, (Frederick) Louis

Malone, Michael (Christopher)
1942- . . . . **CLC 43**
See also CA 77-80; CANR 14, 32

Malory, (Sir) Thomas
1410(?)-1471(?) . . . . . . **LC 11; DA; DAB;**
DAC
See also CDBLB Before 1660; DAM MST;
DLB 146; SATA 59; SATA-Brief 33

Malouf, (George Joseph) David
1934- . . . . **CLC 28, 86**
See also CA 124; CANR 50

Malraux, (Georges-)Andre
1901-1976 . . . . . . **CLC 1, 4, 9, 13, 15, 57**
See also CA 21-22; 69-72; CANR 34;
CAP 2; DAM NOV; DLB 72; MTCW

Malzberg, Barry N(athaniel) 1939- . . . **CLC 7**
See also CA 61-64; CAAS 4; CANR 16;
DLB 8

Mamet, David (Alan)
1947- . . . . . . **CLC 9, 15, 34, 46, 91; DC 4**
See also AAYA 3; CA 81-84; CABS 3;
CANR 15, 41; DAM DRAM; DLB 7;
MTCW

Mamoulian, Rouben (Zachary)
1897-1987 . . . . **CLC 16**
See also CA 25-28R; 124

Mandelstam, Osip (Emilievich)
1891(?)-1938(?) . . . . . **TCLC 2, 6; PC 14**
See also CA 104; 150

Mander, (Mary) Jane 1877-1949 . . . **TCLC 31**

Mandiargues, Andre Pieyre de . . . . . . **CLC 41**
See also Pieyre de Mandiargues, Andre
See also DLB 83

Mandrake, Ethel Belle
See Thurman, Wallace (Henry)

Mangan, James Clarence
1803-1849 . . . . **NCLC 27**

Maniere, J.-E.
See Giraudoux, (Hippolyte) Jean

Manley, (Mary) Delariviere
1672(?)-1724 . . . . **LC 1**
See also DLB 39, 80

Mann, Abel
See Creasey, John

Mann, (Luiz) Heinrich 1871-1950 . . . **TCLC 9**
See also CA 106; DLB 66

Mann, (Paul) Thomas
1875-1955 . . . . **TCLC 2, 8, 14, 21, 35, 44,**
60; DA; DAB; DAC; SSC 5; WLC
See also CA 104; 128; DAM MST, NOV;
DLB 66; MTCW

Manning, David
See Faust, Frederick (Schiller)

Manning, Frederic 1887(?)-1935 . . . **TCLC 25**
See also CA 124

Manning, Olivia 1915-1980 . . . . . . **CLC 5, 19**
See also CA 5-8R; 101; CANR 29; MTCW

Mano, D. Keith 1942- . . . . **CLC 2, 10**
See also CA 25-28R; CAAS 6; CANR 26;
DLB 6

Mansfield, Katherine
. . . . . **TCLC 2, 8, 39; DAB; SSC 9; WLC**
See also Beauchamp, Kathleen Mansfield
See also DLB 162

Manso, Peter 1940- . . . . **CLC 39**
See also CA 29-32R; CANR 44

Mantecon, Juan Jimenez
See Jimenez (Mantecon), Juan Ramon

Manton, Peter
See Creasey, John

Man Without a Spleen, A
See Chekhov, Anton (Pavlovich)

Manzoni, Alessandro 1785-1873 . . **NCLC 29**

Mapu, Abraham (ben Jekutiel)
1808-1867 . . . . **NCLC 18**

Mara, Sally
See Queneau, Raymond

Marat, Jean Paul 1743-1793 . . . . **LC 10**

Marcel, Gabriel Honore
1889-1973 . . . . **CLC 15**
See also CA 102; 45-48; MTCW

Marchbanks, Samuel
See Davies, (William) Robertson

Marchi, Giacomo
See Bassani, Giorgio

Margulies, Donald . . . . **CLC 76**

Marie de France c. 12th cent. - . . . . **CMLC 8**

Marie de l'Incarnation 1599-1672 . . . . **LC 10**

Mariner, Scott
See Pohl, Frederik

Marinetti, Filippo Tommaso
1876-1944 . . . . **TCLC 10**
See also CA 107; DLB 114

Marivaux, Pierre Carlet de Chamblain de
1688-1763 . . . . **LC 4**

Markandaya, Kamala . . . . **CLC 8, 38**
See also Taylor, Kamala (Purnaiya)

Markfield, Wallace 1926- . . . . **CLC 8**
See also CA 69-72; CAAS 3; DLB 2, 28

Markham, Edwin 1852-1940 . . . . . **TCLC 47**
See also DLB 54

Markham, Robert
See Amis, Kingsley (William)

Marks, J
See Highwater, Jamake (Mamake)

Marks-Highwater, J
See Highwater, Jamake (Mamake)

Markson, David M(errill) 1927- . . . . **CLC 67**
See also CA 49-52; CANR 1

Marley, Bob . . . . **CLC 17**
See also Marley, Robert Nesta

Marley, Robert Nesta 1945-1981
See Marley, Bob
See also CA 107; 103

Marlowe, Christopher
1564-1593 . . . . . **LC 22; DA; DAB; DAC;**
DC 1; WLC
See also CDBLB Before 1660;
DAM DRAM, MST; DLB 62

Marmontel, Jean-Francois
1723-1799 . . . . **LC 2**

Marquand, John P(hillips)
1893-1960 . . . . **CLC 2, 10**
See also CA 85-88; DLB 9, 102

Marquez, Gabriel (Jose) Garcia
See Garcia Marquez, Gabriel (Jose)

Marquis, Don(ald Robert Perry)
1878-1937 . . . . **TCLC 7**
See also CA 104; DLB 11, 25

Marric, J. J.
See Creasey, John

Marrow, Bernard
See Moore, Brian

Marryat, Frederick 1792-1848 . . . . **NCLC 3**
See also DLB 21, 163

Marsden, James
See Creasey, John

Marsh, (Edith) Ngaio
1899-1982 . . . . **CLC 7, 53**
See also CA 9-12R; CANR 6; DAM POP;
DLB 77; MTCW

Marshall, Garry 1934- . . . . **CLC 17**
See also AAYA 3; CA 111; SATA 60

Marshall, Paule
1929- . . . . **CLC 27, 72; BLC; SSC 3**
See also BW 2; CA 77-80; CANR 25;
DAM MULT; DLB 157; MTCW

Marsten, Richard
See Hunter, Evan

Martha, Henry
See Harris, Mark

Martial c. 40-c. 104 . . . . **PC 10**

Martin, Ken
See Hubbard, L(afayette) Ron(ald)

Martin, Richard
See Creasey, John

Martin, Steve 1945- . . . . **CLC 30**
See also CA 97-100; CANR 30; MTCW

Martin, Valerie 1948-. . . . . **CLC 89**
See also BEST 90:2; CA 85-88; CANR 49

Martin, Violet Florence
1862-1915 . . . . **TCLC 51**

Martin, Webber
See Silverberg, Robert

Martindale, Patrick Victor
See White, Patrick (Victor Martindale)

Martin du Gard, Roger
1881-1958 . . . . **TCLC 24**
See also CA 118; DLB 65

Martineau, Harriet 1802-1876. . . . **NCLC 26**
See also DLB 21, 55, 159, 163; YABC 2

Martines, Julia
See O'Faolain, Julia

Martinez, Jacinto Benavente y
See Benavente (y Martinez), Jacinto

Martinez Ruiz, Jose 1873-1967
See Azorin; Ruiz, Jose Martinez
See also CA 93-96; HW

Martinez Sierra, Gregorio
1881-1947 . . . . **TCLC 6**
See also CA 115

Martinez Sierra, Maria (de la O'LeJarraga)
1874-1974 . . . . **TCLC 6**
See also CA 115

Martinsen, Martin
See Follett, Ken(neth Martin)

Martinson, Harry (Edmund)
1904-1978 . . . . **CLC 14**
See also CA 77-80; CANR 34

Marut, Ret
See Traven, B.

Marut, Robert
See Traven, B.

Marvell, Andrew
1621-1678 . . . . . . **LC 4; DA; DAB; DAC;**
PC 10; WLC
See also CDBLB 1660-1789; DAM MST,
POET; DLB 131

Marx, Karl (Heinrich)
1818-1883 . . . . **NCLC 17**
See also DLB 129

Masaoka Shiki. . . . . **TCLC 18**
See also Masaoka Tsunenori

Masaoka Tsunenori 1867-1902
See Masaoka Shiki
See also CA 117

Masefield, John (Edward)
1878-1967 . . . . **CLC 11, 47**
See also CA 19-20; 25-28R; CANR 33;
CAP 2; CDBLB 1890-1914; DAM POET;
DLB 10, 19, 153, 160; MTCW; SATA 19

Maso, Carole 19(?)- . . . . **CLC 44**

Mason, Bobbie Ann
1940- . . . . **CLC 28, 43, 82; SSC 4**
See also AAYA 5; CA 53-56; CANR 11,
31; DLBY 87; INT CANR-31; MTCW

Mason, Ernst
See Pohl, Frederik

Mason, Lee W.
See Malzberg, Barry N(athaniel)

Mason, Nick 1945-. . . . . **CLC 35**

Mason, Tally
See Derleth, August (William)

Mass, William
See Gibson, William

Masters, Edgar Lee
1868-1950 . . . . . . **TCLC 2, 25; DA; DAC;**
PC 1
See also CA 104; 133; CDALB 1865-1917;
DAM MST, POET; DLB 54; MTCW

Masters, Hilary 1928- . . . . **CLC 48**
See also CA 25-28R; CANR 13, 47

Mastrosimone, William 19(?)-. . . . . . **CLC 36**

Mathe, Albert
See Camus, Albert

Matheson, Richard Burton 1926- . . . **CLC 37**
See also CA 97-100; DLB 8, 44; INT 97-100

Mathews, Harry 1930-. . . . . **CLC 6, 52**
See also CA 21-24R; CAAS 6; CANR 18,
40

Mathews, John Joseph 1894-1979. . . **CLC 84**
See also CA 19-20; 142; CANR 45; CAP 2;
DAM MULT; NNAL

Mathias, Roland (Glyn) 1915-. . . . . . **CLC 45**
See also CA 97-100; CANR 19, 41; DLB 27

Matsuo Basho 1644-1694. . . . . **PC 3**
See also DAM POET

Mattheson, Rodney
See Creasey, John

Matthews, Greg 1949- . . . . **CLC 45**
See also CA 135

Matthews, William 1942-. . . . . **CLC 40**
See also CA 29-32R; CAAS 18; CANR 12;
DLB 5

Matthias, John (Edward) 1941-. . . . . . **CLC 9**
See also CA 33-36R

Matthiessen, Peter
1927- . . . . **CLC 5, 7, 11, 32, 64**
See also AAYA 6; BEST 90:4; CA 9-12R;
CANR 21, 50; DAM NOV; DLB 6;
MTCW; SATA 27

Maturin, Charles Robert
1780(?)-1824 . . . . **NCLC 6**

Matute (Ausejo), Ana Maria
1925- . . . . **CLC 11**
See also CA 89-92; MTCW

Maugham, W. S.
See Maugham, W(illiam) Somerset

Maugham, W(illiam) Somerset
1874-1965 . . . . . . **CLC 1, 11, 15, 67; DA;**
DAB; DAC; SSC 8; WLC
See also CA 5-8R; 25-28R; CANR 40;
CDBLB 1914-1945; DAM DRAM, MST,
NOV; DLB 10, 36, 77, 100, 162; MTCW;
SATA 54

Maugham, William Somerset
See Maugham, W(illiam) Somerset

Maupassant, (Henri Rene Albert) Guy de
1850-1893 . . . . . **NCLC 1, 42; DA; DAB;**
DAC; SSC 1; WLC
See also DAM MST; DLB 123

Maurhut, Richard
See Traven, B.

Mauriac, Claude 1914-. . . . . **CLC 9**
See also CA 89-92; DLB 83

Mauriac, Francois (Charles)
1885-1970 . . . . **CLC 4, 9, 56**
See also CA 25-28; CAP 2; DLB 65;
MTCW

Mavor, Osborne Henry 1888-1951
See Bridie, James
See also CA 104

Maxwell, William (Keepers, Jr.)
1908- . . . . **CLC 19**
See also CA 93-96; DLBY 80; INT 93-96

May, Elaine 1932- . . . . **CLC 16**
See also CA 124; 142; DLB 44

Mayakovski, Vladimir (Vladimirovich)
1893-1930 . . . . **TCLC 4, 18**
See also CA 104

Mayhew, Henry 1812-1887 . . . . . . **NCLC 31**
See also DLB 18, 55

Mayle, Peter 1939(?)-. . . . . **CLC 89**
See also CA 139

Maynard, Joyce 1953-. . . . . **CLC 23**
See also CA 111; 129

Mayne, William (James Carter)
1928- . . . . **CLC 12**
See also CA 9-12R; CANR 37; CLR 25;
JRDA; MAICYA; SAAS 11; SATA 6, 68

Mayo, Jim
See L'Amour, Louis (Dearborn)

Maysles, Albert 1926- . . . . **CLC 16**
See also CA 29-32R

Maysles, David 1932-. . . . . **CLC 16**

Mazer, Norma Fox 1931- . . . . **CLC 26**
See also AAYA 5; CA 69-72; CANR 12,
32; CLR 23; JRDA; MAICYA; SAAS 1;
SATA 24, 67

Mazzini, Guiseppe 1805-1872 . . . . **NCLC 34**

McAuley, James Phillip
1917-1976 . . . . **CLC 45**
See also CA 97-100

McBain, Ed
See Hunter, Evan

McBrien, William Augustine
1930- . . . . **CLC 44**
See also CA 107

McCaffrey, Anne (Inez) 1926-. . . . . . **CLC 17**
See also AAYA 6; AITN 2; BEST 89:2;
CA 25-28R; CANR 15, 35; DAM NOV,
POP; DLB 8; JRDA; MAICYA; MTCW;
SAAS 11; SATA 8, 70

McCall, Nathan 1955(?)-. . . . . **CLC 86**
See also CA 146

McCann, Arthur
See Campbell, John W(ood, Jr.)

McCann, Edson
See Pohl, Frederik

Meredith, William (Morris)
1919- . . . . **CLC 4, 13, 22, 55**
See also CA 9-12R; CAAS 14; CANR 6, 40;
DAM POET; DLB 5

Merezhkovsky, Dmitry Sergeyevich
1865-1941 . . . . **TCLC 29**

Merimee, Prosper
1803-1870 . . . . **NCLC 6; SSC 7**
See also DLB 119

Merkin, Daphne 1954- . . . . **CLC 44**
See also CA 123

Merlin, Arthur
See Blish, James (Benjamin)

Merrill, James (Ingram)
1926-1995 . . . . **CLC 2, 3, 6, 8, 13, 18, 34,
91**
See also CA 13-16R; 147; CANR 10, 49;
DAM POET; DLB 5; DLBY 85;
INT CANR-10; MTCW

Merriman, Alex
See Silverberg, Robert

Merritt, E. B.
See Waddington, Miriam

Merton, Thomas
1915-1968 . . **CLC 1, 3, 11, 34, 83; PC 10**
See also CA 5-8R; 25-28R; CANR 22;
DLB 48; DLBY 81; MTCW

Merwin, W(illiam) S(tanley)
1927- . . . **CLC 1, 2, 3, 5, 8, 13, 18, 45, 88**
See also CA 13-16R; CANR 15, 51;
DAM POET; DLB 5; INT CANR-15;
MTCW

Metcalf, John 1938- . . . . **CLC 37**
See also CA 113; DLB 60

Metcalf, Suzanne
See Baum, L(yman) Frank

Mew, Charlotte (Mary)
1870-1928 . . . . **TCLC 8**
See also CA 105; DLB 19, 135

Mewshaw, Michael 1943- . . . . **CLC 9**
See also CA 53-56; CANR 7, 47; DLBY 80

Meyer, June
See Jordan, June

Meyer, Lynn
See Slavitt, David R(ytman)

Meyer-Meyrink, Gustav 1868-1932
See Meyrink, Gustav
See also CA 117

Meyers, Jeffrey 1939- . . . . **CLC 39**
See also CA 73-76; DLB 111

Meynell, Alice (Christina Gertrude Thompson)
1847-1922 . . . . **TCLC 6**
See also CA 104; DLB 19, 98

Meyrink, Gustav . . . . **TCLC 21**
See also Meyer-Meyrink, Gustav
See also DLB 81

Michaels, Leonard
1933- . . . . **CLC 6, 25; SSC 16**
See also CA 61-64; CANR 21; DLB 130;
MTCW

Michaux, Henri 1899-1984 . . . . . . **CLC 8, 19**
See also CA 85-88; 114

Michelangelo 1475-1564 . . . . **LC 12**

Michelet, Jules 1798-1874 . . . . **NCLC 31**

Michener, James A(lbert)
1907(?)- . . . . **CLC 1, 5, 11, 29, 60**
See also AITN 1; BEST 90:1; CA 5-8R;
CANR 21, 45; DAM NOV, POP; DLB 6;
MTCW

Mickiewicz, Adam 1798-1855 . . . . . **NCLC 3**

Middleton, Christopher 1926- . . . . . . **CLC 13**
See also CA 13-16R; CANR 29; DLB 40

Middleton, Richard (Barham)
1882-1911 . . . . **TCLC 56**
See also DLB 156

Middleton, Stanley 1919- . . . . **CLC 7, 38**
See also CA 25-28R; CAAS 23; CANR 21,
46; DLB 14

Middleton, Thomas 1580-1627 . . . . **DC 5**
See also DAM DRAM, MST; DLB 58

Migueis, Jose Rodrigues 1901- . . . . . **CLC 10**

Mikszath, Kalman 1847-1910 . . . . . **TCLC 31**

Miles, Josephine
1911-1985 . . . . **CLC 1, 2, 14, 34, 39**
See also CA 1-4R; 116; CANR 2;
DAM POET; DLB 48

Militant
See Sandburg, Carl (August)

Mill, John Stuart 1806-1873 . . . . . **NCLC 11**
See also CDBLB 1832-1890; DLB 55

Millar, Kenneth 1915-1983 . . . . **CLC 14**
See also Macdonald, Ross
See also CA 9-12R; 110; CANR 16;
DAM POP; DLB 2; DLBD 6; DLBY 83;
MTCW

Millay, E. Vincent
See Millay, Edna St. Vincent

Millay, Edna St. Vincent
1892-1950 . . . . . . **TCLC 4, 49; DA; DAB;
DAC; PC 6**
See also CA 104; 130; CDALB 1917-1929;
DAM MST, POET; DLB 45; MTCW

Miller, Arthur
1915- . . . . **CLC 1, 2, 6, 10, 15, 26, 47, 78;
DA; DAB; DAC; DC 1; WLC**
See also AAYA 15; AITN 1; CA 1-4R;
CABS 3; CANR 2, 30;
CDALB 1941-1968; DAM DRAM, MST;
DLB 7; MTCW

Miller, Henry (Valentine)
1891-1980 . . . . **CLC 1, 2, 4, 9, 14, 43, 84;
DA; DAB; DAC; WLC**
See also CA 9-12R; 97-100; CANR 33;
CDALB 1929-1941; DAM MST, NOV;
DLB 4, 9; DLBY 80; MTCW

Miller, Jason 1939(?)- . . . . **CLC 2**
See also AITN 1; CA 73-76; DLB 7

Miller, Sue 1943- . . . . **CLC 44**
See also BEST 90:3; CA 139; DAM POP;
DLB 143

Miller, Walter M(ichael, Jr.)
1923- . . . . **CLC 4, 30**
See also CA 85-88; DLB 8

Millett, Kate 1934- . . . . **CLC 67**
See also AITN 1; CA 73-76; CANR 32;
MTCW

Millhauser, Steven 1943- . . . . **CLC 21, 54**
See also CA 110; 111; DLB 2; INT 111

Millin, Sarah Gertrude 1889-1968 . . **CLC 49**
See also CA 102; 93-96

Milne, A(lan) A(lexander)
1882-1956 . . . . **TCLC 6; DAB; DAC**
See also CA 104; 133; CLR 1, 26;
DAM MST; DLB 10, 77, 100, 160;
MAICYA; MTCW; YABC 1

Milner, Ron(ald) 1938- . . . . **CLC 56; BLC**
See also AITN 1; BW 1; CA 73-76;
CANR 24; DAM MULT; DLB 38;
MTCW

Milosz, Czeslaw
1911- . . . **CLC 5, 11, 22, 31, 56, 82; PC 8**
See also CA 81-84; CANR 23, 51;
DAM MST, POET; MTCW

Milton, John
1608-1674 . . . . . . **LC 9; DA; DAB; DAC;
WLC**
See also CDBLB 1660-1789; DAM MST,
POET; DLB 131, 151

Min, Anchee 1957- . . . . **CLC 86**
See also CA 146

Minehaha, Cornelius
See Wedekind, (Benjamin) Frank(lin)

Miner, Valerie 1947- . . . . **CLC 40**
See also CA 97-100

Minimo, Duca
See D'Annunzio, Gabriele

Minot, Susan 1956- . . . . **CLC 44**
See also CA 134

Minus, Ed 1938- . . . . **CLC 39**

Miranda, Javier
See Bioy Casares, Adolfo

Mirbeau, Octave 1848-1917 . . . . **TCLC 55**
See also DLB 123

Miro (Ferrer), Gabriel (Francisco Victor)
1879-1930 . . . . **TCLC 5**
See also CA 104

Mishima, Yukio
. . . . **CLC 2, 4, 6, 9, 27; DC 1; SSC 4**
See also Hiraoka, Kimitake

Mistral, Frederic 1830-1914 . . . . . . **TCLC 51**
See also CA 122

Mistral, Gabriela . . . . **TCLC 2; HLC**
See also Godoy Alcayaga, Lucila

Mistry, Rohinton 1952- . . . . . . **CLC 71; DAC**
See also CA 141

Mitchell, Clyde
See Ellison, Harlan (Jay); Silverberg, Robert

Mitchell, James Leslie 1901-1935
See Gibbon, Lewis Grassic
See also CA 104; DLB 15

Mitchell, Joni 1943- . . . . **CLC 12**
See also CA 112

Mitchell, Margaret (Munnerlyn)
1900-1949 . . . . **TCLC 11**
See also CA 109; 125; DAM NOV, POP;
DLB 9; MTCW

Mitchell, Peggy
See Mitchell, Margaret (Munnerlyn)

Mitchell, S(ilas) Weir 1829-1914 . . **TCLC 36**

Morris, William 1834-1896 . . . . . . **NCLC 4**
See also CDBLB 1832-1890; DLB 18, 35,
57, 156

Morris, Wright 1910- . . . **CLC 1, 3, 7, 18, 37**
See also CA 9-12R; CANR 21; DLB 2;
DLBY 81; MTCW

Morrison, Chloe Anthony Wofford
See Morrison, Toni

Morrison, James Douglas 1943-1971
See Morrison, Jim
See also CA 73-76; CANR 40

Morrison, Jim . . . . **CLC 17**
See also Morrison, James Douglas

Morrison, Toni
1931- . . . . **CLC 4, 10, 22, 55, 81, 87;**
BLC; DA; DAB; DAC
See also AAYA 1; BW 2; CA 29-32R;
CANR 27, 42; CDALB 1968-1988;
DAM MST, MULT, NOV, POP; DLB 6,
33, 143; DLBY 81; MTCW; SATA 57

Morrison, Van 1945- . . . . **CLC 21**
See also CA 116

Mortimer, John (Clifford)
1923- . . . . **CLC 28, 43**
See also CA 13-16R; CANR 21;
CDBLB 1960 to Present; DAM DRAM,
POP; DLB 13; INT CANR-21; MTCW

Mortimer, Penelope (Ruth) 1918- . . . . **CLC 5**
See also CA 57-60; CANR 45

Morton, Anthony
See Creasey, John

Mosher, Howard Frank 1943- . . . . . . **CLC 62**
See also CA 139

Mosley, Nicholas 1923- . . . . **CLC 43, 70**
See also CA 69-72; CANR 41; DLB 14

Moss, Howard
1922-1987 . . . . **CLC 7, 14, 45, 50**
See also CA 1-4R; 123; CANR 1, 44;
DAM POET; DLB 5

Mossgiel, Rab
See Burns, Robert

Motion, Andrew (Peter) 1952- . . . . . **CLC 47**
See also CA 146; DLB 40

Motley, Willard (Francis)
1909-1965 . . . . **CLC 18**
See also BW 1; CA 117; 106; DLB 76, 143

Motoori, Norinaga 1730-1801 . . . . **NCLC 45**

Mott, Michael (Charles Alston)
1930- . . . . **CLC 15, 34**
See also CA 5-8R; CAAS 7; CANR 7, 29

Mountain Wolf Woman
1884-1960 . . . . **CLC 92**
See also CA 144; NNAL

Moure, Erin 1955- . . . . **CLC 88**
See also CA 113; DLB 60

Mowat, Farley (McGill)
1921- . . . . **CLC 26; DAC**
See also AAYA 1; CA 1-4R; CANR 4, 24,
42; CLR 20; DAM MST; DLB 68;
INT CANAR-24; JRDA; MAICYA;
MTCW; SATA 3, 55

Moyers, Bill 1934- . . . . **CLC 74**
See also AITN 2; CA 61-64; CANR 31

Mphahlele, Es'kia
See Mphahlele, Ezekiel
See also DLB 125

Mphahlele, Ezekiel 1919- . . . . . **CLC 25; BLC**
See also Mphahlele, Es'kia
See also BW 2; CA 81-84; CANR 26;
DAM MULT

Mqhayi, S(amuel) E(dward) K(rune Loliwe)
1875-1945 . . . . **TCLC 25; BLC**
See also DAM MULT

Mr. Martin
See Burroughs, William S(eward)

Mrozek, Slawomir 1930- . . . . **CLC 3, 13**
See also CA 13-16R; CAAS 10; CANR 29;
MTCW

Mrs. Belloc-Lowndes
See Lowndes, Marie Adelaide (Belloc)

Mtwa, Percy (?)- . . . . **CLC 47**

Mueller, Lisel 1924- . . . . **CLC 13, 51**
See also CA 93-96; DLB 105

Muir, Edwin 1887-1959 . . . . **TCLC 2**
See also CA 104; DLB 20, 100

Muir, John 1838-1914 . . . . **TCLC 28**

Mujica Lainez, Manuel
1910-1984 . . . . **CLC 31**
See also Lainez, Manuel Mujica
See also CA 81-84; 112; CANR 32; HW

Mukherjee, Bharati 1940- . . . . **CLC 53**
See also BEST 89:2; CA 107; CANR 45;
DAM NOV; DLB 60; MTCW

Muldoon, Paul 1951- . . . . **CLC 32, 72**
See also CA 113; 129; DAM POET;
DLB 40; INT 129

Mulisch, Harry 1927- . . . . **CLC 42**
See also CA 9-12R; CANR 6, 26

Mull, Martin 1943- . . . . **CLC 17**
See also CA 105

Mulock, Dinah Maria
See Craik, Dinah Maria (Mulock)

Munford, Robert 1737(?)-1783 . . . . **LC 5**
See also DLB 31

Mungo, Raymond 1946- . . . . **CLC 72**
See also CA 49-52; CANR 2

Munro, Alice
1931- . . . **CLC 6, 10, 19, 50; DAC; SSC 3**
See also AITN 2; CA 33-36R; CANR 33;
DAM MST, NOV; DLB 53; MTCW;
SATA 29

Munro, H(ector) H(ugh) 1870-1916
See Saki
See also CA 104; 130; CDBLB 1890-1914;
DA; DAB; DAC; DAM MST, NOV;
DLB 34, 162; MTCW; WLC

Murasaki, Lady . . . . **CMLC 1**

Murdoch, (Jean) Iris
1919- . . . . . . **CLC 1, 2, 3, 4, 6, 8, 11, 15,**
22, 31, 51; DAB; DAC
See also CA 13-16R; CANR 8, 43;
CDBLB 1960 to Present; DAM MST,
NOV; DLB 14; INT CANR-8; MTCW

Murnau, Friedrich Wilhelm
See Plumpe, Friedrich Wilhelm

Murphy, Richard 1927- . . . . **CLC 41**
See also CA 29-32R; DLB 40

Murphy, Sylvia 1937- . . . . **CLC 34**
See also CA 121

Murphy, Thomas (Bernard) 1935- . . . **CLC 51**
See also CA 101

Murray, Albert L. 1916- . . . . **CLC 73**
See also BW 2; CA 49-52; CANR 26;
DLB 38

Murray, Les(lie) A(llan) 1938- . . . . . **CLC 40**
See also CA 21-24R; CANR 11, 27;
DAM POET

Murry, J. Middleton
See Murry, John Middleton

Murry, John Middleton
1889-1957 . . . . **TCLC 16**
See also CA 118; DLB 149

Musgrave, Susan 1951- . . . . **CLC 13, 54**
See also CA 69-72; CANR 45

Musil, Robert (Edler von)
1880-1942 . . . . **TCLC 12; SSC 18**
See also CA 109; DLB 81, 124

Muske, Carol 1945- . . . . **CLC 90**
See also Muske-Dukes, Carol (Anne)

Muske-Dukes, Carol (Anne) 1945-
See Muske, Carol
See also CA 65-68; CANR 32

Musset, (Louis Charles) Alfred de
1810-1857 . . . . **NCLC 7**

My Brother's Brother
See Chekhov, Anton (Pavlovich)

Myers, L. H. 1881-1944 . . . . **TCLC 59**
See also DLB 15

Myers, Walter Dean 1937- . . . **CLC 35; BLC**
See also AAYA 4; BW 2; CA 33-36R;
CANR 20, 42; CLR 4, 16, 35;
DAM MULT, NOV; DLB 33;
INT CANR-20; JRDA; MAICYA;
SAAS 2; SATA 41, 71; SATA-Brief 27

Myers, Walter M.
See Myers, Walter Dean

Myles, Symon
See Follett, Ken(neth Martin)

Nabokov, Vladimir (Vladimirovich)
1899-1977 . . . . . **CLC 1, 2, 3, 6, 8, 11, 15,**
23, 44, 46, 64; DA; DAB; DAC; SSC 11;
WLC
See also CA 5-8R; 69-72; CANR 20;
CDALB 1941-1968; DAM MST, NOV;
DLB 2; DLBD 3; DLBY 80, 91; MTCW

Nagai Kafu . . . . **TCLC 51**
See also Nagai Sokichi

Nagai Sokichi 1879-1959
See Nagai Kafu
See also CA 117

Nagy, Laszlo 1925-1978 . . . . **CLC 7**
See also CA 129; 112

Naipaul, Shiva(dhar Srinivasa)
1945-1985 . . . . **CLC 32, 39**
See also CA 110; 112; 116; CANR 33;
DAM NOV; DLB 157; DLBY 85;
MTCW

North Staffs
 See Hulme, T(homas) E(rnest)

Norton, Alice Mary
 See Norton, Andre
 See also MAICYA; SATA 1, 43

Norton, Andre 1912- . . . . **CLC 12**
 See also Norton, Alice Mary
 See also AAYA 14; CA 1-4R; CANR 2, 31;
 DLB 8, 52; JRDA; MTCW

Norton, Caroline 1808-1877 . . . . . . **NCLC 47**
 See also DLB 21, 159

Norway, Nevil Shute 1899-1960
 See Shute, Nevil
 See also CA 102; 93-96

Norwid, Cyprian Kamil
 1821-1883 . . . . **NCLC 17**

Nosille, Nabrah
 See Ellison, Harlan (Jay)

Nossack, Hans Erich 1901-1978 . . . . . **CLC 6**
 See also CA 93-96; 85-88; DLB 69

Nostradamus 1503-1566 . . . . **LC 27**

Nosu, Chuji
 See Ozu, Yasujiro

Notenburg, Eleanora (Genrikhovna) von
 See Guro, Elena

Nova, Craig 1945- . . . . **CLC 7, 31**
 See also CA 45-48; CANR 2

Novak, Joseph
 See Kosinski, Jerzy (Nikodem)

Novalis 1772-1801 . . . . **NCLC 13**
 See also DLB 90

Nowlan, Alden (Albert)
 1933-1983 . . . . **CLC 15; DAC**
 See also CA 9-12R; CANR 5; DAM MST;
 DLB 53

Noyes, Alfred 1880-1958 . . . . **TCLC 7**
 See also CA 104; DLB 20

Nunn, Kem 19(?)- . . . . **CLC 34**

Nye, Robert 1939- . . . . **CLC 13, 42**
 See also CA 33-36R; CANR 29;
 DAM NOV; DLB 14; MTCW; SATA 6

Nyro, Laura 1947- . . . . **CLC 17**

Oates, Joyce Carol
 1938- . . . . . . **CLC 1, 2, 3, 6, 9, 11, 15, 19,
 33, 52; DA; DAB; DAC; SSC 6; WLC**
 See also AAYA 15; AITN 1; BEST 89:2;
 CA 5-8R; CANR 25, 45;
 CDALB 1968-1988; DAM MST, NOV,
 POP; DLB 2, 5, 130; DLBY 81;
 INT CANR-25; MTCW

O'Brien, Darcy 1939- . . . . **CLC 11**
 See also CA 21-24R; CANR 8

O'Brien, E. G.
 See Clarke, Arthur C(harles)

O'Brien, Edna
 1936- . . . **CLC 3, 5, 8, 13, 36, 65; SSC 10**
 See also CA 1-4R; CANR 6, 41;
 CDBLB 1960 to Present; DAM NOV;
 DLB 14; MTCW

O'Brien, Fitz-James 1828-1862 . . . **NCLC 21**
 See also DLB 74

O'Brien, Flann . . . . **CLC 1, 4, 5, 7, 10, 47**
 See also O Nuallain, Brian

O'Brien, Richard 1942- . . . . **CLC 17**
 See also CA 124

O'Brien, Tim 1946- . . . . **CLC 7, 19, 40**
 See also AAYA 16; CA 85-88; CANR 40;
 DAM POP; DLB 152; DLBD 9;
 DLBY 80

Obstfelder, Sigbjoern 1866-1900 . . . **TCLC 23**
 See also CA 123

O'Casey, Sean
 1880-1964 . . . . . . **CLC 1, 5, 9, 11, 15, 88;
 DAB; DAC**
 See also CA 89-92; CDBLB 1914-1945;
 DAM DRAM, MST; DLB 10; MTCW

O'Cathasaigh, Sean
 See O'Casey, Sean

Ochs, Phil 1940-1976 . . . . **CLC 17**
 See also CA 65-68

O'Connor, Edwin (Greene)
 1918-1968 . . . . **CLC 14**
 See also CA 93-96; 25-28R

O'Connor, (Mary) Flannery
 1925-1964 . . . . **CLC 1, 2, 3, 6, 10, 13, 15,
 21, 66; DA; DAB; DAC; SSC 1; WLC**
 See also AAYA 7; CA 1-4R; CANR 3, 41;
 CDALB 1941-1968; DAM MST, NOV;
 DLB 2, 152; DLBD 12; DLBY 80;
 MTCW

O'Connor, Frank . . . . **CLC 23; SSC 5**
 See also O'Donovan, Michael John
 See also DLB 162

O'Dell, Scott 1898-1989 . . . . **CLC 30**
 See also AAYA 3; CA 61-64; 129;
 CANR 12, 30; CLR 1, 16; DLB 52;
 JRDA; MAICYA; SATA 12, 60

Odets, Clifford
 1906-1963 . . . . **CLC 2, 28; DC 6**
 See also CA 85-88; DAM DRAM; DLB 7,
 26; MTCW

O'Doherty, Brian 1934- . . . . **CLC 76**
 See also CA 105

O'Donnell, K. M.
 See Malzberg, Barry N(athaniel)

O'Donnell, Lawrence
 See Kuttner, Henry

O'Donovan, Michael John
 1903-1966 . . . . **CLC 14**
 See also O'Connor, Frank
 See also CA 93-96

Oe, Kenzaburo
 1935- . . . . **CLC 10, 36, 86; SSC 20**
 See also CA 97-100; CANR 36, 50;
 DAM NOV; DLBY 94; MTCW

O'Faolain, Julia 1932- . . . . **CLC 6, 19, 47**
 See also CA 81-84; CAAS 2; CANR 12;
 DLB 14; MTCW

O'Faolain, Sean
 1900-1991 . . . . **CLC 1, 7, 14, 32, 70;
 SSC 13**
 See also CA 61-64; 134; CANR 12;
 DLB 15, 162; MTCW

O'Flaherty, Liam
 1896-1984 . . . . **CLC 5, 34; SSC 6**
 See also CA 101; 113; CANR 35; DLB 36,
 162; DLBY 84; MTCW

Ogilvy, Gavin
 See Barrie, J(ames) M(atthew)

O'Grady, Standish James
 1846-1928 . . . . **TCLC 5**
 See also CA 104

O'Grady, Timothy 1951- . . . . **CLC 59**
 See also CA 138

O'Hara, Frank
 1926-1966 . . . . **CLC 2, 5, 13, 78**
 See also CA 9-12R; 25-28R; CANR 33;
 DAM POET; DLB 5, 16; MTCW

O'Hara, John (Henry)
 1905-1970 . . . . **CLC 1, 2, 3, 6, 11, 42;
 SSC 15**
 See also CA 5-8R; 25-28R; CANR 31;
 CDALB 1929-1941; DAM NOV; DLB 9,
 86; DLBD 2; MTCW

O Hehir, Diana 1922- . . . . **CLC 41**
 See also CA 93-96

Okigbo, Christopher (Ifenayichukwu)
 1932-1967 . . . . . **CLC 25, 84; BLC; PC 7**
 See also BW 1; CA 77-80; DAM MULT,
 POET; DLB 125; MTCW

Okri, Ben 1959- . . . . **CLC 87**
 See also BW 2; CA 130; 138; DLB 157;
 INT 138

Olds, Sharon 1942- . . . . **CLC 32, 39, 85**
 See also CA 101; CANR 18, 41;
 DAM POET; DLB 120

Oldstyle, Jonathan
 See Irving, Washington

Olesha, Yuri (Karlovich)
 1899-1960 . . . . **CLC 8**
 See also CA 85-88

Oliphant, Laurence
 1829(?)-1888 . . . . **NCLC 47**
 See also DLB 18

Oliphant, Margaret (Oliphant Wilson)
 1828-1897 . . . . **NCLC 11**
 See also DLB 18, 159

Oliver, Mary 1935- . . . . **CLC 19, 34**
 See also CA 21-24R; CANR 9, 43; DLB 5

Olivier, Laurence (Kerr)
 1907-1989 . . . . **CLC 20**
 See also CA 111; 150; 129

Olsen, Tillie
 1913- . . . . . **CLC 4, 13; DA; DAB; DAC;
 SSC 11**
 See also CA 1-4R; CANR 1, 43;
 DAM MST; DLB 28; DLBY 80; MTCW

Olson, Charles (John)
 1910-1970 . . . . . **CLC 1, 2, 5, 6, 9, 11, 29**
 See also CA 13-16; 25-28R; CABS 2;
 CANR 35; CAP 1; DAM POET; DLB 5,
 16; MTCW

Olson, Toby 1937- . . . . **CLC 28**
 See also CA 65-68; CANR 9, 31

Olyesha, Yuri
 See Olesha, Yuri (Karlovich)

Ondaatje, (Philip) Michael
 1943- . . . **CLC 14, 29, 51, 76; DAB; DAC**
 See also CA 77-80; CANR 42; DAM MST;
 DLB 60

Oneal, Elizabeth 1934-
 See Oneal, Zibby
 See also CA 106; CANR 28; MAICYA;
 SATA 30, 82

Parson Lot
  See Kingsley, Charles

Partridge, Anthony
  See Oppenheim, E(dward) Phillips

Pascoli, Giovanni 1855-1912 ...... **TCLC 45**

Pasolini, Pier Paolo
  1922-1975 .... **CLC 20, 37**
  See also CA 93-96; 61-64; DLB 128;
  MTCW

Pasquini
  See Silone, Ignazio

Pastan, Linda (Olenik) 1932- ...... **CLC 27**
  See also CA 61-64; CANR 18, 40;
  DAM POET; DLB 5

Pasternak, Boris (Leonidovich)
  1890-1960 ...... **CLC 7, 10, 18, 63; DA;**
                   DAB; DAC; PC 6; WLC
  See also CA 127; 116; DAM MST, NOV,
  POET; MTCW

Patchen, Kenneth 1911-1972 ... **CLC 1, 2, 18**
  See also CA 1-4R; 33-36R; CANR 3, 35;
  DAM POET; DLB 16, 48; MTCW

Pater, Walter (Horatio)
  1839-1894 .... **NCLC 7**
  See also CDBLB 1832-1890; DLB 57, 156

Paterson, A(ndrew) B(arton)
  1864-1941 .... **TCLC 32**

Paterson, Katherine (Womeldorf)
  1932- .... **CLC 12, 30**
  See also AAYA 1; CA 21-24R; CANR 28;
  CLR 7; DLB 52; JRDA; MAICYA;
  MTCW; SATA 13, 53

Patmore, Coventry Kersey Dighton
  1823-1896 .... **NCLC 9**
  See also DLB 35, 98

Paton, Alan (Stewart)
  1903-1988 ...... **CLC 4, 10, 25, 55; DA;**
                   DAB; DAC; WLC
  See also CA 13-16; 125; CANR 22; CAP 1;
  DAM MST, NOV; MTCW; SATA 11;
  SATA-Obit 56

Paton Walsh, Gillian 1937-
  See Walsh, Jill Paton
  See also CANR 38; JRDA; MAICYA;
  SAAS 3; SATA 4, 72

Paulding, James Kirke 1778-1860 .. **NCLC 2**
  See also DLB 3, 59, 74

Paulin, Thomas Neilson 1949-
  See Paulin, Tom
  See also CA 123; 128

Paulin, Tom .... **CLC 37**
  See also Paulin, Thomas Neilson
  See also DLB 40

Paustovsky, Konstantin (Georgievich)
  1892-1968 .... **CLC 40**
  See also CA 93-96; 25-28R

Pavese, Cesare
  1908-1950 ..... **TCLC 3; PC 13; SSC 19**
  See also CA 104; DLB 128

Pavic, Milorad 1929- .... **CLC 60**
  See also CA 136

Payne, Alan
  See Jakes, John (William)

Paz, Gil
  See Lugones, Leopoldo

Paz, Octavio
  1914- .... **CLC 3, 4, 6, 10, 19, 51, 65;**
               DA; DAB; DAC; HLC; PC 1; WLC
  See also CA 73-76; CANR 32; DAM MST,
  MULT, POET; DLBY 90; HW; MTCW

Peacock, Molly 1947- .... **CLC 60**
  See also CA 103; CAAS 21; DLB 120

Peacock, Thomas Love
  1785-1866 .... **NCLC 22**
  See also DLB 96, 116

Peake, Mervyn 1911-1968 ...... **CLC 7, 54**
  See also CA 5-8R; 25-28R; CANR 3;
  DLB 15, 160; MTCW; SATA 23

Pearce, Philippa .... **CLC 21**
  See also Christie, (Ann) Philippa
  See also CLR 9; DLB 161; MAICYA;
  SATA 1, 67

Pearl, Eric
  See Elman, Richard

Pearson, T(homas) R(eid) 1956- .... **CLC 39**
  See also CA 120; 130; INT 130

Peck, Dale 1967- .... **CLC 81**
  See also CA 146

Peck, John 1941- .... **CLC 3**
  See also CA 49-52; CANR 3

Peck, Richard (Wayne) 1934- ...... **CLC 21**
  See also AAYA 1; CA 85-88; CANR 19,
  38; CLR 15; INT CANR-19; JRDA;
  MAICYA; SAAS 2; SATA 18, 55

Peck, Robert Newton
  1928- .... **CLC 17; DA; DAC**
  See also AAYA 3; CA 81-84; CANR 31;
  DAM MST; JRDA; MAICYA; SAAS 1;
  SATA 21, 62

Peckinpah, (David) Sam(uel)
  1925-1984 .... **CLC 20**
  See also CA 109; 114

Pedersen, Knut 1859-1952
  See Hamsun, Knut
  See also CA 104; 119; MTCW

Peeslake, Gaffer
  See Durrell, Lawrence (George)

Peguy, Charles Pierre
  1873-1914 .... **TCLC 10**
  See also CA 107

Pena, Ramon del Valle y
  See Valle-Inclan, Ramon (Maria) del

Pendennis, Arthur Esquir
  See Thackeray, William Makepeace

Penn, William 1644-1718 .... **LC 25**
  See also DLB 24

Pepys, Samuel
  1633-1703 ..... **LC 11; DA; DAB; DAC;**
                  WLC
  See also CDBLB 1660-1789; DAM MST;
  DLB 101

Percy, Walker
  1916-1990 .... **CLC 2, 3, 6, 8, 14, 18, 47,**
                 65
  See also CA 1-4R; 131; CANR 1, 23;
  DAM NOV, POP; DLB 2; DLBY 80, 90;
  MTCW

Perec, Georges 1936-1982 .... **CLC 56**
  See also CA 141; DLB 83

Pereda (y Sanchez de Porrua), Jose Maria de
  1833-1906 .... **TCLC 16**
  See also CA 117

Pereda y Porrua, Jose Maria de
  See Pereda (y Sanchez de Porrua), Jose
  Maria de

Peregoy, George Weems
  See Mencken, H(enry) L(ouis)

Perelman, S(idney) J(oseph)
  1904-1979 ... **CLC 3, 5, 9, 15, 23, 44, 49**
  See also AITN 1, 2; CA 73-76; 89-92;
  CANR 18; DAM DRAM; DLB 11, 44;
  MTCW

Peret, Benjamin 1899-1959 .... **TCLC 20**
  See also CA 117

Peretz, Isaac Loeb 1851(?)-1915 ... **TCLC 16**
  See also CA 109

Peretz, Yitzkhok Leibush
  See Peretz, Isaac Loeb

Perez Galdos, Benito 1843-1920 ... **TCLC 27**
  See also CA 125; HW

Perrault, Charles 1628-1703 .... **LC 2**
  See also MAICYA; SATA 25

Perry, Brighton
  See Sherwood, Robert E(mmet)

Perse, St.-John .... **CLC 4, 11, 46**
  See also Leger, (Marie-Rene Auguste) Alexis
  Saint-Leger

Perutz, Leo 1882-1957 .... **TCLC 60**
  See also DLB 81

Peseenz, Tulio F.
  See Lopez y Fuentes, Gregorio

Pesetsky, Bette 1932- .... **CLC 28**
  See also CA 133; DLB 130

Peshkov, Alexei Maximovich 1868-1936
  See Gorky, Maxim
  See also CA 105; 141; DA; DAC;
  DAM DRAM, MST, NOV

Pessoa, Fernando (Antonio Nogueira)
  1888-1935 .... **TCLC 27; HLC**
  See also CA 125

Peterkin, Julia Mood 1880-1961 .... **CLC 31**
  See also CA 102; DLB 9

Peters, Joan K. 1945- .... **CLC 39**

Peters, Robert L(ouis) 1924- .... **CLC 7**
  See also CA 13-16R; CAAS 8; DLB 105

Petofi, Sandor 1823-1849 .... **NCLC 21**

Petrakis, Harry Mark 1923- .... **CLC 3**
  See also CA 9-12R; CANR 4, 30

Petrarch 1304-1374 .... **PC 8**
  See also DAM POET

Petrov, Evgeny .... **TCLC 21**
  See also Kataev, Evgeny Petrovich

Petry, Ann (Lane) 1908- ...... **CLC 1, 7, 18**
  See also BW 1; CA 5-8R; CAAS 6;
  CANR 4, 46; CLR 12; DLB 76; JRDA;
  MAICYA; MTCW; SATA 5

Petursson, Halligrimur 1614-1674 .... **LC 8**

Philips, Katherine 1632-1664 .... **LC 30**
  See also DLB 131

Philipson, Morris H. 1926- .... **CLC 53**
  See also CA 1-4R; CANR 4

Phillips, David Graham
1867-1911 . . . . **TCLC 44**
See also CA 108; DLB 9, 12

Phillips, Jack
See Sandburg, Carl (August)

Phillips, Jayne Anne
1952- . . . . **CLC 15, 33; SSC 16**
See also CA 101; CANR 24, 50; DLBY 80;
INT CANR-24; MTCW

Phillips, Richard
See Dick, Philip K(indred)

Phillips, Robert (Schaeffer) 1938-... **CLC 28**
See also CA 17-20R; CAAS 13; CANR 8;
DLB 105

Phillips, Ward
See Lovecraft, H(oward) P(hillips)

Piccolo, Lucio 1901-1969 . . . . **CLC 13**
See also CA 97-100; DLB 114

Pickthall, Marjorie L(owry) C(hristie)
1883-1922 . . . . **TCLC 21**
See also CA 107; DLB 92

Pico della Mirandola, Giovanni
1463-1494 . . . . **LC 15**

Piercy, Marge
1936- . . . . **CLC 3, 6, 14, 18, 27, 62**
See also CA 21-24R; CAAS 1; CANR 13,
43; DLB 120; MTCW

Piers, Robert
See Anthony, Piers

Pieyre de Mandiargues, Andre 1909-1991
See Mandiargues, Andre Pieyre de
See also CA 103; 136; CANR 22

Pilnyak, Boris . . . . **TCLC 23**
See also Vogau, Boris Andreyevich

Pincherle, Alberto 1907-1990 . . . **CLC 11, 18**
See also Moravia, Alberto
See also CA 25-28R; 132; CANR 33;
DAM NOV; MTCW

Pinckney, Darryl 1953- . . . . **CLC 76**
See also BW 2; CA 143

Pindar 518B.C.-446B.C. . . . . **CMLC 12**

Pineda, Cecile 1942- . . . . **CLC 39**
See also CA 118

Pinero, Arthur Wing 1855-1934 . . . **TCLC 32**
See also CA 110; DAM DRAM; DLB 10

Pinero, Miguel (Antonio Gomez)
1946-1988 . . . . **CLC 4, 55**
See also CA 61-64; 125; CANR 29; HW

Pinget, Robert 1919- . . . . **CLC 7, 13, 37**
See also CA 85-88; DLB 83

Pink Floyd
See Barrett, (Roger) Syd; Gilmour, David;
Mason, Nick; Waters, Roger; Wright,
Rick

Pinkney, Edward 1802-1828 . . . . . **NCLC 31**

Pinkwater, Daniel Manus 1941- . . . . **CLC 35**
See also Pinkwater, Manus
See also AAYA 1; CA 29-32R; CANR 12,
38; CLR 4; JRDA; MAICYA; SAAS 3;
SATA 46, 76

Pinkwater, Manus
See Pinkwater, Daniel Manus
See also SATA 8

Pinsky, Robert 1940- . . . . . **CLC 9, 19, 38, 91**
See also CA 29-32R; CAAS 4;
DAM POET; DLBY 82

Pinta, Harold
See Pinter, Harold

Pinter, Harold
1930- . . . . . **CLC 1, 3, 6, 9, 11, 15, 27, 58,
73; DA; DAB; DAC; WLC**
See also CA 5-8R; CANR 33; CDBLB 1960
to Present; DAM DRAM, MST; DLB 13;
MTCW

Pirandello, Luigi
1867-1936 . . . . . . **TCLC 4, 29; DA; DAB;
DAC; DC 5; WLC**
See also CA 104; DAM DRAM, MST

Pirsig, Robert M(aynard)
1928- . . . . **CLC 4, 6, 73**
See also CA 53-56; CANR 42; DAM POP;
MTCW; SATA 39

Pisarev, Dmitry Ivanovich
1840-1868 . . . . **NCLC 25**

Pix, Mary (Griffith) 1666-1709 . . . . . . **LC 8**
See also DLB 80

Pixerecourt, Guilbert de
1773-1844 . . . . **NCLC 39**

Plaidy, Jean
See Hibbert, Eleanor Alice Burford

Planche, James Robinson
1796-1880 . . . . **NCLC 42**

Plant, Robert 1948- . . . . **CLC 12**

Plante, David (Robert)
1940- . . . . **CLC 7, 23, 38**
See also CA 37-40R; CANR 12, 36;
DAM NOV; DLBY 83; INT CANR-12;
MTCW

Plath, Sylvia
1932-1963 . . . . . **CLC 1, 2, 3, 5, 9, 11, 14,
17, 50, 51, 62; DA; DAB; DAC; PC 1;
WLC**
See also AAYA 13; CA 19-20; CANR 34;
CAP 2; CDALB 1941-1968; DAM MST,
POET; DLB 5, 6, 152; MTCW

Plato
428(?)B.C.-348(?)B.C. . . . . **CMLC 8; DA;
DAB; DAC**
See also DAM MST

Platonov, Andrei . . . . **TCLC 14**
See also Klimentov, Andrei Platonovich

Platt, Kin 1911- . . . . **CLC 26**
See also AAYA 11; CA 17-20R; CANR 11;
JRDA; SAAS 17; SATA 21, 86

Plautus c. 251B.C.-184B.C. . . . . **DC 6**

Plick et Plock
See Simenon, Georges (Jacques Christian)

Plimpton, George (Ames) 1927- . . . . . **CLC 36**
See also AITN 1; CA 21-24R; CANR 32;
MTCW; SATA 10

Plomer, William Charles Franklin
1903-1973 . . . . **CLC 4, 8**
See also CA 21-22; CANR 34; CAP 2;
DLB 20, 162; MTCW; SATA 24

Plowman, Piers
See Kavanagh, Patrick (Joseph)

Plum, J.
See Wodehouse, P(elham) G(renville)

Plumly, Stanley (Ross) 1939- . . . . . . **CLC 33**
See also CA 108; 110; DLB 5; INT 110

Plumpe, Friedrich Wilhelm
1888-1931 . . . . **TCLC 53**
See also CA 112

Poe, Edgar Allan
1809-1849 . . . . **NCLC 1, 16, 55; DA;
DAB; DAC; PC 1; SSC 1; WLC**
See also AAYA 14; CDALB 1640-1865;
DAM MST, POET; DLB 3, 59, 73, 74;
SATA 23

Poet of Titchfield Street, The
See Pound, Ezra (Weston Loomis)

Pohl, Frederik 1919- . . . . **CLC 18**
See also CA 61-64; CAAS 1; CANR 11, 37;
DLB 8; INT CANR-11; MTCW;
SATA 24

Poirier, Louis 1910-
See Gracq, Julien
See also CA 122; 126

Poitier, Sidney 1927- . . . . **CLC 26**
See also BW 1; CA 117

Polanski, Roman 1933- . . . . **CLC 16**
See also CA 77-80

Poliakoff, Stephen 1952- . . . . **CLC 38**
See also CA 106; DLB 13

Police, The
See Copeland, Stewart (Armstrong);
Summers, Andrew James; Sumner,
Gordon Matthew

Polidori, John William
1795-1821 . . . . **NCLC 51**
See also DLB 116

Pollitt, Katha 1949- . . . . **CLC 28**
See also CA 120; 122; MTCW

Pollock, (Mary) Sharon
1936- . . . . **CLC 50; DAC**
See also CA 141; DAM DRAM, MST;
DLB 60

Polo, Marco 1254-1324 . . . . **CMLC 15**

Polonsky, Abraham (Lincoln)
1910- . . . . **CLC 92**
See also CA 104; DLB 26; INT 104

Polybius c. 200B.C.-c. 118B.C. . . . . **CMLC 17**

Pomerance, Bernard 1940- . . . . **CLC 13**
See also CA 101; CANR 49; DAM DRAM

Ponge, Francis (Jean Gaston Alfred)
1899-1988 . . . . **CLC 6, 18**
See also CA 85-88; 126; CANR 40;
DAM POET

Pontoppidan, Henrik 1857-1943 . . . **TCLC 29**

Poole, Josephine . . . . **CLC 17**
See also Helyar, Jane Penelope Josephine
See also SAAS 2; SATA 5

Popa, Vasko 1922-1991 . . . . **CLC 19**
See also CA 112; 148

Pope, Alexander
1688-1744 . . . . . . **LC 3; DA; DAB; DAC;
WLC**
See also CDBLB 1660-1789; DAM MST,
POET; DLB 95, 101

Porter, Connie (Rose) 1959(?)- . . . . . **CLC 70**
See also BW 2; CA 142; SATA 81

Porter, Gene(va Grace) Stratton
1863(?)-1924 . . . . TCLC 21
See also CA 112

Porter, Katherine Anne
1890-1980 . . . . . . CLC 1, 3, 7, 10, 13, 15,
27; DA; DAB; DAC; SSC 4
See also AITN 2; CA 1-4R; 101; CANR 1;
DAM MST, NOV; DLB 4, 9, 102;
DLBD 12; DLBY 80; MTCW; SATA 39;
SATA-Obit 23

Porter, Peter (Neville Frederick)
1929- . . . . CLC 5, 13, 33
See also CA 85-88; DLB 40

Porter, William Sydney 1862-1910
See Henry, O.
See also CA 104; 131; CDALB 1865-1917;
DA; DAB; DAC; DAM MST; DLB 12,
78, 79; MTCW; YABC 2

Portillo (y Pacheco), Jose Lopez
See Lopez Portillo (y Pacheco), Jose

Post, Melville Davisson
1869-1930 . . . . TCLC 39
See also CA 110

Potok, Chaim 1929- . . . . CLC 2, 7, 14, 26
See also AAYA 15; AITN 1, 2; CA 17-20R;
CANR 19, 35; DAM NOV; DLB 28, 152;
INT CANR-19; MTCW; SATA 33

Potter, Beatrice
See Webb, (Martha) Beatrice (Potter)
See also MAICYA

Potter, Dennis (Christopher George)
1935-1994 . . . . CLC 58, 86
See also CA 107; 145; CANR 33; MTCW

Pound, Ezra (Weston Loomis)
1885-1972 . . . . . . CLC 1, 2, 3, 4, 5, 7, 10,
13, 18, 34, 48, 50; DA; DAB; DAC; PC 4;
WLC
See also CA 5-8R; 37-40R; CANR 40;
CDALB 1917-1929; DAM MST, POET;
DLB 4, 45, 63; MTCW

Povod, Reinaldo 1959-1994 . . . . CLC 44
See also CA 136; 146

Powell, Adam Clayton, Jr.
1908-1972 . . . . CLC 89; BLC
See also BW 1; CA 102; 33-36R;
DAM MULT

Powell, Anthony (Dymoke)
1905- . . . . CLC 1, 3, 7, 9, 10, 31
See also CA 1-4R; CANR 1, 32;
CDBLB 1945-1960; DLB 15; MTCW

Powell, Dawn 1897-1965 . . . . CLC 66
See also CA 5-8R

Powell, Padgett 1952- . . . . CLC 34
See also CA 126

Power, Susan . . . . CLC 91

Powers, J(ames) F(arl)
1917- . . . . CLC 1, 4, 8, 57; SSC 4
See also CA 1-4R; CANR 2; DLB 130;
MTCW

Powers, John J(ames) 1945-
See Powers, John R.
See also CA 69-72

Powers, John R. . . . . CLC 66
See also Powers, John J(ames)

Pownall, David 1938- . . . . CLC 10
See also CA 89-92; CAAS 18; CANR 49;
DLB 14

Powys, John Cowper
1872-1963 . . . . CLC 7, 9, 15, 46
See also CA 85-88; DLB 15; MTCW

Powys, T(heodore) F(rancis)
1875-1953 . . . . TCLC 9
See also CA 106; DLB 36, 162

Prager, Emily 1952- . . . . CLC 56

Pratt, E(dwin) J(ohn)
1883(?)-1964 . . . . CLC 19; DAC
See also CA 141; 93-96; DAM POET;
DLB 92

Premchand . . . . TCLC 21
See also Srivastava, Dhanpat Rai

Preussler, Otfried 1923- . . . . CLC 17
See also CA 77-80; SATA 24

Prevert, Jacques (Henri Marie)
1900-1977 . . . . CLC 15
See also CA 77-80; 69-72; CANR 29;
MTCW; SATA-Obit 30

Prevost, Abbe (Antoine Francois)
1697-1763 . . . . LC 1

Price, (Edward) Reynolds
1933- . . . . CLC 3, 6, 13, 43, 50, 63
See also CA 1-4R; CANR 1, 37;
DAM NOV; DLB 2; INT CANR-37

Price, Richard 1949- . . . . CLC 6, 12
See also CA 49-52; CANR 3; DLBY 81

Prichard, Katharine Susannah
1883-1969 . . . . CLC 46
See also CA 11-12; CANR 33; CAP 1;
MTCW; SATA 66

Priestley, J(ohn) B(oynton)
1894-1984 . . . . CLC 2, 5, 9, 34
See also CA 9-12R; 113; CANR 33;
CDBLB 1914-1945; DAM DRAM, NOV;
DLB 10, 34, 77, 100, 139; DLBY 84;
MTCW

Prince 1958(?)- . . . . CLC 35

Prince, F(rank) T(empleton) 1912- . . CLC 22
See also CA 101; CANR 43; DLB 20

Prince Kropotkin
See Kropotkin, Peter (Aleksieevich)

Prior, Matthew 1664-1721 . . . . LC 4
See also DLB 95

Pritchard, William H(arrison)
1932- . . . . CLC 34
See also CA 65-68; CANR 23; DLB 111

Pritchett, V(ictor) S(awdon)
1900- . . . . CLC 5, 13, 15, 41; SSC 14
See also CA 61-64; CANR 31; DAM NOV;
DLB 15, 139; MTCW

Private 19022
See Manning, Frederic

Probst, Mark 1925- . . . . CLC 59
See also CA 130

Prokosch, Frederic 1908-1989 . . . . CLC 4, 48
See also CA 73-76; 128; DLB 48

Prophet, The
See Dreiser, Theodore (Herman Albert)

Prose, Francine 1947- . . . . CLC 45
See also CA 109; 112; CANR 46

Proudhon
See Cunha, Euclides (Rodrigues Pimenta) da

Proulx, E. Annie 1935- . . . . CLC 81

Proust, (Valentin-Louis-George-Eugene-)
Marcel
1871-1922 . . . . TCLC 7, 13, 33; DA;
DAB; DAC; WLC
See also CA 104; 120; DAM MST, NOV;
DLB 65; MTCW

Prowler, Harley
See Masters, Edgar Lee

Prus, Boleslaw 1845-1912 . . . . TCLC 48

Pryor, Richard (Franklin Lenox Thomas)
1940- . . . . CLC 26
See also CA 122

Przybyszewski, Stanislaw
1868-1927 . . . . TCLC 36
See also DLB 66

Pteleon
See Grieve, C(hristopher) M(urray)
See also DAM POET

Puckett, Lute
See Masters, Edgar Lee

Puig, Manuel
1932-1990 . . . CLC 3, 5, 10, 28, 65; HLC
See also CA 45-48; CANR 2, 32;
DAM MULT; DLB 113; HW; MTCW

Purdy, Al(fred Wellington)
1918- . . . . CLC 3, 6, 14, 50; DAC
See also CA 81-84; CAAS 17; CANR 42;
DAM MST, POET; DLB 88

Purdy, James (Amos)
1923- . . . . CLC 2, 4, 10, 28, 52
See also CA 33-36R; CAAS 1; CANR 19,
51; DLB 2; INT CANR-19; MTCW

Pure, Simon
See Swinnerton, Frank Arthur

Pushkin, Alexander (Sergeyevich)
1799-1837 . . . . . NCLC 3, 27; DA; DAB;
DAC; PC 10; WLC
See also DAM DRAM, MST, POET;
SATA 61

P'u Sung-ling 1640-1715 . . . . LC 3

Putnam, Arthur Lee
See Alger, Horatio, Jr.

Puzo, Mario 1920- . . . . CLC 1, 2, 6, 36
See also CA 65-68; CANR 4, 42;
DAM NOV, POP; DLB 6; MTCW

Pym, Barbara (Mary Crampton)
1913-1980 . . . . CLC 13, 19, 37
See also CA 13-14; 97-100; CANR 13, 34;
CAP 1; DLB 14; DLBY 87; MTCW

Pynchon, Thomas (Ruggles, Jr.)
1937- . . . . . CLC 2, 3, 6, 9, 11, 18, 33, 62,
72; DA; DAB; DAC; SSC 14; WLC
See also BEST 90:2; CA 17-20R; CANR 22,
46; DAM MST, NOV, POP; DLB 2;
MTCW

Qian Zhongshu
See Ch'ien Chung-shu

Qroll
See Dagerman, Stig (Halvard)

Quarrington, Paul (Lewis) 1953- . . . . CLC 65
See also CA 129

Quasimodo, Salvatore 1901-1968 . . . **CLC 10**
See also CA 13-16; 25-28R; CAP 1;
DLB 114; MTCW

Queen, Ellery. . . . . **CLC 3, 11**
See also Dannay, Frederic; Davidson,
Avram; Lee, Manfred B(ennington);
Sturgeon, Theodore (Hamilton); Vance,
John Holbrook

Queen, Ellery, Jr.
See Dannay, Frederic; Lee, Manfred
B(ennington)

Queneau, Raymond
1903-1976 . . . . **CLC 2, 5, 10, 42**
See also CA 77-80; 69-72; CANR 32;
DLB 72; MTCW

Quevedo, Francisco de 1580-1645 . . . . **LC 23**

Quiller-Couch, Arthur Thomas
1863-1944 . . . . **TCLC 53**
See also CA 118; DLB 135, 153

Quin, Ann (Marie) 1936-1973 . . . . . . **CLC 6**
See also CA 9-12R; 45-48; DLB 14

Quinn, Martin
See Smith, Martin Cruz

Quinn, Peter 1947- . . . . **CLC 91**

Quinn, Simon
See Smith, Martin Cruz

Quiroga, Horacio (Sylvestre)
1878-1937 . . . . **TCLC 20; HLC**
See also CA 117; 131; DAM MULT; HW;
MTCW

Quoirez, Francoise 1935- . . . . **CLC 9**
See also Sagan, Francoise
See also CA 49-52; CANR 6, 39; MTCW

Raabe, Wilhelm 1831-1910 . . . . **TCLC 45**
See also DLB 129

Rabe, David (William) 1940- . . . **CLC 4, 8, 33**
See also CA 85-88; CABS 3; DAM DRAM;
DLB 7

Rabelais, Francois
1483-1553 . . . . . . **LC 5; DA; DAB; DAC;**
WLC
See also DAM MST

Rabinovitch, Sholem 1859-1916
See Aleichem, Sholom
See also CA 104

Racine, Jean 1639-1699 . . . . . . **LC 28; DAB**
See also DAM MST

Radcliffe, Ann (Ward)
1764-1823 . . . . **NCLC 6, 55**
See also DLB 39

Radiguet, Raymond 1903-1923 . . . . **TCLC 29**
See also DLB 65

Radnoti, Miklos 1909-1944 . . . . . . **TCLC 16**
See also CA 118

Rado, James 1939- . . . . **CLC 17**
See also CA 105

Radvanyi, Netty 1900-1983
See Seghers, Anna
See also CA 85-88; 110

Rae, Ben
See Griffiths, Trevor

Raeburn, John (Hay) 1941- . . . . **CLC 34**
See also CA 57-60

Ragni, Gerome 1942-1991 . . . . **CLC 17**
See also CA 105; 134

Rahv, Philip 1908-1973 . . . . **CLC 24**
See also Greenberg, Ivan
See also DLB 137

Raine, Craig 1944- . . . . **CLC 32**
See also CA 108; CANR 29, 51; DLB 40

Raine, Kathleen (Jessie) 1908- . . . **CLC 7, 45**
See also CA 85-88; CANR 46; DLB 20;
MTCW

Rainis, Janis 1865-1929 . . . . **TCLC 29**

Rakosi, Carl. . . . . **CLC 47**
See also Rawley, Callman
See also CAAS 5

Raleigh, Richard
See Lovecraft, H(oward) P(hillips)

Raleigh, Sir Walter 1554(?)-1618 . . . . **LC 31**
See also CDBLB Before 1660

Rallentando, H. P.
See Sayers, Dorothy L(eigh)

Ramal, Walter
See de la Mare, Walter (John)

Ramon, Juan
See Jimenez (Mantecon), Juan Ramon

Ramos, Graciliano 1892-1953 . . . . . **TCLC 32**

Rampersad, Arnold 1941- . . . . **CLC 44**
See also BW 2; CA 127; 133; DLB 111;
INT 133

Rampling, Anne
See Rice, Anne

Ramsay, Allan 1684(?)-1758 . . . . **LC 29**
See also DLB 95

Ramuz, Charles-Ferdinand
1878-1947 . . . . **TCLC 33**

Rand, Ayn
1905-1982 . . . . . . **CLC 3, 30, 44, 79; DA;**
DAC; WLC
See also AAYA 10; CA 13-16R; 105;
CANR 27; DAM MST, NOV, POP;
MTCW

Randall, Dudley (Felker)
1914- . . . . **CLC 1; BLC**
See also BW 1; CA 25-28R; CANR 23;
DAM MULT; DLB 41

Randall, Robert
See Silverberg, Robert

Ranger, Ken
See Creasey, John

Ransom, John Crowe
1888-1974 . . . . **CLC 2, 4, 5, 11, 24**
See also CA 5-8R; 49-52; CANR 6, 34;
DAM POET; DLB 45, 63; MTCW

Rao, Raja 1909- . . . . **CLC 25, 56**
See also CA 73-76; CANR 51; DAM NOV;
MTCW

Raphael, Frederic (Michael)
1931- . . . . **CLC 2, 14**
See also CA 1-4R; CANR 1; DLB 14

Ratcliffe, James P.
See Mencken, H(enry) L(ouis)

Rathbone, Julian 1935- . . . . **CLC 41**
See also CA 101; CANR 34

Rattigan, Terence (Mervyn)
1911-1977 . . . . **CLC 7**
See also CA 85-88; 73-76;
CDBLB 1945-1960; DAM DRAM;
DLB 13; MTCW

Ratushinskaya, Irina 1954- . . . . **CLC 54**
See also CA 129

Raven, Simon (Arthur Noel)
1927- . . . . **CLC 14**
See also CA 81-84

Rawley, Callman 1903-
See Rakosi, Carl
See also CA 21-24R; CANR 12, 32

Rawlings, Marjorie Kinnan
1896-1953 . . . . **TCLC 4**
See also CA 104; 137; DLB 9, 22, 102;
JRDA; MAICYA; YABC 1

Ray, Satyajit 1921-1992 . . . . **CLC 16, 76**
See also CA 114; 137; DAM MULT

Read, Herbert Edward 1893-1968 . . . . **CLC 4**
See also CA 85-88; 25-28R; DLB 20, 149

Read, Piers Paul 1941- . . . . . . **CLC 4, 10, 25**
See also CA 21-24R; CANR 38; DLB 14;
SATA 21

Reade, Charles 1814-1884 . . . . **NCLC 2**
See also DLB 21

Reade, Hamish
See Gray, Simon (James Holliday)

Reading, Peter 1946- . . . . **CLC 47**
See also CA 103; CANR 46; DLB 40

Reaney, James 1926- . . . . **CLC 13; DAC**
See also CA 41-44R; CAAS 15; CANR 42;
DAM MST; DLB 68; SATA 43

Rebreanu, Liviu 1885-1944 . . . . **TCLC 28**

Rechy, John (Francisco)
1934- . . . . **CLC 1, 7, 14, 18; HLC**
See also CA 5-8R; CAAS 4; CANR 6, 32;
DAM MULT; DLB 122; DLBY 82; HW;
INT CANR-6

Redcam, Tom 1870-1933 . . . . **TCLC 25**

Reddin, Keith. . . . . **CLC 67**

Redgrove, Peter (William)
1932- . . . . **CLC 6, 41**
See also CA 1-4R; CANR 3, 39; DLB 40

Redmon, Anne. . . . . **CLC 22**
See also Nightingale, Anne Redmon
See also DLBY 86

Reed, Eliot
See Ambler, Eric

Reed, Ishmael
1938- . . . **CLC 2, 3, 5, 6, 13, 32, 60; BLC**
See also BW 2; CA 21-24R; CANR 25, 48;
DAM MULT; DLB 2, 5, 33; DLBD 8;
MTCW

Reed, John (Silas) 1887-1920 . . . . . . **TCLC 9**
See also CA 106

Reed, Lou. . . . . **CLC 21**
See also Firbank, Louis

Reeve, Clara 1729-1807 . . . . **NCLC 19**
See also DLB 39

Reich, Wilhelm 1897-1957 . . . . **TCLC 57**

Reid, Christopher (John) 1949- . . . . . **CLC 33**
See also CA 140; DLB 40

Reid, Desmond
See Moorcock, Michael (John)

Reid Banks, Lynne   1929-
See Banks, Lynne Reid
See also CA 1-4R; CANR 6, 22, 38;
CLR 24; JRDA; MAICYA; SATA 22, 75

Reilly, William K.
See Creasey, John

Reiner, Max
See Caldwell, (Janet Miriam) Taylor
(Holland)

Reis, Ricardo
See Pessoa, Fernando (Antonio Nogueira)

Remarque, Erich Maria
1898-1970 . . . . **CLC 21; DA; DAB; DAC**
See also CA 77-80; 29-32R; DAM MST,
NOV; DLB 56; MTCW

Remizov, A.
See Remizov, Aleksei (Mikhailovich)

Remizov, A. M.
See Remizov, Aleksei (Mikhailovich)

Remizov, Aleksei (Mikhailovich)
1877-1957 . . . . **TCLC 27**
See also CA 125; 133

Renan, Joseph Ernest
1823-1892 . . . . **NCLC 26**

Renard, Jules   1864-1910 . . . . **TCLC 17**
See also CA 117

Renault, Mary . . . . **CLC 3, 11, 17**
See also Challans, Mary
See also DLBY 83

Rendell, Ruth (Barbara)   1930- . . **CLC 28, 48**
See also Vine, Barbara
See also CA 109; CANR 32; DAM POP;
DLB 87; INT CANR-32; MTCW

Renoir, Jean   1894-1979 . . . . **CLC 20**
See also CA 129; 85-88

Resnais, Alain   1922- . . . . **CLC 16**

Reverdy, Pierre   1889-1960 . . . . **CLC 53**
See also CA 97-100; 89-92

Rexroth, Kenneth
1905-1982 . . . . . . **CLC 1, 2, 6, 11, 22, 49**
See also CA 5-8R; 107; CANR 14, 34;
CDALB 1941-1968; DAM POET;
DLB 16, 48; DLBY 82; INT CANR-14;
MTCW

Reyes, Alfonso   1889-1959 . . . . **TCLC 33**
See also CA 131; HW

Reyes y Basoalto, Ricardo Eliecer Neftali
See Neruda, Pablo

Reymont, Wladyslaw (Stanislaw)
1868(?)-1925 . . . . **TCLC 5**
See also CA 104

Reynolds, Jonathan   1942- . . . . **CLC 6, 38**
See also CA 65-68; CANR 28

Reynolds, Joshua   1723-1792 . . . . **LC 15**
See also DLB 104

Reynolds, Michael Shane   1937- . . . . **CLC 44**
See also CA 65-68; CANR 9

Reznikoff, Charles   1894-1976 . . . . **CLC 9**
See also CA 33-36; 61-64; CAP 2; DLB 28,
45

Rezzori (d'Arezzo), Gregor von
1914- . . . . **CLC 25**
See also CA 122; 136

Rhine, Richard
See Silverstein, Alvin

Rhodes, Eugene Manlove
1869-1934 . . . . **TCLC 53**

R'hoone
See Balzac, Honore de

Rhys, Jean
1890(?)-1979 . . . . **CLC 2, 4, 6, 14, 19, 51;**
SSC 21
See also CA 25-28R; 85-88; CANR 35;
CDBLB 1945-1960; DAM NOV; DLB 36,
117, 162; MTCW

Ribeiro, Darcy   1922- . . . . **CLC 34**
See also CA 33-36R

Ribeiro, Joao Ubaldo (Osorio Pimentel)
1941- . . . . **CLC 10, 67**
See also CA 81-84

Ribman, Ronald (Burt)   1932- . . . . **CLC 7**
See also CA 21-24R; CANR 46

Ricci, Nino   1959- . . . . **CLC 70**
See also CA 137

Rice, Anne   1941- . . . . **CLC 41**
See also AAYA 9; BEST 89:2; CA 65-68;
CANR 12, 36; DAM POP

Rice, Elmer (Leopold)
1892-1967 . . . . **CLC 7, 49**
See also CA 21-22; 25-28R; CAP 2;
DAM DRAM; DLB 4, 7; MTCW

Rice, Tim(othy Miles Bindon)
1944- . . . . **CLC 21**
See also CA 103; CANR 46

Rich, Adrienne (Cecile)
1929- . . . . **CLC 3, 6, 7, 11, 18, 36, 73, 76;**
PC 5
See also CA 9-12R; CANR 20;
DAM POET; DLB 5, 67; MTCW

Rich, Barbara
See Graves, Robert (von Ranke)

Rich, Robert
See Trumbo, Dalton

Richard, Keith . . . . **CLC 17**
See also Richards, Keith

Richards, David Adams
1950- . . . . **CLC 59; DAC**
See also CA 93-96; DLB 53

Richards, I(vor) A(rmstrong)
1893-1979 . . . . **CLC 14, 24**
See also CA 41-44R; 89-92; CANR 34;
DLB 27

Richards, Keith   1943-
See Richard, Keith
See also CA 107

Richardson, Anne
See Roiphe, Anne (Richardson)

Richardson, Dorothy Miller
1873-1957 . . . . **TCLC 3**
See also CA 104; DLB 36

Richardson, Ethel Florence (Lindesay)
1870-1946
See Richardson, Henry Handel
See also CA 105

Richardson, Henry Handel . . . . **TCLC 4**
See also Richardson, Ethel Florence
(Lindesay)

Richardson, John
1796-1852 . . . . **NCLC 55; DAC**
See also CA 140; DLB 99

Richardson, Samuel
1689-1761 . . . . . . **LC 1; DA; DAB; DAC;**
WLC
See also CDBLB 1660-1789; DAM MST,
NOV; DLB 39

Richler, Mordecai
1931- . . . . **CLC 3, 5, 9, 13, 18, 46, 70;**
DAC
See also AITN 1; CA 65-68; CANR 31;
CLR 17; DAM MST, NOV; DLB 53;
MAICYA; MTCW; SATA 44;
SATA-Brief 27

Richter, Conrad (Michael)
1890-1968 . . . . **CLC 30**
See also CA 5-8R; 25-28R; CANR 23;
DLB 9; MTCW; SATA 3

Ricostranza, Tom
See Ellis, Trey

Riddell, J. H.   1832-1906 . . . . **TCLC 40**

Riding, Laura . . . . **CLC 3, 7**
See also Jackson, Laura (Riding)

Riefenstahl, Berta Helene Amalia   1902-
See Riefenstahl, Leni
See also CA 108

Riefenstahl, Leni . . . . **CLC 16**
See also Riefenstahl, Berta Helene Amalia

Riffe, Ernest
See Bergman, (Ernst) Ingmar

Riggs, (Rolla) Lynn   1899-1954 . . . . **TCLC 56**
See also CA 144; DAM MULT; NNAL

Riley, James Whitcomb
1849-1916 . . . . **TCLC 51**
See also CA 118; 137; DAM POET;
MAICYA; SATA 17

Riley, Tex
See Creasey, John

Rilke, Rainer Maria
1875-1926 . . . . **TCLC 1, 6, 19; PC 2**
See also CA 104; 132; DAM POET;
DLB 81; MTCW

Rimbaud, (Jean Nicolas) Arthur
1854-1891 . . . . . **NCLC 4, 35; DA; DAB;**
DAC; PC 3; WLC
See also DAM MST, POET

Rinehart, Mary Roberts
1876-1958 . . . . **TCLC 52**
See also CA 108

Ringmaster, The
See Mencken, H(enry) L(ouis)

Ringwood, Gwen(dolyn Margaret) Pharis
1910-1984 . . . . **CLC 48**
See also CA 148; 112; DLB 88

Rio, Michel   19(?)- . . . . **CLC 43**

Ritsos, Giannes
See Ritsos, Yannis

Ritsos, Yannis   1909-1990 . . . . . **CLC 6, 13, 31**
See also CA 77-80; 133; CANR 39; MTCW

Ritter, Erika   1948(?)- . . . . **CLC 52**

Rostand, Edmond (Eugene Alexis)
1868-1918 ..... **TCLC 6, 37; DA; DAB; DAC**
See also CA 104; 126; DAM DRAM, MST; MTCW

Roth, Henry 1906-1995 ...... **CLC 2, 6, 11**
See also CA 11-12; 149; CANR 38; CAP 1; DLB 28; MTCW

Roth, Joseph 1894-1939 .... **TCLC 33**
See also DLB 85

Roth, Philip (Milton)
1933- ...... **CLC 1, 2, 3, 4, 6, 9, 15, 22, 31, 47, 66, 86; DA; DAB; DAC; WLC**
See also BEST 90:3; CA 1-4R; CANR 1, 22, 36; CDALB 1968-1988; DAM MST, NOV, POP; DLB 2, 28; DLBY 82; MTCW

Rothenberg, Jerome 1931- ...... **CLC 6, 57**
See also CA 45-48; CANR 1; DLB 5

Roumain, Jacques (Jean Baptiste)
1907-1944 .... **TCLC 19; BLC**
See also BW 1; CA 117; 125; DAM MULT

Rourke, Constance (Mayfield)
1885-1941 .... **TCLC 12**
See also CA 107; YABC 1

Rousseau, Jean-Baptiste 1671-1741 ... **LC 9**

Rousseau, Jean-Jacques
1712-1778 ..... **LC 14; DA; DAB; DAC; WLC**
See also DAM MST

Roussel, Raymond 1877-1933 ..... **TCLC 20**
See also CA 117

Rovit, Earl (Herbert) 1927- .... **CLC 7**
See also CA 5-8R; CANR 12

Rowe, Nicholas 1674-1718 .... **LC 8**
See also DLB 84

Rowley, Ames Dorrance
See Lovecraft, H(oward) P(hillips)

Rowson, Susanna Haswell
1762(?)-1824 .... **NCLC 5**
See also DLB 37

Roy, Gabrielle
1909-1983 ..... **CLC 10, 14; DAB; DAC**
See also CA 53-56; 110; CANR 5; DAM MST; DLB 68; MTCW

Rozewicz, Tadeusz 1921- .... **CLC 9, 23**
See also CA 108; CANR 36; DAM POET; MTCW

Ruark, Gibbons 1941- .... **CLC 3**
See also CA 33-36R; CAAS 23; CANR 14, 31; DLB 120

Rubens, Bernice (Ruth) 1923- ... **CLC 19, 31**
See also CA 25-28R; CANR 33; DLB 14; MTCW

Rudkin, (James) David 1936- ...... **CLC 14**
See also CA 89-92; DLB 13

Rudnik, Raphael 1933- .... **CLC 7**
See also CA 29-32R

Ruffian, M.
See Hasek, Jaroslav (Matej Frantisek)

Ruiz, Jose Martinez .... **CLC 11**
See also Martinez Ruiz, Jose

Rukeyser, Muriel
1913-1980 .... **CLC 6, 10, 15, 27; PC 12**
See also CA 5-8R; 93-96; CANR 26; DAM POET; DLB 48; MTCW; SATA-Obit 22

Rule, Jane (Vance) 1931- .... **CLC 27**
See also CA 25-28R; CAAS 18; CANR 12; DLB 60

Rulfo, Juan 1918-1986 .... **CLC 8, 80; HLC**
See also CA 85-88; 118; CANR 26; DAM MULT; DLB 113; HW; MTCW

Runeberg, Johan 1804-1877 ...... **NCLC 41**

Runyon, (Alfred) Damon
1884(?)-1946 .... **TCLC 10**
See also CA 107; DLB 11, 86

Rush, Norman 1933- .... **CLC 44**
See also CA 121; 126; INT 126

Rushdie, (Ahmed) Salman
1947- .... **CLC 23, 31, 55; DAB; DAC**
See also BEST 89:3; CA 108; 111; CANR 33; DAM MST, NOV, POP; INT 111; MTCW

Rushforth, Peter (Scott) 1945- ..... **CLC 19**
See also CA 101

Ruskin, John 1819-1900 .... **TCLC 63**
See also CA 114; 129; CDBLB 1832-1890; DLB 55, 163; SATA 24

Russ, Joanna 1937- .... **CLC 15**
See also CA 25-28R; CANR 11, 31; DLB 8; MTCW

Russell, George William 1867-1935
See A. E.
See also CA 104; CDBLB 1890-1914; DAM POET

Russell, (Henry) Ken(neth Alfred)
1927- .... **CLC 16**
See also CA 105

Russell, Willy 1947- .... **CLC 60**

Rutherford, Mark .... **TCLC 25**
See also White, William Hale
See also DLB 18

Ruyslinck, Ward 1929- .... **CLC 14**
See also Belser, Reimond Karel Maria de

Ryan, Cornelius (John) 1920-1974 ... **CLC 7**
See also CA 69-72; 53-56; CANR 38

Ryan, Michael 1946- .... **CLC 65**
See also CA 49-52; DLBY 82

Rybakov, Anatoli (Naumovich)
1911- .... **CLC 23, 53**
See also CA 126; 135; SATA 79

Ryder, Jonathan
See Ludlum, Robert

Ryga, George 1932-1987 ..... **CLC 14; DAC**
See also CA 101; 124; CANR 43; DAM MST; DLB 60

S. S.
See Sassoon, Siegfried (Lorraine)

Saba, Umberto 1883-1957 .... **TCLC 33**
See also CA 144; DLB 114

Sabatini, Rafael 1875-1950 ...... **TCLC 47**

Sabato, Ernesto (R.)
1911- .... **CLC 10, 23; HLC**
See also CA 97-100; CANR 32; DAM MULT; DLB 145; HW; MTCW

Sacastru, Martin
See Bioy Casares, Adolfo

Sacher-Masoch, Leopold von
1836(?)-1895 .... **NCLC 31**

Sachs, Marilyn (Stickle) 1927- ..... **CLC 35**
See also AAYA 2; CA 17-20R; CANR 13, 47; CLR 2; JRDA; MAICYA; SAAS 2; SATA 3, 68

Sachs, Nelly 1891-1970 .... **CLC 14**
See also CA 17-18; 25-28R; CAP 2

Sackler, Howard (Oliver)
1929-1982 .... **CLC 14**
See also CA 61-64; 108; CANR 30; DLB 7

Sacks, Oliver (Wolf) 1933- .... **CLC 67**
See also CA 53-56; CANR 28, 50; INT CANR-28; MTCW

Sade, Donatien Alphonse Francois Comte
1740-1814 .... **NCLC 47**

Sadoff, Ira 1945- .... **CLC 9**
See also CA 53-56; CANR 5, 21; DLB 120

Saetone
See Camus, Albert

Safire, William 1929- .... **CLC 10**
See also CA 17-20R; CANR 31

Sagan, Carl (Edward) 1934- .... **CLC 30**
See also AAYA 2; CA 25-28R; CANR 11, 36; MTCW; SATA 58

Sagan, Francoise .... **CLC 3, 6, 9, 17, 36**
See also Quoirez, Francoise
See also DLB 83

Sahgal, Nayantara (Pandit) 1927- ... **CLC 41**
See also CA 9-12R; CANR 11

Saint, H(arry) F. 1941- .... **CLC 50**
See also CA 127

St. Aubin de Teran, Lisa 1953-
See Teran, Lisa St. Aubin de
See also CA 118; 126; INT 126

Sainte-Beuve, Charles Augustin
1804-1869 .... **NCLC 5**

Saint-Exupery, Antoine (Jean Baptiste Marie Roger) de
1900-1944 .... **TCLC 2, 56; WLC**
See also CA 108; 132; CLR 10; DAM NOV; DLB 72; MAICYA; MTCW; SATA 20

St. John, David
See Hunt, E(verette) Howard, (Jr.)

Saint-John Perse
See Leger, (Marie-Rene Auguste) Alexis Saint-Leger

Saintsbury, George (Edward Bateman)
1845-1933 .... **TCLC 31**
See also DLB 57, 149

Sait Faik .... **TCLC 23**
See also Abasiyanik, Sait Faik

Saki .... **TCLC 3; SSC 12**
See also Munro, H(ector) H(ugh)

Sala, George Augustus .... **NCLC 46**

Salama, Hannu 1936- .... **CLC 18**

Salamanca, J(ack) R(ichard)
1922- .... **CLC 4, 15**
See also CA 25-28R

Sale, J. Kirkpatrick
See Sale, Kirkpatrick

Schnackenberg, Gjertrud 1953-..... **CLC 40**
See also CA 116; DLB 120

Schneider, Leonard Alfred 1925-1966
See Bruce, Lenny
See also CA 89-92

Schnitzler, Arthur
1862-1931 .... **TCLC 4; SSC 15**
See also CA 104; DLB 81, 118

Schopenhauer, Arthur
1788-1860 .... **NCLC 51**
See also DLB 90

Schor, Sandra (M.) 1932(?)-1990 ... **CLC 65**
See also CA 132

Schorer, Mark 1908-1977 .... **CLC 9**
See also CA 5-8R; 73-76; CANR 7;
DLB 103

Schrader, Paul (Joseph) 1946-...... **CLC 26**
See also CA 37-40R; CANR 41; DLB 44

Schreiner, Olive (Emilie Albertina)
1855-1920 .... **TCLC 9**
See also CA 105; DLB 18, 156

Schulberg, Budd (Wilson)
1914-.................... **CLC 7, 48**
See also CA 25-28R; CANR 19; DLB 6, 26,
28; DLBY 81

Schulz, Bruno
1892-1942 .... **TCLC 5, 51; SSC 13**
See also CA 115; 123

Schulz, Charles M(onroe) 1922-.... **CLC 12**
See also CA 9-12R; CANR 6;
INT CANR-6; SATA 10

Schumacher, E(rnst) F(riedrich)
1911-1977 .... **CLC 80**
See also CA 81-84; 73-76; CANR 34

Schuyler, James Marcus
1923-1991 .... **CLC 5, 23**
See also CA 101; 134; DAM POET; DLB 5;
INT 101

Schwartz, Delmore (David)
1913-1966 ... **CLC 2, 4, 10, 45, 87; PC 8**
See also CA 17-18; 25-28R; CANR 35;
CAP 2; DLB 28, 48; MTCW

Schwartz, Ernst
See Ozu, Yasujiro

Schwartz, John Burnham 1965-.... **CLC 59**
See also CA 132

Schwartz, Lynne Sharon 1939-..... **CLC 31**
See also CA 103; CANR 44

Schwartz, Muriel A.
See Eliot, T(homas) S(tearns)

Schwarz-Bart, Andre 1928-....... **CLC 2, 4**
See also CA 89-92

Schwarz-Bart, Simone 1938-........ **CLC 7**
See also BW 2; CA 97-100

Schwob, (Mayer Andre) Marcel
1867-1905 .... **TCLC 20**
See also CA 117; DLB 123

Sciascia, Leonardo
1921-1989 .... **CLC 8, 9, 41**
See also CA 85-88; 130; CANR 35; MTCW

Scoppettone, Sandra 1936-........ **CLC 26**
See also AAYA 11; CA 5-8R; CANR 41;
SATA 9

Scorsese, Martin 1942-........ **CLC 20, 89**
See also CA 110; 114; CANR 46

Scotland, Jay
See Jakes, John (William)

Scott, Duncan Campbell
1862-1947 .... **TCLC 6; DAC**
See also CA 104; DLB 92

Scott, Evelyn 1893-1963........... **CLC 43**
See also CA 104; 112; DLB 9, 48

Scott, F(rancis) R(eginald)
1899-1985 .... **CLC 22**
See also CA 101; 114; DLB 88; INT 101

Scott, Frank
See Scott, F(rancis) R(eginald)

Scott, Joanna 1960-.............. **CLC 50**
See also CA 126

Scott, Paul (Mark) 1920-1978.... **CLC 9, 60**
See also CA 81-84; 77-80; CANR 33;
DLB 14; MTCW

Scott, Walter
1771-1832 .... **NCLC 15; DA; DAB;**
DAC; PC 13; WLC
See also CDBLB 1789-1832; DAM MST,
NOV, POET; DLB 93, 107, 116, 144, 159;
YABC 2

Scribe, (Augustin) Eugene
1791-1861 .... **NCLC 16; DC 5**
See also DAM DRAM

Scrum, R.
See Crumb, R(obert)

Scudery, Madeleine de 1607-1701..... **LC 2**

Scum
See Crumb, R(obert)

Scumbag, Little Bobby
See Crumb, R(obert)

Seabrook, John
See Hubbard, L(afayette) Ron(ald)

Sealy, I. Allan 1951-............. **CLC 55**

Search, Alexander
See Pessoa, Fernando (Antonio Nogueira)

Sebastian, Lee
See Silverberg, Robert

Sebastian Owl
See Thompson, Hunter S(tockton)

Sebestyen, Ouida 1924-........... **CLC 30**
See also AAYA 8; CA 107; CANR 40;
CLR 17; JRDA; MAICYA; SAAS 10;
SATA 39

Secundus, H. Scriblerus
See Fielding, Henry

Sedges, John
See Buck, Pearl S(ydenstricker)

Sedgwick, Catharine Maria
1789-1867 .... **NCLC 19**
See also DLB 1, 74

Seelye, John 1931-................ **CLC 7**

Seferiades, Giorgos Stylianou 1900-1971
See Seferis, George
See also CA 5-8R; 33-36R; CANR 5, 36;
MTCW

Seferis, George .... **CLC 5, 11**
See also Seferiades, Giorgos Stylianou

Segal, Erich (Wolf) 1937- .... **CLC 3, 10**
See also BEST 89:1; CA 25-28R; CANR 20,
36; DAM POP; DLBY 86;
INT CANR-20; MTCW

Seger, Bob 1945-................ **CLC 35**

Seghers, Anna .... **CLC 7**
See also Radvanyi, Netty
See also DLB 69

Seidel, Frederick (Lewis) 1936-..... **CLC 18**
See also CA 13-16R; CANR 8; DLBY 84

Seifert, Jaroslav 1901-1986..... **CLC 34, 44**
See also CA 127; MTCW

Sei Shonagon c. 966-1017(?) ...... **CMLC 6**

Selby, Hubert, Jr.
1928-.......... **CLC 1, 2, 4, 8; SSC 20**
See also CA 13-16R; CANR 33; DLB 2

Selzer, Richard 1928-............. **CLC 74**
See also CA 65-68; CANR 14

Sembene, Ousmane
See Ousmane, Sembene

Senancour, Etienne Pivert de
1770-1846 .... **NCLC 16**
See also DLB 119

Sender, Ramon (Jose)
1902-1982 .... **CLC 8; HLC**
See also CA 5-8R; 105; CANR 8;
DAM MULT; HW; MTCW

Seneca, Lucius Annaeus
4B.C.-65.............. **CMLC 6; DC 5**
See also DAM DRAM

Senghor, Leopold Sedar
1906-................. **CLC 54; BLC**
See also BW 2; CA 116; 125; CANR 47;
DAM MULT, POET; MTCW

Serling, (Edward) Rod(man)
1924-1975 .... **CLC 30**
See also AAYA 14; AITN 1; CA 65-68;
57-60; DLB 26

Serna, Ramon Gomez de la
See Gomez de la Serna, Ramon

Serpieres
See Guillevic, (Eugene)

Service, Robert
See Service, Robert W(illiam)
See also DAB; DLB 92

Service, Robert W(illiam)
1874(?)-1958 ...... **TCLC 15; DA; DAC;**
WLC
See also Service, Robert
See also CA 115; 140; DAM MST, POET;
SATA 20

Seth, Vikram 1952-............ **CLC 43, 90**
See also CA 121; 127; CANR 50;
DAM MULT; DLB 120; INT 127

Seton, Cynthia Propper
1926-1982 .... **CLC 27**
See also CA 5-8R; 108; CANR 7

Seton, Ernest (Evan) Thompson
1860-1946 .... **TCLC 31**
See also CA 109; DLB 92; DLBD 13;
JRDA; SATA 18

Seton-Thompson, Ernest
See Seton, Ernest (Evan) Thompson

Settle, Mary Lee 1918- .... **CLC 19, 61**
See also CA 89-92; CAAS 1; CANR 44;
DLB 6; INT 89-92

Seuphor, Michel
See Arp, Jean

Sevigne, Marie (de Rabutin-Chantal) Marquise
de 1626-1696 . . . . LC 11

Sexton, Anne (Harvey)
1928-1974 . . . . CLC 2, 4, 6, 8, 10, 15, 53;
DA; DAB; DAC; PC 2; WLC
See also CA 1-4R; 53-56; CABS 2;
CANR 3, 36; CDALB 1941-1968;
DAM MST, POET; DLB 5; MTCW;
SATA 10

Shaara, Michael (Joseph, Jr.)
1929-1988 . . . . CLC 15
See also AITN 1; CA 102; 125; DAM POP;
DLBY 83

Shackleton, C. C.
See Aldiss, Brian W(ilson)

Shacochis, Bob . . . . CLC 39
See also Shacochis, Robert G.

Shacochis, Robert G. 1951-
See Shacochis, Bob
See also CA 119; 124; INT 124

Shaffer, Anthony (Joshua) 1926- . . . . CLC 19
See also CA 110; 116; DAM DRAM;
DLB 13

Shaffer, Peter (Levin)
1926- . . . . . . CLC 5, 14, 18, 37, 60; DAB
See also CA 25-28R; CANR 25, 47;
CDBLB 1960 to Present; DAM DRAM,
MST; DLB 13; MTCW

Shakey, Bernard
See Young, Neil

Shalamov, Varlam (Tikhonovich)
1907(?)-1982 . . . . CLC 18
See also CA 129; 105

Shamlu, Ahmad 1925- . . . . CLC 10

Shammas, Anton 1951- . . . . CLC 55

Shange, Ntozake
1948- . . . . CLC 8, 25, 38, 74; BLC; DC 3
See also AAYA 9; BW 2; CA 85-88;
CABS 3; CANR 27, 48; DAM DRAM,
MULT; DLB 38; MTCW

Shanley, John Patrick 1950- . . . . CLC 75
See also CA 128; 133

Shapcott, Thomas W(illiam) 1935- . . CLC 38
See also CA 69-72; CANR 49

Shapiro, Jane . . . . CLC 76

Shapiro, Karl (Jay) 1913- . . CLC 4, 8, 15, 53
See also CA 1-4R; CAAS 6; CANR 1, 36;
DLB 48; MTCW

Sharp, William 1855-1905 . . . . TCLC 39
See also DLB 156

Sharpe, Thomas Ridley 1928-
See Sharpe, Tom
See also CA 114; 122; INT 122

Sharpe, Tom . . . . CLC 36
See also Sharpe, Thomas Ridley
See also DLB 14

Shaw, Bernard . . . . TCLC 45
See also Shaw, George Bernard
See also BW 1

Shaw, G. Bernard
See Shaw, George Bernard

Shaw, George Bernard
1856-1950 . . . TCLC 3, 9, 21; DA; DAB;
DAC; WLC
See also Shaw, Bernard
See also CA 104; 128; CDBLB 1914-1945;
DAM DRAM, MST; DLB 10, 57;
MTCW

Shaw, Henry Wheeler
1818-1885 . . . . NCLC 15
See also DLB 11

Shaw, Irwin 1913-1984 . . . . . . CLC 7, 23, 34
See also AITN 1; CA 13-16R; 112;
CANR 21; CDALB 1941-1968;
DAM DRAM, POP; DLB 6, 102;
DLBY 84; MTCW

Shaw, Robert 1927-1978 . . . . CLC 5
See also AITN 1; CA 1-4R; 81-84;
CANR 4; DLB 13, 14

Shaw, T. E.
See Lawrence, T(homas) E(dward)

Shawn, Wallace 1943- . . . . CLC 41
See also CA 112

Shea, Lisa 1953- . . . . CLC 86
See also CA 147

Sheed, Wilfrid (John Joseph)
1930- . . . . CLC 2, 4, 10, 53
See also CA 65-68; CANR 30; DLB 6;
MTCW

Sheldon, Alice Hastings Bradley
1915(?)-1987
See Tiptree, James, Jr.
See also CA 108; 122; CANR 34; INT 108;
MTCW

Sheldon, John
See Bloch, Robert (Albert)

Shelley, Mary Wollstonecraft (Godwin)
1797-1851 . . . . NCLC 14; DA; DAB;
DAC; WLC
See also CDBLB 1789-1832; DAM MST,
NOV; DLB 110, 116, 159; SATA 29

Shelley, Percy Bysshe
1792-1822 . . . . NCLC 18; DA; DAB;
DAC; PC 14; WLC
See also CDBLB 1789-1832; DAM MST,
POET; DLB 96, 110, 158

Shepard, Jim 1956- . . . . CLC 36
See also CA 137

Shepard, Lucius 1947- . . . . CLC 34
See also CA 128; 141

Shepard, Sam
1943- . . . . CLC 4, 6, 17, 34, 41, 44; DC 5
See also AAYA 1; CA 69-72; CABS 3;
CANR 22; DAM DRAM; DLB 7;
MTCW

Shepherd, Michael
See Ludlum, Robert

Sherburne, Zoa (Morin) 1912- . . . . . . CLC 30
See also AAYA 13; CA 1-4R; CANR 3, 37;
MAICYA; SAAS 18; SATA 3

Sheridan, Frances 1724-1766 . . . . LC 7
See also DLB 39, 84

Sheridan, Richard Brinsley
1751-1816 . . . . NCLC 5; DA; DAB;
DAC; DC 1; WLC
See also CDBLB 1660-1789; DAM DRAM,
MST; DLB 89

Sherman, Jonathan Marc . . . . CLC 55

Sherman, Martin 1941(?)- . . . . CLC 19
See also CA 116; 123

Sherwin, Judith Johnson 1936- . . . CLC 7, 15
See also CA 25-28R; CANR 34

Sherwood, Frances 1940- . . . . CLC 81
See also CA 146

Sherwood, Robert E(mmet)
1896-1955 . . . . TCLC 3
See also CA 104; DAM DRAM; DLB 7, 26

Shestov, Lev 1866-1938 . . . . TCLC 56

Shevchenko, Taras 1814-1861 . . . . NCLC 54

Shiel, M(atthew) P(hipps)
1865-1947 . . . . TCLC 8
See also CA 106; DLB 153

Shields, Carol 1935- . . . . CLC 91; DAC
See also CA 81-84; CANR 51

Shiga, Naoya 1883-1971 . . . . CLC 33
See also CA 101; 33-36R

Shilts, Randy 1951-1994 . . . . CLC 85
See also CA 115; 127; 144; CANR 45;
INT 127

Shimazaki Haruki 1872-1943
See Shimazaki Toson
See also CA 105; 134

Shimazaki Toson . . . . TCLC 5
See also Shimazaki Haruki

Sholokhov, Mikhail (Aleksandrovich)
1905-1984 . . . . CLC 7, 15
See also CA 101; 112; MTCW;
SATA-Obit 36

Shone, Patric
See Hanley, James

Shreve, Susan Richards 1939- . . . . . . CLC 23
See also CA 49-52; CAAS 5; CANR 5, 38;
MAICYA; SATA 46; SATA-Brief 41

Shue, Larry 1946-1985 . . . . CLC 52
See also CA 145; 117; DAM DRAM

Shu-Jen, Chou 1881-1936
See Lu Hsun
See also CA 104

Shulman, Alix Kates 1932- . . . . . . CLC 2, 10
See also CA 29-32R; CANR 43; SATA 7

Shuster, Joe 1914- . . . . CLC 21

Shute, Nevil . . . . CLC 30
See also Norway, Nevil Shute

Shuttle, Penelope (Diane) 1947- . . . . . CLC 7
See also CA 93-96; CANR 39; DLB 14, 40

Sidney, Mary 1561-1621 . . . . LC 19

Sidney, Sir Philip
1554-1586 . . . . . LC 19; DA; DAB; DAC
See also CDBLB Before 1660; DAM MST,
POET

Siegel, Jerome 1914- . . . . CLC 21
See also CA 116

Siegel, Jerry
See Siegel, Jerome

Sienkiewicz, Henryk (Adam Alexander Pius)
1846-1916 . . . . TCLC 3
See also CA 104; 134

Sierra, Gregorio Martinez
See Martinez Sierra, Gregorio

Sierra, Maria (de la O'LeJarraga) Martinez
See Martinez Sierra, Maria (de la O'LeJarraga)

Sigal, Clancy 1926-.............. **CLC 7**
See also CA 1-4R

Sigourney, Lydia Howard (Huntley)
1791-1865 .... **NCLC 21**
See also DLB 1, 42, 73

Siguenza y Gongora, Carlos de
1645-1700 .... **LC 8**

Sigurjonsson, Johann 1880-1919... **TCLC 27**

Sikelianos, Angelos 1884-1951 .... **TCLC 39**

Silkin, Jon 1930- .... **CLC 2, 6, 43**
See also CA 5-8R; CAAS 5; DLB 27

Silko, Leslie (Marmon)
1948- ...... **CLC 23, 74; DA; DAC**
See also AAYA 14; CA 115; 122;
CANR 45; DAM MST, MULT, POP;
DLB 143; NNAL

Sillanpaa, Frans Eemil 1888-1964... **CLC 19**
See also CA 129; 93-96; MTCW

Sillitoe, Alan
1928- .... **CLC 1, 3, 6, 10, 19, 57**
See also AITN 1; CA 9-12R; CAAS 2;
CANR 8, 26; CDBLB 1960 to Present;
DLB 14, 139; MTCW; SATA 61

Silone, Ignazio 1900-1978 .... **CLC 4**
See also CA 25-28; 81-84; CANR 34;
CAP 2; MTCW

Silver, Joan Micklin 1935- .... **CLC 20**
See also CA 114; 121; INT 121

Silver, Nicholas
See Faust, Frederick (Schiller)

Silverberg, Robert 1935- .... **CLC 7**
See also CA 1-4R; CAAS 3; CANR 1, 20,
36; DAM POP; DLB 8; INT CANR-20;
MAICYA; MTCW; SATA 13

Silverstein, Alvin 1933- .... **CLC 17**
See also CA 49-52; CANR 2; CLR 25;
JRDA; MAICYA; SATA 8, 69

Silverstein, Virginia B(arbara Opshelor)
1937- .... **CLC 17**
See also CA 49-52; CANR 2; CLR 25;
JRDA; MAICYA; SATA 8, 69

Sim, Georges
See Simenon, Georges (Jacques Christian)

Simak, Clifford D(onald)
1904-1988 .... **CLC 1, 55**
See also CA 1-4R; 125; CANR 1, 35;
DLB 8; MTCW; SATA-Obit 56

Simenon, Georges (Jacques Christian)
1903-1989 ...... **CLC 1, 2, 3, 8, 18, 47**
See also CA 85-88; 129; CANR 35;
DAM POP; DLB 72; DLBY 89; MTCW

Simic, Charles 1938-... **CLC 6, 9, 22, 49, 68**
See also CA 29-32R; CAAS 4; CANR 12,
33; DAM POET; DLB 105

Simmons, Charles (Paul) 1924-..... **CLC 57**
See also CA 89-92; INT 89-92

Simmons, Dan 1948-.............. **CLC 44**
See also AAYA 16; CA 138; DAM POP

Simmons, James (Stewart Alexander)
1933- .... **CLC 43**
See also CA 105; CAAS 21; DLB 40

Simms, William Gilmore
1806-1870 .... **NCLC 3**
See also DLB 3, 30, 59, 73

Simon, Carly 1945-............. **CLC 26**
See also CA 105

Simon, Claude 1913-...... **CLC 4, 9, 15, 39**
See also CA 89-92; CANR 33; DAM NOV;
DLB 83; MTCW

Simon, (Marvin) Neil
1927- .... **CLC 6, 11, 31, 39, 70**
See also AITN 1; CA 21-24R; CANR 26;
DAM DRAM; DLB 7; MTCW

Simon, Paul 1942(?)-............. **CLC 17**
See also CA 116

Simonon, Paul 1956(?)- .... **CLC 30**

Simpson, Harriette
See Arnow, Harriette (Louisa) Simpson

Simpson, Louis (Aston Marantz)
1923- .... **CLC 4, 7, 9, 32**
See also CA 1-4R; CAAS 4; CANR 1;
DAM POET; DLB 5; MTCW

Simpson, Mona (Elizabeth) 1957-... **CLC 44**
See also CA 122; 135

Simpson, N(orman) F(rederick)
1919- .... **CLC 29**
See also CA 13-16R; DLB 13

Sinclair, Andrew (Annandale)
1935- .... **CLC 2, 14**
See also CA 9-12R; CAAS 5; CANR 14, 38;
DLB 14; MTCW

Sinclair, Emil
See Hesse, Hermann

Sinclair, Iain 1943-.............. **CLC 76**
See also CA 132

Sinclair, Iain MacGregor
See Sinclair, Iain

Sinclair, Mary Amelia St. Clair 1865(?)-1946
See Sinclair, May
See also CA 104

Sinclair, May................... TCLC 3, 11
See also Sinclair, Mary Amelia St. Clair
See also DLB 36, 135

Sinclair, Upton (Beall)
1878-1968 ...... **CLC 1, 11, 15, 63; DA;**
DAB; DAC; WLC
See also CA 5-8R; 25-28R; CANR 7;
CDALB 1929-1941; DAM MST, NOV;
DLB 9; INT CANR-7; MTCW; SATA 9

Singer, Isaac
See Singer, Isaac Bashevis

Singer, Isaac Bashevis
1904-1991 .... **CLC 1, 3, 6, 9, 11, 15, 23,**
38, 69; DA; DAB; DAC; SSC 3; WLC
See also AITN 1, 2; CA 1-4R; 134;
CANR 1, 39; CDALB 1941-1968; CLR 1;
DAM MST, NOV; DLB 6, 28, 52;
DLBY 91; JRDA; MAICYA; MTCW;
SATA 3, 27; SATA-Obit 68

Singer, Israel Joshua 1893-1944... **TCLC 33**

Singh, Khushwant 1915-........... **CLC 11**
See also CA 9-12R; CAAS 9; CANR 6

Sinjohn, John
See Galsworthy, John

Sinyavsky, Andrei (Donatevich)
1925-..................... **CLC 8**
See also CA 85-88

Sirin, V.
See Nabokov, Vladimir (Vladimirovich)

Sissman, L(ouis) E(dward)
1928-1976 .... **CLC 9, 18**
See also CA 21-24R; 65-68; CANR 13;
DLB 5

Sisson, C(harles) H(ubert) 1914-..... **CLC 8**
See also CA 1-4R; CAAS 3; CANR 3, 48;
DLB 27

Sitwell, Dame Edith
1887-1964 .... **CLC 2, 9, 67; PC 3**
See also CA 9-12R; CANR 35;
CDBLB 1945-1960; DAM POET;
DLB 20; MTCW

Sjoewall, Maj 1935-.............. **CLC 7**
See also CA 65-68

Sjowall, Maj
See Sjoewall, Maj

Skelton, Robin 1925-............. **CLC 13**
See also AITN 2; CA 5-8R; CAAS 5;
CANR 28; DLB 27, 53

Skolimowski, Jerzy 1938-......... **CLC 20**
See also CA 128

Skram, Amalie (Bertha)
1847-1905 .... **TCLC 25**

Skvorecky, Josef (Vaclav)
1924-........... **CLC 15, 39, 69; DAC**
See also CA 61-64; CAAS 1; CANR 10, 34;
DAM NOV; MTCW

Slade, Bernard................. CLC 11, 46
See also Newbound, Bernard Slade
See also CAAS 9; DLB 53

Slaughter, Carolyn 1946-.......... **CLC 56**
See also CA 85-88

Slaughter, Frank G(ill) 1908- ...... **CLC 29**
See also AITN 2; CA 5-8R; CANR 5;
INT CANR-5

Slavitt, David R(ytman) 1935-.... **CLC 5, 14**
See also CA 21-24R; CAAS 3; CANR 41;
DLB 5, 6

Slesinger, Tess 1905-1945 .... **TCLC 10**
See also CA 107; DLB 102

Slessor, Kenneth 1901-1971........ **CLC 14**
See also CA 102; 89-92

Slowacki, Juliusz 1809-1849 ..... **NCLC 15**

Smart, Christopher
1722-1771 .... **LC 3; PC 13**
See also DAM POET; DLB 109

Smart, Elizabeth 1913-1986........ **CLC 54**
See also CA 81-84; 118; DLB 88

Smiley, Jane (Graves) 1949- .... **CLC 53, 76**
See also CA 104; CANR 30, 50;
DAM POP; INT CANR-30

Smith, A(rthur) J(ames) M(arshall)
1902-1980 .... **CLC 15; DAC**
See also CA 1-4R; 102; CANR 4; DLB 88

Smith, Anna Deavere 1950-........ **CLC 86**
See also CA 133

Smith, Betty (Wehner) 1896-1972... **CLC 19**
See also CA 5-8R; 33-36R; DLBY 82;
SATA 6

Sting
See Sumner, Gordon Matthew

Stirling, Arthur
See Sinclair, Upton (Beall)

Stitt, Milan 1941-............... **CLC 29**
See also CA 69-72

Stockton, Francis Richard 1834-1902
See Stockton, Frank R.
See also CA 108; 137; MAICYA; SATA 44

Stockton, Frank R. .... **TCLC 47**
See also Stockton, Francis Richard
See also DLB 42, 74; DLBD 13;
SATA-Brief 32

Stoddard, Charles
See Kuttner, Henry

Stoker, Abraham 1847-1912
See Stoker, Bram
See also CA 105; DA; DAC; DAM MST,
NOV; SATA 29

Stoker, Bram
1847-1912 .... **TCLC 8; DAB; WLC**
See also Stoker, Abraham
See also CA 150; CDBLB 1890-1914;
DLB 36, 70

Stolz, Mary (Slattery) 1920-....... **CLC 12**
See also AAYA 8; AITN 1; CA 5-8R;
CANR 13, 41; JRDA; MAICYA;
SAAS 3; SATA 10, 71

Stone, Irving 1903-1989............ **CLC 7**
See also AITN 1; CA 1-4R; 129; CAAS 3;
CANR 1, 23; DAM POP;
INT CANR-23; MTCW; SATA 3;
SATA-Obit 64

Stone, Oliver 1946-............... **CLC 73**
See also AAYA 15; CA 110

Stone, Robert (Anthony)
1937- ....CLC 5, 23, 42
See also CA 85-88; CANR 23; DLB 152;
INT CANR-23; MTCW

Stone, Zachary
See Follett, Ken(neth Martin)

Stoppard, Tom
1937- ...... **CLC 1, 3, 4, 5, 8, 15, 29, 34,
63, 91; DA; DAB; DAC; DC 6; WLC**
See also CA 81-84; CANR 39;
CDBLB 1960 to Present; DAM DRAM,
MST; DLB 13; DLBY 85; MTCW

Storey, David (Malcolm)
1933- ....CLC 2, 4, 5, 8
See also CA 81-84; CANR 36;
DAM DRAM; DLB 13, 14; MTCW

Storm, Hyemeyohsts 1935-......... **CLC 3**
See also CA 81-84; CANR 45;
DAM MULT; NNAL

Storm, (Hans) Theodor (Woldsen)
1817-1888 .... **NCLC 1**

Storni, Alfonsina
1892-1938 .... **TCLC 5; HLC**
See also CA 104; 131; DAM MULT; HW

Stout, Rex (Todhunter) 1886-1975 ... **CLC 3**
See also AITN 2; CA 61-64

Stow, (Julian) Randolph 1935- .. **CLC 23, 48**
See also CA 13-16R; CANR 33; MTCW

Stowe, Harriet (Elizabeth) Beecher
1811-1896 ..... **NCLC 3, 50; DA; DAB;
DAC; WLC**
See also CDALB 1865-1917; DAM MST,
NOV; DLB 1, 12, 42, 74; JRDA;
MAICYA; YABC 1

Strachey, (Giles) Lytton
1880-1932 .... **TCLC 12**
See also CA 110; DLB 149; DLBD 10

Strand, Mark 1934-...... **CLC 6, 18, 41, 71**
See also CA 21-24R; CANR 40;
DAM POET; DLB 5; SATA 41

Straub, Peter (Francis) 1943- ...... **CLC 28**
See also BEST 89:1; CA 85-88; CANR 28;
DAM POP; DLBY 84; MTCW

Strauss, Botho 1944-............ **CLC 22**
See also DLB 124

Streatfeild, (Mary) Noel
1895(?)-1986 .... **CLC 21**
See also CA 81-84; 120; CANR 31;
CLR 17; DLB 160; MAICYA; SATA 20;
SATA-Obit 48

Stribling, T(homas) S(igismund)
1881-1965 .... **CLC 23**
See also CA 107; DLB 9

Strindberg, (Johan) August
1849-1912 ...... **TCLC 1, 8, 21, 47; DA;
DAB; DAC; WLC**
See also CA 104; 135; DAM DRAM, MST

Stringer, Arthur 1874-1950 .... **TCLC 37**
See also DLB 92

Stringer, David
See Roberts, Keith (John Kingston)

Strugatskii, Arkadii (Natanovich)
1925-1991 .... **CLC 27**
See also CA 106; 135

Strugatskii, Boris (Natanovich)
1933- .... **CLC 27**
See also CA 106

Strummer, Joe 1953(?)-........... **CLC 30**

Stuart, Don A.
See Campbell, John W(ood, Jr.)

Stuart, Ian
See MacLean, Alistair (Stuart)

Stuart, Jesse (Hilton)
1906-1984 .... **CLC 1, 8, 11, 14, 34**
See also CA 5-8R; 112; CANR 31; DLB 9,
48, 102; DLBY 84; SATA 2;
SATA-Obit 36

Sturgeon, Theodore (Hamilton)
1918-1985 .... **CLC 22, 39**
See also Queen, Ellery
See also CA 81-84; 116; CANR 32; DLB 8;
DLBY 85; MTCW

Sturges, Preston 1898-1959 .... **TCLC 48**
See also CA 114; 149; DLB 26

Styron, William
1925- .... **CLC 1, 3, 5, 11, 15, 60**
See also BEST 90:4; CA 5-8R; CANR 6, 33;
CDALB 1968-1988; DAM NOV, POP;
DLB 2, 143; DLBY 80; INT CANR-6;
MTCW

Suarez Lynch, B.
See Bioy Casares, Adolfo; Borges, Jorge
Luis

Su Chien 1884-1918
See Su Man-shu
See also CA 123

Suckow, Ruth 1892-1960.......... **SSC 18**
See also CA 113; DLB 9, 102

Sudermann, Hermann 1857-1928 .. **TCLC 15**
See also CA 107; DLB 118

Sue, Eugene 1804-1857 .... **NCLC 1**
See also DLB 119

Sueskind, Patrick 1949-.......... **CLC 44**
See also Suskind, Patrick

Sukenick, Ronald 1932-..... **CLC 3, 4, 6, 48**
See also CA 25-28R; CAAS 8; CANR 32;
DLBY 81

Suknaski, Andrew 1942- .... **CLC 19**
See also CA 101; DLB 53

Sullivan, Vernon
See Vian, Boris

Sully Prudhomme 1839-1907...... **TCLC 31**

Su Man-shu .... **TCLC 24**
See also Su Chien

Summerforest, Ivy B.
See Kirkup, James

Summers, Andrew James 1942-..... **CLC 26**

Summers, Andy
See Summers, Andrew James

Summers, Hollis (Spurgeon, Jr.)
1916- .... **CLC 10**
See also CA 5-8R; CANR 3; DLB 6

**Summers, (Alphonsus Joseph-Mary Augustus)
Montague** 1880-1948....... **TCLC 16**
See also CA 118

Sumner, Gordon Matthew 1951-.... **CLC 26**

Surtees, Robert Smith
1803-1864 .... **NCLC 14**
See also DLB 21

Susann, Jacqueline 1921-1974....... **CLC 3**
See also AITN 1; CA 65-68; 53-56; MTCW

Su Shih 1036-1101 .... **CMLC 15**

Suskind, Patrick
See Sueskind, Patrick
See also CA 145

Sutcliff, Rosemary
1920-1992 .... **CLC 26; DAB; DAC**
See also AAYA 10; CA 5-8R; 139;
CANR 37; CLR 1, 37; DAM MST, POP;
JRDA; MAICYA; SATA 6, 44, 78;
SATA-Obit 73

Sutro, Alfred 1863-1933........... **TCLC 6**
See also CA 105; DLB 10

Sutton, Henry
See Slavitt, David R(ytman)

Svevo, Italo .... **TCLC 2, 35**
See also Schmitz, Aron Hector

Swados, Elizabeth (A.) 1951-....... **CLC 12**
See also CA 97-100; CANR 49; INT 97-100

Swados, Harvey 1920-1972 .... **CLC 5**
See also CA 5-8R; 37-40R; CANR 6;
DLB 2

Swan, Gladys 1934- .... **CLC 69**
See also CA 101; CANR 17, 39

Swarthout, Glendon (Fred)
1918-1992 . . . . CLC 35
See also CA 1-4R; 139; CANR 1, 47;
SATA 26

Sweet, Sarah C.
See Jewett, (Theodora) Sarah Orne

Swenson, May
1919-1989 . . . . **CLC 4, 14, 61; DA; DAB;
DAC; PC 14**
See also CA 5-8R; 130; CANR 36;
DAM MST, POET; DLB 5; MTCW;
SATA 15

Swift, Augustus
See Lovecraft, H(oward) P(hillips)

Swift, Graham (Colin) 1949- . . . . **CLC 41, 88**
See also CA 117; 122; CANR 46

Swift, Jonathan
1667-1745 . . . . . . **LC 1; DA; DAB; DAC;
PC 9; WLC**
See also CDBLB 1660-1789; DAM MST,
NOV, POET; DLB 39, 95, 101; SATA 19

Swinburne, Algernon Charles
1837-1909 . . . . . . **TCLC 8, 36; DA; DAB;
DAC; WLC**
See also CA 105; 140; CDBLB 1832-1890;
DAM MST, POET; DLB 35, 57

Swinfen, Ann . . . . **CLC 34**

Swinnerton, Frank Arthur
1884-1982 . . . . **CLC 31**
See also CA 108; DLB 34

Swithen, John
See King, Stephen (Edwin)

Sylvia
See Ashton-Warner, Sylvia (Constance)

Symmes, Robert Edward
See Duncan, Robert (Edward)

Symonds, John Addington
1840-1893 . . . . **NCLC 34**
See also DLB 57, 144

Symons, Arthur 1865-1945 . . . . **TCLC 11**
See also CA 107; DLB 19, 57, 149

Symons, Julian (Gustave)
1912-1994 . . . . **CLC 2, 14, 32**
See also CA 49-52; 147; CAAS 3; CANR 3,
33; DLB 87, 155; DLBY 92; MTCW

Synge, (Edmund) J(ohn) M(illington)
1871-1909 . . . . **TCLC 6, 37; DC 2**
See also CA 104; 141; CDBLB 1890-1914;
DAM DRAM; DLB 10, 19

Syruc, J.
See Milosz, Czeslaw

Szirtes, George 1948- . . . . **CLC 46**
See also CA 109; CANR 27

Tabori, George 1914- . . . . **CLC 19**
See also CA 49-52; CANR 4

Tagore, Rabindranath
1861-1941 . . . . **TCLC 3, 53; PC 8**
See also CA 104; 120; DAM DRAM,
POET; MTCW

Taine, Hippolyte Adolphe
1828-1893 . . . . **NCLC 15**

Talese, Gay 1932- . . . . **CLC 37**
See also AITN 1; CA 1-4R; CANR 9;
INT CANR-9; MTCW

Tallent, Elizabeth (Ann) 1954- . . . . . **CLC 45**
See also CA 117; DLB 130

Tally, Ted 1952- . . . . **CLC 42**
See also CA 120; 124; INT 124

Tamayo y Baus, Manuel
1829-1898 . . . . **NCLC 1**

Tammsaare, A(nton) H(ansen)
1878-1940 . . . . **TCLC 27**

Tan, Amy 1952- . . . . **CLC 59**
See also AAYA 9; BEST 89:3; CA 136;
DAM MULT, NOV, POP; SATA 75

Tandem, Felix
See Spitteler, Carl (Friedrich Georg)

Tanizaki, Jun'ichiro
1886-1965 . . . . . . **CLC 8, 14, 28; SSC 21**
See also CA 93-96; 25-28R

Tanner, William
See Amis, Kingsley (William)

Tao Lao
See Storni, Alfonsina

Tarassoff, Lev
See Troyat, Henri

Tarbell, Ida M(inerva)
1857-1944 . . . . **TCLC 40**
See also CA 122; DLB 47

Tarkington, (Newton) Booth
1869-1946 . . . . **TCLC 9**
See also CA 110; 143; DLB 9, 102;
SATA 17

Tarkovsky, Andrei (Arsenyevich)
1932-1986 . . . . **CLC 75**
See also CA 127

Tartt, Donna 1964(?)- . . . . **CLC 76**
See also CA 142

Tasso, Torquato 1544-1595 . . . . **LC 5**

Tate, (John Orley) Allen
1899-1979 . . . . **CLC 2, 4, 6, 9, 11, 14, 24**
See also CA 5-8R; 85-88; CANR 32;
DLB 4, 45, 63; MTCW

Tate, Ellalice
See Hibbert, Eleanor Alice Burford

Tate, James (Vincent) 1943- . . . **CLC 2, 6, 25**
See also CA 21-24R; CANR 29; DLB 5

Tavel, Ronald 1940- . . . . **CLC 6**
See also CA 21-24R; CANR 33

Taylor, C(ecil) P(hilip) 1929-1981 . . . **CLC 27**
See also CA 25-28R; 105; CANR 47

Taylor, Edward
1642(?)-1729 . . . **LC 11; DA; DAB; DAC**
See also DAM MST, POET; DLB 24

Taylor, Eleanor Ross 1920- . . . . **CLC 5**
See also CA 81-84

Taylor, Elizabeth 1912-1975 . . . **CLC 2, 4, 29**
See also CA 13-16R; CANR 9; DLB 139;
MTCW; SATA 13

Taylor, Henry (Splawn) 1942- . . . . . . **CLC 44**
See also CA 33-36R; CAAS 7; CANR 31;
DLB 5

Taylor, Kamala (Purnaiya) 1924-
See Markandaya, Kamala
See also CA 77-80

Taylor, Mildred D. . . . . **CLC 21**
See also AAYA 10; BW 1; CA 85-88;
CANR 25; CLR 9; DLB 52; JRDA;
MAICYA; SAAS 5; SATA 15, 70

Taylor, Peter (Hillsman)
1917-1994 . . . . . **CLC 1, 4, 18, 37, 44, 50,
71; SSC 10**
See also CA 13-16R; 147; CANR 9, 50;
DLBY 81, 94; INT CANR-9; MTCW

Taylor, Robert Lewis 1912- . . . . **CLC 14**
See also CA 1-4R; CANR 3; SATA 10

Tchekhov, Anton
See Chekhov, Anton (Pavlovich)

Teasdale, Sara 1884-1933 . . . . **TCLC 4**
See also CA 104; DLB 45; SATA 32

Tegner, Esaias 1782-1846 . . . . **NCLC 2**

Teilhard de Chardin, (Marie Joseph) Pierre
1881-1955 . . . . **TCLC 9**
See also CA 105

Temple, Ann
See Mortimer, Penelope (Ruth)

Tennant, Emma (Christina)
1937- . . . . **CLC 13, 52**
See also CA 65-68; CAAS 9; CANR 10, 38;
DLB 14

Tenneshaw, S. M.
See Silverberg, Robert

Tennyson, Alfred
1809-1892 . . . . **NCLC 30; DA; DAB;
DAC; PC 6; WLC**
See also CDBLB 1832-1890; DAM MST,
POET; DLB 32

Teran, Lisa St. Aubin de . . . . **CLC 36**
See also St. Aubin de Teran, Lisa

Terence 195(?)B.C.-159B.C. . . . . . . **CMLC 14**

Teresa de Jesus, St. 1515-1582 . . . . . . **LC 18**

Terkel, Louis 1912-
See Terkel, Studs
See also CA 57-60; CANR 18, 45; MTCW

Terkel, Studs . . . . **CLC 38**
See also Terkel, Louis
See also AITN 1

Terry, C. V.
See Slaughter, Frank G(ill)

Terry, Megan 1932- . . . . **CLC 19**
See also CA 77-80; CABS 3; CANR 43;
DLB 7

Tertz, Abram
See Sinyavsky, Andrei (Donatevich)

Tesich, Steve 1943(?)- . . . . **CLC 40, 69**
See also CA 105; DLBY 83

Teternikov, Fyodor Kuzmich 1863-1927
See Sologub, Fyodor
See also CA 104

Tevis, Walter 1928-1984 . . . . **CLC 42**
See also CA 113

Tey, Josephine . . . . **TCLC 14**
See also Mackintosh, Elizabeth
See also DLB 77

Thackeray, William Makepeace
1811-1863 . . . . **NCLC 5, 14, 22, 43; DA;
DAB; DAC; WLC**
See also CDBLB 1832-1890; DAM MST,
NOV; DLB 21, 55, 159, 163; SATA 23

Thakura, Ravindranatha
See Tagore, Rabindranath

Tharoor, Shashi 1956- . . . . **CLC 70**
See also CA 141

Thelwell, Michael Miles 1939- . . . . . **CLC 22**
See also BW 2; CA 101

Theobald, Lewis, Jr.
See Lovecraft, H(oward) P(hillips)

Theodorescu, Ion N. 1880-1967
See Arghezi, Tudor
See also CA 116

Theriault, Yves 1915-1983 . . . . **CLC 79; DAC**
See also CA 102; DAM MST; DLB 88

Theroux, Alexander (Louis)
1939- . . . . **CLC 2, 25**
See also CA 85-88; CANR 20

Theroux, Paul (Edward)
1941- . . . . **CLC 5, 8, 11, 15, 28, 46**
See also BEST 89:4; CA 33-36R; CANR 20,
45; DAM POP; DLB 2; MTCW;
SATA 44

Thesen, Sharon 1946- . . . . **CLC 56**

Thevenin, Denis
See Duhamel, Georges

Thibault, Jacques Anatole Francois
1844-1924
See France, Anatole
See also CA 106; 127; DAM NOV; MTCW

Thiele, Colin (Milton) 1920- . . . . **CLC 17**
See also CA 29-32R; CANR 12, 28;
CLR 27; MAICYA; SAAS 2; SATA 14,
72

Thomas, Audrey (Callahan)
1935- . . . . **CLC 7, 13, 37; SSC 20**
See also AITN 2; CA 21-24R; CAAS 19;
CANR 36; DLB 60; MTCW

Thomas, D(onald) M(ichael)
1935- . . . . **CLC 13, 22, 31**
See also CA 61-64; CAAS 11; CANR 17,
45; CDBLB 1960 to Present; DLB 40;
INT CANR-17; MTCW

Thomas, Dylan (Marlais)
1914-1953 . . . **TCLC 1, 8, 45; DA; DAB;
DAC; PC 2; SSC 3; WLC**
See also CA 104; 120; CDBLB 1945-1960;
DAM DRAM, MST, POET; DLB 13, 20,
139; MTCW; SATA 60

Thomas, (Philip) Edward
1878-1917 . . . . **TCLC 10**
See also CA 106; DAM POET; DLB 19

Thomas, Joyce Carol 1938- . . . . **CLC 35**
See also AAYA 12; BW 2; CA 113; 116;
CANR 48; CLR 19; DLB 33; INT 116;
JRDA; MAICYA; MTCW; SAAS 7;
SATA 40, 78

Thomas, Lewis 1913-1993 . . . . **CLC 35**
See also CA 85-88; 143; CANR 38; MTCW

Thomas, Paul
See Mann, (Paul) Thomas

Thomas, Piri 1928- . . . . **CLC 17**
See also CA 73-76; HW

Thomas, R(onald) S(tuart)
1913- . . . . **CLC 6, 13, 48; DAB**
See also CA 89-92; CAAS 4; CANR 30;
CDBLB 1960 to Present; DAM POET;
DLB 27; MTCW

Thomas, Ross (Elmore) 1926-1995 . . **CLC 39**
See also CA 33-36R; 150; CANR 22

Thompson, Francis Clegg
See Mencken, H(enry) L(ouis)

Thompson, Francis Joseph
1859-1907 . . . . **TCLC 4**
See also CA 104; CDBLB 1890-1914;
DLB 19

Thompson, Hunter S(tockton)
1939- . . . . **CLC 9, 17, 40**
See also BEST 89:1; CA 17-20R; CANR 23,
46; DAM POP; MTCW

Thompson, James Myers
See Thompson, Jim (Myers)

Thompson, Jim (Myers)
1906-1977(?) . . . . **CLC 69**
See also CA 140

Thompson, Judith . . . . **CLC 39**

Thomson, James 1700-1748 . . . . . . **LC 16, 29**
See also DAM POET; DLB 95

Thomson, James 1834-1882 . . . . . . **NCLC 18**
See also DAM POET; DLB 35

Thoreau, Henry David
1817-1862 . . . . . **NCLC 7, 21; DA; DAB;
DAC; WLC**
See also CDALB 1640-1865; DAM MST;
DLB 1

Thornton, Hall
See Silverberg, Robert

Thucydides c. 455B.C.-399B.C. . . . . **CMLC 17**

Thurber, James (Grover)
1894-1961 . . . . **CLC 5, 11, 25; DA; DAB;
DAC; SSC 1**
See also CA 73-76; CANR 17, 39;
CDALB 1929-1941; DAM DRAM, MST,
NOV; DLB 4, 11, 22, 102; MAICYA;
MTCW; SATA 13

Thurman, Wallace (Henry)
1902-1934 . . . . **TCLC 6; BLC**
See also BW 1; CA 104; 124; DAM MULT;
DLB 51

Ticheburn, Cheviot
See Ainsworth, William Harrison

Tieck, (Johann) Ludwig
1773-1853 . . . . **NCLC 5, 46**
See also DLB 90

Tiger, Derry
See Ellison, Harlan (Jay)

Tilghman, Christopher 1948(?)- . . . . . **CLC 65**

Tillinghast, Richard (Williford)
1940- . . . . **CLC 29**
See also CA 29-32R; CAAS 23; CANR 26,
51

Timrod, Henry 1828-1867 . . . . **NCLC 25**
See also DLB 3

Tindall, Gillian 1938- . . . . **CLC 7**
See also CA 21-24R; CANR 11

Tiptree, James, Jr. . . . . **CLC 48, 50**
See also Sheldon, Alice Hastings Bradley
See also DLB 8

Titmarsh, Michael Angelo
See Thackeray, William Makepeace

**Tocqueville, Alexis (Charles Henri Maurice
Clerel Comte)** 1805-1859 . . . . . **NCLC 7**

Tolkien, J(ohn) R(onald) R(euel)
1892-1973 . . . . . . **CLC 1, 2, 3, 8, 12, 38;
DA; DAB; DAC; WLC**
See also AAYA 10; AITN 1; CA 17-18;
45-48; CANR 36; CAP 2;
CDBLB 1914-1945; DAM MST, NOV,
POP; DLB 15, 160; JRDA; MAICYA;
MTCW; SATA 2, 32; SATA-Obit 24

Toller, Ernst 1893-1939 . . . . **TCLC 10**
See also CA 107; DLB 124

Tolson, M. B.
See Tolson, Melvin B(eaunorus)

Tolson, Melvin B(eaunorus)
1898(?)-1966 . . . . **CLC 36; BLC**
See also BW 1; CA 124; 89-92;
DAM MULT, POET; DLB 48, 76

Tolstoi, Aleksei Nikolaevich
See Tolstoy, Alexey Nikolaevich

Tolstoy, Alexey Nikolaevich
1882-1945 . . . . **TCLC 18**
See also CA 107

Tolstoy, Count Leo
See Tolstoy, Leo (Nikolaevich)

Tolstoy, Leo (Nikolaevich)
1828-1910 . . . . . . **TCLC 4, 11, 17, 28, 44;
DA; DAB; DAC; SSC 9; WLC**
See also CA 104; 123; DAM MST, NOV;
SATA 26

Tomasi di Lampedusa, Giuseppe 1896-1957
See Lampedusa, Giuseppe (Tomasi) di
See also CA 111

Tomlin, Lily . . . . **CLC 17**
See also Tomlin, Mary Jean

Tomlin, Mary Jean 1939(?)-
See Tomlin, Lily
See also CA 117

Tomlinson, (Alfred) Charles
1927- . . . . **CLC 2, 4, 6, 13, 45**
See also CA 5-8R; CANR 33; DAM POET;
DLB 40

Tonson, Jacob
See Bennett, (Enoch) Arnold

Toole, John Kennedy
1937-1969 . . . . **CLC 19, 64**
See also CA 104; DLBY 81

Toomer, Jean
1894-1967 . . . . . . **CLC 1, 4, 13, 22; BLC;
PC 7; SSC 1**
See also BW 1; CA 85-88;
CDALB 1917-1929; DAM MULT;
DLB 45, 51; MTCW

Torley, Luke
See Blish, James (Benjamin)

Tornimparte, Alessandra
See Ginzburg, Natalia

Torre, Raoul della
See Mencken, H(enry) L(ouis)

Torrey, E(dwin) Fuller 1937- . . . . **CLC 34**
See also CA 119

Torsvan, Ben Traven
See Traven, B.

Torsvan, Benno Traven
See Traven, B.

Torsvan, Berick Traven
See Traven, B.

Wambaugh, Joseph (Aloysius, Jr.)
1937- .... CLC **3, 18**
See also AITN 1; BEST 89:3; CA 33-36R;
CANR 42; DAM NOV, POP; DLB 6;
DLBY 83; MTCW

Ward, Arthur Henry Sarsfield 1883-1959
See Rohmer, Sax
See also CA 108

Ward, Douglas Turner 1930- .... CLC **19**
See also BW 1; CA 81-84; CANR 27;
DLB 7, 38

Ward, Mary Augusta
See Ward, Mrs. Humphry

Ward, Mrs. Humphry
1851-1920 .... TCLC **55**
See also DLB 18

Ward, Peter
See Faust, Frederick (Schiller)

Warhol, Andy 1928(?)-1987........ CLC **20**
See also AAYA 12; BEST 89:4; CA 89-92;
121; CANR 34

Warner, Francis (Robert le Plastrier)
1937- .... CLC **14**
See also CA 53-56; CANR 11

Warner, Marina 1946- .... CLC **59**
See also CA 65-68; CANR 21

Warner, Rex (Ernest) 1905-1986.... CLC **45**
See also CA 89-92; 119; DLB 15

Warner, Susan (Bogert)
1819-1885 .... NCLC **31**
See also DLB 3, 42

Warner, Sylvia (Constance) Ashton
See Ashton-Warner, Sylvia (Constance)

Warner, Sylvia Townsend
1893-1978 .... CLC **7, 19**
See also CA 61-64; 77-80; CANR 16;
DLB 34, 139; MTCW

Warren, Mercy Otis 1728-1814... NCLC **13**
See also DLB 31

Warren, Robert Penn
1905-1989 .... CLC **1, 4, 6, 8, 10, 13, 18,
39, 53, 59; DA; DAB; DAC; SSC 4; WLC**
See also AITN 1; CA 13-16R; 129;
CANR 10, 47; CDALB 1968-1988;
DAM MST, NOV, POET; DLB 2, 48,
152; DLBY 80, 89; INT CANR-10;
MTCW; SATA 46; SATA-Obit 63

Warshofsky, Isaac
See Singer, Isaac Bashevis

Warton, Thomas 1728-1790........ LC **15**
See also DAM POET; DLB 104, 109

Waruk, Kona
See Harris, (Theodore) Wilson

Warung, Price 1855-1911........ TCLC **45**

Warwick, Jarvis
See Garner, Hugh

Washington, Alex
See Harris, Mark

Washington, Booker T(aliaferro)
1856-1915 .... TCLC **10; BLC**
See also BW 1; CA 114; 125; DAM MULT;
SATA 28

Washington, George 1732-1799...... LC **25**
See also DLB 31

Wassermann, (Karl) Jakob
1873-1934 .... TCLC **6**
See also CA 104; DLB 66

Wasserstein, Wendy
1950- .... CLC **32, 59, 90; DC 4**
See also CA 121; 129; CABS 3;
DAM DRAM; INT 129

Waterhouse, Keith (Spencer)
1929- .... CLC **47**
See also CA 5-8R; CANR 38; DLB 13, 15;
MTCW

Waters, Frank (Joseph)
1902-1995 .... CLC **88**
See also CA 5-8R; 149; CAAS 13; CANR 3,
18; DLBY 86

Waters, Roger 1944- .... CLC **35**

Watkins, Frances Ellen
See Harper, Frances Ellen Watkins

Watkins, Gerrold
See Malzberg, Barry N(athaniel)

Watkins, Paul 1964- .... CLC **55**
See also CA 132

Watkins, Vernon Phillips
1906-1967 .... CLC **43**
See also CA 9-10; 25-28R; CAP 1; DLB 20

Watson, Irving S.
See Mencken, H(enry) L(ouis)

Watson, John H.
See Farmer, Philip Jose

Watson, Richard F.
See Silverberg, Robert

Waugh, Auberon (Alexander) 1939- .. CLC **7**
See also CA 45-48; CANR 6, 22; DLB 14

Waugh, Evelyn (Arthur St. John)
1903-1966 ...... CLC **1, 3, 8, 13, 19, 27,
44; DA; DAB; DAC; WLC**
See also CA 85-88; 25-28R; CANR 22;
CDBLB 1914-1945; DAM MST, NOV,
POP; DLB 15, 162; MTCW

Waugh, Harriet 1944- .... CLC **6**
See also CA 85-88; CANR 22

Ways, C. R.
See Blount, Roy (Alton), Jr.

Waystaff, Simon
See Swift, Jonathan

Webb, (Martha) Beatrice (Potter)
1858-1943 .... TCLC **22**
See also Potter, Beatrice
See also CA 117

Webb, Charles (Richard) 1939- ...... CLC **7**
See also CA 25-28R

Webb, James H(enry), Jr. 1946- .... CLC **22**
See also CA 81-84

Webb, Mary (Gladys Meredith)
1881-1927 .... TCLC **24**
See also CA 123; DLB 34

Webb, Mrs. Sidney
See Webb, (Martha) Beatrice (Potter)

Webb, Phyllis 1927- .... CLC **18**
See also CA 104; CANR 23; DLB 53

Webb, Sidney (James)
1859-1947 .... TCLC **22**
See also CA 117

Webber, Andrew Lloyd............. CLC 21
See also Lloyd Webber, Andrew

Weber, Lenora Mattingly
1895-1971 .... CLC **12**
See also CA 19-20; 29-32R; CAP 1;
SATA 2; SATA-Obit 26

Webster, John 1579(?)-1634(?) .... DC **2**
See also CDBLB Before 1660; DA; DAB;
DAC; DAM DRAM, MST; DLB 58;
WLC

Webster, Noah 1758-1843 .... NCLC **30**

Wedekind, (Benjamin) Frank(lin)
1864-1918 .... TCLC **7**
See also CA 104; DAM DRAM; DLB 118

Weidman, Jerome 1913- .... CLC **7**
See also AITN 2; CA 1-4R; CANR 1;
DLB 28

Weil, Simone (Adolphine)
1909-1943 .... TCLC **23**
See also CA 117

Weinstein, Nathan
See West, Nathanael

Weinstein, Nathan von Wallenstein
See West, Nathanael

Weir, Peter (Lindsay) 1944- .... CLC **20**
See also CA 113; 123

Weiss, Peter (Ulrich)
1916-1982 .... CLC **3, 15, 51**
See also CA 45-48; 106; CANR 3;
DAM DRAM; DLB 69, 124

Weiss, Theodore (Russell)
1916- .... CLC **3, 8, 14**
See also CA 9-12R; CAAS 2; CANR 46;
DLB 5

Welch, (Maurice) Denton
1915-1948 .... TCLC **22**
See also CA 121; 148

Welch, James 1940- .... CLC **6, 14, 52**
See also CA 85-88; CANR 42;
DAM MULT, POP; NNAL

Weldon, Fay
1933- .... CLC **6, 9, 11, 19, 36, 59**
See also CA 21-24R; CANR 16, 46;
CDBLB 1960 to Present; DAM POP;
DLB 14; INT CANR-16; MTCW

Wellek, Rene 1903-1995.......... CLC **28**
See also CA 5-8R; 150; CAAS 7; CANR 8;
DLB 63; INT CANR-8

Weller, Michael 1942- .... CLC **10, 53**
See also CA 85-88

Weller, Paul 1958- .... CLC **26**

Wellershoff, Dieter 1925- .... CLC **46**
See also CA 89-92; CANR 16, 37

Welles, (George) Orson
1915-1985 .... CLC **20, 80**
See also CA 93-96; 117

Wellman, Mac 1945- .... CLC **65**

Wellman, Manly Wade 1903-1986 .. CLC **49**
See also CA 1-4R; 118; CANR 6, 16, 44;
SATA 6; SATA-Obit 47

Wells, Carolyn 1869(?)-1942 ...... TCLC **35**
See also CA 113; DLB 11

Wittgenstein, Ludwig (Josef Johann)
1889-1951 . . . . **TCLC 59**
See also CA 113

Wittig, Monique 1935(?)- . . . . **CLC 22**
See also CA 116; 135; DLB 83

Wittlin, Jozef 1896-1976 . . . . **CLC 25**
See also CA 49-52; 65-68; CANR 3

Wodehouse, P(elham) G(renville)
1881-1975 . . . **CLC 1, 2, 5, 10, 22; DAB;**
DAC; SSC 2
See also AITN 2; CA 45-48; 57-60;
CANR 3, 33; CDBLB 1914-1945;
DAM NOV; DLB 34, 162; MTCW;
SATA 22

Woiwode, L.
See Woiwode, Larry (Alfred)

Woiwode, Larry (Alfred) 1941- . . . **CLC 6, 10**
See also CA 73-76; CANR 16; DLB 6;
INT CANR-16

Wojciechowska, Maia (Teresa)
1927- . . . . **CLC 26**
See also AAYA 8; CA 9-12R; CANR 4, 41;
CLR 1; JRDA; MAICYA; SAAS 1;
SATA 1, 28, 83

Wolf, Christa 1929- . . . . **CLC 14, 29, 58**
See also CA 85-88; CANR 45; DLB 75;
MTCW

Wolfe, Gene (Rodman) 1931- . . . . **CLC 25**
See also CA 57-60; CAAS 9; CANR 6, 32;
DAM POP; DLB 8

Wolfe, George C. 1954- . . . . **CLC 49**
See also CA 149

Wolfe, Thomas (Clayton)
1900-1938 . . . . . **TCLC 4, 13, 29, 61; DA;**
DAB; DAC; WLC
See also CA 104; 132; CDALB 1929-1941;
DAM MST, NOV; DLB 9, 102; DLBD 2;
DLBY 85; MTCW

Wolfe, Thomas Kennerly, Jr. 1931-
See Wolfe, Tom
See also CA 13-16R; CANR 9, 33;
DAM POP; INT CANR-9; MTCW

Wolfe, Tom . . . . **CLC 1, 2, 9, 15, 35, 51**
See also Wolfe, Thomas Kennerly, Jr.
See also AAYA 8; AITN 2; BEST 89:1;
DLB 152

Wolff, Geoffrey (Ansell) 1937- . . . . . **CLC 41**
See also CA 29-32R; CANR 29, 43

Wolff, Sonia
See Levitin, Sonia (Wolff)

Wolff, Tobias (Jonathan Ansell)
1945- . . . . **CLC 39, 64**
See also AAYA 16; BEST 90:2; CA 114;
117; CAAS 22; DLB 130; INT 117

Wolfram von Eschenbach
c. 1170-c. 1220 . . . . **CMLC 5**
See also DLB 138

Wolitzer, Hilma 1930- . . . . **CLC 17**
See also CA 65-68; CANR 18, 40;
INT CANR-18; SATA 31

Wollstonecraft, Mary 1759-1797. . . . . . **LC 5**
See also CDBLB 1789-1832; DLB 39, 104,
158

Wonder, Stevie . . . . **CLC 12**
See also Morris, Steveland Judkins

Wong, Jade Snow 1922- . . . . **CLC 17**
See also CA 109

Woodcott, Keith
See Brunner, John (Kilian Houston)

Woodruff, Robert W.
See Mencken, H(enry) L(ouis)

Woolf, (Adeline) Virginia
1882-1941 . . . . . . **TCLC 1, 5, 20, 43, 56;**
DA; DAB; DAC; SSC 7; WLC
See also CA 104; 130; CDBLB 1914-1945;
DAM MST, NOV; DLB 36, 100, 162;
DLBD 10; MTCW

Woollcott, Alexander (Humphreys)
1887-1943 . . . . **TCLC 5**
See also CA 105; DLB 29

Woolrich, Cornell 1903-1968 . . . . **CLC 77**
See also Hopley-Woolrich, Cornell George

Wordsworth, Dorothy
1771-1855 . . . . **NCLC 25**
See also DLB 107

Wordsworth, William
1770-1850 . . . . **NCLC 12, 38; DA; DAB;**
DAC; PC 4; WLC
See also CDBLB 1789-1832; DAM MST,
POET; DLB 93, 107

Wouk, Herman 1915- . . . . **CLC 1, 9, 38**
See also CA 5-8R; CANR 6, 33;
DAM NOV, POP; DLBY 82;
INT CANR-6; MTCW

Wright, Charles (Penzel, Jr.)
1935- . . . . **CLC 6, 13, 28**
See also CA 29-32R; CAAS 7; CANR 23,
36; DLBY 82; MTCW

Wright, Charles Stevenson
1932- . . . . **CLC 49; BLC 3**
See also BW 1; CA 9-12R; CANR 26;
DAM MULT, POET; DLB 33

Wright, Jack R.
See Harris, Mark

Wright, James (Arlington)
1927-1980 . . . . **CLC 3, 5, 10, 28**
See also AITN 2; CA 49-52; 97-100;
CANR 4, 34; DAM POET; DLB 5;
MTCW

Wright, Judith (Arandell)
1915- . . . . **CLC 11, 53; PC 14**
See also CA 13-16R; CANR 31; MTCW;
SATA 14

Wright, L(aurali) R. 1939- . . . . **CLC 44**
See also CA 138

Wright, Richard (Nathaniel)
1908-1960 . . . . **CLC 1, 3, 4, 9, 14, 21, 48,**
74; BLC; DA; DAB; DAC; SSC 2; WLC
See also AAYA 5; BW 1; CA 108;
CDALB 1929-1941; DAM MST, MULT,
NOV; DLB 76, 102; DLBD 2; MTCW

Wright, Richard B(ruce) 1937- . . . . . . **CLC 6**
See also CA 85-88; DLB 53

Wright, Rick 1945- . . . . **CLC 35**

Wright, Rowland
See Wells, Carolyn

Wright, Stephen Caldwell 1946- . . . . **CLC 33**
See also BW 2

Wright, Willard Huntington 1888-1939
See Van Dine, S. S.
See also CA 115

Wright, William 1930- . . . . **CLC 44**
See also CA 53-56; CANR 7, 23

Wroth, LadyMary 1587-1653(?) . . . . . **LC 30**
See also DLB 121

Wu Ch'eng-en 1500(?)-1582(?) . . . . **LC 7**

Wu Ching-tzu 1701-1754 . . . . **LC 2**

Wurlitzer, Rudolph 1938(?)- . . . **CLC 2, 4, 15**
See also CA 85-88

Wycherley, William 1641-1715 . . . . **LC 8, 21**
See also CDBLB 1660-1789; DAM DRAM;
DLB 80

Wylie, Elinor (Morton Hoyt)
1885-1928 . . . . **TCLC 8**
See also CA 105; DLB 9, 45

Wylie, Philip (Gordon) 1902-1971. . . **CLC 43**
See also CA 21-22; 33-36R; CAP 2; DLB 9

Wyndham, John . . . . **CLC 19**
See also Harris, John (Wyndham Parkes
Lucas) Beynon

Wyss, Johann David Von
1743-1818 . . . . **NCLC 10**
See also JRDA; MAICYA; SATA 29;
SATA-Brief 27

Xenophon
c. 430B.C.-c. 354B.C. . . . . **CMLC 17**

Yakumo Koizumì
See Hearn, (Patricio) Lafcadio (Tessima
Carlos)

Yanez, Jose Donoso
See Donoso (Yanez), Jose

Yanovsky, Basile S.
See Yanovsky, V(assily) S(emenovich)

Yanovsky, V(assily) S(emenovich)
1906-1989 . . . . **CLC 2, 18**
See also CA 97-100; 129

Yates, Richard 1926-1992 . . . . . **CLC 7, 8, 23**
See also CA 5-8R; 139; CANR 10, 43;
DLB 2; DLBY 81, 92; INT CANR-10

Yeats, W. B.
See Yeats, William Butler

Yeats, William Butler
1865-1939 . . . . . **TCLC 1, 11, 18, 31; DA;**
DAB; DAC; WLC
See also CA 104; 127; CANR 45;
CDBLB 1890-1914; DAM DRAM, MST,
POET; DLB 10, 19, 98, 156; MTCW

Yehoshua, A(braham) B.
1936- . . . . **CLC 13, 31**
See also CA 33-36R; CANR 43

Yep, Laurence Michael 1948- . . . . . . **CLC 35**
See also AAYA 5; CA 49-52; CANR 1, 46;
CLR 3, 17; DLB 52; JRDA; MAICYA;
SATA 7, 69

Yerby, Frank G(arvin)
1916-1991 . . . . **CLC 1, 7, 22; BLC**
See also BW 1; CA 9-12R; 136; CANR 16;
DAM MULT; DLB 76; INT CANR-16;
MTCW

Yesenin, Sergei Alexandrovich
See Esenin, Sergei (Alexandrovich)

Yevtushenko, Yevgeny (Alexandrovich)
1933- . . . . **CLC 1, 3, 13, 26, 51**
See also CA 81-84; CANR 33;
DAM POET; MTCW

Literary Criticism Series
Cumulative Topic Index

This index lists all topic entries in Gale's *Classical and Medieval Literature Criticism, Contemporary Literary Criticism, Literature Criticism from 1400 to 1800, Nineteenth-Century Literature Criticism,* and *Twentieth-Century Literary Criticism.*

Topic Index

Topic Index

Topic Index

NCLC Cumulative Nationality Index

Nationality Index

AMERICAN

Alcott, Amos Bronson **1**
Alcott, Louisa May **6**
Alger, Horatio **8**
Allston, Washington **2**
Audubon, John James **47**
Barlow, Joel **23**
Beecher, Catharine Esther **30**
Bellamy, Edward **4**
Bird, Robert Montgomery **1**
Brackenridge, Hugh Henry **7**
Brentano, Clemens (Maria) **1**
Brown, Charles Brockden **22**
Brown, William Wells **2**
Brownson, Orestes **50**
Bryant, William Cullen **6, 46**
Calhoun, John Caldwell **15**
Channing, William Ellery **17**
Child, Lydia Maria **6**
Chivers, Thomas Holley **49**
Cooke, John Esten **5**
Cooper, James Fenimore **1, 27, 54**
Crockett, David **8**
Dana, Richard Henry, Sr. **53**
Dickinson, Emily (Elizabeth) **21**
Douglass, Frederick **7**
Dunlap, William **2**
Dwight, Timothy **13**
Emerson, Ralph Waldo **1, 38**
Field, Eugene **3**
Foster, Stephen Collins **26**
Frederic, Harold **10**
Freneau, Philip Morin **1**
Fuller, Margaret **5, 50**
Halleck, Fitz-Greene **47**
Hamilton, Alexander **49**
Hammon, Jupiter **5**

Harris, George Washington **23**
Hawthorne, Nathaniel **2, 10, 17, 23, 39**
Holmes, Oliver Wendell **14**
Irving, Washington **2, 19**
James, Henry, Sr. **53**
Jefferson, Thomas **11**
Kennedy, John Pendleton **2**
Lanier, Sidney **6**
Lazarus, Emma **8**
Lincoln, Abraham **18**
Longfellow, Henry Wadsworth **2, 45**
Lowell, James Russell **2**
Melville, Herman **3, 12, 29, 45, 49**
Parkman, Francis **12**
Paulding, James Kirke **2**
Pinkney, Edward **31**
Poe, Edgar Allan **1, 16**
Rowson, Susanna Haswell **5**
Sedgwick, Catharine Maria **19**
Shaw, Henry Wheeler **15**
Sheridan, Richard Brinsley **5**
Signourney, Lydia Howard (Huntley) **21**
Simms, William Gilmore **3**
Smith, Joseph, Jr. **53**
Southworth, Emma Dorothy Eliza Nevitte **26**
Stowe, Harriet (Elizabeth) Beecher **3, 50**
Thoreau, Henry David **7, 21**
Timrod, Henry **25**
Trumbull, John **30**
Tyler, Royall **3**
Very, Jones **9**
Warner, Susan (Bogert) **31**
Warren, Mercy Otis **13**
Webster, Noah **30**
Whitman, Sarah Helen (Power) **19**
Whitman, Walt(er) **4, 31**
Whittier, John Greenleaf **8**

ARGENTINIAN

Echeverria, (Jose) Esteban (Antonino) **18**
Hernandez, Jose **17**

AUSTRALIAN

Adams, Francis **33**
Clarke, Marcus (Andrew Hislop) **19**
Gordon, Adam Lindsay **21**
Kendall, Henry **12**

AUSTRIAN

Grillparzer, Franz **1**
Lenau, Nikolaus **16**
Nestroy, Johann **42**
Sacher-Masoch, Leopold von **31**
Stifter, Adalbert **41**

CANADIAN

Crawford, Isabella Valancy **12**
Haliburton, Thomas Chandler **15**
Lampman, Archibald **25**
Moodie, Susanna (Strickland) **14**
Traill, Catharine Parr **31**

CZECH

Macha, Karel Hynek **46**

DANISH

Andersen, Hans Christian **7**
Grundtvig, Nicolai Frederik Severin **1**
Jacobsen, Jens Peter **34**
Kierkegaard, Soren **34**

ENGLISH

Ainsworth, William Harrison **13**
Arnold, Matthew **6, 29**
Arnold, Thomas **18**

487

Nationality Index

Title Index

ISBN 0-8103-6437-9

90000

9 780810 364370